THE DEATH OF THE MESSIAH

Volume One

THE ANCHOR YALE BIBLE REFERENCE LIBRARY is designed to be a third major component of the Anchor Yale Bible group, which includes the Anchor Yale Bible commentaries on the books of the Old Testament, the New Testament, and the Apocrypha, and the Anchor Yale Bible Dictionary. While the Anchor Yale Bible commentaries and the Anchor Yale Bible Dictionary are structurally defined by their subject matter, the Anchor Yale Bible Reference Library will serve as a supplement on the cutting edge of the most recent scholarship. The series is open-ended; its scope and reach are nothing less than the biblical world in its totality, and its methods and techniques the most up-to-date available or devisable. Separate volumes will deal with one or more of the following topics relating to the Bible: anthropology, archaeology, ecology, economy, geography, history, languages and literatures, philosophy, religion(s), theology.

As with the Anchor Yale Bible commentaries and the Anchor Yale Bible Dictionary, the philosophy underlying the Anchor Yale Bible Reference Library finds expression in the following: the approach is scholarly, the perspective is balanced and fair-minded, the methods are scientific, and the goal is to inform and enlighten. Contributors are chosen on the basis of their scholarly skills and achievements, and they come from a variety of religious backgrounds and communities. The books in the Anchor Yale Bible Reference Library are intended for the broadest possible readership, ranging from world-class scholars, whose qualifications match those of the authors, to general readers, who may not have special training or skill in studying the Bible but are as enthusiastic as any dedicated professional in expanding their knowledge of the Bible and its world.

David Noel Freedman
GENERAL EDITOR

THE ANCHOR YALE BIBLE REFERENCE LIBRARY

THE DEATH
OF THE MESSIAH

From Gethsemane to the Grave

A COMMENTARY
ON THE PASSION NARRATIVES
IN THE FOUR GOSPELS

Volume One

By

Raymond E. Brown, S.S.

Yale University Press   New Haven and London

First published in 1994 by Doubleday, a division of Random House, Inc. First paperback edition published in 1998. First Yale University Press impression 2008.

Printed in the United States of America.

The Library of Congress has cataloged the hardcover edition as follows:
Brown, Raymond Edward.
The death of the Messiah : from Gethsemane to the grave : a commentary on the
Passion narratives in the four Gospels / Raymond E. Brown. — 1st ed.
p. cm. — (The Anchor Bible reference library)
Includes bibliographical references and indexes.
1. Passion narratives (Gospels) I. Title. II. Series.
BS2555.3.B7633   1994
226′.07—dc20   93-9241
CIP

Nihil obstat
Myles M. Bourke, S.T.D., S.S.L.
Censor deputatus
Imprimatur
Patrick J. Sheridan, D.D.
Vicar General, Archdiocese of New York
April 30, 1993
The *nihil obstat* and *imprimatur* are official declarations that a book or pamphlet is free
of doctrinal or moral error. No implication is contained therein that those who have granted
the *nihil obstat* and *imprimatur* agree with the contents, opinions, or statements expressed.

ISBN 978-0-300-14009-5 (pbk. : alk. paper) (Volume 1)
ISBN 978-0-300-14010-1 (pbk. : alk. paper) (Volume 2)

A catalogue record for this book is available from the British Library.

To
Union Theological Seminary (N.Y.C.)
and
Auburn Seminary (N.Y.C.)
as an inadequate expression of my gratitude
for encouragement, support, and friendship
during twenty years of teaching
from one who is privileged to have been
the Auburn Distinguished Professor
of Biblical Studies
at Union Theological Seminary

PREFACE AND ACKNOWLEDGMENTS

The Passion Narrative (henceforth PN), as it proceeds from arrest through trial to condemnation, execution, and burial (thus from Gethsemane to the grave), constitutes in each Gospel the longest consecutive action recounted of Jesus. Aesthetically, more than any other section of the Gospels, indeed even more than the infancy narrative, it has captured the attention and imagination of dramatists (passion plays), artists, and musicians. Literarily, passion vignettes have left their mark on language and imagery: thirty pieces of silver, Judas kiss, cockcrow, washing one's hands of blood. Historically, Jesus' death was the most public moment of his life as figures known from Jewish or secular history (Caiaphas, Annas, Pilate) crossed his path. Indeed, alongside "born of the virgin Mary," the other phrase that made its way into the creed, "suffered under Pontius Pilate," has become a marker anchoring Christian belief about the Son of God to a Jesus who was a human figure of actual history. Theologically, Christians have interpreted the death of Jesus on the cross as the key element in God's plan for the justification, redemption, and salvation of all. Spiritually, the Jesus of the passion has been the focus of Christian meditation for countless would-be disciples who take seriously the demand of the Master to take up the cross and follow him. Pastorally, the passion is the centerpiece of Lent and Holy Week, the most sacred time in the liturgical calendar. The custom of Lenten preaching has made it a most favored subject for homilies. In sum, from every point of view the passion is the central narrative in the Christian story.

This centrality is recognizable in the immense literature devoted to the passion, studying it from every angle. Although I wrote commentaries on the Gospel and Epistles of John and on the Gospel infancy narratives, no previous work has required research so lengthy or a bibliography so ample. If I totaled my time, at least ten years of consistent work have gone into it. The bibliographies (which take up some seventy pages) constitute a testament of my gratitude to all those from whom I have learned about the PN. And yet, despite my efforts to be comprehensive in calling attention to previous work, I am certain that there are contributions I have missed—unintentional oversights for which I apologize in advance to my reviewers, who surely will render me the service of pointing them out.

Paradoxically, the very mass of PN writing creates need for a work that will bring together the scattered views and proposals, sift them for the truly worthwhile, and organize them (with new contributions, I trust). I am not aware of a full-scale commentary on the four Gospel PNs of the sort attempted here—an undertaking not without peril and perhaps even foolhardy. There have been many commentaries on the PNs of the Gospels studied individually; but instead of producing another such consecutive or "vertical" treatment of each PN, I made the controversial decision to work through the passion "horizontally," studying each episode in all four Gospels simultaneously. Personally I found such a reading absorbing, and it brought to light important insights and nuances that I feared would be lost if I commented on one whole PN before I turned to the next. (Let me assure those alarmed by the thought of such a procedure that my "horizontal" readings have no harmonizing goal, and I have made a major effort not to lose the "vertical" chain of thought peculiar to each Gospel read consecutively.) The introductory chapter will sketch the extremely difficult problems presented by the PNs. How many of them I have solved I do not know. Nevertheless, I hope to have made available in one place insights of past and present that render study of the passion a uniquely rewarding endeavor. Despite the taxing magnitude of the project, the time consumed has been the most enriching of my life. I shall be happy if I can share my enthusiasm.

A major concern has been to do justice to both scholarship and intelligibility and thus to serve a variety of audiences: scholars, preaching clergy, students of religion or theology and of the Bible, interested Christians, and those of any persuasion who seek knowledge about the passion and death of Jesus. So that this commentary may be widely useful, I have endeavored to treat complicated subjects in a readable way, even if that required greater length. For instance, in cross-references to biblical books, many commentaries simply list the relevant passages by chapter and verse numbers, expecting the readers who wish to follow the discussion to flip through the Bible, looking them up. In an age that demands more user-friendly communication, such an expectation is unrealistic. Most often I have preferred to give the wording of the key cross-referenced passages, thereby making certain that readers are aware of the biblical background. Although I have used a number of abbreviations (all of them given in the list below), in the instance of esoteric ancient works, texts, and versions I have preferred to write out titles rather than frighten away readers who would otherwise be faced with the biblical equivalent of stock-market listings. The dating of years as BC and AD, the pattern followed in *The Birth of the Messiah,* was followed here as well, both for consistency and for general intelligibility and recognition (which BCE and CE still lack).

Some pointers to the way I have arranged the material and a few preliminary suggestions may aid comprehension. *First,* whether one is planning to read the commentary through or to consult it about particular passages, it is essential to read the introductory §1 to understand my perspective and presuppositions. Readers should know what the author thinks he is doing. *Second,* after the INTRODUCTION, the passion is divided into four "Acts," several of which have two "Scenes." The quadruple division (Prayer/arrest; Jewish trial; Roman trial; Crucifixion/burial) surely does justice to the sequence in the Synoptic Gospels, even if one can debate whether John's briefer material in Acts I and II would warrant such a dividing line there. The use of "Act" and "Scene" to designate the divisions reflects my understanding of the Gospel accounts as dramatic narratives, as will be explained in §1. *Third,* beginning with the actual commentary on the text of the PN in §5, I always present first a literal translation of the passages under discussion. May I emphasize my awareness of how painfully literal is this translation—at times to the point of awkwardness. Probably most readers will not be students of the Greek NT, and therefore without such a literal translation important variations in the different Gospel descriptions of the same scene would be lost on them. For instance, my mechanical translation of the particles *kai* and *de* as "and" and "but" does not do justice in English to the subtleties of the Greek language; but it does enable readers to detect sentence patterns that scholars find important for discussions of source. The translations of OT passages, whether from Hebrew or Greek, are also very literal (even in passages where one would have preferred to be freer in order to respect modern sensibilities about pronominal references to God); the goal of such fidelity is to highlight the background that such passages offer for the Gospel PNs. A translation of either the PNs or the OT into more idiomatic English would disguise such patterns and parallels. Please consider the PN translation as only a study tool, not to be read publicly and not to be evaluated on its literary merit. (In order to appreciate the constraints of literalness imposed here, where four Gospel accounts of the same scene must be compared exactly, readers are invited to contrast the translation of the Johannine narratives in this book with those offered in my Anchor Bible commentary on John [BGJ].) *Fourth,* in discussing the actual Gospel text of a passage, I have divided my remarks into COMMENT and ANALYSIS. (The pattern of initial informational NOTES, followed in *The Birth of the Messiah,* proved impractical in this book since passages from four different Gospels were being commented on in most sections. Footnotes cover the appropriate information just as effectively.) The COMMENT seeks to discover and explain what the evangelist wanted to convey by the passage; it is by far the most important part of my treatment and receives primary attention. After the COMMENT in each section (or at the end of a related group of sections) comes the much shorter ANALYSIS. It studies possible dependence of one Gospel on another, proposed preGospel traditions, and factors pertinent to historicity—unavoidable questions, answered of necessity by theorizing, but scarcely the heart of a commentary. Examination of the arrangement or structure of the passage, which I consider very important, may play a role both in the COMMENT and (more abstractly) in the ANALYSIS. *Fifth,* the GENERAL BIBLIOGRAPHY, which constitutes §3, lists writings pertinent to the passion in general or to the whole PN of an individual Gospel. Before each major division (Act, Scene) of the commentary there is a SECTIONAL BIBLIOGRAPHY covering all sections therein. To facilitate usage of the latter, the final line of each section indicates where in the appropriate SECTIONAL BIBLIOGRAPHY pertinent literature may be found. Citation of a writing listed in one of the bibliographies is given by using the author's family name and an abbreviation of the title (usually the first word). If the cited work is not going to appear in a bibliography (because, while pertinent to a particular point, it is only tangentially related to the passion and will not be cited again), full information is given at the moment of citation. The BIBLIOGRAPHICAL INDEX, the first of the indexes supplied at the very end of this book, enables readers to find all works that have been cited in either format. *Sixth,* the last of those indexes is designed to be helpful in different ways. For commentary purposes I have divided the PN into forty-eight sections, sometimes with a whole section devoted to a passage found in only one Gospel. To find a continuous translation of a particular Gospel, readers should turn to the GOSPEL PASSAGE INDEX, where *the complete PN of each Gospel is printed consecutively.* In a column next to that translation I have indicated the pages in the commentary where each verse or group of verses receives its principal treatment. Therefore anyone desiring information about a section of the PN can find directions very quickly through this index.

By way of acknowledgments let me recall that over the years I have given many short series of lectures and retreats on the PN and have taught semester courses on them, once at the Roman Pontifical Biblical Institute and several times at Union Theological Seminary. Never have I failed to be instructed by the questions and papers of hearers and students. Two sabbatical semesters were spent day in and day out reading in the library of the Pontifical Biblical Institute in Rome; and the splendid librarians and staff of that institution, especially Henry Bertels, S.J., and Sister Colette Auger, P.M., helped most hospitably as I worked through bibliography. Dr. Cecil White, the librarian of St. Patrick's Seminary (Menlo Park, California), and Seth Kasten, reference librarian at Union Seminary, have been most adept in tracing what I found untraceable. Eileen Tobin and Julie Galas retyped sections of my own typescript while I was teaching at Union. In an earlier incarnation as my student, Professor Jennifer Glancy of Le Moyne College moved my bibliography from bulky files of cards to a much more flexible computerized list. Angela Bauer, a doctoral student at Union, checked the biblical references in my typescript for accuracy. To all these friends who always did more than I had a right to expect, warm thanks.

As a student writing a paper for a seminar that I was giving on the PN, Professor Marion Soards of the Louisville Presbyterian Theological Seminary composed in preliminary form a survey of theories of a preMarcan PN that he has graciously consented to have appear in its fully developed form as APPENDIX IX of this book. I have learned much also from his doctoral dissertation on the Lucan PN, his continued contributions to the field, and his friendly advice. Professor David Noel Freedman, who supplied sage advice as editor of my Anchor Bible commentaries, most generously helped here again by reading my ms. and supplying, in reference both to style and content, an abundance of significant observations that I have incorporated. I am greatly in debt to him. Professor John Kselman of Weston School of Theology, selflessly rendering a service he has so often done for me before, also read through the 2,700 pages of my typescript. There are many smoother sentences and far fewer mistakes because of his keen perception. I regard this Preface and §1 of the Introduction as crucial for setting the intended tone; and when they had reached that stage of familiarity where I could no longer see their defects, Professor Phyllis Trible of Union, looking with a fresh eye, improved them significantly. There are many others who responded to my requests for information and references, including the members of seminars on the passion at the annual Society of Biblical Literature and Society of New Testament Studies meetings. Although I shall not attempt to name them, it would be an injustice to overlook two who helped significantly: Joseph A. Fitzmyer, S.J., a friend for forty years and always a model of precision; and Professor Burton L. Visotzky of the Jewish Theological Seminary in New York, who over the years has been truly a rabbi to me in matters of Judaica. The folk at Doubleday, Robert Heller and Theresa D'Orsogna in earlier times, Thomas Cahill and Michael Iannazzi more recently, with Susan Higgenbotham as copy editor, have contributed patience, encouragement, assistance, and editing in producing this book that over a decade ago I agreed to write. To one and all, sincere gratitude.

The Birth of the Messiah appeared in 1977. I found great encouragement in the many letters from readers and clergy, both Protestant and Catholic, who told me that the volume had given them a greater appreciation of the wealth of the infancy narratives for spirituality, preaching, and an understanding of Jesus. I would like to think that this companion work, *The Death of the Messiah,* will bear similar fruit. But whatever the judgment of others,

I thank God's providence that has permitted me to spend so many years of my life in commenting on the biblical accounts of Jesus' birth and death. Not only have I learned more of the one for whom "Messiah" (*Christos*) became a second name, but I have come to respect deeply the skill of the evangelists without whose contribution that name would not be known in all its profundity. In a small way may my work make their work better known. As for the seeming antipodes represented by *The Birth of the Messiah* and *The Death of the Messiah,* I am not the first writer to think that the two constitute a compatible subject. A poem by John Donne, "Upon the Annunciation and the Passion,"[1] celebrated the coincidence that in 1608 the 25th of March, the Feast of the Annunciation to Mary, was also Good Friday, so that the conception and the crucifixion of the Messiah came together. A perceptive friend of college days in Baltimore, Marco Gnerro, who called the poem to my attention, marked off this stanza that is so expressive of the continuity of the events:

> All this, and all betweene, this day hath showne,
> Th'Abridgement of Christs story, which makes one
> (As in plaine Maps, the furthest West is East)
> Of the 'Angels *Ave*' and *Consummatum est.*

A surprising number of people have asked if I plan a trilogy to conclude with *The Resurrection of the Messiah.* Responding with mock indignation that I have written two books on the resurrection (a response that conveniently ignores the fact that neither is truly a commentary), I tell them emphatically that I have no such plans. I would rather explore that area "face to face."

Ash Wednesday
February 24, 1993

---

[1]*The Divine Poems of John Donne,* ed. N. Gardner (2d ed.; Oxford: Clarendon, 1966), 29.

CONTENTS OF VOLUME ONE

(Before the Introduction and each "Act" and "Scene" of the Commentary,
a more detailed table will be given breaking the sections [marked by §]
into subsections.)

COMMENTARY (in Four Acts)

ACT I: JESUS PRAYS AND IS ARRESTED IN GETHSEMANE ON THE MOUNT OF OLIVES ACROSS THE KIDRON
(Mark 14:26–52; Matt 26:30–56; Luke 22:39–53; John 18:1–11)

SCENE ONE: Jesus Goes to the Site and Prays There (Mark 14:26–42; Matt 26:30–46; Luke 22:39–46; John 18:1)

ILLUSTRATIVE TABLES

ABBREVIATIONS

AB	Anchor Bible
AER	*American Ecclesiastical Review*
AJBI	*Annual of the Japanese Biblical Institute*
AJEC	*Anti-Judaism in Early Christianity; Vol. 1: Paul and the Gospels,* ed. P. Richardson (Waterloo, Ont.: Canadian Corp. for Studies in Religion and Wilfred Laurier Univ., 1986)
AJINT	*Antijudaismus im Neuen Testament?* eds. W. P. Eckert et al. (Munich: Kaiser, 1967)
AJSL	*American Journal of Semitic Languages and Literature*
AJT	*American Journal of Theology*
AnBib	Analecta Biblica
AnGreg	Analecta Gregoriana
ANRW	Aufstieg und Niedergang der römischen Welt
Ant.	The *Antiquities* of Flavius Josephus
AP	*Apocrypha and Pseudepigrapha of the Old Testament,* ed. R. H. Charles (2 vols.; Oxford: Clarendon, 1913)
AsSeign	*Assemblées du Seigneur*
ASTI	*Annual of the Swedish Theological Institute*
ATANT	Abhandlungen zur Theologie des Alten und Neuen Testaments
ATR	*Anglican Theological Review*
A.U.C.	*anno urbis conditae* or *ab urbe condita* (a specified year from the founding of Rome)
AUSS	*Andrews University Seminary Studies*
BA	*Biblical Archaeologist*
BAA	M. Black, *An Aramaic Approach to the Gospels and Acts* (3d ed.; Oxford: Clarendon, 1967)
BAG	W. Bauer, W. F. Arndt, and F. W. Gingrich, *Greek-English Lexicon of the New Testament and Other Early Christian Literature* (Cambridge Univ., 1957)
BAGD	BAG revised by F. W. Danker (Univ. of Chicago, 1979)
BARev	*Biblical Archaeology Review*

BBM	R. E. Brown, *The Birth of the Messiah* (Garden City, NY: Double-day, 1977; new ed., 1993)
BDF	F. Blass, A. Debrunner, and R. W. Funk, *A Greek Grammar of the New Testament* (Univ. of Chicago, 1961). Refs. to sections.
BEJ	R. E. Brown, *The Epistles of John* (AB 30; Garden City, NY: Doubleday, 1982)
BeO	*Bibbia e Oriente*
BETL	Bibliotheca Ephemeridum Theologicarum Lovaniensium
BExT	P. Benoit, *Exégèse et Théologie* (4 vols.; Paris: Cerf, 1961–82)
BGJ	R. E. Brown, *The Gospel According to John* (2 vols.; AB 29, 29A; Garden City, NY: Doubleday, 1966, 1970)
BHST	R. Bultmann, *History of the Synoptic Tradition* (New York: Harper & Row, 1963)
BibLeb	*Bibel und Leben*
BibLit	*Bibel und Liturgie*
BJG	P. Benoit, *Jesus and the Gospel* (2 vols.; New York: Herder, 1973)
BJRL	*Bulletin of the John Rylands Library, University of Manchester*
BK	*Bibel und Kirche*
BR	*Biblical Research*
BS	Biblische Studien
BSac	*Bibliotheca Sacra*
BSSNT	K. Beyer, *Semitische Syntax im Neuen Testament* (Göttingen: Vandenhoeck & Ruprecht, 1962)
BT	*The Bible Translator*
BTB	*Biblical Theology Bulletin*
BU	Biblische Untersuchungen
BVC	*Bible et Vie Chrétienne*
BW	*Biblical World*
BWANT	Beiträge zur Wissenschaft vom Alten und Neuen Testament
ByF	*Biblia y Fe*
BZ	*Biblische Zeitschrift*
BZNW	Beihefte zur ZNW
CB	*Cultura Bíblica*
CBQ	*Catholic Biblical Quarterly*
CC	Corpus Christianorum (Series Latina)
CCat	*Civiltà Cattolica*
CCER	*Cahiers du Cercle Ernest Renan*
CD	Cairo (Genizah text of the) Damascus (Document)

CH	*Church History*
CKC	*Chronos, Kairos, Christos,* eds. J. Vardaman and E. M. Yamauchi (J. Finegan Festschrift; Winona Lake, IN: Eisenbrauns, 1989)
ColB	*Collationes Brugenses*
ConNT	*Coniectanea Neotestamentica*
CQR	*Church Quarterly Review*
CR	*Clergy Review*
CSA	*Chicago Studies* (Anniversary Volume) 25 (#1; 1986: Passion, Death, and Resurrection of Jesus)
CSEL	Corpus Scriptorum Ecclesiasticorum Latinorum
CT	*Christianity Today*
CTM	*Concordia Theological Monthly*
CTom	*Ciencia Tomista*
CurTM	*Currents in Theology and Mission*
DACL	*Dictionnaire d'Archéologie Chrétienne et de Liturgie*
DBG	M. Dibelius, *Botschaft und Geschichte* (2 vols.; Tübingen: Mohr, 1953, 1956)
DBS	H. Denzinger and C. Bannwart, *Enchiridion Symbolorum,* rev. by A. Schönmetzer (32d ed.; Freiburg: Herder, 1963). Refs. to sections.
DBSup	*Dictionnaire de la Bible, Supplément*
DJ	*The Digest of Justinian,* ed. T. Mommsen (4 vols.; Philadelphia: Univ. of Pennsylvania, 1985)
DJD	Discoveries in the Judaean Desert
DJS	A. Denaux, ed. *John and the Synoptics* (BETL 101; Leuven Univ., 1992). Analyzed by Denaux in ETL 67 (1991), 196–203.
DNTRJ	D. Daube, *The New Testament and Rabbinic Judaism* (London: Athlone, 1956)
DRev	*Downside Review*
DSNT	J.D.M. Derrett, *Studies in the New Testament* (4 vols.; Leiden: Brill, 1977–86)
DSS	Dead Sea Scrolls
DSSW	G. Dalman, *Sacred Sites and Ways* (New York: Macmillan, 1935; German orig. 3d ed., 1924)
EBib	Études Bibliques
EH	Eusebius, *Ecclesiastical History*
EJMI	*Early Judaism and its Modern Interpreters,* eds. R. A. Kraft and G.W.E. Nickelsburg (Atlanta: Scholars, 1986)
EKKNT	Evangelisch-katholischer Kommentar zum Neuen Testament

EQ	*Evangelical Quarterly*
ErbAuf	*Erbe und Auftrage*
EspVie	*Esprit et Vie* (later *L'Ami du Clergé*)
EstBib	*Estudios Bíblicos*
EstEcl	*Estudios Eclesiásticos*
ETL	*Ephemerides Theologicae Lovanienses*
ETR	*Études Théologiques et Religieuses*
EvT	*Evangelische Theologie*
ExpTim	*Expository Times*
FANT	J. Finegan, *The Archaeology of the New Testament* (Princeton Univ., 1969)
FAWA	J. A. Fitzmyer, *A Wandering Aramean* (SBLMS 25; Missoula, MT: Scholars, 1979)
FB	Forschung zur Bibel
FESBNT	J. A. Fitzmyer, *Essays on the Semitic Background of the New Testament* (London: Chapman, 1971)
FGN	*The Four Gospels 1992*, eds. F. Van Segbroeck et al. (F. Neirynck Festschrift; BETL 100; 3 vols.; Leuven Univ., 1992)
FRLANT	Forschungen zur Religion und Literatur des Alten und Neuen Testaments
FTAG	J. A. Fitzmyer, *To Advance the Gospel* (New York: Crossroad, 1981)
FV	*Foi et Vie*
FZPT	*Freiburger Zeitschrift für Philosophie und Theologie*
GCS	Die Griechischen Christlichen Schriftsteller (Berlin)
GPet	*The Gospel of Peter* (see APPENDIX I)
GVMF	*Gottesverächter und Menschenfeinde? Juden zwischen Jesus und frühchristlicher Kirche*, ed. H. Goldstein (Düsseldorf: Patmos, 1979)
HeyJ	*Heythrop Journal*
HibJ	*Hibbert Journal*
HJPAJC	E. Schürer, *The History of the Jewish People in the Age of Jesus Christ* (rev. by G. Vermes et al.; 3 vols.; Edinburgh: Clark, 1973–87)
HPG	*The Holy Places of the Gospels* by C. Kopp (New York: Herder and Herder, 1963)
HSNTA	E. Hennecke and W. Schneemelcher, *New Testament Apocrypha* (2 vols.; Philadelphia: Westminster, 1963, 1965; rev. ed., vol. 1, 1991)

HTR	*Harvard Theological Review*
HUCA	*Hebrew Union College Annual*
IBS	*Irish Biblical Studies*
IEJ	*Israel Exploration Journal*
IER	*Irish Ecclesiastical Record*
ILS	*Inscriptiones Latinae Selectae,* ed. H. Dessau (3 vols.; Berlin: Weidmann, 1892–1916). Cited by inscription number.
ITQ	*Irish Theological Quarterly*
JAAR	*Journal of the American Academy of Religion*
JANT	M. R. James, *The Apocryphal New Testament* (2d ed.; Oxford: Clarendon, 1953)
JBap	John the Baptist
JBL	*Journal of Biblical Literature*
JBR	*Journal of Bible and Religion*
JE	*Jewish Encyclopedia*
JES	*Journal of Ecumenical Studies*
JETS	*Journal of the Evangelical Theological Society*
JEWJ	J. Jeremias, *The Eucharistic Words of Jesus* (2d ed.; New York: Scribners, 1966)
JJC	*Josephus, Judaism, and Christianity,* eds. L. H. Feldman and G. Hata (Leiden: Brill, 1987)
JJS	*Journal of Jewish Studies*
JJTJ	J. Jeremias, *Jerusalem in the Time of Jesus* (Philadelphia: Fortress, 1969)
JPFC	*The Jewish People in the First Century,* eds. S. Safrai and M. Stern (2 vols.; Philadelphia: Fortress, 1974)
JPHD	*Jesus and the Politics of His Day,* eds. E. Bammel and C.F.D. Moule (Cambridge Univ., 1984)
JQR	*Jewish Quarterly Review*
JRS	*Journal of Roman Studies*
JSJ	*Journal for the Study of Judaism in the Persian, Hellenistic and Roman Period*
JSNT	*Journal for the Study of the New Testament*
JSNTSup	Journal for the Study of the New Testament—Supplement Series
JTS	*Journal of Theological Studies*
KACG	H. Koester, *Ancient Christian Gospels* (Philadelphia: Trinity, 1990)
KBW	Katholisches Bibelwerk (Verlag, Stuttgart)
KJV	*King James Version* or *Authorized Version of the Bible*

KKS   W. H. Kelber, A. Kolenkow, and R. Scroggs, "Reflections on the
            Question: Was There a Pre-Markan Passion Narrative?" SBLSP
            (1971), 2.503–86.

Kyr   *Kyriakon,* eds. P. Granfield and J. A. Jungmann (J. Quasten Fest-
            schrift; 2 vols.; Münster: Aschendorff, 1970)

LB   *Linguistica Biblica*

LD   Lectio Divina

LFAE   *Light from the Ancient East* by A. Deissmann (rev. ed.; New York:
            Doran, 1927)

LKS   H. Lietzmann, *Kleine Schriften II* (TU 68; Berlin: Akademie,
            1958)

LS   *Louvain Studies*

LumVie   *Lumière et Vie*

LXX   (The) Septuagint Greek Translation of the OT

MACM   H. Musurillo, *The Acts of the Christian Martyrs* (Oxford:
            Clarendon, 1972)

MAPM   H. Musurillo, *The Acts of the Pagan Martyrs* (Oxford:
            Clarendon, 1954)

MGNTG   J. H. Moulton (and N. Turner), *Grammar of New Testament Greek*
            (4 vols.; Edinburgh: Clark, 1908–76)

MIBNTG   C.F.D. Moule, *An Idiom-Book of New Testament Greek* (Cam-
            bridge Univ., 1960)

MM   J. H. Moulton and G. Milligan, *The Vocabulary of the Greek New
            Testament Illustrated from the Papyri and Other Non-Literary
            Sources* (repr.; Grand Rapids: Eerdmans, 1963)

MNTS   *Die Mitte des Neuen Testaments,* eds. U. Luz and H. Weder
            (E. Schweizer Festschrift; Göttingen: Vandenhoeck & Ruprecht,
            1983)

ms., mss.   manuscript(s)

MT   (The) Mas(s)oretic Text of the OT or standard Hebrew Bible

MTC   B. M. Metzger, *A Textual Commentary on the Greek New Testa-
            ment* (New York: United Bible Societies, 1971)

MTZ   *Münchener Theologische Zeitschrift*

NAB   *New American Bible* (1970; Revised NT 1986)

NDIEC   *New Documents Illustrating Early Christianity*

NEB   *New English Bible* (1961)

NEv   F. Neirynck, *Evangelica, Gospel Studies—Études d'Évangile* (2
            vols.; Louvain: Peeters, 1982, 1991). Vol. 1 covers articles written
            in 1966–81; vol. 2, 1982–91.

NHL	*The Nag Hammadi Library,* ed. J. M. Robinson (3d ed.; New York: Harper & Row, 1988)
NICOT	New International Commentary on the Old Testament
NJBC	*New Jerome Biblical Commentary,* eds. R. E. Brown et al. (Englewood Cliffs, NJ: Prentice-Hall, 1990). Refs. to articles and sections.
NKZ	*Neue Kirchliche Zeitschrift*
NorTT	*Norsk Teologisk Tidsskrift*
NovT	*Novum Testamentum*
NovTSup	Novum Testamentum, Supplements
NRSV	*New Revised Standard Version of the Bible*
NRT	*Nouvelle Revue Théologique*
NS	new series (of a periodical)
NT	New Testament
NTA	*New Testament Abstracts*
NTAbh	Neutestamentliche Abhandlungen
NTS	*New Testament Studies*
NTT	*Nederlands Theologisch Tijdschrift*
OL	The Old Latin Version of the Bible
OS	The Old Syriac Version of the Bible
OS^{cur}	The Curetonian tradition of the OS
OS^{sin}	The Sinaitic tradition of the OS
OT	Old Testament
OTP	*The Old Testament Pseudepigrapha,* ed. J. H. Charlesworth (2 vols.; Garden City, NY: Doubleday, 1983–85)
par.	parallel(s) in one or both of the other Synoptic Gospels to the passage cited
PBI	The Pontifical Biblical Institute (Rome)
PEFQS	*Palestine Exploration Fund, Quarterly Statement*
PEQ	*Palestine Exploration Quarterly*
PG	Patrologia Graeca-Latina (Migne)
PGJK	*Der Prozess gegen Jesus,* ed. K. Kertelge (QD 112; Freiburg: Herder, 1988)
PIBA	Proceedings of the Irish Biblical Association
PILA	*Political Issues in Luke-Acts,* eds. R. J. Cassidy and P. J. Scharper (Maryknoll: Orbis, 1983)
PL	Patrologia Latina (Migne)
PMK	*The Passion in Mark. Studies on Mark 14–16,* ed. W. H. Kelber (Philadelphia: Fortress, 1976)

PN	Passion Narrative. Most often the Passion Narratives of the canonical Gospels that this book considers to be Mark 14:26–15:47; Matt 26:30–27:66; Luke 22:39–23:56; John 18:1–19:42.
PNT	*Peter in the New Testament,* eds. R. E. Brown et al. (New York: Paulist, 1973)
Q	*Quelle* or source for material shared by Matt and Luke but absent from Mark
QD	Quaestiones Disputatae
RA	*Revue Apologétique*
RArch	*Revue Archéologique*
RB	*Revue Biblique*
RBen	*Revue Bénédictine*
RDLJ	*Reimaging the Death of the Lukan Jesus,* ed. D. D. Sylva (Bonner Biblische Beiträge 73; Frankfurt: Hain, 1990)
REA	*Revue des Études Anciennes*
RechBib	Recherches Bibliques
RechSR	*Recherches de Science Religieuse*
REJ	*Revue des Études Juives*
RevExp	*Review and Expositor*
RevQ	*Revue de Qumran*
RevSR	*Revue des Sciences Religieuses*
RHPR	*Revue d'Histoire et de Philosophie Religieuses*
RHR	*Revue de l'Histoire des Religions*
RivB	*Rivista Biblica*
RQ	*Römische Quartalschrift für Christliche Altertumskunde und Kirchengeschichte*
RSJ	G. Richter, *Studien zum Johannesevangelium,* ed. J. Hainz (BU 13; Regensburg: Pustet, 1977)
RSV	*Revised Standard Version of the Bible*
RThom	*Revue Thomiste*
RTL	*Revue Théologique de Louvain*
RTP	*Revue de Théologie et de Philosophie*
RTPL	*Redaktion und Theologie des Passionsberichtes nach den Synoptikern,* ed. M. Limbeck (Wege der Forschung 481; Darmstadt: Wissenschaftliche Buch., 1981)
RV	*The Revised Version of the Bible*
SANT	Studien zum Alten und Neuen Testament
SB	Sources Bibliques
SBB	Stuttgarter Biblische Beiträge

SBE	Semana Bíblica Española
SBFLA	Studii Biblici Franciscani Liber Annuus
SBJ	*La Sainte Bible de Jérusalem*
SBLA	Society of Biblical Literature Abstracts
SBLDS	Society of Biblical Literature Dissertation Series
SBLMS	Society of Biblical Literature Monograph Series
SBLSBS	Society of Biblical Literature Sources for Biblical Studies
SBLSP	Society of Biblical Literature Seminar Papers
SBS	Stuttgarter Bibelstudien
SBT	Studies in Biblical Theology
SBU	Symbolae Biblicae Upsalienses
SC	Sources Chrétiennes
ScEsp	*Science et Esprit*
SEA	*Svensk Exegetisk Årsbok*
SGM	*Secret Gospel of Mark*
SJT	*Scottish Journal of Theology*
SNTSMS	Society for New Testament Studies Monograph Series
SO	Symbolae Osloenses
SPAW	*Sitzungsberichte der (königlichen) Preussischen Akademie der Wissenschaften*
SPNM	D. P. Senior, *The Passion Narrative According to Matthew* (BETL 39; Leuven Univ., 1975)
SRSTP	*Society and Religion in the Second Temple Period*, eds. M. Avi Yonah and Z. Baras (World History of the Jewish People 8; Jerusalem: Massada, 1977)
ST	*Studia Theologica*
St-B	H. L. Strack and P. Billerbeck, *Kommentar zum Neuen Testament aus Talmud und Midrasch* (6 vols.; Munich: Beck, 1926–61)
StEv	Studia Evangelica (I = TU 73 [1959]; II = TU 87 [1964]; III = TU 88 [1964]; IV = TU 102 [1968]; V = TU 103 [1968]; VI = TU 112 [1973]; VII = TU 126 [1982])
SuS	*Sein und Sendung*
SWJT	*Southwestern Journal of Theology*
TalBab	The Babylonian Talmud
TalJer	The Jerusalem Talmud
TBT	*The Bible Today*
TCSCD	*Theologia Crucis—Signum Crucis*, eds. C. Andresen and G. Klein (E. Dinkler Festschrift; Tübingen: Mohr, 1979)
TD	*Theology Digest*

TDNT	*Theological Dictionary of the New Testament,* eds. G. Kittel and G. Friedrich (10 vols.; Grand Rapids: Eerdmans, 1964–76; German orig. 1928–73)
TG	*Theologie und Glaube*
TJCSM	*The Trial of Jesus—Cambridge Studies in Honour of C.F.D. Moule,* ed. E. Bammel (SBT, 2d series 13; London: SCM, 1970)
TJT	*Toronto Journal of Theology*
TLOTC	*The Language of the Cross,* ed. A. Lacomara (Chicago: Franciscan Herald, 1977)
TLZ	*Theologische Literaturzeitung*
TNTSJ	*The New Testament and Structuralism,* ed. A. M. Johnson, Jr. (Pittsburgh Theol. Monograph 11; Pittsburgh: Pickwick, 1976)
TPNL	V. Taylor, *The Passion Narrative of St Luke* (Cambridge Univ., 1972)
TPQ	*Theologisch-Praktische Quartalschrift*
TQ	*Theologische Quartalschrift*
TS	*Theological Studies*
TSK	*Theologische Studien und Kritiken*
TTK	*Text and Testimony,* eds. T. Baarda et al. (A.F.J. Klijn Festschrift; Kampen: Kok, 1988)
TToday	*Theology Today*
TTZ	*Trierer Theologische Zeitschrift*
TU	Texte und Untersuchungen
TV	*Theologische Versuche,* eds. J. Rogge and G. Schille (Berlin: Evangelische Verlag). In this annual a Roman numeral distinguishing the volume is part of the title.
TZ	*Theologische Zeitschrift*
UBSGNT	*United Bible Societies Greek New Testament*
VC	*Vigiliae Christianae*
VCaro	*Verbum Caro*
VD	*Verbum Domini*
VInt	*Vie Intellectuelle*
VSpir	*Vie Spirituelle*
VT	*Vetus Testamentum*
WD	*Wort und Dienst*
WUNT	Wissenschaftliche Untersuchungen zum Neuen Testament
WW	*Wort und Wahrheit*
ZAGNT	M. Zerwick and M. Grosvenor, *An Analysis of the Greek New Testament* (2 vols.; Rome: PBI, 1974, 1979)

ZAW   *Zeitschrift für die Alttestamentliche Wissenschaft*
ZBG   M. Zerwick, *Biblical Greek* (Rome: PBI, 1963)
ZBTJ   *Zur Bedeutung des Todes Jesu,* ed. F. Viering (Gütersloh: Mohn, 1967)
ZDMG   *Zeitschrift der Deutschen Morgenländischen Gesellschaft*
ZDPV   *Zeitschrift des Deutschen Palästina-Vereins*
ZKT   *Zeitschrift für Katholische Theologie*
ZNW   *Zeitschrift für die Neutestamentliche Wissenschaft*
ZTK   *Zeitschrift für Theologie und Kirche*
ZWT   *Zeitschrift für Wissenschaftliche Theologie*

Standard abbreviations are used for the biblical books and the Dead Sea Scrolls. (For information about the major scrolls, see NJBC 67:82–95.) The OT in general and the psalms in particular are cited according to Hebrew chapter and verse numbers. This holds true even when the LXX is under discussion. It will help readers to know that in the psalms the LXX number is frequently one lower than the Hebrew number, e.g., Hebrew Ps 22 is LXX Ps 21. The KJV and RSV number of a psalm *verse* is frequently one number lower than the Hebrew, e.g., Hebrew Ps 22:2 is RSV Ps 22:1.

The names Mark, Matt, Luke, and John are used both for the writings and the writers. No supposition is made about the identity of the individual evangelists; thus when used for the writer, John means whoever was the principal writer of the Gospel according to John. Mark/Matt is used where Mark and Matt (Gospels or evangelists) are so close that they may be considered as presenting the same data or view.

An asterisk after the name of a ms. of the Bible indicates a reading in the hand of the original copyist as distinct from later additions or changes. Sections (= chapters) in this book are marked by the § sign plus a numeral from 1 to 48 (see the list of Contents above). Cross-references within the book will employ that sign with the appropriate section number; see the running head at the top of pages for easy access to the section indicated.

INTRODUCTION

A description of the interpretative perspective from which this commentary has been written, and a discussion of some general issues about the inter-relationships of the Four Gospels and their Passion Narratives. A bibliography is presented that deals with works on the passion in general and the whole Passion Narrative in each of the individual Gospels.

CONTENTS OF THE INTRODUCTION

§1. THE PERSPECTIVE OF THIS COMMENTARY

Let me express in one clause (with no pretension that it is elegantly enunciated or philosophically profound) the primary aim of this book: *to explain in detail what the evangelists intended and conveyed to their audiences by their narratives of the passion and death of Jesus.* Examining phrase by phrase this statement of goal can serve to introduce the problems of the PN. Then we shall discuss the relationship of this statement to issues of history and theology.

A. *Explaining What the Evangelists Intended and Conveyed to Their Audiences by Their Narratives*

1. The Evangelists

The subject for discussion is the passion of Jesus. Understandably there is a desire to know what Jesus himself said, thought, and did in the final hours of his life. Yet Jesus did not write an account of his passion; nor did anyone who had been present write an eyewitness account. Available to us are four *different* accounts written some thirty to seventy years later in the Gospels of Mark, Matthew, Luke, and John,[1] all of which were dependent on tradition that had come down from an intervening generation or generations.[2] That intervening preGospel tradition was not preserved even if at

---

[1]The dating is approximate, but it is likely that all four Gospels were written in the last half of the 1st cent. AD. The majority of scholars date Mark in the late 60s before the destruction of the Jerusalem Temple, but the number of those who would date it shortly after 70 is increasing (Ernst, Gnilka, Pesch, Schmithals). The dating of Luke-Acts is more disputed than the dating of Matt, but ca. 85 is the most often suggested date for both. John is customarily assigned to the 90s, with final redaction in 100–110. (Occasionally there is a revisionist attempt to move all the Gospels back much earlier, but none has been persuasive enough to gain much following in the scholarly world.) There are also accounts in the "apocryphal gospels" such as *GPet* and *The Gospel of Nicodemus* (*Acts of Pilate*). As will be maintained in the commentary (see APPENDIX I for *GPet*), these are later than the canonical Gospels and do not add a single historical fact to what we can know of the passion from the canonical Gospels. They are important witnesses, however, to how the passion was perceived and narrated at a later period.

[2]Any standard critical introduction to the NT will give the reasons for this conclusion. No Gospel identifies its author. The common designations placed before the Gospels, e.g., "The Gospel according to Matthew," stem from the late 2d cent. and represent an educated estimate of authorship by church scholars of that period who were putting together traditions and guesses pertinent to attribution. To this a caution must be added: The ancient concept of authorship was often less rigor-

times we may be able to detect the broad lines of its content. When we seek to reconstruct it or, even more adventurously, the actual situation of Jesus himself, we are speculating. On the other hand, when we work on the level of the evangelists, we are on much more solid ground, for their accounts need not be reconstructed.

The overall view of the passion presented by each evangelist is a major factor in our study. Comparing the four PNs, we see a general similarity in narrative sequence but considerable difference in content. Each evangelist has organized the material to serve a different presentation of the passion. Interpreting that view must take precedence over speculation about earlier tradition or the situation of Jesus. Thus, for instance, Mark/Matt, Luke, and John[3] report three different sayings as Jesus' last words from the cross. It is tempting to speculate about the preGospel situation, going all the way back to Jesus. Was he responsible for all three sayings (although only one can have been last), or for only one, or for none (in which cases the origin must be sought in the intervening tradition)? Despite that uncertainty, the primary task of the commentator is to explain how the last words reported by Mark/ Matt, by Luke, and by John fit into the presentation of Jesus in PNs of those Gospels.

The background of each evangelist may also affect what he was trying to communicate. All four knew the Jewish Scriptures, but in what language? The Hebrew Scriptures differ considerably at times from the LXX or ancient Greek translation, and from the targums or Aramaic translations (most of which were made later than the LXX). There is evidence that Matt and John may have known Aramaic and/or Hebrew, while Mark and Luke may have known only Greek. The PNs mention places in Jerusalem, e.g., the praetorium, Golgotha. How many of the evangelists had ever been in Jerusalem?[4] Those who had may have written with knowledge; those who had not presumably wrote with imagination. We can see the importance of this issue from the example of the rent veil of the Temple sanctuary, mentioned in three Gospels. There were a number of Temple veils with different functions and decorations (described by Josephus); and scholars have developed different interpretations of the scene, depending on which veil they think was rent and the significance of that veil. But did any evangelist or all of them know that there were different sanctuary veils; had any one of them ever

---

ous than our own, at times amounting to identifying only the authority behind a work (however distant) rather than the writer.

[3]Between Mark and Matt there is less difference than one finds in comparisons among Mark/ Matt, Luke, and John; and so very often there will be three distinct forms of a verse. On the use of these names see the explanation at the end of ABBREVIATIONS.

[4]Among the four, John manifests the most detailed knowledge of Palestine (BGJ 1.xlii).

seen the Temple building or the decorated veil? If one writer had seen the decorated veil while the others had not, the evangelists may have had different understandings of the rending of the veil. In commenting on four presentations of the same scene, therefore, similarities must not blind us to the individuality of each evangelist.

2. Intended and Conveyed

The evangelists wrote some nineteen hundred years ago in a social and thought world quite different from our own. Literalist interpreters of the Bible seem to think that the Gospel texts can be read as if Jesus were addressing himself to audiences today. In fact, however, Jesus was a Jew of the first third of the 1st cent. AD who spoke, thought, and acted as such.[5] From the literature of his time we may acquire some knowledge of his likely mindset, but we cannot understand it in the way we understand our own thought world. The same would be true of our relationship to the evangelists, although with added difficulties, for we know more of Jesus than we know of them. For instance, we know with probability that they lived in the last half of the 1st cent., but whether they were Jews or Gentiles we are not sure.[6] Granted those limitations, what the evangelists intended or conveyed by their writings is not an unintelligible mystery. Their words and sentences for the most part make sense, and the story is not complicated. Occasionally we have to guess at motives or rationale, but it is possible to understand a good part of what the evangelists intended to convey to their 1st-cent. audiences.

As for the relevance of knowing that, most today are interested in what the Gospels mean for their own lives. Through the centuries Christian theology and proclamation have sought to translate to new times and situations the message proclaimed in the Gospels, and I hope this commentary will help in that task. In the best of all possible worlds a commentary might itself

---

[5]Some might consider this a suspect thesis of historical criticism; yet it reflects the most orthodox Christian understanding of the incarnation whereby God's Son became man at a particular period of history and was like all his contemporaries in everything except sin. Christian orthodoxy would not have problems with what I have written above unless the adjective "only" were added before "a Jew." The Bible, as word of God, is believed to have meaning for all and in that sense to "speak" to all; but the historical words of Jesus were spoken at a particular time in a particular language (Aramaic) to a particular audience, and reported in writing at a later time in another language (Greek) to another audience, and are being read today in still another language by another audience. One must take into account all those differences as they affect meaning.

[6]I am judging the Gospel authors from the traces left in the texts they wrote, not from any traditions about their identity. I see no major reason to think that those who wrote Mark, Matt, and John were not Jews. The author of Luke knows the Greek Bible well but seemingly not family Jewish customs (in 2:22 he indicates that both parents were purified after the birth of a male child); he might have been a convert to Judaism before coming to believe in Jesus.

do the task of modernizing, not only by elucidating the ancient message but also by theologizing and proclaiming to meet current needs. Certainly commentators cannot afford to ignore the more general contemporary issues; indeed those issues often shape questions they pose to the texts. (For instance, this commentary will not ignore the way in which guilt and punishment for the crucifixion of Jesus have been inflicted on Jews by Christians, not the least in our own times.) Yet the readers of a commentary are diverse; they live in different situations and perhaps even in different decades of rapidly shifting times. No single commentator can imagine the needs and interests of all who would read about the passion and death of Jesus. Therefore my primary goal is to offer solid understanding of the meaning intended and conveyed by the evangelists themselves in the 1st cent. and thus to supply material for reflective interpretation of the passion by the readers themselves.

In that goal I am firmly resisting the idea that the only meaning is contemporary relevance. Instead, the meaning that current audiences take from the Gospels must be related to (but not confined to or necessarily identical with) the meaning intended and conveyed by the evangelists to their audiences. This relationship belongs to the self-understanding of the religious groups that gave us the Scriptures. Perhaps continuity with Shakespeare's world is not an essential factor in the interpretation of Shakespeare's plays; but the theological status of the Bible is quite different. Jews look on themselves as being in continuity with the Israelites addressed by Moses and the prophets and sages of the Hebrew Scriptures, and so they are bound by the same divine word. Similarly, the theological insistence of Christians on apostolicity implies continuity with the generation that proclaimed the content of the Gospels in the 1st cent.—the distrust of a totally other gospel goes far back (Gal 1:6–9). Those who believe that the biblical writers were inspired by God to convey a message in writing will be all the more insistent that the meaning for today has to be related to the meaning intended and conveyed by the inspired authors. (Indeed, they may have to be convinced that there can be a plus value, i.e., a meaning for today that goes beyond what was envisaged in the 1st cent. because questions are being posed to the Scriptures that never entered the minds of the ancient writers.)

In insisting that it is both possible and important to know the ancient message, I have consistently used the two verbs "intend" and "convey." This is an attempt to do justice to a complex situation. The importance of "convey" is relatively obvious. The evangelists certainly knew more of the Christian tradition about Jesus than they chose to convey in their Gospels; John 21:25 affirms that. Therefore we should maintain a certain distrust of negative arguments from silence, as if the failure to write meant the failure to know. Yet exegesis can expound only what the evangelists conveyed in writing. The rest is speculation.

A more delicate issue is the relationship between what the written words convey and what the evangelists intended. There is a span of possibilities: According to the skill of the writer, a writing may convey what the author wished it to convey, or something less, or the opposite, or something other than the author wished or foresaw. The last instance is often exemplified in what was called above the "plus value"—new generations see possibilities in the text that are harmonious with but also beyond the author's intention. Though important, plus values are not a primary focus of this commentary. My concern is above all with the meaning that emerges from positing a general correspondence between what the author intended and what he conveyed. It is by exception, then, that I shall have to alert readers to instances where what the words seem to convey may not be what the author intended. One may well object, "How can a modern interpreter know that ancient authors intended something different from what their words convey?" Sometimes the only key is in other passages. For example, Luke does not report a scourging of Jesus by Roman soldiers as do Mark/Matt; accordingly, the antecedent of the "they" in 23:26 who led Jesus away to be crucified is grammatically "the chief priests and the rulers and the people" of 23:13. Many commentators would read this passage as a deliberate Lucan attempt to make the Jews the agents of the crucifixion and to exculpate the Romans. Yet careless use of antecedents is not infrequent in writing. Indeed, Luke is sometimes a careless editor: In omitting the Roman scourging, he has not noticed that Jesus' own prophecy that he would be scourged (18:33) now remains unfulfilled. Moreover, Luke eventually makes clear that there were (Roman) soldiers involved in the crucifixion (23:36), and elsewhere he indicates that the Gentiles killed Jesus (18:32–33; cf. Acts 4:25–27). Thus the grammatical sense of what Luke wrote very likely was not what he intended to convey. The commentator must take that difference into account.

Nevertheless, one should resort only rarely to such interpretation distinguishing between what was written and what was intended. Too often commentators detect contradictions in the Gospel narratives and assume that one writer could not have been responsible for the text as it now stands or that the writer combined diverse sources without recognizing that they were irreconcilable. Such a solution is not impossible, but probabilities lie in another direction: The account as it now stands made sense to someone in antiquity, and so what seems contradictory to modern interpreters may not be really contradictory. For instance, some commentators contend that the events placed by Mark/Matt between the arrest of Jesus and the crucifixion are too crowded to have happened in one night. Yet does not rearranging that material over a longer period of time undo the intention of the evangelists to describe the whole procedure as hasty and crowded because the authorities wanted to have Jesus executed without any chance that the people would react and thus cause a disturbance (Mark 14:2; Matt 26:5)? Again, some would find a contradiction between Mark 14:50, which says of the disciples, "And having left him, they all fled," and Mark 14:51, which still has a certain young man following Jesus, and Mark 14:54, which has Peter following him from a distance. In this type of narrative are these really contradictory, or are they cumulative ways of illustrating the failure of the disciples? All fled or went away denying Jesus, including even those who, by still following, attempted not to flee.

What the evangelists "intended and conveyed" is the key to the meaning of their PNs and thus the primary concern of this commentary. Although we can be quite positive about the possibility of determining that meaning, the examples that I have given were meant to alert the readers to pitfalls and to gain sympathy for what may seem lengthy attempts to avoid them.

3. To Their Audiences

Another part of the description given above of the aim of the book pertains to the audiences[7] envisaged by the evangelists. Although it is difficult to identify the locale of each Gospel's audience, sometimes their background or outlook can be detected from the evangelists' presuppositions in dealing with them.[8] Working along those lines, I would argue that comprehensibility by the ancient audience should play a role in our interpretative judgments. If we may return to an example given above, I doubt that Luke's audience

---

[7]Since the Gospels are written works, we may think of "readers." However, since few copies of the Gospels would have been available, probably most early Christians heard them read, hence "hearers." Hearing the Gospels read publicly rather than reading them personally and privately was, arguably, the majority situation throughout most of Christian history. I use the word "audience" (despite its root meaning) to cover both readers and hearers.

[8]Among the most frequently suggested sites for the addressees are *Rome* or Syria for Mark; the *Antioch* area for Matt; Antioch or Asia Minor or *Greece* for Luke; and *Ephesus* or Syria for John. The italicized sites would represent my preferences, but nothing in this commentary depends on choosing one over another. Nevertheless, I shall point out that Rome, as the site where we know there had been a major persecution of Christians before 70 (with some Christians betraying others), would make great sense of Mark's stress on failure in the testing provided by Jesus' passion (see R. H. Smith, "Darkness" 325–27). And it is important to ask how, given the address to Theophilus in Acts 1:1, Luke's PN would sound to an educated Hellenized audience in the Greco-Roman world (see Kany, "Lukanische," who would envisage Luke being read by someone in Ephesus ca. AD 170). In literary criticism a distinction is made between "implied" readers (those envisaged by the text) and the actual or historical audience. If the evangelists knew something about those addressed, there would have been a certain coalescence of these potentially diverse readers. In almost all instances I discern the audience from the text.

would have understood 23:26 ("They led him away [to the place where they crucified him]") to mean that the Jews crucified Jesus, despite the antecedent thirteen verses earlier; for I think it plausible that all Christians learned from the start that Jesus was crucified by the Romans. In defense of this view I am not presupposing that Luke's audience had Mark's Gospel to fall back on, but I do contend that the first time they read/heard what Luke wrote to them was scarcely their initial encounter with the outline of Jesus' passion. Passages like I Cor 11:23 and 15:3 show that when Paul converted people at Corinth, he shared with them some of the early tradition about Jesus' death, and surely that would have included crucifixion by the rulers of this age (2:8). Modern church audiences, hearing "They led him away [to the place where they crucified him]," would never think of Jews as the "they" unless the issue of an antecedent were called to their attention. They would interpret what they hear through what they already know. I doubt that it was different in antiquity, and so there will be many instances where the issue of plausible audience comprehension helps us to decide which interpretation is more likely.

By way of another example, let me recall the issue of different Temple veils with their functions and symbolisms. I warned that one had to ask whether a particular evangelist knew of such plurality. One also has to ask whether an evangelist's audience would know of it. In the case of Mark, since simple Jewish customs had to be explained to the audience (7:3–4), surely his audience did not. Therefore, in that Gospel I doubt that one can interpret the rending of the veil of the sanctuary to mean more than the words themselves would imply to anyone who had ever been in a temple, namely, that a veil which partitioned off the sacred place in the Temple of Jerusalem had been rent from top to bottom, thus depriving that place of what made it God's sanctuary, set off from other places in the enclave. Thus once again the likely comprehension attributable to the audience affects exegesis.

A particular debate centers on the extent to which the audiences of the individual evangelists understood "Scripture," i.e., the sacred Jewish writings of the period before Jesus to which the evangelists frequently appeal.[9] Would they catch a subtle allusion? If a passage is cited, would they be aware of the OT context, so that more of the pericope than the cited line would spring to mind? Would vocabulary used by the evangelist in a cited Scripture passage evoke in the readers' minds other passages of Scripture containing the same vocabulary, as scholars sometimes assume in their comments?

[9]Most of these writings would be known by Christians as OT (provided that the term includes the Roman Catholic deuterocanonical books or the Protestant apocrypha); yet occasionally there may be an appeal to works of the intertestamental period that would be considered apocrypha by Christians and Jews both.

Would the audiences know living Jewish tradition that had expanded the meaning of a biblical text? (See, for instance, APPENDIX VI and the redemptive aspect in the Aqedah theme that would reinterpret the sacrifice of Isaac.) One cannot simply assume affirmative answers; and the answer may be different for each Gospel, since early Christian audiences were not uniform. Nevertheless, the authors of NT epistles often write as if they expect their Gentile Christian audiences to possess a wide knowledge of the Scriptures; and by analogy, therefore, interpretations of the PNs based on an audience awareness of scriptural background deserve consideration. Overall, then, combing the Gospel to detect the likely mentality of its audience is not an easy task (and on a particular issue may be an impossible task); but it must be attempted to supply a control on the tendency of scholarly commentators to assume that what they have learned about Judaism in NT times was surely known by the ancient audience to whom a Gospel was directed.

4. By Their Narratives of the Passion and Death of Jesus

Readers of this commentary will be reminded repeatedly that we are dealing with narratives. The division of the commentary into acts and scenes is meant to underline my view that the passion accounts are truly dramatic narratives. Lunn, "Christ's," argues that the PNs fit into the theatrical category of "tragedy." Indeed, at times John even supplies elements of staging, e.g., in the outside-inside organization of the Pilate trial. The passion "from Gethsemane to the grave," as I alerted readers in the opening line of this book, is the longest consecutive action recounted of Jesus, quite different from the series of vignettes that constitute the ministry.[10] That fact must play a role in our interpretative judgments. For instance, an impressive number of happenings occur in threes. In Mark/Matt at Gethsemane, he first comes with the body of disciples and speaks to them; second, he takes along Peter, James, and John and speaks to them; last, he goes off by himself and speaks to God. After he has prayed, Jesus returns three times to find the disciples sleeping. In all the Gospels Peter denies Jesus three times. In Mark the crucifixion scene involves the third, sixth, and ninth hours; and in the Synoptics Jesus is mocked three times as he hangs on the cross, even as in John three groups of people deal with the crucified Jesus. The use of "three" is a well-known feature in storytelling, most familiar to English-speaking audiences

---

[10]Occasionally a Synoptic evangelist has a theme connecting several episodes, e.g., Mark narrates miracle stories as a way of pointing out the difficulty the disciples have in understanding. Yet the people who are the subjects of the stories are not interrelated, and there is no development of their characters. The long episodes in John (Samaritan woman, man born blind, raising of Lazarus) come closer to being short narratives.

in jokes (English-Irish-Scot, priest-minister-rabbi; etc.). Scholars rightly assume that it is unlikely that everything happened so conveniently in threes and so seek to reconstruct the preGospel history. On the Mount of Olives Luke has Jesus come back only once to find the disciples sleeping. Was that original, and do the three times of Mark/Matt represent a conforming to storytelling patterns? Or has Luke simplified down to one to avoid portraying the disciples in such a bad light? A factor to be considered in answering is whether this episode ever circulated other than as a narrative. Is it likely that the earliest preachers simply mentioned that the disciples slept? What evangelistic function would such a report have? Or was the earliest reference to it in a narrative form that brought out human inability to accept the cross? If the latter, there may never have been in circulation a report that was not already influenced by the rule of three that governs narratives. This type of answer, it should be noted, does not solve the issue of history; it establishes the oldest preGospel form traceable.

Neglecting the narrative form of the passion[11] can give rise to questions that miss the mark, e.g., how can the evangelist know what the Synoptic Jesus prayed for in Gethsemane when the disciples were asleep? Such a question (at times asked with a sneer) fails to understand the literary nature of what is being related. In most narratives the omniscient narrator tells the readers things about the protagonists without ever explaining where this information was gained. In the instance cited, the more apropos question would concern the relationship of the Gethsemane prayer to wider traditions about the way Jesus prayed, because a memory that Jesus cried out to God when facing death (Heb 5:7) may, to suit the conventions of narrative, have been filled in dramatically from memories of Jesus' style of praying. To take another example, in Mark/Matt as soon as Pilate sees Jesus, he asks, "Are

---

[11]Although I shall stress the narrative aspect, I do not pretend to apply in my study the technicalities of structural and/or literary criticism. I have read literature on the passion from experts in those fields, and I am not overly impressed by the results some have achieved. To my embarrassment, at times the jargon of the hermeneutical specialization leaves me behind. Bucher, "Elements," castigates traditional exegesis for not caring about the interaction of significant elements within the global context of the PN. Then he explains (p. 836) what his structural analysis will do: "The analysis would thus lead toward the construction of several homogeneous levels of meaning, corresponding even, in certain cases, to the superposition of several partially autonomous layers of narratives. Following Greimas' method it will be furthermore necessary to describe the paradigmatic relations existing at each level, or in other words to locate the structuring or disjunctive presence of the positive and negative terms of the semic categories that analysis will be able to identify. The existence of partially independent layers of narrative will find its main verification in the discovery of places of diachronic transformation. These places of transformation that [sic] make it possible for narrative to generate a before vs. an afterwards. The second step would then consist in elucidating the reciprocal places and function of these diachronic transformations. The concrete complex narrative would then finally find its representation as an abstract system of interrelated levels." Despite my deep concern for narrative and its structure, I have no idea whether I meet what is envisaged in those words.

you the King of the Jews?" How did Pilate find this out? Presumably he had never encountered Jesus before, and we are told nothing of a report having been made to him by the Jewish authorities. But is this a serious objection in such a fast-flowing narrative that does not supply elaborate connectives? Are not the readers expected to assume (as audiences have for centuries) that the Jewish leaders supplied Pilate with material against Jesus (something that Luke and John spell out in different ways)? These examples lead into the next subsection, since a failure to recognize the thrust of narrative is often based on a confused understanding of the role of history in the PN.

B. *The Role of History*

The statement is often made that Christianity is a historical religion, meaning that it is not based on myths about gods who never existed but on the story of someone who lived at a particular time in a particular place among real people.[12] (In application to the passion one can characterize as bedrock history that Jesus of Nazareth was crucified at Jerusalem at the end of the first third of the 1st cent. AD when Pontius Pilate was governor.) Too often, however, that truth has led people to assume that everything related in the NT about Jesus has to be historical. The problem is compounded when it is assumed that the Gospels, the NT writings centered on his life, are historical biographies, despite the fact that two of them tell us nothing about Jesus' birth and relatively nothing about his parentage,[13] and none of them tell us about the many years of his life before he began his ministry. In this commentary I shall work with the understanding that the Gospels are distillations of earlier Christian preaching and teaching about Jesus.[14] The individual evangelists organized what they took over from such a background in order to communicate to their audiences an interpretation of Jesus that would nourish faith and life (as John 20:31 states explicitly).

[12]A sense attested in the oldest ecumenical creed, which speaks of the Son of God as one who was born of the virgin Mary and suffered under Pontius Pilate.

[13]Mark never gives the name of Jesus' father; John never gives the name of his mother. I recognize that Luke-Acts has something of the form and style of ancient biographies and histories; but that structure does not mean that Luke's goal is genuinely biographical or historical in the way we understand those terms in contemporary literature. While the structure matches Luke's professed purpose in 1:3 to write an orderly account, that very statement of purpose indicates that Luke is dealing with the same kind of tradition dealt with by other writers and that his purpose is evangelistic (1:2,4).

[14]In John another factor is detectable. During arguments with synagogue leaders and trials that led to the expulsion of Johannine Christians from the local synagogue (9:22; 16:2), the Jesus tradition was organized as testimony or witness to respond to questioning, e.g., 1:19–27; 5:16–47.

1. Is There History Underlying the Gospel Passion Narratives?

If this origin is true, what relationship have the Gospel reports to what actually happened in Jesus' lifetime? One can focus that question by asking about the historical implications of insisting on the narrative form of the passion. Opposite ends of the spectrum of contemporary Christian attitudes toward the Bible often agree that the language of "narrative" (or of "story") means that what actually happened becomes irrelevant. For that reason ultraconservatives tend to distrust stress on narrative and ultraliberals tend to embrace it. I see no need for such a dichotomy between acknowledging the narrative form of the passion and maintaining a respect for historical issues.

I have already said that I do not think of the evangelists themselves as eyewitnesses of the passion; nor do I think that eyewitness memories of Jesus came down to the evangelists without considerable reshaping and development. Yet as we move back from the Gospel narratives to Jesus himself, ultimately there were eyewitnesses and earwitnesses who were in a position to know the broad lines of Jesus' passion. He was accompanied in his ministry by a group of disciples known as the Twelve,[15] and there is no reason whatsoever to doubt that the arrest of Jesus was the occasion of his being separated from them. It is inconceivable that they showed no concern about what happened to Jesus after the arrest. True, there is no Christian claim that they were present during the legal proceedings against him, Jewish or Roman; but it is absurd to think that some information was not available to them about why Jesus was hanged on a cross. The whole purpose of crucifixion, after all, was to publicize that certain crimes would be severely punished. (That is the sense in which I include "earwitness": hearing what was publicly said about the condemnation of Jesus.) The crucifixion itself was public, and nothing suggests that the burial was secret. Thus from the earliest days available historical raw material could have been developed into a PN extending from the arrest to the burial, no matter what form it might receive in the course of evangelistic use[16] and how it might have been embellished and added to by Christian imagination.

---

[15]Their existence at the time of the resurrection is fixed in a tradition that Paul received most likely in the 30s (I Cor 15:5).

[16]Let us look at a possible instance of the form being given to material. There is clear parallelism between Mark's account of the Jewish trial and his account of the Roman trial: Each has a chief interrogator and a key "Are you . . . ?" question, followed at the end by a mockery. One group of scholars would regard the contents of each as pure Marcan creation; another group would regard the Jewish trial as a Marcan creation based on the pattern of Roman trial which embodied earlier tradition; still another group (with whom I agree) would regard both trial scenes as Christian composi-

Some scholars, however, insist that the evangelistic enterprise means that Christians had no interest in historical raw material whether or not it was available. In a series of important contributions, Dibelius gave primary attention to the formative role of OT Scripture in the development of the PNs. Such a role is quite understandable if we remember that followers of Jesus were interested in the significance of what happened: How was Jesus' death on the cross meaningful in the divine plans for God's people? The only language in which they could answer that question was scriptural, i.e., the descriptions of the suffering just one in the psalms and the prophets. Too often we tend to speak of the early Christians "turning to" Scripture, implying that they turned to the Bible to look up relevant passages even as we do.[17] Rather their minds were imbued with biblical images and phrases, so that scriptural motifs naturally oriented their interest and understanding. The first followers of Jesus would have known many things about crucifixion in general and almost surely some of the details about Jesus' crucifixion, e.g., what kind of cross was employed. Nevertheless, what is preserved in the narrative is mostly what echoes Scripture (division of garments, offering of vinegary wine, final words of Jesus).

The issue of scriptural background becomes more debatable in views like those of Koester and J. D. Crossan, who have gone beyond Dibelius. While he allowed the existence of tradition, these scholars dismiss any rooting of the passion in Christian memory. Koester[18] states with assurance that in the beginning there was only belief that Jesus' passion and resurrection happened according to the Scriptures so that "the very first narratives of Jesus' suffering and death would not have made any attempt to remember what actually happened." Crossan (*Cross* 405) goes even further: "It seems to me most likely that those closest to Jesus knew almost nothing about the details of the event. They knew only that Jesus had been crucified, outside Jerusalem, at the time of Passover, and probably through some conjunction of imperial and sacerdotal authority." He does not explain why he thinks this "most likely," granted the well-founded tradition that those closest to Jesus had followed him for a long period of time, day and night. Did they suddenly

tions (Marcan or pre-Marcan) based on a relatively simple tradition that involved in the death of Jesus both the high priest and Pilate and that reported *with translation* the basic issues that worried those two worthies (Messiah in relation to God, and Messiah equaling king).

[17]Actually, in some circles and sometimes at a later NT stage there does seem to have been a studied inquiry of Scripture, as visible in the formula citations of Matt and John: All these things happened in order to fulfill the words written by the prophet (followed by citation). Where in a series, e.g., in Matt's infancy narrative, those citations vary among the LXX and the MT (and perhaps an unknown popular text), study is implied.

[18]"Apocryphal" 127; see also Denker, *Theologiegeschichtliche* 58–77.

lose all interest, not even taking the trouble to inquire about what must have been a most traumatic moment of their lives?

Frequently appeal is made to Paul in I Cor 15:3–5: "For I gave over to you as of first importance what I received: that Christ died for our sins according to the Scriptures, and that he was buried, and that he was raised on the third day according to the Scriptures, and that he appeared to Cephas, then to the Twelve . . ." Yet how does this passage support the thesis that the earliest followers of Jesus knew or cared nothing about what happened and created the whole narrative according to the Scriptures? Two of the basic four facts mentioned in the passage (burial, appearances) are not designated as "according to the Scriptures"; and so events without scriptural support were indeed recalled. Paul's listing of those to whom Jesus appeared was presumably based in whole or part on their own testimony, and so there was a place for eyewitness memories. As for the fact that Jesus "died for our sins according to the Scriptures," the proponents of scripturally oriented invention cannot seriously maintain that Jesus' death on the cross was invented. Is it not likely, then, that what was interpreted through the Scriptures is the salvific aspect of the death—a horrible death that was paradoxically part of God's plan?[19] And again is it not the "on the third day" aspect of the resurrection rather than the underlying event that has called forth the reference to the Scriptures? In other words there is no evidence in the Pauline formula that scriptural reflection caused the creation of the basic incidents of the passion; far more plausibly it caused the selection and interpretation of certain features in an outline of death, burial, resurrection, and appearance that had been dictated by the early Christian memory of what happened.[20] Moreover, this appeal to I Cor 15 often overlooks the parallel Pauline passage in 11:23ff.: "For I received from the Lord what I also gave over to you: that the Lord Jesus in the night in which he was given over took bread and, having given thanks, broke . . ." No reference to Scripture is made; yet there is a tradition of a eucharistic meal on the same night in which Jesus was given

[19]See Bartsch, "Bedeutung" 88–90; he insists that from I Cor 15:3–5 we can learn about the preGospel passion, for the Pauline formula is meant to identify the risen one with the *crucified*.

[20]In studying the Gospel use of Scripture there has always been an issue of "Which came first, the chicken or the egg?" Did narrators create incidents to give scriptural flavor, or from incidents that occurred did narrators select and dramatize those capable of echoing the Scriptures? Conceivably there were instances of each procedure, but several factors point to the latter as the dominant practice. In the *pesharim* or commentaries of the Dead Sea Scrolls, which represent contemporary Jewish procedure, actual events in the history and life of the Dead Sea community (verifiable from their other works and elsewhere) are seen as fulfilling Scripture. In inner Synoptic comparisons there are controllable examples where facts have been dramatized by the addition of a scriptural reference. For instance, few scholars would deny the historicity of the tradition that Jesus started a ministry of proclaiming the kingdom of God in Galilee, in the Capernaum area near the lake (Mark 1:14,16,21). Matt (4:13–16) sees this happening to fulfill the Isaian passage (8:23–9:1) about Galilee of the Gentiles. Observably he did not use the Scripture to invent the occurrence but to gloss and explain it.

over, i.e., the basic Synoptic outline of the Last Supper and the arrest. The early Christians, then, not only could but did remember basic items in sequence about the death of Jesus.

2. Difficulties in Detecting History

Nevertheless, as we seek to uncover aspects of how Jesus' death actually occurred, we must recognize that there are difficulties flowing both from limitations in our methodology and from the subject matter itself.

Methods Used for Detecting Historical Material Underlying the Gospels. Scholars have developed a number of criteria for judging what comes from Jesus' ministry as distinct from developments of the picture of that ministry attributable to early preaching and writing. Some of these criteria are of use in studying the passion, provided we keep carefully in mind their limitations. More of the Gospel PNs is likely to have been historical than our methods allow us to prove; in particular the methods break down where the content is substantially historical but the vocalization of the contents has been adapted in the subsequent course of preaching to new generations.

(1) Multiple Attestation. The criterion I shall invoke most frequently[21] is the appearance of an event or saying in many of the available independent witnesses to the passion. This criterion has limitations, however. If besides the NT writings one were to include under the rubric of independent witnesses Jewish and Roman writings (see §18E below), scarcely any aspect of the passion except the crucifixion is attested by all witnesses.[22] For instance, neither Paul nor TalBab *Sanhedrin* 43a mention Pilate's activity in the execution,[23] and Tacitus (*Annals* 15.44) and I Tim 6:13 do not mention the Jewish role. The use of this criterion is hindered by the fact that it is not easy to determine which witnesses of the passion are truly independent. Among the Gospels, in §2 below I shall explain why I accept the thesis that Matt and Luke are dependent on Mark but John is not. Mark and John often narrate the same event but with a significant difference that is hard to explain as a deliberate change by the evangelists, and so their agreement may indicate an early tradition that had developed in different directions by the time the Gos-

---

[21]For the moment, let me speak of criteria that point to the preGospel period without being specific as to whether they point to early tradition or, beyond that, to history. Later, I shall emphasize that these are different stages, so that early preGospel tradition is not necessarily history.

[22]In digesting that fact one should remember that silence does not necessarily mean denial or ignorance.

[23]This silence may be of limited significance. The postPauline passage in I Tim 6:13 does mention Pilate (perhaps indicating knowledge of Pilate's role within earlier Pauline tradition), and one may doubt that TalBab *Sanhedrin* 43a is truly independent of the Gospels.

pels were written. Yet there are scholars who think John drew from Mark and who accordingly would dismiss these agreements as not meeting the criterion of multiple attestation.

(2) Coherence. Sometimes a pertinent incident reported by a Gospel does not have multiple attestation but is coherent with another element that does. In my judgment this criterion needs to be used with extreme care since coherence could explain why the incident was imaginatively created. For instance, when Jesus is arrested, John alone identifies as Simon Peter the person who cuts off the servant's ear. Such solitary bravado is coherent with Peter's speaking and acting on many other occasions as attested in all the Gospels. That coherence gives the identification of Peter as the sword-wielder verisimilitude:[24] It is the kind of thing that Peter would do. All that may mean, however, is that if one were going to guess who the unnamed sword-wielder was, one might well guess Peter; it is not a real argument that in fact Peter did wield the sword. There are times, however, where coherence and multiple attestation can be helpfully combined. For example, in very different ways Mark/Matt, John, and Acts agree in relating to Jesus' death his threatening attitude toward the Temple sanctuary. That is coherent with solid historical evidence that in the period before AD 70 disputes over the Temple constituted the most frequent single factor in religious violence among Jews.

(3) Embarrassment. If something reported about Jesus was embarrassing to the early church, the early preachers or the evangelists are not likely to have invented it. That Judas, one of the Twelve, gave Jesus over to his enemies, that (most of) the disciples did not remain with Jesus during the passion, and that Peter denied him were all embarrassing to early Christians. Consequently, it is argued that these elements, which are also multiply attested, are likely to have been historical. While there may be truth in that, one must always allow that it could have been useful to develop one or the other scene of failure as a theological illustration. For instance, it seems embarrassing to have Jesus as he faced death praying to be delivered from the cup or the hour;[25] yet one of the goals of the description may have been to teach Christians that facing death constitutes a trial that may challenge even sincere commitment.

(4) Discontinuity or Dissimilarity. If an item pertinent to Jesus has no parallel in Judaism or in early Christian thought, history is the most plausible

---

[24]Readers should be alerted that I shall use the term "verisimilitude" with the understanding that it is not the same as historical likelihood.

[25]Determining what was embarrassing in the PNs becomes less subjective if we begin with items fastened on by Jewish or pagan polemic against the plausibility of Christianity. The flight of the

origin for it. This is a criterion I hesitate to invoke since one must allow for creativity. There is little evidence in the nonGospel literature of the NT that early Christians confessed Jesus as the Son of Man or that there was a set Jewish expectation centered on that title. Accordingly, some scholars would argue that the appearance of "Son of Man" on the lips of Jesus in Mark, Q, and John is best explained by positing that he himself did use the title. Yet there is no way of knowing that Jesus' usage was not magnified within the development of the Gospel traditions, thus giving the title in the written Gospels a frequency and applications that are not historical. A greater problem about this criterion is that it is inapplicable to a very high percentage of material that might well be historical. Since Jesus was a Jew of the first third of the 1st cent., it is inconceivable that much of his language and symbolism would not have had parallels in the Judaism of that time. Since those who accompanied him later went forth to proclaim him and thus to shape much of early Christian thought, it is to be expected that there would be much in common between Jesus' historical words and attitudes and those of the early Christians. Exclusion of such common material from our discussion of the historical Jesus (even under the rubric of being careful to the extreme) has to distort the results. A particular problem concerns the use of Scripture. Both Jews who did not believe in Jesus and early Christians who did believe in him appealed to Scripture to interpret significant happenings. If we used the criterion of discontinuity, it would mean that no use of Scripture involved in the Gospel accounts of the passion could be attributed to Jesus with certitude. Yet I judge it inconceivable that historically Scripture did not supply background and vocabulary for Jesus' self-understanding. Accordingly when a particular scriptural theme, e.g., the mocked and despised suffering just one, is widely and multiply attested in NT writings, there is reason to think that the theme may well be in continuity with Jesus' historical self-understanding. I admit that certitude may not be possible; but in the matter of historicity probability or likelihood is an important factor, protecting the picture of Jesus from the distortions and unlikelihoods produced by too rigorous a quest for certitude.

Limitations in Our Knowledge of the Times in Which Jesus Died. Not surprisingly, detailed information about Palestine two thousand years ago is necessarily limited; but in treating the passion we encounter a special set of problems. I have tried to treat these problems with proper sensitivity, but it would be impossible to be expert in all. Let me illustrate in three key areas.

---

disciples, denials by Peter, betrayal by Judas, and Jesus' prayer for deliverance were all objects of scorn in such polemic.

(1) Roman law certainly played a role when Jesus was tried and executed by a Roman prefect of Judea. While later jurists of the empire supply us with ample information about procedure in capital cases, virtually all of that documentation comes under the heading of "ordinary law" dealing with the treatment of Roman citizens, especially in Italy or well-established senatorial provinces. Jesus was not a Roman citizen; Judea was a newly established imperial province. Rules guiding the actions of a Roman governor would have been spelled out in the emperor's edicts setting up the province of Judea (an event of Jesus' lifetime), but no copy of those edicts was preserved. Thus even such an essential question as "Who in Judea held the right to execute and for what crimes?" is subject to debate. From Josephus one gets the impression that in handling the Jews Roman governors did whatever they deemed necessary to preserve good order and Roman authority—correctable only later if the emperor thought the behavior of the officials had been abusive. "Extraordinary law" (never codified) is the term often used to cover the procedures they adopted. In analyzing the Roman legalities in the treatment meted out to Jesus, then, we must proceed not so much from codified Roman law[26] as from analogies in historical accounts of the 1st cent. AD that illustrate how governors acted.

(2) Jewish law played a role in the execution of Jesus (see John 19:7: "We have a law"). The Mishna (codified ca. AD 200) offers detailed information about matters that are quite pertinent in a discussion of the passion, e.g., about the Passover meal and the legal procedure for trying capital cases. Yet we are hampered at the moment by a major controversy among Jewish scholars as to the applicability of mishnaic law to the period before AD 70.[27] Indeed, almost every aspect of Jewish polity in the time of Jesus is debated. Were the Pharisees a major force? What relationship did the Pharisees have to the later rabbis who produced the Mishna? To what extent were Galilean peasants influenced by the religious authorities in Jerusalem? How fixed a body was the Sanhedrin and what was its makeup? By what legal outlook, Pharisee or Sadducee, did it judge? Was there another official Jewish executive and Jewish body, the Beth Din or Boulē, consisting of scholars and thus closer in makeup to the Sanhedrin described in the Mishna? How histori-

[26]Where appropriate the *Digest* of Justinian (DJ) will be cited, but with caution. There are unhappy examples of experts in Roman law reading the Gospel accounts of Jesus' trial and judging it historical on the basis of much later opinions assembled in DJ. Beyond the danger inherent in finding parallels between situations separated by centuries, insufficient attention is paid to the Gospel genre and the possibility that in a retelling of the story, the picture of the trial of Jesus before Pilate might have been made conformable to well-known practices of the ordinary law.

[27]Beyond the Mishna some commentators on the passion invoke examples from every stage in the development of Jewish law and lore, bringing into the discussion examples from a period a thousand years after Jesus' time, on the grounds that often later documents reflect earlier situations. I shall alert readers to the likely inapplicability of such later "parallels."

cally reliable was Josephus in matters in which he was trying to influence Roman polity, and are the differences between accounts in the *War* and the *Antiquities* (written some twenty-five years later) accidental or deliberate? To what extent was Philo writing propaganda when he criticized Pilate? Christian critical scholars have spent a century and a half probing the tendencies and reliability of the Christian records. The moment in which this commentary is being written happens to be a time when the critical Jewish examination of Jewish records has reached high tide.

(3) The importance of the political and social scene has become a major issue in the study of the Gospel PNs. Indeed, social study has reached a very scientific level, involving social facts (information from archaeology and various kinds of historical research), social history (combining the facts with the history of the community known from literature), and social analysis (discerning the forces that shaped the social history). Such a highly scientific approach lies beyond the possibilities of this commentary, but I shall try to take cognizance of some of the results applicable to the PNs. The issue is of importance because books drawing on social studies of Palestine in Jesus' time have been the subject of excited discussion even in the popular press, especially when the picture of Jesus that emerges from these studies is found sympathetic by movements on our contemporary scene, e.g., Jesus the revolutionary executed by an oppressive regime because of the ferment produced among ordinary people by what he advocated socially and politically for the poor. However, analyzing the social and political scene in Jesus' time is complex; and some of the most popular books are, in my judgment, unreliable in their generalizations. I shall keep reminding readers that there were two periods in the direct Roman governance of Jerusalem, the early prefecture of Judea (AD 6–41) and the later prefecture of all Palestine (AD 44–66), separated by the four-year reign of the Jewish king Herod Agrippa I. The political atmosphere of those two periods was quite different, and so one is not warranted to bring into the first period (when Jesus lived and died) political groups and revolutionary movements attested only in the second period. Judgments on the Roman governance of Judea in the first period should not mix actions done by the Herodian princes outside Judea with those done by the Roman prefect (a frequent phenomenon in the discussion), all as part of judging the attitude of Jewish subjects toward the Romans. Nevertheless, once proper care is exhibited, the detectable social and political atmosphere in AD 30 or 33 helps to make intelligible what happened to Jesus. The way he was treated was certainly motivated by religious issues; but contributing factors, for instance, were the distrust on the part of the Jerusalem authorities for outside or country religious figures, the economic dependence of a good portion of the Jerusalem populace on the Temple, and the past relations be-

tween the Herodian kings of the Palestine area and the Roman prefect of Judea, as well as the interplay between the Pharisees and the Sadducees.

3. History and PreGospel Tradition in Interpreting the PNs

I have accepted the likely existence of history and tradition behind the heavily scripturally reflective, kerygmatically oriented, and theologically organized PNs of the Gospels, but have also acknowledged that there are severe limitations imposed by method and matter in our ability to acquire certitude about that history. Given that, what stance should be taken in a commentary toward searching for history and preGospel tradition? Let me make several observations.

First, we should keep clear that there is a difference between history and tradition. What Paul reports in I Cor 11:23ff. about the tie-in between the Last Supper and the giving over of Jesus is a tradition; but not all traditions about what happened are historical. The implication that Paul received it early and from those who would have been in a position to know makes it probable that this is a historical tradition; but that very judgment suggests greater certitude about the existence of the tradition than about the history behind it. Readers of this commentary should not jump to conclusions about historicity when they read my judgment that there is preGospel tradition underlying some detail mentioned in the narrative. Such a judgment may bring us back to the period of the late 30s to the 50s, but not necessarily to Jerusalem of 30 or 33.

Second, there will be a range of judgments: certain, very probable, probable, possible, not impossible. "Certain" has nothing to do with the certitude of mathematics or the physical sciences; it refers to the certitude we have in ordinary experience about the things we encounter or are reported to us in writing or orally. When we are dealing with accounts written over nineteen hundred years ago by noneyewitnesses about a death that had occurred some thirty to seventy years before, certitude about the historicity of details is understandably infrequent. Indeed, the fact that there is some certitude and a good deal of probability is remarkable and encouraging.[28]

Third, the primary concern of a commentary is making sense of what the biblical writers have given us, not in reconstructing preGospel traditions or in detecting history. Nevertheless, since the Gospels have to be compared,

---

[28]I recognize that this positive judgment may seem inadequate and even skeptical to those who assume that everything in the Gospels is historically certain—an assumption that is not factually sustainable or, even for the most orthodox of Christians, theologically necessary. One can believe that the Scriptures are the word of God without thinking that God chose to communicate only in historical accounts. Imaginative poetry, parables, and didactic historical fiction are other possibilities.

the issue of preGospel traditions is much closer to the goal of the commentary than is the more difficult issue of historicity. As the next section will stress, we do not have the tools to reconstruct *detailed* preGospel traditions; and so even when the existence of preGospel tradition can be detected, I shall practically never attempt to be precise about its wording. (See AP-PENDIX IX for the many attempts to determine the contents of a preMarcan PN down to the half-verse; the sharp differences among them suggest that the project is self-defeating, for no theory will ever get wide or enduring acceptance. I have no intention to add my views to the list.) We can learn much about early Christian reflection on Jesus' passion by moving from even broadly outlined preGospel traditions to the existing Gospel accounts.

Fourth, the approach taken here will be very wary about harmonizing the Gospel accounts of the passion. The tendency to harmonize is ancient, traceable to Tatian and the mid-2d cent. In recent scholarship Bornhäuser is incessant in his attempts to harmonize every disagreement in the passion, while Benoit harmonizes at least major differences. Part of the justification for such an approach is the thesis that each evangelist has preserved historical memories, so that putting their accounts together will produce a fuller picture, closer to what happened historically.[29] To the contrary, I would argue that although the individual Gospels often do preserve memories of what happened, changes and adaptations that occurred in the course of preaching and writing about the passion usually mean that the end products are not simply historical and that harmonizing them can produce a distortion. For instance, after the arrest of Jesus, John has an interrogation by the high priest Annas alone, Mark/Matt have a whole Sanhedrin trial at night (Matt: involving Caiaphas), and Luke has a Sanhedrin trial/interrogation in the morning—none shows clear awareness of the other two portrayals. Harmonizers will try to fit together all three (or at least two of them), usually by positing that the interrogation by Annas was followed at night by a Sanhedrin trial which was resumed/repeated in the morning. Working with the criterion of multiple attestation, I would note that all four Gospels agree that Jesus was subjected to a Jewish legal inquiry (involving Temple priesthood) after he was arrested and before he was given over to Pilate. All four also agree that a Sanhedrin was involved in Jesus' death, even though John places that many days before he was arrested. Accordingly we must face the possibility that

---

[29]Sometimes underlying the tendency to harmonize is a theory of inspiration in which God guarantees the historicity of each Gospel account. Logically, however, it is dangerous to invoke inspiration to support harmonization: If a harmonized account of the passion were the divine intent, God could have inspired one such account instead of the four different accounts that actually exist. Moreover, since the canon of Scripture is related to the recognition of inspiration, it must be remembered that the large church did not give public acceptance to Tatian's *Diatessaron,* and that the Syrian church which did ultimately abandoned its position in favor of the four Gospels.

the Synoptic accounts (stemming from Mark) have joined into one scene all the significant Jewish legal action against Jesus, including charges gathered from memories of objections raised during the public ministry—a simplified picture, effective for preaching, but not a historical unit to be joined to John's theologized presentation of the brief interrogation of Jesus after his arrest.

Fifth, I know that some who consult this commentary will be more interested in historicity than in either what the evangelist conveyed or preGospel traditions. While I have a deep respect for historical investigation, I regard an obsession with the historical to be as great an obstruction to understanding the Gospel PNs as the cavalier assumption that Christians knew nothing about what happened. It is not tautological to insist that the Gospels are primarily evangelistic; to make them dominantly reportorial is a distortion.[30] I shall not avoid reflecting on historicity, but I have had to debate how I might avoid pandering to that distortion. (I have no objection to studying the history of the passion; I am objecting to confusing that study with discovering the meaning of the Gospel PNs, which is the function of a commentary.) In my commentary on the infancy narratives (BBM) I thought I had the solution: I put studies of historicity in the APPENDIXES, only to find that some reviewers read nothing but the APPENDIXES and evaluated my commentary only on that issue.[31] I have decided in this book to put discussions of history in the short sections called ANALYSIS that follow the much longer COMMENTS on the individual sections of the PNs. That should make more difficult obsessive history-hunting and make clear that such discussions, while a part of legitimate analysis, do not represent commentary on the text.

C. The Role of Theology

The Gospel PNs, in and through the story they tell, present theological views of the suffering and death of Jesus, and so it is the duty of a commentary to

---

[30]In its "Instruction on the Historical Truth of the Gospels" (1964, section X) the Roman Pontifical Biblical Commission observed: "The doctrine and the life of Jesus were not simply reported for the sole purpose of being remembered but were 'preached' so as to offer the church a basis of faith and morals."

[31]It is sadly amusing that this distorted perception still goes on. Every year before Christmas I am phoned by newspaper reporters who have hit on the bright idea of writing a Christmas column on the stories of Jesus' birth and have learned that I wrote a long commentary on them. Almost unfailingly they tell me that the only focus of the article will be, "What actually happened?"; and they insert this statement in an explanation that it might be nice at Christmas to further understanding of the birth stories. With little success I try to convince them that they could further understanding of the birth stories by concentrating on the message of those stories instead of on an issue that was very far from primary in the detectable mind of the evangelists. That effort usually leaves the reporters convinced that they have been misdirected to a pious preacher who knows nothing about the important issues.

explain the theology involved. Some may object to the term "theology" and prefer "christology" since the PNs give portraits of Jesus. Yet what happens to Jesus in the passion and the way he responds to it are revelatory of the God whose rule or presence he proclaimed, and so "theology" is an appropriate term. We must be clear, however, about the specific focus of the passion theology with which we are concerned, namely, how *the evangelists* understood the death of Jesus, not how Jesus understood his own death or how his death was understood in the broad range of early Christianity. Because such distinctions are not always made, let me begin with brief remarks about those other issues in the theology of the passion before turning to the theological outlook of the individual evangelists that will be the focus of this commentary.

1. Jesus' Own Theology and General NT Theologies of the Passion

A considerable body of literature has been devoted to how Jesus understood his own death,[32] especially as to whether he understood it salvifically, i.e., understood that he was laying down his life for others or for sins. APPENDIX VIII will treat of a somewhat different issue: whether Jesus foresaw that he would die a violent death. There I shall list Jesus' predictions of his death in the Gospels and point out how few times salvific phrases are included, e.g., Mark 10:45 (= Matt 20:28); John 10:15. Yet one should not confine the discussion of Jesus' understanding of his death to whether or not the salvific language of the NT appeared on his lips. Other questions would include whether he foresaw his death as a martyr prophet; and if so, did that have a salvific tone? (Thus Gnilka, *Jesu;* see APPENDIX VIII.) Did he interpret his own death as an essential step in the coming of the kingdom? If so, the NT language of "he died for us" may represent a rephrasing of his own insight, since the coming of God's reign over all would bring salvation.

A considerable literature has also been devoted to the range of 1st-cent. Christian understandings of Jesus' death,[33] e.g., apocalyptic event, messianic

[32]See A. George, "Comment Jésus a-t-il perçu sa propre mort?" LumVie 20 (101; 1971), 34–59; H. Schürmann, *Jesu ureigener Tod* (2d ed.; Freiburg: Herder, 1975), esp. 16–65; G. O'Collins, "Jesus' Concept of His Own Death," *Way* 18 (1978), 212–23; X. Léon-Dufour, *Face à la mort. Jésus et Paul* (Paris: Seuil, 1979), esp. 53–167; J. P. Galvin, "Jesus' Approach to Death: An Examination of Some Recent Studies," TS 41 (1980), 713–44; G. Segalla, "Gesù e la sua morte: Rassegna bibliografica," RivB 30 (1982), 145–56. A special area of research has been Jesus' understanding of his death exhibited in the Last Supper: R. Pesch, "The Last Supper and Jesus' Understanding of His Death," *Biblebhashyam* 3 (1977), 58–76, and *Das Abendmahl und Jesu Todesverständnis* (QD 80; Freiburg: Herder, 1980); F. Hahn, "Das Abendmahl und Jesu Todesverständnis," *Theologische Revue* 76 (1980), 256–72; R. J. Daly, "The Eucharist and Redemption: The Last Supper and Jesus' Understanding of His Death," BTB 11 (1981), 21–27.

[33]For example, E. Lohse, *Märtyrer und Gottesknecht: Untersuchungen zur christlichen Verkündigung vom Sühntod Jesu Christi* (Göttingen: Vandenhoeck & Ruprecht, 1955); H. Conzelmann (ed.),

"birthpangs," atonement, justification, redemption, sacrifice, salvation, vicarious suffering, death for sins, death for all, death as a martyr, death as a king, death as a priest, death as a prophet, death as a servant. An individual NT writer may hold several of these views but not exhibit knowledge of the others; later NT strata may have interpretations absent from the earliest strata.[34] Possibly there were views of the passion in the preGospel traditions that have no prominence in the Gospels themselves; and while sometimes the evangelists had views of the passion found in other NT writings, we cannot always extrapolate.

2. The Passion Theology of the Evangelists

As for the theology in the Gospel PNs proper, although the commentary will study the accounts horizontally (i.e., comparing the four Gospels scene by scene), I shall make a major effort not to neglect the vertical impact (i.e., of the consecutive thought from scene to scene within the same Gospel[35]). Running through each PN a consistent theological outlook is discernible. Because I wish to orient readers to theological issues that are appropriate to this commentary, I shall offer here a short preview of those outlooks, i.e., a guideline that readers are urged to fill in and enrich as the commentary moves from episode to episode.

Mark and Matt. These two Gospels present a Jesus who is abandoned by his followers and has to face his hour alone, thus enduring the cross in a particularly agonizing way. They come very close to the theology of Heb 5:8: "Despite his being Son, he learned obedience from the things that he suffered." Both Gospels have a Jewish trial of Jesus and a Roman trial. After false testimony the Jewish authorities seek to convict Jesus of planning to destroy the sanctuary. When he does speak, acknowledging that he is the

---

Zur Bedeutung des Todes Jesu: Exegetische Beiträge (Gütersloh: Mohn, 1967); W. Schrage, "Das Verständnis des Todes Jesu Christi im Neuen Testament," in *Das Kreuz Jesu Christi als Grund des Heiles* (Gütersloh: Mohn, 1967), 49–90; K. Kertelge (ed.), *Der Tod Jesu: Deutungen im Neuen Testament* (QD 74: Freiburg: Herder, 1976); K. Grayston, *Dying, We Live: A New Enquiry into the Death of Christ in the New Testament* (Oxford Univ., 1990).

[34]See G. Delling, *Der Kreuzestod Jesu in der urchristlichen Verkündigung* (Göttingen: Vandenhoeck & Ruprecht, 1972); J. Roloff, "Anfänge der soteriologischen Deutung des Todes Jesu (Mk. x.45 und Lk. xxii.27)," NTS 19 (1972–73), 38–64; M.-L. Gubler, *Die frühesten Deutungen des Todes Jesu* (Fribourg: Universitätsverlag, 1977). Bartsch, "Bedeutung," studies the earliest preSynoptic emphases in the death. De Jonge, "Jesus," reflects on the relationship of the early conception of Jesus' death for others to the death of the Maccabean martyrs.

[35]I remind the readers that the individual PNs are written out consecutively one by one in the PASSAGE INDEX at the end of the book. In the GENERAL BIBLIOGRAPHY (§3) there is a section on the PN of each Gospel, and many of the writings cited there pertain to the passion theology of the respective evangelist.

Messiah, the Son of God (Mark: of the Blessed), they accuse him of blasphemy and abuse and mock him as a false prophet. Yet at that very moment his various prophecies about his followers, especially about Peter (and Judas in Matt), are proving true. The Roman trial is centered on Jesus' being the King of the Jews. Pilate knows he has been handed over out of envy (and in Matt that he is a just man); yet he releases a criminal and gives Jesus over to be crucified, allowing Roman soldiers to flog, mock, and abuse him as King of the Jews. Thus neither authority, Jewish or Roman, grants Jesus justice; and both parties physically maltreat him. No friend or supporter stands at the cross; rather the three groups who are there (including passersby who should have had nothing against him) mock him about the issues of the Jewish trial (destroying the sanctuary, being the Messiah [the Son of God]), even as an inscription picks up the Roman motif of "The King of the Jews."

Jesus' own pilgrimage through all this is brought out by his two prayers with which Mark/Matt have framed the passion. At the beginning in Gethsemane Jesus prays in Aramaic and Greek to his Father to let this cup pass from him, a prayer that receives no overt answer. At the end on Golgotha Jesus prays a second time in Aramaic and Greek but this time simply to "My God" (the only time in all the Gospels), asking why he has been forsaken. And even that heartrending cry is greeted with mockery by those present. Finally, uttering a loud cry similar to that with which the vanquished demons left the possessed, Jesus expires, seemingly vanquished by his enemies. But then Jesus' Father acts, the God who to all appearances had not answered Jesus' prayers and had forsaken him; and we learn that God was not absent at all. God vindicates the Son who bore the cross by fulfilling the words for which Jesus was mocked by the authorities of the Jewish people as a false prophet. In the Jewish trial Jesus was accused and on the cross he was mocked about destroying the sanctuary; at his death the veil of the sanctuary is rent in two from top to bottom. Also in the Jewish trial Jesus was accused and on the cross he was mocked about being the Messiah, the Son of the Blessed God; at his death a Roman centurion says, "Truly this man was God's Son."

A strong theme that occurred earlier in Mark and in Matt was the double necessity for the Son of Man to suffer and for his disciples to take up the cross to follow him. If Jesus proclaims the kingdom or rule of God, both in life and in death he manifests a God whose very being is not acquisitive but self-giving.[36] In their PNs Mark/Matt dramatize how difficult it is for Jesus to go through his crucifixion and how he is clearly recognized as belonging

---

[36]D. A. Lee-Pollard, "Powerlessness as Power: A Key Emphasis in the Gospel of Mark," SJT 40 (1987), 173–88, stresses that the Marcan God's ultimate power is the power to renounce power.

to God only after he has suffered to the full. This is meant both as a graphic warning and a consolation to the readers of these Gospels. If the master found it difficult, if the closest disciples all failed to follow Jesus in bearing the cross, the readers too will find it difficult and will flee. Yet the God who vindicated Jesus, though at times seeming to have forsaken them, will ultimately be their vindicator as well when their final hour has come and their Golgotha looms before them, if like him they get up and have the courage to say "Let us go."

I have discussed Mark and Matt together; their PNs are remarkably close, and so inevitably the theological import is quite similar. Yet there are significant differences, for the larger context of each Gospel differs. Let us look briefly at the distinctive aspects, first of Mark, then of Matt. In Mark's relatively short Gospel, even if the demons can recognize who Jesus is, no human being understands him to be the Son of God before his death on the cross. More than any other Gospel, during the ministry Mark is insistent on the failure of the disciples to understand Jesus because they have not understood the necessity that he suffer. Thus the Marcan PN, where from the moment of leaving the supper until the moment of death Jesus receives no visible assistance, by its very starkness fits in with a consistent vision of what must happen before one can come to faith in following Jesus. Mark is the most graphic Gospel in describing both Jesus' anguish in Gethsemane and the disciples' failure, culminating in the naked flight of the young man. Eventually the women who used to follow him in Galilee and who have observed his death from a distance fail too (see 16:8). One suspects strongly that Mark's addressees must include Christians who have suffered and failed—a community to whom this Gospel offers hope since it points out that Jesus himself did not want to drink the cup and that even his most intimate disciples failed. Since evangelistic theology is geared to spiritual response, this is a PN narrative that will have special meaning for those who have sought to follow Christ but find insupportable the cross that they are asked to bear in life, i.e., to those who at some time have been reduced to asking from the bottom of their hearts, "My God, my God, for what reason have you forsaken me?"

The starkness of the Marcan picture is partially attenuated in Matt when we consider that Gospel's PN in sequence with its account of the ministry. I say "partially" because on the one hand some of the contrasts are even sharper than in Mark. The very fact that in Matt (14:33) all the disciples once confessed Jesus as God's Son makes their flight from Gethsemane more reprehensible. Similarly, that in his personal confession Peter, the rock of faith, had hailed Jesus as "the Messiah, the Son of the living God" (16:16–18) heightens the irony of his denying Jesus at the very moment the high priest is adjuring Jesus by "the living God" to say if he is "the Messiah, the Son of God." In Matt, when after Jesus' death the centurion (accompanied by other guards) confesses Jesus as truly God's Son, he is no longer the first human being to confess Jesus thus, but rather the first of the Gentiles, taking up the faith of the disciples as expressed in their ministry confessions. On the other hand, compared to Mark's picture, the Matthean Gethsemane picture both of Jesus' inner agony and of the disciples' failure is softened; Jesus' foreknowledge of what will happen to him is clearer, illustrating his sovereignty; and Peter is not singled out for failing to stay awake.

Yet the major Matthean difference from Mark is the introduction into the PN of a haunting issue of responsibility, graphically portrayed in the OT language of being guilty of the blood of the innocent who is wrongly condemned to death. In scenes peculiar to Matt, Judas, who gave Jesus over, tries to shake responsibility for that deed by bringing back the thirty pieces of silver; the chief priests do not want to be contaminated by the price for blood and try to free themselves by buying with it the "Field of Blood"; Pilate's wife, moved by a dream, warns her husband not to have anything to do with the just Jesus who is standing before him, and so Pilate declares his innocence of the blood of this man by washing his hands. While none of these attempts at escape is successful and all the characters involved are marked by their part in shedding blood, clearly Matt thinks divine retribution falls most clearly on "all the people" who volunteer: "His blood on us and on our children." We shall see from Josephus how the fall of Jerusalem and the destruction of the Temple in 70 caused self-examination among God's people as to what they had done that could have caused God to punish them thus.[37] Matt, writing after 70 (§2 below), vocalizes a causal judgment that arose among Jewish believers in Jesus, namely, that the decisive factor contributing to the catastrophe was the giving over of the innocent Son of God to crucifixion by the Romans. (A needed evaluation of such antiJewish judgments will be given on pp. 63, 383–97, 526 below; but there is nothing to be gained by denying that Matt and other Christians made them.[38]) In other words, Matt's PN, composed later than Mark's, responds to the theological

[37]In the commentary I shall point out that an answer in terms of purely political realities such as, "We made a tactical mistake in revolting; the Roman armies were stronger than we were; that is why the Temple was destroyed," would not have been adequate for Jews imbued with an understanding that their history was guided by a just God. Such a political answer was not offered by the chronicler of Israel's history for the fall of the first Temple (II Chron 36:11–21).

[38]The crucial text, Matt 27:25, will be discussed in the commentary; but to those who may impatiently judge that I am being careless since Matt says nothing in the scene about the destruction of Jerusalem forty years after Jesus' death, I call attention to the care of that text to include a subsequent generation in the responsibility for the death of Jesus. See also Luke 23:28, which includes a subsequent generation in the punishment that God will send.

(and apologetic) concerns of the later era. That response is also apparent in the peculiarly Matthean account of the guard at the sepulcher, which serves to refute a false story that "has been spread about among the Jews until this day."

Still another element marking Matt's theology of the passion is a correspondence with the Matthean infancy narrative. There the remarkable phenomenon of a rising star proclaimed the birth of the King of the Jews and brought the Gentile magi to faith, while the destructive plans of Herod, the chief priests, and the scribes were frustrated by divine providence. So too the death of the King of the Jews is marked by remarkable phenomena (earth shaken, rocks rent, tombs opened, bodies raised) that bring to faith Gentiles, namely the centurion and those with him. The destructive plans of Pilate, the chief priest, and the Pharisees to block the resurrection (27:62–66) are frustrated by divine providence. God is consistent from beginning to end in planning the story of the Son.

Luke. Most major episodes of the Lucan passion have a parallel in Mark with the notable exceptions of Jesus before Herod, the women on the way to the place of crucifixion, and the "penitent thief." Nevertheless, both in structure and tone Luke diverges far more from Mark than does Matt. I mentioned above that Mark/Matt are characterized (in varying degrees) by the isolation of Jesus and the failure of the disciples. Not so Luke. Absent from the episode on the Mount of Olives are the Marcan references to Jesus' being troubled and sorrowful unto death; indeed, his prayer to his Father receives a strengthening angelic response. Readers are given the sense that Jesus is in communion with his Father throughout, so that appropriately the last words of the crucified are not an anguished cry to his God by one who feels forsaken, but a tranquil "Father, into your hands I place my Spirit." As for Jesus' followers, Peter is assured that Jesus has prayed for him in order that his faith might not fail; and when Peter denies Jesus, the Master is there looking on to remind him of that. The disciples as a whole are congratulated and rewarded for having remained with Jesus in his trials (22:28–30); only a discreet silence about them after Jesus' arrest gives evidence that Luke knows they fled.

These differences mean that there is much less of the negative in Luke's presentation of the passion. If for Mark/Matt victimization and failure dominate a passion where sudden reversal by God comes only after Jesus' death, for Luke the healing and forgiving power of God is already active in the passion before Jesus' death. The Jesus who healed throughout the ministry, as he goes to death, heals the ear wound of one who has come to arrest him, as well as the antagonism that had existed between his judges (Pilate and

Herod). The Jesus who forgave throughout the ministry, as he goes to death, forgives those who crucify him not knowing what they do, and rewards with the promise of paradise a co-crucified wrongdoer who requests remembrance. Similarly in the Lucan passion there is less of the negative among the Jewish participants. In the ministry of all the Gospels there were some who accepted Jesus and some who rejected him; in the Mark/Matt PNs, however, except for Jesus' own followers, the Jews, whether authorities or crowds, are hostile. In Luke a multitude of the people follow Jesus to the place of execution, take no part in any mockery, and return striking their breasts. The Daughters of Jerusalem beat themselves and lament for him. Thus there are Jewish figures at the end of the Gospel to match the Jewish figures at the beginning who were sympathetic to the child Jesus. If Luke's infancy narrative was more positive about Jews than Matt's, so also his PN. Nothing is said in the PN about the destruction of the Jewish sanctuary (even though Jesus warns the Daughters of Jerusalem of oncoming punishment that will affect them and their children), for this Gospel which began with praise of God in the Jerusalem Temple will in its final verse (24:53) end there with praise of God.

In discerning the message that Luke hopes to convey to his audience through this outlook on the passion, we get help from Acts. There Luke takes pains to portray the legal trials of Stephen and Paul as parallel to the trials of Jesus. (Indeed, the appearance of Jesus before Herod as well as Pilate, which is peculiar to Luke, is matched by Paul's appearance before both a Herodian king and a Roman governor.) Stephen dies forgiving his enemies and entrusting his spirit to the Lord Jesus, even as Jesus forgave his enemies and entrusted his spirit to his Father. In other words, Christians will be persecuted just as Jesus was persecuted; and if they are truly his followers, they must manifest forgiveness and a sense of unbroken union with God and Jesus. Their suffering and death then become salutary (for themselves and others) even as were his. The success of the Lucan message is seen in what most people mean when they speak of a "Christian death," namely, the kind of death, forgiving others and at peace with oneself, that the Lucan Jesus died.

The Lucan PN also portrays Jesus as prophet and martyr. More than in Mark, Jesus speaks and acts as prophet throughout Luke (4:24–27; 7:16; 9:8,19; 24:19), with frequent resemblances to Elijah and Elisha.[39] That prophetic role comes with foreboding, for the ancestors of the present generation persecuted and killed the prophets (6:23; Acts 7:52). Jesus goes to Jeru-

---

[39]The prophetic role is emphasized in A. Hastings, *Prophet and Witness in Jerusalem: A Study of the Teaching of Saint Luke* (Baltimore: Helicon, 1958). See also Fitzmyer, *Luke* 1.213–15.

salem because a prophet cannot perish away from Jerusalem, the city that kills the prophets (Luke 13:33–34). Indeed, Jesus' death (terminating in his ascension in 24:51) is referred to as his being taken up in imitation of Elijah (9:51). Martyrdom is envisaged in 12:49–53; and the repeated Lucan PN emphasis on Jesus as innocent means that he came to his death for God's cause as the suffering just and holy one (also Acts 7:52; 13:35).[40] Arrayed against him were not only kings and rulers (Acts 4:25–27), but also Satan who has come back at this opportune time (*kairos*), embodying the power of darkness (Luke 4:13; 22:3,31,53). Even though, unlike some roughly contemporary Jewish martyrs, Jesus does not cry out in defiance of his persecutors or call God's vengeance down on them,[41] his death has the effect of bringing the onlookers, both Gentile and Jew, to recognize the justice of his cause. That the martyr image is intentional can be seen from the parallels that Luke has established between the death of Jesus and the death of Stephen.

Considerable discussion has centered on another theological aspect of Luke's passion. The Lucan Jesus heals and forgives as he suffers and dies (Luke 22:51; 23:12,34a,43), but in Luke's mind was Jesus' death in itself atoning or expiatory for sin? F. C. Baur and the Tübingen school charged that Luke had emptied the cross of its salvific value and made Jesus only a parenetic model of forgiving. When Schneider still held the thesis that there was a special preLucan PN, he wrote: "The oldest account of the crucifixion, as the earliest step in the Passion tradition, was not acquainted with the meaning of the death of Jesus on the cross as an expiatory offering or expiatory death" (*Passion* 26).[42] A key factor in this view is that Luke does not copy Mark 10:45b, that the Son of Man came to give his life as a ransom for many. Nor in his references to Isaiah's fourth Suffering Servant song (52:13–53:12) does Luke (22:37; Acts 3:13; 8:32–33) ever cite 53:5: "By his bruises we were healed." Nevertheless, there are many Lucan scholars

---

[40]Dibelius stressed Luke's portraying Jesus' death as martyrdom; good expositions are found in Beck, "Imitatio"; Stöger, "Eigenart"; Talbert, *Reading* 212–20; and a balanced critique in Green, "Jesus" 39–41. Some scholars react against the martyrdom approach because often Jesus' death as a martyr is claimed to be Luke's substitute for Jesus' atoning death, but that is not a necessary implication. *IV Macc* 6:27–30; 17:21–22 shows that the two ideas can be combined. More widely Bartsch, "Bedeutung" 93, would reject a preGospel theology of Jesus' martyrdom if that was understood as a guarantee of glory, but again that is not a primary or necessary implication. The martyr is first of all one who by accepting death bears witness to God's supremacy, and that would fit a Jesus who proclaimed God's rule or kingdom.

[41]When Jesus speaks of the inevitable divine chastisement to fall on Jerusalem because of what has been done, he does so with reluctance and regret.

[42]Those who hold that atonement is absent from the Lucan picture of the death (also phrased as an absence of the *theologia crucis*) include with variations Conzelmann, Creed, Dodd (absent from the sermons in Acts), Haenchen, Käsemann, Kümmel, Marxsen, Rese, Vielhauer, Voss, and Wilckens.

who would maintain that there is an atoning outlook in the Lucan PN, even if the stress is not strong and is not formulated in the language to which Paul has accustomed us.[43] From the beginning of his life Jesus was set "for the rise [*anastasis*] of many in Israel" (2:34); the Lucan Jesus' own words speak of "my blood which is poured out for you" (22:20); and the Lucan Paul speaks of "the church of God which He obtained with the blood of His own Son" (Acts 20:28). Salvific value is implied in the passion prediction that "the Son of Man *must*" suffer many things, be killed, and raised (Luke 9:22).[44] But I do not plan to enter into this debate in any detail. It is a discussion of theology that springs not directly from the Lucan PN but from a comparison of Luke to Paul. I suspect that if one had Luke without Paul, the issue would not occur to many.

John. In content the Johannine PN[45] differs notably from the Marcan PN, for only about 50 percent of the material can be considered the same; yet often earlier in the Gospel story John has passages that match the other 50 percent in Mark. Therefore, perhaps more insistently than for any other Gospel, one must interpret the theology of John's PN in relation to preceding episodes of hostility toward Jesus. The Jerusalem authorities have tried to seize or kill Jesus several times. In the face of such hostility the Johannine Jesus set the sovereign tone that governs the final attempt on his life: "I lay down my life . . . no one has taken it away from me; rather I lay it down of my own accord" (John 10:17–18). After the raising of Lazarus and before the PN there was a session of the Sanhedrin where the high priest won a decision that Jesus must be killed (11:47–53). Jesus had given life; those

[43]See Feldkämper, *Betende;* Fitzmyer, *Luke* 1.22–23, 27–29; Fusco, "Valore"; George, "Sens"; Zehnle, "Salvific." There are intermediate views as well. D.A.S. Ravens, ExpTim 97 (1985–86), 291–94, holds that the Lucan Jesus' death was not sacrificially atoning (because Luke distrusted such Jewish religious concepts); but through Jesus' role God did the required atonement. Pilgrim (*Death,* esp. 374ff.) admits that Luke does not think of the passion as atoning or directly salvific or of the death as vicarious, but contends that Luke does think of the passion and death as part of God's plan for the salvation of the world. M. Hengel, BJRL 62 (1980), 454–75, distinguishes the expiatory sacrifice of Christ from the ideas of atonement in the ancient world; it was an eschatological act reconciling fallen creation. See also Hengel's updated views in *The Atonement* (Philadelphia: Fortress, 1981). Decrying the concentration on atonement as if it were the only model for interpreting Jesus' death, Garrett ("Meaning") contends that Luke pictured Jesus dying as the "prophet like Moses" leading an exodus from bondage to Satan, and as the second Adam who removed the curse of death put on the descendants of the first Adam.

[44]Schweizer (*Luke* 338–39) would explain away most of these as not really referring to expiation; but on 363 he has a halfway recognition that Luke's writing in the Gospel medium makes analysis of his thought on this point difficult: "In this sense he [Jesus] is crucified 'for' this criminal. One may well ask whether a narrative can show this. Without the reserve of Mark and the didactic explanation given by Paul, it would remain too vague."

[45]I use the term "passion narrative" for John as I do for the other Gospels, even though I suspect John would not think of it as a narrative of suffering (passion). For him it would be the narrative of the lifting up of the Son of Man in victorious return to the Father.

opposed to the light would respond by giving him death. He and the Father are one, and so Jesus cannot, as in the Synoptics, request that the hour or cup of the passion pass from him; rather his whole purpose is to come to this hour and drink this cup in order to glorify God's name and fulfill the Scriptures (12:27; 18:11). Entirely in control of all that will happen, Jesus gives Judas instructions to do quickly what he is going to do, and Jesus is waiting for Judas when he comes with the arresting party (13:27; 18:4). In the garden across the Kidron the Johannine Jesus does not lie or kneel on the earth as does the Synoptic Jesus; rather, as Jesus says, "I am," those who come to arrest him, Roman soldiers led by a tribune of the cohort and Jewish attendants from the chief priests and Pharisees, fall back to the ground helpless.

The Johannine Jesus is the Son of Man come down from heaven to whom the Father has turned over all judgment; he can scarcely be judged by human beings. When he is interrogated by the high priest Annas, Jesus turns the interrogation back: "Why do you question me?" He tells Pilate, "You have no power over me at all"; and Pilate is afraid when he hears that Jesus claims to be God's Son. Indeed, that scene is much more the trial of Pilate before Jesus than vice versa. Everyone who is of the truth hears Jesus' voice, and the only suspense is whether Pilate will listen. As he shuttles back and forth between "the Jews" who are outside the praetorium and Jesus who is inside, Pilate is a man who tries to avoid making a decision for the truth and so eventually decides for falsehood. But "the Jews" have not won, for Pilate does not condemn Jesus until they have had to deny their messianic hope: "We have no king but Caesar." And in condemning Jesus at noon, the very hour when the Passover lambs began to be killed in the Temple precincts, Pilate fulfills at the end of the Gospel the word about Jesus spoken at the beginning by John the Baptist, identifying him as the lamb of God who would take away the world's sin.

Whereas the Jesus of Mark/Matt is mocked on the cross, and the Jesus of Luke is forgiving, the Jesus of John is triumphant. Indeed, this is the kind of death that he foresaw: the Son of Man lifted up in return to the Father. The title on the cross affirmed by Pilate becomes a trilingual proclamation of Jesus' kingship. The Roman soldiers fulfill Scripture by dividing his garments exactly as the psalmist foretold. Jesus does not die alone, for gathered near the cross are followers, including the beloved disciple and his mother. He relates them to one another in family bonds and thus leaves behind a community of believers. Then, knowing that he has completed the Scriptures and all that the Father has given him to do, Jesus says "It is finished" and gives over his spirit to those believers, thus laying down his life of his own accord as he said he would. And even after his death he remains active.

Paradoxically, the request of his Jewish enemies for his bones to be broken leads a Roman soldier to stab his side from which come out blood and water. This fulfills his own word that from within him would come rivers of living water and the word of Scripture that not a bone of the paschal lamb should be broken. He said that when the Son of Man was lifted up, he would begin to draw all to himself; and now formerly timid adherents like Joseph from Arimathea and Nicodemus come publicly and give him a magnificent burial. The Synoptic Jesus is buried in haste, but the Johannine Jesus in a manner worthy of a king who has ruled from the cross. It has been said that until the moment he dies, the Marcan Jesus is a victor only in the eyes of God; the Lucan Jesus is a victor in the eyes of his believing followers; but the Johannine Jesus is a victor for all to see.

Readers who could identify with the other Gospel portraits of Jesus in his passion may find it difficult to identify with the triumphant Jesus whose power from God annuls all that his enemies can do to him. For some it may seem scarcely a human way to die. Yet this is the narrative that has made Good Friday good. It is a narrative for all those who in the course of history have been persecuted by the powerful, but whose sense that God is with them has made them realize how little power any worldly authority really has. Those who believe in Jesus have eternal life, and like him they can say, "No one takes it from me." It is a passion seen so totally with the eyes of faith that the victim has become the conqueror. An eloquent sentence from I John (5:4) has caught the theological message that the fourth evangelist would convey to readers through his portrayal of the elevation of the Son of God on the cross: "Whoever is begotten by God conquers the world, and the victory that conquers the world is our faith."

(*Bibliography for this section of the* INTRODUCTION *is found in §3.*)

§2. GENERAL GOSPEL ISSUES PERTINENT TO THE PASSION NARRATIVES

In the preceding section we discussed the Gospel PNs from the viewpoint of hermeneutical perspective, history, and theology. Before beginning the actual commentary, however, another introductory section devoted to the Gospels is necessary, treating such topics as: What is the extent of the PN in each Gospel, and how does it fit into the overall Gospel plan? How are the three Synoptic PNs interrelated? Was there a preMarcan PN, and what were Mark's sources? Despite Matt's dependence on Mark, how is Matt's PN affected by the special material added to the PN by Matt? Did Luke have as a source another PN different from Mark's? How are the PNs of John and Mark related? I shall deal with these questions only in general here, laying out the positions that I shall adopt. A few examples illustrating my reasoning will be supplied, but the detailed proof for the reasonableness of those positions is in the commentary to follow. I recognize the danger that such a sequence gives the impression that I might have taken positions a priori and bent the subsequent interpretation to suit; and so let me assure readers that although this section is printed at the beginning of the book and thus will normally be read before the commentary, it was the very last chapter of the book to be written. Only after I had studied and commented on every line of the PNs did I draw together my conclusions about the issues discussed here. Indeed, in several instances my a posteriori positions differed from those that I had held before I began.[1]

A. *The Extent and Context of the Gospel Passion Narratives*

I have chosen to write this commentary on that section of the Gospels that begins with Gethsemane[2] (the place of the arrest of Jesus) and ends with the

---

[1]In writing the second volume of my commentary on John (published 1970), I had to adopt certain stances about the genesis of the Synoptic PNs. There (BGJ 2.787–90) I accepted the thesis shared by Bultmann, Taylor, and Jeremias that Mark's PN represented an amalgamation of two pre-Marcan sources or traditions which could be reconstructed. I also thought it probable that Luke used (in addition to Mark) a consecutive preLucan PN. After a decade of intensive work on all the PNs it is now my opinion that neither of those positions offers the most likely explanation of the phenomena encountered.

[2]Mark/Matt use this place-name; Luke speaks of the Mount of Olives, and John of a garden across the Kidron—all referring to the same general locale where Jesus was arrested.

grave (the burial of Jesus' body), thus Mark 14:26–15:47; Matt 26:30–27:66; Luke 22:39–23:56; John 18:1–19:42. Whether or not they posit a longer PN, almost all scholars would accept that material as belonging to the passion. My choice, however, was not dictated by scholarly consensus but by practicality. To begin any earlier in the Gospel sequence would require a treatment of the Last Supper; to continue further would require a treatment of the resurrection. Each of those would necessitate a volume in itself and so lengthen my task beyond feasibility. My choice to limit the PN was also affected by perceived utility. Those who wish to reflect, study, or preach about the passion generally do not think of the Last Supper or the resurrection as part of the subject matter—"passion" means suffering, and Jesus' "agony in the garden" marks the beginning of his suffering which leads to the finale of his death and burial. Another argument for commencing the PN with Gethsemane comes from within the flow of the Gospel story: throughout the ministry, including the Last Supper, Jesus has held the initiative and proclaimed God's kingdom as he deemed best; but now, at least on the visible level, others take the initiative, for the Son of Man is given over into their hands.[3] Despite the defensibility of delimiting the area on which this book comments, I would caution the readers that the evangelists themselves may have had a different understanding of what constituted Jesus' passion. One can detect that in part from the way the passion fits into the structure of each Gospel, as we shall now see.

John comes closest of all to presenting the sequence from the arrest to the burial as a distinct unit.[4] Most interpreters recognize that the second half of this Gospel begins with 13:1 and ends with 20:31, i.e., the long hour in which Jesus showed his love for his own as he passed from this world to the Father. Within 13:1–20:31 there are three subdivisions: Chaps. 13–17 describe the supper of Jesus with his own where he delivers the Last Discourse; chaps. 18–19 begin with the arrest of Jesus in the garden across the Kidron and end with his burial in the garden tomb; chap. 20 portrays different reactions of belief in the risen Jesus by people at the empty tomb and in the locked room. Thus the lines of demarcation on either side of what I call the passion (chaps. 18–19), distinguishing it from the Last Supper and the resurrection, are relatively clear. Alas, that is not true of the Synoptic Gospels.

Mark. Discussions of the contours of the Marcan PN (which I am treating as 14:26–15:47) are complicated by theories about a reconstructible preMar-

---

[3]It is no accident that two of the three detailed Synoptic predictions of the passion (see APPENDIX VIII, A2) begin with this giving over of the Son of Man, which happens at the arrest.

[4]The ancient division of the Gospel into chapters is not a definitive guide to structure, but only in John does this sequence constitute complete chapters (18–19).

can PN (see below under C). Pesch, for instance, positing virtual coextension between the two, would idiosyncratically begin the passion with 8:27 (when Jesus sets out for Caesarea Philippi to utter his first prediction of the suffering death of the Son of Man). He ends it with the departure of the women from the empty tomb after having heard that Jesus is risen. Accepting the same terminus, a number of scholars would start the PN with 11:1 when Jesus draws near for the first time to Jerusalem, the city where he will die.[5] The majority, however, start the passion with Mark 14:1, a verse that, with Passover approaching, has the chief priests and scribes seeking to arrest Jesus and put him to death.[6] Extending the PN that far back into the Gospel story brings the Last Supper (14:17–25) into the passion. Certainly there is continuity between the Gethsemane scene and the Last Supper; indeed, I call attention to that below (§5) by calling the opening section on which I comment (14:26–31) a "Transitional Episode," as Jesus goes with his disciples from the supper to the Mount of Olives. As for the end of the Marcan PN, I agree with the majority of scholars in placing it at the end of chap. 15. Some would extend it to include the story of the women coming to the empty tomb (16:1–8), treating the burial account in 15:42–47 simply as a connective to the proclamation of the resurrection in 16. The first part of the burial account, namely, 15:42–46 which describes the interment of Jesus' body by Joseph of Arimathea, is primarily a terminus for the passion and death that have preceded. The assurance in 15:47 that Mary Magdalene and Mary of Joses saw where Jesus was placed and then rested on the Sabbath is indeed transitional to the resurrection proclamation because when the Sabbath has passed, these same dramatis personae arrive to find the tomb empty (16:1ff.). But I would treat what happens at the empty tomb as a new subdivision that despite its brevity points forward to seeing Jesus in Galilee (16:7).

Matt. I am treating the Matthean PN as 26:30–27:66. Although there are various theories as to how Matt should be divided, most recognize that chaps. 26–28 belong together as dramatic action after the long discourse of chaps. 24–25.[7] Matt 26:1–2 is a parallel for Mark 14:1, and so starting the PN there once again includes the Last Supper.[8] More difficult is discerning

[5]For instance, M. Black ("Arrest" 19) thinks of Mark 10:46–16:8 as a compressed unit.

[6]D. A. Priebe, "The Woman who Anoints Jesus with Oil in Mark's Passion Narrative," SBLA 1989, p. 26, S17, argues that 14:3–9 opens Mark's PN by providing the framework for a soteriological interpretation of Jesus' death.

[7]Yet Kingsbury, *Matthew*, in his tripartite division of the Gospel starts at 16:21 the section dealing with the suffering, death, and resurrection of Jesus the Messiah. This is not unlike Pesch's approach to the Marcan PN.

[8]One should notice that 26:1–2 makes a tight connection between the oncoming passion and what has gone before: Only when Jesus has finished all the words of the public ministry does he announce that within two days the Son of Man will be handed over to be crucified.

where Matt draws the demarcation between the passion and the resurrection. Chap. 28 is longer than Mark 16:1–8 and more clearly able to stand as a separate subdivision, so that many would treat chaps. 26–27 as the passion, comparable to Mark 14–15. Although (for practical reasons, as I explained) I shall stop my commentary with 27:66, which ends the chapter, and thus I include the burial account in the passion, I doubt that Matt saw the structural relationship of the passion to the burial and resurrection in that fashion. In Table 9 (§48) I shall show that a pattern of five alternating episodes constitutes an inclusion[9] between the infancy narrative at the beginning of Matt (1:18–2:23) and the burial-resurrection at the end (27:57–28:20). By interweaving the story of the guard at the tomb (material peculiarly his own), Matt has bound the burial to the resurrection in a way that goes beyond Mark, so that one can argue for 26:1–27:56 as the passion unit in Matt's own view of the structure of the Gospel, with the burial (27:57ff.) beginning the resurrection.

Luke. I am treating Luke 22:39–23:56 as the Lucan PN. The large amount of nonMarcan material that Luke offers in the second part of his Gospel means that scholars must go beyond Synoptic parallelism to determine the Lucan conception of where the passion begins. In 9:51 Jesus sets his face toward Jerusalem because the days are drawing near when he is to be taken up (to heaven). In a certain sense the movement toward passion begins with this journey to Jerusalem, as Jesus reminds his disciples at midpoint (13:33) by affirming that no prophet must die outside Jerusalem. The termination of his discourses given on the journey (19:27) leads into days of teaching at Jerusalem (19:28–21:38) filled with controversies and predictions of coming disasters. (Thus Blevins, "Passion," begins the Lucan PN with 19:28.) Despite all that preparation, most scholars would speak of chaps. 22–23 as the Lucan PN proper; for 22:1–2 is the Lucan parallel to Mark 14:1, concerned with the approach of Passover and the desire of the chief priests and scribes to put Jesus to death. Once again this brings the Last Supper into the passion, even though the division in Luke between the Last Supper and episode on the Mount of Olives is sharper than in Mark/Matt.[10] At the other end, Luke 24 dealing with the risen Jesus is a very long chapter that more clearly than the resurrection in Mark/Matt is a self-contained unit (similar in this to John 20) and so is distinguishable from the PN.

---

[9]"Inclusion" refers to a technique in writing whereby whole works or sections of a work are "packaged" by having a theme or a structure at the end match a theme or structure at the beginning.

[10]Of the three negative predictions by Jesus about the fate of those who have followed him (Judas, his disciples, and Peter), Mark has the first at the supper and the other two in the transition from the supper to the Mount of Olives (§5 below). The three predictions (less negative) are all placed by Luke at the Last Supper, and there is no transitional dialogue on the way to the Mount of Olives. The Johannine equivalents are also all at the Last Supper.

After these very general remarks on the diverse Gospel outlines and thus the diverse ways in which the individual evangelists have treated the units or subunits dealing with the passion, we are ready to broach the thorny issues of interGospel relationships, beginning with the Synoptic problem.

B. *Interdependence among the Synoptic Gospels*

This is a very complex and disputed issue. Some argumentation involves evidence gleaned from comparing the Gospels in their entirety (e.g., the respective order of episodes), and for that readers should consult standard NT introductions.[11] I am concerned here only with the way in which discussion of the Synoptic problem impinges on the PNs. Moreover, as I warned readers at the beginning of the section, this will be a *general* discussion of the theories that I have found most workable; detailed reasoning as to why I have rejected some theories and found others more satisfactory will appear in the commentary itself. In particular, in this subsection I am concentrating on PN passages *shared* by the Synoptics since material peculiar to Matt or to Luke will be discussed in subsections to follow. In the shared material the wording among the Synoptics is so much the same that we must posit a relationship based in large part on one author's having seen a written form of the other's work. Therefore, when I speak below of dependence, I am referring to written dependence unless otherwise specified.

Amid a myriad of theories about Synoptic interdependence, the following hypotheses are the most important when we consider the PNs:

- Marcan priority.[12] Mark is the oldest of the Synoptic Gospels and was written independently of the others. Matt and Luke drew the outline, substance, and much of the wording of their PNs from Mark's, making adaptations (grammatical, stylistic, theological) and adding some special material. This is clearly the majority view among scholars.
- (Modified) Griesbach hypothesis.[13] Matt is the oldest of the Synoptic Gospels; Luke wrote in dependence on Matt; and Mark depended on both, conflating them and frequently omitting passages where the other two showed disagree-

---

[11]A concise survey with bibliography through 1987 is given by Neirynck, NJBC §40.

[12]Applied to the whole Gospels, this is often called the Two-Source theory. In order to explain the large body of sayings material shared by Matt and Luke but absent from Mark, it is proposed that they used independently a second source (Q) alongside Mark.

[13]J. J. Griesbach proposed this theory in 1789, but was not clear (as are most exponents today) that Luke depended on Matt.

ment. Prominent contemporary spokesmen for this hypothesis are W. R. Farmer, B. Orchard, and D. L. Dungan.[14]

- ProtoGospel theories. The assumption that there existed earlier, unpreserved forms of the Gospels known to us, and that the canonical evangelists drew on these as well as on the other canonical Gospels, has many variants, of which I shall mention four. First, L. Vaganay posits a *protoMatt*[15] or the *"logia"* that was used by Mark. Matt and Luke would then have drawn both on protoMatt and on Mark. Second, while B. H. Streeter argued that Matt and Luke were dependent on Mark, he posited that Luke first wrote *protoLuke* (by combining Q and special Lucan material) and then years later added passages influenced by Mark (whence differences in the Matthean and Lucan uses of Mark).[16] Third, the theory of C. Lachmann and H. J. Holtzmann that Matt and Luke drew on a *protoMark* (*Urmarkus*) rather than on the canonical Mark known to us still has followers. Fourth, sometimes the proposals based on detectable early editions of Gospels can become quite complicated, as in the theories of X. Léon-Dufour and M.-É. Boismard.[17]
- Influence of oral tradition. In addition to the written Gospels, the oldest reference to Gospel composition (Papias in EH 3.39.4) points to the perdurance well into the 2d cent. of oral tradition about Jesus. As I have indicated, the amount of virtually identical parallelism among the Synoptics forces us to think of written interdependence; but some theories would add to that as a modifying factor the influence of orally transmitted remembrances. Scholars differ on how much of this was memorized (on a rabbinic model) as distinct from repeated word-of-mouth transmission, and on whether a written Gospel was an attempt (perhaps unconscious) to control the vagaries of oral tradition or simply a untendentious preservation. In different ways the names of B. Gerhardsson and W. Kelber have been associated with the emphasis on orality.[18]

[14]For critical evaluation, see C. M. Tuckett, *The Revival of the Griesbach Hypothesis* (SNTSMS 44; Cambridge Univ., 1982); S. E. Johnson, *The Griesbach Hypothesis and Redaction Criticism* (Atlanta: Scholars, 1990). In defense: H. Riley, *The Making of Mark* (Macon: Mercer, 1989).

[15]Often the justification for this is the statement of Papias (EH 3.39.16) that Matthew collected the *logia* ("sayings") of the Lord in the Hebrew (Aramaic?) language. Generally, however, protoMatt is thought to have been a Greek translation of that work.

[16]The thesis that there were temporal stages in the composition of Luke is wider than the proto-Luke hypothesis, e.g., the idea that the infancy chaps. 1–2 were prefixed in the last stage of Lucan Gospel composition (BBM 239–40) or that within the infancy narratives, the canticles (*Benedictus, Magnificat*, etc.) were added by Luke later (BBM 349).

[17]For a PN instance of Boismard's approach (in conjunction with P. Benoit), see p. 553 below. For an evaluation of Léon-Dufour's theory, see NEv 1.724–28. Subsequently Léon-Dufour associated himself with the theory of A. Gaboury, *La structure des évangiles synoptiques* (NovTSup 22; Leiden: Brill, 1970), evaluated in NEv 1.691–723.

[18]For debate between the two, see B. Gerhardsson, *The Gospel Tradition* (ConNT 15; Lund: Gleerup, 1986). On orality see *Jesus and the Oral Gospel Tradition*, ed. H. Wansbrough (Sheffield: Academic Press, 1991).

From writing this commentary, I have come to the following general conclusions pertinent to the interrelationship of the Synoptic Gospel PNs:

(1*) In dealing with the Synoptic problem we are asking ourselves how
nineteen hundred years ago unknown evangelists composed their Gospels.
The only pertinent traditions about that composition are from a later period,
often secondhand, and perhaps not designed to answer the precise question
that concerns us. We have no firm knowledge of how in the 1st cent. the
evangelists physically composed (writing, dictation), what authority they
gave to their sources (a question related to how exactly they would have used
them), how and how many copies of their Gospel circulated. We can speculate about oral tradition but have available only vague indications of its contents. From personal experience, in terms of read, annotated, and remembered sources and of stages of editing, I can scarcely reconstruct how a book
of mine published twenty years ago was composed. Therefore, I, for one,
cannot hope to reconstruct with great exactitude the interrelationships of the
Synoptic Gospels.[19]

(2*) For that reason I am wary of overcomplicated Synoptic theories that
posit a new source or stage of editing to solve every difficulty. In all probability the 1st-cent. composition of the Gospels was not simple; indeed, it
may have been more complicated than our most complex theory. But I think
that our chances of determining exactly the complex original process of
composition are so slim that it is better to adopt a simpler overall approach
that solves most difficulties and leaves some minor difficulties unsolved.
"What works best most of the time" has emerged in this commentary as
my standard attitude to Gospel interrelationships, and Marcan priority fits
that standard.

(3*) Some advocates of the Griesbach hypothesis have aggressively complained that the theory of Marcan priority is so entrenched that their voices
are not heard and that the implausibilities of Marcan priority are suppressed
in a conspiracy of silence. For that reason, both in teaching the PN and in
preparing this commentary, I have for my own benefit tried over and over
again to see if I could explain the existing situation better by assuming the
modified-Griesbach premises, namely, that Luke drew on Matt while Mark
used Matt and Luke. I have come away utterly convinced that this hypothesis
produces more problems than it solves. In terms of Luke's dependence on
Matt, I knew already from working with the infancy narratives that it takes
immense imagination stretched to the point of utter implausibility to contend
that Luke wrote knowing Matt's infancy narrative. The difficulties are less

---

[19]This judgment is put in the first-person singular, for other scholars think that they can reconstruct the relations quite exactly. Boismard does this down to the half-verse at times.

obvious in the PN; but the failure of Luke to reproduce *any* of the vivid Matthean special material (the casting of blood money into the sanctuary, the dream of Pilate's wife, Pilate's washing his hands, "His blood on us and on our children," the earthquake, the tombs opening and the emergence of the holy ones, the guard at the sepulcher), combined with Acts' presentation of a death of Judas that in details contradicts Matt's account, militates most strongly against Lucan dependence on Matt. Positing the dependence of Mark on Matt and Luke means that in many individual verses, having read in those Gospels a passage written in a Greek and in a sequence that made comprehension easy, Mark proceeded to recast the phrasing in a less grammatical, jumbled, and even obscure way. Having corrected the term papers of many students who in relation to their sources exhibited such a tendency to the *n*th degree, I cannot rule out that possibility. Nevertheless, I remain convinced that the greater likelihood is the vice-versa situation: Matt and Luke read the uneven passages of Mark and improved them in copying. Also I find weak the explanation that although Mark had read Matt and Luke and knew all the PN material *peculiar to each,* he chose to report none of it from either Gospel because it was material not reported by both. Why then does he report items that neither Matt nor Luke report: the flight of the naked young man, the names of the sons of Simon the Cyrenian, Pilate's amazement that Jesus had already died? When years ago I dealt with the infancy narratives (BBM), I could not explain why Mark, if he knew both Matt and Luke, failed to report at the beginning of his Gospel at least those important items about Jesus on which both Gospels agreed, e.g., angelic annunciation before his birth, virginal conception, and birth at Bethlehem, and indeed presented a view of Jesus' relatives virtually irreconcilable with such knowledge. As for the PNs, although there are no major episodes or smaller informational items common to Matt and Luke not reported in Mark, Matt's and Luke's "minor agreements" of word and phrase have not been included by Mark. If Matt and Luke were Mark's main guide, why has Mark changed words and omitted phrases used by both?

(4*) Those who know the field may be amused (or annoyed) that I have used the "minor agreements" of Matt and Luke over against Mark as an argument to controvert Griesbach, for the advocates of that hypothesis often regard such Matt-Luke agreements as their strongest argument against Marcan priority. If *independently of each other* Matt and Luke were both using Mark, how could it happen that they agreed negatively in omitting something that Mark reports, or positively in using words and phrases different from those found in Mark? This is a key point; and my standard of "what works best most of the time" forces me to interpret differently these two types of Matt-Luke agreements over against Mark.

In some ways, the Matt-Luke *negative* agreements in omitting Marcan material are easier to deal with, especially when what was omitted offended against the overall outlook of both Matt and Luke. For instance, at the arrest of Jesus Matt and Luke omit the Marcan episode of the naked flight of the young man who until he was seized would have followed Jesus. Consistently throughout their Gospels these two evangelists are kinder to the disciples of Jesus than is Mark, and independently both of them could have rejected this as too scandalous a scene. Other instances where an attributable reason for omission by Matt and Luke is less obvious will be treated in the commentary and possible explanations proposed.[20] Those explanations are certainly no less convincing than the ones offered by Griesbachians as to why Mark would have included items not in Matt and Luke (3* above).

(5*) The Matt-Luke *positive* agreements over against Mark are more important. A few may be explained relatively easily. For instance, Matt and Luke may have happened independently on the same common word to replace a term in Mark that they found awkward or unusual. Thus, in describing how Joseph from Arimathea buried the body of Jesus, Mark 15:46 uses *eneilein* ("to tie up"), a hapax legomenon in the NT; both Matt 27:59 and Luke 23:53 replace it with *entylissein* ("to wrap"), perhaps independently finding this verb more customary and reverent (since for them Joseph was more unambiguously good than he was for Mark). Yet coincidence has limited appeal as an explanation for many of the Matt-Luke "minor agreements."

We need not expect in every instance to understand the motivation of ancient authors (1* above); but in my judgment some of the positive agreements of Matt and Luke over against Mark force us to modify the thesis of Marcan priority through the introduction of orality. Neirynck, an ardent exponent of Marcan priority who has studied the "minor agreements" in detail,[21] greatly distrusts the introduction of oral dependence into explanations of the phenomenon, as does his student Senior in reference to the PNs.[22] However, despite my agreement with their rejection of the Griesbach hypothesis and of the appeal to dubiously reconstructed protoGospels, I would argue against them both on a general level and in reference to particular PN passages that orality is a factor that cannot be excluded. On the gen-

---

[20]Omissions by Matt and Luke of items in Mark include the cock crowing *twice* in Peter's denials; names of the sons of Simon the Cyrenian; Pilate's amazement that Jesus had already died.

[21]*The Minor Agreements of Matthew and Luke* (BETL 37; Louvain Univ., 1974); NEv, esp. 1.769–810; 2.3–18. Yet R. H. Stein, "The Matthew-Luke Agreements Against Mark: Insight from John," CBQ 54 (1992), 482–502, esp. 501, traces John's agreements with the Synoptics not to a direct use of them but to knowledge of common, oral traditions used independently by the evangelists.

[22]See his "Matthew's Special Material." As we shall find, Matt raises acutely the issue of oral tradition.

eral level, to imagine that Matt and Luke worked only with writings (Mark, Q, perhaps the special material), much in the manner a modern scholar works with copies of Mark, Matt, and Luke, staggers the imagination. Can one seriously believe that Matt and Luke knew nothing of the passion before they read Mark, and that what they already knew was not blended (perhaps unconsciously) with what they read?[23] Sealing off the evangelists by confining them to written dependence contradicts the ethos from which the Gospel material came to them: from a Jesus whose message was oral and who never recorded a word in writing, and from decades of preaching about Jesus which gave rise to bodies of Jesus tradition. It conflicts with the kerygmatic nature of what the evangelists were doing: Through the written word they were preaching to communities; and, as we shall see, their writing still bears the marks of orality. As for particular passages, I shall argue in the commentary that an appeal to oral influence makes better sense than ad hoc hypotheses about written sources. For instance, in the Jewish mockery of Jesus Matt 26:68 and Luke 22:64 have the question, "Who is it that hit you?" which is absent from Mark. To explain this Neirynck and Senior have to suppose that after Luke added the question to what he took over from Mark, later copyists, influenced by what they saw in Luke, added it to Matt who like Mark did not originally have it. None of this ad hoc creation of the history of scribal copying is necessary.[24] We know that the game of blindman's buff existed in Greek antiquity, and according to the Marcan story Jesus was being subjected to a brutal form of that game. It is not unusual for such a game to be known popularly by its key question (as one can hear on a playground the invitation to a tag game phrased as "Let's play 'Who's it?' "), and "Who hit you?" may have been the set question in this game. Independently, without any influence from written documents but affected by oral ambience, the two evangelists may have supplied that question instinctively as they recognized the game, or in order to help reader recognition of the game, or both. Obviously I cannot prove that, but I suggest the tone of the solution is closer to the plausible living ambience in which the Gospels were produced than are the overly bookish explanations demanded by attributing everything to desktop copying. We shall see more of this issue of the orality of the Gospels in the commentary and in the discussion of *GPet* in APPENDIX I. For

[23]Similarly in §1, A3 I argued that the respective audiences of the evangelists knew of the passion before they read the Gospels addressed to them and that this previous background colored the way they would have understood Gospel passages.

[24]The forced character of the approach is increased when in relation to the preceding verse (Matt 26:67), to explain why Matt does not have the phrase about covering Jesus' face which appears in Mark, Senior has to appeal to another exceptional history of copying: The original Mark that Matt read did not have the phrase, but later copyists added it to Mark to make the description more intelligible! Full discussion of these verses is found in the commentary below.

the moment I contend that the dimension it adds makes overall adherence to Marcan priority more defensible.[25]

C. *Mark as a Gospel and the Issue of a PreMarcan Passion Narrative*

Mark has a major role in the study of the PN, not only as the first of the Synoptics (for those of us who accept Marcan priority) but as the Gospel most frequently compared with John. Two major issues need to be considered here: the basic character of Mark as a Gospel and the issue of a preMarcan PN.

1. **Mark as a Gospel**

Inevitably the interpretation of a Gospel PN is strongly influenced by one's understanding of the Gospel as a whole. This is particularly a problem in Mark where, unlike Luke and John, there is no statement of purpose, and where, unlike the situation of Matt and Luke using Mark, we cannot see the changes the evangelist has made in copying from an earlier written source and be instructed by the thrust of those changes. Our ignorance of what preceded Mark has allowed widely divergent theorizing about the Gospel's import. A number of theories see Mark as constituting a radical change compared to what went before, e.g., Mark as the initiator of the gospel genre and thus the first work to put together Jesus' words, deeds, and passion (the "Perrin school" and others); Mark as the first *written* Gospel and thus a break with the previous orality of the message (W. Kelber); Mark the creator of the (fictional) content of the story of Jesus and the inventor of the myth of the redeemer over against an original "Jesus movement" about which we know little or nothing (B. Mack); Mark as antiapostolic apologetic (showing the Twelve as men who failed to take up the cross and thus lost their faith in Jesus) that has the goal of correcting a triumphalist presentation of Christ and the church preached by those who invoked the authority of the apostles (T. J. Weeden, W. Kelber); Mark as a later composition based on *Secret Mark* (see p. 295 below) or on an early form of that apocryphon, bowdlerizing the wilder, more gnostic character of the original by omitting potentially scandalous passages about Jesus (H. Koester; M. Smith). Over against these theories is an approach that sees Mark in considerable continuity with what went before (namely, a Jesus tradition, preached by those who had known

---

[25]Soards (*Passion*) found that he could explain intelligibly the Lucan PN as largely drawn from Mark (with Lucan composition and some items of special material) by allowing for the influence of oral tradition.

him and by others, which was already being shaped into an oral or written Gospel format)—a development that was in part harmonious with that preceding tradition and yet had its own corrective thrust.[26]

It would be unreasonable to expect a PN commentary to discuss all these theories about Mark, but let me explain why a developmental approach is preferable to one that posits radical innovation and why that preference has import for interpreting the passion. The originality of the gospel genre is overstressed in the radical innovation theories. Judging from the Marcan outline, we see that a gospel narrates a career in which Jesus preaches the kingdom (rule) of God and works miracles, suffers violence from those who reject his preaching, and is vindicated by God who raises him up. If we leave aside the unique Christian feature of the resurrection, antecedent patterns for a gospel can be found in the prophetic books of the OT and the intertestamental genre of the "lives of the prophets." In what is related of OT prophets there are collected proclamations of the word of God, cycles of miraculous deeds (Elijah and Elisha, including healings, multiplication of loaves, raising the dead), and a passion narrative where Jeremiah suffers violence from those who oppose his teaching (see p. 396 below). The apocryphal *Lives of the Prophets*[27] extends the pattern of suffering and a martyr's death to many of the prophets. Since from an early stage Jesus was compared to the prophets, it would not have been a great innovation to think that his preaching, miracles, and suffering belonged together.

In part the contention that Mark was the first Gospel to have been composed stems from the thesis that Matt and Luke made independent use of it (and in the mind of some, so did John). Why was Mark so important and influential unless it was the first writing to join the words and deeds of Jesus? In its own figurative language antiquity offered a different reason for Mark's importance: Papias (EH 3.39.15) portrays Mark as the interpreter of Peter's proclamation of what was said and done by the Lord. Few today would accept that explanation taken literally, but with ancient traditions sometimes one must go beneath surface vocalization to a more basic implication. Given the tendency of the late 1st cent. to have Peter serve as the spokesman of the Twelve, this may be an overly simplified way of acknowledging Mark as a preeminent distillation of the way Jesus was proclaimed in apostolic or, at least, traditional preaching.[28] Paul (I Cor 15:11) offers us evidence that there

---

[26]A good diagnosis of the debate, especially with regard to Kelber and Mack, is offered by L. Hurtado, "The Gospel of Mark: Evolutionary or Revolutionary Document?" JSNT 40 (1990), 15–32. He rejects the understanding of Mark as revolutionary and, without minimizing its distinctiveness, sees Mark as an evolution of what went before.

[27]Difficult to date but thought by some to be of 1st-cent.-AD Jewish origin; see OTP 2.379–99.

[28]I take for granted, as I indicated in §1, that the formative process of the Gospels involved decades of preaching and teaching, giving shape to units and collections of miracles stories, sayings,

was a common apostolic preaching about Jesus: Having given a traditional sequence about Jesus (died, buried, raised, appeared) and having mentioned Cephas (Peter), the Twelve, James (the brother of the Lord), and all the apostles, Paul says, "Whether then I or they, so do we preach [*kēryssein*] and so do you believe." Although he does not quote Jesus or cite his individual deeds, many have pointed to echoes of the Jesus tradition in Paul; and R. B. Hays has argued that in Pauline argumentation one can see a basic narrative pattern similar to that in the canonical Gospels.[29] The older thesis that Mark (particularly in its emphasis on the crucifixion) reflects Pauline theology may be an inexact way of recognizing that Mark reflects the emphases of the common "I or they" preaching that Paul spoke of in reference to the death, burial, and resurrection of Jesus.[30] That Matt and Luke, writing in different places in the last third of the 1st cent., independently took Mark as their basic guide is well explained if Mark reflected the gospel of the larger church,[31] i.e., the church that thought of itself as having been evangelized by those who were now known as "the apostles." For the purposes of our study the key element in this approach to Mark does not lie in the precision of the adjective "apostolic" but in an insistence that this Gospel embodied a traditional or widely accepted pattern, i.e., that *Mark constituted a good summary of the main lines of the Jesus tradition familiar to major Christian communities from earlier preaching.*[32]

Is such a thesis defensible in the light of evidence offered by Weeden, Kelber, and others (with variations) that Mark was highly critical of the twelve apostles and was attempting to discredit the invocation of their memory? Indisputably Mark does not report some significant positive passages praising the disciples' faith and constancy that are found in the later

---

parables, etc. Consequently, when I speak of "apostolic or traditional preaching," I am referring to such a complex process but one that was associated in some way (perhaps in its origins) with important apostolic figures of whom Paul, the Gospels, and Acts speak.

[29]*The Faith of Jesus Christ* (SBLDS 56; Chico, CA: Scholars, 1983), 256–58.

[30]C. H. Dodd (ExpTim 43 [1931–32], 396–400) related the skeletal outline of Mark's Gospel to the kerygmatic outline of Jesus' ministry attributed to Peter in Acts 10:37–39. That view probably has the dependence reversed: Luke, who had read Mark, may well have supplied in the Acts sermon an outline derived from Mark. Yet even in the latter explanation, we note that Luke's association of the Marcan outline with apostolic preaching may reflect an early attestation of the way in which Mark was appreciated.

[31]While the following fact is open to different interpretations, it is intriguing that neither later Gospel dares to copy the way Mark opens: "Beginning of the Gospel [*euaggelion*] of Jesus Christ." (The Gospel of Luke never uses *euaggelion;* Matt 24:14; 26:13, using "this gospel," may be referring to Jesus' proclamation as Matt was making it known.) If one used the phrase "The Gospel of Jesus Christ" in association with a written document (even if one did not understand "gospel" to be the content of the document; see H. Koester, NTS 85 [1989], 361–81), was it associated with Mark's presentation? Drawing on I John 1:5, I have suggested that the technical name for John's Gospel within the Johannine community may have been *aggelia* rather than *euaggelion* (BEJ 193).

[32]Tradition associates Mark with Rome; Matt, writing in the Antioch area, knew Mark; Luke, writing in an area where the Pauline heritage was respected, also knew Mark. See n. 8 in §1.

Synoptics (e.g., Matt 16:17; Luke 22:28). According to the Marcan-priority thesis the later Gospels would have introduced these passages in order to modify episodes describing the failure of the Twelve. Such passages are harmonious with the positive postresurrectional career of those who had followed Jesus during the ministry; and Mark is characteristically different from Matt and Luke in having a less *overtly* postresurrectional atmosphere. By not including such ameliorating touches was Mark denying that the Twelve[33] had a subsequent positive career, and did he wish readers to think of the apostles as total failures who abandoned Jesus definitively? That is a highly exaggerated interpretation nullifying an essential element of Mark's presentation of Jesus. As his first action in the ministry the Marcan Jesus chooses Simon, Andrew, James, and John to make them fishers of men (1:16–20). Surely, then, readers are meant to think that their presence and activity is an important part of what he will accomplish. This is confirmed in 3:13 where others are added to make up the Twelve under the rubric that Jesus "called to himself those whom he wanted." In 3:34 they are designated as Jesus' family constituted by doing the will of God.

True, at the time of the arrest and passion of Jesus, Mark shows with brutal clarity the failure of the Twelve, who are scattered and stumble in their faith (14:27–29,50–52), and of Peter, who denies Jesus. That this is a definitive failure, however, is impossible in the logic of what has gone before, for then Jesus' whole purpose in having selected companions would have been definitively frustrated, and there would be no encouragement for thinking that he would call others to himself whom he wanted. One of them, Judas, did fail definitively; and that is spelled out by Jesus in 14:21: "Woe to the man by whom the Son of Man is given over; it would have been better for that man if he had not been born." But how different is Jesus' attitude toward the future of the other disciples enunciated at the very moment when their failure is most strongly predicted! He assures them that when the passion is over and he is raised, he will go before them to Galilee (14:28). Jesus first called them together there, and there he will call them together again after this scattering. And since Peter failed in particular, the (angelic) young man at the tomb who reminds the women of this promise specifies that it is to be told to the disciples "and Peter" (16:7).[34] Mark wishes to show his readers

---

[33]Without doubt, when Mark writes of the disciples, he is using figures from Jesus' ministry to make his audience think of a wider Christian discipleship; nevertheless in the story flow he does this through describing the Twelve as disciples.

[34]Many scholars think that Mark added to earlier material the two verses containing the promise that Jesus would go before them to Galilee where they would see him. That approach gives the verses even greater importance for discerning Mark's mind. For a balanced overall view of discipleship in Mark, see Best, *Following*, esp. 199–203 on these verses.

that without the strengthening made possible through Jesus' victory over crucifixion, even those closest to Jesus failed; yet with the resurrection they will be brought back.[35] If there were false missionaries who had proclaimed to the Marcan community a Christ without a cross (the adversaries attacked by Mark in the hypothesis under discussion) and if they had invoked the authority of the apostles for this "gospel," let them learn that without the cross the apostles were a failure. But what makes the Marcan message truly a gospel (good news) is the indication that after Jesus died on the cross and with the strengthening that came from the reversal of that death by God, the Twelve would once more become disciples and could serve as fishers of men as Jesus intended. To leave out the positive postresurrectional role promised and given to the Twelve (minus Judas) is to rewrite Mark as a jeremiad and to reduce the Marcan Jesus to a failure in a primary project for proclaiming the kingdom.[36]

Understanding Mark as a standardized presentation of the Jesus tradition stemming from a chain of preaching that began in the early days of the Christian mission is in conflict with another thesis of Kelber, namely, that Mark as the first written Gospel embodies a sharp break between orality and textuality. In a laudable effort to remind scholars of the impact of orality on Gospel background, Kelber pictures a very flexible, diversified oral communication about Jesus that was drastically narrowed down by Mark's putting the Gospel into writing. The relationship of textuality to orality varies, however. Kelber's models of orality are taken from a preliterate society, whereas Jesus and those who proclaimed him lived in a Judaism where the paradigm for preserving God's word was Scripture, and thus in a religious context where orality and textuality were combined.[37] Moreover, in positing great flexibility in the oral stage, Kelber underplays the control exercised by the apostolic norms attested by Paul's "Whether I or they, so do we preach" (I Cor

[35]Mark ends in 16:8 without telling us that the disciples did go to Galilee and see the risen Jesus, but this is a suspended ending where the readers are expected to complete the story from the hint in the text. Mark affirms and communicates a postresurrection reunion without narrating it; see Magness, *Sense.*

[36]The importance of the Twelve in Mark is a reason for thinking that in some way Mark is related to apostolic preaching. (Contrast John who knows of the Twelve but never describes a calling of them and never speaks of "apostles.") In giving the Twelve even greater import by added positive verses and by removing negative statements about them, Matt and Luke would be recognizing the overall thrust of the Gospel they took over and adapting it to a more reverential atmosphere. Surely that is more credible than that they took over Mark as their major source, either failing to understand its antiapostolic intentions or wanting to correct them. The fact that Matt and Luke preserved so much from Mark and with remarkable fidelity militates against an adversarial stance on such a key issue.

[37]Hurtado, "Gospel" (n. 26 above) 11, points to models of combined orality and textuality in the Greco-Roman world; see also P. J. Achtemeier, JBL 109 (1990), 3–27; R. Scholes and R. Kellogg, *The Nature of Narrative* (New York: Oxford, 1966), esp. 1–56; and in rejection of Kelber's outlook, Boomershine, "Peter's" 61.

15:11).[38] Certainly there must have been a variety of stories about Jesus' passion, and below I shall maintain that a strain of popular, imaginative presentation of the PN came into Matt; but Paul shows us the existence of a traditional, standardized sequence in the passion that served as a guide to preaching, and I would see Mark in continuity with that. One cannot state with assurance that Mark was the first written Gospel, and most scholars would insist that at least blocks of Jesus tradition existed in writing before Mark. If so, Mark would have been in continuity with preGospel writing on the level of textuality. There was also continuity on the oral level, for signs of orality are evident in Mark's writings, as J. Dewey has argued convincingly.[39] This lends support to a point I made in §1, n. 7, that we should think of a Marcan *audience,* i.e., not merely readers but hearers, so that orality is manifested not only in what Mark took over but in the way he presents it.

A factor in this orality may have been cultic celebration. Without accepting the elaborate thesis of P. Carrington that Mark consists of a series of lessons used in the church according to a primitive Christian liturgical calendar, scholars like Bertram, Schille, and Trocmé have detected in the Marcan PN signs of liturgical recitation, perhaps at the eucharist. It is introduced by a Last Supper that has eucharistic words. The narrative dealing with Jesus' sufferings opens on the way to the Mount of Olives with a reference to hymns (14:26). Of particular interest is a time framework of one day (Thursday evening to Friday evening), where from the beginning of the supper to the burial almost every three-hour period is marked off (14:17,72; 15:1,25,33,34,42). Could these be Christian hours of prayer on an annual sacred day recalling the death of the Lord? And could the context of a reading during the eucharist on that day be where the recalled sequence of events began to become a PN?

The appreciation of the influence of orality on Mark is very important in giving nuance to the Gospel's historicity, namely, that although it is the oldest preserved Gospel, at times its PN is not historical in a precise or narrow sense. In §1B I argued that there is history underlying the Gospel PNs—there was no massive Christian indifference as to what actually happened at the end of Jesus' life; the PNs were not simply made up out of Scripture; there was a core of memory that governed the shaping of the tradition, and we have traces of that memory in the kerygmatic formulas of the preGospel

---

[38]Probably also by his rejection of any other gospel, even though there is no way to show that in the relevant passages (Gal 1:8; II Cor 11:4) Paul was thinking of his own gospel in terms of the sequence made part of the preaching in I Cor 15:11.

[39]*Interpretation* 43 (1989), 32–44; CBQ 53 (1991), 221–36. This is maintained also by T. P. Haverly in his doctoral dissertation, "Oral Traditional Narrative and the Composition of Mark's Gospel" (Edinburgh Univ., 1983).

period. At the same time I attempted to be forthright about the difficulties in detecting history. In Mark's PN (and the PNs of Matt and Luke influenced by Mark) the heritage from oral proclamation and the continued goal of oral communication even when the Gospel was written have honed down and simplified drastically the picture that is given of the passion.

Let me illustrate that by reasoning from the larger context of Jesus' public ministry to the smaller context of his passion. For the ministry in general John's picture of Jesus going back and forth between Galilee and Jerusalem and of many conflicts with the Jerusalem authorities may be closer to history than Mark's picture of Jesus' entire ministry in the North with only one trip to Jerusalem (set at the end of his life) and only one major conflict with the Jerusalem authorities that begins the moment he arrives. Mark's simpler outline would have been easy to preach, as Acts 10:37–40 testifies, while John's outline would not; but then in my judgment, John was not a Gospel primarily shaped by preaching.[40] Concentrating on the small area of the Gospel containing the passion, when I stressed its narrative element (§1, A4 above), I pointed to the presence of dramatic arrangements and of storytelling features (such as the pattern of three, far more dominant in Mark's PN than in John's). Those features, which could only occasionally have been historical, facilitated oral communication and were continued in written communication that retained an oral thrust. For example, it is quite unlikely that historically the Jewish trial and the Roman trial were so neatly balanced as Mark presents them: each centered on one crucial question ("Are you the Messiah?" in the first and "Are you the King of the Jews?" in the second) and each ending in mockery of Jesus (the first over a religious issue, the second over a political issue). I am not implying that the stylization of the Marcan presentation means that none of the content is historical. To the contrary, one can make a decent case for the historicity of an antagonism centered on such issues as messiahship and kingship and for the likelihood of Jesus having been mocked. Yet the way that material has been shaped for effective oral communication cautions us against easily taking the Marcan arrangement as historical. In disputes scattered through the Gospel, John reports that issues were raised by "the Jews" about Jesus being a king, Messiah, and Son of God; and, although, of course, John has embedded those disputes and issues in his own theologically structured outline, that disper-

---

[40]In the earlier stages of the Johannine tradition preaching may have played a role, but the need to arrange the material for testimony when challenged in synagogue disputes was a more important formative factor in the later stages. Moreover, as 20:30–31; 21:25 show, John is quite consciously a written document that will be read. Many Johannine connectives assume that readers will remember things that occurred some chapters before.

sion may be more historical than Mark's concentration of them.[41] Yet were John read aloud, people would find it hard to remember the scattered debates.

Again, before Jesus is finally arrested, John has several Sanhedrin sessions with attempts to seize him and a decision on his death. That presentation, which may have been closer to reality, lacks the brilliant simplicity of Mark's one Jewish trial on the night before Jesus died, a trial in which the whole spectrum of christological issues is brought together. Heb 5:7 vocalizes a tradition that as Jesus faced death, he prayed to the One who had the power to save him. John has distributed over several chapters the motifs of Jesus' praying about death, his soul being disturbed, the oncoming hour, the cup the Father had given him to drink, the forthcoming scandalizing and scattering of his disciples. Mark has those dramatized in one scene. Indeed, Mark divides up Jesus' prayer to his Father and his God and uses it to frame the passion by placing one form at the beginning and the other at the end (14:36: *Abba, ho patēr;* 15:34: *Elōi . . . ho theos mou*—each time in transliterated Aramaic and in Greek). An essential step, then, in appreciating the import of Mark's PN is to recognize the effects of selection, compression, simplification, sharpening, and dramatization—processes initiated in oral communication and preserved in a written narrative for those who through hearing would have to comprehend the Marcan Gospel read aloud.

2. A PreMarcan Passion Narrative

I have argued for the strong likelihood that Mark was in continuity with a preached tradition about the death of Jesus and have pointed to elements of sequence in that preached tradition, e.g., from I Cor 11:23; 15:3–5, that the eucharistic words were spoken on the night that Jesus was given over (= Last Supper, then the giving over of Jesus to his enemies) and that Jesus died (on the cross), was buried, raised, and appeared. I Thess 2:14–15 speaks of the Jews who killed the Lord Jesus, and references to death by crucifixion (I Cor 1:23 and passim) suggest Roman involvement. Thus Paul mentions a sequence and participants close to some of the main elements in Mark 14–16.[42] Before Mark wrote, how fleshed out was that sequence? In answering we need to recognize that in the passion, unlike the ministry, a certain logical order was inevitable: Giving over or betrayal would have

---

[41]See Brown, "Incidents," an early article I did on this phenomenon.

[42]Beyond the Pauline evidence one might invoke as possibly reflecting early tradition the references to Jesus' prayer before death in Heb 5:7, and to Pontius Pilate in I Tim 6:13.

to precede arrest; arrest would have to precede trial; trial would have to precede sentencing; sentencing would have to precede execution (crucifixion); etc. Thus there would have been a tendency to fill in the sequence.[43] Moreover, some of the episodes that expand the sequence in Mark cannot have circulated independently without a connection to the passion. The episode of the physical abuse of Jesus had to have a context in which Jesus had been taken into custody; because of the cockcrow element the denials of Peter had to be set late on the night in which Jesus was given over; the episodes involving Simon of Cyrene and Joseph of Arimathea were localized by what these men did.

Yet the last point directs us to the heart of the problem. Those episodes could not have circulated outside a passion context, but a passion sequence could have circulated without those episodes, e.g., John's sequence without Simon of Cyrene carrying the cross. While the main sequence could have been established by preaching, there could have been various ways of fleshing out that sequence (e.g., in short or long narratives). Therefore, while one might judge that probably there were narratives of the passion before Mark wrote his, that does not necessarily settle the question of a preMarcan PN, since that question concerns the particular PN that *Mark* would have used. We can speak of the preMarcan PN in the strict sense only if there was one PN (or several PNs) that Mark edited (or combined) to produce his PN. An alternative is that on the model of a general sequence that had been fleshed out in different ways in different places, Mark constructed his own PN without copying from a source.[44] If there was a preMarcan PN in the strict sense, was it written or oral; and if there were more than one, could one have been written and the other oral? If plural, could one have been more stereotyped and the other more popular involving a vivid use of the imagination?[45] Could one of the sources have been more heavily influenced by reflection on Scripture than the other?

Today scholars may be almost evenly divided on whether or not to posit the existence of the preMarcan PN(s), although I suspect that the majority

[43]Occasionally the scholarly literature speaks of the outline being "historicized" into a narrative (see Lescow, "Jesus in Gethsemane" 141–43). That terminology can be misleading or ambiguous. First, it creates the impression that there was nothing of history before the narrative was developed. Whatever gave rise to the outline and for whatever purpose it served, it may have represented with reasonable accuracy what happened. Second, the terminology gives the impression that the end product was historical or had the appearance of history, an impression that need not be true.

[44]Another alternative is proposed in terms of various "free-floating" traditions that Mark combined; but my argument above is that the situation could not have been that free. Many of the traditions had to be somehow related to linchpins in a general sequence.

[45]Both Taylor and Bultmann posited that the Marcan PN was composite, combining (A) a primitive sequential account with (B) a collection of more vivid episodes. For Bultmann the material in B was largely legendary; for Taylor it was the reminiscences of Peter and thus of great historical value.

still posit it (them).[46] Those who do not posit Mark's dependence on a pre-Marcan PN often fail to distinguish this issue from the question of whether there were PNs before Mark wrote his, even if he did not use them. Those who do posit Mark's dependence on a preMarcan PN (or PNs) often fail to deal with the possibility that a modern scholar might not be able to recover it (or them) in detail. Although I am convinced that there were sequential narratives of the passion before Mark wrote, I have no intention of recon-structing the preMarcan PN(s); for such an interest would deflect me from the goal of this commentary, which is to interpret what *Mark* wrote. More controversially, I am not sure that anyone can reconstruct the preMarcan PN(s) or the exact sources that Mark used. Both a posteriori and a priori reasoning lead me to this position.

The a posteriori reasoning is amply expounded in the charts supplied by Soards in APPENDIX IX below. There thirty-four scholars' views of the pre-Marcan situation are surveyed; not only are the reconstructions different, but there is scarcely one verse that all would assign to the same kind of source or tradition. Truly a staggering amount of scholarly energy has gone into these reconstructions, some of them detailed to the half-verse; and none has won wide, enduring agreement. That fact should make us at least skeptical about the possibility of reconstructing the preMarcan PN in detail.

The a priori reasoning consists of doubts about the applicability of the criteria employed by scholars in the process of determining what Mark con-tributed to the no longer extant source(s) he is supposed to have used in writing the existing PN.[47] A debate on the applicable criteria would be lengthy (and gratuitous, since I have decided not to attempt a preMarcan reconstruction), so let me just sketch the problems.

(a) A simple and attractive criterion would be agreement between Mark and John. Since, like many others, I think that John did not draw his PN from Mark (or vice versa), agreement between them should point most of the time to preGospel material. Yet there are many scholars who argue for Johannine dependence on Mark, and that weakens the criterion. Moreover, as I have mentioned above, often John has incidents scattered that Mark pre-sents together; thus we would still have to determine which Gospel is more likely to represent the preGospel tradition. Or if there were different preGos-pel traditions and even written sources, did a particular difference observable between Mark and John go back as far as we can trace? In other words, even for those who hold Johannine independence of Mark, this criterion which

---

[46]Those who tend to reject the existence of a preMarcan PN would include K. E. Dewey, Donahue, Kelber, Matera, Perrin, and Schille.

[47]A convenient survey of these criteria in reference to the whole Gospel is offered by R. H. Stein, "The Proper Methodology for Ascertaining a Markan Redaction History," NovT 13 (1971), 181–98.

points to the preGospel level does not necessarily establish the contents of the preMarcan PN.

(b) There have been very careful studies of Marcan style, vocabulary, and syntax,[48] and they are most helpful in discussions of the Synoptic problem in order to distinguish Mark's writing from that of Matt and Luke. It is far more difficult to be certain how to use the information gained from them in recognizing Mark's putative sources. If there was a written preMarcan PN, was its style different from Mark's style? It is not inconceivable that Mark acquired his religious writing style from that of a source he considered authoritative (and even sacred) enough to use, even as some modern English-speaking evangelists consciously or unconsciously pick up their oratorical phrasing and style from the KJV. If the style of the source was different from Mark's, did Mark copy it slavishly, thus enabling us to distinguish it from his own additions? Or having read what was in the source, did he rephrase its contents in his own style? The latter technique would make it virtually impossible to distinguish between what he took over and what he originated.

(c) The presence of material in different styles and the signs of joining (seams) are often appealed to as a guide to what is Marcan and what is preMarcan. But this criterion too has its perils. In a context where orality and textuality were mixed, was Mark always consistent in the way he treated his putative source(s), or did he sometimes copy and sometimes rephrase, especially where he was joining material from an oral background to material from a written background? Did he deliberately vary his style according to what he was describing?[49] If Mark was not always consistent, the presence of different styles is not a certain guide for distinguishing between the pre-Marcan and the Marcan. Nor are "seams" as satisfactory an indicator as many assume. Looking at Mark (or any Gospels), we can see that a certain sequence is awkward because at a particular spot the transition from one section to another is poor. If the material on either side of this "seam" is somewhat dissonant, we might judge that the awkwardness comes not from

---

[48]For instance, J. C. Hawkins, *Horae Synopticae* (2d ed.; Oxford: Clarendon, 1909), 10–15 on Marcan vocabulary; C. H. Turner, "Marcan Usage: Notes, Critical and Exegetical," JTS 25 (1923–24), 377–86; 26 (1924–25), 12–20, 145–56, 225–40, 337–46; M. E. Thrall, *Greek Particles in the New Testament* (New Testament Tools and Studies 3; Leiden: Brill, 1962); E. J. Pryke, *Redactional Style in the Marcan Gospel* (SNTSMS 33; Cambridge Univ., 1978); F. Neirynck, "The Redactional Text of Mark," ETL 57 (1981), 144–62, repr. in NEv 1.618–36; 2.339–46.

[49]Mark 14:61–62, in phrasing the Jewish high priest's question to Jesus and the response it receives, uses two very unusual Semitic-sounding expressions: "Son of the Blessed" (never attested elsewhere) and "at the right of the Power" (such an inactive use of "Power" for God unattested). In describing the Roman governor's giving over of Jesus to be crucified, Mark 15:15 uses a heavy concentration of Latinisms: *hikanon poiein* (= *satisfacere*, "to satisfy") and *fragelloun* (= *flagellare*, "to flog"). Is Mark adjusting the vocabulary to fit the ethos of the main protagonist?

poor writing but because someone has joined two bodies of material that originally did not go together. But here the questions begin. Was it Mark who did the joining, or was the awkward union already in the source? Is the joining really awkward, or is the awkwardness in the eye of the beholder? On that point, one must recognize that the present text, which is deemed awkward, made sense to Mark whether he copied it or composed it. Might we be judging the awkwardness from a standpoint that never occurred to the evangelist? (Once again, if we remember orality, a speech delivered without notes often makes perfect sense and indeed appears eloquent; but when transcribed from an audiotape, the written product may be marked by very awkward transitions and grammatical joinings.) In §11, A2 I shall discuss the theory of K. G. Kuhn that two sources (each with a different theological thrust) are combined in the Marcan Gethsemane scene, a theory based on the amount of awkward duplication. Beyond the fact recognized by Neirynck and others that duality is often a feature of Marcan style, I am far from certain that there is a telltale sign of joining in a duplication where Jesus first separates himself from the body of disciples, saying "Sit here," and then from Peter, James, and John, saying "Remain here." This could be simple narrative designed to illustrate the increasing isolation of Jesus, awkward by our standards of writing, perhaps, but not necessarily by the standards of oral/textual narrative used in evangelistic communication in early Christianity.

These are problems I see about the criteria used for detecting preMarcan sources; others will not deem them so serious.[50] In any case they are not meant to depreciate the intensive study that has gone into establishing the preMarcan PN(s). APPENDIX IX should help those who are interested in pursuing the issue, for Soards explains both the rationale of each of the thirty-four reconstructions and the contents. Also where a particular unit has been seen as key in the debate, I shall in the ANALYSIS summarize some of the main positions. My main concern is that the COMMENT on Mark, which is the substance of this book, be useful to all regardless of the position they take on what preceded Mark.

D. *The Matthean Passion Narrative and Its Special Material*

In discussing Synoptic interdependence in B above, I explained briefly my acceptance of the thesis that Matt knew Mark's PN and followed it so closely that many times there is no major difference in what they narrate. However,

---

[50]Those who regard as unlikely the complications implied in questions I ask are often judging Mark's procedure from the way a modern scholar uses sources; the mixture of what goes into a sermon that is not a smooth composition might be a better parallel for judgment.

the meaning of what otherwise would be the same episode in Mark and in Matt may be influenced and differentiated by the context or outlook supplied by the respective Gospel as a whole. Often even Matt's minor changes of Mark help us to diagnose the attitudes of the evangelist, both as to style[51] and theology. Accordingly in §1, (C2) I presented the theology of the Matthean PN with its unique aspects. Here I am concerned with the broader aspects of the Matthean Gospel and of its PN special material relevant to our study.

While Mark lists the "scribes" among those who were arrayed against Jesus, Matt tends to leave them out. In what I have defined as the Matthean PN the chief priests are mentioned fifteen times; and mentioned alongside them in seven of those are the elders—but the scribes, only in two.[52] Such relative silence about scribes hostile to Jesus during his passion is often explained by the contention that the evangelist had himself been a Jewish scribe. Now, however, as a believer in Jesus, he was no longer one of "their scribes" who could not teach with authority (7:29); he was a scribe learned in the kingdom of God because he could combine the new and the old (13:51–52). Such a scribal mind-set may be attested in the Matthean pattern of citing the Scripture by formally writing out a passage that sometimes seems to echo the Hebrew OT, sometimes the Greek, and perhaps sometimes even an Aramaic targum (translation).[53] As for other aspects of the Gospel's background, Jesus' differences from the Jewish authorities over interpretations of the Law are strongly emphasized in the ministry,[54] a fact that suggests that the Matthean Christian audience, whether predominantly Gentile or Jewish, lived in an ambience where Jewish practices were known (unlike the audience envisioned in Mark 7:3–4). Dahl ("Passion" 38) would place Matt close to the Palestinian milieu; or more precisely, we might say, close to a Greek-speaking Jewish milieu geographically near Palestine.[55] In sup-

---

[51]For example, Matt avoids Mark's duplications, drops unintelligible words, rearranges to get a smoother sequence. Punnakottil ("Passion") summarizes in each scene the thrust of the Matthean changes of Mark; SPNM comments on the Matthean redaction of the Marcan PN verse by verse. Dahl ("Passion" 45–50), while wisely cautioning that not every Matthean change of Mark was motivated ideologically, gives a useful survey of Matthean theological differences from Mark.

[52]Mark mentions scribes alongside the chief priests in five out of twelve PN instances.

[53]It was Matt's pattern of formula citations that caused K. Stendahl to name his famous work: *The School of St. Matthew* (2d ed.; Philadelphia: Fortress, 1968).

[54]In material absent from Mark, many of the views of the Matthean Jesus are explicitly or implicitly different from legal views held by others: 5:17–48; 8:21–22; 17:24–27; 23:1–26 (cf. Mark 12:28–39). Overman (*Matthew's*) is helpful in setting Matt in the context of the Jewish attitudes of the period.

[55]Dahl argues that Matt's community also knew the Marcan Gospel or at least some passages of Mark, so that the Matthean reworking of Mark took place in the setting of the community rather than as the isolated work of an individual. Although I am sympathetic to this insistence on setting, I would prefer to speak of the *community's* knowledge of the larger Jesus tradition (of which Mark was an effective summary), without positing knowledge of Mark.

port of this Dahl (pp. 43–44) points to Matthean Semitisms (26:51: "having stretched out his hand"); and probable "historical" touches[56] (26:57: naming the high priest as Caiaphas; 27:16–17: personal name of Barabbas as "Jesus"; 27:28: scarlet color of the soldier's cloak put on Jesus). To these may be added etiological explanations of a local Jerusalem place-name and of a Jewish polemical story (27:8; 28:15: still known "to/until this day").

This brings us into the arena of Matt's special material scattered through the PN—the approximately one-sixth of the PN not found in Mark.[57] *This material would include: the episode of Judas' hanging himself* (27:3–10) with its thirty pieces of silver and the insensitivity of the chief priests and the elders who care nothing for the guilt involved in giving over an innocent man to death but are scrupulous about blood money, using it to buy what is known as the "Field of Blood" to this day; *Pilate's wife's dream* about a just man (27:19); *Pilate's washing his hands* of the blood of an innocent man, while all the people say, "His blood on us and on our children" (27:24–25); after the death of Jesus *the poetic quatrain* that has the earth shake, the rocks rent, the tombs opened, and the many bodies of the fallen-asleep holy ones raised (27:51b–53); and *the guard-at-the-sepulcher story* with the chief priest and Pharisees conspiring with Pilate to seal the tomb and thus prevent the prophesied resurrection, only to be checked by an earthquake and an angel, a check ultimately leading the Jewish leaders to pay silver pieces to the soldiers to have them spread a lie known among the Jews until this day (27:62–66; 28:2–4,11–15).

On the level of general Matthean practice, since Matt drew most of his Gospel from two bodies of fixed Jesus tradition (Mark and Q), one would assume that this body of special material came from a third fixed tradition. Against that position, Senior (SPNM), who stresses almost exclusively Matt's written dependence on Mark in PN, would regard this nonMarcan material as a Matthean creation, perhaps on the basis of vague tradition. Yet is it likely that Matt, who elsewhere has worked in an almost scribal manner with sources, suddenly releases a creative urge producing a product quite

[56]I have put "historical" in quotation marks to hint at the issue raised by Broer ("Prozess" 86–87), who rightly warns of the danger of considering as historical what seems to us plausible and indeed only that. We should not assume that the evangelists' measure was the same as ours. Yet plausibility (in our eyes) has to enter the picture when we ask what is historical since the question is being posed from our point of view. Matt's inclusion of popular material of a nonhistorical nature shows that the evangelist had no strict historical interest in writing. Where he added de facto historical items absent from Mark, he probably got them from the milieu in which he wrote (Dahl, "Passion" 44–45).

[57]As for what is found in Mark, Matt lacks only a few significant items: the naked flight of the young man (Mark 14:51–52), the second cock crow (Mark 14:30, [68b], 72); the identifications of the sons of Simon the Cyrenian (Mark 15:21b), and Pilate's amazement that Jesus had died already and his questioning the centurion about it (Mark 15:44–45a). Some would add the indirect form of Jesus' prayer about the hour in Gethsemane (Mark 14:35b), but Matt has that reused in 26:42.

different in tone from his changes of Mark? I find in the special material
that Matt has grouped around the birth and the death of Jesus a consistency
that suggests a source, but one of another nature than Mark and Q—a source
that reflects popular dramatization through storytelling, much like expanded
infancy and passion narration ever since.[58] The PN special material is distinctively vivid and imaginative in its portrayals, e.g., the unprincipled behavior by the Jewish authorities, the plotting against Jesus and the lies, silver
as a bribe, dream revelations, sympathetic Gentiles (Pilate's wife, Pilate),
earthquakes and other extraordinary terrestrial phenomena, and the intervening angel of the Lord. Many of these same features are found in the Matthean
infancy narrative (1:18–2:23, which is quite unlike Luke's narrative): dream
revelations, interventions of the angel of the Lord, sympathetic Gentile magi,
extraordinary celestial phenomenon, plotting against Jesus and lies. I argued
in BBM 109–17 that for this infancy material Matt had tapped a vein of
popular stories wherein basic Christian perceptions about Jesus' relation to
Israel's past and his christological identity had been fleshed out through reflection on OT themes: the patriarch Joseph's dreams, the birth of Moses, a
wicked Pharaoh slaying the Hebrew male children, Balaam the magus and
his companions. The term "popular" seemed to fit this peculiarly Matthean
material because the marvelous, vivid, and imaginative are so much stronger
there than in the body of Matthean ministry account drawn from Mark and
Q, which had been honed by a more formal transmission in preaching. I
would contend that this same vein of popular tradition supplied Matt material for the PN. Once again there has been reflection on OT themes: the
patriarch Joseph sold at the suggestion of one of the twelve (Judah) for
pieces of silver, David betrayed by Ahithophel who hanged himself (after he
was outwitted), Jeremiah and/or Ezekiel (innocent blood; the potter's field
bought with silver pieces), Ezekiel and Daniel (the raising of the bodies
of the fallen-asleep saints). In BBM I judged that the preMatthean popular
tradition that was the raw material for the infancy narrative consisted of stories already quite fixed in their format; and the same may be true of the
special preMatthean material that has found its way into the Gospel PN.[59]
Yet in both the infancy narrative and the special PN material, as they now
stand in Matt, one can also recognize elements of Matthean style and overall
vision. This is because Matt rewrote the popular tradition even as he rewrote

---

[58]One might think of subsequent examples where the career and motives of the characters in the
canonical story are filled in, e.g., the magi, the shepherds, the villagers, Judas, Barabbas ("Amahl
and the Night Visitors," passion plays).

[59]Punnakottil ("Passion" 45–47) contends that there is no reason to posit the presence of a written
story between the oral tradition and the appearance of the special material in Matt.

Mark. Matthean style, then, does not tell us that Matt created the special material any more than it tells us that he created the material that he has drawn and rewritten from Mark. APPENDIX I, which discusses *GPet,* will offer supporting reasons for positing the existence of this body of popular PN tradition. That apocryphal gospel, besides drawing on remembrances of canonical Gospels orally proclaimed, has tapped into this popular PN tradition at a later level, e.g., in a more elaborate story of the guard at the sepulcher.[60]

In discussing Mark I stressed the preservation in that Gospel of signs of orality reflecting the preached stage of the preMarcan passion tradition. Matt, despite its somewhat bookish scribal overlay of Mark, did not erase all marks of orality in what was taken from Mark. Indeed, in the body of the Gospel Matt's introduction of the material from Q, a sayings source, has had the effect of increasing the atmosphere of orality. Similarly, Matt increased the orality of its PN through the addition of the special material just discussed. By recounting the suicide of Judas and the blood money, the raising of the fallen-asleep holy ones, and the frustration of the guards at the sepulcher, Matt has made the whole PN a more memorable story, even if he has at the same time submerged the basic PN outline that he had borrowed from Mark, who in turn had taken it from the preaching. With regard to the common Synoptic PN material I argued that OT allusions or citations did not create the basic PN sequence but helped to fill in the established, skeletal preaching outline. In the instance of the Matthean special material, however, the OT background may have actually generated the stories, e.g., of the manner of Judas' death.

One final aspect of the Matthean special material needs to be discussed: its strongly antiJewish character. Above we saw that Matt seems to reflect a milieu more aware of Jewish issues than does Mark. The polemic in some of the debates between Jesus and Pharisees plus the reference to being scourged in "their synagogues" suggests that the Matthean community history involved struggles between Jewish Christians and other Jews over implications for the Law involved in adhering to Jesus. These struggles produced a separation in which the Jewish Christians now had their own synagogue(s). The puzzling references in Matt 16:1,6, and 12 that join the Pharisees and Sadducees, as if they had one teaching, may reflect the confused period after 70 where the Jewish leaders at Jamnia (Yavneh), though closer to the Phari-

---

[60]At this later date of composition the author of *GPet* was not aware of how Judea was governed in the early 1st cent. (he has Herod supreme over Pilate) or of the precise way in which Jewish feasts were celebrated (he seems mixed up on the length of the Feast of Passover/Unleavened Bread).

sees in their intellectual heritage, gained the public authority for the populace represented before 70 by the Sadducee chief priests.[61] With oversimplicity Jewish Christians could now couple their enemies as a conglomerate.

A dispute as to which Jews were the true Israel, those who believed in
Jesus or those who rejected him, is reflected in the Matthean special PN
material in several ways. The Gospel from the beginning has shown Jesus
fulfilling the prophets *and the Law,* and that role of fulfilling what was written is highlighted in his death as well (26:24,54,56). Thus, even as Joseph,
his legal father, was acknowledged as a "just man" (Law-abiding) at the
beginning of the Matthean story (1:19), so at the end Jesus, despite his condemnation for blasphemy by the Jewish authorities, is a just man, as acknowledged by Judas, by Pilate's wife, and by Pilate (27:4,19,24: the theme
of "innocent blood"). The Jewish authorities are particularly malevolent, for
the chief priests and the elders are not concerned with innocence but only
with the thirty silver pieces ("the price of blood") being spent in a legal way;
and later the chief priests and the Pharisees, foiled in their attempt to prevent
the fulfillment of Jesus' promise to be raised after three days, pay silver to
have a lie spread about what happened (27:62–66; 28:11–15). The portrayal
of antagonists, however, includes more than the authorities. The Jewish
crowd is brought by the priests and elders to demand the crucifixion of "Jesus called the Messiah" (27:22), thus rejecting him under the very title with
which Jewish Christians hailed him; and "all the people" accept legal responsibility for putting Jesus to death as a criminal by saying, "His blood on
us and on our children" (27:25), thus inviting the divine punishment that in
the Jewish Christian outlook was embodied in the destruction of Jerusalem
and its Temple sanctuary. Yet despite the antiJewish polemic, the evangelist
does not forget that the God of Israel always holds out the possibility of
repentance for the convenanted people. The peculiarly Matthean theme of
the shedding of innocent blood does not erase Jesus' last words about his
blood: it is poured out "for many [all] for the forgiveness of sins."

Beyond the inner-Jewish issue, however, the Matthean special PN material has a particular interest in the Gentiles. Jesus' last directive, given in
face of the lie against the resurrection spread among the Jews, involves the
Gentiles. He instructs his followers to make disciples of all nations
(28:19)—a modification of the directive during the ministry to go only to
the lost sheep of the house of Israel (10:6). If Matt's community has a strong
heritage from Jewish Christianity, many Gentiles have joined as well; and

----

[61]Of the two names associated with early days of Jamnia, Yoḥanan ben Zakkai may have been a
priest while Rabban Gamaliel II represented the (Pharisee?) tradition of Hillel.

the special material in its storytelling anticipates that. In the infancy narrative, besides Joseph the just Jew who is obedient to the Law and to God's angelic revelation over against the wicked Herod, the chief priests, and scribes[62] of the (Jewish) people who want to destroy Jesus, there are the Gentile magi who, by divine guidance through the star, look for the King of the Jews and hasten to worship him, once they are taught by the Scriptures where the Messiah is to be born. In the special PN material the Gentile wife of Pilate receives revelation in a dream; and so, at the very moment that the chief priests and elders are persuading the crowds to demand that Jesus should be destroyed, she tells her husband that she wants nothing done to that just man (27:19–20). Later the Gentile governor himself washes his hands to symbolize that he is innocent of the blood of Jesus, prompting all the people to accept responsibility for that blood (27:24–25). If before Jesus dies the chief priests with the scribes and the elders challenge God to deliver Jesus who said he was God's Son (27:43), as soon as Jesus has died the centurion and those guards who are with him form a Gentile chorus proclaiming, "Truly this was God's Son." Thus the Matthean PN, far more than the Marcan, sets Gentiles over against Jews as those who recognize the truth about Jesus. Such broad polemics against "the Jews" (not just against the Pharisees), combined with enthusiasm for Gentiles, go beyond what is found in the body of Matt's Gospel. In my opinion, they reflect the unnuanced, prejudiced theological judgments found among the ordinary people who are the source of the stories that make up the Matthean special material. In the later *GPet,* where one finds a popularization freer from the controls of the standardized preaching and teaching discernible in much of Matt, the anti-Jewish feeling is even more unnuanced. For instance, as in Matt, the scribes, Pharisees, and elders get Pilate's soldiers to guard the burial place lest the disciples steal Jesus away (8:28–30). Beyond that, however, although present with the Jewish crowd in the night when immense angels come down and take Jesus from the tomb, they persuade Pilate to lie about it, acknowledging that they are committing the greatest sin before God (11:47–49). It is not clear whether such enmity reflects continued hostile contacts with Jews or is now simply unexamined, accepted tradition vocalized even by Christians who have no personal experience of Jewish hostility. In any case both the Matthean special material and *GPet* suggest that at least in certain areas on the popular level (perhaps for both Jews and Christians) intolerance may have been more rampant than we can learn from the official spokesmen—a sociological phenomenon that should not surprise us.

[62]Notice the plural in 2:20: "those who sought the child's life."

E. *The Lucan Passion Narrative and Its Possible Sources*

The theory of Marcan priority (B above) posits Luke's dependence on Mark and on Q. The dependence on Q is detected through the fact that in some 230 verses Luke and Matt share material lacking in Mark.[63] As for dependence on Mark, over half the verses of that Gospel (350 out of 661) are represented substantially in Luke. Luke at times transposes the order of individual verses taken from Mark, mostly in order to improve the logic of the narrative; but he does not split up the Marcan material into small units to be sprinkled throughout his Gospel. Rather in his account of the public ministry Luke takes over the Marcan material in four substantial blocks and uses them in the same order in which they are found in Mark.[64] The Lucan narrative of the Last Supper, passion, and resurrection would constitute a fifth block taken over from Mark, but here the end product is different. Mixed in with passages that are very close to Mark are passages different or absent from Mark. How do we explain those different or new passages?

1. **General Observations on the Lucan Special Material**

In part the answer to the special Lucan PN material must be related to judgments passed on the rest of the material, constituting about one-third of the Lucan Gospel, that prima facie cannot be explained as borrowing from Mark and Q. In Luke's account of the public ministry the best example of this is found in the "Big Interpolation,"[65] namely, the lengthy journey to Jerusalem in Luke 9:51–18:14. There peculiar to Luke one finds about a dozen parables, a number of healings, and a few short episodes of connecting narrative.[66] Overall the healings and parables are not unlike what one finds in

---

[63]The statistics for much of what follows are documented conveniently in Fitzmyer, *Luke* 1.66ff. That Luke and Matt put this common material in entirely different contexts makes it unlikely that one evangelist borrowed it from the other. (Note also that Luke shows no knowledge of the Matthean special PN scenes involving innocent blood.) The alternative, that they both borrowed it from a common source (Q), is fortified by the fact that if one isolates this common material, frequently it appears in the same order in both Gospels.

[64]Mark 1:1–15 = Luke 3:1–4:15; Mark 1:21–3:19 = Luke 4:31–6:19; Mark 4:1–9:40 = Luke 8:4–9:50; and Mark 10:13–13:32 = Luke 18:15–21:23.

[65]"Interpolation" because it is placed between two blocks of material borrowed from Mark; "Big" to distinguish it from the "Little Interpolation" of Luke 6:20–8:3. Much of the material in the Little Interpolation is found also in Matt and can be explained as stemming from Q. Peculiar to Luke in the Little Interpolation, however, are the resuscitation of the son of the widow of Nain (7:11–17), the forgiving of the woman who weeps over and anoints Jesus' feet (7:36–50: but is that a Lucan variant of the woman's anointing Jesus' head at Bethany in Mark 14:3–9 just before the Last Supper?), and the listing of women (including Magdalene) who go with Jesus in Galilee and provide for him (8:1–3). These last two items are important for PN discussions.

[66]Important for the PN are the description of a group of disciples wider than the Twelve who follow Jesus in Galilee ("the seventy": 10:1,17), the report that Pilate had mingled the blood of

Mark and Q, so that some of them could have arisen from free Lucan composition imitating those sources. However, the large amount of peculiarly Lucan material causes many scholars to posit a third source of Jesus material that Luke utilized along with Mark and Q—an L source.[67] Another substantial body of peculiarly Lucan material appears in the infancy narrative (Luke 1–2, which has only a few themes in common with Matt's infancy narrative). These two chapters are written in a highly Semitized style, at times noticeably different from the style(s) in the Lucan account of the public ministry, even from the style of the special material in that account. Thus scholars who posit an L source for the latter are divided as to whether to attribute the infancy material to it or to opt for a number of special Lucan sources. There are parallels to the motifs and style of the infancy narrative in the opening two chapters of Acts, which are also set in Jerusalem; and this has caused some to think of a special Jerusalem source.[68] On the other hand, Luke is generally conceded to have been adept in using different writing styles to capture the setting of what he narrates. Although Luke probably drew on a collection of hymns that supplied him with the canticles of the infancy narrative,[69] in my judgment Luke himself composed most of the infancy story in Semitized Greek imitative of the LXX, precisely because he intended the characters to resemble OT characters whose fidelity to the Law and the Prophets made them open to the coming of Jesus. With the exception of the canticles, then, loose traditions rather than a fixed source preceded his efforts there.

Turning to the PN, we find that the nonMarcan material here differs from that discussed in the preceding paragraph. Unlike the infancy narrative, the Lucan PN does not stand as a completely nonMarcan block, nor is it written in noticeably Semitized Greek. Unlike the account of the public ministry, the Lucan PN interweaves small amounts of Marcan material with the non-

---

Galileans with their sacrifices (13:1–3), and the indication of Herod's desire to kill Jesus met by Jesus' affirmation that a prophet cannot perish away from Jerusalem (13:31–33).

[67]Sometimes called S. Other factors invoked to justify positing this source include style, points of disagreement with material taken from Mark and Q, seams left by joining, a strong theology of God's forgiveness, and an antagonism toward riches. Since most of these features could have come from Luke himself whether he composed creatively without a source or rewrote L, not all scholars find the criteria convincing. Schweizer ("Zur Frage" 84–85), in advancing seven factors supporting a special Lucan source or sources, admits that they fall short of proof. Rehkopf (*Lukanische*) produced a list of seventy-eight words and four constructions characteristic of the preLucan special source. Despite sympathy for the L-source theory, Taylor (TPNL 24–27) warns that the list has defects; and H. Schürmann (BZ 5 [1961], 266–86) reduces the word list to twenty-nine, most of which he does not find to be totally convincing indicators.

[68]In some theories there is a family source (e.g., Mary, the main character of the infancy story, is present at the beginning of Acts [1:14]); and/or a JBap source (given the detailed story of his conception and birth in Luke 1).

[69]BBM 346–55: perhaps the hymns of the early Christian community responsible for some of the traditions in the first chapters of Acts.

Marcan. Although stylistic details will be discussed in the commentary on individual verses, overall the nonMarcan material in the PN is not startlingly distinct from the style of the surrounding material that Luke borrowed from Mark. If one had only Luke's PN without a copy of Mark, I doubt that one could successfully isolate two distinct sources behind it (Mark and another).

Before I describe different approaches to the special preLucan PN material, let me list some preliminaries by way of clarification. To avoid confusion about references to "source" and "tradition(s)," it will be clearer if we confine "source" to a sequential (most likely written) account of the whole passion or a good portion of it, and "tradition(s)" to isolated items of information or brief episodes of various derivation, many of which would have circulated orally. Unless one wishes to contend that everything in the Lucan PN that is not of Marcan derivation was created ex nihilo by Luke, a nonsource approach will posit (in varying degrees) Luke's use of tradition(s). While Luke might have rewritten and reshaped in his own style what he took over from a special source (even as he reshaped material from Mark) and/or from traditions, presumably he would have followed the sequence of the source, whereas he could have inserted traditions wherever they fit best into his story flow. Many discussions tend to treat the Lucan PN as including the Last Supper and Empty Tomb stories whereas I am not treating either in this commentary; that difference may explain variant statistics quoted about the PN. An issue in positing a special preLucan PN source is a number of PN similarities between Luke and John that might be explained by a common antecedent. While I shall note the similarities below, discussion of how to explain them will be left to the next subsection when we look at the Johannine PN. Let us turn now to the two opposing approaches to the origin of the nonMarcan material in the Lucan PN: use of a PN source other than Mark or free use of Mark's PN combined with miscellaneous traditions.

Many scholars posit that beyond Mark's PN, there was a second PN source used by Luke, whether they think that it was the PN once attached to Q (which Matt has not copied), or a PN that was part of L, or simply a PN on its own (distinct from sources Luke used elsewhere in the Gospel).[70] But then why has Luke combined this source with Mark differently from the way he has combined material from the L source earlier? The difficulty in the special-source hypothesis is visible when one compares reconstructions of it. Some (e.g., J. Weiss) tend to attribute to the source only Lucan material that has no parallel in Mark; others (e.g., Taylor), in order to get a consecu-

---

[70]Scholars who posit a special Lucan PN source beyond Mark include Bacon, Bammel, Bartlet, Black, Burkitt, Easton, Ernst, Feine, F. Grant, Green, Grundmann, Haenchen, Hawkins, Jeremias, Kuhn, Lagrange, Lescow, Marshall, Perry, Rehkopf, Sanday, Schlatter, Schürmann, Schweizer, Spitta, Streeter, Taylor, B. Weiss, J. Weiss, and Winter.

tive story, attribute to the source Lucan material parallel to Mark but appearing in a changed form.[71] In the latter approach sometimes Luke has copied almost verbatim from Mark's PN; other times he has copied (almost verbatim, one assumes) from the special source; other times he has interwoven in the same scene words from each (at times percentage-wise favoring the Marcan wording, at times the source wording).

Other scholars contend that Luke had no special source for the PN but simply edited Mark, rephrasing, transposing, deleting, and expanding (with some elements from special traditions).[72] But then why has Luke edited and expanded here to a degree far beyond his editing of Mark elsewhere? For instance, elsewhere when Luke is working with Marcan material he tends to use slightly over 50 percent of Marcan wording, even as he does within the PN in certain areas where there are Marcan parallels, e.g., the three denials of Peter. But in other parts of the PN (where in this hypothesis Luke had no nonMarcan source) Luke uses Marcan wording in a range of about only 30 to 10 percent.[73] Transpositions of Marcan material in the Lucan PN are estimated to be about four times more frequent than elsewhere.

The difficulty of deciding which approach is better (since each has problems) is illustrated by the fact that some scholars (including Hawkins and myself) in their earlier writings posited a special Lucan PN source and then gave up the hypothesis. The journey of Schneider, a major commentator on the Lucan PN, has been particularly interesting. In the early 1960s in *Verleugnung,* representing his postdoctoral (*Habilitation*) research, he supported a special PN source. By 1973, when he published *Passion* on the three Synoptic PNs, he argued that there was not a special source for Luke 23. His article "Verfahren" in 1988, dealing with the Jewish and Roman legal proceedings against Jesus, seems to have abandoned the source altogether.

2. Survey of the Special Lucan Features in the Passion Narrative

There is no way to solve the source issue with any certitude, but let us look at the differences between Luke's PN and Mark's PN in order to see if one can explain them without positing a Lucan special PN source. Such a

[71]In chap. 23 J. Weiss would attribute to the source vv. 6–9, 11–12, 27–31, 34–35, 39–43. Taylor would attribute vv. 1–2, 4–24, 27–34a, 35–37, 39–43, 46–48, 55.

[72]Scholars who think that there was no separate Lucan PN source include Blinzler, Büchele, Dibelius, Finegan, Fitzmyer, Holtzmann, Lietzmann, Lightfoot, Linnemann, Matera, Schmidt, Schneider, Soards, and Untergassmair. They vary greatly in the amount of preLucan traditional elements they posit, and in some proposals the line between source and traditions seems vague.

[73]The figures provided by Hawkins were 53 percent and 27 percent respectively. Barr ("Use") points out that Luke tends to agree with Mark more closely in sayings than in narrative, and the passion is mostly narrative. On this, see the precisions in TPNL 32–33.

quest is not prejudiced, for it recognizes the validity of Occam's razor: We should not posit the existence of entities that are not necessary.[74] Leaving aside the minor stylistic tinkering that would be expected in one major author's use of another, we find four significant types of differences between Luke's PN and Mark's: additions, omissions, transpositions, and substitutions. To discuss these I shall go through the Lucan PN, following the division into four acts used in this book.

ACT I: *Scene One: Jesus Goes to Gethsemane/Olivet and Prays There (Luke 22:39–46; Mark 14:26–42).* On the way to the place Luke does not record the predictions of the Marcan Jesus about the negative future of the disciples and of the denials by Peter. This is not an omission but a transposition, for the corresponding themes appeared earlier at the Last Supper (22:28–34).[75] There, in a more benevolent context, sayings about the immediate future of the disciples and of Peter were phrased in a gentler form. The Lucan disciples, instead of being told they would be scattered and scandalized (as in Mark), were congratulated for having remained with Jesus. Before being warned that he would three times deny Jesus, Peter was assured that Jesus would pray for him that his faith would not fail. Such a shift of emphasis in the predictions befits a general Lucan outlook in which the disciples are treated more kindly than in Mark, an outlook consonant with Acts, which shows the apostles as faithful confessors of Christ. In the prayer scene itself there are Lucan omissions. The failure to mention the place-name Gethsemane and the "Abba" of Jesus' prayer is harmonious with Luke's avoidance of Aramaic expressions. Luke's description of the disciples asleep only once (not three times) and his explanation that they were doing this "from sorrow" can be seen as another example of the benevolent outlook on apostleship. Unlike Mark, Luke is silent about Jesus being "greatly distraught and troubled" and his saying "My soul is very sorrowful unto death"—an omission consonant with a Lucan christology that does not tolerate the human weaknesses allowed by Marcan christology. If Luke 22:43–44 (the sole major addition to Mark's account) was composed by the evangelist as I suspect, it may be compared to other suggestions that angelic assistance was given to Jesus in his hour of need (Matt 26:53; John 12:28b–29)—an element of preGospel tradition that Luke has interpreted in light of his theology of a Father who would always respond to Jesus and support

[74]We must apply this principle with care, however. It may well be used against positing written sources of whose existence we have no outside indication. But the principle cannot be so easily used against positing preGospel oral tradition, since in one form or another that certainly existed.

[75]John also has them at the Last Supper, a situation that may be more original than the Marcan; and so we shall have to include that issue under John.

him. These verses also are harmonious with the Lucan presentation of the temptations of Jesus at the beginning of the Gospel where Mark's "and the angels ministered to him" was *not* reported; the ministering angel has been kept until Gethsemane.

Scene Two: Jesus Is Arrested (Luke 22:47–53; Mark 14:43–52). Luke's account is shorter. He never states clearly, as does Mark, that Judas had planned the kiss as a signal identifying Jesus or that Judas actually kissed him. Nor does Luke narrate the naked flight of the young man who would have followed Jesus. Both these omissions would once again be harmonious with Luke's greater benevolence toward the disciples of Jesus. As for additions, Luke has a word of Jesus to Judas showing that he knew what Judas was about (harmonious with "higher" Lucan christology); Jesus' reprimand to the disciples for drawing a sword in defense and his healing the servant's ear (items harmonious with Luke's picture of the gentle Jesus who always remains a forgiving savior); and Jesus' reference to "the power of darkness" pertinent to Judas' coming (harmonious with Lucan theology that Satan entered into Judas [22:3]). The most difficult Lucan addition is the presence on the Mount of Olives of "the chief priests and captains of the Temple and elders," come out against Jesus with swords and clubs. Is this to be compared to John's sequence where between the coming of Judas and the denials by Peter, Jesus was interrogated by the high priest Annas with police present? In both Gospels this takes place before Jesus is delivered to the Sanhedrin (Luke) and Caiaphas (John).

ACT II *(Luke 22:54–23:1; Mark 14:53–15:1).* Mark has simultaneous scenes in which Jesus is interrogated and abused by the Sanhedrin authorities, while in another locale Peter denies Jesus three times. Despite the drama of the Marcan contrast, the crowding of concurrent major events (including a trial!) into the one-night period and the switching from the Sanhedrin to Peter and back again has created the thesis that Mark narrated two legal sessions in the trial of Jesus[76]—a misinterpretation, in my judgment. As previously in several instances in the public ministry, Luke's reorganized presentation of the same material improves on Marcan sequence and plausibility.[77] Peter's denials take place first, at night with Jesus present (in harmony with the Lucan Jesus' concern at the Last Supper that Peter's faith would not fail); then those who hold Jesus (not members of the Sanhedrin as in Mark) abuse him; and the Sanhedrin session comes at the end, taking

---

[76]The second of these, narrated in one verse (15:1), appears to have taken place in the morning.

[77]Not a few interpreters have assumed that the more plausible sequence should be accepted as historical, but that may be confusing verisimilitude with fact.

place in the morning.[78] In the prologue to his Gospel (1:3) Luke promised to write an orderly account of what had been accomplished, and this reordering through transposition is most likely an example of that. More intriguing is Luke's treatment of the Jewish interrogation of Jesus. First, compared to Mark there are omissions: no references to false witnesses, or to a statement by Jesus about the destruction of the Temple sanctuary, or to blasphemy by Jesus.[79] It is scarcely accidental that all these features appear, even if in slightly altered form, in Acts 6:11–14 in reference to Stephen, the first Christian to die for (and in imitation of) Jesus. We must, therefore, take into consideration that writing both a Gospel and Acts, Luke had more flexibility than Mark as to where he would report these motifs. As for what Luke does report in the Jewish legal action against Jesus, the basic christological issue featured in Mark (the Messiah, the son of the Blessed) remains but now split into two questions posed to Jesus, with the first (whether he is the Messiah) given the very ambiguous response, "If I shall say to you, you will never believe." No motif of Lucan christology or of orderly arrangement that I know really explains this as an adaptation of Mark. The same splitting of the two issues,[80] greeted by an ambiguous answer to the first, occurs in John 10:24–25,36; and this has to be brought into our explanation of where Luke got his special material.

ACT III *(Luke 23:2–25; Mark 15:2–20a).* In the opening of the Pilate trial Luke 23:2 adds to the Marcan picture that the Sanhedrin leaders listed three charges against Jesus. Not only is this more orderly, but it matches the Sanhedrin leaders' listing of charges against Paul when he was brought before the prefect Felix (Acts 24:5–6). Only one of the three charges is selected by Pilate for investigation, so that in 23:3 Luke rejoins Mark very closely in the question, "Are you the king of the Jews?" There follows a major Lucan addition (23:6–16) wherein, not finding Jesus guilty, Pilate sends him to

---

[78]Fitzmyer (*Luke* 1.71) is correct: "Here one can see Luke's concern to unite the material about Peter . . . and to depict only one appearance of Jesus before the Sanhedrin." Schweizer ("Zur Frage" 58) objects that there is a sign that two different bodies of material have been joined: the "him" in 22:63 who is abused is logically Jesus, but the antecedent in the preceding verse (terminating the denials) is Peter. That is just as easily explained as an awkwardness created when Luke transposed Marcan material.

[79]Before the interrogation Luke 22:65 has blasphemy *against* Jesus by those who hold him. Luke also omits Mark's "they all judged against him [Jesus] as being guilty, punishable by death." Much has been made of this as indicating that Luke did not think that the Sanhedrin had decided that Jesus should die. Such an interpretation is refuted by 24:20 and a number of statements in Acts (3:17; 4:8–10; 5:30; etc.) that attribute responsibility for Jesus' death to Jewish leaders. This is another instance to be added to those given in the text above where Luke's longer work has enabled him to spread more widely what Mark has concentrated.

[80]See the splitting of David's heir and Son of God when in the infancy narrative Gabriel announces Jesus' conception to Mary (Luke 1:32b,35).

Herod (Antipas) for evaluation only to have him sent back, found not guilty by the Jewish ruler as well—a sequence that makes Pilate want to let Jesus go. Once more this is almost an exact parallel to the trial of Paul (Acts 25:13–26:31) where the Roman governor, not finding him guilty of a serious crime, refers his case to (Herod) Agrippa II only to have Paul declared not guilty by the Jewish ruler—a sequence that makes the Roman governor wish he could let Paul go. Those who posit a special preLucan PN source, unless they think that it continued in Acts and had a very similar Roman trial of Paul, have to admit heavy Lucan conforming of the two trials. If one thinks that Luke had some information about Paul's arrest and trial, one may well posit that to match it, he adapted Mark's account of Jesus' Roman trial in order to show readers that the following of Jesus involves a fate similar to his. Rather than a PN source that narrated a trial of Jesus by Herod, then, Luke may simply have had a tradition of Herodian involvement[81] that he introduced here to create the parallelism. Another item in the Lucan additions to the Roman trial beyond Mark's description is a pattern of three "not guilty" statements (23:4,14,22). A similar pattern is found in John (18:38b; 19:4,6) and will be treated in the next subsection. If we turn to omissions, the Lucan abbreviation of Marcan Barabbas information (about the custom to release a prisoner at the feast) is interesting. In Acts Luke betrays a good knowledge of the Greco-Roman world: Did he recognize the implausibility of such a custom? The most serious Lucan omission is the failure to report Mark's account (15:15c–20a) of the scourging, mockery, and abuse of Jesus by Roman soldiers at the end of the trial. This is really a transposition rather than an omission, however. Earlier in the PN Luke moved the Jewish mockery of Jesus from the end of the Sanhedrin trial (where it appears in Mark) to the nighttime procedures in the courtyard before the morning trial. Now he has moved the mockery by the Roman soldiers to the cross (23:36) for a reason I shall explain in the next paragraph. This editing produced problems that Luke did not notice, e.g., the scourging is never narrated, and so Jesus' prediction that the Gentiles would not only mock him but spit on him and scourge him (Luke 18:32–33) is never fulfilled![82]

ACT IV: *Scene One: Jesus Is Crucified and Dies (Luke 23:26–49; Mark 15:20b–41).* The Lucan omissions are minor: the names of Simon the Cyre-

[81]As I pointed out on pp. 64–65 above, Luke had such a Herod tradition in his special Gospel material from L; and it recurs in Acts 4:25–28 where it is glossed with Scripture. See §33 below for an expanded treatment of this issue.

[82]Another awkwardness produced by the transposition is that in handing Jesus over to "them," Pilate seems to hand Jesus over to the Jewish authorities and people (the last antecedent) to be crucified; see the similar problem in n. 78 above. In §35 I shall argue that Luke did not intend to convey such an antiJewish picture and that his audience probably would not have interpreted the scene in that way—it was too well established that the Romans crucified Jesus.

nian's sons (presumably because they would not be of interest to the Lucan audience), the place-name Golgotha (avoidance of Aramaic expressions), and Mark's very early time indication of the third hour (9:00 A.M.) for the crucifixion (presumably because it conflicted with Luke's chronology of a morning Sanhedrin trial). Luke's dislike for Marcan duplications probably explains his reduction of Mark's two wine offerings to one. Four Lucan additions are significant here. (1) On the way to the place of execution, Luke has an episode that joins to Mark's Simon of Cyrene a multitude of people and lamenting women. He thus has a group of three parties favorable to Jesus before the crucifixion, comparable to the group of three favorable parties after Jesus' death (23:47–49). At the beginning of his Gospel Luke showed Jewish people favorable to Jesus; despite the hostility of the crucifixion he wants to present the same picture at the end of the Gospel. The warning about the fate of the Daughters of Jerusalem in the oncoming divine punishment on that city is harmonious with previous Lucan warnings on this subject (11:49–50; 19:41–44; 21:20–24). (2) There is also a Lucan addition in the setting of the crucifixion:[83] a prayer of Jesus for his crucifiers: "Father, forgive them, for they do not know what they are doing." If this textually dubious passage is authentically Lucan, it is another instance of a christology where Jesus distributes forgiveness and grace during (not simply after) the crucifixion. The theme of crucifixion through ignorance is found in Acts (3:17); and the first believer to die for Jesus, Stephen, utters a similar prayer (Acts 7:60). (3) The mocking of Jesus on the cross (Luke 23:35–43) exhibits the skill of Lucan addition combined with transposition. Mark had three mockers (passersby, authorities, co-crucified bandits). Luke wants to present the Jewish people in a more favorable light, and so he does not have the passersby mock Jesus. Rather his three mockers are the authorities, the soldiers (whom he has moved here from the Roman trial to take the place of the passersby), and one of the co-crucified wrongdoers. As framework for this hostile triad Luke has dramatis personae favorable to Jesus before and after the mockings, namely, the people who do not participate but only watch and the other co-crucified who speaks on Jesus' behalf. The promise of Jesus that this unlikely champion would this day be with him in paradise is a most dramatic instance of continuing forgiveness during the PN. Dante (*De monarchia* 1:18) was perceptive in calling Luke *scriba mansuetudinis Christi*, i.e., the writer who gave expression to the gentleness of Christ. (4) After Jesus dies, to the presence of Mark's centurion and the women at a distance,

---

[83]Otherwise, through the transpositions and omissions described above, Luke's setting is shorter than the Marcan setting.

Luke adds the crowds striking their breasts in penance[84]—thus a triad favorable to Jesus matching the triad before the crucifixion, on the way to the place of execution. The rending of the sanctuary veil that Mark places after Jesus' death is transposed by Luke to before Jesus' death in order to clear the way for this entirely favorable scene after death. As for the death itself, a very visible substitution distinguishes Luke from Mark. The Marcan Jesus' citation of Ps 22:2, "My God, my God, for what reason have you forsaken me?" would be intolerable in Luke's christology.[85] Instead Jesus quotes another psalm (31:6), "Father, into your hands I place my spirit," last words that are harmonious with Luke's understanding of a Jesus at peace with himself and with God. These words also make Jesus' death parallel to Stephen's death in Acts 7:59–60 ("Lord Jesus, receive my spirit"). Luke's final substitution in this scene is to have the centurion confess Jesus as "just" rather than as "the Son of God" (Mark), presumably in order to offer after Jesus' death another outsider's certification of Jesus' innocence, comparable to the certifications before he died (by Pilate [three times] and by the co-crucified wrongdoer).

Scene Two: Jesus Is Buried (Luke 23:50–56; Mark 15:42–47). Luke clarifies the Marcan picture of Joseph from Arimathea by stating that he had not been in agreement with the decision and course of his fellow Sanhedrin members. Luke omits Mark's information that Pilate, amazed to hear that Jesus was already dead, checked on his death. Perhaps Luke feared that this would cast doubt on the reality of Jesus' death and thus fuel the late-1st-cent. apologetics against the resurrection that were developing among those opposed to Christianity. Reorganization of the burial sequence and an added reference to the preparation of spices and myrrh on the Sabbath help Luke to point the role of the Galilean women followers more directly toward the empty tomb to which they would go on Sunday to anoint the body. The invocation of the Sabbath rest not only portrays them as pious Jews but helps Gentile readers to understand why they waited a day to act on Jesus' behalf.

If we work with the hypothesis that Luke had at his disposal only one PN (Mark's), the above survey shows that the *omissions* of Marcan PN material can be explained without much difficulty: They are deliberate excisions of

---

[84]Luke expands the group at a distance by placing alongside the women males known to Jesus (not the Twelve but a broader group of disciples); by the addition of Joanna he also has the women correspond more closely to those already mentioned in the Galilean public ministry—changes picking up on the L material of that ministry (nn. 65 and 66 above).

[85]Also the Aramaic words of the psalm cited in Mark would not fit into Luke's habit of sparing his audience foreign words.

items that do not fit in with the Lucan picture of the disciples or of Jesus. The same motivations explain significant Lucan *substitutions* for what is found in Mark.[86] Luke's changing (*transposing*) the Marcan order of events generally fits easily into Luke's stated preference for (logical) order and achieves greater narrative coherence.

More difficulty is presented by Lucan *additions* to or expansions of Mark, and probably they are to be explained in different ways. (1) Some are the results of Lucan creativity, as the evangelist sought to illustrate theological insights. Plausible examples in this category are Luke's having Jesus present while Peter denies him, and the introduction of multitudes/crowds favorable to Jesus before, during, and after the crucifixion. (2) Some are random items stemming from tradition known to Luke (most often, probably, in oral form),[87] which he reshaped and wove imaginatively into the main narrative borrowed from Mark. Good examples would be traditions about Herod's hostility and about words of forgiveness uttered by the suffering Jesus. A special subdivision in this category consists of items found also in the (pre)-Johannine tradition (which will be discussed in the next subsection), e.g., the division of the Jewish inquiry about "the Messiah, the Son of the Blessed [= God]" into two questions with an ambiguous answer to the first, and Pilate's triple affirmation of "not guilty." (3) Some are related to Luke's desire to establish a parallel between Jesus' arrest/trials and death and the arrest/trials of Paul,[88] the great missionary proclaimer of Jesus, and the death of Stephen, the first Christian martyr. These parallels serve pastoral pedagogy, teaching Christians that it may be necessary literally to take up the cross and follow Jesus (Luke 9:23). As for the significant details that the scenes involving Stephen and Paul share with the Jesus scene, it is very difficult to know which way the influence went: from what Luke's tradition(s)

---

[86]Of course, knowing the motivation for the substitution does not tell us whence the substituted material came; what I write in the next paragraph about additions would apply to that issue. For instance, Schweizer (*Luke* 355) maintains that the Ps passage substituted in Luke for Jesus' last words (replacing Mark's Ps 22:2) did not stem from Luke himself since he "often ignores references to specific verses." The vagueness of that reasoning makes it weak; but it is possible that before Luke's Gospel was written, Ps 31:6 was being employed as the dying Jesus' sentiments and thus constituted a tradition that Luke drew upon for his substitution.

[87]In the previous subsection I argued that Matt drew on a consistent body of tradition, heavily marked by orality and imaginative reflection on the OT, that contained popular narrative expansions pertinent to Jesus' infancy and passion. I cannot trace the same consistency in the traditions that Luke has added to Mark's passion or relate most of them to traditions he used in the infancy narrative. (The Daughters of Jerusalem on the way to the place of execution might be related to Simeon and Anna greeting the child Jesus in Jerusalem.)

[88]This is an important motif; see A. J. Mattill, Jr., "The Jesus-Paul Parallels and the Purpose of Luke-Acts," NovT 17 (1975), 15–46. O'Toole (*Unity* 62–71) gives tables of the parallels both to Stephen and to Paul.

told him about the death of Stephen and the trials of Paul to his description of Jesus, or vice versa.[89]

These suggestions about Lucan differences from Mark agree substantially with the results that Soards (*Passion* 116) obtained through his detailed study of Luke 22. He found much material taken over from Mark, some with little or no redaction, some thoroughly redacted. This was combined with material that Luke himself composed and with oral tradition drawn on by him. He found no compelling reason to posit that Luke used another PN besides Mark's; nor did Matera ("Passion") in his short study of Luke 23:44–48; nor do I.

Parenthetically, I might add that the Lucan special material, not found in Mark, presents a particular historical difficulty. Obviously incidents or details asserted by only one evangelist are always a problem for the historian because they do not meet the criterion of multiple attestation, discussed in §1, B2 above. Nevertheless, more than any other evangelist Luke has the mien of a popular Hellenistic historian, in no small part because of his authorship of Acts. Moreover, his additional material, whether in the infancy narrative or the PN, does not have the folkloric character of Matt's special material. Yet scholars are sharply divided on how to evaluate him. On the one side, Gaston ("Anti-Judaism" 153) holds that there was an early version of Luke-Acts before the Lucan Gospel was influenced by Mark; and so if we can recover that source, it is extremely important for reconstructing historical circumstances. On the other side, Millar ("Reflections" 355) contends that among the evangelists "Luke has the weakest grasp on the realities of Palestine under Roman domination." John "can bring us closer to the historical context and overall pattern of Jesus' activities." Faced with such disagreement, I shall insist on evaluating Luke's special material on its own merits without any supposition about "Luke the historian."

F. *The Origin of the Johannine Passion Narrative*

The origin of the Fourth Gospel itself is vigorously disputed by scholars, and here I attempt only to give a respectable rationale for the way I treat the origin of the Johannine PN. (I remind readers that since this book concentrates on the text as it now stands, the issue of origins affects only some items in the ANALYSIS of the sections, not the much more important COM-

---

[89]It is not impossible that a similar significant detail may have been present in early Christian tradition both about Jesus and about Stephen or Paul; but such coincidence would hardly explain all the parallels.

MENT.) From early days (Clement of Alexandria in EH 6.14.7) until the 1930s the dominant thesis was that John knew the Synoptic Gospels. What was disputed is how the fourth evangelist related to them. According to the view accepted for many centuries, he respected them and sought to supplement them with his Gospel, which contained other valid tradition. According to more recent theories, especially those that treat John as a sectarian or gnostic work, the fourth evangelist represented a different and even hostile outlook and sought to replace the Synoptics with his Gospel.[90] The question was also raised whether he composed a pseudo-gospel by imaginative reflection on Synoptic information without any valid tradition of his own. Then a chain of Johannine studies (Bultmann, Gardner-Smith, Dodd) created a new majority view that held the field for the second half of the 20th cent.: The Fourth Gospel was written without substantial use of the Synoptic Gospels.[91]

Yet there have remained scholars who dissented and posited Johannine dependence on the Synoptics or at least on Mark.[92] In a thorough survey summarizing the different theories, D. Moody Smith (*John,* esp. chap. 6) judges that one can no longer speak of a consensus against Johannine dependence on the Synoptics or, at least, on Mark. The reasons for the revival of interest in favor of John's dependence are varied. Some argue on the basis of the (dubious) supposition that Mark invented the gospel genre, and therefore John, if a Gospel, had to be imitating Mark. In particular, the view of Perrin, Donahue, Kelber, and others (sometimes called the Chicago school) that Mark created the *narrative* of the passion has implied to many that John's PN, with its narrative similarities to Mark's, had to be derivative from Mark. Neirynck, Sabbe, Denaux, and others (sometimes called the Leuven school)

[90]H. Windisch, *Johannes und die Synoptiker* (Leipzig: Hinrichs, 1926), was a major proponent of the replacement theory.

[91]Scholars holding this view would include Baum-Bodenbender, Becker, R. E. Brown, Buse, Cullmann, Edwards, Fortna, Goodenough, Haenchen, Hahn, Higgins, Käsemann, H. Koester, Kysar, Maddox, Martyn, Menoud, Nicol, Noack, Reim, Richter, J. M. Robinson, Schnackenburg, Schulz, von Wahlde, and Wilkinson. Some of these posit that a final redactor, in touching up the work of the evangelist, added minor touches from Mark. (I myself made that allowance in BGJ 1.xlvii; but as I have become more aware of the continuing influence of oral recitation and tradition after the Gospels were written, I have become dubious whether the redactor had to have known written Mark.) Others think that John was influenced by a putative preMarcan source. Unfortunately sometimes the thesis of Johannine independence of the Synoptics has been confused (not the least by Dodd, *Historical*) with a defense of Johannine historicity. Johannine independence of Mark can serve to show only the antiquity of certain traditions shared by John and Mark. Yet D. M. Smith is correct in pointing out that on select points where John differs from Mark, John may well be historical ("Historical Issues and the Problem of John and the Synoptics," in *From Jesus to John,* ed. M. C. de Boer [M. de Jonge Festschrift; JSNTSup 84; Sheffield: Academic, 1993], 252–67).

[92]For example, Barrett, Boismard, Feuillet, Freed, Guthrie, Kelber, Kümmel, R. H. Lightfoot, Mendner, Neirynck, Perrin, and Sabbe. Dauer posits dependence on the preJohannine-source level. F. Neirynck, "John and the Synoptics: 1975–1990," DJS 3–62, surveys the last years from the viewpoint of one thoroughly committed to Johannine dependence.

have worked with more classic arguments employed in discussing the Synoptic problem to argue for John's dependence; and DJS has articles exemplifying their reasoning.

I cannot enter the debate in exhaustive detail here, even in regard to the PN; but I shall discuss the evidence for the relationship of John's PN to the PNs respectively of Mark, of Matt, and of Luke. In those three discussions (particularly the first) the alternative theory of Johannine independence will be expounded.

1. John and Mark

Between the opening material pertaining to JBap in chap. 1 and the final six days of the prePassover period beginning with chap. 12 (and so during the whole account of the public ministry), John is truly close to Mark only in chap. 6 (the multiplication of the loaves and the walking on the water) and in some individual verses (cf. John 5:8; 6:7; 12:3; and Mark 2:9,11; 6:37; 14:3). The greater closeness of John to Mark in the PN therefore must be explained.

The argumentation for Johannine dependence on Mark is based on similarities (a few verbatim) and on parallelism of order. Frequently those who advocate dependence ignore a third issue that Gardner-Smith and Dodd made important: If John drew on Mark, one should be able to offer a rational explanation for at least many of the changes he made in producing so different a Gospel and PN.[93] Let me now compare the Johannine and Marcan PNs, bringing out the similarities in order and content and the dissimilarities as well. Because there are important similarities in the PN Preliminaries I shall begin with those, even if I refer to what I have written elsewhere on the episodes.

PASSION PRELIMINARIES:

- *Order:* Marcan order: (a) 11:1–10: Jesus acclaimed as he enters Jerusalem; (b) 11:15–19: Jesus drives out sellers from Temple; (c) 14:3–9: Woman anoints Jesus; (d) 14:17–25: Jesus' Last Supper. From the time that Jesus comes to Jerusalem (Mark 11:1) until his passion (Mark 14:26) these are the only scenes that Mark has in common with John, so that if John used Mark he has been

---

[93]In the preceding subsection I offered rational explanations for a large number of Lucan changes of Mark's PN, but the Lucan end product is much closer to Mark in the PN than is John.

highly selective.[94] The Johannine order of the scenes is (b), (c), (a), (d) and thus quite different.[95]

- *Content:* (a) BGJ 1.459–61 offers a comparative study of the accounts of Jesus entering Jerusalem and judges that John probably has not drawn from Mark and indeed is closer to Matt in spots.[96] (b) BGJ 1.116–20 compares the Synoptic and Johannine cleansings of the Temple and judges that the material in John 2:13–22 is not taken from the Synoptic Gospels. Yet there is room for scholarly difference.[97] (c) BGJ 1.449–52 compares the anointing of Jesus in John 12:1–8 with both Mark 14:3–9 and Luke 7:36–38. It concludes "that the Johannine form of the story represents a somewhat confusing amalgamation of details from two originally separate incidents," i.e., an incident in Galilee at the house of a Pharisee where a penitent woman weeps on Jesus' feet and wipes away her tears with her hair (originally no anointing) and an incident in Bethany at the house of Simon the leper where a woman named Mary anoints Jesus' head. Between Mark 14:3–9 and John 12:1–8 there are both verbatim agreements and significant differences.[98] It is hard to find another passage that has so confounded theories of Gospel relationship. (d) BGJ 2.557–58 compares the Last Supper in John and in the Synoptics; but John's account is about eight times as long as Mark's, so that any comparison limps. The most prominent difference is the lack of eucharistic words in John, and the closest parallel is in the prediction that one of those present would hand him over. In summary, although there may be an unusual number of similarities between Mark and John in these select sections of Passion Preliminaries, the differences between Mark 11:1–14:25 and John 12:1–17:26 are formidable; and any theory of relationship must account for them.

ACT I: JESUS PRAYS AND IS ARRESTED:

- The prayer scene before the arrest appears in Mark but not in John, but the situation is more complicated than first glance implies. The Johannine Jesus,

---

[94]John has no major parallel to Mark's cursing of the fig tree, parable of the tenants in the vineyard, conflicts with Herodians and Sadducees, question about the commandment, warning about the scribes, episode of the widow's mite, eschatological discourse, bribing of Judas, and preparations for the house in which to eat the Passover—an immense amount of the material in chaps. 11, 12, 13, and 14:1–25 that constitutes most of Mark's account of Jesus' Jerusalem ministry.

[95]To be specific: (b) John 2:13–22 (at the beginning of the public ministry); (c) 12:1–8; (a) 12:12–15; (d) 13:1–17:26.

[96]E. D. Freed, JBL 80 (1961), 329–38, argues that here John has simply rewritten the Synoptics; see the refutation by D. M. Smith, JBL 82 (1963), 58–64. This scene is featured in an important debate between P. Borgen and F. Neirynck on "John and the Synoptics" in *The Interrelations of the Gospels*, ed. D. L. Dungan (BETL 95; Leuven Univ., 1990), 408–58, esp. 432–36, 447–50. In his defense of Johannine independence of Mark, Borgen offers a theory of development of John and Mark from oral tradition very close to the one I espouse in this section.

[97]S. Mendner, ZNW 47 (1956), 93–122, thinks John drew on the Synoptics; E. Haenchen, ZTK 56 (1959), 34–46, thinks he did not.

[98]Agreements: "Bethany"; "ointment made from real nard"; "300 denarii"; "leave her alone"; "poor always with you"; "for burial." Differences: anointing head (Mark) vs. feet and drying with

like the Marcan, goes with his disciples from the supper to the area east of the city; the place-names, however, are different: Mount of Olives and Gethsemane in Mark, and "across the Kidron" in John. The predictions about the disciples and Peter, placed by Mark on the way to the Mount of Olives, as well as "Get up; let us go" at the end of the prayer (14:42), are found in John at the Last Supper (16:1,32; 13:36–38; 14:31). Mark's sorrow of Jesus' soul and the prayer to the Father about the hour are not found here in John but in 12:23,27–29 at the end of the public ministry.[99] In Mark 14:36 and John 18:11, but in different contexts, Jesus mentions drinking the cup.

- In the arrest scene there is general similarity between Mark and John in having Judas come with a party from the chief priests that takes Jesus into custody and in having the ear of a servant of the high priest cut off. But numerically more noticeable are the differences of John from Mark: In John the arresting party consists of a cohort of (Roman) soldiers and (Jewish) attendants; the recognition is accomplished by Jesus himself rather than by Judas with a kiss; the initial dialogue is totally different and it is not with Judas, but with the whole arresting party; the arresting party falls to the ground; the one who cuts off the servant's ear is Simon Peter and the servant is Malchus; Peter is reprimanded; Jesus arranges the departure of the disciples rather than having them flee (one of them naked). Overall, then, the agreement is in a very small area.

ACT II: JEWISH INTERROGATION; PETER'S DENIALS:

- In the Jewish legal procedure Mark's account is about twice as long as John's. Between the two there is a small general similarity: A question is asked by a high priest and Jesus is abused. In detail, however, virtually nothing is the same. By contrast with Mark, here John has no Sanhedrin trial (cf. John 11:47–53), no witnesses, nothing about the destruction of the Temple sanctuary (cf. John 2:19; 11:48) or about Jesus as the Messiah, the Son of the Blessed (cf. John 10:24,36; 19:7), and a very different description of the abuse.
- Peter's denials are synchronic with the Jewish interrogation in both Gospels, but in different sequences (Mark: three denials afterward; John: one before and two after). Overall the denials are reasonably alike except for Johannine touches absent in Mark: the involvement of another disciple known to the high priest (probably = the disciple whom Jesus loved) and the identification of the third interrogator as a relative of the one whose ear Peter had cut off.

---

hair (John and Luke). And there are points where Mark agrees with Luke ("Simon," "alabaster") against John.

[99]There in the response to Jesus' prayer involving an angel there is also a parallel to Luke's Mount of Olives scene.

ACT III: THE PILATE TRIAL:

- The details common to Mark and John are Pilate's question "Are you the King of the Jews?"; Jesus' answer "You say . . ."; a custom of releasing a person at the feast/Passover; a choice for Barabbas rather than Jesus that involves rejecting "the King of the Jews"; the giving over of Jesus; a flogging/scourging and a mocking of Jesus by Roman soldiers in the praetorium (with a surprising amount of verbal similarity, but placed at the end of the trial by Mark and in the middle by John). However, John's account is more than twice as long as Mark's and has an elaborate setting of outside/inside the praetorium, much dialogue, and dramatic episodes ("Behold the man"; "not a friend of Caesar"; Pilate on the judgment seat; "Look, your king") that are lacking in Mark.

ACT IV: CRUCIFIXION AND BURIAL:

- In the crucifixion Mark and John agree on the place (Golgotha), and that Jesus is crucified between two criminals (different vocabulary) and offered vinegary wine just before he dies. John makes major scenes (with added information) of three items that are only details in Mark: the title on the cross, the division of clothes, and the women.[100] John lacks the Marcan organization of the scene, including the central episode of three mockeries of the crucified Jesus, as well as a multitude of Marcan details: Simon the Cyrenian, the offering of wine with myrrh, the third- and ninth-hour time notices,[101] the darkness over the whole earth, the scream in Aramaic quoting Ps 22:2, the misunderstanding that Jesus is crying to Elijah, the rending of the sanctuary veil, the centurion's confession of God's Son. John has three unique "words" of Jesus from the cross embodying a vision of his death as triumphant completion, almost the opposite of Mark's picture of abandonment. The nonbreaking of the legs and the flow of blood and water from the side of Christ are unique to John.
- In the burial, late on this preparation day before the Sabbath, John agrees with Mark in having Joseph from Arimathea ask Pilate for the body of Jesus and bury it. However, by way of difference in John: Joseph becomes a disciple; there is no hesitation on Pilate's part; Nicodemus appears with a hundred pounds of spices; the place of burial is identified as a new tomb in a garden near where Jesus died; there is no reference to its being hewn out of rock, to a stone being rolled against the door, or to the women observing where Jesus is placed.

Evaluation: The same *general outline* is shared by John and Mark. After the supper, given over by Judas, Jesus is arrested in the area of the Mount of

---

[100]The women are mentioned in Mark after the death, observing from a distance; but in John before the death, near the cross, and with the addition of two major figures: the mother of Jesus and the disciple whom Jesus loved.

[101]Both Gospels mention the sixth hour: John 19:14 as the hour when Pilate sentences Jesus; Mark 15:33 as the time when darkness comes, after Jesus has been on the cross since the third hour.

Olives across the Kidron. He is brought to the high priest for questioning during which Jesus is abused and Peter denies him three times. Then Jesus is led to Pilate who questions him about being the King of the Jews, a question to which Jesus replies with "You say (so)." In the context of the customary festal release of a prisoner the Jewish crowd chooses Barabbas over Jesus; so under pressure Pilate gives Jesus over to crucifixion. He is scourged/flogged, mocked, and abused by Roman soldiers and then led to Golgotha. There he is crucified between two others, as his clothes are divided up and a notice mentioning "The King of the Jews" is put on the cross. Having been offered vinegary wine, Jesus dies. Some Galilean women are in the vicinity; Joseph from Arimathea asks Pilate for Jesus' body and buries him late on the preparation day before the Sabbath.

There are relatively few details mentioned in that outline, and the dissimilarities of items and wording between John's PN and Mark's far outnumber the similarities. (Peter's denials and the Roman mockery of Jesus would be the exceptions.) In Acts I and II of the PN there is much difference of order as well, with John having earlier in his Gospel what Mark has in the PN. No one can doubt that many of the differences that separate John from Mark fit into Johannine theology; but the same may be said on the other side: The differences that separate Mark from John fit into Marcan theology. Each evangelist has written a PN adapted to his own Gospel plan, and conformity with the respective theology does not inform us about the origin of the material peculiar to one or the other. For instance, if one looks back to the Passion Preliminaries, John's localization of the cleansing of the Temple at the beginning of the public ministry fits into a Johannine theological pattern of having a fundamental controversy with Judaism and its authorities run through the Gospel. Yet such conformity does not show whether or not John knew (and changed) the Marcan order where the cleansing of the Temple comes at the end of Jesus' life.[102] That order fits into Mark's plan, which has a prediction about destroying the sanctuary appear in the Jewish trial of Jesus a few days later. Yet this conformity does not show whether or not Mark knew and changed an order resembling John's where the event had occurred much earlier. Independently both evangelists could have known a basic tradition about the cleansing of the Temple, and each could have adapted it into his own vision of the Gospel narrative.

If we concentrate on John, how can we know whether the evangelist differs from Mark because he changed Mark or because he had an independent tradition? We cannot know; we can only judge what is more likely. The simi-

---

[102]If John did know Mark's account of the Preliminaries, the switch of (a) and (c) is hard to explain in terms of Johannine theological preference.

larities of Matt's PN and Luke's PN to Mark's PN are so strong that they are most logically explained if the two authors knew Mark's PN and used it. True, some instances in which Matt and Luke agree with each other against Mark are difficult to explain according to the theory of dependence on Mark; but these instances are so few when compared with the overwhelming similarities that they can be written off as examples of our ignorance of how ancient authors worked. In the Johannine situation, however, the differences outweigh the similarities, so that an inability to offer a logical explanation for many of them as deliberate changes of Mark becomes a formidable objection to the theory of dependence. Throughout the commentary I shall come again and again to what I regard as a completely illogical result if John knew Mark.[103] For that reason I shall work with the thesis that John wrote his PN independently of Mark's.

Yet then how would I explain the similarities between the two? If readers will look back three paragraphs to the general outline shared by Mark and John, they may recognize that its skeleton contains items attested or plausible in the early preGospel traditions about Jesus' death, as discussed earlier in this chapter (p. 48 above), namely, that Jesus was given over after a supper with his disciples; there was Jewish and Roman involvement; he was crucified and buried. In other words one could get the elementary outline of the four basic acts of the PN from what would be known widely by Christians. Moreover, differences between the Marcan and Johannine *sequence* are explicable if we pay attention to where the tradition did not establish a fixed order. If Heb 5:7 reports prayers of Jesus to the One who had the power to save him from death, it leaves open whether the prayers could have been uttered before the supper (John), before the arrest (Mark 14:35–36), and/or just before he died (Mark 15:34). The early Pauline statement that Jews were involved in the death of Jesus (I Thess 2:14–15), given the politics of the Jerusalem situation, could easily mean that the high priest and a Sanhedrin session were involved.[104] But the time of the session was not necessarily fixed in the Christian tradition. Accordingly Mark could place it on the night before Jesus' death (as part of his simplified outline shaped by preaching), and John 11:47–53 could place it days before the Last Supper and arrest (connecting it with the raising of Lazarus).

My comments thus far do not explain all the similarities visible when one looks at the general outline of Mark and John. It is not implausible to suppose that short informational items could have been part of a widely known tradition and thus available independently in Marcan and Johannine circles,

---

[103]Those who wish to anticipate may look at pp. 125–26, 143, 154, 177, 554 below for examples.
[104]See Josephus, *Ant.* 20.9.1; #200, on the execution of James, the brother of Jesus. A full discussion of the Sanhedrin issue will be presented in §18 below.

e.g., place memories (site of the arrest, Golgotha), persons (Judas as the one who gave Jesus over; Joseph from Arimathea as the one who buried him), and key phrases ("The King of the Jews" as the Roman charge against him). But if John did not draw on Mark, the similarity between them in the three-fold denial of Peter and the Roman mockery would have to mean that certain stories (and not just a general outline) had been shaped into a relatively fixed form before the Gospels were written.[105] Once again, however, we should notice that the evangelists would have had freedom in arranging these stories. The denials of Peter (because of the cockcrow) had to be placed during the night; but the evangelists could weave them around the Jewish interrogation (placed in the same night) in different ways, as Mark and John have done. The Roman mockery had to be somehow connected to the Roman section of the passion; but it could be narrated at different moments of that trial, as Mark and John have done.[106] That, before the evangelists took them over, such stories had been orally recited in different ways in different places would account for the fact that the substance and some of the wording is the same in Mark and John, but some of the details differ. Whether all the differences were already present when the story was first brought into Marcan or Johannine circles, whether some differences developed as it was re-told within the particular community circle, or whether some differences were introduced in a final stage when the evangelist himself wrote is often impossible to know. Nevertheless, such a projected history of widely circu-lating stories and of independently developing variants (some of them hap-hazard, others deliberate) is far more plausible in my judgment than the pic-ture of the Johannine evangelist working directly on the written Marcan PN, making dozens of inexplicable changes of order and words, and thus produc-ing the very different PN that appears in John.[107]

To summarize, then, I would postulate that (as discernible from Pauline and other nonGospel NT references to Jesus' death) there was a basic se-quence in early Christian tradition that connected supper to arrest, condem-nation, crucifixion, and burial. Alongside this sequence, which guided ker-ygmatic preaching and liturgical (eucharistic) memories, stories about figures and incidents in the passion were told. At the early stages the se-

---

[105]The importance of Peter in the one and echoes of the OT in the other may have been contribut-ing factors in such a process. But it is hopeless to attempt to decipher why, while other episodes remained fluid, relatively minor episodes of the passion became so widely known and relatively fixed, e.g., the role of Barabbas.

[106]I contend that Luke depends on the Marcan PN and at times has purposefully changed the Marcan order. But one wonders whether the different Lucan placing of Peter's denials (before the Sanhedrin session) and of the Roman mockery (while Jesus is on the cross) was not facilitated by the memory that the placement was not fixed in early tradition.

[107]I have postulated that the Matthean and Lucan evangelists did work directly on Mark's PN, but they emerged with end products far closer to Mark than is John.

quence need not yet have been fleshed out into a consecutive narrative, and the stories need not have been connected to precise points in it. Since I think of this as a widespread *tradition,* it may be called "preGospel" in the sense that it had not begun to be channeled toward any of the Gospels that would emerge. Only when a form of it had entered into the particular community and evangelistic history that led to the Gospels of Mark and John would I speak specifically of features as belonging to preMarcan or preJohannine tradition as distinct from preGospel tradition.

In the final preGospel stages before that step, were there already fleshed-out passion sequences so that one can speak of "preGospel passion *narrative(s)*" that came already formed into Marcan or Johannine circles? Story-telling instincts may well have produced such early PNs; but if they existed, I do not think that we have the tools to reconstruct them, although many scholars have attempted to do so. In the next stage of development, within the particular Marcan and Johannine history, was there a "preMarcan PN" and a "preJohannine PN" that could be worked on by the evangelists to produce the respective PNs now known to us?[108] Subsection C above has discussed this question in regard to Mark; it called attention to limitations in the criteria used to establish what is preMarcan and took note of the very divergent results produced by attempted reconstructions. The same criteria (with their serious limitations) have been used to establish preJohannine sources, including a preJohannine PN.[109] Most who attempt this do so by stripping off from the present Gospel what is distinctively Johannine by way of wording, style, and theology and emerge with a source much closer to the Synoptic Gospels. Some argue the other way around: The source was distinctively Johannine and the final Gospel has been more thoroughly adapted to the Synoptics.[110]

In BGJ 1.xxxiv–xxxix I presented my own approach. Material taken from the preGospel traditions (called Stage 1) was taken over and shaped within the life of the Johannine community through preaching and teaching and the influence of developing christology (Stage 2). Contributing factors in that

---

[108]Mohr (*Markus*) not only answers affirmatively but contends that the preJohannine PN represents an earlier stratum than the preMarcan.

[109]Those who think they can reconstruct in whole or in part the text of a preJohannine gospel, book of signs, collection of discourses, or PN include Becker, Bultmann, Dauer, Fortna, Haenchen, Kysar, Nicol, Schnackenburg, Thyen, and von Wahlde. D. M. Smith, *John,* gives a good survey of the efforts and results; in an earlier study (JBL 95 [1976], 231–41) he offered reasons for thinking that a collection of miracles or signs could scarcely have functioned as a missionary document to prove to Jews that Jesus was the Messiah without having contained a PN, since the passion would have been the point most controverted by the intended audience. W. J. Bittner, *Jesu Zeichen im Johannesevangelium* (WUNT 2.26; Tübingen: Mohr, 1987), rejects the preJohannine signs source.

[110]Thus Thyen and his disciples. Bultmann maintained that the final contributor, the Ecclesiastical Redactor, added material that would give John greater resemblance to the Synoptics.

stage would have been the entrance into the community of new members from different backgrounds (probably including Samaritans) and the ejection of community members from the synagogue amid disputes over the openly divine way they described Jesus.[111] In the course of the ejection, community members had to appear before synagogue authorities and give reasons for their Christian assertions; and those trials gave a strong legal tone to the Johannine tradition, marking it with an atmosphere of witness and testifying as well as hostility toward "the Jews." Eventually (Stage 3) this tradition was gathered into the consecutive narrative that we call "the Gospel according to John,"[112] and it was here that the skill of the evangelist showed itself in dramatic organization and dialogue. (The Pilate trial, with an outside/inside locale used to catch the opposing moods of the dramatis personae, and face-to-face dialogue used to bring out the theological issues, is an excellent example of the way the fourth evangelist outdistances the Synoptists in organizing a scene.) In reference to the period preceding the written Gospel of John (Stages 1 and 2), I prefer to speak of "traditions" (both preJohannine and preGospel) rather than "sources." Perhaps those traditions were organized into what could be called a consecutive source—I see no way to be sure—but in either case I would argue that what the evangelist took over was already very much shaped by Johannine community life and theology. There is no convincing reason to posit an alien source that the evangelist spent his time correcting.

Thus far I have been discussing the relationship of John's PN to Mark's, favoring the conclusion that John did not use Mark. That still leaves open the possibility of Johannine use of the Matthean and/or the Lucan PNs. Let us turn our attention to that issue now, comparing John to Matt very briefly and to Luke at length.

2. John and Matthew

One should distinguish between the material that Matt took over from Mark and the material peculiar to Matt. Usually those who do not think that John drew on Mark's PN find little reason to think that John is closer to Matt's presentation of the Marcan material. True, there are a number of small items where Matt and John share PN information lacking in Mark, e.g., in the arrest both have a reprimand by Jesus about the sword but in different

[111]This whole history is sketched and the supporting evidence marshaled in R. E. Brown, *The Community of the Beloved Disciple* (New York: Paulist, 1979).

[112]To accommodate what looked like interruptive additions to the text, I allowed a secondary editing and a final redaction (Stages 4 and 5), but they need not concern us here since I did not attribute anything major in the PN to those stages.

wording (John 18:11: "Put the sword into the scabbard"; Matt 26:52: "Return your sword to its place"); both name the high priest Caiaphas (but have him function differently); both include the name "Jesus" in the title on the cross (but do not have the same wording for that title); both use disciple language for Joseph from Arimathea (one using a verb, the other a noun); both refer to Jesus' tomb as "new" (but they differ on other information about it). These few items could have come from the preGospel tradition, or they could represent independent conclusions by the two evangelists;[113] and the fact that in every case the ambience is different works against a theory of Johannine dependence on Matt.[114]

As we saw (p. 59), Matt has a body of separate material in the passion. In my judgment, the fact that there is not a single plausible echo of that material in John makes it extremely unlikely that John was aware of Matt's PN.

3. John and Luke

When above under "Luke" we considered areas in which the Gospel differed from Mark, Lucan parallels to John were noted but discussion of them was postponed until here.[115] Scholars who accept a special relationship between the two PNs have most often resolved the dependency in one of three ways:[116] (a) John's knowledge of Luke or of the special preLucan PN (if one

[113]For instance, many think that Joseph from Arimathea's name was remembered because later he became a Christian; it would not have been unusual to simplify this and present him as a disciple from the beginning when he did this burial service for Jesus' body. Dahl ("Passion" 42) thinks of preMatthean and preJohannine parallels or of the possibility that some Matthean features passed into oral tradition and came to John that way. Buse ("St. John . . . St. Matthew" 65–68) is not impressed by the parallels between John and Matt.

[114]Nor are there really good examples of close relationship in the body of the Gospel. Changing the Marcan description (6:3) of Jesus as carpenter, Matt 13:55 has: "Is not this the carpenter's son? Is not his mother called Mary?" That is only partially close to John 6:42: "Is not this Jesus, the son of Joseph, whose father and mother we know?" These descriptions may be independent rephrasings of the tradition that some Galileans did not accept Jesus because they knew the ordinary status of his parentage. "A servant is not greater than his master" (John 13:16; 15:20) only partially resembles Matt 10:24: "A disciple is not above his teacher" (see Luke 6:40), and again we may be dealing with independent variants.

[115]Bibliography comparing the PNs of Luke and John is found in the GENERAL BIBLIOGRAPHY (§3), under John. See there the contributions of Buse, Cribbs, Klein, Osty, and Schniewind. Besides those treatments of the PNs, overall comparisons of John and Luke include J. A. Bailey, *The Traditions Common to the Gospels of Luke and John* (NovTSup 7; Leiden: Brill, 1963); F. L. Cribbs, "St. Luke and the Johannine Tradition," JBL 90 (1971), 422–50; A. Dauer, *Johannes und Lukas* (FB 50; Würzburg: Echter, 1984); Fitzmyer, *Luke* 1.87–89; F. C. Grant, "Was the Author of John Dependent upon the Gospel of Luke?" JBL 56 (1937), 285–307; H.-P. Heerekens, *Die Zeichen-Quelle der Johanneische Redaktion* (SBS 113; Stuttgart: KBW, 1984); R. Maddox, *The Purpose of Luke-Acts* (FRLANT 126; Göttingen: Vandenhoeck & Ruprecht, 1982), 158–79. See also P. Parker, "The Kinship of John and Acts," in *Christianity, Judaism, and Other Graeco-Roman Cults,* ed. J. Neusner (M. Smith Festschrift; 4 vols.; Leiden: Brill, 1975), 1.187–205.

[116]Without finely tuned cautions ("seemingly," "sometimes"), I assign scholars on the basis of their views about the *principal* evangelist, not on whether they posit that at the last moment there was minor assimilation of Luke to John or vice versa by another hand. One should note that for

is posited), e.g., Bailey, Barrett, Boismard, Heerekens, Kümmel, F. C. Grant, Parker, Streeter, Thyen; a variant is Dauer's thesis that John's *source* drew on Luke; (b) Luke's knowledge of a preJohannine PN source or traditions,[117] e.g., Cribbs, Schniewind; (c) Luke's and John's common knowledge of an independent (oral) source or tradition(s), e.g., Hahn, Günther Klein, Maddox, Soards.

Arguments invoked for a special relationship between John and Luke in the PN involve their having affinities in items or information, parallels in order, and similarities of thought.

Affinities in PN items or information[118] include the following:

ACT I: JESUS PRAYS AND IS ARRESTED:

- The place across the Kidron on the Mount of Olives as a customary meeting place (John 18:2: "many times Jesus had come there"; Luke 22:39: "according to his custom").
- God answers Jesus' prayer: In John 12:28–29 (at the end of the ministry) some mistake God's voice out of heaven for that of an angel; in Luke 22:43–44 an angel appears from heaven to strengthen Jesus.
- The presence in the arresting party of some type of Jewish officers: (John 18:3,12: "attendants of the Jews"; Luke 22:52: "captains of the Temple").
- The sword cuts off the *right* ear of the servant of the high priest (John 18:10; Luke 22:50: different words for "ear").

ACT II: JEWISH INTERROGATION OF JESUS; PETER'S DENIALS:

- A reference to starting a fire in the court of the high priest (John 18:18: "having made a charcoal fire"; Luke 22:55: "when they had kindled a fire").
- John mentions the high priest Annas, otherwise known only to Luke (John 18:13; Luke 3:2; Acts 4:6).
- Unlike Mark/Matt, which make Jesus' (attested) prediction of the destruction

---

Thyen and his disciples (Langbrandtner, Heerekens) the final redactor of John is the principal evangelist.

[117]Most scholars think that Luke was written before John and therefore do not posit Lucan dependence on John itself.

[118]Those to be presented in the list involve only the PNs. In the accounts of the public ministry, the most significant affinities between John and Luke are the miraculous catch of fish (John 21:4–13; Luke 5:4–11) and the mention of only one multiplication of loaves and fish. In the Passion Preliminaries, John and Luke have these parallels: a knowledge of Mary, Martha, and Lazarus (John 12:1–3; Luke 10:38–42; 16:20); the anointing of Jesus' feet (not head) by the woman (John 12:3; Luke 7:38); Satan's activity in or on Judas (John 13:2,27; Luke 22:3); and at the Last Supper, John 13:16, "A slave is not greater than his master," comparable to Luke 22:26, "Let the leader be as one who serves." After the burial, the two Gospels have Simon Peter go to the tomb (John 20:3–6; Luke 24:12 [textually dubious]), and Jesus' appearance to members of the Twelve in Jerusalem on Easter Sunday night.

of the Temple sanctuary a major factor in the Jewish proceeding against Jesus just before he dies, John and Luke do not mention it here. (But both introduce the theme elsewhere: John 2:19–21; 11:48; Acts 6:13–14).
- The christological issue is split into two questions (Messiah, Son of God) with an ambiguous answer to the first (John elsewhere: 10:24–25,33–36; Luke here: 22:67,70).
- Neither John nor Luke reports that Peter cursed and swore, as affirmed in the third denial in Mark/Matt.

ACT III: THE PILATE TRIAL:

- Pilate three times says that he finds no case against Jesus or finds nothing guilty in him (John 18:38b; 19:4,6; Luke 23:4,14,22).
- The Jews or the people are the first ones to mention Barabbas, choosing not "this fellow" (Jesus) but Barabbas (John 18:40; Luke 23:18).
- Pilate uses or proposes to use scourging as a halfway step toward releasing Jesus (John 19:1,4; Luke 23:22).
- The double cry to crucify (John 19:6: "Crucify, crucify"; Luke 23:21: "Crucify, crucify him").
- "Caesar" is mentioned by the Jewish adversaries of Jesus in speaking to Pilate (at the end in John 19:12: "If you release this fellow, you are not a friend of Caesar"; at the beginning in Luke 23:2: "We have found this fellow . . . forbidding the giving of taxes to Caesar").

ACT IV: CRUCIFIXION AND BURIAL:

- The naming of the place (different nomenclature) is immediately followed by the notice that there "they crucified him."
- The crucified Jesus speaks three times, although the words are different (John 19:26–27,28,30; Luke 23:34a,43,46).
- Jesus is offered wine (vinegary) only once (John 19:29; Luke 23:36).
- Both John and Luke mention spices and myrrh in relation to the burial on Friday; John's Nicodemus already has them, while Luke has the women get them ready when they return (home).

Evaluation of affinities of items or information: The most impressive of these parallels are the splitting of the christological question in Act II and Pilate's three affirmations of innocence in Act III. The others, often in very different contexts, involve small items, some of which may be accidental. In none of them is there any significant vocabulary similarity.[119] No knowledge

---

[119]The fact that in the resurrection narratives there is so much vocabulary similarity between John 20:3–6 and Luke 24:12 has made many scholars suspect that Luke did not write 24:12 and that a later scribe copied it from John! In comparing the whole of John to the whole of Luke, scholars like Neirynck and Dauer who do micro-comparisons of vocabulary will sometimes point out as characteristically Lucan (perhaps as stemming from Lucan redaction of Mark) a verb or noun form,

is shown by John of major peculiarly Lucan PN features: an actual angel that strengthens Jesus, the presentation to Pilate of three charges against Jesus, Jesus appearing before Herod, the Daughters of Jerusalem on the way to the place of execution, the forgiveness of one wrongdoer. Luke shows no knowledge of peculiarly Johannine features: a garden across the Kidron, a Roman cohort in the arrest, the role of the disciple whom Jesus loved, the dialogue between Pilate and Jesus, the presence at the crucifixion of the mother of Jesus, blood from the side of Jesus, and the arrival of Nicodemus.

Parallels in PN order are exemplified by the following:
- While Mark/Matt have the prediction of Judas' betrayal before the eucharistic words, Luke (22:21–23) has it afterward; John (13:10–11,18–19), without eucharistic words, places the prediction of betrayal (not in the same words) after the washing of the feet.
- During the night (after Jesus is led away from the place where he has been arrested), *before* he is sent to Caiaphas, John (18:13–14,19–23) has Jesus interrogated by Annas with attendants present; Jesus says that he always taught in a synagogue and in the Temple. During the night (on the Mount of Olives before Jesus is arrested and led away), *before* Jesus is led away to the Sanhedrin session, Luke (22:52) has the chief priests, captains of the Temple, and elders arrive against Jesus; Jesus says that day after day he was with them in the Temple. Notice that John and Luke disagree about the relationship to the arrest.
- John and Luke do not report a session of the Sanhedrin during the night of Jesus' arrest, as Mark/Matt do. In fact, however, John reports no Sanhedrin session at all between Jesus' arrest and the Pilate trial, while Luke does. (We do not know what John 18:24 envisaged during the night in having Jesus sent bound to Caiaphas the high priest; and Luke's sequence with a morning Sanhedrin session most likely stems from rearranging Mark's order.)
- Both have Peter deny Jesus *before* the Jewish interrogation (but John once and Luke three times).
- Neither John nor Luke ends the Roman trial with scourging or mocking as do Mark/Matt. But John has a scourging of Jesus, and Luke does not. John has a mockery by Roman soldiers in the middle of the Roman trial; Luke has a partial mockery by Roman soldiers while Jesus hangs on the cross.

---

a preposition, a placement of a word in a sentence—the appearance of these in John proves to them Johannine dependence on Luke. Other scholars do not always have confidence in our ability to determine exactly Lucan redaction and style that could come from no other source. Pointing to such a small feature when the rest of the wording of a passage (the macro-comparison) is different also casts doubt on the claim for dependence. In this book such detailed comparisons of Luke and John are reserved for the commentary on the individual verses.

Evaluation of parallels in PN order: They are extremely fragile, as my comments indicate. Sometimes Luke follows the Marcan order whereas John differs, e.g., in not having Jesus pray to his Father in the garden across the Kidron. At other times both Luke and John differ from the Mark/Matt order, but are not much like each other! At still other times they differ in ordering from Mark/Matt and are like each other; but that need not mean that one evangelist is being guided by the other's sequence, since Mark's order is not necessarily the most ancient Christian order. A good case, for instance, can be made that originally all Jesus' passion predictions about his disciples were set in the context of the Last Supper (where Luke and John have them) and that Mark created his own order by moving two of the negative predictions to fill in the transitional scene where Jesus was making his way to the Mount of Olives. The fact that John and Luke have very different wordings in these predictions suggests that one evangelist did not borrow from the other, but in terms of order they may be independently reflecting an older tradition.

Similarities of PN thought are in general attitudes rather than in specific descriptions or identical passages:

- When compared with Mark/Matt, Luke and John do not report that the disciples fled when Jesus was arrested. Luke is silent, and John shows Jesus in control, arranging for them to be let go. One should note that not only the description but also the rationale is different. Preparation for the Book of Acts, in which disciples like Peter and John become major heroes, suggested that Luke should not be harsh on them in the immediately preceding PN. John's christology could not allow a failure that would imply Jesus' enemies had real power to undo his work.

- Luke and John give a briefer (but very different) account of the Jewish proceedings against Jesus, so that the Roman trial (longer in both, but again different in content) gets the focus. In it Pilate becomes a major spokesman for Jesus' innocence. Again the tonality is different. Luke wants to show his readers that a series of objective witnesses testified that Jesus was not guilty: Jesus was not a crucified criminal. John is interested in Pilate as an archetype, i.e., the man who does not have the courage to decide for the truth and hear Jesus' voice (18:37) even though he knows Jesus is innocent.

- In the PNs of John and Luke one does not have the extreme turmoil, unanswered prayers, and abandonment by God found in Mark/Matt. Jesus remains united with his Father. If one were to put Gospel christologies on a spectrum showing the extent to which they allow the human weakness or the divine power of Jesus to become apparent, Mark would be at one end and John at the other, and in between Matt would be closer to Mark and Luke closer to John. Yet the portrayal of Jesus in John and in Luke is not the same. The Johannine

Jesus does not manifest the forgiveness and healing bestowed by the Lucan Jesus; the Lucan Jesus does not exhibit the hauteur and the power evident in the Johannine Jesus.

Evaluation of the similarities of thought: It is not surprising that a passing of time and growing perception within the Christian movement would produce similarities of thought. However, the different nuances in the PNs of John and Luke that I have indicated above caution against assuming that the similarities were taken over from one Gospel to the other. In other aspects the Gospels are quite diverse, e.g., Luke departs from Mark/Matt in showing Jewish crowds or the multitude sympathetic to Jesus and penitent for what was done to him; John makes no distinction between the hostility of the authorities and that of "the Jews" and has all of them willing to deny their messianic hopes rather than accept Jesus (19:15).

The evaluations I have given of the three types of evidence mean that I see no convincing reason to think that the author of John knew the Lucan Gospel (or vice versa). Furthermore, the parallels or similarities are not close or consecutive enough to demand dependence respectively on a preLucan or preJohannine continuous narrative (source) if either existed.[120] In the discussion of the Lucan PN under subsection E above, I judged it likely that Luke drew his special PN material from oral traditions. The best way to explain the parallels between John's PN and Luke's PN is to assume that the traditions that John drew on were at times similar to those that Luke drew on.

How could this contact have arisen? John differs from the Synoptics in picturing that the first following of Jesus begins in Judea among disciples of JBap, and that most of the ministry of Jesus takes place in Jerusalem. In chap. 4 John pictures a second following of Jesus among Samaritans, who are not brought to Jesus by the initiative of his Judean followers but by the proclamation of the Samaritan woman who has heard Jesus affirm that a time is at hand when God will not be worshiped in Jerusalem. If we take into account the infancy narrative, Luke speaks more about JBap than do Mark/Matt. The first five chapters of Acts are devoted to the initial following of the risen Jesus in Jerusalem. Chaps. 6–8 concentrate on the Hellenist Jerusalem Christians (distinct from the Hebrew Christians among whom the Twelve are prominent). Their first spokesman is Stephen, who denounces the Jerusalem Temple on the grounds that God does not dwell in houses made by hands (7:48). After Stephen is martyred, the Hellenist Philip brings the proclamation of Jesus to Samaria, and is so successful that the apostles

---

[120]In the previous subsection dealing with Lucan PN, I favored the thesis of those scholars who did not think there was evidence for a special preLucan PN. There may have been a preJohannine PN, but I do not think one can reconstruct it *in detail.*

at Jerusalem send Peter and John to investigate this mass conversion for which they have not been responsible. In other words, Acts relates a history of early Christian missionary expansion remarkably parallel to John's unique account of Jesus' missionary activity that in all likelihood is by double exposure the story of Johannine community history.[121] Many scholars maintain that Luke had special traditions about JBap and about the Jerusalem stage of early Christianity,[122] and so it is not at all farfetched that the traditions on which Luke and John drew had certain similarities and cross-fertilization. In my judgment this is more plausible than that Luke wrote his PN supplementing what he took from Mark with additions from a written Johannine source, or that John had access to a written Lucan source.

To summarize, the thesis with which I shall work in this commentary is that on the preGospel level (before tradition had been channeled into lines of development leading to any one of the four Gospels) there existed at least a sequence of the principal stages in the death of Jesus, along with some stories about episodes or figures in that death. There may have been one or more preGospel *narratives* of the passion composed from this material, but neither the fact nor the wording of the contents of such a narrative can be established persuasively. There was channeling of that traditional material toward Mark (the preMarcan stage), but whether or not there was a shaped preMarcan PN is uncertain. Mark wrote his PN without use of any of the other canonical PNs. The Matthean PN drew heavily on Mark's PN; yet Matt has incorporated into the material taken from Mark a body of popular and imaginative tradition (exemplified in the theme of the responsibility for innocent blood that runs through several episodes and in the eschatological incidents that follow the death of Jesus). The Lucan PN also drew heavily but more freely on Mark's PN. No other PN was used by Luke; but there were oral traditions (e.g., about the hostility of Herod) that he combined in orderly fashion with the material drawn from Mark. Some of those preLucan traditions (perhaps in a preGospel form) were also known to John. John did not use any of the Synoptic PNs in writing his own account, even though some of the preGospel tradition on which he drew resembled material on which Mark and Luke drew. Whether or not a preJohannine PN had already been shaped is not possible to determine. Since Mark and John wrote independently of each other, the agreement of their PNs is often an important

[121]See R. E. Brown, *Community*, 25–54.

[122]As I noted in subsection E above, I have proposed that Luke drew the hymns found in his infancy narrative from a collection of early Christian hymns, perhaps those of the Jerusalem community. Parker has argued strongly for parallels between John and Acts.

indicator of preGospel order and stories. Nevertheless, this criterion must be used with caution, for accidentally similar developments in the preMarcan and preJohannine situation are possible.

(Bibliography for this section of the INTRODUCTION *is found in §3.)*

§3. GENERAL BIBLIOGRAPHY

Information pertinent to *all* bibliographies in this book: The primary concern is with what the evangelists wrote, intended, and understood about the passion and death of Jesus. An immense bibliography about how his death was understood by Jesus himself, by Paul and other NT writers, by the Church Fathers, and by modern theologians will not be represented. Works dedicated to the Gospel PNs that are elementary explanations or principally spiritual or homiletic will also not be included. In both areas I have found judgments about what to include difficult, not only because the lines of demarcation are blurred, but also because of a personal interest in what is thus excluded. Yet the number of writings on the Gospel PNs is very large, and utility suffers if the tangential is included.

Authors' names beginning with the prepositions *de, di, du, van,* or *von* are found under "d" and "v" respectively. With rare exception, works by the same author are listed alphabetically rather than chronologically.

In the present bibliography, Part 1 covers writings on the passion in general. Some works using "Trial" in the title belong under this general rubric, for they treat the whole passion; others use that designation more literally for the Jewish and/or Roman legal process against Jesus and will be included under §17 and/or §30. Parts 2–5 cover writings on the PN respectively in Mark, Matt, Luke, and John. When a writing treats of two PNs, it is listed under the first Gospel in the order just named, with the exception that treatments comparing the Lucan and Johannine PNs are treated under John.

Part 1: The Passion Narratives in General
Aletti, J.-N., "Mort de Jésus et théorie du récit," RechSR 73 (1985), 147–60.
Avanzo, M., "El arresto, el juicio y la condena de Jesús. Historia y presente," *Revista Bíblica* 35 (1973), 131–50.
Bartsch, H.-W., "Die Bedeutung des Sterbens Jesu nach den Synoptikern," TZ 20 (1964), 87–102.
———, "Historische Erwägungen zur Leidensgeschichte," EvT NS 22 (1962), 449–59.
Beauchamp, P., "Narrativité biblique du récit de la Passion," RechSR 73 (1985), 39–59.

Belser, J. E., *History of the Passion* (St. Louis: Herder, 1929). Free adaptation of German orig. 1903, 1913 (2d ed.).

Benoit, P., *The Passion and Resurrection of Jesus Christ* (New York: Herder and Herder, 1969).

Bertram, G., *Die Leidensgeschichte Jesu und der Christuskult* (FRLANT 32 NS 15; Göttingen: Vandenhoeck & Ruprecht, 1922).

Bishop, E. F. F., "With Jesus on the Road from Galilee to Calvary: Palestinian Glimpses into the Days Around the Passion," CBQ 11 (1949), 428–44.

Bornhäuser, K., *The Death and Resurrection of Jesus Christ* (Bangalore: C.L.'s Press, 1958; German orig. completed in 1946).

Bovon, F., *Les derniers jours de Jésus* (Neuchâtel: Delachaux & Niestlé, 1974).

Brown, R. E., *A Crucified Christ in Holy Week* (Collegeville: Liturgical Press, 1986).

Calloud, J., "Entre les écritures et la violence. La passion du témoin," RechSR 73 (1985), 111–28.

Chabrol, C., "An Analysis of the 'Text' of the Passion," TNTSJ 145–86. French orig. in *Langages* 22 (1971).

Conzelmann, H., "History and Theology in the Passion Narratives of the Synoptic Gospels," *Interpretation* 24 (1970), 178–97. German orig. in ZBTJ 35–53.

Czerski, J., "Die Passion Christi in den synoptischen Evangelien im Lichte der historisch-literarischen Kritik," *Collectanea Theologica* 46 (Special Fascicle, 1976), 81–96.

de Jonge, M., "Jesus' Death for Others and the Death of the Maccabean Martyrs," TTK 142–51.

Delorme, J., "Sémiotique du récit et récit de la Passion," RechSR 73 (1985), 85–109.

Dibelius, M., *From Tradition to Gospel* (London: Nicholson and Watson, 1934; German orig. 1919, 1933), esp. 178–217 on the PN.

———, "Das historische Problem der Leidensgeschichte," ZNW 30 (1931), 193–201. Also in DBG 1.248–57, and in RTPL 57–66.

———, "La signification religieuse des récits évangéliques de la Passion," RHPR 13 (1933), 30–45.

Evans, C. F., "The Passion of Christ" (four sections), *Explorations in Theology 2* (London: SCM, 1977), 1–66.

Finegan, J., *Die Überlieferung der Leidens- und Auferstehungsgeschichte Jesu* (BZNW 15; Giessen: Töpelmann, 1934).

Flusser, D., *Die letzen Tage Jesu in Jerusalem* (Stuttgart: Calwer, 1982).

Garland, D. E., *One Hundred Years of Study on the Passion Narratives* (Macon: Mercer, 1990). The most complete bibliography, but with many misprints.

Girard, R., "The Gospel Passion as Victim's Story," *Cross Currents* 36 (1986), 28–38.

Green, J. B., *The Death of Jesus: Tradition and Interpretation in the Passion Narrative* (WUNT 33; Tübingen: Mohr, 1988).

Guillet, J., "Les récits de la Passion," LumVie 23 (119; 1974), 6–17.

Harvey, A. E., *Jesus and the Constraints of History* (Bampton Lectures 1980; Philadelphia: Westminster, 1982).

Haulotte, E., "Du récit quadriforme de la Passion au concept de Croix," RechSR 73 (1985), 187–228.

Hendrickx, H., *The Passion Narratives of the Synoptic Gospels* (2d ed.; London: Chapman, 1984).

Hillmann, W., *Aufbau und Deutung der synoptischen Leidensberichte* (Freiburg: Herder, 1941).

Horbury, W., "The Passion Narratives and Historical Criticism," *Theology* 75 (1972), 58–71.

Innitzer, T., *Kommentar zur Leidens- und Verklärungsgeschichte Jesu Christi* (4th ed.; Vienna: Herder, 1948).

Janssen, F., "Die synoptischen Passionsberichte," BibLeb 14 (1973), 40–57.

Kümmel, W. G., "Jesusforschung seit 1965. VI. Der Prozess und der Kreuzestod Jesu," *Theologische Rundschau* 45 (1980), 293–337.

Léon-Dufour, X., "Autour des récits de la Passion," RechSR 48 (1960), 489–507. Survey of literature.

———, "Autour de la mort de Jésus," RechSR 66 (1978), 113–24. Survey of literature.

———, "Passion, Récits de la," DBSup 6 (1960), cols. 1419–92.

Limbeck, M. (ed.), *Redaktion und Theologie des Passionsberichtes nach den Synoptikern* (Wege der Forschung 481; Darmstadt: Wissenschaftliche Buchgesellschaft, 1981). Abbreviated as RTPL.

Linnemann, E., *Studien zur Passionsgeschichte* (FRLANT 102; Göttingen: Vandenhoeck & Ruprecht, 1970).

Lohse, E., *History of the Suffering and Death of Jesus Christ* (Philadelphia: Fortress, 1967).

Lunn, A. J., "Christ's Passion as Tragedy," SJT 43 (1990), 308–20.

Marin, L., *The Semiotics of the Passion Narrative* (Pittsburgh: Pickwick, 1980; French orig. 1971).

Martinez, E. R., *The Gospel Accounts of the Death of Jesus* (Rome: Gregorian, 1970).

Matera, F. J., *Passion Narratives and Gospel Theologies* (New York: Paulist, 1986).

Mode, E., "Der Passionsweg Jesu Christi: Vom 'Hosianna' zum 'Kreuzige,'" *Forum Katholische Theologie* 7 (1991), 61–72.

Morgan, R., "'Nothing more negative . . .' A Concluding Unscientific Postscript to Historical Research on the Trial of Jesus," TJCSM 135–46.

O'Collins, G., "The Crucifixion," *Doctrine and Life* 26 (1976), 247–63.

Peddinghaus, C. D., *Die Entstehung der Leidensgeschichte* (Dissertation, Heidelberg, 1965).

Pesch, R., "Die Überlieferung der Passion Jesus," in *Rückfrage nach Jesus,* ed. K. Kertelge (Freiburg: Herder, 1974), 148–73. Also in RTPL 339–65.

Pesch, R., and R. Kratz, *So liest man synoptisch* (7 vols.; Frankfurt: Knecht, 1975–80). Vols. VI (1979) and VII (1980) treat the PN, respectively Mark 8:27–13:2 par.; and Mark 14:1–16:8 par.

Ramsey, (A.) M., "The Narratives of the Passion," StEv II, 122–34. Also *Contemporary Studies in Theology* 1 (London: Mowbray, 1962).

Richardson, P., "The Israel-Idea in the Passion Narrative," TJCSM 1–10.

Ricoeur, P., "Le récit interprétatif. Exégèse et Théologie dans les récits de la Passion," RechSR 73 (1985), 17–38.

Riedl, J., "Die evangelische Leidensgeschichte und ihre theologische Aussage," BibLit 41 (1968), 70–111.

Rinaldi, B., "Passione di Gesù Cristo. Appunti di storia e di teologia," *Scuola Cattolica* 114 (1986), 716–28.

Schelkle, K. H., *Die Passion Jesu in der Verkündigung des Neuen Testaments* (Heidelberg: Kerle, 1949).

Schenk, W., "Der derzeitige Stand der Auslegung der Passionsgeschichte," *Der Evangelische Erzieher* 36 (1984), 527–43.

———, "Leidensgeschichte Jesu," *Theologische Realenzyklopädie* 20 (1990), 714–21.

Schille, G., "Das Leiden des Herrn," ZTK 52 (1955), 161–205. Also in RTPL 154–204.

Schmauch, W., "Auslegungsprobleme der Leidensgeschichte," *Zu Achten aufs Wort* (Göttingen: Vandenhoeck & Ruprecht, 1967), 56–64.

Schmidt, K. L., *Der Rahmen der Geschichte Jesu* (Berlin: de Gruyter, 1919), esp. 303–9 on the PN.

Schneider, G., *Die Passion Jesu nach den drei ältern Evangelien* (Biblische Handbibliothek 11; Munich: Kösel, 1973).

———, "Das Problem einer vorkanonischen Passionserzählung," BZ 16 (1972), 222–44.

Schubert, K., "*Studien zur Passionsgeschichte* [von E. Linnemann]," BibLit 45 (1972), 33–41.

Soards, M. L., "Oral Tradition Before, In, and Outside the Canonical Passion Narratives," in *Jesus and the Oral Gospel Tradition,* ed. H. Wansbrough (JSNTSup 64; Sheffield: Academic, 1991), 334–50.

Suggs, M. J., "The Passion and Resurrection Narratives," in *Jesus and Man's Hope,* eds. D. G. Miller and D. Y. Hadidian (2 vols.; Pittsburgh Theological Seminary, 1971), 2.323–38.

Surkau, H. W., *Martyrien in jüdischer und frühchristlicher Zeit* (FRLANT 54; Göttingen: Vandenhoeck & Ruprecht, 1938), esp. 82–105 on the PN.

Taylor, V., "Modern Issues in Biblical Studies: Methods of Gospel Criticism," ExpTim 71 (1959–60), 68–72. (Special ref. to the PN.)

Theissen, G., *The Gospels in Context* (Edinburgh: Clark, 1992), 166–99 on the passion.

Trocmé, É., *The Passion as Liturgy* (London: SCM, 1983).

Vanhoye, A. (et al.), *La Passion selon les quatres Évangiles* (Lire la Bible 55; Paris: Cerf, 1981).

———, *Structure and Theology of the Accounts of the Passion in the Synoptic Gospels* (Collegeville: Liturgical Press, 1967).

Zehrer, F., "Jesus, der leidende Gerichte, in der Passion," BibLit 47 (1974), 104–11.

———, *Das Leiden Christi nach den vier Evangelien* (Vienna: Mayer, 1980).

Part 2: The Passion Narrative of Mark

Commentaries on the whole Gospel of Mark are cited by the use of the author's name and the equivalent of "Mark" in the respective language. In particular, I used these commentators in the publication or edition of the indicated year: R. G. Bratcher and E. A. Nida (1961); J. Gnilka (1978–79); W. Grundmann (1959); R. H. Lightfoot (1950); E. Lohmeyer (1967); D. Lührmann (1987); R. Pesch (1976); E. Schweizer (Eng. 1970); V. Taylor (1959); J. Weiss (in *Die Schriften des Neuen Testaments,* 1905; cited as *Schriften*); and J. Wellhausen (1909).

Anderson, C. P., "The Trial of Jesus as Jewish-Christian Polarization: Blasphemy and Polemic in Mark's Gospel," AJEC 107–25.

Best, E., *The Temptation and the Passion: The Markan Soteriology* (SNTSMS 2; 2d ed.; Cambridge Univ., 1990).

Black, C. C., *The Disciples according to Mark* (JSNTSup 27; Sheffield: Academic, 1989).

Buckley, E. R., "The Sources of the Passion Narrative in St. Mark's Gospel," JTS 34 (1932–33), 138–44.

Burkill, T. A., "St. Mark's Philosophy of the Passion," NovT 2 (1958), 245–71.

Bussmann, W., *Synoptische Studien* (3 vols.; Halle: Waisenhaus, 1925–31), esp. 1.192–205 on preMarcan PN.

Chordat, J.-L., *Jésus devant sa mort dans l'évangile de Marc* (Paris: Cerf, 1970).

Cook, M. J., *Mark's Treatment of the Jewish Leaders* (NovTSup 51; Leiden: Brill, 1978).

Dewar, F., "Chapter 13 and the Passion Narrative in St Mark," *Theology* 64 (1961), 99–107.

Donahue, J. R., "From Passion Traditions to Passion Narrative," PMK 1–20. A history of Marcan PN research.

Dormeyer, D., *Die Passion Jesu als Verhaltensmodell. Literarische und theologische Analyse der Traditions- und Redaktionsgeschichte der Markuspassion* (NTAbh NS 11; Münster: Aschendorff, 1974).

————, *Der Sinn des Leidens Jesu. Historisch-kritische und textpragmatische Analysen zur Markuspassion* (SBS 96; Stuttgart: KBW, 1979).

Ernst, J., "Die Passionserzählung des Markus und die Aporien der Forschung," TG 70 (1980), 160–80.

Fenton, J., "The Passion Narrative in St Mark's Gospel," in *The Reality of God. Essays in honour of Tom Baker,* ed. J. Butterworth (London: Severn House, 1986), 21–32.

Genest, O., *Le Christ de la Passion. Perspective structurale. Analyse de Marc 14,53–15,47 des parallèles bibliques et extra-bibliques* (Tournai: Desclée, 1978).

Heil, J. P., "Mark 14,1–52: Narrative Structure and Reader-Response," *Biblica* 71 (1990), 305–32. For Mark 14:53–16:8, see *Biblica* 73 (1992), 331–58.

Houlden, J. L., *Backward into Light: The Passion and Resurrection of Jesus according to Matthew and Mark* (London: SCM, 1987).

Jeremias, J., "A Comparison of the Marcan Passion Narrative with the Johannine," JEWJ 89–96.

Kelber, W. H., "From Passion Narrative to Gospel," PMK 153–80.

————, *The Oral and Written Gospel* (Philadelphia: Fortress, 1983), esp. 184–99.

———— (ed.), *The Passion in Mark* (Philadelphia: Fortress, 1976). Abbreviated as PMK.

Kelber, W. H., A. Kolenkow, and R. Scroggs, "Reflections on the Question: Was There a Pre-Markan Passion Narrative?" SBLSP (1971), 2.503–86. Abbreviated as KKS.

Kingsbury, J. D., "The Religious Authorities in the Gospel of Mark," NTS 36 (1990), 42–65.

Kolenkow, A., "Healing Controversy as a Tie between Miracle and Passion Material for a Proto-Gospel," JBL 95 (1976), 623–38.

Léon-Dufour, X., "Mt et Mc dans le récit de la Passion," *Biblica* 40 (1959), 684–96.

Lull, D. J., "Interpreting Mark's Story of Jesus' Death: Toward a Theology of Suffering," SBLSP 1985, 1–12.

Luz, U., "Theologia Crucis als Mitte der Theologie im Neuen Testament," EvT 34 (1974), 116–41. Compares Paul's and Mark's view of the passion.

McVann, M., "The Passion in Mark: Transformation Ritual," BTB 18 (1988), 96–101.

Malbon, E. S., "The Jewish Leaders in the Gospel of Mark," JBL 108 (1989), 259–81.

Mann, D., *Mein Gott, mein Gott, warum hast du mich verlassen? Eine Auslegung der Passionsgeschichte nach Markus* (Neukirchen-Vluyn: Neukirchener, 1980).

Matera, F. J., *The Kingship of Jesus: Composition and Theology in Mark 15* (SBLDS 66; Chico: Scholars, 1982).

Maurer, C., "Knecht Gottes und Sohn Gottes im Passionsbericht des Markusevangeliums," ZTK 50 (1953), 1–38. Also in RTPL 112–53.

Mohr, T. A., *Markus- und Johannespassion* (ATANT 70; Zurich: Theologischer Verlag, 1982).

Myllykoski, M., *Die letzten Tage Jesu: Markus und Johannes, ihre Traditionen und die historische Frage, Band 1* (Annales Academiae Scientiarum Fennicae B/256; Helsinki: Suomalainen Tiedeakatemia, 1991); *Band 2* (1994).

Navone, J., "Mark's Story of the Death of Jesus," *New Blackfriars* 65 (1984), 123–35.

Neirynck, F., "L'Évangile de Marc II. À propos de R. Pesch, *Das Markusevangelium*, 2 Teil," ETL 55 (1979), 1–42. Reprinted in NEv 520–64.

Nickelsburg, G.W.E., "The Genre and Function of the Markan Passion Narrative," HTR 73 (1980), 153–84.

Oberlinner, L., "Die Botschaft vom Kreuz als die Botschaft vom Heil nach Markus," BibLit 61 (1988), 56–65.

Patte, D. and A., *Structural Exegesis: From Theory to Practice. Exegesis of Mark 15 and 16* (Philadelphia: Fortress, 1978).

Schenk, W., "Die gnostisierende Deutung des Todes Jesu und ihre kritische Interpretation durch den Evangelisten Markus," in *Gnosis und Neues Testament*, ed. K.-W. Tröger (Gütersloh: Mohn, 1963), 231–43.

————, *Der Passionsbericht nach Markus. Untersuchungen zur Überlieferungsgeschichte der Passionstraditionen* (Gütersloh: Mohn, 1974).

Schenke, L., *Der gekreuzigte Christus: Versuch einer literarkritischen und traditions-geschichtlichen Bestimmung des vormarkinischen Passionsgeschichte* (SBS 69; Stuttgart: KBW, 1974).

————, *Studien zur Passionsgeschichte des Markus: Tradition und Redaktion in Markus 14,1–42* (FB 4; Würzburg: Echter, 1971).

Schlier, H., *Die Markuspassion* (Einsiedeln: Johannes, 1974).

Schreiber, J., *Die Markuspassion* (Hamburg: Furche, 1969). Brief history of PN research.

————, *Theologie des Vertrauens. Eine redaktions-geschichtliche Untersuchung des Markusevangeliums* (Hamburg: Furche, 1967), esp. 22–86.

Scroggs, R., aspects of and scenes in the Marcan PN in KKS: 2.505–36, 543–50, 556–85.

Senior, D., *The Passion of Jesus in the Gospel of Mark* (Wilmington: Glazier, 1984).

Smith, R. H., "Darkness at Noon: Mark's Passion Narrative," CTM 44 (1973), 325–38.

Soards, M. L., "The Question of a Pre-Markan Passion Narrative," *Biblebhashyam* 11 (1985), 144–69. Reprinted and updated in APPENDIX IX below.

Telford, W. (ed.), *The Interpretation of Mark* (Issues in Religion and Theology 7; Philadelphia: Fortress, 1985), esp. 1–41.

Temple, S., "The Two Traditions of the Last Supper, Betrayal, and Arrest," NTS 7 (1960–61), 77–85. PreMarcan PNs.

Vellanickal, M., "The Passion Narrative in the Gospel of Mark (Mk. 14:1–15:47)," *Biblebhashyam* 9 (1983), 258–78.

White, J. L., "The Way of the Cross. Was There a Pre-Markan Passion Narrative?" *Forum* 3 (#2; 1987), 35–49.

Wrege, H.-T., *Die Gestalt des Evangeliums* (Beiträge zur biblischen Exegese und Theologie 11; Frankfurt: Lang, 1978), esp. 49–96 on the Marcan PN.

Zeller, D., "Die Handlungsstruktur der Markuspassion," TQ 159 (1979), 213–27.

Part 3: The Passion Narrative of Matthew

Commentaries on the whole Gospel of Matt are cited by the use of the author's name and the equivalent of "Matthew" in the respective language. In particular, I used these commentators in the publication or edition of the indicated year: J. Gnilka (1986–88); R. H. Gundry (1982); J. D. Kingsbury (Proclamation, 1977); M.-J. Lagrange (1948); J. P. Meier (1980); and E. Schweizer (Eng. 1975). Also G. Strecker, *Der Weg der Gerechtigkeit* (FRLANT 82: Göttingen: Vandenhoeck & Ruprecht, 1971).

Bartsch, H.-W., "Die Passions- und Ostergeschichten bei Matthäus," reprinted in his *Entmythologisierende Auslegung* (Theologische Forschung 26; Hamburg: Reich, 1962), 80–92.

Bligh, J., "Matching Passages 2: St. Matthew's Passion Narrative," *The Way* 9 (1969), 59–73.

Broer, I., "Bemerkungen zur Redaktion der Passionsgeschichte durch Matthäus," in *Studien zum Matthäusevangelium,* ed. L. Schenke (Festschrift W. Pesch; SBS; Stuttgart: KBW, 1988), 25–46.

Bucher, G., "Elements for an Analysis of the Gospel Text: The Death of Jesus," *Modern Language Notes* 86 (1971), 835–44. Structural analysis of Matt 26–28.

Buck, E., "Anti-Judaic Sentiments in the Passion Narrative According to Matthew," AJEC 165–80.

Dahl, N. A., "The Passion Narrative in Matthew," *Jesus in the Memory of the Early Church* (Minneapolis: Augsburg, 1976), 37–51. German orig. 1955.

Descamps, A., "Rédaction et christologie dans la récit matthéen de la Passion," in *L'Evangile selon Matthieu,* ed. M. Didier (BETL 29; Gembloux: Duculot, 1972), 359–415.

Fischer, K. M., "Redaktionsgeschichtliche Bemerkungen zur Passionsgeschichte des Matthäus," TV-II (1970), 109–28.

Gerhardsson, B., "Jésus livré et abandonné d'après la Passion selon saint Matthieu," RB 76 (1969), 206–27. In German in RTPL 262–91.

Heil, J. P., *The Death and Resurrection of Jesus. A Narrative-Critical Reading of Matthew 26–28* (Minneapolis: Augsburg Fortress, 1991).

Lambrecht, J., "Het matteaanse lijdensverhaal," *Collationes* 30 (1984), 161–90.

LaVerdiere, E., "The Passion Story as Prophecy," *Emmanuel* 93 (1987), 84–98.

Lodge, J. C., "Matthew's Passion-Resurrection Narrative," CSA 3–20.

Martin, F., and L. Panier, "Dévoilement du péché et salut dans le récit de la passion selon Saint Matthieu," LumVie 36 (1987), 72–88.

Miyoshi, M., "Die Theologie der Spaltung und Einigung Israels in der Geburts- und Leidensgeschichte nach Matthäus," AJBI 15 (1989), 37–52.

Overman, J. A., "Heroes and Villains in Palestinian Lore: Matthew's Use of Traditional Polemic in the Passion Narrative," SBLSP 1990, 592–602.

———, *Matthew's Gospel and Formative Judaism* (Minneapolis: Fortress, 1990).

Przybylski, B., "The Setting of Matthean Anti-Judaism," AJEC 181–200.

Punnakottil, G., "The Passion Narrative According to Matthew. A Redaction-critical Study," *Biblebhashyam* 3 (1977), 20–47.

Rieckert, S.J.P.K., "The Narrative Coherence in Matthew 26–28," *Neotestamentica* 16 (1982), 53–74. Volume published as *Structure and Meaning in Matthew* (Stellenbosch, R.S.A., 1983).

Senior, D., "Matthew's Special Material in the Passion Story," ETL 63 (1987), 272–94.

———, *The Passion Narrative According to Matthew* (BETL 39; Louvain Univ., 1975). Abbreviated as SPNM.

———, *The Passion of Jesus in the Gospel of Matthew* (Wilmington: Glazier, 1985).

Trilling, W., "Die Passionsbericht nach Matthäus," *Am Tische des Wortes* 9 (1965), 33–44.

van Tilborg, S., *The Jewish Leaders in Matthew* (Leiden: Brill, 1972).

Witherup, R. D., *The Cross of Jesus: A Literary-Critical Study of Matthew 27,* Union Theological Seminary, Richmond, Ph.D. Dissertation (Ann Arbor: University Microfilms International, 1986).

Part 4: The Passion Narrative of Luke

Commentaries on the whole Gospel of Luke are cited by the use of the author's name and the equivalent of "Luke" in the respective language. In particular, I used these commentators in the publication or edition of the indicated year: J. A. Fitzmyer (1981–85); W. Grundmann (1981); I. H. Marshall (1978); A. Plummer (1922); G. Schneider (1977); and E. Schweizer (Eng. 1984). Treatments comparing the Lucan and Johannine PNs are found under Part 5.

Barr, A., "The Use and Disposal of the Marcan Source in Luke's Passion Narrative," ExpTim 55 (1943–44), 227–31.

Beck, B. E., "'Imitatio Christi' and the Lucan Passion Narrative," in *Suffering and Martyrdom in the New Testament*, eds. W. Horbury and B. McNeil (Studies for G. M. Styler; Cambridge Univ., 1981), 28–47.

Blevins, J. L., "The Passion Narrative. Luke 19:28–24:53," RevExp 64 (1967), 513–22.

Blinzler, J., "Passionsgeschehen und Passionsbericht des Lukasevangeliums," BK 24 (1969), 1–4.

Brawley, R. L., *Luke-Acts and the Jews* (SBLMS 33; Atlanta: Scholars, 1987).

Büchele, A., *Der Tod Jesu im Lukasevangelium. Eine redaktionsgeschichtliche Untersuchung zu Lk 23* (Frankfurter Theologische Studien 26; Frankfurt: Knecht, 1978).

Carlson, R. P., "The Role of the Jewish People in Luke's Passion Theology," SBLSP 1991, 82–102.

Cassidy, R. J., "Luke's Audience, the Chief Priests, and the Motive for Jesus' Death," PILA 146–67.

———, "The Trial and Death of Jesus," *Jesus, Politics, and Society: A Study of Luke's Gospel* (Maryknoll, NY: Orbis, 1978), 63–76, 165–75.

Chance, J. B., "The Jewish People and the Death of Jesus in Luke-Acts," SBLSP 1991, 50–81.

Fransen, I., "Le baptême de sang (Luc 22,1–23,56)," BVC 25 (1959), 20–28.

Fusco, V., "Il valore salvifico della croce nell' opera lucana," in *Testimonium Christi. Scritti in onore di J. Dupont* (Brescia: Paideia, 1985), 205–36.

Garrett, S. R., "The Meaning of Jesus' Death in Luke," *Word and World* 12 (1992), 11–16.

Gaston, L., "Anti-Judaism and the Passion Narrative in Luke and Acts," AJEC 127–53.

George, A., "Le sens de la mort de Jésus pour Luc," RB 80 (1973), 186–217. Reprinted in his *Études sur l'oeuvre de Luc* (SB; Paris: Gabalda, 1978), 185–212.

Gollwitzer, H., *The Dying and Living Lord* (London: SCM, 1960; German orig. 1941). A commentary on Luke 22:39–24:53.

Hawkins, J. C., "St. Luke's Passion Narrative Considered with Reference to the Synoptic Problem," ExpTim 15 (1903–4), 122–26, 273–76.

Kany, R., "Der lukanische Bericht von Tod und Auferstehung Jesu aus der Sicht eines hellenistischen Romanlesers," NovT 28 (1986), 75–90.

Karris, R. J., *Luke: Artist and Theologian: Luke's Passion Account as Literature* (New York: Paulist, 1985).

Kiddle, M., "The Passion Narrative in St Luke's Gospel," JTS 36 (1935), 267–80.

Kloppenborg, J. S., *"Exitus clari viri:* The Death of Jesus in Luke," TJT 8 (1992), 106–20.

Kodell, J., "Luke's Use of *Laos,* 'People,' Especially in the Jerusalem Narrative (Lk 19,28–24,53)," CBQ 31 (1969), 327–43.

LaVerdiere, E., "The Passion-Resurrection of Jesus According to St. Luke," CSA 35–50.

Matera, F. J., "The Death of Jesus according to Luke: A Question of Sources," CBQ 47 (1985), 469–85.

———, "Responsibility for the Death of Jesus according to the Acts of the Apostles," JSNT 39 (1990), 77–93.

Moule, C.F.D., Review of G. Schneider, *Verleugnung,* JTS NS 22 (1971), 194–97.

Mowery, R. L., "The Divine Hand and the Divine Plan in the Lukan Passion," SBLSP 1991, 558–75.

Neyrey, J., *The Passion According to Luke* (New York: Paulist, 1985).

O'Toole, R. F., *The Unity of Luke's Theology* (Good News Studies 9; Wilmington: Glazier, 1984), esp. 62–71.

Perry, A. M., *The Sources of Luke's Passion Narrative* (University of Chicago, 1920).

———, "Luke's Disputed Passion-Source," ExpTim 46 (1934–35), 256–60.

Pilgrim, W. E., *The Death of Christ in Lukan Soteriology* (Princeton Theol. Seminary Th.D. Dissertation, 1971).

Rehkopf, F., *Die lukanische Sonderquelle: ihr Umfang und Sprachgebrauch* (WUNT 5; Tübingen: Mohr, 1959). See also Taylor, "Rehkopf's," below.

Rese, M., *Die "Stunde" Jesu in Jerusalem (Lukas 22,1–53). Eine Untersuchung zur literarischen und theologischen Eigenart des lukanischen Passionsberichts* (Münster Univ., 1970–71).

Rice, G. E., "The Role of the Populace in the Passion Narrative of Luke in Codex Bezae," AUSS 19 (1981), 147–53.

Richard, E., "Jesus' Passion and Death in Acts," RDLJ 125–52, 204–10.

Schneider, G., *Verleugnung, Verspottung, und Verhör Jesu nach Lukas 22,54–71* (Munich: Kösel, 1969).

Schütz, F., *Der leidende Christus: Die angefochtene Gemeinde und das Christuskerygma der lukanischen Schriften* (BWANT 89; Stuttgart: Kohlhammer, 1969).

Schweizer, E., "Zur Frage der Quellenbenutzung durch Lukas," *Neues Testament und Christologie im Werden* (Göttingen: Vandenhoeck & Ruprecht, 1982), esp. 33–85.

Senior, D., *The Passion of Jesus in the Gospel of Luke* (Wilmington: Glazier, 1989).

Soards, M. L., *The Passion According to Luke. The Special Material of Luke 22* (JSNTSup 14; Sheffield: JSOT, 1987).

Stöger, A., "Eigenart und Botschaft der lukanischen Passionsgeschichte," BK 24 (1969), 4–8.

Sylva, D. D. (ed.), *Reimaging the Death of the Lukan Jesus* (Bonner Biblische Beiträge 73; Frankfurt: Hain, 1990). Abbreviated as RDLJ.

Talbert, C. H., *Reading Luke: A Literary and Theological Commentary on the Third Gospel* (New York: Crossroad, 1982), esp. 212–25.

Taylor, V., *The Passion Narrative of St. Luke* (SNTSMS 19; Cambridge Univ., 1972).

————, "Rehkopf's List of Words and Phrases Illustrative of Pre-Lukan Speech Usage," JTS ns 15 (1963), 59–62.

Tyson, J. B., *The Death of Jesus in Luke-Acts* (Columbia: University of South Carolina, 1986).

Untergassmair, F. G., *Kreuzweg und Kreuzigung Jesu. Ein Beitrag zur lukanischen Redaktionsgeschichte und zur Frage nach der lukanischen "Kreuzestheologie"* (Paderborn: Schöningh, 1980). On Luke 23:26–49.

————, "Thesen zur Sinndeutung des Todes Jesu in der lukanischen Passionsgeschichte," TG 70 (1980), 180–93.

Via, E. J., "According to Luke, Who Put Jesus to Death?" PILA 122–45.

Vööbus, A., *The Prelude to the Lukan Passion Narrative: Tradition-, Redaction-, Cult-, Motif-Historical and Source-Critical Studies* (Stockholm: ETSE, 1968).

Walaskay, P. W., "The Trial and Death of Jesus in the Gospel of Luke," JBL 94 (1975), 81–93.

Wilson, S. G., "The Jews and the Death of Jesus in Acts," AJEC 155–64.

Winter, P., "The Treatment of His Sources by the Third Evangelist in Luke xxi–xxiv," ST 8 (1954), 138–72, esp. 158–66 on the PN.

Winter, P., and V. Taylor, "Sources of the Lucan Passion Narrative," ExpTim 68 (1956–57), 95.

Zehnle, R., "The Salvific Character of Jesus' Death in Lucan Soteriology," TS 30 (1969), 420–44.

Part 5: The Passion Narrative of John

Commentaries on the whole Gospel of John are cited by the use of the author's name and the equivalent of "John" in the respective language. In particular, I used these commentators in the publication or edition of the indicated year: C. K. Barrett (2d ed. 1978); J. H. Bernard (1928); M.-E. Boismard (*Jean = Synopse III*, 1977); R. E. Brown (BGJ, 1966–70); R. Bultmann (Eng. 1971); E. Haenchen (Eng. 1984); E. Hoskyns (1947); M.-J. Lagrange (1948); A. Loisy (1921); R. Schnackenburg (Eng. 1968–82); B. F. Westcott (1880). Also the reconstructions of R. T. Fortna, *The Gospel of Signs* (SNTSMS 11; Cambridge Univ. 1970); *The Fourth Gospel and Its Predecessors* (Philadelphia: Fortress, 1988).

Blank, J., "Die Johannespassion. Intention und Hintergrunde," PGJK 148–82.

Borgen, P., "John and the Synoptics in the Passion Narrative," NTS 5 (1958–59), 246–59. Reprinted in his *Logos was the True Light* (Trondheim: Tapir, 1983), 67–80.

Braun, F.-M., "La passion de Notre Seigneur Jésus Christ d'après saint Jean," NRT 60 (1933), 289–302, 385–400, 481–99.

Buse, I., "St. John and the Marcan Passion Narrative," NTS 4 (1957–58), 215–19.

————, "St. John and the Passion Narratives of St. Matthew and St. Luke," NTS 7 (1960–61), 65–76.

Cribbs, F. L., "A Study of the Contacts That Exist between St. Luke and St. John," SBLSP 1973, 2.1–93, esp. 46–81.

Dauer, A., *Die Passionsgeschichte im Johannesevangelium* (SANT 30; Munich: Kösel, 1972).

de la Potterie, I., *The Hour of Jesus: The Passion and the Resurrection of Jesus According to John* (New York: Alba, 1989; French orig. 1983–84).

———, *La passion de Jésus selon l'évangile de Jean* (Lire la Bible 73; Paris: Cerf, 1986).

Dodd, C. H., *Historical Tradition in the Fourth Gospel* (Cambridge Univ., 1963), esp. 21–151 on the PN.

———, *The Interpretation of the Fourth Gospel* (Cambridge Univ., 1953), esp. 423–43 on the PN.

Fenton, J. C., *The Passion According to John* (London: SPCK, 1961).

Fuller, R. H., "The Passion, Death and Resurrection of Jesus According to St. John," CSA 51–63.

Granskou, D., "Anti-Judaism in the Passion Accounts of the Fourth Gospel," AJEC 201–16.

Haenchen, E., "History and Interpretation in the Johannine Passion Narrative," *Interpretation* 24 (1970), 198–219. German orig. in ZBTJ 55–78.

Harvey, A. E., *Jesus on Trial: A Study in the Fourth Gospel* (Atlanta: Knox, 1977).

Janssens de Varebeke, A., "La structure des scènes du récit de la passion en Joh. xviii–xix," ETL 38 (1962), 504–22.

Klein, H., "Die lukanisch-johanneische Passionstradition," ZNW 67 (1976), 155–86. Also in RTPL 366–403.

Koester, C. R., "The Passion and Resurrection According to John," *Word and World* 11 (1991), 84–91.

Kurichianil, J., "The Glory and the Cross: Jesus' Passion and Death in the Gospel of John," *Indian Theological Studies* 20 (March 1983), 5–15.

Lacomara, A., "The Death of Jesus as Revelation in John's Gospel," TLOTC 103–27.

L'Eplattenier, C., "La Passion dans l'évangile de Jean," FV 81 (#4; 1982), 25–30.

Lindars, B., "The Passion in the Fourth Gospel," in *God's Christ and His People*, eds. J. Jervell and W. A. Meeks (N. A. Dahl Festschrift; Oslo: Universitetsforlaget, 1977), 71–86.

McHugh, J., "The Glory of the Cross: The Passion According to St John," CR 67 (1982), 117–27.

Meeks, W. A., *The Prophet-King* (NovTSup 14; Leiden: Brill, 1967), esp. 55–80 on John's PN.

Müller, U. B., "Die Bedeutung des Kreuzestodes Jesu im Johannesevangelium," *Kerygma und Dogma* 21 (1975), 49–71.

Osty, E., "Les points de contact entre le récit de la passion dans saint Luc et dans saint Jean," RechSR 39 (1951: *Mélanges J. Lebreton*), 146–54.

Pfitzner, V. C., "The Coronation of the King—Passion Narrative and Passion Theology in the Gospel of St. John," *Lutheran Theological Journal* 10 (1976), 1–12.

Riaud, J., "La gloire et la royauté de Jésus dans la Passion selon saint Jean," BVC 56 (1964), 28–44.

Richter, G., "Die Deutung des Kreuzestodes Jesu in der Leidensgeschichte des Johannesevangelium (Jo 13–19)," BibLeb 9 (1968), 21–36. Reprinted in RSJ 58–73.

Schniewind, J., *Die Parallelperikopen bei Lukas und Johannes* (orig. 1914; reprint Hildesheim: Olms, 1958), esp. 37–85 on PN.

Schwank, B., SuS 29 (1964), a series of eight articles commenting section by section on the Johannine PN.

Senior, D., *The Passion of Jesus in the Gospel of John* (Collegeville: Liturgical Press, 1991).

Smith, D. M., *John among the Gospels: The Relationship in Twentieth-Century Research* (Minneapolis: Fortress, 1992), esp. chap. 5 comparing the PNs.

Staley, J., "Reading with a Passion: John 18:1–19:42 and the Erosion of the Reader," SBLSP 1992, 61–81.

Stanley, D. M., "The Passion according to St. John," *Worship* 33 (1958–59), 21–30.

Summers, R., "The Death and Resurrection of Jesus: John 18–21," RevExp 62 (1965), 473–81.

Talavero Tovar, S., *Pasión y Resurrección en el IV Evangelio* (Salamanca Univ., 1976).

Zumstein, J., "L'interprétation johannique de la mort du Christ," FGN 3.2119–38.

COMMENTARY
ON ACT I:

JESUS PRAYS AND IS ARRESTED IN GETHSEMANE ON THE MOUNT OF OLIVES ACROSS THE KIDRON

(Mark 14:26–52; Matt 26:30–56; Luke 22:39–53;
John 18:1–11)

The first Act of the Passion Narrative describes how Jesus, having left the Last Supper with his disciples, went across the Kidron to a place (Gethsemane) on the Mount of Olives and prayed there to his Father while his disciples slept. Judas arrived with an armed party; and, during an incident where the ear of the servant of the high priest was cut off, Jesus was arrested.

CONTENTS OF ACT I, SCENE ONE

§4. SECTIONAL BIBLIOGRAPHY
for Scene One of Act I:
Jesus Praying in Gethsemane (§§5–11)

The subdivision into three parts is outlined in the immediately preceding list of Contents. A separate SECTIONAL BIBLIOGRAPHY in §12 deals with the *arrest* of Jesus in Gethsemane, but writings that cover *both* prayer and arrest are listed in Part 2 below.

Part 1: Jesus Goes across the Kidron to the Mount of Olives (§5)

Best, E., *Following Jesus: Discipleship in the Gospel of Mark* (JSNTSup 4; Sheffield Univ., 1981), esp. 199–203 on Mark 14:28; 16:7.

Curtis, J. B., "An Investigation of the Mount of Olives in the Judaeo-Christian Tradition," HUCA 28 (1957), 137–80.

Evans, C. F., "I Will Go Before You into Galilee," JTS NS 5 (1954), 3–18.

Glasson, T. F., "Davidic Links with the Betrayal of Jesus," ExpTim 85 (1973–74), 118–19.

Grass, K., "Zu Mc 14,28," ZNW 13 (1912), 175–76.

Hoskyns, E. C., "Adversaria Exegetica," *Theology* 7 (Sept. 1923), 147–55 (on Mark 14:28).

Joüon, P., "Marc 14,31: *ho de ekperissōs elalei*," RechSR 29 (1939), 240–41.

Lightfoot, R. H., "A Consideration of Three Passages in St. Mark's Gospel," in *In Memoriam Ernst Lohmeyer,* ed. W. Schmauch (Stuttgart: Evangelisches Verlag, 1951), 110–15 (on Mark 14:28).

Magness, J. L., *Sense and Absence* (Semeia Studies; Atlanta: Scholars, 1986; in ref. to Mark 16:7 and 14:28).

Muñoz León, D., "'Iré delante de vosotros a Galilea' (Mt 26,32 y par). Sentido mesiánico y posible sustrato arameo del logion," EstBib 48 (1990), 215–41.

Odenkirchen, P. C., "'Praecedam vos in Galilaeam' (Mt 26,32 [par])," VD 46 (1968), 193–223.

Orge, M., "'Percutiam pastorem et dispergentur oves,'" *Claretianum* 7 (1967), 271–91 (on Mark 14:27).

Pieper, K., "Einige Bemerkungen zu Mt. 26.31 und Mk. 14.27," BZ 21 (1933), 320–23.

Schmauch, W., "Der Ölberg. Exegese zu einer Ortsangabe besonders bei Matthäus und Markus," TLZ 77 (1952), 391–96.

Schroeder, R. P., "The 'Worthless' Shepherd: A Study of Mark 14:27," CurTM 2 (1975), 342–44.

Soards, M. L., "Understanding Luke 22,39," BT 36 (1985), 336–37.

Stein, R. H., "A Short Note on Mark xiv. 28 and xvi. 7," NTS 20 (1973–74), 445–52.

Trudinger, L. P., "Davidic Links with the Betrayal of Jesus: Some Further Observations," ExpTim 86 (1974–75), 278–79.

van Iersel, B.M.F., "'To Galilee' or 'in Galilee' in Mark 14,28 and 16,7?" ETL 58 (1982), 365–70.

Part 2: The Prayer and Agony of Jesus in Gethsemane (§§6–11)

Aagaard, A. M., "Doing God's Will. Matthew 26:36–46," *International Review of Mission* 77 (1988), 221–28.

Aars, J., "Zu Matth. 26, 45 und Marc. 14, 41," ZWT 38 (1895), 378–83.

Andrews, M., "Peirasmos—A Study in Form-Criticism," ATR 24 (1942), 229–44.

Anonymous (F. A. Bornemann), "Erklärung einiger dunklen Stellen des Neuen Testaments," TSK 16 (1843), 103–40, esp. 103–6 on Mark 14:41.

Armbruster, C. J., "The Messianic Significance of the Agony in the Garden," *Scripture* 16 (1964), 111–19.

Baldwin, E.S.G., "Gethsemane: The Fulfillment of a Prophecy," BSac 77 (1920), 429–36.

Barbour, R. S., "Gethsemane in the Tradition of the Passion," NTS 16 (1969–70), 231–51.

Beck, B. E., "Gethsemane in the Four Gospels," *Epworth Review* 15 (1988), 57–65.

Bernard, J. H., "St. Mark xiv. 41,42," ExpTim 3 (1891–92), 451–53.

———, "A Study of St. Mark x 38,39," JTS 28 (1927), 262–70 (in ref. to Mark 14:36).

Black, M., "The Cup Metaphor in Mark xiv. 36," ExpTim 59 (1947–48), 195.

Blaising, C. A., "Gethsemane: A Prayer of Faith," JETS 22 (1979), 333–43.

Boman, T., "Der Gebetskampf Jesu," NTS 10 (1963–64), 261–73.

Bonnetain, P., "La cause de l'agonie de Jésus," RA 50 (1930), 681–90.

———, "La crainte de la mort en Jésus agonisant," RA 53 (1931), 276–95.

Boobyer, G. H., "*Apechei* in Mark xiv. 41," NTS 2 (1955–56), 44–48.

Brandenburger, E., "Texte und Vorlagen von Hebr. V 7–10. Ein Beitrag zur Christologie des Hebräerbriefs," NovT 11 (1969), 190–224 (in ref. to Mark 14:33–35).

Braumann, G., "Hebr 5:7–10," ZNW 51 (1960), 278–80 (in ref. to Mark 14:35–37).

———, "Leidenskelch und Todestaufe (Mc 10.38f.)," ZNW 56 (1965), 178–83 (in ref. to Mark 14:36).

Brongers, H. A., "Der Zornesbecher," *Oudtestamentische Studiën* 15 (1969), 177–92.

Brown, R. E., "Incidents that are Units in the Synoptic Gospels but are Dispersed in St. John," CBQ 23 (1961), 143–60, esp. 143–52 on Gethsemane and the trial. Reprinted in his *New Testament Essays* (New York: Paulist, 1982), 192–203.

———, "The Pater Noster as an Eschatological Prayer," TS 22 (1961), 175–208. Reprinted in his *New Testament Essays* (New York: Paulist, 1982), 217–53.

Brown, S., *Apostasy and Perseverance in the Theology of Luke* (AnBib 36; Rome: PBI, 1969), esp. 5–25 on *peirasmos*.

Carmignac, J., "'Fais que nous n'entrions pas dans la tentation,'" RB 72 (1965), 218–26 (in ref. to Luke 22:40; Mark 14:38 and par.).

Cavallin, A., "*(tò) loipon*. Eine bedeutungsgeschichtliche Untersuchung," *Eranos* 39 (1941), 121–44 (in ref. to Mark 14:41).

Chase, T., "*To loipon*, Matt. xxvi.45," JBL 6 (June 1886), 131–35.

Couchoud, P.-L., "Notes de critique verbal sur St Marc et St Matthieu," JTS 34 (1933), 113–38, esp. 129–31 on *apechei* in Mark 14:41.

Cranfield, C.E.B., "The Cup Metaphor in Mark xiv. 36 and Parallels," ExpTim 59 (1947–48), 137–38.

Daube, D., "Death as a Release in the Bible," NovT 5 (1962), 82–104 (in ref. to Mark 14:34).

———, "A Prayer Pattern in Judaism," StEv I, 539–45.

———, "Two Incidents after the Last Supper," DNTRJ 330–35, esp. 332–35 ("The Sleeping Companions").

Davies, W. D., "Paul and the Dead Sea Scrolls: Flesh and Spirit," in *The Scrolls and the New Testament*, ed. K. Stendahl (New York: Harper, 1957), 157–82 (in ref. to Mark 14:38).

Delling, G., "*Baptisma, baptisthenai*," NovT 2 (1957–58), 92–115 (in ref. to Mark 14:36).

de Tuya, M., "La 'agonía' de Jesucristo en Gethsemaní," CTom 82 (1955), 519–67.

de Zwaan, J., "The Text and Exegesis of Mark xiv. 41 and the Papyri," *Expositor* 6th Ser., 12 (1905), 459–72.

Dibelius, M., "Gethsemane," *Crozer Quarterly* 12 (1935), 254–65. In German in DBG 1.258–71, and in RTPL 67–80.

Feldkämper, L., *Der betende Jesus als Heilsmittler nach Lukas* (Bonn: Steyler, 1978), esp. 224–50 on Luke 22:39–46; and 251–84 on 23:34,46.

Feldmeier, R., *Die Krisis des Gottessohnes. Die Gethsemaneerzählung als Schlüssel der Markuspassion* (WUNT 2.21; Tübingen: Mohr, 1987).

Feuillet, A., *L'agonie de Gethsémani* (Paris: Gabalda, 1977).

———, "La coupe et le baptême de la Passion (Mc, x,35–40; cf. Mt, xx,20–23; Lc, xii,50)," RB 74 (1967), 356–91 (in ref. to Mark 14:36).

———, "L'évocation de l'agonie de Gethsémani dans l'Épître aux Hébreux (5,7–8)," EspVie 86 (1976), 49–53.

———, "Le récit lucanien de l'agonie de Gethsémani (Lc xxii.39–46)," NTS 22 (1975–76), 397–417.

Fiebig, P., "Jesu Gebet in Gethsemane," *Der Geisteskampf der Gegenwart* 66 (1930), 121–25.

Fitzmyer, J. A., "Abba and Jesus' Relation to God," in *À cause de l'évangile* (Mélanges J. Dupont; LD 123; Paris: Cerf, 1985), 1.15–38 (in ref. to Mark 14:36).

Flusser, D., "The Dead Sea Sect and Pre-Pauline Christianity," in *Scripta Hierosolymitana IV: Aspects of the Dead Sea Scrolls*, eds. C. Rabin and Y. Yadin (2d ed.; Jerusalem: Magnes, 1965), 215–66, esp. 252–63 on flesh and spirit (in ref. to Mark 14:38).

Friedrich, G., "Das Lied vom Hohenpriester im Zusammenhang von Hebr. 4,14–5,10," TZ 18 (1962), 95–115 (in ref. to Mark 14:35–37).

Galizzi, M., *Gesù nel Getsemani* (Biblioteca di Scienze Religiose 4; Zurich: Pas, 1972).

Giblet, J., "La prière de Jésus [Mc 14,32–42]," in *L'Expérience de la Prière dans les*

Grandes Religions, eds. H. Limet and J. Ries (Homo Religiosus 5; Louvain-la-Neuve: Centre d'Histoire des Religions, 1980), 261–73.

Grassi, J. A., *"Abba,* Father (Mark 14:36): Another Approach," JAAR 50 (1982), 449–58.

Green, J. B., "Jesus on the Mount of Olives (Luke 22.39–46): Tradition and Theology," JSNT 26 (1986), 29–48.

Hanson, A. T., *The Wrath of the Lamb* (London: SPCK, 1957), esp. 27–39 in ref. to Mark 14:36.

Heitmüller, F., "Gethsemane," *Jesu Dienst* 17 (1938), 314–18.

Héring, J., "Simples remarques sur la prière à Gethsémané," RHPR 39 (1959), 97–102. Also in German in *Neotestamentica et Patristica* (O. Cullmann Festschrift; NovTSup 6; Leiden: Brill, 1962), 64–69.

Holleran, J. W., *The Synoptic Gethsemane* (Analecta Gregoriana 191; Rome: Gregorian Univ., 1973).

Hudson, J. T., "Irony in Gethsemane? (Mark xiv. 41)," ExpTim 46 (1934–35), 382.

Huppenbauer, H., *"Bśr* 'Fleisch' in den Texten von Qumran (Höhle I)," TZ 13 (1957), 298–300 (in ref. to Mark 14:38).

Hutton, W. R., "The Kingdom of God Has Come," ExpTim 64 (1952–53), 89–91, on Matt 26:45.

Indemans, J.H.H.A., "Das Lukas-Evangelium xxii, 45," SO 32 (1956), 81–83.

Jannaris, A. N., "Misreadings and Misrenderings in the New Testament," *Expositor* 5th Ser., 8 (1898), 422–32, esp. 428–31 on Mark 14:41.

Jeremias, J., "Hbr 5.7–10," ZNW 44 (1952–53), 107–11 (in ref. to Mark 14:33–35).

Kelber, W. H., "The Hour of the Son of Man and the Temptation of the Disciples (Mark 14:32–42)," PMK 41–60.

———, "Jesus in Gethsemane," KKS 2.537–43.

———, "Mark 14:32–42: Gethsemane," ZNW 63 (1972), 166–87.

Kenny, A., "The Transfiguration and the Agony in the Garden," CBQ 19 (1957), 444–52.

Kiley, M., " 'Lord Save My Life' (Ps 116:4) as Generative Text for Jesus' Gethsemane Prayer (Mark 14:36a)," CBQ 48 (1986), 655–59.

Kruse, H., " 'Pater Noster' et Passio Christi," VD 46 (1968), 3–29.

Kuhn, K. G., "Jesus in Gethsemane," EvT NS 12 (1952–53), 260–85. Also in RTPL 81–111.

———, "New Light on Temptation, Sin, and Flesh in the New Testament," in *The Scrolls and the New Testament,* ed. K. Stendahl (New York: Harper, 1957), 94–113, 265–70. German orig. in ZTK 49 (1952), 200–22.

Le Déaut, R., "Goûter le calice de la mort," *Biblica* 43 (1962), 82–86.

Léon-Dufour, X., "Jésus à Gethsémani. Essai de lecture synchronique," ScEsp 31 (1979), 251–68.

———, " 'Père, fais-moi passer sain et sauf à travers cette heure' (Jn 12,27)," in *Neues Testament und Geschichte,* eds. H. Baltensweiler and B. Reicke (Mélanges O. Cullmann; Zurich: Theologischer Verlag, 1972), 157–65.

Lescow, T., "Jesus in Gethsemane," EvT NS 26 (1966), 141–59.

———, "Jesus in Gethsemane bei Lukas und im Hebräerbrief," ZNW 58 (1967), 215–39.

Lods, M., "Climat de bataille à Gethsémané," ETR 60 (1985), 425–29.

Lövestam, E., *Spiritual Wakefulness in the New Testament* (Lund: Gleerup, 1963), esp. 65–67, 90–91 in ref. to Mark 14:38.

Lotz, W., "Das Sinnbild des Bechers," NKZ 28 (1917), 396–407 (in ref. to Mark 14:36).

McMichael, W. F., J. Ross, and R. E. Wallis, "Our Lord's Prayer in Gethsemane," ExpTim 7 (1895–96), 502–5.

Manns, F., "Le symbolisme du jardin dans le récit de la passion selon St Jean," SBFLA 37 (1987), 53–80.

Marchel, W., "'Abba, Pater!' Oratio Christi et christianorum," VD 39 (1961), 240–47.

Martin, F., "Literary Theory, Philosophy of History and Exegesis," *Thomist* 52 (1988), 575–604 (on Mark 14:32–42).

Mees, M., "Die Bezeugung von Mt. 26,20–40 auf Papyrus (P[64], P[53], P[45], P[37]) und ihre Bedeutung," *Augustinianum* 11 (1971), 409–31.

Mohn, W., "Gethsemane (Mk 14:32–42)," ZNW 64 (1973), 194–208.

Müller, K. W., "*Apechei* (Mk 14:41)—absurda lectio?" ZNW 77 (1986), 83–100.

Neyrey, J. H., "The Absence of Jesus' Emotions—the Lucan Redaction of Lk 22,39–46," *Biblica* 61 (1980), 153–71.

Omark, R. E., "The Saving of the Savior. Exegesis and Christology in Hebrews 5:7–10," *Interpretation* 12 (1958), 39–51 (in ref. to Mark 14:33–35).

Ott, W., *Gebet und Heil* (SANT 12; Munich: Kösel, 1965), esp. 82–90 on Luke 22:39–46.

Parrish, G., "In Defence of the Eleven," *Faith and Freedom* 40 (119; 1987), 91–94.

Pelcé, F., "Jésus à Gethsémani. Remarques comparatives sur les trois récits évangéliques," FV 65 (4; 1966), 89–99.

Phillips, G. A., "Gethsemane: Spirit and Discipleship in Mark's Gospel," in *The Journey of Western Spirituality,* ed. A. W. Sadler (Annual Publication College Theology Society; Chico, CA: Scholars, 1981), 49–63.

Popkes, W., *Christus Traditus* (ATANT 49; Zurich: Zwingli, 1949), on *paradidonai,* esp. 152–69, 180–81 (in ref. to Mark 14:41).

Radl, W., *Paulus und Jesus im lukanischen Doppelwerk: Untersuchungen zu Parallelmotiven im Lukasevangelium und in der Apostelgeschichte* (Europäische Hochschulschriften 23/49; Bern: Lang, 1975), esp. 159–68 on Luke 22:39–46, and 211–20 on 22:47–23:25.

Robinson, B. P., "Gethsemane: The Synoptic and the Johannine Viewpoints," CQR 167 (1966), 4–11.

Robson, J., "The Meaning of Christ's Prayer in Gethsemane," ExpTim 6 (1894–95), 522–23.

Sabbe, M., "The Arrest of Jesus in Jn 18,1–11 and its Relation to the Synoptic Gospels. A Critique of A. Dauer's Hypothesis," in *L'Évangile de Jean. Sources, rédaction, théologie,* ed. M. de Jonge (BETL 44; Gembloux: Duculot, 1977), 203–44. Also in his *Studia Neotestamentica: Collected Essays* (BETL 98; Leuven Univ., 1992), 355–88.

Schille, G., "Erwägungen zur Hohepriesterlehre des Hebräerbriefes," ZNW 46 (1955), 81–109, esp. 95–104 in ref. to Mark 14:33–35.

Schrage, W., "Bibelarbeit über Markus 14,32–42," in *Bibelarbeiten* (Bad Godesberg: Rheinischen Landessynode, 1967), 21–39.

Schürmann, H., "Lk 22,42a das älteste Zeugnis für Lk 22,20?" MTZ 3 (1952), 185–88. Reprinted in his *Traditionsgeschichtliche Untersuchungen zu den synoptischen Evangelien* (Düsseldorf: Patmos, 1968), 193–97.

Schwartz, J. W., "Jesus in Gethsemane," *Lutheran Quarterly* 22 (1892), 267–71.

Simpson, M. A., "The Kingdom of God Has Come," ExpTim 64 (1952–53), 188 (on Matt 26:45; Mark 14:41).

Skard, E., "Kleine Beiträge zum Corpus hellenisticum Novi Testamenti," SO 30 (1953), 100–3, esp. 100–1 on Luke 22:45.

Smisson, E. A., "Mark xiv. 41: *apechei*," ExpTim 40 (1928–29), 528.

Söding, T., "Gebet und Gebetsmahnung Jesu in Getsemani. Eine redaktionskritische Auslegung von Mk 14,32–42," BZ 31 (1987), 76–100.

Speier, S., "'Das Kosten des Todeskelches' im Targum," VT 13 (1963), 344–45.

Stanley, D. M., *Jesus in Gethsemane* (New York: Paulist, 1980).

Staples, P., "The Kingdom of God Has Come," ExpTim 71 (1959–60), 87–88 (on Matt 26:45; Mark 14:41).

Starkie, W.J.M., "Gospel According to St. Matthew xxvi. 45, and xxviii. 2," *Hermathena* 19 (1922), 141–43, esp. 141 on 26:45.

Strobel, A., "Die Psalmengrundlage der Gethsemane-Parallele Hebr. 5.7ff.," ZNW 45 (1954), 252–66.

Summerall, H., Jr., "What Was the Cup That Jesus Had to Drink?" CT 14 (1969–70), 937–40.

Szarek, G., "A Critique of Kelber's 'The Hour of the Son of Man and the Temptation of the Disciples: Mark 14:32–42,'" SBLSP 1976, 111–18.

Thomson, A. E., "The Gethsemane Agony," BSac 67 (1910), 598–610. Reprinted as "Our Lord's Prayer in the Garden," BSac 97 (1940), 110–16.

Trémel, Y.-B., "L'agonie de Jésus," LumVie 13 (68; 1964), 79–103.

van Unnik, W. C., "'Alles ist dir möglich' (Mk 14,36)," in *Verborum Veritas*, eds. O. Böcher and K. Haacker (Festschrift G. Stählin; Wuppertal: Brockhaus, 1970), 27–36.

von der Goltz, E. F., *Das Gebet in der ältesten Christenheit* (Leipzig: Hinrichs, 1901), esp. 16–30 on the prayers of the PN.

Wiens, D., "The Passion History as Holy War," *Direction* 13 (1984), 26–32.

Wilson, W. E., "Our Lord's Agony in the Garden," ExpTim 32 (1920–21), 549–51.

Zeydner, H., "Apechei, Mark. xiv.41," *Theologische Studiën Tijdschrift* 23 (1905), 439–42.

Part 3: The Strengthening Angel in Luke 22:43–44 (§8)

Arthus, M., and V. Chanson, "Les sueurs de sang," RThom 6 (1898–99), 673–96.

Aschermann, H., "Zum Agoniegebet Jesu, Luk. 22,43–44," *Theologia Viatorum* 5 (1953–54), 143–49.

Brun, L., "Engel und Blutschweiss, Lc 22,43–44," ZNW 32 (1933), 265–76.

Duplacy, J., "La préhistoire du texte en Luc 22:43–44," in *New Testament Textual Criticism,* eds. E. J. Epp and G. D. Fee (B. M. Metzger Volume; Oxford: Clarendon, 1981), 77–86.

Ehrman, B. D., and M. A. Plunkett, "The Angel and the Agony: The Textual Problem of Luke 22:43–44," CBQ 45 (1983), 401–16.

Gamba, G. G., "Agonia di Gesù," RivB 16 (1968), 159–66 (on Luke 22:44).

Harnack, A. (von), "Probleme in Texte der Leidensgeschichte Jesu," SPAW (1901), 251–66, esp. 251–55 on Luke 22:43–44. Reprinted in his *Studien zur Geschichte des Neuen Testaments und der Alten Kirche* (Berlin: de Gruyter, 1931), 1.86–104.

Holzmeister, U., "Exempla sudoris sanguinei (Lc. 22,44)," VD 18 (1938), 73–81.

Keen, W. W., "The Bloody Sweat of Our Lord," *Baptist Quarterly Review* 14 (1892), 169–75.

———, "Further Studies on the Bloody Sweat of our Lord," BSac 54 (1897), 469–83.

Larkin, W. J., "The Old Testament Background of Luke xxii. 43–44," NTS 25 (1978–79), 250–54.

Moffatt, J., "Exegetica: Luke xxii.44," *Expositor,* 8th Ser., 7 (1914), 90–92.

Paton, W. R., "*Agōnia* (Agony)," *Classical Review* 27 (1913), 194 (on Luke 22:44).

Schneider, G., "Engel und Blutschweiss (Lk 22,43–44)." BZ NS 20 (1976), 112–16.

Smith, H., "Acts xx.8 and Luke xxii.43," ExpTim 16 (1904–5), 478.

van Lopik, T., "Tekstkritiek: telt het wegen of weegt het tellen," *Nederlands Theologisch Tijdschrift* 45 (1991), 101–6, esp. 103–4 on Luke 22:43–44.

§5. TRANSITIONAL EPISODE: JESUS GOES WITH DISCIPLES TO THE MOUNT OF OLIVES

(Mark 14:26–31; Matt 26:30–35; Luke 22:39; John 18:1a)

Translation

Mark 14:26–31: ²⁶And having sung a hymn/hymns, they went out to the Mount of Olives. ²⁷And Jesus says to them that: "You will all be scandalized because it is written, 'I will strike the shepherd, and the sheep will be scattered.' ²⁸However, after my resurrection I shall go before you into Galilee."

²⁹But Peter said to him, "Even if all are scandalized, yet not I." ³⁰And Jesus says to him, "Amen, I say to you that today, this very night, before a cock crows twice, three times you will deny me." ³¹But he was saying vehemently, "Even if it be necessary for me to die with you, I will not deny you." And they were all saying the same.

Matt 26:30–35: ³⁰And having sung a hymn/hymns, they went out to the Mount of Olives. ³¹Then Jesus says to them, "All of you will be scandalized in me this night, for it is written, 'I will strike the shepherd, and the sheep of the flock will be scattered.' ³²But after my resurrection I shall go before you into Galilee."

³³But in answer Peter said to him, "If all are scandalized in you, I will never be scandalized." ³⁴Jesus said to him, "Amen, I say to you on this very night, before a cock crows, three times you will deny me." ³⁵Peter says to him, "Even if it be necessary for me to die with you, I will not deny you." And so said all the disciples.

Luke 22:39: And having gone out, he proceeded according to his custom to the Mount of Olives; and the disciples too followed him.

[22:28–34 (at supper, Jesus speaking): ²⁸"Now you are the ones who have remained with me in my trials; ²⁹and so I appoint for you, even as my Father appointed for me, a kingdom, ³⁰so that you may eat and drink at my table in my kingdom, and you will sit on thrones judging the twelve tribes of Israel.

³¹"Simon, Simon, behold Satan asked to test you (pl.) like wheat." ³²But I have prayed for you (sg.) that your faith might not fail. And you, when you have turned around, strengthen your brothers." ³³But he (Peter) said to him, "Lord, I am ready to go with you both to prison and to death." ³⁴But he said, "I say to you, Peter, a cock will not crow today until you have three times denied knowing me."]

John 18:1a: Having said these things, Jesus went out with his disciples across the Kidron valley. [²ᵇ . . . many times Jesus had come there together with his disciples.]

[16:1,32 (at supper, Jesus speaking): ¹"I have said these things to you lest you be scandalized." . . . ³²"Why, an hour is coming—indeed has already come—for you to be scattered, each on his own, leaving me all alone. Yet I am never alone because the Father is with me."]

[13:33,36–38 (at supper, Jesus speaking): ³³"My little children . . . where I am going, you cannot come." . . . ³⁶Simon Peter says to him, "Lord, where are you going?" Jesus answered, "Where I am going you cannot follow me now; but you will follow later." ³⁷Peter says to him, "Lord, why can I not follow you now? I will lay down my life for you." ³⁸Jesus answers, "So you will lay down your life for me? Amen, amen, I say to you, 'A cock will not crow until you deny me three times.'"]

COMMENT

Since this is the first section of the book in which there is actual commentary on PN texts, let me remind readers of the notification in the PREFACE that the translation supplied is deliberately kept very literal.[1] Bracketed para-

---

[1]An instance is the exact, even if awkward, rendition of the historical present. Without that, in comparing Mark 14:27,30 to Matt 26:31,34, one would not see that while Matt preserves the first

graphs in the translation signal parallels *found in another sequence* that are relevant to the text under discussion. Thus the Lucan dialogue parallel to Mark 14:27–31 consists of the bracketed 22:28–34; but that dialogue is spoken at the Last Supper, not when Jesus is going with his disciples to the Mount of Olives, which is the setting of this episode.

As indicated in §2 above, I have chosen to begin the PN immediately after the Last Supper. However, to provide context for such a beginning, let me report briefly on what has preceded in each Gospel by way of immediate preliminaries to the passion. Then I shall turn to comment verse-by-verse on the present episode. The sequence of subsections is given in the list of Contents that precedes §4.

PASSION PRELIMINARIES IN EACH GOSPEL

Mark 14 and Matt 26, the chapters that introduce the present episode, have the same sequence. In previous chapters hostile encounters, debates, admonitory parables, and forebodings of present and future destruction have marked Jesus' coming (for the first time) to Jerusalem.[2] Now, with the Passover (Mark: "and Unleavened Bread") coming "after" only two days, the Jewish authorities seek to seize and kill Jesus[3]—by stealth and not on the feast lest there be a disturbance among the people (Mark 14:1–2; Matt 26:1–5). Meanwhile at Bethany (Mark 14:3–9; Matt 28:6–13)[4] a woman pours a vessel of myrrh (*myron*) over the head of Jesus. Although some of the disciples judge this a waste, Jesus sees it as a "beautiful deed" that will be told in memory of her, for it represents an anointing (Mark: *myrizein*), preparing his body for burial. Readers thus learn from Jesus' own lips that the efforts of the authorities to kill him will be successful. In confirmation of this (and perhaps as part of a stubborn rejection of Jesus' condoning the waste), Judas, one of the Twelve, goes to the chief priests and helps their plot by offering

---

historical present ("says"), he shifts the second to an aorist—a warning against generalizations about Matt's style. Or again, the issue of whether a set of hymns was sung would be obscured if the Greek verb *hymnein* in Mark 14:26; Matt 26:30 were not rendered "sung a hymn/hymns" to preserve the ambiguity, even though that rendering lacks grace.

[2]Respectively Mark 11:1 and Matt 21:1. Thus there are three Marcan chaps. (11–13) and five Matthean (21–25) dedicated to Jesus' activities in Jerusalem before the passion. These chaps. have many relationships to the PN; see, e.g., R. H. Lightfoot (*Mark* 48–59) connecting Mark 13 to the PN.

[3]Matt has Jesus himself call attention to the oncoming Passover and predict that in it the Son of Man will be given over—a touch that heightens Jesus' awareness and control of what will happen. Matt also formalizes the plot of the authorities by having them brought together in the court of the high priest Caiaphas, and thus anticipates the place, personnel, and context in which Jesus will shortly be sentenced to death (26:57–58).

[4]This is an instance of the Marcan "sandwich" technique: He inserts the Bethany episode to fill in the time between the plotting of the authorities in vv. 1–2 and the activation of that plan through Judas' treachery in vv. 10–11. See APPENDIX II, B2.

to give Jesus over, a betrayal for which he is promised silver (Mark 14:10–11; Matt 26:14–16).[5] After this foreboding background, Mark/Matt jump ahead a day or two (see APPENDIX II, B2) to the first day of Unleavened Bread when Jesus sends his disciples into the city to prepare the Passover meal in a large upper room (Mark 14:12–16; Matt 26:17–19) to which he comes at evening with the Twelve and eats at table. In that (Last) Supper (Mark 14:17–25; Matt 26:20–29) Jesus speaks twice. He announces that one of the Twelve eating with him is going to give him over. Accordingly the Son of Man goes as it is written of him, but it would be better if the one who is giving him over had not been born.[6] Then, taking bread and a cup, Jesus speaks of them as his body and as his blood of the covenant poured out for many (Matt: for the forgiveness of sins); and he states (Mark: with an "Amen") that he will not drink again of the fruit of the vine until he drinks of it new in the kingdom of God (Matt: "of my Father"). Clearly this brief account of the supper continues and heightens the foreboding and imminence of Jesus' death. Yet despite the misunderstanding by the Twelve (disciples) of the anointing with myrrh and the fact that one of them is giving him over, Jesus shows a desire to eat his last meal, the Passover meal, with them. He shares with them bread and wine symbolically related to his death.[7]

Luke's chapter (22) that contains the beginning of the PN (22:39) has a sequence partially similar to that of Mark/Matt. Once more it follows a period of controversy that greets Jesus' appearance in Jerusalem,[8] and opens (22:1–6) with the nearness of Passover/Unleavened Bread and the Jewish authorities seeking to put Jesus to death. But there is no interlude of an anointing at Bethany, for Judas comes immediately on the scene offering to give Jesus over to the authorities—an example of Luke's sense of a more clearly ordered narrative (Luke 1:3). Then, as in Mark/Matt, on the day of

---

[5]Matt dramatizes the iniquity of Judas: He asks for money rather than having the priests propose it; and he is given *thirty* silver pieces.

[6]I pointed out in n. 4 above that Mark has left his mark in the organization of the first part of chap. 14. Nevertheless, F. W. Danker (JBL 85 [1966], 467–72) points to a literary unity in Mark 14:1–25, relating the anointing by the woman (objected to because the money could have been given to the poor) and the betrayal by Judas predicted at the meal. In his judgment both echo Ps 41:2 ("The one who has regard for the poor is blessed"); and 41:10 (The trusted friend who partook of the just man's bread raises his heel against him). Once more Matt heightens both Jesus' sovereignty and Judas' iniquity. While the other disciples say, "Is it I, Lord?" Judas uses a forbidden term, "Is it I, Rabbi?" (see Matt 23:8); and Jesus indicates that he knows it is Judas who will give him over, an identity left vague in Mark.

[7]This makes incredible that their failure in Gethsemane represents a permanent rejection; the eucharistic words include them in the "many" for whom Jesus' death will be salvific.

[8]That occurs in Luke 19:28–29. Thus Luke has two and a half chaps. of Jerusalem activity; cf. n. 2 above.

the Feast of Unleavened Bread Jesus sends his disciples into the city to prepare the Passover meal in a large upper room (22:7–13) where, when the
hour comes, he eats with his apostles. The Lucan account of the Last Supper
(22:14–38) is three times as long as that of Mark/Matt, with only 22:14–23
parallel to their account (in reversed order, however: the eucharist preceding
the warning about the one to give him over). Then follow predictions about
the disciples and Peter (22:24–34) that, as we shall see below, Mark/Matt
place in the transitional episode on the way to the Mount of Olives. The
Lucan predictions have a more positive tone, so that the supper dialogue
taken as a whole is less foreboding and tilts toward victory where the disciples will sit on thrones in the kingdom of Jesus, and Simon Peter will turn
and strengthen his brothers. Finally (22:35–38), using symbolic language
Jesus warns the disciples to prepare themselves for the coming conflict, since
he is about to be counted among the lawless. The response that they have
two swords prepares readers for their wielding a sword against the arresting
party on the Mount of Olives (22:49–50).

John's preliminaries to the PN are more complex. Jesus has come to Jerusalem or its environs many times (2:13; 5:1; 7:10; 11:17; 12:1); and scattered
over these visits are events similar to those that the Synoptics place during
Jesus' single coming to Jerusalem, or on the last two days before Passover,
or even early on Friday after Jesus had been arrested. A Sanhedrin session
led by Caiaphas (11:45–53) takes place considerably more than a week before Passover (see 12:1); in it the authorities decide that the number of
people whom Jesus is attracting because of raising Lazarus presents a danger
that the Romans might destroy the sacred place (Temple sanctuary), and so
Jesus must be put to death. Then, at Bethany six days before Passover (12:1–
8), Mary the sister of Lazarus uses myrrh to anoint the feet of Jesus; Judas
protests, but Jesus speaks of her keeping it for the day of his burial. In
12:20–36 the coming of some Greeks indicates to Jesus that the hour has
come for the Son of Man to be glorified; his soul is troubled, but he
refuses to pray to the Father to be saved from the hour. The Last Supper
begins in 13:1 with Jesus knowing that the hour has come for him to
cross from this world to the Father; and it lasts through five chaps. (13–
17)—about eight times longer than Mark's account. There is a prediction
of Judas' iniquity (13:10–11,18–19), but no eucharistic words. A prediction of Peter's three denials (13:36–38) and sayings pertinent to the fate
of the disciples (16:1,32: scandal and scattering) occur during the supper,
as in Luke. Overall the atmosphere at the supper is one of Jesus' love for
his own (13:1).

After these somewhat similar and somewhat different accounts of what led up to the Last Supper and of the supper itself, in all four Gospels Jesus sets out to meet his death and thus begins his passion.

OPENING, TRANSITIONAL VERSE (MARK 14:26; MATT 26:30; LUKE 22:39; JOHN 18:1A)

In each Gospel the episode under discussion here constitutes the transition just described—from a supper that had taken place somewhere in Jerusalem to a site east of the walled city, across the Kidron (John) on the Mount of Olives (Synoptics), a place called Gethsemane (Mark/Matt: §6 below). The initial verse of this section is so transitional that, at least in Mark/Matt, some interpreters would put it with the Last Supper as a termination. The grammatical connection with what precedes is apparent in the fact that in the Synoptics the subject ("they" or "he") does not need to be identified. In Mark the immediately preceding verses (14:22–25) contain the eucharistic words spoken by Jesus to his disciples over the bread and cup. Wellhausen (*Marcus* 119) would connect our transitional verse 14:26 to 14:21 because he regards the intervening eucharistic passage as a later stratum. While Wellhausen's arrangement would place the prediction of Judas' betrayal (14:18–21) adjacent to this scene's predictions of the scattering of the disciples and the denials by Peter, the theory is too strongly dependent on reconstructing an original, sequential preMarcan account through excisions. The present sequence offers no major difficulty, for 14:25 (with its implication that the kingdom of God is not far off) conveys a sense of impending destiny that this scene develops.

Using exactly the same Greek, Mark and Matt begin with an aorist plural participle from the verb *hymnein,* a form that does not permit surety as to whether there was one hymn or more. In the only other NT instances of the verb (Acts 16:25; Heb 2:12) God is the object of the sung praise. Many scholars connect the usage here with the thesis that the Last Supper was a Passover meal after which the second group of Hallel psalms of praise (Pss 114/115–118) would have been sung. Indeed, although this is not the normal verb that one would use for chanting those psalms, NEB translates *hymnein* as "sung the Passover hymn"; and J. Ellington (BT 30 [1979], 445–46) suggests such an identification: "the Psalms [of the feast or Passover]."[9] D.

---

[9]Other candidates have been proposed for the *hymnein* of Mark 14:26. D. Cohn-Sherbok (NTS 27 [1980–81], 704–9), relying on the account of the Passover meal in Mishna *Pesaḥim* 10:1–7, rejects the frequent identification of the eucharistic drink with the third Passover cup ("the cup of blessing"), which would be followed by the Hallel psalms in relation to still a fourth cup. He identifies the fourth cup as the eucharistic drink, after which the benediction song (*brkh hšyr*) would be recited. H. Rusche (*Wissenschaft und Weisheit* 51 [1988], 210–12) suggests Ps 136 because of v. 23: God remembered us in our low estate, for God's mercy endures forever.

Daube points out that the rabbis allowed finishing the Passover meal in one place and moving elsewhere to praise God.[10] All this theorizing assumes that: (1) the Mishna is a safe guide to Passover practice 150 years earlier in Jesus' time;[11] (2) the Last Supper was factually a Passover meal; (3) Mark/ Matthew were giving a precise description evocative of the ceremonies of that meal; and (4) the Marcan readers would have recognized such a Passover reference without further explanation, despite their ignorance of Jewish customs as indicated in Mark 7:3–4. Such a conglomeration of uncertainties suggests that instead of identifying the *hymnein* of Mark/Matt with Passover hymnology (or other variants) and of developing a theology or eschatology based on the identification, one should recognize more simply and surely that *hymnein* indicates a prayerful context as the meal closed. Mark's first readers/hearers (even as readers today) would have thought of hymn(s)-singing familiar to them[12] without reflecting about the historical situation many years before.

In setting out from the place of the supper Jesus was accompanied by his disciples, as indicated explicitly by Luke and John, and implicitly by the plural subject in Mark/Matt.[13] If one looks back to the Last Supper, it is clear from Mark 14:17 and Matt 26:20 that the Twelve (minus Judas, as we shall discover) are those who "went out" (*eiserchesthai*) with Jesus. Luke has changed the Marcan expression to: "having gone out [*eiserchesthai*], he proceeded [*poreuesthai*]." Attention is thus focused on the initiative of Jesus; and by the addition of *poreuesthai*[14] Luke has connected this action to the central geographical movement of the Gospel previously described by this

[10]"Two" 332. For an excellent summary of Daube's connecting the Last Supper (and the PN) with the Passover, see D. B. Carmichael, JSNT 42 (1991), 45–67.

[11]B. M. Bokser, *The Origins of the Seder* (Berkeley: Univ. of California, 1984) cautions on this point, insisting that with the destruction of the Temple there was a major change in the manner in which the Passover was celebrated since the sacrificial lamb, which was the centerpiece, was no longer slaughtered in the Temple. Hymns in the Temple would have been sung by experts in connection with the sacrifice of the lambs. Philo (*De specialibus legibus* 2.27; #148), writing in the diaspora in Jesus' time, mentions hymns at table during Passover; and Bokser (p. 45) is willing to allow that the Hallel psalms may have had a place in the pre-70 rite. (See also J. Tabory, *Immanuel* 12 [1981], 32–43, esp. p. 42). Stemberger ("Pesachhaggada" 154–55), however, maintains that we cannot be sure that the Hallel psalms were used in Jesus' time *in Jerusalem*.

[12]Christian singing of hymns (Col 3:16; Eph 5:19) may have taken place at eucharistic meals and have influenced the Gospel portrayal of the meal at which Jesus performed the eucharistic action.

[13]C. H. Turner, JTS 26 (1924–25), 225–26, 231, cites Mark's tendency to use the plural to describe Jesus' movement (in which practice Mark is not usually followed by Matt, as he is here). Schenke (*Studien* 350) sees the plural as a generalization used to pull together diverse traditions.

[14]A Lucan favorite: 51 times in Luke, 37 in Acts, compared to 3 in Mark, 29 in Matt, 13 in John. I shall on many occasions give vocabulary statistics; and to avoid getting the wrong impression, readers should keep in mind throughout that the compared works are of different length: Mark about 11,000 words, Matt 18,000, Luke 19,000, Acts 18,000, John 15,000. Therefore, a word that occurs 3 times in Mark, 5 in Matt, 10 in Luke-Acts, and 4 in John would be used with roughly the same proportionate frequency by each writer.

verb: Jesus' proceeding to Jerusalem where prophets must die (9:51,53; 13:33; 17:11) and where the Son of Man will go his way as destined (22:22). As for the disciples who follow him, Luke 22:14 mentioned "the apostles" at the supper; and 22:30, by envisioning them as judges of the twelve tribes of Israel, made it clear that here as elsewhere, for Luke "apostles" means the Twelve.[15] Luke, anticipating the designation of these as disciples in Mark 14:32, writes "the disciples too followed him," with a verb chosen to underline their character as disciples.[16] The apostles and specifically members of the Twelve were also called "disciples" when Jesus was proceeding with them to Jerusalem (see 9:54 with 9:51–53; and 17:1,5 with 17:11).[17]

Again many scholars, imagining the Last Supper to have been a Passover meal, point out that Jewish customs demanded that this holy night should be spent within the confines of Jerusalem.[18] Jeremias (JEWJ 43) presents evidence that in order to accommodate large crowds, the city confines were enlarged for Passover to include the environs as far as Bethphage on the Mount of Olives,[19] but not Bethany (Jesus' normal residence in the area). The four Gospels, however, use here *exerchesthai*, "to go out," the same verb Mark 11:11 used for going out to Bethany; and thus they show no explicit awareness of Passover extensions. Luke 21:37 has Jesus regularly lodging on the Mount of Olives, whence the reference to "his custom" here.[20]

Is there theological import in Jesus' "going out" of Jerusalem here? Schmauch ("Ölberg" 392–94) invokes the theme of the red heifer being slaughtered outside (*exō*) the camp (Num 19:2–3), which Heb 13:11–13 relates to the sufferings of Jesus (and of Christians). That theme, however, is more plausible background for another verse, namely, Mark 15:20: "They lead him out [*exagein*] in order that they might crucify him." Neither does

---

[15]Soards ("Understanding" 336, n. 2) is justified in stating that the claim that Luke thought of a larger group at the Supper than just the Twelve "goes directly against the plain sense of the text." Acts 1:15–26 shows how, although Judas will not be among them, the apostles will be able to judge the *twelve* tribes: Matthias will take Judas' place.

[16]"Follow" is associated with the activity of disciples some eighteen times, beginning in 5:11.

[17]This is surely more likely than the suggestion that by "the disciples *too*" Luke is suddenly introducing another group of people, without explaining where they came from. Soards ("Understanding") is correct that Luke does know of disciples beyond the Twelve (6:13) and that at a distance from the cross in 23:49 he will mention "all those known to him"; but neither of those points justifies reading another cast of characters into the Mount of Olives scene. Luke does speak in this scene (22:49) of "those about him [Jesus]"; but those are not a different group from the apostles who had been present at the supper since they ask, "Lord, shall we strike with sword?" referring back to the supper dialogue of 22:36–38.

[18]This interpretation embodies an exegesis of Exod 12:22 (none of those involved in the Passover could go outdoors before morning) and Deut 16:7 (in the morning they could return to their tents), combined with Neh 13:19 insisting that one could not leave Jerusalem during the Sabbath.

[19]Yet Tosepta *Pesahim* 8:8 indicates that to go out to Bethphage means not to spend the night in Jerusalem, at least in regard to certain legal obligations; for a contrary view see Tosepta *Menaḥot* 11:1.

[20]For Acts 1:12 the Mount of Olives is within a Sabbath's day journey of Jerusalem.

the present verse plausibly echo an earlier saying of Jesus (Matt 10:14), "And if anyone will not receive you or listen to your words, as you go out [*exerchesthai*] from that house or town, shake the dust from your feet," for there is no indication of anger at Jerusalem as Jesus leaves the supper.

The theology here is not attached to the verb but to the destination, the Mount of Olives. In Luke particularly, Jesus has gone to mountains to pray (6:12; 9:28), but this site has greater symbolism. There are six OT references (II Sam 15:30; I Kings 11:7; II Kings 23:13; Ezek 10:23; Neh 8:15 [?]; Zech 14:4) to the spur of the mountain range that has three summits or mounts running parallel to Jerusalem for some two and a half miles on the east, separated from the city by the Kidron valley and rising some 300 ft. higher than the Temple area. Although "Mount of Olives" can designate the whole, often it is used for the central section, with Mount Scopus to the north and the Mount of Offense to the south-southwest.[21] Two of the six OT references (the two that use the name "Olives") function actively in NT thought. The only explicit occurrence of the name "*Mount* of Olives" is in the apocalyptic context of the great battle on the day of the Lord in Zech 14, when the feet of the Lord stand on the Mount in the scene of judgment. That scene offers background for Acts 1:9,12 where Jesus ascends to heaven from the Mount with the promise that he will come back in the same way, and for Mark 13:3 where Jesus sits on the Mount to deliver his apocalyptic discourse about the fate of Jerusalem. As we shall see below, Zech 14 is in mind implicitly in the present Marcan scene as well.

More obviously, however, several of the evangelists are echoing the Ascent of Olives reference in II Sam 15:30. Absalom had led Jerusalem to revolt against David with the help of Ahithophel, David's trusted counselor who deserted him; and so David went out (15:16: *exerchesthai*), crossed "the winter-flowing" Kidron (LXX 15:23), went up the Ascent of Olives, wept there, and prayed to God. As Glasson ("Davidic"), Trudinger ("Davidic"), and others have pointed out, this David narrative in II Sam 15 constitutes the background of the Synoptic scene where Jesus goes to the Mount of Olives, soul sorrowful, praying to God, betrayed by a trusted member of the Twelve (a parallelism that Matt 27:5 heightens by having Judas hang himself, even as did Ahithophel in II Sam 17:23—the only two biblical figures to do so). John, who does not mention the Mount of Olives, echoes II Sam 15 as well, since "across the Kidron valley" is literally "across the winter-flowing Kidron," i.e., a wadi or arroyo that has flowing water only in the winter when it rains. We shall see other instances of where John and the Synoptics echo

---

[21]For the geography, see J. B. Curtis, "Investigation" 137–38; also *Le Monde de la Bible* 55 (Aug.–Sept. 1988).

the same OT traditions but in ways so different that only with great difficulty can one imagine deliberate change of the Synoptic account by John. In the independent development of the Synoptic and Johannine Gospels an older appeal to II Sam's picture of David has been articulated in different ways.

As we turn now to the contents of this episode that moves the scene from the supper to the Mount of Olives, we find that it consists of two predictions by Jesus, the first concerning the fate of the disciples, the second concerning the fate of Peter.

FATE OF THE DISCIPLES (MARK 14:27–28; MATT 26:31–32)

Jesus' words to his disciples as they go out to the mount have both a negative and positive tone. He warns them, citing Scripture, that they will be scandalized and scattered, but then he promises that he will return after the resurrection to go before them into Galilee.

Predicted Scandal and Scattering (Mark 14:27; Matt 26:31). In these two Gospels the first thing that Jesus does upon leaving the supper is to utter a foreboding prediction of the fate of his disciples. Matt's differences from Mark here are almost surely redactional, even in the Scripture citation (SPNM 89–94), so that one is justified in speaking of a Mark/Matt account. For purposes of comparison I have printed as part of the biblical translation at the beginning of this section two passages, John 16:1,32 and Luke 22:28–30, where at the Last Supper Jesus speaks of the fate of his disciples.[22] The Johannine passage, which consists of separated sayings, shares with Mark/Matt the themes of scandal and scattering. Yet in John, while Jesus predicts that the disciples will be scattered, he tries to prevent them from being scandalized. The parallel, then, is only partial; and it is not obvious that John was dependent on Mark (as we shall see when we discuss details). The outlook of the Lucan passage is almost diametrically opposite to that of the other Gospels, for it *congratulates* the disciples on their fidelity! It also predicts a favorable future for them at Jesus' table, but that is partially like the Mark/Matt prediction that after the resurrection Jesus will go before them to Galilee. In both Luke and Mark/Matt the prediction about the disciples precedes the prediction about Peter, and there is no reason to think that here Luke is drawing on a different narrative. Luke is consistently gentler with the disciples than are the other evangelists and presumably is deliberately omitting the Marcan prediction of their being scattered, even as he will omit all reference to their flight. Retaining the tradition of a prediction

---

[22]In the ANALYSIS I shall discuss the composite nature of this scene in Mark and the fact that these predictions are placed by Luke and John at the supper rather than as Jesus exits Jerusalem.

about the disciples, Luke has substituted a Q saying, which Matt (19:28) places elsewhere, about the eschatological future of the Twelve, seated on thrones judging the tribes of Israel. The congratulating of the disciples for having remained faithful, which Luke uses here as a preface to the passion, is postresurrectional in outlook, written from the perspective of what will be narrated in Acts.

As we look at Mark/Matt, as pointed out above, the verse that preceded the prediction of the fate of the disciples was grammatically transitional and could be considered as the terminus of the supper scene. Thus the prediction that introduces the coming failure of the disciples has the tone of starting a new section. In particular Matt's "Then" (*tote*) indicates a break.[23] Unlike the preceding verse in Mark/Matt, the subject here is clearly identified as Jesus. Even the Scripture citation is presented as a statement of Jesus, and this is the only formal, explicit citation of Scripture in the whole Marcan PN.

The prediction begins in Mark/Matt with the theme of the disciples being scandalized. Matt adds "in me," conformable to the Matthean preference for using an "in" phrase to specify an absolute "scandalized": 11:6; 13:57; 26:33; cf. Mark 6:3. This clarifies that their scandal will be focused on Jesus. A further Matthean specification has the scandalizing take place "this night," so that the prophecy becomes parallel to the one to be uttered a few verses later (Matt 26:34) about Peter's denials to take place "on this very night." As for *skandalizein,* while the verb has the general sense of stumbling, falling, and hence sinning, the absolute usage can connote a loss of faith (see Mark 9:42–47; *Didache* 16:5), especially in the face of tribulation or persecution, as in Mark 4:17.[24] Worthy of comparison is the Lucan Jesus' prayer at the supper (22:32) that Peter's faith *not* fail, so that he might turn and strengthen his brothers. The Johannine Jesus speaks beforehand lest his disciples be scandalized in the sense of losing their faith; and in that context (John 15:18–16:4) there is emphatic reference to persecution, hatred, and trials. The next verse in Mark/Matt will define the scandal in terms of being scattered, i.e., fleeing when Jesus is arrested, and so the use of "scandalized" suggests that in the Christian mind the flight of the disciples was on a par with denying Jesus—something later followers did when brought before tribunals.

The theme of scandal is followed by a citation from Zech 13:7 about the

[23]Seemingly this was recognized by the late-2d-cent. scribe of P64(67) who extended the pertinent line of his written text to the left even as he had done at 5:21 (another section beginning); see E. Bammel, JTS NS 24 (1973), 189.

[24]Orge ("Percutiam" 276ff.) argues for the loss-of-faith interpretation in Mark 14:27, citing in support Lohmeyer, Schelkle, and Stählin. In Matt 24:10 *skandalizein* describes the final apostasy. Here Jesus' prediction of the disciples being scandalized would refer to a serious but temporary loss of faith.

scattering of the sheep. Mark 14:27b–28, which contains this citation, is attributed by many scholars to a late stage of redaction, so that 27a, "You will be scandalized," was once followed by Peter's objection in 29: "Even if all be scandalized. . . ." This section of Mark is certainly a collection of material, and the suggested reconstruction reads well. Nevertheless, the tradition history is so complex that such a diagnosis of addenda is perilously uncertain.[25] John 16 has both themes, being scandalized and being scattered—far enough apart to make Johannine dependence on Mark implausible, but in close enough proximity to challenge the thesis that a late Marcan redactor first made the connection. We saw above that the story of David's flight underlay the reference to the Mount of Olives in Mark 14:26 (II Sam 15:30; also the Kidron reference in 15:23 as background for the Johannine parallel). The theme of who would faithfully remain with David as he fled is strong in II Sam 15:19–21, and so there is a scriptural connection in the sequence Mark 14:26–27.

Another background for the Mount of Olives in Mark 14:26 was probably the final judgment scene localized on the Mount in Zech 14. Mark's preceding chapter (13:3) has the Mount of Olives as the setting for Jesus' apocalyptic discourse about the endtimes. In that discourse (13:9–13) the persecution of the disciples is predicted with a warning to endure to the end, a theme related to the verse we are now discussing. Indeed, Dibelius (p. 15 above) has argued that motifs from the last part of Zech were woven together with great ingenuity in the PN so that they contributed to its shaping; see also Bruce, "Book." For instance, the beginning of Zech 13 speaks of a fountain opened for the house of *David,* constituting a possible connection between the mention of the Mount of Olives in Zech 14 and the mention of the Ascent of Olives in the David story of II Sam 15, both used by the Gospels. Chaps. 9–14 of Zech are also in mind in other Gospel passages that precede and follow the Olives/Gethsemane scene in the context of Jesus' passion. In Mark 11:1–10 Jesus entered Jerusalem seated on a colt and was received with hosannas; the background is Zech 9:9: "Shout aloud, O Daughter of Jerusalem: your king comes to you triumphant and victorious . . . riding on a colt." In the Last Supper (Mark 14:24) Jesus said, "This is my blood of the covenant"; Zech 9:11 has the phrase, "the blood of my covenant with you." John has his own use of Zech; for when a soldier stabs the dead Jesus' side with a lance (19:34), this is said (19:37) to fulfill Zech 12:10: "They shall look on him whom they have pierced"—cited in a form that does not correspond to either the MT or the most frequent LXX reading (see also Rev 1:7).

---

[25]For instance, Linnemann and Wilcox think that the contents of 14:27b-28 may be older than the prediction of Peter's denials but, under the influence of that prediction, have been shaped to illustrate the failure of the disciples.

With this awareness of the ways in which Zech 9–14 has influenced the Gospel descriptions of Jesus' last days, let us consider the wording of Zech 13:7, which is cited here by Mark/Matt as "I will strike the shepherd, and the sheep [of the flock: Matt] will be scattered." This is a form that once again does not correspond to the MT or majority LXX reading of Zech 13:7: "'Arise, O sword, against my shepherd [shepherds: LXX] and against the man who stands next to me,' says the Lord of Hosts. 'Strike the shepherd, and the sheep are scattered; I will turn my hand against the little ones.'" (The LXX has "and draw out the sheep" in place of "and the sheep are scattered.") The context in Zech leaves the passage obscure. Earlier, in Zech 11:4–14 God had instructed someone to become a shepherd, ready to care for the sheep and be slain by those who traffic in sheep; yet at the end of Zech 11 (vv. 15–17) God raises up a shepherd who does not take care of the sheep—thus in one chapter a good shepherd and a worthless shepherd.[26] Zech 12 begins with a threat against Jerusalem/Judah but ends with a spirit of compassion being poured out on Jerusalem. The alternation between positive and negative seems to carry over to Zech 13:7–9, the passage that Mark/Matt cite. In itself 13:7 is not a future prophecy but an invocation of destruction against the shepherd and the sheep; yet 13:9 describes a third of the whole as a purified remnant of God's people. In CD 19:8–9 (ms. B) it is evident that the Qumran group read a future reference into Zech 13:7, but a negative one whereby it threatened punishment; yet they also had the notion of a remnant preserved (CD 19:10). As for the Mark/Matt citation, Schroeder ("Worthless") would find Zech's negative aspect preserved in the sense that Jesus' suffering makes him assume the role of the worthless shepherd of Zech 11:15–17 who can no longer protect the sheep, a role to be reversed after the resurrection. More likely, in my judgment, of the two Zech shepherd roles, the NT has concentrated on the positive picture in Zech 11:4–14 for describing Jesus. For instance, John 10:1–18 pictures Jesus as the model shepherd who does not abandon the sheep but lays down his life for them; and John 18:8–9 has Jesus interceding for his disciples that they be allowed to leave the garden peacefully lest they perish. (Jesus' care for the sheep is also exhibited in Luke 12:32; 15:3–7.) Mark 6:34 has Jesus pitying the multitude because they were like sheep without a shepherd—a picture close to the positive view of the shepherd in Zech and unlike the worthless shepherd who does not care for those perishing (11:15–17).

[26]Amid the poetry of Zech 9–14 the more prosaic shepherd section in 11:4–14 is related to the similarly prosaic shepherd section in 13:7–9; and some reconstructions would join them. On the complexities see Josef Kremer, *Die Hirtenallegorie im Buche Zacharias* (Münster: Aschendorff, 1930); A. Gelin, "L'allégorie des pasteurs dans Zacharie," in *Études de critique et d'histoire religieuses* (Offerts à L. Vaganay; Lyons: Facultés Catholiques, 1948), 67–78.

The import of the Mark/Matt citation is that since Jesus the caring shepherd who brought the flock into being is to be struck down,[27] the sheep will no longer receive his care and will be scattered. For "scatter" John uses *skorpizein;* Mark/Matt uses *diaskorpizein* (late Greek with the connotation "scatter about"). While this reading does not agree with the majority LXX tradition (*ekspan,* "draw out"), we are not certain whether "scatter" represents an independent Christian rendering of the Hebrew or a literal Jewish translation into Greek that was already in circulation in NT times. (*Diaskorpizein* appears in certain LXX mss. [Codex Alexandrinus, correction of Sinaiticus, Codex Marchalianus], perhaps the remnant of such an alternative Jewish translation.[28]) The prophecy of Jesus drawn from Zech is seen to be fulfilled when all the disciples flee (Mark 14:50) or are let go (John 18:8–9). This scattering is not primarily geographical in the sense that they leave Jerusalem to go home to Galilee; for in John 20 they remain in Jerusalem, and that is hinted at also in Mark 16:7: "He is going before you to Galilee; *there* you will see him." Rather it is a scattering from Jesus and from one another so that there is no longer one flock, as made explicit by Matt's addition: "the sheep *of the flock* will be scattered."

Promise of Jesus' Postresurrectional Return (Mark 14:28; Matt 26:32). Nevertheless, Jesus' prediction concerning his disciples is not entirely pessimistic in any Gospel. In Luke 22:28–30 the positive has completely suppressed the negative, for Jesus promises that the disciples will be appointed a kingdom and sit on thrones judging Israel. In John, alongside the negative elements of 16:1,32 there are counteracting positive elements both in terms of Johannine christology (Jesus will not be left alone, for the Father is always with him) and in terms of the fate of the disciples: "You cannot follow me now; but you will follow later" (13:36; to be treated below). In Mark 14:28/Matt 26:32 the positive promise, "However, after my resurrection I shall go before you into Galilee," may retain implicitly the majority LXX reading of Zech 13:7 ("draw out the sheep"). The risen Jesus going before (*proagein*) the disciples into Galilee is a reversal of the scattering, as suggested by the Marcan "However" (*alla*). In Mark 10:32, on his

---

[27]In the Zech passage the sword is told by God to strike the shepherd, but in Mark/Matt the "I" who will strike the shepherd is God Himself. Has that reading been influenced by Isa 53:4,10 where the Servant of the Lord is smitten or crushed by God?

[28]For the preservation in Codex Marchalianus of Jewish renditions of the OT into Greek differing from the LXX renditions, see NJBC 68:97. Stendahl and Gundry, who have studied Matthean citations of the OT, doubt that copyists influenced by Mark/Matt produced this variant Greek rendering of Zech 13:7; rather Christian reflection on different Jewish renditions of Zech into Greek may have produced the Mark/Matt text (see SPNM 92–93).

way to die, Jesus went before (*proagein*) the disciples and they walked behind him as a group going up to Jerusalem; after the resurrection he will resume the role of leading, a shepherding role that will reconstitute the flock. Mark does not necessarily mean that Jesus will walk before them on the road back to Galilee (pace J. Weiss); nor does simple temporal priority do justice to the Marcan idea (see the range of meaning in Odenkirchen, "Praecedam"); rather *proagein* here connotes both priority and authoritative leadership (Evans, "Go Before" 9–11). The import of this prediction then fits well a strong interest visible in the Gospel treatments of the postresurrectional activity of Jesus who builds up the community or church. More precisely, however, for Mark 14:28 the issue would be the restoration and renewal of a community or flock that had already existed in Jesus' lifetime. The risen Jesus who had called disciples in 1:16ff. and 3:13ff. would renew his initiative.

The issue of whether that initiative would have new elements is involved in the debate among scholars about the antiquity and meaning of Mark 14:28. The prediction, "After my resurrection I shall go before you into Galilee" (virtually identical in Matt 26:32), is intimately related to the words spoken in Mark 16:7 by the (angelic?) youth at the tomb after he has announced the resurrection of the crucified Jesus: "Go tell his disciples and Peter that he is going before you into Galilee; there you will see him as he told you." (This is expanded and interpreted by the angel's words in Matt 28:7: "Going quickly, tell his disciples that he is risen from the dead, and behold he goes before you into Galilee; there you will see him. Behold I told you.") Various theories about these two verses have been proposed because Mark closes in 16:8 without Jesus going to Galilee and without his being seen there. (For a survey see Stein, "Short.") For instance, van Iersel, "To Galilee," labors to show that *eis* in both verses should be translated as "in" Galilee, instead of "into," so that what is anticipated is the retrieval of a permanent spiritual relationship, not momentary appearances in a physical Galilee. More idiosyncratic is the thesis of Muñoz León ("Iré") based on his ability to recover an Aramaic substratum (in part interpreted through references to targums, the preserved forms of which postdate the NT, sometimes by several centuries). Originally the supposed Aramaic original did not refer to a vision of Jesus in Galilee. (In part, Muñoz León wishes to make room for the appearance of Jesus to his male disciples in Jerusalem, attested by Luke and John, but significantly absent from Mark/Matt who report this statement!) Underlying *proagein* is the pael conjugation of the Aramaic verb *děbar*, which means "to conduct"; and *gelil* was mistranslated, for it does not mean *Galilaia* but a sheepfold or place in Jerusalem. Therefore, what Jesus promised was a messianic gesture to congregate the dispersed. I recognize the element of reassembling the scattered, but that does not require such an unprovable hypothesis of misrendered Aramaic. A frequent proposal (e.g., Bousset, Bultmann, Dibelius, Taylor) is that 16:7 is a very late redactional insert to harmonize Mark with the idea of Jesus' appearing in Galilee (an idea attested in Matt 28:16–20). Some who hold that position argue that 14:28 is older and more original inasmuch as it has no reference to seeing Jesus. Others think that 14:28 and 16:7 were inserted into Mark at the same (late) moment. Still others argue that 16:7 antedated 14:28—we saw above the thesis that 14:27a was once followed by 14:29.[29] We cannot make our interpretation of Mark dependent on such uncertain theorizing and must recognize that the presence in the text of 14:28 followed by 16:7 gives a positive thrust to Jesus' future relationship to his disciples.

Many scholars think that 16:7 in particular refers not to postresurrectional appearances by Jesus but to his parousia in Galilee.[30] The parousia of the Son of Man, however, surely involves a manifestation to the world, and strange indeed would be a parousia selectively directed to the disciples and Peter. Moreover, references to Jesus' resurrection in Mark 16:6 and in 14:28 make it far more plausible that 16:7 refers to the seeing of the risen Jesus by the disciples and Peter (which is the way that Matt interpreted it). The absence of a reference to *seeing* in 14:28 has led some interpreters to stress another aspect of the disciples' predicted encounter with the risen Jesus, namely, hearing and receiving his commission to teach the Gentile world (see articles in §4, Part 1, by Evans, Hoskyns, Lightfoot, and Odenkirchen). The idea would be that the disciples, called together by the risen Jesus, would be empowered to evangelize the world. Various factors are cited to support this interpretation of 14:28, e.g., that Mark 13:10 and 14:9 indicate that the gospel is to be preached to all nations; that Zech 14 envisions the judgment of the nations on the Mount of Olives; that a nations theme is frequent in postresurrectional appearances (Matt 28:19; Luke 24:46–47; Mark 16:15); and that Galilee is associated with Gentiles in Matt 4:15. Nevertheless, I think that finding such a theme in Mark 14:28 is too subtle. Jesus is mentioning Galilee to his disciples simply as a reminder that they were

[29]The absence of Mark 14:28 from the late-2d-cent. Fayum fragment (Rainer papyrus) may be an early attempt to harmonize Mark's presentation of Jesus' postresurrectional career with the portrayal of Luke, John, and the Marcan Appendix where there are Jerusalem appearances of Jesus, not only Galilean ones.

[30]So Lohmeyer, R. H. Lightfoot, Marxsen, Weeden, Kelber. See contrary arguments in Schenke, *Studien* 437–60; Stein, "Short."

originally called together in that place. Now they are being scattered; but in leading them back to Galilee, he shall once more be calling them together as his flock. There, as they shall learn (16:7), they shall see him again.

FATE OF PETER (MARK 14:29–31; MATT 26:33–35)

Peter's Protest (Mark 14:29; Matt 26:33). Although Jesus has spoken to a group of disciples, in Mark/Matt it is Peter alone who vocalizes a challenge to Jesus' statement. (The same group-Peter sequence appears in John 13:33,36, but there Peter asks a *question* of Jesus.) Mark begins the verse: "But Peter said to him"—the "But" here renders *de,* unlike the strong *alla,* "However," in the preceding verse.[31] Matt has the same introduction but specifies that it is an answer to Jesus. It is not unusual that the words of the Marcan Peter are phrased elliptically ("Even if all are scandalized, yet not I"), nor that Matt makes minor redactional, stylistic improvements ("If all are scandalized in you, I will never be scandalized"). The Matthean "in you," besides once more adding an "in" phrase to "scandalize" as happened two verses before, emphasizes again that the scandal or loss of faith will be centered on Jesus.[32] The Matthean "I will never be scandalized" is clearer and more emphatic than Mark's "not I."

The *ei kai* ("Even if") of Mark indicates that the condition is likely to be fulfilled: All (except Peter) will be scandalized. (The reversed *kai ei* reading in the Koine tradition, including Codex Alexandrinus, tends to make the condition more improbable.) Thus Peter is not repudiating the likelihood of Jesus' prophecy, but only insisting on an exception. Speaking out from the body of the Twelve or from the disciples is part of the common Gospel portrait of Peter. In Mark 8:27–34 Peter's protest and Jesus' corrective reaction are not too dissimilar to the pattern here: After being confessed as the Messiah by Peter, Jesus predicts the rejection and suffering of the Son of Man;

[31]There has been considerable debate about the Marcan use of *de.* C. H. Turner, JTS 28 (1927), 152, suggests that at the beginning of a paragraph it marks a significant point in the narrative. The usual interpretation is adversative, indicating contrast; yet *kai* ("and") can also be adversative. Thrall, *Greek* 50–63, points out that in classical and Hellenistic Greek *de* can be purely continuative, and that the use of the definite article *ho* (as here before *Petros*) necessitates *de* rather than *kai* as a connective, so that many or most *ho de* constructions are not truly adversative. Be that as it may, the contrast ("But") here is indicated by the context.

The sequence of tenses used for the verbs of saying in this section of Mark is worth noticing: *legei* (v. 27: pres.), *ephē* (v. 29: aor.), *legei* (v. 30: pres.), *elalei* (v. 31: impf.), *elegon* (v. 31c: impf.). Schenke (*Studien* 409) is probably right that (as with the alternation of *kai* and *de*) the alternation of verbs and tenses is mostly a matter of style and not indicative of subtle nuances (or sources).

[32]Notice a similar prepositional phrase used by Peter in Matt 26:35 (Mark 14:31): "Even if it be necessary for me to die *with you.*"

Peter rebukes him; then Jesus rebukes Peter in return for playing a Satanic role and having too human an outlook.

In his current objection Peter fastens on the "all scandalized" of Mark 14:27a, as if the intervening Scripture citation did not exist. While that has led many to regard the citation as an insertion (see above), psychologically the flow of the Marcan storyline is good. A Peter who overrode Jesus when he said that the Son of Man *must* suffer (a divine plan) does not now hesitate to override him when he quotes Scripture. (Linnemann, "Verleugnung" 17, contends that if there were no Scripture citation, all the disciples would have immediately objected as in 14:19; only Peter is not cowed.) Peter goes straight to the point that threatens him: the "all" in Jesus' prediction about being scandalized. Peter's negative ellipsis, "Yet not I," is not unlike the phrase in Mark 14:2, "Not during the feast." His desire to exclude the "I" resembles 14:19, "Surely not I?"

Jesus' Prediction of Peter's Denials (Mark 14:30; Matt 26:34). All four Gospels (see Luke 22:34; John 13:38) have a solemn prediction by Jesus (an "Amen" saying, except in Luke) of a threefold denial by Peter before the cock would crow. In Mark/Matt this takes place on the way to Gethsemane as Jesus' response to the verse just discussed: Peter's protest that by exception he would not be scandalized. It is followed by Peter's insistence that he is willing to die with Jesus (to be treated in the next subsection). In Luke and John the prediction takes place at the Last Supper and is *preceded* by Peter's declaration that he is willing to die with or for Jesus. Let me first discuss the peculiarities of the Johannine and Lucan passages (printed within brackets in the translation at the beginning of this section) and then turn to the prediction itself.

Johannine and Lucan Settings for the Prediction. As we saw, the Johannine Jesus speaks to his disciples in chap. 16 about being scandalized and scattered. Earlier in the Last Supper discourse (13:33,36–38) come the sayings pertinent to Peter. While phrased in Johannine language, these sayings are evocative of Mark's sequence in their logic. In Mark, following the prediction of the scandalizing and scattering of the disciples, there is the promise, "After my resurrection I shall go before you into Galilee." Then Peter objects that he is an exception. In John, Jesus speaks to all the disciples about their inability to come with him, but Simon Peter objects that he is an exception. The interchange about not following now but following later is similar in its thrust to the image of the risen Jesus going before the disciples to Galilee.

Luke's scene reflects his benevolent outlook on the disciples and on Peter. In the passage 22:31–34, v. 34 about the triple denial reflects dependence on Mark; v. 33 about Peter's willingness to go to prison and death is similar in theme to both Mark 14:31 and John 13:37, but the wording of all three is different. Vv. 31–32 are unique and need discussion. As we saw, Luke 22:28–30 was a prediction of the fate of the disciples, not in terms of being scandalized/scattered but in terms of fidelity and being rewarded; for that Luke used an adapted Q saying of Jesus. Jesus' words to Peter in 31–32 are also positive even if they begin with an acknowledgment of danger for the disciples: Satan has desired to sift them like wheat. The image, which involves the throwing away of the chaff, is even more violent than that of scattering the sheep: Satan entered into Judas (22:3; cf. John 13:27), and now Satan is trying to destroy all the disciples. Jesus' reassuring prayer for Peter that will prevent this (v. 32) may well be from preLucan tradition (see TPNL 65; Fitzmyer, *Luke* 2.1421). An address to Peter as Simon is not typical of Lucan style (24:34 has a preLucan reference to Simon);[33] yet Luke uses a repeated personal name, comparable to "Simon, Simon," as intimate persuasion in 10:41. The import, then, is that just as Matt 16:18 promises Simon Peter a supportive role for the church to be built by Christ, and John 21:15–17 grants him a pastoral role in tending the sheep of Christ, so this Lucan passage looks forward to his strengthening his brothers once he has turned around (*epistrephein* taken intransitively), presumably after he has recovered from the denials about to be predicted. The strengthening role may be related to the leadership he shows among the Twelve in Acts. Thus, even as Luke drew the positive prediction about the fate of the disciples from earlier tradition, so seemingly he has drawn the positive promise from earlier Peter tradition.

Of particular interest is that Luke and John, differing in this passage from each other and from Mark/Matt, may echo in vocabulary and theme the scene in II Sam 15 of the flight of David from Absalom, which we saw as very influential background for the Mount of Olives motif. Just before David crosses the Kidron valley and goes up the Ascent of Olives, he speaks to Ittai the Gittite, warning him that he (David) is not certain *where he will be going,* and so Ittai should *not come along* but *turn around* and take his *brothers* (men) with him. Ittai objects, "Wherever my *lord* shall be, whether *for death* or for life, there will your servant be." Italics point out similarities to Luke and John; but whereas in II Sam 15:22–37 David yields and has Ittai and his companions come with him, only later will Peter and his companions be able to follow Jesus. In the II Sam story another person, Hushai, the Archite, is sent back to Jerusalem to remain there and thus help David.

[33]Some scholars maintain that Luke has preferred "Simon" to "Peter" here because the figure concerned does not yet have the firmness that would justify his being called by a name derivative from *petra* ("rock"); he will get that firmness after he has been strengthened through Jesus' prayer and after his faith has survived the ordeal of the denials. That theory is not justified by other Lucan

The Prediction. The heart of this subsection is the saying common to the four Gospels about Peter's threefold denial before cockcrow. Some differences of phrasing among the accounts deserve attention. Timewise John sets the denials before the next cockcrow. Mark specifies both "today" and "this very night"; Matt has "this very night," and Luke has "today." While the Synoptic picture could favor the Griesbach hypothesis where Mark used both Matt and Luke, combining their differences, it can also be explained in terms of Marcan priority. By a Jewish reckoning in which day begins at sunset, this night would already have been "today" (Passover for Mark? see APPENDIX II B). One suspects that this Jewish reckoning was the first to be attached to the saying. It would not have been intelligible, however, to those who were unfamiliar with this way of calculating; and so a more universally intelligible "this very night" may have been added by Mark (see the pleonastic time indication in Mark 16:1–2). Matt and Luke would each have simplified. The omission of "today" from Codices Bezae and Koridethi of Mark was probably under the influence of the single time reference in Matt and Luke.

The Gospel word for "cock" is *alektōr,* a once poetic but now ordinary short form of the *alektryōn* used in the Fayum papyrus (MM 21). The verb translated "crow" is *phōnein,* which refers simply to producing a sound or tone and can be used of human or animal emissions.[34] (The technical term for the cock's sound was *kokkyzein,* which appears in the Fayum fragment of Mark.)

Mark has the cock crowing twice; the other Gospels lack that detail. The first question is whether the duplication was a genuine part of the Marcan text; the second is what meaning did it have if it was. Within Mark there are four passages involved: 14:30,68,72a,72b. Textually, the most dubious is the reference to the cock crowing (for the first time) in 14:68. One can argue that since three passages mentioned the cock crowing twice and there was no mention of a first crowing, a scribe tried to improve by inserting one in 14:68. Wenham argues the other way: A scribe interpolated a reference to a cock crowing in 14:68 (why?); and since there was already mention of a cock crowing in 14:72a, the idea that this was a second time spread to other passages of Mark. In 14:30,72a,72b, although the phrase supporting the two cockcrows is always omitted by Codex Sinaiticus and some Koine witnesses (whence the UBSGNT rating which stresses the uncertainty of the "twice"

---

usage: Three verses later (22:34) the Lucan Jesus will address "Peter"; on the other hand, it is to "Simon" that the risen Lord appears (24:34).

[34]D. Zuntz, JTS 50 (1949), 152–53, argues, largely on the basis of early papyri evidence, that the original text of Matt 26:34 (and 26:75), instead of the Marcan "a cock crows" (*alektora phonēsai*), read "a cockcrow" (*alektorophōnia*).

evidence), it is supported impressively by Codex Vaticanus and most ancient Syriac, Latin, and Sahidic witnesses. Accordingly, I judge MTC 114 correct in arguing for its originality in these three passages and explaining the omission as an attempt by copyists to assimilate Mark to the other Gospels, which had only one cockcrow. Presumably Matt and Luke omitted the Marcan "twice" as a needless complication or considered such exact numbers poor rhetorical style (so Turner, JTS 26 [1924–25], 338).

A more difficult question is the implication the "twice" had for Mark. Mayo ("St. Peter's" 369–70) suggests that *dis,* "twice," was added by way of assonance with *tris,* "thrice," "three times." Brady ("Alarm" 54) argues that the Marcan pattern "two/three" in reference to the cockcrows and denials is a feature of proverbs or parables, similar to the "three/four" in Prov 30:15,18,21,29. On the other hand, the Marcan "twice" could have been understood as a slight precision equivalent to "before the next dawn," since there is clear evidence in Greco-Roman writing that dawn or the rising sun was associated with the *second* cockcrow (Aristophanes, *Ecclesiazusae* 30–31, 390–91; Juvenal, *Satire* 9.107–8; Ammianus Marcellinus, *Res Gestae* 22.14.4). More will be said about the prediction and its implication in §27 on the denials.

The Synoptics employ for "deny" the compound verb *aparnesthai,* which is often considered stronger than the simple *arnesthai* used by John, so that it could reflect both "disown" and "deny." Yet the simple verb is used by all the Gospels in the accounts of the actual denials (even if the compound verb is kept when the prediction is recalled). There is no evidence that the evangelists saw any difference of meaning.

Luke excepted, the prediction is presented by the Gospels as an Amen-saying of Jesus. The special pattern of "Amen" introducing a saying (rather than constituting a response) is not found in the LXX, and in the Gospels is found only on the lips of Jesus (13 times in Mark; 31 in Matt; 6 in Luke; 25 [always doubled] in John). In Mark/Matt the prediction of denial is the only Amen-saying in the postsupper passion narrative; John has no Amen-saying between the end of the supper and the death of Jesus; Luke has one from the cross. Some have tried to argue that "Amen" guarantees that a particular saying was historically uttered by Jesus; others see some of the Amen-sayings as stemming from early Christian prophets. What is certain is that "Amen" lends solemnity to the saying that follows it.

Peter's Rebuttal (Mark 14:31; Matt 26:35). In Mark/Matt after the solemn cockcrow prediction of Jesus, Peter offers a rebuttal in terms of his willingness to die with Jesus (cf. Luke 22:33; John 13:37); and all (the disciples) chime in like a chorus. While this rebuttal is meant to be recognized by readers as unrealistic bravado, it ends the scene on a pathetically positive note of the desire of Peter and the disciples to stand by Jesus at the price of their own lives. In Luke and John, where Peter professed his willingness to die *before* Jesus' words about denial before cockcrow, that negative prediction terminates the direct dialogue with Peter.

The words that Mark uses to introduce the rebuttal ("But he was saying vehemently") are *ho de ekperissōs elalei*. The need to specify Mark's *ho* ("the one," "he") as Peter is recognized by Matt. Mark's *de*, "But," accompanies these words of Peter even as it accompanied his previous words (14:29). Matt, who usually avoids Mark's historical-present usages (as in the previous verse before Jesus' prediction), curiously substitutes one in 26:35 for Mark's imperfect "was saying" and ignores Mark's *ekperissōs* ("vehemently") because it was either difficult or exaggerated. The word is not found elsewhere in the NT, nor in the LXX; nor is it classical. It is related to a group of *periss*-words with the meaning of being left over or abundant.[35] In 7:37 Mark used the more easily intelligible *hyperperissōs*, "superabundantly." Is then *ekperissōs*, "from abundantly," used here, an ungrammatical mistake? Joüon ("Marc 14,31") contends that it is a learned formation with superlative force, since by this period *perissōs* already had comparative force ("more abundantly," "excessively"). Thus Joüon would have it mean "beyond all measure," a contention that I have acknowledged by rendering it "vehemently."

Peter's actual words to Jesus, "Even if it be necessary [*deē*] for me to die with [*syn*] you," involves a form of *dei*, a word used in the Gospels especially for the divine will pertinent to Jesus. It appears in the first of the three predictions of the sufferings of the Son of Man (APPENDIX VIII, A2). Peter, who once strongly rejected the necessity of that suffering (Mark 8:31–33), is now more strongly professing his willingness to share it; but alas he is no more realistic in one reaction than in the other. "Cosuffering" with other disciples or with Jesus was an ideal of early Christians (II Cor 7:3; II Tim 2:11). A parallel is found earlier in John (11:16) in the Lazarus story: "Let us go too that we may die with [*meta*] him." Peter's generosity in meeting this ideal is contagious in extracting from the other disciples a similar commitment, so that as in times past, Peter has once more served as their spokesman. By the end of the scene on the Mount of Olives the "all" who said the same will have "all fled" (Mark 14:50).

---

[35]Scribes tended to substitute well-known words of that group in Mark 14:31, e.g., *perissōs* ("exceedingly") in Codex Alexandrinus; or *ek perissou* ("from an abundance": Mark 6:51) in the Washington and Koridethi codices.

ANALYSIS[36]

A. Jesus' Predictions about the Disciples and Peter: Placing and Role

Above (§2A) the reader was alerted that I decided on practical grounds to begin the passion narrative discussion with the scene on the Mount of Olives at a place that Mark/Matt calls Gethsemane. While this decision causes a sharper division than the Synoptic evangelists intended between the Last Supper and what followed on the Mount, there is, as we shall see, a coherent viewpoint in the postsupper narrative of all the Gospels. Obviously the difficulty of sharp delineation from the supper is most acute in this transitional scene that moves the action from the supper room to the Mount. Indeed, only in Mark/Matt is it a scene; the other two Gospels are content with a sentence describing the movement from one place to the other. The scene in Mark (on which Matt is dependent) consists of two warning predictions by Jesus, addressed respectively to the disciples (all will be scandalized and scattered) and to Peter (threefold denial before the cock crows). Both Luke and John place the prediction to Peter at the Last Supper, as well as their own variants (very distant in Luke) of the prediction to the disciples.

W. M. Ramsay (ExpTim 28 [1916–17], 278) argued that setting these predictions at the supper rather than on the way to the Mount was more historical because the path down from Jerusalem to the Kidron was narrow and steep, requiring Jesus and his disciples to walk one after the other in "Indian file" and impeding sayings heard by all. The issue is not to be solved by such historicizing, even if it is likely that as part of his somber view on the passion, Mark has fashioned a preface consisting of two negative predictions that more traditionally would have been associated with the supper discourse.

Part of the Last Supper for the Synoptics was the eucharist (matched in John by the washing of the feet) with its language of a covenantal self-sacrifice by Jesus for many. The very positive attitude of Jesus toward his disciples projected by the eucharist (and the foot washing) would inevitably balance and neutralize any negative predictions of their fate.[37] We can see

---

[36]While the COMMENT deals with the Gospel passages verse by verse, the ANALYSIS covers the whole scene; and there is a deliberate attempt to avoid repeating material from the COMMENT pertinent to individual verses. After having worked through the detailed COMMENT, before beginning the ANALYSIS readers might profitably go back and read the Scripture translation given at the beginning of the scene in order to remind themselves of the whole passage.

[37]In the two Gospels where the predictions about the disciples and about Peter are placed at the supper, they become more positive—in Luke 22:28–34 positive in the wording itself; in John positive because of being subsumed in a five-chapter scene where, having loved his own, Jesus "now showed his love for them to the very end" (13:1).

this neutralization at work in regard to a third negative prediction by Jesus concerning his followers, namely, that he would be given over by one of the Twelve (specified as Judas in Matt)—a prediction that Mark/Matt have left in the supper context (in agreement with Luke and John). Since it involved a reference to the betrayer eating with Jesus and dipping a morsel in the dish, it could not easily be moved from the table setting. The whole Last Supper scene in Mark 14:17–25 and Matt 26:20–29 consists, then, of that betrayal prediction followed by the eucharist showing the forgiving response of Jesus. Although before the supper we are told how the chief priests plotted to put Jesus to death, and the pouring out of his blood mentioned in reference to the cup suggests a violent death, the conclusion of the supper is the oracular statement: "I tell you I shall not drink again of the fruit of the vine until that day when I drink it new in the kingdom of God [Matt: "with you in the kingdom of my Father"]," a statement with a triumphant ending.

This supper context scarcely prepares the reader for the agonizing experiences that will follow in Mark/Matt, culminating in a shriek from Jesus on the cross, "My God, my God, for what reason have you forsaken me?" Luke and John do not need especially to prepare their readers, for they do not have such a negative view of the human elements in the passion. In Luke, Jesus is not abandoned by fleeing disciples; he remains composed and forgiving throughout, and his last words are a trusting "Father, into your hands I place my Spirit." In John, the human actors are a foil for a sovereign Jesus who lays down his own life only when he decides to do so (10:18) and whose final words are his majestic decision to do so: "It is finished." For Mark/Matt, however, the passion is a descent into an abyss during which Jesus himself will hesitate as he finds himself with no human support. He will be betrayed, abandoned, denied, and cursed by his disciples; he will be calumniated in the presence of the chief authorities of his people, who are determined to use every artifice to put him to death; he will be sentenced to crucifixion cynically by the representative of Roman justice, who knows he was handed over out of envy. As Jesus hangs on the cross for six hours (Mark), all will mock him; nature will be plunged into darkness; and his only words on the cross, wrenched from the depth of his soul, will be greeted with contemptuous skepticism. It is understandable, then, that Mark, followed by Matt, did not find in the Last Supper an introduction that could prepare the reader for a passion thus conceived.

The present scene serves that purpose admirably. Leaving the supper room, Jesus becomes decisively negative in outlook. Outside of one allusive verse (Mark 14:28; Matt 26:32: "After my resurrection I shall go before you into Galilee"), Jesus never makes another consoling promise to his disciples before his death. The somber mood is established by the opening words,

"You will all be scandalized." Why such pessimism? Why juxtapose two such dire predictions, one about the disciples, the other about Peter? In §2, C1 I rejected the thesis that Mark is hostile to the persons or the memories of the disciples and Peter because of the type of Christianity they or their adherents profess (based on miracles, power, and success), and that Mark wants to demonstrate that they definitively abandoned their vocation before Jesus died. Mark 14:28, just cited above, shows the contrary: Despite the disciples being scandalized, Jesus would not abandon them but reassemble them as his flock. I contend that Mark and his readers, like other early Christians, probably held Jesus' disciples and Peter in esteem as saintly witnesses, especially if by the time of writing Peter had been martyred. But Mark uses the Gospel to stress that such witness to Jesus did not come easily or under the disciples' own impetus. Mark takes very seriously the saying quoted in 8:34 that following Jesus involves taking up the cross, and Mark does not wish the reader to be deceived about the difficulty of that task. When the disciples of Jesus who had walked with him most intimately, who indeed had already begun their following of him, faced the issue of accompanying him to the cross, they were scandalized and even denied him. Peter in particular underestimated the trial that faced him ("Even if all . . . yet not I"), and he led all the others to state assuredly that they would not be scandalized. Only after their failure and only after the death and resurrection of Jesus called them together once more were they able finally to take up the cross—a cross that Jesus had foreseen in 13:9 and that involved being delivered up to courts, beaten in synagogues, and made to stand before rulers for Jesus' sake. Mark is offering a pedagogy of hope based on the initial failure of the most famous followers of Jesus and a second chance for them. He may well have in mind readers who also failed initially or became discouraged by the thought of the cross. He is issuing parenetic warnings against the danger of being scandalized or falling away from faith[38] and against overconfidence.

I pointed out that if Mark has moved these two dire predictions from the supper setting to this scene transitional to the passion, he was not able to move from the supper the prediction about betrayal by one of the Twelve because it involved eating at table. But in light of what I have diagnosed as Mark's pedagogical and parenetic purposes, he may *not* have been interested in relating the prediction about Judas to those about the other disciples and Peter. Judas failed; these others succeeded. All three predictions are negative as to what Jesus' followers will do during the passion, but only in the case of Judas is the ultimate outcome negative. Neither Mark 14:28 nor 16:7

---

[38]The danger of being scandalized (even in the face of lesser dangers than persecution) seems to have been a widespread Christian concern; see Rom 14:21; I Cor 8:13; II Cor 11:29.

holds out any hope that Judas will be among those whom Jesus will reassemble as a flock in Galilee after the resurrection.

The two predictions in this scene serve another purpose for Mark/Matt, casting light not only on the course of discipleship but also on the mystery of Jesus himself. In the next scene we shall be made privy to a remarkable abasement of Jesus as he lies prostrate in Gethsemane begging his Father that the hour might pass from him. That prayer beginning Jesus' suffering, when juxtaposed to the anguished prayer at the end ("My God, my God, for what reason have you forsaken me?"), colors with tones of human weakness and impotence the portrait of one who at the beginning and ending of his ministry is hailed in Mark as the Son of God (1:1; 15:39). The various Gospels present in different balance the combination of the human and more-than-human in Jesus as he goes to his death. For Mark/Matt a counterbalance to his anguished pleading is his prophetic foresight that shows to what extent he is attuned to God's control of all that will happen and knows that the divine plan for victory cannot be frustrated. The two predictions uttered at the beginning of the passion will have been proved true by the halfway mark, at the very moment when Jesus is being tried and mocked as a false prophet (Mark 14:65, followed by the three denials of Peter in 14:66–72). And two prophetic themes introduced at that halfway point (themes of the destruction of the Temple sanctuary and of Jesus' divine sonship) will have been verified by the end of the passion narrative (§§43,44 below). Thus there is an overall atmosphere of Jesus' attunement to the divine plan that is not to be forgotten during Jesus' pleas to God for deliverance—a combination that could be pedagogic for Mark's readers if, as they face their own cross, cries to be spared by God are wrung from their lips.

B. The Origins of the Predictions

We have seen that the two predictions fit very well into Marcan theology, which here is adopted by Matt. The placing of the two predictions as transitional to the scene in Gethsemane is a Marcan arrangement to provide an introduction appropriate in tone to what follows. The wording of this scene reflects what scholars diagnose as Marcan style.[39] It is not surprising, therefore, that some would regard the two predictions (and even the third, about the betrayer) as Marcan creations. In particular, many scholars of various outlooks[40] contend that the biblical quotation in 14:27b and/or the reference

---

[39]For instance, *hoti* recitativum ("that"—some fifty times in Mark) after a verb of speaking, even in 14:27, 30 where there are direct quotations. See n. 31 above in regard to the alternation of *kai* and *de,* and the verbal tenses for "say," including historical presents.

[40]Bultmann, Dibelius, Gnilka, Grass, Marxsen, Schreiber, Scroggs, Suhl, Taylor, to name a few.

to going before the disciples to Galilee in 14:28 are Marcan creations or insertions, with a division as to whether the context that received these created or inserted verses is preMarcan. I have cautioned (p. 131 above) that in general I am skeptical about the absoluteness with which such an issue is decided, especially since contradictory analyses are offered. I pointed to Johannine parallels phrased and situated without discernible dependence on Mark.[41] These incline me to judge that the predictions came to Mark from earlier tradition, even if he reshaped and localized them to fit his own proclamation of Jesus. I would judge that John did the same, drawing from similar (but not necessarily the same) earlier tradition.[42]

If the predictions in some form antedated both Mark and John, what is their historicity? The idea of three predictions (Judas, disciples, Peter) made at approximately the same time on the night before Jesus was arrested seems artificial. For preaching purposes foreboding predictions made at different times may have been gathered into the one Last Supper scene, where there was a setting for Jesus' speaking to his disciples. Only the Peter prediction has an in-built time indication that would make an earlier setting implausible. Some scholars object to the historicity of the predictions on the rationalist grounds that foreknowledge is impossible. In fact, however, such an objection applies only to the Peter prediction. The idea that the disciples would scatter, and not stand up for Jesus were he arrested, could represent a shrewd guess about their likely weakness under pressure. Since the betrayal had been agreed upon before the supper (Mark 14:10–11), Jesus could have got wind of it, without even knowing who the betrayer was (he is not identified in the Marcan prediction [14:18–21]). But the exactness of the Peter prediction (three times before the cock crows) would require foreknowledge. *This whole approach, however, is dubious.* The evangelists do not present any of these predictions as shrewd guesses; all three are presented as indicating Jesus' knowledge of the divine plan. Scholars have come to realize that one cannot dismiss Jesus' miracles simply on modern rationalist grounds,

[41]If John is dependent on Mark, he has changed the Mount of Olives (better known) to "across the Kidron valley" (18:1). From the prediction about the disciples, he has placed the "scandalized" motif in 16:1, the "scattered" motif in 16:32, reformulating both; reshaped the "after my resurrection . . . go before you" as "follow [me] later" in 13:33,36; and then placed the Peter prediction in 13:37–38, in part considerably reworded. Why?

[42]In the preJohannine form of the early tradition the predictions were situated at the Last Supper and, unlike Mark, John left them there. Luke shows no knowledge of the form in which the predictions now appear in John, but there were *preGospel* contacts between Luke and the Johannine tradition (§2, F3 above). That would be one explanation for how Luke, although using Mark, was led to place the predictions at the supper. As for the wording of the supper predictions, Luke drew upon Mark in reference to Peter's denials; but he softened that prediction by prefixing it with a saying from material favorable to Peter's role in the church. For the prediction about the disciples, Luke used a Q saying about their enthronement (see p. 127 above).

for the oldest traditions show him as a healer.[43] Historically, the phenomenon of Jesus is unintelligible unless one acknowledges that from the earliest days he was recognized as one with more than human powers and that within the range of powers attributed to him was prophetical foreknowledge. These observations mean not that the three predictions under discussion must be considered historical, but that their historicity cannot be dismissed on a priori, rationalist grounds.

A discussion of the predictions involves the historicity of the events predicted. Finegan (*Überlieferung* 69–70) thinks that the predictions are not historical but the events are; yet not all would even agree on that. True, relatively few would deny that Judas betrayed Jesus[44] or that the disciples did not support Jesus publicly during the period between his arrest and crucifixion.[45] There is dispute, however, about the historicity of Peter's denying Jesus three times before cockcrow. Some judge the scene theatrical, especially when three evangelists correlate these denials with the moment of Jesus' bravely giving witness before the priests—the chief disciple denies; the master confesses. (A further striking touch is Mark/Matt's having Jesus mocked as a false prophet at the moment his prophecy about Peter is being verified.) This dramatic contrast, however, which may well reflect preaching interests, is not intrinsically related to the issue of the historicity of the denials. Nor are the details of the denials essential to historicity (who asked the question; what was the exact response; where was it given); for, as we shall see in Table 3 (§27), they vary widely in the different Gospel accounts, as might be expected under the influence of oral tradition. The lengthier discussion in §27 will report the views of scholars who argue that the prediction of Peter's denials is ancient tradition and even historical, but the denials never took place, for the narrative concerning them was a creation to fulfill the prediction. Others hold just the opposite: The denials by Peter are ancient or even historical and gave rise to a prediction that was never really uttered. We shall also see the rebuttal argument that the early retention of a prediction that never proved true is hard to explain, as is the gratuitous creation of the denials and/or prediction that would have the effect of vilifying Peter.

[43]See the treatment of miracles in the NJBC 81:89–117.

[44]On the dubious grounds that Judas is consistently reidentified (which may be simply a matter of theological emphasis) Grayston (*Dying* 399) contends that the Judas episodes did not belong to the original PN. Yet I Cor 15:5 suggests that the group of the Twelve truly was in existence at the time of the resurrection, and Judas' name is firmly embedded in the four NT lists of the Twelve. It is extremely unlikely that without basis in fact early Christians would have created a story so damning to one of the Twelve, with no suggestion of rehabilitation. Details in the story of Matthias being chosen to replace Judas (Acts 1:13–26) are old, as is the Field of Blood association which is attested also in Matt 27:8.

[45]This would not be refuted by Luke's benevolent silence about their departure from Jesus' presence during the passion or by the Johannine portrait of the beloved disciple at the cross.

Clearly the *role* of Jesus' predictions in the Gospels is much easier to discern with some consensus than is their origin and historicity.

A key factor in this question is the interplay of OT motifs described at length in the COMMENT (and not repeated here). The account of Jesus' words and behavior in this episode and the next, which take place on the Mount of Olives, has been influenced by the last chapters of Zech and by II Sam 15, both of which are localized on that Mount. The influence is not so direct, however, that one can easily imagine that the *predictions* (or their fulfillment) were simply created from the OT passages. More plausibly the historical arrest of Jesus at Gethsemane involved failure by his disciples, eventually specified in terms of flight, denial, and betrayal. How could one reconcile such failure with God's plan for Jesus? That Gethsemane was on the Mount of Olives called attention to OT passages that had the same locale, and several of those passages offered motifs that cast light on the role played by the disciples (betrayal, departure) and thus contributed to the development of that role into narratives, incorporating key sayings of Jesus. The fact that different motifs from Zech or II Sam 15 appear in diverse ways in Mark and John is best explained if much of the formation of the sayings and of the basic data used in the narratives (but not the shaping of the data) antedated the evangelists.

(Bibliography for this episode is found in §4, Part 1.)

§6. PRAYER IN GETHSEMANE, PART ONE: ENTRY AND PREPARATIONS

(Mark 14:32–34; Matt 26:36–38; Luke 22:40; John 18:1b)

Translation

Mark 14:32–34: 32And they come into the plot of land the name of which was Gethsemane; and he says to his disciples, "Sit here while I pray." 33And he takes along Peter, and James, and John with him, and he began to be greatly distraught and troubled. 34And he says to them, "My soul is very sorrowful unto death. Remain here and keep on watching."

Matt 26:36–38: 36Then Jesus comes with them into the plot of land called Gethsemane; and he says to the disciples, "Sit in this place until, going away, I pray there." 37And having taken along Peter and the two sons of Zebedee, he began to be sorrowful and troubled. 38Then he says to them, "My soul is very sorrowful unto death. Remain here and keep on watching with me."

Luke 22:40: And being at the place, he said to them, "Keep on praying not to enter into trial."

John 18:1b: (after Jesus has gone out with his disciples "across the Kidron valley"): 1bwhere there was a garden into which he entered with his disciples.

[2aJudas . . . knew this place 2bbecause many times Jesus had come there together with his disciples.]

[12:27a (end of the public ministry when Greeks have come, marking the coming of the hour): "Now is my soul disturbed."]

COMMENT

Luke's account of the prayer of Jesus on the Mount of Olives is considerably briefer than that of Mark/Matt and, rather than standing by itself, constitutes a composite scene with the arrest. John has a comparable prayer of Jesus, not here but at the end of the ministry. For Mark/Matt, however, the prayer of Jesus in Gethsemane has its own consistency as a scene in which there is a discrete dramatic development. The structure of that scene is indicated by the evangelists' concentration on movement (see Martin, "Literary Theory" 582–87). In the first half of the scene, in three steps Jesus comes with his disciples into the plot of land, takes along three of them, and finally goes forward a little and prays. In the second half of the scene, three times Jesus comes (back) to his disciples from praying. The prayer is central, for it helps to articulate Jesus' reaction to his fate as well as the reaction of his disciples.

A glance at the Contents listed before §4 will show that I have divided my COMMENTS on Jesus' prayer in Gethsemane into five parts (§§6–10), with one ANALYSIS (§11) covering all five. This first part covers the entry of Jesus with his disciples into "the place" (plot of land, garden) where he will pray and later in the night be arrested.

THE ARRIVAL OF JESUS AND HIS DISCIPLES (MARK 14:32–33A; MATT 26:36–37A; LUKE 22:40; JOHN 18:1B)

The disciples. This episode terminates the transition of Jesus and his disciples from the Last Supper. Wilcox ("Denial" 428) suggests that Mark 14:32, where "they come" into the plot of land named Gethsemane, originally followed 14:26 where "they went out to the Mount of Olives," and that the intervening verses represent inserted independent material. Others who think of Jesus' prayer in Gethsemane as composed through the combination of two separate accounts tend to treat 14:26 and 14:32 as duplication. When we trace the "they" (Jesus and his disciples) from 14:32 back through 14:26 to the Last Supper, then the disciples are equivalent to the Twelve mentioned at the supper in 14:17,20 (but now minus Judas who will come in 14:43). But Mark makes no point of that, and interpreters are being inventive when they speak of the Twelve in 14:32 and the Three in 14:33.[1] In these verses not only does Mark not use the term "Twelve" for Jesus' companions, but after 14:32 he does not use "disciples" again until after the resurrection

---

[1]When Mark mentions Peter, James, and John, he never separates them out of "the Twelve" but always out of the disciples: see 5:31,37; 8:34 with 9:2; 13:1,3. Sometimes Andrew appears with them (1:16–19, 29; 13:3), so that there is nothing fixed about "three."

(16:7). While Jesus prays, they will not act in the manner of disciples; and when he is arrested, they will flee and abandon him.

Matt 26:36 has Jesus coming "with them" into Gethsemane, thus giving a picture of solidarity that is not broken when Jesus goes off from them to pray. In v. 37 Matt speaks of "Peter and the two sons of Zebedee." At the Transfiguration Matt 17:1 named the three disciples: "Peter and James and John"—the language Mark uses here—but for Matt in this scene only Peter is important. In v. 41 the Matthean Jesus will address Peter in the plural, for among the disciples only he has a representative role.

The site. There has been learned speculation about the route Jesus would have followed from the site of the supper[2] to the Mount of Olives and Gethsemane. Suggestions include his coming down through the Temple area and out an eastern gate (DSSW 320–21) or his descending the hill south of the Temple area, using a flight of steps from Roman times that can be detected just north of the church of St. Peter in Gallicantu. There are too many uncertainties to take these suggestions seriously.

As we saw in the preceding scene, Luke reported no conversation while Jesus was proceeding to the Mount of Olives (22:39). Similarly John reported none while Jesus was going out with his disciples across the Kidron valley (18:1a). In neither of those Gospels is a further place-name now given. Luke 22:40 speaks simply of "the place," i.e., not a technical designation but a customary place on the Mount of Olives where Luke 21:37 tells us that Jesus used to go.[3] The same term occurs in John 18:2.

In Mark/Matt intervening dialogue has separated the present verses from Mark 14:26/Matt 26:30, which reported that they went out to the Mount of Olives. (Indeed, Matt's use of "Then" here gives the impression that a separate scene is beginning.) Both these Gospels now introduce a new name, i.e., a plot of land called Gethsemane, which becomes a specification of the general direction "to the Mount of Olives." We saw that such designations as "Mount of Olives" and "winter-flowing Kidron" had scriptural resonance with the story of David's flight from Jerusalem in II Sam 15. "Gethsemane" (Greek *Gethsēmani,* or in Codex Bezae *Gesemanei*) probably reflects Hebrew/Aramaic *Gat-šěmānî,* "oil press," and has no known theological import.[4] Thus there is good reason to regard "Gethsemane" as coming from early tradition and, indeed, as a historical reminiscence. Luke's omission

---

[2]This is generally presumed to have been on the southern summit of the western hill of Jerusalem, i.e., the traditional site of the Cenacle near the place later identified as "the tomb of David."

[3]For topos ("place") as a location where Jesus prays, see Luke 4:42; 11:1. The expression used here, "being at" (*ginesthai epi*), is quite Lucan (3:2; 24:22; Acts 21:35).

[4]To be rejected, in my judgment, are both the ancient attempt by Jerome (CC 72.136; 77.253) to connect a form of the name with "valley of fatness" (Gě'-šěmānîm: Isa 28:1,4), and the modern suggestion of Stanley (Jesus 131) that there is a symbolic relationship between crushing olives and

of the name is consonant with his avoidance of exotic Semitic names and expressions. Mark places two scenes here: Jesus' prayer and the arrest. Those scholars who insist that these two parts had quite separate histories (see ANALYSIS §16A) argue that the name was remembered as the *place of the arrest*. The facts that Mark associates the name primarily with the prayer, that Luke and John describe the general site as a place to which Jesus had gone before (to pray?), and that John's story of the arrest does not contain the name suggest that more caution is required. If the form of the tradition that was known to Mark contained already attached to the story of the arrest at least an indication that Jesus prayed on the night he was given over, "Gethsemane" may have belonged to the compound story.

John refers to the site as a garden (*kēpos*, applicable to a place with vegetables, flowers, or trees). Church Fathers made a connection between this garden and the Garden of Paradise of Gen 1–3, and some modern scholars would maintain that the evangelist had such symbolism in mind; but there is little in the text to encourage such speculation.[5] Combining plausible pre-Marcan and preJohannine traditional elements, one may assume that on the Mount of Olives there was a plot of land or garden with olive trees and an oil press, bearing the name Gethsemane.[6] Josephus (*War* 6.1.1; #6) reports that the trees on the east side of the city were cut down in the Roman siege of Jerusalem (some forty years after Jesus' death), and so it is impossible to be sure exactly where on the Mount of Olives Gethsemane was. Since the 4th cent. a site at the bottom of the Mount (where olive trees grow more abundantly than on the upper slopes) has been venerated and, in particular, a rock formation or cave that might have housed an oil press (DSSW 322–26).

The action. Mark's beginning line, "And they come into the plot of land," illustrates well features of Marcan style. In 14:26,27,30 we have already

---

Jesus' anguish. I see no reason to think that Mark's readers would have understood the etymology of "Gethsemane" to make such connections.

[5]Stanley and B. P. Robinson are among those who advocate this symbolism. If John had such a reference in mind, he could have used the *paradeisos* of Gen 2:8 to indicate it. The contention that Aquila substituted *kēpos* in the Gen description is not really significant: This is the common Greek word for "garden"; every time it is used are we to think of the Garden of Eden? True, John is a Gospel that employs symbolism, but centuries separate John from Fathers like Cyril of Jerusalem and Cyril of Alexandria, and we cannot assume that the evangelist shared their imaginative interpretations. A similar problem bedevils the evidence brought forth by Manns ("Symbolisme" 63ff.) that Jewish thought associated the Garden of Paradise with Jerusalem. The rabbinic evidence he cites is considerably later than the 1st cent., and one cannot show that the evangelist thought in this fashion.

[6]Highly imaginative is the hypothesis that the country villa of John Mark and his mother Mary (Acts 12:12) stood here, a thesis involving the extremely dubious identification of the lightly clad young man of Mark 14:31 (assumed to have been roused from sleeping nearby) as John Mark. Thus E. Petavel, *Expositor* 4th Ser., 3 (1891), 220–32.

encountered the frequent use of the "And" connective (coordinating *kai*); and this feature continues throughout the Marcan prayer scene with a frequency greater than in the accounts of Matt and Luke together. Although Taylor and Black would attribute it to Semitic influence, the *kai* usage is probably popular Greek narrative style (even as "and" is frequent in English oral recounting) and has no special significance. That Mark reports the action in the plural suggests to some (Taylor, Cranfield, Galizzi) that this may be an eyewitness account. As observed in reference to Mark 14:26, however, Mark likes to use this construction to describe Jesus' movements, and it should not be pressed for particular significance. Already we saw the historical present tense in verbs of saying in 14:27,30; now a verb of motion is in that tense. The preference for this tense in narrative style is not peculiar to Mark (over 150 times in LXX I Sam; 160 in John); and in the Greek of this period the tense had become increasingly characteristic for verbs of speaking, seeing, coming, going, bringing, and sending. Matt and Luke generally disdain it as somewhat vulgar, even if in this particular scene Matt imitates the Marcan historical present a surprisingly high percentage of the time. Although it will be impossible to discuss such stylistic features pertinent to every verse of Mark, I have commented on this verse to stress that Marcan style often tells us little about either Mark's theology or his sources.

In the second part of 14:32 Mark moves from a "they" to a "he"; but, avoiding such complication, the other evangelists make Jesus the main subject of the whole action. In the Synoptics, prayer seems to be Jesus' main goal in coming here. As for the disciples, they are to sit where they are while Jesus goes off and prays,[7] or they are to pray themselves (Luke—an instruction that will be repeated after Jesus prays and so constitutes a framework). Mark mentions Jesus praying only in 1:35 and 6:46. One should not move too easily, then, toward the thesis of Marcan creation here and should appreciate how strong are the repeated references to prayer in 14:32,35, and 39. Most of Matt's changes of Mark here are purely stylistic; but Feuillet ("Récit" 416) and SPNM 101–2 call attention to Matt's unusual substitution of "Sit *in this place*" (adv. *autou,* only four times in NT) for Mark's "Sit here" (*hōde*). They point for background to Abraham's words to his servants as he prepares for the sacrifice of Isaac in Gen 22:5: "Sit in this place [*autou*] with the donkey. I and the little boy shall go on farther; and having worshiped, we shall return to you." (See APPENDIX VI on the sacrifice of Isaac.)

---

[7]There is no real reason not to take *kathizein* ("to sit") literally in Mark/Matt, but it could mean "to stay" as in Luke 24:49.

Some scholars would argue that when Jesus "takes along" (*paralambanein*) Peter, James, and John, there is in Mark no movement away from the "here" where the disciples are told to sit (presumably the entrance to the plot of land, an implication clearer in Luke). Part of the reason for theorizing that the three remain in the same place as the rest of the disciples is the desire to simplify where Jesus "comes" after his prayer in 14:37,40,43—he comes to where Peter is and yet some of what he says seems directed to all the disciples. To make a problem of this issue, however, is not to allow for the lack of detail in popular narrative: Mark never expected the reader to ask whether Jesus returned only to the three rather than to all the disciples. If there is separation, it has a dramatic effect; but the behavior and the fate of the three and of all the disciples are the same, so there is no need for differentiation in Jesus' return to them. In diagnosing Mark's mind about farther separation, one must ask whether the verb "take along" implies motion. Noteworthy is the context involving motion in the other Marcan uses of *paralambanein* in relation to the disciples, implicitly (walking) in 10:32, and explicitly in relation to Peter, James, and John in 5:40 (see 5:37) and 9:2. By analogy with those passages, then, Mark likely means that Jesus separated the three from the rest by moving them along farther. This is certainly how Matt 26:36 ("going away") understood Mark. The objection that two separations are illogical, since in Mark 14:35 Jesus *immediately* goes forward from the three and so there is no point in his having taken them along, does not take into account that Mark is dramatizing Jesus as increasingly isolated from effective support, even from those who have been closest to him.

The named disciples. In the ANALYSIS (§11,A3) I shall confess that I think it impossible to decide with surety whether the mention of Peter, James, and John is a Marcan creation, stems from preMarcan tradition,[8] and/or is historical. What is sure and more important is that the three disciples are named because they are very important in the flow of the Marcan narrative. The Gethsemane scene has often been compared with the Transfiguration (Mark 9:2–10), where virtually the same vocabulary is used by Mark (9:2) to describe Jesus taking along Peter, James, and John to a high mountain. He is revealed to them by God as "my beloved Son" (9:7), even as at Gethsemane he addresses God as "*Abba*, Father." The reaction of Peter to the transfigured Jesus is described thus: "for he did not know what to say,

---

[8]Scholars also argue about whether they are preMarcan in the other two passages in which they appear: Mark 5:37; 9:2.

for they were very afraid" (9:6); the disciples' reaction to Jesus later in Gethsemane will be described: "for their eyes were very burdened and they did
not know what they should answer him" (14:40). (Kenny, "Transfiguration"
445–48, points out that Matt's Gethsemane scene has parallels to Matt's
Transfiguration [17:1–9], but not the same ones found in Mark. In Matt Jesus
falls on his face, even as at the Transfiguration the disciples fall on their
faces [17:6]; and "while he was still speaking" is shared by 17:5 and 26:47,
even if the speaker is different. Luke does not mention Peter, James, and
John on the Mount of Olives; and his scene has no *obvious* parallels to his
account of the Transfiguration [9:28–36]; yet 9:32 in Luke's Transfiguration
is parallel to Mark's Gethsemane statement [14:40] about the eyes of the
disciples being "burdened" with sleep.)

How should the parallels between the appearance of Peter, James, and
John in Mark's account of Gethsemane and the previous appearances of
these three in Mark 5:37–43 and 9:2–10 be understood? From the comparison with the other two scenes, some (e.g., Kelber, "Mark 14" 169) relate the
appearance of the three at Gethsemane to the "Marcan secret" as if they were
receiving important revelation. But is that precise? Only in Mark 9:7 were
Peter, James, and John given a revelation by God about Jesus. In 5:37–43
they were witnesses of Jesus' miraculous power over death; but was that
miraculous power so different from other manifestations of power over
storms, ailments, and demons (of which the disciples and others were witnesses) that it should be considered a signal revelation coming under special
secrecy? In the Gethsemane scene there is no revelation at all given to the
three; rather they become witnesses to Jesus' anguish. What is common to
the three scenes is not revelation but witness. Peter, James, and John saw
Jesus acting with full power in 5:41–42; they heard God speak of him as His
Son in 9:7 and they heard Jesus say that the Son of Man must suffer many
things in 9:12; but now they are close by at a time in which he is in anguish
and weakness, in which he is not answered verbally by the One whom he
calls Father, and in which he himself asks to be delivered from the hour or
cup of suffering. More specifically, Peter's being close by is important: He
said he would not be scandalized (14:29); yet he will not be strong enough
to watch one hour. The close presence of James and John is important: They
were the very ones Jesus challenged in 10:35,38 ("Are you able to drink the
cup that I drink?"). Then they said they were able, but now they will find
themselves weak. And the Jesus who challenged them will himself pray,
"Take away this cup from me." Besides portraying Jesus' own struggle in the
face of evil, Mark shows that the best-known disciples never understood
either Jesus' glory or his anguish.

JESUS TROUBLED AND SORROWFUL (MARK 14:33B–34; MATT 26:37B–38)

If we concentrate on Mark/Matt, the atmosphere in the present episode (§6) has suddenly changed from that of §5 which introduced it. There in a series of prophecies Jesus showed himself prescient about the fate of his disciples and thus about what would happen by God's will: They would be scattered and deny him. Now, despite such predictions, he seems to want their human support as well as their prayer. This change is related to an anguish of Jesus that Mark 14:33 describes graphically: "He began to be greatly distraught [*ekthambeisthai*] and troubled [*adēmonein*]." Many times in NT Greek "come to, begin" (*erchesthai*) is virtually a pleonastic auxiliary to an infinitive[9] and need not be translated. Here, however, Mark does not wish simply to report that Jesus was greatly disturbed; he calls attention to the beginning of that disturbance as Jesus faces his fate. (The state now described in Mark/Matt has a partial parallel in the "strong clamor and tears" mentioned in Heb 5:7.)

There are in the OT many descriptions of the sufferings of the just one who pleads to God, especially in the Pss (22; 15; 31; 10; 39; 13; 43:2,5; 55:2–6; 116:10–15). In the next verse of Mark (14:34) Jesus himself will echo such a psalm; but the two verbs employed by 14:33 to describe Jesus' anguish are not derived from these passages. *Ekthambeisthai*, "to be greatly distraught," occurs in the LXX in Sir 30:9, and in the NT is peculiarly Marcan.[10] It indicates a profound disarray, expressed physically before a terrifying event: a shuddering horror. *Adēmonein*, "to be troubled," has a root connotation of being separated from others, a situation that results in anguish. It is not found in the LXX but in the Symmachus version of Ps 61:3, where Aquila reads *thambeisthai*. Not surprisingly, Luke (who would never attribute psychological disarray to Jesus) omits the whole Marcan description; and Matt softens the first verb to *lypeisthai*, "to be sorrowful" (which is consonant with the following verse where Jesus' soul is very sorrowful, *perilypos*).

What is the cause in Mark (and with slight attenuation in Matt) for such deep distress on Jesus' part? It must involve his impending fate that has been planned by his enemies since 14:1,11 and of which he has shown cognizance in 14:20,24,27. While the vocabulary is different, one is close here to the situation described in Ps 55:5–6: "My heart was disturbed within me; and the horror of death fell upon me; fear and trembling came upon me, and terror [LXX: darkness] covered me." But what exact aspect of that fate an-

---

[9]J. W. Hunkin, JTS 25 (1923–24), 390–402.
[10]Mark 9:15; here; 16:5–6; for *thambeisthai (thambein)* see 1:27; 10:24, 32.

guishes Jesus?[11] In the present context Mark/Matt have not spoken of Satan entering into Judas, and so one should not appeal to that. Is it the anticipation of physical pain? The context offers support for centering on Jesus' sense of being abandoned by all who have been close to him. Other scholars focus on the sense of enduring a cursed death (Gal 3:13) and of becoming sin (II Cor 5:21). Still others view the situation synthetically: "The abandonment of the Son of Man who is also the Suffering Servant of Isa 53:1" (Taylor, *Mark* 552), or of Jesus' finding himself without that good that could fill his life, God (Léon-Dufour, "Jésus" 256). Szarek ("Critique" 114) would have Jesus in anguish because of uncertainty about the value or meaning of his death. In my judgment Jesus' distress must be related to the eschatological context of his suffering and death, to be established by 14:53–58 as Jesus prays for deliverance from the hour and the cup and warns about trial (see below).

In Mark 14:34 Jesus expresses his anguish in direct discourse, "My soul [*psychē*] is very sorrowful [*perilypos*] unto death." While Matt has the same words, his initial "Then" gives the impression of another step in the anguish. Earlier, in Mark 14:18–19 when Jesus predicted betrayal, his disciples began "to be sorrowful [*lypeisthai*]"; now, as the result of the betrayal closes in on him, Jesus is "very sorrowful." The "soul" is the whole person, the "I," as can be seen from the parallelism in a psalm verse (42:6; see also 42:12), the first line of which the Marcan Jesus is echoing:

> Why are you very sorrowful [*perilypos*], my soul,
> and why do you disturb [*syntarassein*] me?

The next verse (42:7) continues: "My soul is disturbed [*tarassein*]." (Interestingly, these verses are echoed in a Qumran hymn perhaps written by the Teacher of Righteousness himself: 1QH 8:32: "My soul is downcast within me.") Although Kelber ("Mark 14" 178) questions the connection between Mark and this psalm, it is implicitly confirmed by an echo of Ps 42:7 in John 12:27 (a section of John with several parallels in this scene): "Now is my soul disturbed [*tarassein*]." In §5 we saw that II Sam 15 was the source from which the Marcan tradition drew the motif of the Mount of Olives and John drew "across the winter-flowing Kidron." If here from the same psalm Mark echoes the "very sorrowful" while John echoes the "disturb," most likely we should think of a preGospel association of such Scripture passages with the picture of Jesus' anguish as he faced death. In John 12, of course, Jesus

[11]See Luke 23:3,31 and John 13:2,27. The proposals discussed in the text are culled from a large body of writings on the subject (see already J. W. Schwartz, "Jesus," for a listing of solutions), most of which analyze Jesus in Gethsemane psychologically (taking the PNs as history) or theologically (often drawing on other NT or postNT christology).

overcomes the disturbance instantly, so the scriptural echo becomes a foil for a triumphant self-resolution (see §7 below).

If the first part of Jesus' statement in Mark 14:34 comes from a psalm describing the suffering just one, some like Schenke (*Studien* 546) would trace "unto death" to the same source. Something like the idea can be found, for instance, in Ps 31:10–11: "My eye is disturbed [*tarassein*] . . . also my soul; my life is worn out with grief." But the vocabulary of "unto death" is lacking in such passages. Suggested interpretations of the sense of that phrase include: (a) Degree: sorrow on a level of that produced by an awareness of imminent death, i.e., "so very sorrowful that I could die." Ps 55:5 is interesting in the light of the whole saying of the Marcan Jesus: "My heart was disturbed [*tarassein*] within me, and the horror of death fell upon me." (b) Consecutive: sorrow bringing him close to death, i.e., "so very sorrowful that it is killing me." (c) Final: sorrow leading to a desire of death, i.e., "so very sorrowful that I want to die." In I Kings 19:4 Elijah leaves his servant behind, goes into the wilderness, and states, "It is enough . . . take away my life." (d) Temporal: sorrow lasting till death, i.e., "very sorrowful until at last I shall die." This is reflected in the Vulgate.

In both (c) and (d), which somewhat overlap since a purely temporal sense would be rather banal, death becomes an anticipated and longed-for liberation from suffering. Close to Mark in wording is the LXX of Jonah 4:9 (*lypeisthai heōs thanatou*) where (see 4:8) Jonah means, "I am so weighed down by sorrow, I want to die." Finegan (*Überlieferung 70*) and Boman ("Gebetskampf" 271) do not hesitate to claim that Mark 14:34 is a combination of Ps 42:6 and Jonah 4:9. Supporters of the final sense of "unto death" include Bultmann, Gnilka, Héring, Klostermann, Lohmeyer, Schenke, and Schweizer. Daube ("Death" 96–98) points to the model of the weary prophet who asks for deliverance by death, e.g., Moses (Num 11:15), Elijah (I Kings 19:4), and Jeremiah (Jer 20:14–18). Nevertheless, J. Weiss (*Schriften* 1.194) was correct in objecting that the final interpretation does not fit the context, for Jesus does not go on to pray for death but to be delivered from death (so too Pesch, *Markus* 2.389, rejecting both Héring and Daube). I find unpersuasive Héring's attempt to answer this by claiming that while Jesus feared to die on the cross, he would have been willing to die in Gethsemane.

The other interpretation, favored until recent times by most commentators (Lagrange, Loisy, Swete, Taylor), lies in the range of (a) and (b). This has good biblical support, e.g., we are told in Judg 16:16 that after Delilah persisted in questioning him day after day, Samson's soul was vexed to death. Sir 37:2 asks, "Is it not a sorrow unto death when your companion or friend is turned enemy?" (We remember that Jesus' friend Judas is about to do something hostile.) In the context of being surrounded on all sides by enemies, Sir 51:6 affirms, "My soul has been close to death; my life has gone down to the brink of Sheol." If Jesus is the weary prophet in Mark/Matt, in part it is because he foresees his disciples scandalized and scattered by his arrest and death, after they have betrayed and denied him. The very thought of this is enough to kill him, and he will ask God to be delivered from such a fate.

Accordingly he tells Peter, James, and John, "Remain here and keep on watching," while he goes forward to make his request. "Remain here" matches the "Sit here" addressed to the body of disciples in 14:32—aorist imperatives of durative verbs, carrying in themselves the notion of continued action. "Keep on watching," a present imperative of *grēgorein*[12] putting stress on the necessity of continuance, is an additional demand addressed to the three. (Notice that Matt 26:38 has an added phrase: "watching *with me*," corresponding to the "comes *with them*" in 26:36 and expressing solidarity.) What is the specific reason for which the three are told to watch? Suggestions include: (a) As part of the Passover night watch, even as Exod 12:42 inculcates a "watch" to be kept to the Lord for all generations. Some would appeal to (the later) rabbinic legislation that the Passover group or *habura* could remain intact if some dozed but not if all fell asleep, whence Jesus' concern about the disciples sleeping. However (see APPENDIX II, A), it is dubious to keep finding Passover motifs after the Last Supper, since Mark and Matt seem to forget that feast once the supper is over. Is there any likelihood that Mark's readers, who seem to be ill-informed about Jewish customs, would make this connection? (b) So that they may witness his prayer or his suffering. Although in fact the three disciples do become witnesses of a low moment in Jesus' career after previously having witnessed his glory, "watch" is not clearly associated with that. *Grēgorein* here does involve staying physically awake, but it also has a sense of religious alertness. The words to all the disciples in 14:32, "Sit here while I pray," lead more directly to a witness of Jesus' prayer than do the words "Keep on watching." (c) As a protection against being surprised when Jesus' enemies arrive. Yet in Matt 26:51–54 Jesus will discourage resistance on their part. (d) As a companionable gesture so that Jesus will not be alone. Matt's addition of "with me" turns the phrase in this direction and underlines Jesus' unity with his disciples. (e) As an attitude required by the eschatological context of Jesus' death. Comparable to Mark's triple use here of *grēgorein* (14:34,37,38) is the triple use of that verb in the parable of the doorkeeper that ends the eschatological discourse of Mark 13. The atmosphere is set by the introductory line (13:33):

---

[12]Also in Matt 26:38. There, however, a form from the secondarily constituted verb *egrēgorein* is read by P[37] (ca. AD 300); and J. N. Birdsall, JTS NS 14 (1963), 390–91, argues that this is original.

"Keep your eyes open and stay awake, for you do not know when is the appointed time [*kairos*]." The parable tells of a master who has gone away leaving servants in charge and a doorkeeper admonished to watch. The master may return at any of the four divisions of the night (late evening, midnight, cockcrow, early morning), and he must not find them asleep. Jesus ends the parable (13:37) with the directive, "What I say to you, I say to all, 'Keep on watching.'" Certainly the Gethsemane context in Mark where Jesus will come back three times and find the disciples sleeping (as well as the later scene of Peter at [second] cockcrow) favors a connection with the parable. While here, unlike the parable, there is no reference to the parousia, we are in the atmosphere of the final trial, as will become apparent in the discussion below. If the readers of Mark's Gospel had already experienced another form of the eschatological conflict in terms of Christian martyrdom, this command to keep on watching would have had a special urgency. And even independently of martyrdom, they could share the context of I Pet 5:8: "Be sober and watch, for your adversary, the devil, as a roaring lion walks about seeking whom he will devour."

The Approaching Trial in Luke 22:40b (Peirasmos)

We turn now from the Mark/Matt presentation of Jesus as troubled, sorrowful, and enjoining his disciples to keep on watching to the very different preparation that Luke 22:40 gives to Jesus' prayer. Luke offers no portrait of Jesus in distress; rather, very much in command, Jesus simply instructs his disciples to pray by way of an anticipating accompaniment to his own prayer. Before we discuss the content of their prayer (the *peirasmos* motif), the suppression by Luke of the Marcan portrait of Jesus as troubled deserves comment. Despite John's high christology, that Gospel (12:27) does not hesitate to have Jesus say, "Now is my soul disturbed," precisely in the context of vocalizing his decision about the hour. But Luke refuses any such report as his Jesus prepares to pray about the cup. Luke can acknowledge the suffering of the Son of Man (9:22,44) but refuses to describe Jesus' inner reaction to suffering. This Jesus, who is far from indifferent to the suffering of others (7:13; 7:38 with 47–48; 10:41; 13:11–12), is so at peace with God that he cannot be distraught by the sufferings that are inflicted on him (4:29–30; 6:11–12; 13:31–33). His only concern in that regard is the inevitable divine judgment that such injustice to him will bring on Jerusalem (13:33–34; 23:28).

In part this Lucan portrait is colored by the desire to have Jesus in his passion revealed as a model to Christian sufferers and martyrs. (For the strong martyrological thrust in Luke's PN, see p. 187 below.) In 12:11 Jesus told his disciples, "When they bring you in to the synagogues and the rulers and the powers [*exousia*; cf. 22:53], do not be anxious." Obviously Jesus could not be anxious himself or he would not set a good example. On p. 217 below, I shall show how aspects of the Mark/Matt scene caused scandal and disbelief among Greco-Roman outsiders, and Neyrey ("Absence") has argued persuasively that part of Luke's reason for omitting the emotions of Jesus described in Mark/Matt may have been because of the impact these emotions could make. Neyrey cites Stoic passages, Cicero, and Philo to the effect that passions like sorrow (*lypē*) in the face of suffering were irrational, sinful, and the mark of one out of control. In the same line of thought Kloppenborg (*"Exitus"*) would see Luke conforming Jesus' approach to death to the model of composure established in the Greco-Roman world by the death of Socrates. Without going that far, one can find a dislike for exaggerated sorrow in the LXX, for texts like Gen 3:17 and Isa 1:5 portrayed sorrow as a punishment for sin. In I Macc 6:8 the very wicked King Antiochus Epiphanes was greatly disturbed and *fell* into sickness out of sorrow, even as in Mark 14:35 the very sorrowful Jesus falls on the ground. Luke cannot leave Jesus so open to misunderstanding. Others can weep and be upset by Jesus' suffering (23:27,48), but Jesus himself cannot. Telling his disciples to pray, he kneels down and prays. It is not accidental that Luke describes Paul in a similar way, for that missionary has learned from the Master. Knowing that he is on the way to prison and affliction (Acts 20:22), and surrounded by weeping disciples, Paul kneels down and prays with them (Acts 20:36–37; see Radl, *Paulus* 159–68).

The words of the Lucan Jesus to his disciples in 22:40, "Keep on praying not to enter into trial [*peirasmos*],"[13] show the eschatological tone that Luke found in Mark's (14:34) "Keep on watching." The theme of the disciples' praying about *peirasmos* will come in Mark 14:38 and Matt 26:41 after Jesus himself has prayed; Luke has anticipated it here. "Not to enter into [*eiserchesthai eis*] *peirasmos*" is the *content* of the prayer the Lucan Jesus urges on his disciples. Among the Gospels, only in Luke (11:1) has Jesus received from his disciples a request that he teach them how to pray; and in response he gave them the Lord's Prayer, which has the petition "Do not lead us into *peirasmos*." Now twice, before and after his own praying, the Lucan Jesus does not hesitate to instruct the disciples to make not entering into *peirasmos* their immediate petition. The double use of *eis* ("into") both as part of the verb and a preposition shows that the central issue is not one of help during *peirasmos* but avoiding *peirasmos* altogether. Feldkämper (*Betende* 236),

---

[13]Codices Sinaiticus and Koridethi and minuscule family 13 have "to pray not to enter" with an infinitive functioning for the imperative; and H. N. Bate, JTS 36 (1935), 76–77, argues for that as original and good Lucan style.

who classifies the expression as a Semitism, suggests that "falls into" renders the idea. But Carmignac ("Fais"), from a study of negated Hebrew positive verbs, argues that the phrase means "enter into the object of" and thus "succumb to": In other words, what may happen if they enter into *peirasmos* is in view. Similarly, Léon-Dufour, "Jésus" 253–54, speaks of entering into a trap—a force that can seize.

What is this *peirasmos* that presents such a perilous entanglement? Several possible meanings stem from the word itself (see Holleran, *Synoptic* 37): "temptation" or solicitation to evil; "trial" or testing by affliction; some specific danger. Let us note examples of general biblical usage before turning to Luke in particular. At the beginning of the public career of Jesus, the Synoptic Gospels use the related verb *peirazein* for the tempting of Jesus by the devil during the forty days in the desert. Andrews[14] suggests an OT background, beginning with such passages as Deut 6–8; 9:9; Exod 34:28; I Kings 19:8, which involve Israel's being tested in the desert, or Elijah's trials. It became a familiar view that God tests the righteous and they conquer. Abraham, in particular, gave an example of one who has been faithful in *peirasmos*; and in *Jubilees* 19:1–9 the death of Sarah constitutes the tenth test in his life. In II Chron 32:31, God left King Hezekiah on his own "in order to test [*peirazein*] him and to know all that was in his heart." In addition, there are many biblical examples of *peirasmos/peirazein* used for the temptations met in ordinary or Christian life that test one's fidelity to God (James 1:2,13–14; I Tim 6:9). In the early period God was described as the tester; but gradually other human beings (Wis 3:5; 11:9; Sir 2:1; 33:1; 44:20) or Satan (Job 1:6–2:14; I Thess 3:5) assumed that role. It is probably in the broad sense that Heb 4:15 describes Jesus as "one who in all things has been tempted/tested as we are." Few scholars, however, think that the present context favors the broad interpretation of the word. When the disciples were told to pray not to enter into *peirasmos*, something more dangerous must have been meant.

There are a number of times in the NT where *peirasmos* refers to testing in a specific way, namely, the great eschatological trial or struggle involving divine judgment—a context that began with Jesus' proclamation of the kingdom, that continued in the proclamation of the gospel by his followers, and that will culminate soon, as the Son of Man comes in power to destroy the forces of evil. It is in this eschatological sense that, with different nuances, most scholars interpret the *peirasmos* of the Gethsemane scene (Beasley-Murray, Dibelius, Dodd, Grundmann, Holleran, Kuhn, Lohmeyer, Nineham,

---

[14]"Peirasmos" 230–34, drawing on *Peirasmos* by J. H. Korn (BWANT 72; Stuttgart: Kohlhammer, 1937).

Schniewind, Schweitzer, Taylor, etc.). In Mark the implied and in Luke the explicit agent of the testing is Satan, who struggles with Jesus;[15] but more important, God is involved (Barbour, "Gethsemane" 244–48) by allowing this great struggle so that the Son may be victorious (Heb 4:15; 5:8–9). K. G. Kuhn ("New" 95–101) has pointed to a similarity between NT thought and that of Qumran, where God allows the momentous struggle between the forces of truth and falsehood, light and darkness (1QS 3:20–25; 4:16–19). An example of the eschatological outlook is supplied by II Pet 2:4–9 where, in a context of God's judgment on the evil angels, on the generation of the flood (from which Noah was preserved), and on Sodom (from which Lot was preserved), we hear, "Thus the Lord knows how to rescue the pious from *peirasmos* and to keep the unjust under punishment until the day of judgment." In Rev 3:10, One who is the first and last, and has the keys of death and Hades (1:17–19), directs a message to the church in Philadelphia: "Because you have kept my word of endurance, so I too will keep you from the hour of trial [*peirasmos*] which is coming on the whole world to try [*peirazein*] those who dwell on earth." Using *peirazein*, Rev 2:10 relates the sufferings of the church of Smyrna, especially imprisonment, to testing by the devil; and 2:9 describes all this as *thlipsis*, a term for the tribulations of the last time (Rev 7:14; Mark 13:19,24). I Pet 4:12 refers to "the fiery ordeal that comes upon you for *peirasmos*." In Acts 20:19 Paul speaks of the trials (pl. *peirasmos*) which came upon him through the plots of the Jews. Probably, too, *peirasmos* had an eschatological meaning in the Lord's Prayer (R. E. Brown, "Pater" 248–53); for "Do not lead us into *peirasmos*" (Matt 6:13; Luke 11:4) is parallel to "but free us from the Evil One."

The two basic uses of *peirasmos* just described are not totally independent of each other in the NT, since after the coming of Jesus the trials of ordinary Christian life have a relationship to the final great struggle for the kingdom. (This duality of meaning may explain the tendency to use *peirasmos* without the definite article.) In my "Pater" I argued that while the original focus of "Do not lead us into *peirasmos*" was eschatological, gradually it was de-eschatologized to refer to the temptations of ordinary life. Nevertheless, one must ask where lies the emphasis in the Mount of Olives scene when the Lucan Jesus instructs, "Keep on praying not to enter into *peirasmos*." How

[15]The Satanic presence is more obvious in Luke than in Mark. For Luke this is the more opportune time of Satan's return anticipated in 4:13; Satan has entered Judas (23:3,21); and "the power of darkness" makes itself felt on the Mount of Olives (22:53). In an important study Best (*Temptation* xxiii) argues that Mark transferred to the temptation of Jesus at the beginning of the Gospel the defeat of Satan and the cosmic powers presented by other NT writers in the passion. I do not think that view does justice to the Marcan picture of a ministry marked by struggles with demons who must be dispossessed (see p. 168 below). Although not as emphatically as for Luke, the *peirasmos* in Gethsemane for Mark continues the *peirazein* by Satan in 1:13.

does Luke conceive of *peirasmos*? Conzelmann's famous view of a Satan-free ministry of Jesus in Luke after 4:13 ("When the devil had concluded every *peirasmos*, he departed from Jesus until an opportune time [*kairos*]") is quite unsatisfactory.[16] As in Mark/Matt, so also in Luke there is opposition by the demon to Jesus' proclamation of the kingdom (10:17; 11:14–22; 13:11–17). During the ministry, Satan may not have attempted the same kind of face-to-face frontal attack that constituted the *peirazein/peirasmos* of Luke 4:1–13; but skirmishes with the demons were serious enough to be considered *peirasmoi* by Jesus (22:28)—indeed, fidelity during them won for the Twelve thrones in Jesus' kingdom. Now, in the Lucan account of the passion, Satan has resumed a frontal attack: He has entered into Judas, taking him away from Jesus (22:3–4), and he has sought to have all of the disciples to sift them like wheat (22:31); his activity will make itself felt almost tangibly as "the power of darkness" in the arrest of Jesus (22:53).

The scene on the Mount of Olives, then, is a crucial moment in the great *peirasmos*. I do not find relevant the distinction that some scholars make that this is a *peirasmos* not of Jesus but of the disciples—that distinction really reduces *peirasmos* to personal temptation. If we think of *peirasmos* as the final trial, both Jesus and the disciples are confronted with entering it. Jesus' prayer to the Father (to be treated below), "Take away this cup from me" (Luke 22:42), is a prayer not to enter into *peirasmos*.[17] His request will not be granted; but he will be strengthened by an angel from heaven to go through the trial successfully (22:43–44). His instruction urging his disciples to pray not to enter into *peirasmos* will have an effect. Luke does not tell us that they fled or were let go, as do the other evangelists; but certainly the Lucan silence about them (see discussion in §44 of "all his acquaintances" in 23:49) indicates that here they were not thought to have drunk the cup that Jesus drank. The underlying idea is probably that they were not strong enough before Jesus' resurrection to survive the *peirasmos*, for Luke 8:13 conceives of the time (*kairos*) of *peirasmos* as one in which even those who have heard the word and have received it with joy can fall away. Certainly, passages cited above (II Pet 2:4–9 and Rev 3:10) see *peirasmos* as a superhuman trial, with only God's help protecting Christians from its most

---

[16]S. Brown (Apostasy 5–7) has shown this well. I disagree, however, with Brown's overrefinements, which include confining the *peirasmos* of Jesus to chap. 4 despite 22:28, understanding the present prayer to refer only to a future *peirasmos* of the disciples (not to the struggle of Jesus in his passion), and arguing that the age of the church is not a time of *peirasmos* despite Acts 20:19.

[17]Héring ("Simples" 97–98), reviving a suggestion by Loisy, thinks that originally Jesus told his disciples, "Pray that I do not enter into *peirasmos*," and that the "I" was dropped because of scandal in the idea of Jesus asking for prayer for himself. There is no textual support for this theory; there is no other example of Jesus asking his disciples to pray for him; and the whole idea is unnecessary: Jesus prays for himself in relation to *peirasmos* when he prays about the cup.

destructive aspects (Eph 6:12–13). Mark 13: 19–20 warns that the *thlipsis* is unlike any other since creation; if not shortened, it would destroy all flesh. Divine angelic help, such as that given to the Lucan Jesus, was, as we shall see, a feature of Jewish martyr stories and was to become a feature of Christian martyr stories. Therefore, when in God's plan those who had prayed to be allowed not to enter into *peirasmos* (part of the Lord's Prayer in Luke) were nevertheless forced to enter it, they too received assistance.

(Bibliography for this episode is found in §4, Part 2.)

§7. PRAYER IN GETHSEMANE, PART TWO: JESUS PRAYS TO THE FATHER

(Mark 14:35–36; Matt 26:39; Luke 22:41–42)

Translation

Mark 14:35–36: ³⁵And having gone forward a little, he was falling on the earth and was praying that if it is possible, the hour might pass from him. ³⁶And he was saying, *"Abba,* Father, all things are possible to you: Take away this cup from me. But not what I will but what you (will)."

Matt 26:39: And having gone forward a little, he fell on his face praying and saying, "My Father, if it is possible, let this cup pass from me. Nevertheless, not as I will but as you (will)."

Luke 22:41–42: ⁴¹And he drew away from them as if a stone's throw; and having knelt, he was praying, ⁴²saying, "Father, if you desire, take away this cup from me. Nevertheless, not my will but yours be done."

[John 12:27b-28a: ²⁷ᵇ"And what should I say? Father, save me from this hour? But for this (purpose) have I come to this hour. ²⁸ᵃFather, glorify your name."

18:11 (after Jesus has told Peter to put the sword back into the sheath): "The cup that the Father has given me—am I not to drink it?"]

COMMENT

The forward direction that began when Jesus arrived at the plot of land (Mark/Matt) or place (Luke) on the Mount of Olives is continued in this episode which brings us to the middle point of the scene, i.e., the prayer of

Jesus to the Father. From this prayer he will in subsequent episodes come back to his disciples, whom he has left behind. In discussing this episode we shall begin with the position that Jesus takes in order to pray and then discuss the contents of the prayer. The sequence of subsections is given in the list of Contents that precedes §4.

JESUS GOES FORWARD AND PROSTRATES HIMSELF OR KNEELS (MARK 14:35A; MATT 26:39A; LUKE 22:41)

Following his expression of sorrow and turmoil, the Jesus of Mark/Matt is said to have moved "forward a little" from the three named disciples—an unusual NT meaning for both *proserchesthai*, which normally means "to come toward, approach," and for *mikron*, which adverbially is more often temporal than spatial. Luke describes a similar action ("drew away [*apospan*] from them [all the disciples] as if a stone's throw") in different vocabulary, which for the most part is characteristically Lucan. *Apospan* (three of four NT instances in Luke-Acts) has in classical Greek the sense of tearing away violently. Plummer, Lagrange, and Feuillet would see that meaning here: Jesus tore himself away from his disciples to enter into agony. In the papyri, however (MM 68), *apospan* frequently has no such sense of violence; and in the other, intransitive NT instance (Acts 21:1) there is a peaceful separation, which better fits the Lucan conception of Jesus. "As if" (*hōsei*) is Lucan in sixteen of twenty-two NT usages. "A stone's throw" occurs in classical Greek, but not in the LXX.[1] While that distance would allow the disciples still to have contact with Jesus, it is not possible to judge whether they would both have seen and heard him (Feuillet, "Récit" 400) or just have seen him (Fitzmyer, *Luke* 2.1441), and whether "a stone's throw" implies less distance than indicated by Mark's "a little" and thus solves for Luke how the disciples were able to know how Jesus prayed (see Schrage, "Bibelarbeit" 24). Unconvincing is the attempt of Feldkämper (*Betende* 237) to associate this description of Jesus' distancing himself a stone's throw with the throwing of stones at the prophets (Luke 13:34) or at Stephen, Paul, and Barnabas (Acts 7:58–59; 14:5).

Separation for prayer or contact with God is attested in the OT (Gen 22:5; Exod 19:17; 24:2,14: Lev 16:17), but Mark's description of Jesus moving forward also implies alienation from the disciples, who no longer can come with Jesus as he approaches the hour. Similarly, prostrating oneself on the ground reverentially before the Divine Presence is attested in the OT;[2] but

---

[1] A LXX equivalent might be "as if the distance of a bow shot" in Gen 21:16.

[2] Gen 18:2; also Gen 19:1 and Judg 13:20, which combine "on the earth" with the "on his face" found in Matt.

Mark's "was falling [impf.] on the earth" continues from the preceding verses a portrayal of the distraught attitude of Jesus. (Some cite as a verbal parallel to Mark the words of Jesus in John 12:24: "Unless a grain of wheat falls into the earth and dies . . ."; but that is a very different image.) By substituting "on his face" (equally biblical: Gen 17:3; Luke 17:16) and by using the aorist tense for the verb, Matt 26:39 slightly softens Mark's picture of Jesus' distress. Matt did this previously in 26:37. Luke also softens the Marcan picture by having Jesus kneel (*tithenai ta gonata,* "to place one's knees"), a position that is the more normal one for Christian prayer in Acts 7:60; 9:40; 20:36; 21:5 (contrasted with standing by the Pharisee and publican in Luke 18:11,13). Luke is interested in Jesus as a model of prayer for his future followers.

THE PRAYER CONCERNING THE HOUR AND THE CUP (MARK 14:35B–36; MATT 26:39B; LUKE 22:42)

While the three Synoptics have Jesus offer a prayer in his own words, Mark alone first describes the prayer in indirect discourse and thus gives a double prayer, indirect and direct.

The Twofold Marcan Prayer in Indirect and Direct Discourse. There is a likeness between the indirect and direct descriptions that constitute the heart of Jesus' petition in Mark:

14:35: He was praying that if it is possible, the hour might pass from him
14:36: He was saying, "All things are possible to you: Take away this cup from me"

We saw much the same phenomenon in Mark 14:33–34 where the distress of Jesus was described first indirectly and then in his own words, even if there the vocabulary of the two verses differed. (See also the mixture of the direct and indirect in 6:8–11.) Inevitably there has been speculation whether Mark found the content of both v. 35 and v. 36 separately in earlier tradition and combined them, or found only one and created the other as a commentary. Bultmann, Dibelius, Greeven, Linnemann, and Schrage are among those who opt for the priority of v. 35, while Schenke and Wendling opt for the priority of v. 36.[3] This approach is cast into doubt when one recognizes

---

[3]E. P. Sanders, *The Tendencies of the Synoptic Tradition* (Cambridge Univ., 1969), 252–62, offers statistics that show how difficult it is to guess whether a given evangelist would necessarily prefer direct or indirect discourse. There are elements of Marcan style in both verses, e.g., *hina* introducing indirect discourse and "if it is possible" (see 13:22) in v. 35; *alla* ("but") and an ellipsis in v. 36. Yet in both verses there are also elements not generally found in Mark, e.g., in v. 35 the introductory action and in v. 36 the combination of transliterated Aramaic *"Abba"* with a Greek *ho Patēr.*

that John has both a form of Jesus' prayer about the hour (12:27–28) and a reference to the cup (18:11, in the context of the arrest). Unless one thinks John used Mark and divided the Marcan material in such a strange manner, one should reckon with the possibility that the content of both Marcan verses came from the preGospel tradition, even if Mark reshaped the material to the present indirect/direct pattern. In any case, as in vv. 33–34, the repetitiveness of 35–36 is effective narrative style, impressing readers with the seriousness of Jesus' plight. Indeed, Phillips ("Gethsemane" 52) would contend that there is a type of alternation throughout this whole scene between narrative (vv. 32a,33,35,37a,39–40) and direct discourse (32b,34,36,37b–38,41–42), and that the former brackets and draws attention to the latter. Whether the organization is that perfect one can debate, but certainly Phillips is largely correct in his perception; and in the ANALYSIS (§11) I shall insist that this literary artistry intended by Mark should not be undone.

The indirect petition (v. 35) is tempered by the condition "if it is possible" (see also Mark 13:22); the direct petition in v. 36 has the qualification "not what I will but what you (will)." Both the condition of 35 and the qualification of 36 are necessary, since Jesus has three times indicated that the suffering, rejection, and crucifixion or killing of the Son of Man are by divine plan (8:31; 9:31; 10:33–34). Some scholars find it impossible that having acknowledged that these things must (*dei* in 8:31) happen, Jesus could have prayed that they would "pass," i.e., pass away or disappear (*parerchesthai* in v. 35, as in Matt 5:18). Accordingly, there have been attempts to divorce the hour/cup of 35–36 from the passion and death or to interpret the passage so that Jesus is not trying to avoid crucifixion and death. Robson ("Meaning") reports one such attempt: What Jesus feared was that the suffering in Gethsemane might be too much for him and that he might die before he reached the cross (see also B. P. Robinson, "Gethsemane"; Baldwin, "Gethsemane"). Or, it has been argued (Blaising, "Gethsemane" 337–38) that Jesus did not pray that the hour would not come, but that it would pass quickly and not be prolonged. Similarly, some would argue that the cup does not involve death, but sin or some other bad result.

Such attempts to avoid having Jesus ask God to change the planned suffering and crucifixion of the Son of Man may stem from misunderstanding the relationship between prayer and the divine will. In the biblical outlook, it is not irreverent to ask God for a change of mind.[4] Moses intercedes to change

---

[4]Daube ("Prayer") would even argue for a set Jewish prayer pattern: (a) acknowledgment of God's controlling power and planning; (b) wish that nevertheless God would allow something that is not part of the plan; (c) surrender to or acceptance of God's will if the answer is negative. The evidence for Daube's pattern is later than the NT, and indeed, as the biblical evidence given above indicates, not a necessary postulate.

the Lord's will about Israel after the incident of the golden calf (Exod 32:10–14); Hezekiah prays to change God's will about his death (II Kings 20:1–6). David's action in II Sam 15:25–26 is worth noting, since we have seen that this chapter has definite parallels to Gethsemane. Having crossed the winter-flowing Kidron, David sends Zadok with the Ark back to Jerusalem, implicitly as a prayer that the Lord would bring David back—but if not, "Let him deal with me as he likes." In I Macc 3:58–60 Judas encourages his followers toward victory in battle: "But as His will in heaven may be, so He will do." In such instances, the prayer is not one of rebellion but of confidence in God's love and justice. God will listen and will grant the request if it is reconcilable with overall Providence.

The Hour (Mark 14:35). Let us discuss the wording of the indirect petition of Jesus peculiar to Mark 14:35: "that if it is possible, the hour might pass from him." The condition at the beginning does not reflect Jesus' doubt about God's power, for the next verse will assert "all things are possible to you." Rather the issue is one of reconcilability with God's plan that has been spelled out in the passion predictions. The key is the meaning of "the hour," a theme with which Mark will frame this pericope, since in 14:41 Jesus will say, "The hour has come; behold the Son of Man is given over into the hands of the sinners" and thus will indicate his awareness that God has not granted the petition. In Mark an absolute "the hour" eschatologically used is found previously only in 13:32: "But of that day or the hour no one knows, not even the angels in heaven nor the Son, but only the Father." Despite the fact that 13:32 is offered as a leading example of the genuine sayings of Jesus (since a limitation of the Son was scarcely invented by Christians), the pre-Marcan absolute (eschatological) use of "the hour" has been challenged (see Linnemann, *Studien* 28). Yet if "the hour" were Marcan rather than preMarcan, one would have to explain John's *wide* use of "the hour" as indirectly or directly derivative from Mark's three uses—a derivation that would demand great imagination. Also indicative of preMarcan use is Rom 13:11, where Paul in an eschatological context dealing with salvation, i.e., the end of night and the day being at hand, writes: "You know the appointed time [*ho kairos*], that it is already (the) hour for you to rise from sleep." While *hōra* in the Romans passage does not have the definite article, it is synonymous in meaning with *the* appointed time. See also "the hour" in Rev 9:15.

This leads us into the question of the extent to which "the hour" in Mark 14:35 is eschatological.[5] The *kairos* that is parallel to *hōra* in the Romans

---

[5] Those favoring eschatology include Feldmeier, Grundmann, Phillips, Schrage, and Taylor; negative, Kelber, Kuhn, Linnemann, and Mohn.

passage is clearly eschatological in Dan 11:35,40; 12:1,4, where it describes the endtime with great battles and tribulation (*thlipsis*) and the intervention of Michael to deliver God's people. Mark's use of "the hour" in 13:32 is in specifying apposition with that day when all the eschatological signs are to take place—the following verse (13:33) speaks of it as *kairos*. How much of that atmosphere is carried over to Mark 14:35, or are we dealing here *only* with the hour of Jesus' destiny and the hour of his death in particular? We must remember that the Marcan Jesus, in his predictions of the death of the Son of Man in terms of the divine plan, somehow related this to the coming of the kingdom. (Notice how Acts 1:6–7 translates Mark 13:32: The lack of knowledge about the day or the hour of the endtime has become a lack of knowledge about the restoration of the kingdom to Israel.) The idea that the hour mentioned in Gethsemane is eschatological is reinforced when we note that all through the Marcan Gospel Jesus has encountered the opposition of Satan, of unclean spirits, and of demons while proclaiming the kingdom (1:13,23,32,39; 4:15; 5:8; 6:7,13; 7:25, etc.) Particularly important is 3:22–27 where Jesus envisages a kingdom of Satan and the conquest of that kingdom in terms of the strongest person taking away possessions from the strong, and 8:33 where Peter's idea that the Son of Man need not suffer and die to accomplish his purpose is regarded as a satanic suggestion. (Wiens, "Passion," contends that Mark/Matt saw the passion of Jesus as comparable to the OT idea of holy war, but it cannot be won in a traditional way, without the agony of crucifixion.) A few verses after 14:35 the Marcan Jesus will interpret the hour in terms of the Son of Man being given over to the hands of sinners. While for Mark the death of Jesus is involved in "the hour," the death is part of a struggle with sinners that is an aspect of the coming of the kingdom. Mark is presenting a moment that is both historical and eschatological. The suffering and crucifixion of Jesus are a physical trial for him but also part of a cosmic struggle.

The Cup (Mark 14:36 and par.). The Marcan Jesus' indirect request that the hour pass from him must be seen as parallel to his direct words in the next verse: "Take away this cup [*potērion*] from me." To some extent, as D. N. Freedman pointed out to me, the two requests must have the literary effect of a hendiadys, with the second specifying the first: "The hour when the cup is to be drunk." Nevertheless, we must ask about the tonality contributed by the idea of drinking a cup. Of five OT Hebrew words for "cup," with one exception ("a cup [*sap*] of reeling" in Zech 12:2), only *kôs* is used metaphorically (some twenty times; see Cranfield, "Cup" 137); and it is *kôs* that *potērion* translates in the LXX thirty out of thirty-two times. A. T. Hanson (*Wrath* 27–36) shows that the idea of the cup of wrath is ancient in the

Near East; and seventeen times in the OT *kôs/potērion* describes figuratively God's wrath or punishment to be drunk by the guilty. Usually, concrete historical punishments are meant (Isa 51:17; Jer 25:15–16; 51:7; Ezek 23:33; Ps 75:9); but Rev 14:10 and 16:19 show that an apocalyptic cup of wrath can also be envisaged. Are we to see Jesus as being asked to drink the cup of God's wrath against sin, as if God were going to make him the object of anger?[6] Some argue that by drinking it he changed it to a cup of blessing (I Cor 10:16). Others see here a reflection of the idea that in crucifixion Christ became a curse (Gal 3: 13) or sin (II Cor 5:21); but we have no evidence that such Pauline ideas were known by Mark, and even in Paul such passages do not establish that Jesus himself was the object of God's wrath.

Others have understood the cup about which Jesus prayed as his fate or destiny. There is some OT evidence for *kôs* as the positive good portion allotted to the writer (Pss 16:5; 23:5; 116:13). By analogy, can "cup" also refer to a negative fate, i.e., the cup of suffering and death as one's destiny (so Black, Davies, Fiebig, Surkau)? We find such usage in the targums or Aramaic translations of the Bible, e.g., taste of "the cup of death" in Neofiti of Deut 32:1 and in Neofiti, Yerushalmi II, and Fragmentary Targum of Gen 40:23. (See Le Déaut, "Goûter"; Speier, "Kosten"; Black, "Cup.") "The bitter cup of death" occurs in ms. A (but not in ms. B) of the *Test. of Abraham* 16:12. In the *Martyrdom of Polycarp* 14:2, the cup is a sharing in the martyrdom of Christ leading to resurrection; and the *Martyrdom of Isaiah* 5:13 (late 1st cent. AD?) has the prophet saying in reference to his being sawed in half, "Only for me has God mixed this cup." For earlier evidence of the cup of painful death, some have argued that drinking the cup is equivalent to the expression "taste death" in Heb 2:9; John 8:52; *IV Ezra* 6:26. Even more pertinent would be Jesus' question addressed to James and John in Mark 10:38–39: "Are you able to drink the cup which I drink, or to be baptized with the baptism with which I am baptized?" When they say, "We are able," Jesus promises that they will drink the cup and be baptized. It is very difficult to think that this can be the cup of God's wrath over sin, for the disciples are scarcely invited to drink that. Therefore, many who hold the wrath theory for Mark 14:36 argue that a different cup is involved in 10:38–39.[7] The simplest interpretation of 10:38–39 is that the disciples are being challenged to drink

[6]This wrath interpretation has been held by (among others) Albertz, Blaising, Cranfield, Delling, Feldmeier, Lane, Lotz, Summerall, and Taylor.

[7]E.g., Summerall and Cranfield, but not Delling. For Feuillet ("Coupe") both cup and baptism in Mark 10:38–39 refer to vicarious expiatory suffering, but does Mark think of the disciples playing that role? Bernard ("Study") argues that 10:38–39 must refer to the tribulation the disciples would undergo; and he points to texts using *baptizein* for anguish, sin, or affliction flooding over a person (Isa 21:4).

the cup of suffering that Jesus has already begun to drink (note the present tense in 10:38), a cup of suffering that will culminate in an anguished death as a condemned criminal. They are being asked if they can accept being plunged into the waters of affliction in their proclamation of the kingdom, similar to those that are already beginning to engulf Jesus. (Note that Rom 6:3 speaks of being baptized into the death of Christ; and that Paul speaks of bearing the suffering of Christ in himself.) In this challenge to James and John, Jesus is not far from the earlier demand addressed to the disciples in 8:34, "If anyone would come after me, let him . . . take up his cross and follow me."

As for Mark 14:36, the cup about which Jesus prays would once more be the suffering of a horrendous death as part of the great trial. Some of the connotation of the classical cup of wrath or judgment may be preserved in Mark, not in the sense that Jesus is the object of wrath, but inasmuch as his death will take place in the apocalyptic context of the great struggle of last times when God's kingdom overcomes evil. "Hour" and "cup" thus have the same general range of historical and eschatological meaning and can be related to the idea of *peirasmos* discussed above. By having Jesus in his own words ask to be delivered from the cup that he had challenged James and John to drink with him, Mark is confirming the wrenching crisis that Jesus is undergoing and adding to the picture of him as greatly distraught, sorrowful unto death, and prostrate on the earth.

The vividness of Mark's portrayal of Jesus in Gethsemane praying about the cup is enhanced if we remember a cup reference at the Last Supper. When in Mark 14:36 Jesus says, "Take away this cup [*to potērion touto*] from me," his words echo the description in 14:23–24: Jesus "having taken a cup [*potērion*], gave thanks [*eucharistein*] . . . and said to them, 'This [*touto*] is my blood of the covenant that is poured out for many.'"[8] At the supper a complete self-giving was symbolized by the cup of wine/blood, and now Jesus asks the Father to take away the cup! To some interpreters such an apparent rethinking is scandalous and must be explained away. To others it exemplifies a human process of learning obedience through suffering from which even God's Son was not exempt (Heb 5:8—see ANALYSIS in §11): a desire to avoid a *peirasmos* that involves death on a cross. It is not surprising that Mark 14:36, together with its parallels, especially Luke 22:42,

---

[8]The connection is even closer in Luke between 22:42,"Take away this cup [*touto to potērion*] from me," and 22:20, "This cup [*touto to potērion*] is the new covenant in my blood that is poured out for you." Indeed, Schürmann ("Luke 22,42a") thinks that the Lucan prayer on the Mount of Olives may constitute the oldest witness for the genuineness of the textually disputed chalice saying at the Lucan Last Supper.

has become the classic text in theology for proving that Jesus had a human will as well as a divine will (see Thomas Aquinas, *Summa Theologiae* III, q. 18, a.l).

Overall the accounts of the prayer in Matt and Luke soften the starkness of the Marcan Jesus. Both of them omit the prayer about the hour that was phrased in indirect discourse, perhaps judging Mark to be tautological. (From it Matt does preserve the clause "if it is possible" and makes it the introduction to the cup prayer; he then negates the clause and uses it as a preface to Jesus' second Gethsemane prayer in 26:42: "if it is not possible."[9]) Even though all three Synoptics report Jesus' prayer about the cup, the way in which they preface it shows increasing softening of the demand:

> Mark 14:36: "Abba, Father, all things are possible to you"
> Matt 26:39: "My Father, if it is possible"
> Luke 22:42: "Father, if you desire"

Luke's introduction of "desire" (*boulesthai*; thirty-seven times in the NT of which sixteen are in Luke-Acts) deserves comment. Several authors have studied the difference in tone between "will, wish" (vb. *thelein*; noun *thelēma*), used in other clauses of Jesus' prayer (listed on p. 175 below), and *boulesthai*, used only in the first clause of the Lucan prayer. Luke favors *boulesthai* when God is the subject: It carries the tone of a preordained divine decision, somewhat more deliberate than *thelein* (P. Joüon, RechSR 30 [1940], 227–38; Feldkämper, *Betende* 239). Thus the Lucan Jesus is first of all concerned with the direction of the divine planning before he asks whether in the execution of that plan the cup can be taken from him.[10]

John goes further than any of the Synoptics in modifying the tradition by abolishing the distinction between what Jesus wishes and what is possible or desirable to the Father. Even if, as in Mark/Matt, the Johannine Jesus' soul is disturbed (12:27a), he works out for himself (and the reader) the issue concerning the hour by refusing to pray to be saved from it (12:27b). The reason for this change is that for John the hour is not primarily one of horrendous suffering and death on a cross, but one of the lifting up of the Son of Man who will draw all to himself (12:32).[11] Similarly for the cup: If Mark's Jesus prays to have it taken away, a rebuke is addressed to Peter by John's

---

[9]Also in both the first and second prayers, Matt uses the verb "pass" from Mark's hour prayer, rather than "take away" from Mark's cup prayer.

[10]The mss. are divided on whether to read an imperative or an infinitive of "take away" following "desire," but the choice makes no difference in meaning.

[11]For this affirmative Johannine attitude toward the hour, see Léon-Dufour, "Père" 157–59, 162, even if I cannot accept his translation (165) of John 12:27b: "Father, make me pass safe and sound through this hour."

Jesus (18:11) because use of the sword might interfere with his drinking the cup the Father had given him.

OTHER ASPECTS OF THE PRAYER

Thus far in discussing Jesus' prayer, we have concentrated on the hour and the cup. But there are two other elements in the prayer that require attention: the use of the term "Father" and the motif of God's will being done.

"Abba, Father." John's treatment of Jesus' prayer about the hour and all four Gospels' rendition of the cup saying use "Father"; indeed, Mark combines transliterated Aramaic and Greek forms in the address *"Abba,* Father." An immense literature has concentrated on Jesus' use of the Aramaic term: its historicity, its uniqueness, and its christological implications. The current state of the discussion, especially from the viewpoint of Aramaic evidence, has been presented with precision by Fitzmyer ("Abba"). Aramaic *'abbā'* is not an otherwise unattested special vocative form with an adverbial ending, but an irregular emphatic state of *'ab,* "father" (one would have expected *'ăbā'*). All three NT uses of *abba* (a Greek transliteration of the Aramaic: Mark 14:36; Gal 4:6; Rom 8:15) seem to confirm it as an emphatic form used vocatively, since they accompany it with the Greek equivalent *ho patēr,* a nominative used vocatively.[12] Much of the discussion is in dialogue with the position advocated by J. Jeremias[13] that Jesus' custom of addressing God in Aramaic as *'abbā'* in prayer is distinctive and that the address is a caritative (="Dear Father" or "Daddy") which implies intimate, family relationship. Thus Jesus claimed a special, familiar relationship to God as his Father beyond the general relationship postulated in contemporary Judaism. Other scholars have challenged Jeremias, and qualifications are needed. Let us look at the data.

We have now an example of the author of a Dead Sea Scroll prayer-psalm addressing God in Hebrew as "My Father" (4Q372:*'ābî*), and in the Greek OT there are several instances of Jews speaking to God as "Father" or "My Father" as they prayed.[14] In the Greek of the Gospels various expressions are used by Jesus to address God as "My Father" and "Father" (*pater mou, pater, patēr*), and we cannot simply assume that all represent Aramaic

---

[12]In the Gethsemane prayer, interestingly, Matt and Luke, who do not report the transliterated Aramaic form, prefer the more normal Greek vocative form *pater.*

[13]His most concise treatment is "Abba," in *The Central Message of the New Testament* (London: SCM, 1965), 9–30; see also his *Abba* (Göttingen: Vandenhoeck & Ruprecht, 1966), 15–67; and R. Hammerton-Kelly, *Concilium* 143 (3; 1981), 95–102.

[14]*III Macc* 6:3; Wis 14:3; Sir 23:1. On these and the 4Q passage, see E. M. Schuller, *CBQ* 54 (1992), 67–79, esp.77 .

'*abbā*'.[15] Indeed, in the Gospels the only example of the Aramaic term transliterated into Greek (*Abba*) is the Marcan Gethsemane prayer (14:36) under
discussion. In attested Aramaic for the period 200 BC–AD 200 '*ăbî* is normal
for a child's address, "My father"; and so the "Daddy" interpretation for
Jesus' usage should be dropped.[16] Only in literature to be dated after AD 200
does '*abbā*' replace '*ăbî* in addressing an earthly parent; and even then '*abbā*'
is not used of God in the Mishna, and only once in the Onkelos and Jonathan
targums (Mal 2:10 is a statement, not an address).[17] When all these observations are made, it should be admitted from the available evidence that if
historically Jesus did address God in Aramaic as '*abbā*', this usage was
highly unusual. As Fitzmyer ("Abba" 28) phrases it: "There is no evidence
in the literature of pre-Christian or first-century Palestinian Judaism that
'*abbā*' was used in any sense as a personal address for God by an individual."[18]

Shifting the discussion from the frequency of the Aramaic term, let us
now evaluate the likelihood that Jesus did address God as "Father" and the
theological implication behind such a practice. Most biblical usage (Hebrew
or Greek) of "Father" for God is in relation to corporate Israel (Deut 32:6;
Isa 63:16). Usage by an individual appears very seldom and then only in
the last period before Jesus.[19] Fitzmyer ("Abba" 27) challenges Jeremias's
contention that "heavenly Father" was a widely used prayer form in 1st-
cent.-AD Judaism. How then do we account for the massive frequency of
"Father" used for God in the NT: 170 times in the Gospels alone, with Jesus
speaking of God as "Father" 3 times in Mark, 4 times in Q, 4 times in the
Lucan special material, 31 times in the Matthean special material, and some
100 times in John? On the one hand, those very statistics show that in the
later Gospel material there is a tendency to increase the usage by introducing
"Father" into sayings of Jesus. Yet the widespread attestation suggests that
no evangelist invented the usage and that it stems from preGospel tradition.
The combination of transliterated Aramaic and Greek (*Abba, ho Patēr*) in
Gal 4:6; Rom 8:15 implies that Greek converts learned the Aramaic form as

[15]It is generally thought that the Greek *pater* in Luke 11:2 ("Father" as contrasted with "Our
Father" in Matt's Lord's Prayer) translates '*abbā*', since Luke 22:42 uses *pater* to express the *abba*
of Mark 14:36.

[16]J. Barr, " '*Abbā* Isn't Daddy," JTS NS 39 (1988), 28–47.

[17]Fitzmyer ("Abba" 29–30) challenges two passages proposed by G. Vermes, (*Jesus the Jew*
[Philadelphia: Fortress, 1981], 210–11). The reading in Mishna *Berakot* 5.1 is very uncertain, and
TalBab *Ta'anit* 23b comes from a much later period than the NT.

[18]Nevertheless, Jesus offered to share this relationship with his followers: He taught them to pray
to God as "Abba" (see Luke 11:2 in n. 15 above), and they carried this custom even into the Greek-
speaking world (Gal 4:6; Rom 8:15).

[19]Sir 23:1,4 (Greek; no Hebrew preserved), and in canticles like Sir 51:10 (Hebrew) and 1QH
9:35 where the individual may be speaking collectively.

a venerated expression. Most plausibly, addressing God in Aramaic as '*abbā*' was a historical and memorable (because unusual) practice of Jesus himself, reflecting Jesus' consciousness of what he had received from God. To recognize that the usage had implicit christological content is *not* to state that calling God "Father" in Aramaic was in itself equivalent to Jesus claiming to be God's only Son (*monogenēs*); considerable development in Christian insight led to the latter formulation. J. P. Meier (NJBC 78:31) is appropriately cautious but not minimalistic in assessing the situation: "One is justified in claiming that Jesus' striking use of *Abba* did express his intimate experience of God as his own father and that this usage did make a lasting impression on his disciples."

Some would move from that observation to contend that the prayer attributed to Jesus in Gethsemane with its address "Father," especially in the Marcan form "*Abba*, Father," should be considered Jesus' own words. Often they point for confirmation to the tradition in Heb 5:7–8 that "with a strong cry and tears" Jesus, despite his being Son, brought prayers to "the One having the power to save him from death" and that he was heard "from fear." That is all too simple. In the ANALYSIS (§11) I shall point out that the vocabulary in the Hebrews passage is quite different from that of Gethsemane and that a prayer to be saved from death which is heard is quite different from a prayer to be delivered from the hour/cup which is not granted. To reach a more nuanced judgment on the Gethsemane prayer, a few other simplifications should be identified. Against historicity, skeptics scoff that the only witnesses to it were asleep at a distance (Jesus has moved "forward a little" [Mark/Matt], "as if a stone's throw" [Luke]). If one wishes to answer this "village atheist" objection on its own low level, one can argue that perhaps the disciples were still awake when Jesus prayed about the hour/cup. More important, however, is to understand the setting given to the prayer in Mark/Matt. The separation of Jesus from his disciples portrays symbolically that he has no human support; the sleep of the disciples portrays their unreadiness to face the trial (*peirasmos*). We have no idea whether Mark (or any evangelist) asked himself whether the disciples, as he described them, could have heard or seen Jesus praying. If he were dealing with that question, he might have described the scene quite differently.[20] The Hebrews passage shows at least that the tradition of Jesus praying before death was widespread beyond the Gospels and so has a claim to antiquity; and it is on the level of *an attested tradition of prayer* that one should approach the Gethsemane prayer.

---

[20]A failure to appreciate the nature of the Gospel narrative is no less obvious in those who, in order to answer the skeptical objection, propose that the risen Jesus, when he appeared to the disciples, told them what he had said and done while they were asleep!

Indeed, Giblet ("Prière" 265–66) would see Jesus' words as a standard prayer pattern.

Moving in that direction, we should note that Mark's *Abba, ho Patēr* has gone beyond the ipsissima verba of Jesus, for he certainly did not pray at the same time in Aramaic and Greek. It reflects an Aramaic prayer form that he probably did use, transliterated into Greek to be used in Christian prayers, and then finally translated for those who spoke only Greek[21]—Matt and Luke, who drop Mark's *Abba*, represent a further development where the foreign Semitic term is dispensed with in praying. That exactly the same formula appears in Gal and Rom suggests strongly that Mark has placed on Jesus' lips a Hellenistic Christian prayer formula. A similar indication is supplied by the second clause in the prayer of Mark 14:36, "All things are possible to you," which is parallel to "if it is possible" in the hour prayer of 14:35. Van Unnik ("Alles") has shown that a statement of the potentiality of a god (appropriate to be part of a prayer) is a Greek or Greco-Roman theme rather than a Hebrew one, with examples in Homer, Virgil, and Aelius Aristides. The LXX introduces it at times where it was lacking in the MT, e.g., Zech 8:6: "'Even if this should seem impossible [MT: marvelous] in the eyes of the remnant of the people, in those days shall it also be impossible [MT: marvelous] in my eyes?' says the Lord" (see also Gen 18:14). Philo (*De opificio mundi* 14; #46) affirms: "All things are possible to God." Thus the opening of the prayer in Mark 14:36 would be most familiar to Greek-speaking Christians (van Unnik, "Alles" 36).

God's will be done. The ending of the prayer in 14:36 involves what God wills (the last word in Mark 14:36 is not Jesus' "I" but the "you" of God); and a discussion of that motif furthers our comparison between the Gethsemane prayer and early Christian prayers. Priority is given to what the Father wishes in the three Synoptic forms of Jesus' cup prayer (Luke twice) and in Matt's account of Jesus' going away from his disciples a second time and praying. The statements in reference to the divine will may be listed as follows:

Mark 14:36:   "But [*alla*] not what I will but [*alla*] what you (will)"
Matt 26:39:   "Nevertheless [*plēn*], not as I will but [*alla*] as you (will)"
Matt 26: 42:   "Let your will be done"
Luke 22:42a: "If you desire"
Luke 22:42b: "Nevertheless [*plēn*], not my will but [*alla*] yours be done"

A few remarks about details before I approach the issue of prayer background. Mark and the first Matt form are elliptic, having no verb governed

---

[21]We find a similar bilingual prayer pattern in the *nai amēn* of Rev. 1:7 and in a comparison of the *marana tha* ("Our Lord, come") of I Cor 16:22 and *erchou kyrie* ("Come, Lord") of Rev 22:20.

by "you";[22] Luke has avoided that. Luke has thoroughly cushioned Jesus' "Take away this cup from me" by placing statements of the priority of God's will before and after it. Both Matt and Luke avoid Mark's initial *alla*, perhaps to avoid having that word ("but") twice, a few words apart, within such a short clause.[23] Another agreement is between Luke 22:42b, "But yours [will] be done," and Matt's second prayer (26:42), "Let your will be done": Both employ the noun *thelēma* ("will") and a form of the verb *ginesthai* ("to be, become, be brought about"). Soards (*Passion* 71–72, 98) attributes these agreements between Matt and Luke over against Mark to the influence on the evangelists of common oral prayer tradition.

The Lord's Prayer was surely part of that tradition. There is an enormous literature on that prayer; my own article on its eschatological aspect offers briefly the basic points of comparison between the two forms found in Matt 6:9–13 and Luke 11:2–4. Almost all agree that Luke's "Father" (imperative *Pater*) is more original than Matt's "Our Father in the heavens." We saw that *Abba, ho Patēr* in Mark's cup petition stemmed from an early Christian prayer form attested in Rom and Gal; similarly the imperative *Pater* found in Matt's and Luke's cup prayer may well have been influenced by this usage attested in the Lord's Prayer.[24]

Three parallel petitions constitute the first half of the Lord's Prayer in Matt; two of them (asterisked below) appear also in Luke:

> *Let your name be made holy
> *Let your kingdom come
> Let your will be done, as in heaven so on earth.

All the verbs are aorist forms; the passive implies divine agency; and so a definitive eschatological action is envisaged when God will make the kingdom come, will cause the nations to recognize the holiness of the divine name (Ezek 36:22–23), and will bring about the divine will. We saw that both the hour and the cup have an eschatological dimension in the Gethsemane/Olives prayers. There is visible closeness between Matt's third petition in the Lord's Prayer and the clause in the cup prayer emphasizing

---

[22]Feldmeier (*Krisis* 243) argues that Mark does not mean that Jesus is expressing a willingness to subject his will to that of the Father. The negative is not *mē*, which might connote willingness, but *ou*, which is more factual. The supposition of the prayer is that what God wills is going to come about; and, of course, Jesus wills that. His hopeful prayer is that it does not include the cup. This interpretation fits in with the petition in the Lord's Prayer to which I shall call attention.

[23]Thrall (*Greek* 67–70) comments on their both preferring *plēn* to Mark's *alla*. *Plēn* gives the sense of a possible but not inevitable conflict between the request and God's will, or may even be milder in thrust: "on condition that it be as you will" (LXX of Josh 1:17; Num 36:6).

[24]In the prayer Matt 6:9 added "in the heavens" to "Our Father" in order to make the address to God by Christians more reverential. Such an addition was not necessary here where Jesus is praying. For a treatment of Gethsemane in the light of the Lord's Prayer, see Aagaard, "Doing."

the divine will, especially Luke 22:42b and Matt 26:42, the latter passage being verbatim the same as the petition. In the Johannine passage where Jesus debates about praying to be saved from the hour, what he finally prays in 12:28a is "Father, glorify your name," which is very close to the first Matt and Luke petition in the Lord's Prayer. In other words, the Synoptic equivalents of "Father, let your will be done" and the Johannine "Father, glorify your name," both found in Jesus' prayer about his impending suffering and death, are parallels drawn from early Christian prayer patterns known to us in the Lord's Prayer. (Previously we saw that the Synoptic Mount of Olives and the Johannine winter-flowing Kidron both reflected II Sam 15; and the Mark/Matt "My soul is very sorrowful" and the Johannine "My soul is disturbed" came from parallel lines in Ps 42:6–7.)

The sixth and final petition in Matt's Lord's Prayer has two parallel requests, the first of which is found also in Luke:

*Do not lead us into trial [*peirasmos*]
   but deliver us from the Evil One.

We have already discussed the Lucan preface to the cup prayer where Jesus instructs his disciples, "Keep on praying not to enter into trial [*peirasmos*]." In all three Synoptics after the cup prayer, Jesus instructs his disciples, "Keep on praying lest you enter into trial [*peirasmos*]." A closeness to the first part of the final petition of the Lord's Prayer is obvious. As for John, if we remember that chap. 17 is prayed by Jesus on the night before he dies, even as is the Synoptic cup prayer, then John 17:15, "(I pray) that you keep them from the Evil One," is very close to the second line of the final petition.

Such parallels cannot be accidental; but once more they should not be too simply explained, e.g., by the thesis that Mark had the Lord's Prayer in his preGospel source but, instead of reporting it as a unit, broke it up and used part of it here; or by the thesis that Matt fleshed out his form of the Lord's Prayer by adding the petition "Let your will be done" taken from the ipsissima verba of Jesus in Gethsemane; or by the thesis that historically the Lord's Prayer was composed in Gethsemane (Kruse, "Pater" 8,29). Rather the Lord's Prayer in Matt and in Luke is already a *developed* early Christian prayer drawn from a formula and wording associated with Jesus himself. As I shall explain more fully in the ANALYSIS (§11) when I discuss Heb 5:7–10, there was an early Christian memory or understanding that Jesus struggled with and prayed to God about his impending death. In Hebrews that prayer struggle is phrased in hymnic and psalm language; but in the tradition that led to the Gospels the prayer struggle found expression in terms of his being spared the *peirasmos*, the coming of the hour, and the drinking of the cup. Could not the Father bring about the kingdom in some other way that did not involve the horrendous suffering and crucifixion of the Son delivered to the hands of sinners? As for giving wording to such a prayer, the early Christians did not need to worry whether there were disciples close enough to Jesus and wide awake enough to hear and remember his words. Christians knew how Jesus prayed because some of their prayers were traditionally his prayers, reflecting his style and values.

When such prayers were used in part to phrase Jesus' last prayer, a picture that was highly persuasive for Christian life emerged. The *readers of Matt or of Luke,* for instance, found Jesus telling his disciples during the ministry how to pray and then using the same formulas as he faced death—a pattern of consistency that told the readers how (or even enabled them) to pray in life and death. They had adopted his custom of addressing God as "Father"; so too they must appropriate his obedience, "Let your will be done" (see Marchel, "Abba"). We see exactly this happening in Acts 21:14: Those who loved Paul had begged him not to go to Jerusalem lest he be afflicted there, but they are forced by him to say, "Let the will of the Lord be done." As for *the readers of Mark*, they have seen Jesus challenge James and John in 10:38, "Are you able to drink the cup which I drink?" and yet at the end pray to the Father, "Take away this cup from me." Nevertheless the readers also know that Jesus, just before he gave the disciples the challenge about drinking the cup, had explained to them (when they wondered about the difficulty of entering the kingdom and being saved): "All things are possible with God" (10:27). If Jesus, facing death, has now hesitated about drinking the cup, he poses a petition consistent with that principle: *"Abba,* Father, all things are possible to you." At the beginning of Mark (1:40) a leper placed himself at Jesus' mercy, "If you will, you can cleanse me"; at the end of the Gospel Jesus places himself at the Father's mercy, "Take away this cup from me . . . but what you [will]." As Mark's readers face their trial and find it too much, emboldened by knowing that all things are possible with God, they may find themselves, despite all their previous commitments, asking that this cup be taken away. And they can do that in Jesus' name provided that they add as he did, "But not what I will but what you (will)." The *readers of John*, with its atmosphere of facing expulsion from the synagogue and persecution (9:22; 16:2), have been taught to avoid ambiguity and concealment in confessing Jesus. As they face their moment of trial, it is not "Father, save me from this hour," but "Father, glorify your name" that must (and now can) be their prayer.

(Bibliography for this episode is found in §4, Part 2.).

§8. PRAYER IN GETHSEMANE, PART THREE: THE STRENGTHENING ANGEL

(Luke 22:43–44)

Translation

Luke 22:43–44: ⁴³But an angel from heaven appeared to him, strengthening him. ⁴⁴And being in agony, he was praying more earnestly. And his sweat became as if drops of blood falling down to the earth.

[Matt 26:53: "Do you think that I am not able to call upon my Father, and He will at once supply me with more than twelve legions of angels?"]

[John 12:28b–29: ²⁸ᵇThen a voice came from heaven, "I have both glorified it [my name] and will glorify it again." ²⁹So the crowd that was standing there and had heard was saying that there had been thunder; others were saying, "An angel has spoken to him."]

COMMENT

Since these verses are textually dubious, we shall have to discuss that issue before turning to the content. As extra assistance in this complicated section, let me give a more detailed list of contents:

- Question of Lucan Authorship
    Textual and Stylistic Evidence
    Evidence from Structure and Thought Pattern
    Hypotheses about Scribal Logic
    Problem of the Bloody Sweat
- Import of the Passage
    The Angel
    Jesus' Agony

QUESTION OF LUCAN AUTHORSHIP

These two verses in Luke constitute a famous problem passage. Were they a genuine part of Luke's Gospel or were they added later (2d or 3d cent.) by a copyist? The textual situation that provokes that question will be described below; but even here we may note that the oldest reference to the passage (mid 2d cent. in Justin, *Dialogue* 103.8) does not indicate where it may be found. That is not an irrelevant issue, for it appears after Matt 26:39 in family 13 of minuscule mss. (see n. 4 below); and the 14th–15th-cent. *Historia passionis Christi* attributes it to the *Gospel of the Nazarenes*.[1] Today some Bibles place the verses in the text of Luke; others relegate it to a footnote. For Roman Catholics, at the Council of Trent on May 27, 1546, the Bishop of Jaen named it as a "part" that was meant to come under the definition of the council accepting the Bible "with all its parts"—an indication that the passage was to be considered biblical but not necessarily a decision as to whether it is Lucan. The Roman Pontifical Biblical Commission on June 26, 1912 insisted that the passage had to be considered genuinely Lucan, but a statement of the secretary of that commission in 1955 gave Catholics "full freedom" with regard to such earlier decisions (NJBC 72:25). In short, Lucan authorship is not a confessional issue for Catholics, although it may be for conservative Protestants in whose theology apostolic authorship is an essential element for inspiration or canonicity. Modern scholars are sharply divided.[2] Let us consider the evidence pro and con under several headings.

Textual and Stylistic Evidence. Textually, the passage is omitted from P[69] (apparently), P[75], Codices Vaticanus and Alexandrinus, the first correction of Sinaiticus, Syr[Sin], and the Sahidic Coptic. It appears to have been absent from the text of Luke used by Marcion, Clement of Alexandria, Tertullian, and Origen; yet, as Duplacy ("Préhistoire" 78) points out, the failure of early writers to refer to a passage does not always mean that they did not know of it. The passage is included in Codices Sinaiticus (original and second correction), Bezae, Koridethi, family 1 of minuscules, OL, Vulgate, Syr[Cur], Peshitta, and many Bohairic copies. It was known to Justin, Tatian (seemingly), Irenaeus, and Hippolytus.[3] Thus the Alexandrian witnesses to

---

[1]Of six references to this apocryphal gospel in *Historia,* one at least may be verified from Jerome; see Duplacy, "Préhistoire" 84.

[2]Among those opting for Lucan authorship are Arndt, Bertram, Brun, de Wette, Dibelius, Duplacy, Galizzi, Goguel, Green, Grundmann, Harnack, J. R. Harris, Hirsch, Keim, Klostermann, Knabenbauer, Kuhn, Lagrange, Larkin, Loisy, Marshall, Morgenthaler, Osty, Renan, Rengstorf, Schlatter, J. Schmid, Schneider, Strauss, Surkau, and Zahn. Among those rejecting Lucan authorship are Ehrman, Feldmeier, Fitzmyer, Hauck, Lescow (v. 44), Plunkett, Soards, Wellhausen, and Westcott.

[3]U. Holzmeister, ZKT 47 (1923), 309–14, argues persuasively that Epiphanius knew the passage. T. Baarda, NovT 30 (1988), 289–96, shows that Julian the Apostate knew even variant readings of it.

the NT tend to omit it, while the Western, Caesarean, and Byzantine witnesses tend to include it. It was already absent from some copies of Luke in the late 2d cent., but also known to mid- and late-2d-cent. church writers and translators. On purely textual grounds, because of P⁶⁶ and P⁷⁵, I would judge that the weight of the evidence moderately favors omission.[4]

On the basis of style Harnack ("Probleme" 252–53) and Schneider ("Engel" 113–15) have argued strongly for the Lucan authorship of 22:43–44, but others insist that this criterion does not settle the issue definitively (see Brun, "Engel" 266–67 on Harnack's arguments; also Feldmeier, *Krisis* 12–17). If we consider v. 43, forms of *ōphthē* ("appeared") occur over twelve times in Luke-Acts (in several instances for angelic appearances), as compared with once each in Mark and Matt. The first four Greek words of the verse, translated "But an angel appeared to him," are found verbatim in Luke 1:11 and nowhere else in the NT. *Enischyein* ("strengthen") occurs elsewhere in the NT only in Acts 9:19 where, however, unlike here it is intransitive. "From heaven" is Lucan style (17:29; 21:11); yet nowhere else in Luke-Acts is an angel described as "from heaven" or left silent, without delivering a verbal message. Is the latter feature explicable because God has assigned a peculiar task to the angel here, to strengthen and not to reveal? That would not be true silence.

In v. 44 there are several words that occur nowhere else in the NT: *agōnia* ("agony"), the comparative *ektenesteron* ("more earnestly"), *hidrōs* ("sweat"), and *thrombos* ("drop"); but that statistic may stem from the peculiar character of an event described only here. *Thrombos* and *ektenesteron* never occur in the Greek OT either, and *agōnia* and *hidrōs* occur in it only three times each. Moreover, there are other undoubtedly genuine verses of Luke with a high percentage of hapax legomena (6:38; 10:31). A *ginesthai* ("being") construction is frequent in Luke, several times as here used participially at the beginning of a sentence and several times with *en* ("in"). Acts 22:17, "be in ecstasy," offers a very close parallel. As for *ektenesteron, ektenōs* ("earnestly") is used in Acts 12:5 for a prayer on behalf of Peter, a prayer that receives an answer from God through the appearance of an angel of the Lord; see also *en ekteneia* in Acts 26:7. The verb *proseuchesthai* ("to pray"), used here, occurs in Luke 19 times and in Acts 16 times, compared

---

[4] I say "moderately" because as van Lopik ("Tekstkritiek" 103–4) points out, some of the textual arguments used against Lucan authorship are weak when considered critically. The omission of the verses in many lectionaries reflects Byzantine dislike for liturgical repetition: Luke 22:43–45a was read on Holy Thursday (between Matt 26:21–39 and Matt 26:40–27:2); when it became customary to read 22:39–23:1 as a pericope on Tuesday of the last week before Lent, 22:43–44 was omitted from it to avoid duplication. The placing of Luke 22:43–44 after Matt 26:39 in family 13 of the minuscules (most of which are lectionaries) reflects the Holy Thursday arrangement and is not real evidence of the "floating" character of the Lucan passage.

with 15 in Matt and 10 in Mark. The verb *agōnizesthai*, related to *agōnia*, occurs in the Gospels only in Luke 13:24. In the second half of v. 44 *egeneto* ("became") is frequent in Luke; and Luke-Acts has 15 of a total of 21 NT occurrences of *hōsei* ("as if"). While *katabainein* ("to fall down") occurs 11 times in Matt, and 6 times in Mark, it occurs 32 times in Luke-Acts, including the only other participial usage. Overall, then, in style and vocabulary this passage is closer to Luke than to any other NT author. In the hypothesis that a person other than Luke composed and added the passage, seemingly one would have to posit a conscious or unconscious imitation of Lucan style with the goal of making the passage fit the Lucan context into which it was being inserted—something that, by contrast, the copyist who inserted the story of the adulteress in John 7:53–8:11 did not do. While style may not settle the issue, clearly the passage is more easily explained stylistically if Luke wrote it.

Evidence from Structure and Thought Pattern. Does the scene in Luke 22:40–46 read better with or without the passage? Ehrman and Plunkett ("Angel" 413–14) think that without the passage they can detect a beautifully balanced chiasm; this chiasm, adapted and summarized below, is for them a convincing reason for rejecting Lucan authorship.

(a)	v. 40: prayer about *pei-rasmos*	=	(a')	vv. 45c–46: prayer about *peirasmos*
(b)	v. 41a: Jesus distances himself from disciples	=	(b')	v. 45b: Jesus goes back to disciples
(c)	v. 41b: having knelt	=	(c')	v. 45a: having stood up

(d) vv. 41c–42: prayer to Father

Without wishing to be harsh (for otherwise the Ehrman-Plunkett article is impressive), I judge most of the proposal to be another example of the exaggerated chiasm detection that plagues modern scholarship. I refer in particular to parts b, c, d, c', b'. In a paperback thriller with no literary pretensions one can detect a meaningless chiasm of the same sort: (b) character Z comes in; (c) Z sits down; (d) Z says something; (c') Z gets up; (b') Z goes out. What is valid in the above analysis of 22:40–46 is that Jesus tells his disciples to pray about *peirasmos* before and after his own prayer, which is the centerpiece of the scene—a fact that is visually obvious without reference to chiasm. Does having Jesus' prayer answered in vv. 43–44 add to or detract from the flow of thought? Interestingly, Gamba ("Agonia" 161) detects a chiastic structure that includes 43–44; and Feldkämper (*Betende* 232) argues that structurally 44 is the center of the scene. (For those intrigued by chiasm, it could be adapted thus: [d] vv. 41c–42: Jesus' prayer to his Father; [e] v. 43: Father's response; [d'] v. 44: Jesus' more earnest prayer in reaction.)

Luke stresses Jesus' prayers, giving instances not found in the other Gospels.[5] With this predilection, he may have found it difficult to follow Mark in not having Jesus receive a discernible answer to his prayer about the hour/cup. Consequently Luke may have turned to another tradition (see below) involving an answer through an angel. In that case the Father's answer to the prayer and the resultant strengthening of Jesus for the coming trial become central—a development harmonious with Luke's having Jesus pray successfully that Peter might become a source of strength by means of this crisis (22:32). Schneider ("Engel" 115) suggests that Luke may have felt free to shorten the Marcan Gethsemane structure, cutting from three to one the visits by Jesus to the sleeping disciples, partly because he wanted to introduce 43–44 from his special tradition and thus lengthen the treatment of Jesus' prayer. Brun ("Engel" 273–74) contends that in the passion Luke never shortens Mark without compensating by adding special material of his own, and Green ("Jesus" 33) supports and expands his reasoning. Including vv. 43–44, Schneider ("Engel" 116) finds a parallel between the structure here and that of the Lucan Transfiguration scene, where Jesus' prayer (9:29) is followed by the appearance (form of *ōphthē*) of Moses and Elijah (9:30–31), while Peter and the others were heavy with sleep (9:32).

Hypotheses about Scribal Logic. Would a later Christian copyist have been more likely to add or to delete this passage? The question assumes that the action that led to the present textual situation was deliberate, for the passage is too long to have been omitted by accident. Moreover, the motivation for addition or deletion was probably theological, since it is unlikely that a copier of Luke omitted it simply because he did not find it in Matt or Mark; indeed in the latter part of the 2d cent., when the passage was already known by some writers and ignored by others, all copyists may still not have had the three Gospels for comparison. (If harmonization played any role, it may have been in the insertion of the passage after Matt 26:39 in family 13 of minuscule mss. Because Matt was used most frequently in public reading, it was supplemented from the other Gospels with passages that it hitherto lacked [see n. 4 above and Feuillet, "Récit" 398].) Some arguments proposed under this heading of scribal logic virtually cancel each other out. For example, since angelic assistance plays a role in 2d-cent. Christian martyr stories, some scholars suggest a copyist added the passage to Luke to strengthen the conformity of Jesus' death with that of the martyrs. But others

---

[5]Luke 3:21; 5:16; 6:12; 9:18,28–29; 11:1; 22:32; see Feldkämper, *Betende*.

suggest that a copyist omitted the passage because it departed seriously from the model of how a martyr should die, i.e., with serenity, joy, and a certain imperviousness to pain (see Clement of Alex., *Stromata* 4.4; GCS 15.254).

Those who regard the passage as an addition point out that there were gnostic and docetic movements in the 2d cent., calling into question Jesus' humanity, and so a copyist who knew of a tradition of Jesus' bloody sweat might have included it as a way of stressing that humanity. Both Justin (*Dialogue* 103.8) and Irenaeus (*Adv. Haer.* 3.22.2) cite the passage against docetists. One may wonder, however, how effective such an addition would have been since the Valentinian gnostics, for example, could have countered the humanizing effect of the Gethsemane scene (which already in Matt had Jesus troubled and prostrate) by denying that it was the Savior who was present there (see *Adv. Haer.* 3.16.1). Moreover, would a copyist not have hesitated about adding a passage that apparently made an angel superior to Jesus, strengthening him? Certainly such a passage might have seemed hard to reconcile with NT descriptions of Christ as superior to angels (Col 1:18; 2:15,18; Heb 1:4–7,13–14; 2:5,9—if those passages were known). This last point leads to a plausible reason why a copyist might have dropped the passage from the form of Luke he was copying, namely, fear that this passage might supply comfort to those who challenged the divinity of Jesus. Origen's *Contra Celsum* reflects Jewish and pagan polemic against Christianity dating back at least to the latter half of the 2d cent.; and Celsus (2.24) used the weakness of Jesus in the Gethsemane scene, exemplified in the petition about the cup, as an argument against divine claims for him. Epiphanius (*Ancoratus* 31.4–5; GCS 25.40) knew that Irenaeus used this passage in an anti-docetic way; yet he explains the textual situation not as an addition for the sake of such polemics but as an omission by the *orthodox*. True, Epiphanius (ca. 374) was thinking of later orthodoxy struggling with Arian heresy, but his assertion may reflect on how earlier "orthodoxy" would have reacted to the danger that opponents might find ammunition in this passage.

Problem of the Bloody Sweat. Schneider ("Engel" 116) thinks that some modern rejection of this passage may stem from a distrust of the supernatural. One must be cautious, however, in judging what is described in this passage. (a) In deciding whether or not the passage is Lucan, the primary issue is not the historicity of the event described (which is very difficult to decide without other confirming evidence) but whether Luke would have thought it plausible. Given what Luke says in 1:1–4, we may assume that Luke would not have included what he considered unbelievable. Holzmeister ("Exempla" 74) cites references in antiquity to a bloody sweat, e.g., Aristotle, *Historia animalium* 3:19; #10.[6] "Drops of blood" was ancient medical language, and *katabainein* ("fall down") was used by medical writers to describe the descent of humors. Probably, then, both Luke and his readers would have found plausible what is described in 22:43–44. Holzmeister ("Exempla" 75–78) points out that down to modern times various writers have cited instances of a bloody sweat without any claim that something miraculous was involved. Medical contributions by Keen, Arthus, and Barbet cite instances of hematidrosis, involving intense dilation of subcutaneous capillaries that burst into the sweat glands. The blood then clots and is carried to the surface of the skin by the sweat.

(b) One should ask whether the passage in fact describes a bloody sweat. Whether or not they believe it happened, some scholars answer affirmatively;[7] and that is how Irenaeus understood it (*Adv. Haer.* 3.22.2: "He . . . sweat drops of blood"). Yet others, including ancient writers,[8] argue that the Greek is more subtle, constituting a metaphor or figurative comparison: Jesus sweat as profusely as if he were bleeding. *Hōsei* ("as if, like") can be used to express identity, e.g., "Make me like one of your servants" (*hōs*: Luke 15:19; also 16:1). It can also be used for likeness short of identity, e.g., "tongues as if of fire" (Acts 2:3, a good comparison for the present passage) or "as if a stone's throw," three verses earlier (22:41). Feuillet ("Récit" 403) argues for identity, contending that the blood, not the sweat, fell to the earth; but "falling" modifies *thromboi*, "drops."[9] There is no surety, therefore, that the passage means that Jesus' sweat became bloody; it could mean that the sweat became so profuse that it flowed to the ground as freely as if it were drops of blood. In the narrative Jesus does not appear to have been weakened by this sweat, and there is no indication of pain. This "bloody sweat" issue constitutes no argument against Lucan authorship.

While clearly the evidence available does not settle the issue of whether Luke wrote 22:43–44, in my judgment the overall import of the types of evidence or reasoning discussed above favors Lucan authorship; and henceforth I shall write as if Luke were the author. Let us see now how this passage of Jesus praying more earnestly and being in agony after strengthening fits

---

[6]Aristotle (*Problemata* 2.31) also mentions sweat accompanying an agony.

[7]E.g., Strauss, Dibelius (a divine omen), Feuillet (miraculous).

[8]E.g., Photius, Theophylact, Euthymius Zigabenus: PG 101.991–92; 123.1081; 129.685.

[9]Except in Sinaiticus and some Lat and Syr evidence where "falling" is singular modifying "blood." Barbet (*Doctor* 70) would render *thromboi* as "clots" in harmony with the description of hematidrosis.

into the total Lucan scene—an issue that would be pertinent even if a copyist added it, for presumably he thought the passage appropriate to the context.

IMPORT OF THE PASSAGE

In response to Jesus' request (Luke 22:42), "Father, if you desire, take away this cup from me," an angel is sent from heaven to strengthen him: The cup will not be taken away, but Jesus is fortified to drink it. That the initiative comes from God is underlined by the passive construction, literally, "An angel from heaven was seen by him [Jesus]"or "shown to him." Where did Luke get such a dramatic conception of divine help?

The Angel. In the scene of the temptation (*peirazein*) of Jesus by the devil in the desert, both Mark (1:13) and Matt (4:11) report that angels ministered to him; Luke 4:13 simply has the devil depart until an opportune time. In the present chapter Luke has twice called attention to Satan's work among the disciples (22:3,31); and when the Mount of Olives episode comes to its denouement, Jesus will acknowledge the presence of "the power of darkness" (22:53). Apparently Luke conceives of this as the opportune time of Satan's return for further temptation/testing (*peirasmos*), and so he has placed here the angelic ministering found in Mark's and Matt's accounts of the earlier *peirasmos*. Three times in Luke 4:4,8,12 Jesus answered Satan's testing by citing Deut (8:3; 6:13,16); now Luke 22:43 echoes the language of the Song of Moses in Deut 32:43 (LXX): "Let all the *angels* of the Lord *strengthen* themselves in him" (H. Smith, "Acts xx.8").

Luke may have been encouraged in this by a tradition associating an angelic response with the prayer that Jesus made to the Father concerning the hour/cup. In the range of the Gospel treatments of that prayer, Mark portrays external silence on the Father's part, implying that in this silence Jesus recognized a refusal which he obediently accepted, since shortly afterward he is shown expressing a firm resolve to face the hour (14:41–42). Matt follows Mark; but later in the course of the arrest (26:53) the Matthean Jesus will state his assurance that if he had insisted, the Father would have responded with angelic help: "Do you think that I am not able to call upon my Father, and He will at once supply me with more than twelve legions of angels?" In John 12:27b–28a Jesus answers his own musings about the prayer: He will not ask the Father to save him from the hour because the whole purpose of his life has been to come to this hour. Rather, he prays, "Father, glorify your name." To that prayer the Father responds vocally and positively, a voice that is understood by some as coming from an angel (12:28–29). Thus, here as elsewhere, Luke stands between John and Mark/Matt. Luke preserves the

Marcan Father's silence, but moves more radically beyond Mark than Matt's potential angelic assistance,[10] for an angel is actually sent. That is not as dramatic as John, where the Father speaks; and this assuring confirmation of Jesus, coming from heaven, is heard publicly but mistaken for an angelic response. Luke has the effect of actualizing the angelic assistance that is potential or misunderstood in the accounts of Matt and John. Such actualization may have been influenced by the impact of the earlier *peirasmos* in the desert, where the tradition had angels ministering to Jesus.

We shall see later that Acts 7:55–60 highlights parallels between the death of Stephen, the first Christian martyr, and the death of Jesus. Accounts of the behavior of Christian martyrs during the Roman persecutions also echo the behavior of the Lucan Jesus. Aschermann ("Agoniegebet" 149) and others call attention to Lucan passages portraying Jesus as heir to the martyr prophets of Israel (11:47–51; 13:34; 6:23).[11] Accordingly, let us look at elements in Luke 22:43–44 that have martyrological parallels.[12] We can begin with the stories of the Jewish martyrs of the Maccabean period when the Syrian king Antiochus IV Epiphanes tried to impose Hellenistic religious practices on God's people. *Agōnia* ("agony") appears in II Macc 3:14,16; 15:19; and a related term, *agōn*, occurs in *IV Macc* 13:15; 16:16; 17:11–16. Words related to *ektenōs* ("earnestly") are used in II Macc 14:38; *III Macc* 5:29; 6:41; Judith 4:9,12. In *IV Macc* 6:6 the martyr Eleazar is pictured as "flowing with blood"; in 6:11 his face is "bathed in sweat"; in 7:8 he is held up as an example for others to defend the Law "with their own blood and with their noble sweat in sufferings unto death."

Particularly interesting is the development of the role of the assisting angel in martyrological writing. Of course, there are earlier examples of the motifs of strengthening and of angelic help, e.g., in I Kings 19:5–8 an angel gave Elijah strengthening food; in Ps 91:11–12, cited in the temptation of Jesus (Luke 4:10), "He will put you in his angels' charge to guard you . . . support you."[13] Yet the angel has a special prominence in Daniel and hence in a martyr setting of the Maccabean period. According to Dan 3:20 three

---

[10]In later scenes (e.g., Judas' death in §29 and the postcrucifixion happenings in §43) we shall see that in the passion Matt taps a vein of popular material characterized by vivid imagination. Here the exuberant number of angels ("twelve legions" = about 72,000) may reflect development of the angel tradition within that same popular background.

[11]Surkau (*Martyrien* 90) states quite accurately: "The influence of martyr literature is by far more strongly observable on the third evangelist than on Mark and Matthew" (also Feuillet, "Récit" 413–14).

[12]We saw above the role of Deut 6 and 8 as Jesus responds to the devil from Scripture in Luke's temptation scene, and of Deut 32 (the Song of Moses) in Luke's presentation of a strengthening angel. The Song of Moses was cited in martyr literature (II Macc 7:6; *IV Macc* 18:18).

[13]Isa 42:6 promises the Lord's strengthening (LXX: *enischyein* as in Luke 22:43). Larkin ("Old" 253) argues strongly for Suffering Servant influence on this passage in Luke.

young Israelites were thrown into the fiery furnace for refusing to worship the statue Nebuchadnezzar had erected; but an angel of the Lord joined them (3:49 LXX), so that even the king recognized "God has sent his angel and saved his servants" (3:95 LXX or 3:28). According to 10:16–19 Daniel was troubled by the oncoming time of wrath: "Anguish overcomes me at this vision, and the strength I had deserts me." But the angel to whom he spoke touched him and gave him strength (Theodotion: *enischyein* transitively).[14] In *III Macc* 6:18, when the priest Eleazar is about to be martyred before an Egyptian king, God answers his prayer by opening the gates of heaven from which two angels come down.

The theme of the angel carries over to martyr stories of Christians dying for their faith. In the martyrdom of Stephen (Acts 6:15), when the Sanhedrin members looked at him, his face appeared like that of an angel. In *Martyrdom of Polycarp* 2:5 we are told that the martyrs, because they "were no longer human but angels," could see heavenly mysteries when they looked upward; and (9:1) a voice from heaven strengthened Polycarp as he entered the arena.[15] This martyrological background offers insight as to how Luke's readers may have understood the presence of the strengthening angel in Jesus' passion, i.e., as God's loving response to his servant who was suffering from unjust persecution.

In the Lucan passage some have wondered whether v. 44 follows logically after v. 43: If Jesus has been strengthened by the angel, why does he pray more earnestly and why is he in agony? Brun ("Engel" 273) is correct, however, in resisting the attempt to shift 44 before 43. The sequence in Mark 14:37–38 has Peter, who is not strong enough to watch and pray, urged to do so: If he were stronger, he could pray without being urged. In Col 1:29 Paul agonizes *after* being "energized" by God. The Lucan sequence of a first prayer by Jesus about the cup and a second and more earnest prayer after being strengthened makes perfect sense, provided that one understands the second prayer to have a different focus. In 22:40 Jesus told his disciples to pray not to enter into *peirasmos* ("trial," in particular, the trial brought about by the forces of evil); and according to my interpretation of 22:41–42 he himself prayed not to enter into *peirasmos* when he asked that the cup might be taken from him. The arrival of an angel from heaven (i.e., the presence of a heavenly being, not a vision of someone in heaven) and the consequent strengthening have told Jesus that he must enter the *peirasmos* but not without divine help. Knowing that, he prays "more earnestly," but this time with

---

[14]In the martyrdom story of the seven brothers (II Macc 7:6) there is an explicit reference to divine support as promised in the Song of Moses (Deut 32:36).

[15]In a somewhat broader context *Hermas* (*Simil.* 5.4.4) addresses a specific group: "You who were clothed with strength by the holy angel and received from him the gift of prayer."

respect to the outcome of the *peirasmos*. Luke's use of the comparative of the adverb ("more earnestly"), plus the imperfect of the verb ("was praying"), portrays an inner intensity that is translated externally by profuse sweat.

The approach just taken implicitly rejects a number of proposals that have been made. Medieval exegesis of the passage was contorted by the theory that Jesus could not gain knowledge from the angel's presence since he already had the beatific vision or infused knowledge.[16] Highly curious is the thesis of J. Lightfoot (*Opera Omnia* [1686] 2.561B) that the angel was a manifestation of Satan come to tempt Christ. The frequently heard suggestion that Jesus needed strengthening because he foresaw the sins of the world has no support in the Lucan context. Related to that is Feuillet's point ("Récit" 402–3) that here Jesus was already shedding real blood for redemption.

Jesus' Agony. This is the central point of these Lucan verses. Paton's brief article raises the essential issue: In English "agony" often means extreme pain; is that the idea of the Greek *agōnia*? Crucial in the argument against Lucan authorship of this passage (e.g., Ehrman-Plunkett) is that Luke, who has avoided Mark's description (14:33–34) of a Jesus greatly distraught with a soul very sorrowful unto death, would never portray Jesus in such uncontrolled agony.[17] Paton, however, urges that Greek *agōnia* often meant the kind of agony that a runner in an athletic contest experienced just before the start (see also Neyrey, "Absence" 161–66). *Agōn* originally meant the place of an athletic contest, and then the contest itself. An athletic parallel offers an explanation for the profuse sweat that follows: The runner is tensed up to begin the trial, and sweat breaks out all over his body. In such an interpretation, the *peirasmos* or great trial, which Jesus now knowingly will enter, resembles an athletic contest. Gamba ("Agonia" 162) compares the strengthening role of the angel to that of a trainer who readies the athlete; the prayer of Jesus is the last-minute preparation. Unlike the disciples who sleep, Jesus is now poised at the starting line.

Feuillet ("Récit" 401–2) dismisses the whole approach as a curious and fantastic conjecture. Yet *IV Macc* compares the martyr Eleazar to a noble athlete: 9:8 speaks of the prize of virtue to be won after severe suffering; and 11:20 portrays torture as "a contest [*agōn*] befitting holiness in which so many of our fellows, because of their piety, have been summoned to an arena [*gymnasia*] of suffering." Paul's use of athletic imagery is also apropos. In I Thess 2:2 he writes: "We had courage in our God to proclaim to

---

[16]Aquinas, *Summa Theologiae* III, q.11–12; and still de Tuya, "Agonía" 554–56.

[17]In fact, Luke does not exclude all cognizance of Jesus' suffering: 13:31–33; 22:15,28,37; 24:7,20,26,46.

you the gospel of God in the face of much opposition [*agōn*]"; in I Cor 9:25 *agōnizomenos* is equivalent to an athlete or contender in the games; in I Tim 6:12 and II Tim 4:7 *agōnizesthai agōna* means "fighting the good fight." In the ANALYSIS (§11) we shall study Heb 5:7–10 as a possible parallel to the Mount of Olives prayer; and Heb 6:20 refers to Jesus as a "forerunner," while 12:1 compares the Christian struggle to running the "race [*agōn*] that is before us." Moffatt ("Exegetica . . . xxii"), who challenges Paton by arguing that in the Greek *agōnia* there was an element of fear, presses too far by contending that Luke was portraying Jesus in terror of death. Rather the Paton approach should be seen as consonant with the fear or trepidation of the athlete because of the unpredictable or inscrutable elements in the contest and its outcome: a physical and psychological tenseness. In II Macc 3:16–17 the high priest undergoes *agōnia* of soul that leads to bodily trembling: This is not from fear of death but from anxiety as he faces the impending disaster of the profanation of the Temple by Heliodorus. Stauffer (TDNT 1.139) writes of *agōnia* in terms of a supreme concentration of one's power in face of the impending battle. Neyrey ("Absence" 160) discusses Philo's use of *agōnia*:[18] The good person, like an athlete in *agōnia*, combats a *lypē* ("sorrow") that destroys strength and power. Understood against this background, the *agōnia* in Luke 22:44 is not the same as Jesus' soul being very sorrowful (*perilypos*) in Mark 14:34; it is rather an anguished tension preparatory to entering into the *peirasmos*. The Father cannot spare Jesus from drinking the cup, but the strengthening angel prepares Jesus so that he arises from prayer in tense readiness for the combat with the approaching power of darkness (Luke 22:53). The sweat that breaks forth and flows as freely as blood is the visible sign of that readiness for the cup and hints at martyrdom. (Feldkämper, *Betende* 246–47, points out that the references to cup and blood in the prayer and answer of 22:42,44 come after 22:20: "This cup which is poured out for you is the new covenant in my blood.") Jesus has warned and will again warn his disciples to pray not to enter into this *peirasmos*; but personally, now knowing that he cannot be spared, Jesus has returned to the attitude of 12:50: "I have a baptism to be baptized with, and how I am constrained until it is completed."

(*Bibliography for this episode may be found in §4, Part 3.*)

---

[18]*De virtutibus* 5.24; *De praemiis* 26.148; also *agōn* in *Quod omnis probus* 21.

§9. PRAYER IN GETHSEMANE, PART FOUR: JESUS COMES BACK TO HIS DISCIPLES THE FIRST TIME

(Mark 14:37–38; Matt 26:40–41; Luke 22:45–46)

Translation

Mark 14:37–38: [37]And he comes and finds them sleeping; and he says to Peter, "Simon, are you sleeping? Were you not strong enough to watch one hour? [38]Keep [pl.] on watching and praying lest you [pl.] enter into trial. Indeed the spirit is willing, but the flesh is weak."

Matt 26:40–41: [40]And he comes to the disciples and finds them sleeping, and he says to Peter, "So you [pl.] were not strong enough to watch one hour with me. [41]Keep [pl.] on watching and praying lest you [pl.] enter into trial. Indeed the spirit is willing, but the flesh is weak."

Luke 22:45–46: [45]And having stood up from prayer, having come to the disciples, he found them asleep from sorrow; [46]and he said to them, "Why do you sleep? Having stood up, keep on praying lest you enter into trial."

COMMENT

For Mark/Matt what we treat here is but the first of three times that Jesus returns to find his disciples sleeping. For Luke, however, this one and only time that Jesus comes to find his disciples sleeping terminates the prayer on the Mount of Olives. The subdivisions of the episode are listed in the Contents before §4.

THE LUCAN TERMINATION OF JESUS' PRAYER (LUKE 22:45–46)

Although Luke's text here is parallel to Mark and (despite some stylistic vocabulary changes) is surely drawn from Mark, overall the Lucan passage has a distinctive thrust. In Mark/Matt Jesus' prayer to the Father has received no detectable answer, and so Jesus will pray several more times. This struggle of the Marcan Jesus with his own destiny and that of his disciples develops dramatically, helping to make the Gethsemane prayer episode a unit with its own suspense—a scene distinct from that of the arrest which will follow. In Luke the Mount of Olives prayer has been greatly truncated and leads smoothly into an equally truncated arrest, so that one should probably speak of one Lucan scene involving both prayer and arrest. The shortened Lucan version, besides sparing the disciples, makes Jesus the dominant figure spotlighted in both the prayer and the arrest. This is still not the sovereign Johannine Jesus, but the composed and masterful Jesus of Luke represents a move in that direction from Mark/Matt.

The Jesus of Luke 22:45 who comes (or "comes back" as some would render the *erchesthai* found in all three Synoptics) has had his prayer to the Father answered by the gift of the strengthening angel. Jesus comes "to the disciples,"[1] after "having stood up" and thus terminated his prayer. The standing action is Lucan, not only in vocabulary (*anastas*, intransitive aor. ptcp. of *anistanai*: 34 times in Luke-Acts, 6 in Mark, 2 in Matt, 0 in John) but in outlook. The kneeling (22:41) and standing of Jesus are familiar to Luke's readers as prayer positions. The disciples, however, are sleeping, clearly not a prayer position, even though they were told to pray (22:40). For Mark/Matt sleep means not watching; for Luke it means not praying.[2] We remember that in Luke the disciples have *not* received a dire warning that they will be scandalized and scattered but have been congratulated on their

---

[1]Coincidentally, Luke 22:45 and Matt 26:40 add this *clarificatory* phrase to Mark's vague "he comes"; but for Matt it also has the function of reuniting Peter and Zebedee's sons with the larger group of disciples left behind by Jesus upon arrival at Gethsemane (also 26:45). In the Gospel Luke uses the phrase some ten times, and Matt tends to add to Mark phrases about the disciples.

[2]While Mark/Matt employ *katheudein* for "sleep" three times in the Gethsemane scene, Luke uses *koimasthai* ("asleep") in 22:45 and *katheudein* in 22:46—a touch of elegant variation. As for the significance of sleeping, with regret I must judge as probably misleading the suggestion of Daube, "Two . . . Sleeping," that the disciples' falling asleep presented a danger that the Passover meal might not be resumed. The problem is not only that all the evidence offered for this comes from more than 100 years after Jesus' time (even though he thinks Mishna *Pesaḥim* 10.8 may reflect Exod 12:42 "the night of watchfulness"). There is not a single word in any Synoptic Gospel *after the supper* to remind readers that the night or day of the passion was Passover itself (see APPENDIX II, B2b). Because the Synoptics (for symbolic Christian liturgical purposes) identified the supper as a Passover meal, scholars have vainly sought to reconcile all that follows the supper with Passover practices as known 150 years after Jesus' time. There is no evidence that either the evangelists intended or their first readers would have understood such (often anachronistic) Passover references.

fidelity, with a promise of heavenly thrones (22:28–29). They have not seen Jesus himself distraught and troubled, his soul very sorrowful unto death. Logically, then, it is not clear why they would be asleep "from sorrow." Granted the warning in Luke 22:36–37 that they had to be prepared since Jesus would be reckoned among outlaws, one might be tempted to relate the sorrow of the disciples to a realization that now the reckoning was coming to fulfillment. However, 22:38 and 22:49–51 (see §14) imply that the disciples never really understood that warning; and so it would scarcely play a role in their reaction here. Skard ("Kleine") points out that in some ancient texts (Cicero, *Ep. ad Atticum* 9.10.1) sorrow was said to deprive one of sleep; in response Indemans stresses that the Lucan idea was that when sorrow had exhausted one, sleep came (so Sallust, *Iugurthinum* 71.2). But Luke is not thinking medically. He has drawn on Mark's description of Jesus' soul as "very sorrowful" and shifted the sorrow to the disciples. Even though Luke has suppressed Mark's view of the disciples where they had reason to be upset, he has added this phrase lest they seem too blameworthy in not having prayed. In the Transfiguration (9:32) he had reported that "Peter and those with him were heavy with sleep; but having wakened, they saw his glory"; in those circumstances sleep could be tolerated. But not here, and so Jesus has to correct the disciples. Luke moves that correction away from being a judgment by supplying a forgivable motive for their sleep.

Besides terminating Jesus' prayer, his "having stood up" is a sign of vigor, a clear indication that the *agōnia* and the accompanying sweat were not debilitating but, as explained in §8, reflective of the tenseness of an athlete now ready to enter the trial. The fact that the same "having stood up" is used in Jesus' directive to his disciples, alongside a repetition of the command to pray, represents a desire to communicate his strength to them. (We remember his concern in 22:32 that they be strengthened.) Both physically and spiritually they must be ready. Their prayer not to enter into trial will be granted for this time, but the power of darkness (22:53) is close by as part of the hour that is at hand. (Some scholars [e.g., Ott, *Gebet* 89] see an inclusive play on *eiserchesthai eis,* used for Satan "entering into" Judas in 22:3 and for "entering into" trial here.) We hear in the very next verse, "While he was still speaking, behold a crowd; and the man named Judas . . . was coming in front of them" (22:47).

SLEEPING, WATCHING, AND THE COMING TRIAL (MARK 14:37–38A; MATT 26:40–41A)

Turning from Luke's account to its Marcan counterpart, we find once more that scholars are concerned with how much of this stems from preMarcan tradition. Stylistic features are invoked for different solutions. The beginning of v. 37 is typically Marcan: coordinating *kai* plus the historical present tense ("And he comes and he finds"); yet nowhere else in Mark does Jesus address Peter as "Simon." For older scholarship, that touch of personal address showed that the memory of this scene came from Simon Peter himself. In the opposite direction, while Mohn ("Gethsemane" 200) would posit a preMarcan source for the context established by v. 37, he argues that Mark has secondarily introduced Peter into the scenario. Much of v. 38 would be useful for community parenesis, but Taylor (*Mark* 554) warns, "The obvious parenetic *motif* in no way compromises the tradition." L. Schenke (*Studien* 512–15, 521–22) understands the watching motif in v. 34 to involve a request for friendship, while watching in v. 38a is for the dangerous trial (*peirasmos*); therefore the verses are from different hands, with 34 as preMarcan and 38a as Marcan redaction! As I shall stress when I give a larger survey of such views of composition in the ANALYSIS, they are too fragile to be of real help in diagnosing what Mark means.

Leaving the insoluble unsolved, let me study how the flow of that narrative fits Mark's purpose. The "them" whom Jesus finds sleeping in Mark 14:37 are not clearly identified by what has gone before, whence the need of both Matt and Luke to clarify that they are "the disciples." The other two evangelists, in a sense, answer the question that many microscopic studies of the text would put to Mark. By "them" does he mean the disciples left in 14:32 to sit and pray near the entry to Gethsemane, or Peter, James, and John, whom Jesus had taken along in 14:33–34 and instructed, "Remain here and keep on watching"? The singling out of Peter for address in v. 37 and the stress on watching have led many to assume that the latter group is in focus, but surely by the end of the Gethsemane prayer scene (14:41–42) Jesus is giving directives more universally. The answer may lie in recognizing limitations imposed on microscopic research by Mark's narrative purpose. He separated the two groups in 14:32–33 to portray visually the progressive distancing of Jesus from those who might have been expected to give him support. Now, when a distinction between the two groups no longer serves his purpose, Mark portrays Peter together with all the disciples.

The spotlight on Peter within this Marcan scene must again be understood as part of the storyline. Peter has said that he would not be scandalized in Jesus even if all the others were (14:29), and his bravado led all to affirm that they would be faithful (14:31). Therefore Jesus speaks first to him as embodying the failure of all the disciples. Matt, in changing the words addressed to Peter from the singular to the plural, may be softening the blunt treatment that Mark gives to the first of the Twelve, but he is also diagnosing Mark's meaning—Peter was not strong enough to watch one hour and neither were any of the others. (Luke goes further by eliminating Peter from the dialogue.) The movement in Mark from an address by Jesus in the singular in v. 37 to an address in the plural in v. 38 is by way of continuity, not of contrast. It tells us nothing about different Marcan sources or editorial changes. Having appealed to Peter on the subject of watching, Jesus now appeals to the group on the same subject.

That Peter is addressed as "Simon" in Mark 14:37 and spoken to reproachfully is in the view of some (Swete, Kelber, etc.) a sign that the Marcan Jesus no longer deems him worthy of his apostolic name (Mark 3:14,16): "He made twelve to be with him [whom he also named apostles] . . . and he placed the name Peter on Simon." This is most unlikely. If Mark wanted to make such a distinction between the implication of "Simon" and "Peter," why does he call the man "Peter" in this very verse and then go on calling him by that name in scenes yet to follow (14:54,66–72; 16:7)? Much more likely is that in the Peter tradition of the Gospels, the standard form of Jesus' direct address to him was "Simon" (Luke 22:31; Matt 17:25; John 1:42; 21:15,16,17). That the address has nothing to do with an unfavorable view of this man by Jesus is clear from Matt 16:17, "Blessed are you Simon, son of Jonah." There are only two exceptions where Jesus speaks to him directly as Peter; one is Matt 16:18, where that name is necessitated by the play about to be made associating it with "rock"; the other is Luke 22:34, where two verses previously Jesus has spoken to him as "Simon, Simon." There, when Luke chooses to add a name to what he takes from Mark 14:30, as a touch of elegance he shifts to "Peter."

The key words in the rebuke to Simon for sleeping (v. 37) are: "Were you not strong enough to *watch* one *hour*?" In v. 38a Jesus urges all: "Keep on *watching* and *praying lest you enter into trial* [*peirasmos*]." Already in reference to Mark 14:34 we discussed "Keep on watching" as words directed by Jesus to Peter, James, and John before his prayers about the hour and the cup. We discussed "Keep on praying not to enter into trial [*peirasmos*]" as the Lucan parallel (22:40) to Mark 14:34. (Both of those discussions were under §6 above.) We discussed "hour" in the prayer of the Marcan Jesus in 14:35 (under §7 above). Throughout I contended that "watching," "trial," and "hour" were to be understood both on a historical level (what happened to Jesus on the last night of his life in Gethsemane with real enemies approaching who would arrest him and have him crucified) and on an eschatological level (the great period of final struggle with evil for the establishment of God's kingdom). The fact that here "watch" is repeated in v. 38a from

v. 37 brings the Marcan usage even closer to the eschatological parable in Mark 13:34–37 with its repetition of "watch." And of course Jesus has done exactly what he warned in that parable the master would do (13:36): He has come suddenly and found the disciples sleeping. Matthew does not have the Marcan parable; but his readers too could catch the eschatological meaning of this Gethsemane dialogue by recalling 24:42: "Keep on watching for you do not know on what day your Lord is coming" (also 25:13). The complaint of Jesus about their not being "strong enough" (*ischyein*) may be meant to evoke for the readers Mark 3:27 (Matt 12:29), i.e., the parable of the strong man (*ischyros*) and the one who can bind him, a parable of the struggle between Satan (the strong) and Jesus (the stronger) for the kingdom. Matt's addition of "with me" to the watching in 26:40, besides once more emphasizing solidarity with Jesus (pp. 148, 156 above), echoes a warning in 12:30: "The one who is not with me is against me."

Some would give "onè hour" in Mark/Matt a purely historical meaning, namely the length of time that Jesus prayed. But the Marcan Jesus has just prayed that the hour might pass from him, and within a few verses (Mark 14:41; Matt 26:45) we shall hear Jesus proclaim that there has come (near) the hour for the Son of Man to be given over into the hands of sinners. Surrounded by such references, it is likely that in both Gospels "one hour" also has an eschatological thrust. This particular hour is one of entering into the great trial, the hour Jesus had wanted to escape and about which he will continue to pray. When Jesus wants them to watch this one hour with him, the reference is more than to a short length of time; that is why he will come back several times to press them on the issue. Christian readers who were accustomed to thinking of the trials of their own existence on two levels would have had little difficulty understanding these two levels of the historical and the eschatological. I Pet 5:8–10 gives a good example: "Watch! Your adversary the devil walks about like a roaring lion. . . . After you have suffered a little, the God of all graciousness . . . will Himself restore, establish, and strengthen you."

Turning our full attention to the plural in Mark 14:38a and Matt 26:41a, "Keep on watching and praying," we find that despite the foreknowledge Jesus has shown in Mark/Matt that all his disciples would be scandalized and scattered, he still has plans and hopes for them. By sleeping they have failed to watch while he prayed, but he does not give up on them. Lövestam (*Spiritual* 64–67) has shown that the combination of watching and praying (which is not preserved in Luke) has OT roots in Psalms (42:9; 63:7; 77:3) that speak of praying while staying awake at night, in an ideal attested at Qumran (1QS 6:7–8), and elsewhere in the NT (Luke 2:37; Acts 16:25). Here, however, the combination is dictated not by piety or asceticism, but by the threatening "trial" (the *peirasmos* discussed at length above in §6 in relation to Luke 22:40). Analyzing the Gethsemane situation and using Qumran language, Lövestam (*Spiritual* 90–99) observes that the sons of light have yielded to the darkness (night) and its influence by sleeping, and so must be made even more aware of the dangers of the great trial.

The wording "lest you enter into *peirasmos*" needs special comment. Whereas the very similar command in Luke 22:40 employed a *mē* plus an infinitive construction, here the three Gospels use a *hina mē* with aorist subjunctive.[3] The two different constructions probably do not signal difference of meaning, since the *hina*, besides signifying purpose, can be used epexegetically to indicate the content of the prayer, and that is the role of the infinitive Luke used earlier.[4] If *hina* does signal content, the coordination of the two governing verbs "watch" and "pray" would then have a slightly distinguishing nuance: Not entering into trial would be the purpose of the watching and the object of the praying.

The urgency of the command can be explained by the following sequence. Jesus' own prayer not to have to enter into trial (in terms of the hour and cup) has not been answered affirmatively. The disciples were not able to watch (with him: Matt) while he made that prayerful attempt. If he must enter the *peirasmos* (and he will pray further about that in Mark/Matt), the proved unreadiness of the disciples makes it imperative that they not enter into trial at this time. Kelber ("Mark 14" 183) objects that such a prayer to be spared is not in keeping with the apocalyptic understanding of the scene, for Mark 13:13 insists that "the person who endures to the end will be saved." But Mark 13:20 must not be overlooked: "If the Lord had not shortened the days, no flesh would be saved." The great trial is inevitable and threatening; yet there is an uncertainty about how individuals participate, and so a prayer to be spared is not inconsistent. The same Lord's Prayer that teaches Jesus' followers to say with eschatological intensity, "Let your kingdom come," teaches them also to say, "Do not lead us into *peirasmos*," even though the kingdom cannot come without the great trial. In the highly apocalyptic Book of Revelation (3:10) we hear, "Because you kept my word of endurance, so too I will keep you from the *hour of peirasmos* which is coming on the whole world, to try [*peirazein*] those who dwell on earth." If God can adapt in that way, then Jesus' command to the disciples makes perfect sense in the partially apocalyptic context of Gethsemane.

---

[3]Of *erchesthai* in Mark and of *eiserchesthai* in Matt and Luke. The latter agreement shows the influence on these two evangelists of a fixed oral prayer formula (notice *eispherein* in the Lord's Prayer), an influence stronger than that of their dependence on Mark.

[4]See the debate on Mark 14:38a between C. J. Cadoux (JTS 42 [1941], 172), who argues for an imperative force for *hina*, and H. G. Meecham (JTS 43 [1942], 180).

SPIRIT AND FLESH (MARK 14:38B; MATT 26:41B)

Jesus' words to his disciples continue in Mark 14:38b (and Matt 26:41b, which is identical): "The spirit is willing [*prothymos*], but the flesh is weak [*asthenēs*]." Noteworthy is the early citation of this as a saying by the Lord in Polycarp, *Philip.* 7:2. The context there is one of avoiding heresy and the antichrist (echoes of I John 4:2–3; II John 7), of being sober "unto prayers" (I Pet 4:7), and of the petition, "Do not lead us into *peirasmos*" (Lord's Prayer). Also to be noted is *Hermas, Mand.* 4.3.4: The Lord knew "the weakness [*astheneia*] of human beings and the subtlety of the devil." As for the present context, L. Schenke (*Studien* 521–23), who judges Mark 14:38a to be a Marcan addition, thinks 38b goes well with 37. Linnemann (*Studien* 11) finds that none of this spirit/flesh instruction fits the context of Gethsemane and so cannot be original here. Kelber ("Mark 14" 183) finds it the real motive for the warning to watch and pray: "not the nearness of the *kairos* but the weakness of the flesh." As will become apparent, I find that v. 38b can be read quite plausibly in the Marcan context (plausibility, of course, does not necessarily mean that it was originally spoken here), and I disagree with Kelber's either/or approach: The motive for the watching and praying is the nearness of the *peirasmos*, which is all the more dangerous because of the weakness of the flesh.

As for the saying itself, since this is the only Synoptic instance of the spirit/flesh contrast (see John 6:63) and the only Marcan usage of the two accompanying adjectives, many scholars (e.g., Bousset, Holtzmann, Pfleiderer) were confident that the aphorism came from Hellenistic circles, perhaps through the medium of Pauline theology (Hauck, W. L. Knox, Swete). With the discovery of the Dead Sea Scrolls, the opposite view, that the background for the spirit/flesh contrast was Semitic, has now become almost universal. For the OT and most of intertestamental Judaism, spirit and flesh are not parts of the human being like soul and body, but the whole human being considered under two different aspects. "Spirit" could be used of God and angels and of human beings—but of the latter in their higher functions such as feeling, thinking, and willing. "Flesh" applies to human beings and animals, and represents people in their tangible, perishable, and earthy aspects. In the OT "flesh" connotes weakness but not sinfulness.

The Dead Sea Scrolls add new elements.[5] In the Qumran context of the eschatological battle between the forces of good and evil, between the Spirit

---

[5]Yet one should read carefully in sequence the Qumran studies by Kuhn, Huppenbauer, Davies, and Flusser (SECTIONAL BIBLIOGRAPHY §4, Part 2) to recognize increasing nuance in scholarly affirmations about "the" Qumran theology of spirit/flesh. There are various meanings given to those terms at Qumran even as there are in the NT, and there is no evidence that the Marcan usage is directly dependent on Qumran.

of Truth and the Spirit of Wickedness, flesh (which in itself is not evil, sinful, crassly sexual, or opposed to God) is often the channel through which the Spirit of Wickedness attacks, tests, tempts, or takes over the individual. There are community members whose lives are ruled by the Spirit of Truth but who stumble because of the flesh (1QS 11:12).

Turning to Mark's statement, we do not find there the developed antithesis between spirit and flesh glimpsed in Paul, who uses it to contrast divine power and human weakness. Mark is not close, for instance, to Rom 8:9, where the flesh is so hostile to God that Paul tells believers in Christ: "You are not in the flesh, but in the spirit." The disciples addressed by Jesus are under the influence of both spirit and flesh. The Marcan "willing spirit" is not the Holy Spirit given by Jesus or God to Christians after the resurrection.[6] It is the human spirit through which people can be moved to do what is harmonious with God's plan. It is not far from what is described in 1QH 13:18–19: "I know by the spirit that you have given me . . . that all your works are righteous, and you will not take back your word."[7] Flesh is characteristic of all (1QH 18:23 puts it in parallelism with being born of woman), and in the Marcan statement it is not Satanic or a drive toward sin—otherwise Jesus would not complain that the flesh is weak. But it is the means through which Satan moves to distract people from God's plan; it represents the vulnerability of the human being.

Many commentators assume that since this saying is addressed by Jesus to the disciples, it refers only to them. However, Jesus himself is in turmoil, while praying and facing *peirasmos;* he wants their watching and praying to accompany him. An interpretation of "the spirit is willing, but the flesh is weak" should not exclude Jesus. (Thus Luke had a double reason for omitting it.) "Willing" (*prothymos* = Hebrew *nādîb*) is used in I Chron 28:21 and II Chron 29:31 for those who are ready in knowledge and eager for liturgical service. Ps 51:14 asks God to sustain in the psalmist "a willing spirit" (LXX: *hēgemonikos,* "dominant"), which in the context seems to mean a steadfast spirit that is in holy alignment with God's plans. In Rom 1:15 "willing" describes Paul's eagerness to preach the gospel in Rome. Earlier Jesus was willing in the sense of being eagerly determined to follow God's will by drinking the cup (Mark 10:38–39); indeed at the supper he had taken a cup of wine and identified it as his blood that was already being poured out for many (14:23–24). The disciples were willing: Peter (who has

---

[6]In my judgment Phillips ("Gethsemane" 58), following Schweizer, is wrong on this point: There is no prayer here "for the Spirit to come." The prayer concerns the flesh; Jesus and the disciples already have a willing spirit.

[7]Since the human spirit is given by God, sometimes in postexilic Judaism the lines of distinction between God's spirit and the human spirit were not always clear.

been specifically addressed by Jesus in this scene) said, "Even if it be necessary for me to die with you, I will not deny you"—and they all said the same
(14:31). But now Jesus has experienced the weakness of the flesh, i.e., the
distress, troubling, and sorrow unto death (14:33–34) that has caused him to
ask the Father whether this hour might pass and this cup be taken away. We
are very close here to the atmosphere of Heb 5:7 (see ANALYSIS) where "in
the days of his flesh" Jesus prays with a strong cry and tears to be saved
from death—a situation that Heb 4:15 identifies as sharing our weaknesses
(*astheneia*) and being put on trial (*peirazein*). Knowing that his human
weakness can be used by Satan, who is the strong one (Mark 3:27), as a
weapon in the trial or testing, Jesus is dealing with the weakness of his flesh
by praying to his Father, "But not what I will but what you (will)"—again in
the language of Hebrews (5:8), "Despite his being Son, he learned obedience
through the things he suffered." The disciples have yielded to the weakness
of the flesh by sleeping, and they are so weak that they must pray to avoid
being caught up in the testing of God's Son or they can be destroyed. (Luke
articulated all of this in 22:31–32: "Simon, Simon, behold Satan asked to
test you [pl.] like wheat. But I have prayed for you [sg.] that your faith might
not fail.") For Christian readers, all of this would be a plea to be realistic:
Eager to see the kingdom come, they should be aware of the danger of the
trial that precedes and of their weakness that the evil power will exploit.

(*Bibliography for this episode is found in §4, Part 2.*)

§10. PRAYER IN GETHSEMANE, PART FIVE: JESUS COMES BACK TO HIS DISCIPLES THE SECOND AND THIRD TIMES

(Mark 14:39–42; Matt 26:42–46)

Translation

Mark 14:39–42: ³⁹And again having gone away, he prayed, saying the same word. ⁴⁰And again having come, he found them sleeping; for their eyes were very burdened, and they did not know what they should answer him.

⁴¹And he comes the third time and says to them, "Do you go on sleeping, then, and taking your rest? The money is paid; the hour has come; behold the Son of Man is given over into the hands of the sinners. ⁴²Get up; let us go; behold the one who gives me over has come near."

Matt 26:42–46: ⁴²Again, a second time, having gone away, he prayed saying, "My Father, if it is not possible for this to pass if I do not drink it, let your will be done." ⁴³And having come again, he found them sleeping, for their eyes were burdened.

⁴⁴And having left them, again having gone away, he prayed a third time, saying the same word again. ⁴⁵Then he comes to the disciples and says to them, "Do you go on sleeping, then, and taking your rest? Behold the hour has come near, and the Son of Man is given over into the hands of sinners. ⁴⁶Get up; let us go; behold, there has come near the one who gives me over."

[John 12:23: "The hour has come in order that the Son of Man may be glorified."

14:30–31: ³⁰". . . For the Prince of the world is coming . . . ³¹but as the Father has commanded me, so do I do. Get up; let us go from here."]

COMMENT

This section ends the treatment of the Gethsemane prayer of Jesus in Mark/ Matt, the first scene in Act One of the PN. (John has no prayer here, and the prayer segment of the Lucan scene on the Mount of Olives ended with the previous section.) In it for a second and third time Jesus departs, prays, and returns to find his disciples sleeping. The subdivisions of our treatment are listed in the Contents before §4.

THE PLACE OF THIS EPISODE IN THE STRUCTURE OF THE SCENE

The fact that Jesus departs from his disciples, prays, and returns to them *three* times (more clearly in Matt than in Mark) has been seen by some as a key, to either the structure of the scene or the origin of the material. If we begin with structure, can we organize the whole Mark/Matt prayer scene on a pattern of threes? At the beginning of §6 I called attention to a pattern indicated by the evangelists' six verbs of movement, three before Jesus prays and three after:[1]

#1. Jesus and the disciples come into the plot of land; and he has the dis- ciples sit there (Mark 14:32), while he goes away (Matt 26:36)

#2. Jesus takes along Peter, James, and John and has them remain (Mark 14:33–34; Matt 26:37–38)

#3. Jesus goes forward a little and *prays* by himself (Mark 14:35–36; Matt 26:39)

#4. Jesus comes to the disciples the first time (Mark 14:37–38; Matt 26:40–41)

#5. Jesus comes to the disciples the second time (Mark 14:39–40; Matt 26:42–43)

#6. Jesus comes to the disciples the third time (Mark 14:41–42; Matt 26:44–46)

While the pattern has validity, the symmetry is not perfect. Notice that in #1 it is Matt who most spells out the continuance of the movement. In #5 it is Matt who mentions the "second time," and that phrase really modifies the going away and praying rather than the coming (back). In Mark only by implication do we learn that between #5 and #6 Jesus had gone away again to pray, something that Matt once more spells out. Nevertheless, an intelli-

---

[1] F. Martin ("Literary" 582–87) helpfully calls attention to the role of the verbs of motion as a categorizing factor; but in my opinion his fourfold division, which lumps into one segment (14:32–36) the first three verbs before Jesus prays, does not do justice to the Marcan balance.

gent appeal to a pattern of three movements of Jesus forward to pray and three movements back to his disciples from prayer helps us to see that the prayer that focused Jesus' decision about the hour/cup is the center of the scene. Working with Matt, Gnilka (*Matthäus* 2.409) notes that the significant *tote* ("Then") occurs in 26:36,38,45.

This could suggest a division of Matt into:

26:36–37:   Jesus arrives with the disciples and takes Peter and the two sons of Zebedee with him
26:38–44:   Jesus prays three times with increasing emphasis on God's will
26:45–46:   Jesus comes to the disciples for the last time and gives them instructions

Such an arrangement is close to the thrust of the Matthean scene, but notice the extent to which Jesus' finding the disciples sleeping *three* times has now only minor significance.

Others have found in this episode the key to the origins of the material. In the ANALYSIS (§11) I shall discuss the two-source approach to the Gethsemane prayer. In particular the present episode with plural goings and comings is thought to result from the combination of two different accounts, each of which had *a* coming and going. Others contend that one incidence of praying and coming back to find the disciples asleep was fleshed out to create three. A factor is that Luke has only one incident. Yet, as indicated above, more likely Luke is simplifying to avoid repeating what might appear embarrassing for Jesus and the disciples. In judging all this, one should first be attentive to what the evangelists report. In Mark there are not three prayers but two, and no numerical attention is given to praying. What Mark counts imperfectly ("third" in 14:41 but no second) is Jesus' coming and finding them sleeping; and so the Marcan emphasis is on the failure of the disciples to struggle alongside Jesus. It is Matt who perfects the pattern of three by counting out three prayers and supplying a wording for the second. This may have developed in the evangelist's mind or tradition out of a Jewish pattern of praying three times which was taken over into Christianity.[2] Jesus' proclamation of the kingdom in power meant that he enabled his followers to pray to the one whom he called Father; but the Matthean readers would learn from the Gethsemane scene that Jesus was also the model of how intensely to pray. The Jesus who emerges from the scene is neither stoic nor fanatic. The number of times he withdraws to pray shows that he goes to death only when it is clear that God wills it (Gerhardsson, "Jésus" 216).

[2]E.g., Ps 55:18 (evening, morning, noon); Dan 6:11(10); II Cor 12:8; *Didache* 8:3. See §40, #5 below.

As for the preMarcan situation, however this story may have come into existence, I see no reason to think that it ever existed without a pattern of plural comings to the disciples. That is suggested by the close relationship to Mark 13:33–37, where the master could come at any one of four times and find the servants asleep. There is a highly parabolic character about the dealing of Jesus with his disciples in Gethsemane, and the repetition gives an emphasis that is essential to why the story is being told. Matt has shifted the thrust to a threefold *prayer* pattern; but for analogies to Mark, see I Sam 3:2–8, where Samuel is called three times and only on the third instance does Eli understand, or I Sam 20:20–22,35–39, where Jonathan repeats the instructions about the arrow three times to be sure David will understand. (An example of what happens without the repetition is supplied by Luke's truncation, which has lost its parabolic value.) In Mark the three failures of the disciples are beautifully balanced with the three denials by Peter, soon to be narrated; and both offer a warning to Christians.

SECOND INCIDENCE OF DEPARTURE, PRAYER, AND RETURN
(MARK 14:39–40; MATT 26:42–43)

Whatever may be the origin of this episode, there is a considerable amount of "Marcan style" in 14:39. Mark accounts for one-fifth of the NT uses of *palin* ("again"); and he uses with particular frequency the combination *kai palin* that begins both vv. 39 and 40. The awkwardness of a double participle in the brief v. 39 has been dubbed Marcan by some. Actually the last clause, "saying the same word," is missing in Codex Bezae and the OL, so that scholars like Cranfield, Taylor, and Wellhausen regard it as a gloss. There are good arguments, however, for judging the clause to be genuine (so MTC 114). For instance, the use of *logos* ("word") for sayings of Jesus is frequent in Mark (4:33; 8:32,38; 9:10; 10:24), so that the putative glossator would have had to take the trouble of imitating Mark. Moreover, we shall see the same pattern in the denials of Jesus by Peter in Mark 14:68a,70a: a first denial that consists of a direct statement by Peter and a second that consists of "But again he was denying it" without specifically quoted words. Matt knew of the existence of this clause about "saying the same word" in Mark 14:39; for, although omitting it here, he adopted it verbatim for the third prayer of Jesus in 26:44. As to the Marcan authenticity of the clause, then, copyists who considered Matt authoritative probably omitted it from Mark because in Matt Jesus does not say the same word in his second prayer.

Indeed, here one must pay tribute to Matt (26:42) for having expanded Mark's colorless v. 39 with theological skill to fashion a second prayer. Matt's "a second time" is verbatim the same as Mark's description of the cock crowing "a second time" (14:72), and Matt will not use the phrase there (26:74). From the Marcan prayer that the hour might pass (14:35), Matt has once more taken the clause "if it is possible"; but whereas when Jesus prayed the first time about the cup, Matt left that condition affirmative, now he makes it negative. His "if it is not possible" hints that Jesus has begun to read God's silence in face of the first prayer as a sign that God would not take away the cup from him. This may also be hinted at in the condition "if I do not [*ean mē*] drink it."[3] The heart of the second prayer by the Matthean Jesus, "Let your will be done," is a verbatim quote from Matt's form of the Lord's Prayer (6:10). If Jesus is being offered as a model of prayer, that prayer is uttered in total obedience to God even when the answer is likely to be negative.

In Mark 14:40 we read that "again having come" (another *palin*, omitted by Codex Bezae), Jesus found them sleeping. In reference to 14:37 I commented that some scholars wanted to render *erchesthai* as "comes back"; evidently the same instinct existed in antiquity, for a widely attested variant in the Koine text tradition of this verse reads: "And having returned [*hypostrephein*], he found them again sleeping." Just as Mark did not supply any words for Jesus' second prayer, so he reports no second words of Jesus to his disciples. Not Jesus' reaction but their sleeping is the key issue for Mark. (Although Matt supplied words for Jesus' prayer, he supplies no words of Jesus to the disciples; here Marcan brevity suits Matt, for he is not interested in developing the weakness of the disciples.) Obviously "sleep" is something with symbolic as well as physical import; it makes the disciples unprepared for the ever closer *peirasmos*.

The clause in Mark 14:40 "for [*gar*][4] their eyes were very burdened" (= Matt 26:43[5]) is a periphrastic construction consisting of the imperfect of the verb "to be" plus a present participle.[6] Turner (JTS 28 [1926–27], 349–51) doubts, however, whether this construction meant more for Mark than the ordinary imperfect. In the present scene what would this description reinforce? Is the fact that "their eyes were very burdened" an excuse for the disciples' behavior in Mark? Luke's "asleep from sorrow" (22:45) represents an interpretation in that direction. The fact that Matt omits the next Marcan

[3]BSSNT 1.139–40 argues that the Greek should be translated not as a strong conditional clause, but as virtually equivalent to "unless I should drink it," reflecting the Hebrew exceptive *'al*. The effect would be a greater subordination to the main clause about God's will.

[4]*Gar* clauses in Mark have been the subject of a special study by C. S. Bird, JTS NS 4 (1953), 171–87. They may allude to what is already known.

[5]Mark uses a present participle of *katabarynein* ("to weigh down heavily"), an intensive form of *barynein*, which was replacing the more classical *katabarein*. Matt, who frequently prefers the simple to the compound verb, uses a perfect participle of *barein* that is not quite so strong.

[6]Taylor (*Mark* 45) gives the statistics of such periphrastic constructions as 16 times in Mark, 3 in Matt, 28 in Luke, 10 in John.

clause ("and they did not know what they should answer him") may mean
that he too looked upon the burdened eyes as an excusing factor (Gnilka,
Matthäus 2.413). But for Mark "burdened eyes" are probably an illustration
of the weakness of the flesh. In Gen 48:10 the eyes of Jacob/Israel are said
to be heavy with age, and that is an example of weakness.

Mark complements the burdening of their eyes with the observation that
they did not know what they should answer him. Linnemann (*Studien* 25,
27), taking her cue from "answer," posits that Jesus must have said something; and so she would move "Do you go on sleeping?" from v. 41 back to
the middle of v. 40 before this statement! K. G. Kuhn ("Jesus" 273) holds
that "answer" here has the broad sense of Hebrew '*ānâ*, which can mean
"speak," so that Mark is reporting that the disciples had no idea what to talk
to Jesus about. More simply, Mark probably means that Jesus' return to find
the situation unimproved was itself an implicit rebuke to which the disciples
would have responded if they knew how. There is a parallel in the Marcan
Transfiguration scene (producing the usual debate as to which Marcan passage is the original). In 9:5–6 when Peter has responded to the appearance
of Elijah and Moses talking with Jesus by offering to make three booths,
Mark comments disparagingly, "for [*gar*] he did not know what to say, for
[*gar*] they were very afraid." That parallel suggests that in Mark 14:40 the
human frailty and misunderstanding of the disciples is being highlighted.[7]

THIRD INCIDENCE AND JESUS' WORDS TO HIS DISCIPLES (MARK 14:41–42; MATT 26:44–46)

Mark 14:41 betrays the evangelist's lack of interest in an exact numerical
pattern: Jesus comes (back) the third time without our having been told he
had gone away once more to pray. Tidily, Matt 26:44 fills in the lacuna, using
in this third incident some of the wording Mark had employed in the second
incident, including verbatim Mark's "saying the same word" (14:39). Matt's
addition of "again" at the end of that clause must have puzzled scribes, since
it could imply that the Matthean Jesus had said the same word once before,
which he had not. (Matt probably meant the "again" to refer to the content
of the prayer.) That is why "again" was widely omitted in the Koine textual
tradition. The enumeration "a third time" that Mark attaches to Jesus' coming back and speaking to "them" about sleeping is shifted by Matt to Jesus'

---

[7]If we compare Mark 14:40 to the Transfiguration scene in Luke 9:32, there we have: "Peter and
those with him were burdened [perf. ptcp. of *barein*, as in Matt's Gethsemane account] with sleep
but kept awake [or wakened]." (In reference to §9, n. 2, clearly in the Transfiguration being "awake"
has nothing to do with Passover requirements.) Luke 9:33 describes Peter as "not knowing what he
was saying." Has Luke, seeing the connection between Mark's Transfiguration and Mark's Gethsemane, taken details from the latter for his own description of the former?

praying, a move consonant with Matthean interests. The Marcan coordination in 14:41 with historical present tenses ("and he comes . . . and [he] says") illustrates a strongly narrative style, while Matt's "Then" in 26:45 helps to compartmentalize the two elements in the third episode: departure to pray; then return to find the disciples sleeping. The Matthean "Then" is also a divider from the main scene of prayer to signal that this is Jesus' final coming and his last words. Mark's "them" is correctly interpreted by Matt as "to the disciples"; but Matt's reiterated use of "disciples" in 26:40,45,56 has the effect of emphasizing that despite failures the followers of Jesus have not lost their identity, even as Mark's abandonment of the term may represent an implicit comment upon how they are acting—not like disciples.

Challenge about Sleeping and Resting (Mark 14:41). There has been much scholarly discussion about the words of the Marcan Jesus to "them": *katheudete to loipon kai anapauesthe apechei.* The Greek contains constructions and expressions that are embarrassingly obscure. It is comforting that already Matt seems to have been puzzled, for in 26:45 he has omitted the very difficult *apechei,* reporting only *katheudete loipon kai anapauesthe.*[8] The basic meaning of the second-person-plural verbs *katheudete* and *anapauesthe* as "sleep" and "rest"[9] is clear. What is uncertain is in which of three ways the verbs are used: (1) *indicative,* which would be the normal rendering of the forms unless there is reason to expect otherwise; here there would probably be a touch of exclamation: "You are sleeping . . . and resting!"; (2) *interrogative,* with a touch of irony (Bratcher, Goodspeed, Holleran, Jannaris, Kilpatrick, Klostermann, Manson, Moffatt, Schenke, Taylor): "Are you sleeping . . . and resting?"; (3) *imperative* (KJV, Lagrange, Léon-Dufour, Swete, Vulgate, Weymouth): "Sleep . . . and rest." Some would add a touch of compassion to the imperatives (Augustine, Chrysostom, Bengel): "Sleep on now if you can; take your rest"; others interpret the imperatives as Jesus giving up on the disciples in anger. Certainly in this Gethsemane context Mark uses imperatives: "Keep on watching and praying" (14:38); "Get up; let us go" (14:42); but an imperative translation in 14:41 would inculcate an action just the opposite of the action inculcated by the surrounding imperatives. Even an ironic "Sleep and rest" in 14:41 leads with difficulty into "Get up; let us go" in 14:42. Sometimes to reconcile the two it has been suggested that in a pause taken between the two statements Jesus looked up and suddenly caught sight of Judas coming (see "And imme-

---

[8]There is no *to* before *loipon* in Codexes Vaticanus and Ephraem rescriptus of Matt; there is a *to* in P[37] and Codexes Sinaiticus, Alexandrinus, Bezae, and much of the Koine tradition.

[9]In the noneschatological context of Mark 6:31 Jesus uses *anapauein* to encourage his disciples to rest.

diately, while he was still speaking" in 14:43). Leaving aside such an unwritten stage directive, many scholars (Aars, Boobyer, Gnilka, Jannaris) reject the imperative rendering as impossible or implausible. As for the other two renderings, there is little difference between an indicative expressing exasperation and an interrogative; and so that range of meaning should be favored. Luke's rendition in 22:46 ("Why do you sleep?") is the earliest preserved attempt at interpreting Mark 14:41; it tips the scales in favor of an interrogative.

Uncertainty about the meaning of (*to*) *loipon* complicates the issue.[10] As an adjective or noun *loipos* describes what remains or is left over, the other, or the last of a series (sometimes pejoratively; see Cavallin, "*Loipon*" 130–31). Our primary interest is in the adverbial usage of (*to*) *loipon*—classically with the article (Mark), but at this period frequently without (Matt). A basic meaning is "from now on, henceforth, in addition." While many would render it in Mark 14:41 as "still" ("Are you still sleeping?"), it is not clear that *loipon* has such a meaning, which implies "up to now." Another suggestion is "for the rest of the time," a rendition especially popular with those who translate the verbs imperatively. But then one must face the question of what "time" is meant. If it means the rest of the time before Jesus is arrested, the betrayer appears in the next verse. If it means the rest of the night, the disciples are not shown asleep or resting after this moment. A more eschatological suggestion is the rest of the time until the final trial, but it has been my practice to discuss a meaning on the historical level as well. Moreover, Cavallin ("*Loipon*" 122–23) insists that in Hellenistic times the adverb meant an immediate, not a distant, sequence. Similarly the rendering by Palmer, "Sleep and take your rest in *the future*, but now get up," is rejected by Bernard ("St. Mark xiv") on the grounds that *loipon* does not have such a meaning (see also T. Chase, "*To loipon*" 131–32). A large number of scholars[11] suggest that the adverb be rendered simply as a connective "so then, therefore"—a meaning so vague that it can fit with any interpretation of the verbs. That seems to me best.

The greatest problem about Mark 14:41 is the meaning of *apechei*, the word that Matt omitted. To discuss all the possible translations would be a long distraction here; so I shall place that discussion in APPENDIX III A, drawing here on the conclusions I reached there. No one of the many possible translations is truly convincing, but fortunately almost all of them have the same import. *Apechei* says something harmonious with what follows: "The hour has come; behold the Son of Man is given over into the hands of

---

[10]In the SECTIONAL BIBLIOGRAPHY (§4, Part 2) see the articles dedicated to it by Bernard ("St. Mark xiv"), Cavallin, Chase, Jannaris, and Starkie, plus observations by Thrall, *Greek* 25–30.

[11]Including Aars, Chase, Holleran, Starkie; see Cavallin, "*Loipon*" 140–41; BAGD 480, 3b.

the sinners." It is an expression of urgency, and my translation, "The money is paid," preserves the most frequently attested meaning of *apechei* in ordinary life. Mark is picking up on the promise of payment made by the chief priests to Judas in 14:11. The bargain is completed, and so the machinery has been set in motion to have Jesus arrested; the great *peirasmos* has begun.

The Coming of the Hour. The next statement in Mark 14:41 is "the hour has come [*erchesthai*]"; the next in Matt 26:45 is "Behold the hour has come near [*eggizein*]." Both Mark and Matt will use "behold" twice, once in this verse, once in the next. (Matt will have a third usage in the following verse for the coming of Judas with a crowd.) In Mark the two instances of "behold" emphasize the "give over" motif; in Matt they both emphasize the "come near" motif. In 14:41 Mark speaks of the hour coming (*erchesthai*), while in 14:42 he speaks of the coming near (*eggizein*) of the one who gives Jesus over. Mark uses the verb *eggizein* only three times. In 1:15 he used the same perfect form as here (*ēggiken*) for the coming near of the kingdom of God; in 11:1 he used the verb for Jesus coming near to Jerusalem. Thus the eschatological atmosphere is very strong.

In the corresponding verses of Matt (26:45 and 46) only *eggizein* is used, i.e., not only for the one who gives Jesus over but also for the hour. Is Matt making a theological statement over against Mark's use of *erchesthai:* the hour has only come near rather than fully come? Considerable debate has centered on the existence and meaningfulness of such a distinction.[12] It is part of a larger debate about the use of *eggizein* in passages where Jesus speaks of the advent of the kingdom.[13] C. H. Dodd was a champion of the view that this verb meant that the kingdom had come or arrived, but overwhelmingly other scholars rejected that.[14] They insisted that even though there were already premonitory signs of the imminent coming of the kingdom in the ministry of Jesus, it was near and had not yet come. *Erchesthai* is used of the kingdom in the petition of the Lord's Prayer (Matt 6:10; Luke 11:2), "Let your kingdom come," an eschatological petition. By analogy, then, Mark's "The hour has come" and Matt's "The hour has come near" are not saying the same thing. For Mark, Jesus prayed in 14:35 that the hour

[12]W. R. Hutton ("Kingdom") argues against the dictionaries that most of the forty-two times that *eggizein* occurs in the NT, it does not mean "to approach, come near" but "to arrive, come." He cites Matt 26:45 as meaning that the hour has come, but allows either meaning for 26:46 and the one who gives Jesus over. In response to Hutton, M. A. Simpson ("Kingdom") contends that since Matt 26:45 renders the *erchesthai* of Mark 14:41 by *eggizein*, Matt saw no difference of meaning between the two verbs, so that both should be translated as "has come." Staples has challenged that reading by asking whether we can be sure that Matt, who did not reproduce the Marcan prayer about the hour, had the same attitude toward the hour that Mark had.

[13]Mark 1:15 = Matt 4:17; Matt 10:7 = Luke 10:9; also Matt 3:2.

[14]See W. G. Kümmel, *Promise and Fulfillment* (SBT 23; London: SCM, 1957), 19–25.

might pass (*parerchesthai*); once he acknowledges that the Father has not granted his request, he announces that the hour has come (*erchesthai*), i.e., a type of inclusion. For Matt, who reported no such prayer, the hour will start with the arrival of Judas to arrest Jesus (*erchesthai* will be reserved till that moment); and until that moment the hour and the one who gives him over have only come near.

The Son of Man Given Over. Both Mark 14:41 and Matt 26:45 relate the coming (near) of the hour to "the Son of Man is given over into the hands of (the) sinners." It is interesting that John 12:23 also combines the hour and the Son of Man motifs: "The hour has come in order that the Son of Man may be glorified." The difference between being given over and being glorified (both of them actions by God) reflects the respective outlooks of Mark and John on the passion. We shall speak below of the OT background for the giving over of the Son of Man in Mark/Matt; but in passing we should note that Dan 7:13–14 offers background for John, for there *a* son of man comes to be presented to the Ancient of Days and to be given glory.

Let us discuss briefly "the Son of Man," a designation mentioned here for the first time after the Last Supper, and therefore for the first time in what we have been considering the PN. There is an enormous literature on this term: whether it was a recognized title in Judaism; whether Jesus himself used it and, if so, in what sense; what it meant christologically, etc. There is no way that we can enter the debate in a commentary, although a good deal of background will be presented in §§22 and 23 below. What is interesting for our purpose of understanding the present text is that Jesus, who has just prayed to God as Father, does not hesitate to call himself the Son of Man. We shall encounter a similar phenomenon in the trial before the Jewish authorities where, being asked about his identity as the Son of the Blessed (God), Jesus responds in terms of the Son of Man. Thus the evangelists saw in these two sonships no conflicting evaluation of Jesus. The last previous mention of the Son of Man (Mark 14:21; Matt 26:24) occurred at the Last Supper as a woe on the man who would give over the Son of Man; the reintroduction of the term here prepares the readers for the fulfillment of that prophecy. Also, while there are several types of references to the Son of Man in Mark/Matt, that title has been consistently applied to Jesus in the predictions of the passion (Mark 8:31; 9:31; 10:33 and par.; see APPENDIX VIII, A2). Its use here, after Jesus' prayers to be delivered from the hour and the cup, shows that Jesus now knows that the Father will not deliver him from this fate and so he is resuming the language in which he predicted such a destiny. Indeed, the parallelism between two of the passion predictions and the present affirmation is interesting:

  9:31:   "is given over into the hands of men (*anthrōpoi:* humans)"

10:33:   "will be given over to the chief priests and the scribes"

14:41:   "is given over into the hands of the sinners [*hamartōloi*]"

The "hand(s) of" as an image for "power of" is a biblical expression (II Sam 14:16). Holleran (*Synoptic* 65) points out that in terms of the recipients, 14:41 is intermediary between the specificity of 10:33 and the generality of 9:31. One can find irony here: At the beginning of the ministry Jesus announced that he came to call "sinners" (Mark 2:17); at the end he is given over into their hands. Jesus is the Son of Man; yet being given over into the hands of "men" is an evil fate.

We must discuss *paradidonai,* "to give over." In the Marcan Greek of both v. 41 and v. 42, the "giving over" expression immediately follows "behold"; Matt has changed the word order so that in his two verses (45 and 46) the "coming near" expression immediately follows the "Behold." *Paradidonai* is used frequently in relation to Judas—indeed Mark 3:19 first introduces Judas as "the one who gave over" Jesus—and so there is a tendency to translate it as "betray" (ptcp. = "the traitor"); but such a translation blurs the parallelism to the agency of others expressed by this verb.[15] The important study by Popkes (*Christus*) has helpfully classified uses of *paradidonai* in relation to the passion of Jesus according to whether he is given over by God, by human beings, or by himself.

Let us begin with the giving over of Jesus by human beings (or by evil powers). Popkes (*Christus* 53–55) points out that the verb was a *terminus technicus* in Greek legal procedure for handing criminals over to judgment, judges, and executioners (see Acts 8:3). Some of that remains in the PN; but because Jesus was given over (nay, betrayed) to his judges by his trusted friend and because Jesus was innocent, there is a stigma of guilt in the human chain of those who gave Jesus over: Judas gave him over to the chief priests (Mark 3:19; 14:10–11,21; Matt 27:3–4); the chief priests (or "the Jews") gave him over to Pilate (Mark 10:33b; 15:1,10; John 18:30,36; Acts 3:13); Pilate gave him over to the soldiers to be crucified (Mark 15:15). Jesus, speaking to Pilate in John 19:11, says, "The one who gave me over to you has the greater sin"; but, while this makes clear that sin touches all those who gave Jesus over, we are not certain who is being designated the primary perpetrator. The satanic Prince of this world, the agent behind the scene (John 13:2), may well be meant, as well as Caiaphas.

[15]In our concentration on the passion of Jesus we should not forget that *paradidonai* is used for the giving over of JBap to die at the hands of Herod (Mark 1:14), for the future giving over of Jesus' followers to Sanhedrins (13:9,11,12), for generous self-giving to death (*I Clem.* 55:1), and for God's giving over Israel to punishment (Justin, *Dialogue* 25.4; 135.4).

The concept of God giving Jesus over also enters the picture. Barbour ("Gethsemane") makes an interesting point that just as the *peirasmos* of Jesus (the testing of God's Son) may be understood both as a testing by Satan and a testing by God (cf. II Chron 32:31), so also the giving over: a giving over by wicked human beings and a giving over by the Father. In Mark 14:41 the divine agency is phrased in the passive.[16] This is the most common NT way of describing the divine agency, but Rom 8:32 does not hesitate to mention God: "He gave over him [the Son] for all of us." At times that produces ambiguity, e.g., in the traditional formula cited in I Cor 11:23, "the night in which Jesus was given over," how much of the memory of Judas is involved, or is God the only agent in mind? In the present instance, Jesus' statement reveals the Father's answer to his prayers: God will not deliver the Son from the hour or the cup, but gives him over into the hands of sinners. The background for this concept is not Greek legal language but the literature of Israel, where the destiny of all lies in God's power. *Paradidonai* is frequent in the LXX for God giving over the wicked into the hands of their punishers, even as He delivers the just from the hands of their opponents. The DSS use words from the roots *ntn* and *sgr* (less frequently *msr*) for the giving over of the impious to punishment (1QpHab 9:10; 4QpPs 37 IV 9–10); the just continue to be delivered from the hands of their enemies (4QpPs 37 II 18–19). What is noteworthy about Jesus, however, is that *a just man is being given over by God* into the hands of his enemies. Popkes (*Christus* 258–66) regards this idea as very old in the Christian tradition. He deems Mark 9:31 to be preMarcan and older than Rom 4:25, which has been expanded to include soteriological purpose, "[Jesus] who was given over for our trespasses," under the influence of the Suffering Servant passage in Isa 53:6 (LXX): "And the Lord gave him over for our sins." The Gospel picture of Jesus being given over, besides being shaped by the Isaiah and Psalms portrait of the suffering just one, has a martyrological coloring (see Surkau, *Martyrien* 82–103). A passage like Wis 2–3 is important as background, for it shows the just suffering at the hands of the wicked as part of God's testing (3:5) and with the expectation that God will make them victorious.

A further development of *paradidonai* is Jesus' giving himself over to death, a theme prominent in John in terms of laying down his own life (10:17–18). While Isa 53:10a describes the bruising of the servant to reflect thw will of the Lord, 53:10b seems to have the servant making himself an offering. The insight that Jesus totally accepted God's will would have facilitated the theological movement from God's giving him over to his giving

---

[16]Contrast the active thrust of the verb in reference to Judas in 14:42 and previously (with the Son of Man as object) in 14:21, even though there the construction is passive.

himself.[17] This rich complex of ideas involved in *paradidonai* is inter-mingled in Mark 14:41–42 and Matt 26:45–46 where, in the context of Jesus' obedience to the will of God, the verb is used first for God's action and then for Judas' action. Holleran (*Synoptic* 65, partially citing Tödt) states: "This title [the Son of Man] expresses the real sovereignty of Jesus, even in Gethsemane, where 'the one who subordinates his will to the Father is *in so doing* delivered into the hands of sinners, [and] the one who is not over-whelmed by the power of darkness is delivered up by God.'"

Jesus' Last Words to His Disciples (Mark 14:42; Matt 26:46). The last verse of this Gethsemane prayer scene in Mark/Matt has identical phrasing, differing only in the placing of *ēggiken,* "come near." The opening words of the verse, "Get up; let us go," are also identical with those in John 14:31, which is from a context that echoes the Mark/Matt context in a number of ways. *First,* the Johannine exhortation is preceded in the same verse by "But as the Father has commanded me, so do I do," just as Mark 14:36 has Jesus finish his prayer to the Father with "But not what I will but what you (will)"—a theme strengthened in Luke 22:42 and in Matt's second form of Jesus' prayer (26:42: "Let your will be done"). *Second,* in the immediately preceding verse the Johannine Jesus announces that "the Prince of the world is coming," a warning quite comparable to Mark's "the one who gives me over has come near," especially when we remember that according to John 13:2,27 the devil or Satan has entered into Judas. We are not to think either that the Marcan Jesus can announce that Judas is coming because he has caught sight of the arresting party in the distance or (pace Haenchen, "History" 495) that Jesus is taken by surprise. In both Mark and John (and in any traceable form of the tradition) Jesus is aware of what is about to happen because he is attuned to God's plans. *Third,* chaps. 15–17 of John may have been inserted as part of a redaction (BGJ l.xxxvii; 2.656–57); and so many scholars think that 14:31 once led directly into 18:1 thus: "'Get up; let us go from here.' Having said these things, Jesus went out with his disciples across the Kidron valley." This would mean a sequence leading directly to the arrival of Judas, which is precisely the sequence in Mark.

What is significant about this verse in Mark/Matt is that Jesus still includes the disciples alongside him as he faces the approaching evil. It is interesting that in the antidisciple interpretation of Gethsemane by Kelber ("Hour" 54–56), he treats Mark 14:41 but pays little or no attention to 14:42. "Let us go" is not a call to discipleship, nor an invitation to run away; it

---

[17]A similar movement can be detected in resurrection formulas from Jesus' being raised up to Jesus rising, and finally to his raising himself.

expresses Jesus' desire that he and his disciples be in readiness to encounter *together* the traitor who is coming. At the beginning of the Mark/Matt Gethsemane scene, two imperatives were addressed by Jesus to his disciples: "Sit here while I pray" and "Remain here and keep on watching" (Mark 14:32,34). Mid-scene when Peter and the disciples had by their sleeping clearly failed to carry out his commands, Jesus tried again with two imperatives: "Keep on watching and praying" (14:38). The disciples have failed again by continuing to sleep and take their rest. Jesus has recognized that they are not at this time ready to enter into the *peirasmos* with him, to drink the cup with him, or to share his hour; indeed, he had predicted that they would be scattered when the shepherd was struck. But Jesus has not given up on them. No longer are the commands static like "Sit" and "Remain"; they are dynamic: "Get up, let us go." These final imperatives to the disciples—the last words that Jesus ever speaks to them in Mark, or speaks to the group before the resurrection in Matt—constitute a refutation of the thesis that Mark wrote to discredit the disciples permanently. They may not take their stand at this time with Jesus; yet he still considers them on his side, not on the side of the sinners into whose hands he is given over.

At the beginning of the Gospel (Mark 1:38) Jesus had said to Simon and to those who were with him, "Let us go," as he urged them to set out with him to proclaim the kerygma to the towns of Galilee: "for this purpose have I come out." But now when it is clear that "this purpose" must include entering the hour and drinking the cup, Jesus repeats his "Let us go." Even if the disciples are going to be scattered in flight, after the resurrection he will precede them to Galilee and there they will see him once more (14:28; 16:7). Mark writes this Gospel with the understanding that when the disciples finally came through their experience to comprehend what the suffering and death of Jesus meant, they responded obediently to this "Let us go" by preaching the gospel and giving themselves for Jesus. Mark is inviting his readers to do likewise.[18]

In the PN of all four Gospels the next verse will describe the arrival of Judas to arrest Jesus, and so my COMMENT on the next episode (§13) will open by describing the previous portrayal of Judas in each Gospel. Before we leave the present scene, however, it may be well to remind ourselves that the Jesus who encounters Judas has not had the same experience in all four

---

[18]Phillips ("Gethsemane") is correct in insisting that discipleship is a major theme in the Gethsemane scene, as Mark seeks to convince readers that trial and persecution are to be expected by disciples. That very appeal, however, means that the career of those disciples who followed Jesus during his ministry should not terminate with their failure in Gethsemane but in their ultimately joining Jesus after the resurrection. Against Kelber's view of total failure, see Szarek, "Critique" 117–18.

Gospels. In Mark he has been plunged into the traumatic knowledge of the weakness of his own flesh; out of his anguish prayers have been wrung from his lips begging the Father that he be delivered from the hour and the cup that he once so bravely anticipated; those prayers have not been granted; rather God has given him over to sinners as he himself once predicted would happen to the Son of Man. At the last moment he has aligned his disciples with him to face Judas and the forces of evil, but Jesus does this with the sad experience of their threefold sleeping and the realization that they cannot come with him into this trial. The Marcan Jesus who faces Judas does so with a resolve born of obedience, but with the taste of suffering in his mouth and the sense that in this struggle he will stand alone without human companionship and without visible help from God. The Matthean picture of the Jesus who will encounter Judas is not essentially different, even if the vivid colors of Mark are much muted and subtle tones soften the contrasts. Throughout what has preceded Jesus was more in command; his prayer was less lengthy and less anguished; his unity with his disciples (and they still bear that name) has held together better; but overall God's lack of assistance and the eventual scattering of the disciples have not changed.

The Lucan Jesus has not experienced anguish or weakness. His prayer was uttered in a reverent posture and most cautiously accompanied by a double expression of obedience. The ever-loving Father responded with a strengthening angel. His disciples may have slept for sorrow and not prayed as they should have, but there is no suggestion that they have failed and will not remain true to him in his trial. Thus accompanied by the Father's love and human companionship, Jesus has stood up confidently to face the power of darkness.

The Johannine Jesus who will encounter Judas, nay, go out to meet him, has not shown the slightest hesitation nor uttered a word that could deflect him from the hour which is the very purpose for his existence in this world. Pray he did at the end of the supper (chap. 17); but that prayer was one of loving unity with the Father, untroubled by any impending tragedy. The last time that John's Jesus showed a sign of reflecting on the struggle to come was in 16:33 with a ringing cry of triumph: "Have courage: I have conquered the world." It is Judas who needs to fear this Jesus!

(Bibliography for this episode is found in §4, Part 2.)

§11. ANALYSIS COVERING ALL FIVE PARTS OF JESUS' PRAYER IN GETHSEMANE

(Mark 14:32–42; Matt 26:36–46; Luke 22:40–46; John 18:1b)

In five sections of COMMENT I developed the thought particular to each of the various Gospel presentations of the Gethsemane/Mount of Olives "scene." In fact, John has no prayer scene across the Kidron; rather, motifs of Jesus' prayer pertinent to "the hour" occurred earlier, at the end of the public ministry to Israel. Luke describes a prayer on the Mount of Olives (one answered by a strengthening angel, if we accept 22:43–44 as genuinely Lucan); yet for Luke the prayer is not self-subsistent but contributes to a scene of which the arrest is an equal constituent. Mark/Matt are the Gospels that cause us to think of Gethsemane as a prayer scene with its own drama in which Jesus works out his fate and his disciples fail to join him.

There are questions, however, that could not be dealt with until we had discussed all the sections of the text. How would 1st-cent. hearers/readers interpret such a scene? How much of it represents a dramatization by the evangelists or their immediate preGospel forebears, and how much of it represents old tradition? Are there factors outside the Gospels that cast light on it? It is to these questions that we now turn. (For the outline of this ANALYSIS, see p. 109 above.)

A. *Various Approaches to the Scene*

The scene of Jesus' prayer in Gethsemane has had a special place in Christian piety. Jesus separating himself from his disciples; his anguish of soul in praying to have the cup taken away; the caring response of the Father in sending an angel to strengthen him; the loneliness of the master as three times he finds his disciples sleeping instead of praying with him; the courage expressed by the final resolve to face the betrayer—taken from the various Gospels, this combination of human suffering, divine strengthening, and solitary self-giving has done much to make Jesus loved by those who believe in him. It has served as the subject of art and meditation.

Most Christians, then, are surprised to discover that outsiders have found the scene scandalous and ridiculous. Believers are annoyed to be told that scholars have judged parts of it illogical and the whole awkwardly put together. Without acceding to those judgments, let me explain the difficulties that have given rise to them, especially when the scene has been the object of different hermeneutical approaches (see F. Martin, "Literary" 575–81).

1. Scandal over the Content of the Scene

Educated Greco-Roman pagans would have been familiar with the death of Socrates described by Plato. Execution by self-administered poison was forced upon this philosopher of lofty principles who was innocent of crime. Without tears and without impassioned pleas to be spared, he accepted his fate, nobly encouraging his followers not to grieve since he was going to a world of perfect truth, beauty, and goodness, only the shadows of which were glimpsed here below. Admirers of Socrates would not be familiar with the Judeo-Christian objection that the tranquility of Socrates was based on a wrong evaluation of this life as existence in a world of shadows, with true existence found only in the world of absolutes to which one escapes as from a confining cave. Consequently, hearers/readers imbued with Platonic/Socratic ideals might react disparagingly toward the Mark/Matt picture of a Jesus distraught and troubled, throwing himself prostrate to the earth and begging God to deliver him.[1]

A different reaction might be expected from those dominated by the earlier biblical attitude toward death. Human beings were created for this world, which for them is the only real world; death is an enemy destroying all that is good in life and leaving only a shadowy existence in Sheol. Toward the end of the OT period we find a more positive view of the afterlife (Isaian Apocalypse; Dan; II Macc); but death remains an enemy, even if God enables those who are loyal to overcome it. Thus one may argue that Jesus' anguish in facing death is an attestation of the Jewish sense of the value of life in this world as God's great gift—an attestation that had to be kept alive for Jesus' followers lest their faith in the resurrection lead them to devalue life in this world. Yet even within the framework of Jewish thought the presentation of Jesus in Gethsemane could have caused problems. The Maccabean martyrs were righteous people who had died violent deaths at the hands of unjust authorities, but they had faced their fate with the resolve to give a

---

[1]For comparisons of Christ and Socrates, see J. M. Pfättisch, TQ 90 (1908), 503–23; E. Benz, ZNW 43 (1950–51), 195–244; E. Fascher, ZNW 45 (1954), 1–41.

"noble example of how to die a good death willingly and generously" (II Macc 6:28; see de Jonge, "Jesus"). Eleazar went to the instrument of torture "of his own accord . . . as a man of courage ought to go" (6:19–20); the seven brothers and their mother astonished all with their bravery. Josephus records many examples of contemporary Jews bravely and cheerfully undergoing religious martyrdom (*War* 1.33.3; #653; 2.8.10; #153; 7.10.1; #417–18). Jesus would not compare favorably with such a model unless one understood that his reluctance and anguish were caused not simply by facing suffering and death but also by the knowledge that he was entering a great struggle with Evil, the great trial that preceded the coming of the kingdom. Outsiders would not recognize that, but I am not sure that all Christians do either. The passage may be said to have created an implicit scandal among theologians and preachers who explain away the prayers about the hour and cup so that Jesus is not really asking to be delivered from death or is not thinking of his own suffering but of all the sins of the world.[2]

We have an ancient example of the treatment of Gethsemane as a mark against Jesus in Celsus, a learned pagan of ca. AD 170 who had Jewish sources and whose work against Christianity was refuted by Origen. We hear objections like these: How can one who is divine "mourn and lament and pray to escape the fear of death, expressing himself thus, 'O Father, if it be possible, let this cup pass from me'?" (*Contra Celsum* 2.24). How can he "be deserted and delivered up by those who had been his associates and with whom he had shared all things in common?" (2.9). Why was he caught hiding; and if he foresaw that such things would happen to him, why did he not avoid them? (2.9,17).

2. Problems about the Composition of the Scene

Some scholars have been impressed that Mark's description of Jesus' prayer in Gethsemane is in good order and that little can be removed from it without damage.[3] Indeed, those who consider the PN to be a Marcan cre-

---

[2]In the COMMENT of §7 I gave some examples of attempts to soften the impact of the prayer. The scene offers difficulty for those exponents of the theory that, though human, Jesus knew all things, including the future, or had the beatific vision.

[3]Lohmeyer (*Markus* 313–21) argues for this, but the threefold division he detects (vv. 32–34, 35–41a,41b–42) is hard to justify on a prima facie reading. Fiebig ("Jesu" 122–25) argues that the whole Marcan scene has Hebrew or Aramaic roots and stems from Jesus. Pesch (*Markus* 2.386) points to the number of hapax legomena as an indication that it came to Mark whole from a source. More persuasively, he rejects Bultmann's classification of it as legend and detects a combination of forms: prayer, prophecy, and parenesis. For Mark 14, Heil, "Mark," argues for an (overly) elaborate structure of nine alternating scenes in 14:1–52 of (a) opposition and separation from Jerusalem and (b) union with Jesus. The whole of 14:32–42 is classified as an (a) scene.

ation from disparate traditions often stress the care with which a given section has been assembled as a proof of their redaction theory. I myself am convinced that Mark is deliberately dramatic here: When Jesus separates himself from the body of the disciples and then from Peter, James, and John, he symbolizes his increasing alienation from his disciples. The double prayer about the hour and the cup catches the intensity of the request; the address to God in (transliterated) Aramaic and Greek here at the beginning of the passion is meant to match the prayer in (transliterated) Aramaic and Greek at the end of the PN (15:34), etc. Nevertheless, the Gethsemane prayer scene sets off an alarm for many major indicators that scholars use to detect the composition of a passage. For those who use agreement between John and Mark as a possible indicator of antiquity (since they think John represents a tradition independent of Mark), this whole prayer scene just before the arrest is missing from John's PN. John 18:1–3 has Jesus cross the Kidron to the garden and immediately encounter the arresting party—to get the same effect, one would have to join Mark 14:26 to 14:32a to 14:43b, omitting all the material in between. For those who think that Luke drew here upon an independent source rivaling Mark in antiquity,[4] Luke has a much shorter prayer scene than Mark, without reference to Peter, James, and John, without Jesus being distraught and sorrowful, without a prayer about the hour, and without the second and third departures of Jesus to pray, followed by returning to find the disciples asleep.

Finally, if one uses internal Marcan cohesion as a guide, there is here a remarkable number of seeming doublets, giving support to the thesis that two sources might have been combined. Let me list those, for they fit into most discussions of preMarcan strata of this passage. I put in the left column the part of the doublet mentioned first in Mark's narrative:

Place: Mount of Olives (14:26)	Place: Gethsemane (14:32)
Group of disciples (14:32)	Peter, James, John (14:33)

[4]If we leave aside the episode of the strengthening angel (Luke 22:43–44), the following scholars would consider Luke 22:39–42, 45–46 to reflect in whole or in part a special source independent of Mark: Feldkämper, Grundmann, Holleran, Kuhn, Lagrange, Loisy, and Schlatter. The following would consider these verses to be an abridgement and rewriting of Mark: Creed, Feldmeier, Finegan, Fitzmyer, Klostermann, Neyrey, Schmid, Schneider, and Soards. In the COMMENT I have espoused the latter view with the proviso that one recognizes that in his editing of Mark, Luke has woven into his account material that came to him from oral tradition (e.g., prayer patterns—that proviso also explains vv. 43–44 which, in my judgment, are genuine). As pointed out on p. 147, in Luke this scene is not really separate from the arrest (22:47–53), and the same range of opinion about Lucan sources exists there. Here, in editing Mark, Luke has avoided duplications, Aramaic place-names, the picture of a distressed Jesus, and what would place the disciples in a bad light. Accordingly his Jesus is much more in control, moving with his disciples toward his destiny: an example of prayer to all who are called on to suffer and die for him.

Jesus moves away saying, "Sit here while I pray" (14:32)	Jesus moves away saying, "Remain here and keep on watching" (14:34)
Jesus is greatly distraught and troubled (14:33)	Jesus' soul is very sorrowful unto death (14:34)
Jesus prays, if it is possible to let the hour pass (14:35)	Jesus prays: "All things are possible; take away this cup" (14:36)
Jesus comes and finds them sleeping (14:37)	Jesus comes and finds them sleeping (14:40)
"Simon, are you sleeping?" (14:37)	"Do you go on sleeping, then?" (14:41)
"Behold the Son of Man is given over" (14:41)	"Behold the one who gives me over has come near" (14:42)

To my knowledge no major scholar would propose a Marcan source consisting of the items in the left-hand column, and another consisting of items in the right-hand column; but with great selectivity two-source theories of preMarcan PNs split up these doublets, assigning the parts to different sources, often on the basis of a theological orientation thought to exist in the source. Among those who adopt the two-source approach to the Gethsemane scene are K. G. Kuhn, Léon-Dufour, and Lescow.[5] Since this is our first chance to look closely at source theories, let me do what I shall not have the space to do elsewhere: give examples of competing approaches. I begin by writing out Kuhn's proposed two sources ("Jesus"); they have been rendered in the very literal translation I am using for the commentary:

Kuhn's Source A (14:32,35,40,41)

[32]And they come into the plot of land the name of which was Gethsemane; and he says to his disciples, "Sit here while I pray." [35]And having gone forward a little, he was falling on the earth and was praying that if it is possible, the hour might pass from him. [40]And having come he found them sleeping, for their eyes were very burdened; and they did not know what they should answer him. [41]And he says to them, "Do you go on sleeping then and taking your rest? The money is paid; the hour has come; behold the Son of Man is given over into the hands of the sinners."

In order to make this logical, Kuhn had to do some emendation on vv. 40–41 (removing "again" and "the third time"). He actually translates 41 as an imperative ("Sleep on") as part of his claim that there is no motif of watching

[5]In §2, n. 45, I mentioned the two-source approach to the whole PN, which is somewhat different from the two-source approach to this scene. Taylor (*Mark*, 551), for instance, assigns the whole of the Gethsemane prayer to Source B: 14:32–42 as a vivid eyewitness account, very close to the original facts.

here. The Son-of-Man saying is the whole point of the narrative, the theology of which is eschatological and christological. John is somewhat close to this source. (See also Trémel, "Agonie" 83.)

Kuhn's Source B (14:33,34,36,37,38)

> [33]And he takes along Peter, and James, and John with him, and he began to be greatly distraught and troubled. [34]And he says to them, "My soul is very troubled unto death. Remain here and keep on watching." [35a] *And having gone forward a little,* [36]he was saying, *"Abba,* Father, all things are possible to you: Take away this cup from me. But not what I will but what you (will)." [37]And he comes and finds them sleeping; and he says to Peter, "Simon, are you sleeping? Were you not strong enough to watch one hour? [38]Keep on watching and praying lest you enter into trial. Indeed the spirit is willing, but the flesh is weak."

Notice the passage I have italicized; Kuhn already attributed 35a to the other source, but he reuses it here because it is necessary for the flow. Thus we must posit that the two sources had the same phrase, or if they had different vocabulary for the movement of Jesus, Mark discarded the other wording in favor of this. This source is more parenetic with its stress on watching and trial. As the COMMENT above pointed out, the Dead Sea Scrolls throw light both on "trial" (*peirasmos*) and "flesh and spirit." This may be the older source. Luke's report of the scene is close to this source.

Let me make some observations. The theory that Mark combined these sources requires a paste-and-scissors approach interweaving the lines and ingeniously creating a pattern of three comings of Jesus to the disciples. In the two-source approach to the Synoptic problem whereby Matt combines Mark with Q, would there be a comparable example of this type of interweaving through a ten-verse passage? The theory smacks somewhat of the way modern scholars would work, combining lines from two books propped up on either side of them. Kuhn supposes that Luke drew from a preLucan source; and since there is resemblance of Luke to Marcan source B, that helps to prove that B actually existed. In the COMMENT I agreed firmly with those who think that Luke's account (except for the strengthening angel) came from editing Mark by simplifying some repetitions (which is exactly how Kuhn has produced his sources). Moreover, Luke chose from Mark the group of the disciples rather than Peter, James, and John (who are crucial to Kuhn's Source B). As for the ending of Source A, could not the themes of the hour and the Son of Man just as well go with Source B, joining with the motif of watching? Of course, one may argue that these themes fit into the eschatological and christological thrust of A; yet they also help to constitute that thrust. There is some circular reasoning in most reconstruction, but in a four-verse source the circularity can be too strong if one decides that the theological thrust is eschatological and then includes what makes it eschatological.[6]

Linnemann has been quite critical of Kuhn's analysis; she argues that the PN was constructed for the first time by Mark from various separate traditions which were edited. In the Gethsemane scene she proposes that an earlier tradition underwent two adaptations before Mark (the third redactor) produced the present form. Insisting that her form-critical approach enables her to detect the oldest stage of the tradition but that "oldest" does not necessarily mean historical, she proposes that stage to have consisted of 14:32,35,37a,39a,40ab,41a,40c,41b.[7] This may be written out as follows:

> [32]And they come into the plot of land the name of which was Gethsemane; and he says to his disciples, "Sit here while I pray." [35]And having gone forward a little, he was falling on the earth and was praying that if it is possible, the hour might pass from him. [37a]And he comes and finds them sleeping. [39a]And again having gone away, he prayed; [40ab]and again having come, he found them sleeping, for their eyes were very burdened. [41a]And he comes the third time and says to them, "Do you go on sleeping, then, and taking your rest?" [40c]And they did not know what they should answer him. [41b]"The money is paid; the hour has come; behold the Son of Man is given over into the hands of the sinners."

(In the COMMENT above I discussed her putting v. 41a before v. 40c, observing that I saw no need for this.) In the source as she has reconstructed it, the disciples have no major role; Peter, James, and John have disappeared; Jesus is not distraught or very sorrowful; and the prayer concerns the hour, not the cup. The whole scene concentrates on Jesus' relationship to the Father about the coming of the hour. She is one of the few scholars who opts for a shortened original and yet includes the threefold coming and going of Jesus. The main problem is that other scholars, arguing on other grounds (e.g., style)

---

[6]Lescow ("Jesus in Gethsemane" 145–51), in a favorable summary of Kuhn's view, shows to what extent the reconstructed Sources A and B are centered on one verse, respectively 41 and 38, so that each can be classified as a biographical apophthegm. Notice the different thrust produced by the reconstruction of Léon-Dufour ("Jésus" 251), who, working from doublets, has Source A consist of 14:32,33b,35,40,50, dealing with the horizontal relationship of Jesus to his disciples. The inclusion of v. 50 creates a picture of disciples who, having been told to remain, actually fled. Source B consists of 14:33a,34,36,37 and deals with the vertical relationship between Jesus and the Father.

[7]Linnemann (*Studien* 24–26) regards herself as working in the same line as Bultmann, who posited as original 32,35,37,39,40,41a. Her critique of Kuhn is on pp. 17–23; her cautions about historicity, on pp. 12–13. Illustrating how complicated is such an analysis, a comparison of part of this reconstruction with that of Söding ("Gebet" 80–82) finds that he considers 14:32 to be from the evangelist, 33a to be redactional, 33b–34a to be partly redactional, 35 to be redactional, and 36 to be original.

for excision as the means of reaching a preMarcan source, emerge with quite different results. Schenke (*Studien* 461) is painstaking, and his reconstructed source (14:32a,33b,34,35a,36,37,38b,40b,41a [= "the money is paid"], 42) is about the same length as Linnemann's; but it includes Jesus' being distraught and very sorrowful; a prayer concerning the cup but not the hour; the saying about the flesh being weak, which is interpreted by the immediately following reference to the eyes of the sleepy disciples being burdened; and a final saying about the man who gives him over coming near (omitted by Linnemann), but not one about the Son of Man being given over (included by Linnemann). On the last point Schenke would argue that the Son-of-Man saying is a Marcan editorial addition, corresponding to the references to the Son of Man in the passion predictions.[8] Others opt for a much shorter original, e.g., Mohn ("Gethsemane") proposes 14:32,35,37a,41b, substantially a prayer about an apocalyptic hour, with sleep representing the darkness of evil.[9] The diversity of the results obtained in efforts to establish the exact contents of the preMarcan source (and many more proposals could be mentioned) warns us that we may not have the means to do this project with any probability (see APPENDIX IX). Although some recent scholarship continues to seek the preMarcan source (e.g., Myllykoski), others (Phillips, Feldmeier) resist the dismemberment of the Marcan account.

3. Factors That Are Likely To Be Early Tradition

As I explained in §2, C2, granted such uncertainties I shall not attempt any detailed reconstruction of a preMarcan source. I shall be content with pointing out factors that most likely from a very early period were part of the tradition of Jesus' prayer before death. No precise wording will be suggested for such traditions because I see no way of working back from the wording in which they are now phrased to an earlier wording if that differed.[10] While I gave a chart above of the unusual number of doublets in this scene, they shall play little or no role in my endeavor. One may certainly question whether all the items listed in that chart are truly doublets. Are Peter, James, and John a doublet of the body of the disciples, since really

---

[8]Gnilka (*Markus* 257), however, would attribute the Son-of-Man saying to a preMarcan level that also contained v. 35b (prayer about the hour, a verse treated as Marcan by Schenke).

[9]Briefer still is Finegan (*Überlieferung* 71), who posits as genuine tradition only 14:32,37a,43: Jesus and his disciples come to Gethsemane where he prays alone; when he comes back he finds them sleeping, and then Judas comes with a crowd.

[10]Even if I disagree with his diagnosis of Marcan motives and theology, Kelber ("Mark 14") is correct in pointing out Marcan style and thought patterns throughout the scene; however, as I contended in §2, C2 above, that does not tell us much about whether there was a preMarcan source. If one did exist, Mark either rewrote it in his own style or the source had much of the style and thought that Mark made his own.

the group has to be mentioned for Jesus to call these individuals out? Is it the proximity of the two references that creates the impression of duplication? The triple going, praying, and coming back (which is not reported fully in Mark) has to be broken down in order to find doublets. Moreover, a biblical style where the synonymous parallelism of Hebrew poetry makes it elegant to say the same thing twice in different words weakens the value of doublets for reconstructing the history of composition. In particular, Mark shows a penchant throughout the Gospel for doublets of various types.[11]

More important is the agreement of NT witnesses on certain items contained in the Gethsemane prayer scene. In the COMMENT I have shown how hard it is to derive John's presentation of common material from Mark's account. In the next subsection of this ANALYSIS I shall argue that Heb 5:7–10 is a witness to Jesus' prayer independent of Mark (and there I shall carry the discussion of early tradition further than I do here). Therefore one can make a case for Mark, John, and Hebrews as three independent witnesses to a tradition[12] that in the last period of his life Jesus struggled with and prayed to God about his impending death. In different vocabulary all three mention anguish on Jesus' part over this issue. Hebrews does not specify the precise moment when he prayed; John has material parallel to Mark's account scattered in chaps. 12, 14, and 18; Mark has a prayer scene in 14:32–42 but also a psalm prayer on the cross (15:34). Plausibly the tradition of this prayer by Jesus did not contain within it a precise time or location; and so the two evangelists (or their respective forebears) who had to place it in a narrative sequence inserted it where and how they thought best.

Let me concentrate here on what the agreement between Mark and John might tell us about the detectable preGospel items in the tradition. They both place the cup motif at the site where Jesus was arrested (Mark 14:36; John 18:11); one can also argue that for both the context of the arrest is one of an

---

[11]See F. Neirynck, *Duality in Mark* (BETL 31; Leuven Univ., 1972).

[12]The agreement of three such witnesses would establish the antiquity of the tradition, not necessarily its historicity. Other factors that would enter into that judgment would include the conformity of what is described with other attested behavior of Jesus and whether the thrust of the scene would have fitted the theological interests of the early Christians so that they might have engendered it. On the latter point an argument advanced for historicity is that the early Christians would not have invented a scene so unfavorable to Jesus as one in which he is prostrate on the earth begging to be delivered from the hour and the cup. Gnilka (*Markus* 2.264) and others question that argument on the grounds that the greatness of Jesus is made manifest in his suffering. Obviously Christian writers have made a positive lesson of the scene, but would they have created such awkwardness for the sake of a lesson that they can only draw tortuously from it? If it was not embarrassing, why does Matt tone down Mark's account, and why does Luke completely bowdlerize it? Why does Hebrews betray awareness of a tension between being God's Son and crying out to be saved from death? As I showed at the beginning of the ANALYSIS, outsiders did not read it as a triumph and Christian preachers have been embarrassed by it.

eschatological struggle with evil.[13] Thus part of the tradition about Jesus' last prayer may early have been associated with the place and time where Mark gives us the full-blown Gethsemane scene. That nucleus may have been what attracted the Marcan tradition to assemble at Gethsemane other elements of Jesus' prayer into a dramatic portrayal.[14] Those elements to which I refer are found in John in a scene at the end of the public ministry (12:23,27,28,29).[15] They include the idea that the hour has come, a reference to the destiny of the Son of Man, an echo of Ps 42:6–7 whereby Jesus speaks of his soul as very sorrowful or disturbed, a prayer about Jesus being delivered from the hour, and an acknowledgment that he accepted God's plan or will.[16] In both traditions, but in different ways, part of this prayer was assimilated to early Christian prayer forms, most often to those associated with the memory of Jesus' style of praying, e.g., the Lord's Prayer. From early Christian prayer one hears the following motifs echoed: *Abba* (Mark), Father (Mark, John), let your will be done (adapted in Mark), let your name be glorified (John), lead us not into trial (Mark), and (probably) all things are possible to you. The influence of Ps 42 and of early Christian prayer has been expressed differently in each tradition, and so it probably antedates the formation of both.

To recapitulate, I posit that early Christians had a tradition that before he died Jesus struggled in prayer about his fate. I do not know whether they retained or claimed to retain accurate memories of the wording he used; more probably they did not. But they understood his prayer in terms like the hour and the cup, which in the tradition of his sayings he had used to describe his destiny in God's plan. They fleshed out the prayer tradition in light of the psalms[17] and of their own prayers, both of which they associated with

[13]Mark's themes of "watching" and *peirasmos* are interpreted eschatologically in the COMMENT. John 14:30 describes the Prince of this world as coming. (Earlier in 12:31, in the context of the prayer parallels of 12:23–29, John's Jesus spoke of casting out the Prince of this world.) In the next verse (14:31) John has the words "Get up; let us go" (words that originally may have led into 18:1–3, where Jesus goes to the garden to meet Judas); these are the same words with which Mark 14:42 terminates the Gethsemane prayer and leads into the appearance of Judas.

[14]Luke and John describe the site where Jesus went after the Last Supper as a place to which he had gone before with his disciples. In Mark 13 it is in this area on the Mount of Olives that Jesus gives his long eschatological discourse. It is not surprising that Jesus' last prayer would be associated with a site where in the tradition he had gone before. I warned in the COMMENT against associating Gethsemane *solely* with the arrest. See Gnilka, *Markus* 2.264.

[15]I am not suggesting that John's placing of these items is more historical than Mark's placing; both accounts have undergone theological and dramatic developments.

[16]In the exalted Johannine christology Jesus refuses to pray to be saved from the hour since it is God's purpose and his own that he come to this hour. In Mark Jesus leaves the passing of the hour in the Father's hands.

[17]Many have reacted against Dibelius's contention that psalm reflection gave rise to the event described (see Schrage, "Bibelarbeit" 27–28; L. Schenke, *Studien* 544–45). The fact that Hebrews and Mark/John use different psalms (respectively 116 and 42) suggests that a basic tradition was being developed, not created.

Jesus' way of praying. Each evangelist (and his tradition before him) knew different forms of that tradition,[18] and each developed it differently both before and in the course of fitting it into his narrative. Some may find this approach to the Gethsemane scene too vague and allusive; but I would argue that it does more justice to the early Christian ethos and to the limits of our own investigatory methods than do the overly bookish, scribal processes implied in some of the theories of composition described earlier, where one has to imagine the meticulous interweaving of phrases from two different sources or the creation of a long verse by each of four different redactors adding a phrase to it. Readers may wonder whether, when I speak of each evangelist developing the tradition before incorporating it into the Gospel, I can avoid supposing some bookish process of working with texts. Of course, some of that must have gone on; but in the case of Mark and John I do not think we can discern the details of that process. However, the broad lines of what went on before the specific developments within a Gospel-writing stage may be discernible and really be of more importance.

Thus far I have not dealt with the role of Jesus' prayer *in relation to the disciples* (their watching, praying, sleeping). Hebrews and John are silent about this, but it constitutes at least half of Mark's description. Was the reaction of the disciples part of a more general early tradition, or did it spring from the interaction between the prayer and the context where Mark (or his forebears) placed that prayer? (In the present Marcan sequence the disciples have stated that they are willing to share Jesus' fate, but this interaction with his prayer shows they are not.) I know of no way to decide.[19] What is obvious is the parenetic thrust of the parts pertaining to the disciples; we are being given almost a parabolic lesson. The parabolic nature of the material is confirmed by close similarities to the eschatological parable in Mark 13:34–37 with its injunctions to watch (three times) and not to sleep, for the master

[18]When I speak of each evangelist, I think primarily of Mark and John. However, while Matt (very closely) and Luke (very loosely) drew on Mark's account of the prayer, each probably had access to a wider oral tradition than Mark reported. A tradition of an angelic response, completely absent in Mark, appears in Luke 22:43–44; Matt 26:53; John 12:29. See §8.

[19]Schenke (*Studien* 548) thinks that Mark developed parenetically the role of the disciples, which was preMarcan. But Barbour ("Gethsemane") makes a strong case that a parenetic warning about watching and *peirasmos* was part of the earliest preMarcan tradition; and Boman ("Gebetskampf" 262–64) argues that the motif of sleep was preMarcan and helped to fix the time of the scene as the *night* before Jesus died. Many who have a two-source approach attribute Peter, James, and John to the preMarcan level, whereas most defenders of the one-source approach attribute their appearance to Mark in imitation of 5:37 and 9:2. Yet Mohn ("Gethsemane" 197) thinks that those two appearances of the three disciples, as well as the present one, represent Marcan redaction; Linnemann judges only 5:37 to have resulted from Marcan redaction; and Schenke (*Studien* 480) holds that the role of the three disciples is scarcely historical. Braumann ("Leidenskelch" 179–81) discusses the theory that these three are mentioned because by the time Mark wrote they had all died a martyr's death. (Also E. W. Stegemann, TZ 42 [1986], 366–74.) Certainly their failure to watch with Jesus here is a play on their promises in Mark 10:38–39 and 14:31.

may come at a number of times. This observation causes me to join Linnemann in arguing that the threefold character of the interchange between Jesus and the disciples belongs to the earliest detectable form of the Marcan narrative. It is an example of the rule of three that is operative in oral narrative forms of tradition and is not a pastiche from two separate sources, each mentioning a coming.

Having discussed much of this in terms of the material in Mark and John, let us turn to the very important witness of Hebrews.

B. *The Contribution of Heb 5:7–10*

A surprising amount of the discussion of the Synoptic Gethsemane prayer scene is in dialogue with this passage in Hebrews; see in the Gethsemane BIBLIOGRAPHY (§4, Part 2) articles by Brandenburger, Braumann, Feuillet ("Évocation"), Friedrich, Jeremias, Lescow, Omark, Schille, Strobel, and Trémel.

1. The Prayer of Jesus in Hebrews and Its Origins

In Heb 4:14–16 Christians are told to gain confidence in their time of need because they have a high priest who is able to sympathize with their weaknesses: "one who in all things has been tempted/tested [*peirazein*] as we are, [but] without sin." To illustrate this the author insists in 5:5 that Christ's being made into a high priest was not a matter of self-glorification; rather he was appointed by God. He was one

> [7]who in the days of his flesh, *having brought prayers and supplications,* with a strong *clamor* and *tears* to the One having the power to save him from death, and *having been heard* from fear, [8]despite his being Son, *learned obedience* from the things that he *suffered.* [9]And having been *made perfect,* he became to all who obey him the cause of eternal salvation, [10]being *designated* by God a *high priest* according to the order of Melchizedek.

A study of the Greek vocabulary in this passage shows that the author of Hebrews did not make up the passage from wording that he found in any of the canonical Gospels, nor did any evangelist make up his PN account of Jesus' prayer(s) from this passage. The words I have italicized in the passage describe key actions of Jesus or things done to him as he faced death; yet not one of them describes anything done by or to Jesus in the PN of any

Gospel, or indeed (with the exception of "suffer") throughout the whole Gospel accounts of the ministry. (Note: a verb related to "tears" is used of Jesus in John 11:35; the verb "to suffer" [*paschein*] is used in the passion predictions [Mark 8:31; 9:12] and at the Last Supper [Luke 22:15].)

Where, then, did the author of Hebrews get the description given in 5:7–9 of Jesus' struggle with death and his being perfected? Many scholars point to parallels with the early Christian hymn in Philip 2:6–11, especially with 2:8–9, which describes Jesus becoming obedient unto death and being exalted by God. The Philippians hymn and this passage in Hebrews both begin with the relative pronoun "who" (*hos*), a characteristic of hymns contained in epistles (also Col 1:15). Characteristic, too, is the addition of clarifying or theologically modifying clauses that were not in the original form of the hymn. Lescow ("Jesus ... Hebräerbrief" 223, 229) posits such clauses in the Hebrews passage, e.g., the awkward "and having been heard from fear" in 5:7. When understood as reverential fear, this addition prevented the reader from thinking that Jesus' prayer was not answered. Friedrich ("Lied" 107–10) would regard that clause as original but judges "in the days of his flesh" to be an addition. Notable too in 5:7 are the sets of parallel nouns, "prayers and supplications" and "clamor and tears," which may reflect poetic style. Four words in that verse occur only here in Hebrews ("prayers," "supplications," "cry," "tears"); Hebrews, then, may be copying the phrasing of an already composed work, like a hymn. There is paronomasia in 5:8 between "learned" and "suffered" (*emathen ... epathen;* see J. Coste, RechSR 43 [1955], 481–523, esp. 517–22).

Early Jewish-Christian hymns, like the Jewish hymns known from the Books of the Maccabees and Qumran, were often a pastiche of OT motifs (see BBM 346–66 on the Lucan infancy hymns), and that may also be true of the Hebrews passage. Boman ("Gebetskampf" 266) points out that in the OT a prayer uttered in deep anxiety is frequently phrased in terms of crying out to God (Exod 2:23; Num 12:13; Judg 3:9) and shedding tears before God (Judg 20:26; II Sam 12:22; Joel 2:12,17). Many authors detect psalm motifs (abundant elsewhere in Hebrews) in 5:7. Dibelius ("Gethsemane") posits the influence of the Greek of Ps 31:23, where God listens "because of my prayers," and of Ps 39:13, "Hear, O Lord, my supplication and my prayer; attend to my tears." P. Andriessen (NRT 96 [1974] 286–91) shows that several words of Heb 5:7 occur in Ps 22:24 ("prayer" and "heard"; *kraugē,* "clamor," is used in Hebrews and the verb *krazein* is used in the Greek of the psalm).

Several have pointed to the first verse of Ps 116 (= Greek Pss 114–15); and Strobel ("Psalmengrundlage") has gone further to show that most of the vocabulary of Heb 5:7 may be found scattered throughout the psalm: in the days of (116:2); prayer (116:1); tears (116:8); save (116:6); from death (116:8); heard (116:1). (Note that some of this vocabulary is from clauses that scholars who are mentioned above judge as later additions to the hymn. Either that theory is wrong, or the person making the additions imitated the psalm upon which the hymn drew.) At the end of 116 (vv. 17–19) the psalmist thanks God for listening to his prayer and tears and for saving his life from the snares of death; and he promises to offer a sacrifice of praise in the courts of the house of the Lord in Jerusalem—a not inappropriate preparation for the Jesus of Hebrews who, having been saved from death, went as a Melchizedek-like priest to minister in the heavenly sanctuary (Heb 5:10; 8:1–2; 9:12).[20] Thus one can make a plausible case that the description in Hebrews of Jesus' prayer to be saved from death (which was heard) came from an early Christian hymn of praise, constructed of a mosaic of psalm motifs. Among those who have accepted the passage as stemming from a hymn are Brandenburger, Braumann (baptismal hymn), Friedrich, Lescow, Schille, and Strobel.

2. Hebrews and the Prayers of Jesus in the Passion Narratives

Does this Hebrews passage, which originated independently of the Gospels, cast light on their descriptions of Jesus' prayers in the PN? Let me summarize the Gospel PN pictures discussed in the COMMENT. Foreseeing his being given over to death at the hands of his enemies, a distraught, sorrowful, and troubled Jesus (Mark/Matt) prayed that the hour might pass from him (Mark) or that the Father would take away the cup from him (Mark, Matt, Luke). According to John 12:27b–28a, at the end of the ministry when the hour had come, Jesus debated about asking the Father to be saved from this hour. He rejected that in favor of a prayer, "Father, glorify your name," a close parallel to the thrust of the Synoptic termination of the cup prayer, "Let your will be done." In John 18:11, in the garden across the Kidron, Jesus asked the rhetorical question, "The cup that the Father has given me— am I not to drink it?"[21] As for the prayer being answered, no response from

[20]While I find plausible Strobel's parallels between Heb 5:7–8 and Ps 116, I find implausible the attempt of Kiley ("Lord") to make Ps 116:4, "Lord, rescue my soul," generative of the Marcan Gethsemane scene. "Soul" is really the only word shared by the two, and that word is found in Mark's citation of Ps 42:6! Other parallels between Ps 116 and Mark that Kiley mentions, besides requiring imagination, do not concern the Gethsemane prayer scene, e.g., 116:11 ("Every man is false") is compared to the flight of the disciples; 116:13 ("a cup of salvation") is closer to the Last Supper cup than to the cup Jesus does not wish to drink in 14:36; 116:15 ("Precious . . . is the death of the saints") is associated with the money promised to Judas (Mark 14:11).

[21]Probably, anterior to the Fourth Gospel, there stood a tradition close to that of Mark about praying in reference to the hour and the cup; but now this has been modified in the light of a Johannine higher christology where the Father and Jesus are one, so that the thought of Jesus praying for a change in the hour on which he and the Father have one mind is no longer tolerable.

the Father by way of voice or action is recorded in Mark/Matt; but having taken the Father's silence as a sign that the hour must now come, Jesus showed resolve in facing it. If Luke 22:43–44 is genuine (and I favor that view), the Father answered by sending an angel to strengthen Jesus. In John 12:28b–29 the Father answered by voice (mistaken by some for an angel's voice): "I have both glorified (my name) and will glorify it again." The "will glorify" consists in the glorification of Jesus after crucifixion (17:1,4–5).

There is another Gospel prayer of Jesus before death that should also be taken into consideration for comparison with Hebrews. In Mark 15:34 and Matt 27:46, just before dying, Jesus is described as having shouted or shrieked in Aramaic with a loud voice, "My God, my God, for what reason [purpose] have you forsaken me?" a quotation of Ps 22:2. As soon as Jesus died, a type of response was given; for the Temple sanctuary veil was torn and a centurion confessed Jesus as God's Son, constituting a sign that God had not forsaken Jesus.

In order to compare Heb 5:7–10 with any or all of this, we must be clear as to what that passage is describing. "In the days of his flesh" has its time range limited by the urgency of the prayer about death and the reference to suffering: The author is speaking of the period of Jesus' last days or his passion. Although the grammatical relationship of the "from fear" phrase and whether it means "because of (reverential) fear" or "(delivered) from (anxious) fear" is not clear,[22] the author seems to be describing an anguished prayer, uttered aloud and wrung from the depths of Jesus' humanity. The author has a very high evaluation of Jesus' divinity (Jesus is greater than the prophets, Moses, and the angels, and can be called "God" [1:8]); and so he is making a sharp contrast between Jesus' being Son and Jesus in his flesh facing death with anguish and urgently praying to be saved from it. His having to learn obedience through such suffering is a clear example of his being tested or tempted even as we are (Heb 4:15). Jesus' prayer was heard, so he was "saved" from death. The emphasis that Hebrews places on Jesus' blood and sacrifice means that being saved from death cannot mean that he was spared dying.[23] Rather Jesus was spared from being conquered by death, as in 2:14. His "being made perfect" means that after death he entered into the heavenly tabernacle (9:11–12) and was seated at God's right hand (1:13). Much the same sequence appears in Heb 2:9: "We see Jesus, who for a little while was made lower than the angels, raised with glory and honor because he suffered death."

With that understanding of Heb 5:7–10, let me list points comparing the

---

[22]See the grammatical discussion in APPENDIX III B.

[23]It is possible, of course, that Jesus prayed not to die, but that God saved him from death in the sense of giving him victory through death.

passage with two prayers of Jesus in the PN described above. The first, by shorthand, will be called the Gethsemane prayer (even if neither Luke nor John use the designation Gethsemane, and John places at the end of the ministry the prayer concerning the hour); the other, the prayer on the cross (primarily the citation of Ps 22:2 in Mark/Matt).

(a) *Hebrews and the Gethsemane prayer:*
- Hebrews speaks of Jesus as Son; the Synoptic prayer about the cup is addressed to the Father, as is John's discussion of this prayer.
- Hebrews sets the prayer "in the days of his flesh," perhaps to establish a contrast between Jesus' weak human state and "the One having the power." A parallel is: "The spirit is willing, but the flesh is weak" (Mark/Matt). The relationship of the two passages is close if the Marcan statement is meant to flow from Jesus' experience of his own weak flesh (see COMMENT), even as Heb 4:15 speaks of Jesus being tested because he shared our "weaknesses."
- Hebrews speaks of "tears"; none are mentioned in the Gospels, but Mark/Matt have Jesus' soul "very sorrowful" and John 12:27 has his soul "disturbed."
- Hebrews has Jesus praying to be *saved* from death; the Johannine Jesus debates whether he should say, "Father, save me from this hour." The Synoptic prayers about the cup (or hour) do not use the word "save."
- Hebrews has the prayer addressed to "the One having the power" (*dynasthai*); this verb is used in Jesus' second Gethsemane cup prayer in Matt 26:42, and the related *dynastos* is used in the Mark/Matt first prayer.
- Hebrews speaks of Jesus being heard; Luke's account portrays a divine answer but Jesus is not spared death; John's account in 12:28 has an answering divine voice in terms of glorification which involves Jesus' death.
- Hebrews uses the phrase "from fear" to describe the context in which he was heard, and may mean that Jesus was delivered from anxious fear; in Mark/Matt Jesus is severely troubled, but he emerges from his prayer resolved; in Luke an angel strengthens him. It is tempting to relate Luke to Heb 2:9, "We see Jesus who for a little while was made lower than the angels, crowned with glory and honor because he suffered death."
- Hebrews speaks of Jesus' learning obedience from the things he suffered; the three Synoptics have Jesus affirm what God wills. In Heb 10:9 Jesus' attitude is described as "here I am to do your will [*thelēma*]," the word used in Jesus' prayer in Matt 26:42; Luke 22:42.
- Hebrews speaks of Jesus' being made perfect; John 12:28 has the Father say that he will glorify His name again, which may be connected with giving Jesus the glory he had before the world began (17:4–5).
- Hebrews, in the introductory context of 4:15, speaks of Jesus' being tempted/tested (*peirazein*); the Synoptics place Jesus' prayer in the context of his disciples being instructed to pray not to enter into trial (*peirasmos*).

One should also notice some important differences. Hebrews speaks of a "strong clamor" to God, and this does not occur in the Gethsemane prayer. In Hebrews Jesus' prayer to be saved from death is heard, presumably in the sense that he emerges from death victoriously; that does not apply readily to the Gethsemane prayer despite Omark's attempt ("Saving" 43–49) to argue that Luke's strengthening angel can be interpreted as a savior from death. The answer to the prayer about the hour or cup in all four Gospels confirms that Jesus must face death; the issue of whether or not he will be annihilated by death does not come to the fore. Moreover, at this stage in the passion Jesus has not really learned obedience through the things he *has suffered,* even if in Mark/Matt he is in the process of doing so.

(b) *Hebrews and the prayer on the cross:*
- Hebrews speaks of a strong clamor (*kraugē*); Mark/Matt describe Jesus as shouting (*boan*) his words to God with a loud cry (*phonē*).
- Hebrews is widely thought to echo a psalm such as 116; in Mark/Matt Jesus' words consist of Ps 22:2.
- Hebrews has Jesus cry to be saved from death; in Mark/Matt it is just before Jesus dies that he expresses his sense of being forsaken by God, presumably because he has been allowed to die such a wretched death without any visible support.
- Hebrews has Jesus made perfect after his suffering, i.e., taken into the heavenly sanctuary; the Synoptics have Jesus vindicated after his death by the tearing of the sanctuary veil of the Temple (Mark/Matt) and the centurion's confession (all three); John has life-giving signs of blood and water flow from the corpse on the cross; all four have Jesus raised from the dead (which is presumably what Hebrews means by stating that his prayer to be saved from death was heard; see 2:9). In terms of the vocabulary of being made perfect (*teleioun*), John 19:28,30 uses *teleioun* and *telein* to describe Jesus' last moments on the cross as he completes (perfects) the Scriptures and finishes the work the Father has given him to do.
- Elsewhere in Hebrews (9:12, 10:12) the being made perfect is interpreted as moving from death on the cross to the heavenly tabernacle carrying his blood, with little mention of burial among the dead (13:20); John portrays the crucifixion as a stage in the lifting up of the Son of Man, as Jesus passes from this world to the Father (12:32; 13:1; 17:11).

One should also notice some important differences. The prayer in Gethsemane about the hour/cup is closer than is the prayer on the cross to being a prayer to be "saved from," even if intrinsic to Jesus' citing Ps 22:2 on the cross is the plaintive hope that in the end "my God" will really not forsake "me." If by "fear" Hebrews means anxious fear, that resembles the Gethsemane prayer more than the prayer on the cross.

Overall there may be more similarities in Heb 5:7–10 to the Gethsemane prayer than to the prayer on the cross; yet I firmly disagree with those, like Feuillet and Omark, whose discussion would relate Hebrews only to Gethsemane. (That approach *sometimes* reflects an assumption that Mark's account of Gethsemane retains so much history that any reflection on Jesus' praying to be delivered would have to be related to it.) Schille and Brandenburger are more accurate in relating Hebrews to both Gospel prayers; but in my judgment the relationship is complicated and is not one of direct dependence of Hebrews on the Gospels or of the Gospels on Hebrews.

3. Development of the Different Prayers of Jesus

That Jesus struggled with and prayed to God about his impending death was an early Christian memory or understanding. As I explained in the first part of this ANALYSIS, the prayer struggle phrased in terms of the coming of the hour, of drinking the cup, and of being abandoned by God was taken over in the preMarcan and preJohannine traditions. Each tradition developed the theme in light of a different christology, and the respective evangelists continued that development in the process of fitting the sayings into a Gospel sequence. *Mark* has dramatically placed together at the beginning of the PN, in the context of the failure of the disciples, prayers about being delivered from the hour and the cup (modified by an acceptance of the divine will), and at the end of the PN, when no one has helped Jesus, a melancholy cry that he has been forsaken by his God, phrased in terms of Ps 22:2. This arrangement has the effect of drawing out Jesus' struggle concerning death[24] and reserving to the moment of his expiring God's response clarifying that it all ends in the victory of the Son.

In *John* even before the Last Supper Jesus himself resolves the issue of the hour by insisting that he does not want to be saved from it (12:27); toward the end of the supper he denies that during the hour he is ever left alone by the Father, even though the disciples will be scattered (16:32); and after the supper, at the beginning of the PN, when the disciples are let go by his own arrangement, Jesus insists that he must not be prevented from drinking the cup (18:11). Thus not struggle but victory in that struggle is emphasized throughout the sequence—a victory certain from the beginning because God always answers the prayer of a Jesus who says, "I and the Father are one."

Hebrews also draws upon the early theme that Jesus struggled with and prayed to God about his impending death but not in the "hour-cup-

---

[24]It is tempting to speculate that the lengthy struggle at the end of Jesus' life in Mark may be the functional equivalent of the testing of Jesus that Matt and Luke had in a lengthier form in the account of the three "temptations" by the devil at the beginning.

abandoned" phrasing known to the preGospel traditions. Rather Heb 5:7 draws upon the phrasing of an early Christian hymn which has described the theme in the language of the suffering, plaintive psalmist (e.g., Ps 116). Hebrews has used that phrasing of crying out from fear to the powerful One to be saved from death to emphasize its own christology that Jesus learned obedience through suffering and thus shared the trial of all of us before going to the heavenly sanctuary as the pioneer of salvation perfected through suffering (2:10; 12:2), the "forerunner on our behalf" (6:20).

The relationship of the Gospel presentations to each other and to Hebrews stems from their common dependence on the early theme that Jesus struggled with and prayed to God about his impending death. A discussion of historicity must center on that theme and not on the dramatic and theologically developed presentations of the theme in the Gospels and Hebrews, presentations intended not simply to report facts but to make the theme relevant to the lives of respective readers. APPENDIX VIII will deal with an extensive body of literature on Jesus' knowledge of his forthcoming death. *That, in the last days of his life in Jerusalem as the leaders of his people showed unremitting hostility,* both rejecting his proclamation and desiring to get rid of him, *Jesus would have struggled in prayer with God about how his death fitted into the inbreaking of God's kingdom is, in my judgment, so extremely plausible as to warrant certainty.* The objection that he already knew all the details of how his death fitted into the victory will be convincing to those whose theology can afford to ignore the many NT indications to the contrary. The opposite objection, that he could not have foreseen his death at the hands of his enemies, will be convincing to those who think that all reflection on the Scriptures (including Jeremiah, Deutero-Isaiah, and the psalms of the suffering just one) belongs to the early Christians and not to Jesus. That in his struggle and prayer Jesus could or would have prayed to be delivered from the death of an outlaw at the hands of his enemies will not shock those who give sufficient attention to Jesus' view that the inbreaking of God's kingdom involved a massive struggle with diabolic opposition in whose arsenal death had hitherto served as a mighty weapon. Heb 2:14 speaks of the enemy Jesus overcomes through death as "him who has the power of death, that is, the devil."

(*Bibliography for this* ANALYSIS *is found in §4, Part 2 or in the* GENERAL BIBLIOGRAPHY *[§3].*)

CONTENTS OF ACT I, SCENE TWO

§12. SECTIONAL BIBLIOGRAPHY
for Scene Two of Act I:
The Arrest of Jesus (§§13–16)

Part 1 covers the arrest scene in general (§§13,14,16); Part 2 concentrates on the Marcan episode of the naked flight of the young man (§15). General treatments of Jesus in Gethsemane, some of which include the arrest scene as well, are found in §4, Part 2. Bibliography on Judas Iscariot is found in §25, Part 3, and APPENDIX IV.

Part 1: The Arrest of Jesus (§§13,14,16)

Argyle, A. W., "The Meaning of *kath hēmeran* in Mark xiv. 49," ExpTim 63 (1951–52), 354.

Bartina, S., "'Yo soy Yahweh'—Nota exegética a Jn. 18,4–8," SBE 18 (1959), 393–416.

Belcher, F. W., "A Comment on Mark xiv.45," ExpTim 64 (1952–53), 240.

Charbonneau, A., "L'arrestation de Jésus, une victoire d'après la facture interne de Jn 18.1–11," ScEsp 34 (1982), 155–70.

Crossan, R. D., "Matthew 26:47–56—Jesus Arrested," in *Tradition as Openness to the Future,* eds. F. O. Francis and R. P. Wallace (Honor of W. W. Fisher; Lanham, MD: University Press of America, 1984), 175–90.

Deissmann, A., "'Friend, wherefore art thou come?'" ExpTim 33 (1921–22), 491–93.

Derrett, J.D.M., "Peter's Sword and Biblical Methodology," BeO 32 (1990), 180–92.

Dibelius, M., "Judas und der Judaskuss," DBG 1.272–77 (orig. pub. 1939).

Doeve, J. W., "Die Gefangennahme Jesu in Gethsemane. Eine traditionsgeschichtliche Untersuchung," StEv I, 458–80.

Droge, A. J., "The Status of Peter in the Fourth Gospel: A Note on John 18:10–11," JBL 109 (1990), 307–11.

Eltester, W., "'Freund, wozu du gekommen bist,' (Mt xxvi 50)," in *Neotestamentica et Patristica,* ed. W. C. van Unnik (O. Cullmann Festschrift; NovTSup 6; Leiden: Brill, 1962), 70–91.

Emmet, P. B., "St. Mark xiv.45," ExpTim 50 (1938–39), 93.

Giblin, C. H., "Confrontations in John 18,1–27," *Biblica* 65 (1984), 210–31.

Gillman, J., "A Temptation to Violence: The Two Swords in Lk 22:35–38," LS 9 (1982), 142–53.

Hall, S. G., "Swords of Offence," StEv I, 499–502.

Hingston, J. H., "John xviii. 5,6," ExpTim 32 (1920–21), 232.

Joüon, P., "Luc 22,50–51: *to ous, tou ōtiou,*" RechSR 24 (1934), 473–74.
Klostermann, E., "Zur Spiegelbergs Aufsatz 'Der Sinn von *eph ho parei* in Mt 26,50,'" ZNW 29 (1930), 311.
Kosmala, H., "Matthew xxvi 52—A Quotation from the Targum," NovT 4 (1960), 3–5.
Krieger, N., "Der Knecht des Hohenpriesters," NovT 2 (1957), 73–74.
Lampe, G.W.H., "The Two Swords (Luke 22:35–38)," JPHD 335–51.
Lee, G. M., "Matthew xxvi.50: *Hetaire, eph ho parei,*" ExpTim 81 (1969–70), 55.
Limbeck, M., "'Stecke dein Schwert in die Scheide . . . !' Die Jesusbewegung im Unterschied zu den Zeloten," BK 37 (1982), 98–104.
MacDonald, D., "Malchus' Ear," ExpTim 10 (1898–99), 188.
McVann, M., "Conjectures About a Guilty Bystander: The Sword Slashing in Mark 14:47," *Listening* 21 (1986), 124–37.
Mazzucco, C., "L'arresto di Gesù nel vangelo di Marco (*Mc* 14,43–52)," RivB 35 (1987), 257–82.
Mein, P., "A Note on John xviii.6," ExpTim 65 (1953–54), 286–87.
Minear, P. S., "A Note on Luke xxii 36," NovT 7 (1964–65), 128–34.
Nestle, Eb., "Zum Judaskuss," ZNW 15 (1914), 92–93.
Owen, E.C.E., "St Matthew xxvi 50," JTS 29 (1927–28), 384–86.
Peri, I., "Der Weggefährte," ZNW 78 (1987), 127–31 (on Matt 26:50).
Rehkopf, F., "Mt 26.50: *Hetaire eph' ho parei,*" ZNW 52 (1961), 109–15.
Reynen, H., "*Synagesthai,* Joh 18,2," BZ NS 5 (1961), 86–90.
Richter, G., "Die Gefangennahme Jesu nach dem Johannesevangelium (18,1–12)," *Bibel und Leben* 10 (1969), 26–39. Reprinted in RSJ 74–87.
Rostovtzeff, M., "*Ous dexion apotemnein,*" ZNW 33 (1934), 196–99 (Mark 14:47 and par.).
Schneider, G., "Die Verhaftung Jesu. Traditionsgeschichte von Mk 14.43–52," ZNW 63 (1972), 188–209.
Schwank, B., "Jesus überschreitet den Kidron (Joh 18,1–11)," SuS 29 (1964), 3–15.
Spiegelberg, W., "Der Sinn von *eph ho parei* in Mt 26,50," ZNW 28 (1929), 341–43.
Suggit, J., "Comrade Judas: Matthew 26:50," *Journal of Theology for Southern Africa* 63 (1988), 56–58.
Suhl, A., "Die Funktion des Schwertstreichs in den synoptischen Erzählungen von der Gefangennahme Jesu (Mk 14,43–52; Mt 26,47–56; Lk 22,47–53)," FGN 1.295–323.
Viviano, B., "The High Priest's Servant's Ear: Mark 14:47," RB 96 (1989), 71–80.
Wilson, J. P., "Matthew xxvi.50: 'Friend, wherefore art thou come?'" ExpTim 41 (1929–30), 334 (response to Deissmann).
Zorell, F., "'Amice, ad quod venisti!'" VD 9 (1929), 112–16.

Part 2: Mark 14:51–52 on the Naked Flight of a Young Man (§15)
Brown, R. E., "The Relation of 'The Secret Gospel of Mark' to the Fourth Gospel," CBQ 36 (1974), 466–85.
Cosby, M. R., "Mark 14:51–52 and the Problem of the Gospel Narrative," *Perspectives in Religious Studies* 11 (1984), 219–31.

Fleddermann, H., "The Flight of a Naked Young Man (Mark 14:51–52)," CBQ 41 (1979), 412–18.

Fuller, R. H., "Longer Mark: Forgery, Interpolation, or Oral Tradition," in Colloquy 18 of the Center for Hermeneutical Studies (Berkeley, CA: Graduate Theological Union, 1976), 1–11.

Gourgues, M., "À propos du symbolisme christologique et baptismal de Marc 16.5," NTS 27 (1981), 672–78 (in ref. to Mark 14:51–52).

Gundry, R. H., *Mark: A Commentary on His Apology for the Cross* (Grand Rapids: Eerdmans, 1993), 603–23 (on the *Secret Gospel of Mark*).

Jenkins, A. K., "Young Man or Angel?" ExpTim 94 (1982–83), 237–40.

Knox, J., "A Note on Mark 14:51–52," in *The Joy of Study*, ed. S. E. Johnson (F. C. Grant Volume; New York: MacMillan, 1951), 27–30.

Koester, H., "History and Development of Mark's Gospel (From Mark to *Secret Mark* and 'Canonical Mark')," in *Colloquy on New Testament Studies*, ed. B. Corley (Macon, GA: Mercer, 1983), 35–57.

McIndoe, J. H., "The Young Man at the Tomb," ExpTim 80 (1968–69), 125 (in ref. to Mark 14:51–52).

Meyer, M. W., "The Youth in the *Secret Gospel of Mark*," *Semeia* 49 (1990), 129–53.

Monloubou, L., "L'étonnant destin d'un personnage évangélique," *Chronique. Supplément au Bulletin de Littérature Ecclesiastique* 1 (1984), 25–28.

Neirynck, F., "La fuite du jeune homme en Mc 14,51–52," ETL 55 (1979), 43–66. Reprinted in NEv 1.215–38.

Nolle, L., "The Young Man in Mk. xiv,51," *Scripture* 2 (1947), 113–14.

Ross, J. M., "The Young Man who Fled Naked," IBS 13 (1991), 170–74.

Saunderson, B., "Gethsemane: The Missing Witness," *Biblica* 70 (1989), 224–33.

Schenke, H.-M., "The Mystery of the Gospel of Mark," *The Second Century* 4 (1984), 65–82.

Schnellbächer, E. L., "Das Rätsel des *neaniskos* bei Markus," ZNW 73 (1982), 127–35.

Scroggs, R., and K. I. Groff, "Baptism in Mark: Dying and Rising with Christ," JBL 92 (1973), 531–48, esp. 536–40.

Smith, M., *Clement of Alexandria and a Secret Gospel of Mark* (Cambridge, MA: Harvard Univ., 1973).

———, "Clement of Alexandria and Secret Mark: The Score at the End of the First Decade," HTR 75 (1982), 449–61.

———, "Merkel on the Longer Text of Mark," ZTK 72 (1975), 133–50.

Vanhoye, A., "La fuite du jeune homme nu (Mc 14,51–52)," *Biblica* 52 (1971), 401–6.

Waetjen, H., "The Ending of Mark and the Gospel's Shift in Eschatology," ASTI 4 (1965), 114–31, esp. 114–21 on Mark 14:51–52; 16:5.

§13. THE ARREST OF JESUS, PART ONE: THE INITIAL ENCOUNTER

(Mark 14:43–46; Matt 26:47–50; Luke 22:47–48; John 18:2–8a)

Translation

Mark 14:43–46: [43]And immediately, while he was still speaking, there arrives Judas, one of the Twelve, and with him a crowd with swords and wooden clubs, from the chief priests and the scribes and the elders. [44]The one who was giving him over had given them a signal, saying, "Whomever I shall kiss, he is (the one). Seize him and lead him away securely." [45]And having come, immediately having come up to him, he says, "Rabbi," and he kissed him warmly. [46]But they laid hands on him and seized him.

Matt 26:47–50: [47]And while he was still speaking, behold Judas, one of the Twelve, came, and with him a numerous crowd with swords and wooden clubs, from the chief priests and elders of the people. [48]But the one who was giving him over gave them a sign, saying, "Whomever I shall kiss, he is (the one). Seize him." [49]And immediately having come up to Jesus, he said, "Hail, Rabbi," and he kissed him warmly. [50]But Jesus said to him, "Friend, that's what you are here for." Then, having come up, they laid hands on Jesus and seized him.

Luke 22:47–48: [47]While he was still speaking, behold a crowd; and the man named Judas, one of the Twelve, was coming in front of them; and he came near Jesus to kiss him. [48]But Jesus said to him, "Judas, with a kiss do you give over the Son of Man?"

John 18:2–8a: [2]But Judas too, the one who was giving him over, knew this place because many times Jesus had come there together with his disciples. [3]So Judas, having taken the cohort and, from the chief priests and the Pharisees, attendants, comes there with lanterns and torches and weapons. 4So Jesus, having known all the things to come upon him, came out and says to them, "Whom are you seeking?" 5They answered him, "Jesus the Nazorean." He says to them, "I am (he)." Now standing there with them was also Judas, the one who was giving him over. 6So as Jesus said to them, "I am (he)," they went backward and fell to the ground. 7So again he asked them, "Whom are you seeking?" But they said, "Jesus the Nazorean." 8aJesus answered, "I told you that I am (he)."

COMMENT

The arrest scene will be divided into three parts. Part One (§13), after recounting the previous role of Judas in each Gospel, discusses his arrival along with those who will arrest Jesus. To identify Jesus the Synoptic Judas approaches him with a kiss; in the larger Johannine account Jesus identifies himself and incapacitates the arresting party. Part Two (§14) treats a set of incidents that occur just after the arresting party has taken custody of Jesus in Mark/Matt and just before that seizure in Luke and John. Most prominent among them are the cutting off of the servant's ear and Jesus' words and citation of Scripture to the arresting party. Part Three (§15) covers a puzzling event reported by Mark alone: A young man who attempts to follow Jesus flees away naked. A common ANALYSIS will be offered in §16 for all three parts, discussing composition. The SECTIONAL BIBLIOGRAPHY on the arrest is found in §12.

As for Part One, which we now begin, the subsections are listed on p. 235 above.

PREVIOUS PORTRAYAL OF JUDAS IN EACH GOSPEL

Later in this book, APPENDIX IV will be devoted to Judas, the meaning of Iscariot, and Judas' possible motives for acting against Jesus. Here I am concerned with what each evangelist has already told his reader that would make Judas' action in this scene intelligible.

Mark. In 14:1–2 Mark states that the chief priests and scribes are seeking to seize Jesus and kill him, employing a stealthy maneuver that would not cause the people to riot during the festival. Shortly afterward (14:10–11) Mark reports that Judas Iscariot, one of the Twelve, goes to the chief priests in order to give him over. Presumably Judas' appearance before them is not by happenstance; but the reader is left to surmise how Judas found out that the chief priests were seeking help—their desire to avoid a riot meant that they could not have sought help publicly. No reason is offered by Mark why Judas wants to give Jesus over. But in response to his offer, the chief priests rejoice and promise to give him money. No sum is specified, and we are never actually told that they did so, although that may be the most plausible meaning of *apechei* in 14:41 (APPENDIX III A). The scene finishes with Judas seeking how he could give over Jesus opportunely. At the Last Supper (14:18–21) Jesus announces, *"One of you* [the Twelve] eating with me *will give me over."* In response to the "Is it I?" posed by one after the other, Jesus says it is one of the Twelve who is *dipping* bread in the same dish with him and warns this one who is giving over the Son of Man that it would have been better for him if he had not been born. (The phrases that I have italicized are common to Mark, Matt, and John; and a variant of the first is in Luke.) Notice that the Marcan Jesus never mentions who the betrayer is. Judas, in fact, is never mentioned by name at the Synoptic Last Supper; and so his departure from the supper is never indicated. Theoretically in the flow of the narrative, as Judas arrives with the arresting party, it might come as a surprise to the reader that Judas had not accompanied his fellow disciples when they came with Jesus to Gethsemane; for 14:26 would give the impression that those who were at the supper went to the Mount of Olives. Moreover, since Mark never indicates that Jesus had gone to Gethsemane before, it is not apparent how Judas knew where to find Jesus.

I have just noted many illogicalities, but none of these gaps in the Marcan story should be pressed seriously. The ordinary reader of Mark's fast-flowing narrative would not dream of asking many of the above questions; and if some ancient forerunner of the modern biblical critics pressed the readers of Mark about these points, they would have made plausible guesses to fill in the lacunae. And that is surely what Matt and Luke did as they rewrote their version of Mark's account, where some of those very questions I posed are answered. Also one must imagine that a mysterious, villainous figure like Judas would have been the subject of Christian popular imagination and folkloric tales. (The death he is assigned by Matt 27:3–10, discussed in §29 below is but one of the three demises recounted by early Christians.) Therefore, Matt and Luke may have had other popular information, as well as their own guesses, to fill in Marcan lacunae—an observation that is respectable so long as we realize that such other information need not represent fact. Little factual information may have been known about this man.

Matt. Taking over Marcan information, Matt adds a few details to the immediate presupper dealings between the chief priests and Judas. In Matt 26:3–5 we find the elders of the people (in place of the Marcan scribes) plotting with the chief priests against Jesus, and we are told that they gathered together in the *aulē* ("court, palace, courtyard") of the high priest Caiaphas. Matt will bring us to that *aulē* again when Jesus is taken for trial before the same Caiaphas (mentioned by Matt, not by Mark) and when Peter denies Jesus (26:57–58,69). Intriguingly, Matt 26:14–16 adds that Judas was paid thirty pieces of silver. We shall hear more of that as a scriptural motif in 27:3 when Matt (and he alone) stops the PN to narrate the death of Judas. At the Last Supper in 26:21–25 there is an expansion beyond Mark's account: When Judas too asks "Is it I, Rabbi?"[1] Jesus answers, "You have said so." Now the reader has been informed not only that Jesus was aware of the precise identity of the betrayer, but also that Judas knew Jesus was aware! This touch is both dramatic and protective of christology.

Luke. In the immediate presupper material Luke 22:2 follows Mark closely and more concisely in the plotting of the chief priests and scribes against Jesus; but without any interlude[2] Luke (22:3–6) presents an adapted form of Judas' coming to them. Money is mentioned by Luke, but no specific sum (see also Acts 1:18). Luke's chief addition is to explain why Judas went to the chief priests and *stratēgoi* ("captains [of the Temple]"), namely, that Satan entered into him. At the Last Supper Luke 22:21–23 follows Mark closely, but again more concisely. He omits the "Is it I?" formulation of the disciples' question and the reference to dipping bread in the same dish, but keeps the statement that Jesus will be handed over by one who is at table with him. This abbreviation may be another reflection of Luke's tendency to play down unfavorable memories of the Twelve. As in Mark, Judas is never mentioned by name at the supper, nor is his departure.

John. Any comparison between what John has told his readers about Judas and what the Synoptics have told theirs is complicated by the scattered placement of the Johannine parallels. Between the plotting of the priests two days before Passover and the arrival of Judas to offer his services just before Passover, Mark 14:3–9 and Matt 26:6–13 place a scene where a woman anoints Jesus' head with expensive ointment. In that scene "some" (Mark) or the disciples (Matt) complain about the waste, but Jesus explains that she has anointed his body for burial. John's parallel (12:1–8) occurs six days before Passover after he has described how the chief priests and Pharisees, who gathered together with the Sanhedrin, at Caiaphas' instigation planned

---

[1]Matt makes a distinction between Judas, who calls Jesus "Rabbi," and the others, who call him "Lord"; disciples should not use "Rabbi" (23:7–8). All this goes beyond Mark's "Is it I?"

[2]Between the plot (Mark 14:1–2) and the coming of Judas to take part in the plot (14:10–11), Mark intercalates the story of the woman anointing Jesus' head (14:3–9). Luke's rearrangement is an example of his writing an account more orderly than that found in the narratives compiled before his (1:1,3).

to kill Jesus (11:47–53).[3] When Mary, the sister of Martha and Lazarus, anoints Jesus' feet, Judas Iscariot is the disciple who protests. The evangelist supplies an evaluation: "Not because he was concerned for the poor did he say this, but because he was a thief. He held the money box and could help himself to what was put in." This is the only Johannine mention of money in relation to Judas; it is not the chief priests' payment for betrayal but the fruits of his own habitual theft. Thus John gives Judas a bad character and makes the soon-to-come unfaithfulness less surprising.

In the Johannine Last Supper Judas is mentioned twice. At the beginning (13:2) we are told that the devil had already put it into the heart of Judas, son of Simon the Iscariot, to give Jesus over. This explanation of Judas' wickedness was foreshadowed in John 6:70–71 when Jesus said that one of the Twelve was a devil and the evangelist supplied a note identifying the figure as Judas. In this motif John is close to Luke (22:3), who has Satan entering into Judas called Iscariot before the supper, and both are probably reflecting a popular Christian evaluation of the betrayer as doing diabolic work. Later in the supper, John 13:18–30 constitutes an account of Jesus' prediction of the betrayal that is much more lengthy than any in the Synoptics. Besides an oracular statement by Jesus about one who eats bread with him lifting his heel against him (conformed to Ps 41:10[4]), there is an interchange between Simon Peter and the beloved disciple as to whom Jesus means. Jesus identifies the betrayer by dipping a morsel of bread into the dish and giving it to Judas. "And then, after the morsel, Satan entered into that man" (12:27). John reports that Jesus told Judas to do what he was going to do quickly, and so Judas went out into the night. In another helpful note, the evangelist explains that none of the others understood what was happening because they thought that Jesus was telling Judas to draw on the common money box to buy something. Here, whether or not John knew Mark's account, many of the lacunae in the behavior of the Marcan Judas are filled in, including the departure from the supper. (Yet a new lacuna is created: Since John has told us nothing about Judas' dealings with the chief priests, we are left to wonder how so quickly that night Judas could get together a Roman cohort and some attendants from the chief priests and Pharisees.) How much of what is used to make the story flow better in John represents historical memory and how much represents a better storytelling sense? Was Judas in fact the treasurer for the community of those who followed Jesus, or does this description supply context for a

---

[3]Despite the time differences in relation to the Passover, both Mark and John place the anointing scene after the chief priests and their allies have decided on Jesus' death.

[4]Glasson ("Davidic") points out that Ps 41 is entitled "A psalm of David," and so the perfidy described therein would be seen as a reference to Ahithophel, who for Matt serves as a type of Judas.

popular denigration of Judas as a thief? So much skepticism is not warranted, even if we cannot be certain.

THE ARRIVAL OF JUDAS (MARK 14:43A,44A; MATT 26:47A,48A; LUKE 22:47A; JOHN 18:2)

In John's account of the scene in the garden across the Kidron to which Jesus came after the Last Supper, Jesus has spoken no words or prayer. Thus one gets the impression that the Johannine Jesus, who had sent Judas out from the supper to do quickly what he was going to do, has come to this place which Judas knows well in order to encounter the betrayer and the hostile forces aligned with him. Reynen ("*Synagesthai*") argues that the verb used by John in 18:2 implies that Jesus had often gathered his disciples there and stayed with them in that place; see *synagesthai* in Acts 11:26. In the Synoptics, even though Jesus has predicted betrayal by one of the Twelve (by Judas in Matt), there is an artistic touch of suddenness in having Judas arrive while Jesus is still speaking—especially since we have *not* been told that Judas had left the supper and therefore was not with the disciples in Gethsemane.

Matt has a logical progression in the verbs used in 26:45,46,47. The hour and the one who was going to give over Jesus were both said to have "come near" (*ēggiken*); now Judas is said to have "come" (*ēlthen*). Mark's sequence in 14:41,42,43 is less smooth: The hour has "come" (*ēlthen*); the giver-over has "come near" (*ēggiken*); Judas arrives (*paraginetai*). In both Gospels, however, the appearance of Judas fulfills Jesus' words at the end of the prayer scene: "Behold the one who gives me over has come near." Mark heightens the fulfillment by using his beloved *euthys* ("immediately"; forty-one of fifty-three NT uses are Marcan). Matt inserts an *idou* ("behold"), thus offering a sequence of three verses, each using that word. That technique underlines the insight that the arrival of Judas in 26:47 marks the beginning of the hour identified as coming near in 26:45. Luke too has an *idou;* but it calls immediate attention to the crowd, not to Judas as in Matt.[5] Indeed, in Luke what Jesus was saying when he was interrupted by this arrival did not deal with the betrayer as in Mark/Matt but with the disciples' praying lest they enter into trial. For Luke the presence now of the crowd is a significant sign that the great trial is beginning.

[5]Granted that Matt and Luke use *idou* differently here, the fact that they both have that word versus Mark's *euthys* is not a significant agreement. *Idou* is frequent in both Matt (61 times) and Luke (56), not in Mark (8). The thesis of Doeve ("Gefangennahme" 462) that they are translating an Aramaic *hā'* that Mark omitted is an illustration of unnecessarily positing a Semitic original. In particular, Matt is following Mark closely here but ameliorating Mark's overly long and grammatically awkward opening sentence.

In all four Gospels at the opening of this arrest scene a phrase identifies Judas: either "one of the Twelve" (Synoptics) or "the one who was giving him over" (John[6]). Some scholars (e.g., K. G. Kuhn, "Jesus" 261) who think that the preGospel PN originally began with the arrest (perhaps preceded only by a geographical notice now embedded in the preceding arrival and prayer scenes) have observed that in that original PN this would have been the first time Judas was mentioned, whence the need to identify him for the readers. In particular, Luke's "the man named [*ho legomenos*] Judas" might seem to point in that direction, since that phrase when employed elsewhere by Luke (22:1 and Acts 3:2) introduces something to the readers. As for previous uses of "one of the Twelve," Schneider ("Verhaftung" 196) would see Mark 14:10,20 as back-formations from the identification here. Yet caution is required in evaluating this thesis. Since "one of the Twelve" is a designation for Judas that occurs in all four Gospels, one may well argue that it was preMarcan; but one can also doubt that even on that preMarcan level it was merely an identification of Judas. Why were not other members of the Twelve also so introduced to readers? In the Synoptics, outside the lists of the Twelve, the designation "one of the Twelve" was applied to Judas every time he has been mentioned up to this point except in Matt 26:25 (where "the Twelve" appears in the context: 26:20). Can all these be back-formations from a primary identification here? Indeed, of nine NT uses of the phrase, eight apply to Judas, one to Thomas (John 20:24). I suggest that already in the tradition this fixed designation vocalized Christian distress that Jesus was betrayed by one of his chosen Twelve (see Dibelius, "Judas" 272). Certainly, that motif and not identification is the import of the phrase as it now occurs in Mark 14:43 (and par.), following two previous uses of it in chap. 14.

THE ARRESTING PARTY (MARK 14:43B; MATT 26:47B; [LUKE 22:52]; JOHN 18:3)

The Synoptics portray a crowd (Matt: "numerous") coming with Judas. Matt has used "numerous" before (8:18; 15:30; 19:2) but for crowds favorable to Jesus. In APPENDIX V I shall discuss the varied vocabulary used by the evangelists to describe those hostile to Jesus, both the collectivity (crowd, people) and the Jewish authorities; but here let me concentrate on how each Synoptic evangelist portrays the components of the crowd and on John's picture of soldiers and police attendants.

---

[6]Six times previously John identified Judas as the one giving Jesus over (6:64,71; 12:4; 13:2,11,21), but see "one of the Twelve" in 6:71 and "one of his disciples" in 12:4.

Mark's portrayal is closely followed by Matt. Many commentators have judged that these two evangelists give the impression that an armed rabble has come "with" (*meta*) Judas. This impression needs to be modified by the indication that the crowd has delegation "from" (*para* in Mark; *apo* in Matt) Jewish authorities who make up the Sanhedrin. No vigilantism or lynch mentality is implied, then; and there is no suggestion that the arrest at night is illegal. The Marcan readers will not be surprised by the involvement of chief priests, scribes, and elders. Jesus had predicted that in 8:31, and they plotted with Judas in 14:1–2,10.[7] The effort may have been hastily arranged, but the night setting is harmonious with Mark 14:2 and the desire to prevent a commotion during the feast. Bickermann ("Utilitas" 172–74) warns that we may not be reading "crowd" with sufficient awareness that in the Empire the whole community had responsibility for the maintenance of order. If there were danger of banditry (Mark 14:48 and par.), the Sanhedrin could have forcibly recruited the populace and given them small arms for the occasion. In any case, "rabble" or "mob" is an overinterpretation.

What coloring do the weapons mentioned in Mark/Matt give to the picture? Machaira, while it can refer to a large knife, normally means "sword"; and Matt 26:52 will indicate that the *machaira* drawn to cut off the servant's ear came from a scabbard or a sheath. Thus the reader is led to think of military or paramilitary arms. *Xylos* covers a range of wooden articles (in this instance: clubs, poles, staves) and might give the impression of "pickup" weapons.[8] Mark/Matt give no hint of the presence of regular military or of police in Gethsemane, although *hypēretai* (attendants of the priests with police duties) will be present when Jesus is brought to the court(yard) of the high priest to be interrogated (Mark 14:54; Matt 26:58). Presumably "the servant [*doulos*] of the high priest" who had his ear cut off (all four Gospels) is conceived by Mark/Matt as part of the crowd from the chief priests.

Luke's portrayal has a different impact. The arrival of a crowd is mentioned even before Judas; that may be a touch of Lucan logic, since a crowd would be seen before the individual. More orderliness is implied by the statement that Judas came in front of them (as a guide in Acts 1:16). There is no reference to weapons. Later in the Lucan scene (22:52) Jesus addresses "the chief priests and captains [*stratēgoi*] of the Temple and elders who were arrived against him." Once again I refer the reader to APPENDIX V for an overall discussion of these authorities, including the "captains," who are pe-

---

[7]Similarly the Matthean readers: Matt 16:21; 26:3,14. For Matt's omission of "scribes" here, and the specification "elders *of the people*," see APPENDIX V.

[8]Yet Blinzler (*Trial* 70–72) points to an instance in Josephus (*War* 2.9.4; #176) where Roman soldiers were armed with these wooden clubs.

culiar *in the PN* to Luke. This is the only time Luke makes a triad out of
those three groups (but see Acts 4:1–3 and 4:5). Normally paired against
Jesus or the Christians are the chief priests and the (Temple) captain(s),[9]
while the Sanhedrin triad is "the chief priests, the scribes, and the elders."[10] Although we know such officials had plotted Jesus' death (Luke
22:2,4) and so are extremely hostile, their presence as all or part of the
crowd removes any tone of irregular rabble. In all three Synoptics Jesus
will challenge the arresting party by asking why they have come out as
if against a bandit with swords and clubs. (In Mark/Matt the mention of
swords and clubs at the beginning may be editorial preparation for those
words of Jesus.) Only then does Luke acknowledge the presence of these
weapons in the arresting party; but since the Lucan Jesus addresses those
words to a group containing Temple captains who supervise order, the
presence of the weapons also seems less disorganized than in Mark/Matt.
In a certain sense Luke's account, which has a crowd consisting in part
of Temple captains, forms a bridge between Mark/Matt's account of a
crowd and John's account which has no crowd but soldiers and police-
like attendants.

John's portrayal of the arresting party begins with "Judas, having taken
the cohort." The verb is probably not meant to imply that Judas had authority
over the cohort (pace Winter, *On the Trial* 62), since the presence of a commander will be mentioned in 18:12. Rather it means that Judas took the
cohort with him, acting as a guide (BAGD 464[1a]; BDF 418[5]). Actually once
on the scene Judas is passive, "standing there" with the arresting party in
18:5. Although there are instances of Greek *speira* rendering Latin *manipulus* (two hundred troops), it is the normal word for the Roman cohort (one-
tenth of a legion, six hundred troops). That John means the latter is suggested by the title *chiliarchos* given to the commander in 18:12, the normal
Greek rendering of the *tribunus militum* who was over a cohort. (Those who
reduce the cohort to a *manipulus* have to reduce him to a *decurio,* a type of
corporal.) Some have tried to argue that John could have been thinking of a
Jewish force rather than a Roman one.[11] Yet the evangelist clearly distinguishes these troops, for whom he uses technical Roman terminology, from
the attendants supplied by "the chief priests and the Pharisees" (18:3) or "of
the Jews" (18:12)—a distinction that indicates the cohort is not Jewish or
under the direct command of Jewish authorities. Below in §31, n. 64 I shall

[9]Luke 22:4; Acts 4:1; 5:24.
[10]Luke 22:66; 9:22; 20:1; cf. Acts 6:12 and 7:1.
[11]Blinzler, *Trial* 64–70; Benoit, *Passion* 46. One can appeal to the LXX (Judith 14:11; II Macc
8:23) and to Josephus (*War* 2.1.3; #11; *Ant.* 17.9.3; #215), where Roman military terms are used for
non-Roman troops.

caution, however, that the troops under the command of the prefect of Judaea were not crack legionaries or necessarily ethnic Romans; many of them would have been recruits from the Syro-Palestinian area. The use of six hundred soldiers to arrest Jesus seems to some to make the Johannine narrative quite implausible.[12] If one does posit tradition behind it, we may have here the (confused) memory of a *speira* that Mark 15:16 and Matt 27:27 locate at the praetorium of Pilate when the full cohort is called together to see the mockery and flagellation of Jesus.

John has a second group in the arresting party, hypēretai "from [*ek;* cf. Mark*'s para;* Matt's *apo*] the chief priests and the Pharisees," also identified as "of the Jews" in 18:12.[13] While this is John's last reference to the Pharisees (see APPENDIX V) and therefore they are not *by name* active in the PN, we should not underestimate the psychological importance of this reference, which connects the arrest of Jesus with previous attempts of "the chief priests and the Pharisees" to seize Jesus through "attendants" and with their Sanhedrin decision to arrest him (7:32,45; 11:47,57). Probably from the viewpoint of the readers who had lived through the Johannine community history, the Pharisees were the main opponents in the synagogues at the time when the Gospel was being written. The combination "the chief priests and the Pharisees" was a way of juxtaposing the enemies of Jesus and the enemies of the community. On a historical level, in Jesus' time surely there were scribes of Pharisee persuasion in the Sanhedrin constituency, but we have no way of knowing whether John was evoking that.

While *hypēretēs* (literally "under-rower") can cover a wide range of servants and helpers (as in I Cor 4:1; Acts 13:5; 26:16), NT usage of the term is most frequently in policing situations.[14] Blinzler (*Trial* 62–68; *Prozess* 126–28) would make a sharp distinction between two groups with policing powers: (a) the Temple Levites or police, who maintained order within the Temple precincts and only in great crises were used outside; (b) court servants at the disposal of the Sanhedrin when necessary for police purposes. One can doubt that the evangelists knew the situation with such precision (if such precision existed at Jesus' time); but Blinzler is surely right in claiming that the second group is closer to what is in mind here, whence my transla-

---

[12]Acts 23:23 has almost five hundred soldiers assigned to conduct Paul to Caesarea, but that is understandable as a measure to protect against a planned ambush on the journey.

[13]The ms. evidence is divided about inserting "from the" before "Pharisees" (as in John 7:32; 11:47,57) or omitting it (7:45). The presence of the phrase may be a corrective to avoid the impression that the chief priests and Pharisees (often unfriendly to each other) were one group. Josephus, *Life* 5; #21, mentions them together but as separate groups.

[14]In Matt 5:25 the judge hands a convicted offender over to the attendant. In Acts 5:22,26 the attendants are sent to find the apostles in prison and then go out with the Temple captain to arrest them. Josephus (*Ant.* 4.8.14; #214), drawing on the OT, gives a picture of "attendants from [*ek*] the Levites" being assigned to local magistrates in carrying out justice.

tion "attendants" rather than the more specific "police," even in John's PN where they have a clear policing function.

The arresting party in John comes with "lanterns and torches and weapons." Some (e.g., Winter) have harmonized with the Synoptics by claiming that the Roman soldiers carried swords and the Jewish attendants carried batons (clubs), but that is unnecessary. John does not specify the weapons of the arresting party; the first reference to a sword (*machaira*) will come when Simon Peter uses his to cut off the servant's ear. The lanterns and torches could have had a simple, practical use on a dark night.[15] John's stress in 13:30 that it was night, however, was theologically symbolic, as Judas went over to the realm of darkness (see John 1:5; 3:20; 12:35,46). Accordingly, there could be bitter irony that these forces need illumination because they cannot see the light of the world (3:19; 8:12; 9:5).

That leads us into the question of whether John's description of the arresting party is historical, theological, or both. That it is theologically symbolic should be evident. Both Roman and Jewish troops have come to take Jesus of Nazareth, and despite their apparent power they will be forced to the ground before him (18:6). Does that mean the participation of Roman troops in the arrest cannot be historical? Acts 4:1–3 and 5:26 show arrests of Peter and John made by the Jewish authorities without Roman involvement (but also without any hint that these men were to be put to death). Acts 21:27–36 shows a "crowd" seizing and trying to kill Paul in the Temple precincts, interrupted by a tribune of the cohort who himself with his soldiers arrested Paul. Thus Roman participation in an arrest desired by Jews might depend on circumstances. Those who opt for the historicity of the Johannine picture often come to this view from very different scholarly backgrounds, e.g., Bruce, Goguel, Winter. A wide range of scholars from Mommsen through Blinzler to Barrett and Lohse reject historicity. Besnier ("Procès" 198) estimates that there were too few Roman troops in Jerusalem for a cohort or any sizable number to have been sent out against an unarmed man. Others contend that Roman soldiers would never have delivered a prisoner to a Jewish high priest (as in 18:13). But is that so certain if Pilate had ordered such a delivery and wanted to know how the highest Jewish authorities evaluated this man? A Roman cohort under a Roman centurion would not have joined in a planned arrest without being ordered to do so by the Roman prefect. Most of the Gospel evidence, including John's account in 18:29ff., would give no hint that Pilate became involved with Jesus before

---

[15]The fact that the paschal moon would be nearly full is scarcely an objection, for the night could have been cloudy.

the Jewish authorities delivered him.[16] It would be a fascinatingly different picture if Pilate was consulted by the high priest about the arrest of Jesus and cooperated in it with Roman troops because he wanted Jesus investigated by the Sanhedrin. In John's Roman trial Pilate is rather sympathetic to Jesus and plots to have him released; and so one could argue that John would not have invented Roman participation in the arrest scene because it really does not fit his own view of Pilate's role.

All that probably is too subtle. Except for using Roman military terms (which he may be using in a popular, inexact way to supply color, somewhat the way we speak of Roman legions, no matter the quality or quantity of the troops), John has done nothing to help the reader recognize Pilate's participation here. Jesus' power even over Roman troops is the evangelist's interest; he may never have seen that as a conflict with the portrait of Pilate he will paint, since Jesus will frighten the Roman prefect as well (19:8). No matter how fascinating the historical implications of the Johannine scene, we have no way of confirming or denying it.

While the Gospels vary on the constituency of the arresting party, they agree that Judas was able to gain the assistance of this group swiftly and at night. In the Synoptics that is more easily explained, for even before the Last Supper (Mark 14:1–2,10–11 and par.) Judas had been plotting with the chief priests and others who would eventually play a role in the Sanhedrin trial. John tells us nothing about Judas' involvement in a plot (but see 11:57), and his decision to betray seems to have come during the supper (John 13:2,26–30). Yet Judas did leave the supper early and was instructed to act quickly. As for the necessity of having Judas' help and the precise assistance he rendered in the procedure against Jesus, I shall leave to APPENDIX IV scholarly speculations. If we confine ourselves to what is stated in the Synoptics, Judas' function as a betrayer is twofold. First, he goes before or with the (armed) arresting party, showing them how to seize Jesus on the Mount of Olives at night, thus *where* and *when*. This information fulfills the desire of the Jewish authorities to arrest Jesus by stealth and not cause a riot among the people (Mark 12:12 and par.; Mark 14:1–2; Matt 26:4–5; cf. Luke 22:2). Second, in that setting he identifies Jesus amid his disciples, thus *who*. As I stressed in discussing *paradidonai* (p. 211 above), the primary meaning is not "to betray" but "to give over." Judas gave Jesus over by making it possible to arrest him; there is no evidence he betrayed secrets. Curiously some (e.g., Hendrickx, *Passion* 6–7) question the identifying role of Judas on the

---

[16]Yet H. Conzelmann (*The Theology of St. Luke* [New York: Harper, 1960], 90–91) contends that in Acts 3:13–14; 4:27; 13:28 there is evidence for preLucan formulas that attribute to Pilate great responsibility in the death of Jesus.

grounds that Jesus had taught publicly in the Temple and it is improbable that the arresting party would not have known him. Factually in Mark, as we shall see, Jesus has *not* taught in the Temple often. Moreover, this is the first mention in Mark of the crowd hostile to Jesus (see APPENDIX V), so there would be no reason for the readers to think this crowd knows him. The readers also know that it is night and Jesus is surrounded by his disciples. It is interesting that both the Synoptic tradition and the Johannine report that Jesus had to be identified. The Synoptics have Judas do it with a kiss; John has Jesus identify himself. These two different accounts of identification are our next concern.

IDENTIFICATION OF JESUS BY JUDAS' KISS (MARK 14:44B–45; MATT 26:48B–49; LUKE 22:47B)

While the three Synoptics refer to a kiss by Judas, the idea that the kiss was a prearranged sign for identifying is stated in Mark/Matt, but only implied in Jesus' question in Luke 22:48. Mark (14:44) uses the pluperfect "had given," thus making the moment of the actual kiss the focus of the narrative. Matt's "gave" makes the narrative more sequential, with each action of Judas (gave, said, kissed) having its own importance. The somewhat unusual Marcan *syssēmon* ("signal") is replaced by Matt with the more common *sēmeion* ("sign"). I have rendered literally Mark's *autos estin*, "he is" (although it is unexceptional Greek for "it is he" or "he is the one") because of its resemblance to the answer John puts in direct discourse, "I am," and of which he makes theological use (see below).

Leaving a discussion of the import of the kiss to the enactment in Mark 14:45, let me discuss the preliminaries. In 14:44 the instruction to the arresting party is "Seize him and lead him away *asphalōs*." The second part of that instruction is reported neither by Matt, who follows Mark closely, nor by Luke, who abbreviates. The noun *asphaleia* can mean "safety" in the sense of without harm; it is combined with "peace" in I Thess 5:3. The idea that the Marcan Judas wanted to be sure that Jesus was led away safely has sparked romantic speculation about Judas having a secret plan whereby Jesus or his cause would emerge triumphant (see APPENDIX IV). Indeed, some would find NT confirmation of this in Matt 27:3, where Judas repents when he sees that Jesus had been condemned by the Sanhedrin—did he never wish things to go that far? While Mark/Matt use *philein* in the planning of the kiss, both use *kataphilein* (intensive: kiss warmly) in describing the action. Belcher ("Comment") would argue that by the time he kissed Jesus, Judas was already repenting and trying to show his love in the very act. (Matt's ambiguous answer by Jesus [to be discussed below at length] would then mean: Don't stop; go on and do that for which you are here.) At the opposite extreme, Emmet ("St. Mark") would interpret the warmth of *kataphilein* to mean that Judas puts his arms around Jesus and thus stops him from escaping! I see all of this as overinterpretation and the *kataphilein* as no more than vivid narrative. Similarly, I prefer the dominant meaning of *asphaleia* (and the adjective and adverb associated with it): "security." In Acts 16:23 *tērein asphalōs* means to guard prisoners securely. Mark's Judas is not interested in the safety of Jesus but in his not getting away. Perhaps the reason why Matt does not include this section of Mark's directive is that while the seizing part of Judas' command will be implemented immediately (next verse), the leading away securely will not take place until Mark 14:53/Matt 26:57; and so Mark's double command is a bit awkward. SPNM 123 alludes to Matt's "typical simplification."

The approach of Judas to Jesus in Mark 14:45 is described with confusing repetitiveness ("having come" [*elthōn*]; "having come up to" [*proselthōn*]). The "having come" is reiterative of the arrival in 14:43 after the parenthetical 14:44. Again Matt simplifies (also clarifying by inserting Jesus' name), and Luke abbreviates. A word needs to be said about *proserchesthai* ("to come up to or near"), which occurs here for the first time in the PN. Of some 90 NT uses of this verb, about 52 are in Matt and almost three-quarters of those have Jesus as the person approached. Because a great number of the 115 LXX uses are cultic inasmuch as worshipers approach God, often to sacrifice, J. R. Edwards (JBL 106 [1987], 65–74) has argued that Matt uses the term deliberately most often to exalt the messianic status of Jesus as the one now approached. While Edwards may be right in his main thesis, his attempt to make the Matthean usage consistent leads him to explain as cultic or especially reverential usages which need mean no more than approach.[17] In any case, Edwards recognizes that Mark does not use the verb "cultically"; and presumably, therefore, in Mark 14:45 (and Matt 26:49, which draws upon it) we need posit no special awe in Judas' "coming up" to Jesus.

After his approach to Jesus, the greeting "rabbi" is Judas' first step in Mark.[18] This title has been used previously for Jesus in the relationship be-

[17]For instance, Edwards (67–68) explains ten instances where people approach Jesus to trap him as implicit recognitions of his exalted status as a teacher! But since one often approaches another person for a reason, an implicit recognition of special status is being attributed to what by normal standards are pedestrian uses of the verb. The Jewish deuterocanonical writings, close in time to the Greek of the NT, offer examples of this, e.g., Judith 7:8; *I Esdras* 5:65(68); 8:65(68).

[18]In the Gospels Jesus is addressed or referred to as "Rabbi" or as the caritative "Rabbouni" ("My dear Rabbi"; Rabbōni is a Western ms. variant) a total of fourteen times (Mark 4, Matt 2, John 8). JBap is thus addressed in John 3:26. The term means "my great one [lord, master]." The sense of the "my" was lost, and in Judaism it came to be a title for a recognized or ordained teacher of the Law. When? The Epistle of Sherira Gaon (10th cent.) reports that the first person to bear the title "Rabban" was Gamaliel (ca. mid-1st cent.); and the general impression is that only post–AD 70 with

tween him and the disciples (Mark 9:5; 11:21), and it should be looked on in Mark as the normal respectful address. It is not, therefore, an unusual, especially ingratiating address by a hypocritical Judas, but is meant to disarm Jesus as if all were normal.[19] There is a special tone, however, in the Matthean usage. Matt 23:7–8 shows that Jesus does not approve of the use of "rabbi" as a salutation by the scribes and Pharisees, and forbids his disciples to imitate it. At the Last Supper while the other disciples ask, "Is it I, Lord?" Judas asks, "Is it I, Rabbi?" Thus Judas' usage of this term betrays one who is already outside the company of Jesus' disciples.

Matt prefixes "Rabbi" by *chaire,* the normal salutation in secular Greek ("Hail, hello, good day, greetings"). W. Michaelis (*Der Kirchenfreund* 76 [1942], 189ff.) proposed that Judas actually used the Greek greeting in Gethsemane, but there is no need to think that: The functional Hebrew equivalent would have been *shālôm.* Matt's readers speak Greek, and the presence of *chaire* helps to underline the idea that Judas is trying to act normally. With a stereotyped word (some twelve times as a greeting in the NT) one never knows if readers remain aware of the derivational meaning (e.g., would we easily catch a play on "Good-bye" being from "God be with you"?); but there could be irony in having a word from the verb "to rejoice" (*chairein*) used in these circumstances. See also the ironic use of *chaire* in Matt 27:29; Mark 15:18.

We come now to what in Mark/Matt is the prearranged signal/sign, the kiss itself. Once it was depicted in this context the Judas kiss, a sign of affection or love used to betray, entered the repertory of Christian imagery; and the evangelists were surely aware of that possibility when they described it. Already Prov 27:6 had inculcated distrust of the kisses of an enemy, and in the flow of the Gospels the readers know that Judas is now an enemy. But on the level of history or of verisimilitude, how are we to understand Judas' use of the kiss? If it was a normal greeting that could be used by any acquaintance or a customary greeting between Jesus and the disciples, then it could fit into the plot of those who had paid Judas to avoid noisy resistance and hence into Judas' desire to appear disarmingly normal.[20] If it was not a normal greeting but an unusual gesture implying special affection, then Judas

---

the school at Jamnia did "rabbi" come into regular use as a title. However, E. L. Sukenik discovered a pre-70 ossuary on the Mount of Olives where *didaskalos* ("teacher," the Greek word John uses to translate both rabbi and rabbouni) is used as a title (plate 3 in *Tarbiz* 1 [1930]; Frey, *Corpus Inscriptionum Judaicarum* 1266). The NT may constitute more evidence of the titulary use of "rabbi" before 70 if the "Rabbi" address to Jesus is a title.

[19]The fact that the Koine Greek textual tradition doubles the "Rabbi" in Mark 14:45 for emphasis (cf. Codex Vaticanus of Acts 19:34) has the effect of making the address more hypocritical.

[20]That is more plausible an understanding than Origen's suggestion (*Contra Celsum* 2.11) that the kiss displayed a certain sincerity on the part of Judas, who could not utterly despise what he had learned from Jesus.

was a malevolent hypocrite. Dibelius ("Judas" 277) opts for the former: Judas greeted the master as he always greeted him. Some have argued against this on the grounds that having been with Jesus at the Last Supper, Judas would not so soon afterward be giving him a greeting. In fact, however, the frequency of extending normal greetings, e.g., a handshake, varies greatly among peoples; and we have very little idea of how often Palestinian Jews made such an exchange.

Nowhere else are Jesus and his disciples shown exchanging a kiss, but that silence may be accidental. The kiss as a greeting is well attested in the Bible. In II Sam 20:9 Joab, planning to kill Amasa, greets him, "Are you well, my brother," and holds Amasa's beard as if to kiss him. The kiss is a sign of forgiveness between Jacob and Esau in Gen 33:4 (even if the later rabbis wondered whether it was sincere; see Nestle, "Zum Judaskuss"), as it is between father and son in Luke 15:20. There was reticence about public kisses in Greco-Roman society; mostly they are described in scenes of reconciliation or of relatives meeting after separation. A type of sacred kiss developed among Christians.[21] For the kiss as a sign of respectful hospitality, see Luke 7:45; for it as a sign of Christian fellowship, see Rom 16:16; I Pet 5:14, etc. We do not know whether it is appropriate to invoke the evidence of rabbinic Judaism whereby pupils greeted rabbis with a kiss as a sign of respect, and the rabbi could return it. The kiss might be on the hand, head, or foot but not normally mouth to mouth (Dibelius, "Judas" 276). Such evidence is of a period later than the NT, but we saw the possibility that the use of "rabbi" for Jesus by his disciples might have anticipated later practice. In any case one need not appeal to that in the instance of Judas; there is enough evidence of the kiss as a normal greeting among acquaintances to make plausible the theory that what Judas did would not have aroused suspicion.

On the question of historicity scholars are divided. In part A of the ANALYSIS (§16) I shall mention some minimalistic reconstructions of a preMarcan source that would regard the kiss as a Marcan creation. Others would allot it to an early source without settling the question of historicity. Klauck (*Judas* 421) thinks the kiss was imported from the liturgy. As I shall point out below, it is curious that John shows no knowledge of the kiss although that Gospel does echo the context. Yet even some scholars who are very cautious about acknowledging historicity place the kiss in that category (e.g., Gnilka). I see no way to establish historicity (within the usual range of plausibility), even though there is no serious reason to reject it. Similarly Fitzmyer (*Luke* 2.1449): "One is hard put to establish the historicity of Judas' kiss."

[21]W. Klassen, "The Sacred Kiss in the New Testament," NTS 39 (1993), 122–35.

Jesus' Response to the Kiss (Matt 26:50a; Luke 22:48)

Mark leaves Judas' greeting and kiss unanswered by Jesus, even as later in the arrest he will leave unanswered the cutting off of the servant's ear. The other evangelists seem to have felt the need to supply a response, perhaps because they found such a response in their tradition and/or because they felt the need for theological commentary. Certainly, here the responses supplied by Matt and Luke would have the effect of countering any suggestion that Jesus did not know what Judas planned and thus of safeguarding the exalted character of Jesus.

Matt. Most of our attention will be focused on the response of Jesus in Matt, *hetaire eph ho parei,* words that, as SPNM 125 correctly observes, have "provoked an enormous amount of discussion but little certitude."[22] There are some minor textual variants, giving us the consolation that ancient scribes also wrestled with the meaning.

Hetairos means "friend, companion, comrade." While it could be used as an address for someone whose name the speaker did not know (BAGD 314), the Matthean Jesus not only has called Judas as one of his Twelve but also knows what he is about by way of betrayal (26:25). There is irony, then, in Jesus' use of the term, but with what tone? Would *hetairos* have been accepted by Matt's readers as a normal greeting of Jesus to a member of the Twelve, having a tone of intimate companionship? *Hetairos* is not a common word in the LXX. In later Judaism it could serve as the Greek rendition of the designation for rabbinical candidates qualified to be teachers but not yet ordained (K. H. Rengstorf, TDNT 2.699–701); but that can scarcely be invoked here. There is no example of *hetairos* used within Jesus' discipleship in the canonical Gospels, but *GPet* 7:26 has Peter employ the term for his fellow disciples after Jesus' death: "I was sorrowful with the *hetairoi*." Noteworthy too is John 15:15, "No longer do I call you servants . . . but I have called you friends [*philos*]." Even if intimacy in the relationship between Jesus and the Twelve was implied by the use of *hetairos,* two previous uses by Matt where there was irony involved may be of use in diagnosing the irony here and may cast light on why Jesus would use it now of Judas, not positively but negatively. In Matt 20:13, although the householder had paid the agreed wage to those who worked all day long, they grumble that they did not get more; so he addresses a reproach to one of them, "*Hetaire,* I am not wronging you." In Matt 22:12 the king, who courteously has invited guests to a wedding banquet and sees a man who has come without a wed-

---

[22]In the Sectional Bibliography in §12, Part 1, see the articles by Deissmann, Eltester, Klostermann, Lee, Owen, Peri, Rehkopf, Spiegelberg, and Zorell.

ding garment, addresses a reproachful question, *"Hetaire,* how did you get in here not wearing a wedding garment?" In both instances the speaker has done a good action; the person addressed should have responded with friendly gratitude but is not doing so. That may be the irony in the address to Judas as well.

Beyond that, two other uses of *hetairos* may offer background. First, in II Sam 15, in the context of Ahithophel's joining the conspiracy against King David and of David's flight across the Kidron to the ascent of Olives, Hushai, who remains loyal to the king, is spoken of as David's *hetairos* (15:37) and later suspected by Absalom as such (16:17). We saw (p. 125 above) that this David story offers background for the whole Gethsemane scene, and the use of *hetairos* for the loyal follower in that story may increase the irony of Judas being addressed here as *hetairos* by the Son of David. The other use, stressed by Eltester and especially Peri, involves the OT horror of being reviled by a close acquaintance whose harsh words are like drawn swords.[23] Sir 37:2 laments: "Is it not a sorrow [*lypē*] unto death when your companion [*hetairos*] and friend [*philos*] is turned enemy?" Earlier in Gethsemane (Matt 26:38) Jesus has said, "My soul is very sorrowful [*perilypos*] unto death"; the first words of that saying echo Ps 42:6, while Sir 37:2 has been suggested as a parallel for the last part. Is the rest of the Sir passage being invoked here as the cause of Jesus' sorrow unto death, namely, that the one who has turned enemy and is leading him to death is his *hetairos* or "companion" (in the Hebrew original, his bosom friend)?[24]

The heart of the difficulty in fully understanding Jesus' response to Judas in Matt 26:50, however, lies in the meaning not of *hetairos* but of *eph ho parei.* To stop here to discuss the grammatical problems and the varied proposed solutions would be a distraction, and so I shall reserve that discussion for APPENDIX III C. There I conclude that the various interpretations of *eph ho parei* actually cover a narrow range of meaning. As it now functions in Matt, the clause is probably Jesus' way of indicating that he knows what Judas is about, whence my choice of "That's what you are here for." It may be part of a standard greeting to convivial friends, "Rejoice; that's what you are here for"; consequently, Jesus' countergreeting may be just as ironical as Judas' "Hail, Rabbi." Matt cannot allow the ambiguous silence of the Marcan Jesus to stand; his Jesus appears more clearly as master of the situation.

---

[23]E.g., Pss 41:10; 55:13–15,22. It is noteworthy that Mishna *'Abot* 6:3 and *Sanhedrin* 10:2 relate Ps 55:14 to Ahithophel, who turned against David. Yet the LXX of these passages does not employ *hetairos* or *machaira.*

[24]Romantically Peri speaks of a "death companion"; and he and Eltester point to a form of gnostic thought cited by Ps-Tertullian (*Adv. Omnes Haereses* 2.6; CC 2.1404) where Judas renders

The *tote* ("Then") that follows Jesus' words in Matt helps to give the impression that now that Jesus has spoken, the arrest can proceed. The "having come up" in 26:50 (see the discussion of *proserchesthai* above in relation to Mark 14:45 and Matt 26:49) gives a somewhat choreographed effect. First Judas comes up and kisses him; then the arresting party comes up and lays hands on him; all are playing their preassigned roles. Having begun the process of handing Jesus over, Judas is now on a fixed path; he will not be able to turn back (see 27:3–10).

Luke. The response of the Lucan Jesus to Judas is clear, albeit subtle. Christological development leads both Matt and Luke (and John, *suo modo*) not to have Jesus passively silent, but for each evangelist the response functions differently. Luke did not report the second and third prayers of Jesus in Gethsemane and thus had no parallel to the Marcan Jesus' statements: "Behold *the Son of Man is given over* into the hands of the sinners . . . behold the one who gives me over *has come near* [*ēggiken*]" (Mark 14:41–42). Now, however, Luke draws upon those sayings, as indicated by my italicized English. At the end of 22:47 we are told that Judas "*came near* [*ēggisen*] Jesus to kiss him." There has been no reference in Luke to the kiss as a prearranged sign; but the Lucan Jesus knows about it (notice the emphatic position of "kiss" in the question he asks) and what it signifies for the Son of Man, "Judas, with a kiss do you *give over the Son of Man?*" The incorporation of "the Son of Man" into the words to Judas echoes the Lucan passion predictions (9:44; 18:31–33) and the Last Supper prediction (22:22, "as it has been determined") and thus hints at the inevitability of what Judas is doing.

The brevity of the Lucan account, harmonious with Luke's abbreviation of the prayer scene, leaves a tantalizing question: In Luke's portrayal did Judas actually kiss Jesus? Codex Bezae[25] has a longer text of Luke 22:47, not *all* of which can be identified as scribal amplification on the basis of Mark or Matt: "But while he was still speaking, behold a numerous crowd; and the man called Judas Iscariot was going ahead of them; and having come near, he kissed Jesus. This one had given them a sign: 'Whomever I shall kiss, he is (the one).'" Obviously the Bezae reading is one way of solving Luke's ambiguities. On the other hand, some modern commentators affirm that Jesus repelled the kiss (see Schneider, *Lukas* 461).

The delicacy of deliberate silence, not spelling out the unmentionable, is more typical of Luke as he closes his eyes to the scene; and subtlety colors even the portrayal of Judas. (Note that Luke uses *philein* for "kiss" and thus

---

service by making salvation possible when the powers of this world might have prevented Jesus from dying (see I Cor 2:7–8).

[25]And in part P69, the OS, and some Latin witnesses. The longer Western recension of Luke represented by Bezae is a famous problem beyond our concern here; see Fitzmyer, *Luke* 1.128–33.

avoids the added warmth of Mark's *kataphilein*.) Judas has been mentioned by name previously only twice in Luke: in the list of the Twelve (6:16) and as one into whose heart Satan entered (22:3). The standard reference here, "one of the Twelve," catches the horror that one so close to Jesus would give him over to his enemies, but that is softened when Jesus speaks to Judas by name (only here among all the Gospels!), even as at the supper he spoke to Simon by name (22:31). The agent of Satan is still a human individual with the possibility of decision, and one whom Jesus acknowledges personally. The question addressed by Jesus combines foreknowledge with an implicit appeal for repentance. Throughout the PN the Lucan Jesus remains one who reaches out in forgiveness to sinners. The reader, who will find out in Acts 1:18 the horrible fate of Judas, knows that the Savior tried one final time to touch his heart and to persuade him not to "turn aside" (Acts 1:25). Alas, "the Scripture had to be fulfilled, which the Holy Spirit spoke beforehand by the mouth of David, about Judas who served as guide to those who took Jesus with them" (Acts 1:16). In the Lucan account of Judas' part in the arrest there is no need to posit a special Lucan source (pace Taylor, *Passion* 74); Luke has reused Marcan material with finesse to describe the scene in a way consonant with his own theology.

JESUS' SELF-IDENTIFICATION ("I AM") IN JOHN 18:4–8A

The Johannine identification scene has also gone its own way theologically, but so radically that here the relationship to the kind of tradition found in Mark or to any earlier tradition is very uncertain. (See above on the question of whether the presence of Roman troops has a basis in fact.) Let us take the absence of any reference to the Judas kiss, for instance. Did John's tradition not know of so vivid an image, which would have spread quickly and widely in Christian storytelling? Or is John's silence, combined with the presumption that John did not know Mark, an indication that Mark created the image and that it had no base in early tradition? Or, more likely, did John excise from the tradition the Judas kiss, which gave a human being initiative in determining Jesus' destiny (even as later in the PN John almost surely excised the memory of Simon the Cyrenian as compromising Jesus' carrying his own cross)? Was it seen as a detraction from the principle of sovereignty that governs the Johannine PN: "I lay down my life . . . no one has taken it away from me; rather I lay it down of my own accord" (10:17–18)?

That governing principle would explain the remarkably inactive role of Judas in John's account of the arrest. Once he comes (*erchetai* in 18:3; compare *ēlthen* in Matt 26:47), he seems to do nothing. Much more important is Jesus' matching action of coming out (*exēlthen* in 18:4) and taking the initiative of speaking first—quite unlike the Synoptics. All four Gospels have Jesus foresee the giving over; but the Johannine comment, fitting the theme of sovereignty, is far more sweeping: Jesus "having known all the things to come upon him." To the arresting party brought by "one of his disciples" (a designation for Judas in 12:4), Jesus addresses a question: "Whom are you seeking?" (*tina zēteite*), hauntingly reminiscent of the first words Jesus ever addressed to those who would be disciples in this Gospel, "What are you seeking?" (*ti zēteite;* 1:38). The language of seeking, drawn from the sapiential literature of Israel, is very strong in John, where Jesus is incarnate divine wisdom (BGJ 1.78–79). While people "seek" Jesus because he has the gift of life, much more frequently, as irony would have it, people "seek" him to put him to death (5:18; 7:1,11,19,25,30; 8:37,40; 10:39; 11:8,56). Because he is going away, several times Jesus has said, "You will seek me and not find me" (7:34–36; 8:21; 13:33, with variants). But the hostile seeking (and finding with Judas' help) in the arrest scene is not the final word. The ultimate "Whom are you seeking?" (*tina zēteite*) of the Fourth Gospel, forming an inclusion with the first, will be addressed to a woman disciple, Mary Magdalene (20:15), who will proclaim to the other disciples, "I have seen the Lord" (20:18).

To Jesus' question about their search, the arresting party answers, "Jesus the Nazorean." The Nazorean designation is probably used by John in both the geographical and theological senses.[26] The arresting party is searching for a Jesus; but since that is a common name, they specify the Jesus from Nazareth.[27] But for the evangelist "Jesus the Nazorean" has christological value; it will appear again on the cross triumphantly (19:19), and so Jesus can answer "I am (he)" with an affirmative in a sense that the believing reader will appreciate.

Another meaning of the response *egō eimi*, however, is paramount. This is good Greek for "I am the one" or "It is I"; but throughout the Gospel John has played on *egō eimi* without an expressed predicate giving voice to Jesus' divine claims: "Before Abraham was, I am."[28] While in the hymn of Philip 2:6–11, "the name that is above every other name" is bestowed on Jesus after his death on the cross and his exaltation (2:9), in John before death Jesus

---

[26]Two gentilic adjectives applied to Jesus in the NT are *Nazarēnos* (Nazarene: Mark 4 times, Luke 2, Matt 0, John 0) and *Nazōraios* (Nazorean: Luke-Acts 8 times, John 3, Matt 2, Mark 0). In BBM 209–13 I argued that despite philological difficulties, Matt 2:23 is not wrong in claiming that Jesus was called a Nazorean because he came from Nazareth, but that the term had taken on theological value related to *Nāzîr* (Nazirite, an ascetic holy person) and *nēṣer* ("branch," a description of a figure from the House of David in Isa 11:1).

[27]If further specification were needed, e.g., if there were several men named Jesus at Nazareth, the designation "Jesus son of Joseph" could be used, as in John 1:45; 6:42.

[28]John 8:58; also 8:24,28; 13:19. For the evidence that *egō eimi* may have served as a type of divine name in early Judaism, see BGJ 1.535–38.

speaks to the Father of "your name which you have given me" (see BGJ 2.759 for that as the better translation of John 17:11–12). There the name seems to have the power to keep the disciples safe; here the name seems to have the power to paralyze his enemies; for as soon as he speaks it the arresting party is forced backward (*eis ta opisō*) and falls [*piptein*] to the ground [*chamai*]!

OT antecedents for this reaction have been proposed, e.g., Ps 56:10(9): "My enemies will be turned back [*eis ta opisō*] in the day when I shall call upon you"; Ps 27:2: "When evildoers come at me . . . my foes and my enemies themselves stumble and fall [*piptein*]"; Ps 35:4: "Let those be turned back [*eis ta opisō*] and confounded who plot evil against me." Falling down (*piptein*) as a reaction to divine revelation is attested in Dan 2:46; 8:18; Rev 1:17; and that is how John would have the reader understand the reaction to Jesus' pronouncement. *Piptein chamai* is combined with the verb "to worship" in Job 1:20. No matter what one thinks of the historicity of this scene, it should not be explained away or trivialized.[29] To know or use the divine name, as Jesus does, is an exercise of awesome power. In Acts 3:6 Peter heals a lame man "in the name of Jesus of Nazareth," i.e., by the power of the name that Jesus has been given by God; and "there is no other name under heaven given among human beings by which we must be saved." Eusebius (*Praeparatio Evangelica* 9.27.24–26; GCS 43¹.522) attributes to Artapanus, who lived before the 1st cent. BC, the legend that when Moses uttered before Pharaoh the secret name of God, Pharaoh fell speechless to the ground (R. D. Bury, ExpTim 24 [1912–13], 233). That legend may or may not have been known when John wrote, but it illustrates an outlook that makes John's account of the arrest intelligible.

This same Jesus will say to Pilate, "You have no power over me at all except what was given to you from above" (19:11). Here he shows how powerless before him are the troops of the Roman cohort and the police attendants from the chief priests—the representatives of the two groups who will soon interrogate him and send him to the cross. Indeed, an even wider extension of Jesus' power may be intended. Why does John suddenly, in the midst of this dramatic interchange, mention the otiose presence of Judas, "Now standing there with them was also Judas, the one who was giving him over" (18:5)? Is it because the devil has induced the giving over (13:2) and Satan has entered into Judas (13:27)? John 17:12 calls Judas "the son of perdition," a phrase used in II Thess 2:3–4 to describe the antichrist who exalts himself to the level of God. Is the idea that the representative of the power of evil

---

[29]As, for instance, by Hingston ("John" 232), who would interpret John to mean "they went behind (him)," for in fact they had pushed Judas forward; or by J. H. Bernard (his *John* commentary, 2.586–87), who would understand figuratively that they were "floored" or astounded.

must also fall powerless before Jesus?[30] I have already pointed out a close Johannine parallel to the Mark/Matt saying about the coming near of the one who gives Jesus over, namely, John 14:30: "For the Prince of this world is coming" (p. 213 above). In John 12:31, in the context of proclaiming the coming of the hour (12:23) and of praying about that hour (12:27), Jesus exclaims, "Now will the Prince of this world be driven out" (or "cast down," a textual variant; see also 16:11).

Is there historicity in this extraordinarily triumphal Johannine scene of Jesus' self-identification during the arrest, as compared with the Synoptic account of the Judas kiss? On the one hand, we should recognize that John's account is not without likenesses to the Synoptic tradition. Although the absolute use of *egō eimi* is distinctively Johannine, it is not totally foreign to the Synoptic tradition.[31] Is it purely accidental that the Judas of Mark 14:44 says, "Whomever I shall kiss, *he is*," the third person equivalent of John's "I am"? Also one is tempted to see an ironic contrast between Jesus' enemies falling to the ground (*piptein chamai*) in John, and Jesus himself falling to the earth (*piptein epi tēs gēs*) in Mark. The tradition of prostration is the same, but the roles are reversed. On the other hand, we need to avoid literalistic simplifications in judging John. Bartina ("Yo soy") regards the falling to the ground as an example of Jews prostrating themselves out of habit at the mention of the divine name. One would need contemporary proof that prostration was an automatic Jewish response, and such an explanation does not account for the action of the Roman troops. Haenchen ("History" 201) thinks that story is a preJohannine creation using some of the OT antecedents mentioned as background above. Elsewhere when John has retold a scene in the light of his unique theological outlook, he has rarely departed from verisimilitude. This seems to be a major exception. Even if John might be historical in indicating that Roman soldiers took part in the arrest of Jesus, critical standards would suggest that he has moved from history to parable in reporting that those soldiers plus the Jewish police attendants fell back to the ground when Jesus spoke to them.

THE SEIZURE OF JESUS (MARK 14:46; MATT 26:50B)

After this extraordinary introduction of Jesus to the arresting party, the Johannine narrative continues smoothly into Jesus' gaining the release of the

---

[30]In BGJ 2.810 I regarded 18:5b as a "very awkward editorial insertion," and Charbonneau ("Arrestation" 159) associates de la Potterie and Schnackenburg with the view that 5b is an interruption. I now see the verse as having theological significance.

[31]See BGJ 1.538. Important texts are Matt 14:27 with 14:33; a variant in Luke 24:36; and Mark 14:62 (which will be discussed below).

disciples and Simon Peter's cutting off the servant's ear. Luke too shows no break in the continuity between the Judas kiss and the attack on the servant. In neither John nor Luke does anyone take physical control of Jesus until this scene on the Mount of Olives is over and the arresting party moves to take him to the Jewish authorities (John 18:12–13; Luke 22:54). Mark, on the contrary, breaks the sequence by telling us that after the Judas kiss, in obedience to the traitor's instruction to seize Jesus and lead him away securely, the arresting party "laid hands on him and seized him" (14:46). The vivid expression "laid hands on him" reflects LXX language for doing harm to someone (Gen 22:12; II Sam 18:12). While here it implies physical seizure, it carries with it a tone of hostile intent. Luke 20:19 and John 7:30,44 have reported previous attempts to lay hands on Jesus; but neither Gospel uses that expression in the arrest.

Mark's description of the seizure of Jesus means that in the events to follow, including the attack on the servant and Jesus' response to the arresting party, we must picture him being held physically by his captors, until finally as a transition from the arrest to the trial he is led away (14:53—only then fulfilling the second part of Judas' instructions). The awkwardness of this has caused some to argue that 14:46 was originally continued by 14:53, with all the intermediary incidents as secondary insertions (including the cutting off of the servant's ear—the best attested single section of the whole Mount of Olives sequence!). In any case, Taylor (*Mark* 559) is correct in speaking of a loose attachment of what follows the Judas kiss. Matt has the same picture as Mark but with somewhat better flow since the command to lead Jesus away securely has been eliminated from Judas' instruction. Yet the physically restrained Jesus of Matt speaks at greater length than in Mark and speaks openly to his disciples. Matt may have recognized the awkwardness of having Jesus seized in the middle of the arrest scene; for at the terminus of the scene Matt 26:57 repeats the reference to seizure ("And having seized Jesus, they led him away") almost as if Jesus were free up to that time.

Having taken cognizance of this difference in sequence, let us now consider those incidents in the arrest scene that take place before Jesus is led away.

(*Bibliography for this episode is found in §12, Part 1.*)

§14. THE ARREST OF JESUS, PART TWO:
ACCOMPANYING INCIDENTS

(Mark 14:47–50; Matt 26:51–56; Luke 22:49–53;
John 18:8b–11)

Translation

Mark 14:47–50: ⁴⁷But a certain one of those standing by, having drawn the sword, hit at the servant of the high priest and took off his ear. ⁴⁸And in answer Jesus said to them, "As if against a bandit have you come out with swords and wooden clubs to take me? ⁴⁹Day after day I was with you in the Temple teaching, and you did not seize me. However—let the Scriptures be fulfilled!" ⁵⁰And having left him, they all fled.

Matt 26:51–56: ⁵¹And behold one of those with Jesus, having stretched out his hand, drew out his sword; and having struck the servant of the high priest, he took off his ear. ⁵²Then Jesus says to him, "Return your sword to its place, for all who take the sword, by the sword will perish. ⁵³Do you think that I am not able to call upon my Father, and He will at once supply me with more than twelve legions of angels? ⁵⁴How then would the Scriptures be fulfilled that it must happen thus?" ⁵⁵In that hour Jesus said to the crowds, "As if against a bandit have you come out with swords and wooden clubs to take me? Day after day in the Temple I was sitting teaching, and you did not seize me. ⁵⁶But this whole thing has happened in order that the Scriptures of the prophets might be fulfilled." Then all the disciples, having left him, fled.

Luke 22:49–53: ⁴⁹But those about him, having seen what would be, said, "Lord, shall we strike with the sword?" ⁵⁰And a certain one of them struck the servant of the high priest and took off his right ear. ⁵¹But in answer Jesus said, "Let that be enough!" And having touched the ear, he healed him. ⁵²But Jesus said to the chief priests and captains of the Temple and elders who were arrived against him, "As if against a bandit have you come out with swords and wooden clubs? ⁵³Even though day after day I was with you in the Temple, you did not stretch out your hands against me; however, this is your hour and the power of darkness!"

John 18:8b–11: ⁸ᵇ"If therefore you are seeking me, let these go away, ⁹in order that the word may be fulfilled which says that 'those whom you have given me, I have not lost one of them.'" ¹⁰So Simon Peter, having a sword, pulled it out and hit at the servant of the high priest, and cut off his right ear. (The name of the servant was Malchus.) ¹¹So Jesus said to Peter, "Put the sword into the scabbard. The cup the Father has given me—am I not to drink it?"

COMMENT

The four Gospels place a series of incidents between the identification of Jesus to the arresting party and his being led away by that party. The subdivisions of my COMMENT (listed on p. 235 above) will treat one by one the various actions and sayings involved. Despite frequent identity of content among the respective Gospels, there is often difference of vocabulary and detail in describing the incidents; and all that needs careful attention. It is not easy to decide in what sequence to comment on them: Not only are they narrated in different order if one compares John to the Synoptics; but also, as noted at the end of the preceding section (§13), the evangelists have different portrayals of the way in which this part of the arrest scene fits into what has preceded. With the realization that I have left John's sequence in the middle of a verse and promising not to forget that sequence, I have made the decision that the incidents can be more easily commented upon if we follow the Marcan order, supplemented by Matt and Luke.

CUTTING OFF THE SERVANT'S EAR (MARK 14:47; MATT 26:51; LUKE 22:49–50; JOHN 18:10)

Along with the coming of Judas, this is the incident in the arrest scene most commonly shared by the evangelists. Matt 26:51 marks it off with an *idou* ("behold") as a way of making it parallel in importance to the beginning of the arrest scene in 26:47. In Mark/Matt where Jesus has been seized, the sword blow serves as a reaction to that seizure. In Luke, where there has been no seizure, action against Jesus has to be foreseen by the disciples (22:49: "having seen what would be"), i.e., foresight by prudent calculation,[1] not the more exalted, divinely derived knowledge of "all the things to come upon him" exhibited by Jesus in John 18:4. In John the action against the servant (by Simon Peter) comes after Jesus has laid down the condition that his disciples must be allowed to go away (safely); and so the attack on the servant must be understood as defiance by Peter, who is determined to be faithful to his words in 13:37: "Lord, why cannot I follow you now? I will lay down my life for you."

Who acted against the servant? Mark is vague: "a certain one [*heis tis*] of those standing by" drew out his sword.[2] BDF 247[2] points to *heis tis* with the classical function of distinguishing "this one" from the rest of the group. Theissen (*Gospels* 185–89, 199) considers the anonymity to be deliberate, stemming from the context of the preMarcan PN in Jerusalem before 40 when the sword-wielder would still have faced punishment by the authorities. Although others have found in the Marcan phrase a suggestion that a well-known person is meant, that emphasis is not necessary. Despite the fact that the man is not identified as a follower of Jesus, Suhl ("Funktion" 301) contends that he was one, for the use of the sword illustrates the disciples' characteristic failure to understand. Yet in the context the only ones thus far mentioned as having swords are those in the crowd from the chief priests, and so the readers would not immediately associate a sword with those on Jesus' side. Some who think that Mark is referring to a disciple invoke the contention of Jeremias (JEWJ 95) that disciples were not referred to by that title in the preMarcan PN but only as "those who stood by." Without debating the wording of the preMarcan PN (about which I am very uncertain), I note that in the four remaining uses of the verb "to stand by" in the Marcan PN, those so designated are *not* disciples (14:69,70; 15:35,39). It is true that in the Marcan PN there is no reference to "disciples" after 14:32; but there are other ways that Mark could have indicated that the sword-wielder was a companion of Jesus if he thought the man to be such. Moreover, in reaction to the sword thrust, Jesus rebukes those who have come out against him (Mark 14:48), not his disciples. If for Mark this man is not a disciple (a view that solves several historical problems, as we shall see), he is either one of the arresting party (Schenke) or one of a third group, the bystanders. The fact that he has a sword favors his being of the arresting

---

[1]Codex Bezae and some Latin and Syriac witnesses are not far from Luke's mind with their alternative text: "having seen what was happening."

[2]A number of textual witnesses drop the *tis* ("a certain"); but that probably is an "improvement" by scribes who judged it to be redundant (or perhaps a haplography since both *heis* and *tis* end in *is*). Luke (22:50) has *heis tis,* which apparently he read in Mark.

party; but that identification makes it hard to understand why he would draw the sword and cut off the ear of one of his companions. (The description given by Mark does not favor the thesis of a cutting by accident.) The most likely inference from Mark is that the sword-wielder belonged to a third group.

Matt and Luke have gone beyond Mark in making the sword-wielder a disciple. (We shall see exactly the same phenomenon in the case of Joseph of Arimathea.) Luke's "those about him" of which the man is one, while not far from Mark's vague wording, is clarified by the address to Jesus as "Lord" and by the plea to have Jesus decide what to do—the people so described are disciples even as "those about Paul" in Acts 13:13 are Paul's companions and have a certain solidarity with him. Indeed, the progression from Mark's "one of those standing by" to Matt's and Luke's disciple and then to John's Simon Peter is probably a reflection of the popular tendency to identify or clarify the unnamed by giving them a known identity. Yet this identification also helps to individualize the theme of incomprehension. Some have found an act of armed resistance by a disciple incongruous (especially in Matt) with the picture of disciples who thus far have shown little initiative, e.g., they slept while Jesus prayed, and soon they will all flee (Matt 26:56). Yet since the assault on the servant is presented as a *misunderstanding* of what a disciple should do, one could argue for a consistency of failure on the part of the disciples throughout the Mount of Olives scene.

If John's identification of the sword-wielder as Simon Peter is historically correct, the Synoptic silence about Peter's brave action is hard to explain. Some would respond by contending that Mark's formula is *deliberately* vague: Mark knew the man was Peter but did not want to identify him for prudential reasons (Taylor, *Mark* 560). This prudence could be more plausible if Mark was written at Rome, where Peter had been (or would be) executed by Nero, and the evangelist did not want to supply evidence that could be used against him or his memory. Yet that is more speculation than "a certain one of those standing by" should be made to bear. To the contention that this type of bravado would be consonant with Peter's character as illustrated elsewhere in the Gospels, one may reply that such verisimilitude may be precisely why John or John's tradition chose to dramatize Peter as the sword-wielder. Peter bravely defending Jesus here (18:10) and Peter denying that he is a disciple of Jesus seven verses later (18:17) fit John's sense of drama. Peter's obstreperous refusal to have his feet washed (13:8) is continued by his intervention here, and in each case the Johannine Jesus rebukes him for misunderstanding. In speaking to Pilate (18:36), Jesus will argue that any struggle of his attendants to stop him from being given over to the Jews would have shown that his kingdom was of this world. By struggling that Jesus not be given over, therefore, Peter is betraying a basic misunderstanding about the kingdom of Jesus.[3] Thus there is serious reason to doubt that John's identification of the sword-wielder as Simon Peter need stem from history.

Where did the sword-wielder get the sword? G. Dalman, *Jesus-Jeschua* (Leipzig: Hinrichs, 1922), 89–90, discusses the issue of carrying a weapon in the light of an added chronological problem. For the Synoptics, since the supper was a Passover meal, this activity took place on the first day of Passover/Unleavened Bread, which like the Sabbath was a day on which pious Jews should not work or burden themselves with weapons (Exod 12:16; I Macc 2:34–36,41; Josephus, *Ant.* 13.1.3; #12). But Dalman argues that on such a day Jews could put on weapons for self-defense (Josephus *Ant.* 14.4.2; #63; 18.9.2; #319–23); and (appealing to talmudic literature) he claims that in a border area like Galilee sword-carrying would be necessary and almost the same as being clothed. We have evidence from Josephus (*War* 2.8.4; #125) that the Essenes carried weapons when traveling because of highway robbers. However, may we not leave aside the Passover issue since after the supper there is no clear evidence that the Synoptics present the night and the following day as Passover itself? (See APPENDIX II B below.) Moreover, none of the evidence about highways and border areas helps to establish that the disciples of Jesus normally went about Jerusalem or dined together carrying swords.

Mark has the least problem since he does not describe the sword-wielder as a disciple, and a bystander might have had a sword (legally or illegally) for reasons that have nothing to do with Jesus. If the bystanders in Mark

---

[3]Kelber and others press the Marcan picture of Gethsemane to argue that the disciples completely and permanently failed, so that even after the resurrection they were not to be considered true followers of Jesus. Similarly Droge ("Status") would argue that John completely rejects Peter so that in the end he is not a subject of Jesus' heavenly kingdom. In part, this view, which I regard as a serious misunderstanding, results from considering John in isolation from the rest of Christianity as we know it, almost as a sectarian Gospel, even though it has the very unsectarian outlook of Jesus insisting that he has other sheep that are not of this fold (10:16) and praying that all his followers may be one (17:20–21). There is no way to understand John unless the evangelist knew the larger Christian tradition about Jesus; and there is no way to understand the Gospel unless one understands his desire to qualify it on certain issues, e.g., by properly circumscribing the importance of Peter's role. But the unity passages that I have just cited mean "qualify" the common Christian tradition, not destroy it. Destroying it would be manifested in the contention of Droge that although Peter is mentioned at the Johannine Last Supper, for John he is not really one of Jesus' own mentioned in 13:1 (i.e., those with whom Jesus desired to share the supper); or that although John mentions the Twelve, he never gives a list of them in order to make it dubious who constitute the Twelve and thus whether Peter is one of them. I would contend that there is no evidence in the 1st cent. that any Christian would have denied that Peter was one of the Twelve, including the author of John, who in 6:67–71 explicitly describes Peter as the spokesman of the Twelve who did not leave Jesus because he thought that Jesus had the words of eternal life. In that passage Jesus specifies that *one* of the Twelve is a devil, namely, Judas son of Simon Iscariot, with whom Simon Peter is clearly contrasted.

were neither disciples nor the arresting party, this bystander's assault on the servant of the high priest needs not have been in defense of Jesus. *John* has the greatest problem: Swords have never been mentioned in that Gospel. Did Peter, the most prominent member of the Twelve, regularly carry a sword? Was he or were all armed during that meal where Jesus, having loved his own, showed his love for them to the very end (13:1)? True, at the supper Peter learned through the beloved disciple as intermediary that the one who would lift his heel against Jesus, the one who would give him over, was Judas (13:18–30). Having acquired this knowledge, Peter had promised that he would lay down his life in following Jesus (13:37). Are we to think that having seen Judas leave the supper, instructed to do what he was going to do quickly (13:27–30), Peter went out and got a sword for protection? John gives no hint of that. In this particular instance the evangelist, who often thinks out lacunae in the story, does nothing to explain Peter's sword.

As for the identification of the sword-wielder as a disciple in *Matt,* there is little point in invoking as background purely figurative NT references to a sword in Jesus' ministry.[4] Matt seems to offer no reason why a disciple would be carrying his own (material) sword, especially when the disciples had just come from the Last Supper.

Apparently *Luke* was the only evangelist who considered the problem. He offers a dialogue with the twelve apostles (see 22:14,30) at the Last Supper that makes intelligible the presence of a sword in the arrest scene (22:35–38):

> [35]And he [Jesus] said to them, "When I sent you without purse or bag or sandals [9:3; 10:4—the latter containing instructions to the seventy!], did you lack anything?" But they said, "Nothing!" [36]But he said to them, "Now, however, let the one who has a purse take it, and similarly a bag; and let the one who does not have sell his cloak and buy a sword. [37]For, I say to you, this that is written must be completed in me: 'And with outlaws was he reckoned' [Isa 53:12]. For, indeed, the things that refer to me have (their) completion." [38]But they said, "Lord, behold, here are two swords." But he said to them, "Enough of that!"

Although Finegan (*Überlieferung* 16) regards this passage as a Lucan composition to prepare for the sword in the Mount of Olives scene, most scholars think that Luke took it from an earlier source in whole or in part (e.g.,

---

[4]For instance, Jesus had said, "I have not come to bring peace but a sword" (Matt 10:34); and Simeon had said to Jesus' mother, "Indeed a sword [*romphaia*] will pass through your own soul" (Luke 2:35).

vv. 35–36 for Schürmann and Schneider—an original that did not refer to the passion).[5]

The exegesis is not uncomplicated; but in the part that can be related to the use of a sword against the servant, the translation of v. 36b is crucial. Although many render it: "Let the one who does not have a sword sell his cloak and buy one," the Greek gives no object for the negated verb "to have"; rather "sword" follows the verb "to buy." (See Fitzmyer, *Luke* 2.1431–32, for the translation options; he favors the literal one I have chosen.) The idea is *not* that everyone should have a sword and that those who do not should sell even the clothes they have to get one. Rather, everyone should be prepared, e.g., by having the very things that previously they did not need, such as a purse and bag. Those who do not have such necessary preparations for a journey (or flight) should sell even a valuable piece of clothing and buy a sword. All this is in light of the completion of God's plan concerning Jesus, including his forthcoming crucifixion. There is considerable debate about how Luke understood Jesus being reckoned among outlaws (*anomoi*). But whether it is a reference to those who arrested Jesus (Luke 22:52), or to the wrongdoers crucified on either side of him (23:32–33), or to the lawless men who put him to death (*anomoi* in Acts 2:23), the arrest and crucifixion are in mind.[6] During Jesus' ministry when the disciples were sent out on a journey, God would provide and protect; but Jesus' death inaugurates times of struggle and persecution (such as Acts will narrate), and they need to be prepared for travel and defense. The foreboding in this Lucan scene at the supper is parallel in thrust to the words Jesus speaks on the way to the Mount of Olives in Mark 14:27 and Matt 26:31, quoting Scripture to show God's plan, "I will strike the shepherd and the sheep will be scattered." Luke has no scattering at the time of the arrest, but he has later scattering from Jerusalem amid persecution in Acts (8:1–4; 12:17). The items mentioned as preparation, namely, purse, bag, and sword, are quasi-symbolic ways of concretizing the necessary readiness for such contingencies. The response of the disciples that they have in their possession two swords shows that they have (mis)understood literally.[7] The disciples' misunderstanding leads Jesus to use the phrase *hikanon estin. Hikanos* means "sufficient, enough, fitting." "It

---

[5] Farfetched is Hall's suggestion ("Swords") that this passage and that of the cutting off of the servant's ear form a type of midrash on Ps 40:7b (cf. Heb 10:5), "Ears you have opened for me" (with the verb form from *krh* "to open, pierce," read as *krt*, "to cut off").

[6] Minear ("Note" 132–34) thinks that these "outlaws" for Luke are the disciples since they have swords and will use one; but Luke has no such pejorative view of the disciples elsewhere.

[7] One may add that they have not been the only ones to misunderstand: This text has been (mis)used as a general declaration of the right of Christians to bear arms; as support for the right of the medieval papacy to exercise both material and spiritual power (two swords); and as a proof that Jesus encouraged armed revolution!

is fitting" would be a highly ironic rendition, equivalent to "That's the way you normally misunderstand." More characteristic of the Lucan Jesus would be resignation: "That's enough."[8] One must be wary not to translate the phrase as if Jesus were saying that two swords were enough for the task (pace A. Loisy). Fitzmyer (*Luke* 2.1434) insists correctly "the irony concerns not the number of the swords but the whole mentality of the apostles."

This dialogue at the Lucan Last Supper is meant to be remembered by the reader when on the same night (and only eleven verses later) those about him on the Mount of Olives ask, "Lord, shall we strike with the sword?" The literalistic misunderstanding that Jesus wanted them armed with swords continues: This is one of the two swords they said they had.

The action of striking with the sword and cutting off the servant's ear. All the Gospels use the same word for "sword" (*machaira*) and speak of "the servant of the high priest." Otherwise there is an interesting variety in vocalizing the commonly described action: (a) Taking out the sword: Mark uses *span;* Matt uses *apospan* (prefaced by "having stretched out his hand"); John uses *helkein.* (b) Delivering a blow: Mark and John use *paiein;* Matt and Luke use *patassein* (previously used in Mark 14:27; Matt 26:31). (c) Cutting action: Synoptics use *aphairein;* John uses *apokoptein.* (d) Ear: Mark and John 18:10 use *ōtarion* (double diminutive of *ous*); Matt, Luke 22:51, John 18:26, and P[66] of John 18:10 use *ōtion* (diminutive of *ous*); Luke 22:50 uses *ous* (an atticization according to BDF 111[3]). (e) Specification of the *right* ear: in Luke and John.

The presence of such vocabulary variations is to be explained by different factors. In regard to the word "ear," since the same author uses different words (Luke 22:50,51; John 18:10,26), we must allow for a touch of elegance in avoiding repetition. Diminutives had "faded" or lost much of their force in Hellenistic Greek;[9] and the words for "ear" were probably synonymous, although some use "earlobe" for the diminutive, and Benoit (*Passion* 37, note 1) thinks that the diminutive clarifies that the external part of the ear was meant. Joüon ("Luc 22") has probably the soundest observations on this point, distinguishing between Luke, which does not shy away from the abnormal declension of *ous,* and the other Gospels, which are not consistent but use *ous* as the most general term. As for the specification "right ear," Luke (6:6) has previously specified "right hand" in contrast to "hand" in the Marcan parallel (3:1), and so we may be facing editorial activity. Yet Rostovtzeff cites an Egyptian papyrus of 183 BC (Tebtunis III, 793, xi. 1)

---

[8]To back this there are examples in the LXX of *hikanoun* used impersonally to mean "It is enough" (Deut 3:26; I Kings 19:4).

[9]BDF 111[3]; D. C. Swanson, JBL 77 (1958), 146–51.

where cutting off the right ear is a deliberate choice to render a shameful lesson to someone and points out that damage to an organ on the right side was considered more serious than damage to an organ on the left (see Mishna, *Baba Qamma* 8:6 for the general principle that dignity increases the offense). Therefore the agreement between Luke and John on this point need not reflect a common source of preGospel influence; more vivid story-telling may have influenced both accounts independently.[10] Many of the other vocabulary differences may represent redactional preferences of the evangelists and can be explained on a literary level. However, since there are odd combinations of agreement between evangelists who did not nec-essarily know each other's work (Mark and John; Matt and Luke), one should take into account that with a vivid scene like this, likely to catch the popular imagination, the way he had heard the story told may have influenced an evangelist's expression as much as a written source he was copying.

Was the servant a known figure? John speaks of Malchus, a name not uncommon in this era.[11] Some have tried to discover symbolism in the name, e.g., Aileen Guilding in her theory of lectionary background for John in-vokes Zech 11:6 (read before Passover): "I will deliver . . . each into the hands of his king [*malkô*]." Appeal to historicity is less demanding than such an imaginative solution (so Bruce, "Trial" 10). Many suggest that "Malchus" may simply be another example of the tendency of storytelling to supply names (with no particular theological symbolism). Wherever the name came from, the identification fits John's pattern of person-to-person encounters: Two named figures, Simon Peter and Malchus, face one another here; and later in the denials Peter will face the relative of Malchus (18:26). In the garden by hitting at Malchus Peter defends Jesus; before Malchus' relative Peter will deny that he was even in the garden with Jesus.

Tied in with John's naming the servant is the fact that in all four Gospels we hear of "*the* servant of the high priest."[12] As BDF 252 (see ZAGNT 1.158) points out, one does not expect the definite article when a hitherto unknown person is being introduced in a narrative. Accordingly some (La-

---

[10]Storytelling continued after the written Gospels: Since a right-handed man would have had difficulty cutting off the right ear of an opponent facing him (that ear would normally be shielded by the angle of the face), in some popular traditions Peter emerged as a left-hander. Apparently the thought that Peter could have been a right-hander who struck the servant from behind did not occur or was deemed unworthy since it could hint at cowardice!

[11]"Malchus" is found five times in Josephus and is known from Palmyrene and Nabatean inscrip-tions (whence the suggestion that Malchus was an Arab).

[12]The designation "of the high priest" is surprising in Luke, who thus far has mentioned nothing about the high priest as having any involvement with the crowd that has come out to the Mount of Olives; that mention will come only two verses later! This is a Lucan inconsistency that has arisen from changing the Marcan order.

grange, Taylor) have assumed that even as with "a certain one of those standing by," Mark knew who the servant was and expected his readers to do so as well—perhaps the Malchus of John who might have become a Christian. Krieger ("Knecht") suggests that Judas is meant, for he had made himself the servant of the high priest; and it was to punish him for his betrayal that another disciple struck at him. Moving away from the biographical approach, one could appeal to "the servant of the king" in I Sam 29:3. Gnilka (*Matthäus* 2.419) thinks that the article signifies that this servant is the most important figure, the leader of the crowd. That explanation would not work for Luke and John, however, where more important figures than the servant are in the arresting party. Doeve ("Gefangennahme" 462) proposes a literal translation from Aramaic where the determined state could have an undetermined meaning. More simply, could this be a usage bordering on the generic article where the whole class or group is subsumed under the person being introduced (BDF 252, 263), so that the servant of the high priest is looked upon as representative of the hostile crowd that comes from the chief priests? Josephus (*Ant.* 20.8.8; #181) mentions, in the context of the period AD 60, that the chief priests would send their servants to demand tithes that really belonged to the ordinary priests. In that atmosphere the servant of the high priest could be looked on as his agent, carrying out what he wanted.[13]

Viviano ("High") argues that the servant is the prefect of the priests, the *sagan*, i.e., the chief assistant or deputy of the high priest. He combines this identification with other elements of a thesis that fills in the story (e.g., that Mark's anonymous sword-wielder carefully cut off the servant's earlobe) and argues that this was a deliberate mutilation of an important priest so that he could never function ritually. He points to examples of cutting off priests' ears to disqualify them ritually (Josephus, *Ant.* 14.13.10; #365–66; Tosepta, *Para* 3.8). What Mark is recounting, then, is a symbolic action that equivalently states the unworthiness of this priest-servant and the high priest whom he represents to be a mediator between God and humankind, an unworthiness exhibited in coming here to lay violent hands on the anointed holy one of God. I regard this as an implausible interpretation of what Mark meant. As already noted, diminutives like *ōtarion* are very imprecise at this period; and Mark could scarcely have hoped to get his readers to understand a carefully planned, almost surgical action simply by using a diminutive. (Apparently Matt and Luke did not notice the precision Viviano postulates, for they substituted other terms for "ear.") If Mark has to explain to his readers ele-

---

[13]Others cite the later evidence of TalBab *Pesaḥim* 57a, which criticizes the behavior of the high priests of Jesus' period (including the house of Annas [Ḥannin]), employing what is thought to have been a street ballad: "They are the high priests, and their sons are the treasurers; their sons-in-law are the Temple officers, and their servants beat the people with staves."

mentary laws of Jewish purification (7:3–4), he can scarcely have expected them to recognize under the designation "the servant of the high priest" one of the most important priests of the Temple. And it is highly dubious that "servant" meant that. Viviano defends his interpretation by pointing to Luke's "captain of the Temple," who is possibly equivalent to the *sagan* of mishnaic literature (see APPENDIX V B4). But he does not point out that in the Lucan arrest scene the cutting off of the servant's ear is mentioned before the reported arrival of the captains (pl.) of the Temple (22:50,52), so that Luke certainly does not associate the two. The three evangelists who present a scene beyond the Marcan bare bones (Matt, Luke, and John) all see this as an act in defense of Jesus and give no suggestion whatsoever that it was the cultic disabling of a priest. Indeed, their reports of Jesus' attempt to *forbid* the action scarcely helps Viviano's effort to place the incident in the context of Jesus' critique of Temple abuses.

To conclude this discussion of "the servant of the high priest," all that we can say with surety is that the readers of Mark, Matt, and Luke (and even John) would have envisaged a figure hostile to Jesus and might have tended to rejoice at his fate. We now turn to how the evangelists portray Jesus' reaction to the cutting off of this servant's ear.

JESUS' RESPONSE TO THE SWORD-WIELDER (MATT 26:52–54; JOHN 18:11; LUKE 22:51)

In Mark Jesus makes no response to the person who cut off the servant's ear, a silence that fortifies the possibility that for Mark this person was not a disciple. As we shall see, after the incident Jesus speaks only "to them" (14:48), i.e., to the crowd from the chief priests. (It is unlikely that Mark considered the sword-wielder to be one of "them.") In the other Gospels where a disciple or even Peter has done this violent deed, Jesus addresses the perpetrator. Some have wondered whether the impetus to supply a response was not the fear that otherwise Christians could be looked on as lawbreakers, carrying weapons and resisting an authorized arresting party (especially in John where Roman soldiers were involved). Hall ("Swords") points to the *Lex Iulia de maiestate* with its penalties against instigators of armed riot and Ulpian's application of it to those who carried arms against the public good (DJ 48.4.1; see §31, D3a below). But how concerned were the evangelists that their Gospels would be read by hostile Gentile outsiders? (The same query is applicable to the thesis that Mark hid the name of the sword-wielder.) An explanation based on inner Christian community concerns is always more plausible. Christians who were themselves persecuted and arrested would need to know if Jesus approved of such armed resistance.

Should they too resist with a sword? Matt, John, and Luke all indicate Jesus' disapproval, but in different wording.

The Response in Matt 26:52–54. This is "one of the first clear examples of Matthean *Sondergut*" in the PN (SPNM 130–31), i.e., of material peculiar to Matt; and so we must look carefully at theories about where it came from. Rejecting dependence on an independent written source known to Matt (so also Punnakottil, "Passion" 31), Senior argues strongly that Matt created vv. 52–53 from material in his own Gospel, his own "seedbed." I think a third possibility may be more plausible: Matt drew on Christian tradition (not a written source) for his material and to some extent rewrote it in his own style. While SPNM 132–42 shows in detail that the style and thought of vv. 52–53 is consonant with Matt's style and thought, it does not pay much attention to the parallels between Matt and John or between Matt and Luke on such themes as putting the sword back or angelic help, parallels (in this same context of facing the hour) that make likely the existence of such Christian tradition. Some of it could have reached the evangelist orally, and SPNM's concentration on literary dependence does not facilitate appeal to oral tradition. But let us move from generalities to the verse involved.

The key response of Jesus, introduced by Matt's favorite "Then" (*tote*), is in v. 52a: "Return your sword to its place." By way of content the Johannine Jesus, as we shall see, gives exactly the same command, "Put the sword into the scabbard"; but in vocabulary only the word "sword" is the same. One could argue that by hazard both evangelists created spontaneously a brief imperative statement of Jesus with the same message. But is it not more likely that in circles where the arrest story was told with a disciple as the sword-wielder, a response had developed in which Jesus told the disciple to put the sword back, and that each evangelist is reflecting this tradition? The difference in wording would stem from rephrasing by each evangelist in his own style. I see no way of telling about rephrasing by John; SPNM offers sufficient reason for thinking that Matt rephrased.[14]

The Matthean Jesus' concise command about returning the sword to its place is bolstered by a general poetic (chiastic) assertion, "For all who take the sword, by the sword will perish." Again SPNM (134–36) stresses that the wording is not foreign to Matt's style and that the sentiment is harmonious with Matt 5:39, where Jesus forbids his followers to answer violent action by violent action, and with 10:39, which encourages them to be willing

---

[14]Already in 26:51 Matt expanded Mark's account of the assault by adding "having stretched out his hand," a clause with OT resonance—seventy-five times in the OT, e.g., Judg 3:21; 15:15; and esp. Gen 22:10. However, the imperative in 26:52 to return the sword to its place is the reversal of the action of drawing the sword common to Mark/Matt, not of the peculiarly Matthean stretching out of the hand.

to lose their lives for his sake. Such harmony, of course, is not surprising; if 26:52b were not in harmony with Matt's view of Jesus, he would not have reported it. Yet there are no previous words of the Matthean Jesus about his disciples using a sword; and v. 52b goes beyond the do-not-return-violence principle, for it warns that in the divine plan violence by a human being will be punished by equal violence. Thus the case for Matt having created v. 52b out of material previously reported in the Gospel is extremely weak.

In this statement about perishing by the sword a warning is being extended beyond the sword-wielding disciple and addressed to Jesus' followers in general. (A few minor textual witnesses read "to them" instead of "to him" in 26:52.) Therefore, a plausible source from which Matt may have derived it is Christian moral teaching reflecting Jewish moral teaching. Gen 9:6 offers a type of *ius talionis* (also in chiastic poetry): "Whoever sheds the blood of a fellow human being shall by a human have his own blood shed." In the context of calling for endurance and faith, Rev 13:9–10 has the same moral principle but phrased in terms of a sword, "If anyone kills with a sword, with the sword must that person be slain." This type of poetic axiom, brought to Matt's mind by the key word "sword," may have been adapted by him to fit the present scene. Kosmala ("Matthew") has argued for a different source, namely the Aramaic targum of Isa 50:11, which has added the image of a sword to that passage in the Hebrew Bible: "*All* you (that) kindle a fire, (that) *take a sword,* go *fall* into the fire that you have kindled and into *the sword* that you have taken. From my Memra [personified Word] you have this: You shall return to your *destruction.*" He contends that Matt has selected words (my italics) from this to make a general statement. Notice, however, that this procedure would require ingenuity and a poetic feeling, for to emerge with Matt 26:52 one would almost have to assume the compositor was influenced by Gen 9:6 or something similar. There is no proof, moreover, that this targum or its thought existed when Matt wrote; its chief utility is to show that the sword motif also became a popular motif in Judaism in the *ius talionis* pattern.

Besides warning his disciples what will happen if they resort to the sword, the Matthean Jesus (v. 53) points out that he has no need of their paltry military assistance: If he called upon his Father, more than twelve legions of angels would be supplied. The statement reflects the OT imagery of angelic armies or "hosts" (Josh 5:14; Ps 148:2; etc.), who in the postexilic period were thought to intervene militarily in human affairs (Dan 12:1; II Macc 5:2–3; 10:29–30; 1 QM 12:8), especially when prayed for (II Macc 15:22–23). Once more there is ample evidence that this verse is consonant with Matthean thought and style. Matt uses *angelos* some twenty times and likes hyperbole (a legion would be six thousand!). The idea of angels helping Jesus was proposed by Satan in 4:6. Jesus has just spoken of the Son of Man being given over into the hands of sinners (26:45), and angels are associated with the Son of Man (13:41; 16:27; 24:30–31; 25:31). Was the number twelve suggested by contrast with the insignificant human help of the Twelve?[15] This time, unlike v. 52b, the Gospel offers respectable material that might have influenced Matt in shaping the statement. But why would he shape it and introduce it here? Probably because tradition guided him, as we can discern from Luke and John where (in entirely different vocabulary) angelic intervention is mentioned in relation to Jesus' prayer about the cup/hour. I already proposed above (pp. 186–87) that this motif of angelic response was shaped by the three evangelists, each in his own way. As another indication of what may have been in the tradition, in relation to Matt's implication that Jesus did not need the use of the sword by his disciples to defend him, we should note Jesus' words to Pilate in John 18:36: "If my kingdom were of this world, my attendants [*hypēretai*] would have struggled [*agōnizein*] lest I be given over to the Jews."

As for the next verse in Matt (v. 54), "How then would the Scriptures be fulfilled that it must happen thus?" I agree with SPNM 142–48 that Matt has drawn this theme from Mark 14:49. The "How then" introduction is Matthean style, as we see from comparing Matt 22:43–44 and Mark 12:36.[16] In Mark the Scripture-fulfillment theme comes after Jesus' statement about teaching daily in the Temple. There Matt (v. 56) will have a reference to fulfilling the prophets, so that by anticipating the theme here, Matt has Jesus twice signal the fulfillment of what was written. That is appropriate in a Gospel where fulfillment citations of Scripture are a leitmotif: "All this happened to fulfill what the Lord had spoken by the prophet who said . . ." (see BBM 96–104). Some scholars have proposed that it was for apologetic purposes that Matt added to the Gospel some fourteen citations introduced by such formulas; but a didactic, theological purpose explains them better (since some of them do not pertain to points that would have been sharply debated between Christians and those Jews who did not believe in Jesus). Scripture reflection helped those who believed in Jesus to understand the way in which he fulfilled God's plan, not only in the great events of his life but even in minor incidents. His being arrested and dying at the hands of sinners are part of that plan, and the Matthean Jesus wants his disciples to realize this lest they continue to interfere.

The element of "must" (*dei*) appears in the fulfillment reference of v. 54: "It must happen thus." In the first passion prediction (Matt 16:21): "Jesus began to show his disciples that it is necessary [*dei*] for him to go away to

---

[15]Yet now, without Judas, they are the Eleven (Matt 28:16).

[16]Throughout these verses Matt is composing not by freely creating, but by reshaping and rewriting. In 26:52–53 Matt was reshaping tradition (not a written source); in 26:54 he is reshaping Mark.

Jerusalem and suffer many things from the elders and chief priests and scribes." Now Jesus makes explicit what was implicit there: His knowing what he must do was related to what the Scriptures said. The PN began in Matt 26:31 with Jesus citing Zech 13:7; it will come to its climax in Matt 27:46 with Jesus citing Ps 22:2. For Matt, God has written from beginning to end what must be. The traditional passage for showing the Jewish sense of the divine plan as a "must" is Dan 2:28–29 (Theodotion version, also 2:45), where Daniel explains to King Nebuchadnezzar what must come to pass in the last days. SPNM 148, following H. E. Todt, wants to make a sharp distinction between such an apocalyptic or eschatological "must-formula" and a fulfillment-of-Scripture "must-formula." Granted that these formulas may have had different origins, can one think that Matt kept them distinct or expected his readers to? The Scriptures that say "it must happen thus" are being fulfilled, but the "it" consists of the passion of the Son of Man who belongs to the last days.

The Response in John 18:11. This is much briefer than the response in Matt, and indeed we have already discussed the two segments that constitute it. In the first, even though the arresting party makes no objection to letting the disciples go, Peter strikes off the servant's ear. Jesus tells him peremptorily, "Put the sword into the scabbard," a message identical in content but not in wording to the message of the Matthean Jesus.

The second segment of v. 11 also stems from tradition. There the Johannine Jesus asks a rhetorical question (BDF 365[4], even as Matt 26:54 was a rhetorical question): "The cup the Father has given me—am I not to drink it?" I treated this in §11, A3 as parallel to Mark 14:36 (Matt 26:39; Luke 22:42), "*Abba*, Father . . . Take away this cup from me."[17] There I also considered John 12:27b, "And what should I say? Father, save me from this hour? But for this (purpose) have I come to this hour," as a parallel to the preceding verse in Mark (14:35), "He . . . was praying that, if it is possible, the hour might pass from him." In other words, Mark has two prayers in Gethsemane, for the passing of the hour and for the taking away of the cup. John has two rhetorical questions, one earlier in the ministry and one in the garden across the Kidron: the first indicating that Jesus does not want to be saved from the hour; the second, that he must not be prevented from drinking the cup. Mark's christology in which the Son could ask the Father to change the plan if He willed to do so differs from that in John, where Jesus and the Father are one (10:30) and there can be no suspense in prayers (11:41–42). While in Matt the disciples should not interfere with the arrest by using the

---

[17]See also Mark 10:38: "Are you able to drink the cup which I drink?"

sword because the Scriptures must be fulfilled, the Johannine Peter should not interfere with the drinking of the cup because (like the coming of the hour) that represents Jesus' own purpose (which is the same as the Father's). Again we are seeing the influence of the Johannine principle of sovereignty: "I lay down my life . . . of my own accord" (10:17–18).

I have suggested that these clear parallels between Mark and John and between Matt and John involve so much diversity that literary dependence is quite implausible. If the components came to the evangelists independently from earlier tradition, I would estimate using the analogy of Hebrews (§11B above) that the prayer for the *passing* of the hour and cup as reflected in Mark is closer to the most ancient form of the tradition than is John's transformation of it into a rhetorical question under the impact of a higher christology. In Mark Jesus' mind is made up in conformity to the Father's will but *after* the prayer has been made, and not before as it is in John, when the prayer becomes unnecessary. Yet John's separation of the hour and cup themes, with only the cup belonging to the PN, may be closer to the original disposition than Mark's joining them in the Gethsemane scene. (Mark, despite its antiquity, often gives a simplified, kerygmatic sequence.) John's response to the sword-wielder, reflecting elements in the tradition, is less elaborate and less rewritten than Matt's.

The Response in Luke 22:49–51. As I indicated above, the preparatory question presented by "those about him," asking the Lord, "Shall we strike with the sword?" is a Lucan creation connecting the dialogue at the Last Supper about having two swords (22:35–38) with the cutting off of the servant's ear and Jesus' reaction to such sword-wielding. Fitzmyer (*Luke* 2.1448) points out that stylistically a direct question such as this, introduced by *ei* ("whether"), is frequent in Luke. Those whom Jesus has praised as having remained with him in his trials (Luke 22:28) show their willingness to resist. Functionally this is a stage-setting question like that of the disciples in Acts 1:6, "Lord, will you at this time restore the kingdom to Israel?"; it enables Jesus to give an answer that Luke wants his readers to hear. A few scholars have tried to trace a radical development in Jesus' outlook from 22:35–38 to 22:49–51. Included would be those who try to render the *hikanon estin* of v. 38 to mean that Jesus thought two swords were enough to meet the oncoming danger,[18] or who render it as an undecided answer. Jesus

---

[18]Or "long enough": W. Western, ExpTim 52 (1940–41), 357. K. H. Rengstorf (TDNT 3.295–96) offers several bewilderingly subtle interpretations, e.g., the swords are not forbidden, but those who use them have calculated erroneously. Bornhäuser (*Death* 73–74) calls on the LXX use of *hikanos* as a divine name rendering Hebrew *šadday,* meaning "the Mighty One" (Ruth 1:20,21; Job 21:15; 31:2). However, his suggested translation, "It is sufficient power," makes little sense in the context.

then would have seriously contemplated armed resistance at the supper; but now that he has actually seen bloodshed, he would be pulling back and calling a halt (see Gillman, "Temptation" 150–52). However, such a theory involves not only a very dubious exegesis of vv. 35–38 but also a portrait of Jesus quite unlike that found elsewhere in Luke. Rather there is consistency on the part both of Jesus and of the disciples in the two Lucan passages. The disciples misunderstood when he spoke about the need for being prepared for flight and danger and took the need for a sword literally; here they misunderstand even more seriously by wishing to use the sword. They have been told twice to pray not to have to enter into trial (*peirasmos:* 22:40,46); yet they are still wondering whether they should enter violently. Jesus' "Enough of that" at the supper was an expression of frustration at their inability to understand, and now he must be even more firm.

Like the *hikanon estin* of v. 38, the command Jesus gives in v. 51, *eate heōs toutou,* is brief and difficult to translate. *Eate* is the second-person-plural present imperative of the verb *ean,* so that although "a certain one" of those who stood by struck the sword blow, Jesus addresses the group of disciples. The verb means "to allow, let, let go, leave alone"; and of eleven NT uses, nine are in Luke-Acts. It is not clear who or what is the object of "let." *Heōs toutou* means "as far as this."[19] It is not clear whether "as far as this" refers to the assault or the arrest. Nor is it clear whether these are to be taken as two separate, almost repetitive phrases, or united into one. Some suggested renderings include, "Stop! That's far enough!"; "Let them [the arresting party] be, even to the point of arresting me"; "Let him [the servant] alone. That's far enough." But most of the proposals have the same emphatic import: Let that be enough!

Luke does not spell out why Jesus did not want the arrest interrupted; that was done in the earlier dialogue (22:37): "This that is written must [*dei*] be completed in me." Notice how similar that motif is to the words Matt gives (26:54) as a response to the sword-wielder: he must stop, otherwise "How then would the Scriptures be fulfilled that it must [*dei*] happen thus?" As background for Matt's use of *dei* for the divine plan, I mentioned the Theodotion version of Dan 2:45: "The great God had made known . . . what must [*dei*] happen after this." The LXX of that passage is: "The great God has signified . . . what would be [*ta esomena*] in the last days." When the Lucan disciples asked Jesus about using the sword, the request was on the basis of their "having seen what would be [*to esomenon*]," namely, an arrest leading to an execution. Jesus in response forbids the sword because the Scriptures

---

[19]See II Sam 7:18, where David asks the Lord, "Who am I or what is my house that you have brought me this far [*heōs toutōn*]?"

give a deeper knowledge of the meaning of "must" and "would be" (*dei* = *to esomenon*). After the resurrection he will explain: "Was it not a must [*dei*] that the Messiah suffer these things and (so) come into this glory?" (Luke 24:26–27). "It is written thus: The Messiah is to suffer and rise from the dead on the third day, and there is to be preached in his name repentance for the forgiveness of sins to all the nations" (24:46–47).

But the Lucan Jesus responds to the cutting off of the servant's ear not only by reprimanding word but also by action: touching the ear and healing the servant.[20] Most scholars regard the account of the healing as a Lucan composition (Soards, *Passion* 100). MacDonald ("Malchus'") argues for historicity because unless the servant had been healed, this act of violent resistance would have been brought up against Jesus before Pilate. For some this incident in Luke explains John's identification of the servant: Because Jesus healed him, the servant eventually became a Christian, and that is how his name "Malchus" was known and preserved. The combination of the verb "to touch" with *iasthai*, "to heal," is good Lucan style, e.g., Luke 6:19. With a modern sense of lessening the miraculous, some modern scholars have stressed the "earlobe" rendition of *ōtion* (p. 271 above). They imagine that Jesus stopped the bleeding after a small part of the ear had been cut off. More traditionally this has been a text exploited for the picture of a medically concerned Luke the physician. The evangelist's outlook, quite far from either of those two approaches, was expressed in 5:17: "The power of the Lord [God] was for the purpose of his [Jesus] healing." Not simply remedying ailments but healing people was a major part of Jesus' great task in the midst of his own troubles. This is another example of the special Lucan theology of Jesus acting as savior during the passion itself. Jesus is faithful to his own words: "Love your enemies and do good . . . expecting nothing in return." In the dialogue that led to the mention of the two swords, Jesus cited the Suffering Servant passage of Isa 53:12 (Luke 22:37). Here we are not far from Isa 53:5, "By his bruises we are healed [*iasthai*]."[21]

JESUS' COMPLAINT (MARK 14:48–49A; MATT 26:55; LUKE 22:52–53A)

The three Synoptics have a complaining statement of Jesus addressed to the arresting party. Each evangelist gives it a slightly different setting. *In Mark* the sword attack has just taken place; Jesus says nothing to the by-

---

[20]As in 22:47, the brevity of the Lucan sentence about the healing in v. 51 is expanded in Codex Bezae: "Having stretched out his hand [see Matt 26:51], he touched him and restored his ear."

[21]Tenuous is the Scripture background offered by Doeve ("Gefangennahme" 470) in Amos 3:12: "As the shepherd rescues from the mouth of the lion two legs or the lobe [*lobos*] of an ear, so shall the people of Israel who dwell in Samaria be rescued."

stander who did it and indeed makes no mention of it. Rather in 14:48–49 his only reaction is to address a statement ("answer" can mean that) of complaint "to them" about *their* behavior in seizing him, i.e., presumably to the "crowd with swords and wooden clubs, from the chief priests and the scribes and the elders." It is not clear that his statement has anything to do with the sword attack, unless we are to think that the bystander was a member of the crowd, which seems unlikely. The very vagueness of the connection with the sword blow and the tone of injured innocence make sense if the bystander was not a disciple. Neither Jesus nor any of his followers have done anything to offend.

In Matt Jesus has reprimanded one of his disciples for using the sword, and now he turns to reprimand "the crowds." Matt has a fondness for speaking of "crowds" and has no problem with switching back and forth between the singular and the plural (13:2; 14:13–15; 15:30–31; 21:8,9,11). One need not think, therefore, that another crowd has arrived beyond the one described (in agreement with Mark) in 26:47. The two reprimands, one to the disciple who struck the servant of the high priest and the other to the crowd(s) from the chief priests, show a Jesus who judges that neither friend nor foe understands God's plan. Dramatically, Matt 26:55 introduces the second reprimand "in that hour"—an hour last mentioned in 26:45 as coming near, in parallelism with the coming near of his being given over (26:46).

In Luke there is also the pattern of two reprimands, one for his disciple, one for his foes. In the Lucan sequence, however, the reprimand to the disciple has been followed by the healing of a foe. Thus Jesus first shows those opposed to him that he wishes to heal them; only then does he correct them. It is at this moment that Luke becomes specific about the foes; hitherto (22:47) he has spoken only of "a crowd," but now we hear of "the chief priests and captains of the Temple and elders" who are there against Jesus. Luke uses an aorist participle; and it is not clear whether he would have us think that these "had arrived" as part of the crowd previously mentioned, or "arrived" just now as a new group—whence my ungrammatical "were arrived" which leaves both options open. In either case Luke has probably drawn his cast of characters from the triad mentioned in Mark 14:43, substituting "captains of the Temple" for Mark's "scribes" and shaping an introduction for them to bring them into contact with Jesus.[22] The idea that such dignitaries have come out carrying swords and wooden clubs (as Jesus' statement implies) in the night that is Passover to arrest a criminal amid armed resistance is simply staggering. Not only is there the usual problem (APPEN-

---

[22]*Paraginesthai* ("to arrive, be present"), although used by Mark 14:43 of Judas, is very Lucan: twenty-eight times in Luke-Acts.

DIX II, B2ab) that, having mentioned that the Last Supper was a Passover meal, the Synoptics ignore the actual feast day in what follows; but also Luke's simplification of Mark has created a new problem by switching the reference to the chief priests and companions from its Marcan place at the beginning (as the authorization of the crowd) to here (as the audience). Albeit more dramatic, from the viewpoint of logic this may be one of the less successful instances of putting things in order of which the Lucan Prologue boasts (1:3). We shall see below in discussing John what may have pushed Luke in this direction.

The three Synoptics show remarkable agreement on the first part of Jesus' complaint: "As if against a bandit have you come out with swords and wooden clubs to take me?" The only variant is Luke's omission of "to take me," which Fitzmyer (*Luke* 2.1451) would explain as Luke's wanting to depict Jesus in charge. Yet just two verses later (22:54), in exactly the same vocabulary Luke will describe the taking of Jesus by his adversaries. More likely, then, the omission is simply more of Luke's abbreviation, avoiding repetition.

This is the first PN reference to *lēstēs* ("bandit"; pl. *lēstai*), which will be a significant term in crucial scenes. It designates violent, armed men (not of official police or military status) who were often no better than marauders or thugs.[23] Mark 11:17 and par. recall a contemptuous objection to making the Temple a den of *lēstai*. In the countryside *lēstai* often functioned as brigands preying on villages or travelers, so that in the parable of the man going down from Jerusalem (through a desert region) to Jericho, he can be said to fall among *lēstai* who strip and beat him (Luke 10:30,36). In the cities they could be troublemakers who produced civic disturbance. Thus Barabbas, whom Mark 15:7 and par. associate with a riot in Jerusalem, is called a *lēstēs* in John 18:40. This riot may also be connected with the fact that Mark/Matt call *lēstai* the two men crucified alongside Jesus. In the present scene, then, Jesus is protesting that the arms employed in arresting him give the absurd impression that he has been a man of violence.

Parenthetically, let me remark that the attempt to use the present passage or the other PN references to *lēstai* to show that historically Jesus was or was considered to be a revolutionary is simplistic and anachronistic. In §31,A2e I shall survey the usage of *lēstēs* in Josephus and point out that there is no

---

[23]Illustrating the anarchy ca. 40 BC that colored Herod the Great's rise to power, Josephus, *War* 1.10.5; #204, speaks of a hoard of *lēstai* ravaging the Syrian frontier, led by Ezekias, an *archilēstēs*, while in 1.16.2; #304 he uses *lēstai* to designate cave-dwelling marauders who preyed on villages near Sepphoris in Galilee. Inevitably such lawless men could be persuaded to lend their services to schemers or visionaries, almost as mercenaries with the hope of booty. At Herod's death Simon of Perea, who took a crown for himself, collected *lēstai* and with them burned down the Herodian palace in Jericho (*War* 2.4.2; #57). In 2.8.4; #125 and 2.12.2; #228–29 *lēstai* are highway robbers; Essenes on a journey carrying weapons to protect themselves against such.

remembrance of revolutions against the prefects of Judea in Jesus' adulthood, and that even in the politically more disturbed period of the post-44 Roman prefecture Josephus does not simply equate *lēstai* with revolutionaries, Zealots, or *sicarii*.[24] Nevertheless, we must remember that the Gospels were written, read, and heard in the period of 70 to 100, after the Jewish revolt against the Romans. Popular mindsets of that time may well have blended together the various groups whom Josephus distinguished explicitly or implicitly. Therefore, it is not impossible that the instances of *lēstēs* in the PNs were envisioned anachronistically to refer to the kind of violent men who functioned in the Jewish Revolt, so that Jesus was "heard" to protest that he was being treated like a revolutionary (not simply a "bandit"). Similarly, in this post-70 period Barabbas and the co-crucified might have been thought of as equivalent to those who had just revolted against Rome. We are touching here on a delicate and almost uncontrollable hermeneutical area where a misapprehension may have become the real meaning, conveyed and understood; but we should not compound the difficulty by reconstructing earlier history on the basis of that misunderstanding.

There is also broad Synoptic agreement in the second part of Jesus' complaint to the arresting party, which Mark phrases as "Day after day I was with [*pros*] you in the Temple teaching, and you did not seize me." Matt moves "in the Temple" forward in the sentence to emphasize it; and both Matt and Luke in different ways avoid Mark's periphrastic "was" plus the participle "teaching" (BDF 353). Matt substitutes "I was sitting teaching," presumably offering a more vivid picture, since sitting was the normal position for authoritative teaching (Matt 5:1–2; 13:1–3; 23:2–3). Luke substitutes a more elegant participial clause that literally translated clearly heightens the contrast: "(Although) being with [*meta*] you." Notice too the different Lucan preposition; Mark's *pros* had more of a directional sense: Jesus was speaking with and to them. More difficult to discern is the reason why Luke substitutes "you did not stretch out your hands against me" for the Marcan "and you did not seize me."[25] These words in Luke are directed to the chief priests with the elders; did Luke think it incongruous that they themselves would seize him and therefore prefer a more indirect description? (Yet the captains of the Temple, who are also addressed, could quite congruously have seized him.)

The last question brings us into some problems of technical or logical accuracy in this statement, granted the envisaged audience. *Kath hēmeran* appears in the three Synoptic forms of Jesus' complaint, and the normal

---

[24]In discussing whether Jesus was a revolutionary, §31, A2 will describe these and other groups who figured in the political and social scene of 1st-cent.-AD Judea.

[25]Matt earlier had the sword-wielder stretch out his hand, but that is probably an accidental similarity to Luke, reflecting OT language (n. 14 above).

translation would be "day after day." Thus understood, Jesus' claim is imprecise. In Mark, for example, when was Jesus in the Temple?[26] He was there
in Mark 11:11; 11:15,17; and 11:27–13:1 (esp. 12:35), i.e., a total of three
days on only two of which he is said to have taught. This statement is often
advanced as proof that the Marcan outline (followed by Matt and Luke)
whereby Jesus comes to Jerusalem only once in his public ministry, namely,
at the time of his death, has been simplified for preaching purposes and that
John is more accurate in describing many journeys to Jerusalem and a long
history of Temple encounters. Argyle ("Meaning") raises the interesting
possibility of avoiding the difficulty by translating *kath hēmeran* as "by day,"
a translation that would fit into Jesus' objection about the manner in which
they have come to arrest him, namely, by night—which, of course, was part
of the strategy to avoid public trouble (Mark 14:1–2). In his description of
Jesus' Temple activities, Luke has established a case for either rendering of
the term: 19:47–20:1 makes clear that Jesus did teach day after day, while
21:37 speaks of this as a daytime activity, following which at night Jesus
used to go and lodge on the Mount of Olives.

Pursuing the issue of logic, we note that while Luke seems implausible in
bringing the chief priests and elders to the Mount of Olives to take part
themselves in the arrest (the captains of the Temple are not a problem), Jesus' statement makes better sense addressed to them than it does to the
Mark/Matt crowd. That pickup crowd has been quickly deputized this very
night for the arrest. How can Jesus tell its members that he was with *them* day
by day in the Temple and they did not seize him (as if they had existed before
and would have had the authority to do this)? Of course, one can rightly say
that this is the imprecise logic of a popularly described tale and scene. But is
Luke attempting to be more "orderly" (1:3) in having the words addressed precisely to those priestly authorities who (with scribes or elders, as previously
reported in 19:47; 20:1,19) were with Jesus when he taught on different days
in the Temple and who had sought to destroy him at that time?

The key to that Lucan orderliness may lie in John's report of a similar
complaint addressed by Jesus *to the high priest,* just after, not before (as in
Luke) his being arrested. (This scene in John 18:19–23 will be discussed in
detail in §19 below. Luke and John in a different sequence agree that during
the night of the arrest, before Jesus was taken to the authorities [Sanhedrin
for Luke; Caiaphas for John] who would give him over to the Romans, Jesus
stood before the chief priests [Luke] or the high priest [John] and made this
complaint.) In John 18:19 the high priest (Annas: 18:13) will question Jesus

[26]*To hieron* (the holy site) describes the whole Temple enclave, including those outer precincts
that a layman like Jesus could enter.

about his disciples and about his *teaching;* and Jesus will answer (18:20): "I have spoken openly to the world. I always taught in a synagogue and in the Temple, where all the Jews come together, and in secret I spoke nothing." Did very early tradition place a statement of this sort in defensive remarks made by Jesus before the priestly authorities? John then would have adapted it ("the world"; "openly"; "a synagogue"; "the Jews"; etc.) and reported it where Jesus encountered the high priest on the night before Jesus died. Mark (followed by Matt) would also have adapted it to become an address to a crowd *from the chief priests.* Luke, while rearranging and abbreviating Mark's account, may have been led into some of his awkward presentation by trying to do justice to the tradition that the chief priests were the original audience. This would exemplify Schneider's contention (*Passion* 54) that Luke and John drew not on a common source, but on a common tradition, so that Luke's redactional activity on Mark was not simply haphazard.

FULFILLMENT OF SCRIPTURE; DEPARTURE OF DISCIPLES
(MARK 14:49B–50; MATT 26:56; JOHN 18:8B–9)

Mark 14:49b–50:"However—let the Scriptures be fulfilled!" The last words that the Marcan Jesus speaks to the arresting party (indeed the last words of his life to his people) express his summary understanding of all that has happened, including his being seized as if he were a *lēstēs,* and his impatience to get on with the affair. In a way this reference to fulfilling the Scriptures answers a question that Mark does not raise explicitly (nor does any evangelist) but which readers might well raise, and certainly the opponents of Christianity did. Jesus *does* nothing in this scene. Why? This is a man who raised the dead (Mark 5:35–43), calmed raging storms (4:36–41; 6:47–52), and drove out legions of wild demons (5:1–13). If he shows no such power now, it is because the Scriptures that point to suffering and death must be fulfilled. The opening *alla* ("but, however") is strong, thrusting the thought forward but in another direction; ZAGNT 1.158 suggests the translation "Come." An abrupt *hina* introduces what follows: "in order that the Scriptures be fulfilled." Taylor and others agree with Matt 26:56 in fleshing out the clause to constitute a sentence: "All this happened in order that . . ." But others by appealing to an imperatival *hina* (BDF 387) preserve the abruptness of the Marcan Greek: "Let the Scriptures be fulfilled." This translation has the advantage of affirming that what fulfills is not only what has happened but what will follow, namely, that having left him, all flee.

Bultmann (BHST 269) thinks that this statement about fleeing follows awkwardly on the theme of Scripture fulfillment and wonders whether v. 50 did not once follow v. 46 and the seizure of Jesus. Bultmann, Schenke (*Stu-*

dien 358), and others observe that the Marcan "all" is vague since Jesus has just been talking to the crowd and wonder if once it did not refer to others besides (or in place of) the disciples. On the other hand, Linnemann (*Studien* 79) judges that the word for "disciples" may have been in the original tradition. Some of these difficulties about vv. 49b and 50 can be lessened if one recognizes that the logic of the Marcan sequence at the end of the Mount of Olives scene is dictated by an inclusion with the beginning of the scene. The first words of Jesus spoken as he and his disciples went to the Mount of Olives was a scriptural reference to the disciples being scattered once the shepherd was struck (Mark 14:26–28); the last words that he speaks on the Mount concerning the fulfillment of the Scriptures include in their reference the disciples fleeing. At the beginning of the scene, Peter reacted to Jesus' prophecy of the forthcoming scandalizing and scattering of the disciples by asserting, "I will not deny"; then Mark 14:31 added: "And they were all saying the same." That is echoed here in Mark's "And having left him, all fled." The sequence in Jesus' three prophecies (see ANALYSIS of §5) was that one of the Twelve would give him over (Mark 14:18–20, Last Supper), all the disciples would be scattered (14:27), and Peter would deny him three times before the cock crowed twice. Two of the prophecies have been fulfilled (in order) in the arrest; the third will soon be fulfilled (14:66–72). Not only the Scriptures but his own prophecies must be fulfilled!

Indeed there is also an inclusion between Mark's description of the call of the first disciples at the beginning of the ministry and these last actions of all the disciples at the end of the ministry. We are told in Mark 1:18 that having been called by Jesus, Simon (Peter) and Andrew "left [*aphienai*] their nets and followed him" and then in 1:20 that James and John "left [*aphienai*] their father . . . and went after him." At the end, "Having left [*aphienai*] him, all fled." ("Fled" may be too weak a translation, for there is a note of abandonment.) Their internship in being disciples during the ministry has ended in failure because they have not yet learned the lesson of Mark 8:34: "If anyone wishes to follow after me, let him deny himself and take up his cross and follow me."

Matt 26:56 represents some minor modifications of Mark 14:49b–50.[27] In Jesus' rebuke to his disciple who attacked the servant (26:54), Matt already introduced the theme of the fulfillment of Scripture. The repetition of the theme in the rebuke to the crowds means that all the actions of the arrest, both by disciple and by foes, come under God's already indicated plan. Matt

---

[27]Although some interpreters think that Jesus ceased to speak at the end of Matt 26:55 and that therefore 26:56a is the evangelist's comment, I see no reason for suspecting that; analogies with Mark 14:49b and Matt 26:54 suggest that it is Jesus speaking about the fulfillment of the prophetical Scriptures.

solves Mark's hiatus by supplying a grammatical preparation for the *hina:* "But this whole thing has happened in order that . . ." This formula that Matt uses to introduce the penultimate fulfillment citation in his Gospel is verbatim the same as the formula that introduced his first fulfillment citation (1:22—his only other use of it), an inclusion signaling the comprehensiveness of God's plan stretching from the conception of Jesus by a virgin through the Holy Spirit to his arrest at the hands of sinners "in that hour" (26:55). This inclusive outlook explains why two verses later (26:58) Matt will describe Peter as anticipating "the end." The first citation was a fulfillment of "what the Lord had spoken through the prophet"; here Matt expands the Marcan words to specify the fulfillment of the *prophetical* Scriptures. Almost every formula citation in Matt has in whole or in part been from a prophet (not only the writing prophets, but the "former prophets" stretching from Joshua through Kings). In the one exception (13:35, which cites Ps 78[77]:2) he still speaks of "the prophet," so that in his thought all Scripture may have taken on a prophetical aura pointing to Jesus (so SPNM 154).

Is Matt thinking of a specific text? That question may be asked about Mark, but more appropriately about Matt, whose fulfillment citations generally do point to specific texts. Probably the majority of scholars think that no one text is meant and point for support to the generalized "Christ died for our sins in accordance with the Scriptures" in I Cor 15:3. And certainly a whole group of psalm passages pertaining to the suffering just one could be invoked, dealing with seizing the one whom God has forsaken (71:11), using the sword (37:14), flight of friends (38:12), and insincere betrayal (41:7,10). But even if a larger number of Scriptures are meant, is one or the other in the foreground of Matt's reference? In part that depends on the direction of "this whole thing" that has happened—does it point exclusively back to what has just happened or been said? Since Jesus has complained about being treated as a *lēstēs,* some (e.g., Schreiber, Schweizer) point to Isa 53:12, "And among outlaws [*anomos*] will he be reckoned," arguing that the citation of that text in Luke 22:37 shows that it was in the early Christian arsenal. But Luke does not clearly refer that text to the arrest (he does not appeal to the Scriptures in the arrest scene), and the vocabulary for the criminal(s) is different. Thinking of the betrayal by Judas as the focus, Dibelius ("Judas" 272–73) points to Ps 41:10, where the sufferer complains that the trusted friend who partook of bread with him has raised his heel against him. Dibelius contends that this psalm text was already influential in the Last Supper prediction of Judas' betrayal (Matt 26:20–25), but in fact only John (13:18) makes the reference explicit. Others argue from the "Then" (*tote*) which introduces Matt's sentence describing the flight of "all the disciples," maintaining that this connective points to the flight as the focus of the Scripture fulfillment. In that case Matt, like Mark, could have had in mind Zech 13:7, which Jesus cited explicitly as he began the Mount of Olives scene: "I will strike the shepherd and the sheep of the flock will be scattered" (Matt 26:31). I pointed out above that Mark may have meant an inclusion between the action taken by the disciples at the beginning of the scene and at its end: There *all* said that they would not deny; here *all* have fled. In Matt 26:35 (the parallel to Mark's beginning of the scene) a reference to "the disciples" was added: "And so said all disciples"; so here too in Matt 26:56 that addition has been made: "All the disciples . . . fled." Even in flight they remain Jesus' disciples.

Matt 26:45–46 constituted Jesus' last words before his death spoken directly "to the disciples"; 26:52–54 constituted his last words to an individual disciple; and 26:55–56 constitute his last words "to the crowds." Since both 54 and 56 have Jesus himself emphasize that what is happening is fulfilling the Scriptures, we see dramatically the extent to which, even though his cup prayer was not granted, Jesus meant, "Let your will be done."

John 18:8b–9, with its concentration on fulfillment and letting the disciples go, is closer to Mark 14:49b–50 (and Matt 26:56) than is Luke 22:53b, which mentions neither detail. Even though John has the tradition of the disciples being scattered (16:32) and mentions the danger of their being scandalized (16:1), the disciples in John's arrest scene do not flee; rather Jesus arranges for their release. Bickermann ("Utilitas" 213–16) would explain this as John's narrative reflecting a different legal situation. Jesus was officially tried and sentenced by the Sanhedrin in John 11:47–53; yet he hid himself and fled (11:54; 12:36), thus making himself officially a fugitive. Origen (*Commentary on John* 28.21–23 [18–19]; GCS10 [Origen 4].419–20), pertinent to John 11:54, used the term *anachorēsis,* which in the papyri appears as a technical term for flight from the authorities. Evidently Celsus also read Jesus' action this way, for he accuses Jesus of shameful hiding (Origen, *Contra Celsum* 2.9). Flight led to proscription (*prographē*), and anyone who knew where he was should have denounced him, as Judas was doing. Therefore Jesus had to bargain for the release of his disciples who could have been arrested. In my judgment Bickermann is reading the account through the technicalities of Roman ordinary law, which, as we shall see (§31, D3 below), was not so simply applicable to an imperial province like Judea, administered by extraordinary law. Certainly in John's mind (18:30) the Sanhedrin did not have legal authority to execute Jesus, and so it is doubtful that in hiding himself from them he was officially proscribed.

The ancient authorities Bickermann describes are reading John through their own experiences of official Roman decrees against Christians where harboring a proscribed fugitive was indeed a crime.

The solution of why the Johannine Jesus tells the arresting Roman soldiers and Jewish police attendants, "If therefore you are seeking me, let these go away," is simpler: It is another instance of the principle of Jesus' sovereignty that governs the Johannine PN. If the disciples fled, they would be acting on their own. Just as Judas could not leave the Last Supper without Jesus controlling the action (13:27: "What you are going to do, do quickly"), so what the other disciples will do in the PN is under Jesus' control. He has already shown the arresting party that he has the power to throw them back to the ground; and so when he states the condition on which he will allow himself to be arrested, he is not offering his would-be captors any choice. Indeed, since John's *hina* clause ("in order that the word may be fulfilled") is addressed to the arresting party, it is made clear that their real role in Jesus' eyes is to further the fulfillment of God's plan by letting the disciples go. As a more profound instance of sovereignty, "the word" expressing God's plan that they must help to fulfill is not from the Scriptures of Israel but a word of Jesus himself![28] The Johannine Jesus cites himself in the same way as he has previously cited an OT book (John 13:18). The citation, "Those whom you have given me, I have not lost one of them," was not actually said verbatim in John but echoes closely 17:12: "I have kept them with your name which you have given me. I kept watch and not one of them was lost" (also 6:39). The evangelist does not feel it necessary to tell us that this demand of the all-powerful Jesus was granted. The absence of the disciples (except for Simon Peter and the unique beloved disciple) in the story that follows is a tacit indication that despite Simon Peter's undiplomatic intervention with his sword *after* Jesus had thus arranged for his disciples' safety, Jesus' wish was implemented.

Critics have raised the question of why the disciples were not arrested with Jesus. A similar issue evidently arose in antiquity as well, for *GPet* 7:26, in describing the events surrounding Jesus' death, has Peter say, "We were in hiding, for we were sought after by them as wrongdoers [*kakourgos*] and as wishing to set fire to the [Temple] sanctuary." The closest passage to that in the canonical Gospels is John 20:19: On Easter the doors of the place where the disciples were are closed "for fear of the Jews." The fact that the canonical Gospels did not discuss the issue here in the arrest scene is indicative that in the evangelists' minds what pro-

---

[28]In John's view (17:8) Jesus' words have been given him by God and have the same divine authority as the Scriptures of Israel.

voked this arrest was not a "Jesus movement" of determined followers, but only the person, claims, and actions of Jesus himself.

In particular, critics object, there is a lack of logic in having no attempt to seize the one who attacked the servant of the high priest with a sword. In Mark this is not an issue because the sword-wielder is not portrayed as a disciple, and the Gospel would not interest itself in the fate of outsiders. As for Matt, where the sword-wielder is a disciple, perhaps we are meant to assume that he escaped with "all the disciples" as they fled. The issue is more complicated in John where Simon Peter, the principal member of the Twelve, has perpetrated an aggression that leaves enduring hostility, as we see in the question posed by the relative of Malchus in 18:26. Presumably the evangelist would have us think that Simon Peter could not be touched because of the protective power of Jesus' word and name. However, in all this, the evangelists' outlook might be shaped by a scriptural background that would be natural to them and foreign to us. I have already noted many parallels between this scene of Jesus on the Mount of Olives in the garden across the Kidron and the scene that begins in II Sam 15 as David has to flee across the Kidron to the Ascent of Olives because of the conspiracy of Absalom joined by Ahithophel. In II Sam 17:1–2 Ahithophel seeks permission from Absalom to pursue David that very night: "I will come upon him while he is weary and discouraged . . . and all the people who are with him will flee. I will strike down the king only." The evangelists might well find there the reason why in the tradition when Judas came with his arresting party, only Jesus was seized.

LUKE 22:53B: "YOUR HOUR AND THE POWER OF DARKNESS"

Luke's version of the end of the arrest scene is quite different from that of the other Gospels since he makes no reference to Scripture or to a flight/ departure of the disciples. (It has been observed that he preserves from Mark 14:49b only the introductory *alla*, "However.") The omission of the flight motif is sometimes explained on the grounds that Luke is going to narrate appearances to these disciples in Jerusalem three days hence. It is not certain, however, that flight/departure for any Gospel means physically going away from Jerusalem. The disciples who are "let . . . go away" in John 18:8b are in Jerusalem on Sunday (John 20), and Mark 16:7 supposes that all the disciples who fled are nearby and have yet to go to Galilee. (See also *GPet* 14:59.) Rather, just as Luke omitted the contents of Mark 14:27–28 that predicted the scandal and scattering of the disciples, so here he omits their flight and for the same reason: He will not have them put in a bad light. Luke will not grossly violate the tradition by portraying the disciples as present during the period between the arrest and the death; he simply remains silent about them (see commentary on 23:49). That they wavered is suggested very delicately in Luke 24:21 as two of them comment on the import of the crucifixion: "We *were hoping* that he was the one who was going to redeem Israel."

As for the fulfillment of Scripture that Mark mentions in relation to the arrest and the flight of the disciples, Luke has anticipated that at the Last Supper in the dialogue that led to the mention of the two swords: "This that is written must be completed in me" (22:37). At the end of the arrest Luke prefers to deal with the divine plan using another term, "hour" (see pp. 167, 209 above). Thus far in the PN Mark and Matt have each twice mentioned the hour of God's plan and of Jesus' fate (or even a third time if one counts the double-meaning question posed by Jesus in Mark 14:37; Matt 26:40: "Were you not strong enough to watch one hour [with me]?"). First Mark 14:35 has Jesus pray that the hour might pass, and then 14:41 has him proclaim that the hour has come. Matt's first PN usage is when Jesus proclaims that the hour has come near (26:45); his second introduces Jesus' rebuke to the crowd for treating him as a *lēstēs* (26:55): "In that hour Jesus said." Luke has not mentioned the hour in the PN, but he alone among the Synoptics introduced the Last Supper with "When the hour came" (22:14, after having described the chief priests' plot against Jesus involving Judas into whom Satan had entered: 22:1–6). In discussing the difference between Mark and Matt about the hour having "come" or "come near," we saw that the two evangelists may have had a different view about precisely at what point in Jesus' movement toward crucifixion the hour could be said to have come. Luke sees the hour having come as Jesus begins to give himself at the Last Supper, when Satan has already set the plot to kill him in motion through Judas. (John sees it having come even earlier, in 12:23 following the arrival of Gentiles who want to see Jesus—a sign that his ministry to "the Jews" is over and he has not been able to bring them to belief.)

Luke has his second reference to "hour" not before Jesus' words to the arresting party as Matt does, but at the end of those words, as he refers to "your hour and the power of darkness." Preparation for the expression "this is your hour" can be found in Luke 20:19, where the scribes and chief priests, having perceived that Jesus had told a parable against them, "were seeking to lay hands on him in this hour, but they feared the people." Luke has previously mentioned "darkness" (*skotos;* synonym *skotia*) parabolically as a sphere contrasted with the goodness of light (1:79; 11:35; see Acts 2:20); but some of the Lucan references overlap an attitude toward darkness found widely elsewhere in the NT (and at Qumran), where it is the domain of sin and ignorance presided over by Satan, a domain opposed to Jesus, who is light and whose followers must walk in light.[29] In Acts 26:18 turning "from *darkness* to light" is equated with turning "from *the power of Satan* to God." The reference to "the power of darkness" in the arrest scene is related to the presence of Satan in Judas, who has led the arresting party, and to Satan's request to test the disciples like wheat (Luke 22:31), so that here Luke comes close to the outlook in John 16:32–33, where the hour (of the scattering of the disciples and thus implicitly of the arrest) is a time of struggle between Jesus and the world whose Prince he overcomes.[30] Thus for Luke the "hour" has two sides: It is the hour of Jesus, which begins with his self-giving at the Last Supper and will culminate as he delivers his spirit into the hands of his Father; it is also the hour of Satanic domination through enemies who will crucify him. The devil, who after testing Jesus at the beginning of the ministry [4:13] left him until "an opportune time [*kairos*]," has at last his hour. This double aspect is caught in the complex theological attribution of agency vocalized in Acts 2:23 addressed to the men of Israel: "This Jesus, given up according to the determined will and foreknowledge of God, you nailed up and killed through the hands of outlaws."

(Bibliography for this episode is found in §12, Part 1.)

---

[29] I Thess 5:4–5; Col 1:13; Eph 5:8–14; I Pet 2:9; John 1:5 and passim.

[30] Also John 12:23,31–32; and 13:30 combined with 14:30. Yet John would not speak of "your hour"; it remains Jesus' hour.

§15. THE ARREST OF JESUS, PART THREE: NAKED FLIGHT OF A YOUNG MAN

(Mark 14:51–52)

Translation

Mark 14:51–52: ⁵¹And a certain young man was following with him, clothed with a linen cloth over his nakedness; and they seize him. ⁵²But he, having left behind the linen cloth, fled naked.

COMMENT

This brief scene, narrated only by Mark, has been the subject of an extraordinary amount of speculation. If the evangelist terminated with the young man alone and naked and did not spell out the implication of the scene, ingenious preachers and scholars have been eager to make up for his silence. The young man has been given an identity (John of Zebedee, James the brother of the Lord, John Mark, Christ himself). His nudity has been the subject of inquisitive speculation (he had just been aroused from sleep; as the Christ he wears the skimpy garments of the flesh; he was a homosexual initiate who had come for a tryst with Jesus); and he has been clothed anew (with the garments of the risen Christ; with the white robe of the postresurrectional messenger; and/or with the garment of the newly baptized). Well does Monloubou entitle his tongue-in-cheek survey of this: "The astonishing fate of a Gospel personage."

ANCIENT INTERPRETATIONS BY COPYISTS AND BY THE *Secret Gospel of Mark*

Evidently efforts to decipher the passage or to explain it away began early. An interesting number of textual variants appear, often a sign of the puzzlement of the copyists. In an attempt to clarify, copyists added "from them" after "fled" in v. 52. Since the "they" of "they seize" in v. 51 would have as its nearest antecedent the disciples who fled in v. 50, scribes inserted "the young men" to identify the seizers (an addition that is not particularly helpful since it does not point clearly to the subject Mark surely intended: the members of the armed crowd). Modern scholars query the correctness of the phrase *epi gymnou* (literally, "over naked") in v. 51, pointing out that there is little evidence that this adjective in the singular can be used without a substantive.[1] Both Taylor and Neirynck are happy to follow the lead of Codex Washingtonensis, the Lake family of minuscules, Syr[sin], Sahidic Coptic, and some Latin witnesses by dropping the phrase, thus removing some of the mystery about the youth—his nakedness is then not called to our attention until his garment has been snatched. And some go further still in making him modest by appealing to examples where *gymnos* is used for the lightly clad and those wearing only underclothes (BAGD 167). However, the ancient textual omission (which does not have impressive support) is surely an attempt by early scribes to get rid of a difficulty. It is safer scholarship to wrestle with the best attested text and all its difficulties than to emend or explain it away. The fact that Matt and Luke omitted the passage and scribes emended it suggests strongly that it was understood to refer to complete nakedness and thus was a bit scandalous.

Another example of an early attempt to interpret the passage appears in the *Secret Gospel of Mark (SGM)*, a fragment of which is quoted in an 18th-cent. copy of a (presumably genuine) letter of Clement of Alexandria, discovered by M. Smith of Columbia University in 1958. The letter would have been written ca. AD 200 to a certain Theodore, who had requested advice about a strange gospel that was being circulated. Clement responds that during Peter's stay in Rome Mark wrote an account of the "Acts of the Lord" (canonical Mark), but after Peter's martyrdom (mid 60s) Mark brought his notes to Alexandria and expanded the earlier work into "a more spiritual gospel" for the use of those being brought to perfection—a guide to the mysteries that would lead into the inner sanctuary of the truth hidden by the seven veils. Mark left this second edition to the Alexandrian church, in the archives of which it was kept and read only to those being initiated into the great mysteries. Unfortunately a church presbyter gave to Carpocrates (whom Church Fathers identify as a very early gnostic heretic) a copy of *SGM*, which that unworthy misinterpreted for the use of his "blasphemous and carnal doctrine." To illustrate his point Clement quotes two passages from *SGM*, one of which he says occurs after the end of Mark 10:34 (the third passion prediction). In what follows I italicize the words pertinent to our study of Mark 14:51–52:

---

[1]Lucian (*Navigium* 33) uses the neuter plural for "the naked body."

And they come into Bethany, and a certain woman was there whose brother had died. And, having come, she bowed before Jesus and says to him: "O Son of David, have mercy on me." But the disciples rebuked her. And Jesus, angered, went away with her into the garden where the tomb was; and immediately a loud voice was heard from the tomb. And coming forward, Jesus rolled away the stone from the door of the tomb; and immediately going in to where the young man was, he stretched out his hand and raised him up, having taken his hand. Now the young man having looked upon him, loved him and began to beg that he might be with him. And coming out of the tomb, they came into the house of the young man, for he was wealthy. After six days Jesus commanded him; and when it was evening, *the young man* comes to him *clothed with a linen cloth over his nakedness.* And he remained with him that night, for Jesus taught him the mystery of the kingdom of God. Then arising, he went from there to the other side of the Jordan. (2:23–3:11)

Despite the brevity of this passage cited by Clement,[2] major hypotheses involving *SGM* have been offered. Smith himself proposes that there had existed in Aramaic an esoteric common source resembling in content *SGM* and antedating the canonical Gospels. Then came canonical Mark, produced when Mark translated the common source into Greek and omitted certain passages. *SGM* resulted when an editor supplemented canonical Mark with passages that had been omitted from the common source, passages that he translated into a Greek imitative of Mark's style. Koester ("History" 54–57) proposes that *SGM* was written before canonical Mark, which, when composed in the late 2d cent., eliminated from *SGM* passages deemed unfit to be read in public.[3] H.-M. Schenke suggests that the (nonextant) gospel used by the Carpocratians preceded *SGM,* and that in turn preceded canonical Mark. I shall not attempt here to debate these proposals. I still hold the views expressed in my 1974 article "Relation," namely, that part of Smith's thesis is correct: *SGM* did not precede; it is an expansion of Mark in imitative Marcan style (which is what Clement recognizes in his too simplified thesis that Mark supplemented his own Gospel). I disagree with Smith, however, as to the source of the content used in the expansion of Mark: not a hypothetical

---

[2]The other passage that Clement cites from *SGM* is even shorter, consisting of only three lines that refer to Jesus coming to Jericho, where there were the sister of the young man whom Jesus loved, Jesus' mother, and Salome. Meyer ("Youth" 138) contends that Clement's remarks suggest that *SGM* closely resembled Mark except for these two additions. I interpret Clement in a directly opposite way: Mark transferred into his first book (canonical Mark) things suitable for making progress in *gnōsis* and thus composed a more spiritual gospel. How could these two small passages, if they were the only additions, accomplish that purpose? More plausibly, from the considerably longer *SGM* Clement has chosen two passages that deal with the young man because his behavior was the heart of the Carpocratian corruption of the message.

[3]For the thesis that *SGM* preceded the canonical Gospels, see also J. D. Crossan, *Four* 91–121.

common Aramaic source, but material picked up from hearing or reading at times past other canonical Gospels, especially John (the Lazarus story). In my judgment *SGM* was composed considerably before Clement came to Alexandria in 175, most likely ca. 125 when Carpocrates was active (Hadrian's time). The licentious possibilities that Smith sees in the *SGM* passage, with its picture of an almost naked youth who loved Jesus coming to him at night to be taught mysteries, may well be similar to the interpretation that the Carpocratians put on *SGM* (so also J. D. Crossan, *Four* 118). Without that sexual twist, *SGM* may have served Christians of an esoteric mindset as accompaniment to a ritual that was thought of as more advanced than baptism and the eucharist—or, as Clement puts it, initiation into the great mysteries. As we know from other literature, there was a strong interest, even among those who would be judged orthodox at Alexandria, in going beyond the Christianity of the masses through special knowledge and initiation. In any case the document shows an early use of the image of the young man clothed with a linen cloth over his nakedness, a use that will enter our discussion below.

IDENTITY OF THE YOUNG MAN UNDERSTOOD AS A REAL PERSON

The first question in the exegesis of the Marcan passage is whether Mark is thinking of a disciple of Jesus when he describes "a certain young man . . . following with him." Clearly *SGM* understood him to be a disciple. But Pesch (*Markus* 2.402) thinks of a curiosity seeker who lives in the neighborhood and, having been roused by the noise of the crowd, has thrown a piece of clothing on to come down and see what is happening. However, why would the arresting party seize him? And why would Mark bother reporting this? If we survey the Marcan use of *akolouthein*, the most general verb "to follow," while the reason for following is not always sharply defined, it pertains to following by disciples or would-be disciples twelve times, and to more general walking after five times. The compound verb *synakolouthein* found here is employed elsewhere in the NT only in Mark 5:37 and in Luke 23:49, in both instances referring to action by disciples. According to Mark 14:51 the arresting party tried to "seize" the young man, the same verb used throughout chap. 14 for apprehending Jesus (14:1,44,46,49); and so he was treated as one on Jesus' side.

There are two reasons advanced for thinking that he might not be a disciple. The first is the statement in the preceding verse indicating that all the disciples had fled. However, after making that statement, Mark 14:54 is not troubled in describing Peter's attempt to follow Jesus. It is quite possible that in Marcan logic the flight of this young man is further illustrative of the flight of disciples rather than an exception to it, even as Peter's denials are seen as ultimately confirming that they all fled. The second reason is his clothing; in the logic of the narrative surely he has not been at the Last Supper with the other disciples of Jesus wearing only a *sindōn* over his nakedness.[4] The imperfect "was following" may well be conative (BDF 326), expressing what he was trying to do. Is Mark describing someone who has been attracted to the scene, and who from watching Jesus' behavior and hearing Jesus' words wants to follow, not out of curiosity but out of sympathetic interest? In Mark disciples who are called by Jesus usually follow him or wish to follow after very short contact with him (1:18,20; 2:14; 10:17–21,52). If this man was visibly sympathetic to Jesus and showed it by following him, in the logic of the story the arresting party might well try to seize him. Then it would become understandable why Mark narrates the story: This is the last person to be attracted to the following of Jesus even when all the others have fled. This would-be follower becomes "the last disciple."

If Mark does mean to describe a disciplelike following, what does the wording "a certain [*tis*] young man" suggest? The reasoning just given would suggest that the *tis* be taken literally: "someone" whose name is not known and who is of no importance to the reader. But others contend that Mark was thinking of a significant figure[5] or of someone known by name to him or his readers. We faced the same problem regarding "a certain one [*heis tis*] of those standing by" in Mark 14:47; but there at least (even if in my judgment the figure was *not* someone known) the evidence of John could be invoked, explicitly identifying the sword-wielder as Simon Peter. Some would invoke John as implicitly supplying evidence here; for in that Gospel, after Jesus insisted that the disciples be let go (18:8b–9) and after Jesus was taken and bound (18:12), it is reported that "following Jesus was Simon Peter and another disciple" (18:15, i.e., the beloved disciple; see §27 below). Mark's "a certain young man" is taken as parallel to John's "another disciple," who in turn is taken to be John son of Zebedee (Ambrose, Gregory). One would think that the garb of the young man would offer a difficulty to advocates of this theory, when one thinks of the beloved disciple at the Last Sup-

---

[4]Saunderson ("Gethsemane") contends that the *sindōn* mentioned by Mark referred to the linen material from which was made the *chitōn* that the young man was wearing, and thus he was not improperly dressed. However, no *chitōn* is mentioned here by Mark.

[5]E.g., Dibelius, Taylor, and Lohmeyer. The latter suggested that he was the eyewitness guarantor of the tradition. Such a witness would answer the objection against the historicity of the Gethsemane scene that none of the disciples was awake to know what Jesus prayed (p. 174 above). Elaborating the eyewitness motif, and continuing her thesis about the young man's being properly dressed (n. 4 above), Saunderson contends that plausibly he was one of the Passover pilgrims who were camping out on the Mount of Olives. In my judgment this reconstruction, based almost entirely on what Mark does *not* mention, obscures the theme of shame that is much more obvious in the naked flight of a would-be follower.

per. Moreover, Mark's young man runs away naked, and the beloved disciple is still with Jesus at the foot of the cross (John 19:26). If anything, John's ideal beloved disciple who remains faithful should have been introduced as a *contrast* to the image of discipleship supplied by the young man!

Another source for identifying the young man has concentrated on his light garb: He was aroused from sleep by the noisy arresting party and so must have lived nearby; accordingly he must have been someone who lived in Jerusalem. An ancient identification (Epiphanius) is James the brother of the Lord, who is pictured as being in Jerusalem in the years after the resurrection (Gal 1:18–19; 2:1,9; Acts 12:17; 15:13; 21:18). A more recent guess is John Mark, whose mother Mary had a house in Jerusalem (Acts 12:12). If "was following with him" in 14:50 means the young man followed him from the Last Supper (!), then according to this proposal his light garb indicates he lived in the supper house; and one can imagine that Mark's mother owned that house (McIndoe) or with verve that Mark's father did since he was "the householder" of Mark 14:14 (and also owned the arrest site: Nolle). Indeed, one can regard John Mark's failure and rapid departure here as anticipating his later failure and departure when he abandoned Barnabas and Saul in Acts 13:13. If one guesses further that this John Mark was the author of Mark's Gospel, then we have a self-flagellating but also self-concealing autobiographical nugget in the evangelist's inclusion of the passage. The omission by Matt and Luke can be regarded as noblesse oblige on their part, not wishing further to embarrass the author of their source. In my judgment these suggestions are nothing other than imaginative flights of fancy.

THE YOUNG MAN AS A SYMBOLIC FIGURE

Eschewing such flights of imagination without inner Gospel proof, others (not less imaginatively) have appealed for identification to another passage in Mark (16:5), where in the tomb of the risen Jesus, telling the women not to be amazed, is "*a young man* seated on the right side, *clothed* in a white robe." The two Greek words indicated by my italicized translation occur in Mark only in 14:50 and 16:5, leading many scholars[6] to contend that the same young man (*neaniskos*) is involved in both; only in the tomb he has been clothed again, even if the garment is not the same (*sindōn* in 14:50, but in 16:5 *stolē leukē*). It is not impossible to argue for significance in the fact that *neaniskos* is found only in these two passages in Mark. But

---

[6]E.g., Groff, J. Knox (?), McIndoe, M. W. Meyer, Schnellbächer, Scroggs, Vanhoye, and Waetjen.

the word "clothed" (participle of *periballein*), although it does not appear elsewhere in Mark, is a normal word for being dressed (Matt 6:29; 25:36; Luke 23:11; John 19:2) and probably would have no distinctive resonance for the reader.

There is no prima facie reason to think of the *neaniskos* in 14:51–52 as other than a human being, but is the *neaniskos* in 16:5 a human being or an angel? Matt 28:2–5 understood the figure at the tomb to be angelic. The two men (*andres*) at the tomb in Luke 24:4 are identified as angels in 24:23. The garment of the young man in Mark 16:5 is appropriate for a celestial figure, for it clothes the saints who stand before the throne of the Lamb in Rev 7:9. The opening line of his message, "Do not be amazed," resembles the standard opening line of the biblical angel-revealer, "Do not be afraid" (BBM 156–58). Although Hebrew angelology is complex, in general angels are regarded as males, frequently identified with "the sons of God."[7] In Dan 8:15 (Theodotion) and 9:21 Gabriel has the appearance of a male (*anēr*). In the Codex Sinaiticus of Tobit 5:5,7,9(10) the archangel Raphael is addressed as *neaniskos*. The angel who appears to the wife of Manoah in Judg 13:3 is described by Josephus (*Ant.* 5.8.2; #277) as being in the likeness of a beautiful youth (*neanias*). II Macc 3:26,33 describes the heavenly figures who prevent Heliodorus from robbing the Temple treasury as strikingly beautiful youths (*neanias*).[8] I would judge from all this that more likely Mark is thinking of an angel at the tomb in 16:5. Thus there is a serious problem about the thesis that a disciple who ran away nude in 14:51–52 has found new garments and turned up again in 16:5 to interpret the empty tomb and give commands in the name of the risen Jesus, constituting an example of a failed disciple who has been rejuvenated in his faith.

Yet scholars who identify the *neaniskos* of Mark 14 with the *neaniskos* of Mark 16 appeal to other symbolism for interpreting one or both aspects of the figure. For instance, it is contended that in chap. 16 the young man has taken on the aspects of a triumphant Christian martyr wearing the clothes of the martyred saints in Rev 7:13–14.[9] More adventurously, the young man is sometimes thought to represent Jesus (Knox, Schnellbächer, Vanhoye). On the level of brute fact Jesus is led away to be put to death, but in the eyes of faith his captors will not be able to hold him. As the young man escapes, they are left holding a *sindōn* or linen cloth, the very term Mark (15:46) will

---

[7]In Gen 6:1–4 the sons of God have intercourse with earthly women and beget children.

[8]Jenkins ("Young Man" 238) queries whether these are angels or the Dioscuri—but if the latter, would they not still be heavenly beings rather than simple mortals?

[9]The three who are thrown into the fiery furnace in Dan 3 are identified as *neaniskoi* in Dan 1:4; both *neaniskos* and *neanias* are used for the martyred brothers in II Macc 7.

use for the garment in which Jesus will be buried, a garment he will leave behind when he is raised from the dead. (In fact, however, Mark never mentions that the *sindōn* was left behind by the risen one; John 20:6–7 cannot be invoked, for that Gospel does not use *sindōn*.) In chap. 16 the risen Jesus is represented symbolically once more as this young man, only now clothed in heavenly garments, even as the transfigured Jesus appears in garments that have been made white in Mark 9:3. A gnostic variation of this symbolism would involve a distinction between the Christ (the heavenly principle) and Jesus (the earthly shell or human appearance). The captors have seized Jesus, but the incident of the young man symbolizes the escape of Christ, who is not crucified. Schenke thinks that the Carpocratian form of *SGM* may represent this type of thought, and Irenaeus (*Adv. haer.* 1.26.1–2) tells us that Cerinthus, who was associated with Carpocrates, had such a theology.

Another variation of the Jesus interpretation of the *neaniskos* appeals to a typology relating Jesus and the OT Joseph who was sold into captivity by his brother (p. 658 below). Church Fathers already made a connection between Mark 14:52 and Gen 39:12, which describes Joseph's escape from Potiphar's wife: "Having left behind his clothes in her hands, he fled." Waetjen ("Ending" 120) adds that the young man in Mark 16 is described in an exalted posture ("on the right side"), clothed in a white *stolē*, just as the Pharaoh honored Joseph and dressed him in a *stolē* of fine quality (Gen 41:42). Eventually the Joseph of Egypt came together with his brothers once more, even as Jesus will rejoin his disciples, who in postresurrectional language are his brothers (Matt 28:10; John 20:17). A. Farrer, *The Glass of Vision* (London: Dacre, 1948), 136–45, adds to the picture that a Joseph (of Arimathea) buried Jesus just as Joseph of Egypt buried Jacob/Israel. My difficulty is that some of this Joseph imagery stands at cross-purposes—if Jesus is Joseph, then being buried by Joseph does not help. Some of the imagery is very tenuous—seated at the right side of a tomb is scarcely comparable to being seated at the right hand of one's Lord (Ps 110:1); and there is no evidence elsewhere of Marcan interest in Joseph imagery.

Some scholars see the young man not so much as Jesus but as the Christian undergoing baptismal initiation in the Marcan community. This is not too far from the bold proposal of B. Standaert (*L'évangile selon Marc* [Paris: Cerf, 1983]) that the whole Gospel is a Christian haggada[10] for an Easter-eve liturgy, with time indications for the celebration (Mark 15:25,33,42;

---

[10]I.e., a meditative retelling of the exodus story associated with the Jewish Passover.

16:1–2). In following Christ the initiate was stripped of clothes, entered the water naked to be baptized, and emerged to be clothed with a white garment—the initiate died with Christ and rose with him (Scroggs and Groff). But in disagreement Gourgues ("À propos" 675) objects that the unclothing/clothing aspect of baptism by immersion is not clearly attested before AD 150, since II Cor 5:3 and Eph 4:22–24 are metaphorical. When the practice does begin, the Christian who is baptized divests clothes to be with Christ; the young man in Mark 14 divests to get away from him.[11] After baptism the one who emerges is reborn as a child; in Mark 14 the figure symbolically representing the unbaptized is already a young man. If positive Christian symbolism was intended in Mark 14, why did both Matt and Luke omit the passage? Did they fail to understand Mark? Those who hold the baptismal interpretation have been heartened by the discovery of *SGM* (p. 295 above) as proof that one early interpreter did see a sacramental symbolism. Undoubtedly some ritualistic interpretation of the young man is involved in *SGM;* but there he starts out in a tomb and *after* being raised appears with a *sindōn* over his nakedness. Is this a postbaptismal nakedness? Moreover, how safe a guide to the mind of canonical Mark is such a professedly esoteric secret gospel? Those who claimed special knowledge (gnostics, orthodox or heterodox) often exploited the less significant characters of the Gospels for revelatory purposes—the less known about them, the freer one is to be creative with them.

EVALUATION AND SUGGESTED INTERPRETATION

Giving due respect to the erudition invoked on behalf of the symbolic exegesis of Mark 14:51–52, I join Gnilka, Gourgues, Monloubou, Neirynck,

---

[11]With acidity, M. Smith ("Clement" [1982], 457) remarks, "This interpretation neglects only the main facts: this young man deserted Christ and saved himself." Meyer ("Youth" 145–46) turns the sequence around: As in *SGM* (immediately after Mark 10:34), the young man had previously clothed himself with the baptismal linen cloth [*sindōn*] over his nakedness; and now he abandons this linen cloth and flees, unwilling to participate in Jesus' passion and death. (Yet if Mark 14:51 were referring to a young man previously mentioned, one would scarcely have expected him to speak of "a certain young man.") Meyer assumes that the *neaniskos* of Mark 16:5 is the same young man who has reaffirmed his baptismal loyalty and donned the ritual white robe. (Yet Meyer offers no satisfactory explanation why Mark has now shifted from a *sindōn,* which in this hypothesis he used twice before for baptismal clothing, to a *stolē*—a shift that obscures the continuity of the imagery.) My parentheses indicate skepticism about Meyer's thesis, especially as an interpretation of canonical Mark. I think its only possibility would be as an interpretation of *SGM* if the full form of that gospel offered readers much more help in following the continuity of the young man's career as a symbolic disciple who underwent conversion, failure in the face of suffering, and reconversion. Meyer ("Youth" 149) cites my contention that John's beloved disciple symbolizes the Christian; and so conceivably *SGM* could have developed the same symbolism around the *neaniskos.* The great likelihood that John is the latest of the canonical Gospels, completed (with chap. 21) perhaps as late as AD 110, would then constitute another argument for dating *SGM* and its parallel development to the early 2d cent.

Pesch, and especially Fleddermann in judging it quite foreign to what the evangelist intended to convey. These symbolic interpretations do little justice to the Marcan context of the verses (the arrest scene) and to the issue of flight. The flight of this young man has to be parallel to the flight of the disciples and therefore ignominious. (See also the flight in Mark 16:8). Therefore he cannot symbolize Christ or the model Christian initiate. There is nothing mystical about this *neaniskos;* a would-be disciple is described by that term in Matt 19:20–22. That he is described as being "clothed with a linen cloth over his nakedness" is to prepare the reader for the denouement, for when his garment is abandoned, he will be naked. His attempt to follow exemplifies his wanting to be true to Jesus and not flee like the others. But the disciples had been warned by Jesus in 14:38 to pray not to enter into *peirasmos,* i.e., the great struggle that he himself was going to have to face. This young man's attempt to follow Jesus into *peirasmos* is a miserable failure; for when seized as Jesus had been, he is so anxious to get away that he leaves in the hands of his captors the only clothes he wears and chooses the utter disgrace of fleeing naked—an even more desperate flight than that of the other disciples. Nakedness is not something good, as it is in the symbolic interpretation; it is something to be avoided, as in Matt 25:36; John 21:7; James 2:15; Rev 3:17; 16:15. The *sindōn* mentioned in the narrative was usually of fine linen and therefore expensive (Prov 31:24; Judg 14:12); if Mark's readers understood that, leaving it behind had even more force in depicting the young man's desperate flight. The moment of Jesus' passion is an eschatological battle with evil. Amos 2:16 warns what can happen under the pressures of such a time: "The one who is stout of heart among the mighty shall flee away naked on that day."[12] If such can happen to the stout of heart, why be surprised when it happens to this would-be follower who was not prepared for the trial? During the ministry an enthusiastic would-be disciple left when he heard how demanding discipleship was (Mark 10:17–22); the failure of the would-be disciple at the end of Jesus' life is even greater.

In discussing Mark 14:50 above we saw the ironic contrast made between the disciples at the beginning of the public ministry, leaving things to follow Jesus, and at the arrest, leaving Jesus to flee away. Here with "the last disciple" the irony is even more biting. In Mark 10:28 Peter described to Jesus a model of discipleship that Jesus praised: "We have left all things and have followed you." This young man has literally left all things to flee from Jesus. Neither Matt nor Luke could bring themselves to be this harsh. If Mark did

---

[12]J. M. Ross ("Young") lists five theories about the young man but favors the thesis (Nineham, Hoskyns and Davey) that an episode with a basis in fact was cited as fulfillment of Amos 2:16 (Hebrew; the LXX has "will hasten, pursue").

intend the reader of 16:5 with its reference to *neaniskos* to recall the figure who had the same designation in 14:51–52, it was to establish a contrast. The Jesus who was abandoned disgracefully by the last disciple and left to face his hour of arrest and death alone is in 16:5–6 served by an angel who proclaims his victory over death.

(Bibliography for this episode is found in §12, Part 2.)

§16. ANALYSIS COVERING ALL THREE PARTS OF THE ARREST OF JESUS

(Mark 14:43–52; Matt 26:47–56; Luke 22:47–53; John 18:2–11)

In the previous ANALYSIS section (§11) I concentrated on various approaches to the Gethsemane prayer scene. In part, that was because I wanted to give readers a taste just once of the incredible diversity of scholarly opinions and thus to show that any attempt on my part to produce a new reconstruction of the "original" PN would be a waste of effort. From another aspect, though, the Gethsemane prayer scene is complicated and under any circumstances the composition would need discussion. Much less of that is required here, not only because henceforth I do not plan to list in detail the range of scholarly theories, but also because there is more consensus. Let us for the moment think of this scene as consisting of two basic components: I. Initial Encounter (Mark 14:43–46); and II. Incidents during the Arrest (Mark 14:47–52).[1] How were these composed? I shall begin with various theories proposed by scholars and then discuss the common elements in the four Gospels as a possible key to older tradition.

A. *Theories of Composition*

Component I (Mark 14:43–46). Taylor (*Mark* 658) attributes this component to Source A, which is a sequential narrative, while he assigns component II to Source B, consisting of separate items appended by Mark. Although most recent scholars would not agree with Taylor's understanding of these sources or their origin, there is much agreement that a substantial part of I is preMarcan in origin, whether one considers it to have come from a tradition or a source. Two items provoke differences. The first is the opening in v. 43. Did the PN begin here, standing free from all that precedes?[2] Or was some of

---

[1] I give the verses in Mark because many of the analyses consider no other Gospel. In the COMMENT I separated the story of the naked flight of the young man (14:51–52) as Part Three because of the abundant literature on it and the required length of the discussion.

[2] One would then posit that Mark added connecting phrases, e.g., "while he was still speaking," perhaps at the same time suppressing the opening phrase in the source.

the Gethsemane prayer scene joined to the arrest in the putative source?[3] Or did the arrest scene follow immediately after the Last Supper (as in John), with only a geographical transitional sentence to get Jesus to Gethsemane (elements of Mark 14:26 and 32)? A refinement of that thesis would be that it followed after certain elements in the Last Supper scene, which itself was composite.[4] Or did the arrest scene follow the plotting of Judas with the Jewish authorities described in Mark 14:1–2, 10–11?[5] The second focus of different views is the prearrangement of the kiss as a sign in v. 44 (missing in Luke) and the enactment of the Judas kiss in v. 45 (missing in John). Doeve omits v. 44, and Finegan omits both verses; but the majority of scholars retains the preMarcan unity of the content of 44–46 (e.g., Bultmann, Gnilka, Lohmeyer, Linnemann, Schneider, Schweizer, Taylor). The judgment of Dibelius ("Judas" 275) is notable: "The arrest of Jesus is described in an especially believable way." Yet BHST (268) speaks of a narrative "coloured by legend in the motif of the betrayal by a kiss." It is worth recalling that already by the mid-50s for Paul there was an old tradition that mentioned "the night he [Jesus] was given over" (I Cor 11:23), which at least implies the arrest.

Component II (Mark 14:47–52). There is less agreement here among scholars. A few like Finegan (*Überlieferung* 71–72) would assign to the earliest tradition only the flight in v. 50. Linnemann (*Studien* 41–52) sees none of it belonging to the main arrest narrative, but speaks of Mark having combined other preMarcan material, such as biographical apophthegmata in vv. 48,49b and fragments pertaining to opposition and flight in vv. 47,50,51–52. Schneider ("Verhaftung" 201–5) differs from Linnemann in details, but he too sees 14:47–52 as a Marcan collection of disunified material that was not originally part of the preMarcan arrest sequence. Gnilka (*Markus* 2.267) would connect vv. 47 (sword stroke) and 50–52 (flight, including naked young man) to the preMarcan arrest story.[6] Here, then, as in the Gethsemane scene, a comparison of authors makes it obvious that determination of the preMarcan source with any surety simply defies our methods. In particular, the arguments that Linnemann advances against the unity of the material in

---

[3]Consult §11 for those who attribute part of the prayer to the source.

[4]BHST 268–69 would have it follow 14:27–31, the predictions of the fate of the disciples and of Peter. Those predictions may originally have been localized at the Last Supper.

[5]See Linnemann (*Studien* 48–49), who excludes 14:11b and suggests that Judas came to the arrest with the authorities mentioned in those earlier verses.

[6]Viviano ("High" 72) would separate the sword stroke of Mark 14:47 from the surrounding verses. It does not belong to the earliest PN stratum, but neither is it free Marcan composition. Viviano would prove the latter by pointing to Marcan hapax legomena such as "*drawing* a sword," "*hitting at*," "*taking off* his *ear*." I do not find these convincing since Mark is describing here an action that he has never described elsewhere in the Gospel, and so he had to use language not employed previously.

14:47–52 are weak in my judgment, e.g., that the one who struck Jesus is not identified even though Judas was identified as one of the Twelve, that the authorities do not react to or punish the sword stroke, that Jesus' claim to teach day after day in the Temple is not verified in Mark's account of Jesus' ministry, that the flight of all is contradicted by the young man who had not fled. These are inconsistencies in the light of a modern microscopic quest for logic. Are they really illogicalities in a swift-flowing, impressionistic narrative such as Mark has given us? Scroggs (KKS 511) and Mazzucco ("Arresto") are quite right in questioning the probatory value of such inconsistencies.

B. *Common Elements in the Gospels*

Let us now pursue the more profitable enterprise of looking at some common elements in the Gospels that may have come independently to the respective evangelists. There is virtually no reason to think that Mark is the source of John's account, for the two Gospels agree only on the presence of Judas and an arresting party, and the sword incident.[7] There is every reason to think that Matt drew on Mark, but Matt has supplemented the story with some elements that have functional parallels in Luke. In the COMMENT I have indicated why I think it likely that the basic Lucan account is an editing of Mark, abbreviating the initial encounter and expanding the subsequent efforts.[8] Yet the agreements of Luke with Matt suggest that both evangelists had access to (oral?) developments of the story not apparent in Mark (Soards). Working with that understanding, we notice the following points:

Component I (Initial Encounter: Mark 14:43–46 and parallels). There are two basic items shared by all the Gospels. The first is the appearance of Judas with an arresting party authorized by the Jewish authorities. Luke's report that the chief priests themselves came to the Mount of Olives probably stems from Luke's conflating the episode of the arrest with the episode of Jesus' encountering one or more of the chief priests that the other Gospels

---

[7]Sabbe devotes "Arrest" to refuting Dauer's thesis that John drew on a written preJohannine source that had been influenced orally by the Synoptic Gospels (a thesis that I also would reject). Sabbe argues that the Synoptic influence was directly on John rather than on the Johannine source. However, in this article Sabbe is simply supposing, not proving, Synoptic influence, something that is much in doubt in my judgment (pp. 75–93 above). For example, a cohort of Roman soldiers appears in different circumstances in Mark 15:16 and John 18:3; that fact may be explained by seeing these as two different reflections of preGospel tradition rather than as John's drawing on Mark and changing it drastically (as Sabbe posits).

[8]I side with Creed, Finegan, Fitzmyer, Schmid, Schneider, and Soards over against Green, Grundmann, Rehkopf, Rengstorf, and Taylor who think Luke had a source for this scene separate from Mark.

place after the arrest when Jesus has been brought back to Jerusalem. There are other minor differences among the Gospels as to the makeup of the arresting party and those who authorized the arrest. John alone portrays Roman troops in the arresting party, and in the COMMENT I found it impossible to decide the antiquity or historicity of that portrayal.

The second shared item is the identification of Jesus. In the Synoptics that is done by Judas with a kiss; in John Jesus identifies himself dramatically, forcing the arresting party backward to the ground. The latter is surely a Johannine dramatization of the power of the name that Jesus possesses, "I am." Something with a partial resemblance to the Marcan account may lie behind the Johannine dramatization (notice the "he is" in Mark 14:44); but the Marcan account with its dramatic Judas kiss has surely also undergone development. Matt and Luke agree over against Mark in having Jesus speak in reaction to the kiss. The difference in their respective wording means that independently they offer witness that storytelling and reflectional development of this scene continued independently of the version set down in writing by Mark.

Component II (Incidents during the Arrest: Mark 14:47–52 and par.). The four Gospels have in common the cutting off of the servant's ear; and there is good reason to think that an ancient detail. The fact that Matt, Luke, and John in independent wording have Jesus comment negatively on the action shows that Christians found this incident puzzling, and indeed scandalous once the perpetrator was identified as a disciple. Both the suggestion of Schneider ("Verhaftung" 202) that the tale of the sword stroke was originally narrated to exonerate the disciples (someone, at least, stood up for Jesus) and the other suggestion that it was a Marcan addition to illustrate the misunderstanding of the disciples run against major difficulties. As I insisted in the COMMENT, in the Marcan account the perpetrator was seemingly not a disciple (and that may have been the oldest tradition); and the Marcan Jesus offers no comment to tell the reader whether this action was something praiseworthy or not. (The identification of the perpetrator is one more example of the continued development of the story beyond Mark.) The incident may be a puzzling memory from the early tradition that acquired theological significance. Is there any persuasive reason to think it was not part of the arrest story when it could scarcely fit elsewhere?

Another incident is a short speech of protest by Jesus that such an arrest was not necessary since he had taught frequently in public in the Temple area. John's arrest scene lacks such a speech, but it appears later the same night before Annas (18:20–22). The wording is different, but the theme of frequent public teaching in the Temple is the same. Therefore in Christian tradition this defense was an early development to emphasize the justice of

Jesus' cause. Unlike the sword stroke there would have been little in this defense argument to localize it precisely, and the Synoptic and Johannine traditions have taken two different options. Another common aspect is that Jesus' words explain the *necessity* of what is happening[9] as fulfilling what had been spoken beforehand by divine authority: the Scriptures for Mark/ Matt and Jesus' own word for John.[10] Obviously early Christians did fasten upon the scriptural explanation. Certainly a pious Jew like Jesus would have reflected on the way things were turning out and use the Scriptures to do so. But there is no way to be sure at what point he did that and when Christians introduced such scriptural reflection into their narratives.

Component II ends with the flight of the disciples (Mark/Matt) or their implied departure arranged by the all-powerful Jesus (John). The latter portrayal shows the influence of Johannine christology, even as the absence of this scene in Luke reflects Luke's consistent unwillingness to report things derogatory to the memory of the disciples. Most critics see no reason to doubt that this belonged to the earliest tradition of the PN, and indeed there is little reason for doubting factuality.[11] Obviously Mark developed a theology of discipleship by meditating on the meaning of this and other failures by the disciples, but that theology would have had no credibility if it were widely thought or known they had stood with Jesus in his last hours.

In the COMMENT I treated separately (as Part Three: Naked Flight of a Young Man) a scene found only in Mark 14:51–52. The flight of all the disciples constitutes for Mark an ironic inclusion with the call of the disciples at the beginning of Jesus' public ministry and with their brave, but naive, promises at the beginning of the PN to remain faithful to Jesus. This young man who was following Jesus was a would-be disciple—indeed, the last disciple—and so his disgraceful, naked flight is a culminating example of the failure of the disciples. It was omitted by Matt and Luke as too harsh for their outlook on the followers of Jesus. For Mark's community, however, such grave failure offered a way of understanding its own lapses in following Jesus during periods of suffering (and perhaps of persecution), especially since there was also the implicit promise that those who failed could be gathered once more into the flock of Jesus (Mark 14:28; 16:7).

---

[9]I use the phrase "what is happening" because the Gospels differ as to which precise event represents the fulfillment: the betrayal or the arrest.

[10]Luke does not have the Scripture fulfillment theme here but earlier, in the discussion that leads to the reference to the two swords (22:37–38).

[11]Pesch (*Markus* 2.403) lists points he considers historical: Judas came from the high priest and by the signal of a kiss gave Jesus over to the arresting party who seized him. In the melee a servant of the high priest lost his ear. Jesus made a protest. The disciples fled as did a young man. Parrish ("Defence") is rather solitary in defending the loyalty of the Eleven by questioning the historicity of their flight in Mark 14:50.

I see no way of being certain whether the incident of the young man had preMarcan origins and, of course, no way of testing its historicity. The flight of all the disciples, including the best known, could scarcely have been invented without demur; but that argument cannot apply to such an unknown and isolated figure. To modern sensibilities the creation of an especially disgraceful incident without historical basis might seem unlikely; but it is best to practice modesty in every sense by leaving this young man wrapped in mystery, if naught else.

COMMENTARY
ON ACT II:

JESUS BEFORE THE JEWISH AUTHORITIES

(Mark 14:53–15:1; Matt 26:57–27:10; Luke 22:54–23:1; John 18:12–28a)

The second Act of the Passion Narrative describes how Jesus, having been led to the high priest (and other authorities), was tried/interrogated by him/them, and how Jesus' answers caused him to be given over to the Roman governor. Related to Jesus' trial/interrogation was a mockery by Jewish authorities/police, three denials by Peter, and an attempt by Judas to render back to the Jewish authorities the price of innocent blood.

CONTENTS OF ACT II, SCENE ONE

§17. SECTIONAL BIBLIOGRAPHY
for Scene One of Act II:
The Jewish Trial/Interrogation of Jesus
(§§18–24)

Some writings treat the trial under the rubric of "The Trial and Death of Jesus" and thus become general treatments of the PN, whence my inclusion of them in §3 above. Bibliography for the Roman trial of Jesus is found under §30 below, but contributions covering both Jewish and Roman trials are listed here. The subdivision of this bibliography into five parts is outlined in the immediately preceding Contents.

Part 1: Overall Treatments of the Jewish Legal Procedures against Jesus

Abrahams, I., "The Tannaitic Tradition and the Trial Narratives," *Studies in Pharisaism and the Gospels* (2 vols.; Cambridge Univ., 1917–24), 2.129–37.

Aguirre, R., "Los poderes des Sanhedrín y notas de crítica histórica sobre la muerte de Jesús," *Estudios de Deusto* 30 (1982), 241–70.

Aicher, G., *Der Prozess Jesu* (Kanonistische Studien und Texte 3; Bonn: Schroeder, 1929).

Aron, R., "Quelques réflexions sur le procès de Jésus," LumVie 20 (101; 1971), 5–17.

Bammell, E., "Die Blutgerichtsbarkeit in der römischen Provinz Judäa vor dem ersten jüdischen Aufstand," JJS 25 (1974), 35–49.

———, "'*Ex illa itaque die consilium fecerunt* . . . ,'" TJCSM 11–40 (on John 11:47–53).

———, "Der Tod Jesu in einer 'Toledoth Jeschu'-Überlieferung," ASTI 6 (1967–68), 124–31.

———, (ed.), *The Trial of Jesus—Cambridge Studies in Honour of C.F.D. Moule* (SBT, 2d series 13; London: SCM, 1970). Abbreviated as TJCSM.

Barton, G. A., "On the Trial of Jesus before the Sanhedrin," JBL 41 (1922), 205–11.

Bartsch, H.-W., "Wer verurteilte Jesus zum Tode?" NovT 7 (1964–65), 210–16. Reaction to Winter and Stauffer.

Beavis, M. A., "The Trial before the Sanhedrin (Mark 14:53–65): Reader Response and Greco-Roman Readers," CBQ 49 (1987), 581–96.

Beilner, W., "Prozess und Verurteilung Jesu," *Christus und die Pharisäer* (Vienna: Herder, 1959), 235–38.

Benoit, P., "Jesus Before the Sanhedrin," BJG 1.147–66. French orig. in *Angelicum* 20 (1943), 143–65.

———, "The Trial of Jesus," BJG 1.123–46. French orig. in VInt (Feb. 1940), 200–13; (March 1940), 372–78; (April 1940), 54–64.

Besnier, R., "Le procès du Christ," *Tijdschrift voor Rechtsgeschiedenis; Revue d'Histoire du Droit* 18 (1950), 191–209.

Betz, O., "Jesus and the Temple Scroll," in *Jesus and the Dead Sea Scrolls,* ed. J. H. Charlesworth (New York: Doubleday, 1992), 75–103, esp. 79–91 on Jewish legal use of crucifixion for blasphemy.

———, "Probleme des Prozesses Jesu," ANRW II/25.1 (1982), 565–647.

Bickermann, E., "Utilitas Crucis. Observations sur les récits du procès de Jésus dans les Évangiles canoniques," RHR 112 (1935), 169–241. Reprinted with a *Postscriptum* in E. J. Bickerman, *Studies in Jewish and Christian History* (3 vols.; Leiden: Brill, 1976–86), 3.82–138.

Bisek, A. C., *The Trial of Jesus Christ* (Chicago: Progressive Press, 1925).

Blinzler, J., "Geschichtlichkeit und Legalität des jüdischen Prozesses gegen Jesu," *Stimmen der Zeit* 147 (1950–51), 345–57.

———, "Probleme um den Prozess Jesu," BibLit 35 (1961–62), 204–21.

———, *Der Prozess Jesu* (4th ed.; Regensburg: Pustet, 1969). For Eng. trans. of the much shorter 2d ed., see Blinzler, *Trial.*

———, "Das Synedrium von Jerusalem und die Straffprozessordnung der Mischna," ZNW 52 (1961), 54–65.

———, *The Trial of Jesus* (from 2d German ed.; Westminster, MD: Newman, 1959). See Blinzler, *Prozess.*

Bowker, J. W., "The Offence and Trial of Jesus," *Jesus and the Pharisees* (New York: Cambridge, 1973), 42–52.

Brandon, S.G.F., "The Trial of Jesus," *History Today* 16 (1966), 251–59.

———, *The Trial of Jesus of Nazareth* (London: Batsford, 1968).

Braumann, G., "Markus 15,2–5 und Markus 14,55–64," ZNW 52 (1961), 273–78.

Broer, I., "Der Prozess gegen Jesus nach Matthäus," PGJK 84–110.

Bruce, F. F., "The Trial of Jesus in the Fourth Gospel," in *Gospel Perspectives: Studies of History and Tradition in the Four Gospels,* eds. R. T. France and D. Wenham (2 vols.: Sheffield: JSOT, 1980–81), 1.7–20.

Büchsel, F., "Die Blutgerichtsbarkeit des Synedrions," ZNW 30 (1931), 202–10.

———, "Noch Einmal: Zur Blutgerichtsbarkeit des Synedrions," ZNW 33 (1934), 84–87. Answers Leitzmann, "Bemerkungen II."

Burkill, T. A., "The Competence of the Sanhedrin," VC 10 (1956), 80–96.

———, "The Condemnation of Jesus: a critique of Sherwin-White's thesis," NovT 12 (1970), 321–42.

———, "The Trial of Jesus," VC 12 (1958), 1–18.

Burkitt, F. C., "Review: *Der Prozess Jesu* by H. Lietzmann," JTS 33 (1931–32), 64–66.

Buss, S., *The Trial of Jesus Illustrated from Talmud and Roman Law* (London: SPCK, 1906).

Campbell, W. A., *Did the Jews Kill Jesus? and the Myth of the Resurrection* (New York: Peter Eckler, 1927).

Cantinat, J., "Jésus devant le Sanhédrin," NRT 75 (1953), 300–8.

Catchpole, D. R., "The Problem of the Historicity of the Sanhedrin Trial," TJCSM 47–65.

———, *The Trial of Jesus* (Studia Post-Biblica 18; Leiden: Brill, 1971).

Chandler, W. M., *The Trial of Jesus from a Lawyer's Standpoint* (2 vols.; New York: Empire, 1908).

Cheever, H. M., "The Legal Aspects of the Trial of Christ," BSac 60 (1903), 495–509.

Cohn, H., *The Trial and Death of Jesus* (New York: Harper & Row, 1967).

Cooke, H. P., "Christ Crucified—And By Whom?" HibJ 29 (1930–31), 61–74.

Dąbrowski, E., "The Trial of Jesus in Recent Research," StEv IV, 21–27.

Danby, H., "The Bearing of the Rabbinical Criminal Code on the Jewish Trial Narratives in the Gospels," JTS 21 (1920), 51–76.

Dauer, A., "Spuren der (synoptischen) Synedriumsverhandlung im 4. Evangelium— Das Verhältnis zu den Synoptikern," DJS 307–40.

Delorme, J., "Le procès de Jésus ou la parole risquée (Lc 22,54–23,25)," RechSR 69 (1981), 123–46.

Derrett, J.D.M., "The Trial of Jesus and the Doctrine of Redemption," *Law in the New Testament* (London: Darton, Longman & Todd, 1970), 389–460.

Dodd, C. H., "The Historical Problem of the Death of Jesus," *More New Testament Studies* (Grand Rapids: Eerdmans, 1968), 84–101.

Doerr, F., *Der Prozess Jesu in rechtsgeschichtlicher Beleuchtung* (Berlin: Kohlhammer, 1920).

Donahue, J. R., *Are You the Christ? The Trial Narrative in the Gospel of Mark* (SBLDS 10; Missoula: Scholars, 1973).

———, "Temple, Trial, and Royal Christology (Mark 14:53–65)," in PMK 61–79.

Dormeyer, D., "Die Passion Jesu als Ergebnis seines Konflikts mit führenden Kreisen des Judentums," GVMF 211–38.

Drucker, A. P., *The Trial of Jesus from Jewish Sources* (New York: Bloch, 1907).

Easton, B. S., "The Trial of Jesus," AJT (1915), 430–52.

Ebeling, H. J., "Zur Frage nach der Kompetenz des Synhedrion," ZNW 35 (1936), 290–95. Critique of Büchsel.

Fiebig, P., "Der Prozess Jesu," TSK 104 (1932), 213–28.

Flusser, D., "A Literary Approach to the Trial of Jesus," *Judaism* 20 (#1; 1971), 32–36.

France, R. T., "Jésus devant Caïphe," *Hokhma* 15 (1980), 20–35.

Fricke, W., *The Court-Martial of Jesus* (New York: Grove Weidenfeld, 1990). German ed. (*Standrechtlich gekreuzigt*), 1986. See review by A. Kolping, *Theologische Revue* 83 (1987), 265–76.

Garnsey, P., "The Criminal Jurisdiction of Governors," JRS 58 (1968), 51–59.

Gerhardsson, B., "Confession and Denial before Men: Observations on Matt. 26:57–27:21," JSNT 13 (1981), 46–66.

Gnilka, J., "Die Verhandlungen vor dem Synhedrion und vor Pilatus nach Markus 14,53–15,5," EKKNT *Vorarbeiten* 2 (1970), 5–21.

Goguel, M., "À propos du procès de Jésus," ZNW 31 (1932), 289–301. Reaction to Lietzmann.

Goldin, H. E., *The Case of the Nazarene Reopened* (New York: Exposition, 1948).

Goodenough, E. R., *The Jurisprudence of Jewish Courts in Egypt. Legal Administration by the Jews under the Early Roman Empire as described by Philo Judaeus* (New Haven: Yale, 1929), esp. 1–29.

Gorman, R., *The Trial of Christ: a Reappraisal* (Huntington, IN: Our Sunday Visitor, 1972).

Grant, F. C., "*On the Trial of Jesus* [P. Winter]: A Review Article," *Journal of Religion*, 44 (1964), 230–37.

Groupe d'Entrevernes, "Analyse de la véridiction. Procès de Jésus devant le Sanhedrin (Marc 14,55–65)," *Sémiotique et Bible* 27 (1982), 1–11.

Grundmann, W., "The Decision of the Supreme Court to Put Jesus to Death (John 11:47–57) . . . ," JPHD 295–318.

Hasler, V., "Jesu Selbstzeugnis und das Bekenntnis des Stephanus vor dem Hohen Rat," *Schweizerische Theologische Umschau* 36 (1966), 36–47.

Haufe, G., "Der Prozess Jesu im Lichte der gegenwärtigen Forschung," *Die Zeichen der Zeit* 22 (1968), 93–101.

Herranz Marco, M., "El proceso ante el Sanhedrín y el Ministerio Público de Jesús," EstBib 34 (1975), 83–111; 35 (1976), 49–78, 187–221; 36 (1977), 35–55.

Hill, D., "Jesus before the Sanhedrin—On What Charge?" IBS 7 (1985), 174–86.

Holzmeister, U., "Zur Frage der Blutgerichtsbarkeit des Synedriums," *Biblica* 19 (1938), 43–59, 151–74.

Horbury, W., "The Trial of Jesus in Jewish Tradition," TJCSM 102–21.

Husband, R. W., *The Prosecution of Jesus* (Princeton Univ., 1916).

Imbert, J., *Le procès de Jésus* (Qui sais-je? 1896; Paris: Presses Universitaires, 1980).

————, "Le procès de Jésus," *Revue de l'Institut Catholique de Paris* 19 (1986), 53–66.

Innes, A. T., *The Trial of Jesus Christ: a Legal Monograph* (Edinburgh: Clark, 1899).

Isorni, J., *Le vrai procès de Jésus* (Paris: Flammarion, 1967).

Jaubert, A., "Les séances du Sanhédrin et le récits de la passion," RHR 166 (1964), 143–69; 167 (1965), 1–33.

Jeremias, J., "Zur Geschichtlichkeit der Verhörs Jesu vor dem Hohen Rat," ZNW 43 (1950–51), 145–50.

Judaism 20 (#1; 1971). Whole issue on *The Trial of Jesus in the Light of History*. Brief articles by J. Blinzler, S.G.F. Brandon, H. Cohn, D. Flusser, R. M. Grant, S. Sandmel.

Juel, D., *Messiah and Temple: The Trial of Jesus in the Gospel of Mark* (SBLDS 31; Missoula: Scholars, 1977).

Kamelský, J., "Über den Prozess und die Lehre Jesu," *Internationale Dialog Zeitschrift* 3 (1970), 149–62.

Kastner, K., *Jesus vor dem Hohen Rat* (Breslau: Goehrlich, 1929).

Kempthorne, R., "Anti-Christian Tendency in pre-Marcan Traditions of the Sanhedrin Trial," StEv VII, 283–85.

Kennard, J. S., Jr., "The Jewish Provincial Assembly," ZNW 53 (1962), 25–51.

Kertelge, K. (ed.), *Der Prozess gegen Jesus* (QD 112; Freiburg: Herder, 1988). Abbreviated as PGJK.

Kilpatrick, G. D., *The Trial of Jesus* (London: Oxford, 1953).

Klövekorn, P. B., "Jesus vor der jüdischen Behörde," BZ 9 (1911), 266–76.

Koch, W., *Der Prozess Jesu* (Cologne: Kiepenheuer & Witsch, 1966).

———, *Zum Prozess Jesu. Mit Beiträgen von J. Blinzler, G. Klein, P. Winter* (Weiden Kr. Cologne: Der Löwe, 1967).

Kosmala, H., "Der Prozess Jesu," *Saat auf Hoffnung* 69 (1932), 25–39.

Kremer, J., "Verurteilt als 'König der Juden'—verkündigt als 'Herr und Christus,'" BibLit 45 (1972), 23–32.

Lapide, P. E., "Jesu Tod durch Römerhand," GVMF 239–55.

———, *Wer war schuld an Jesus Tod?* (Gütersloh: Mohn, 1987).

Légasse, S., "Jésus devant le Sanhédrin. Recherche sur les traditions évangéliques," RTL 5 (1974), 170–97.

Lengle, J., "Zum Prozess Jesu," *Hermes* 70 (1935), 312–21.

Leroux, M., "Responsabilités dans le procès du Christ," *Cahiers Sioniens* 1 (1947), 102–21.

Lietzmann, H., "Bemerkungen zum Prozess Jesu," ZNW 30 (1931), 211–15; "Bemerkungen . . . II," 31 (1932), 78–84. Also in LKS, 2.264–68, 269–76.

———, "Der Prozess Jesu," SPAW XIV Philos-Hist Klasse (1931), 313–22. Also in LKS, 2.251–63.

Lohse, E., "Der Prozess Jesu Christi," in *Ecclesia und Res Publica*, eds. G. Kretschmar and B. Lohse (K. D. Schmidt Festschrift; Göttingen: Vandenhoeck & Ruprecht, 1961), 24–39. Reprinted in his *Die Einheit des Neuen Testaments* (Göttingen: Vandenhoeck & Ruprecht, 1973), 88–103.

McLaren, J. S., *Power and Politics in Palestine* (JSNTSup 63; Sheffield: JSOT, 1991), esp. 88–101 on the trial of Jesus.

McRuer, J. C., *The Trial of Jesus* (London: Blandford, 1965).

Maier, P. L., "Who Was Responsible for the Trial and Death of Jesus?" CT 18 (1973–74), 806–9.

———, "Who Killed Jesus?" CT 34 (1990), 16–19.

Mantel, H., *Studies in the History of the Sanhedrin* (Cambridge, MA: Harvard, 1961), esp. 254–90.

Massenet, J., "Sanhédrin," DBSup 11 (1991), cols. 1353–1413.

Matera, F. J., "Luke 22,66–71: Jesus before the *Presbyterion*," ETL 65 (1989), 43–59.

———, "The Trial of Jesus: Problems and Proposals," *Interpretation* 45 (1991), 5–16.

Meyer, F. E., "Einige Bemerkungen zur Bedeutung des Terminus 'Synhedrion' in den Schriften des Neuen Testaments," NTS 14 (1967–68), 545–51.

Millar, F., "Reflections on the Trials of Jesus," in *A Tribute to Geza Vermes: Essays on Jewish and Christian Literature and History*, eds. P. R. Davies and R. T. White (Journal for the Study of the Old Testament—Supplement Series 100; Sheffield: Academia, 1990), 355–81.

Mommsen, T., *Römisches Strafrecht* (Leipzig: Duncker & Humblot, 1899).

Müller, K., "Jesus und die Sadduzäer," in *Biblische Randbemerkungen*, eds. H. Merklein and J. Lange (R. Schnackenburg Schülerfestschrift; Würzburg: Echter, 1974), 3–24.

————, "Möglichkeit und Vollzug jüdischer Kapitalgerichtsbarkeit im Prozess gegen Jesus von Nazaret," PGJK 41–83.

Nörr, D., "Problems of Legal History in the Gospels," in *Jesus in His Time,* ed. H. J. Schultz (Philadelphia: Fortress, 1971), 115–23.

O'Meara, T. F., "The Trial of Jesus in an Age of Trials," TToday 28 (1971–72), 451–65.

Ostrow, J., "Tannaitic and Roman Procedure in Homicide," JQR 48 (1957–58), 352–70; 52 (1961–62), 160–67, 245–63.

Pesch, R., *Der Prozess Jesu geht weiter* (Herder Taschenbuch 1507; Freiburg: Herder, 1988).

Philippson, L., *Haben wirklich die Juden Jesum gekreuzigt?* (2d ed.; Leipzig: Kaufmann, 1901; orig. 1866).

Powell, F. J., *The Trial of Jesus Christ* (Grand Rapids: Eerdmans, 1949).

Powell, M. A., "The Plot to Kill Jesus from Three Different Perspectives: Point of View in Matthew," SBLSP 1990, 603–13.

Quispel, G., "The Gospel of Thomas and the Trial of Jesus," TTK 193–99.

Radin, M., *The Trial of Jesus of Nazareth* (University of Chicago, 1931).

Radl, W., "Sonderüberlieferungen bei Lukas," PGJK 131–47, on Luke 22:67–68; 23:2,6–12.

Regnault, H., *Une province procuratorienne au début de l'Empire romain. Le procès de Jésus-Christ* (Paris: Picard, 1909).

Reichrath, H., "Der Prozess Jesu," *Judaica* 20 (1964), 129–55.

Ritt, H., "Wer war Schuld am Tod Jesu?" BZ NS 31 (1987), 165–75.

Rivkin, E., "Beth Din, Boulé, Sanhedrin: A Tragedy of Errors," HUCA 46 (1975), 181–99.

————, *What Crucified Jesus?* (Nashville: Abingdon, 1984).

Rosadi, G., *The Trial of Jesus* (New York: Dodd, Mead, 1905).

Rosenblatt, S., "The Crucifixion of Jesus from the Standpoint of the Pharisaic Law," JBL 75 (1956), 315–21.

Safrai, S., "Jewish Self-government," JPFC 1.377–419.

Sanders, E. P., *Jesus and Judaism* (Philadelphia: Fortress, 1985), esp. 243–318 on conflicts related to his death.

————, *Jewish Law from Jesus to Mishnah* (London: SCM, 1990), esp. 84–96 on conflicts related to his death.

————, *Judaism: Practice and Belief 63BCE–66CE* (Philadelphia: Trinity, 1992), esp. 315–494 on Jewish groups and parties.

Schalit, A., "Kritische Randbemerkungen zu Paul Winters 'On the Trial of Jesus,'" ASTI 2 (1963), 86–102.

Schinzer, R., "Die Bedeutung des Prozesses Jesu," *Neue Zeitschrift für systematische Theologie und Religionsphilosophie* 25 (1983), 138–54.

Schneider, G., "Gab es eine vorsynoptische Szene 'Jesus vor dem Synedrium'?" NovT 12 (1970), 22–39.

————, "Jesus vor dem Synedrium," BibLeb 11 (1970), 1–15.

————, "Das Verfahren gegen Jesus in der Sicht des dritten Evangeliums (Lk 22,54–23,25)," PGJK 111–30.

Schreiber, J., "Das Schweigen Jesu," in *Theologie und Unterricht,* ed. K. Wegenast (Gütersloh: Mohn, 1969).

Schubert, K., "Die Juden oder die Römer? Der Prozess Jesu und sein geschichtlicher Hintergrund," WW 17 (1962), 701–10.

———, "Die Juden und die Römer (zum Kaiphasprozess)," BibLit 36 (1962–63), 235–42.

———, "*Kritik der Bibelkritik.* Dargestellt an Hand des Markusberichtes vom Verhör Jesu vor dem Synedrion," WW 27 (1972), 421–34. Also in RTPL 316–38. In English in JPHD 385–402.

———, "Das Verhör Jesu vor dem Hohen Rat," in *Bibel und zeitgemässer Glaube II,* ed. J. Sint (Klosterneuberg, 1967), 97–130.

Schumann, H., "Bemerkungen zum Prozess Jesu vor dem Synhedrium," *Zeitschrift der Savigny-Stiftung für Rechtsgeschichte* (Romantische Abteilung, Weimar) 82 (1965), 315–20.

Scroggs, R., "The Trial before the Sanhedrin," KKS 2.543–50.

Sherwin-White, A. N., *Roman Society and Roman Law in the New Testament* (Oxford: Clarendon, 1963), esp. 1–47 on the trial of Jesus.

———, "The Trial of Christ," in *History and Chronology in the New Testament* (Theological Collections 6; London: SPCK, 1965), 97–116.

Sloyan, G. S., *Jesus on Trial* (Philadelphia: Fortress, 1973).

———, "Recent Literature On The Trial Narratives of The Four Gospels," in *Critical History and Biblical Faith: New Testament Perspectives,* ed. T. J. Ryan (Villanova Univ., 1979), 136–76.

Smallwood, E. M., "High Priests and Politics in Roman Palestine," JTS NS 13 (1962), 14–34.

———, *The Jews under Roman Rule* (Studies in Judaism and Late Antiquity 20; Leiden: Brill, 1976), esp. 145–80.

Sobosan, J. G., "The Trial of Jesus," JES 10 (1973), 70–93.

Söding, T., "Der Prozess Jesu. Exegetische, historische und theologische Fragestellungen," *Herder Korrespondenz* 41 (1987), 236–40.

Steinwenter, A., "Il processo di Gesù," *Jus* NS 3 (1952), 471–90.

Stern, M., "The Province of Judea," JPFC 1.308–76.

———, "The Status of Provincia Judaea and Its Governors in the Roman Empire under the Julio-Claudian Dynasty," *Eretz-Israel* 10 (1971; Z. Shazar vol.), 274–82 (in Hebrew).

Stewart, R. A., "Judicial Procedure in New Testament Times," EQ 47 (1975), 94–109.

Stonehouse, N. B., "Who Crucified Jesus?" *Paul before the Areopagus and Other New Testament Studies* (London: Tyndale, 1957), 41–69. Reply to Zeitlin.

Strobel, A., *Die Stunde der Wahrheit. Untersuchungen zum Strafverfahren gegen Jesus* (WUNT 21; Tübingen: Mohr, 1980).

Tcherikover, V. A., "Was Jerusalem a 'Polis'?" IEJ 14 (1964), 61–78.

Trilling, W., "Der 'Prozess Jesu,'" *Fragen zur Geschichtlichkeit Jesu* (Düsseldorf: Patmos, 1966), 130–41.

Tyson, J. B., "The Lukan Version of the Trial of Jesus," NovT 3 (1959), 249–58.

Valentin, P., "Les comparutions de Jésus devant le Sanhédrin," RechSR 59 (1971), 230–36.

Verdam, P. J., "Sanhedrin and Gabbatha," *Free University Quarterly* (1960–61), 259–87. Orig. in Dutch (Kampen: Kok, 1959).

Wallace, J. E., "The Trial of Jesus: A Legal Response," TToday 28 (1971–72), 466–69. Answer to O'Meara.

Watson, F., "Why Was Jesus Crucified?" *Theology* 88 (1985), 105–12.

Wilson, W. R., *The Execution of Jesus* (New York: Scribners, 1970).

Winter, P., "The Marcan Account of Jesus' Trial by the Sanhedrin," JTS NS 14 (1963), 94–102.

———, "Marginal Notes on the Trial of Jesus," ZNW 50 (1959), 14–33, 221–51.

———, "Markus 14,53b.55–64 ein Gebilde des Evangelisten," ZNW 53 (1962), 260–63. Response to Braumann.

———, *On the Trial of Jesus* (2d ed.; Studia Judaica 1; Berlin: de Gruyter, 1974).

———, "The Trial of Jesus and the Competence of the Sanhedrin," NTS 10 (1963–64), 494–99. Response to Derrett, ibid, 1–26.

———, "Zum Prozess Jesu," AJINT 95–104. Also in *Das Altertum* 9.3 (Berlin: Akademie, 1963), 157–64.

Yamauchi, E. M., "Historical Notes on the Trial and Crucifixion of Jesus Christ," CT 15 (1970–71), 634–39.

Zeitlin, S., "The Dates of the Birth and Crucifixion of Jesus: II. The Crucifixion, a Libelous Accusation against the Jews," JQR 55 (1964), 1–22.

———, *Who Crucified Jesus?* (4th ed.; New York: Bloch, 1964).

Part 2: AntiJewish Tone in the Gospel Accounts of the Passion
(From the broad field of literature that could be included, a selection has been made to form a background appropriate for a commentary, especially for §18F. See also bibliography in §30, Part 6.)

Éliás, J., "Erwählung als Gabe und Aufgabe (Eine Analyse des Jesus-Prozesses)," *Judaica* 11 (1955), 29–49, 89–108.

Ernest, K. J., "Did the Jews Kill Jesus? A Reply [to Sizoo]," *Interpretation* 1 (1947), 376–78.

Evans, C. A., "Is Luke's View of the Jewish Rejection of Jesus Anti-Semitic?" RDLJ 29–56, 174–83.

Flannery, E. H., *The Anguish of the Jews* (2d ed; New York: Paulist, 1985).

Flusser, D., "The Crucified One and the Jews," *Immanuel* 7 (1977), 25–37.

Johnson, L. T., "The New Testament's Anti-Jewish Slander and the Convention of Ancient Polemic," JBL 108 (1989), 419–41.

Leistner, R., *Antijudäismus im Johannesevangelium? Darstellung des Problems in der neueren Auslegungsgeschichte und Untersuchung der Leidensgeschichte* (Frankfurt: Lang, 1974).

Lindeskog, G., "Der Prozess Jesu im jüdisch-christlichen Religionsgespräch," in *Abraham unser Vater*, eds. O. Betz et al. (O. Michel Festschrift; Leiden: Brill, 1963), 325–36.

Michl, J., "Der Tod Jesu. Ein Beitrag nach Schuld und Verantwortung eines Volkes," MTZ 1 (1950), 5–15.

Pawlikowski, J. T., "The Trial and Death of Jesus: Reflections in Light of a New Understanding of Judaism," CSA 79–94.

Sizoo, J. R., "Did the Jews Kill Jesus? Historical Criticism in the Pulpit," *Interpretation* 1 (1947), 201–6.

Skoog, Å., "The Jews, the Church, and the Passion of Christ," *Immanuel* 21 (1987), 89–98.

Part 3: Transferral of Jesus to the Jewish Authorities; Interrogation by Annas (§19)

Charbonneau, A., "L'interrogatoire de Jésus, d'après la facture interne de Jn 18,12–27," ScEsp 35 (1983), 191–210.

Chevallier, M.-A., "La comparution de Jésus devant Hanne et devant Caïphe (Jean 18:12–14 et 19–24)," in *Neues Testament und Geschichte,* eds. H. Baltenweiser and B. Reicke (O. Cullmann Festschrift; Zurich: Theologischer Verlag and Tübingen: Mohr, 1972), 179–85.

Church, W. R., "The Dislocations in the Eighteenth Chapter of John," JBL 49 (1930), 375–83.

Farquhar, J. N., "The First Trial of Christ," ExpTim 6 (1894–95), 284–88, 429–31 (on John 18:12–28).

Findlay, G. G., "The Connexion of John xviii.12–28," ExpTim 6 (1894–95), 335–36, 478–79 (responses to Farquhar).

Flusser, D., ". . . To Bury Caiaphas, Not to Praise Him," *Jerusalem Perspective* 4 (#4–5, 1991), 23–28.

Fortna, R. T., "Jesus and Peter at the High Priest's House," NTS 24 (1977–78), 371–83.

Gardiner, F., "On the aorist *apesteilen* in Jn. xviii.24," JBL 6 (1886), 45–55.

Hahn, F., "Der Prozess Jesu nach dem Johannesevangelium," EKKNT *Vorarbeiten* 2 (1970), 23–96.

Mahoney, A., "A New Look at an Old Problem (John 18,12–14,19–24)," CBQ 27 (1965), 137–44.

Matera, F. J., "Jesus before Annas: John 18:13–14,19–24," ETL 66 (1990), 38–55.

Schneider, J., "Zur Komposition von Joh 18,12–27. Kaiphas und Hannas," ZNW 48 (1957), 111–19.

Thom, J. D., "Jesus se verhoor voor die Joodse Raad volgens Joh 18:19–24," *Nederuits Gereformeerde Teologiese Tydskrif* 25 (1984), 172–78.

Vicent Cernuda, A., "Jesús ante Anás," in *Cum Vobis et Pro Vobis,* eds. R. Arnau-Garcia et al. (Homenaje a M. Roca Cabanellas; Valencia: Facultad de Teologia San Vicente Ferrer, 1991), 53–71.

Wright, A., "The First Trial of Jesus," ExpTim 6 (1894–95), 523–24 (response to Farquhar).

Part 4: Synoptic Sanhedrin Proceedings: Jesus Destroying the Temple Sanctuary (§20)

Betz, O., "The Temple Scroll and the Trial of Jesus," SWJT 30 (#3; 1988), 5–8.

Biguzzi, G., "Mc. 14,58: un tempio *acheiropoētos*," RivB 26 (1978), 225–40.

———, *Io distruggerò questo Tempio* (Rome: Pontificia Università Urbaniana, 1987).

Bissoli, G., "Tempio e 'falsa testimonianza' in Marco," SBFLA 35 (1985), 27–36.

Dupont, J., "Il n'en sera pas laissé pierre sur pierre (Marc 13,2; Luc 19,44)," *Biblica* 52 (1971), 301–20 (in ref. to Mark 14:58).

Evans, C. A., "Jesus' Action in the Temple: Cleansing or Portent of Destruction?" CBQ 51 (1989), 237–70.

Flusser, D., "Two Notes on the Midrash on 2 Sam vii," IEJ 9 (1959), 99–109.

Gärtner, B., *The Temple and the Community in Qumran and the New Testament* (SNTSMS 1; Cambridge Univ., 1965), esp. 105–22 in ref. to Mark 14:58.

Gaston, L., *No Stone on Another* (NovTSup 23; Leiden: Brill, 1970), esp. 66–243 in ref. to Mark 14:58.

Hoffmann, R. A., "Das Wort Jesu von der Zerstörung und dem Wiederaufbau des Tempels," in *Neutestamentliche Studien* (G. Heinrici Festschrift; Leipzig: Hinrichs, 1914), 130–39.

Hooker, M. D., "Traditions about the Temple in the Sayings of Jesus," BJRL 70 (1988), 7–19 (in ref. to Mark 14:58).

Jeremias, J., "Die Drei-Tage-Worte der Evangelien," in *Tradition und Glaube*, eds. G. Jeremias et al. (K. G. Kuhn Festschrift; Göttingen: Vandenhoeck & Ruprecht, 1971), 221–29, esp. 221–26 on Mark 14:58. French in *Herméneutique et Eschatologie*, ed. E. Castelli (Paris: Aubier, 1971), 189–95.

Kleist, J. A., "The Two False Witnesses (Mk. 14:55ff)," CBQ 9 (1947), 321–23.

Lührmann, D., "Markus 14,55–64: Christologie und Zerstörung des Tempels im Markusevangelium," NTS 27 (1980–81), 457–74.

McElvey, R. J., *The New Temple* (Oxford Univ., 1969), esp. 67–79 on Mark 14:58.

Plooij, D., "Jesus and the Temple," ExpTim 42 (1930–31), 36–39, on Mark 14:58–59.

Prete, B., "Formazione e storicità del detto di Gesù sul tempio secondo Mc. 14,58," BeO 27 (1985), 3–16.

Schlosser, J., "La parole de Jésus sur la fin du Temple," NTS 36 (1990), 398–414.

Simon, M., "Retour du Christ et reconstruction du Temple dans la pensée chrétienne primitive," in *Aux sources de la tradition chrétienne* (Mélanges M. Goguel; Neuchâtel: Delachaux & Niestlé, 1950), 247–57.

Sweet, J.P.M., "A House Not Made with Hands," in *Templum Amicitiae*, ed. W. Horbury (E. Bammel Festschrift; JSNTSup 48; Sheffield: JSOT, 1991), 368–90.

Theissen, G., "Die Tempelweissagung Jesu. Prophetie in Spannungsfeld von Stadt und Land," TZ 32 (1976), 144–58.

Vögtle, A., "Das markinische Verständnis der Tempelworte," in *Die Mitte des Neuen Testaments*, eds. U. Luz and H. Weder (E. Schweizer Festschrift; Göttingen: Vandenhoeck & Ruprecht, 1983), 362–83. Reprinted in his *Offenbarungsgeschehen und Wirkungsgeschichte* (Freiburg: Herder, 1985), 168–88.

Weinert, F., "Assessing Omissions as Redaction: Luke's Handling of the Charge against Jesus as Detractor of the Temple," in *To Touch the Text,* eds. M. P. Horgan and P. J. Kobelski (J. A. Fitzmyer Festschrift; New York: Crossroads, 1989), 358–68.

———, "Luke, Stephen, and the Temple in Luke-Acts," BTB 17 (1987), 88–90.

Wenschkewitz, H., *Die Spiritualisierung der Kultusbegriffe Tempel, Priester und Opfer im Neuen Testament* (Angelos-Beiheft 4; Leipzig: Pfeiffer, 1932), esp. 96–101 in rel. to Mark 14:58.

Wood, H. G., "A Mythical Incident in the Trial of Jesus," ExpTim 28 (1916–17), 459–60, on Mark 14:55.

Young, F. M., "Temple Cult and Law in Early Christianity," NTS 19 (1972–73), 325–38 (in ref. to Mark 14:57–58).

Part 5: "Are You the Messiah?"; Jesus' Response; Blasphemy; Condemnation (§§21–23)

Beasley-Murray, G. R., "Jesus and Apocalyptic: With Special Reference to Mark 14,62," in *L'Apocalypse johannique et l'Apocalypse dans le Nouveau Testament,* ed. J. Lambrecht (BETL 53; Gembloux: Duculot, 1980), 415–29.

Borsch, F. H., "Marx xiv.62 and I Enoch lxii.5," NTS 14 (1967–68), 565–67.

———, *The Son of Man in Myth and History* (London: SCM, 1967), esp. 391–94 on Mark 14:62.

Burkitt, F. C., "On Romans ix 5 and Mark xiv 61," JTS 5 (1903–04), 451–55, esp. 453–54.

Catchpole, D. R., "The Answer of Jesus to Caiaphas (Matt. xxvi.64)," NTS 17 (1970–71), 213–26.

———, "'You have heard His Blasphemy,'" *Tyndale House Bulletin* 16 (April 1965), 10–18.

Dahl, N. A., *The Crucified Messiah and Other Essays* (Minneapolis: Augsburg, 1974), 10–36.

de Jonge, M., "The Use of *ho Christos* in the Passion Narratives," in *Jésus aux Origines de la Christologie,* ed. J. Dupont (BETL 40; Louvain: Duculot, 1975), 169–92 (in ref. to Mark 14:61).

———, "The Use of the Word 'Anointed' in the Time of Jesus," NovT 8 (1966), 132–48 (in ref. to Mark 14:61).

Derrett, J.D.M., "Midrash in the New Testament: The Origin of Luke xxii 67–68," ST 29 (1975), 147–56. Reprinted in DSNT 2.184–93.

Duplacy, J., "Une variante méconnue du texte reçu: '. . . ē apolysēte' (Lc 22,68)," in *Neutestamentliche Aufsätze,* eds. J. Blinzler et al. (J. Schmid Festschrift; Regensburg: Pustet, 1963), 42–52.

Dupont, J., "'Assis à la droite de Dieu'. L'interprétation du Ps 110,1 dans le Nouveau Testament," in *Resurrexit,* ed. É. Dhanis (Rome: Vatican, 1974), 340–422, esp. 347–72 on Mark 14:62 and par.

Feuillet, A., "Le Triomphe du Fils de l'homme d'après la déclaration du Christ aux Sanhédrites," in *La Venue du Messie* (RechBib 6; Desclée de Brouwer, 1962), 149–71.

Flusser, D., "'At the Right Hand of the Power,'" *Immanuel* 14 (1982), 42–46, on Luke 22:69.

Glasson, T. F., "The Reply to Caiaphas (Mark xiv.62)," NTS 7 (1960–61), 88–93.

Goldberg, A. M., "Sitzend zur Rechten der Kraft. Zur Gottesbezeichnung Gebura in frühen rabbinischen Literatur," BZ NS 8 (1964), 284–93.

Hay, D. M., *Glory at the Right Hand. Psalm 110 in Early Christianity* (SBLMS 18; New York: Abingdon, 1973), esp. 64–70 on Mark 14:62 and par.

Heil, J. P., "Reader-Response and the Irony of Jesus before the Sanhedrin in Luke 22:66–71," CBQ 51 (1989), 271–84.

Héring, J., *Le Royaume de Dieu et sa venue* (Paris: Alcan, 1937), 111–20 (on Mark 14:62).

Hofrichter, P., "Das dreifache Verfahren über Jesus als Gottessohn, König und Mensch. Zur Redaktionsgeschichte der Prozesstradition," *Kairos* NS 30–31 (1988–89), 69–81.

Kempthorne, R., "The Marcan Text of Jesus' Answer to the High Priest (Mark xiv 62)," NovT 19 (1977), 197–208.

Kingdon, H. P., "Messiahship and the Crucifixion," StEv III, 67–86.

Lamarche, P., "Le 'blasphème' de Jésus devant le sanhédrin," RechSR 50 (1962), 74–85. Reprinted in *Christ Vivant* (LD 43; Paris: Cerf, 1966), 147–63.

Linton, O., "The Trial of Jesus and the Interpretation of Psalm cx," NTS 7 (1960–61), 258–62.

Lövestam, E., "Die Frage des Hohenpriesters (Mark.14,61, par. Matt.26,63)," SEA 26 (1961), 93–107.

Maartens, P. J., "The Son of Man as a Composite Metaphor in Mark 14:62," in *A South African Perspective on the New Testament*, eds. J. H. Petzer et al. (B. M. Metzger Festschrift; Leiden: Brill, 1986), 76–98.

McArthur, H. K., "Mark xiv.62," NTS 4 (1957–58), 156–58.

Marcus, J., "Mark 14:61: 'Are You the Messiah-Son-of-God?'" NovT 31 (1989), 125–41.

Meloni, G., "'Sedet ad dexteram patris' [Mark 14:62 et par.]," *Saggi di Filologia Semitica* (Rome: Italiana, 1913), 283–87. Orig. in *Rivista Storico-Critica delle Scienze Teologiche* 5 (1909), 341–44.

Moule, C.F.D., "The Gravamen against Jesus," in *Jesus, the Gospels, and the Church*, ed. E. P. Sanders (Honor of W. R. Farmer; Macon: Mercer, 1987), 177–95.

Mussner, F., "Die Wiederkunft des Menschensohnes nach Markus 13,24–27 und 14,61–62," BK 16 (1961), 105–7.

O'Neill, J. C., "The Charge of Blasphemy at Jesus' Trial before the Sanhedrin," TJCSM 72–77.

———, "The Silence of Jesus," NTS 15 (1968–69), 153–67 (on Mark 14:62).

Perrin, N., "The High Priest's Question and Jesus' Answer (Mark 14:61–62)," in PMK 80–95.

———, "Mark xiv.62: The End Product of a Christian Pesher Tradition?" NTS 12 (1965–66), 150–55.

Plevnik, J., "Son of Man Seated at the Right Hand of God: Luke 22,69 in Lucan Christology," *Biblica* 72 (1991), 331–47.

Robinson, J.A.T., "The Second Coming—Mark xiv.62," ExpTim 67 (1955–56), 336–40.

Scott, R.B.Y., "'Behold, He Cometh with Clouds,'" NTS 5 (1958–59), 127–32.

Seitz, O.J.F., "The Future Coming of the Son of Man: Three Midrashic Formulations in the Gospel of Mark," StEv VI, 478–94 (in ref. to Mark 14:62).

Stauffer, E., *Jesus and His Story* (London: SCM, 1960), esp. 142–59 on Mark 14:62.

———, "Messias oder Menschensohn?" NovT 1 (1956), 81–102.

Vanni, U., "La Passione come rivelazione di condanna e di salvezza in Matteo 26,64 e 27,54," *Euntes Docete* 27 (1974), 65–91.

van Unnik, W. C., "Jesus the Christ," NTS 8 (1961–62), 101–16 (in ref. to Mark 14:61).

Winter, P., "Luke xxii 66b–71," ST 9 (1955), 112–15.

Winterbotham, R., "Was, Then, Our Lord Mistaken?" ExpTim 29 (1917–18), 7–11.

§18. INTRODUCTION: BACKGROUND FOR THE JEWISH TRIAL/INTERROGATION OF JESUS BY THE PRIESTLY AUTHORITIES

Before commenting on the Gospel accounts of this scene, we need to survey some general information. It may help the readers to have an itemized outline of this long section:

A. Roman Governance in Judea ca. AD 30
  1. Developments in Governance at the Beginning of the Empire
  2. Governance in Palestine
  3. Special Issues Pertinent to the Governance of Judea
    (a) Relationship between the legate of Syria and the governor of Judea
    (b) Title of the governor
    (c) Power to execute criminals
B. Jewish Self-governing Bodies, Including the Sanhedrin
  1. Before the Creation of the Roman Province of Judea in AD 6
  2. The Jewish Ruling Body under the Roman Prefecture
    (a) The New Testament
    (b) Josephus
    (c) The Mishna
C. The General Functioning of a Sanhedrin
  1. Membership and Meeting Place
  2. Dominant Influence on a Sanhedrin: Pharisee or Sadducee?
  3. The Trial of Jesus in the Gospels and Its Relation to Mishnaic Law
    (a) Conflicts between the Gospel accounts and later rabbinic procedure
    (b) These conflicts and Gospel accuracy
D. A Sanhedrin's Competence to Condemn to Death and Execute
  1. General Picture of Roman Control of the Death Penalty
  2. Proposed Examples of Executions by Jewish Authorities
  3. Conclusions
E. Evidence of Action against Jesus by Jewish Authorities
  1. Jewish Evidence
    (a) Josephus' *Testimonium Flavianum*
    (b) The Babylonian Talmud

Throughout I shall employ the traditional word "trial" for the appearance of Jesus before the Jewish authorities (and also before the Roman prefect), but my usage does not reflect a prejudgment that this was a trial in a technical sense. Indeed, by modern standards, "hearing" or "legal proceeding" might be a more appropriate designation. Inevitably a discussion of this "trial" as to legality and historicity will be quite detailed since it involves Jewish judicial practice and the interplay with Roman jurisdiction, as well as disputes about how to interpret the pertinent Christian sources. Another factor is the highly sensitive issue of the passion as a source of antiJewish antagonism (which shall be treated in subsection F below).

In §24 I shall outline the development of modern scholarship on how the account of the Jewish trial was composed and how much depends on the detectable presence of preGospel traditions (whether or not they be historical). But here I shall try to help readers to appreciate the necessity for detailed knowledge by giving a brief report on just one part of the research into the Jewish trial of Jesus, the legal research. Historians, biblical scholars, and theologians have studied the trial; but a special part of the pertinent bibliography (§17) constitutes evaluations by those trained in law.[1] Advocates, judges, magistrates, and professors of ancient and modern law have all produced studies of the Jewish trial of Jesus prefaced by the disclaimer that they are studying the biblical evidence simply from a legal viewpoint. (Most of these treat the Roman trial as well, but the legality of that procedure will be considered under §31 below.) As Schinzer ("Bedeutung") points out, this approach may be more complex than many who participate in it realize, given the great differences between the biblical view of law and modern jurisprudence. (Many of the judges and lawyers constantly appeal to the legal system in which they have practiced, e.g., Powell's references to English

---

[1]Similarly, the bibliography on the crucifixion (§37, Part 9) will contain studies of the death of Jesus by medical doctors. Often such contributions are made with a confidence about enlightening scientifically or professionally the somewhat backward biblical scholars. Alas, often the "outside" contributors are unaware of the extent to which their analysis is dependent on a simplistic reading of the NT evidence.

law in his *Trial* 47, 72.) For instance, Israelite law is thought to be revealed by God, even to specified punishments. The community has the primary right and duty to try homicides, and those who are judges function as representatives of the community. (This may cast light on the involvement of "the people" in Gospel accounts of the trial of Jesus.) Witnesses play a part not only in the trial but in the execution (Deut 17:7), where they are the first to cast stones. (This may cast light on why the Sanhedrin judges who, having been called on *to witness* at the trial of Jesus and having found him deserving of death, participated in chastising him.) Moreover, it may not be possible to understand the trial of Jesus legally without understanding the sociopolitical complexities of the Roman province of Judea with all the interplay of conflicting forces—any more than it is possible really to understand the Dreyfus trial without a knowledge of the antisemitism and rivalries in the French army and state. With those cautions let me sample legal approaches to the Jewish trial of Jesus.

Already in the 19th cent. there was a famous controversy in France between A. M. Dupin, an advocate, and J. Salvador, a Jewish historian. In 1828 Salvador argued that Jesus was legally and justly condemned to death by Jews in good faith because they thought that his claims were blasphemous and that he had misled the people—an opinion that exposed Salvador to criminal action. Dupin counterargued that the Jewish trial was illegal because of subornation of witnesses and procedures that violated the law of the Mishna, Roman restrictions, and justice. S. Greenleaf, a Harvard professor and famous American jurist (1846), deemed the treatment of Jesus to be murder perpetrated under the pretense of a legal sentence. Since 1899 *legal* studies of the Jewish trial of Jesus[2] available in English have been published by Scots or English (Innes, Buss, Powell), by Americans (Chandler, Cheever, Bisek, Goldin, Radin), by a Canadian (McRuer), an Italian (Rosadi), and an Israeli (H. Cohn)—as well as studies in French by Isorni, Besnier, and Imbert; and in German by von Mayr, Doerr, and Fricke.[3] Among the authors, Goldin, Isorni, and Cohn identify themselves as Jewish, while many of the others are clearly Christian believers. Only in a few instances (e.g., Radin, Goldin, Cohn, Besnier, Imbert, Fricke) is there indication of treating the Gospel evidence critically rather than at simple face value with harmoni-

[2]Besides those authored by scholars I mention above, there may be other works in my bibliography that would fit into this category, but whose authors I do not think of (or remember) as primarily specialists in law.

[3]Fricke was involved in a war-crimes trial of a Nazi who claimed as justification for obeying orders to kill Jews the way that according to the NT accounts Jews treated Jesus. For an evaluation of Fricke's rather journalistic attempt to deny all Jewish role in the death of Jesus, see Kolping's corrective review (#17, Part 1, under Fricke). Söding ("Prozess" 237) characterizes Fricke as indulging in much speculation bordering on fantasy.

zation.[4] All these writers bring to the discussion a knowledge of the Jewish legal procedure described in the Mishna, which, in general, they assume to be applicable to the time of Jesus. Yet most divergent results emerge from their studies. A large group (Innes, Cheever, Buss, Chandler, Rosadi, McRuer, Isorni) consider the Jewish trial of Jesus as described in Mark/Matt to have been irregular and formally illegal. The Christians in that group assume that the Jewish authorities were proceeding ignobly for political or self-protective purposes, rather than as men forced in difficult times to use improper means because they were honestly convinced that Jesus deserved to die (as Isorni would contend). A smaller group considers the Jewish trial to have been legal and formally correct under the rubric of treating Jesus as a blasphemer (Radin) and/or as a false prophet (Doerr). Other theories contend that the Jewish legal procedure was not a trial but only a preliminary investigation for the Roman trial (Bisek, Powell, Besnier), or that it never resulted in a sentence (Imbert), or that the Gospel accounts are fictitious and there was only a Roman trial (Goldin, Fricke), or that the intention of the Jewish authorities toward Jesus was benevolent (H. Cohn).[5] Biblical scholars are just as divided as the lawyers and have arrived at an even wider range of possibilities. To evaluate them we need to be aware of the complexities of the evidence.

A. *Roman Governance in Judea ca.* AD *30*

We shall begin with a discussion of the developments of governance under Augustus as the empire was established. Then we shall turn to Roman governance in Palestine, and finally to some specific questions concerning Judea where Jesus was put to death.

1. Developments in Governance at the Beginning of the Empire

A fundamental issue is the concept of *imperium:* "The supreme administrative power, involving command in war and the interpretation and execu-

---

[4]Indeed Bisek (*Trial* 231) even appeals to *The Acts of Pilate*; and Cheever ("Legal" 507–8) follows a text of "The Sentence Rendered by Pontius Pilate" inscribed on a copper tablet found ca. AD 1200 at Aquila (ancient Amiturnum; see p. 855 below).

[5]Cohn's book attracted attention because of his career in Israel as an attorney general and supreme court justice. Yet one must characterize as benevolently imaginative fiction his thesis that the Sanhedrin was called to protect Jesus against the Romans, seeking false witnesses who would be disproved so that Pilate could be made to see that Jesus was innocent. An earlier version of the revisionist approach to Jewish participation was offered by Rabbi A. P. Drucker (*Trial*) who, by combining extraordinary interpretations of the NT with Jewish legends, maintained that Jesus was a hero for ordinary Jews and opposed only by Zealots and by Caiaphas, a corrupt high priest who feared that Jesus would get Pilate to remove him. Caiaphas spread rumors that Jesus was an idolater to discredit him among other Jews.

tion of the law (including the infliction of the death penalty) which belonged at Rome . . . to consuls, military tribunes with consular powers (from 445–367 BC), praetors, dictators, and masters of the horse."[6] By extension, *imperium* could be granted to a substitute (pro-official, e.g., a proconsul) for a period of time (often a year) or until a specific commission expired. The way in which and by whom *imperium* was exercised affected the provinces, for by definition a province was the sphere of action of a magistrate possessing *imperium.* An area where a war was being fought could be a province because a Roman general had *imperium* there even before it was annexed; gradually, however, "province" came to refer to possessions of Rome outside Italy where inhabitants paid taxes to Rome—the Italian confederacy paid no taxes. When a province was annexed by Rome, a law was drawn up laying down the principles (usually financial and judicial) by which it would be governed; subsequently a new governor on entering office supplemented the law of the province by issuing an edict. (Unfortunately we have no copy of the law or the edicts pertinent to the establishment of the province of Judea.) Before Augustus' time the Senate was normally responsible for the allocation of provinces.[7]

When we come to the time of Octavian (Augustus), we must remember that under his leadership (30 BC–AD 14) Rome moved from being a republic to becoming an empire. Consequently, during Jesus' lifetime new governance structures were emerging both in the empire and in Palestine. In the process of eliminating the claimants to the heritage of Julius Caesar and solidifying his own position, Octavian held various types of *imperium.*[8] In 27 BC, after purging the Senate and restoring the republic, Octavian was awarded the title Augustus; and functioning under the umbrella of annually renewed consulships, he received a number of provinces for ten years (including Egypt and Syria). Thus there was created a new type of province, namely, the imperial province, eventually about a dozen in number, which Augustus did not own but administered for Rome. For this purpose he was given proconsular *imperium,* which he exercised through governors who were his legates. Frequently these legates were taken from the equestrian

---

[6]*The Oxford Classical Dictionary,* eds. M. Cary et al. (Oxford: Clarendon, 1949), 451; also 741 on "province."

[7]Former consuls and former praetors were often granted the *imperium* in these provinces by prorogation (of the twelve senatorial or public provinces two were consular, ten praetorian).

[8]A. H. M. Jones, "The *Imperium* of Augustus," JRS 41 (1951), 112–19, warns that the constitutional basis of Augustus' power was important precisely because his status was resisted by the Italian middle class, who venerated the republican traditions of Rome. As Jones shows in his discussion, we are dependent on later writers who did not describe the complicated situation with meticulous accuracy, whence scholarly disputes about the type of *imperium.*

class (the lower nonsenatorial nobility that had supported Octavian[9]), although the senatorial class supplied legates both for the imperial and for the senatorial provinces. In 23 BC Augustus resigned his annual consulship, while the Senate increased his proconsular *imperium* so that it affected not only the provinces assigned to him but other provinces if he disagreed with their proconsuls. In Rome itself he got the *imperium* of the tribune for life, including the right to veto, and thus complete control of the Senate—truly the end of an effective Roman republic that could withstand the emperor! The combination of powers enabled him to rule the imperial provinces directly and the senatorial provinces indirectly.[10] In 19 BC he became what was tantamount to a permanent consul, i.e., one whose *imperium* had no territorial limitations. In AD 13 the proconsular *imperium* over the provinces was extended to Tiberius, who one year later succeeded Augustus as emperor.

2. Governance in Palestine

There were related changes in Palestine before and during Jesus' lifetime. I plan to discuss here the structures of government, while the political atmosphere, including the quality of the governors and instances of stability and unrest, will be treated in §31 below.

In 63 BC, at a time when the princes of the Hasmonean priestly family were squabbling fiercely to be high priest and king, Pompey came to Jerusalem with troops. Thus he ended Jewish independence and brought Palestine into the Roman sphere of control, which was exercised through the Roman province of Syria and client local rulers. In 47 BC the Hasmonean high priest Hyrcanus II was made an ethnarch by Julius Caesar for his help in the Roman civil wars and was given authority over most of Palestine (except Samaria and the coast). Another powerful figure in the area was the Idumean Antipater II; and after his death in 43 BC his son Herod, to be known as the Great, came to the fore. By 37 he had become the master of Palestine, both marrying into and killing off the Hasmonean family. In 31 Octavian (Augustus), who had outlasted all other claimants to Roman supremacy, confirmed Herod's status as an ally king (*rex socius*) of Rome. Herod's reign was marked by splendid building; he began a monumental restoration of the Jerusalem Temple ca. 20 BC; Samaria was rebuilt and named Sebaste (the Greek equiv-

---

[9]G. H. Stevenson, *Roman Provincial Administration till the Age of the Antonines* (Oxford: Blackwell, 1939), 85 and 115, points out that the Roman republic never developed a civil service, and in a way Augustus began to fill that gap through his use of equestrians.

[10]Appeals from the imperial provinces were made to the emperor; appeals from the senatorial provinces were made to the emperor or another consul.

alent of "Augustus"); and Caesarea (Maritima), a town named after Augustus Caesar, was constructed on the coast. Yet there was brutal repression of any sign of opposition, and homicidal extermination of family members whom Herod suspected of disloyalty. An atmosphere of madness made him hated in his last years.

After the death of Herod the Great, ca. 4 BC, his sons went to Rome to implore Augustus to grant them rule of Herod's kingdom (Josephus, *Ant.* 17.9.3–7; #213–49). In Palestine, where the legate of Syria, Varus, and the imperial procurator or financial administrator, Sabinus, were keeping a close eye on the situation until Augustus would decide the case, there were major disturbances. Even though a delegation of Jews came to Augustus petitioning an end to the reign of the Herod family (*Ant.* 17.11.1–2; #299–314), Augustus' decision was to appoint (Herod) *Archelaus* ethnarch of Judea, Samaria, and Idumea; (Herod) *Antipas* ruler of Galilee and Perea (Transjordan); and (Herod) *Philip* ruler of the territories NE of the Lake of Galilee.[11]

A major change in that arrangement took place ten years later, ca. AD 6, when, at the petition of leading Jews and Samaritans, Augustus banned Archelaus to Gaul. The territory subject to him "was added to Syria, and Quirinius, a man of consular rank, was sent by Caesar to take a census of property in Syria and to sell the estate of Archelaus" (*Ant.* 17.13.2,5; #342–44,355). This description by Josephus given at the end of *Ant.* 17 is not totally clear (and will need to be clarified by what he says at the beginning of *Ant.* 18); but certainly in AD 6 Quirinius became legate in Syria with special census authority in Judea and Samaria. Coponius, a man of equestrian rank, was sent along with him to rule over the Jews with full authority (*exousia* = *imperium*), including the death penalty (*Ant.* 18.1.1; #1–2).[12]

Thus the government that Jesus knew in his lifetime was established. In the Galilee area where he grew up (Nazareth) and preached (Lake of Galilee) and in the Transjordan (opposite where John baptized), Antipas, the son of Herod the Great, was tetrarch (4 BC–AD 39) or "king" in popular parlance. The (ten) cities of the Decapolis (including Gadara and Gerasa), which he sometimes visited, were under the Roman legate of the province of Syria. When Jesus moved from Capernaum east-northeast to Bethsaida and Chorazin, he was crossing into the territory of another son of Herod the Great, the

---

[11]*Ant.* 17.11.4; #317–20. In addition some cities are mentioned as having special status, e.g., Sebaste in Samaria and the Decapolis (added to the province of Syria).

[12]Later we shall discuss the transition and relationship between Quirinius (Syria) and Coponius (Judea); some would even argue that they were successive, not simultaneous. Part of the ambiguity probably lies in the reality that an emerging province with a new system of taxation (an added head tax) required support (both by way of experience and armed backup) from an established province (see Smallwood, *The Jews* 151).

tetrarch Philip (4 BC–AD 34). When Jesus passed into Samaria (only in the Fourth Gospel) or Judea, visiting Jerusalem, he came under the authority of the Roman governor of the province of Judea (including Idumea), who resided at Caesarea on the coast.

3. Special Issues Pertinent to the Governance of Judea

Three topics need to be discussed: (a) What was the relationship between the legate of Syria and the governor of Judea? (b) What title did the governor of Judea have? (c) How extensive was his *imperium* in regard to executing capital sentences passed on criminals?

(a) *The relationship between the legate of Syria and the governor of Judea.* Although both were imperial provinces, Syria was an older (from 64–63 BC under Pompey) and more important province, often assigned to governors of a higher social status and more distinguished past career. The Syrian legate had at his disposition as many as four legions of soldiers, of a more professional military quality than those of the five cohorts assigned to the governor of Judea (see §31, n. 64). The Judean cohorts (consisting of nonJewish local recruits, mostly from the Samaria region) were meant to keep general order; the legionaries from Syria were brought in at times of rebellion or invasion.[13] The ambiguous description quoted above from the end of *Ant.* 17 stating that the territory of Archelaus was added to Syria, plus the special census task assigned to Quirinius with regard to Judea, has caused some scholars to think that the governor of Judea was directly subject to the governor of Syria, even to the point of considering Judea a subdivision of the Syrian province. An argument favoring this view has been drawn from the fact that Jews and Samaritans appealed to the legate of Syria when they were dissatisfied with the behavior of a Roman governor in Palestine, e.g., the Samaritan complaint to the legate Vitellius, which caused the removal of Pilate (*Ant.* 18.4.1–2; #85–89). This argument, however, is complicated. Lémonon (*Pilate* 59–69) points out that the legates of Syria had occasionally intervened in the affairs of the kingdom of Herod the Great, mediating delicate situations by advice (*Ant.* 16.9.1; #277–78, 280; 16.11.3; #368). This tradition may have influenced occasional actions later when Judea became a Roman province,[14] but

---

[13]See Smallwood, *The Jews* 146–47; Stern, "Status" 278–79.

[14]One must recognize that the four years (AD 36/37–40/41) between the removal of Pilate and the addition of Judea to the realm of Agrippa I are not carefully explained by Josephus. In *Ant.* 18.4.2; #89 he says that besides ordering Pilate to return to Rome, Vitellius dispatched his friend Marcellus as administrator or caretaker (*epimēlētēs*) of Judean affairs. This seems to have been a temporary arrangement, and we know nothing of what Marcellus did. A year later (*Ant.* 18.6.10; #237) Caligula sent Marullus as "commander of the cavalry" in Judea. Thus the direct imperial authority was restored, but the designation of the official is curious. Why in AD 40 was it to Petro-

the interference of the legate of Syria was more de facto than de jure. It does not show that the governor in Judea lacked full *imperium* or political independence. Most scholars (e.g., Regnault, *Province* 42) recognize that according to *Ant.* 18.1.1; #1–2 the powers of Coponius, the first governor of Judea, included full *imperium*.[15]

(b) *Title of the governor.* If the governor of Judea had independent *imperium*, what title was given to him by the emperor? This question may throw light on his functioning. The reference in Tacitus (*Annals* 15.44) is clear: "The originator who gave the group its name, Christ, had been executed in the reign of Tiberius by the *procurator*, Pontius Pilate." The view that Pilate was a procurator (approximate Greek equivalent: *epitropos*) has dominated in scholarship until recent times; for Josephus (*War* 2.9.2; #169) and Philo (*Ad Gaium* 38; #299) use that same term of Pilate.[16] Once again, however, one must recognize development.[17] During the republic the procurator was a figure in private not public law: the personal agent of an individual. There remained an element of the personal even when, after empire began, procurators entered into the public domain; they were imperial agents in fiscal matters but not general administrators. Administration was the function of an *eparchos* or *praefectus*. A prefect had a supervisory role, originally most often at the head of auxiliary troops (especially equestrian or cavalry troops), and was part of the entourage of a proconsul or tribune. As Augustus developed the organization for exercising his proconsular *imperium*, he enlarged the leadership functions of the prefects to include administration of the newly designated imperial provinces. The prefect serving as the emperor's legate was given *imperium* for civil and criminal jurisdiction. In a small imperial province[18] the same person could be both the prefect who governed

---

nius, the legate in Syria, and not to Marullus, that Caligula gave orders to set up statues of himself in the Jerusalem Temple (*War* 2.10.1–5; #184–203)? Was it that he suspected the legions might be needed, or did Marullus not have full *imperium*? But all these complications took place after Jesus' lifetime.

[15]The evidence of *Ant.* 18 agrees closely with the earlier account Josephus had written in *War* 2.8.1; #117: "The territory of Archelaus was now reduced to a province [*eparcheia*], and Coponius, a Roman of the equestrian order, was sent as procurator [*epitropos*], receiving from Caesar power [*exousia=imperium*] even to the point of executing."

[16]Presently we shall discuss variations in Josephus. Philo's usage is stereotyped, for he uses the same *epitropos* for the governor of Egypt (*Ad Gaium* 20; #132), who was clearly a prefect (*eparchos*).

[17]Helpful here is Jones, *Studies* 117–25 ("Procurators and Prefects in the Early Principate"). An earlier major study was by Hirschfeld, *Kaiserlichen.*

[18]Jones, *Studies* 120, observes that the tasks assigned to the prefect of a small province were much the same as those assigned to a legate in a large province; the difference was one of the provincial scale and the rank of the holders. Legates had to be senators; the lower, equestrian prefect was often a prolegate ("in place of a legate") in a small province. Pflaum, *Essai* 6, points out that the equestrian prefects were in a sense the emperor's servants; limitations placed on them were in terms of independently raising money or soldiers.

and the procurator who protected the financial rights of the emperor to money gained by taxation. In larger provinces the procurator could be a separate figure. The situation changed in the mid-40s during the reign of the emperor Claudius, when most governors began to be designated as procurators.[19]

In calling Pilate a procurator Tacitus was reflecting the later terminology of the 1st cent., still in vogue at the time of his writing. A similar explanation may be offered for Josephus' use of *epitropos*, although one should note that he is not consistent in his terminology for the governors of Judea. Both Josephus and the NT are giving popular designations rather than technical ones.[20] Technically the governors of Judea in the period AD 6–41 would probably have been designated prefects, with a secondary title of procurator for tax-collecting purposes.[21] The first part of this surmise has now been confirmed for Pilate by the discovery of an inscription in which he designates himself as *praefectus Iudaeae* (p. 695 below). When Roman rule was restored after Agrippa I (AD 44–66), the governors of Judea presumably had "procurator" as their primary title. In referring to the total period of Roman provincial rule from AD 6 to 66 (with the interstice of Agrippa I in 41–44), I shall use the terminology "prefect" and/or "procurator" with the nuances recounted above.

(c) *Power to execute criminals.* If the governor of the province of Judea had the full *imperium* of a prefect, independent of the legate of Syria, a question of special concern for our treatment of the death of Jesus is the applicability of that power in executing capital sentences. *Ius gladii* ("the

---

[19]For the still later situation (Nero's time) Tacitus, *Annals* 15.25, is interesting: In reference to the Roman governance of areas around Syria, he mentions some prefects of troops; for others (including probably Judea), procurators. Already under Augustus Egypt got exceptional treatment because its food supply was so important to Rome and Augustus did not want a senator in control of it. After the change under Claudius it seems to have remained exceptional, being ruled by a prefect with three legions under his control.

[20]See Lémonon, *Pilate* 46–47. Philo, Josephus, and the NT fail to describe Pilate as *eparchos* (=*praefectus*, the term that Pilate himself used in his Latin inscription [§31, B1 below]). Indeed, the NT does not use either *eparchos* or *epitropos* for any Roman governor (although John 19:38 employs *epitrephein* for Pilate). Besides calling Pilate an *epitropos* and using that term in general to refer to the Roman governors of Judea (*War* 2.16.4; #348, 350), Josephus thus entitles Pilate's predecessor Coponius (2.8.1; #117) and Pilate's successors: Cuspius Fadus, Tiberius Alexander (2.11.6; #220), Ventidius Cumanus (*Ant.* 20.6.2; #132) and Felix (*War* 2.12.8; #247). Josephus uses *eparchos* of Pilate's two immediate predecessors (*Ant.* 18.2.2.; #33), and of Festus and Albinus, successors of Pilate (*Ant.* 20.8.11; #193; *War* 6.5.3; #303; for *eparcheia* cf. Acts 25:1). Both Josephus (*Ant.* 18.3.1; #55) and the NT (Matt 27:2; Luke 20:20) describe Pilate as *hēgemōn* (= Latin *praeses*), "governor" of Judea. *Epimēlētes* ("administrator, caretaker") is used implicitly of Pilate in *Ant.* 18.4.2; #89, but not in the NT. The verbal form related to *prostatēs* ("superintendent, commander") is used of Felix, a successor of Pilate, in *Ant.* 20.7.1; #137.

[21]ILS 1358–59 shows that the Sardinian governor was entitled *procurator Augusti (et) praefectus.* Imbert, *Procès* 60, points out that the emperor might have other procurators or fiscal agents for areas of special concern.

right of the sword"; DJ 1.18.6.8) is sometimes used to cover this power to execute, but that is debatable terminology.[22] The argumentation of one school of classicists stems from Mommsen but is most articulately represented by A.H.M. Jones. The latter contends that *ius gladiii* referred to the right to put to death (without appeal to the emperor) a soldier who was a Roman citizen; it was an aspect of army discipline. The term first appears in the reign of Domitian (ILS 9200; Jones, *Studies* 61), although the right may have existed much earlier. Only in certain cases were governors delegated a *ius gladii* over other Roman citizens, e.g., the execution of Saint Perpetua in AD 203 (*Passion of Perpetua and Felicitas* 6.3; MACM 112). Later, just after AD 200, Septimius Severus extended the right to executing any Roman citizen (see DJ 1.18.6.8). Thus the *ius gladii* would not have covered the execution of those who were not Roman citizens; that was an extension of military *imperium*. All this has been sharply challenged by P. Garnsey: "The governor had the power to impose the death sentence on all provincials except for the aristocracy, who had been specifically exempted. This power was the *ius gladii* . . . the *ius gladii* was available to all governors from the Julio-Claudian period at least."[23] This was not a specially delegated power but was inherent in the governor's office. The point is a technical one, but ordinary parlance would seem to favor Garnsey's view whereby *ius gladii* was not so specialized, e.g., Romans 13:3–4: The ruler [*archōn*] is the minister of God, and he does not "bear the sword [Vulgate: *gladium*]" in vain.

In any case, according to Josephus (*War* 2.8.1; #117), the first Roman prefect (called here a procurator) of Judea, Coponius (AD 6–9), was sent by Augustus with power, "including the power to execute" (*mechri tou kteinein exousia*). There is no convincing reason to think that his successors in the prefecture of Judea had any less power, and so it is entirely reasonable to suppose that within the prefect's *imperium* was a full *coercitio* (right to coerce or punish) for the protection of Roman interests, limited only by the special exemptions granted to the Jews by Julius Caesar. When we discuss the Roman trial of Jesus (§31), we shall call attention to the way the later prefects/procurators of Judea treated criminals accused of capital crimes; there is nothing in Josephus' descriptions of them to suggest that they did not have the power of execution.[24] A far more difficult question is whether in the Roman governance of Judea *only* the prefect/procurator had this power legally; but that will be discussed later in this chapter.

---

[22]See the strong objections by Winter, "Trial . . . Competence" 494–95.
[23]"Criminal" 51–59, esp. 55.
[24]Philo (*Ad Gaium* 38; #302), by criticizing Pilate for executions without trial, implicitly testifies to Pilate's authority to execute with trial.

B. *Jewish Self-governing Bodies, Including the Sanhedrin*

All the Gospels mention the Sanhedrin by name as having a contributory role in the death of Jesus (Mark 15:1; Matt 26:59; Luke 22:66; John 11:47).[25] This harmonizes with the affirmation of Josephus (*Ant.* 14.9.3; #167): ". . . our law, which forbids us to slay someone, even an evildoer, unless this person has first been condemned by the Sanhedrin to suffer this fate." The root meaning of the Greek *synedrion* (Sanhedrin) involves the idea of sitting together; the term can cover the *place* of doing this, the *assembly* of those involved, and even their *functioning* as council, court, or governing body. Thus in secular Greek *synedrion* is not truly a technical term; and this variety of meaning is also reflected in LXX usage and at times in Philo and Josephus, even if in 1st-cent. Judaism "Sanhedrin" was (also) a technical designation for a specific Jewish assembly. Let me begin before Jesus' time and continue through the period of his ministry in order to give a brief account of the historical background of the assemblies or councils that had authority in Jerusalem.

1. Before the Creation of the Roman Province of Judea in AD 6

In postexilic Judea under foreign control (Persian and then Hellenistic), the priests and the elders or nobles, i.e., especially the heads of the leading families, had a leadership role as well as a judging function. For instance, Neh 5:17 refers to 150 "Jewish magistrates" who sat at the table of Nehemiah, the Jewish governor of Judea. A decree of the Seleucid (Syrian) King Antiochus III (223–187 BC), cited by Josephus (*Ant.* 12.3.3; #138), describes how he was met by the Gerousia (senate of elders) of the Jews. (BAGD 156 points to an inscription juxtaposing *synedrion* and *gerousia*.) Antiochus goes on to proclaim (#142): "All the members of the nation shall be governed in accordance with the laws of their country; and the Gerousia, the priests, the scribes of the Temple, and the Temple-singers shall be relieved from the poll tax. . . ."

In the troubled 2d cent. BC the Seleucid kings sought to tighten their control of Judea by frequently changing the high priest; but the Gerousia of

---

[25]Millar ("Reflections" 369) makes the unusual claim that only in Luke's Gospel "something which is clearly a meeting of 'the Sanhedrin' is represented as taking place." He bases the claim on Luke 22:66, where Jesus is led away to the Sanhedrin. But certainly Mark 14:55; Matt 26:59 speak of "the whole Sanhedrin," and the description of the trial that follows (witnesses, questioning, and sentencing) is more detailed than in Josephus' description of Sanhedrin meetings. (See also McLaren, *Power* 92–93.) Below I shall argue against too fixed a notion of "the Sanhedrin" in Jesus' lifetime.

the nation, where the elders constituted an ongoing factor, was mentioned solemnly in the address of letters from and to Judea (II Macc 1:10; 11:27; I Macc 12:6—also I Macc 13:36 and 14:20, which mention "presbyters" or "elders"). Occasionally it is clear that the Gerousia resented the behavior of the puppet high priests (II Macc 4:44). By the end of the 2d cent. BC, the Maccabees/Hasmoneans not only had restored the hereditary high priesthood (by substituting their own family) but had become kings; yet "the elders of the Jews" remained a potent force to be reckoned with (Josephus *Ant.* 13.16.5; #428). Under Queen Alexandra (76–67 BC) the Pharisees gained a strong voice (*Ant.* 13.16.2; #408–9).[26] Perhaps for a short period the Pharisees became the majority in the Sanhedrin or Gerousia; but after Pompey's conquest of Jerusalem in 63 BC, while Rome terminated the monarchical aspect of the high priesthood, it left to that priesthood "the primacy/leadership of the nation" (*prostasia:* Josephus, *Ant.* 20.10.4; #244). It would seem that at least by Herod's time the Sadducee adherents with their strong base in the priests and the elders represented the majority in governance once more. (See pp. 350–57 below.)

The proconsular governor of Syria, Aulus Gabinus (57–55 BC), reorganized the governance of Palestine, dividing it into five synods or *synedria* (one of them in Jerusalem); and Josephus' reference to this (*War* 1.8.5; #170 [dubious]; *Ant.* 14.5.4; #91) constitutes his first use of the Greek word for a Sanhedrin in Palestine. A decade later (47 BC) Julius Caesar appointed the priest Hyrcanus II ethnarch of the Jews, and the Sanhedrin at Jerusalem seems to have assumed juridical responsibility for all Palestine including Galilee, with the power to put even Herod to death (*Ant.* 14.9.4–5; #168–80). When Herod became king, the Sanhedrin of Jerusalem (purged of his enemies and now at his disposal) continued as a juridical body with the power to execute (*Ant.* 15.6.2; #173). Tcherikover ("Was" 73) suggests that under Herod this Sanhedrin may have dealt mainly with religious matters. When Herod died ca. 4 BC, Palestine was divided under his three sons (see A2 above). Our primary concern here is how this responsibility was exercised after AD 6, when the son who ruled Judea, Archelaus, was replaced by a Roman prefect whose headquarters was at Caesarea on the coast.

2. The Jewish Ruling Body under the Roman Prefecture

Our history thus far has portrayed a Gerousia or Sanhedrin in Jerusalem dominated by the chief priests, with other priests, wealthy nobles or elders,

---

[26]In NT designations of the constituency of the Sanhedrin as "the priests, the elders, and the scribes," there may have been Pharisees among the last-mentioned group (see n. 52 below; and APPENDIX V, B2).

and Pharisees (scribes?).[27] This assembly, administrative and judicial, had responsibility in religious and some secular matters. Before AD 6 the ruler had dealt with and through this body, at times being reproached by it over matters of justice, at times ordering it to accomplish what he wanted. Is there evidence that such a situation continued in the 1st cent. AD and thus in Jesus' time?

(a) The New Testament. The situation just described certainly matches the picture given by the NT of the Sanhedrin procedures relating to Jesus, Stephen, and Paul. According to John 11:47–53 the chief priests and Pharisees, disturbed by Jesus' raising of Lazarus, convene the Sanhedrin, which is addressed by Caiaphas the high priest. They take counsel (*boulesthai*) on how to put Jesus to death. The Jewish trial of Jesus, which in Mark, Matt, and Luke takes place just before his crucifixion, involves a Sanhedrin of chief priests, scribes, and elders. In Mark/Matt there are witnesses against Jesus; the issue is blasphemy, and the sentence urges death; the Sanhedrin leaders deal with Pilate over this, and he deals with them.[28] Acts 4:5–6,15 has Peter and John, who have been charged with religious issues such as preaching about the risen Jesus, appear before the Jerusalem Sanhedrin consisting of chief priests, rulers, elders, and scribes. To judge these apostles Acts 5:21,34 has the high priest and those with him calling together "the Sanhedrin and all the Gerousia of the sons of Israel," in which there are also Pharisees. There is a movement toward effecting the apostles' death (5:33), but dismissal after beating is the outcome (5:40). Stephen is brought before the Jerusalem Sanhedrin, which involves elders and scribes; witness is given accusing him of inflammatory statements about the Temple and the Law of Moses (6:12–14); Stephen's defense fails, and he is stoned to death (7:54–58). A Roman centurion commands a meeting of the chief priests and all the Sanhedrin and brings Paul before them (22:30). In this meeting there are Pharisees as well as Sadducees (23:6–9), who dispute over religious issues such as the resurrection and questions of the law (23:28–29). The centurion takes Paul away from them and sends him to the Roman governor, but the Sanhedrin leaders (chief priests and elders) go to Caesarea to present their charges against Paul (24:1). According to the Western text of Acts 24:6 they

[27]No claim is made that this is the total picture of Jewish administration in Palestine: There may have been other courts, but our concern here is only with Judea. As we turn to Jewish administration under the Romans, readers will notice the extent to which the chief priests continue to play a role. James (*Trial*), who is simplistically literal in interpreting the biblical accounts but offers a serious presentation of Greco-Roman evidence, points out (1.181) that most Roman-controlled assemblies involved the priests of the local religion: "Political authority in ancient times always wore a cloak of sanctity."

[28]In light of the discussion of Josephus to follow, it is noteworthy that although the three Synoptics have used "Sanhedrin" to describe the assembly before whom Jesus stood, Luke 23:50–51 and Mark 15:43 use "Boulē" [or *bouleutēs*] in describing Joseph from Arimathea, a member of that body.

state that if they had not been interrupted, "we would have judged according to our law."

(b) *Josephus*. When we turn to Josephus, we find a similar picture of the Sanhedrin. At the beginning of the Roman period, he states (*Ant.* 20.10.5; #251), "After the death of these kings [Herod the Great and Archelaus, his son] the form of government became an aristocracy, and the chief priests were entrusted with the leadership of the nation." (See also *Against Apion* 2.21–22, #185–86,188.) To describe the assembly brought together by the priests Josephus uses two terms, "Sanhedrin" and "Boulē" ("senate, council [of a city-state]"),[29] just as he had two terms of description in the preRoman period, namely "Sanhedrin" and "Gerousia." Let me give a summary analysis of eight illustrative passages, the first three of which use "Sanhedrin" and the second five "Boulē." These are Josephus' only uses of those terms for the Jerusalem assembly during the Roman prefecture of Judea (AD 6–66).[30]

(1*) Ca. 62 (*Ant.* 20.9.1; #200–3). The Sadducee high priest Ananus (Annas) II, at the moment of the change between the procurators Festus and Albinus, convened (*kathizein:* made sit) a Sanhedrin of judges and brought before it a man named James (the brother of Jesus called the Christ) and certain others. He accused them of transgression of the Law, and he gave them to be stoned. Some complained that Ananus had acted illegally because he had no authority to convene a Sanhedrin without the procurator's consent, and so he was removed from office.

(2*) Ca. 64 (*Ant.* 20.9.6; #216–17). In the time of the procurator Albinus, Agrippa II convened a Sanhedrin to get permission for dressing in robes the levites who were singers. Those who attended the Sanhedrin agreed.

(3*) Late 60s (*Life* 12; #62). When Josephus arrived in Galilee, he wrote to the Sanhedrin of Jerusalem, asking for instructions on how to proceed.

(4*) Ca. 44–45 (*Ant.* 20.1.2; #11). The emperor Claudius wrote "to the rulers [*archontes*], Boulē, and populace of Jerusalem,[31] to the whole nation of the Jews." For *archontes*, see APPENDIX V, B6, below.

---

[29]Like *synedrion*, *boulē* can mean the place or chamber of assembly as well as the assembly itself (Josephus, *War* 5.4.2; #144). *Bouletērion* is also the place of assembly (*War* 6.6.3; #354).

[30]Unfortunately, nowhere does Philo describe the governing group in Jerusalem by using either "Sanhedrin" or "Boulē." In some of his allegorical descriptions, however, one can see that there is for him no sharp distinction between the two terms, e.g., the meeting place (*synedrion*) and council chamber (*bouleutērion*) of the soul (*De vita contemplativa* 3; #27); also the combination of senators (*bouleutēs*) and *synedrion* with symbolic import in *De confusione linguarum* 18; #86. Comparable to Josephus' description of convening a Sanhedrin is Philo's summoning a council: *boulēn synagein* (*Quis rerum heres* 50; #244). "Boulē" is used for the Roman senate and for town councils.

[31]Although he does not think that Jerusalem was a Greek *polis* (city-state), Tcherikover ("Was" 62–63) points out that this was the normal form of imperial address for such a city. (This letter itself militates against the thesis that Jerusalem was like other Greek city-states, for it takes care to mention the right of the Jews to live according to their ancestral traditions.) Like the Romans, Josephus used standard Greek names for peculiar Jewish institutions; but both they and he knew the difference

(5*) Mid-60s (*War* 2.15.6; #331). The procurator Florus sent for the chief priests and the Boulē and told them he intended to leave the city of Jerusalem. By studying the context of this passage (*War* 2.14.8 and 15.3; #301,318), Tcherikover ("Was" 68) shows that in describing those who made up the Boulē, Josephus makes no distinction among the *archontes* ("rulers"), the *dynatoi* ("powerful or influential"), and the *gnōrimoi* ("notable or prestigious"). They are all Jerusalem aristocracy (and probably equivalent to the NT "chief priests and elders").

(6*) Mid-60s (*War* 2.16.2; #336). The chief priests of the Jews, the influential citizens (*dynatoi*), and the Boulē came to Jamnia to welcome King Agrippa II and complain about Florus. This is scarcely the action of a local city council, but of a body whose authority extended over the whole of Jewish Palestine.

(7*) Late 60s (*War* 5.13.1; #532). Aristeus is described as the Scribe of the Boulē. He is from Emmaus (near present-day Latroun), even as the NT *Bouleutēs*, Joseph, is from Arimathea—if those cities represent present domicile rather than birthplace, the presence of non-Jerusalemites would be another indication of the wide-range of the Boulē.

(8*) (*War.* 5.4.2; #142–44). The first and oldest north wall of Jerusalem went past the Xystus or gymnasium, then joined the chamber of the Boulē before terminating in the western portico of the Temple. (See also *War* 6.6.3; #354: *Bouleutērion.*)

The similarities between Josephus' descriptions of the Sanhedrin/Boulē and the NT descriptions of the Sanhedrin are quite clear. Tcherikover's meticulous study ("Was" 71) concludes: "The council [Boulē] in Josephus and the Sanhedrin in the New Testament were one and the same institution." The assembly described in both involves the presence of chief priests, scribes, and rulers or influential citizens (= elders), constitutes the supreme Jewish authority in dealings with Roman prefects/procurators, and sentences lawbreakers. Thus most scholars have little difficulty in positing that during the Roman prefecture in Judea a Sanhedrin (Gerousia, Boulē) of priests, elders, and scribes, led by the chief priests, played a major administrative and judicial role in Jewish self-governance in Judea.

(c) *The Mishna.* A minority of scholars[32] would drastically correct this picture in light of the mishnaic tractate *Sanhedrin*. There the assembly,

---

in the reality beneath the terminology. Tcherikover (74–75) argues that the archons of Jerusalem were not archons in the Greek sense; the Boulē of Jerusalem was not similar to the Boulē of the Greek city-state, and the people of Jerusalem did not function like the Hellenistic *demos.*

[32]See especially A. Büchler, "Das Synedrion in Jerusalem und das grosse Beth-Din in der Quaderkammer des jerusalemischen Tempels," *Jahresbericht der isr.-theol. Lehranstalt in Wien* 9 (1902), 1–252; J. Z. Lauterbach, "Sanhedrin," JE 2.41–44. Also Mantel, *Studies,* 54–101; Zeitlin, *Who,* 68–83; and bibliography in HJPAJC 2.199.

called the (Great) Sanhedrin or, more frequently, the Beth-Din,[33] consists of
scholars who are expert in the written Law of Moses and in the oral
interpretation/law that was developed through rabbinic debates. The functions of this assembly are more legal or judicial than political; but there
are legislative and executive elements as well. Although secular matters are
treated, the overall tone is strongly religious. Mishna *Ḥagiga* 2.2 gives a list
of rabbinic scholars who served as president (*nāśî*, "patriarch") or as father
of the Beth-Din, while *Sanhedrin* 2.1 gives no special prestige there to the
high priest. Despite the date of codification of the Mishna (ca. AD 200), in
its self-understanding it is describing a Sanhedrin that had functioned in
Jerusalem in antiquity. Because of that some Jewish scholars (Abrahams,
Büchler, Hoenig, Lauterbach, Mantel, Zeitlin) have argued that there were
two assemblies in Jesus' time:[34] a political Sanhedrin, such as described in
the NT and in Josephus, which was the cynical instrument of the Roman
prefect and of the high priest; and a religious Sanhedrin of scholars sincerely
interested in the Law. Jesus would have been tried by the political rather than
by the religious Sanhedrin.

There are several variants of this thesis. (Beyond those discussed here, see
Tcherikover, "Was" 59–60,71.) The one proposed by F. E. Meyer ("Einige")
uses the mishnaic term Beth-Din ha-Gadol (i.e., the Great Beth-Din) for the
Sanhedrin in Jerusalem, of which he finds an example in Acts 5:21ff., where
the Pharisees are present. He argues that what is described in Acts 4:1,5–6
is just a priestly investigation with no Pharisees involved and should be seen
as preparatory for the Sanhedrin trial of the next chapter. Since Pharisees
are not mentioned in the Jewish process against Jesus,[35] it too was only preparatory for a trial, but in that instance for a Roman trial. Thus Jesus was
not tried by the Sanhedrin or Beth-Din ha-Gadol but investigated by a
smaller court. Kennard's variant ("Jewish" 35–37) contends that the Phari-

---

[33]"House of judgment/justice" or "tribunal." In the LXX of Prov 22:10 *synedrion* translates Hebrew *dîn*. Mishna *Sanhedrin* 4.1 also mentions smaller courts of twenty-three judges known as the
Lesser Sanhedrins, presumably of a more local character and/or for lesser crimes. For the confusing
rabbinic information on the Greater and Lesser Sanhedrin, see J. M. Baumgarten, "The Duodecimal
Courts of Qumran, Revelation and the Sanhedrin," JBL 95 (1976), 59–78, esp. 72–75.

[34]I shall not discuss the variant that proposes three Sanhedrins (see HJPAJC 2.207–8). For a
careful refutation of Zeitlin's two-Sanhedrin thesis, see Stonehouse, "Who" 45–52; he examines and
refutes seven examples of the political Sanhedrin. Stonehouse also denies the claim that Luke described a political Sanhedrin, for Lucan language points to a *presbyterion* of the people.

[35]See, however, John 11:47–53. As I shall point out in n. 52 below, some of the scribes described
as present at the trial would probably have been Pharisees, even though Christian memory gives the
Pharisees no prominent role in the actual death of Jesus. Rivkin (*What*) hyphenates Scribes-
Pharisees as if one body, e.g. (53): "It is evident that in Jesus' day the Scribes-Pharisees coexisted
peacefully on the religious plane and held similar views on the political plane." Safrai ("Jewish"
384), whose views differ significantly from those of Rivkin, agrees on this point: The sages or
teachers of the Torah, often called scribes, were the backbone of the Pharisee movement.

sees had their own assembly in Jesus' time, but it was simply a Beth ha-Midrash or interpretative school, and that later Jewish documents exaggerated its role by speaking of a Beth-Din ha-Gadol. The major assembly for the province of Judea was the Sanhedrin, the successor to the preRoman assembly of priestly nobility. Pharisees participated even if they distrusted the priestly leaders; it was not merely political but was concerned with the sanctity of the Temple ("Jewish" 26–27). Jesus stood before this ethnic assembly for the nation, which was executive and had authority to sentence to death. Thus Meyer's and Kennard's theses about two assemblies are virtually contradictory. Another variant has been proposed in several writings on the subject by Rivkin, who points out that in the Mishna, at a proportion of nineteen to three, "Beth-Din" is a term favored over "Sanhedrin," despite the name of the tractate. He thinks that "Beth-Din" was the Hebrew designation of what Josephus calls the Boulē, which in Jesus' time was distinct from the Sanhedrin dominated by the chief priests.[36] The Boulē of the interpreters of the law was Pharisee in leaning, while the Sanhedrin was Sadducee. According to Rivkin, the Boulē originated in the early Hasmonean period, over 100 years before Jesus, and it met in the Bouleutērion on the Temple Mount. After AD 70, the high-priestly Sanhedrin ceased; but Vespasian authorized a reconstituted Beth-Din in Javneh (Jamnia) and gave it some autonomy. The only post-70 body, then, was a Beth-Din functioning in part as the Sanhedrin had done in the pre-70 period.

In my judgment, two observations may be made. First, most likely, the theory of two *major* assemblies in the Jerusalem of Jesus' time is a wrong interpretation of the evidence whether in Josephus or the NT. With even greater surety, nothing in Jewish or Christian memory of the treatment of Jesus encourages us to believe that more than one Jewish assembly dealt with him—an assembly of the type that the Romans dealt with in negotiating with the Jews.[37] Second, the Mishna must be understood as anachronistic in attempting to read back the Beth-Din of scholars into this earlier period.[38] Supporting this judgment are the following observations:

[36]"Beth-Din" 189; at greater length in his book *What* (p. 35: "We are therefore not dealing with a sanhedrin that possessed some permanent religious or political status, but rather with a privy council that functioned as an adjunct to the political authority").

[37]McLaren (*Power* 192ff.) shows painstakingly the extent to which the Roman prefecture ruled Judea through negotiations with the Jewish group whom both sides regard as authoritative. That group consisted of priests and other prominent figures, and most often they, not the Romans, were the ones who initiated the negotiations. In a further section of the book (211–18) that I admit I do not find clear, McLaren states that the Boulē of Jerusalem (which he quite rightly recognizes is the successor of the older Gerousia) is not to be confused with two (!) further institutions described by the term *synedrion* (Sanhedrin; p. 213) but never really explains why. (Much of what he describes could be the Boulē functioning as a Sanhedrin; see n. 49 below).

[38]Despite the view cited in the previous note, McLaren (*Power* 217–18) is firm on this point: "It is now apparent that the institution depicted in Mishna *Sanhedrin* did not exist during the period

(i) Neither source of information, Josephus/NT or the Mishna, affirms that two overall Jewish authoritative assemblies or Sanhedrins existed at the same time in the 1st cent.[39] This is a modern proposal based on the fact that these sources have used several terms (Josephus: "Sanhedrin" and "Boulē"; Mishna: "Beth-Din" and "Sanhedrin").[40] In *Against Apion* 2.21–22; #185, 188–89, Josephus clearly envisions only one governing body (dominated by priests) administering the affairs of the community. Similarly the Mishna (*Soṭa* 9.11) knows of one body, for the earlier Sanhedrin had ceased.

(ii) If the great assembly of scholars who judged religious matters (as it is described in the late-2d-cent. Mishna) really existed in the 1st cent., why is there no indication of it in the 1st-cent. witnesses, Christian or Jewish? Why do these witnesses assign not only political but religious functions to the Sanhedrin of priests, elders, and scribes? As for the NT, the trial of Jesus concerns the survival of the Temple sanctuary, divine sonship, and blasphemy; the trial of Stephen concerns blasphemies, speaking against the Temple and the Law, and changing the customs given by Moses (Acts 6:12–14); the trial of Paul (22:30–23:10) is understood by the centurion to concern questions of Jewish law (24:29). Transgressions of the Law and levitical matters come before the Sanhedrin described by Josephus (nos. 1*,2* above).

(iii) As for the Mishna's claim that the scholarly Beth-Din it describes is an ancient institution, the Mishna is very often anachronistic in its assumptions, indeed even in the most basic assumption claiming great antiquity for the oral law stemming from Moses himself. The work of many recent Jewish scholars shows how hard it is to establish authentic pre-70 situations from the Mishna. (The numerous writings of J. Neusner eloquently illustrate this.) The burden of proof is made much more heavy when 1st-cent. witnesses, both Christian and Jewish, describe a situation different from that envisaged by the Mishna.

(iv) Meyer's variant explained above has little support in Acts and the Gospels. Blinzler (*Prozess* 138) is perfectly correct in arguing that there is not an iota of difference in the Lucan presentation of the functioning of the Jewish authorities in chaps. 4 and 5 of Acts, except that Acts 5 gives the

---

examined [100 BC-AD 70]. It remains debatable whether we should even attempt to associate this institution with any historical period."

[39]The Lesser Sanhedrins mentioned in n. 33 above were not involved in overall administration. On this, see Tcherikover, "Was" 71, n. 17. He states: "The religious-legal situation in Israel does not allow for any division of authority between institutions with political functions on the one hand and religious functions on the other. . . . Those learned in the Torah (Pharisees, scribes) also participated in the Sanhedrin."

[40]Safrai ("Jewish" 382), who is relatively conservative in arguing that mishnaic evidence has value in determining 1st-cent. customs and institutions, is clear: "We have no choice but to assume the presence of one 'Sanhedrin' that appears under different names."

final session. Moreover, Luke would surely see this assembly as continuous with the group that acted against Jesus. Nothing in the Mark/Matt account of the proceedings against Jesus suggests a Sanhedrin more restricted than that described by Josephus.

(v) There is not adequate basis for Rivkin's distinction between the Sanhedrin and the Boulē in Josephus' description of Judea under the Roman prefects, for the Boulē is nothing other than the Jewish Sanhedrin of priests, elders or nobles, and scribes.[41] The Josephus passages nos. 4*–7* given above mention all those components.[42] If the Boulē were simply a religious assembly of scholars, why would it be addressed along with the whole nation of the Jews by the Roman emperor? (The later rabbis might think that religious scholars were important enough to be treated by the emperor as a primary dialogue partner, but would that be true during the Roman prefecture?) Compare 4* in Josephus with the official address to the Gerousia (or Sanhedrin) of priests and elders in II Macc 11:27 (see I Macc 13:36; 14:20). Why would the prefect inform a Boulē of scholars that he was leaving the city, as in 5*? If Sadducees or priests had no major role in it, why is it associated with priests, as in 5*,6*? Compare Mark 14:55: "the chief priests and the whole Sanhedrin" with Josephus, *War* 2.15.6; #331: "the chief priests and the Boulē." Finally, why would Josephus have chosen "Boulē" to represent the religious rather than the political assembly when it is a term that he uses elsewhere for the Senate of Rome (*War* 1.14.4; #284; *Ant.* 19.4.5; #266) and the governing body of Tyre (*Ant.* 14.12.4; #314)?[43] In presenting the Jerusalem Sanhedrin, the one and only high council of the Jews, Josephus has used the term "Boulē," which would be familiar to his Greek-reading audience since it was the common name for the council of their city-states. If there is any difference in Josephus' mind between "Boulē" and "Sanhedrin," it may be that he thought of the latter almost as the proper name or title of the Jerusalem Boulē (see *Life* 12; #62).

---

[41]Safrai ("Jewish" 389): "One ought to emphasize that the boule is identified with the Sanhedrin." We have already seen two names for the same assembly (Sanhedrin and Gerousia) in the pre-1st-cent. period. The Sanhedrin references in John 11:53 (see 12:10) and Acts 5:33 use the verb *boulesthai*; and Luke 23:50–51 clearly relates Joseph, a *bouleutēs* ("member of the Boulē"), to the Sanhedrin session against Jesus.

[42]The Boulē in 4* should not be interpreted as if it had nothing to do with the priests and leading citizens, for 6* associates such authorities with the Boulē.

[43]See also the term "Sanhedrin" for assemblies held at Berytus (Beirut: *Ant.* 16.11.1; #357) and at Rome (*Ant.* 17.11.1,4; #301, 317). I have confined the discussion to the use of "Sanhedrin" and "Boulē" during the Roman prefecture; but given that there is no major distinction in Josephus' description of the Sanhedrin under the Herodians and under the Romans, it is most implausible to read *Ant.* 14.9.3–5; #163–84 as if a purely political body were involved (much less "a privy council"). There it is a body that exercises judgment (#168, 172) about a violation of the Law (#167), before whom the name of God is invoked (#174), and whose members are aware that later Herod may kill them (#173, 175). The less detailed account in *War* 1.10.6–7; #208–11 speaks of this as an

Two citations, then, sum up this discussion. Danby, "Bearing" 75, states: "The Mishna fails to agree with the earlier accounts [Josephus, NT, Macc] of the Sanhedrin because the historical Sanhedrin had ceased to exist, and the Sanhedrin which it did know, on which it based its description, was a purely academic institution, having purely academic powers and purely academic interests." Similarly, HJPAJC 2.208 is correct in affirming: "If by 'the Great Sanhedrin' is meant a body officially recognized by the occupying power and endowed with competence in judicial and administrative powers and in legal exegesis, there was a single institution under the presidency of the High Priest."

C. *The General Functioning of a Sanhedrin*

The references to the Sanhedrin (or Boulē) in the New Testament and Josephus are not detailed enough to tell us how the Sanhedrin functioned. Even if the Beth-Din of the Mishna describes a different assembly that came later and succeeded the 1st-cent. Sanhedrin, are any legitimate memories of the earlier period preserved? We shall answer that question first by dealing with general issues (number of members, those eligible, place of meeting) and then by discussing the dominant thought (Pharisee or Sadducee).

1. Membership and Meeting Place

Many accept as applicable to the Sanhedrin of Jesus' time the statement of Mishna *Sanhedrin* 1:6, "The Great Sanhedrin consisted of seventy-one members," because that number would have been suggested to Jews in the pattern of Num 11:16 where Moses is joined by the seventy elders of Israel.[44] The seventy-one in the Sanhedrin are conjectured to have consisted of the seventy priests, elders, and scribes in three groups, led by the high priest. (R. Judah in the Mishna passage counts only seventy.) However, such a numerical constituency in the 1st cent. AD is not substantiated by any contemporary evidence. If one looks back at the Josephus citations above, the language of convening *a* Sanhedrin appears;[45] and so one may wonder whether

---

action of Hyrcanus, the high priest, whom *Ant.* makes part of the Sanhedrin. Similarly the Gospels heighten the role of the high priest to the point where the Sanhedrin rubber-stamps his decisions.

[44] For the idea of seventy men, see Josephus, *War* 2.18.6; #482; 2.20.5; #570–71 (Blinzler, *Prozess* 90–92). On the question of a seventy-two member Sanhedrin, see HJPAJC 2.210.

[45] However, as Betz ("Probleme" 646–47) points out, in the longest story told by Josephus about a Sanhedrin, dealing with Herod ca. 47 BC, the definite article occurs six times (*Ant.* 14.9.3–5; #163–84). Consequently one should not exaggerate the indefiniteness as if a nondescript meeting were being called. The Sanhedrin was a definite enough body for a letter to be addressed to it (see 3*).

in the 1st cent. there was such a fixed number of members. Might it not be that in order to deal with a problem the high priest convened Sanhedrin members who were available? Surely the Josephus texts do not encourage us to think of a fixed body regularly in session, like the U.S. Senate.

Still, were there members of the Sanhedrin in the sense of a list of known people who constituted it? (I summarize here the treatment in APPENDIX V, B1–3.) In Jesus' time the Roman prefect designated the high priest, and he was surely the prominent figure. The "chief priests" (pl.), who are mentioned, were probably former high priests, along with the prominent members of families from which the recent high priests had been drawn and some who had been entrusted with special sacerdotal duties. The "elders" may have been for the most part from wealthy or distinguished families (although rabbinic literature often considered them to be scholars). These two groups could explain Josephus' remark, cited above, about a government dominated by aristocracy. As for the "scribes," their position may have reflected excellence in intelligence and learning. Yet in none of these instances do we necessarily have to think of a fixed list beyond the expected and frequent presence of the better-known priests and nobles. (The list of names in Acts 4:6, whether historical or not, supports the latter part of that suggestion, for at least it betrays a view of what Luke thought should have been the case.) Rather than assigned members, we may have to think of the expected attendance of representatives of particular groups when a Sanhedrin was called.

Where did the Sanhedrin meet (or "sit," to use Josephus' imagery)? In reference to the trial of Jesus, Mark 14:53–55 speaks of the court(yard) or palace (*aulē*) of the high priest (presumably, an old Hasmonean palace on the side of the western hill facing the Temple). Neither Josephus nor the Mishna envisages a session of the Sanhedrin in such a palace.[46] Josephus describes the meeting place as the *Boulē* or the *Bouleutērion*. According to *War* 5.4.2; #144 (see 6.6.3; #354) this place stood in the region where the first or older city wall of Jerusalem came from the Xystus (gymnasium?) to join the west wall of the Temple area, thus in or above the Tyropoeon valley, outside the Temple.[47] Mishna *Middot* 5.4 describes the Sanhedrin meeting place as the *Liškat ha-Gāzît,* most often understood as the Chamber of Hewn

---

[46]Luke 22:66 has Jesus led from the high priest's courtyard or palace to the Sanhedrin without making clear where the latter was assembled. John describes no Sanhedrin session on the night before Jesus died, but 18:24 has Jesus led from Annas to Caiaphas without specifying whether that involves a building different from the *aulē* of the high priest (18:15). If, as I shall suggest, historically there were two Jewish legal actions, namely, a Sanhedrin meeting that led to the arrest of Jesus with the intention of condemning him and an interrogation of Jesus by the high priest before he was handed over to the Romans, the latter may have been associated in the preGospel tradition with the *aulē* of the high priest.

[47]On all this see Blinzler, *Prozess* 166–70. Acts 22:30–23:10 imagines a Roman tribune present at a Sanhedrin session; that favors a site outside the Temple area. Also Acts 22:30 and 23:10 use

Stone, which Mishna *Sanhedrin* 11.2 places in the inner courts of the Temple.[48] *Middot* 5.4 describes it as a southern chamber of the Temple courts. HJPAJC 2.224, however, understands the *Gāzît* as the Xystus (thus, "the Chamber beside the Xystus") and argues that it stood where Josephus places the Bouleutērion outside the Temple. Yet another mishnaic tradition (*Yoma* 1.1) associates the high priest with the Hall of the Proedroi, which may be also the Hall of the Bouleutai or Councilors (TalBab *Yoma* 8b; on various names for the Hall, see Tosepta *Yoma* 1.1–3; TalJer *Yoma* 38c [1.1.17]). This was in the outer court of the Temple, opening to the exterior, a description that might with imagination agree with Josephus' localization.

A TalBab tradition of dubious reliability has the Sanhedrin moved or expelled from the *Liškat ha-Gāzît* forty years before the Temple was destroyed (thus ca. AD 30) to the Bazaars (*Sanhedrin* 41a; *Šabbat* 15a; *'Aboda Zara* 8b). Some would associate these Bazaars (*Ḥanut*) with the high priestly family of Annas (*Ḥănanyâ*); there is a dispute whether the Bazaars were on the Mount of Olives or on the Temple Mount. Further confusion is caused by TalBab *Roš Haššana* 31a, which has a subsequent move of the Sanhedrin in the opposite direction, from the Bazaars to Jerusalem. In short, we cannot be sure where the Sanhedrin usually met at the time of Jesus' death, but a place adjacent to rather than in the Temple may be more correct. Quite probably anachronistic for Jesus' time would be the rule found in TalBab *Sanhedrin* 41a and *'Aboda Zara* 8b, which would consider illegal a sentence of death passed outside the *Liškat ha-Gāzît*.

2. Dominant Influence on a Sanhedrin: Pharisee or Sadducee?

It has been customary to think of the Sanhedrin as a court acting like judge and jury. Before the time of the Roman prefecture in Judea, the Sanhedrin of Jerusalem judged whether Herod the Great should die (*Ant.* 14.9.4–5; #168–80). During the Roman prefecture the NT reports trials of Jesus, Stephen, and Paul on capital offenses; and Josephus (1* above) reports a high priest and a Sanhedrin of judges giving over James, "the brother of Jesus called the Christ," to be stoned. (The courtlike atmosphere receives support from the later rabbinic description of the Sanhedrin, for by the time of the

---

verbs of going *down* to a meeting with the Sanhedrin, presumably from the Fortress Antonia, which would have been on a level with the Temple esplanade. (Occasionally, however, biblical Greek usage reflects Hebrew expressions; and in Hebrew "to go up" and "to go down" may reflect an established traditional description rather than an exact indication of direction.) Cantinat ("Jésus . . . Sanhédrin" 300) thinks the Sanhedrin met in the Xystus itself (see Josephus, *War* 2.16.3; #344), but Josephus' description of the wall seems to have the meeting place adjacent to the Xystus.

[48]TalBab *Yoma* 25a envisions a great basilica, standing half within and half without the Temple forecourt.

Mishna the Sanhedrin had become a body of experts in the Law.) The picture of the Sanhedrin as a court may be too simple for Jesus' time, however, for the instances of Sanhedrin/Boulē activity given above under B2 show *role of* administrative and executive activity as well.[49] In literature written before *סנהדרין* AD 100, when the Sanhedrin does sentence to death, there is little evidence of courtlike procedures to protect the defendant. Below I shall spend time discussing the traditional question, "According to what interpretation of Jewish law would the Sanhedrin of Jesus' time have judged cases, especially capital crimes?" Nevertheless, I strongly suspect that as a quasi-legislative and executive body with interests that we would call religious and political hopelessly intertwined, a Sanhedrin when called often acted according to what seemed prudent and expeditious. Not all of those attending may have worried about systems of legal interpretation, unless such a concern was opportune and advantageous. Having issued that caution, let me discuss in a more traditional manner the Sanhedrin as a judicial body.

We are going to be discussing Sadducees and Pharisees, and might well begin with some general remarks about both. Many brief treatments of the Sadducees describe them as a priestly caste who were very Hellenized, pro-Roman, and worldly rather than religious. In a book describing the Jewish sects, however, A. J. Saldarini correctly cautions: "The task of reconstructing the Sadducees from the sources is daunting and in many respects impossible."[50] Josephus (who during the Roman prefecture identifies few figures as Sadducees, viz., the high priests Ananias and Ananus II: *War* 2.17.10; #451; *Ant.* 20.9.1; #199) never states that all the Jewish leaders or all the priests were Sadducees. They may have constituted an elite drawn from the noble priestly groups and the aristocratic laity. Defending rabbinic authority, later Jewish works like the Mishna and Tosepta painted the Sadducees as traditional adversaries; but in truth the authors may have known little about the historical Sadducees. Factually Sadducees would have followed the written Law of Moses (*Ant.* 13.10.6; #297). Perhaps one should add "at least," for inevitably the Sadducees would have developed some customs that went beyond the written Law. Seemingly, however, they did not have a system of interpretation/law that they acknowledged as going beyond the

---

[49]Of the three uses of "Sanhedrin" cited there, 1* involves a trial, whereas 2* and 3* do not. A Sanhedrin that functioned in different ways is more plausible in my judgment than McLaren's contention (n.37 above) that there were two different institutions, both called a Sanhedrin. Although none of the uses of "Boulē" cited there involve a judicial function, Luke 23:50–51 shows a *bouleutēs* who had been involved in a trial.

[50]*Pharisees, Scribes and Sadducees in Palestinian Society: A Sociological Approach* (Wilmington: Glazier, 1988), 299. Similarly L. H. Schiffman (*From Text to Tradition* [Hoboken: KTAV, 1991], 110–11) maintains: "The Sadducean party cannot be said to have come into being at any particular point." Indeed, he posits that there were two groups of Sadducees, some more Hellenized, others more faithful to older traditions.

written Law (whereas the Pharisees did acknowledge the more-than-biblical character of some of their laws/interpretations).[51] Nevertheless, we know little or nothing of the postbiblical Sadducee customs, and we must settle for their adherence to the written Law. Certainly they rejected the oral traditions that the Pharisees considered to be from the Fathers, and thus disputed "with the teachers of wisdom" (*Ant.* 18.1.4; #16).

As for the Pharisees, in order to correct the many hostile Gospel references, Christian scholars have struggled to present a benevolent portrayal of the Pharisees on the assumption that their views were those of the 2d-cent. rabbis who composed the Mishna and whose piety and legal benevolence were undeniable. Leaving open the possibility of a favorable picture of the Pharisees, scholars have now come to recognize that there were differences between the Pharisees and the rabbis. Saldarini (*Pharisees* 3) plaintively reports: "Recent research on the Pharisees has paradoxically made them and their role in Palestinian society more obscure and difficult to describe." In a paper given at the August 1991 Catholic Biblical Association meeting, J. Sievers pointed out that in the NT, Josephus, and the Mishna only a dozen men were ever identified by name as Pharisees. As I shall stress more than once, the Gospels attribute the Sanhedrin action against Jesus largely to the chief priest(s), the elders, and the scribes. Presumably some of these scribes would have been Pharisees,[52] learned in traditions that applied the written Law often in a more lenient way. Nevertheless, if there were Pharisees among the Sanhedrin scribes, the Gospels do not stress that allegiance. In the Jewish legal proceedings that specifically led to Jesus being handed over to the Romans for execution, the Pharisees are mentioned only in John 11:46,47,57; 18:3.[53] The general hostility between Jesus and the Pharisees reported by the Gospels (to the extent that such hostility is not read back

---

[51]See E. P. Sanders, *Jewish Law* 107–10. There is still a realistic opportunity for learning more about the Sadducees. L. H. Schiffman (BA 53 [1990], 64–73) contends that a 2d-cent. BC Qumran document denoted as "Legal Rulings Pertaining to the Torah" (4QMMT), which is addressed to the Jerusalem (priest?) authorities, would place the Qumran group closer to opinions designated (three centuries) later as Sadducee and locate the Jerusalem authorities closer to opinions designated later as Pharisee. (At the time of Schiffman's writing, the text had not been published.) The disputes are largely ritual; and we should be careful in moving from this to judgments about the law that would have been followed by Jerusalem Jewish authorities in judging Jesus.

[52]Certainly that is the impression gained from the Synoptic joining of scribes and Pharisees (some fifteen times). Yet there are even more times when scribes are joined with the chief priests, and there were surely scribes of Sadducee persuasion as well. Ezra, the biblical scribe par excellence, was a priest (Neh 8:1–2). There were "scribes of the Temple" from his time (*Ant.* 11.5.1; #128) and later (2d cent. BC: *Ant.* 12.3.3; #142). The Qumran group was dominated by Zadokite priests, yet its scribes produced numerous interpretations of the Law. Saldarini (*Pharisees* 241–76) shows that scribes have a diversified role in the range of Jewish literature, but that more than in any other source they are seen as a unified group in the NT (266: a picture that may not be historical).

[53]There is a postmortem mention of the Pharisees in Matt 27:62. That Pharisees were part of a Sanhedrin is noticed in John 11:47 and Acts 5:34; 23:6.

from later Christian experience) would make it intelligible that there was no Pharisee opposition to or complaint about a Jew like Jesus being handed over to foreigners for execution. Nevertheless, the Gospels do *not* suggest that the legal matters which constituted the subject of dispute between Jesus and the Pharisees were specifically alluded to in the decision that found him guilty.[54]

Moving beyond these general issues, we encounter the contention that the Sanhedrin would have had to judge capital cases according to Pharisee rules (with the further jump in dubious logic that the Pharisee rules were the same as those of the Mishna). This is often advocated on the basis of some generalizing texts in Josephus' *Ant.* which speak of the dominant influence of the Pharisees. "All prayers and sacred rites of divine worship are performed according to their interpretation" (*Ant.* 18.1.3; #15); whenever the Sadducees come into office, "they submit, although unwilling and under duress, to what the Pharisees say, because otherwise the masses would not tolerate them" (*Ant.* 18.1.4; #17).[55] Such statements cannot be accepted uncritically. Josephus, although of a priestly family, had chosen to live by the rules of the Pharisees (*Life* 1.1–2; #1,12). More important, there is a notable difference between what he says in the *War* (written in the 70s and early 80s) and the *Ant.* (90s) about the influence of the Pharisees in the 1st cents. BC and AD. The theory of Morton Smith[56] explaining this difference has gained considerable following: When Josephus wrote the later work, he was anxious to gain from the Romans a recognition of and commitment to incipient rabbinic authority in Palestine. This was the period after the destruction of Jerusalem during the Jewish Revolt when the rabbinic school at Jamnia was emerging as the major force in Palestinian Jewish life. Since (to some extent) the Pharisees were the intellectual forerunners of the rabbis, and had gained some

[54]I find little to support the thesis of H. Falk (*Jesus the Pharisee* [New York: Paulist, 1985]) that the Shammai school of Pharisees would have been bitterly opposed to Jesus who was a Pharisee of Hillel persuasion and would have joined in the plot of the Sadducees against him. It is difficult to be certain how much role Hillel-Shammai debates would have played in Jesus' lifetime. More important, it is most unlikely that Jesus can be classified as a Pharisee, despite the fact that some of his positions were similar to those that later Jewish tradition would associate with the Pharisees. There has been debate about the appropriateness of the title of the book by J. P. Meier: *A Marginal Jew: Rethinking the Historical Jesus* (3 vols.; New York: Doubleday, 1991–). Yet on the implicit point that Jesus was not identifiably an adherent of any of Josephus' three sects of the Jews (Pharisees, Sadducees, Essenes) Meier (1.8, 345–49) is surely right.

[55]The much later evidence of TalBab has also been invoked, e.g., a remark of a Sadducee to his son, "Although we are Sadducees, we are afraid of the Pharisees" (*Yoma* 19b); also the affirmation that the wives of the Sadducees had to follow the Pharisee rules in reference to menstruation (*Niddah* 33b).

[56]"Palestinian Judaism in the First Century," in *Israel: Its Role in Civilization*, ed. M. Davis (New York: Harper, 1956), 67–81. Also J. Neusner, "Josephus' Pharisees: A Complete Report," JJC 274–92, esp. 282–83 where he judges it unbelievable that Sadducees had to follow Pharisees in cult and prayers—that is a post-70 view.

favor with the Romans (see below), Josephus in the *Ant.* desired to portray the Pharisees as having been most influential for some two centuries, indeed so influential that it would be difficult to rule Palestine efficiently if they were antagonized.

Let us look at some of the differences between the *Ant.* and the *War* in order to see how the picture is changed from relative silence about the influence of the Pharisees[57] to one of their dominance. Those scholars who advocate Pharisee moral control of the Sanhedrin often begin their argument with the report in *Ant.* 13.15.5 to 16.3 (#399–417) of the deathbed advice given by the priest-king Alexander Jannaeus in 78 BC to his wife Salome Alexandra. He had hated the Pharisees; and presumably they were among the 800 men he crucified, since later they sought the death of the one who had advised him to do this cruel act (*Ant.* 13.16.2; #410). Yet he now recognized that they had such influence over the Jewish people that anyone whom they opposed could not rule without conflict. Accordingly he told his wife to yield power to them, since his own failure to do so had brought the land to a sad impasse. She did this as soon as he died, and in return they publicly honored the deceased Jannaeus. Although she appointed her son Hyrcanus to be high priest, she told the people to obey the Pharisees and their tradition (*paradōsis*). Yet the *War* (1.5.1–3; #107–14) gives a much less romantic picture. There is no deathbed instruction by Jannaeus[58] or statement that Palestine is ungovernable without the Pharisees. They are described as exacting exponents of the Law who gained too much influence over the religiously inclined Alexandra. Taking over the state, they ruthlessly exterminated their enemies, causing hatred.[59] One gets the impression that this was not a good time and that it was unwise to let such fanaticism loose.

After the Salome era we hear little of the Pharisees until the time of Herod the Great; and even in the Herodian period they are certainly not as prominent as they were under Jannaeus and his wife. Some have treated the relative silence as a mystery (or even a plotted silence on the part of Josephus); but with greater Roman influence after 63 BC when Pompey became "the first Roman to subdue the Jews and set foot in their Temple by right of conquest" (Tacitus, *History* 5.9), and with the advent of a strong ruler like Herod, there

---

[57]Notice that even the *War* (2.8.14; #162) speaks of them as "the leading sect (*hairesis*)." But that judgment may be subjective, reflecting Josephus' choice to follow them.

[58]TalBab *Qiddušin* 66a gives Simeon ben Sheṭaḥ a (reconciling?) role in the troubles between the Pharisees and Jannaeus.

[59]E. J. Bickerman, *The Maccabees* (New York: Schocken, 1947), 103: "Early Pharisaism was a belligerent movement that knew how to hate." See also Sanders, *Jewish Law* 85–86, for instances of early Pharisee belligerence. We hear relatively little of them on the political scene after the early days of Herod, and some have thought that they withdrew from an active national role. In terms of strife neither Herod the Great nor the Romans would have permitted the internecine bickering that flourished during the period of Judean independence.

was probably less tolerance for meddling by religious figures who had no public office. Ca. 20 BC an oath of loyalty to Caesar and Herod's government was demanded, but both Pharisees and Essenes did not take it (*Ant.* 15.10.4; #370–72). From that description one could get the impression that the Essenes were the more important group; but later (*Ant.* 17.2.4; #41–45) Josephus describes six thousand Pharisees as having been involved and adds the notice that they could have been of great help to the king. Because of their refusal he killed some of them. The *War* 1.29.2; #571 reports nothing of their influential potentialities. (In any case, they were not influential enough to stop the Jewish people as a whole from taking the oath.) Yet if the Roman patrons of Josephus read *Ant.*, the passages cited above could give the impression that it was better to work with the Pharisees than to have them opposed.

Having presented the evidence behind M. Smith's thesis, parenthetically I should mention that a number of scholars disagree with it. A strong dissenting voice is D. R. Schwartz,[60] who would reverse Smith's proposal: In the *War* Josephus suppressed Pharisee involvement in politics and rebellion, while in the *Ant.* he told more of the facts. Would that really account for the difference concerning Salome Alexandra, however? The picture in the *Ant.*, were it included in the *War,* could have given a favorable picture of the Pharisees without involving them in a blameworthy way in the Revolt. D. Goodblatt[61] has made a careful comparison of Smith and Schwartz and decided that Smith's case is much more convincing. If Josephus wanted to spare the Pharisees in the *War,* he could have treated them as he did the priests, i.e., have shown them as politically important but against the Revolt. In any case, on pp. 164–65, Schwartz seems to agree that the claims of dominant Pharisee political influence and overwhelming popular support are spurious propaganda.[62] E. P. Sanders (*Judaism* 409–11) in discussing Josephus' biases raises the possibility that the confused picture may stem from the fact that

---

[60]"Josephus and Nicolaus on the Pharisees," JSJ 14 (1983), 155–71.

[61]"The Place of the Pharisees in First century Judaism: The State of the Debate," JSJ 20 (1989), 12–30.

[62]There is a growing body of literature on the debate that M. Smith originated. G. Stemberger (*Pharisäer, Sadduzäer, Essener* [SBS 144; Stuttgart: KBW, 1991], 23) points out complexities in the overall comparison of *War* and *Ant.*, for even in the latter Josephus shows some negative aspects of the Pharisees. S. Schwarz, *Josephus and Jewish Politics* (Leiden: Brill, 1990), treats the Pharisees on 170–208. He contends that Josephus in *Ant.* was not precisely supporting the Pharisees but the characteristics that favored the emerging rabbinic movement. S. Mason, *Flavius Josephus on the Pharisees* (Studia Post-Biblica 39; Leiden: Brill, 1991), 193–95, doubts that Josephus changed his purpose from Roman propaganda in the *War* to Jewish apologetics in the *Ant.*, even if there is a difference in the presentation of the Pharisees. Actually, for Mason, Josephus was antipathetic to the Pharisees though he consistently presented them as the dominant religious group (356, 372–73). In *Josephus and the New Testament* (Peabody, MA: Hendrickson, 1992), 142–43, Mason denies that Josephus was a Pharisee.

in *Ant.* Josephus copied more from Nicolaus of Damascus than he did in the *War.* However, that does not mean that *Ant.* is to be followed uncritically. In a carefully nuanced evaluation pertinent to this whole dispute, Sanders (*Judaism* 393–409) maintains that the Pharisees lacked power both direct and indirect. In the 1st cent. BC and at the time of Judas the Galilean (AD 6) the Pharisees may have supported insurrections; but the majority of people did not follow the Pharisees in an insurrection unless they were persuaded that the cause was right and the chances for success were good. Sanders denies that Sadducees would have had to submit to the Pharisees and that the high priest and his associates had to work according to Pharisee dictation. The Pharisees did not control the synagogues, and there were three times as many priests and levites as there were Pharisees. It may well be that the Pharisees were popular, since the Essenes were too exclusive and the Sadducees too aristocratic; but their support would have been among the well-educated, especially the merchants, traders, and landowners, not among the masses or the common laborers.

To return to our survey of Pharisee influence, even at the time of the Jewish Revolt in the late 60s, it is not clear that the Pharisees were a dominant voice, although they were active in political issues, especially in the person of Simon, son of Gamaliel I, who negotiated with the Romans for power.[63] Their dominance in Palestine came only with Yohanan ben Zakkai and the movement to Jamnia from Jerusalem; it was the son of Simon, Gamaliel II (in a type of Pharisee dynasty[64]), who became head of the Jamnia academy-government, often thought to have been recognized by the Romans with the proviso that there be no support for subversion.[65]

Other arguments of diverse value have been advanced for laying aside the assumption that in Jesus' time the Sanhedrin had to judge capital cases according to Pharisee rules (derived from the Mishna) and for recognizing that the successful imposition of Pharisee (= mishnaic) standards came later. A reference in the ancient Jewish *Fasting Scroll* (2d cent. AD or earlier)

---

[63]Josephus, *Life* 38; #190–91, specifically calls this Simon a Pharisee; in *War* 4.3.9; #159 he gives the name as Symeon. His father, Gamaliel I, is called a Pharisee in Acts 5:34.

[64]In Josephus and the Mishna, Yohanan ben Zakkai (who has a priestly name) is, in fact, never called a Pharisee. On the surface Mishna *Yadayim* 4.6 seems to distance him from the Pharisees: "Have *we* not against the Pharisees [other causes of complaint] save only this?"; but that may be meant ironically and thus highlight closeness to the Pharisees in most things. Gamaliel II is a safer link between Pharisees and rabbis.

[65]Neusner, "Josephus" 280. Some contend that after 70 the Romans appointed Gamaliel II to power. See D. Goodblatt, "The Jews in the Land of Israel during the Years 70–132," in *Judea and Rome—the Jewish Revolts,* ed. U. Rappaport (Tel Aviv: 'Am 'Obed, 1983), 155–84 (art. and book in Hebrew). D. R. Schwartz, "Josephus and Nicolaus" 167–68, challenges as without real evidence the theory that the Pharisee dominance in Jamnia was negotiated with the Romans. Yet S. Schwarz (*Josephus* 201) argues that Yohanan ben Zakkai had to have Roman approval because Jamnia was an imperial estate with a procurator in residence.

rejoices that on the 4th (or 14th) of Tammuz "The Book of the Code was abrogated." Some have seen this as an allusion to the end of the Sadducean penal code, but both that reference and the date of the abrogation are unclear.[66] The Mishna indicates that there was another form of the death penalty to be imposed besides those mentioned in the Bible, namely, strangulation (*Sanhedrin* 9.3; 11.1). Many think that this was a concession to Pharisee expectation of bodily resurrection, for strangulation was less mangling than stoning. Strangulation would also have been appropriate to the period of foreign domination, for it was less public. Yet no instance of strangulation is cited in the 1st cent. AD, and Josephus clearly thinks that stoning was the punishment in relevant instances (*Ant.* 4.8.23; #248; 20.9.1; #200—although one must be cautious about "stoning" as a generic term for execution, as sometimes in rabbinic writings). Another argument is that in one case of capital punishment (1* above) Josephus portrays the high priest (clearly identified as a Sadducee) able to impose his will on the Sanhedrin even if some were not happy about that. The Gospels show Caiaphas imposing his views on a Sanhedrin that dealt with Jesus (Mark 14:63–64; Matt 26:65–66; also John 11:49–53 where the Pharisees follow his lead). In the matter of resurrection, which constituted a major difference between Pharisees and Sadducees, Acts 23:7–10 portrays a paralyzing dispute in the Sanhedrin. Yet in the aftermath of the meeting, the high priest and some elders are described as formulating the case before the Roman procurator (24:1–2), perhaps as a sign of who dominated.

3. The Trial of Jesus in the Gospels and Its Relation to Mishnaic Law

The 2d-cent. Mishna describes the Beth-Din as observing practices that came down through oral interpretation/law. On the presumption that the Pharisees ruled the 1st-cent. Sanhedrin, some scholars have tried to argue that the mishnaic precepts would have governed the trial of Jesus were it conducted by the Sanhedrin. I phrase the preceding sentence with the subjunctive "were" because many of these scholars go on to contend that since the mishnaic precepts were not observed in the trial recounted by the Gospels, those very accounts must be fictional and in fact Jesus was never tried by the Sanhedrin. In discussing this thesis let me first list the main conflicts between the Gospel accounts and rabbinic law (particularly as found in the Mishna), and second make comments on the thesis of fictive Gospel reporting that is related to this theory.

---

[66]Blinzler, Dalman, Jeremias, Olmstead, and Strack are among those who argue for AD 66 and the beginning of the uprising against Rome. See n. 87 below.

(a) *Conflicts between the Gospel accounts of the trial and later rabbinic procedure.* These have sometimes been estimated at twenty-seven.[67] The following are among the most frequently cited:

- In the four Gospels the legal proceedings against Jesus are dated to the eve of the Sabbath. In John the actions of Annas and Caiaphas against Jesus take place on the day before the Passover meal was eaten; in the Synoptics the trial of Jesus before the Sanhedrin takes place on the day that began with the eating of the Passover meal (see APPENDIX II, B). Mishna *Sanhedrin* 4.1 forbids the trying of capital cases on the eve of the Sabbath or the eve of a feast day.
- In John the high priest Annas alone interrogates Jesus, seemingly without other judges present. Mishna *'Abot* 4.8 cites R. Ishmael b. Jose against judging alone.
- Both the interrogation described in John and the Sanhedrin trial before Caiaphas narrated in Mark and Matt take place at night. In Mark/Matt the verdict is given at night. Mishna *Sanhedrin* 4.1 stresses that capital cases must be tried by day and a decision reached during the daytime.
- In Mark and Matt, the trial begins with the chief priests and the whole Sanhedrin seeking testimony against Jesus (false testimony according to Matt) that they might put him to death. The witnesses are not admonished to speak the truth, nor are witnesses for Jesus brought forward. Indeed nothing is offered on his behalf. Mishna *Sanhedrin* 4.1 insists that capital cases begin with reasons for acquittal. According to Tosepta *Sanhedrin* 7.5, Jewish figures as harsh as those portrayed by the Gospels would be disbarred from acting as judges in capital cases. Mishna *Sanhedrin* 4.5 requires in capital cases special care in admonishing witnesses about the necessity to speak the truth, and 5.4 assumes that there have been witnesses brought in for the defense.
- In Mark and Matt, although the testimony of the witnesses is false and does not agree, no action is reported against them by the Sanhedrin. Mishna *Sanhedrin* 5.2 stresses that when witnesses contradict one another, their evidence is nullified. *Sanhedrin* 11.6 holds that all false witnesses must suffer the penalty that the accused would have had to suffer if he were found guilty.
- In Matt and Mark, the words Jesus speaks about himself are blasphemy which the Sanhedrin members have heard for themselves. According to Mishna *Sanhedrin* 7.5, one is not guilty of blasphemy unless one has expressly pronounced the divine name (something Jesus has not done). Hearing such blas-

---

[67]Blinzler, "Geschichtlichkeit" 352; see also Danby, "Bearing" 54–55. In my list of examples I shall most often cite the Mishna and only occasionally the Tosepta. Scholars debate whether the Tosepta embodies mostly postmishnaic developments or complementary interpretations of the same date as those of the Mishna, with the latter as the majority opinion. See J. Neusner in *Approaches to Ancient Judaism III*, ed. W. S. Green (Chico, CA: Scholars, 1981), 1–17, esp. 11–12; and R. Neudecker, *Frührabbinisches Ehescheidungsrecht* (Biblica et Orientalia 39; Rome: PBI, 1982), esp. 11–16. For an intelligible explanation of the rationale behind the mishnaic rules on homicide, see Ostrow, "Tannaitic."

phemy would cause the Sanhedrin members to become witnesses, and people may not act as judges in a case wherein they are witnesses (*Sanhedrin* 5.4).

- In Mark and Matt (see also John 11:49–53), the high priest speaks first in finding Jesus guilty and urging the other judges to find him so, with the immediate result that "they all judged against him as being guilty, punishable by death" (Mark 14:64). Mishna *Sanhedrin* 4.2 insists that in capital cases judges with less seniority should vote before those who have more seniority (obviously to prevent undue influence). Mishna *'Abot* 4.8 does not want one judge to say to the others, "Adopt my view." Mishna *Sanhedrin* 4.1 states that a unanimity of judges voting for condemnation nullifies the conviction in capital cases (in order to prevent collusion or "railroading"). Moreover, according to 4.1, a verdict for condemnation in a capital trial cannot be arrived at on the same day as the trial (to allow maturity of decision).[68]

(b) *These conflicts and Gospel accuracy.* Obviously the trial or interrogation of Jesus as described in the Gospels was not conducted according to the rabbinic rules. Conclusions from that fact take one of two possible directions. First, if one thinks that the 1st-cent. Sanhedrin was bound by such rules, either the Gospel accounts are fictional, or they are factual and the Sanhedrin acted illegally and corruptly. Second, if one thinks that the 1st-cent. Sanhedrin was not bound by such rules, the Gospel accounts may be describing a trial that was legal by another set of rules.[69] Perhaps, however, these alternatives phrase the possibilities too starkly. Since there are in the Gospels at least three different presentations of the Jewish proceedings against Jesus, the question of Gospel accuracy cannot be solved solely in terms of the applicability of rabbinic rules to a Sadducee-controlled Sanhedrin. Even if one wants to concentrate on the scribes and assume that they were Pharisees, we are not certain about the extent to which 1st-cent. Phari-

[68]Some have sought to find the rule of two sessions observed in the Gospels by reading Mark 15:1 (Matt 27:1–2) as a second session in the morning distinct from the night session. That is dubious exegesis, and in any case the verdict is passed at the first session at night. Others would find two sessions being honored in 40 BC when Hyrcanus II postpones the Sanhedrin trial of Herod to another day (Josephus, *Ant.* 14.9.5; #177), but that is simply a shrewd tactic in a campaign to spare Herod's life. The story in *Ant.* 15.7.4; #229–30 suggests that in the time of Herod the execution could have been on the same day, were there not a special reason to delay.

[69]The surface evidence of the NT favors the latter. Acts 23:3 charges that the trial of Paul was illegal; but although the Gospel writers indicate that the Jewish authorities were dishonest and callous, they never state that in trying and condemning Jesus the authorities were acting illegally according either to Roman law or the Law of Moses. The evangelists never call attention to even one of the conflicts with mishnaic procedures that I have indicated above. The charge, were it made, should have become a major factor in antiJewish polemic. I reject the view of Regnault (*Province* 103–15) that Pilate treats the Jewish trial as illegal when he questions Jesus about an issue (King of the Jews) different from that of the Jewish trial (Messiah, Son of God). The different titles are simply a way of dramatizing that the Jewish and Roman authorities were concerned with different issues (or different aspects of the same issue).

sees already practiced 2d-cent. rabbinic rules in judicial proceedings.[70] Modern Jewish scholarship recognizes that there were important differences between the more sectarian Pharisees of the pre-70 period and the 2d-cent. rabbis.[71] (Indeed, in judging the mishnaic code itself, one has the problem of whether even the rabbis ever observed all the rules, since some of the legislation is clearly theoretic: an idealized legal theory that is scarcely practical. For instance, the Mishna has rules for the king and for a whole tribe that falls into idolatry—scarcely problems of the 2d cent. Danby ["Bearing" 71–72] warns against taking the Mishna too simply as an active working code.) Certainly, there was a continuity from the Pharisees to the rabbis in giving authority to an oral interpretation that went beyond the written Law and in a tendency to add specifications that protected the defendant. But it is very difficult, if not impossible, to be sure that many of the mishnaic specifications had been reached by the Pharisees of Jesus' time. Thus, even if the Pharisees dominated the Sanhedrin (which is very dubious), we are not sure what the Pharisee law pertinent to trying capital crimes would have been. Indeed, some of the mishnaic theory and practice may have developed precisely to correct 1st-cent. jurisprudence which was so imprecise as to produce injustice.[72]

Let me comment briefly on some of the differences listed above between the Gospel accounts and rabbinic law. Already in the written law there was a tendency to postpone verdicts against the violators until one was sure that the verdict corresponded to God's will (Num 9:8; 15:34; and specifically in the case of blasphemy in Lev 24:11–12). One cannot be sure, however, that already by Jesus' time this had led anyone, even the Pharisees, to the preciseness of the mishnaic law which demands separate sessions so that the verdict can be given at a later time. Would the immediacy of the verdict described in Mark and Matt be illegal for the Pharisees, especially when the oncoming feast might have offered reason for haste? As for trying Jesus at night, nocturnal trials of serious offenses are suspect in most jurisprudence,

---

[70]Rosenblatt ("Crucifixion" 317–20), thinking that mishnaic rules did bind 1st-cent. Pharisees, attributes participation in Jesus' death to pseudo-Pharisees who were hypocrites, of the type criticized by Jannaeus in TalBab *Sota* 22b.

[71]See S.J.D. Cohen, "The Significance of Yavneh: Pharisees, Rabbis, and the End of Jewish Sectarianism," HUCA 55 (1984), 27–53. Stemberger (*Pharisäer* 40–41) argues against the general tendency of Neusner to think that *pre*rabbinic traditions are Pharisee. In fact, very few people of the Second Temple period are ever identified by name as Pharisees, and Stemberger (45) wonders if they are all Pharisees of the same type.

[72]Abrahams, "Tannaitic" 137: "So great, indeed, is the discrepancy between the Rabbinic and the Gospel trials, that the Mishnah (*Sanhedrin*) almost looks like a polemic of the former against the latter." Whether or not the rabbis knew the details of the Gospel accounts of the Jewish trial/interrogation of Jesus, they would have known of other trials by the Sanhedrin under Sadducee leadership of which they would have disapproved.

for they are often the mark of "kangaroo justice." That they were not normal in the Judaism of the 1st cent. is attested by Acts 4:3–5 where Peter and John, although arrested in the evening, are not tried before the Sanhedrin until the following daytime. Similarly, when Paul is arrested, the trial before the Sanhedrin is on the morrow (22:30). But had Pharisee jurisprudence reached the stage that no night trial could be held even if the oncoming feast day made haste imperative because there would be obligations on the priests in the daytime?[73] Such uncertainties explain Blinzler's strong admonition (*Trial* 154): "We do not have a single documentary proof the Great Sanhedrin adhered to a specifically pharisaic view of the law in criminal trials."

Can we be certain, on the other hand, that the Sanhedrin adhered to Sadducee rules in the trial or interrogation described in the Gospels? Blinzler and others have insisted that nothing of the written Law found in the Pentateuch was violated in the trial of Jesus described in the Gospels; and on the assumption that Sadducee law was the written Law,[74] they have answered affirmatively the question just posed. Blinzler italicizes the following statement (*Trial* 157; *Prozess* 227): "Everything that has hitherto been attacked as an illegality in the trial of Jesus, in view of the criminal code outlined in the Mishna, was completely in accordance with the criminal code then in force, which was a sadducean code, and did not know or recognize those pharisaic, humanitarian features of the Mishna code which were not founded on the Old Testament." Nevertheless, a major objection to Blinzler's claim has been raised by Lohse (*History* 81–82; also TDNT 7.869), namely, that the written Law itself would militate against the Sanhedrin having tried a capital case on the feast day that began with the Passover meal (Synoptic chronology) or even on the Day of Preparation before the Passover meal or before the Sabbath (Johannine chronology).[75] Unfortunately, Lohse does not offer a detailed defense of his position; and Blinzler (*Prozess* 229) denies it by asserting that capital trials on a feast day were not demonstratively forbidden in Jesus' time.[76] Among those who disagree with Lohse are Catchpole

[73]E.g., if Friday daytime were the eve of Passover, they would be busy slaughtering lambs for the festival meal (Josephus, *War* 6.9.3; #423).

[74]Haufe ("Prozess" 95) is one of a number of scholars who has found Blinzler overoptimistic in stating what we know about the "sadducean code," but it seems likely that they would have followed the written Law no matter what other customs they had. The issue, then, is whether the trial of Jesus offended against Penteuchal laws.

[75]Lengle ("Zum Prozess" 320) and Millar ("Reflections" 375–76) argue that the Jewish authorities knew that their own trial of Jesus and the death sentence emerging from it were illegal because of the date (and that restriction is what is meant in John 18:31b: "It is not permitted us to put anyone to death"). Consequently they gave him over to the Romans, who could put him to death even during a feast on a political charge. There is no Gospel suggestion, however, of calendric difficulties about the Jewish trial of Jesus, and the Gospels are our only source for that trial.

[76]Certainly they were forbidden in the Mishna (see above), but Ostrow ("Tannaitic" 362–64) connects that prohibition with another mishnaic principle: If a person were condemned on the eve

(*Trial* 258) and JEWJ 78–79. The latter interprets Deut 17:12–13 to mean that certain evils, such as insulting the priests, were to be punished before all the people when they came to Jerusalem on pilgrimage feasts (see Tosepta *Sanhedrin* 11.7; TalBab *Sanhedrin* 89a—passages that Lohse, "Prozess" 34, regards as purely theoretical). Overall the evidence is really not clear. Acts 12:1–4 portrays Agrippa I as having Peter arrested during the days of Unleavened Bread/Passover but holding him until after the feast to bring him before the people. Josephus (*Ant.* 16.6.2; #163), in citing a decree of Caesar Augustus allowing Jews to follow their own customs, states that they need not appear in court to give bond on the Sabbath or after 3:00 P.M. on the day of preparation for it (*paraskeuē*). If one followed this analogy, much depends on which day was considered the actual feast day of Passover (see APPENDIX II, B1e): the day that began with the meal (Synoptic chronology for the day on which Jesus died) or the day on which the lambs were sacrificed preparatory for the meal (John's chronology for the day on which Jesus died). If the former calculation was used for the feast day, then John (19:14) would have Jewish participation in the Roman trial come to a conclusion at noon on the preparatory day. (Nevertheless, according to 19:21 the chief priests continued to be active in the afternoon when they should have been in the Temple sacrificing the animals for the oncoming meal!) Interestingly, a talmudic passage (to be cited under E below) without any indication of calendric impropriety places the hanging of Jesus on the eve of Passover and thus on the Day of Preparation (even though it implies that the trial of Jesus had taken place forty days earlier). Perhaps all that can be said is that the trial of Jesus recounted in the Gospels would not clearly violate the written Law in most of its details. (That statement is technically correct but does not catch the spirit of the Gospel accounts that deliberately portray the high priest as insensitive to legal niceties, since he has already determined on the death of Jesus and in Mark/Matt employs false witnesses.) In retrospect on the period of Gentile domination, the much later TalBab, *Sanhedrin* 46a, shows a tolerant attitude toward capital-crime procedures not warranted by the written Law "because the times required it."[77]

Let me add that most of this discussion about possible illegality in the timing of the Jewish trial would be irrelevant to a nuanced theory of the sequence of events, i.e., one that takes seriously both John's information and

---

of a holiday, the verdict, which as a general rule could not be promulgated the same day, now could not be promulgated the next day either but would have to be postponed until after the feast day. Are we to think that both these rules were in effect in Jesus' time?

[77]Blinzler (*Prozess* 204–5) challenges Stauffer's approach that this was virtually a legal principle that governed practice in Jesus' time and so would justify proceeding against him at times forbidden by the Law. Rather it is a postfactum evaluation of irregularities.

the simplified character of the preaching outline found in Mark. All the Gospels agree that a Sanhedrin session discussed Jesus' activities and decided that he should die. All the Gospels have Jesus interrogated by a high priest or priests during the last hours before the Romans executed him. John may well be more accurate in portraying these as two separate actions, with the Sanhedrin session a good number of days before Jesus was arrested; and Mark may have elided the once-distinct actions into one easily remembered final scene. In that case the only procedure on a feast day or the eve of a feast day would have consisted of questions posed to the accused—not a trial that might have infringed on the law protecting feasts.

D. *A Sanhedrin's Competence to Condemn to Death and Execute*

Both Christian and Jewish documents portray Jewish authorities as involved in the death of Jesus (see E below). Nevertheless, all the canonical Gospels (but not *GPet*) affirm that the Roman prefect of Judea both tried and executed this Galilean Jew who was temporarily in his jurisdiction. They betray no awareness of conflict in there having been a previous trial of Jesus by the Sanhedrin, resulting in a death sentence.[78] Only John 18:31 offers an explanation for why the Jewish authorities did not themselves execute Jesus: "the Jews" state to Pilate, "It is not permitted to us to put anyone to death."[79] Is that explanation historically correct? In 1914 a Jewish writer, J. Juster, investigating the situation of Jews in the early Roman empire, challenged John's explanation by arguing that during the Roman prefecture the Jewish authorities did have the power to apply the death penalty. Consequently, the fact that Jesus was executed by the Romans shows that Jesus was not condemned by the Jewish authorities and that the Gospel accounts are not historically accurate.[80] The propagation of Juster's view by Lietzmann in the

[78]Phraseology to be interpreted as a sentencing of Jesus is found in the trial accounts of Mark 14:64; Matt 26:66; 27:1 (see Winter, "Marginal" 229); also John 11:53. Luke may not report a sentence in his Gospel account of Jesus' trial, but Acts 13:27 states that those who lived in Jerusalem and their rulers judged/condemned (*krinein*) him. See n. 141 below.

[79]Even though Pilate has sarcastically invited them, "Take him yourselves and according to your law judge him," this response given to him by the Jews most likely means that it is not permitted them *by Roman law* to put anyone to death—the Jewish law recorded in the Pentateuch makes it not only lawful but obligatory to put some criminals to death. Nevertheless, in evaluating this passage in John, one should remember that the evangelist had no primary interest in giving a historical solution; elsewhere he reports attempts to kill Jesus without reference to such a limitation (5:18; 7:30; 8:59; 10:31). Yet in those scenes the Romans were not involved.

[80]That there was no Sanhedrin trial of Jesus is advocated on grounds other than the competence of the Sanhedrin, with which we are concerned here, e.g., disagreements among the Gospel accounts and inconsistencies in the basic Marcan account. These will be discussed in the appropriate sections of the COMMENT on individual passages.

1930s won attention, and basically it has been accepted by Aguirre, Burkill, Ebeling, Guignebert, R. H. Lightfoot, Loisy, Winter, and others. A strong challenge to it has been issued by Benoit, Blinzler, Büchsel, Catchpole, Fiebig, Goguel, Holzmeister, Jeremias, Kosmala, Lagrange, Lengle, Oepke, Schalit, Schubert, and Strobel among many. (Worthy of special attention is the short treatment by Schumann, "Bemerkungen," whose disagreement with Juster is much less heavy-handed than that of others.) In dealing with this issue let me begin by describing what we know about the death penalty in general and then turn to specific cases that have been invoked.

1. General Picture of Roman Control of the Death Penalty

We saw at the end of A above that the first prefect of Judea, Coponius, was sent with the power to execute capital sentences, and that nothing recounted by Josephus causes us to think that later prefects/procurators had less power. What information do we have as to how this power of the governor related to the judicial authority of a Jewish Sanhedrin? Already in the 19th cent. Mommsen in his study of Roman penal law insisted that especially in the East, the Romans respected the competence of local courts in criminal matters, even if they imposed certain restrictions. In the province of Egypt the Roman prefect made a judicial circuit to decide cases prepared in advance for him by lesser officials (see Danby, "Bearing" 56–59). E. R. Goodenough[81] draws on Philo's *De specialibus legibus* to show that in this system the Egyptian Jews had their own courts, with a Jewish ethnarch as the chief officer. They could judge their fellow Jews in matters civil and criminal according to their own law, but in crimes against society at large the accused had to be treated according to Roman norms. As for execution, Jewish courts could sentence to death, subject to the approval of the Roman ruler. In religious issues that the Romans did not regard as capital, seemingly there was not always a Roman reaction when Jews slew another Jew; but in a public issue that the Romans considered important, a Jewish sentence had to be ratified by the prefect.

A better analogy for Judea than the larger, older province of Egypt is supplied by the small province of Cyrenaica, which also came under Augustus' empowering edicts. While Judea was created by Augustus as an imperial province in AD 6, Cyrenaica in 27 BC was assigned the status of a senatorial province united to Crete. In 7–6 BC Augustus issued edicts on the administra-

---

[81]*Jurisprudence* 1–29. On pp. 21–26 he rejects Juster's contention that Philo is theoretical rather than factual in his description.

tion of justice, a delicate operation in an area where many Hellenes (Greeks) lived alongside wealthy Romans. The edicts to the proconsuls (*stratēgoi*) of Cyrene were discovered in 1927 (and thus were not available to Juster). Local provincial courts were to judge many cases according to their own (Greek) law, but in capital cases jurisdiction did not have to be delegated to them by the proconsul. Just how capital cases were treated is not totally clear.[82] Edict I deals with capital cases involving Hellenes; the jury was to be one-half Hellene and one-half Roman. Edict IV deals with another group of capital cases to be judged by the governor himself and where he chooses the jury: "In capital cases the one in charge of the province shall personally institute proceedings, or assign a panel of justices."[83] The latter was an alternative to the prefect's own *cognitio* or investigation.[84] The superior right of the governor is treated not as novel but as fundamental and traditional.

Overall, then, analogies from other provinces do not refute the possibility that there were Jewish procedures against Jesus, and yet Pilate had the final say, as described in the Gospels. A Sanhedrin convened by the high priest could have presented the prefect with a criminal they had judged worthy of death with an understanding that such a presentation did not remove the final sentencing from the prefect's hands.

As for evidence about what was customary in Palestine, there are some references to a change of law that point to Roman control of the death penalty.[85] A tradition preserved in a *baraita* (early tradition) in TalJer *Sanhedrin* 18a and 24b (related to Mishna *Sanhedrin* 1.1 and 7.2) states that the right of pronouncing sentences of life and death was taken from Israel forty years before the destruction of the Temple (thus AD 30). Since we know of no reason why such a change would have come in the midst of the prefecture of Pilate (26–36), some scholars like Jeremias ("Geschichtlichkeit" 148) would argue that forty was a round number and that the change came in AD 6 with the founding of the province. Even though there is a chance that this tradition stems from Tannaitic times (2d cent. AD), the absence of the tradition from some of the corresponding places in TalBab, and the use of the same date

[82]The nuanced differences among the edicts are carefully discussed by F. de Visscher, *Les édits d'Auguste découverts à Cyrene* (Louvain Univ., 1940), esp. 44–69.

[83]V. Ehrenberg and A.H.M. Jones, *Documents Illustrating the Reigns of Augustus and Tiberius* (2d ed.; Oxford: Clarendon, 1955), #311. Also Goodenough, *Jurisprudence* 20.

[84]Sherwin-White, *Roman* 15–19, points out that if Roman citizens were involved as accuser/accused and the province were under ordinary law (*ordo*), e.g., of *lex de maiestate* (see §31, D3a below), there would be fewer options open to the prefect. But *extra ordinem* the prefect could make a personal *cognitio*.

[85]At an earlier period the Seleucid (Antiochene Greek) control of Palestine during much of the 2d cent. BC had already raised the issue of Jews being handed over to Gentile justice. In the DSS death is threatened to anyone who vows another to destruction by the law of the Gentiles (CD 9:1).

(forty years before the destruction of the Temple) for other events, e.g., the moving of the Sanhedrin to the Bazaars (p. 350 above),[86] has made the historicity of the claim suspect. What is clear is that it is not alien to Jewish memory that the Jewish courts lost the power to execute capital sentences. Another statement about change of law is found in the very early Jewish *Fasting Scroll* with the report that on the 17th of Elul (Sept. of AD 66) the Roman soldiers were driven out of Jerusalem, and five days later (22d Elul) "They began again to execute evildoers." This seems to mean that Jewish authorities regained the right to punish by death and that the first executions according to Jewish justice took place.[87] Mishna *Sanhedrin* 9.6 envisions some executions done by zealots, and Schubert ("Verhör" 110) sees such an appeal to irregular executions as a proof that the Sanhedrin did not have the right to impose a death penalty.

Some concrete examples have also been cited to show that during the prefecture (AD 6–66) the death penalty was kept under Roman control, and it is to those that we now turn. Josephus (*War* 5.5.2; #193; *Ant.* 15.11.5; #417; also Philo, *Ad Gaium* 31; #212) tells us of slabs with Greek and Latin writing warning foreigners against crossing from the outer Court of the Gentiles to the inner section of the Temple compound under threat of the penalty of death. The text of a notice discovered by Clermont-Ganneau contains the warning and shows the mindset: "No foreigner is to enter within the forecourt and the enclosure around the Temple, and whoever is caught will have himself to blame that his death ensues." In other words, there is a divinely ordained penalty for polluting the holy place for which the judges cannot be held responsible.[88] In *War* 6.2.4; #124–26, Josephus makes clear that these notices about the enclosure were the work of Jewish authorities *with Roman permission,* for Titus says, "Did we not permit you to put to death anyone who passed it, even were he a Roman." Obviously such permission would

---

[86]In two passages in the TalBab the removal of the right to pronounce capital sentences forty years before the destruction of the Temple is an interpretative comment on that same dating for the movement of the Sanhedrin to the Bazaars. In *Sanhedrin* 41a the comment appears as an anonymous gloss, probably to be dated ca. 500; in *'Aboda Zara* 8b it is reported as something said by R. Naḥman b. Isaac (ca. 325). See Fiebig, "Prozess" 217–20; Burkill, "Competence" 83–85. Lengle ("Zum Prozess" 321) thinks that the forty-year reference did apply to capital punishment, but *de facto,* not *de jure,* i.e., from Pilate's time on, with few exceptions, in practice the Jewish authorities had to get Roman approval for executions.

[87]See H. Lichtenstein, "Die Fastenrolle: eine Untersuchung zur Jüdisch-Hellenistischen Geschichte," HUCA 8–9 (1931–32), 257–307, esp. 305–6; also Bammel, "Blutgerichtsbarkeit." Winter, "Trial . . . Competence" 495, argues that this was only a usurpation by revolutionaries, not a change of governance. Some doubt that such a passing usurpation would explain why the day became a holiday free from fasting; but this document gives attention to what might seem minor events.

[88]P. Segal, "The Penalty of the Warning Inscription from the Temple of Jerusalem," IEJ 39 (1989), 79–84, makes a good case that the automatic penalty is an example of "death at the hands of God" (*myth bydy šmym;* see examples in Mishna *Sanhedrin* 9.1).

not be necessary were there not Roman-imposed restraints on the death penalty.[89] Perhaps the agreement of Roman authorities about certain automatic death penalties for Temple violations explains the report in Philo (*Ad Gaium* 39; #307) that any Jew or priest lower than the high priest who entered the Holy of Holies would suffer death without appeal.

According to Acts 21:27ff., about the year 58 Paul was seized by Jews in the Temple who would have killed him for violating the Mosaic Law and defiling the Temple. A Roman tribune stopped them, and on the next day he commanded the chief priests and the whole Sanhedrin to meet in order to try Paul's case (22:30). When he saw the dissension in the Sanhedrin, the tribune sent Paul to Caesarea to the procurator Felix, for in the tribune's judgment they had charged Paul with nothing deserving death (23:29). The high priest Ananias came down with elders and a spokesman to present the case against Paul (24:1), but he was never returned to their jurisdiction.[90] Clearly, in this instance the Romans overrode a Sanhedrin on a capital case. The next procurator, Festus (Acts 25), also refused to turn Paul over to a Jewish Sanhedrin.

In *Ant.* 20.9.1; #200–3, Josephus describes how in AD 62, after the death of the procurator Festus, and before the new procurator, Albinus, arrived, the high priest Ananus II convened "a Sanhedrin of judges" and brought before them James, the brother of Jesus, and others whom he accused of transgressing the Law. He delivered them to stoning. Citizens of Jerusalem "who were meticulous about the laws," knowing that Ananus had not been correct in his first step of convening a Sanhedrin without the procurator's consent, reported him to King Agrippa II (who appointed high priests at this time) and to Albinus, so that the high priest was removed from office. This instance shows the tight Roman control over a Sanhedrin, particularly in capital cases.[91] Evidently the lesson had its effect. Shortly afterward in AD

---

[89]When was this permission given? At the beginning of the Roman prefecture in AD 6, under Coponius, Samaritans profaned the Jerusalem Temple by placing human bones there; in response there were new measures taken by the priests to protect the Temple, including the exclusion of people (Josephus, *Ant.* 18.2.2; #29–30). McLaren (*Power* 80–81) points out that this could exemplify Roman policy, allowing local inhabitants responsibility for the peace and order of an institution that involved them.

[90]We see the opposite in *War* 2.12.7; #246; *Ant.* 20.6.3; #136 where the Roman tribune Celer, who functioned under the prefect Cumanus (AD 48–52), is sent back to Jerusalem from Rome by the Emperor Claudius "to be delivered over to Jewish outrage" for crimes he had committed against Jews.

[91]Although the precise issue was the convoking of a Sanhedrin (to mete out capital sentences), surely the situation was aggravated by the executions for which this Sanhedrin was responsible (Strobel, "Stunde" 35). Burkill ("Competence" 92), along with Lietzmann, assumes that the crimes were purely political and that is why the procurator was upset. There is no evidence for that in the text: Josephus specifies that the accusation against James concerned violation of the Law. Lengle ("Zum Prozess" 316), assuming that mishnaic rules were applicable, contends that this was not the whole Sanhedrin of seventy-one members, but a smaller group selected by the high priest, who

62 (*War* 6.5.3; #300–9) a certain Jesus, son of Ananias, began crying out in the Temple referring to a voice of doom against Jerusalem, against the sanctuary, and against all the people. Some of the prominent citizens arrested and flogged him, but finally the leaders (*hoi archontes*) led him to Albinus, the Roman prefect. Jesus refused to answer the prefect's questions, and so Albinus let him go as a maniac. Thus despite their anger, the Jewish leaders, who could arrest and flog, did not dare execute this Jesus as they had executed James.

2. Proposed Examples of Executions by Jewish Authorities

There are also examples that in the eyes of some scholars raise the possibility of the right of Jewish authorities to execute independently of the Romans. Let us evaluate those suggestions.

The Adulterous Woman. Inserted in the Gospel of John (7:53–8:11) is the story of a woman caught in the act of adultery. The scribes and the Pharisees state to Jesus, "Moses in the law ordered such women to be stoned.[92] But you—what have you to say about it?" Jesus' answer is: "The man among you who has no sin—let him be the first to cast a stone at her." The story does not assume that those who seized the woman or Jesus would have had to bring her to the Roman authorities before they executed her. Although some have described the scene as a trap forcing Jesus to decide between Mosaic Law and the Roman prohibition of executions, Schumann ("Bemerkungen" 318) is perfectly correct in observing that the alternatives are the Mosaic Law and Jesus' own moral stance toward sinners. True, the passage is a late insertion, found after Luke 21:38 in other textual witnesses. Nevertheless, as I have argued elsewhere (BGJ 1.335–36), although not written by the fourth evangelist, it may well be an early story. Nothing in it suggests a lynch-mob mentality; and while it is not clear that a Sanhedrin had judged the woman, the story suggests indirectly that the Jewish authorities could condemn and execute for adultery—a suggestion of uncertain value, however, since the point of the story to which all else is subordinated is Jesus' clemency. The passage calls those authorities scribes and Pharisees, but this

---

excluded Pharisees, so that the complaint against the action was partly based on the makeup of the Sanhedrin.

[92]The punishment by stoning is interesting (if it is truly specific and not simply to be equated with execution). Deut 22:21–22 orders stoning for a woman who before marriage has lost her virginity through fornication or adultery; it commands that a woman who has committed adultery after marriage should die but does not specify the type of execution. Ezek 16:38–40 shows stoning being used as a punishment in the latter case as well. Mishna *Sanhedrin* 11.1 specifies strangulation as the punishment; yet there is no clear instance of strangulation being prescribed before the 2d cent., and certainly John's Pharisees are not thinking of it. See J. Blinzler, NTS 4 (1957–58), 32–47.

may be a post-70 simplification when all the opponents of Jesus' lifetime were being reduced to those who still remained significant.

The Priest's Daughter. Mishna *Sanhedrin* 7.2 reports a statement of Rabbi Eleazar ben Zadok: It once happened in the case of a priest's daughter who committed adultery that they placed a bundle of branches around her and then burned her. The Sages responded that this was because there was not at that time a court that was properly trained. This explanation may mean that the court had treated the woman under Sadducee rather than Pharisee standards, namely, following the written law of Lev 21:9 (also Josephus *Ant.* 4.8.23; #248), which would burn a priest's daughter to death, rather than the mishnaic law of strangulation. TalBab *Sanhedrin* 52b adds the detail that at that time R. Eleazar was a child riding on his father's shoulders (also Tosepta *Sanhedrin* 9.11). Eleazar as a teacher is traditionally dated in the second generation of the Tannaim, thus in the period 90–130. This execution in Eleazar's childhood (TalJer *Sanhedrin* 24b, related to Mishna *Sanhedrin* 7.2: an age less than ten) Jeremias places during the reign of King Agrippa I in Palestine (41–44)—a period when there was no Roman prefect and the king could allow Jewish courts to impose the death penalty (see Agrippa's execution of James the brother of John in Acts 12:1–4 which "pleased the Jews"). Other scholars have tried to place the execution in 62–63 in the period between the procuratorships of Festus and Albinus when, as we have seen above, James the brother of Jesus was put to death. These datings would remove the problem of such an execution taking place without the approval of a Roman governor. If one does not resort to such datings (which are highly speculative), the story may offer another indication that Jewish authorities on their own could execute for adultery. Even if the Roman governor kept the death penalty in his own hands, we have seen that he allowed the Jewish authorities to execute anyone who went into the forbidden area of the Temple. Perhaps he also did this for cases of adultery (thus Nörr, "Problems" 117), confining Roman supervision to public and political crimes, not to such moral or cultic offenses. It is precisely in response to a question of how the Jews in captivity could have had the authority to put Susanna to death when they thought that she had committed adultery (Dan 13:28) that Origen (*Ep. ad Africanum* 20 [14]; SC 302.564–66) pointed out that it was not unusual for kings to concede to subject people their own laws and judgments— a reply that he justifies from his knowledge of Jews under 3d-cent. Roman rule.

Stephen. In Acts 6:11ff. the people and the elders and the scribes are aroused by those who claim that they have heard Stephen speak blasphemously against Moses and God, and they bring him before the Sanhedrin. False witnesses testify that Stephen speaks incessantly against this holy place and the Law, saying that Jesus of Nazareth will destroy this place and will change the customs given by Moses. In responses to the chief priests' question, Stephen speaks at length; but his antiTemple affirmation that the Most High does not dwell in houses made with hands enrages the hearers so that they cast him out of the city and stone him to death. There is a tone of violence, and some have argued that this execution was an instance of lynch law and thus illegal. Yet Acts 26:10 has Paul casting his vote for putting Christians to death, so that a judicial procedure was envisaged by the author of Acts. Since the incident is related to Paul's conversion which may be dated in AD 36, others suggest that while not a lynching, it happened in the troubled time when Pilate had been removed (see n. 14 above). In that period, they propose, the Sanhedrin would have taken the opportunity to act against Stephen, even as in the early 60s during the absence of a Roman procurator a Sanhedrin acted illegally against the life of James the brother of the Lord. Another solution stays closer to the text: Stephen was violating the law of Temple sanctity and the Romans had given the Jews the right to execute in such cases. A parallel instance in Acts 21:27ff. (discussed above) describes an attempt to execute Paul for having violated the Temple by bringing Gentiles where they did not belong, but that time the Romans interfered. However, one must wonder whether speaking against the Temple, as Stephen was charged with doing, would come under a Roman grant of capital jurisdiction, since, as we have seen, in the case of Jesus son of Ananias who warned of doom for the sanctuary, the Jewish authorities handed him over to the Roman governor. Probably the best solution is to recognize that the stoning of Stephen may have been an example of the inevitable tension that occurred in instances when Jews believed that the Law received by Moses from God demanded capital punishment but Roman polity prohibited them from executing that punishment. Naturally there would have been a tendency for Jews to take the law into their own hands, especially when the offense was regarded as horrendously impious. Whether the Roman governor reacted by punishing such illicit procedure may have depended on whether he heard about it and, if he did, whether the execution had popular support so that intervention would have caused an uproar.[93] The Roman governor, for example, removed the high priest Ananus II for killing James the brother of Jesus (and others) precisely because Ananus was denounced by

---

[93]Jeremias ("Geschichtlichkeit" 146–47) is important on this point. He denies that the stoning of Stephen was lynch justice or took place during a prefectural interstice (arguing correctly that Pilate lasted through most of 36 [probably leaving Judea in Dec. 36]). He thinks that the Jewish authorities overstepped their competence; yet the persecution that followed had to have Roman approval, even if tacit. It was in Pilate's interest that the Christians be kept under control. But were Christians that important a group in Roman eyes already in the 30s?

fellow Jews observant of the Law (presumably Pharisees). The citation from Origen mentioned in the preceding paragraph in regard to adultery goes on to affirm that in his experience private trials according to Jewish law were conducted even to the point of a death sentence, not indeed with full liberty granted by the Romans but also not without the knowledge of the Roman prefect.[94]

3. Conclusions

If I may return to the question with which I opened this D subsection, namely, whether John 18:31 is accurate in having the Jews exclaim, "It is not permitted us to put anyone to death," I would say that the prevailing evidence supports historicity but only when the statement is understood in a nuanced sense. The Romans permitted the Jews to execute for certain clear religious offenses,[95] e.g., for violating the prohibitions against circulating in certain quarters of the Temple, and perhaps for adultery. Beyond this specified religious sphere the Jewish authorities were supposed to hand over cases to the Romans, who would decide whether or not to pass and execute a death sentence. This corresponds to what we saw above (A3c) about the Roman prefect/procurator being given the *imperium* to execute when the province of Judea was set up. Inevitably there were tensions between the Jews and the Romans over crimes that would have brought a death penalty under Jewish law but not under Roman law.[96] When Jews took it into their own hands to execute criminals for such crimes,[97] the Romans upon hearing of this judicial action might or might not punish those involved, depending on the notoriety of the crime or of the criminal. Great notoriety would not permit the Romans to pass over the issue in silence, nor would complaints by respectable citizens. Such a nuanced conclusion rules against Juster's claim that a Sanhedrin had the power of execution and that since Jesus was executed by the Romans, a Sanhedrin could not have been involved in condemning him.

If the complicated situation I have just described is accurate, one may still wonder why the Jewish authorities who condemned Jesus would not have

---

[94]DNTRJ 307 suggests that strangulation was gradually substituted for stoning as a capital punishment because it attracted less public attention.

[95]Josephus (*War* 6.6.2; #333–34) has Titus say: "We maintained the ancestral laws, and allowed you a way of life as you willed, not only among yourselves but toward others." See Smallwood, *The Jews* 150–51.

[96]If we can judge from the Gospels and the instance of Jesus son of Ananias reported by Josephus, the Jewish Sanhedrin could pronounce that someone deserved death for what the Romans did not consider capital (e.g., for apostasy, blasphemy, infanticide) before handing the criminal over.

[97]Josephus (*War* 2.8.9; #145) tells of meticulously careful Essene courts (clearly not exercising lynch justice) that punished blasphemies with death. The Romans could not control all executions in remote places.

taken a chance and executed him, trusting that Pilate might choose not to make trouble. That question can be answered only by speculation, but the following factors should not be forgotten. Caiaphas lasted as high priest the whole length of Pilate's prefecture; perhaps the two of them had worked out a modus vivendi that would allow some Jewish actions to be overlooked so long as they would not endanger Roman governance or be publicly embarrassing to Pilate. Execution at Passover time when hordes of pilgrims were in Jerusalem[98] and Pilate himself was there could scarcely have been overlooked. Pilate could have been all the more sensitive about this because, as we shall see in §31, he had had conflicts with the Jews in Jerusalem during a feast. The Gospels indicate that the Jewish authorities feared the ire of the crowds if they moved against Jesus, and so it may have suited their purpose to have the Romans carry out the execution so that they themselves would not be the direct target if there was an angry reaction. In addition, the Romans would crucify Jesus and that manner of death, equivalent to the hanging on a tree mentioned in the Law, would place Jesus under a curse and thus discredit him (see pp. 381, 533, 535 below).[99] In any case, one should recognize that the procedure of the Jewish authorities in dealing with Jesus of Nazareth as described in the Gospels can scarcely be considered unusual; Josephus describes almost the same procedure thirty years later in dealing with Jesus son of Ananias.[100]

E. *Evidence of Action against Jesus by Jewish Authorities*

What we have seen thus far shows that it was possible for the Sanhedrin authorities to have tried or interrogated Jesus, to have sentenced him as deserving death, and then to have turned him over to Pilate to be crucified. The

[98]Scholars guess at the number who came for Passover, but most think exaggerated the three million given by Josephus, *War* 2.14.3; #280. There were riots at Passover in 4 BC under Archelaus (*Ant.* 17.9.3; #213–18), and ca. AD 48 under the procurator Cumanus (*Ant.* 20.5.3; #105–12).

[99]A further implication has been suggested but has little scriptural backing: Giving him over to the Romans would exclude him from God's people and have him die as an outsider (Bornhäuser, *Death* 106). I find completely unsubstantiated in the text the suggestion of Aguirre ("Poderes" 266) that although the Sanhedrin had the jurisdiction to stone Jesus, they had to give him over to the Romans because they could not agree among themselves about him. See also the imaginative suggestion in n. 75 above about the calendric necessity of giving him over to the Romans.

[100]Notice also a parallel pattern much later. In the late 2d cent., although the Christian martyrs were interrogated in the forum of Lyons by the local tribunes and city magistrates, they were imprisoned until the arrival of the governor for his approval of the execution (1.8; MACM 62; see also MACM 156, 206). In the instance of the martyrdom of Pionius at Smyrna, the local officials say that the *fasces* do not allow them to exercise the *imperium* of execution until the proconsul comes— a proconsul who, when he does come, judges and then pronounces a sentence in Latin from a tablet (MACM 148, 162).

move from possibility to historical plausibility, however, is complicated. The evangelists, because they lived in the Roman Empire, would have been aware of how Roman governors acted in the provinces; and so a priori it is unlikely that they would have described an impossible situation (pace Juster). Yet were they in a position to know in detail what had actually happened in Jerusalem thirty to seventy years before they wrote? Did the fact that often in Jerusalem a Sanhedrin was involved in religious questions of public import cause Christian tradition to assume that it was involved in the death of Jesus? Was a less structured Jewish involvement dramatized into a formal Sanhedrin involvement? In fact, no detailed legal court record of Jesus' trial was preserved, and so surely the Gospel narratives involve dramatization and simplification—but how much? We shall never be able to answer these questions with certainty, but let us survey the evidence for authoritative Jewish involvement in the death of Jesus.[101] The evidence is derived from Jewish, Christian, and pagan sources.

1. Jewish Evidence

Two items are of major importance: the witness of Josephus and of the Babylonian Talmud.

(a) Josephus' *Testimonium Flavianum* (*Ant.* 18.3.3; #63–64) is the famous reference to Jesus[102] which the Jewish historian, writing in the 90s, includes among the events that took place in the early part of Pilate's prefecture (AD 26–36):

> Now about this time there was [appeared] a wise man named Jesus—**if indeed one ought to speak of him as a man**, for he was a doer of astonishing deeds, a teacher of people who gladly receive what is true.[103] He won over many Jews and many of the Greeks. **He was the Messiah [*Christos*].** When/Although Pilate had condemned him to the cross upon indictment [*endeixis*] of the first-ranking men [*prōtoi andres*] among us, those who had loved him from the first did not cease (to do so), **for he appeared to them once more alive on the third day. The divine proph-**

---

[101]Blinzler (*Trial* 10–20) lists at least five grades of involvement and the scholars who have advocated them: (1) Jews were totally responsible for the death of Jesus, with the Romans reduced to mere implementation; (2) Jews had the decisive role and the Romans a lesser share; (3) Jews and Romans were equally involved; (4) the Romans had the decisive role and the Jews a lesser share; (5) the Romans were totally responsible and there was no Jewish involvement.

[102]The presence of the *Testimonium* contributed significantly to the role Christians played in the preservation of Josephus' works. As I shall explain, **the words in boldface are probably post-Josephus additions.**

[103]A frequently suggested emendation (*ta aēthē* for *talēthē* [a contraction involving *alēthē*]) would read "what is novel/extraordinary." It is unnecessary, for Josephus is capable of deliberate ambiguity: "They receive gladly what (they think) is true."

ets had spoken these and other marvelous things about him. The clan
of the Christians [*Christianoi*], named after him, has still not disappeared
even up to now.

Suspect is such fulsome praise of Jesus when we reflect that Josephus was a
Pharisee of priestly descent who courted Roman favor and who lived in
Rome after Nero's persecution of the Christians and was writing in the time
of the distrustful Domitian. Accordingly from the 16th cent. (J. J. Scaliger)
to the 20th cent. the authenticity of this passage has been questioned, either
as entirely a Christian interpolation or as a Christian substitution for a genuine, uncomplimentary reference to Jesus by Josephus.[104] That is not the majority view, however. Even if few scholars today would argue that Josephus
wrote the whole passage as quoted,[105] most would contend that Josephus
wrote a basic text to which Christians made additions. In vocabulary and
style large parts of it are plausibly from the hand of Josephus; and the context in which the passage appears in *Ant.* (i.e., among the early unpleasant
relations involving the Jewish leaders and Pilate) is appropriate. The passage
that follows it speaks of another arbitrary or outrageous action, thus indicating Josephus' attitude toward the treatment of Jesus by Pilate. Although
some statements in the *Testimonium* are fulsome and fit a Christian pen,
other statements would scarcely have originated (in the 2d cent. or later)
with those who believed that Jesus was the Son of God, e.g., "a wise man"
seems an understatement. Granted how Christians came to vituperate the
Jewish authorities for their role in the death of Jesus, "upon indictment of the
first-ranking men among us" seems bland. Moreover, we have no evidence of
Christians in the 1st cent. referring to themselves as a tribe or clan.[106] The
Testimonium is found in all mss. of *Ant.* and was cited in full in the early 4th
cent. by Eusebius (EH 1.11.7–8; also *Demonstratio Evangelica* 3.5.105;
GCS 23.130–31). It may have been known in some form in the early 3d cent.
by Origen, who discussed the fact that Josephus mentioned Jesus *without
believing* that he was the Messiah.[107]

That comment of Origen led already in the 17th cent. (R. Montague) to
the contention that Josephus did indeed describe Jesus, but that very early
Christian scribes glossed the passage, e.g., by adding: "He was the Mes-

---

[104]Those who regard it as totally inauthentic would include Battifol, Birdsall, Burkitt, Conzelmann, Hahn, L. Herrmann, Lagrange, Norden, and Zeitlin. Thackeray changed from this view to
that of Christian additions to an authentic text.

[105]Exceptions are F. Dornseiff, ZNW 35 (1936), 129–55; ZNW 46 (1955), 245–50; and E. Nodet,
RB 92 (1985), 320–48; 497–524.

[106]For genuine Josephus usage, see *War* 3.8.3; #354: "the tribe of the Jews."

[107]See *Contra Celsum* 1.47; also *Comm. in Matt.* 10.17 on 13:55 (GCS 40.22). We are not certain
of Origen's knowledge of the *Testimonium*, however, for there is another Josephus reference to Jesus
in *Ant.* 20.9.1; #200: James "the brother of Jesus who was called the Christ."

siah."[108] The partial interpolation or gloss theory finds support also among Jewish scholars.[109] In the translation given above I put in boldface the most plausible Christian glosses.[110] Even with these removed, the Josephus passage gives in nonGospel language a picture of Jesus as a religious teacher and miracle-worker who was crucified by the Roman prefect but only after the involvement of the Jewish authorities—a presentation that agrees substantially with the portrait painted by the NT.

S. Pines[111] reports a citation of the *Testimonium* by a 10th-cent. Christian, Agapius of Mabbug, writing in Arabic and deriving his information from earlier chronicles. The citation omits many of the more obvious Christian phrases:

> At this time there was a wise man who was called Jesus. And his conduct was good, and he was known to be virtuous. And many people from among the Jews and other nations became his disciples. Pilate condemned him to be crucified and to die. And those who had become his disciples did not abandon his discipleship. They reported that he had appeared to them three days after his crucifixion and that he was alive; accordingly he was perhaps the Messiah concerning whom the prophets have recounted wonders.

One omission is "upon indictment of the first-ranking men among us"; accordingly some have hastened to acclaim this as the orginal text of Josephus. Pines himself (pp. 35, 70) is more cautious about whether the omissions might not have come from scribal negligence. Overall, he suggests the possiblity that Agapius may have preserved a form of the *Testimonium* less modified by Christians than the Eusebius form. Reviewers[112] have been less gen-

---

[108]There is traceable a hardening between Origen's reports and what Eusebius reports about the relation between the high priest's execution of James (the brother of Jesus) and the fall of Jerusalem/ Israel. Z. Baras (JJC 338–48) makes a good case that Eusebius himself added to the *Testimonium* and that it was his form that became standard for the text of Josephus. In the 3d cent. the Josephus text would have circulated without the Christian additions found in Eusebius (p. 341).

[109]E.g., L. H. Feldman in the Loeb translation (9.49); and the important article of P. Winter, "Josephus on Jesus," *Journal of Historical Studies* 1 (1968), 289–302. That this is now the view of most scholars is documented by J. P. Meier, "Jesus in Josephus, a Modest Proposal," CBQ 52 (1990), 76–103, which is defensibly the best treatment in recent years. As Meier insists, the complete interpolation theory does not explain satisfactorily that there are two styles in the passage, with some lines demonstrably in the style of Josephus and other lines demonstrably not.

[110]See the helpful discussion in HJPAJC 1.428–41, with an ample bibliography. Also Z. Baras's survey of research and bibliography on the *Testimonium* in SRSTP 303–13, 378–85. I had already composed this analysis of the glosses when I read Meier, "Josephus"; and these are exactly the glosses that he detects with much added argumentation.

[111]*An Arabic Version of the Testimonium Flavianum and Its Implications* (Jerusalem: Israel Academy, 1971), translation on p. 16. See the preliminary reactions of R. McL. Wilson, "The New *Passion of Jesus* in the Light of the New Testament and Apocrypha," in *Neotestamentica et Semitica*, eds. E. E. Ellis and M. Wilcox (M. Black Festschrift; Edinburgh: Clark, 1969), 264–71.

[112]E. Bammel, ExpTim 85 (1973–74), 145–47; M. Smith, JBL 91 (1972), 441–42.

erous in their evaluation of the importance of the quotation, pointing out that it is not attested until very late, that Agapius is not particularly rigorous in citations, and that there have been seemingly anti-Islamic modifications, e.g., in the added phrase "and to die." (For the common Islamic view that Jesus did not die on the cross, see p. 1094 below.) The Agapius citation helps, however, to confirm that Christian copyists did feel free to modify the *Testimonium*.[113]

(b) The Babylonian Talmud (*Sanhedrin* 43a) records a *baraita* or older tradition that I quote from the London Soncino translation (*Nezikin* volume 3.281):[114]

> On the eve of Passover Yeshu was hanged. For forty days before the execu-
> tion took place, a herald went forth and cried, "He is going forth to be
> stoned because he has practised sorcery and enticed Israel to apostasy.
> Anyone who can say anything in his favour, let him come forward and
> plead on his behalf." But since nothing was brought forward in his favour
> he was hanged on the eve of Passover.

In reaction to this, TalBab gives the comments of the Babylonian Ulla (ca. 300?) indignantly asking whether Yeshu was one for whom a defense could be made. Was he not a *mesith* (deceiving enticer) concerning whom Scripture says, "You shall neither spare nor conceal him" (Deut 13:9[8])? The Talmud continues: "With Yeshu, however, it was different, for he was connected with the government." In other words, apparently there was a 5th-cent. perception that Romans as well as Jews were involved, thus modifying the earlier *baraita* reference. The extent to which the *baraita* draws upon Christian sources is not clear, e.g., the chronology in it is Johannine. The use of "hanging" for crucifixion is attested in the NT and

---

[113]E. Bammel, "Zum Testimonium Flavianum," in *Josephus-Studien,* eds. O. Betz et al. (70 Geburtstag O. Michel; Göttingen: Vandenhoeck & Ruprecht, 1974), 9–22, posits emendations rather than omissions, so that he emerges with an original Josephus text that would be closer in length to the standard one.

[114]Only very rarely does the Talmud refer to "Yeshu" without further identification. Some scholars (Dalman, Jeremias) deny that Jesus of Nazareth is involved and suggest a Jesus who was a disciple of Joshua b. Perahiah, an early 1st-cent.-BC teacher, at the time of Alexander Jannaeus. However, the comment that follows in the tractate *Sanhedrin* refers to Yeshu's disciples, including Matthai (Matthew), and indicates that it took place during foreign ("government" = Roman?) rule. For a careful analysis of this passage and a defense of its pertinence to Jesus of Nazareth, see Betz, "Probleme" 570–80. That it was thought to refer to the Christians' Jesus explains the frequent suppression of it in the censored editions of the Talmud. In correspondence Rabbi B. L. Visotzky indicated emendations that he would make on the basis of a Munich ms.: The two references would be enlarged from "Yeshu" to "Yeshu ha-Nosri," who would be described as having "*misled and* enticed Israel." Visotzky believes that here "stoned" is generic for "executed."

the DSS.[115] It is perhaps this reference to crucifixion (a punishment associated with the Romans) that led to the talmudic comment about Gentile involvement—unless we are seeing simply a post-325 Jewish equation of Christianity with Roman rule. The charge that Jesus was a sorcerer fits very well with 2d-cent. Jewish charges against Jesus reported in Origen.[116] No matter what the origins of the tradition in TalBab, the *baraita* shows that ancient Jews thought that their ancestors were involved in and even responsible for the death of Jesus. M. Goldstein, *Jesus in the Jewish Tradition* (New York: Macmillan, 1950), 22ff., would date the TalBab tradition before 220.

If we try to move backward from that approximate date, we find that in the late 100s the Jew cited by Celsus says, "We punished this fellow (Jesus) who was a cheater," and "We had convicted him, condemned him, and decided that he should be punished."[117] Even earlier in that 2d cent. Justin in his *Dialogue* speaks to the Jew Trypho, "You (pl.) crucified him" (17.1). Of course, Justin is reporting views Christians thought Jews to hold; nevertheless, Trypho is often portrayed as qualifying or rejecting what Justin says, and nowhere in the *Dialogue* does Trypho question this charge. Rather, Jewish involvement in the death of Jesus seems to be taken for granted by both sides; and indeed Trypho turns it around theologically: "If the Father wanted him to suffer these things . . . we did no wrong"(95.3).

Origen's *Contra Celsum* and Justin's *Dialogue* supply only indirect (and often prejudiced) evidence about Jewish thought. Nevertheless, whether we appeal to direct or indirect evidence, there is no ancient indication of any Jewish tradition that calls into doubt the involvement of Jewish authorities in the death of Jesus. (Indeed, if Jesus were killed by the Romans alone, one might wonder why he was not remembered to some extent as a Jewish hero.) That the Jewish authorities or Jews were not involved is a modern idea. In Catchpole's study of Jewish historiography on this issue, he traces to 1866 and L. Philippson[118] the pattern of denying all Jewish juridical action and attributing the death of Jesus entirely to the Romans. In three editions of his famous *Geschichte der Juden*, between 1856 and 1878, H. Graetz moved

---

[115]Gal 3:13; Acts 5:30; 10:39; and 4QpNah 3–4, col. 1.7–8; 11Q Miqdaš (Temple Scroll) 64.8–12.

[116]*Contra Celsum* 1.28,71. H. Chadwick, *Origen: Contra Celsum* (Cambridge Univ., 1965), xxviii, judges, "On balance, therefore, probability lies with the view that Celsus' date is to be assigned to the period 170–80." Celsus cites a Jew for some of his views of Jesus.

[117]*Contra Celsum* 2.4 and 2.9; also 2.5: "As an offender he was punished by the Jews."

[118]In his *Haben,* 11–14, Philippson is conscious of being revisionistic in denying the classic Jewish position that Jesus' divine claims would have caused him to be considered guilty of blasphemy, for which the penalty had to be death.

from defending the Jews of Jesus' time for executing him to defending them as not having executed him.

2. Christian Evidence Independent of the Gospels

All the Gospels, written in the period 70–100, portray Jewish involvement in the death of Jesus, and in so doing they draw upon preGospel traditions which certainly antedate 60. One must debate whether such a massive fiction could have been created within thirty years of Jesus' death. In terms of pre-Gospel and pre-60 evidence, the sermons in Acts (3:14–15; 4:10; 5:30; 7:52; 13:27–28) attribute to Jews and/or Jewish authorities a role in the death of Jesus. Many scholars would argue that elements of early tradition are involved in those sermons, especially in kerygmatic formulas like "You killed him, but God raised him up." Nevertheless, the fact that "Luke" has edited that Acts material removes it from the category of evidence independent of the Gospels.

Very important is the passage in I Thess 2:14–16 meant as encouraging words to the Thessalonian Christians who have endured persecution:

> [14]For you became imitators, brothers, of the churches of God which are in Judea in Christ Jesus because you too endured the same things from your own countrymen as they did from *the Jews* [15]*who killed both the Lord Jesus* and the prophets, and who persecuted us, and who are not pleasing to God, and who are opposed to everyone, [16]hindering us from preaching to the Gentiles that they may be saved. This has the result of always filling up their sins, but the wrath has come upon them to the end.

It is generally agreed that I Thess was written about 50, and certainly Paul would have had the idea that Jews killed the Lord Jesus long before he wrote this letter. Indeed, since Paul was in Jerusalem and hostile to Christians shortly after Jesus' death (Gal 1:13,18), this passage is a very serious challenge to the thesis that there was no Jewish involvement in the death of Jesus. The evidence has been questioned, however.

Despite the fact that the passage is not missing from any ms. of the epistle, some scholars would argue that Paul could not have written this.[119] Let me list one by one the difficulties they see and at the same time report the rebut-

---

[119]Among earlier scholars: Baur, Holtzmann, Ritschl, Schmiedel; recently, B. A. Pearson, HTR 64 (1971), 79–94; H. Boers, NTS 22 (1975–76), 140–58; D. Schmidt, JBL 102 (1983), 269–79. For a review of the literature, see G. E. Okeke, NTS 27 (1980), 127–36.

tals by a larger group of scholars who defend the passage as genuinely Pauline:[120]

- Here Paul seems to divorce himself from his own people in the generalized hostile use of "the Jews," which is characteristic of later NT writings, e.g., John. Yet in I Thess Paul is addressing chiefly Gentiles and may well be using their terminology ("the Jews"), which was gradually becoming his own. The usage here is no more difficult than that of the undoubtedly genuine II Cor 11:24,26, which shows clearly that the use of "the Jews" did not divorce Paul from them: "Five times I received from the Jews thirty-nine lashes . . . in danger from my own countrymen (*genos*)." As for hostility, anger toward Jews in writing to Thessalonica is understandable if Acts 17:5–15 is correct in reporting that Jews rioted against Paul in that city and were responsible for driving him out, even pursuing him to Beroea.

- Here there is a suppression of the Roman role in the death of Jesus, and that is a mark of later writing, e.g., *GPet*. Such an objection distorts the evidence by equating silence with suppression. If Paul was making an analogy between the way the Jews had acted in Thessalonica and the way they acted toward Jesus, there would have been no reason to mention the Roman role in the death of Jesus. Notice that Paul attributes responsibility to the Jews by speaking of their "killing" Jesus, not of their crucifying him, which would have been normal Pauline vocabulary, so that he was not trying to substitute the Jews as the ones who physically put Jesus on the cross. For Paul Jews were the moving force in the action against Jesus. Indeed, one might even suspect that the general Pauline practice of speaking about the crucifixion (commonly thought of as a Roman punishment) meant that all his converts knew of Roman involvement, so that there was no need to call attention to it.[121]

- The reference in I Thess to the Jews "who killed . . . the prophets, and who persecuted us" echoes the post-70 language of the murdering of the prophets in Matt 23:29–31. However, the likelihood that Matt was written after 70 does not mean that the material preserved therein arose after 70. Moreover, there is

[120]See R. F. Collins, *Studies on the First Letter to the Thessalonians* (BETL 66; Leuven Univ., 1984), 135; K. P. Donfried, *Interpretation* 38 (1984), 242–53; J. C. Hurd, AJEC 21–36; R. Jewett, *The Thessalonian Correspondence* (Philadelphia: Fortress, 1986), 35–46; S. G. Wilson, "The Jews" 168; J. A. Weatherly, JSNT 42 (1991), 79–98; and F. Gilliard, NTS 35 (1989), 481–502, who adds plausibly that while genuine, the passage is restrictive, referring to those specific Jews who killed the Lord Jesus.

[121]The noun "cross" and verb "to crucify" occur some fifteen times in the undoubtedly genuine Pauline letters. There may be more direct allusion to a Roman role in I Cor 2:8, which has the rulers of this eon crucifying the Lord Jesus. Even if the "rulers" are supernatural forces who control events in this world, that does not exclude a reference to the earthly agents they used (see the duality in Daniel's attitude toward the angelic prince/king of Persia: 10:13,20; 11:2). In any case, I judge simplistic the argument that the failure to include the Romans as a factor in the death of Jesus is a sign of lateness. I Tim 6:13 was written *later* than I Thess, and there Romans are mentioned and Jews are not: "Christ Jesus in his testimony before Pontius Pilate made the good confession."

a perfectly good Pauline parallel. In Rom 11:3 Paul uses Elijah in I Kings 19:10 to speak of his contemporary Israelites: "Lord, they have killed your prophets . . . and they seek my life."

- The affirmation of I Thess that the wrath of God has come upon the Jews "to the end" would seem to suppose the destruction of Jerusalem or some very dramatic sign of divine punishment that could not have occurred by the date I Thess was written. Rather, this is flexible apocalyptic language and is perfectly at home in the overall apocalyptic context of I Thess. It is quite capable of being applied to something that happened just before Paul wrote I Thess in 50—something that might be interpreted as divine punishment, e.g., the expulsion of Jews from Rome by Claudius in 49.

- The divine rejection of the Jews suggested by the last line of the Thess passage in terms of a wrath that has come upon them to the end contradicts what Paul writes in Rom 9–11 concerning the ultimate conversion of Israel (11:25–26). However, Romans speaks of the wrath of God ten times, addressing Jew and Gentile alike with the warning: "You are storing up wrath for yourself on the day of wrath" (2:5; also 1:18; 9:22). This is a wrath from which ultimately all will be saved through Christ (5:9). Also in Romans Paul asks his fellow Jews, "Shall we say God is unjust, humanly speaking, to inflict wrath? By no means!" (3:5–6; also 4:15). The idea of I Thess that the wrath has come upon the Jews matches Rom 11:14–15, which speaks of the rejection of those related to Paul according to the flesh in order to make them jealous. (See also Rom 11:7,11,21 for the hardening and stumbling of Israel which is not spared.) The coming of wrath upon Israel in I Thess, therefore, is not a contradiction of Rom 11:25–26 but reflects the first part of that sentence: "A hardening has come upon Israel in part, until the full number of the Gentiles comes in, and so all Israel will be saved."

- I Thess 2:13 hooks smoothly into 2:17, so that 2:14–16 can easily be a secondary insertion. This is the weakest argument that can be offered, for on almost any page of the Bible one can omit some verses and find a smooth sequence without them. Hurd (AJEC 27–30) points out that it is perfectly good Pauline structure to have 2:14–16 returning, after an interruption, to the theme of affliction introduced in 1:2–10.

In my judgment none of the arguments against the Pauline authorship of I Thess 2:14–16 is persuasive, and the passage must be deemed to represent a very early Christian testimony to Jewish involvement in the death of Jesus.[122] It is perfectly harmonious with Gal 3:13, which reports that "Christ

[122]Lindeskog ("Prozess" 330–31) contends that the passion comes to us in two forms: *the early Christian kerygma,* especially in its Pauline form where the death of Christ is an act of God, and *the Gospel presentation,* with an emphasis on Jewish responsibility. The kerygma, stemming from Jewish-Christian sources, is primary and clearer; the Gospel presentation reflects later history (including Gentile experience) of relations to the synagogue. That is too simple an analysis, for it judges early Christian preaching about the passion on the basis of some kerygmatic formulas. I

redeemed us from the curse of the law by having become a curse for us" inasmuch as his death fulfilled Deut 21:23: "Cursed every one who hangs on a tree." That reasoning, which looks on Jesus' death in terms of the Mosaic Law, would make little sense if the death was simply the result of a Roman intervention without Jewish involvement. Similarly Paul's references to the crucifixion or death as a *skandalon* to the Jews (I Cor 1:23; see Gal 5:11), and the statement that he was crucified in "weakness" are not easily reconcilable with a death that was only Roman civil punishment. Schinzer ("Bedeutung" 152) would carry further the argument about the theological meaninglessness of exclusive Roman responsibility: Paul's thesis that Christ's death frees us from the Law (Rom 7:1–6) and that Christ (through his death) is the end of the Law makes sense because the Sanhedrin acting according to the Law sentenced Jesus to death. Indeed, Paul's own testimonies to his blameless status as a Jew and a Pharisee and his persecution of the followers of Jesus (Gal 1:13; Philip 3:5)[123] help to illustrate how pious Jews could have been involved in the death of Jesus.

3. Pagan Evidence

Some of this is of little utility for our purposes here. Explicit ancient Roman evidence about the death of Jesus was supplied ca. AD 120 by Tacitus, *Annals* 15.44.[124] This passage does not concern itself with the issue of Jewish participation since it seeks to explain to the Romans about "the depraved group who were popularly called Christians—the originator who gave the group its name, Christ, has been executed in the reign of Tiberius by the procurator, Pontius Pilate."[125] Various patristic references to documents about the trial of Jesus supposedly preserved in the Roman archives (Justin, *Apology* 1.35.9; 1.48.3; Tertullian, *Apology* 5.2; 21.24 [CC 1.94–95, 127]) either reflect an anticipation that such documentation should have existed or

---

Thess shows that Paul told those to whom he preached that there was Jewish involvement in the death of Jesus.

[123]One might add to these the reports of Acts 8:3 and 9:1–2 about Saul's (Paul's) hostility to Christians and his functioning as an emissary of the (Sadducee) high priest.

[124]For a defense of the genuineness of the passage, see K. Linck, *De antiquissimis quae ad Jesum Nazarenum spectant testimoniis* (Giessen: Töpelmann, 1913), 67–81. The contention that this is a Christian interpolation (e.g., S. Cohen, "Jesus of Nazareth," *Universal Jewish Encyclopedia* 6 [1942], 83) has had little following. Tacitus had been in the Near East and knew Pliny (who dealt with Christians) and thus could easily have known this detail. Unfortunately, there is a gap in the *Annals* for the period AD 29–31 that might have mentioned Pilate.

[125]Another ancient pagan testimony to the death of Jesus, written some years later by Lucian of Samosata, adds nothing to the picture. He wrote about Peregrinus, who had for a while become a Christian and whose coreligionists in Palestine "still worship the man who was crucified in Palestine" (*De morte Peregrini* 11).

are echoes of Christian apocryphal writings (e.g., *Acts of Pilate*; see HSNTA 1.444ff) that have no independent historical value.[126]

More helpful, but problematic, is the letter of the Syrian Mara bar Serapion from the region of Samosata (where he was in Roman imprisonment) to his son studying in Odessa.[127] Mara asks rhetorically how it helped the Athenians to have killed Socrates, or the people of Samos to have burned Pythagoras, "or the Jews to have crucified their wise king, since from that time the kingdom was taken from them." Mara then speaks of how God took vengeance on each; in particular: "The Jews were deported and driven out of their kingdom, living thereafter in diaspora." In fact, each of the three victims has survived: Socrates through Plato's writings; Pythagoras through the statue of Hera; "and the wise king through the new law that he gave." The date of Mara's letter is determined from the events described therein, especially in terms of the deportation of Jews from Judea, which is presumably a reference to the aftermath of the destruction of the Temple in AD 70 or to the construction of the Roman city of Aelia Capitolina on the site of Jerusalem after 135. Some scholars date the letter to AD 72–74 (Blinzler, *Trial* 34–38; *Prozess* 52–57); others opt for the end of the 2d cent. at the latest; Léon-Dufour (DBS 6.1422–23) proposes a date ca. 260. There is no evidence of a direct dependence of this writer on Christian Gospels; but the later the date, the more possible indirect dependence. Yet "wise king" is not a detectably Christian designation.

When the Jewish, Christian, and pagan evidence is assembled, the involvement of Jews in the death of Jesus approaches certainty. Notice that I have not specified in what way, for the commentary will examine various Gospel portrayals of involvement. All the Gospels agree that the Jewish authorities, particularly the priests, disliked Jesus and that there were earlier attempts to stop his teaching. All agree on a judicial action by the Sanhedrin,[128] and (if we join Acts to Luke) all agree that one of the issues against Jesus was the threatened destruction of the Temple sanctuary. All agree that the Jewish authorities gave Jesus over to Pilate, who sentenced him to death. It is interesting to compare the agreement of the Gospels with that of scholars. Bartsch (*Wer*) evaluates the views of Stauffer and Winter on the historic-

---

[126]Neither does the medieval "Epistle of Lentulus" to the Roman senate involving a command for the arrest of Jesus. Also see n. 4 above.

[127]Ed. W. Cureton, *Spicilegium syriacum* (London: Rivingtons, 1855), 70–76, esp. 73–74; F. Schulthess, *Zeitschrift der Deutschen Morgenländischen Gesellschaft* 51 (1897), 365–91; A. Baumstark, *Geschichte des syrischen Literatur* (Bonn: Marcus & Webers, 1922), 10.

[128]The Synoptics describe the Sanhedrin hearing in the period after the arrest of Jesus (Mark/Matt, at night; Luke, in the morning), while John has it days or weeks earlier, with only an interrogation by the high priest after the arrest.

ity of the passion—views that Bartsch considers to be at opposite (and exaggerated) ends of the spectrum. All three scholars agree on the historicity of the arrest of Jesus on the Mount of Olives and on some involvement of the Sanhedrin; Stauffer and Bartsch agree against Winter that the issue was partly religious (Temple and/or christological) rather than simply political.

Before we move on to consider verse by verse the Gospel accounts of the involvement, let me point out the import of their overall picture by comparing two relevant Roman judicial actions described by Josephus. In a case concerning Galileans, Josephus (*Ant.* 20.5.2; #102–3) reports that the procurator Tiberius Alexander (AD 46–48) crucified two sons of Judas, who had led an earlier revolt. In the case of Jesus son of Ananias who cried out against Jerusalem and the sanctuary, Josephus (*War* 6.5.3; #300–4) reports that the Jewish leaders arrested him and handed him over to the procurator Albinus. The first case, which entailed no Jewish legal action against the crucified, exemplifies Roman treatment of political revolutionaries; the second case, which had strong Jewish involvement, exemplifies combined Jewish/Roman treatment of a religious figure who was a public concern. It is no accident that the treatment of Jesus of Nazareth described in the Gospels resembles the second rather than the first. In §31 below, as part of the discussion of the background of the Roman trial, we shall see that Jesus cannot be classified simply as a political revolutionary. He was a troublesome religious figure and was treated as such.

F. *Responsibility and/or Guilt for the Death of Jesus*

Given the conclusion just reached, the issues of responsibility and guilt are inevitable. Reading the Gospels will convince most that at the least, although troublesome, Jesus was a sincere religious figure who taught truth and helped many,[129] and that therefore crucifying him was a great injustice. Believers in the divinity of Jesus will have a magnified sense of injustice, which

---

[129]Of course, opponents of Jesus had and have a different view. In terms of Jewish reaction through the centuries, except for the relatively few who came to believe in him, there were in the first millennium presentations of Jesus as illegitimate, a magician, one who seduced Israel by false teaching, and a blasphemous pretender to divinity. In recent centuries the portrait is kinder; e.g., he was well-intentioned but picked up wrong ideas from Gentiles (in Galilee); or he was a good teacher, but his disciples misinterpreted him (especially those disciples who had lived among Gentiles, as had Paul). Now some would argue that if Jesus came today, he could be accepted or tolerated among Jews because basically he was faithful to Judaism. (E. P. Sanders [who is not Jewish] holds that the Synoptic Jesus lived as a law-abiding Jew whose differences from others lay within the parameters of 1st-cent. legal debate [*Jewish Law* 90–96].) Others, however, like J. Neusner (*A Rabbi Talks with Jesus* [New York: Doubleday, 1993]), would regard some of Jesus' teaching as irreconcilable with the Torah revealed to Moses.

at times has been vocalized as deicide.[130] Since by their very nature the Gospels are meant to persuade (evangelize), the PNs will arouse resentment toward the perpetrators of the injustice. As for the Roman perpetrators, Rome ceased to function as a world power some fifteen hundred years ago, and so anger toward Pilate for having made a mockery of the vaunted Roman reverence for law and justice has no ongoing effects. Unto this day, however, the Jews as a people and Judaism as a religion have survived; and so the observation that factually Jewish authorities (and some of the Jerusalem crowds) had a role in the execution of Jesus—an execution that Christians and many nonChristians regard as unjust[131]—has had an enduring effect.

Very early the destruction of the Jerusalem Temple in AD 70 by the Romans was seen as divine retribution for what Jews had done to Jesus. Beyond that event, Matt 27:25 where "all the people" accept legal responsibility for the execution of Jesus ("His blood on us and on our children") has been interpreted to mean that Jews of later generations and even of all time are guilty and should be punished. Origen (*In Matt* 27:25; #124; GCS 38.260) was an early voice in a series of patristic statements that would grow in intensity: "Therefore the blood of Jesus came not only on those who existed at that time but also upon all generations of Jews who would follow afterwards till the endtime." Flannery's *Anguish of the Jews* is one of several books that document through centuries the many deeds and words directed against Jews because of the part their ancestors played in the crucifixion.[132] Some of the greatest names in Christian history (Augustine, Chrysostom,

---

[130]Melito of Sardis (ca. 170) would be one of the first to speak clearly of deicide: "God has been murdered; the King of Israel has been removed by an Israelite hand" (*On the Pasch* 96). E. Werner (HUCA 37 [1966], 191–210) places him in a chain with *The Gospel of Nicodemus* leading to the 7th-cent. Latin *Improperia*, or reproaches that God addresses to the Good Friday liturgical audiences over the crucifixion of Jesus; he believes that the *Improperia* have been malevolently shaped on the Jewish liturgical prayer *Dayenu*, which he would date to the 2d cent. BC.

[131]Jewish explanations of the actions of the Jewish authorities that led to crucifixion have varied according to the outlooks on Jesus listed in n. 129 above. When Jesus was looked on as an evil man, crucifixion (or at least death) was considered a just punishment, since the authorities were doing what the law required as punishment for a blasphemer or a seductive magician. When Jesus was looked on as misled or even good, the authorities were thought to have been forced by the Romans to do their bidding against one whom the Romans considered a revolutionary. I discussed above the relatively recent contention that there was no Jewish involvement.

[132]Also Kampling, *Blut*; Lapide, *Wer* 95–101. Note that I speak here of hostility toward the Jews on the basis of *the crucifixion*. In a total picture other contributing factors would need to be mentioned. For instance, there was a strong antiJudaism among pagans, and this was carried over when pagans became Christians in large numbers. See W. Klassen, "Anti-Judaism in Early Christianity," AJEC 1–19, esp. 1–6; M. Stern, *Greek and Latin Authors on Jews and Judaism* (3 vols.; Jerusalem: Israel Academy of Sciences and Humanity, 1974–84); J. N. Sevenster, *The Roots of Pagan Antisemitism in the Ancient World* (NovTSup 41; Leiden: Brill, 1975). In subsequent centuries there were economic, ethnic, and nationalistic components; and these have contributed to modern antisemitism. Hannah Arendt (*The Origins of Totalitarianism* [New York: Harcourt Brace, 1951], 9) states, "Modern antisemitism must be seen in the more general framework of the development of the nation-state." S.J.D. Cohen (*From the Maccabees to the Mishnah* [Philadelphia: Westminster, 1987], 47–48)

Aquinas, Luther, etc.) are quoted there as advocating with frightening feroc-
ity the right and even duty of Christians to dislike, hate, and punish the Jews.
In writing on responsibilities in the trial of Jesus, Leroux begins by referring
to a Zionist article published just after the foundation of the State of Israel
that declared: "The universal predisposition to antisemitism proceeds from
the accusation of deicide leveled against the Jewish people by the Christian
church."[133] As Leroux points out, whether or not one agrees with that historical judgment, both the suffering and sincerity behind it must be faced.[134]

Thinking Christians have come belatedly to recognize that an underlying
hostile attitude toward Jews because of the crucifixion is religiously unjustified and morally reprehensible. An indication of this realization found solemn expression at the Second Vatican Council: "What happened in Christ's
passion cannot be blamed without distinction upon all the Jews then living,
nor upon the Jews of today. Although the Church is the new people of God,
the Jews should not be presented as rejected or accursed by God, as if such
views followed from the Holy Scriptures."[135] To those Christians who had
long before reached such a conclusion this statement may have seemed obvious, but a very traditional Church was authoritatively and publicly contra-
dicting attitudes toward the Jews uttered by some of its most venerated Fathers and Doctors.

Quite rightly, however, there has been a continuing search to ameliorate
the situation and to block any recurrence of hatred of the Jews because of
the crucifixion. The most common effort is to insist that Jesus died for all or
for sins, and thus it is irrelevant to speak of Jewish responsibility or guilt.
Although such a salvific evaluation of the death of Jesus is good Christian
theology, it really does not deal with the historical situation. No matter what
good came out of the death of Jesus, some human beings put him to death;

---

points out that "antisemitism" is a term coined in Germany in the 19th cent. to bestow 'scientific'
respectability on hatred of the Jews by arguing that the Germans and the Jews belonged to different
species or races of humanity and that the ancients did not have anything resembling a racial theory.
Thus one should not use the term for the 1st-cent. situation.

[133]The reference he gives is *La Terre retrouvée* (April 1, 1947). Blinzler (*Trial* 4–5) comments
on the oversimplicity of the equation in this article since antisemitism (he means antiJudaism) existed before Christianity. Yet Blinzler does acknowledge (8): "The story of the passion of Jesus has
truly become a story of the suffering of Jewry; the Lord's Way of the Cross has become a *via dolorosa* of the Jewish people down the centuries."

[134]Leroux's own solutions are not satisfactory, in my judgment. He quite rightly points out that
antisemitisim is complicated and that much of it is not rooted in the NT accounts of the passion
(n. 132 above). Nevertheless, drawing on Jewish traditions and taking the NT pictures at face value
he attributes to Annas, Caiaphas and their partisans not only responsiblity for the death of Jesus but
a "secret sinful tendency" (117), namely, malice and pride which tends of its own drive to suppress
God; "its basic tendency is deicide." How does Leroux know all this? Even the NT with its picture
of the scheming high priests does not go into their relationship to God and their own consciences.

[135]*Nostra aetate* ("Declaration on the Relationship of the Church to Non-Christian Religions,"
approved Oct. 28, 1965), 4.

and the issue of their responsibility and/or guilt remains. Another path has been to deny that there was any Jewish participation in the crucifixion.[136] My judgment, as explained in the preceding subsection (and with more detail in the commentary below), is that historical evidence does not warrant this thesis. Accordingly I think it is required of me to discuss the ways (some of them strongly antiJewish) in which the Gospels have described the Jewish role in the death of Jesus, and then to offer some observations that may help readers to deal constructively with that role.

Frankly, some have advised me against devoting even these few pages to the issue. They have warned me that whatever I write will be dismissed as Christian self-justification or as inadequate. I would do better, they tell me, to treat the antiJewish issue as I treated the implications of the passion for Christian spirituality and for the systematic theology of the redemption, namely, as very important subjects that lie outside the scope of a book dedicated to commenting on what the Gospels report. I know that what I write below is inadequate. Given the history of antisemitism in the 20th cent., even whole books devoted to two millennia of antiJewish attitudes derived from the PNs are inadequate. And in a real way the subject does lie beyond the scope of this book. Yet since I am a Christian commentator, readers are likely to trust my affirmation that I am sincerely interested in the spiritual implications of the passion and its import for the theology of the redemption, even though those topics lie outside the task of my commentary. NonChristians need more tangible evidence that a Christian commentator is aware of and concerned about the harmful way in which the PNs have been misused against Jews; and Christian readers need to be forcefully reminded of hostile elements in their own reading of the PNs. As for Christian self-justification, these remarks are aimed only at intelligibility. I would not dare to justify or condemn the attitudes either of 1st-cent. Christians or of their opponents, about whose motives and consciences we are ill informed. However, if we can more clearly perceive and understand those 1st-cent. attitudes, we may be able to judge our own attitudes and self-justifications.

1. AntiJudaism in the Passion Narratives of the Four Gospels

At the end of E above, I described what all the Gospels agree on: Because they disliked Jesus and what he did and said, Sanhedrin authorities were

---

[136]Sobosan ("Trial") provides an interesting survey of proposed interpretations that would exonerate historically the Jewish authorities and/or the Jewish crowds of participating in the death of Jesus. In the course of the commentary every one of them will be examined. Maier ("Who Killed" 17) complains about the wild swing of the pendulum from illogically blaming Jews of all times for the death of Jesus to implausibly denying all Jewish involvement. Such a swing bypasses the most

involved in seizing him and giving him over to the Romans to be put to death. However, the Gospels differ in the degree of malevolence attributed to these authorities and the way in which they are representative of or associated with the people ("the Jews"). Undoubtedly the context in which each evangelist wrote and the amount of conflict with synagogues experienced by him or his Christian community have influenced the presentation.

Mark shows the chief priests and the scribes determined on the death of Jesus and willing to give Judas money for the opportunity of accomplishing this without a disturbance among the people (14:1–2, 10–11). They seek testimony against Jesus; but when it proves false and inconsistent, they condemn him for blasphemy on the basis of his own words[137] and give him over to Pilate (14:65–66; 15:1). While that portrayal is highly unsympathetic, it is primarily one of fanatical intolerance rather than of hypocrisy or of knowingly rejecting God. The chief priests anticipate that the people might be an obstacle to their plans, and the crowd present at the Roman trial has to be won over to prefer Barabbas to Jesus (15:11). Although from that moment on the crowd is hostile in calling for Jesus' crucifixion, and passersby blaspheme him on the cross, there is no emphatic or sweeping antiJudaism. Nor is there a tremendous contrast with Roman behavior. Pilate realizes that "the King of the Jews" issue does not really fit Jesus and that he was given over out of Jewish zeal and intrareligious fighting; yet Pilate yields to the cries of the crowd without much resistance (15:10,15). One gets the impression that the Marcan Jesus receives just treatment from no one in authority.[138]

---

plausible thesis, namely, involvement by some. The debate between Sizoo and Ernest on "Did the Jews Kill Jesus?" is, in my judgment, not only unhappily phrased but also unhappily reasoned. Sizoo argues that most Jews loved Jesus, so that only a few politicians of the Sanhedrin were involved in his being killed by Pilate. Ernest says that the many cannot be excused if they allowed the few to perpetrate a crime, even as the mass of Germans cannot be excused for having allowed Hitler to do what he did.

[137]The Sanhedrists in Mark (and even more clearly in Matt) spit on Jesus, slap him, and mock his ability to prophesy. In Israelite law witnesses are to be the first to cast a stone against the condemned, and the Sanhedrists have been called on to witness Jesus' blasphemy; that principle might lend justification to the procedure. I doubt, however, that the readers of Mark (or even of Matt) are expected to know such a fine point, and so this brutality would add to the image of fanatical dislike of Jesus.

[138]My overall evaluation of Mark's PN on the score of antiJudaism differs from that of C. P. Anderson, "Trial," who deals with blasphemy and polemic in Mark's Gospel. In large part that is because I am reading the impression made by the account as it now stands, while Anderson is evaluating it on the basis of presuppositions about the origins and historical value of Mark's account: e.g., that the sanctuary saying came to Mark by way of antiChristian polemic, that Rivkin's reconstructions of the role of Sanhedrin and Boulē are correct, that Mark created the Jewish trial scene (without analyzing how much ancient tradition might have been reshaped). Readers will discover that I think those are very dubious presuppositions. Moreover, I reject Anderson's thesis that would drive a wedge between the PNs as accounts of the trial of Jesus and the PNs as accounts of Christian reactions to Jews and Romans at the time of Gospel writing. The second stage has influenced the portrayal of the first, but one must respect the important influence of preGospel evidence about what happened to Jesus.

Matt. There is increased and widened malevolence in Matt's picture of Jewish involvement in the death of Jesus.[139] Picking up what was at most a Marcan implication, Matt 26:59 has the chief priests and the whole Sanhedrin "seeking *false* testimony against Jesus." When Judas tries to return the thirty pieces of silver, the chief priests and elders say, "What is that to us?" Having been told it is the price of innocent blood, they cynically observe the law against putting blood money in the Temple treasury by purchasing a potter's field (27:3–10). Because of a dream revelation, Pilate's wife can tell him that Jesus is a just man; and Pilate washes his hands to show that he is innocent of the blood of this man (27:19, 24). Although that action demonstrates that a hitherto uninformed Gentile will recognize Jesus' innocence while the scheming Jewish authorities blind themselves to it, it scarcely exculpates the Roman governor; for Pilate still gives over to be crucified a man who he knows is innocent. Besides portraying the Jewish authorities as dishonest and thoroughly malevolent, Matt broadens the blame, since "all the people" take the legal responsibility for condemning Jesus to death: "His blood on us and on our children" (27:25). As I shall explain in §35, this is not a bloodthirsty cry or a self-curse, but an affirmation that despite Pilate's judgment of innocence, they regard Jesus as guilty and are willing to be responsible before God for the shedding of his blood. Unlike the authorities, "all the people" are not dishonest, but in Matt's judgment they have cooperated and are held responsible. The antiJewish tone continues after Jesus' death (27:62–66; 28:2–4,11–15). The chief priests and the Pharisees obtain a Roman custodial guard to counteract the promised resurrection on the third day; and when the guards are overpowered by the events surrounding the resurrection, the chief priests and the elders give them money to lie that the body was stolen. This lying word that Jesus' body was stolen has been spread about "among the Jews" to this day. One gets the impression that all the Jews are against Jesus, but have been lied to by their malevolent leaders. The "to this day" implies that the antiJudaism in Matt's portrayal of the trial and death of Jesus has been influenced by the current situation, with his

---

[139]See the articles of Buck and Przybylski, and on a larger scale Overman's *Matthew's Gospel* (p. 101 above). Unfortunately Buck, in usefully listing the peculiarly Matthean antiJewish touches that go beyond Mark, dismisses too easily all passion historicity in them on the assumption that they all reflect the Matthean life situation. Why is it inconceivable that since Matt's community was in conflict with the synagogue, Matt preserved earlier elements of hostility that were of no interest to Mark? Millar ("Reflections" 357) wisely cautions that all the Gospels derive from "an environment in which the *concerns* of pre-70 Jewish society were still significant, whether we think of the High Priests and 'the Sanhedrin', of Pharisees and Sadducees." Przybylski argues against using the anti-Jewish elements to support the thesis of Clark, Nepper-Christensen, Strecker, and Trilling that the evangelist was a Gentile. Matt's roots are Jewish-Christian, separated from the synagogue but not geographically remote; the antiJudaism reflects a church retaining elements of what was once an internal Jewish debate, in order to define itself against the synagogue.

depiction of the Jewish authorities of Jesus' time colored by a dislike for Pharisaic synagogue authorities who were active when Matt was writing.

Luke. Diagnosing the extent to which Luke's PN is antiJewish is complicated and has produced an abundant literature.[140] On the one hand, Winter and others have preferred Luke's account of the Jewish trial in which there are no false witnesses and apparently no condemnatory sentence as more original and a proof of a less antiJewish stage of early Christian thought. Others, while attributing this difference to Luke's editing of the Marcan scene, have added to the picture his more favorable portrayal of the role of the Jewish people in the crucifixion. As I pointed out in §1C under "Luke," he alone among the evangelists describes a Jewish group who during the crucifixion are on Jesus' side: A multitude of people accompany Jesus to the place of execution and return beating their breasts, and the "Daughters of Jerusalem" beat themselves and lament for Jesus (23:27–28, 48). Another group of scholars have a diametrically opposite interpretation. They point out (correctly, in my judgment) that Luke has moved the false witnesses to the trial of Stephen (Acts 6:12–14); moreover, scattered statements show that Luke thought that the Jewish authorities condemned Jesus to death and that elements of the Jewish population shared in responsibility for the crucifixion,[141] even if they acted in ignorance. I shall enter into this issue in appropriate sections of the commentary below, but I find particularly exaggerated Walaskay's interpretation of Luke's antiJudaism. He describes Luke's Sanhedrin interrogation of Jesus as "the chaotic prelude to a lynching which even Roman jurisprudence could not overcome"! Compared to Mark's account, at most Luke's account would give the impression of a less formal Jewish legal procedure.[142] If there is antiJudaism in the *Gospel,* readers would find

[140]Under §3, Part 4, see the writings of Brawley, Carlson, Cassidy ("Trial"), Chance, Gaston, Kodell, Matera ("Responsibility"), Rice, Richard, Tyson, Via, and Walaskay. A judicious overview beyond the issue of the Lucan passion is supplied by M. Rese, "'Die Juden' im lukanischen Doppelwerk," in *Der Treue Gottes trauen. Beiträge zum Werk des Lukas,* eds. C. Bussman and W. Radl (G. Schneider Festschrift; Freiburg: Herder, 1991), 61–79.

[141]Via ("According" 141) is correct in her analysis of Luke's texts: "That the Jewish people as a whole were in *no* way involved in Jesus' death simply does not stand up in light of the evidence of these passages." See esp. Acts 13:27–28, where *krinein* involves a negative judgment against him, pace Harvey, *Jesus . . . Constraints,* 174–75, who would ignore the context and reduce the verb to a neutral "made a decision." Catchpole (*Trial* 183–89) is helpful in showing what not to conclude from comparing Luke's Jewish interrogation to Mark's Jewish trial.

[142]At times I shall speak of an "interrogation" of Jesus in Luke to do justice to this less formal situation, but I do not thereby imply agreement with the thesis that Luke (or his putative source) intended to convey there was really no Jewish trial of Jesus. Tyson, "Lukan" 254, and Matera, "Trial" 7–8, think that; Müller ("Jesus" 124) contends that Luke changed Mark because he had a more realistic view of the competence of the Sanhedrin; and Bickermann ("Utilitas" 202) would argue that in Luke's mind the Sanhedrin did not function here as a court. Yet Catchpole (*Trial* 202) is more persuasive in arguing that Luke thinks of the Jewish procedure as a trial. In 22:66 there is brought together "the assembly of the elders [*presbyterion*] of the people"; the venue involves a movement "to their Sanhedrin [hall]"; in 22:71 "testimony" is mentioned; in 23:50–51 the body that judged

it in the Roman trial, where a charge reported by the Jewish accusers such as "forbidding the giving of taxes to Caesar" is patently false (granted 20:21–25), and where, despite the judgments of Pilate (reiterated) and of Herod that Jesus is not guilty, the chief priests, rulers, and people press for a death sentence. The primary motive in this portrayal is not the exculpation of the Romans;[143] rather we learn from the examples of Pilate, Herod,[144] the wrongdoer on the cross, and the centurion that anyone (Jew or Gentile) who judges in an unprejudiced manner could immediately see that Jesus was a just man.

There can be no doubt that a series of passages in Acts hardens the picture of Jewish involvement in the death of Jesus,[145] even as increasing Jewish hostility to the Christian preaching is portrayed, culminating in a harsh evaluation of the future of all mission to the Jews, using Isaian language: They shall never understand or perceive (Acts 28:25–28). Part of the solution probably lies in an evolving evaluation of the situation. Luke's understanding is that the Jewish role in the death of Jesus was serious but able to be forgiven if they accepted apostolic preaching. Their refusal to do so and their harsh treatment of figures like Peter, John, Stephen, James (brother of John), and Paul magnified the element of malevolence in what they contributed to the crucifixion of Jesus. Nevertheless, as Matera ("Responsibility" 89) points out, this more somber picture in Acts is not presented for the purpose of denigrating the Jews; in a missionary context it is intended to summon people (Gentiles) to the repentance necessary to accept the Gospel.

John. Struggle with Jerusalem authorities, synagogue authorities, and simply "the Jews" marks the whole Gospel of John, so that the antiJewish picture in the PN[146] does not change or startlingly magnify the hostility that Jesus has hitherto encountered and provoked. If one works within the confines of the PN, by comparison to Mark's account of the Sanhedrin trial, John's picture of an interrogation by Annas is mild. But in 11:47–53 John has already shown us the chief priests and the Pharisees cynically deciding

---

Jesus is referred to as a Boulē that had taken a decision or course of action (or had judged: Acts 13:27).

[143]Acts 2:23 seemingly designates the Romans as lawless, and Acts 4:25–28 has Pilate and the Gentile Romans raging against Jesus.

[144]Walaskay sees Luke's introduction of Herod into the Roman trial as an antiJewish feature, despite 23:14–15 where Pilate states that Herod found Jesus not guilty of the proffered charges. As for Luke's attitude toward the Romans, Cassidy and Via, despite their disagreements, agree that Luke was not interested in depicting Jesus as loyal to Rome or in praising Rome (see 21:12–16; 22:25–26; Acts 4:25–27). Via ("According" 138–39) puts her finger on the precise goal: Neither Jesus nor his disciples should be thought guilty of a crime against the Roman government or of anything deserving imprisonment or death.

[145]Acts 2:23,36; 3:13–17; 4:10,25–28; 5:30; 7:52; 10:39; 13:27–29. Going beyond the idea condemning Jesus, some of these texts have the Jews killing him.

[146]On this topic see the article by Granskou in §3, Part 5.

on the death of Jesus to avert danger to "the place [Temple] and the nation." A more theological reason will be offered by "the Jews" in 19:7: "According to the law he ought to die because he has made himself God's Son." Pilate's statements that he finds no case against Jesus are not meant to exculpate the Romans. Quite the contrary, the Johannine Pilate is meant to typify the person who tries to avoid deciding between truth and falsehood and who, in failing to decide for truth, in effect decides for falsehood. This Roman is not "of the truth," for he fails to hear the voice of Jesus (18:37c). His hesitation, however, culminates in a very antiJewish scene where the chief priests deny the messianic hopes of their people in order to obtain Jesus' death: "We have no king but Caesar" (19:15b). The malevolence continues when the "chief priests of the Jews" try to get Pilate to change the title on the cross that proclaims Jesus to be "the King of the Jews" (19:21–22); and even after Jesus' death some would find implicit malice in the request of "the Jews" to Pilate to have the legs broken (19:31), since that would disfigure Jesus' body. The appearance of the risen Jesus will be in an atmosphere of "fear of the Jews" (20:19).

I have attempted to give a sober presentation of the extent to which each Gospel PN gives an antiJewish picture of the Sanhedrin authorities and/or of a larger group of the people or "the Jews." The following observations are intended as at least a small contribution (especially to those who treasure the Gospels) in reflecting on such a portrayal, which involves not only the relations between Jesus and some major leaders of his people, but the relations in the last third of the 1st cent. between those who believed in Jesus and Jews who did not—and indeed even relations between Christians and Jews today.

2. Observations about Jewish Involvement in the Death of Jesus

(a) *One must understand that religious people could have disliked Jesus.* For different reasons some Christians and Jews have argued that one can settle the question of Jewish involvement by allowing that a few priests and nobles conspired with the Romans to have Jesus put to death. Beyond that Jesus' death had nothing to do with Judaism. Obviously early Christian preachers like Paul thought differently: Christ crucified was proclaimed to be a stumbling block to the Jews (I Cor 1:23) and the rejection of Christ a major stumbling of Israel (Rom 9–11). To reflect on such a difference of thought, let us leave aside the issue of whether it is a historically correct evaluation that only a negligible and irresponsible few in Judaism were involved and deal with a more fundamental question: If Jesus was the kind of person described in the Gospels, could he have presented an offense of such a magnitude that an official Jewish religious body would judge him to be intolerable?[147] Christians think of Jesus as an ideally noble figure, caring for the sick, reaching out to the poor and outcast, rejecting hypocrisy, and preaching love. How then could Jewish authorities have handed Jesus over to the Romans to be crucified? A traditional Christian answer has been that these authorities were not truly religious but were hypocrites, or political sycophants, or intolerant ultra-legalists, and so did not hesitate to be callously brutal. That answer is not satisfactory, even though in most "religious" groups there are usually some who would fit all those descriptions. Historically we know of teachers and leaders in the Judaism of Jesus' time who were genuinely religious. Rather than blaming the authorities, one must reflect more carefully on the reaction produced by Jesus, a sharply challenging figure who could not always have been received sympathetically even by the truly religious. On the one hand, Jesus is portrayed as consorting frequently and pleasantly with public sinners who take no offense at him. On the other hand, he criticizes scathingly a religious outlook that many would judge laudable, e.g., condemning as unjustified before God a Pharisee who has taken care not to break the commandments, who observes pious practices and prays, and who is generous to religious causes (Luke 18:11–14). To the accumulated teaching of his era Jesus at times offers a sovereign challenge, the sole authority for which seems to be his claim that he can speak for God. If one takes the Gospels at face value (and even if one examines them through the microscope of historical criticism), there emerges a Jesus capable of generating intense dislike.[148] Indeed, that is the usual result of asking self-consciously religious people to change their minds (which is what is meant literally by *metanoia*). Those Christians who see Jesus as offensive only in the context of (what they think of as) legalistic Judaism fail to grasp that mutatis mutandis, he would be offensive on any religious scene if he told people that God wants something different from what they know and have long striven to do, and if he

---

[147]Lindeskog ("Prozess" 329, 333–36), citing the issue raised by S. Ben Chorin, is helpful on this point.

[148]Kamelský ("Über") would argue that the Jewish authorities had a duty to put Jesus to death. Jesus had prophesied that he would be given over to the Gentiles, put to death, and raised after three days. If he was a false prophet, he had to be put to death according to Deut 18:20–22; if by any chance he was speaking God's word, they would be responsive by giving him over to the Gentiles, who would put him to death and thus supply God with the opportunity to raise him up. As we shall see in APPENDIX VIII, the historicity of such an exact prophetic prediction is hard to verify. (Kamelský rejects all such objections by making no distinction between Jesus' historical career and that described in the Gospels, despite their diversities!) Moreover (see §23), the evidence that Jesus was condemned as a false prophet according to Deut is relatively late in the attested 1st-cent. tradition, and there is no historical evidence that any of the authorities were waiting to see if he would be verified by being raised from the dead.

challenged established sacred teaching on his own authority as self-designated spokesman for God.

Besnier ("Procés" 191) relates that on April 25, 1933, at 2:00 PM there was enacted a retrial in the case of Jesus of Nazareth by a special tribunal in Jerusalem.[149] The vote of the judges was four to one for innocence. This vote may tell us that modern judges, to their credit, would be more sensitive about legal niceties (although I have indicated above that the procedure against Jesus was *not* clearly illegal by the detectable standards of his time). However, if the retrial was meant to have religious implications, the result is not in agreement with the import of the Gospels (even though the evangelists also thought Jesus innocent). The Gospel portrait implies that Jesus would be found guilty by the self-conscious religious majority of any age and background. More than likely, however, were Jesus to appear in our time (with his challenge rephrased in terms of contemporary religious stances) and be arrested and tried again, most of those finding him guilty would identify themselves as Christians and think they were rejecting an impostor—someone who claimed to be Jesus but did not fit into their conception of who Jesus Christ was and how he ought to act. To use Johannine language, if the Word became flesh again, the Prologue would still be true: "He came unto his own, and his own did not accept him" (John 1:11). The makeup of "his own" would be different.

(b) *In Jesus' time religious opposition often led to violence.* I have just suggested that Jesus could be found guilty by sincerely religious people in any era; but whether or not the guilty verdict would involve a death sentence would depend on how seriously religious issues were taken at the time, and on the civil law's attitude toward death penalties. In the First World today governments restrict sharply public expressions of religious antagonism, and religious tolerance of others is deemed a virtue by many who themselves have strong religious convictions about the rightness of their own views. That makes it difficult for modern readers to understand the religious mindset of the 1st cent. Often the writings of the NT are considered strongly antiJewish; but as Johnson ("New Testament's") has shown, if we look to the historical and social context of the time and situate the NT among religious and philosophical writings, its attacks on the Jews are surprisingly

---

[149]Blinzler (*Trial* 4) warns, however, of great uncertainty about the date and details of this affair. There have been other attempted legal reevaluations. Blinzler (*Trial* 3) and Haufe ("Prozess" 93) recount that in spring 1949, scarcely twelve months after the founding of the State of Israel, a Dutch jurist, known simply as H. 187, presented a fifteen-page brief to the Israeli Ministry of Justice requesting the reconsideration of the trial of Jesus. Blinzler (*Trial* 4) reports that in the same year members of the Faculty of Law of the University of Paris reexamined this trial and found that because of a technical error the death sentence passed on Jesus appeared to lack legal validity. Lapide ("Wer" 93) reports another request for retrial in 1974.

mild. Beyond polemic, however, parallels suggest that truly religious Jews of the 1st cent. in their opposition to Jesus could have gone to the extreme of wanting him dead. Evidence for the period 130 BC to AD 70 shows irrefutably that Jews hated and killed one another over religious issues (sometimes admixed with self-interest, as religious issues frequently are).

Let me list some examples from Jewish sources like Josephus and the DSS. High priests (perhaps representative of the *Sadducees*) were responsible for many violent deeds. Probably in the late 2d cent. BC an unnamed high priest sought the death of the Essene Teacher of Righteousness on the Day of Atonement celebrated on a date peculiar to the Essene calendar;[150] in 128 BC John Hyrcanus destroyed the sanctuary of the Samaritans on Mt. Gerizim where the Hebrew patriarchs had worshiped God (*Ant.* 13.9.1; #255–56); a few decades later Alexander Jannaeus massacred 6,000 Jews at the feast of Tabernacles over a challenge (by Pharisees?) to his legal qualifications to hold the priestly office (*War* 1.4.3; #88–89; *Ant.* 13.13.5; #372–73); later he crucified 800 (seemingly including Pharisees) while their wives and children were butchered before their eyes (*War* 1.4.6; #97; 1.5.3; #113; *Ant.* 13.14.2; #380); and in AD 62–63 Ananus II together with the Sanhedrin executed James the brother of Jesus and others for transgressing the Law of Moses (*Ant.* 20.9.1; #200). In the early 60s (AD) leading Jews in Jerusalem (probably elders and priests) sought to have the Romans kill the prophetic Jesus son of Ananias because he proclaimed doom for the city and the sanctuary (*War* 6.5.3; #300–9). In the period 135–67 BC *Pharisees* incited hatred among the masses against the high priests John Hyrcanus (*Ant.* 13.10.5–6; #288, 296) and Alexander Jannaeus (*Ant.* 13.15.5; #402); and, once let loose on their enemies by the Jewish queen Salome Alexandra, they executed and exiled their religious/political enemies (*Ant.* 13.16.2; #410–11). Later, religious teachers (presumably Pharisees) urged youths to pull down the eagle which Herod the Great placed above the Temple gate, even if they had to die for observing the law against graven images (*War* 1.33.2; #648–50).[151] The Dead Sea Scroll writers, presumably *Essenes,* railed against the (Sadducee?) hierarchy in Jerusalem, condemning them as wicked priests who broke the commandments, criticizing one as "the furious young lion . . . who hangs

---

[150] 1QpHab 11:2–8. E. P. Sanders, in his partly necessary but partly overdone effort not to exaggerate the lethal character of Jewish disputes (e.g., over points of the Law), states that after that the Essenes lived in peace (*Jewish Law* 85). We do not know that, for our accounts of DSS Essene existence derived from commentaries on the prophets are not consecutive; and we have only a limited section of the DSS library. From the fact that Essenes composed a letter (was it sent?) to the Jerusalem high priest about differences of cultic law (4QMMT) Sanders argues that the relations were somewhat amicable! Extremely hostile relations between groups can allow one document that has the appearance of reasoned dissent.

[151] Sanders, *Jewish Law* 87–88, lists rabbinic accounts of strong intraPharisee disputes of this general period.

men alive" (4QpNah 1.5–6) and another as a scoffer and liar who persecuted the backsliders (seemingly the Pharisees; CD 1.14–21). I realize that most of these incidents and attitudes belong to the period before the Roman prefecture in Judea. That temporal distribution, however, means that the Romans put restraints on internecine religious behavior, not necessarily that the attitudes had changed. Indeed, with the outbreak of the First Revolt and the loss of Roman control in AD 66, fierce fights among Jewish factions broke out, fights where religious idealism was mixed with visions of how God's people should be ruled.[152] In such a context of hostile interJewish feelings, how can one dismiss as unthinkable a desire on the part of some fellow Jews for severe action against Jesus, a troubling religious figure, and eventually against those in Judaism who came to accept him? Lest anyone think that this paragraph written by a Christian is a covert attempt to deprecate Judaism, let me acknowledge clearly that Christians, motivated by the "love" of God and the defense of "truth," have matched or surpassed in intensity such religious hostility during two millennia of hating and killing fellow Christians.

(c) *Responsibility, not guilt.* In discussing developments traceable within the Gospel PNs, scholars have spoken of a tendency "to exculpate the Romans and inculpate the Jews"—in other words, to make the Jews more guilty or blameworthy than they actually were. I would urge that we use the term "guilty" with great care in referring historically to the crucifixion.[153] According to later Jewish records the high priesthood of the period during which Jesus lived was not of high moral quality. It is perfectly possible that in a Sanhedrin that had been called together to consider Jesus, some may have decided to effect his death on the basis of their own self-interest and without real religious concerns. For them "culpable" or "guilty" may be an appropriate adjective, even if only on the level of their callous treatment of a human being. But for those (surely the majority) who thought they were rendering service to God in prosecuting Jesus,[154] it is far better to speak of "responsibility" for Jesus' death. At any time and in any place those who contribute to the execution of an accused are responsible for that death; they

---

[152]An important contribution of rabbinic Judaism of the post-70 era was to have moved away from the more vicious forms of sectarianism, so that important religious issues became a matter for judicial debate rather than for violence.

[153]I find Haufe ("Prozess" 97) a particularly extravagant example of interpreting everything in the Roman trial as a Christian attempt to remove responsibility from Pilate (including features with parallels thirty years later in the treatment of Jesus bar Ananias by a Roman procurator!). Yet (p. 101) he is correct in urging that "guilt" be dropped from Christian consideration of the Jewish role.

[154]See John 16:2 for a begrudging Christian recognition that this attitude existed among Jews. Herranz Marco ("Proceso" 85–92) argues that the recognition in Mark 15:10 that the chief priests had given Jesus over to the Romans out of *phthonos* refers to their zeal for the Law.

are guilty only if they know that the accused is undeserving of such punishment or have been negligent in discerning innocence.

(d) *The religious dispute with Jesus was an inner Jewish dispute.* The Gospel accounts of the passion have been made particularly inflammatory by a reading that has "those Jews" doing violence to "Jesus, the Christian." It is true that in the PNs of Matt and John, written after 70, "the Jews" appear as an alien group over against Jesus; but on the level of history Jews were dealing with a fellow Jew.

The import of that becomes clear when we study a parallel that had occurred six centuries earlier. The prophet Jeremiah was a just man and a spokesman for God, but also a disturbing challenger of the religious structures of his time. In particular, his warning "Reform your ways" lest God bring about the destruction of the Jerusalem Temple ("a den of thieves"), even as God had destroyed the Shiloh tabernacle (Jer 7:1–15), won Jeremiah the lethal enmity of the authorities of Judea. Priests and (false) prophets tried to persuade the people that Jeremiah deserved death, although Jeremiah warned them that his innocent blood would be on them (26:1–15). The wealthy nobles tried to persuade the king to execute him, and the king put Jeremiah into their hands (38:1–5). Although he did not perish at that moment, in later times the destruction of the Jerusalem Temple was seen by some as God's vindication of Jeremiah; and in apocryphal tradition Jeremiah was ultimately killed by his fellow Jews.

Both Jews and Christians read the story of Jeremiah as Scripture. Jewish leaders persecuted Jeremiah; yet, even though the language of blood guilt appears in the account, no one suggests that the blood of Jeremiah needs to be avenged. Rather for both Jews and Christians Jeremiah is an outstanding example of the innocent just one made to suffer by the leaders of God's own people; and the prophet's sufferings offer the opportunity for self-examination on what *we* who consider ourselves God's people do to *our* prophets whom God raises up among us. Although much the same story is told of Jesus (with a pagan governor in place of a Jewish king as the one who ultimately decides), the case is emotionally different because those who thought that Jesus was right ultimately became another religion. Jews and Christians were not able to say in this instance that one of *our* own whom God raised up was made to suffer by *our* leaders. Rather Christians spoke to Jews of *your* leaders doing this to our savior, while for Jews (in centuries past) it was our leaders doing this to *their* (false) prophet.[155] Perhaps the "our," "your," and "their" outlook cannot be overcome, but it will help

---

[155]Notice that I have spoken in one instance of "your" and in the other of "their." Christian evangelism over the centuries has forced on Jews direct debate about the crucifixion because it was an issue of importance for Christians. Jews have not looked on the issue as of key Jewish importance,

readers of this commentary if they can remember that it was not thus when the crucifixion was taking place and even when the story was first taking shape.

(Bibliography for A to E of this section may be found in §17, Part 1; bibliography for F may be found in §17, part 2.)

---

and until recent times Jewish writing about the crucifixion has often been for inner consumption by way of (explicit or implicit) comment on Christian accusations.

§19. TRANSITIONAL EPISODE: JESUS TRANSFERRED TO THE JEWISH AUTHORITIES; INTERROGATED BY ANNAS

(Mark 14:53–54; Matt 26:57–58; Luke 22:54–55; John 18:12–25a)

Translation

Mark 14:53–54: [53]And they led Jesus away to the high priest, and there (now) come together all the chief priests, and the elders, and the scribes. [54]And Peter followed him from a distance until inside the court of the high priest, and he was seated together with the attendants and warming himself near the blazing flame.

Matt 26:57–58: [57]And having seized Jesus, they led him away to Caiaphas the high priest where the scribes and the elders were brought together. [58]But Peter was following him from a distance until the court(yard) of the high priest; and having entered inside, he sat with the attendants to see the end.

Luke 22:54–55: [54]But having taken (him), they led and brought him into the house of the high priest, but Peter was following at a distance. [55]But when they had kindled a fire in the middle of the court and had sat down together, Peter sat down in their midst.

John 18:12–25a: [12]Thereupon the cohort and the tribune and the attendants of the Jews took Jesus and bound him. [13]And they led (him) first to Annas, for he was father-in-law of Caiaphas who was high priest that year. ([14]Now Caiaphas was the one who had advised the Jews that "It is better that one man die for the people.") [15]But following Jesus was Simon Peter and another disciple. But that disciple was known to the high priest, and he entered together with Jesus into the court of the high priest. [16]But Peter was standing at the gate outside. Accordingly the other disciple, the one known to the high priest, came out and spoke to the gatekeeper and brought Peter in. [17]And so the servant woman, the gatekeeper, says to Peter,

"Are you too one of the disciples of this man?" He says, "I am not." [18]But the servants and the attendants were standing around, having made a charcoal fire because it was cold; and they were warming themselves. But Peter too was with them, standing and warming himself.

[19]Thereupon the high priest questioned Jesus about his disciples and about his teaching. [20]Jesus answered him, "I have spoken openly to the world. I always taught in a synagogue and in the Temple, where all the Jews come together; and in secret I spoke nothing. [21]Why do you question me? Question those who have heard what I spoke to them. Behold these know what I said."

[22]But when he had said these things, one of the attendants who was standing by gave Jesus a slap, saying, "In such a way do you answer the high priest?" [23]Jesus answered him, "If I have spoken badly, give testimony about what is bad. If (I have spoken) well, why do you beat me?"

[24]Thereupon Annas sent him bound to Caiaphas the high priest. [25a]But Simon Peter was standing there and warming himself.

COMMENT

We turn now to a detailed treatment of the PN scene where Jesus is brought for interrogation or trial before the authorities of his people—obviously a dramatic moment in all the Gospels.[1] The Mark and Matt sequence is roughly the same (with the exception of Matt's additional episode where Judas returns the silver to the chief priests). While Luke has much of the same material, his sharply different sequence exhibits considerable rearrangement. (I shall try consistently to remind the reader of the Lucan thought-flow, although overall treatment follows the Marcan sequence.) John's content is quite different in the Jewish interrogation of Jesus, even if the material pertinent to Peter's denials is roughly the same as that of the Synoptics. The divergences among the Gospels as to the content and se-

[1]The episodes on the Mount of Olives consisted of 27 verses in Mark; the episodes before the Jewish authorities consist of 21; in Matt the ratio is 27 to 29; in Luke 15 to 19; in John 11 to 17. Of the verses each Gospel allots to the latter, about 7 or 8 concern the denials by Peter.

quence of the trial/interrogation raise important questions to be treated in the ANALYSIS of this section; the historicity of the elements of the Sanhedrin trial will be treated in later sections.

The present episode is clearly transitional, although in John the transition cannot be distinguished from what happens before the high priest Annas. The inevitable denouement of the arrest of Jesus on the Mount of Olives is that he must come before those who had him seized, especially the chief priests, so that the theological cause of their hostility toward him can be made clear and his fate sealed. In Mark 14:10 Judas contracted to give Jesus over to the chief priests, and this episode fulfills the contract exactly. Prominent in all the narratives of the arrest was "the servant of the high priest"; not surprisingly it is to the dwelling of the high priest that the arrested Jesus is brought. In three Gospels the flight or dismissal of the disciples, predicted by Jesus, was a result of the arrest. Now the scene is set for the threefold denial by Peter, also predicted by Jesus. The subdivisions of the COMMENT on this episode are outlined on p. 312 above.

DETAILS OF THE TRANSFER

While the material that opens the scene is remarkably similar in the four Gospels, each evangelist has left his own stylistic marks on the initial verses. In each the first verse is a connective to what has preceded, employing an appropriate particle (Mark/Matt: *kai,* "and"; Luke: *de,* "but"; John: *oun,* "thereupon"). In the Synoptic Gospels it is presumed that the reader knows who the "they" are who lead Jesus away. Yet one must go back ten verses to find that the "they" are the crowd who in Mark 14:43 and Matt 26:47 came with swords and clubs. Luke has a closer antecedent but one that shows the awkward effects of his editing. While in 22:47 (parallel to Mark 14:43) Luke too mentioned a crowd, those whom Mark identified as the authorizers of the crowd were brought in Luke 22:52 to the Mount of Olives to face Jesus and were described as the chief priests, the captains of the Temple, and the elders. These are the logical antecedents for the "they" of 22:54. Perhaps one could imagine the chief priests physically taking possession of Jesus and bringing him along to the house of the high priest, but the thought that then this Lucan "they" kindled a fire and sat down with Peter in the middle of the court (22:55) is a bit much.[2] John is clear as to who takes Jesus to the high priest (Annas). In 18:3 we were told that Judas came with "the cohort" and (from the chief priests and the Pharisees) "attendants"—implicitly Roman

---

[2]Not only in this way did Luke's writing skill lapse in 22:52; see Fitzmyer (*Luke* 2.1464) for the careless grammar and inexact use of verbs here, an awkwardness producing in the textual witnesses a spate of scribal improvements.

and Jewish soldiers/police. Here (18:12) John speaks of "the cohort and the tribune" (clearly Roman) and "the attendants of the Jews."

In the midst of the arrest scene, Matt 14:46 and Matt 26:50 reported that the arresting party "laid hands on him [Jesus] and seized [*kratein*] him." As we begin the present scene, Matt 26:57 reminds us that Jesus has been seized, a repetition that may reflect the evangelist's unease about having Jesus constrained through all the activity of 26:51–56. (It may also help to clarify the antecedent of the "they": As I mentioned in the preceding paragraph the antecedent is the crowd that came in 26:47 and that *seized* Jesus in 26:50.) In Luke and John, Jesus has remained unshackled throughout the arrest. Neither uses *kratein* in the PN, but both Luke 22:54 and John 18:12 speak of Jesus being taken (*syllambanein*), the verb that Mark/Matt employed in Jesus' complaining question, "As if against a bandit have you come out . . . to take me?" (Luke did not use it in that question but saved it for here to describe the transfer; also Acts 1:16: "those who took Jesus.") Only John at this stage of the PN mentions the binding of Jesus as he is taken to Annas; he will be bound also when he is sent by Annas to Caiaphas (18:24). Binding is mentioned by Mark (15:1) and Matt (27:2) *after* the Sanhedrin session as Jesus is led away to Pilate. Luke does not have Jesus bound during the PN.[3] Is a key to John's having Jesus bound so early in the proceedings that for the fourth evangelist the Sanhedrin session had taken place weeks before and the decision that Jesus was to die was taken then by the Jewish authorities? In any case Jesus is being treated like a common criminal throughout!

The four Gospels speak of Jesus being led (away) to the high priest (*apagein* in Mark/Matt, Koine textual tradition of John; *agein* in Luke and [best text of] John). Most textual witnesses of Luke 22:54 have a second verb, *eisagein* ("lead into; bring into"), which goes with Luke's mention of "the house [*oikia*] of the high priest."[4]

Mark 14:53 describes a coming together (*synerchesthai*) of "all the chief priests, and the elders, and the scribes." Codices Vaticanus and Alexandrinus and the Koine tradition read "to him" (i.e., to the high priest) after "come together"; and some scholars use that to argue that Mark is describing simply a consultation, not a meeting of the Sanhedrin. However, 14:55 mentions "the whole Sanhedrin."[5] Moreover, Josephus (*War* 2.8.9; #145), uses *syner-*

---

[3]By way of comparison, it is of interest that in the riot that will break out over Paul's presence in the Temple, the tribune who arrests him will order him to be bound with chains (Acts 21:33) and will unbind Paul again before he brings him to the Sanhedrin (22:30).

[4]This second verb is absent from Codices Bezae and Koridethi, from the Latin and OS. Cf. the use of *agein eis* when Stephen is brought into the Sanhedrin in Acts 6:12.

[5]Both "all" and "the whole" are generalizing and impressionistic (see also "the whole cohort" in 15:16). We are scarcely meant to treat them as exact historical memories. Flusser ("Literary") recog-

chesthai for the coming together of the members of the courts of the Essenes, so it can have just as technical a sense as the *synagein* that Matt uses here and throughout the PN (see also Luke 22:66) and that echoes psalms of the suffering just one (22:17; 86:14).

Mark is repetitive within 14:53 in mentioning "the high priest" and "all the chief priests," especially when 14:55 will open with "the chief priests." Presumably it was for the sake of simplification that Matt's initial verse (26:57) has only "Caiaphas the high priest," and "the chief priests" is kept till 26:59 (there without an "all," since "the whole Sanhedrin" is mentioned). This simplification has the effect of heightening the role of Caiaphas. Despite the agency John attributes to the cohort and the tribune, these Roman troops do not bring Jesus to Pilate as might have been expected. John wants the arrest associated with the Sanhedrin session in 11:47–53, which was led by Caiaphas; and so Jesus is taken to the father-in-law of Caiaphas and ultimately to Caiaphas himself. The fact that Acts 22:30 shows a Roman tribune bringing Paul before the Sanhedrin should caution us against the claim that John is describing a patent impossibility.

In all four Gospels a verse associated with the transfer of Jesus to the high priest mentions Peter's following him.[6] I shall leave *entirely* until §27 the discussion of Peter's role and his denials of Jesus. From Mark 14:54 and par. pertaining to Peter, I am concerned here only with information pertinent to Jesus. Bruce ("Trial") notes that synchronization is built into the picture of attendants and servants sitting around a fire in the middle of the night: Something is going on, and they are on duty until it is over. Luke would be the weakest on that score, for no trial is being held. All four Gospels mention the *aulē* of the high priest. In §27 I shall explain that this term can refer to the court of a prince, a palace building, a major room therein, or the courtyard of such a building. The evangelists have different images of where Jesus was in relation to Peter and therefore in relation to the *aulē*, a term that does not mean the same for each writer.

John has already mentioned police "attendants" (*hypēretēs*) as part of the arresting party in 18:3; they appear again in 18:12–13 as transferring Jesus to Annas; and so it is not surprising that when Peter stands around the fire in the *aulē* (18:18) there are attendants present warming themselves. There are also attendants guarding Jesus as he stands before Annas; one of them

---

nizes that Mark is talking about a Sanhedrin meeting, but thinks that the Marcan source (as he reconstructs it) was not.

[6]More precisely John 18:15 describes as following Jesus both Simon Peter and "another disciple." Their arrival just after Jesus has been led to Annas has a certain parallel to the arrival of Judas just after Jesus comes to the garden in John 18:1–3.

will slap him for speaking arrogantly (18:22).[7] For Mark/Matt the first mention of the attendants is when Peter sits with them. In Mark 14:65 they join the Sanhedrin judges who are physically abusing Jesus, and they give him slaps. One may be meant to think that the attendants who appear at the high priest's court in Mark/Matt were part of the group who came out to Gethsemane to arrest Jesus. Pesch (*Markus* 2.426), however, thinks they are servants who just now had come along with the Sanhedrin members—this explains their being left in the *aulē,* and also how Peter can mingle with such outsiders without creating suspicion. But that is never made clear, and their role is nebulous. (Luke omits them altogether from the PN, perhaps for that very reason.) In John they have a clear police role throughout, indeed now the principal police role since we hear no more of Roman soldiers. All the Gospels mentioned the servant of the high priest in the arrest scene; John 18:18 has servants standing with the attendants around the fire. All the Gospels will mention a servant woman (*paidiskē*) in the account of Peter's denials.

Thus, putting together the Gospel pictures of where Jesus goes, one has the impression of a palace with a gateway, courtyard, and large room—a complex where servants and (police) attendants are at hand. Only Luke mentions the house of the high priest, but such an image is probably in the mind of the other three evangelists. This would mean that Mark/Matt are not thinking of the Sanhedrin as meeting in one of the buildings mentioned in Josephus or the Mishna (*Bouleutērion, Liškat ha-Gāzît;* see above §18C). Of course, this is a night session when the regular meeting hall might be closed. Those who support the Synoptic dating of these events whereby this night is already 15th Nisan, the Passover, often point to Josephus (*Ant.* 18.2.2; #29), who says that at midnight the priests opened the gates of the Temple. This is irrelevant for several reasons. First, the Synoptics themselves show not the slightest concern after the supper about any Passover details (see APPENDIX II, B). Second, the gates were opened so people could come crowding into the Temple courts (Mishna *Yoma* 1:8), and it is precisely public attention that the priests were anxious to avoid in handling Jesus. Third, it is not clear that the regular meeting hall of the Sanhedrin was within the Temple. Leaving such problematic historicizing aside, we may wonder whether the less formal locus of the meeting is not another indication that the Synoptics simplified facts by placing a Sanhedrin session in this se-

---

[7]Charbonneau ("Interrogatoire" 200) argues, wrongly in my judgment, that the presence of attendants both in the *aulē* and at the interrogation of Jesus means that for John, Annas questioned Jesus in the courtyard. More likely we are meant to envision that a larger body of attendants who were in the garden for the arrest had split up, with some remaining in the *aulē* while others took Jesus to Annas.

quence. John may be more accurate in describing on this night before Jesus died only an interrogation by the high priest that would quite plausibly be held at "the court [= palace] of the high priest." The picture is complicated, however, since both Luke and John have Jesus moved from where he was first brought: Luke 22:66 from the *aulē* of the high priest to where the Sanhedrin met; John 18:24 from Annas to Caiaphas.

Where was the high priest's palace or house? Presumably we should think of the Hasmonean palace on the West Hill of Jerusalem, overlooking the Xystus (gymnasium) and facing the Temple (Josephus, *War* 2.16.3; #344). Since the 4th cent. the "house of Caiaphas" has been localized in the southern section of the West Hill, just outside the Zion gate and near the traditional site of the Cenacle (see E. Powers, *Biblica* 12 [1931] 411–46); but the historicity of this tradition is quite dubious (see HPG 352–57). Because of John's indication that Jesus was sent from Annas to Caiaphas, in the 13th cent. the local tradition of Jerusalem began to distinguish between the "house of Annas" and the "house of Caiaphas"; previously no attention had been paid to where Annas lived. Some would harmonize John with Luke 22:66 and have the sending to Caiaphas mean a sending to where Caiaphas had convened the Sanhedrin and thus not to a house but a meeting place— in that case one could imagine that Annas lived in the palace of the high priest (as did Caiaphas). A host of scholars argue that Annas and Caiaphas lived in different wings of the same palace. This is all guesswork based on Gospel descriptions that may have been included to facilitate the flow of the story and may reflect no historical memory of the locale.

THE HIGH PRIESTS ANNAS AND CAIAPHAS

Mark mentions no high priest by name throughout the Gospel. At the extremes of the spectrum, some scholars wonder whether Mark (whom they presume to have known little about Jerusalem) would have known his name, while Pesch (*Markus* 2.425) contends that the narrative was taking shape among the Jerusalem community so early that the high priest was still in office and unnecessary to identify. All that we know for certain is that Mark's "the high priest" has a stylized effect. Matt mentions only Caiaphas by name, in the plot against Jesus (26:3) and here. Luke uses no name throughout the PN and employs the singular title only in the set phrases "the servant of the high priest" (22:50) and "the house of the high priest" (here). Since the chief priests (pl.) act in the Lucan PN, it is not extremely important to know whom Luke would think of as he used those set phrases. Too often, however, it is assumed that Luke like Matt would read "the high priest" in Mark to mean Caiaphas; in fact Luke always mentions Annas before Caiaphas (Luke 3:2: "In the priesthood of Annas and Caiaphas"; Acts 4:6: "Annas the high priest and Caiaphas").

John clearly mentions *both* Annas (two times) and Caiaphas (five times) in the Jewish proceedings against Jesus, even if there are difficulties about determining their respective roles. In 11:49,51 and 18:13 Caiaphas is designated as "high priest that year." Bultmann (*John* 410) exemplifies the judgment that the evangelist mistakenly thought the high priest was changed every year, as were the pagan priests in Asia Minor. I do not agree with that reading of John, both because the evangelist shows a very adequate knowledge of Jewish liturgical and festal customs and because the phrase can have the implication "high priest that fateful year." It is associated with Caiaphas' ability to prophesy about Jesus, and John is emphasizing not the length of the high priestly term of office but its synchronism with the time of Jesus' death.

Did John think Annas could also be called "the high priest"? A priori such an idea offers no major problem, as we have just seen from the Lucan references. Annas had been high priest some fifteen years before; and Josephus (*Ant.* 18.4.3; #95) still calls him high priest at the end of Caiaphas' reign. Moreover, in *War* 2.12.6; #243, he refers to Jonathan and Ananias as "the high priests" fifteen years after Jonathan had been deposed. (See also Mishna *Horayot* 3.4, which speaks of a former living "high priest.") The problem of whether in fact John made use of this terminology arises from the ambiguity of the Johannine sequence. Caiaphas was first mentioned in 11:45 and unambiguously functioned as "the high priest that year" in obtaining a decision from the Sanhedrists to put Jesus to death (11:47–53). Therefore, when at the beginning of the Johannine PN (18:10) we heard of "the servant of *the high priest*," if there were a tendency to identify the hierarch, Caiaphas would have come to mind. Only after the arrest does Annas appear on the scene (18:13: "They led him [Jesus] first to Annas"); he is not identified as a high priest but as "father-in-law of Caiaphas who was high priest that year." In the episode that follows (involving Peter's first denial and the interrogation of Jesus) "the high priest" is mentioned five times (18:15,16,19,22) without an identifying personal name. On the one hand, since only Caiaphas has been called high priest, one might think he was meant.[8] However, it was never made clear that he was present in the episode, especially during the interrogation. Moreover, at the end of the episode (18:24) we are told "Annas sent him bound to Caiaphas the high priest," with the clear implication that Caiaphas was (and had been) elsewhere. The

---

[8]Yet Vicent Cernuda ("Jesús"), as we shall see in n. 15 below, argues that because of his patriarchal role in a family of high priests, Annas was known par excellence as "*the* high priest." Consequently, as soon as John 18:13a mentioned his name, allusions to "the high priest" should be understood as referring to him unless specified otherwise (Caiaphas was "high priest that year").

majority interpretation, therefore, has been that John considered (also) Annas "the high priest," that Peter and the other disciples were admitted to Annas' terrain when they came "into the court of the high priest," and that Jesus was interrogated by Annas in 18:19–23. Yet that interpretation, on the surface, leaves Caiaphas virtually inactive.[9] Not only was he not present during the whole episode 18:13–23; but he did nothing with Jesus after that prisoner had been sent bound to him from Annas (18:24), for only three verses later (18:28a) we are told, "They lead Jesus from Caiaphas to the praetorium [of Pilate]." One might ask why, if Annas was the high priest who did the interrogation, did he not send Jesus directly to Pilate without bothering with Caiaphas as a transit agent or middleman. The answer may be simply that Annas was not the high priest *that* year and therefore could not deal on an official basis with Pilate in the way in which Caiaphas could.

Some find the present Johannine arrangement so awkward that they contend that originally only one priest was involved in interrogating Jesus and giving him over to Pilate.[10] Which priest? One group (e.g., Schnackenburg, *John* 3.230–34) thinks that only Annas was mentioned in John's source, with Caiaphas being added in later Johannine editing. Such a proposal suffers from the usual uncertainty about the putative source, since others think Caiaphas' role dominated in the source (and the Johannine redactor mixed things up by moving the reference to Caiaphas that originally followed 18:13 to 18:24), and Dauer insists that both Annas and Caiaphas were in the source. Moreover, most forms of the source theory assume that inexplicably a redactor changed a lucidly clear original to produce (what the source-theorizers regard as) the thoroughly confused text that stands before us. Without resorting to sources, many would harmonize the Gospels by contending that John's report of Jesus being sent to Caiaphas was meant to leave room for the account of the trial of Jesus before the high priest(s) related by the Synoptics. There is not one iota of evidence in John, however, to show that he or his readers knew about the Synoptic Sanhedrin session on the night before Jesus died (or cared about it, if they knew). Indeed, John's equivalent of the Synoptic Sanhedrin session appeared already in 11:47–53.

From antiquity to modern times there have been attempts to rearrange or

[9]The "modesty" of the role assigned to Caiaphas in this Johannine scene where the high priest is an adversary of Jesus is explained by Vicent Cernuda ("Jesús" 60–65) by an appeal to his theory (expounded in "Condena II") that Caiaphas eventually resigned his office and had become a Christian. As I shall explain when I discuss Caiaphas, I judge that explanation totally implausible.

[10]As support two later passages have been invoked. A minor variant in 18:35 has Pilate say, "Your nation and the chief priest [sg.] have given you over to me"; and in 19:11 Jesus speaks of "the one who gave me over to you." (Actually, 19:11 may be responsible for scribes introducing the singular into 18:35.) Nevertheless, both those passages come after 18:28a, "Then they lead Jesus from Caiaphas to the praetorium," and because of that may be concentrating on Caiaphas. They cast no light on whether another high priest (Annas) interrogated Jesus in 18:13–24.

rewrite John so that Caiaphas becomes the interrogating high priest of the present episode (18:12–23).[11] The 2d-cent. scholar who translated the Greek of John into the Syriac of the OS[sin] moved 18:24 to after 18:13 so that Jesus was sent on immediately from Annas to Caiaphas and everything happened before Caiaphas. Since this Syriac translator also presents John's form of Peter's denials so that the first is joined to the second and third as in the Synoptics, most likely throughout the episode he was simply harmonizing John's account with the Mark/Matt presentation. (For additional evidence of the OS[sin] as a shrewd modifier of texts to solve difficulties, see BBM 64, 130.) Further transposition theories have also been proposed,[12] and the hundred-year-old debate between Farquhar and Findlay shows both the erudition and weaknesses of such an approach. Other scholars reinterpret or rephrase. A number have proposed translating the aorist 18:24 as a pluperfect: "Annas had sent him bound to Caiaphas the high priest," namely, before anything narrated in 18:15ff. This rendition is unusual but not impossible in an independent clause (Gardiner, "Aorist"). Yet the Johannine *oun*, which I have translated "thereupon," does not favor it; and such an obscurely phrased afterthought containing what was very necessary to interpret the twelve preceding verses would be uncharacteristically careless writing for John. A. Mahoney ("New . . . Old") resorts to textual emendation. In 18:24, in place of *dedemenon* ("bound"), he would read *de menōn:* "But Annas, *remaining* (after the departure of Caiaphas) sent him to Caiaphas." To support this Mahoney must implausibly suppose unmentioned details: Caiaphas was with Annas when Jesus was interrogated, but after the interrogation he went on to where the Sanhedrin was assembling.

I agree with those scholars who distrust all such rearrangement and rewriting and accept the text as it now stands. Indeed, in Johannine logic there is no insurmountable problem about the prominent role attributed to Annas in 18:13–23 and the mention (without detailed narrative) of Caiaphas in 18:24,28a. Throughout John we hear of dramatis personae who have no (or no significant) role in the Synoptics. The references to Annas alongside Caiaphas in Luke 3:2 and Acts 4:6 may well mean that Christian tradition considered both those high priests significant in the Jesus story, and John may have developed in his own way the significance of Annas. Indeed, if, as I have suggested above, there was no formal Sanhedrin trial of Jesus on the

---

[11]The thesis that Caiaphas was the high priest throughout the interrogation has been supported (with varied explanations) by Cyril of Alexandria, Erasmus, Luther, Calvin, Beza, Bengel, Calmes, Westcott, Gardiner, Spitta, Farquhar, Lagrange, Streeter, Durand, Joüon, Vosté, Sutcliffe, and Fortna. A much larger group from antiquity (Augustine, Chrysostom) to modern times follows the surface indication of John in positing that Annas was the interrogator.

[12]E.g., Greek ms. 225 (copied AD 1192) placed v. 24 in the middle of v. 13; Spitta placed 19–24 before 14–18; Farquhar placed v. 24 after v. 14.

night before he died but only an interrogation, historically Annas might have been the interrogator. (That possibility need not blind us to the distinctively Johannine cast of the scene as it now stands.) The role of Annas in John and the absence there of a Sanhedrin trial before Caiaphas offer major difficulty only to those who assert Johannine dependence on Mark. Nor are the sending of Jesus to Caiaphas in 18:24 and the transfer of him by Caiaphas to Pilate in 18:28a (without information as to what happened in the brief interval) obstacles, given John's penchant for dramatic symbolism. John wants to emphasize that the last Jewish official to deal with Jesus is the Caiaphas who was the first named Jewish official to demand his death. While Annas may have been the high priest who interrogated Jesus this night, Caiaphas was the "high priest *that (fateful) year*," who had the ability to prophesy. When Jesus was led from Caiaphas to the praetorium, readers are invited to recognize that the oracle enunciated by that high priest in 11:50 is now being fulfilled: 'It is better . . . to have one man die for the people, rather than to have the whole nation perish."

Thus John attributes to Annas and Caiaphas, both of them high priests, an important role in the Jewish proceedings against Jesus. It will be helpful, then, before we proceed in the discussion, to have information about both those men.

Annas. In AD 6 P. Sulpicius Quirinius, legate in Syria, appointed Annas (Greek: Ananos; Hebrew: *Ḥănanyâ*) high priest.[13] In 15 Valerius Gratus, prefect in Judea, deposed Annas.[14] He remained a powerful force, however, for in the fifty years after his deposition five of his sons became high priests (*Ant.* 20.9.1; #198: "something that never happened before to any other of our high priests"), as well as a son-in-law and a grandson. By the late 60s the tomb of Annas stood near the south wall of Jerusalem.[15] Many have suggested that the propertied family of Annas was involved with the obscure moving of the Sanhedrin to the Bazaars ca. AD 30 (p. 350 above); and some would relate this hint of merchandising to Jesus' attack on the Temple

---

[13]Josephus, *Ant.* 18.2.1; #26. Annas was the son of Seth and replaced Jesus son of See (? or Seth—Jesus and Annas may have been brothers).

[14]*Ant.* 18.2.2; #34. For a list and the dating of the twenty-seven high priests in the time of Herod and the Roman prefects, see HJPAJC 2.229–32; and NJBC p. 1246.

[15]Josephus (*War* 5.12.2; #506) calls it simply the tomb of "Annas the high priest"; but, as Vicent Cernuda ("Jesús" 55–57) argues convincingly, Josephus surely means Annas (Ananos) I, not Annas (Ananos) II, the son. In AD 67–68, at a particularly vicious moment in the Jewish revolt against Rome, the (deposed) high priest Ananos II was killed in Jerusalem by the Idumeans and Zealots (*War* 4.5.1–2; #305–25); and in describing that Josephus (#317) comments that the Idumeans took no care to bury corpses. Consequently it is unlikely there would have been a honorary tomb for Ananos II. Moreover, Vicent Cernuda argues that because of his patriarchal role in the greatest of the priestly families of this period, Annas (I) was, by way of autonym, known as "*the* high priest" par excellence.

money changers. Josephus (*Ant.* 20.9.2; #205–7) tells how Ananos II (Annas, son of Annas) ca. 62 bribed the procurator of Judea, Albinus, with money raised by extortion at the threshing floors. (Caution: earlier *Ant.* 20.8.8; #101 attributed much the same abuse to the reign of Ishmael, not of the house of Annas.) Midrash *Sifre* on Deut 14:22; #105 (also the *baraita* or ancient tradition in TalBab *Baba Meṣi'a* 88a) reports that the produce stalls of the "Sons of Ḥanan" (which were on the Mount of Olives) were destroyed ca. 67 because their owners failed to tithe; they may have been involved in overpricing the requisites for sacrifice at the Temple. Rabbinic documents criticize (perhaps with prejudice) the Sadducee high priests of the Roman era, but there seems to be a special animosity toward the house of Annas as greedy and repressive.[16] TalBab *Pesaḥim* 57a; Tosepta *Menaḥot* 13.21 criticize the priests of the house of Ḥanin because of their secret conclaves. Surely not all this evidence is accurate; nor are all agreed that the various Jewish references to Ḥan(n)in or Ḥanan pertain to Annas and his descendants; but some of the negative evaluation seems to be historical.

As far as Christians are concerned, is it accidental that Jesus, Stephen (the first martyr), and James the brother of the Lord were all put to death during the tenure of priests of the house of Annas? Indeed, since Matthias, son of Annas, was high priest in 42/43 under Herod Agrippa I (*Ant.* 19.6.4; #316), possibly James the brother of John (the first of the Twelve to be martyred) also perished under the house of Annas (Acts 12:1–3). That would mean that every famous Christian who died violently in Judea before the Jewish Revolt suffered in the tenure of a priest related to Annas.[17] Be that as it may, among the Sadducee high priests the house of Annas may have had a special antipathy toward the followers of the man whose crucifixion they promoted in 30 or 33. Even though only John gives Annas a role in the death of Jesus, there is no persuasive reason to doubt that memory, especially since no discernible theological reason would have caused the Johannine tradition to introduce this figure.

Caiaphas. Josephus (*Ant.* 18.2.2; #34–35) tells us that after the prefect Valerius Gratus removed Annas from office (ca. 15), in rapid succession no more than a year apart he appointed four different high priests, the last of whom was Joseph surnamed Caiaphas (Hebrew *Qayyapâ*; John 18:13 identifies him as son-in-law of Annas). Then Valerius Gratus retired to Rome

---

[16]St-B 2.569–71; P. Gaechter, "The Hatred of the House of Annas," TS 8 (1947), 3–34.

[17]J. J. Ensminger, "The Sadducean Persecution of Christians in Rome and Jerusalem, A.D. 58–65," SWJT 30 (#3; 1988), 9–13, has tried to make a case that *priestly* opposition followed Paul from Jerusalem to Rome when he was taken there as a captive (ca. 60), since Josephus (*Ant.* 20.8.11; #194–95) mentions a delegation at Rome under Nero that included the high priest Ishmael and lasted several years.

(after eleven years in Judea), and Pontius Pilate came as his successor. That compressed notice is a bit confusing, for Caiaphas seems to have been appointed about the year 18, while Pilate replaced Gratus about 26. It is a testimony to the staying power of Caiaphas that after such a revolving-door high priesthood between the years 15 and 18, he remained high priest not only during the last eight years of the rule of Valerius Gratus, but also throughout eleven years of the rule of Pontius Pilate. Josephus (*Ant.* 18.4.1–2; #85–89) reports that the legate in Syria, Vitellius, intervened in Palestine after trouble between Pilate and the Samaritans and ordered Pilate to return to Rome. One calculation is that Pilate left Judea in Dec. 36. By Passover of 37 Vitellius had come to Jerusalem and removed Caiaphas, replacing him with Jonathan, a son of Annas (*Ant.* 18.4.3; #90,95). This pontificate of eighteen to nineteen years, which outlasted Pontius Pilate, means that Caiaphas ruled by far the longest of the nineteen high priests in Jerusalem in the 1st cent. AD, rivaled only by the nine-year tenure of Annas. Since (§31, B3 below) there were public incidents during Pilate's time that caused friction between the prefect and the populace (and its leaders), one can guess that Caiaphas was a shrewd strategist and no mean politician if he was able to survive in office. One may suspect also that Pilate, a rare long-presiding governor who never removed a high priest, was not as obdurate and intractable as he is sometimes portrayed.

As for what Caiaphas did while in office, Josephus supplies no information. Most scholars are willing to assume that the silence is because he (and his sources) had little information about this figure; but inevitably some would argue that Josephus was trying to conceal something embarrassing about Caiaphas. The most adventurous step in the latter direction is the thesis advanced in 1991 by Vicent Cernuda ("Condena II") that Caiaphas resigned his office and became a Christian![18] As fate would have it, the thesis seems to have been refuted indirectly at the very moment it was being proposed. In Nov. 1990 near Abu Tor, south of the walled portion of Jerusalem (in the region where Josephus had placed the tomb of Annas), to all appearances the family tomb of Caiaphas was discovered;[19] and it evidenced a re-

[18]Why do the Gospels and Acts not mention this triumphantly? Vicent Cernuda appeals to Acts 6:7 (in Jerusalem "a great crowd of the priests became obedient to the faith") and to the fact that Mark and Luke leave his name out of the hostile context of the passion and John 18–19 assigns him only a modest role (outside of reiterating that [in 11:49–52] Caiaphas had prophesied that Jesus would die for the people). It is not credible that the conversion of the Jewish high priest to the following of Jesus (which arguably would have been the most prominent conversion before Constantine) would have been hinted at so indirectly in Christian sources.

[19]What follows draws on Z. Greenhut, "Burial Cave of the Caiaphas Family," BARev 18 (#5; Sept./Oct. 1992), 28–36, 76; and R. Reich, "Caiaphas' Name Inscribed on Bone Boxes" (ibid.), 38–44, 76. See also the series of articles on Caiaphas by Z. Greenhut, R. Reich, J. Zias, and D. Flusser in 'Atiqot 21 (1992), 63–87.

vered Jewish burial given to the former high priest—scarcely consonant with his having become a follower of Jesus. The name of Caiaphas (if the same person is meant) is represented in the Mishna (*Para* 3.5) in Hebrew as *Qwp* or *Qyyp* (*Qayyap[â]*); but on one of the twelve ossuaries found in the collapsed burial cave the family name appears in Aramaic as *Qp'* (*Qapā'*). On the most elaborately decorated ossuary are found two inscriptions, presumably the name of the sixty-year-old man whose bones were found inside:[20] *Yhwsp br Qp'* and *Yhwsp br Qyp'*, thus "Joseph son of *Qapā'* or *Qaypā'*."[21]

Even with the new finds history would remember Caiaphas as little more than a name in the list of high priests were it not for his being "high priest that (fateful) year" (John 11:49; 18:13). In the NT only John 11:47–53 supplies an indication of why Caiaphas would want Jesus dead: "Do you not realize that it is better for you to have one man die for the people, rather than to have the whole nation perish?" Éliás ("Erwählung" 34) comments that in his own way Caiaphas is patriotic, but that is scarcely the impression John wishes to convey. Rather, Caiaphas is presented as having a political motive, agreeing with the general worry of the chief priests and Pharisees about Jesus, "If we permit him (to go on) thus, all will believe in him. And the Romans will come and take from us both the (holy) place and the nation." But in John's eyes the office of high priesthood (especially in that fateful year) carried with it the power to prophesy (see Josephus, *Ant.* 11.8.4; #327–28; 13.10.7; #299). In pronouncing that one man should die for the people (meant by Caiaphas as "in place of the people"), the high priest uttered a profound truth: Jesus would die for (on behalf of) the nation, and not for the nation alone but to gather into one as well the dispersed children of God (11:50–52). John reminds the reader of that prophecy (18:14) when he mentions Caiaphas in the scene following the arrest of Jesus.

THE QUESTION POSED TO JESUS BY THE HIGH PRIEST (JOHN 18:19)

In the Synoptics the transition from the Mount of Olives to the *aulē* of the high priest can be kept distinct from the trial/interrogation of Jesus before

[20]Along with those of five other people: two infants, two children, and an adult woman—perhaps the immediate family of the elderly man.

[21]If there is good reason to think that this is the Joseph Caiaphas of Josephus, and the Caiaphas of the Gospels, recent reflections look on "Caiaphas" as a family name. Two other high priests of this period are Simon Cantheras and Elionaeus son of Cantheras, representing Hebrew *Qntrs* (or perhaps with assimilation *Qtrs* [*Qatros*], the name of a priestly family found inscribed on a stone weight in Jerusalem and in TalBab *Pesaḥim* 57a as parallel to the House of Annas). Drawing on R. Brodi and others, Reich ("Caiaphas'" 42) suggests that Caiaphas, Cantheras, and Qatros may be three different versions of the same family name etymologically related to the idea of "basket" or "carrying," in regard to grapes and vines.

the Sanhedrin. But John has written his transition in such a way that it is intermingled with the questioning of Jesus by Annas (18:19–21). Before this questioning Jesus is led to Annas (18:13), and we get a description of the *aulē* (18:18). In 18:24 after the questioning Jesus is sent to Caiaphas (who was introduced before the questioning). Also, while the other Gospels place the denials of Peter either before the Sanhedrin session (Luke) or concurrent with it, even if narrated afterward (Mark/Matt), John's account of the denials is both concurrent with the questioning and intermingled with it. Accordingly it seems best to treat the Johannine questioning by Annas and the movement of Jesus to the high priests that surround it in this same scene where I am discussing the movement of Jesus to the high priest's *aulē* in the Synoptics. Perforce, in the translation of John given at the beginning of the section, I have included part of Peter's denials because they are intrinsic to the scene, but the discussion of those denials as such will be postponed until §27 below.

To understand how the questioning fits into the Johannine scene, we must note that just as the evangelist began the transition in v. 12 with a postpositive *oun* ("Thereupon"), so he uses an *oun* to begin the questioning in 18:19 and to mark the terminus of the questioning and the transfer to Caiaphas in 18:24. This technique identifies three segments in the scene:

- 18:12–18: Transfer of Jesus to Annas; the other disciple and the first denial by Peter.
- 18:19–23: Interrogation of Jesus by the high priest (Annas); slapping of Jesus by an attendant.
- 18:24–27: Transfer of Jesus to Caiaphas; the second and third denials by Peter.

Although later on (18:22) we shall find out that there are attendants present, v. 19 portrays the high priest interrogating Jesus on a one-to-one basis. The evangelist was aware that in a Sanhedrin session Caiaphas would have guided the members to a decision (11:47–53); and so his presentation of Annas without the trappings of witnesses, a jury, or a sentence refutes the thesis of Bultmann (*John* 647) and JEWJ 78[4] that John thought of this as a Sanhedrin trial. Indeed, Jesus twice calls attention to the lack of witnesses or testimony (18:21,23). The Gospel has insisted that the presence of Jesus, the light, in the world constitutes an occasion of judgment, according to the reaction of people to the light (3:17–21). Therefore, John likes to portray an individual standing alone before Jesus and having to make a decision about him (see Giblin, "Confrontation," 225). Chevallier ("Comparution" 179, 182) is right both in rejecting all rearrangements designed to conform John to the Synoptic Sanhedrin trial (before Caiaphas) and in drawing a parallel between Annas before Jesus in 18:19–21 and Pilate before Jesus in 18:28ff. (Note that I speak of "before Jesus," for that is the theological thrust of these scenes where the one who seems to be judging is himself on trial as to whether he is of the truth [see 18:37–38].) John's readers already know that Caiaphas has made up his mind, as have the Sanhedrin members, but here is one final Jewish leader, Annas, the patriarch of the family of high priests.[22] Pilate will at least ask questions and try to understand. Annas' silence in the face of Jesus' response and the slap by the attendant show a decisive rejection of the truth. Also throughout what follows one must be very aware that while on the surface John is describing a scene involving Jesus on the night before he died, he is also describing the Johannine Christian experience of being brought before Jewish authorities who were conducting trials leading to expulsion from the synagogue. In John's judgment these Christians receive little satisfaction when they complain about the injustice of the proceedings as Jesus did. The questioning of Peter by various servants of the high priest, simultaneous with the questioning of Jesus by the high priest, emphasizes the double level of the proceedings: What happens to Jesus happens to his disciples.

The question of the high priest centers on Jesus' disciples and on his teaching. Let us seek to interpret this question in light of what the Gospel has told us about Jesus. As for his *disciples,* in 11:48 there was a worry that those who believed in him were so numerous as to constitute a threat: "If we permit him (to go on) thus, all will believe in him. And the Romans will come and take from us both the (holy) place and the nation." Just before Annas speaks, the servant woman who is the gatekeeper challenges Peter, "Are you too one of the disciples of this man?" (18:17); and we heard about another disciple who is known to the high priest (but not necessarily as a disciple). On the level of Jesus' ministry, the authorities may have been annoyed when he attracted crowds. On the level of John's community history, the presence of too many disciples of Jesus would have been disturbing in synagogues. For comparison see Josephus *Ant.* 18.5.2; #118, who tells us that when others joined those who were crowding about JBap, Herod Antipas became alarmed and put him to death.

As for Jesus' *teaching,* we have many examples of his having offended: He was calling God his own Father, making himself equal to God (5:18); he claimed to be the Messiah (10:24–25); he blasphemed in saying, "I am God's Son" (10:36). Eventually "the Jews" will be most specific, "We have a law,

---

[22]As seen above (n. 15) Vicent Cernuda would make him "*the* high priest." In "Jesús" 60–65 Vicent Cernuda, on the basis of external evidence, maintains that Jesus and Annas represented two different ways of life, poverty and wealth. Would John's readers recognize that, since John never tells them that Jesus was poor or that Annas was wealthy?

and according to the law he ought to die, because he has made himself God's Son" (19:7). By implication, then, one could find in a question about Jesus' disciples and teaching the motifs of Temple destruction and of being the Messiah, the Son of the Blessed, that are expressed clearly in the Synoptic Sanhedrin session (e.g., Mark 14:58,62). But such a harmonizing is not plausible, for elsewhere John has phrased those issues quite specifically. The general question asked here, if it came from tradition, might be seen as reflecting the high priest's concern that Jesus was the type of false prophet condemned by Deut 13:2–6; 18:20, one who leads others astray (disciples), and falsely presumes to speak in God's name (teaching). It may be wiser, however, to recognize that in a synagogue of the post-70 period Jesus would be evaluated as a rabbi—for John an inadequate category.[23] A rabbi would be judged by his disciples and by his teaching.

THE RESPONSE BY JESUS TO THE HIGH PRIEST (JOHN 18:20–23)

I have already discussed the content of 18:20–21 in relation to the Synoptic Jesus' response to the arresting party (which included chief priests in Luke; see §14 above): "Day after day I was with you in the Temple teaching; and you did not seize me" (Mark 14:49 and par.). Even though the similar theme in the two responses suggests an older Christian tradition, John's phrasing reflects his own theology. Fortna ("Jesus" 38) posits a source behind John in this scene, but admits that it has been so rewritten that one can scarcely reconstruct the wording in the source. The perfect "I have spoken" in 18:20 is the verb *lalein,* the usual Johannine word for giving voice to Jesus the revealer of God. Mark's Jesus argues that he was present daily; John's Jesus argues that he spoke "openly."[24] For John, Jesus is personified divine wisdom; and in the OT, Wisdom speaks in public places as she invites all to hear her message (Prov 8:2–3; 9:3; Wis 6:14,16). In making his defense is John's Jesus protesting that he is not subversive, or that he is not esoteric? The historic setting of seeking evidence to bring him to Pilate fits best with

[23]See John 3:2, where "rabbi" is applied to Jesus by Nicodemus, who thinks he is flattering Jesus, but is told that he does not understand at all (3:10).

[24]John uses *parrēsia* 9 times (Mark 1, Matt 0, Luke 0, Acts 5). In this Johannine usage, as a figure from above, Jesus may speak "in public" and still not be speaking clearly by the standards of this world. In 7:26 people see that Jesus is speaking "publicly" in Jerusalem, but in 11:54 we are told that he no longer walked about "openly" now that the Sanhedrin was trying to have him put to death. He was challenged in 10:24 to answer "clearly" whether he was the Messiah; but only in 16:25 does he finally speak clearly to his disciples of the Father without figures of speech. The disciples acknowledge this gratefully in 16:29–30, exclaiming that now they understand; but Jesus calls that into question (16:31).

the nonsubversive understanding, but the later battle with the synagogue fits best with the nonesoteric.[25]

John's Jesus goes on to say, "I always taught in a synagogue and in the Temple, where all the Jews come together" (18:20). More frequently than in any other Gospel, John's Jesus has taught in the Temple (2:14; 7:14,28; 8:20; 10:23). Whereas in the Synoptics Jesus mentions only the Temple, in John he adds the synagogue even though the Gospel (6:59) reports only one instance of that locale for teaching.[26] Clearly the evangelist is enlarging the tradition to meet the community synagogue experiences of his own time, a period also reflected in the reference to "the Jews" almost as if Jesus were not one. Moreover, the high priest would scarcely need to be informed as to where "the Jews" come together. (In 18:20 Jesus claims to speak openly "to the world," and he mentions "the Jews." On the level of Johannine community life both terms refer to outsiders: The Johannine Christians are not of this world [17:14] and they have been thrown out of the synagogue [9:22; 12:42; 16:2].) The "in secret I spoke nothing" appropriately echoes the God of the LXX of Deutero-Isaiah, who says (45:18–19): "I am [*egō eimi*] the Lord, and there is no other. Not in secret have I spoken . . . I am I am, the Lord who speaks righteousness." Also 48:16: "Not from the beginning have I spoken in secret; when it took place there was I." The Jesus who answers Annas is majestic, even as was the Jesus who said "I am" to the arresting party and drove them backward to the ground.

"Why do you question me?" indicates the objectionable character of what is happening, comparable to the Synoptic question about coming out against him with swords and clubs. In the Jewish law of later times (e.g., Maimonides), it was improper to have an accused person convict himself; but we need not invoke such a law here to explain the challenge "Question those who have heard what I spoke to them." On the level of history Jesus is demanding that there be witnesses before he is condemned. On the level of the evangelist's message, this serves also as a defiant statement to the synagogue leaders of John's time that if they want to know what Jesus said, his Christian disciples speak for him. And those disciples are to speak as defiantly before their synagogue judges as Jesus speaks before Annas.

Josephus (*Ant.* 14.9.4; #172) tells us that whoever came before the Sanhe-

---

[25]I mentioned above the issue of whether the high priest's questioning about Jesus' disciples and teaching reflected a concern that Jesus was the false prophet of Deut who leads others astray. In Mishna *Sanhedrin* 7.10 the *mēsît* who leads others astray can be trapped by witnesses who pretend to be interested (disciples) and so hear what he says in private. Catchpole (*Trial* 8–9) argues that John 18:19 is preJohannine in origin and fits the theme of the false prophet.

[26]That reference to teaching in a synagogue is closely followed by a reference to Simon Peter's confession of Jesus. Here the reference to teaching in a synagogue is surrounded by Simon Peter's denials (Charbonneau, "Interrogatoire" 207).

drin for trial showed himself humble and assumed the manner of one who is fearful and seeks mercy. It is no wonder then that one of the (policing) attendants considers Jesus' behavior to be an effrontery and slaps him for his arrogance in addressing the high priest thus. (If the soldiers of the Roman cohort were present at the beginning [18:12–13], halfway through the scene they seem to have disappeared completely.) The Synoptics have a more elaborate scene of abuse and mockery of Jesus as a would-be prophet (Mark/Matt by the Sanhedrin judges; Luke by those who hold him) that will be considered in detail under §26 below. Let me note here only that while in the mockery Mark 14:65 (cf. Matt 26:67) has the attendants take Jesus with *slaps* and Luke 22:63 has those who hold him *beat* him, both terms appear in John 18:22–23. Only John associates the abuse of Jesus with his sovereign attitude toward the Jewish authorities, and the slap administered is more an insult than a physically damaging blow.

A scene similar to John's occurs in Acts 23:1–5, where Paul is struck on the mouth during a Sanhedrin trial. He insults the high priest Ananias for this behavior, but the bystanders protest, "Would you insult the high priest of God?" Paul apologizes, "I did not know, brothers, that he was a high priest; for it is written, 'You shall not speak badly [*kakōs*] of a ruler of your people'" (Exod 22:27[28]). That same Scripture passage may well be in mind in the Johannine Jesus' answer to the attendant who slapped him (18:23). Paul apologized because he had spoken "badly," but Jesus insists that there is no evidence or testimony that he has spoken "badly." In his ministry (John 8:46) Jesus asked defiantly, "Can any of you convict me of sin? If I am telling the truth, why do you not believe me?" Now this same spirit of defiance calls attention to the lack of witnesses and legal behavior. (Jesus is silent throughout the Synoptic accounts of the Jewish mockery and abuse, but not in John; we shall see the same phenomenon in the Pilate trial.) In John 15:25 Jesus calls attention to the Scripture passage "They hated me without cause" (Pss 35:19; 69:5[4]; 119:161; *PsSol* 7:1). Is a Scripture passage also in mind here? The Suffering Servant of Isa 50:6 says, "I gave my cheeks to slaps." (We shall see under §26 that this Isaian passage is surely echoed in the Mark/Matt accounts of the mockery of Jesus.) At the beginning of the ministry Jesus was hailed as "the Lamb of God" (John 1:29)—a polyvalent symbol pointing not only to elements of the paschal lamb in his death but also to his role as a servant who goes to his death as a lamb led to slaughter (Isa 53:7; see BGJ 1.60–63).

ANALYSIS

A. The Order of Events

In all the Gospels Jesus is led away from the place of arrest (Gethsemane, on the Mount of Olives, across the Kidron) to the *aulē* (court or courtyard) of the high priest. This transfer is always coupled with a reference to Peter following Jesus to that *aulē*. These two items constitute #1 and #2 in the accompanying table; the numbers 3 through 6 show what follows in the differing sequences of the Gospels. While there is much similarity, that difference in sequence and some difference in content cause a number of questions. I shall discuss those questions primarily on the level of what the Gospels are telling their readers, even though issues of source and historicity are of necessity intermingled in such a discussion.

WHAT TOOK PLACE AT NIGHT AND WHAT EARLY IN THE MORNING? All the Gospels place #1, the giving over of Jesus to the custody of the high priest, at night. Probably the tradition of "the night in which he was given over" (I Cor 11:23) was so strong as to leave little choice. All the Gospels place Peter's following and his three denials at night; for since they ended at cockcrow, there was no choice. The problem centers on two other items: legal proceedings against Jesus involving the high priest or chief priests, and some physical abuse and mockery of Jesus. In relation to the first item, the legal proceedings, readers should be alerted that probably the most common solution (at least in times past) has been to harmonize the individual Gospel presentations with the presumption that each is historically true but reporting only part of a much larger scene. Often much imagination has gone into such harmonizations, e.g., that of Valentin ("Comparutions"):

- a night interrogation of Jesus by Annas (John);
- a night trial of Jesus before Caiaphas (John 18:24, with first part of Mark/Matt);
- a morning Sanhedrin session (rest of Mark/Matt, with Luke).

Since the individual Gospels offer no encouragement to make such a harmonization, it is better to consider separately the three arrangements that have come down to us in Mark/Matt, Luke, and John. No matter how it arose, each arrangement would give the impression of being the full picture of what happened, not a part of a considerably larger whole.

Mark/Matt in #3 and 4 have the main legal proceeding (witnesses, questioning, response, charge of blasphemy, sentence) and the abuse/mockery at night, but then in #6 have further reference to a legal proceeding in the morning. Peter's denials occur simultaneously with the nighttime legal proceed-

TABLE 1. THE ORDER IN WHICH THE GOSPELS DESCRIBE INCIDENTS
FROM THE ARREST OF JESUS TO THE TRANSFER TO PILATE

Mark 14:53–15:1	Matt 26:57–27:2	Luke 22:54–23:1	John 18:12–28a
#1. Jesus (= J.) is led away to h.p. (= high priest); coming together of chief priests, elders, scribes.	#1. J. is seized, led away to h.p. Caiaphas where scribes, elders brought together.	#1. J. is taken, led to house of h.p.	#1. J. is taken by cohort and tribune, bound, led first to Annas, father-in-law of Caiaphas, h.p. that year.
#2. Peter follows inside *aulē* of h.p. and sits with attendants near blazing flame.	#2. Peter following until *aulē* of h.p., enters inside, and sits with attendants to see the end.	#2. Peter following; they kindle fire in middle of *aulē*; Peter sits in their midst.	#2. Peter and another disciple following; other disciple enters *aulē* of h.p.; gets Peter in; FIRST DENIAL; servants and attendants make charcoal fire at which Peter stands.
#3. Whole Sanhedrin seeks testimony against J.; many testify falsely, inconsistently; falsify J.'s sanctuary warning; h.p. standing, says: "Are you the Messiah, Son of Blessed?"; J. says: "I am; you will see Son of Man"; h.p. tears garments; charges blasphemy; all judge J. punishable by death.	#3. Whole Sanhedrin seeks false testimony; many testify falsely; two testify about J.'s sanctuary warning; h.p. standing, adjures: "Are you the Messiah, Son of God?"; J. says: "*You* have said it; you will see Son of Man"; h.p. tears clothes; charges blasphemy; they answer: J. to be punished by death.	#3. Peter's THREE DENIALS.	#3. H.p. questions J. about his disciples and teaching; J. answers that he taught openly; challenges h.p. to question those who heard him.

#4. Some spit at J., cover his face, strike him, saying "Prophesy"; attendants slap him.	#4. Men holding him (J.) mock and beat him; covering him, they ask, "Prophesy; who hit you?"; blaspheming, they speak against him.	#4. An attendant, standing by, slaps and rebukes J. for answering h.p. thus; J. answers that he did not speak badly, so "Why do you beat me?"	
#5. Peter's THREE DENIALS.	#5. As day comes, an assembly of elders of the people, chief priests, and scribes brought together; they lead J. away to their Sanhedrin.	#5. Annas sends Jesus bound to Caiaphas, the h.p.; Peter standing there, warming himself; Peter's SECOND AND THIRD DENIALS.	
#6. Early a.m., chief priests with elders, scribes, and whole Sanhedrin, having made consultation and having bound J., take him away and give him over to Pilate.	#6. They say, "If you are the Messiah, say to us"; J. says, "If I shall say to you, you will never believe . . . the Son of Man will be sitting at right of God's power"; they all say, "Are you then the Son of God?"; J. says: "You yourselves say that I am"; they say, "What further need of testimony?"; whole multitude leads him to Pilate.	#6. They lead J. from Caiaphas to the praetorium; it is early.	

ing. Scholars differ as to whether #6 is meant to be a second proceeding or simply the terminus of the first (#3–4). In §28 below I shall opt firmly for the latter position. Simultaneity in narrative is not an easy effect to achieve. Mark/Matt interrupt the night trial/abuse to narrate the denials of Peter, which took place synchronically and ended at (second) cockcrow; and then Mark/Matt come back to report that at this same moment when night was passing into morning the Sanhedrin finished its trial of Jesus with the decision to give him over to Pilate. Thus all the action takes place at night and terminates as morning begins.

John. The Johannine order of events is much the same as that of Mark, even if the content of the legal proceeding (#3) is quite different, and there is a much simpler abusive action without mockery (#4). In #3 there are no witnesses, no judges, no interrogation about the sanctuary or about Jesus' christological identity, no charge of blasphemy, and no sentence. The high priest who asks the questions is Annas[27]—not an unnamed as in Mark, and not Caiaphas as in Matt. The simultaneity of the denials by Peter is shown with greater artistry: one denial placed before the questioning of Jesus, and the other two after it. Once again the denials and the questioning of Jesus come to an end with the beginning of morning, i.e., cockcrow (18:27) and "early" (18:28, as Jesus is led from Caiaphas to Pilate).

The similarity of order between John and Mark has supplied an interesting test case for theories about the origin of John's PN. Matera ("Jesus") recognizes that sharp differences of content and language in this episode have caused prominent scholars to deny Johannine dependence on Mark and to posit a separate passion source (e.g., Bultmann, Dodd, Hahn, Lindars). Disagreeing, he thinks that the basic structural likeness is best accounted for if John drew on Mark and substituted some redactional material of his own. However, Matera assumes what needs to be proved, namely, that the Marcan structural pattern was created by Mark and did not come from earlier tradition. As shall be seen below, I think most of the elements of parallel structure (taking Jesus to the high priest's *aulē,* nighttime interrogation of Jesus by one of the chief priests and abuse of him, and denials by Peter during the same night) were preMarcan and preJohannine—that is why the two Gospels have the same structure. This early tradition underwent independent development in the processes that led to Mark's Gospel and to John's Gospel. Matera is right that a basic outline of a Jewish interrogation of Jesus has been adapted, redacted, and filled in by the introduction of Johannine motifs to produce the hearing before Annas on the night Jesus was arrested. It is

---

[27]Annas is mentioned in #1 and is the antecedent for the high priest in #3. Caiaphas is mentioned four times but is not the subject of any actions against Jesus on the night before he died.

just as true, however, that such an outline has been adapted, redacted, and filled in by the introduction of Marcan motifs to produce the trial before the Sanhedrin on the night Jesus was arrested.

Luke represents among the Gospels the only departure from a total night-time action that would end at the beginning of morning. While #1 and #2 cover the same events in Luke as in the other Gospels, Luke does not have simultaneity between Peter's denials and the legal proceeding. In #3 and 4 the denials and the abuse/mockery take place at night (and in this Luke agrees with the other Gospels); but the whole legal proceeding (#5 and 6), including moving Jesus from the *aulē* to a gathering Sanhedrin, takes place when it is day. By way of harmonizing many have argued that Luke (#5 and 6) does not narrate the trial session that Mark #3 puts during the night, but an enlarged form of the morning session in Mark #6. That thesis should be rejected on three grounds: First, Luke in narrating the morning trial gives no indication of a previous night session and has left no room for one; second, the contents of the Lucan morning session are quite similar to a major part of the Marcan night session, but not to what Mark reports in the morning; and third, Mark #6 does not describe a morning session but simply the termination of the one and only session which took place at night. Accepting, then, that Luke has the same one session as Mark but in a different order, other scholars prefer Luke's arrangement (whereby the Jewish interrogation of Jesus did not take place at night) as more original and/or even historical.[28] I disagree but wish to comment on the arguments often advanced.

First, the Mishna (*Sanhedrin* 4.1) states that capital cases must be tried in the daytime. I pointed out under §18, C3 above that there is little or no solid evidence that mishnaic rules governed Sanhedrin proceedings in this period.[29] Second, universal jurisprudence prefers daytime trials; juridical bodies who sentence people to death at night are often suspected of being kangaroo courts. This objection presumes something that is contradictory to what the Gospels tell us, namely, that this was to be a normal trial open to public scrutiny. Mark 14:1–2 (and par.) reports that the Jewish authorities wanted Jesus arrested and put to death by stealth and with as little public attention as possible. Nighttime proceedings fit that desire very well. Third, Mark/Matt are illogical in reporting two sessions of the Sanhedrin, one at night and a second in the morning. I would contend, however, that the reading of

---

[28]These would include scholars with very different overall stances: Benoit, Black, Bousset, Burkitt, Fitzmyer, Hauck, Husband, Kastner, Klausner, W. Knox, Lagrange, Lebreton, Loisy, Rengstorf, Ricciotti, Schweizer, Taylor, Vosté, and J. Weiss.

[29]The ameliorated procedures of the Mishna were shaped by scholars with legal skill describing an ideal court procedure, perhaps in reaction to how 1st-cent. high priests had conducted affairs under foreign rulers, i.e., acting "as the times required." See p. 362 above.

Mark 15:1 and Matt 27:1 as referring to a second session is both unnecessary and unlikely (§28). When, as suggested above, those verses are read as a notice that the Sanhedrin trial (interrupted to recount the denials) ended in the morning as did the denials, this whole argument disappears. Fourth, the proceedings described in Luke are more plausible than those described in Mark/Matt. An investigation (which is the way some interpret Luke), rather than a trial with witnesses and a sentence, is more plausible, granting that a Roman trial will follow. Under B. below I shall discuss whether or not Luke intends to describe a trial and, if he does, why he has omitted those features. Here let me discuss in relation to Luke the plausibility of what Mark/Matt describe and the issue of sequence.

As for *plausibility*, there are polemic elements in the Mark/Matt description, but here I am not trying to decide historicity. Nevertheless, at the heart of the question is the Mark/Matt description (also in Luke-Acts when taken as a whole) of authorities who did not give Jesus an impartial trial because they had already made up their minds that he deserved to die. Some who opt for the account of the proceedings in Luke 22:66–71 (and ignore other passages in Luke-Acts) do so because they think it does not describe so prejudiced a treatment of Jesus. They argue that all the authorities in Jesus' time cannot have been so villainous. Those who hold the opposite view cite rabbinic evidence pointing to the corruption of the house of Annas. While there may well have been corruption among the high priests, much of this misses the point that if genuinely religious men decided that the law of God demanded the death of someone like Jesus, they would not have been villainous in finding the surest way to accomplish that. Acts 26:10 does not regard Paul as a dishonest villain but as a misguided zealot when it has him say that by authority from the chief priests he put saintly Christians in prison, punished them in synagogues, tried to make them blaspheme, and in raging fury persecuted them even to foreign cities. Josephus (*War* 6.5.3; #300–9) is not describing villains when he says the rulers (*archontes*) of Jerusalem, who were annoyed at the bad omen in the prophecies of Jesus son of Ananias about the destruction of Jerusalem and the Temple sanctuary, even though they thought he might have some more-than-human impulse, brought him before the Roman governor. Thus an ethical judgment that favors the Lucan account over that of Mark/Matt as less prejudicial should be ruled out of the discussion.[30]

As for the *sequence*, is not Luke once more following Mark but rearranging to put things "in an orderly manner" (Luke 1:3)? Why bother the readers

---

[30]I think such a qualitative evaluation affected the judgment of P. Winter, who strongly favored Luke in his otherwise often very perceptive treatments of the trial.

with Mark's complicated sequence of Jesus (#1), Peter (#2), Jesus (#3,4), Peter (#5), Jesus (#6)? Why not more simply have *Jesus* brought to the high priest's house (#1), *Peter* following and denying Jesus three times (#2,3), and then *Jesus* mocked and interrogated (#4,5,6)? Why bother with complicated simultaneity, interrupting the interrogation of Jesus to narrate the denials of Peter, and then retracing one's steps to the interrogation to tell the readers that it was finishing about the same time as the denials, namely, morning?[31] Why not tell the Peter story as an undivided whole that took place at night? (This would have the added advantage that Jesus could be mentioned at the end, both as a transition to the interrogation and by implication as present during the denials and thus able to extend forgiveness to Peter on the spot: §27 below). And why not describe the legal procedure against Jesus as an undivided whole, taking place in the morning where it finished in any case? A Luke who did not hesitate to improve on Mark's order at the beginning of the Gospel, finishing the story of JBap to his arrest before telling the story of Jesus, and placing the history of Simon Peter's mother-in-law before Simon followed Jesus rather than afterwards,[32] did not hesitate to improve on it at the end of the Gospel, especially when the improvement would match the pattern in Acts (4:3,5) where Peter and John, arrested at night, were kept in custody till the next day.

B. The Legal Event: Trial or Interrogation?

Even if Luke's sequence, placing the whole legal proceeding in the morning, is a simplification of Mark, there are still the questions of whether all the Lucan *content* is borrowed from Mark and whether Luke is describing a trial. Although the proceedings in Mark/Matt do not meet the mishnaic requirements for trials of capital offenders (§18, C3 above) certainly the contents would give readers the impression of a trial: convening of the judging authorities, appearance of witnesses with specific testimony about Jesus' threat to destroy the Temple sanctuary, interrogation by the high priest, an admission by Jesus that he claimed to be the Messiah, instruction to the judges that the accused was guilty of blasphemy, and a condemnation by all as deserving death. Luke, on the other hand, has no witnesses, no reference to the high priest as an interrogator, a very vague answer by Jesus to the Messiah issue, no charge of blasphemy, and no death sentence. Understand-

---

[31]The observations above are based on the presumption that Luke understood Mark 15:1 to be a resumption of the one Sanhedrin session. If Luke understood Mark to be opening a second session of the trial, Luke's desire to simplify and avoid repetition makes his sequence easily explicable.

[32]On JBap, cf. Luke 3:1–20 and Mark 3:1–8; 6:17; on Peter's mother-in-law, cf. Luke 4:38–39; 5:9–11 and Mark 1:16–20,29–31: Luke's placing the miracle first and joining to it the miraculous catch of fish made the disciples' following of Jesus more intelligible.

ably, some would argue that Luke here does not draw on Mark but on another source that had only an interrogation. Would not a Jewish interrogation lead more plausibly into a Roman trial than does the somewhat tautological Jewish trial described by Mark/Matt? In §21–22 below when we discuss Luke's account, I shall agree with the possibility that Luke has combined *some* independent material (similar to that found elsewhere in John) with guidelines borrowed from Mark. But here let me point out that despite his omissions, Luke may have intended to describe a trial (see also §18, n. 142).

Probably the most serious trial element omitted by Luke is the condemnation of Jesus to death by the Sanhedrin. Yet in Luke 9:22 Jesus predicted: "It is necessary for the Son of Man . . . to be rejected by the elders and chief priests and scribes and to be killed" (much the same as Mark 8:31). In Luke 24:20 the disciples on the road to Emmaus say: "The rulers and our chief priests gave him over to a death sentence [*krima*] and crucified him." Stephen, speaking in Acts 7:52 in the Sanhedrin before the people, elders, and scribes, and addressing the high priest, says that they have become those who gave over and killed the Just One (Jesus). In Acts 13:27–28 we hear (from Paul) that those who dwell in Jerusalem and their rulers fulfilled the prophecy by "having judged [*krinein*] him; and though they found no charge really deserving of death, they asked Pilate to have him killed." Thus the readers of the whole of Luke-Acts are told that the Sanhedrin authorities charged Jesus, judged him, rejected him, and though they did not have an adequate case, gave him over to die. That sounds very much like the Mark/Matt trial and death sentence. The absence of witnesses who testify that Jesus threatened to destroy the Temple sanctuary is another factor in judging whether Luke intended a trial. Yet the Sanhedrin members say, "What further need of testimony [witness] do we have?" (22:71); and Stephen is supposed to have said that Jesus would destroy the holy place (Acts 6:13–14).[33] The very passage that Luke put on Paul's lips in Acts 13:27–28, cited above, may mean that Luke took for granted that the standard Christian preaching had informed all Christians that Jesus was tried and condemned by the rulers in Jerusalem and that he wrote his brief account in the Gospel (22:66–71) without any compulsion to spell that out.

The legal proceeding described in John is not ambiguous, for nothing suggests a trial—not even by a small Sanhedrin as suggested by Doerr (*Prozess* 23ff.). A one-sentence question is put to Jesus by the high priest Annas; but there are no judges or judgment, and Jesus himself twice notices the lack of witnesses. Later Jesus is sent to Caiaphas, but we are not told that anything

---

[33]We shall see in §20 that Luke's desire to create a resemblance between the trial of Stephen and the trial of Jesus probably led him to flesh out the Stephen story with details that Mark had in the trial of Jesus.

happens while he is with Caiaphas before he is sent to Pilate. Any parallelism in content or format with the Synoptic Sanhedrin trial before the high priest (or priests—Caiaphas for Matt) is in the eye of the interpreter, not in the text of John.[34] We see from 11:47–53 that John knows how to describe a Sanhedrin session with Caiaphas presiding, wherein the threat that Jesus poses to the holy place is prominent: Caiaphas urges death, and the other members agree. That Johannine scene, not the Annas questioning, is parallel to the Synoptic picture. Yet for John that scene took place weeks before Passover. John 11:47–53 lies outside the area of the Gospel PNs on which I am commenting in this book, and so only in passing do I make comparisons to it. Grundmann, however, in his careful study of the passage ("Decision" 300–1) argues convincingly that John's Sanhedrin scene is not dependent on that of the Synoptics but represents independent tradition.

To sum up what we have discussed, the following points would be well attested in the different Gospel traditions:

- a Sanhedrin session was called to deal with Jesus (all four, but John places the session weeks before Passover);
- an issue in that session was the threat Jesus posed to the Temple/sanctuary (Mark, Matt, John; in Luke-Acts that issue is mentioned in the Sanhedrin trial of Stephen);[35]
- the one who urged the others to decide Jesus' death was the high priest (unnamed by Mark; Caiaphas for Matt and John);
- there was a judgment equivalent to a death sentence (all four; but in Luke-Acts we learn this from others, not from the direct account of the Sanhedrin session);
- there was a high-priestly investigation of Jesus on the night he was arrested (all four; but for John this was different from the Sanhedrin session).

A serious possibility is that John's arrangement is more original and perhaps even more historical. If there was a Christian memory of a Sanhedrin called to deal with Jesus, only John, which has multiple visits of Jesus to Jerusalem, would have been free to date the Sanhedrin session to any period

---

[34]John mentions that Jesus was sent to Caiaphas, not to leave room for a trial before Caiaphas but to show that fittingly the one who wanted Jesus put to death (11:47–53) was the one who handed him over to Pilate and thus to crucifixion. A failure to pay attention to this makes dubious the position of Giblin ("Confrontations" 221–25) that John reports they took him to Annas *first* (18:13) because he knew of an additional hearing before Caiaphas. (Would John's readers be expected to know about such a hearing?) That expression means only that they took him to Caiaphas later (18:24).

[35]The issues of christology (Messiah, Son of God) and of blasphemy that Mark/Matt have in this Sanhedrin session are found in John but not in the presence of the Sanhedrin. Luke has the christological issue as Jesus stands before the Sanhedrin but phrases it in wording close to John's. He has the blasphemy issue in the Stephen trial.

other than the last days of Jesus' life. Mark (followed by Matt and Luke) could have run together that memory with another, namely, that on the night before he died, Jesus was interrogated by the high priest before being handed over to the Romans.[36] Historically, having a Sanhedrin session weeks before Passover would be more plausible than one gathered hastily in the middle of the night.[37] Moreover, as mentioned before, an interrogation just before handing Jesus over to the Romans for a trial makes better sense than a full-scale Sanhedrin trial. On the other hand, John is not a secure guide, since he had a theological reason for placing the Sanhedrin session in chap. 11 directly following the raising of Lazarus: Immediately after Jesus has given life, the Sanhedrin meets to give him death.

C. Evaluation of Mark 14:53–54

A factor in judging the material I have assembled above is whether one thinks that it is Mark who for the first time joined in the same night Peter's denials and a Jewish legal proceeding against Jesus. In the approach of what has been called the "Perrin school,"[38] there was no consecutive preMarcan PN; Mark shaped the flow of events, and John adapted Mark. While I have been very uncertain that we can reconstruct a consecutive preMarcan source, I have argued that the preMarcan traditions already contained a certain sequence and that there is little cogent evidence that John knew or used Mark.[39] Accordingly when Mark and John present a common sequence, that sequence may well be quite old in Christian tradition. In this scene, therefore, I would argue for a preMarcan joining of Peter's denials and a Jewish legal proceeding on the night before Jesus was taken to Pilate. (Mark's main contribution[40] may have been to identify the legal proceeding with another tradition of a Sanhedrin trial that determined Jesus' death—a tradition without a fixed time designation.)

Let me discuss here a particular aspect of the "Perrin school" approach

[36]In Mark 14:1, *before* the Last Supper, we are told that the chief priests and the scribes were seeking how to seize him by stealth. The parallel in Matt 26:3–4 says that the chief priests and the elders of the people were gathered (same verb as in 26:57) in the *aulē* of the high priest who was called Caiaphas. Did Mark/Matt retain a memory of a Sanhedrin session held earlier?

[37]I have argued that the nighttime setting fits well the stealth motif of the Gospels: Jesus' adversaries wanted him arrested without an uproar (Mark 14:1; John 11:53,57). Yet the nighttime setting does not demand a session of the Sanhedrin—a simple questioning of Jesus by the high priest in his own house would have been less conspicuous.

[38]The late Prof. Norman Perrin of the Univ. of Chicago and those who worked or studied with him; see the authors collected in PMK.

[39]There is the possibility that the final redactor of John knew Mark and embellished John with minor touches drawn from Mark (BGJ 1.xxxvi–xxxviii), but I prefer not to appeal to that.

[40]Mark has rewritten in his own style much of the material in 14:53–15:1, but he worked with earlier elements.

that rests on a careful study of the trial narrative in Mark, *Are You the Christ?*, by Perrin's student J. R. Donahue. He would prove that Mark has joined the legal proceeding and the denials of Peter by detecting a Marcan pattern of intercalation[41] in the scene. Mark 3:21–35 exemplifies intercalation. In 3:21, disturbed by reports of the intensity of Jesus' ministry, "his own" set out to seize him, for they said, "He is beside himself." Then in 3:22–30 we are told how Jesus dealt with the hostile scribes who came from Jerusalem with the charge, "He is possessed by Beelzebul." It is thought that this was once freestanding material that Mark intercalated between the setting out of "his own" in 3:21 and the arrival of his mother and brothers to call for him, as described in 3:31–35. The intercalation allows time for the journey. Another example is found in 5:22–43. In 5:22–24 Jairus asks Jesus to come and heal his dying daughter, and Jesus sets out with him. In 5:25–34 there is a scene of what happens on the way as a woman with a flow of blood touches Jesus and is healed. Jesus' arrival at Jairus' house and his raising the daughter from the dead is narrated in 5:35–43. Once again we have once freestanding material inserted to take up the time of the journey. Finally we may consider Mark 14:1–11. In 14:1–2 we have the chief priests and the scribes seeking how to take Jesus by stealth so that they can kill him. Then in 14:3–9 we have the story of a woman anointing Jesus' head, an action that Jesus interprets as anointing his body beforehand for burial. Finally in 14:10–11 Judas comes to the chief priests with a plan to hand Jesus over to them. The story of the woman gave time for the search inaugurated by the chief priests to turn up someone who could help them. Donahue is right: If this clear Marcan pattern is found in 14:53–72, there is every reason to think that Mark put that whole scene together and, since John has some of the same sequence, perhaps to think that John drew on Mark.

Donahue's suggestion for the intercalation is as follows: Peter seated in the *aulē* in 14:54; an intercalated scene of the Sanhedrin proceeding in 14:55–65; and resumption of the Peter scene in 14:66–72. I disagree on several scores. Mark is not filling in between the beginning of Peter's denial scene and its conclusion; he is describing two simultaneous actions, and that is not a feature of intercalation. Moreover, Donahue's schema really does not account for 14:53, which does not fit the pattern. My suggestion would give 14:53 and 14:54 equal value. Wanting to describe as simultaneous the Jewish legal proceeding and Peter's denials, Mark gives us side by side two topical sentences: v. 53 provides the setting for the Sanhedrin trial, which will be narrated first; v. 54 provides the setting for Peter's denials, which will

---

[41]Sometimes this is called the Marcan "sandwich" technique: The intercalated scene is the filler between the two slices of "bread." J. R. Edwards, "Marcan Sandwiches," NovT 31 (1989), 193–216, treats this passage as a "sandwich" (211–13). See APPENDIX II, B2 below.

be narrated second.[42] As the Sanhedrin proceeding is narrated in 14:55–65, the initial verse (55) picks up the cast of characters and setting from the introductory topical sentence in v. 53; similarly as the denials are narrated in 14:66–72, the initial verse (66) picks up the characters and setting from the introductory topical sentence in v. 54. Then, at the end of these two parallel scenes of similar length and value (neither of which is intercalated), Mark 15:1 returns to the Sanhedrin scene to show that it terminated at the same time as the denials. I am perfectly willing to concede (and not only on the dubious basis of "Marcan language") that the whole arrangement stems from Mark. But it is far more elaborate than Marcan intercalation, and represents an ingenious way to do justice to the tradition that these two scenes happened at the same time. John has to do the same, but the very fact that his solution is different from Mark's helps to show his independence.[43] While he has a similar introduction in which Jesus is led to the high priest and Peter follows, John tells at the outset the story of the first denial by Peter, only then bringing him into the *aulē* (18:15–18). Then John tells the story of the interrogation of Jesus and gets Jesus off the scene (18:19–24) before he returns to tell of Peter's second and third denials. I find little evidence here of Johannine dependence on Mark.[44] I would judge that both Mark and John are dependent on earlier traditions that had in common Jewish legal proceedings against Jesus and Peter's denials. Each evangelist has rewritten his respective tradition, perhaps more heavily in the Jewish proceedings than in the denials.

(*Bibliography for this episode is found in §17, Part 3.*)

---

[42]Schneider ("Gab" 34) also recognizes that vv. 53–54 introduce two scenes; one does not form a framework for the other. Similarly Gerhardsson ("Confession" 50), for Matt 26:57–58.

[43]Fortna ("Jesus") thinks that he can reconstruct the preJohannine PN with considerable exactness, and he accepts some of Donahue's discernment of Marcan source and redaction. Nevertheless, after painstaking comparisons between John and Mark, he comes to virtually the same conclusion to which I have come: The denials and the trial were joined on a preMarcan level, so that John's joining of them does not necessarily display dependence on Mark.

[44]Under §27 I shall discuss similarities between Mark and John in the denials. Evans ("Peter" 246–47) points to the greatest parallel: the words "Peter . . . warming himself" are found in Mark 14:54 and are picked up again at the beginning of the report of the denials in 14:67. Similarly these words are found at the end of the first denial in John 18:18 and are picked up again as the denials resume in 18:25. (In Mark Peter is seated; in John, standing.) As Evans admits, however, from this parallel "seam" (words used to resume), it is very hard to deduce John's dependence on Mark— perhaps it was a set phrase from an earlier form of the story.

§20. SANHEDRIN PROCEEDINGS, PART ONE: THE GATHERED AUTHORITIES, WITNESSES, AND THE CLAIM THAT JESUS WOULD DESTROY THE SANCTUARY

(Mark 14:55–59; Matt 26:59–61; Luke 22:66)

Translation

Mark 14:55–59: 55But the chief priests and the whole Sanhedrin were seeking testimony against Jesus in order to put him to death, and they were not finding (any). 56For many were giving false testimony against him, and the testimonies were not consistent. 57And some, having stood up, were giving false testimony against him, saying 58that "We have heard him saying that 'I will destroy this sanctuary made by hand, and within three days another not made by hand I will build.'" 59And even so their testimony was not consistent.

Matt 26:59–61: 59But the chief priests and the whole Sanhedrin were seeking false testimony against Jesus so that they might put him to death. 60And they did not find (any), although many false testifiers came forward. But at last two, having come forward, 61said, "This person stated, 'I am able to destroy the sanctuary of God, and within three days I will build (it).'"

Luke 22:66: And as it became day, there was brought together the assembly of the elders of the people, both chief priests and scribes; and they led him away to their Sanhedrin.

[Acts 6:12–14: 12And they stirred up the people and the elders and the scribes; and having come upon him [Stephen], they snatched him and led him away to the Sanhedrin. 13And they set up false testifiers who said, "This man does not cease speaking words against this holy place and the Law; 14for we have heard him saying that this Jesus the Nazorean will destroy this place and will change the customs that Moses gave over to us."]

[John 2:19: Jesus answered them [the Jews], "Destroy this sanctuary, and in three days I will raise it up."

11:47–48: ⁴⁷So the chief priests and the Pharisees gathered together a Sanhedrin; and they were saying, "What are we doing? Because this man does many signs, ⁴⁸if we permit him (to go on) thus, all will believe in him. And the Romans will come and take from us both the place and the nation."]

COMMENT

The Sanhedrin proceedings, as I have divided them, consist of at least four parts (§§20–23) and a conclusion (§28). I say "at least" because in Mark/ Matt one would have to enumerate more parts; both those Gospels place within the framework of the Sanhedrin trial the Jewish abuse and mockery of Jesus (§26) and Peter's denials (§27). In Luke, however, those episodes precede the Sanhedrin trial. See the listed Contents on pp. 313–14 above for the arrangement of my treatment. In the ANALYSIS of the preceding section (§19) I have already discussed issues of sequence and which episodes are placed at night.

There are Johannine parallels in the PN to the Synoptic accounts of Peter's denials and of the Jewish abuse of Jesus, but the Johannine parallels to the contents of the Synoptic Sanhedrin sessions are found outside the PN. In particular, John narrates in 11:47–53 a Sanhedrin session that decided against Jesus, but this takes place considerably before Passover. There are also scattered pieces of Johannine dialogue that I shall quote as parallels.

OPENING OF THE SANHEDRIN MEETING AND THE WITNESSES

Mark/Matt set the Sanhedrin scene upstairs or inside the *aulē* of the high priest, while Peter is downstairs or outside in the *aulē* (Mark 14:66; Matt 26:69) denying Jesus. The whole scene takes place at night, ending in the early morning. When Luke opens his scene, however, he has already described the nighttime denials by Peter in the *aulē*, along with the mockery and abuse of Jesus there (22:54–65); now that it is day Jesus is led *away* to the Sanhedrin. To avoid such a conflict in timing, some would translate Luke's aorist in 22:66 as a pluperfect: "had been brought together." The suggestion that here, for Luke, "Sanhedrin" does not refer to the body of men but their meeting or council (Bousset, Hauck, Holtzmann, Schmid, J. Weiss) somewhat softens the conflict in locale because that council could be held in the same house of which the *aulē* would be the forecourt.[1] Perhaps Luke knew that the Sanhedrin met in a special hall across the Tyropoeon valley from the Temple (see Acts 22:30; also §18, C1 above) and is incorporating a transfer to that place in his description of this scene where "Sanhedrin" is aggregate, i.e., the ruling body in session at their meeting place. But now let us examine the derivation of this Lucan description, and whether we need posit a special source for 22:66.

In what I have called a topical sentence (p. 427 above) introducing the Jewish legal proceeding, Mark 14:53 and Matt 26:57 have already described Jesus being led away to the high priest and the coming or gathering together of the chief priests (Matt: Caiaphas) with the elders and the scribes. Mark 14:55 and Matt 26:59 use "the chief priests and the whole Sanhedrin" to sum up that group.[2] (The claim of McLaren, *Power* 92–93, that Mark [followed by Matt] would make a distinction between "the chief priests, and the elders, and the scribes" in 14:53 and "the chief priests and the whole Sanhedrin" in 14:55 represents a failure to understand the resumptive relation of 14:55 to 14:53.) Luke has been abbreviating Mark throughout the PN. Accordingly in 22:66, which opens the Jewish legal proceeding, Luke can be explained as both abbreviating the Marcan opening in 14:53,55 and combining it with elements from the Marcan termination in 15:1 ("And immediately, early, having made their consultation [*symboulion*], the chief priests with the elders and scribes and the whole Sanhedrin . . ."). The Lucan setting "As it became day" may be a rewriting of Mark's time setting in 15:1. The three Sanhedrin component groups found in Mark 14:53 and 15:1[3] appear in a modified form in Luke 22:66, with the chief priests and scribes almost in apposition to "the assembly [*presbyterion*] of the elders of the people."[4] Codex Bezae would harmonizingly draw Luke 22:66 closer to Mark by breaking down the apposition and making a threesome of the *presbyterion*, "and

[1]In Acts 4:15 and 6:12 "Sanhedrin" seems local, i.e., the meeting *and* the Sanhedrin meeting place.

[2]One finds a similar expression in Josephus (*War* 2.15.6; #331), where the procurator Florus sends for "the chief priests and the Boulē."

[3]Known to Luke, as we can see in 20:1–2 where "the chief priests and the scribes with the elders" ask Jesus questions.

[4]The Lucan *presbyterion* (also Acts 22:5) is virtually a combination of Mark's *presbyteroi* and *symboulion*. In Ignatius of Antioch (*Magn.* 13:1; *Trall.* 7:2; et passim) *presbyterion* is a common term for a church assembly or grouping with the bishop, and some have wondered whether Luke has not used an Antiochene Christian term to describe the council or assembly at Jerusalem. Luke's description, "the assembly of the elders of the people," is probably meant to underline the official status of the body (see Jer 19:1). Curiously, however, it has the side effect of aligning "the people" against Jesus, whereas normally Luke does not portray "the people" in a hostile manner (APPENDIX V, A2).

the chief priests, and the scribes"; but 20:19–20 shows that Luke thinks of the chief priests and the scribes as the major elements *within* the Sanhedrin hostile to Jesus. The Lucan "brought together" (*synagein*)[5] is a synonym for Mark's "come together" (*synerchesthai*) in 14:53. The Lucan "and they led him away" is found in Mark 14:53, while "the Sanhedrin" picks up a term Mark used in 14:55 and 15:1.[6] In the ANALYSIS of §19B I argued that Mark's elaborate interweaving of the Jewish interrogation with Peter's denials in order to achieve simultaneity—an interweaving that took three separate passages to describe the Sanhedrin session—was simplified by Luke. I would see this verse in Luke as the product of that simplification; no separate source need be posited. Légasse ("Jésus" 192–94) studies painstakingly the Lucan vocabulary in 22:66 and comes to the same conclusion. In diagnosing Luke's composition, however, we should not forget the comparison between Luke and Acts. This Sanhedrin which will eventually give Jesus over to Pilate resembles the group of Jews at Corinth who will attack Paul and bring him before the tribunal of Gallio (Acts 18:12–13).

Missing from Luke's overall account of the Sanhedrin proceeding is one of the two principal themes of the Mark/Matt account, namely, witnesses[7] who testify that Jesus made a statement about the destruction of the Temple sanctuary "made by hand [Mark]." Luke has false witnesses appear in another Sanhedrin proceeding where the charge that Jesus would destroy the holy place is a major issue, namely, the Stephen trial of Acts 6:13; and he has the theme of the Most High not dwelling in houses "made with hands" in the Stephen speech of Acts 7:48.[8] Has Luke shifted material from this Marcan episode to the Stephen setting, and why? We shall return to that question after looking at what Mark/Matt tell us.

An emphasis on testimony dominates the Marcan account of the first section of the Jewish proceeding against Jesus, with five words of the stem *martyr-* in 14:55–59 (plus one in the high priest's summation [v. 60] and one in his inclusive reference [v. 63]). It is the only explicit juridical element

---

[5]See also Matt 26:57, but more importantly Acts 4:5.

[6]Luke avoids, however, Mark's adjective "whole," twice used to describe the Sanhedrin. He wishes to leave space for Joseph from Arimathea, whom in 23:50–51 he will describe as "a member of the council [*bouleutēs*] . . . not in agreement with their decision and course of action."

[7]Although in describing a court trial, English prefers the verb "testify" and the noun "testimony" to the verb and noun "witness," it prefers for the person involved "witness" to "testifier." Yet my *translation* will use the latter to show that words of the same Greek stem are being employed throughout: *martyrein, martyria, martys*. In my comments, on the other hand, I shall employ the less awkward "witness" for the person who testifies.

[8]"The holy place" of Acts 6:13 and "this place" of 6:14 are the (Second) Temple, the existing form of the house built by Solomon for God, as described in 7:47–49. See Hasler, "Jesu," for the close tie between the trial of Jesus in Luke 22 and the trial of Stephen in Acts 6–7.

that Mark narrates in these verses.[9] As Wood ("Mythical") points out, many commentators create a false problem by translating Mark 14:55 as "seeking testifiers [witnesses]," as if in the middle of the night the Sanhedrists were supposedly rounding up people to speak against Jesus! Mark actually says that they were "seeking testimony" in the sense of evidence, not people. In 11:18 the chief priests and scribes began "seeking" to destroy Jesus; in 12:12 they *sought* to seize him; in 14:1 they *sought* in stealth to seize and kill him; in 14:11 Judas *sought* how to give him over; now that he is both given over and seized, the authorities *seek* testimony to accomplish what has been the goal from the beginning: to destroy him.

From the first time that the testimony is given in v. 56 to the conclusion of this testimony in v. 59, the Marcan emphasis is on its false character (two uses of false testimony; two statements that the testimony was not consistent). The whole case against Jesus is false for Mark, and he tells the readers that. (In the next section he will not need to comment on the truthfulness of Jesus' testimony to the high priest; Mark's readers know that Jesus always speaks the truth.) Matt 26:59–61 simplifies Mark's redundancies (which have a storytelling power), and in so doing changes the picture. He preserves two references to false testimony, but places them in vv. 59–60a as an initial and unsuccessful part of the trial. He has the harsh statement, "The chief priests and the whole Sanhedrin were seeking *false* testimony against Jesus," but SPNM (163) is correct in pointing out that this is really a summation of Mark's total picture; and even if Mark did not say that they sought false testimony, that is the import.

Frustrating as it may be to a modern wish for impartiality, Mark and Matt portray polemically a Sanhedrin that is against Jesus from the outset of the trial—a not surprising bias given that ancient literary accounts of famous trials are most often narrated with a bias. Already, close to the beginning of Jesus' ministry (Mark 3:6) the Pharisees and the Herodians took counsel to destroy Jesus; and the chief priests and their cohorts have been "seeking" to do the same. That the testimony used against Jesus was false, as were interpretations placed on his words and deeds by his opponents in his lifetime and in synagogues of the 1st cent., was a Christian judgment that surfaces in the evangelists' account of the trial. If we move back from the Gospel picture toward history, to what extent Jesus' opponents made a conscious use of distortions we can never know—in religious polemic, distortions are not uncommon, but conscious use of them may be less common.

---

[9]Blinzler (*Trial* 98–99) speculates on the witnesses having the function of prosecutors; other scholars, commenting on the Gospel accounts, fill in aspects of the court and trial from Mishna references to legal proceedings. All that is uncertain and largely irrelevant.

As for the hostility attributed to the Sanhedrin, see my remarks in §18, F2a above insisting that religious men might have thought it their duty to remove such a person as Jesus. In a Sanhedrin where the high priests (present and past) were Roman appointees, and these were combined with aristocrats and scribes, there was surely an admixture of insincerity, self-protective cunning, honest religious devotion, conscientious soul-searching, and fanaticism.

We must recognize, moreover, that the evangelists are depicting the trial of Jesus in an atmosphere colored by Psalms and other OT passages describing the plots against the righteous, wherein the wicked "stand up," give false testimony to accuse the righteous man of things he knew not, and seek to put him to death.[10] Prov. 6:17, in the context of "a heart that plots wicked plans," joins together "a lying tongue and hands that shed innocent blood," even as in this trial "against" Jesus, Mark puts together false witnesses and the condemnation of Jesus to death. We note that in Acts 6:13–14 Luke will use much the same stereotyped language to depict the tactics of Stephen's opponents. An additional factor is an allowance for the narrative flow that governs the description. To detect a contradiction between the statement in Mark 14:55 that they were not finding any testimony and the statement in the next verse that many were giving false testimony is to misunderstand a repetitious writing style that is reporting vividly a frustrated failure to find adequate legal testimony. Nor need we raise questions of how witnesses were available in the middle of the night.[11] Given the Marcan storyline, the need to take advantage of Judas' help in getting rid of Jesus quickly and without causing a riot has produced a hurried trial with ill-prepared, inconsistent testimony. The failure of false witnesses to agree in their testimony is a novelistic touch, as in the story of Susanna (Dan 13:52–59). But in the Susanna story the judges are honest, and the demonstration that the testimony is false brings an end to the trial. Here the trial will be continued.

We have noted that in Mark 14:56–59 all the testimony is false; in Matt 26:59–61 only the first part of the testimony is false. Now we come to the testimony concerning the destruction of the Temple sanctuary, which Mark and Matt describe and evaluate differently.

DESTRUCTION OF THE SANCTUARY: MATT, ACTS, AND JOHN

Mark 14:58 supplies a concrete example of the testimony against Jesus: "We have heard him saying that 'I will destroy this sanctuary made by hand,

---

[10]Pss 27:12; 35:11; 37:32; 38:13; 54:5; 71:10; 86:14; Wis 2:12–20.

[11]In the ANALYSIS of §19B we saw that Mark may have placed here a Sanhedrin session that in the tradition carried no precise date but in fact occurred earlier, and that historically John may be more plausible in describing only a priestly interrogation in the night before Jesus was given over to the Romans.

and within three days another not made by hand I will build.'" Mark prefaces the quotation attributed to Jesus with an indication that the witnesses *were giving false testimony* against Jesus.[12] Mark (v. 59) follows with the statement that "even so their testimony was not consistent." Ironically the trial against Jesus has violated the Law against false testimony (Exod 20:16; Deut 5:20—one of the Ten Commandments, reiterated by Jesus in Mark 10:19). The influence of Mark on Luke is apparent in Acts 6:13–14 where *false* witnesses say, "We have heard him [Stephen] saying that this Jesus the Nazorean will destroy this place."[13] The Marcan form of the destruction statement is very difficult to interpret; and so before I treat Mark, let me first discuss the other, less difficult forms: Matt, Acts (dependent on Mark), and John (perhaps independent).

Matt. The changes in Matt's account are considerable. The false testimony seems to end in 26:60a. Then "at last" *two* witnesses come forward (26:60b). The number is not simply a literary touch, making more specific Mark's "many"; it is an indication that the testimony was legal according to the required number of witnesses (see Deut 17:6; 19:15; Num 35:30; Qumran *Temple Scroll* 61:6–12). While these witnesses are surely hostile, there is no indication that what they say is false. Matt drops Mark's "We have heard him saying," so there is no issue of whether this testimony depends on personal hearing. But the main changes are in Matt's form of the statement itself: "I am able to destroy the sanctuary of God, and within three days I will build (it)." Mark's "I will destroy" becomes "I am able to destroy." Some have interpreted Matt's statement as being more carefully qualified, changing from futurity to potentiality (cf. John 21:22–23). But Senior, Gnilka, and others are probably right that the "I am able" (*dynasthai*) is primarily a statement of power. Some passages in Mark (1:45; 3:20; 6:5; 7:24; 9:22–23) seem to put limitations on what Jesus was able to do; Matt modifies or eliminates all those passages, and so the Matthean reader would have the impression that Jesus' power was limitless. The awesomeness of that power is underlined here by Matt's substitution of "the sanctuary of God" for Mark's "this sanctuary made with hands." The statement "I am able to destroy the sanctuary of God" could be an impiety worthy of the antiGod or antichrist figure, "one who opposes and exalts himself against . . . every object of worship, so that he seats himself in the sanctuary of God, proclaiming himself

---

[12]The Greek of v. 58 involves a compound verb, making it very difficult to hold that Mark referred only to the contents, not to the intention.

[13]In agreement with commentators on Acts (e.g., Schneider) I judge Acts 6:14 to represent a Lucan editing of Mark 14:58. See S. Arai, "Zum 'Tempelwort' Jesu in Apostelgeschichte 6.14," NTS 34 (1988), 397–410, esp. 398–99; A. Weiser, "Zur Gesetzes- und Tempelkritik der 'Hellenisten,'" in *Das Gesetz im Neuen Testament,* ed. K. Kertelge (QD 108; Freiburg: Herder, 1986), 146–68, esp. 159, 162.

to be God" (II Thess 2:4). Perhaps that is the way any such claim sounded to Jews who did not believe in Jesus, whether in his lifetime or later in the 1st cent. But the statement attributed to Jesus in Matt has a second half that for the believer would remove it from impiety: "and within three days I will build (it)"—notice, not "another not made by hand" as in Mark but the sanctuary of God once more. The Matthean Jesus who makes this claim is joining himself very closely with God's final plans for Israel and the world, since (see p. 441 below) in apocalyptic thought God would intervene to replace the earthly Temple with one of divine design or building. The Jesus who makes this claim is one who has spoken of being "greater than the Temple" (Matt 12:6). In the flow of the Matthean narrative the failure of Jesus to deny having made such an extraordinary claim to power will provoke the high priest to demand if he thinks he is the Messiah, the Son of God. In summation, then, while for Mark the sanctuary statement constitutes false witness (for reasons yet to be explored), for Matt it seems to be a true statement of Jesus consonant with his role as the one endowed with God's power to inaugurate the kingdom.

Yet the Christian reader knows that Jesus has bound himself by the Father's will about drinking the cup, and so he is not going to do at this moment all the things he is able to do. Just as he is able to destroy the sanctuary, so he said in 26:53 that he was able to call on his Father for the more than twelve legions of angels. He did not call for such assistance, and he will begin to destroy the sanctuary only later.

Luke. Still a third reaction to the statement is given by Luke, who omits it from the Jesus trial. Why? Did Luke think it was not important for the outcome of the proceedings (Blinzler, *Trial* 101)? Did he have another source in which it was not found and which he preferred to follow here, cautiously moving the material that he saw in Mark to the Stephen trial in Acts? Did he make a historical judgment that debate about destruction of the sanctuary was more appropriate to the context of the first Christians? The issue is complicated because, as in Mark, the testimony concerning Stephen (and what he says about Jesus destroying the holy place) comes from false witnesses. Nevertheless, one gets the impression that the idea of Temple destruction related to Jesus was a genuine issue in the Stephen trial and that he has been heard repeating or interpreting Jesus. (See P. Doble, NTS 31 [1985], 73.) Does Luke's effort to have Stephen made the spokesman of Jesus stem from Luke's theological outlook combined with his sense of order, wanting to make it clear to the readers that in his own lifetime Jesus was not against the Temple? Jesus had warned about divine judgment on the Jerusalem Temple (Luke 13:35; 19:44; 23:28–31), but it was not something in which he would have a personal role. Situating this particular threat in

Acts might highlight that the sanctuary destruction (which was already a physical reality when Luke wrote) was punishment for what was done by the chief priests and Temple captains not only to Jesus but also to Peter, Stephen, and Paul. Brawley (*Luke-Acts* 117) is quite right that for Luke the primary opponents of earliest Christianity were the high priestly party and the Sadducees.

The form of the statement that the false witnesses attribute in Acts 6:14 to Stephen is only the negative part of the Marcan trial statement, "This Jesus the Nazorean will destroy this place." Whatever Stephen may have stood for in terms of Christian rejection of the Temple,[14] the Lucan Jesus said that the Temple belonged to his Father (2:49; 19:46), and Jesus' earliest disciples were not hostile to the Temple (24:53; Acts 2:46; 3:1). Even in the late 50s the Paul of Acts (25:8) is heard proclaiming that he has not offended against the Temple at all. That sentiment was surely the way Luke understood Jesus as well, even though both Jesus and Paul were brought before Jewish authorities on that very charge.

John. To the differences among the Synoptics just described must be added the evidence of John. First, in the Johannine account (11:47–48), weeks before Jesus' death during a Sanhedrin session led by Caiaphas, the destruction of the holy place comes up when the chief priests and the Pharisees express their fears that if what Jesus is doing is not somehow checked, there will be a Roman reaction that will "take from us" the Jewish holy place. It is important to note that what will be done to the Temple is reported by Jesus' enemies in the Sanhedrin, just as in Mark/Matt and Acts. Second, John (2:19) is the only canonical Gospel in which Jesus himself makes a direct statement about the sanctuary (one clearly related to what the witnesses at the Mark/Matt trial claim he made): "Destroy this sanctuary and in three days I will raise it up." Helpfully the evangelist explains that although the Jews thought he was speaking of the Jerusalem Temple and took the time indication literally, Jesus was actually speaking of the sanctuary of his body. His statement then was a warning to "the Jews" that if they put him to death

---

[14]Luke places on Stephen's lips the ancient prophetic argument against the Temple: "The Most High does not dwell in houses made by hand" (Acts 7:48). Weinert ("Luke" 90) would interpret it as no more definitive than the prophetic complaint, i.e., a critique of any automatic concept of God's presence but not a rejection of the Temple. However, I would suggest that because of the rejection and the persecution of Stephen, Christian thought was now moving toward a more definitive rejection of the Temple than in the prophetic past, and indeed Luke records no promise of replacement. Nevertheless, I agree overall with the series of writings by Weinert on the Lucan view of the Temple showing that through most of Luke-Acts there was no polemic against the Temple, but only against abuses. J. M. Dawsey, *Perspectives in Religious Studies* 18 (1991), 5–22, argues that the positive Lucan attitude toward the standing Temple and its possible role in the eschatological age of the kingdom was very ancient in Christianity, perhaps reflecting the earliest church in Jerusalem. Differences in Christian attitudes toward the Temple will be discussed later in this section.

as they would be inclined to, he would raise himself from the dead in three days.[15]

THE MARCAN FORM OF THE SANCTUARY STATEMENT

Before any exploration of different Gospel treatments of the sanctuary statement, more attention must be paid to Mark's account because it is not clear what Mark thought was false and why. We shall begin by commenting on *the Marcan wording* and then in the next section try to pinpoint the falsehood. I forewarn the reader that what follows, dealing with the sanctuary (and then, in the next section, with the christological titles) will be a long treatment. In the 1st cent. AD the issues involved became the most important points in debates between Jews who believed in Jesus and Jews who did not, and also in debates among believers, all of whom did not hold that same view. Thus this trial scene is a major opportunity to understand Gospel development (which mirrors the various levels of the debate) and the growth of Christian thought.

Mark 14:58 uses *naos*, "sanctuary," i.e., the most sacred, inner part of the Temple buildings. The word occurs 20 times in the Gospels and Acts (Mark 3, Matt 9, Luke 4, Acts 2, John 3), compared to some 67 uses in these writings of *hieron*, "Temple." Biguzzi[16] insists on a very sharp distinction between the Temple being destroyed in Mark 13:2,7–8,19–20 and Jesus saying, "I will destroy the sanctuary" in 14:58. Certainly the material Temple could be left standing while the sanctuary could be spiritually destroyed in the sense that God's presence had left and it was no longer a holy place (15:38). On the other hand, the Temple could scarcely be destroyed without a destruction of the earthly sanctuary. Mark, Matt, and John are harmonious in using "sanctuary" in the statement we have been discussing and in their later PN references to it; indeed such usage accounts for almost half of the twenty occurrences of *naos*. Mark's three uses are connected: the testimony here in 14:58; the mockery by those who passed by the cross making fun of the claim by Jesus (15:29); and the tearing of the sanctuary veil as Jesus dies

---

[15]Cf. John 10:17–18. For this conditional understanding of "destroy," see BSSNT 1.252. See notes 40 and 45 below for the debate about John's different setting for the saying. It is very difficult to know whether John's form of the saying (2:19) is independent of Mark 14:58. John's verb "raise up" reflects Johannine theological interpretation and is probably secondary to the "build" that appears in Mark. John's "in [*en*] three days" is probably a meaningless variant of Mark's "within [*dia*] three days," although Schlosser ("Parole" 401–2) thinks it could be a very slight indication of Johannine dependence on Mark. Much depends on whether there was a preMarcan form of 14:58 and how it was phrased (n. 37 below).

[16]"Mc. 14" 236; *Io distruggerò* 112–13. Schlosser ("Parole" 405–14) also argues for two basic sayings (Temple and sanctuary) represented by 13:2 and 14:58.

(15:38), which is a symbolic destruction of the sanctuary. The fact that "Temple" is not used may be important, especially as regards the rebuilding.

In 14:58 Jesus is supposed to have said "I will destroy." The Greek has an *egō*, so the agency is not unimportant. The verb is future, as also in Acts 6:14. Yet probably no distant future is meant, for in the mockery of Mark 15:29 the participles are in the present: "Aha! O one destroying the sanctuary and building (it) in three days."[17] That the destruction of the sanctuary has already begun (or, indeed, is done) is underlined in 15:38 by God's tearing the sanctuary veil.

Mark 14:58 distinguishes between two sanctuaries: The one to be destroyed is *cheiropoētos* ("made by hand") and the "another" to be built is *acheiropoētos*. Neither Matt nor John make this distinction, nor does Luke in the claim attributed to Jesus in Acts 6:14 (although Luke is aware of it, as Acts 7:48 shows). In Mark itself the distinction is not repeated in the mockery of 15:29. The paired positive and negative adjectives are a good Greek construction, but very difficult to retrovert into Hebrew or Aramaic. We can be relatively certain, then, that any statement made historically by Jesus about the destruction and rebuilding of the sanctuary did not contain these two distinguishing words—they are interpretations that arose among Greek speakers. The contrast does not exist in the LXX because there is no matching contrast in the Hebrew Bible to translate. *Acheiropoētos* never occurs, and LXX *cheiropoētos* translates the Hebrew contempt for idols, i.e., worthless gods made by human beings (see Biguzzi, "Mc. 14" 226–29). Indeed, it is possible that Christians were the first to formulate the negative adjective. While Philo sometimes follows the LXX usage, in *De vita Mosis* 2.18; #88 he uses *cheiropoētos* to describe the tabernacle constructed by Moses, without a pejorative tone. Secular Greek uses the *cheiropoētos* to distinguish what is made by human beings from what stems from nature.

"Made by hand" was taken over in the NT, in part to contrast what is of human origin and what is of divine origin. But Juel[18] insists that "not made by hand" is not simply a divine redoing of the human but a replacement of a different order, e.g., a contrasted circumcision in Eph 2:11 and Col 2:11. Paul states in II Cor 5:1 that if our earthly house or tent is destroyed, we have a building by God, not made by hand, eternal in the heavens—seemingly a contrast between an earthly body and a heavenly one, but phrased in terms of two buildings. The other NT uses of *cheiropoētos* concern "sanctuary," "Temple," and "tabernacle." Acts 7:48 and 17:24 affirm that God does not

---

[17]Perhaps the present participle in Mark 15:29 explains why in Mark 14:58 Codex Alexandrinus and Origen read the present tense "I destroy"; yet Hoffmann ("Wort" 130) opts for that reading as original because it is more difficult.

[18]*Messiah* 146–51 offers a good treatment of the two adjectives.

dwell in houses or sanctuaries made by hand, respectively the Jerusalem Temple and pagan sanctuaries. Against the liturgical Atonement Day background of the Hebrew high priest entering the sanctuary (Holy of Holies) of the Israelite tabernacle, Heb 9:11 has Christ the high priest entering into the heavenly holy place through the greater and more perfect tabernacle or tent not made by hand (*ou cheiropoētos*). Heb 9:24 says that he has entered not into a holy place made by hand but into heaven itself.[19]

If the Marcan contrast between the two sanctuaries comes from adjectives inserted to interpret Jesus' words, the Christian usage of those two adjectives and of Temple/sanctuary imagery may be an important key to what Mark wants his readers to understand (even if he dubs the pertinent statement false). There is little doubt that the "sanctuary made by hand" that Jesus is said to destroy is the innermost holy place of the Jerusalem Temple. It may be that by using this first adjective (which is LXX language for idols) Mark is expressing contempt for that sanctuary. But what is "another (sanctuary) not made by hand" that Jesus will build within three days? Three major suggestions have been made.

(1) One suggestion identifies this sanctuary as *the Christian community or church* (Cullman, Donahue, Gaston, Juel, Sweet, Vielhauer—scholars who approach the Marcan narrative in very different ways). Wenschkewitz and Vielhauer maintained that any such interpretation of "Temple" or "sanctuary" did not come into Christianity from Hebrew origins, but from Greek (specifically Stoic) thought. That view has been eroded by the Dead Sea Scrolls, which show that the idea of community as Temple or sanctuary was perfectly at home in Palestinian Judaism.[20] The Qumran group is described in 1QS 9:6 as a sanctuary, a house for Israel, and a Holy of Holies for Aaron (also CD 3:19). 4Q *Florilegium* interprets II Sam 7:10 to refer to the Qumran community: In implicit contrast to the existing Temple, this is the "house" that God will build in the last days, a "sanctuary consisting of human beings" fulfilling Exod 15:17–18: "In the sanctuary, O Lord, that your hands have established the Lord will be king forever and ever." The interpretation (pesher) goes on to comment on II Sam 7:12 (the promise of a Davidic dynasty): The Branch of David shall arise with the Interpreter of the Law in Zion at the end of time. Next the interpretation turns to Ps 2:1 but unfortu-

---

[19]The second Heb passage suggests that the tabernacle/tent not made by hand is the *heavenly realm*, whereas the first Heb passage has led some to identify it with the *glorified body* in which Christ has gone to the heavenly realm. See A. Vanhoye, Biblica 46 (1965), 1–28. The ambivalence of the language may be related to Paul's outlook in II Cor, where the ideas of heavenly body and heavenly house are intermingled.

[20] Gärtner, *Temple;* G. Klinzing, *Die Umdeutung des Kultus in der Qumrangemeinde und im Neuen Testament* (Göttingen: Vandenhoeck & Ruprecht, 1971). Here I am especially indebted to Flusser, "Two Notes," dealing with 4Q *Florilegium.*

nately breaks off, so that we do not know if it continued to Ps 2:7 where God says to the king, "You are my son." Even without that it has associated a sanctuary built by God's hands in the last days (the community) and the Davidic Messiah. If we move on to the NT, Paul considers the individual Christian God's sanctuary (I Cor 3:16–17; 6:19) and can say, "We are the sanctuary of the living God" (II Cor 6:16). Eph 2:21 speaks of "a holy sanctuary in the Lord," and I Pet 2:5 imagines "living stones" built as "a spiritual house." In Acts 15:16 James associates rebuilding the dwelling of David with the coming of Gentiles to believe in Jesus. Yet while "not made by hand" is used of the circumcision that Christians receive, it is never used in the NT of the Christian community as sanctuary, even though such a use would not be far from what is said about the community.

(2) A different proposal (Jeremias, Pesch, E. P. Sanders, etc.) is that "another (sanctuary) not made by hand" in Mark 14:58 refers *to the sanctuary of divine origin* that Jewish apocalyptic expected *in the last times* to replace the earthly Temple. Already the Song of Moses (Miriam) in Exod 15:17 anticipated a divinely established sanctuary: "You planted them on the mountain of your inheritance . . . the sanctuary, O Lord, which your hands established" (whether that sanctuary will be in Jerusalem, or is on top of a sacred mountain like Sinai, or in heaven). The pattern of Temple destruction and rebuilding became part of Israel's religious imagery, flowing from the bitter 6th-cent.-BC experience of the Babylonian destruction and the rebuilding some seventy years later. In the idealistic descriptions of the Temple in Ezek 40–44; 46:19–47:2, and Trito-Isaiah 60:7,13, the expected replacement almost surpasses human building. In the Sinaiticus form of Tobit (read in the light of the OL) we hear in 14:4: "The house of God will be burned down and will be in ruins for a time." Tobit 13:14[12] puts a curse on all who destroy Jerusalem and its buildings but a blessing on all who build it up. Tobit 13:11[10] speaks of the tent of God being built with joy, and 13:17[16] has Jerusalem built up as the great King's house forever. Inevitably, as even the rebuilt sanctuary became impure in the eyes of some Israelites, the anticipation of a heavenly sanctuary grew stronger. *Jubilees,* looking forward from the time of the exodus, predicts the exile of Israel from the land (1:13) and then a recovery when, as God promises, "I will build my sanctuary in their midst and I shall dwell with them" (1:17)—a sanctuary for all eternity (1:27) in Jerusalem on Mount Zion (1:29). *I Enoch* 90:28–29 looks into the future and pictures the removing of the old house of God, and the Lord of the sheep bringing a new house greater and loftier than before. *IV Ezra (II Esdras)* 10:54, envisioning a city of the Most High to be revealed, states that no building of human construction can stand in it. Rev 21:10 has the holy city of Jerusalem coming down out of heaven from God; but 21:22

makes clear that there is no sanctuary in the city, for the Almighty and the Lord constitute the sanctuary.[21] In the post-NT Midrash *Mekilta* (Shirata 10) on Exod 15:17 God is expected to build [tense disputed] the sanctuary with His hands. In the much later Midrash on Ps 90:16 (#19), now that the Temple built by flesh and blood is destroyed, God promises, "I myself will build it," and it will last forever. On the Christian side, *Barnabas* 16 attacks the Jews for putting their hope in the Temple as a building rather than in the true house of God. The edifice, like the city and the people of Israel, has been "given over" to destruction; but the sanctuary of God exists and is being built up gloriously—a spiritual sanctuary being built for the Lord. (This image combines the language of the eschatological sanctuary with that of the community constituted by divine indwelling.)

These last passages illustrate the difficulty in employing the idea of the eschatological sanctuary to interpret Mark 14:58, namely, God is the normal builder of that sanctuary, not the Messiah.[22] Bornhäuser's observation (*Death* 45) that kings like Hezekiah and Josiah took responsibility for refurbishing the Temple cannot without further evidence be transferred to the Messiah. Indeed, apocalyptic strains often concentrate on divine intervention without envisioning a major human agent. Pesch (*Markus* 2.435) tries to cite Jewish texts for the Messiah as the builder of the sanctuary; but in fact there is no pre-NT text to support that. One might think it logical that since David and his son Solomon were involved with Temple building, the Davidic Messiah would rebuild it. Actually, however, the opposite emerges from 4QFlor 1:1–13, which is our earliest attestation of the application of the Davidic dynastic oracle (II Sam 7:8–16) to the Messiah. That text speaks of a house that will not be laid waste like the former sanctuary—a sanctuary to be built among human beings for the pure ones of Israel; yet that building is not ascribed to the Messiah. Indeed, II Sam 7:13a, which speaks of David's son building a house for God's name, is omitted from the interpretation! *PsSol* 17:32(30) foresees the anointed king, the Son of David, purging Jerusalem and making it holy as of old; but he is not said to build the Temple. *Sibylline Oracle* 5:414–33 (ca. AD 100–120?), having reflected on the destroyed Second Temple, speaks of a blessed man who comes from heaven and makes a holy house with a beautiful sanctuary; yet it hails God as the founder of the great Temple. Eventually Zech 6:12–13, which spoke of the Davidic Offspring (Zerubbabel) building the Temple (i.e., the Second Temple in 515 BC), was reinterpreted to apply to the Messiah as we see in the Targum of that passage.

---

[21]Notice once again (n. 19) the ambivalent combining of celestial sanctuary with the risen Christ.

[22]Another difficulty is detected by Schlosser ("Parole" 411–12). Despite the evidence in Jewish and Christian apocalyptic eschatology of the expectation of a sanctuary of the last times, this idea is not found elsewhere in Jesus' own preaching of the kingdom of God.

Similarly, once the Targum of Isa 52:13 identified the servant of the Lord as God's Messiah, the Targum of Isa 53:5 could affirm: "He will build the [already destroyed] sanctuary that was polluted because of our transgressions." But the written form of this Targum is from about the 5th cent. AD. Still later is *Midrash Rabba* 9.6 on Leviticus 7:12 that also has the Messiah king rebuilding the sanctuary. Such later works scarcely constitute evidence for interpreting Mark, and none of them have the Messiah destroying the Temple.

(3) A final possibility for the Marcan sanctuary "not made by hand" is the *body of the glorified Christ* raised on the third day (Cole, Gärtner, Gaston [plus the community], Lamarche, Nineham, Simon). Indeed, Prete ("Formazione" 16) would argue that "within three days" was not part of the original statement but was added to make it applicable to the resurrection. John 2:19 interprets the replacement sanctuary in that way but has only *one* sanctuary destroyed and raised (not built). Self-raising by Jesus is at home in a Johannine christology where Jesus lays down his life and takes it up again; it is less easy to justify for Mark. In support of the sanctuary as the body of Christ some cite Mark 12:10–11 where, in the context of the son and heir being killed by the vineyard tenants, Jesus speaks seemingly of himself as a cornerstone rejected by the builders. In an addition in some mss. of Mark 13:2 (which speaks of the throwing down of the stones of the Jerusalem Temple), we find that "within three days another will *rise* without hands"—clearly an early resurrection interpretation. Perhaps the two interpretations of Mark's sanctuary (heavenly sanctuary and glorified body) are combinable, as we see in II Cor 5:1 and Heb 9:11,24 (see n. 19 and n. 21 above).

There are variations of the three interpretations just discussed and other interpretations as well, e.g., Biguzzi[23] speaks of the sanctuary as a new salvific economy introduced by Jesus' death; and in an intricately argued essay Vögtle ("Markinische" 373) understands Mark 14:58 to refer to the end of OT cult and community and, implicitly through Jesus' death, to the founding of a community for Jew and Gentile in God's presence.[24] To some extent the plausibility of all interpretations depends on how strictly the "I will build" demands action traceable to Jesus—a question not to be divorced from the literalness of "I will destroy."

Tied in with the issue of "another sanctuary not made by hand" is the precise meaning in Mark 14:58 of *dia triōn hēmerōn,* which can refer to "a

[23]"Mc. 14" 292; *Io distruggerò* 114–64.

[24]Schlosser ("Parole" 414) is very close to Vögtle in his interpretation: not an eschatological Temple, for God will be all in all. But one has a hard time recognizing such a conception in "another sanctuary" if that wording is original.

space of three days *within* which" (i.e., the time it will take to build the sanctuary) or "the moment *after* the extent of three days" (the time for the completion of the building). The force of *dia* is time through which something happens. The fact that later Mark 15:29 will use "in [*en*] three days," as does John 2:19, seems to me to point toward the "within" meaning. Yet Jeremias ("Drei" 222–23) argues that *dia* and *en* are variant translations of Hebrew *lĕ*, and he favors the "after" translation. Perhaps we are trying to be too precise. "Three days," expressed in the Bible in various ways, sometimes means a short time.[25] In particular it can refer to the limited endurance of a time of calamity from which God delivers.[26] It heightens the tone of prophecy here (and at the end of the trial Jesus will be mocked as a false prophet). Thus the Marcan statement could envisage the building of another sanctuary *shortly* after the destruction of the physical sanctuary. If one looks at the passion predictions (APPENDIX VIII), the standard language in Mark (8:31; 9:31; 10:34) is "after [*meta*] three days," while in Matt (16:21; 17:23; 20:19) it is "on the third day." Would "within [*dia, en*] three days" suggest the resurrection to Marcan readers, despite the difference of vocabulary, and thus favor the interpretation of "another sanctuary" as the glorified body of Jesus?

Much of this discussion of what Mark means by the sanctuary statement of 14:58 inevitably draws on thought found elsewhere in Mark. Nevertheless, a major objection to all such diagnoses of meaning is the fact that Mark describes this statement attributed to Jesus as embodying *false* testimony. How does that condition our interpretation?

THE FALSITY OF THE SANCTUARY TESTIMONY

Various explanations have been offered of what Mark means when, before the words reporting what Jesus said, he writes of "false testimony" and after those words he comments that even so, the testimony of the witnesses was not *isos*. One approach is that Mark is not really thinking of objectively false testimony. A noun related to the Marcan *pseudomartyrein* is found in I Cor 15:15, where Paul is accused of *misrepresenting* by having testified that God raised Christ (see Wenschkewitz, *Spiritualisierung* 99). Some have argued that "false" means no more than "unjust," in the sense that the witnesses were prejudiced against Jesus, even if their report was true. Burkill ("Trial" 7) and Prete ("Formazione" 11) see the falsehood in the opposition

[25]II Kings 20:5; Hos 6:2; Luke 13:33; see G. M. Landes, JBL 86 (1967), 446–50.
[26]See K. Lehmann, *Auferweckt am dritten Tag nach dem Schrift* (QD 38; Freiburg: Herder, 1968), 181.

to Jesus and the failure to understand his mysterious words. Several psalm passages could be important background here. The MT of Ps 27:12 is: "False witnesses have risen up against me and such as breathe out violence"; but the LXX reads: "Unjust witnesses have risen up against me, and their injustice is false." Ps 35:11 is also interesting: "Violent [LXX: unjust] witnesses have risen up; things I knew not of, they ask of me." One should point out, however, that only at times does the LXX equate "unjust" with Hebrew "false"; and when it does, there is usually a hint of falsehood in the context. Certainly Mark means that the witnesses are unjust to Jesus, but he also indicates that part of the injustice is their false reporting.

As for *isos,* twice used of the witnesses' testimony and translated by me as "consistent," it means "equal" in number, size, or quality. The thrust here is, in part, that their testimony is not equal to the task of convicting Jesus, and so "adequate" would not be an impossible translation. Plooij ("Jesus") presses the interpretation too far in one direction when he suggests that the basic difficulty is that to say "I will destroy the sanctuary" is not a punishable offense (for there were others who condemned the Temple). The inadequateness of the testimony is, after all, related to its being false (even if that was not the only problem with it). One gets the impression that because they do not agree, the falsity of the witnesses has become patent and rendered their testimony useless to the Sanhedrin. That is why the high priest will now intervene. I have already called attention to the Susanna Story involving both false and inconsistent testimony (Dan 13). If fidelity to Mark, then, does not permit us easily to explain away falsity as injustice or prejudice, in what precise point in 14:58 is the falsity found?

(1) Is it in the claim by the witnesses, "We have heard him saying," a claim peculiar to Mark? In a modern court, if witnesses had not heard the accused themselves but were relying on what someone had told them, the evidence could be rejected as hearsay. In a story such as Mark's, however, this would seem too much a technicality if Jesus had actually made the statement. Mark wants his readers to think more is wrong than a point of criminal procedure. Kleist ("Two") has a refinement of this: What Mark's overly abbreviated account means to report is that one witness said, "I have heard him say, 'I will destroy this sanctuary . . . ,'" while the other said, "I have heard him say, 'I will build another sanctuary. . . .'" It was because of these two different renderings of Jesus' words that their testimony did not agree. Still another theory is that because their testimony did not agree, the court did not have two witnesses (in agreement) as demanded by Deut 17:6. In my judgment all such approaches that find the flaw solely in the witnessing (rather than in the statement itself) are refuted by Mark 15:29, where those who pass by

the cross mock Jesus about destroying and building the sanctuary. That suggests a claim widely attributed to Jesus and not dependent on a few false
hearers.

(2) Is the statement attributed to Jesus false in the sense that Mark thinks
or wants the readers to think that Jesus never said anything like this at all?
Let us leave to (3) below the possibility that Mark regards one or the other
aspect of the statement as false. First we shall discuss it on this more global
level.[27] Lührmann ("Markus 14" 459–60) is one who makes a strong case
for understanding falsity to mean that Mark wants his readers to think the
statement in 14:58 was a total fabrication by the witnesses. The basic argument is simple: Even though chaps. 11–12 of Mark raised the Temple issue
several times, Jesus never made *this* statement. If one objects that 14:58 is a
digest of Jesus' attitudes, why did Mark have to resort to a digest? Why was
the statement not made by Jesus during the cleansing of the Temple (as it is
in John 2:19) and then quoted (correctly or incorrectly) by the witnesses?
(See how Mark 16:7 quotes 14:28, and Mark 14:72 quotes 14:30.) Lührmann regards it as a change of tack when the high priest asks Jesus in 14:60,
"Are you the Messiah, the Son of the Blessed?"; for the readers would recognize that this was now a true issue: Peter said that Jesus was the Messiah in
8:29, and God said that Jesus was his Son in 1:11; 9:7; see 1:1.

Overall, however, I am convinced that this approach to the falsity is not
correct. The two issues in the trial find a parallel in the mockeries of Jesus
as he hangs on the cross: The passersby mock Jesus as the one who destroys
and builds the sanctuary within three days, and the chief priests mock him
as the Messiah. One finds no suggestion in the twofold mockery that one
charge is completely false and the other is true. How are readers to think
that passersby knew about the sanctuary statement? Scarcely from the false
witnesses! Would not the readers of Mark assume that the reason that even
passersby knew about the sanctuary statement was that in fact Jesus had said
something like that? Moreover, still a further parallel to the two trial issues
is found the moment Jesus dies on the cross. There the vindication of Jesus
on both issues is shown triumphantly as the sanctuary veil is torn from top
to bottom and the centurion confesses that Jesus was truly God's Son (15:38–
39). Would Mark see any victory in having a statement fulfilled that Jesus
never made and that existed only in the created fiction of false witnesses?
Matt certainly did not read Mark as meaning that Jesus never made such a
statement; nor is that meaning supported by John's presentation in which

[27]The issue of whether historically Jesus made some form of this statement will be treated in the
ANALYSIS; what is of concern here is what Mark wants the reader to suppose.

Jesus actually makes the sanctuary statement, constituting further evidence of widespread Christian awareness. Does the trial accusation have to quote rather than digest? Would Mark's readers really think that *in globo* a threat to destroy the sanctuary had never been made by Jesus when he predicted that the Temple buildings would be thrown down in 13:2, using the same verb (*katalyein*) as in 14:58?[28] Also Mark surrounds Jesus' cleansing of the Temple with the cursing and withering of the fig tree (11:12–14 and 20–21 around 11:15–19) as a symbolic interpretation of how he will treat the Temple.[29] My judgment, then, is that when Mark wrote that this was false testimony, he did not expect readers to say, "Ah yes, because the statement is totally foreign to the Jesus we have been reading about." Rather they were expected to say, "Well, Jesus did say something about the Temple being destroyed but not in the way the witnesses are claiming."

(3) For Mark, then, falsity lies in a particular aspect of the statement attributed to Jesus in 14:58. One can wonder whether the actual phrasing of the statement is false or only the witnesses' understanding of it (and some would take *isos* in 14:59 in that way: Their understandings of it were not consistent). The misunderstanding approach—a correct statement badly understood—was already held by Jerome and is probably the most common among scholars, e.g., Gnilka (*Markus* 2.280). Yet Mark gives us no clue as to how the witnesses understood the statement and no clue for distinguishing between their understanding and a correct understanding. In my judgment one should follow the more difficult course of seeing if the statement is being phrased falsely, which is what Mark seems to say. Since neither Matt nor John treat their corresponding statement as false, attention has focused on those ways in which Mark's phrasing of the statement differs from theirs.

(a) Only in Mark is Jesus reported to say "I [*egō*] will destroy." John 2:19 attributes the destruction of the sanctuary to "the Jews"; John 11:48 raises the possibility that the Romans might take away the Jewish holy place; Mark 13:2 treats the coming destruction of the Temple buildings as a divine action. It might be, then, that the witnesses have falsified Jesus' intention by making him the agent of the destruction. It is dubious, however, that this could be the whole point of falsity. In the *Gospel of Thomas* 71 (Nag Hammadi II.2.45:34–35) Jesus says, "I shall destroy [this] house, and no one will be

---

[28]Ancient scribes saw the close connection between 13:2 and 14:58; Codices Bezae and Washingtonensis, the OL, and Cyprian read at the end of Mark 13:2: ". . . thrown down, and within three days another will rise without hands."

[29]See W. L. Telford, *The Barren Temple and the Withered Tree* (JSNTSup 1; Sheffield: JSOT, 1980). On p. 238 he finds Jesus' action against the fig tree "a proleptic sign prefiguring the destruction of the Temple cultus."

able to rebuild it." If that refers to the Temple, some early Christians saw no problem in attributing agency to Jesus.[30] Mark 11:15–17 has Jesus take personal, violent action to correct Temple abuses, so he does not imagine Jesus to be uninvolved. As I explained, in the interpretative framework of the Temple cleansing, the Marcan Jesus curses the fig tree and it withers, surely a prophetic action of destructive judgment. The tearing of the sanctuary veil in Mark 15:38 occurs just as Jesus has died and is God's angry reaction to what has been done to the Son (15:39). Jesus did not tear the sanctuary veil, but who he is and what he has done is so much a part of the scene that to describe it in terms of "I will destroy" would be more inexact than false. Moreover, Matt, who changes Mark's phrasing and drops the suggestion of falsity, leaves Jesus as agent, "I am able to destroy." Matt 27:39–40 also preserves the Marcan mockery by the passersby which makes Jesus the agent, the destroyer of the sanctuary.

(b) Another unique aspect of Mark's form of the statement on which many have fastened is the distinction between two different sanctuaries, one made by hand, another not. I mentioned above that this is clearly an interpretation that would have been added in the Greek-speaking development of the saying and that it is lacking in the mockery of Mark 15:29. Some have found the solution to the problem of falsity in this addition, but in a way that is almost the opposite of the direction we have been moving. Juel, Vielhauer, and others suggest that the statement of destroying and building the sanctuary *without* those adjectives was false (in other words, as it is phrased in the mockery of 15:29) and that Mark has supplied those adjectives to tell the readers how to interpret the statement correctly. These adjectives, then, become the neutralizers of falsity. That runs up against significant objections. Mark becomes an almost impossible pedagogue. He has rephrased a false statement so that it is now true, but he still calls it false and suggests incoherence. Second, both Matt and John, who think the statement true, do so without the adjectives! Those arguments would almost suggest the opposite: The statement is false because it has those adjectives! But have we not seen that they are probably Christian interpretation, and so how can they be false?

THE SANCTUARY STATEMENT, TRUE AND FALSE IN VARIOUS WAYS

Obviously it is time to attempt an answer to the conundrum represented by Mark 14:57–59, an answer that may not solve everything but brings to

[30]But Gaston (*No Stone* 153) thinks that the gnostic editor of this gospel is talking about the body as the prison of the soul. Quispel ("Gospel" 197–99), judging it impossible that the *Thomas* form of the saying was derived from Mark/Matt, where the statement is attributed to false witnesses, would argue for Jewish-Christian origin. He sees echoes of that background in the use of "this

the fore factors that must enter into a solution. Let me list some reasons why, at the start, one should take for granted that *Christian tradition* contained a statement of Jesus on the theme of sanctuary destruction and rebuilding.[31] If Mark dubs the statement as false, obviously some people had been giving voice to the basic theme. John 2:19 may be an independent witness to the statement. (The Q saying in Luke 13:35/Matt 23:38–39 contrasts the house of God forsaken with a positive return of Jesus; this shows that the outlook is found in the tradition.) Looking at similar statements in the tradition that involve a future element (pertaining to the kingdom, the Son of Man, the endtime), we find that Jesus' imprecision about the future often left both foe and friend puzzled. (Modern scholars puzzle over Mark 9:1; 13:30,32; 14:62; Matt 10:23; John 21:22.) What Jesus' destruction-of-the-sanctuary proclamation meant for Jewish cult and sanctuary could therefore be a subject of dispute for decades between Jews who did not believe in Jesus and Jews who did, and also of dispute among his followers. Acts portrays the hostility of Jewish leaders against both Stephen and Paul as focused on Temple issues. Among Christians, Acts (2:46; 3:1) shows some going to the Temple for the hours of prayer and sacrifice, even though Stephen is heard to say that the Most High does not dwell in such a house made by hand (7:48). Radical challenges to the ongoing validity of sanctuary cult practiced by levitical priests or at Jerusalem are mounted in Hebrews and John.

Given such a volatile situation, it is not surprising to find a statement of Jesus about sanctuary destruction and rebuilding treated as true in some documents (Matt, John) and false in others (Mark, Acts). Much would depend on how the statement was understood and phrased; moreover, attitudes could change when increasing numbers of Gentiles entered the following of Jesus, when the Jerusalem Temple was destroyed, etc. Weeden ("Cross" 123–29) and Lührmann ("Markus 14" 466–69) would argue that Mark thought the sanctuary statement as phrased in 14:58 false because of the way it was being used by other Christians, e.g., by those who expected Jesus to build a Temple not made with hands by miraculous power (Weeden: a divine-man outlook on Jesus) or by those who linked the parousia with the fall of Jerusalem (Lührmann: already kept distinct in Mark 13). While that general approach is quite persuasive, the attempt to interpret the sanctuary statement only on an inner-Christian level makes the Marcan setting of Jewish opposi-

---

house" for the Temple and in the claim that no one will rebuild it. Quispel thinks that the saying in the *Thomas* form originally meant that God would be the agent of destruction, for it quoted God in the first person even as did Jer 7:14: "I will do to this house . . . as I have done to Shiloh." Thus part of the offense was Jesus' daring to speak for God.

[31]Once more I am reserving to the ANALYSIS whether plausibly Jesus made such a statement.

tion to Jesus merely a transparency through which to see church debate. In the PN the struggle between Jesus and the Jewish authorities is too basic a theme, in my judgment, to disappear so totally, especially when we have evidence that Jews who did not believe in Jesus continued to struggle with Christians over Temple issues throughout the first century, and even later. Mark 15:29 is just as important a key to the evangelist's outlook as 14:58, and there nonbelieving Jewish passersby mock Jesus as the destroyer and builder of the Temple, without the "made by hand" clauses. If it is plausible that Christians (and Jews) developed false interpretations of the sanctuary statement, it is equally plausible that Jews mocked Christians over the outlandish claims of their master. Mark, then, would not be giving us simply a transparency but a story of Jewish failure to believe Jesus that also has meaning in a situation where Christians fail to believe him (because they distort his words).

It may be helpful to illustrate the sense of flow and diversity that I am proposing for interpreting this statement, not only in Mark but also in the other Gospels. (1) Let us begin by supposing that *in his lifetime* Jesus made a warning proclamation about the destruction and replacement of the sanctuary. Such a proclamation could have been a Jeremiah-like attitude (attested elsewhere in the tradition) sharpened by a sense of eschatological urgency that accompanied the advent or inbreaking of the kingdom. Those in Jerusalem who distrusted rural religious figures with reforming tendencies might well see in such a statement a dangerous apocalyptic fanaticism. If Jesus included in his statement a figurative indication of brevity ("within three days," not meant literally), he could have been the object of mockery as well as the source of alarm. Jesus' claim is subject to mockery both in Mark 15:29 and in John 2:20, where the three days are taken literally, and in the latter he is reminded that Herod's rebuilding has taken forty-six years! What I am projecting here would not have been foreign to the 1st cent. Josephus (*Ant.* 20.8.6; #169–70) describes a prophet who in the 50s came from Egypt to Jerusalem, and from the Mount of Olives thought he could command the wall of Jerusalem to fall. The procurator sent troops against him. In the 60s Josephus (*War* 6.5.3; #300–9) tells of the apocalypticist Jesus son of Ananias who announced the coming destruction of the Jerusalem sanctuary; the Jewish authorities tried to get the Romans to execute him.

(2) Let us move to the years between 30/33 and 70, between Jesus' lifetime and the Roman destruction of the Jerusalem Temple. Christians would have had to wrestle with the meaning of Jesus' sanctuary statement because his death and resurrection had not destroyed the Temple sanctuary. (During this period Christians struggled with other eschatological statements attributed to Jesus about the endtime, e.g., that this generation would not pass

away before all these things took place.) How could they answer non-believing Jews who, if they heard of the statement, would point to the still-standing, magnificent buildings? One answer would have been to search out incidents serviceable as omens that the Temple would soon be destroyed.[32] Matt 27:51–52 joins the tearing of the sanctuary veil to an earthquake, splitting of rocks, and opening of tombs; presumably these were signs of the endtime. Ultimately Jesus the Messiah would show his power by destroying the sanctuary of God and building it. More radically, Mark 15:29 probably sees the tearing of the veil as a sign from God that *from that moment on* the sanctuary no longer had salvation history value. Although the Temple stood, the sanctuary was destroyed; it was no longer the holy place, for God had left.[33] Even those who awaited the literal destruction of the sanctuary building may have begun in this period to reinterpret its replacement, e.g., a heavenly tabernacle, or the Christian community, interpretations that have left their traces in NT thought. At the same time, because of development in christology wherein the closeness of the risen Lord to the Father became more and more articulated, any vagueness of agency in the earliest form of Jesus' statement may have begun to disappear, moving perhaps from "destroyed" and "built" to "I will destroy" and "I will build."[34] But the NT also describes others (Jews, Romans, God) as agents in the statement about Temple or sanctuary destruction. Another type of change could have occurred as some believers in Jesus because more hostile to Jewish cult and priesthood. The boldness shown in Stephen's claim that the Most High would not dwell in such a place as the Temple, a house made by hand (echoing an OT expression for the worthless human-made idols) may in Luke's mind have led to the false charge that Stephen hoped to execute Jesus' threat to destroy the holy place, a statement made even more polemic (and thus falsified) by losing the positive motif of rebuilding.

(3) Finally, let us move to the period after the destruction of the Temple in 70, a period when most likely three canonical Gospels were written. Those Christians who understood the saying to refer literally to the Jerusalem sanctuary could regard themselves as verified, for in their faith they could see behind the Roman eagles of Titus' army the cross of Jesus. This was for

---

[32]When I discuss the tearing of the sanctuary veil in Mark 15:38 (§43), I shall mention the strange occurrences that Josephus saw as omens and precursors of the destruction of the Temple in 70.

[33]Another approach would have been to reinterpret the statement of Jesus by giving his use of "sanctuary" a different meaning—not the Jerusalem building but Jesus' own body. This bodily sanctuary was destroyed by "the Jews" and raised in three days, just as Jesus said. Such is the interpretation in John 2:21–22, so that the statement becomes a symbolic passion prediction.

[34]A similar movement is often traced in resurrection statements: Jesus was "raised up" yielding to Jesus "rose"—a movement not in any simplistic chronological sense but in attested frequency of use.

them the long-delayed judgment of God exercised because of what was done to Jesus.[35] Some Christians may still have yearned for a new physical building that could meet God's standards. Hebrews finds it necessary to disparage an earthly tabernacle as if some Christians longed for it; and both Irenaeus (*Adv. Haer.* 1.26.2) and Jerome (*In Isa.* 13 on 49:14; CC 73A.543) testify to an enduring yearning for the Jerusalem Temple among Jewish Christians. Yet surely most Christians would have interpreted the rebuilt sanctuary not literally but symbolically, different from the first. But they might differ on whether this second sanctuary was already in place (the Christian community or the risen body of Christ) or soon to come (a heavenly tabernacle descending as part of the end of the world). Many Jews would have argued that the Roman destruction of Jerusalem flowed from a combination of Roman brutality and Jewish fanaticism. Josephus (*Ant.* 20.8.5; #166), having described murders and profanations that took place in Jerusalem in the 50s, states: "For this reason, I think, even God Himself, hating their impiety, turned away from our city, and no longer judging the Temple to be a clean house for Him, brought the Romans upon us and a cleansing fire on the city." Just as after the Babylonian destruction, Jews now prayed for the rebuilding of the physical Temple in the same spot. Simon ("Retour" 247–48) points to *Shemoneh Esreh* 14 with its prayer for God to return and dwell in the city which would be built as an everlasting building; he compares it with the Christian *Maranatha* or "Come, Lord Jesus" (Rev 22:20). When Jews encountered the "prophecy" by Jesus, they would have mocked the claim that he was the cause of the destruction, and have trusted that when the Temple was rebuilt, his arrogance would be refuted. It is interesting that centuries later one of the tactics of the apostate Emperor Julian, in his attempt to discredit Christianity, was a plan to rebuild the Jewish Temple.

In such an array of fluctuating interpretations and arguments against the sanctuary saying, how are we to understand Mark? Surely he wrote against the unbelieving mockery typified by the passersby of 15:29 who regarded Jesus as a powerless charlatan. But there is also evidence that he rejected any strain of Christian interpretation that would have seen the destruction of the Jerusalem Temple as a sign that Jesus was about to act immediately to build another not made by hand. In 13:2 Jesus predicts that the buildings of the Temple will be thrown down, not one stone left upon another. But when in 13:4 he is asked when this will take place and when all things will be completed, Jesus makes a distinction. In 13:5–23 he describes apocalyptically the things that precede and surround the setting up of the abomination

---

[35]For the continuation of this judgment in early Christianity, see Justin, *Dial.* 108; Origen, *Contra Celsum* 1.47; 4.22.

of desolation where it should not be (13:14: Danielic language for the profanation of the Temple); but that is not the end, for there is still more time until the Son of Man comes in the clouds (13:26), a period that Mark treats symbolically in 13:24–37. He says specifically that the Son does not know of that day or that hour (13:32). This is over against a set of false messiahs and false prophets who come in his name and lead people astray (13:5–6,21–22). Lührmann ("Markus 14" 466–68) invokes this plausibly to illustrate how a statement like "I will destroy this sanctuary made by hand, and within three days another not made by hand I will build" might have served as a supporting text for the false prophets.

Suggestions from Vögtle ("Markinische" 373–75) can also be woven into the discussion if we turn to Mark 15:37–39 as a sign of what Mark thinks is true about sanctuary destruction and replacement. On the occasion of Jesus' death on the cross, God rends the veil of the sanctuary and leads a Roman centurion to confess Jesus as Son of God. This is Mark's interpretation of the "I will build": The power of Jesus to do this lies in his death. His is not the power of a false messiah who shows signs and wonders (13:22) but the power of the cross. Having drunk the cup and gone through the hour, the crucified Christ shares in God's power to reject unbelief and beget belief. What replaces the empty sanctuary of the Jerusalem Temple as the holy place of God is a community of believers such as the centurion, whose true confession of Jesus as the Son of God comes from having comprehended his death on the cross—a community willing to take up the cross and follow Jesus. All those who think that the kingdom will come and the sanctuary be established simply because the Jerusalem Temple has been destroyed have not understood that they too must suffer before all these things come to pass, that they too must go through tribulations (13:24). God's action is not automatic in any way that removes having to drink the cup that Jesus drank, a cup drunk to its dregs on the cross.

The understanding just enunciated is harmonious with the evidence of the Marcan text and attested Marcan thought.[36] Nevertheless, as readers of Mark at this point in the flow of the story, we must not overly anticipate what Mark will show to be the truth about sanctuary destruction and building. In 14:58 the readers are meant to see the depth of the hostility toward Jesus in such false testimony that makes him appear like an apocalyptic fanatic. Even so the ploy of his opponents fails, for the testimony is not consistent; and so now the high priest himself will have to intervene.

Matt is the only other evangelist to have the sanctuary saying in the PN.

---

[36]Other interpretations, e.g., that Mark rejected totally any eschatological sanctuary, while possible, go beyond the available evidence.

He has simplified both the statement and the context he received from Mark (perhaps because he found 14:57–59 as difficult as modern interpreters find it). What becomes in Matt a clear affirmation of power, "I am able to destroy the sanctuary of God, and within three days I will build (it)," is attributed to Jesus without a suggestion of falsehood. The thought that Jesus may have made such an extraordinary claim provokes the high priest, Caiaphas, to intervene, and it is to his intervention we shall turn in the COMMENT of the next section (§21).

ANALYSIS

Two major issues must be discussed in relation to the trial/investigation of Jesus by the Jewish authorities before he was given over to the Romans. Overall there is the issue of *composition:* How were the accounts in the various Gospels put together? I shall reserve the discussion of the myriad proposals about composition until I have commented on the whole trial/interrogation, and so it will come in the ANALYSIS that will constitute a separate section (§24) below. More immediately there is the issue of *historicity.* In the ANALYSIS of each of the four parts into which I have divided my treatment of the Sanhedrin proceedings (§§20–23) I shall raise historical questions pertinent to the material commented on therein. Accordingly in this ANALYSIS of Part One the topic is the historicity of what is attributed to Jesus concerning the Temple/sanctuary.

In discussing Mark 14:58 and par. above, we saw that the saying attributed to Jesus about the destruction and rebuilding of the sanctuary is preserved by the different evangelists in varied wordings, and that this statement is evaluated as false testimony by Mark and Acts. In the COMMENT, attempting to deal with that situation in terms of what the Gospels might wish to convey, I used scattered NT evidence to trace experimentally through three periods of the 1st cent. AD (before 30, 30–70, after 70) how followers of Jesus and those who opposed him *might have* understood a claim about sanctuary destruction and rebuilding. That effort showed that the different Gospel ways of understanding the claim do not contradict the possibility that in his lifetime Jesus uttered a prophetic warning that the sanctuary would be destroyed and replaced. It is important to insist on the word "sanctuary" here, for Jesus is not recorded to have promised the replacement of the whole Temple. Moreover, I shall speak of "the" sanctuary; for, although Mark indicates that the replacement will be of a different kind, I agree with Hooker ("Traditions" 17) that such a distinction is a precision that does not go back to Jesus' time. Ultimately it may not be possible to establish with certitude whether or in what precise form Jesus made the claim.[37] Yet it is useful to test briefly whether a claim that if his proclamation of the kingdom was not heeded, the sanctuary would be destroyed and replaced by something more pleasing to God[38] could be consonant with other attitudes of Jesus attested in the tradition.

We may begin with the action, attributed to Jesus in all four Gospels, of cleansing the Temple precincts from commerce.[39] If we look on that as a historical action,[40] would not the underlying hope of reform conflict with the idea that the Temple or its sanctuary must be destroyed? Did Jesus want a purified worship or did he want a total replacement of the Temple? (In fact, Mark 11:17 specifies more than purification: not simply "a house of prayer" but one "for all the nations" [Isa 56:7].) Jesus' recorded attitude toward the Temple is nothing like that of the Essenes, who had a whole program for matters of priestly descent, sacrifice, those to be admitted, etc. He was not from Jerusalem or the priestly class, and so he had no vested interest in the continued building of the Temple and its material survival as a way of life. The Gospel writers understood Jesus' hostility toward the Temple, when he manifested it, to be similar to that of the ancient prophets; for they cite Jer 7:11; Zech 14:21 on the purity that should be found there. Yet the evangelists did not forget that the prophets who sought to purify the Temple could eventually begin to predict destruction if the decried abuses were not corrected (Jer 7:14; 26:6,9; see also Micah 3:12).

[37]Many scholars accept the substance of the saying as stemming from Jesus, but for others Mark 14:57–59 is totally a Marcan creation. For Bultmann, even if the saying is preMarcan, it is secondary. For Lührmann ("Markus 14" 466) one can scarcely reconstruct the original behind Mark 14:58 and John 2:19 or say that it goes back to Jesus. Lohmeyer and Donahue note that the first part of the sanctuary saying (destruction) is better attested than the second part (rebuilding—missing in Acts); but Gaston thinks the destruction part arose with Stephen. Yet form-critically the antithetical, bipartite pattern underlying both Mark and John has a claim to be considered old. See n. 48 below for those who regard Jesus' opposition to the Temple as the most basic factor in the Sanhedrin's antagonism toward him.

[38]It is better not to try to specify the destroying agent (God, Jesus, the priestly authorities) or the replacement (a new sanctuary, a heavenly place of worship, a community of believers, etc.). Given Israelite thought about God's presence among the covenanted people, there would surely have been a notion of replacement of some sort. That is true even in the radical outlook of John 4:21–24, where neither in Jerusalem nor on Gerizim will people worship the Father, but in Spirit and truth.

[39]I shall use the term "cleansing," even though I respect the thrust of W. W. Watty, "Jesus and the Temple—Cleansing or Cursing?" ExpTim 93 (1981–82), 235–39, who argues that this was, even historically, a symbolic action pointing to the destruction of the Temple.

[40]Theissen ("Tempelweissagung") offers a context for accepting as historical Jesus' actions (and words) against the Temple. Yet inner-NT disagreements present problems. In John 2:13–17 the cleansing takes place early in the public ministry; in the Synoptics (Mark 11:15–17; Matt 21:12–13; Luke 19:45–46) it comes in the last days. See BGJ 1.117–19 for which timing is preferred by which scholars and why, and for which account is more original. Were oxen and sheep allowed in the Temple precincts? Were not coins necessary for continued support of sacrificial offerings?

One gets the impression from Mark that Jesus' disenchantment with the Temple was cumulative.[41] In 11:11 Jesus' first action on entering Jerusalem is to visit and inspect the Temple precincts. He returns the next day; and, offended at the buying and selling, attempts to stop it (11:15–17). Yet he speaks of the Temple as God's house. Theissen ("Templeweissagung" 146–47) points out that his general attitude is perfectly plausible in the history of the time. The rural populace was attached to the Temple, of which they had an idealized view. When the Emperor Caligula wanted a statue of himself placed in the Temple, farmers left their fields, even though it was seeding time, to protest (Josephus, *Ant.* 18.8.3; #272). As for Jesus, the immediate reaction of the chief priests and the scribes is to seek to destroy him (Mark 11:18; cf. Jer 26:8); evidently they see in his actions a critique of their administration of God's house.[42] Mark interprets all of this through the imagery of the fig tree with which he frames the cleansing of the Temple. Before Jesus entered the Temple, he had looked for fruit from the fig tree but found none (11:12–14); after the reaction of the authorities the fig tree is found withered (11:20–21). Only when faced with obdurate irreformability does Jesus say (13:1–2) that not one stone will be left on another from the wonderfully built Temple.[43]

Of course there are strong elements of Marcan theology in such a development; but it is noteworthy that Luke in material peculiar to him has a similar progression with regard to the destruction of Jerusalem,[44] which included the destruction of the Temple. As a newborn baby Jesus is presented in the Temple; and he visits it at age twelve—all in obedience to the Law. It is for him a place peculiarly related to his Father (Luke 2:49). Certainly then there is nothing in his background that should a priori make Jesus hostile to the Temple during his ministry. Only as he turns his face to Jerusalem on his great journey (9:51–19:27) does the theme of chastising judgment begin to appear. In 13:31–35 Jesus apostrophizes Jerusalem in the language of the prophetic oracles against the nations; yet the fate of the city is not totally

[41]So McElvey, *New* 70. Hooker ("Traditions" 17–18) also moves in this direction when she argues against E. P. Sanders that Jesus did not immediately want the Temple destroyed; he wanted it to serve God's purposes. C. A. Evans, "Jesus," gives a major rebuttal of Sanders's views.

[42]That the Jerusalem authorities reacted violently to what they regarded as attacks on the Temple will be shown on pp. 539–41 below.

[43]There is considerable debate among scholars about the relationship between Mark 13:2 and 14:58. Many think that the substance of both is preMarcan. Dupont ("Il n'en sera" 304–6) thinks that the localization of 13:2 comes from Mark himself. Pesch formerly thought 13:2 to be a Marcan composition based on 14:58. Bultmann, Grundmann, and Nineham are among the many who think the opposite, giving priority to 13:2. Lambrecht thinks 13:2 secondary to John 2:19; Hartmann thinks it secondary to Luke 19:44.

[44]Giblin (*Destruction*) has demonstrated this with care; see also Neyrey, "Jesus."

fixed. As he nears Jerusalem, he tells a parable threatening to take away what was given to the unprofitable servant and warning that the enemies of the king would be slain (19:11–27). Even closer to the city (19:41–44: material from Luke's own source), he still yearns that Jerusalem would listen; but he combines this with an oracle of impending violent destruction. There follows the cleansing of the Temple and the hostile reaction of the chief priests, scribes, and principal men (19:45–48). Then, in a Lucan redaction (21:20–24) of Mark we hear a definitive word of doom: days of retribution to fulfill all that is written. The same motif will be seen on the way to crucifixion (23:27–31). Thus the evangelists saw no contradiction between an action intended to purify the Temple and an apocalyptic threat of destroying the sanctuary.[45] Such a change toward more dire treatment is comparable to the attitude we find in the parables of an opportunity offered and refused (banquet, vineyard, etc.).

If there are no serious obstacles refuting the possibility that Jesus made a statement about the destruction of the sanctuary, there are positive factors that lend plausibility. The several NT attestations with varied wording mean that the saying surely existed before AD 70 (also Sanders, *Jesus* 74). Earlier, it is hard to think that Christians invented a prediction involving Jesus in the destruction and rebuilding of the sanctuary when he was dead and the Temple was still standing untouched.[46] The different wordings that have been preserved ("I will destroy . . ."; "I am able to destroy . . ."; "(You) destroy . . .") are more likely Christian attempts at reformulating a difficult dominical saying than free creations. The fact that Mark, Matt, and Acts place the saying about destroying the sanctuary (holy place) on the lips of enemies of Jesus militates against Christians having made it up. And certainly if Jesus spent any time in Jerusalem he could scarcely have ignored the Temple. In a sense the Second Temple (515 BC to AD 70) was of greater importance than the First, for there were no Davidic monarchy and palace to compete with it as the visible center of Jerusalem and even of Judaism. Whether we look at Ezra and Nehemiah, I–II Macc, or Josephus, we find that the Temple, the priesthood, and the cult constitute a major focus in what is narrated. Jesus, who had commented so piercingly on the religious atti-

[45] John's view is different since the Temple cleansing, placed earlier, is more violent and is combined with the destruction-of-the-sanctuary statement. That combination gives the impression that from the very beginning of his ministry Jesus threatened the destruction of the Temple, and thus removes any objections to the authenticity of the sanctuary statement based on its disagreement with earlier attitudes. Yet John's portrayal has probably been influenced by the sharp break of the Johannine community from the synagogue, so that Jesus spells out a message of incompatibility from the start.

[46] Theissen ("Tempelweissagung" 144–45) is correct that this is not *vaticinium ex eventu*. He raises the issue of how Herod the Great reshaped the Zerubbabel Temple: Did people think of that as renovation or as a destruction/rebuilding?

tudes of his contemporaries, would have had to reflect on whether what he
saw in the Temple had validity for his conception of God's kingdom.[47] I
would join those scholars, then, who give very high probability to Jesus having spoken about the forthcoming destruction and rebuilding of the sanctuary.

If it is probable that Jesus engaged in a prophetic dramatic action against
improprieties in the Temple and uttered a prophetic threat that the coming
of the kingdom would involve a destruction and rebuilding of the sanctuary,
there are still two questions. First, is it historically likely that such an attitude
perceived as antiTemple entered into the desire of the authorities that he die?
Second, is it historical that Jesus' saying about the sanctuary was actually
cited in a Sanhedrin proceeding against him? The likelihood of the first is
easier to evaluate. It is nigh-certain that the high priesthood was the moving
agent on the Jewish side in the final proceedings against Jesus; and if one
has to explain what disturbed that group about Jesus, something that could
be interpreted as presenting a danger to the Temple/sanctuary would be the
most plausible factor.[48] Many theological factors could have caused the Sadducee priests to dislike Jesus (K. Müller, "Jesus . . . Sadduzäer" 9–12): his
stance on an afterlife (Mark 12:18–27) and on angels; his rejection of some
purity rules and his qualification of the Qorban obligations (Mark 7:1–15);
his criticism of oaths, especially those based on the Temple and the altar;
etc. Some of these points were not peculiar to Jesus and featured in Pharisee
versus Sadducee debates as well; at most they could have been aggravating
factors but scarcely serious enough to raise the dislike or distrust of Jesus to
a lethal level. The Temple, however, was the key institution of civic and
religious life in Judea and the treasury of the nation; action against it or
threats to it reached beyond theological concerns to the socioeconomic and
political realms. Drastic changes could affect employment of the masses in
Jerusalem, priestly livelihood and power, and the sphere of public order that
involved the Romans. Apprehension engendered by threats of destruction
may well have been aggravated by religious and economic uncertainty about
what an apocalyptic prophet like Jesus would substitute for the present functioning of the Temple, given his distrust of wealth and stress on total dependence on God. Thus the agreement of John, Mark/Matt, and Acts in different

[47]S.J.D. Cohen (*From* 106–7) makes the point that debate over the Temple was a main factor in
the Judaism of this period.

[48]Goguel, Hooker, Simon, Theissen, and E. P. Sanders are among those who concentrate on the
sanctuary/Temple issue as a main cause for the desire of the authorities to have Jesus dead. Some
would reconstruct from the limited evidence a whole scenario. For example, Watson ("Why Was"
107–9), after discarding too facilely the historicity of much in the Gospel accounts of the Jewish
trial, proposes as historical what is not attested in the Gospels: By his actions in the Temple announc-
ing an imminent destruction and rebuilding, Jesus caused a riot.

ways that the Temple or holy place or sanctuary issue aroused lethal priestly hostility toward Jesus has plausibility indeed. The Gospels in their description of the Sanhedrin proceedings do not agree, however, on the second question: whether Jesus' saying was actually cited in the Sanhedrin session that caused the Jerusalem leaders to promote his death. John and Luke do not have the saying there; Mark/Matt do. Thus there is no way to decide the point: The appearance of the saying on the lips of (false) witnesses in Mark/Matt could be a way of dramatizing an issue that was involved factually, although not by verbatim quoted words.

Let me end this whole discussion on a caution. Even if it is probable that the Temple/sanctuary issue was a factor in the decision to try to get rid of Jesus, in the Gospels that factor is seen through the filter of what happened later in Judea. We must be careful, for instance, in judging the historicity of the way John describes the apprehensions of the Sanhedrin authorities about Jesus (11:48): "If we permit him (to go on) thus, all will believe in him. And the Romans will come and take from us both the (holy) place and the nation." During the Roman prefecture in Judea up to the time of Jesus' death (AD 6–30/33), Josephus records no parallel example of religious enthusiasm for an individual bringing about Roman intervention. (The argument that surely such incidents occurred and the silence is accidental is not very convincing.) I shall discuss the political situation under the Romans in §31A,B and show that charismatic leaders and false prophets in Judea, arousing large groups of followers and thus provoking Roman military action, were characteristic of *the second half of the prefecture* (AD 44–46).[49] Josephus (*War* 2.15.2; #315–17) tells us how in 66 the most powerful nobles and chief priests pleaded with the people not to provoke the Roman procurator Florus, and later on that year (2.17.2; #408–10) how a refusal at the Jerusalem Temple to continue offering sacrifices for Rome and the emperor caused the war that ultimately led to the destruction of the Temple. Thus any recollection about Jesus' threat to the holy place possibly constituting an occasion of Roman intervention may have been rephrased in John in the language and imagery of the 50s and 60s.[50]

All this suggests to me a modest phrasing of what at its core has high

---

[49]We know of one earlier instance in Samaria in AD 36 (note: after Jesus' time) where a false prophet caused a gathering of people to go to Mount Gerizim, only to be blocked by Pilate's troops. But this overreaction by the prefect caused Vitellius, the legate in Syria, to dismiss Pilate back to Rome (Josephus, *Ant.* 18.4.1–2; #85–89). The severity of the legate's intervention fortifies the suspicion that this was a new and unusual movement among the people. After 44 there were many parallel instances.

[50]This is pointed out by Bammel, "Ex illa," esp. 25. This probing article on the historicity of John's account of the Sanhedrin session is complicated by Bammel's frequent appeal to the *Toledoth Yeshu* as verification.

historical probability: Something done and/or said by Jesus prognostic of Temple/sanctuary destruction was at least a partial cause of the Sanhedrin's decision that led to his death.

(Bibliography for this episode is found in §17, Part 4.)

§21. SANHEDRIN PROCEEDINGS, PART TWO: QUESTION(S) ABOUT THE MESSIAH, THE SON OF GOD

(Mark 14:60–61; Matt 26:62–63; Luke 22:67–70a)

Translation

Mark 14:60–61: [60]And having stood up, the high priest in (their) midst questioned Jesus, saying, "Have you nothing at all to answer to what these are testifying against you?" [61]But he stayed silent and answered nothing at all. Again the high priest was questioning him and says to him, "Are you the Messiah, the Son of the Blessed?"

Matt 26:62–63: [62]And having stood up, the high priest said to him, "Have you nothing to answer to what these are testifying against you?" [63]But Jesus stayed silent. And the high priest said to him, "I adjure you according to the living God that you say to us if you are the Messiah, the Son of God."

Luke 22:67–70a: [[66]. . . there was brought together the assembly of the elders of the people, both chief priests and scribes; and they led him away to their Sanhedrin] [67]saying, "If you are the Messiah, say to us." [But he said to them . . .] [70a]But they all said, "Are you then the Son of God?"

[John 10:24,36: [24]So the Jews surrounded him and were saying to him, ". . . If you are the Messiah, say to us openly." ([25]Jesus answered them . . .) [36]. . . "Do you say that, 'You are blaspheming,' because I said, 'I am God's Son'?"]

[19:7: The Jews answered him [Pilate], "We have a law, and according to the law he ought to die, because he made himself God's Son."]

COMMENT

Continuing our commentary on the Sanhedrin proceedings, we deal here with "christological" questions posed to Jesus by the high priest in Mark/Matt[1] and by the Sanhedrin members in Luke. (In John there are similar christological questions posed to Jesus during the ministry by "the Jews.") In Mark/Matt there is only one question and it combines "the Messiah" and "the Son of the Blessed/God." In Luke (as in John) the titles, although in close proximity, are in questions separated by Jesus' (ambivalent) response to the Messiah title. For the subdivision of this section, see p. 313 above. We shall begin with a part of the scene that is peculiar to Mark/Matt as the high priest stands up and challenges Jesus about his refusal to answer.

INTERVENTION OF THE HIGH PRIEST; SILENCE OF JESUS (MARK/MATT)

In both Mark and Matt the standing up of the high priest marks a definitive turn in the proceedings. One gets the impression that the trial is moving toward what is really of concern.[2] Above (p. 434) I pointed to the OT motif of the evil plotters who stand up against the just one. Previously (Mark 14:57) the witnesses stood up but they were not effective; the high priest will be more persistent. Jesus was led to him at the beginning (Mark 14:53; Matt 26–57), and he must bring the matter to a conclusion. For Mark, he takes his stand *in their midst* or *before them*, positioning himself to speak for the whole Sanhedrin to Jesus.[3] The high priest also plays the key role in the Sanhedrin session of John 11:47–53 (Caiaphas) and in the interrogation of 18:19–23 (Annas). Christian tradition mentions the involvement of others as decision makers, witnesses, and attendants, but the high priest was remembered as the main opponent of Jesus. (This could even be historical, but

---

[1] In Matt this high priest has been identified as Caiaphas, who also takes the initiative in John's account of the Sanhedrin proceedings against Jesus in 11:47–53. (For the English translation of the latter, see §§20 and 23.)

[2] On a historical level some (e.g., Schumann, "Bemerkungen" 319) would contend that if the witnesses who testified about Jesus destroying the sanctuary had not proved false and inconsistent, Jesus would have been condemned to death on that charge without further ado. However, on the literary level in Mark/Matt one gets the impression that the christological question posed by the high priest was the more serious issue and the one that most concerned the authorities. Clearly Luke read Mark in this fashion because he reports in the Sanhedrin trial only the christological issue. In the Roman trial "the King of the Jews," echoing in some way the Messiah question, is the focal point without any reference to the Temple/sanctuary.

[3] Although Strobel thinks this positioning implies that the Sanhedrin is seated in a semicircular room, Broer ("Prozess" 87–88) is correct in disagreeing. Standing "in the midst" or advancing to that position to speak or pray is found several times in Josephus without any implication about the shape of the site in which this takes place: *Life* 27; #134; *Ant.* 3.1.4; #13; 19.4.4; #261; etc.

we must remember that in a dramatic narrative it is characteristic to have the protagonist face one major antagonist; cf. Amos and Amaziah in Amos 7:10–17.) It is surprising, then, that the "high priest" plays no role in Luke's account of the Jewish proceedings against Jesus. Once more, apparently, Luke has moved material to the Stephen trial of Acts 6:9–7:1ff. There false witnesses have testified against Stephen, charging him with claiming that Jesus of Nazareth would destroy "this holy place." After those seated in the Sanhedrin had seen that Stephen's face was like that of an angel, the *high priest* said, "Are these things so?"[4]

In Mark/Matt the high priest first speaks of the preceding testimony against Jesus.[5] Mark uses the theme of "against" (*kata*) to structure the proceedings. The chief priests and the whole Sanhedrin begin in 14:55 by seeking testimony *against* Jesus in order to put him to death; the midway point in 14:60 is when the high priest calls attention to what these men have testified *against* Jesus; the conclusion in 14:64 will come after there is no more need of testimony and they all will judge *against* Jesus as punishable by death. By dropping the "judge against" of Mark 14:64, Matt 26:66 will lose the inclusion.

As for what the high priest says at the beginning, Mark 14:60–61a and Matt 26:62–63a are not far apart in wording, although Matt simplifies Mark's redundancies, thus losing some of the intensity about Jesus' silence and his answering nothing at all. Despite the similar wording, the logic of the sequence in the two Gospels is different. In Mark the testimony has been false and inconsistent throughout; and so the high priest's question as to whether Jesus has an answer to the testimony is a bluff, trying to save the awkward situation. The emphatic silence of the Marcan Jesus is a contemptuous rebuke for the low quality of the charade. In Matt, while the first testimony was false, the second testimony (26:60b-61) was given by a legal number of witnesses and was a revelation of Jesus' claim to power: "I am able to destroy the sanctuary of God, and within three days I will build (it)." The high priest in 26:63a, testing whether Jesus denies such an extraordinary claim, evidently takes Jesus' silence as tacit consent.

In Mark 14:61 we hear that Jesus "stayed silent and answered nothing at all." The Greek of the latter uses the classical middle tense, very rare in the

---

[4]The Western text of Acts 6:15 heightens the parallelism by inserting "And having stood in their midst" before "the high priest said." The parallelism so impressed J. R. Harris, ExpTim 39 (1927–28), 456–58, that he suggested that a verse had fallen out of Mark wherein the Sanhedrin members looked on Jesus' face and saw that it was like an angel's!

[5]What he asks can be phrased as *one* question, "Have you nothing to answer to what these are testifying against you?" (my translation; also Lagrange, Lohmeyer, Senior), or as two, "Have you nothing to answer? What are these testifying against you?" There is a difference of meaning, but it is not of major importance; see BDF 298[4]; 299[1].

NT, but common as a technical legal term for response (MM 64). "Answer nothing at all" or "not answer," i.e., language used here to describe Jesus' failure to cooperate with the high priest who has asked why he has not responded to the testifiers, will reappear in Mark 15:5 and Matt 27:14 as Jesus fails to cooperate with Pilate (who will ask why he has not responded to the many charges brought against him); but the verb "to be silent" will not be repeated. Luke 23:9 will tell us that Jesus answered nothing to Herod who questioned him. In John, Jesus speaks both to Annas and to Pilate; but in one passage (19:9) we hear: "Jesus did not give him [Pilate] an answer."

Schreiber ("Schweigen" 81–83) points to the majestic behavior of Jesus throughout the Marcan PN. He did not speak to Judas nor to the sword-wielder who cut off the ear of the servant. His silence before the high priest and Pilate is in Schreiber's words "the silence of the eschatological judge before the final passing of judgment." Without going that far, we could see it as more contempt for the hostile proceedings. The Matthean Jesus has been much more vocal before the arrest. In both Gospels one gets the impression that now Jesus is resigned to his fate, knowing that words spoken to those who are so against him will not change the outcome.[6] Many interpreters see here the impact on Christian tradition of psalm passages about the suffering just one who did not open his mouth or in whose mouth there were no rebukes (38:13–15; 39:10; also Lam 3:28–30 where his being silent is combined with his giving his cheek to be hit). Acts 8:32–35 applies to Jesus part of the Suffering Servant passage of Isa 53:7, which in its completeness reads: "And despite being afflicted he does not open his mouth, as a sheep led to slaughter; and as a lamb before its shearers is without voice, so he opens not his mouth." Yet, as Kosmala ("Prozess" 28) insists, the vocabulary of silence and giving no answer in the PN is not the same as in any of those OT passages.[7] One wonders if a tradition of Jesus' silence did not exist first, eventually to be compared to the Deutero-Isa and psalm passages. Some would take the silence back to historical fact, e.g., Rengstorf, K. L. Schmidt; and it should be noted that Jesus son of Ananias, who spoke against the sanctuary, answered nothing on his own behalf both before Jewish magistrates and the Roman governor (Josephus, *War* 6.5.3; #302, 305—on all this see Schreiber, "Schweigen"). What is certain is that the silence of Jesus became a model for others. I Pet 2:21,23 speaks of the suffering of Christ

---

[6]On the level of the storyline one finds little to support Blinzler's contention (*Trial* 101–2) that legally Jesus' silence stopped the court from using the (false) testimony that had been presented.

[7]In particular, Luke 22:71, "We ourselves have heard from his own mouth," is almost the opposite of "he does not open his mouth."

"who, though reviled, did not revile; suffering, did not threaten; he was giving himself to the One judging justly."[8]

THE CHRISTOLOGICAL QUESTION: THE MESSIAH, THE SON OF GOD

Just as different sequences gave a different tone in Mark and Matt respectively to the high priest's first question to Jesus and to Jesus' silence, so also with the high priest's second question. As for Mark, Juel (*Messiah* 170) and others interpret *palin* ("Again") in 14:61b as possibly relating the second question on christology to the sanctuary motif that was the topic of the first question when the high priest asked about testimony (14:60). However, *palin* will also introduce Pilate's second question to Jesus in Mark 15:4, and that is not the same as his first question. Thus *palin* seems to mean "another time" and to underline the persistence of the high priest who "was questioning" Jesus. He has found no way to move further with the false testimony, so now he tries another tactic to see if he can get Jesus to speak. The use of the historical present tense ("says") for the high priest's key question and response in vv. 61,63 reflects the strongly narrative quality of Mark here.

In Matt 26:63, which omits the *palin* of Mark, the high priest puts Jesus under oath, "I adjure [*exorkizein*] you according to the living God." Some have speculated that this might be a standard oath formula administered in court; others point to Mishna *Shebu'ot* 4:13, which states that if one is put under oath by the divine name or a recognized divine attribute, one is bound.[9] The "living God" or "God who lives (forever)" is an OT term (Deut 5:26; Josh 3:10; Dan 4:31[34]) and is appropriate in oaths (I Sam 14:39) since it invokes One who will be active in punishing the perjurer. Here "the living God" echoes Peter's confession of Jesus as "the Messiah, the Son of the living God" in Matt 16:16, and Matt intends to draw attention to the parallelism between that scene and the present one. Such an oath does increase the courtroom flavor of this scene, but it fits into more popular patterns as well. *Exorkizein* and *orkizein* are used in exorcisms, e.g., "I adjure you by the Jesus whom Paul preaches" (Acts 19:13; also Mark 5:7). According to Josephus (*Ant.* 2.8.2; #200) Joseph had put his brethren under oath to take his bones to Canaan (see also Gen 24:3). In I Kings 22:16, although Ahab, the king of Israel, has had unhappy experience with the neg-

---

[8]See also the more problematic Ignatius, *Eph.* 15:2; *Test. Benjamin* 5:4.

[9]Van Tilborg (*Jewish* 80) suggests that the wording of the high priest's demand under oath to Jesus contained a violation of the Law; but Broer ("Bemerkungen" 35) shows from the Qumran literature that oaths in the name of "the Most High God, Lord of heaven and earth, the Holy Great One" were used (1QapGen 2:4,14; 22:20–21).

ative prophecies of Micaiah ben Imlah, he insists, "How many times shall I adjure you to speak to me nothing but the truth?" In fact, the Matthean Jesus has shown a dislike for oaths, instructing his disciples to avoid them (5:33–37). Yet ironically, at the very moment when at the end of his life Jesus is ordered by the highest authority of his people to take an oath, Peter, his most important disciple, is voluntarily taking an oath. Jesus is told to take an oath that he is the Messiah, the Son of God, while Peter, who made that very confession in 16:16, is now volunteering an oath that he does not even know Jesus (26:74).

An almost endless flow of articles has treated the high priest's question or demand in Mark/Matt and Jesus' response. The Lucan variation with its Johannine parallel would not be far behind in abundant literature. Many discussions blend what may have happened in AD 30/33 and what the evangelists are describing. I find that confusing and shall try to resist it. Pp. 472–83, 530–47 (below) will discuss whether in Jesus' lifetime it is likely that titles like "the Messiah" or "the Son of God" would have been applied to him and with what meaning; whether, even if titles were not involved, there was an issue about the identity of Jesus caused by his prominence in the advent or inbreaking of the kingdom; and whether any of this could plausibly have annoyed the high priest to the point of handing him over to the Romans for crucifixion. Here I wish to discuss what each evangelist is communicating to Christian readers anywhere from thirty to seventy years later. I assume that when that Christian audience heard "the Messiah" or "the Son of God," those expressions had the same meaning as in familiar creedal expressions and liturgical praise—a meaning that surely was different from any usage in Jesus' lifetime. Moreover, I assume that for the readers of the Gospel the high priest embodied in his question all the skepticism and hostility that they had encountered or had been told about in years of Jewish rejection of the Christian proclamation. In other words, the high priest's evaluation of Jesus was assimilated to what contemporary Jews who did not believe in Jesus thought of the Christian gospel. The readers are *Christianoi* (Acts 11:26), i.e., those who believe Jesus is the Messiah (*christos*); and that issue divides them from Jews who do not believe (see de Jonge; "Use of *Christos*" 182–87).

Thus, for example, in the question of whether Jesus is the Messiah, it is irrelevant for our purpose to talk *simply* of an anointed king of the House of David. The readers' understanding of the Messiah (*ho christos*) would have been shaped by the fact that *christos* had become Jesus' second name—what Jesus was, the Messiah was.[10] Nor are we to confine "Son of God" here

---

[10] W. Kramer, *Christos, Kyrios, Gottessohn* (ATANT 44; Zurich: Zwingli, 1963), 203–14, shows how closely connected this title was, even in the prePauline days, to faith formulas used in preaching and baptism.

to a reflection of Nathan's promise to David that every king of his House would be treated by God as a son. For the readers of Matt and Luke "the Son of God" means one not begotten by a human father but by the Holy Spirit, so that God is his only Father. For the readers of John, "the Son of God" is one who is always in the Father's presence (1:18), even before the creation of the world. These readers may have been aware that the vocabulary in which they expressed their faith differed in content from an earlier use, but they scarcely divorced what was being asked of Jesus from what they confessed him to be. Several texts (Mark 12:35–37; Rom 1:3–4) show that Christians knew that the Messiah could not be adequately described as Son of David.

With that premise, let us look at issues in each Synoptic Gospel's treatment of the christological question. (John's parallels are mostly not in the PN and will be cited for comparison rather than made the subject of direct comment.) Jesus' answer in terms of the Son of Man will be reserved for the next section (§22).

Mark. The high priest's question in 14:61 begins, "Are you the Messiah?" In Greek this is *sy ei ho Christos*. The formula *sy ei* with a title is frequent in Mark (1:11, 3:11; 8:29; 15:2), but we should not assume it is a Marcan creation. Despite the quite different treatments of the crucial Messiah question in Mark/Matt and Luke/John, the formula in all four is *sy ei ho Christos*, suggesting that such titulary formulas are the fixed language of early confessions identifying and praising Jesus. As the high priest continues, there is nothing in the Marcan form of his interrogative (or for that matter in Matt's demanded oath) to suggest that he is asking two separate questions, "Are you the Messiah?" and "Are you the Son of the Blessed?" The natural implication, then, is to take the two terms in apposition. In an important contribution Marcus ("Mark") argues that this is a restrictive apposition where the second term supplies essential information for understanding the first. There were various types of Messiah expected by Jews of Jesus' time, e.g., Messiahs of Aaron and of Israel at Qumran.[11] Against that background the high priest is depicted as asking Jesus whether he is the Messiah-Son-of-God. Because of an unfortunate tendency to mix the levels of history and of Gospel description, and because on the historical level the high priest would not have understood "Son of the Blessed/God" literally, many argue that the messianic question in Mark/Matt pertains only to whether Jesus is the (or an) anointed king of the House of David, whose monarchs God promised to

---

[11]In this commentary I leave aside the expectation of the Messiah the son of Joseph since it is not clearly attested in the 1st cent. AD; see M. Barker, TJCSM 40–46. That figure is a suffering and/or dying Messiah. A Qumran fragment, 4Q285, mentions a killing in relation to the (messianic) Branch of David; but it is not clear whether he kills (an evil enemy) or is killed.

treat as sons (II Sam 7:14). If interpretation is kept on the Gospel level, however, such a weak reading of Messiah-Son-of-God is clearly refuted by Mark 12:35–37 and Matt 22:41–46. There the issue of defining the Messiah was specifically broached ("Whose son is he?"), and "Son of David" was declared by Jesus to be an inadequate description. Here Jesus will answer affirmatively to the high priest, and so "the Messiah, the Son of the Blessed/ God" must mean more. It means what the Christian readers of Mark and Matt understood by such terminology when those Gospels were written. It means what the opening verse of Mark's Gospel proclaims: "The beginning of the Gospel of *Jesus Christ, Son of God*" (best attested text). And so there is no surprise when Jesus says, "I am"; he is affirming what the whole Gospel was written to proclaim.

Because we are working on the Gospel level, we must take into account previous passages, e.g., in Mark 8–9. (There is a deliberate parallelism between the middle and end of the Gospel.) In 8:29 the most important of Jesus' Twelve confessed him as the Messiah. (This was not an adequate confession because Peter did not allow for suffering, and Jesus had to correct him by speaking of the Son of Man even as here he will speak of the Son of Man—but it was a correct confession as the reader knows from the opening line.) God personally complemented that confession seventeen verses later (9:7) by speaking of Jesus as "my beloved Son" (the same information given the reader at the beginning of the Gospel in 1:11).

There is also a connection between the present scene and Mark 13, which we saw to be of great importance for understanding the saying on the destruction of the sanctuary.[12] There the issue of the destruction of the Temple (sanctuary) led into christology, as it does here. In 13:21–22 Jesus warned against false messiahs who would announce the end of time. (Once again he followed this by speaking of the Son of Man in 13:26.) Ten verses later (13:32) he said that of that day or hour no one knows, not even *the Son* but only the Father. Thus one should complement the notion of the Messiah with the notion of Jesus as God's Son to get the whole Christian picture. Well does de Jonge ("Use of *Christos*" 180) insist that "the Messiah" was part of the essential Christian confession when complemented by the glorious relation of the Son to his Father. The royal aspect of the Messiah remains, for in 15:32 Jesus will be mocked as the Messiah, the King of Israel. But the divine element is very strong in "the Son of God," and the whole complex is being challenged by the high priest.

Nevertheless, we must note meticulously that Mark does not actually use

---

[12]A strong linkage between Mark 13 and the PN is brought out by Dewar, "Chapter," even if his application of every detail is overdone.

"the Son of God" in the trial narrative but "the Son of the Blessed [*ho eulo-gētos*]." Why? *Eulogētos* appears in the NT eight times. Whether Rom 9:5 applies it to Christ or to God is not certain, but elsewhere it always describes God. With the exception of the present passage, *eulogētos* is used in benedictions like "Blessed is the Lord, the God of Israel" (Luke 1:68; II Cor 1:3; Eph 1:3; I Pet 1:3) or in modifiers of praise like "the Creator who is blessed forever" (Rom 1:25; 9:5; II Cor 11:31). This is the only NT instance of "the Blessed" as a *title* for God.[13] Despite the tendency of some to state that *ha-barûk,* the Hebrew equivalent of *ho eulogētos,* was a recognized substitute for the divine name (often citing the much later rabbinic references offered by Dalman or St-B), there is no real evidence of that. "The Son of the Blessed" is not found elsewhere in either the NT or Jewish literature; *neither is "the Blessed" as a title for God found.* A predicate adjectival use ("He who is blessed forever") appears in *I Enoch* 77:1; there is also usage as a complement in early Jewish prayers ("The Holy One, Blessed be He"). Mishna *Berakot* 7.3 and the talmudic commentaries on it (TalBab 50a; TalJer 7.11) have another predicate adjectival use. These resemble the general NT use of *eulogētos,* but they do not offer evidence for a substitute divine name.[14]

A judgment on why Mark uses "the Blessed" must also involve the name for God that Jesus uses in his response, "sitting at the right of the Power [*hē dynamis*]" (14:62). I shall discuss "the Power" in the next section, which treats Jesus' response about the Son of Man (p. 496 below); but if I may anticipate, "the Power" is never used as a title for God's own self (as distinct from God working in the world or revealing). In one short interchange, then, instead of "God" Mark has used "the Blessed" and "the Power," neither of

[13]Far too speculative is the thesis of F. C. Burkitt (JTS 5 [1903–4], 451–55) that *ho ōn . . . eulo-gētos* in Rom 9:5 echoes the LXX form of the tetragrammaton (*ho ōn* in Exod 3:14), so that there and here *eulogētos* would have been recognized as a substitute for YHWH.

[14]Nevertheless, as E. E. Urbach, *The Sages* (2 vols.; Jerusalem: Magnes, 1979), in his chaps. 3 and 5 on epithets suggests, there is a thin line between epithets and titles. Urbach's example (1.41) from a later period compares *bārûk* ("Blessed be") and *ha-mĕbōrāk* ("the Blessed"). In DJD 2.160, document 43 (from Murabba'at) is a letter of Simon ben Kosiba (leader of the Second Jewish Revolt) to Yeshua' ben Galgula and "to the men of *hbrk.*" The first two letters in the last word are unclear, and some have read *hkrk,* "the fortress." The editor, J. T. Milik, prefers to find here a reference to the place Ha-Baruk, a shortened form of the name of a village east of Hebron, Kaphar ha-Baruk (village of the blessed). Although *kephar* ("village of," "estate of") is a common component of talmudic place names, only seldom does one find a definite article before the governed component, e.g., Kephar ha-Babli ("Village of the Babylonian"). The more normal pattern would be Kephar Nahum (= Capernaum). In the present instance, drawing on F.-M. Abel, *Géographie de la Palestine* (2 vols.; Paris: Gabalda, 1967), 2.288, Milik identifies the site as the Caphar Barucha mentioned by Jerome, who interpreted the name as *villa Benedictionis,* where Abraham stood before God (Gen 18:22). Milik takes it to mean the "Village of the Blessed [Abraham]." The question has been posed, however, whether, like Bethel ("House of God"), "the Blessed" here might not be a title of God. The evidence is uncertain, and so in my comments above I work with the thesis that we still do not have a firm example of "the Blessed" as a divine title.

them really accurate Jewish terminology according to the evidence now available. Why? Accurate or not, there is no doubt that these titles in their Greek translation lend a "Jewish atmosphere" to the interchange. The custom of using surrogates instead of the divine name could have been well known to anyone familiar with Greek-speaking Judaism.[15] Juel (*Messiah* 77–79) speaks of a pseudoJewish impression attempted by Mark, and the use of these words may be a literary touch to give atmosphere. It would not be unlike letting Jesus "lapse" into Aramaic, his native language, just before he dies (Mark 15:34). Throughout we have seen that the Marcan PN is a skillful, effective narrative with good popular touches. The fact that seemingly the surrogates for the divine name were not quite accurate would make little difference if they had the flavor of how it was thought Jews would speak.

If one queries why this touch occurs here but not widely elsewhere, the answer could be that only at especially dramatic moments was the trouble taken to achieve linguistic plausibility, precisely as a way of heightening the importance of those moments. That is certainly true for the last words of Jesus' life, and is probably true for the only direct exchange between Jesus and the highest authority of his people, especially when the exchange touched on the basic gospel issue of christology that divided Christians (Jewish and Gentile) from Jews who did not believe in Jesus.[16] I think Pesch (*Markus* 2.437) is very wrong in contending that the use of "the Son of the Blessed" instead of "the Son of God" shows that Mark does not want his readers to understand the titles in their ordinary confessional sense but on a lower level of simply the Davidic Messiah. That would assume incredible sophistication. Surely Mark's readers ca. 70 would think that David in his reference to "Messiah" (Ps 2:2) meant what they had come to believe Messiah meant applied to Jesus. As I pointed out above, they would hear the titles in the question as the equivalent of those in Mark 1:1. Otherwise Jesus could not answer, "I am."

Matt. More interested in pedagogical clarity than in drama, Matt 26:63 prefers "the Messiah, the Son of God" over Mark's "the Messiah, the Son of the Blessed" in order to have readers think back to apostolic confessions of

---

[15]Here I shall not enter the question of whether the LXX preserved by Christians always reflects the Jewish practice of Jesus' time, and whether in certain issues (like *Kyrios* for YHWH) the great LXX codices of the 4th and 5th cents. have the original wording of the LXX translators of five hundred years before.

[16]Other factors have been suggested as entering into Mark's choice of "the Blessed" and "the Power," e.g., the desire to avoid the blasphemy of pronouncing the divine name (very dubious; see n. 9 above and p. 523 below), or a desire to preserve verisimilitude by not putting on the lips of the Jewish high priest the full Christian confessional formula "Jesus Christ, the Son of God" (a dubious historical sensitivity).

faith, e.g., "Truly you are God's Son" in 14:33, and especially to the virtually identical confession by Peter in 16:16, "You are the Messiah, the Son of the living God." (Here the high priest adjures by "the living God.") It would help the readers to know that while Peter and the high priest proposed the same titles, one spoke in faith and the other in incredulity; and so the reactions of Jesus were different. Also "the Son of God" supplies for Matt a bond with the previous theme in the sense that the one who spoke about destroying the sanctuary "of God" is now being asked if he thinks he is the Son of God. Matt will retain the Marcan picture of the Son of Man sitting at the right hand of "the Power" (*dynamis*), for the Matthean Jesus had said, "I am able [*dynamai*] to destroy the sanctuary of God," and Matt wants to make the connection. It is harder to decide whether in dispensing with "the Blessed" and keeping "the Power," Matt, who apparently knew synagogue thought in the late 1st cent., was opting for the second as closer to Jewish usage.

Of course, in changing from Mark's "the Son of the Blessed" to "the Son of God," Matt was not differing from the Marcan understanding of the term. In the fulfillment scene as Jesus dies on the cross, both evangelists will have the centurion confess that Jesus was "truly *God's Son*" (Mark 15:39; Matt 27:54). For both evangelists the Messiah king is understood in the Christian sense of the glorified Son of God even on the lips of a disbelieving high priest. Matt, as we shall see, is not unaware of the incongruity, for he will qualify Jesus' reply.

Luke. Unlike Mark/Matt, who have the high priest ask about the one, combined title "the Messiah, the Son of the Blessed/God," Luke 22:67[17] and 70a have the priestly investigators separate the two titles, similar to the separation in John 10:24 and 36. We saw that the combined title in Mark/Matt is meant to be read on the level of Christian understanding in the last third of the 1st cent. whereby "Messiah" is the divine Son of God. Luke too believes that (Acts 9:20,22), but with a greater sense of what was appropriate earlier. His separation has the historicizing effect of suggesting a distinction between "Messiah" as understood by Jews and the Christian understanding of "the Son of God." Jesus will give a noncommittal response to the former, but a positive answer to the latter. (It is interesting that for the demons in Luke 4:41 "the Son of God" and "the Messiah" are equivalent terms, so that even if malevolent, they have supernatural perception lacking among the Jewish authorities.) The first christological passage in Luke (1:32,35) kept

---

[17]To avoid confusion one should note that Luke 22:67 has been versified in three different ways. The pattern I have followed ([67]saying, "If you are the Messiah, say to us." But he said to them, "If I shall say to you, you will never believe.") is accepted by most. Tischendorf's Greek NT, however, puts the first half of my v. 67 as the end of v. 66, while the NEB Greek NT has the second half of my v. 67 as the first part of v. 68.

distinct but complementary the Davidic Messiah ("the Lord God will give him the throne of his father David") and the Son of God (conceived through the Holy Spirit, "the power of the Most High"). The Messiah designation of Jesus comes indirectly through JBap in Luke 3:15–16, but the Son of God designation directly from the divine voice in 3:22. The Messiah is confessed by Peter in 9:20 while the Son of God is proclaimed by a heavenly voice in 9:35. Thus for Luke, one seems to need divinely revealed knowledge to interpret "the Messiah" correctly as a title that fully identifies Jesus as the Son of God. (In the Johannine parallel to Luke, the Messiah question-and-answer of 10:24–25 is followed in 10:26–28 by an explanation given by Jesus [the Davidic shepherd-Messiah] that only the sheep the Father has given him can hear his voice and believe.)

This history of the Lucan distinction between the titles may help to explain why, although Luke certainly knew the Marcan form of the high priest's question, he chose to follow it only in part (chiefly in Jesus' answer in 22:69) and particularly in 22:67–68 preferred to follow another tradition. Since the discussion of that, however, involves Jesus' response to the Messiah question, I shall leave it to the next section.

ANALYSIS

The Synoptic Gospels in their account of the Sanhedrin trial of Jesus have in different ways an interrogation of Jesus about his being the Messiah, the Son of God (and in the next section [§22] an affirmative response in which he speaks of the Son of Man). In the COMMENT I insisted on dealing with these titles on the level on which Christian readers of the Gospels in the period 70–100 would have understood them (in the light of their faith in Jesus) and would have thought them to be rejected by Jewish opponents of the Christian gospel. Here I turn the clock back to the year of Jesus' death (AD 30 or 33) and in reference to each title look at the compound issue: Could a Jewish authority have asked Jesus whether he accepted such a title; and if Jesus said yes, what would he and the high priest have understood by this affirmed title? There is no way to establish that the question was asked and the answer given, but possibility and plausibility can be discussed.[18]

---

[18]The bibliography on the christology involved in "Messiah," "Son of God," and "Son of Man" is immense. I digest here my treatment of "Messiah" in NJBC §77, paragraphs 152–63. Beyond the biblography given there, especially pertinent to the present issue are *Judaisms and Their Messiahs at the Turn of the Christian Era*, eds. J. Neusner et al. (Cambridge Univ., 1987); and S. Talmon, "Types of Messianic Expectation at the End of the Era," *King, Cult and Calendar* (Jerusalem: Magnes, 1986), 202–24.

A. **Jesus the Messiah**

The English word "Messiah" is from Aramaic *mĕšîḥā'*, reflecting Hebrew *māšîaḥ;* the Greek translation is *christos,* whence "Christ." Both the Semitic and Greek terms mean "Anointed." As we shall see, various figures were thought to be anointed physically or spiritually, but for our purposes a brief history of the royal anointed figure is useful. The idea of anointing with oil seems first to have been applied to the king and only later to the high priest. When the Davidic monarchy ruled Judah (1000 to 587), each king of the dynasty was an anointed of the Lord and thought of as God's special representative to the people. In Ps 2:2 we find "YHWH and His anointed [= messiah]" working together against the hostile kings and rulers. The literary charter of the messianic dignity of the Davidic dynasty is found in II Sam 7; Ps 89; I Chr 17. In various ways it contained the following ideas: the election of David by Yahweh; promises of victory and wide dominion; adoption of David and his successors as sons; promise of an eternal dynasty not conditioned on the fidelity of the successors of David to Yahweh. The king was to be the instrument for the political safety and welfare of the people.

In the 8th cent. there came a development in royal messianism, after wicked and inept kings had for a long time dimmed the glory of the Davidic line and spoiled the optimistic hope that each king would be a savior of his people. Isaiah in particular gave voice to a more nuanced hope: There would be an inbreaking of the power of Yahweh that would revive the dynasty and ensure its permanence, for in the near future God would raise up a worthy successor of David. Isa 7:14–16 and 9:1ff. are rhapsodical in their description of the heir soon to be born as a sign that God is still with the chosen people (Emmanuel). The heir would establish justice, build a vast empire, bring peace to it, and be worthy of the traditional courtly titles of the monarch (9:5: Wonder-Counselor; God-Hero; Father-Forever; Prince of Peace). In Isa 11:1ff. (perhaps of somewhat later composition) the expected ideal ruler will restore the conditions of Paradise and bring cosmic peace. See also Micah 5:1–4a for another description of the ideal king. Despite the exuberant language which might seem to go beyond history, this expectation was centered on a king of the dynasty to be born in the near future.

In the postexilic period there was a drastic change within this Davidic messianic hope that we cannot fully describe because of the sparsity of documentation. The Davidic dynasty no longer ruled in Jerusalem, and so the expected anointed one could scarcely be the next king in the line. In a shift, the ideal king would come in the indefinite future when the Davidic throne would be restored. Here we get the emergence of the Messiah king in the sense that many have been taught to think of the Messiah. Of course he would still be a human figure within the bonds of history; but his work would be a special manifestation of the power of Yahweh, definitively delivering the people and bringing spiritual as well as material goods. Yet since there was no visible dynasty to produce this figure, other Jewish hopes and expectations appeared alongside the Davidic, e.g., salvation through an ideal priest, or a prophet like Moses, or by God without human assistance.

As we come to the times preceding and during Jesus' life, then, we find diversity of expectation: Not all Jews expected the Messiah, and those who did had different understandings of whom he would be. De Jonge ("Use of Word") emphasizes how few times the Jewish literature between 200 BC and AD 100 actually mentions the term in reference to a future figure. There are more than fifteen occurrences of *mšyḥ* in the Dead Sea Scrolls composed over 150 years, with a very wide range of meaning. 4QPatr 3–4 speaks of the descendant of David as the Messiah of Righteousness, the Branch of David; 1QSa 2:12,14,20 speaks of the possibility of God begetting the Messiah in the Council of the Community, the Messiah of Israel who shall come with the chiefs of the clans. 11QMelch 18 speaks of the Messiah foretold by Dan 9:25. There is also an anointed priest, for 1QS 9:11; CD 12:23–13:1; 19:10-11; and 20:1 speak of the Messiahs of Aaron and Israel. CD 2:12; 6:1 refer to the prophets as the anointed ones. Harder to date are the references in the Parables section of *I Enoch:* In 48:10 we hear of "the Lord of Spirits and His Messiah," who is presumably the same as the Son of Man in 48:2; see also "His Messiah" in 52:4. This Messiah figure would have existed with God in heaven from before creation. The 1st-cent.-BC *Psalms of Solomon* (notice "Solomon": the son of David and Temple-builder) speaks of "the anointed of the Lord" (17:32 [36]), the son of David (17:21–26) who shall break in pieces the godless nations and gather a holy people whom he shall bless with wisdom and shepherd faithfully. Perhaps slightly later, *PsSol* 18 (Title, 6[5], 8[7]) speaks again of the Lord's anointed who shall wield a rod of chastening in a spirit of wisdom, righteousness, and strength. The Fourteenth Benediction of the *Shemoneh Esreh* (1st cent. AD?) speaks of the kingdom of the House of David and "the Messiah of Your justice." At the end of the 1st-cent AD in *IV Ezra (II Esdras)* God refers to "my Son the Messiah" who shall rule for four hundred years and die (7:28–29). *IV Ezra* 12:32 speaks of the Messiah who shall spring from the seed of David, and whom the Most High has kept unto the end of days; he shall rebuke the unrighteous. *II Bar* 29:3 and 30:1 speak of the revelation of the Messiah (from heaven?) and then, seemingly after a temporary reign, a final advent of the Messiah.

To the sparsity of the fewer-than-thirty references in three hundred years (expectations of a Messiah to come) should be added the fact that although Josephus describes all sorts of historical figures (prophets, would-be kings, priests, agitators) in the 1st cent. AD, he never calls one of them a Messiah. Granted that silence, it is remarkable that both of the Josephus references to Jesus allude to him as *christos* (*Ant.* 18.3.3; #63; 20.9.1 #200). If we take at face value later rabbinic references (see §23, n. 26 below), they tell us that Rabbi Aqiba hailed Simon ben Kosiba as the Messiah (AD 130), but before him in these centuries there seems to be no identifiable Jew hailed as the kingly Messiah other than Jesus of Nazareth. I stress this so that in the following discussion some commonly found but erroneous ideas may be discounted. There was *not* a single national expectation of the Messiah; one cannot argue that if Jesus' followers thought he was sent by God, they would have had to say he was the Messiah. He was *not* one among many messianic claimants at this period (indeed we have no proof of any other). In the following discussion of Jesus as "the Messiah," although as we have seen the word could refer to a priest or prophet as well as to a royal figure, we are speaking of the Messiah king. Jesus was not of levitic descent, and so people would not have thought him to be the anointed priest of Aaron. Confessions of him as the Messiah deliberately distinguish that designation from the recognition of him as prophet (Mark 8:28–29 and par.).[19]

The basic historical question is: Was Jesus called the Messiah before his resurrection, and if so by whom and with what acceptance by him? I shall mention a number of theories but in evaluating them three points must be taken into account. Two of these points are facts; the third is a very strong probability.

Fact #1 is that after the resurrection Jesus was called the Messiah (Jesus Christ, Jesus the Christ, the Christ of God) by his followers with astounding frequency as attested in the various genres of early Christian literature. This is true already in prePauline confessions of faith, but massively so in the Pauline writings to the point that "Christ" becomes a second name for "Jesus" and even begins to replace "Jesus."

Fact #2 is that scenes in the Gospels in which Jesus is addressed or acknowledged as the Messiah are very few and acceptance of that title by Jesus is marred by complications. In John 4:25–26 the Samaritan woman mentions the coming of the Messiah, and Jesus says "I am he." Yet Samaritans did not accept the Davidic monarchy; and so if one were to evaluate this scene as

---

[19]O'Neill ("Silence" 156) exaggerates the ambiguity of the term "Messiah" by arguing that since there was no standard interpretation to accept or reject, if Jesus claimed he was the Messiah, he would have had to supply an interpretation of the way in which he meant the title. The combination of his use of kingdom language and his Davidic lineage would have narrowed down possibilities for understanding him as the Messiah.

literal history, she meant by "the Messiah" something other than the anointed king of the House of David—perhaps a Moses-like figure as we find in the later-attested Samaritan belief in the Taheb (BGJ 1.172). In Matt 16:16–17 Jesus responds enthusiastically to Peter's confession of him as "the Messiah, the Son of the living God"; but in the parallel Mark 8:29–30 Peter confesses him only as "the Messiah," and Jesus' response is to tell that to no one. Which should one consider as more likely to have been the historical response? The same question must be asked if one treats the present scene as history; for while the Marcan Jesus answers "I am" to the high priest's' question about being "the Messiah, the Son of the Blessed," the Matthean Jesus answers, "*You* have said it." Luke 22:67–68 and John 10:24–25, if they are taken on the level of history, show no uncomplicated affirmation by Jesus that he is the Messiah. In Luke 4:41 Jesus acts as if he thinks the demons' knowledge that he is the Messiah is correct; but that is Luke's interpretation, not Jesus' own words. Obviously it is going to be difficult to reconcile Facts #1 and #2: a massive postresurrectional confession with a minimal remembered preresurrectional attestation.

Probability # 3 is that Jesus was crucified on a charge involving his being or claiming to be the King of the Jews. Although the wording of the inscription on the cross varies slightly in each Gospel (Mark 15:26 and par.), all have the four Greek words for "The King of the Jews." This was not a title ever used by the followers of Jesus during his ministry, nor was it a commonly attested title in Jewish literature (see p. 731 below), so there is little reason to think that Christians simply created the wording of the charge. In the extraGospel evidence surveyed in §18E above, however, kingship is attested in relation to the death of Jesus only by Mara bar Serapion. High probability, then, is the most we can claim for this as a historical memory. "The King of the Jews" need not mean the anointed king of the House of David; indeed the first attestations of the title are for Alexander Jannaeus and Herod the Great, neither of whom were Davidids. The Romans who made the inscription could have understood it simply as a Jewish king. Nevertheless, it would be harmonious with Jesus being called Messiah in his lifetime.

On the issue of Jesus as the Messiah in his lifetime the following theories have appeared in scholarship. Immediately following the statement of each, I shall indicate in italics my judgment of its value.[20]

(a) Publicly or privately Jesus clearly claimed to be the Messiah. *Unlikely.*

[20]In making such judgments I shall assume that while Christians interpreted, theologized, and qualified the tradition about their master, they did not proclaim or preserve what they *knew* to be false or totally opposed to what Jesus had in fact said. Without that assumption there is no rational control of plausibilities.

While this could explain Fact #1 and Probability #3, it makes Fact #2 virtually unintelligible. One has to suppose some sort of maneuver during Jesus' life to hide what he thought he was. O'Neill ("Silence") proposes without real textual support that Jesus thought of himself as the Messiah but could not say so because *God* was supposed to identify and enthrone the Messiah; the Messiah dare not identify himself. Views about the Messiah were scarcely so uniform as to demand such silence.[21] Totally fictional in my judgment is the attention-attracting theory of S.G.F. Brandon (*Jesus*) that Jesus was a political (indeed revolutionary) Messiah and his followers knew this (see §31, A2 below). One is hard pressed to find a single text that (without an incredibly imaginative interpretation) supports this. History shows none of his followers in the 1st cent. involved in a revolutionary movement (indeed, the contrary);[22] and according to the actual references in Josephus, the Zealot movement postdated Jesus' time by thirty-five years (p. 690 below). Still another thesis that Jesus understood himself to be the Messiah not in his present ministry but in the future parousia at the end of time suffers from lack of evidence in the Gospel texts. One does find something close to that in Acts 3:20 on Peter's lips, but such an approach is precisely the kind of adjustment that Christians in the postresurrectional period had to make in applying "Messiah" to Jesus.

(b) Jesus clearly denied that he was the Messiah. *Most unlikely.* This makes Fact #1 virtually impossible and Probability #3 very difficult to understand; indeed it does not really explain Fact #2. There is no preserved passage where Jesus ever denies he is the Messiah; even Mark 8:29–33 does not mean that. Since a Messiah was not a universal expectation, there is no reason why his followers would have massively proclaimed him the Messiah if he said he was not. That he was crucified as a would-be King of the Jews would have been explained as calumny invented by his enemies instead of being interpreted as partly true (John 18:36–37). Some may be puzzled by my judgments on the two points I have discussed. If Jesus did not claim that he was the Messiah, would he not equivalently have been saying that he was not the Messiah? The key to the logic is once again that Messiah was not a univocal concept. To deny that he was the Messiah could have meant to some

[21]Granted O'Neill's view mentioned in n. 19 above, I find it curious that he regards this poorly attested silence aspect of the Messiah to be indispensable. For the Messiah from the House of David, lineage and birth at Bethlehem could function as *divine identification,* as we see in the Matthean and Lucan infancy stories (plus John 7:41–42).

[22]Jesus was arrested alone; that is not true of the brigands, self-proclaimed kings, and prophets described by Josephus in the 1st cent., i.e., those proposed as parallels for Jesus as a revolutionary. Against them hundreds of soldiers were sent, and in the ensuing armed struggle their followers perished and/or were arrested. The only solitary figure (and the one treated in a manner resembling the treatment of Jesus) was Jesus bar Ananias, who was not patently political or revolutionary.

hearers that Jesus was denying something he would not wish to deny, e.g., that he was God's unique and final agent in establishing God's kingdom—a role of which he was totally convinced. To affirm that he was the Messiah could have meant to other hearers that Jesus was affirming something he had no wish to affirm, e.g., that he would conquer Israel's enemies and establish a Davidic kingdom on earth.

(c) Jesus' opponents (Roman or Jewish) interpreted (honestly or dishonestly) him or his followers as making the claim that he was the Messiah, and that contributed to the charge on which the Romans crucified him. *Very likely.* (Notice that I am leaving aside for the moment whether this interpretation was justified.) This would make Probability #3 intelligible and is harmonious with Facts #1 and #2. That Jews were interested in knowing whether he thought he was the Messiah and that Romans were interested in knowing whether he thought he was the King of the Jews is attested in all four Gospels.

(d) During his lifetime some of his followers thought him to be the Messiah and made that claim/confession whether to him or to others. *Very likely.* This would make Fact #1 perfectly intelligible and indeed is just what is attested in the texts cited under Fact #2 (the Gospel memory would be correct). It would also clarify Proposition #3 and the preceding statement made under (c)—the idea that he was a Messiah king was indeed in circulation to be picked up by his opponents. All the Gospels support such a claim/confession on the part of his disciples.[23] Even if one wants to claim that the charge of the Jewish kingship associated with the crucifixion was false, there had to be some reason for making it, based on what had gone before. (We can scarcely think that it came as a new idea to a Roman soldier as he made the sign to be placed on the cross.) The suggestion that his followers had never thought of him as the Messiah but had to accept that idea because he had been crucified as the King of the Jews deserves the simple answer "Why?" (Dahl, *Crucified* 10–36, is perceptive on this point.) I realize that what I am proposing runs against a "dogma" of modern critical scholarship since Wrede's time: Neither Jesus nor his followers thought he was the Messiah, but postEaster Christians did. More plausible is the theory that postEaster Christians hailed Jesus as the Messiah in part because (at least some of) his preEaster followers had done the same—what changed was not the confession but the content and interpretation given to "Messiah" in the light of the way he died. One may object that the notion of Jesus as the Messiah king would not have come up in his ministry, granting his Galilean origins, the

---

[23]The objection that *christos* does not appear in the Q source betrays a dubious confidence that the total knowledge/faith of the Q author can be known from our reconstruction of the document. Did he/they not believe in Jesus *Christ?*

type of people he associated with, and his disinterest in wealth and power. However, the combination of two factors could have made the issue of Messiahship difficult to evade. First, he preached strongly in the language of kingdom. True, the kingdom of God is not the same as the kingdom of David; but one would need to discover that, and it would be a natural suspicion that the one who made the kingdom already present in his preaching and healing was himself the promised king. Second, very likely Jesus himself was a Davidid (on this point see the discussion in BBM 505–12) and therefore one to whom the role of the anointed king of the House of David might plausibly be attributed by those who accepted his proclamation of the kingdom.

(e) Jesus himself responded to the Messiah issue ambivalently, neither affirming nor denying, partly because he had his own conception of what he must do and partly because he left the ultimate manifestation of his own role in God's hands. *Likely.* Some may wish to theorize that Jesus remained silent and what we have in the Gospels is the interpretation of his silence. Yet the position of ambivalent response (combined with [c] and [d] above) best explains Fact #1 and #2 and Probability #3, as well as all the Gospel Messiah texts. A few qualifications are necessary, however. Although our texts report that some of those who followed Jesus hailed him as the Messiah, it is very difficult to discern how those who did so understood "Messiah," and therefore it is difficult to be sure why Jesus is remembered answering ambivalently. But from Gospel passages one may cull the following as understandings of "Messiah" or "king" that Christians thought Jesus would reject: an understanding in which suffering and death were excluded (Mark 8:31–32); a claim to rule over other nations (Matt 4:8–10; Luke 4:5–8); a public acceptance and coronation (John 6:15); having places of honor and power to assign (Mark 10:37–38); putting an emphasis on Davidic descent and family connections (Mark 12:35–37; 3:31–35). One should also take into account that the tradition supplies scarcely any attempts by Jesus to define his own role. Such reticence may flow from the fact that he did not claim to know exactly what God had in store for him. Jesus appears self-confident in proclaiming God's kingdom in word and deed, but he is remembered as recognizing that in the when and how of the coming of that kingdom God retained sovereignty (Mark 4:26–29; 13:32; see I Cor 15:23–24). If Jesus was ambivalent about the Messiah issue, it may have been that in part the role of a Messiah king in God's kingdom was up to God to design.[24] If Jesus spoke

---

[24]Accepting the Gospel picture that Jesus was self-assured about his identity and role in God's plan, we may suspect that among the hopes attached to the advent of the Messiah (a) some would have matched his own conceptions of himself, e.g., a unique agent in God's definitive plan for Israel; (b) some may not have matched, e.g., a military leader reestablishing the Davidic kingdom; (c) about

of the less defined eschatological Son of Man (see below), in Dan 7:13–14 it is the Ancient of Days who gives kingship to one like a son of man. Even in the most exalted christology in the NT we hear (John 5:19), "The Son cannot do anything of himself; he can only do what he sees the Father doing." And one may add that even in the most orthodox Christian belief, the coming kingship of Jesus is yet to be defined.

Thus, combining (c), (d), and (e) above, I judge it plausible that during Jesus' lifetime some of his followers thought him to be the Messiah, i.e., the expected anointed king of the House of David who would rule over God's people. Jesus, confronted with this identification, responded ambivalently because associated with that role were features that he rejected, and also because God had yet to define the role that he would play in the kingdom beyond what he was already doing. Such an indefinite and ambivalent answer could have constituted the basis on which his enemies gave him over to the Romans as would-be king.

B. Jesus the Son of God

When we turn to the use of "the Son of God" by or about Jesus in his lifetime and its possible appearance in AD 30/33 in Jewish inquiries made about him, there is far less evidence than there was for "the Messiah." In ancient Near Eastern and Greco-Roman polytheism, rulers, heroes, and wonder-workers were entitled "son(s) of god" because mythically or literally they were thought to have been begotten through a god's mating with a human being. In Israelite thought angels could be called figuratively "sons of God" (Gen 6:2; Job 1:6; Ps 29:1; Dan 3:25 [3:92]; etc.). God could speak of Israel as "my son" (Hosea 11:1); and a pious individual could be referred to as "son of God" (Wisdom 2:18) or a "son of the Most High" (Sirach 4:10). Yet in the biblical or extrabiblical Jewish literature before or contemporary with the NT, "the Son of God" *as a title* for a human being is extremely rare and for all practical purposes confined to one obscure instance in the Dead Sea Scrolls. (The Marcan "the Son of the Blessed" does not occur, as we have seen.) In what has been called a pseudo-Danielic fragment preserved in Aramaic at Qumran (4Q246) we read "the Son of God he shall be said to be, and the Son of the Most High they shall call him."[25] The lack of context in this poorly preserved piece from a larger document makes identification

---

some he may have been uncertain, not knowing in full what God had in store (see Mark 10:37–38a). These observations differ in nuance from those proposed by O'Neill (nn. 19 and 21 above).

[25]This text was discussed and disseminated by J. T. Milik in a Harvard lecture in 1972. J. A. Fitzmyer made the crucial lines available in NTS 20 (1973–74), 391–94; republished in FAWA 90–94, 102–7. It was finally published by E. Puech, *RB* 99 (1992), 98–131, and commented on by Fitzmyer *Biblica* 74 (1993), 153–74.

of the "he" difficult, although a king seems to be in mind. Milik, dating it ca. 25 BC, saw a reference to a Syrian king hostile to the Jews; and D. Flusser[26] argued that the use of the titles had an antichrist (antiGod) atmosphere of arrogance exemplified by Antiochus Epiphanes. More scholars now, however, understand the titles positively, often referring them to a future figure on the side of God.[27] This is favored by another Qumran document (1QSa 2:12) which speaks of God begetting the Messiah at an expected moment in the future. In particular, J. J. Collins sees a possible relationship of this "Son of God" to "one like a son of man" in Dan 7:13–14 to whom the Ancient of Days (God) will give dominion, glory, and kingship. I shall discuss the Daniel passage in §22 below, and if the connection proposed by Collins can be sustained, the logic of Jesus' "Son of Man" response to the high priest's question about the Son of God becomes much clearer. Nevertheless, in this ANALYSIS where we are asking historical questions, it would be methodologically unsound to make much depend on the obscure 4Q246.

Leaving aside the issue of recorded instances of the title, many turn to OT texts where the Davidic king is said to be treated by God as a son (II Sam 7:14) begotten by God (Ps 2:7; 110:3), especially since we have confirmatory evidence from Qumran that language of begetting by God was taken over and applied to the Davidic Messiah (1QSa 2:11–12). One may argue, then, that it should have been a simple and obvious step to call the Messiah, the descendant of David, the Son of God. As of yet, however, there is no clear evidence that such a step was taken within Judaism independent of reflection on Jesus. Later Jewish literature does *not* feature the title even where we might expect it, e.g., in Targum Pseudo-Jonathan's rendering of II Sam 7:14. That silence was often explained away as antiChristian prejudice, as not wanting to mention the Davidic Messiah as "the Son of God" because Christians used the title. Now, however, we see that the preNT 4QFlor 1:7–13, which is an interpretation of II Sam 7:11–14, does not emphasize the sonship relationship in 7:14, even though the text was interpreted as a reference to the Davidic Messiah. *PsSol* 17:23 [21] speaks of the Messiah as the Son of David, not as the Son of God.

The frequency and early date of the Christian usage of "the Son of God" for Jesus is impressive, e.g., in the Pauline writings of the 50s ("His Son" in I Thess 1:10; Gal 1:16; I Cor 1:9; and "the Son of God" in Gal 2:20; II Cor 1:19). In a formula in Rom 1:3–4 that Paul assumes to be known to the Romans and that is not phrased in Paul's own style, "the Son of God" is a

---

[26]*Immanuel* 10 (1980), 31–37.

[27]Fitzmyer (= a king), F. García Martínez (= Melchizedek), M. Hengel (= Jewish people). The Messiah is proposed by Puech and by J. J. Collins, "The 'Son of God' Text from Qumran," in *From Jesus to John*, ed. M. de Boer (M. de Jonge Festschrift; JSNTSup 84; Sheffield: JSOT, 1993), 65–82.

title that gives Jesus status beyond Davidic descent; this formula could easily go back to the 40s. The idea of the divine begetting of Jesus as the Son of God through the Holy Spirit, contained in the infancy narratives of Matt and Luke, may also go back to an early Christian period (BBM 160–61; 311–21).[28] Reflection on the psalm passages pertinent to the status of the Davidic Messiah as God's Son was widespread (Acts 13:33; Heb 1:5; 5:5). Had this reflection begun in Jesus' lifetime, so that already then he was thought of as the Son of God?

The Gospel evidence should make us cautious. While Mark, the earliest written Gospel, has Peter, the most important of Jesus' followers, hail Jesus as "the Messiah," it has no human being during his ministry hail him as "the Son of God." The use of that title by Jesus' disciples in Matt 14:33 and 16:16 represents Matthean addition supplementing Mark (even if the addition, particularly in 16:16, has its own early history). The same lack of the use of "the Son of God" by Jesus' disciples during his lifetime is attested by Luke. The tradition that demons called Jesus "the Son of God" (Mark 3:11; 5:7; also Q represented in Matt 4:3 and Luke 4:3), as did an angel (Luke 1:35), and that God spoke to him as "my beloved Son" (Mark 1:11) suggests that this evaluation of Jesus was looked on as a more-than-human insight that had to be revealed to those who would believe—something stated explicitly in Matt 16:17. Mark 15:39 dramatizes this in the case of the first human to make the confession, which took place after he saw how Jesus died. Thus there is reason in the Gospels, read perceptively, to think that unlike "the Messiah," the title "the Son of God" was *not* applied to Jesus in his lifetime by his followers[29] or, a fortiori, by himself.[30] It was a revealed, early post-ministry insight. This would mean that the high priest's question phrased in Mark 14:61, "Are you . . . the Son of the Blessed [= God]?" was *not* the formulation in a Jewish investigation of Jesus in AD 30/33.

If "the Son of God" was not used by Jesus or his followers in his lifetime, why did Christians so soon begin to express [their] faith in him under that title? Why did that title ultimately become a touchstone of baptismal and confessional faith (Matt 28:19; John 20:31). If, from the available evidence, "the Son of God" was not an already existing way of describing the filial relationship of the Davidic king and hence of the Messiah to God (II Sam 7:14; Ps 2:7; 110:3), what made Christians understand Jesus the Davidic

---

[28]M. Hengel, *The Son of God* (Philadelphia: Fortress, 1976), argues forcefully that this title belonged to the earliest kerygmatic proclamation.

[29]The available evidence favors that judgment, but for the contrary see Lövestam, "Frage" 96–99.

[30]In John 10:36 Jesus has said, "I am God's Son," but most would regard that as a Gospel spelling-out of what was implicit—John's equivalent of Mark's having Jesus say "I am" when asked by the high priest about being the Son of the Blessed.

Messiah as "the Son of God"? Mark 12:35–37 betrays a Christian awareness that Jesus' exalted sonship did not come from his Davidic status. Some find another route toward sonship language in Jesus' praying to God as Abba ("Father"), which most probably does stem from his lifetime (p. 174 above) as well as in some statements about himself as "the Son" (found in preGospel traditions). Those factors lead us into the issue of an exalted christology implicit in the way Jesus acted and spoke but not covered by the use of titles—hints of a self-evaluation that other Jews might have considered blasphemous. One would have to ask then, granted that the high priest's "Are you the Son of God?" is the kind of language used in the Jewish-Christian struggles later in the century, does it translate and vocalize a concern of AD 30/33 among the Jewish authorities about Jesus' exalted pretensions that had not yet found such a convenient title? That question will be discussed below in the ANALYSIS of §23, which deals with the historicity of the blasphemy charge.

(*Bibliography for this episode is found in §17, Part 5.*)

§22. SANHEDRIN PROCEEDINGS, PART THREE: JESUS' RESPONSE(S) AND STATEMENT ABOUT THE SON OF MAN

(Mark 14:62; Matt 26:64; Luke 22:67–70b)

Translation

Mark 14:62: But Jesus said, "I am, and you [pl.] will see the Son of Man sitting at the right of the Power and coming with the clouds of heaven."

Matt 26:64: Jesus says to him, "*You* have said it. Yet I say to you [pl.], 'From now on you will see the Son of Man sitting at the right of the Power and coming on the clouds of heaven.'"

Luke 22:67–70: [⁶⁷saying, "If you are the Messiah, say to us."] But he said to them, "If I shall say to you, you will never believe. ⁶⁸But if I shall ask a question, you will never answer. ⁶⁹But from the present there will be the Son of Man sitting at the right of the power of God." [⁷⁰But they all said, "Are you then the Son of God?"] ⁷⁰ᵇBut he said to them, "You (yourselves) say that I am."

[John 10:25: (²⁴So the Jews . . . were saying to him, ". . . If you are the Messiah, say to us openly.") ²⁵Jesus answered them, "I have said to you and you do not believe."]

[10:36: ". . . I said, 'I am God's Son.'"]

[1:51: And he says to him [Nathanael], "Amen, amen, I say to you [pl.], 'You will see the heavens opened and the angels of God ascending and descending on the Son of Man.'"]

COMMENT

As we turn to Jesus' response(s) to the question(s) about being the Messiah, the Son of God (the Blessed), two factors are common to all the Gospels:

When the Son of God is mentioned, Jesus is affirmative in various degrees; and he proclaims positively the role of the Son of Man in relation to God. (Those two factors are present under different circumstances in John 10:36 and 1:51[1] as well.) However, because Luke (like John) separates the Messiah issue as a preliminary question distinct from that about the Son of God, we shall comment first on Jesus' ambiguous response to that question in Luke (and John) before turning to the two common factors. (See outline of the subdivisions on p. 313 above.)

RESPONSE TO THE SEPARATE MESSIAH QUESTION IN LUKE 22:67–68

In having the Sanhedrin members pose to Jesus two questions (about the Messiah and about the Son of God) and in having Jesus respond to each, is Luke simply reorganizing Mark's one question and response? Many would answer yes by analogy with the whole Jewish trial scene, in which Luke is heavily dependent on Mark. In the appropriate sections of my commentary on the Sanhedrin proceedings I contend that Luke's omissions from the Marcan Jewish trial (no witnesses, no destruction-of-the-sanctuary statement, no intervention by the high priest, no blasphemy charge, no formal sentencing) reflect editing in which much of this material is used in the Stephen trial in Acts 6–7. I see no reason to posit that Luke had another account of the trial at his disposal. In the question-and-answer part of the Sanhedrin proceedings, Luke's treatment of the second query concerning the Son of God (22:70) is very close to Mark 14:62a, even as the Lucan form of the Son-of-Man response (22:69) is very close to Mark 14:62b. But such an explanation of Luke 22:69–70 as dependent on Mark does not give assurance that Luke 22:67–68,[2] which has no close parallel in Mark, did not draw on an independent tradition about the way Jesus answered his Jewish adversaries.

Most who posit the existence of special Lucan tradition attribute at least 22:67 to it (Fitzmyer, *Luke* 2.1458: "almost certainly").[3] Schneider ("Verfahren" 117–18), despite a change of heart that has led him to reject most proposed Lucan special traditions, would still see this as a traditional saying, but not one that historically had been part of the Sanhedrin trial. Radl ("Sonderüberlieferungen" 143–47) argues that by working at it, one can find parallels in Luke-Acts for many of the features in 22:67–68, including an

---

[1]Reasons for appealing to this verse will be pointed out below in discussing Mark/Matt, but we should already note that it follows shortly after a confession of Jesus as Son of God in John 1:49.

[2]Matera ("Luke 22") argues that throughout this scene Luke does not possess an independent tradition about Jesus' trial; but he does not seem to recognize that he has not proved the right to jump from Mark as the primary source of Luke to Mark as the *sole* source (p. 58), e.g., he does not discuss 22:67 in detail. Compare Soards's more careful treatment (*Passion* 103–4).

[3]Readers are reminded of n. 17 in §21 and that interpreters define the limits of 22:67 differently.

evasive answer constructed by Luke in 20:1–8. However, Légasse ("Jésus" 183) and others, paying meticulous attention to the wording and grammar of 22:67, point out that there are technical features in the Greek of this conditional sentence that are not the usual Lucan style. Above all there is the fact that John 10:24–25 has an answer to the Messiah question that resembles closely in import Luke 22:67, and that in both Gospels this is soon followed by an affirmative indication on the issue of Jesus as God's Son. We cannot, then, assume Lucan dependence on Mark in 22:67–68 simply because in the rest of the interrogation one finds such dependence; rather we must examine these two verses in detail.

The two conditional sentences of 22:67–68 by which the Lucan Jesus answers the Messiah question have future-more-vivid apodoses and so they emphatically expect a negative response: The authorities will surely never believe or never answer. The same type of conditional answer, showing that the one being questioned is perfectly aware that he is being given no choice, is found in Jer 38:14–15. King Zedekiah says he will pose a question to the prophet and urges him to hide nothing. Jeremiah replies, "If I tell you, will you not be sure to have me put to death? And if I give counsel, you will not listen to me." Probably the tradition underlying both Luke and John has been affected by the experience of believers in Jesus interrogated by those hostile to him. When examined about their faith in Jesus as the Messiah, they have found that their affirmations are ignored and their counterarguments are not answered. This explanation, in my judgment, is far preferable to the complicated theory put forward by Derrett, "Midrash." He draws on the LXX of Isa 41:28 in reference to the idols, "And if I shall ask them, 'Whence are you?' they will not reply." It is true that Luke (22:37 = Isa 53:12) presents Jesus as the Suffering Servant and that therefore there may be a tone here of Isa 53:1, "Who would believe what we have heard?"—a passage applicable both to Jesus' proclamation and to the Christian proclamation of him. But farfetched is the idea that the whole scene is a midrash[4] that polemicizes against the Jewish interrogators of Jesus as if they are idols.

In the narratives of Luke and John the cautious attitude about what will happen if Jesus' Messiahship is affirmed suggests that both are aware that adaptation and translation are necessary for "the Messiah" to become applicable to Jesus as understood in Christian faith. These two evangelists are more self-conscious than Mark and Matt about how Christian faith transformed all the material pertinent to Jesus, supplying understanding for what was not at first understood (Luke 24:25–27; John 2:21–22; 16:12–13). Such

---

[4]Detected by skipping back and forth from Greek to Hebrew and invoking as proof much later rabbinic references, which are very dubiously applicable to the 1st cent.

subtlety in answering a question is not appropriate in legal testimony at a trial, but Luke's Jewish proceedings against Jesus in 22:66–71 are not so clearly a trial (even if we learn Luke's full mind about a trial from elsewhere). John places the Messiah interchange not in a trial but in the general Jerusalem controversies of the ministry.

To be precise, only in 22:67, the first condition on saying and never believing, is Luke close to John 10:24–25. The second condition (22:68), "But if I shall ask a question, you will never answer," is distantly alike in tone but not in word to John 18:23 ("If I have spoken badly, give testimony about what is bad. If [I have spoken] well, why do you beat me?"). One suspects that Luke has shaped this second condition along the lines of the first, which he found in the tradition. The addition of it begins to shift Jesus over from being defendant to being judge who prosecutes with questions, and in that shift Luke has moved closer to Johannine thought. With two conditions serving as the first part of Jesus' answer, we are finding another example of the Lucan Jesus not being overly cooperative with questions by hostile authorities. When he was questioned in 20:1–8 by what authority he did things like cleansing the Temple, he asked the chief priests, and the scribes, and the elders about JBap; since they could not answer him, he said, "Neither will I tell you by what authority I do these things." See also 20:20–26; 20:27–40 for the instances of answering by posing questions and problems. Also we should not forget that Luke sees the trial of Jesus in relation to the trials of Christians described in Acts. Stephen terminates his testimony in Acts 7:51–53 by asking his judges questions, only to provoke rage. At the end of his testimony Paul turns to question Agrippa II (Acts 26:27). If in defending themselves Christians were not to resort to the sword (Luke 22:51), questions born of their sense of innocence could be a potent weapon.

There is an interesting textual variant (which I italicize) in Luke's second condition (22:68) worthy of discussion: ". . . not answer *me or release* (me)."[5] It is lacking in the best Alexandrian witnesses[6] but found in Codex Bezae, the Latin and Syriac versions, and the whole Koine tradition. Fitzmyer (*Luke* 2.1467) dismisses it as a typical clarifying Bezae tradition. Duplacy argues strongly for it, suggesting that scribes dropped it. The omission could have been accidental (homoioteleuton) or deliberate (if read disjunctively, it sounds as if Jesus wishes to be released from dying). If original, it heightens the role of Jesus as judge: He is spelling out for them their alternatives.

---

[5]In such a negative statement "or" is ambiguous: Is it copulative, meaning "and you will not release me"? Or is it truly disjunctive, meaning "or else you will release me"? (See BDF 446 for copulative sense; Duplacy, "Variante" 44.)

[6]P[75], Codices Vaticanus and Sinaiticus, Coptic, Cyril of Alexandria.

Nevertheless, Luke 22:67–68 has not responded with precision to the question whether or in what sense Jesus is the Messiah. Clarification will be given by Jesus as he speaks about the Son of Man (22:69); that in turn will produce another question of whether he is then the Son of God, to which Jesus will respond affirmatively. This reverses the Marcan order where the affirmative response precedes the Son-of-Man clarification. Presumably once more we are seeing an exercise of Lucan logic and sense of order: An obscure response needs a clarification more than does an affirmative response. But let us return to the Marcan order by dealing first with the affirmative response and then with Jesus' Son of Man statement.

FORMS OF JESUS' AFFIRMATIVE RESPONSE TO THE SON-OF-GOD QUESTION

Each Synoptic has a slightly different response by Jesus to the christological question, i.e., to the combined "the Messiah, the Son of the Blessed/God" in Mark/Matt and to "the Son of God" in Luke:[7]

Mark: 14:62:	Jesus said,	"I am" (*egō eimi*)
Matt 26:64:	Jesus says to him,	"*You* have said it. Yet . . ." (*sy eipas plēn*)
Luke 22:70b:	He said to them,	"*You* say that I am" (*hymeis legete hoti egō eimi*)

For each of the Gospels scholars have discussed the extent to which the answer of Jesus is to be considered affirmative and what is being affirmed. Let us consider them one by one.[8]

Mark. The response *egō eimi* is unambiguously affirmative. Notice that Mark does not have Jesus address himself "to him" (i.e., the high priest) as Matt does. This affirmation is addressed to all who read and is not affected by the skepticism or malevolence of the questioner. (The breadth of the response will be explicit in the "you" [pl.] of "will see.") We have already observed (p. 260 above) that in the Johannine tradition "I am" serves virtually as a divine name with the power to cast men to the ground (18:5). Rather than inventing a totally new vocabulary, John was developing the potentialities of expressions already found in the tradition. Our proof of that is the appearance of "I am" at very solemn moments in the Synoptics, e.g., Mark 6:50 and the current passage, where it affirms that Jesus is the Messiah and the Son of God. However, that distant relationship to Johannine usage does

---

[7]In this comparison I have italicized the English "you" to indicate where the Greek has a personal pronoun.

[8]For the purposes of comparison let me present here Jesus' answer to Pilate's question as to whether he was the King of the Jews (Mark 15:2; Matt 27:11; Luke 23:3; John 18:33,37):

Synoptics: "*You* say it" (*sy legeis*)

John 18:37: "*You* say that I am a king" (*sy legeis hoti basileus eimi*).

not mean that here Mark is using "I am" as a divine name,[9] or that in itself it is the cause of the blasphemy charge. Some scholars appeal to another reading of Mark that is poorly attested (Codex Koridethi, family 13 of minuscules): "You said that I am" (*sy eipas hoti egō eimi*) or variants thereof.[10] Kempthorne's detailed refutation ("Marcan") of it is quite convincing on many grounds: not Marcan style; two awkward uses of forms of *eipon* ("said") in a row; switch from singular to plural in almost back-to-back uses of "you"; etc. Rather, as Kempthorne finds in at least ten other passages, the mss. that support the longer reading are harmonizing Matt's *sy eipas* with Mark's *egō eimi*.

There is no real difficulty in having Jesus give an affirmative answer to being the Messiah, the Son of God; for as we saw (p. 468 above), taken in the flow of Marcan Gospel scenes, these two titles together confirm what respectively Peter and the heavenly Father have said about Jesus—and the third component, "the Son of Man," is soon to follow. But even on the Gospel level, some interpreters are surprised that the Marcan Jesus who instructed Peter to tell no one that he was the Messiah (8:30) and ordered the unclean spirits who recognized him as the Son of God not to make him known (3:11–12) should break the code of silence. But silence in those instances was mandated because such confessions would give the wrong impression if they were not accompanied by an appreciation of the necessity to give oneself in suffering. When Jesus speaks to the high priest, his suffering and degradation have already begun. To be able to see him as the Messiah, the Son of God, in *these* circumstances is to understand the mystery.

Matt. In 26:64, whereas the corresponding Marcan verse (14:62) has an aorist ("Jesus said"), Matt has a historical present tense: "Jesus says." That is unusual but not inexplicable stylistically; here it has the impact of giving enduring force to Jesus' response on this all-important issue. While *sy eipas* (aorist), "*You* have said it," used by Matt in that response resembles *sy legeis* (present), which is the Synoptic Jesus' response to Pilate, let us reserve the latter phrase until our discussion of Luke, who uses a present tense (pl.) in this scene as well. These responses involve the Greek use of a personal pronoun; but scholars are not agreed whether that pronoun is used for emphasis, "You yourself have said it" (thus a strong affirmative); or in sarcastic challenge, "You have said it, but you do not believe it"; or by way of contrast,

---

[9]Pace Stauffer ("Messias") and others; see Catchpole, *Trial* 133. Part of the reason Stauffer would have the offense related to "I am" as a divine name is that he cannot accept that statement as an affirmation by Jesus that he was the Messiah. Such an objection confuses the historical level with Mark's intended communication to his readers.

[10]For diverse reasons this reading is favored by Cranfield, Feuillet, Lohmeyer, O'Neill, J.A.T. Robinson, Strecker, Streeter, and Taylor.

"You, not I, have said it" (see BDF 277[1,2]). The latter interpretation could have a whole range of possibilities: I have not said it because I do not agree (negative); I have not said it because I might get into trouble (cautious affirmative); I have not said it because, although there is truth in it, I am not happy with the phrasing (qualified affirmative), etc.

Every one of these interpretations has had supporters, but sometimes the arguments hopelessly intermingle Jesus' attitude in AD 30/33 answering the historical high priest (on the presumption that these are his actual words) with what the evangelist wished his readers to think of Jesus in the post-70 period. I am interested here only in the latter. A study by Irmscher (*"Sy legeis"* 157–58) of the comparable formula used in responding to Pilate argues that little light is thrown on such a formula by classical Greek and by the type of parallels gathered by Wettstein; also the Greek Fathers were not at one in interpreting it. Catchpole ("Answer") has made a thorough survey of the interpretations of the "You have said it" phrase by Jewish scholars, who call upon the speech patterns of the ancient Jewish documents; but no one dominant interpretation emerges. Many hold *sy eipas* to be affirmative; more think it to be equivocal or obscure; and a respectable minority judges it to be ambiguous but affirmative. In other words, Jewish scholarship has not differed greatly from Christian scholarship in the range of views, despite the fact that some of those surveyed were treating it on the level of history and were attempting to show that Jesus did not have the same view of himself that his followers had.

De Wette claimed that *sy eipas* represents an affirmative formula attested in rabbinic documents; but D. Chwolson, a Jewish scholar, in a series of writings between 1892–1910 challenged this (Catchpole, "Answer" 215–16) and favored a disengagement interpretation, e.g.: Whether true or not I leave aside, but it was not I who said it. Catchpole himself argues for an affirmative interpretation, but the Jewish texts he cites are also invoked by Aicher (*Prozess* 71–72), who would find in them neither a yes nor a flat no. It may be helpful to cite an example illustrating the obscurity of "You have said." In Tosepta *Kelim Baba Qamma* 1.6 (65b), we are told that many sages held that one could not enter between the outer court of the Temple and the altar without washing, even though R. Meir (ca. 130) said one could. R. Simeon the Modest did so and reported it to R. Eliezer (ca. 90) who challenged him, Who is beloved, you or the high priest? When R. Simeon was silent, he was asked, Are you ashamed to admit that the high priest's dog is more beloved than you? R. Simeon answered, "You have said it." From what follows it would seem that Simeon is affirming the immediate question about the dog but is insisting that he is correct about the right to walk where he had. Although one might find other Jewish examples that are clearer[11] and in general they do not run against the interpretation of Matt 26:64 that I favor, I am reluctant to invoke such remote evidence from a later period.

Other internal Matthean factors are more helpful than dubious parallels from later Jewish literature. In 26:25, after Jesus had announced that one who dipped bread with him at the Last Supper would give him over, Judas said, "Is it I, Rabbi?"; and Jesus responded, "You have said it" (*sy eipas*). The expression cannot be a negative there. It is an affirmative; but Jesus' answer frees him from taking responsibility for what Judas is about to do, and the reason for the qualification is supplied by the context. Another interpretative aid is that in 26:64 *sy eipas* is followed by *plēn* ("Yet"). Although that particle is not always an absolute adversative,[12] its presence here means that at least the affirmative is conditioned or qualified.

The following summary conclusions can be offered on "You have said it": (a) *Sy eipas* is not a negative (pace Héring, Cullmann), meaning "You have said so, but I disagree, or I would not say it"; nor is *sy eipas* an expression of complete personal uninvolvement: "Whether or not it is true I cannot say"; for Jesus has already affirmed that the confession "the Messiah, the Son of the living God" is a revelation from God (Matt 16:16–17). Moreover, the Sanhedrists understand it as an affirmative since they say to Jesus, "Prophesy for us, O Messiah" (Matt 26:68), a mockery that would make no sense if he denied being the Messiah—similarly for the mockery "the Son of God" in 27:40. Indeed, in 27:43 the chief priests confirm, "He said that 'I am God's Son.'" (b) *Sy eipas* is not an unqualified affirmative, indicating absolute agreement with what has been said. If Matt wanted an unambiguous affirmative, he could have repeated Mark's *egō eimi*. Also justice must be done to *plēn*, "Yet. . . ." (c) *Sy eipas* is a qualified affirmative: There is truth in what the high priest has said, but he must take responsibility for the way he interprets it and the use he plans to make of it. (The *sy eipas* addressed to Judas and the *sy legeis* addressed to Pilate are also qualified affirmatives, but the nuance of the qualification in each case must be drawn from the context.) The hostility shown by the high priest means that the demand imposed on

[11]In *Midrash Rabbah* on Qoheleth 7:12 we are told that Rabbi Judah the Prince was dying, and the people of the town decided to put to death the first one who announced the bad news that the rabbi had died. Bar Kappara announced to them that in the struggle between angels and human beings for tablets of the covenant, the angels were victorious. Catching the symbolism, the people cried, "The rabbi is dead." Bar Kappara stated, "You have said it; I have not said it." In this case the statement made by the people is true, but the respondent does not want to suffer punishment for having said it.

[12]See n. 23 in §7. Here if Matt wanted an absolute adversative, he should have put the contrasting pronoun *egō* before *legō*, thus *sy eipas plēn egō legō*.

Jesus under oath is phrased as a tactic to get incriminating self-witness from Jesus, testimony to be interpreted in harmony with the sanctuary-of-God statement presented as blasphemous arrogance.[13] In the Gethsemane scene, when the Marcan Jesus kept silent as Judas kissed him, the Matthean Jesus spoke, so that there would be no doubt in the readers' minds that Jesus knew what Judas was about. So here too Matthew wants to make clear that the Jesus who answers the high priest affirmatively is perfectly aware of what is intended. Moreover, by putting responsibility on the questioner for what is being said, Jesus as the one questioned turns judgment against the high priest. When Jesus turns from *"You* have said it" to "Yet I say to you," he will invoke the image of the Son of Man coming in judgment. There is irony for the perceptive readers in the issue of who is really being condemned here.

Luke. Occasionally one encounters the observation that Luke's "You [pl.] say that I am" has the appearance of combining Matt's "You [sg.] have said it" with Mark's "I am." Luke's *hymeis legete,* however, is not the same as Matt's *sy eipas* (pace Winter, "Treatment" 164); it is rather the plural of the answer the Lucan Jesus will give to Pilate: *sy legeis* (23:3), which is the same answer that the Marcan Jesus will give. Evidently Luke thinks of "You say" as the basic pattern of Jesus' answer to the authorities, Jewish and Roman, in the interrogations that led to his death. Thus, Luke is combining two Marcan answers (the "I am" to the high priest and the "you say it" to Pilate) to form Jesus' answer to the Jewish Sanhedrin authorities who ask Jesus "Are you then the Son of God?" Notice that we are no longer in the future conditions that phrased the question about the Messiah; the Son-of-God question is phrased in the present tense and not conditional.[14]

Other misunderstandings have plagued the interpretation of Luke's scene. There is the usual confusion caused by blending history and Gospel interpretation, e.g., Aicher (*Prozess* 75–76) argues that the Lucan answer to "Are you then the Son of God?" has to be ambiguous, for otherwise Jesus would be affirming that he is a political Messiah. Yet from 1:35 on the reader has known from an angel that Jesus is the Son of God conceived without a hu-

---

[13]While some would attribute to the sanctuary statement an equal share in the affirmation of Jesus, the fact that Matt 27:63 showed him silent toward it suggests caution. On the other hand, I cannot agree with the judgment that it has no decisive role since it is not mentioned again at the trial (see Broer, "Bemerkungen" 29–30). It is equally an excuse for mocking Jesus in 27:39 and is confirmed by God in 27:51. In the Matthean picture the Sanhedrin authorities are angered by the claim that Jesus has the divine power to destroy the sanctuary, and that leads into a primary focus on who he claims to be.

[14]And, of course, for Luke's Gentile readers it is not phrased in Mark's Jewish (pseudo-Jewish?) style, "Son of the Blessed."

man father—how can the answer be anything other than affirmative? Part of the same problem is a failure to recognize that in the questioning Luke has carefully distinguished between Messiah and Son of God, following in this a tradition similar to John's. Any ambiguity in the answers of the Lucan Jesus concerns the Messiah issue, not the Son-of-God issue. Indeed "the Son of God" title is a *conclusion* from Jesus' identifying himself as "the Son of Man sitting at the right of the power of God" (22:70). "The Son of God" indicates Jesus' divine origin and status.

How then should one interpret "You say that I am" in response to "Are you then the Son of God?" Who is correct, Fitzmyer (Luke 2.1453, 1463), who speaks of "a half-affirmative answer" and translates: "It is you who say I am"; or SBJ with its fully affirmative: "You say well; indeed I am" ("Vous dites bien; Je le suis")? In my judgment the key lies in the fact that Luke, who obviously wanted some conformity between the answer to the Jewish authorities and the answer to Pilate, has chosen here to include Mark's "I am"[15] (unlike Matt who replaced it; also notice that Luke has no contrasting *plēn*). In the question about the Messiah, as we saw, Luke was following a tradition somewhat like John's; if here he has rejoined the pattern of the Marcan scene, he remains close to John's understanding (John 10:36) whereby Jesus states affirmatively that he said "I am God's Son." I see no justification, then, for speaking of a qualified affirmative (as in Matt), precisely because Luke has separated the questions of Messiah and Son of God. I agree with SBJ in seeing a full affirmative: "You yourselves say that I am." Jesus has turned the question of the Jewish authorities into an affirmation of the highest Christian title. While Mark/Matt will have a Roman centurion affirm that Jesus is the Son of God, Luke will change that to a confession of Jesus' innocence (23:47); but here the Lucan Jesus has interpreted affirmatively what was on the lips of *all* the leaders of the Jerusalem Sanhedrin, so that ironically it becomes a confession.[16] Luke begins his Gospel in Jerusalem and ends it in Jerusalem, staying within the confines of Judaism; he will leave Gentile confessions of faith until the Book of Acts. Within Judaism Luke has set up an inclusion between the first words spoken about Jesus by the angel to Mary at the beginning of the Gospel (1:34) and these last words by the Jewish Sanhedrin leaders in 22:70; both identify Jesus as the Son of God.

[15]Such an "I am" is missing from the response to Pilate (n. 8 above): Pilate's query concerns "the King of the Jews," which is not a title that has occurred previously in Luke; but "Son of God" has, and Luke is more positive toward it.

[16]Notice what Luke has done with the "all" that Mark puts at the beginning of the Sanhedrin session (14:53) and repeats at the condemnation (14:64); Luke has used it for this unplanned confes-

JESUS' STATEMENT ABOUT THE SON OF MAN

The three Synoptic Gospels agree that in response to a question posed to him at the trial, Jesus made reference to the Son of Man; John 1:51 is a partially similar statement:

> Mark 14:62: "And you [pl.] will see the Son of Man sitting at the right of the Power and coming with the clouds of heaven."
>
> Matt 26:64: "Yet I say to you [pl.], 'From now you will see the Son of Man sitting at the right of the Power and coming on the clouds of heaven.'"
>
> Luke 22:69: "But from the present there will be the Son of Man sitting at the right of the power of God."
>
> John 1:51: "Amen, amen, I say to you [pl.], 'You will see the heavens opened and the angels of God ascending and descending on the Son of Man.'"

It is noteworthy that a plurality is addressed even though (in Mark/Matt and John) Jesus has been speaking to an individual. In Mark and Matt this Son-of-Man saying continues Jesus' answer to the issue of being the Messiah, the Son of the Blessed (God); in Luke it follows his heavily conditioned response about the Messiah and provokes the authorities to ask if he is the Son of God.[17] In the three Synoptics this is the last Son-of-Man saying that Jesus will utter before he dies (see Luke 24:7), and thus it brings his frequent teaching about the Son of Man to a culmination. Let us consider how each Synoptic evangelist would have his readers understand this reference.

Mark. The "and you will see" continues the fully affirmative "I am"; and so the future sight of the Son of Man confirms the present identity of Jesus as the Messiah, the Son of God, as well as adding to it. But with what nuances or in what way? In Mark 8:31 Jesus' teaching that the Son of Man must suffer was meant to color Peter's confession of him as the Messiah; without that dimension of suffering Peter had so wrong an understanding that he was thinking only human thoughts, not those of God. And that was the first of three predictions that the Son of Man would suffer (9:31; 10:33–34; also 9:12; 10:45; 14:21,41). Inevitably, then, some would contend that once again here Jesus is using the figure of the Son of Man to clarify: He is the Messiah, the Son of the Blessed, but his self-understanding involves

---

sion. Heil ("Reader ... Luke 22") effectively brings out the irony of the Lucan account: The Sanhedrists are thinking of one thing, the Christian readers are thinking of another.

[17]The statement in John 1:51 follows confessions of Jesus as the Messiah (1:41) and the Son of God (1:49).

suffering not envisaged by the high priest. Nothing in the grammar of the Marcan sentence, however, favors such a "but" implication. And in Jesus' circumstances as an arrested criminal whom the authorities wish to destroy, the necessity of suffering really does not need to be emphasized. The term "the Son of Man" is not so univocal in Marcan usage that in isolation it has a set meaning without the coloring given to it by the *functions* mentioned in the context. Maartens ("Son") expresses this in another way when he argues that "Son of Man" is a composite metaphor, containing ideas both of suffering and of exaltation.

In the important christological sequence that runs from Peter's confession of Jesus as the Messiah in 8:29 to God's proclamation of Jesus as "my beloved Son" in 9:7, there are two different Son-of-Man passages. Besides the suffering Son of Man in 8:31 mentioned above, there is in 8:38 the judging Son of Man who will come "in the glory of his Father with the holy angels."[18] In another christological section which runs from 13:21–22, where Jesus speaks of false messiahs who show signs of the endtime, to 13:32, where Jesus says that the Son does not know the day or the hour (thus framed by Messiah and Son-of-God motifs), the Son of Man is mentioned in 13:26: "And then they will see the Son of Man coming in the clouds with much power and glory." This Son of Man will send his angels to gather the elect (13:27).

In evaluating Jesus' Son-of-Man response to the question about the Messiah, the Son of the Blessed, then, we can accept at face value what Mark 14:62 reports about the functioning of the Son of Man in glory and judgment and need not resort to some coded implications of suffering. The high priest has asked what Jesus is (present tense); Jesus has answered in the present tense, "I am"; but now he adds a future element, "you will see," that goes beyond the high priest to all the Sanhedrists. Because of the intrinsic difficulty of understanding how the Sanhedrists will see the glorious things proposed, Perrin ("High Priest's" 92) contends that the "you" refers to the readers, citing Mark 13:14, "But when you see the abomination of desolations standing where it ought not to be (let the reader understand)." Yet there is a clear note to the readers in that passage and there is none here.

---

[18]I am comparing the trial of Jesus in Mark 14 to a section in Mark 8 on the basis of *theological themes.* Beavis ("Trial" 584–86) draws an interesting parallel between 8:27–33 and 14:53–65 on the basis of *structure,* e.g., comparing inadequate initial proposals of who Jesus is in 8:27–28 to inadequate false witness about Jesus as the destroyer of the sanctuary in 14:55–59. Both are corrected by a principal spokesman introducing the theme of the Messiah. And one could continue: Peter's confession of Jesus as the Messiah in 8:29 had to be amplified by Jesus' reference to the Son of Man in 8:31, even as the high priest's question about Jesus as the Messiah in 14:61 has to be amplified by Jesus' reference to the Son of Man in 14:62. Beavis's observations about public reading in antiquity (pp. 594–96) remind us that there would have been more than one reading, and therefore such connections could be recognized.

Perrin's is but one of several attempts to avoid the obvious import of what the Marcan (and Matthean) Jesus says about the Sanhedrists' seeing the Son of Man.

The Son of Man will be seen in two positions. The first, "sitting at the right of the Power," is a description adapted from Ps 110:1, "The Lord said to my Lord, 'Sit at my right until I make your enemies the footstool of your feet.'" Already in Mark 12:35–37 Jesus had used this text to clarify an understanding about the Messiah as the Son of David, and so quite appropriately he uses it here to give a dimension of heavenly glory to himself as the Messiah, the Son of the Blessed.[19] With disbelief the high priest has asked this criminal, soon to be condemned to death, whether he thinks he is God's Messiah (who was expected to exhibit royalty as he set up with power the kingdom of David, destroying Israel's enemies). Jesus replies that the high priest and his fellow Sanhedrists will see him in glory, given a throne by God and (implicitly from the psalm) crushing his enemies beneath his feet. Ironically, the Sanhedrists who condemn Jesus are the enemies he will crush.

We need to consider the unusual term "the Power" that Mark 14:62 (followed by Matt 26:64, and adapted by Luke 22:69[20]) substitutes for "the Lord," the designation one might have expected from the cited Ps 110:1. In a way this term is parallel to the unusual "the Blessed" that the high priest used in Mark 14:61 in the question he posed to Jesus about the Messiah (although in that instance neither Matt nor Luke followed Marcan usage). Flusser ("At the Right") would relate "the Power" here distantly to Isa 9:5, where "God of Power" (*El Gibbôr*) is a title of the Davidic king. Luke 1:49 has "the Mighty One" [*ho dynatos*]" as a subject. For the absolute use *hē dynamis* in Mark/Matt, however, one cannot find a true contemporary parallel. Quite distinct is Philo's hypostatization of the attribute: "God, the highest and greatest *dynamis*" (*De vita Mosis* 1.19; #111), whom he contrasts with the lesser Powers. In the postNT Jewish writings (not the Mishna, but the Tannaitic Midrashim and the Targums), *ha-Gebûra* ("the Power") is used for God, not in all circumstances but as the revealing God, especially at Sinai. The careful study of Goldberg ("Sitzend" 289–91), therefore, disagrees with

---

[19]Meloni, "Sedet," gives Semitic examples of where the right-hand seat is the place for the heir, not simply a mark of honor.

[20]The Lucan form, "the power of God," offers none of the problems we shall see in the Mark/Matt use of "the Power." In Luke 1:35 "the power of the Most High" is placed in parallelism to the Holy Spirit as the agency in the conception of Jesus in the virgin Mary; and Acts 8:10 says of Simon Magus, "This man is the power of God that is called great [*megalē*]." The power of God as a distinctive divine attribute is well attested among Jews in Hebrew and Greek before Jesus' lifetime, e.g., 1QM 1:11; 6:2; I Chron (LXX) 12:23; II Macc 3:38; Wis 7:25.

St-B 1.1007 that "the Power" is a paraphrase of the divine name. In these Jewish writings it is never used for God simply as the divine self; it always refers to God working in the world, and in the revealing passages stresses the agency of God distinct from angels. This is different from the usage in Mark, where the term refers to the majestic God of judgment (Goldberg, "Sitzend" 293).

Overall Mark's localization of the sitting "at the right of the Power" is part of the glorious aspect of Jesus as the Son of Man, for it calls attention to the source of the authority he will wield over his enemies. Truly, in the language of Ps 80:18, the Lord has protected what His right hand planted, namely, the son of man whom the Lord made strong for Himself. Was Ps 80:18 with "the man of Your right hand ... the son of man" the bridge between Ps 110:1, where the Davidic king (i.e., the anointed) is told by God, "Sit at my right hand," and Jesus' answer to the Messiah question in terms of the Son of Man sitting at the right of the Power?

The second position in which the Son of Man will be seen is "coming on the clouds of heaven."[21] While there is a complementarity in the two positions, Mark means us to think of a sequence from one action to the other, for obviously one cannot sit and come at the same time. In Dan 7:13, after the beasts who represent the passing kingdoms of this earth have had their dominion taken away, there is depicted "coming with the clouds of heaven one like a son of man"; and to him is given the dominion, the honor, the kingdom, and an everlasting power. In Dan the "coming" of the figure is *to* the Ancient of Days who gives him these gifts, but the sequence to "sitting" in Mark demands that the coming be *from* the right (hand) of the Power to earth and human beings.[22]

In Dan 7 "one like a son of man" is a symbolic description contrasted with the beasts that precede him; and 7:18,22 clarifies that "the saints of the Most High" are what is meant by the symbolism. Yet by the time of the formative stage of the Gospel tradition "the Son of Man" had become a specific designation that Jesus uses of himself pertaining to moments in his career, whether his ministry, his death on the cross, or his future glory and coming to judge the world. Mark 14:62 and par. have generated numerous studies, tied in with the whole Son-of-Man problem: What caused a development from the imprecise symbolism in Dan to the title in the Gospels? What

---

[21]There is the usual desperate attempt to avoid the problem of how this will be seen by the Sanhedrists, e.g., the contention that "you will see" governs as its object only the "sitting"—yet both "sitting" and "coming" are in the accusative.

[22]Perrin ("Mark" 151) cites two *Midrash Rabba* texts (*Genesis* 13.11 on Gen 2:6; *Numbers* 13.14 on Num 7:13) for proof that Dan was interpreted also in the heaven-to-earth direction: They are both very late and not overly clear.

OT or intertestamental texts played a role? Did Jesus use the title and what did he mean by it? I am reserving all those questions for treatment in the ANALYSIS, for none of them really affect what Mark means his readers to understand.

When, in Mark's conception, does Jesus as the Son of Man sit at the right of the Power? When does he come with the clouds of heaven? Presumably the answer to the first question is the period after the resurrection, and to the second, the parousia. (It is better to speak of the period *after* the resurrection, for *kathēmenon,* "sitting," implies continuance, not simple beginning.[23]) These two "moments" are part of Jesus' continued state and activity. The three passion predictions about the Son of Man end with a reference to his resurrection after three days; in 9:9 silence about what the disciples have seen in the transfiguration is imposed "until the Son of Man be risen from the dead"; also a resurrection denouement seems harmonious with other futuristic promises made at the Last Supper or in the PN (14:25,28). As for understanding the "coming with the clouds of heaven" as the parousia, the future of the verb "to see" is often related to the events of the last times (Mark 9:1; 13:26,29). Mark 8:38 speaks of the Son of Man being ashamed of those who are ashamed of Jesus "when he comes in the glory of his Father with the holy angels." And the eschatological discourse is clearly speaking of the parousia: "And they will see the Son of Man coming in clouds with great power and glory." We find in Rev 1:7 such language almost stereotypic of the parousia: "Behold he is coming with the clouds and every eye will see him, even those who pierced him; and all the tribes of the earth will wail on account of him"—a combination of Dan 7:13 and Zech 12:10.[24]

Will the Sanhedrists *see* the resurrection and the parousia? The Marcan Jesus' words are addressed to the Sanhedrists, but we should not forget that for Mark those Jewish leaders have a representative role. Whatever is predicted concerning them would for Mark's readers have some relation to Jews of their own time who continue to disbelieve and to mock Christian claims. While in what follows I shall wrestle with the difficulty of having the *Sanhedrists* "see," Mark may also (but not principally) include in the "you"

---

[23]Hay (*Glory*) has studied all the NT texts pertinent to Ps 110 and the session of Jesus at God's right hand; he finds there is no consistent interpretation or fixed time for the session other than that all references assume the glorification of Jesus.

[24]Perrin and others argue that the Zech text was the source of Mark's "see" (*opsesthe*) in 14:62, even though the LXX of Zech has "look on" (*epiblepsontai*). Borsch ("Mark" 566) rejects that and traces the "see" to *I Enoch* 62:5, "when they see the Son of Man sitting on the throne of his glory." Gnilka ("Verhandlungen" 14; *Markus* 2.282) also doubts the originality of the Zech derivation and suggests Wis 5:1–2, where the adversaries of the just one are stricken with fear upon "seeing" how he confronts them.

his Christian readers, for whom this sight is triumphal verification.[25] The verb "see" governs both the sitting and the coming of the Son of Man; one should not posit two different kinds of perception, one for the sitting and one for the coming. "Seeing" in an eschatological context can go beyond physical sight. Isa 40:5 proclaims, "The glory of the Lord shall be revealed, and all human beings shall see it together." (Notice also "seeing" salvation in Isa 52:10, and judgment in Micah 7:10,16.) Nevertheless, one should respect the root meaning of the word (in Greek it is related to "eye") and not reduce it simply to meditative knowledge (cf. Vanni, "Passione" 77). Something has to happen to be seen, even if the seeing means the ability to appreciate the significance of what happens. Perhaps the Sanhedrists could be said to "see" the Son of Man sitting at the right of the Power if the public proclamation that Jesus has been raised and been seen in glory forced their attention, as Acts 5:27–34 reports that it did. It is much harder to understand how they could be said to see the parousia. Would the destruction of Jerusalem be a sign of the parousiac judgment upon them? But one does not get the impression from the Marcan passage that forty years would separate the sitting and the coming. Moreover, in 13:26–27 it is part of Jesus' teaching that the coming of the Son of Man in clouds is at a future time that no one knows (13:32); it is the mark of the false messiah and the false prophets to lead people astray on this issue (13:21).

Although Marcan thought about the when and the how of the "you will see" is not clear, these three observations may help. *First,* early Christianity struggled with Jesus' words about what would happen in the future, especially in relation to the parousia. Some of his sayings seem to imply quick return or establishment of the kingdom (Mark 9:1; 14:25; Matt 10:23; Luke 23:43; John 14:3; 21:22–23); other sayings posit an undefined interim (Mark 13:35; Matt 13:31–33; 24:50; 25:13; Acts 1:7); and the famous Mark 13:32 says the Son does not know. In many layers of the NT the result is a combination of future eschatology and present eschatology. Sometimes modern scholarship wants to resolve this problem by dividing the two types of sayings and attributing one to a source and the other to editing. But the both/ and approach is probably intentional. Jesus both is and will be glorified; Jesus is already ruling and will rule more visibly; the judgment he exercises is already taking place and will take place. Feuillet ("Triomphe" 168) observes that the triumph of Jesus had two aspects, present and future (with Jesus' primary interest in the present); Christians translated that into differ-

[25]Pesch (*Markus* 2.438) points out that in the accounts of the martyred just ones, the promise to see who was really right plays a role (Wis 6:2; Rev 11:11–12), and that the place for the victorious just ones is at God's right (*Test. Benjamin* 10:6).

ent events. Therefore, it is not impossible that Mark has several ways to understand the parousiac judgment symbolized by the coming of the Son of Man with the clouds of heaven.

Second, while Jesus is the Son of Man, the answer to the high priest does not have Jesus say, "You will see *me* sitting at the right of the Power and coming. . . ." By speaking of the Son of Man he is not speaking of someone else; rather he is refusing any suggestion that he is exalting himself. The "one like a son of man" in Dan 7 is one to whom the Ancient of Days gives power and dominion. In Ps 110:1 it is the Lord who says, "Sit at my right until I make your enemies the footstool of your feet." Thus the Son-of-Man answer with its biblical echoes is an assurance that *God* will glorify and vindicate Jesus over the Sanhedrists. They will see the signs of what God will do for Jesus.

Third, in Mark's thought the irony about Jesus' sanctuary and Son-of-God claims is that although the Sanhedrists will judge Jesus to be a blasphemer (14:64) and mock him as a false prophet (14:65), everything he says will prove true. As he dies on the cross, the veil of the sanctuary will be torn in two from top to bottom; and (upon *seeing* that Jesus died thus) a Roman centurion will confess Jesus to be the Son of God. Mark regards those two actions in 15:38–39 as the work of God vindicating the Son (and indeed as a response of God to Jesus' agonized cry in 15:34, "My God, my God, for what reason have you forsaken me?"). Is it not likely that Mark regards those actions as also fulfilling the threatening promise Jesus makes to the Sanhedrists at the trial? Is not the acclamation of Jesus as the Son of God the sign that the Lord has enthroned him on high (granted that there is a Davidic royal element in "the Son of God")? Is not the tearing of the veil of the sanctuary the sign of judgment on the Sanhedrists, since their holy place is no longer holy? The fact that Mark reports this as part of the centurion's *seeing* how Jesus died suggests that it is not impossible to interpret these actions as being seen. Such a glorification and parousiac judgment would be in the immediate future (the same day as Jesus' prediction), but of course it would not nullify or substitute for the exaltation involved in the resurrection or the judgment involved in the final parousia. It would be the realization of all that *here and now* for the Sanhedrists.

Matt. The problem of futurity raised by Mark was apparent to the two earliest interpreters of the Gospel; for both Matt and Luke have prefaced the Marcan Son-of-Man statement with a temporal phrase of approximately the same meaning: *ap' arti* ("from [just] now") in Matt; and *apo tou nyn* ("from the now [= present]") in Luke. Attempts to explain such an ideational agreement (against Mark) have been imaginative. Since Matt has used the *ap' arti* phrase earlier in futuristic statements (23:39; 26:29), some have proposed that its presence here in 26:64 is a derivative scribal gloss. Scribal glosses, however, usually make the meaning of a passage more comprehensible; this phrase makes the problem of the Sanhedrists' seeing more difficult. I think Hay (*Glory* 68) is not to be followed in interpreting the phrase as meaning "at a later time" on the grounds that earlier Matthean uses signal the end of a significant period. They denote both the end of one period and *the beginning* of another (a more eschatological one), so that "from now" is perfectly correct. The OS^sin solution of reading the equivalent of *ap' arti* in Mark would normally be acknowledged by all as the harmonization of Mark with Matt (which, I would insist, it is). Yet J.A.T. Robinson ("Second" 339) argues for this as original and thus as the source for Matt's reading.[26] Other scholars contend that here Matt and Luke are not dependent on Mark but on another source, pointing out that they agree once more against Mark in having the Greek phrase for "at the right" after the participle "sitting," while Mark has it before. But in the latter detail they are simply following the Greek word order in Ps 110:1, which shaped the Son-of-Man saying. Also overall in essentials Matt is closer to Mark there than to Luke or the putative common source reflected in Luke (Soards, *Passion* 82); e.g., Matt and Mark have "*you will see* the Son of Man" and have the second clause about the coming, both absent in Luke. The fact that all three Gospels have the unusual "the right of the Power" (not the wording of the psalm) makes extremely unlikely two independent sources, in any case.

If then, rejecting the extraordinary explanations, one argues that both Matt and Luke draw on Mark (but, as usual in the PN, Luke with greater freedom), how is it that they both have a temporal phrase (differently worded) not in Mark? An important key is that exactly the same phrase in the same wording was added respectively by Matt and Luke as they rewrote Mark 14:25, another futuristic statement in which at the Last Supper Jesus says, "Amen, I say to you I shall not drink of the fruit of the vine until that day when I drink it new in the kingdom of God." Matt 26:29 reads, "I say to you I shall not drink from now [*ap' arti*] of the fruit . . ."; Luke 22:18 reads, "I shall not drink at all from the present [*apo tou nyn*] from the fruit. . . ." (There the Lucan context is quite different from that of Matt, and the thought of *both* of them drawing on another source independent of Mark is even more unlikely.) In both that passage and the one under discussion we should see the appended temporal phrase as independent efforts of Matt and of Luke to clarify the imminent futurity of Jesus' triumph as already taking

[26]Despite the enormous difficulty of explaining how such a reading harmonious with Matt fell out of the vast majority of Greek mss. of Mark, Hawkins and Glasson ("Reply") agree with this proposal; and Feuillet ("Triomphe" 157) makes it part of his argument that such a phrase stood in the words of Jesus himself.

place. Each evangelist has done this in his own style: Matt uses *arti* 7 times and *ap' arti* 3 times; Luke/Acts uses neither of those, but *nyn* 39 times (compared to 4 in Matt) and *apo tou nyn* 6 times (0 in Matt).

Let me mention one more attempt (by A. Debrunner[27]) to avoid the import of Jesus saying to the Sanhedrists, "From now on you will see." Since word division was not customary in Greek writing of NT times, *ap' arti* could have been written as *aparti* ("certainly, with security").[28] My preceding paragraph contrasts Mark 14:25 and Matt 26:29, using the reading *ap' arti* in Matt. Is Debrunner correct when he reads *aparti:* "I say to you *certainly* I shall not drink of the fruit," arguing that this is Matt's way of preserving Mark's "Amen"? (Yet Matt is perfectly capable of writing "Amen" when he means it; and the normal position in which to render the "Amen" meaning would be before "I say to you," not six words later, after "I drink.") Debrunner, by analogy with his interpretation of Matt 26:29, wants to read *aparti* in Jesus' response to the high priest: "You will surely see the Son of Man sitting. . . ." Now here there is no "Amen" in the corresponding Mark 14:62, but Debrunner reaches out to "Amen, amen" in John 1:51 for support.[29] I agree with Feuillet ("Triomphe" 156) in rejecting this as another desperate, even if learned, attempt to circumvent a difficult reading. If one regards John 1:51 as a parallel, that is because it is an example of the future fulfilled in the present.

Before we concentrate on Matt's intensified present, some other differences of Matt from Mark need brief attention. The Son of Man comes "on" (*epi*) the clouds in Matt contrasted to Mark's "with" (*meta*). The choice of prepositions may reflect the influence of different Greek texts of Dan 7:13: The LXX has *epi*, while Theodotion has *meta*.[30] A more important difference from Mark is Matt's added "I say to you" (so also John 1:51), an expression that adds solemnity, turning what follows into a pronouncement. Vanni ("Passione" 71–72) analyzed all the usages of this expression in Matt and found that thirty-nine out of forty-seven times it is a revelatory formula. The sense of a revealing proclamation to the Sanhedrists fits in with the "yet" (*plēn*) that prefaces Jesus' statement. Jesus gave a qualified affirmative response to Caiaphas' question about being the Messiah, the Son of God, "*You* have said it," putting responsibility on the high priest. Now Jesus makes his own proclamation, "Yet I say to you [pl.]." This same phrasing occurred

[27]ConNT 11 (1947), 33–49, esp. 45–49; the article discusses Chester Beatty papyri readings.

[28]Beatty papyrus P[47] raises the issue in Rev 14:13: "Blessed are the dead who die in the Lord *aparti.*" Should it be read "from now on" or "with security"?

[29]Ancient scribes related the two passages in the opposite direction, reading Matt's *ap' arti* into the Koine witnesses of John, *added* to the double "Amen."

[30]Also in a very similar "Son of Man on the clouds of heaven" statement, Matt 24:30 preferred *epi* to the *en* in Mark 13:26.

in Matt 11:22,24, where Jesus proclaimed his judgment on Bethsaida and Chorazin: If the mighty works done by Jesus in them had been done in Tyre, Sidon, and Sodom, the people of those three cities would have repented and survived. "Yet I say to you," Jesus affirmed, there will be more tolerance on the day of judgment for Tyre, Sidon, and Sodom than for Bethsaida and Chorazin. Thus the implication is both adversative and intensive. If Jesus has already suggested that the high priest will be judged and held responsible for his motives in seeking a condemnation by forcing him to swear about his identity, Jesus now solemnly proclaims the judgment to be exercised by himself as the glorified Son of Man, even as in a similar manner he warned Bethsaida and Chorazin of severe judgment.

Matt's main thrust, then, is not different from Mark's but is more solemnly intense. There is also greater attention to time in the proclamation that the Sanhedrists will see "*from* now on." While not as strong perhaps as a simple "now," the phrase does signal that a change has *begun* to take place. Capitalizing on that and stressing the negative import of the "Yet I say to you," a group of scholars (SPNM 179–81 cites Hummel, Trilling, Walker) do not think of the sitting and the coming of the Son of Man in Matt as primarily referring to the future resurrection and parousia. The scene has become one of polemical opposition; the judgment of God against the Jewish people and their leaders has begun. The authorities are rejecting Jesus as the Messiah; Jesus is saying they will see him confirmed beginning right now. Jewish prerogatives are at an end. Indeed, some of this proposed polemic is germane to Matt's thought (27:25), but Senior is right in doubting whether it is so apparent in the present scene. Twice before Matt has used *ap' arti*. When Jesus spoke to Jerusalem in a lamentation in 23:39, he said, "For I say to you, you will not see me from now until you say, 'Blessed is he who comes in the name of the Lord.'" Obviously in that saying "from now" did not mean "from this very moment" (since Jesus would be in Jerusalem for days) but "from this crucial time when you are making your decision." Jesus used "from now" also at the Last Supper in his saying that he would not drink of the fruit of the vine (26:29). Thus "from now" is not necessarily an exact, single moment in the trial; but more strongly than in Mark one gets the impression of the end of an era. In the sharply distinct new era that is beginning Jesus will be vindicated and glorified by God. This positive side comes first, but secondarily there is a negative side for the Jewish authorities. The revelation in "I say to you" is that they will see Jesus as the enthroned Messiah, as the Son of Man to whom all power is given; but for them this sight will bring not salvation but judgment. The Christian readers heard Peter blessed when he confessed Jesus as "the Messiah, the Son of the living God"; these were God's words, not merely human words (Matt 16:16–18).

Here in his own affirming words Jesus has intensified the revelation of who he is, and in their discussions with nonbelievers Christians will be expected to profess all this from now on. (See Broer, "Prozess," who emphasizes in Matt the affirmation element over that of judgment.)

As for the moment of seeing, therefore, I would reiterate the points made at the end of the treatment of Mark. The "both/and" of eschatology is more vivid in Matt than in Mark. Although the Son of Man will be sitting at the right of the Power and coming on the clouds, the Matthean Jesus can also say, "Behold I am with you all days until the end of the age/world" (28:20)! As for the possibility that the death of Jesus was a crucial moment of seeing, the case may be even stronger in Matt. According to 27:51–54 much more happened at the death of Jesus than the tearing of the sanctuary curtain: The earth was shaken, rocks were split, tombs were opened, and the dead were raised and appeared to many. The centurion and those with him saw "the (earth)shaking and these happenings." Since these signs of the last times are described as visible actions, in the storyline the Sanhedrists could have seen dramatic signs of Jesus' vindication by God. In addition, after Jesus was raised, there was an earthquake; and an angel descended and rolled back the stone. The guards saw these phenomena and reported them to the chief priests, who assembled the elders (thus a Sanhedrin) to discuss them (28:2–4,11–12). Thus Matt's readers could associate that desperate assembly with Jesus' prediction that they would see the Son of Man exalted.

Luke. The Son-of-Man saying in Luke 22:69 is shorn of the most difficult components in the Mark/Matt form: The Sanhedrists are not told they will *see* anything; there is no reference to the parousia (i.e., the coming of the Son of Man on the clouds of heaven); God is not called "the Power." In the body of the Gospel, Luke allots judging and parousiac roles to the Son of Man (9:26; 12:8). He retains statements of an imminent coming of the kingdom of God (9:27) and does not hesitate to record Jesus' promise, "They will see the Son of Man coming on a cloud with power and much glory" (21:27). Yet the overall Lucan thrust is to profess ignorance of when all this will take place, so that time is not to be spent looking for it (Acts 1:6–11). Through his victory over death Jesus is the exalted Messiah whom heaven is to receive until the time for establishing all that God spoke by the holy prophets; then for those who repent he will be sent as the appointed Messiah (Acts 3:19–21). Thus the words that Jesus speaks to the Sanhedrists concentrate on exaltation, not on the judgment.

By the conditional sentences of Luke 22:67–68 Jesus has in a certain sense refused to answer the question of the Sanhedrists as to whether he is the Messiah; then in 22:69 he gives an affirmative answer. The "But" (*de*) of Luke is not adversative like the *plēn* ("yet") of Matt 26:64; it continues the preceding in a new direction. This new orientation interprets the Messiah as exalted: "From the present there will be the Son of Man sitting at the right of the power of God." Luke equates the Messiah and the Son of Man, for in Acts 2:32–35 this same text is used of the Messiah. There Ps 110:1 is cited explicitly to explain that God has raised up Jesus and exalted him at the divine right (hand), making him both Lord and Messiah. To the Sanhedrists Jesus says that this "will be" from the *present* (*apo tou nyn*). The seemingly contradictory tenses catch the ambivalence of NT eschatology that I mentioned in reference to Mark.[31] The exaltation of Jesus is beginning in the Sanhedrin session; it will be advanced on the cross, where he will speak of being in paradise *this day* (23:43).[32] As Plevnik ("Son") insists, the exaltation is fulfilled in the ascension of Jesus which concludes the Gospel (24:50–51) and is a point of departure for Acts (1:8–11). It may be important to Luke to emphasize the victorious aspect of the "now" because he has already made reference to the negative side when Jesus spoke to the Jewish authorities at the time of the arrest (22:53): "This is your hour and the power [*exousia*] of darkness."

To illustrate the victorious aspect and the power (*dynamis*) of God, Luke 22:69 copies Psalm 110 language from Mark and refers to Jesus "sitting at the right." The sitting posture will be quoted again from Psalm 110 in Acts 2:34, but the accompanying Peter speech that interprets the event there refers simply to Jesus "being exalted at the right of God." That the *exaltation* of Jesus and not simply an enthroned sitting is the important element can be deduced from Acts 7:55–56, where Stephen, full of the Holy Spirit and gazing into heaven, sees the glory of God and Jesus *standing* at the right of God—a vision Stephen himself interprets as "I see the Son of Man standing at the right of God." (In Mark/Matt the Sanhedrists are told they will see the Son of Man at the right of the Power; for Luke it is the first Christian martyr who sees this!) Luke's "at the right *of the power* of God"[33] associates the exaltation of Jesus with a state of divine power. Already in his ministry, after the baptism and the temptation, Jesus returned to Galilee under the influence of "the power of the Spirit" (Luke 4:14; Acts 10:38); in driving out demons and healing, "the power of the Lord" was with him and went out from him (4:36; 5:17; 6:19; 8:46; 9:1). Yet power is particularly associated with the Son of Man in heaven (21:27) so that he can send it down from on high

[31]The distinctions of future and past are only from the viewpoint of a narrative that continues in time; at the right of God there is only the present.

[32]The use of Ps 110:1 in Acts 2:32–35 shows the completion of the exaltation when God has raised up Jesus to the right hand.

[33]We saw in n. 20 above that "the power of God" as a divine attribute is well attested in the OT and offers none of the problems presented by Mark's titulary use of "the Power."

(24:49; Acts 1:8). Those who receive it from him must clearly acknowledge its source (Acts 3:12; 4:7), and for anyone other than Jesus to speak of himself as "the power of God" is blasphemous (Acts 8:10).

The Sanhedrists are portrayed as understanding the implications of Jesus' affirmation that from now on there will be the Messiah exalted as the Son of Man, for in reaction they say, "Are you then the Son of God?" (Notice the "are"; of the two time indications given by Jesus they have understood *apo tou nyn* as the more important.) Walaskay ("Trial" 83) denies that the *oun* ("then") of 22:70 refers to 22:69; he wants to apply it to the Messiah issue of 22:67; but the Messiah and the Son of Man are one and the same. Walaskay is arguing against the notion that Jesus *becomes* the Son of God through exaltation. The issue, however, is not one of becoming. The readers of the Gospel know that Jesus was conceived as the Davidic Messiah and, through "the power of the Most High" overshadowing Mary, as the Son of God (1:32–35). As for when this identity of Jesus is revealed, that happens for different people at different times. For instance, Luke does not hesitate to use the language of "being made" and "being begotten" in reference to the exaltation of Jesus to signify that as a moment which manifests who Jesus is (Acts 2:36; 13:33). As Acts 10:40 phrases it: "God raised him up on the third day and gave him to become manifest." The *oun* in Luke 22:70 is a deduction from what Jesus is revealing about his exalted identity. For Mark/Matt the Son-of-Man saying seems almost to go beyond the dimensions of the asked-about Messiah, Son of God; for Luke it defines the Messiah as the Son of God. Jesus responds very affirmatively to the conclusion that all the Sanhedrists have reached, "You yourselves say that I am." Unfortunately, the Sanhedrists reject (22:71) the conclusion they rightly deduced—or at least most of them do. Luke 23:50–51 will tell of one member of the Boulē (see pp. 340–48 above) who accepted the conclusion and had no part in the rejection, namely, Joseph from Arimathea, who "was looking for the kingdom of God."

ANALYSIS

In the Synoptics, Jesus' portrayal of the Son of Man sitting at the right of the Power and (in Mark/Matt) coming with/on the clouds of heaven has the theological import of stressing majesty and judgment by way of response to the Sanhedrin. As we turn to the issue of historicity, there may be no way to determine whether Jesus spoke the sentence in Mark 14:62 and par. in an interrogation on the night before he died. Yet at least we can discuss *the plausibility of his using "the Son of Man" as a title for himself* (if it is always a title). Even as I begin to survey modern confusion over the title's usage and meaning, it may be a consolation to know there are traces of ancient puzzlement in the words addressed to Jesus in John 12:34, "How can you say that the Son of Man must be lifted up? Just who is the Son of Man?"

The Gospel usage of this title for Jesus presents statistics that are dramatically different from the statistics (§21) discussed in relation to "the Messiah" and "the Son of God." With those titles acceptance or usage during Jesus' lifetime is difficult to discern even from the surface evidence of the texts; but "the Son of Man" appears some 80 times in the Gospels and all but 2 times (Mark 2:10; John 12:34) clearly as self-designation by Jesus. It has been estimated that these constitute some 51 sayings (J. Jeremias, ZNW 58 [1967], 159–64), 14 of which are in Mark and 10 in the Sayings-Source. Outside the Gospels the phrase occurs only 4 times, viz. Heb 2:6; Rev 1:13; 14:14; Acts 7:56; and only in the last of these (which is a Lucan borrowing from Gospel usage) does it have definite articles as in the Gospels. The debate whether the historical Jesus used this title of himself or whether it is a product of early church reflection retrojected into Jesus' ministry has raged throughout the last hundred years. If one takes the latter view, one faces two major difficulties: Why was this title so massively retrojected, being placed on Jesus' lips on a scale far outdistancing the retrojection of "the Messiah," "the Son of God," and "the Lord"? And if this title was first fashioned by the early church, why has it left almost no traces in nonGospel NT literature, something not true of the other titles?

Nevertheless, there remain curious features about this title in the Gospel usage.[34] No person addresses Jesus by this title, and Jesus never explains its meaning. When the question comes up as to who Jesus is, despite his many uses of "the Son of Man," it is never a suggested identification of him. (And it is not used of him by early Christians in their confessions of praise or their creeds.) In what follows in the PN, Jesus will be mocked on the cross about all the details of the trial (the destruction of the sanctuary, the Messiah, the Son of God) but never about his identification of himself as the Son of Man.

---

[34]These observations are drawn from J. D. Kingsbury, *The Christology of Mark* (Philadelphia: Fortress, 1984), 166–79. He contends (174–75) that unlike "Son of God" or titles that focus inwardly on Jesus' identity, "Son of Man" focuses outwardly on Jesus' relation to the world. In the present instance it focuses on what through God's initiative will be given to Jesus by way of status and what he will do—factors that complement and manifest what he is. Thus I would judge that the title had both an outer and an inner dimension.

I shall now mention very briefly below some issues that enter into the debate about the historicity of Jesus' use of the title.[35]

When and how did "the Son of Man" become a title? Since *ho huios tou anthrōpou,* the usual Gospel phrase, is unknown in secular Greek and makes as little sense in Greek as "the son of the man" would make as a title in English conversation, the origins of the usage must lie in a Semitic context. The divine voice that speaks to Ezekiel addresses him over ninety times as "son of man" (= "O human being"), a term that highlights the contrast between the heavenly message and the mortal recipient. More pertinently, "one like a son of man" in the Aramaic of Dan 7:13 enters the discussion, but the designation there simply means one like a human being. Because there is little else in canonical Scripture pertinent to this figure,[36] it became fashionable for a while to appeal to comparative religious evidence and to posit the existence in the Near East of a widely accepted picture of a heavenly man (often thought to be of Iranian origin) as background for what the NT meant by calling Jesus "the Son of Man." When that approach was rejected for lack of evidence, a strong vein of scholarship (e.g., in the years 1965–90: Lindars, Perrin, Vermes) came to deny that there existed in Judaism any expectation of a specific figure known as the Son of Man or the Heavenly Man. Yet through appeal to Jewish apocrypha (rather than comparative nonJewish religion) another vein of scholarship, which now seems to be reviving, has argued that there was a 1st-cent. Jewish expectation that God would make victorious and enthrone over Israel's enemies a specific human figure who would be the instrument of divine judgment—a figure who could be appropriately designated "the Son of Man" because he embodied or exemplified the destiny of all righteous human beings. To respect the uncertainty of the scholarly situation, I have decided to answer the question of the plausibility of Jesus' use of "the Son of Man" within each of these two approaches, namely, if there was a specific Jewish concept of "the Son of Man," and if there was not.

[35]For a good survey of the overly abundant literature on this question, see J. R. Donahue, CBQ 48 (1986), 484–98; also M. Casey, JSNT 42 (1991), 17–43. Casey's own views are marked with a confidence that he can detect which Son-of-Man sayings in the Gospels are original by reconstructing the underlying Aramaic (for which, however, he depends on post-1st-cent. targums). After Jesus' time there was a secondary development of the concept and sayings in the light of Dan 7 and the parousia of Jesus.

[36]Seitz ("Future") has pointed to Ps 80 as complementing the picture of Dan 7. If the latter relates one like a son of man to the holy ones of the Most High, Ps 80:15–16, in a prayer to God, relates a son of man to the vine of Israel: "Take care of this vine, and protect what your right hand has planted, a son of man whom you yourself made strong." The plea continues in 80:18: "May your help be with the man of your right hand, with the son of man whom you yourself made strong." Seitz argues that since this psalm deals with the elevation of an earthly being, it may have constituted the primary background of Mark 14:62.

A. If There Was a Jewish Concept of the Son of Man

In apocalyptic Jewish circles whose voice is echoed in the noncanonical literature of the 2d and 1st cents. BC and 1st cent. AD, there may have developed a strong image of a heavenly Son of Man through reflection on Dan 7[37]—an image not widely attested outside those circles and hence leaving relatively sparse traces, but an image that could well have appealed to Jesus and his early Christian followers because of their own strong apocalyptic bent.[38]

It has long been recognized that the "Parables" (Similitudes) section of *I Enoch* (37–71) contributed to the Son-of-Man issue. Yet the absence of this section from the many fragments of *I Enoch* found at Qumran seemed at first to favor regarding the Parables as a Christian composition that reflected rather than explained NT usage.[39] Lately, however, the arguments for pre-Christian or nonChristian Jewish composition have been recognized as having greater force; and proposals have emerged for why the Qumran sectarians might not have agreed with the theology of the *I Enoch* Parables and so not have preserved them. J. J. Collins ("Son"), judging that a pre-70 (AD) date can scarcely be denied because of the influence of the Parables on Matt 19:28; 25:31 and the absence of a reference to the fall of Jerusalem, proposes a date ca. AD 50 for composition. The references to the Ancient (Head) of Days in *I Enoch* 46:1 and 47:3 indicate that the author used Dan 7:9–10, 13–14, and support the likelihood that his portrayal of the Son of Man arose from reflection on Dan. Indeed, the language of Enoch leaves open the possibility that we are seeing the emergence of a set figure from the vaguer Danielic picture. Danielic imprecision is represented in *I Enoch* 46, which speaks at first only about one "whose face had the appearance of a human being"; yet upon questioning he is explained to be "the Son of Man who has righteousness." Although he is like one of the holy angels, he has a higher

[37]While the supporting evidence has been known for a long time, there have been problems of dating and interpretation. The second half of the 20th cent. has refined scholars' appreciation of the pseudepigrapha, especially as Dead Sea Scroll study has reinforced our grasp of the wide range of contemporary Judaism. In what follows I am indebted for additional insights to J. J. Collins, who allowed me to see a prepublication copy of various articles, including "The Son of Man in First Century Judaism" (NTS 38 [1992], 448–66).

[38]The author of Dan 7 scarcely created ex nihilo his imagery of monsters conquered by a human being; indeed it may go back to long-forgotten roots in Canaanite mythology of Baal conquering the sea monster. Nevertheless, attempts by OT scholars to trace the "son of man" section in Dan 7:9ff. to a preDanielic poetic source are too speculative to serve our purposes here; and all the literature I shall discuss can be explained through reflection on Dan 7 itself rather than on earlier sources.

[39]See the report on the discussion by D. W. Suter, *Religious Studies Review* 7 (1961), 217–21.

rank than that of the angels.[40] The Son of Man is one whose name was named in the presence of the Lord of Spirits before the sun and the stars were created (48:3). He is described as "the Elect One" (the chosen servant of Isa 42:1?), for the two titles are juxtaposed in 62:1,5. Indeed, 48:10 and 52:4 seem to identify him as the Messiah of the Lord.[41] The Son of Man is shown seated on the throne of glory in 62:5 (presumably a deduction that one of the thrones in Dan 7:9 was meant for him [Collins])—an enthronement that could suggest that already in Jewish circles Dan 7 was being joined to Ps 110:1 ("sit at my right") as is reflected in Mark 14:62. There were already in Dan 7:13–14 hints of judgment: "One like a son of man" is brought into the heavenly court where the books are opened that will decide the fate of the great kingdoms represented by the beasts (7:10c). Nevertheless, we are not told specifically what participation this one like a son of man will have when upon the coming of the Ancient of Days judgment is pronounced (7:22).[42] The imagery of Isaiah (11:1–4) that describes the spirit given to the Davidic king to enable him to judge righteously may be echoed in *I Enoch* 62:2, where the spirit of righteousness is poured out on the chosen one to enable him to kill sinners. In *I Enoch* 63:11; 69:27,29 the wicked are brought before the Son of Man to be shamed, while the name of the Son of Man is revealed to the blessed. Collins ("Son" 459) contends that the Parables of *I Enoch* "show how the Danielic text inspired visions of a heavenly savior figure in first century Judaism."

If the author of *I Enoch* specified the Danielic picture to portray a heavenly enthroned human figure as judge, namely the Son of Man, there were

[40]Part of the difficulty of imaging the Son of Man in *I Enoch* is the seeming identification of him with the exalted, celestial Enoch in 71:11–17, especially 71:14. For many that has meant that the Son of Man in *I Enoch* is more a role than a specific figure. To counteract the Enoch identification R. H. Charles deliberately changed the translation, and some have argued that this passage was a secondary addition to the Parables. J. J. Collins ("Son" 455–57) would now argue that in 71:14 Enoch is not identified with the Son of Man but is addressed as a human being who is exalted to share the likeness of the heavenly Son of Man. In 70:1 Enoch's name is lifted up alive to the presence of the Son of Man, imagery that seems to distinguish between the two.

[41]K. Schubert ("Verhör" 121–22) thinks that in the description of the Son of Man in *I Enoch* 48:4–5 he can find traces of Davidic Messiah passages (Gen 49:10; Num 24:17; Isa 9:1); but that is not at all clear.

[42]Sometimes Dan 7 is presented simply as the enthronement of this representative human figure (an ascension to heaven with the clouds) with no indications of future activity related to those on earth, in which case the combination of enthronement and parousia in Mark 14:62 is a major innovation. However, Beasley-Murray ("Jesus" 425–26) makes the point that the scene involves the participation of this human figure in the theophany of the Ancient of Days, and a theophany always involves an intervention in human affairs on earth. He quotes K. Müller that nowhere in the OT or early Jewish and talmudic literature do "clouds" ever play a role when the concern is to express the activity of heavenly beings among one another entirely in the realm of transcendence. Only when they step out of hidden transcendence are clouds brought into play, and so there would be an implication in Dan 7 that the human figure has yet a descending role.

catalysts that could have moved his thought in that direction.[43] Ezekiel the Tragedian (before 150 BC) has God, with crown and scepter, bring Moses to the heavenly throne to be seated there, crowned, and enabled to survey the heavens. P. J. Kobelski has done interesting work on the celestial Melchizedek figure at Qumran, comparing it to Son-of-Man material. He is convinced that "the concept of an enthroned figure who would come to judge the righteous and the wicked existed prior to the NT."[44] A hymnic fragment of the War Scroll from cave 4 published by M. Baillet in DJD 7 (1982), 26–30, has one who had prowess as a teacher and in rendering legal judgment exalted to a seat in the heavens and reckoned with gods in the holy congregation. M. Smith[45] cites this as proof for the thesis that ascent to the heavens was an important part of the 1st-cent. Palestinian background.

Reflection on Dan 7 and the Son of Man appears after *I Enoch* at the end of the 1st. cent. in *IV Ezra* (*II Esdras*) 13, another Jewish apocalypse, composed originally in Hebrew or Aramaic. Daniel (7:1–28) saw four monstrous beasts representing the great kingdoms of Near Eastern history and their power replaced by the authority that God gave to one like a son of man who came with the clouds of heaven. When Ezra sees a monstrous eagle, he is told (12:11) that it is "the fourth kingdom that appeared in a vision to your brother Daniel." In 13:3 one "in the form of a man" comes up from the sea and flies with the clouds of heaven. This superhuman figure destroys the forces of evil with flaming breath from his mouth and gathers a peaceful and joyous multitude. In his commentary M. Stone[46] writes: "The man is interpreted as the Messiah, precreated and prepared in advance, who will deliver creation and direct those who are left." He maintains that the dream vision itself, independent of the interpretation, may have come from a pre-Ezra source; that source would have drawn from Dan 7 even as did the author of *IV Ezra*.

All this evidence suggests that in apocalyptic Jewish circles of the 1st cent. AD the portrayal in Dan 7 had given rise to the picture of a messianic human figure of heavenly preexistent origin who is glorified by God and

---

[43]J. J. Collins will develop this motif in "A Throne in the Heavens: Apotheosis in pre-Christian Judaism," which he plans to publish in *Death, Ecstasy and Otherworldly Journeys*, eds. M. Fishbane and J. J. Collins (Memory of I. Culianu; forthcoming).

[44]*Melchizedek and Melchireša'* (CBQ monograph series 10: Washington: Catholic Biblical Association, 1981), 136.

[45]"Ascent to the Heavens and Deification in 4QMᵃ" in *Archaeology and History in the Dead Sea Scrolls*, ed. L. H. Schiffman (Memory of Y. Yadin; Sheffield: JSOT, 1990), 181–88.

[46]*Fourth Ezra* (Hermeneia; Minneapolis: Fortress, 1990), 397. The term "my son" is used in some versions for the man figure in 13:37,52, even as it was used for the Messiah in 7:28. Other versions read "my servant" as in 13:32, which may echo Isaian servant language. We saw that in the Parables of *I Enoch* the Son of Man had both servant and messianic identification.

made a judge.[47] Against that background Jesus, if he was familiar with apocalyptic thought, could have used Son-of-Man terminology.[48] He need not have read the Parables of *I Enoch*, but only have been aware of some of the burgeoning reflection on Dan 7 that gave or would give rise to the presentation of the Son of Man in the Parables and of the man in *IV Ezra*. Indeed, the setting supplied for Jesus' self-reference to the Son of Man in Mark 14:62 would make good sense: It was used to interpret the Messiah issue, explaining in what sense Jesus was responding affirmatively to that designation proposed by the high priest.[49] As we shall see in §23, Jesus' claim to such an apocalyptic Son-of-Man role would also explain the high priest's indignant charge of blasphemy, if blasphemy be understood as arrogant pretensions infringing on divine prerogatives.

B. If There Was No Jewish Concept of the Son of Man

Although I find the evidence and speculation advanced under A attractive, probably the majority view among scholars is that Jesus or his followers were responsible for the specification of the Son-of-Man concept,[50] for there was no established Jewish portrait or expectation of that figure. There are different theories as to how Christians developed the concept.

[47]Beyond the apocrypha, if Justin (*Dialogue* 32.1) reports Jewish views correctly, the identification of Daniel's "one like a son of man" with the King Messiah was accepted by the mid-2d cent. AD. See also (but with great caution) St-B 1.956–57.

[48]Scholars generally distinguish three types of Son-of-Man sayings found on the lips of Jesus in the Gospels: (1) those that refer to the earthly activity of the Son of Man (eating, dwelling, saving the lost); (2) those that refer to the suffering of the Son of Man; (3) those that refer to the future glory and parousia of the Son of Man in judgment. In APPENDIX VIII, where I treat of Jesus' predictions of his passion and death, I shall have to deal with type 2, since many of the predictions are phrased in terms of "the Son of Man." For the moment I am concerned only with type 3. Donahue (*Are You* 150ff.) would subdivide type 3, for he finds a difference between the future Son-of-Man sayings in Mark, which refer to "coming," "seeing," "glory," "clouds of heaven," and the future sayings in Q, which are devoid of such images. In my judgment this distinction does not hold up well. The Q saying in Luke 12:20 and Matt 24:44 has the Son of Man *coming;* the one in Luke 17:24 and Matt 24:27 has flashes of *lightning* accompanying (Matt: the coming of) the Son of Man, i.e., the functional equivalent of clouds.

[49]Above on pp. 480–81 I discussed the ambivalent Qumran "Son of God" fragment (4Q246) and J. J. Collins's contention that "Son of God" there is to be related to the use of "son of man" in Dan 7. If he is right and there was in apocalyptic Judaism an interpretative chain binding together the Davidic Messiah expectation (in reflection on II Sam 7:11–16), the Danielic "son of man" who was to be taken up to heaven, and the royal one whom God called "son" and had sit at the right of the throne (Ps 2:7; 110:1), then there may have been more connection than hitherto diagnosed between the titles in the high priest's question ("the Messiah," "the Son of the Blessed/God") and Jesus' response in terms of "the Son of Man." Nevertheless, the whole interpretative chain, with Dan 7 as the linchpin, is highly speculative. Moreover, were it true, we would still be uncertain whether Jesus or his early followers were responsible for phrasing the christological dialogue at the trial in terms of one title as a response to a question about the others.

[50]In particular, L. Hartman in *L'Évangile selon Matthieu*, ed. M. Didier (BETL 29; Gembloux: Duculot, 1972), 142–46, argues that the *coming* of the Son of Man to judge the world is a Christian development.

Some who want to attribute that development to the early church would argue that Jesus used the Semitic expression equivalent to the Son of Man but not as a title. G. Vermes points to targumic evidence where Aramaic *bar* *('ĕ)nāš(ā')* ("son of man") serves as a circumlocution for "I"; but J. A. Fitzmyer (FAWA 95–96, 143–60) has insisted, quite correctly, that all the evidence advanced is later than the NT and does not establish proof for this usage in Jesus' time. True, the phrase can mean "someone"; and B. Lindars[51] has argued that in some nine sayings of Jesus that appear to be authentic, "son of man" is used to mean "a man such as I" or "a man in my position." However, when one looks at Mark 8:31 or 8:38, which would be among these sayings, it is hard to see how they make sense thus translated. Accordingly, if Jesus used the expression "the Son of Man," it would seem to have been in the titular sense. The position of Bultmann, Hahn, Tödt, and Fuller, namely, that Jesus did use the title of a future figure who would come to judge but that this figure was not Jesus himself, has lost much of its following. Granted Jesus' conception of the role he himself was playing in making present the rule of God, his anticipation of another unidentified human-like figure to bring the work to a conclusion seems unlikely.

The writings of N. Perrin on the Son-of-Man issue[52] treat the Gospel presentations of the Son of Man as derived from Christian midrashic reflection on Dan 7, employing Ps 110:1 to herald Jesus as the exalted Lord, and Zech 12:10–14 ("looking upon him whom they have pierced") to develop the notion of the Son of Man coming from heaven to be seen below.[53] Of course, these are OT passages that appear in the NT and were clearly in the NT arsenal for interpreting Jesus. But two points should be made in reference to Perrin's thesis. First, if it seems quite likely that the Gospel picture is developed beyond any single OT or known intertestamental passage or expectation, and that this development probably took place through the interpretative combination of several passages, any affirmation that all this development *must have* come from early Christians and none of it from Jesus reflects one of the peculiar prejudices of modern scholarship. A Jesus who did not reflect on the OT and use the interpretative techniques of his time is an unrealistic projection who surely never existed. *The perception that OT passages were interpreted to give a christological insight does not date the process.* To prove that this could not have been done by Jesus, at least incho-

[51]*Jesus Son of Man* (Grand Rapids: Eerdmans, 1983), 25–29.

[52]Gathered in *A Modern Pilgrimage in New Testament Christology* (Philadelphia: Fortress, 1974).

[53]Perrin attributes the combining of the OT texts to preMarcan tradition; Lührmann ("Markus 14" 470) would attribute it to Marcan redaction (in part because of the use of "the Power"). While I shall suggest that the scriptural reflection in its essentials (not necessarily in its wording) *could* go back to Jesus, the Perrin-Lührmann disagreement illustrates the uncertainty of dating.

atively, is surely no less difficult than to prove that it was done by him. Hidden behind an attribution to the early church is often the assumption that Jesus had no christology even by way of reading the Scriptures to discern in what anticipated way he fitted into God's plan. Can one really think that credible? My second point is that Perrin speaks of a *pesher* technique. He means a reading of OT Scriptures and the interpretative application of them to the present situation, as illustrated by Qumran works such as the pesher on Habakkuk, the pesher on the Psalms, etc. Obviously some of that technique would have been used by Jesus and/or by Christians in developing the image of the Son of Man. Yet a pesher is a line-by-line commentary on an OT book where the controlling factor has to be revelation through that sacred writing. It is highly significant that none of the twenty-seven books of the NT is a pesher or a midrash, i.e., a line-by-line commentary on the OT. Rather the Gospels are in a sense commentaries on Jesus. The hermeneutical focus has changed. While OT passages are applied to Jesus, the idea is not primarily that the OT makes sense of the present situation, but that the present situation makes sense of the OT: The control is supplied by Jesus, not by the Scriptures. I mention this because I do not think the christological interpretation of the Son of Man came simply from the interpretation of OT texts; the christology existed from a perception of Jesus (or from Jesus' perception of himself) and found voice and color in phrases from OT passages that were now seen to have a deeper meaning than hitherto recognized.

In sum, I would think *nothing in this approach B rules out the following possibilities:* Jesus reached a firm conviction that if he were rejected and put to death as the prophets of old had been, God would bring about the divine kingdom by vindicating him against those who regarded him as a false spokesman and who rejected as diabolical the power over evil and sin that God had given him. In reflection on Dan 7 and other OT passages (Ps 110:1; perhaps Ps 80:18) Jesus might have expanded the symbolic concept of "one like a son of man" to whom God would give glory and dominion. It became "the Son of Man," the specific human figure whom God glorifies and through whom God manifests his triumph; and Jesus used it of himself seen as the instrument of God's plan. Early Christians, taking their clue from Jesus' own language, developed the idea further, applied it to different aspects of his life, and used it frequently to describe Jesus' self-understanding. But the reason that it appears in the Gospels in a way "the Messiah" and "the Son of God" do not is precisely because this description was remembered to have come from Jesus in a very affirmative manner.

As we reflect on the historicity of Mark 14:62 in approach B, if any of the above paragraph be true, Jesus could have spoken of "the Son of Man" as his understanding of his role in God's plan precisely when he was faced with hostile challenges reflecting the expectations of his contemporaries. Inevitably the Christian record would have crossed the *t*'s and dotted the *i*'s of the scriptural background of his words.[54] Even though *all* of Mark 14: 61–62 and par. is phrased in the Christian language of the 60s (language *not* unrelated to the issues of AD 30/33), there is reason to believe that in 14:62 we may be close to the mindset and style of Jesus himself.[55] Previously we saw that there was also a likelihood that Jesus spoke about the future destruction and rebuilding of the sanctuary.[56] Each of these future statements about God's plan has a threatening element of judgment plus an element in which Jesus, vindicated by God, would have a part in bringing God's plan to its culmination. The threatening element would be quite understandable against the background of the history of the prophets. The second element would be the one that in the ears of his enemies might sound like arrogant blasphemy, and it is to that we now turn.

(*Bibliography for this episode is found in §17, Part 5.*)

---

[54]Catchpole (*Trial* 136–40) argues strongly for deriving Mark 14:62b from Jesus virtually as it now stands. As we shall see when we discuss the historical cause of the blasphemy charge, some (Bruce, Flusser, Héring) relate the blasphemy to Jesus' having in fact spoken of himself at the right of the Power.

[55]The difficulty of determining what Jesus would have meant by "you will see" may favor authenticity. Post factum, Christians producing such a statement might have been clearer. Did "you will see" on Jesus' lips mean that he thought the parousia would come right away? Winterbotham ("Was") thinks so and argues that Jesus could and did make mistakes, even as did the prophets when they became specific about what would happen. Mark 13:30; Matt 10:23; 16:28 all seem to suppose a quick return (see R. E. Brown, *Jesus God and Man* [New York: Macmillan, 1967], 70–79). Others, arguing from the Aramaic of Dan 7, think "the clouds of heaven" would have been understood as the setting for the whole scene (i.e., for a theophany; see Scott, "Behold"), and that Jesus could have thought of himself as going to God, not coming from God (Glasson, "Reply"; see I Thess 4:17). But then one would expect to find the "going" mentioned before the "sitting" (McArthur, "Mark").

[56]Like the difficulty mentioned in the preceding footnote, the problem of understanding how the rebuilding would be fulfilled constitutes an argument for authenticity. Post factum one tends to fashion clearer "prophecies."

§23. SANHEDRIN PROCEEDINGS, PART FOUR: REACTION OF THE JEWISH AUTHORITIES TO JESUS' RESPONSE

(Mark 14:63–64; Matt 26:65–66; Luke 22:71)

Translation

Mark 14:63–64: ⁶³But the high priest, having torn his garments, says, "What further need do we have of testifiers? ⁶⁴You have heard the blasphemy. What does it appear to you?" But they all judged against him as being guilty, punishable by death.

Matt 26:65–66: ⁶⁵Then the high priest tore his clothes, saying, "He blasphemed. What further need do we have of testifiers? Behold now you heard the blasphemy. ⁶⁶What does it seem to you?" But in answer they said, "He is guilty, to be punished by death."

Luke 22:71: But they said, "What further need of testimony do we have? For we ourselves have heard from his own mouth."

[John 10:33,36: ³³The Jews answered him, "Not on account of a good work do we stone you, but on account of blasphemy, and that you, being a man, make yourself God." ³⁶(Jesus answered them . . .) "Do you say that, 'You are blaspheming' because I said, 'I am God's Son'?"]

[11:49–53: ⁴⁹But a certain one of them, Caiaphas, being high priest that year, said to them, "You (people) understand nothing at all! ⁵⁰Do you not realize that it is better for you to have one man die for [= in place of] the people, rather than to have the whole nation perish?" ⁵¹This he did not say of himself; but being high priest that year, he prophesied that Jesus would die for [= on behalf of] the nation. . . . ⁵³So from that day they decided to put him to death.

COMMENT

In Mark 14:63–64 and Matt 26:65–66 Jesus' answer to the high priest's question/demand about the Messiah, the Son of the Blessed (God), and his own statement about the Son of Man bring a reaction from the high priests and from (all) the Sanhedrists. There are four elements in the reaction: *Element A:* The high priest tears his garments/clothes; *Element B:* He indicates through a rhetorical question that there is no further need of testifiers (witnesses); *Element C:* He tells the members of the Sanhedrin that Jesus has blasphemed (Matt) and they have heard Jesus' blasphemy; *Element D:* At his prodding they come to the conclusion that Jesus is guilty and should die.

My comment on these individual elements will incorporate pertinent comparative material from Luke-Acts, i.e., from the denouement of the Sanhedrin interrogation (Luke 22:71: Element B), from general statements about what was done to Jesus (C, D), and from the parallel trial of Stephen in Acts 6–7 (C). Appropriate Johannine passages will also be called upon, e.g., the questioning by "the Jews" in chap. 10 as to whether Jesus considers himself the Messiah, the Son of God (Elements C, D), and the Sanhedrin session in chap. 11 where the high priest Caiaphas takes the lead (D).

ELEMENT A: THE HIGH PRIEST TEARING HIS GARMENTS/CLOTHES

This violent symbolic act is found only in Mark/Matt.[1] The oldest use of deliberately tearing clothes was to symbolize passionate grief, especially on hearing the death of a beloved and/or important figure. Jacob tore his clothes on hearing of the death of Joseph (Gen 37:34), as did David on hearing of the death of Saul and Jonathan (II Sam 1:11–12; see also Josh 7:6; II Kings 2:12). Extrabiblical examples show that Greco-Roman readers would have been familiar with this gesture of grief and anger. In his *History* (54.14.1–2) Cassius Dio tells us of Licinius Regulus who tore his apparel (*esthēta*) publicly in the Roman Senate when he discovered that he was not on the list of selected members. The Emperor Augustus tore his apparel on hearing of the defeat of Varus in Germany (56.23.1).

Tearing one's clothes on hearing something offensive to God indicates that the grief this causes is as great as or greater than that caused by hearing of death. The commander of the Assyrian armies blasphemed in II Kings

---

[1] The closest one comes to it in the Lucan material is where those who testify at the stoning of Stephen lay down their clothes (Acts 7:58).

18:30 by asserting publicly that the Lord God of Israel could not deliver Jerusalem and its king (Hezekiah) from the hand of the king of Assyria; those who reported this to Hezekiah came with their clothes torn (18:37) and the king tore his when he heard it (19:1). Many point to the later mish-naic law in *Sanhedrin* 7.5 as background for the present scene: The judges of a blasphemy trial must tear their clothes on hearing the blasphemy. But the wider biblical custom would make the high priest's action intelligible.[2]

Matt 26:65 speaks of tearing *himatia* ("clothes"), the word used in the LXX of all the biblical texts just cited. Mark 14:63 uses the plural of *chitōn*, a word that if meant technically would refer to an undergarment. (Matt 5:40 distinguishes between a *chitōn* and a *himation*.) Many commentators mention that a well-off person wore two of these garments, citing Josephus, *Ant.* 17.5.7; #136, which refers to the inner *chitōn* of a slave who was wearing two. Some seek a more exotic explanation, pointing out that the description of the high priest's special liturgical vestments (Exod 28:4; Lev 16:4) includes a *chitōn* (Hebrew *kutōnet*). Would Mark have been thinking of the high priest tearing the inner or outer *chitōn*?[3] Josephus (*War* 2.15.4; #321–22) reports that ca. AD 66, in their earnest entreaties to their countrymen not to resist the Romans and bring about the destruction of the Temple, the priests wore in processions the robes in which they performed their priestly offices and knelt; and the chief priests were seen heaping dust on their heads, "their vestments [pl. of *esthēs*] torn." Did the Jewish high priest wear his vestments when convening a Sanhedrin? In part, that might depend on whether the meeting was within the Temple area adjacent to the holy place, for Ezek 42:14, 44:19 specifies that the vestments (pl. *stolē*) used in the liturgies were not to be taken from the holy place. Also in this period the Romans, as Herod before them, kept control of the high priestly vestments. Blinzler (*Prozess* 160) argues that this was because the high priest did wear

---

[2]I remind the readers that in the COMMENT the whole discussion is on the storyline level of what the evangelists intended to convey and/or what the first readers might have understood. The overall issue of historicity (especially of the blasphemy) is reserved for the ANALYSIS. However, for the sake of intelligibility I must comment here on the elementary historical problem raised by the high priest's tearing his garments/clothes in Mark/Matt. In Lev 10:6 Moses tells Aaron and his sons not to tear their clothes (*himatia* as in Matt)—presumably, from the context, their sacred vestments. (On the holiness of the priestly vestments see J. Milgrom, *Leviticus 1–16* [AB 3; New York: Doubleday, 1991], 447–49, 606.) There are rabbinic limitations on and debates about the possibility of the high priest's rending his ordinary garments (Mishna *Horayot* 3.5 and TalBab *Horayot* 12b) that have as their background Lev 21:10, which forbids the high priest to tear his clothes. No matter what the storyline of Mark/Matt may imply (see my discussion above), the *high priest* would never rend the sacred sacrificial garments; the issue of whether he might rend his ordinary garments is not clear.

[3]Josephus (*Ant.* 3.7.2; #153) describes an inner *chitōn* of the high priest descending to the ankles, and over that another *chitōn*, also reaching to the feet, blue/purple in color, with tassels, golden bells, and pomegranates on the hem, not composed of two pieces but woven as one cloth (*Ant.* 3.7.4; #159–61; see Exod 28:31–35).

them when he convened a Sanhedrin and the Romans wanted no Sanhedrin meeting without permission; but Josephus (*Ant.* 15.11.4; #403–8) tells us that the vestment (*stolē*) was taken out of the Fortress Antonia with Roman permission (later with that of Agrippa I and II) the day before the feast, giving the impression that the legitimacy of the requesting high priest (one acknowledged by the Romans) might be the reason for the controls.

I mention all this to give readers data for decision. I have no reason to think Mark knew much of this and even less reason to think his readers did (see Mark 7:3–4 for their level of ignorance of Jewish customs). Matt may have been correct in understanding Mark to mean "clothes," for the plural of *chitōn* can mean that (BAGD 882). As for why Mark used a slightly less common word, it may have been for the storytelling purposes of describing an exotic figure. I suspect many of the readers would have imagined the high priest perpetually in exotic dress, as have artists and many readers ever since.

ELEMENT B: "WHAT FURTHER NEED DO WE HAVE OF TESTIFIERS?"

In John's account of the Sanhedrin session that sentenced Jesus to death *in absentia* (11:47–53) there is no testimony given by witnesses and thus no parallel to this question in Mark/Matt.[4] There is a form of the question about further testimony in Luke's Sanhedrin investigation (22:71)—on the surface a surprising feature since Luke has not reported any witnesses at the investigation, probably because he has moved that part of the proceedings to the Sanhedrin trial of Stephen in Acts 6:13.

The question in Mark/Matt and Luke would imply that Jesus has now incriminated himself. Some scholars have worried about the plausibility of a Sanhedrin allowing a person's self-incrimination to stand as the total evidence, pointing to TalBab *Sanhedrin* 9b and the principle of Raba: "No one can incriminate himself." That issue is not apposite on the historical level, for such later jurisprudence is dubiously pertinent to a 1st-cent. Sanhedrin. On the level of narrative, to have an admission of guilt from the person's own mouth is very persuasive, and that is what the high priest is claiming in Mark/Matt and the Sanhedrin authorities are claiming in Luke. We must remember that all three Synoptics reported previous (unsuccessful) attempts on the part of the Jerusalem Jewish authorities to catch Jesus in his speech (Mark 12:13; Matt 22:15–16a; Luke 20:20), and so clearly for them self-

---

[4]The action of the chief priests and the Pharisees in sending attendants (*hypēretai;* cf. John 19:6) to arrest Jesus in John 7:32, 45–49 and the prejudgment of Jesus involved in this attempt are protested by Nicodemus in 7:51: "Does our law condemn a man unless first it has heard from him and learned what he is doing?"

incrimination would have been effective. Nevertheless, the identical statement about no further need of testifiers may have slightly different nuances in Mark and in Matt. In Mark the testifiers who appeared gave false testimony that was not consistent. All that can be dispensed with, the high priest is saying, in light of Jesus' clear "I am" response to the question about being the Messiah, the Son of the Blessed, and his further boastful claim that the Sanhedrists would see him sitting as the Son of Man at the right hand of the Power and coming as celestial judge. In Matt, even though in response to the demanded oath about his status as the Messiah the Son of God, Jesus' affirmative sought to throw responsibility on the high priest, his own "Yet I say to you" made the unconditioned exalted Son-of-Man claim. This, *plus* the legal testimony of two witnesses about his ability to destroy the sanctuary of God, made further testifiers or legal proceedings unnecessary.

To modern readers who know Mark, Luke's use of virtually the same words, "What further need of testimony do we have?" (slightly different word order), is curious because, unlike Mark, no testifiers have spoken about Jesus.[5] But, of course, Luke's readers would not have had Mark propped up before them; and Luke's use of "testimony" (not "testifiers") would make them think of the testimony given by Jesus. Jesus has answered two questions and spoken on his own, and so no testimony beyond his is necessary. There is an element of triumph in the Sanhedrists' statement, for they had tried previously and less successfully to get Jesus to speak damaging words. The scribes and chief priests, "having watched him closely, sent spies who were pretending to be sincere themselves in order that they might seize on his words, so that they might give him over to the power of the governor" (Luke 20:20). Now by asking him direct questions without subterfuge they had what they needed. Luke's scene ends (22:71) with the Sanhedrists' gloating: "We ourselves have heard it from his own mouth."[6]

ELEMENT C: THE CHARGE OF BLASPHEMY

Luke has substituted the boast just cited for Mark's statement by the high priest: "You have heard the blasphemy." Apparently Luke's sense of propriety would not allow him to report that the highest authority of the Jewish people so directly insulted God's Son. Rather in two ways Luke has reshaped the charge of blasphemy. First, in the mockery of Jesus that preceded the

---

[5] I have argued that Luke is using Mark here, as have Bultmann, Creed, Finegan, Streeter, etc.

[6] The phrase "from his own mouth," peculiar to Luke's account of the Sanhedrin investigation, has appeared three times previously in what many would diagnose as Lucan special source material, but always with the preposition *ek*. The use of *apo* here (normal LXX style) suggests that Luke is composing freely.

Sanhedrin investigation (22:63–65), those holding Jesus "were saying against him many other things, blaspheming"—thus no charge that Jesus blasphemed but a blasphemy against Jesus! Second, in Acts 6:11 Stephen is charged with having spoken blasphemous words against Moses and against God, words that consisted of Stephen's saying that Jesus the Nazorean would destroy this (holy) place and change the customs given over by Moses—an indirect charge of blasphemy by Jesus. That a charge of blasphemy by Jesus was part of the tradition (and not simply created by Mark) is strongly suggested by John 10:33,36 (a tradition, as we saw, with parallels to Luke's account of the Sanhedrin trial). There "you are blaspheming" is the reported Jewish response to Jesus' affirmation "I am God's Son."

The discussion of the blasphemy charge in Mark/Matt has been unduly complicated, not only by the usual admixture of the historical level (see ANALYSIS) but by the issue of what constituted blasphemy in the 1st. cent. AD, an issue that affects the Gospel level as well.[7] The law in Lev 24:16 states, "The one who blasphemes/curses [*nqb*] the name of YHWH shall surely be put to death; all the congregation shall stone him." (This is enunciated in relation to the story of the son of an Israelite mother and an Egyptian father who quarreled with an Israelite and cursed [presumably *qbb*] the Name [26:11]; he was taken outside the camp and stoned.) What does Lev 24:16 mean by using a form of *nqb*: to curse the name of God or to pronounce the divine name YHWH? Lev 24:16 is the only instance of this use of *nqb* in the Hebrew Bible. Is it a variation of *nqb*, "to pierce," or more likely is it a biform of *qbb*, "to curse"? Related are passages like Exod 22:27, "You shall not make little [*qll*] of God, and you shall not curse [*'rr*] a prince among you"; and Num 15:30: "Anyone who sins defiantly insults [*gdp*] YHWH, and this person shall be cut off from among his people." At Qumran we read, "With an insulting [*gdp*] tongue they have opened their mouth against the ordinances of the covenant of God" (CD 5.11). By the time of the Mishna (*Sanhedrin* 7.5) there was a clarification about the application of the death penalty: "The blasphemer [*gdp*] is not guilty unless he pronounces the Name." Easton ("Trial" 437–38) wonders how literally this was meant—would the rabbis have judged someone as not guilty of blasphemy when he said, "I am God," just because he used *'Ĕlōhîm* instead of YHWH for "God"? Remnants of less strict interpretations are found in rabbinic literature, e.g., Tosepta *Sanhedrin* 1.2 lists intervening arbitration on behalf of unworthy people, like a robber, as blasphemy; in TalBab *Sanhedrin* 56a R. Meir argues that the person who curses God blasphemes even if that per-

---

[7]I had finished my study of blasphemy when the careful discussion by Sanders (*Jewish Law* 57–67) appeared; his observations about the import of Jewish usage are not too dissimilar from mine.

son does not mention the divine name; and the Tannaitic Midrash *Sipre* on Deut 21:22 (#221) describes blasphemy as stretching out the hand against God. (To define blasphemy narrowly, however, is being benevolent, since it reduces the number of instances subject to the death penalty.) Earlier than the rabbinic references, we have evidence that to mention the name of YHWH did bring the death penalty (Philo, *De vita Mosis* 2.38; #206). Indeed, the LXX cleared up the ambiguity of the Lev 24 passages cited above by translating not with the verb "to blaspheme," but with the expression "to name the Name of the Lord." That is what brought stoning.

But none of this has much to do with the description in Greek of the charge of blasphemy related to the death of Jesus. In the Greek used by Jewish writers before and during the time of Jesus *one is hard pressed to find even a single example of a word of the stem "blasphēm-" used precisely and specifically for naming the divine Name,* whether one considers the adjective *blasphēmos* ("blasphemous," or substantively "blasphemer"), the noun *blasphēmia* ("blasphemy"), or the verb *blasphēmein* (to "blaspheme"). Readers must be patient if I give statistics here, for often this point is not recognized.

The basic meaning of the Greek is "to abuse, insult." Of some 89 uses of the adjective, noun, and verb in Josephus and Philo, 67 (75 percent) are for the abuse, slander, or libel of *other human beings* or their customs, especially for the abuse of persons of dignity; a patriarch, Moses, a king, a governor, a priest, a handicapped person, or even the Jews in general. Often there is a tone of arrogance in the insult, and in one case the blasphemy consists simply of bragging about ancestors. The uses in the LXX and the other 25 percent of the Josephus and Philo uses pertain to insults *to the deity* or deities. The abuse can be by word or by indecent or demeaning actions. Once in the Greek OT (Theodotion of Bel 9 in the Daniel literature), and some 5 times in Josephus and Philo, the act of insulting the pagan gods is called blasphemy. The rationale is usually that such behavior toward pagan gods might lead the blasphemer or those insulted by his blasphemy to go further and insult the God of Israel (Philo, *De specialibus legibus* 1.9; #53). Sometimes on this issue a reverence is expressed for the name of the God of Israel; but in *De vita Mosis* 2.38; #206 Philo distinguishes between blaspheming the Lord of Gods and daring to utter the Name—both deserve the most serious punishment, but "blaspheming" (insulting) is not confused with naming. Philo (*De decalogo* 19; #93) does not want one who is already a blasphemer to take an oath, for a reviling mouth should not utter the holiest of names— again a differentiation between blasphemy and using the Name. Josephus (*Apion* 2.33; #237) says that Moses the lawgiver forbids blaspheming the gods recognized by others out of respect for the very word "God." We find the same in the LXX, where "naming the Name" is used in the crucial Lev 24:11,16, not *blasphēmein.*

Out of 22 LXX *blasphēm-* usages (adjective, noun, verb), 19 pertain to abusing, deriding, or insulting the *God of Israel,* God's people or possessions, as do some 13 of the Josephus and Philo uses. (A special example of the latter is calling God to witness to perjury.) Once more the tone of arrogance creeps in, as when II Macc 9:28 calls the great antiGod figure Antiochus Epiphanes a blasphemer and II Kings 19:4,6,22 finds blasphemy in the proud words of the Assyrian general exalting his king over the God of Israel. Philo (*De somniis* 2.18; #123–31) writes of a ruler in Egypt who tried to destroy Jewish customs, boasting of his power and daring to liken himself to the All-Blessed God. He would even blaspheme the sun, moon, and stars if what he hoped for at each season did not happen (#131). Philo (*Ad Gaium* 46; #368) speaks of blasphemies uttered against the God of Israel by the crowd in a discussion held before Gaius Caligula as to why Jews failed to recognize that emperor's godhood.

Thus there is no convincing reason to think that when the four evangelists used the Greek words for blasphemy in reference to Jesus, they thought of his naming the Name; nor is there reason why their readers would interpret them in that way. (Some have wondered whether Mark in avoiding *theos* ["God"] in 14:61–62 and using "the Blessed" and "the Power" was avoiding even the impression of mentioning the Name. However, Matt, who would usually be more aware about Jewish sensibilities, saw no problem with Jesus' speaking of *theos.*) From the context of the "*blasphēm-*" word usage given above, Jesus is being accused of arrogantly claiming for himself what belongs to God and thus insulting God. And when others are said to blaspheme Jesus, they are being accused by the evangelists of insulting and calumniating a figure who deserves respect. The same data will be applicable when we discuss the blasphemy issue on the historical level in the ANALYSIS. People could be put to death for insulting the God of Israel through arrogance, *as well as* for naming the Name, before and during the 1st cent. AD according to the mindset of the LXX, Josephus, and Philo.

With that clear, let us turn to the charge associating Jesus with blasphemy (in all four evangelists, but in different ways in the passages we have been considering). In John 10:36, even though earlier Jesus has been asked about being the Messiah, the issue that provokes the blasphemy charge is explicitly Jesus' claim "I am God's Son." (See also John 5:18; 19:7). For Luke-Acts in the trial of Stephen (Acts 6:11–14) his blasphemous words against Moses and God, words against the holy place and the Law, consist of his supposedly having said that Jesus the Nazorean would destroy the "place" and change the customs that Moses gave to the Jews. As for the execution of Stephen, it is when he says that he sees "the Son of Man standing at the right of God" that his hearers are driven to stone him (Acts 7:56–58). Since stoning was the punishment for blasphemy, is this statement presented as blasphemous by Luke?

In Mark the blasphemy they have heard is scarcely the false and inconsistent testimony about destroying the sanctuary, but Jesus' clear "I am" to being the Messiah, the Son of the Blessed, and his self-identification as the exalted Son of Man sitting at the right of the Power and coming on the clouds to judge—the christological claims. In Mark this charge of blasphemy by the high priest (to which all the Sanhedrists will agree), coming at the end of Jesus' life, is particularly dramatic. At the beginning of Jesus' ministry his first encounter with the authorities (scribes) caused them to charge, "He blasphemes" (2:7). From start to finish these authorities have found him arrogantly claiming what belongs to God alone.

Matt, in the trial context, is the most emphatic about the issue, for Caiaphas begins with "He blasphemed" (or even "Behold, he blasphemed" in Codex Sinaiticus and the Syriac Peshitta) and returns after a sentence with "Behold *now* you heard the blasphemy." This double reference is fitting since the blasphemy is twofold: According to legal testimony Jesus said he was "able to destroy God's sanctuary" (clearly an insult to God); and then, placed under oath, he affirmed he was the Messiah, the Son of God. And if one objects that Jesus had put on the high priest the responsibility for making him state that identity ("*You* have said it"), clearly and without reservation Jesus himself claimed ("Yet I say to you") that his hearers would from now on see him as the Son of Man sitting at God's right hand, coming on the clouds of heaven.

Perhaps we can summarize *the views of the evangelists*. In the eyes of the Sanhedrin Jesus was blasphemous or arrogantly insulting God because of one or more of three types of claims:

- "Christological" claims to be the Son of God (John, Mark, Matt [in part]), to be the Messiah (Mark, Matt [in part]), and/or to be the exalted Son of Man (Mark, Matt). For Christian readers all those titles would refer to a Jesus who had a uniquely close relationship to God, a uniqueness the various Gospels phrase differently. The charge of blasphemy against a christology portrayed in titles would be harmonious with the charge of blasphemy found in Synoptic Gospel reports of the ministry when Jesus claimed to forgive sins, a power reserved to God alone.[8] John reports stoning attempts against Jesus (clearly a

---

[8]Mark 2:5–11; Matt 9:2–6; Luke 5:20–24—notice that Luke, who does not report a blasphemy charge in reference to the titles during the trial of Jesus, reports a blasphemy charge in this earlier scene.

punishment for blasphemy) because of his use of "I am" (8:58–59) or his claim that "the Father and I are one" (10:30–31). In the judgment of the evangelists the truth is the opposite of what the Sanhedrists affirm: The real blasphemy is on the part of disbelievers who mock Jesus' divine claims either just before the trial (Luke 22:64: "Prophesy") or on the cross (Matt 27:39–40: "the Son of God"; Luke 23:39: "The Messiah"). The evangelists also use "blasphemy" words during the ministry when disbelievers attribute Jesus' extraordinary power to an unclean spirit (Mark 3:30) and speak against the Holy Spirit (Mark 3:29; Matt 12:32; Luke 12:10).

- Claims to (be able to) destroy the sanctuary of God or the holy place (Matt, Acts). In the trial Matt closely connects this with the christological claims, even as Matt 12:6,8 closely relates Jesus' words "Something greater than the Temple is here" to "The Son of Man is lord of the Sabbath." Mark and John do not use "blasphemy" words in relation to Jesus' sanctuary/Temple claims or attitudes. Yet John 11:47–53 shows the Sanhedrists thinking that the danger posed by Jesus to the holy place is so grave that he should be put to death; and Mark 11:27–28 (also Matt 21:23; Luke 20:1–2) locates in the issue of Jesus' *authority* the offensiveness of his action of cleansing the Temple. Also if one may regard the Christian charge that Jesus' opponents blasphemed him as the mirror image of the blasphemy with which the opponents charged Jesus, Mark 15:29 says that the passersby blasphemed Jesus when they ridiculed his claim to destroy the sanctuary and rebuild it in three days.

- Claims to be able to change the Mosaic Law (Acts in the Stephen trial). While Luke seems to be alone in associating the word "blasphemy" with this, during the ministry all the Gospels show Jesus' attitude toward the Law to be a cause of dislike and hatred to the point of wanting to put him to death.[9] Matt would follow and sharpen this portrayal, since he has the "You have heard it said . . . but I say to you" passages in 5:21ff., illustrating a righteousness greater than that of the scribes and Pharisees without which one cannot enter the kingdom of heaven (5:20). He also has bitter attacks on Pharisees and scribes over legal interpretations in chap. 23, relating their attitudes toward Jesus to the killing of the prophets (23:30–35). Even the gentle Luke in 6:1–11 makes the legal and Sabbath claims of Jesus something that produces fury and the wish to kill Jesus. In John 5:18 the attitude of Jesus in "breaking" the Sabbath is joined (subordinately) to his making himself equal to God as the reason "the Jews were seeking all the more to put him to death." In John 7:19–24 a dispute over the Law of Moses is mentioned as the reason for seeking to kill Jesus. Luke may not be far, then, from the common Christian mind when he reports in the last third of

---

[9]For examples, see Mark 2:16,18,24; 3:2 (culminating in 3:6); 7:5; in 7:6 Jesus condemns the Pharisees and scribes for distorting the religious purpose of the Law.

the 1st cent. that Jesus' claims to be able to change the Law of Moses were part
of what was thought blasphemous about him by his opponents.

Thus, despite minor variations the four evangelists, writing in different
places in different decades between 60 and 100 to different Christian audiences, give almost the same picture of the charge of blasphemy against Jesus. They were telling their readers that Jews who did not believe in Jesus
thought[10] that what Christians proclaimed about Jesus was blasphemous, primarily because of how Christians elevated Jesus when in their confessional
formulas they called him the Messiah, the Son of God, and the Son of Man
(or even portrayed him as employing the divine "I am") and thus attributed
to him a unique relationship to God. To Jewish opponents such a proclamation that involved the God of Israel was an insult to the divine majesty and
uniqueness.[11] A particularly significant aspect of objectionable christological claims was the Christian judgment that the visible destruction of the Jerusalem Temple and the invisible withdrawal of God's presence from the sanctuary or holy place of Jerusalem was a sign of the power of Jesus Christ, in
the sense that God was judging the Jewish leaders for the rejection of God's
Son (pp. 451–52 above). Related too to the christological proclamation were
Christian memories of Jesus' claim to forgive sins and his sovereign attitude
toward statutes and interpretations of the Law of Moses—memories that
governed Christian lifestyles and self-understanding. For Christians these
attitudes did not make him another rabbi debating the Law but one who had
authority over the Law that God revealed to Moses, and thus a greater than
Moses to whom in Jewish thought God had spoken and given revelation as
to no other human being: "There has not arisen a prophet since in Israel like
Moses whom the Lord knew face to face" (Deut 34:10). The evidence suggests that because in this period Christians were increasingly *articulating*

---

[10]Let me stress that I am discussing a *Christian picture of Jewish attitudes* as derived from the
Gospels, because, except for Josephus' *Testimonium Flavianum,* we have practically no Jewish evidence from the period 60–100 that would tell us how Jews looked on Jesus, his followers, and their
claims about him. (By the early 2d cent. there is evidence that some Jews looked on Christians as
minîm or deviants.) It is hypercriticism to contend that the Christian portrayal of Jewish attitudes is
pure fiction, but caution must be urged. For instance, Matt's portrayal of the Pharisees is surely
based on the attitudes of some synagogue authorities of his time. Yet there is exaggerated hostility
in his depiction. Gerhardsson ("Confession" 47) comments: "He cannot even *try* to understand them
or see *anything* defensible in their attitude toward Jesus." Moreover, Matt universalizes his perception by moving from the Pharisees of his acquaintance to Pharisees in general and to "the Jews"
(28:15). (A tendency to universalize from a particular is a basic element in prejudice.) Also, while
there may be a historical connection between opposition to Jesus in the 20s and opposition to the
Matthean Christians in the 70s, we must recognize that Matt's presentation of Jesus is vividly colored
by the post-70 local situation.

[11]A Jewish writer, C. Setzer, "'You Invent a Christ,'" *Union Seminary Quarterly Review* 44
(1991), 315–28, points out that the earliest detectable Jewish objections to Jesus were based on
christological claims by Christians.

their christology in unabashedly divine statements about "the Son of God," [12] for Jews the legal attitudes of Jesus became proportionately less the subject of concern in judging Christian blasphemy. Why bother with implications when explicitations were easily available and opponents could say, "We have heard the blasphemy for ourselves"?

On the opposite side of the controversy, believers in Jesus in the post-70 period considered Jewish adversaries of Jesus guilty of blasphemy because they mocked the Christian faith confessions and were so impious as not to see God's judgment against them in the destruction of the Jewish Temple. After the destruction of the First, Solomonic Temple Belshazzar was "blaspheming," even as God's judging hand wrote on the wall (Josephus, *Ant.* 10.11.2–3; #233, 242); similarly in Christian eyes, despite the warning from the destruction of the Second Temple, by continuing to reject Jesus and to denounce his claims, Jews were blaspheming against the Holy Spirit, the unforgivable sin (Mark 3:29). Read thus, the Gospel texts in the post-70 period affirm that in many places followers of Jesus (Jew and Gentile) and Jews who did not accept their proclamation were two separate communities, each passionate for the honor of the God of Israel and each seeing the other as blaspheming because of the way they understood Jesus.

ELEMENT D: THE SANHEDRIN JUDGMENT INVOLVING GUILT AND DEATH

At the beginning of my treatment of Element C, I observed that the latter part of Luke 22:71 ("For we ourselves have heard from his own mouth") is the functional equivalent of Mark 14:64 ("You have heard the blasphemy") and that Luke had moved the blasphemy motif elsewhere. But the cited clause in Luke is the end of the Jewish interrogation of Jesus, to be followed by "the whole multitude of them, having stood up," leading him to Pilate (23:1). Thus while Mark/Matt have the trial end with the Sanhedrists stating that Jesus is guilty, punishable by death (Mark 14:64; Matt 26:66), and while John concludes his account of the Sanhedrist session against Jesus (11:47–53) by reporting "From that day they decided to put him to death," the Lucan interrogation of Jesus does not state that the Sanhedrists found him guilty or sentenced him to death. Is this silence explicable on the theory that Luke knew of Mark's "They all judged against [*katakrinein*] him as being guilty, punishable by death"? An affirmative response is suggested by the implicit agreement with Mark in Luke 24:20: "The rulers and our chief priests gave him over to a death judgment [*krima*] and crucified him." Luke knew of the

---

[12]For instance, that God spoke to Jesus as "my uniquely beloved Son," that Jesus was conceived without a human father by the direct action of God's Holy Spirit, that he existed before the world began.

Jewish Sanhedrin judgment that Jesus should die, and the sermon in Acts 13:27–28 gives Luke's "orderly" analytic account of what happened: "Having judged [*krinein*] him, . . . though they found no charge really deserving death, they asked Pilate to have him killed." There was a judgment against Jesus by the Sanhedrin authorities; but it was based on inadequate evidence. Overall, then, in this last part of the trial (22:69–71) I would judge that Luke was reshaping Marcan material and had no independent tradition in which the Sanhedrin session ended differently. In the Messiah question (22:67b–68) Luke gave precedence to material similar to that found in John 10:24–25. Whether in that tradition, as in John, the Messiah issue was raised in a simple question posed to Jesus rather than in a Sanhedrin trial and whether that factor influenced Luke to shape the Marcan Sanhedrin trial less formally, I see no way of deciding. Nevertheless, I remind readers that above (§18, n. 142) I agreed with the contention that Luke was still describing a Jewish *trial* of Jesus. Indications scattered through Luke-Acts show that Luke took for granted an essential element of the trial, namely, a Jewish judgment against Jesus, and assumed that such a judgment had been preached by the apostles. As I cautioned in §1A, one cannot interpret a Gospel passage such as Luke 22:66–71 as if it existed entirely as an entity in itself. Both the evangelist and his audience had heard the story of the passion before and therefore had certain assumptions that colored what was written in the Gospel and how it was heard.

In Mark/Matt the high priest has dominated the proceedings against Jesus and virtually told his colleagues what they must judge; yet at the end of the trial he follows the formality of asking for their decision. Matt phrases this as "What does it seem to you?"[13] As we shall see, Mark's "appear" and Matt's "seem" play an important part for some scholars in evaluating the response. Dutifully the Sanhedrin members ("all" in Mark to match the "all" at the beginning of the session in 14:53) tell the high priest what he wants to hear. They had several possibilities in the abstract, as we see from elsewhere in the NT. For instance, they could have released the accused after beating him, as they would do in the case of Peter and John (Acts 5:40);[14] yet these apostles were not accused of blasphemy, which required a death penalty. In searching out alternatives we may be thinking too abstractly, however. The evangelists and their traditions, in describing the sentence against Jesus, would have been influenced by scriptural passages describing how the wicked deal with the just, e.g., Wis 2:20: "Let us condemn [*katadikazein*] him to shameful death"; Jer 26:11: "The priests . . . said to the rulers and to

---

[13]Matt has made a similar insert in 22:42 over against Mark 12:35. Evidently Matt is fond of the "seem to you" question, for he uses it in 17:25; 18:12; 21:28; 22:17—all without parallels.
[14]Also Mark 13:9 associates beatings with Sanhedrins and synagogues.

all the people, 'A judgment of death to this man' [Jeremiah]" (see also Dan 13:53 [Susanna]).

Mark 14:64 phrases the response in terms of the verb *katakrinein*, "to judge against," to harmonize it with the repeated "against" statements that run through the trial (14:55,56,57,60). Bickermann, Lagrange, and Schneider are among those who interpret Mark's *katakrinein* not as a sentence but as a judicial opinion. (Once again we must rigorously keep distinct what Mark meant [our concern here] from what happened historically.) In itself *katakrinein* can mean "to accuse hostilely";[15] but it also means "to condemn, pass judgment against" as in John 8:10–11 where the woman who has already been accused is now open to being condemned. The usual meaning in the papyri seems to be "to condemn" or "to decide against" (MM 328). If one places the verb in the context of Mark's description, after the panoply of summoning the whole Sanhedrin, seeking out witnesses, getting an admission, and the tearing of garments by the high priest with an affirmation of blasphemy, then it becomes almost inconceivable that the climax is an opinion, not a judgment. Some who recognize this suggest that Matt 26:66, by not using *katakrinein*, has weakened the denouement of the session. But that is not true, for immediately after the session Matt alone will report the scene of Judas' death, which he will begin thus: "Then Judas, the one who gave him over, having seen that he was *judged against* . . ." (27:3)—Matt has simply reserved *katakrinein* till there.

In Mark (and Matt) the judgment is phrased as *enochos thanatou*, a phrase difficult to translate, for *enochos* with genitive can mean both "guilty of" and "punishable by or to be punished by." I have tried to get both ideas in my translation: "guilty, to be punished by death." Once more, many would translate so weakly that this is not a death sentence but an opinion that Jesus could justifiably be put to death if another power decides to do so (Husband, Klausner, Montefiore), a view that often presupposes Mark's knowledge of the information supplied in John that the Sanhedrin could not execute criminals. But even without that presupposition, one could argue that this interpretation explains better why Jesus was handed over to the Romans. In itself the phrase *enochos thanatou* does not solve the question. It may well reflect the expression in Deut 21:22 (the law pertaining to blasphemy discussed in the ANALYSIS below): "a crime judged worthy of death" (*ḥēṭ mišpaṭ māwet*). Fiebig ("Prozess" 224) would see here a reflection of rabbinic *ḥyyb mwt*, which involves being held and bound over to death. Other scholars cite various examples in secular Greek that have *enochos thanatō* or *thanatou* as a decree affecting criminals if they are caught: In some the death penalty is

---

[15]As it does in the Q passage of Matt 12:41–42; Luke 11:31–32; also Josephus, *Ant.* 3.14.4; #308.

automatic; in others it is a threatened possibility but can be commuted. In Matt 5:21–22 there are four instances of *enochos* with the dative; in the first three it means "liable to" (to judgment or to the Sanhedrin), but in the last it can scarcely mean "liable to hell fire": The idea there is "punished by hell fire." Surely in the LXX of Gen 26:11 the decision of the Philistine king Abimelech that anyone who harmed Isaac and Rebekah would be *enochos thanatō* means "punished by death," not just "punishable by death."

In my judgment the meaning of the present passage in Mark/Matt is determinable by the wording of the third passion prediction in Mark 10:33; Matt 20:18; there both evangelists say that the chief priests and the scribes "will judge against him to death [*katakrinousin auton thanatō*], and will give him over to the Gentiles." The second clause is important, for evidently neither evangelist sees any problem about a firm death sentence followed by giving Jesus over to the Gentiles for the execution of that sentence. Thus Mark/Matt were describing a death sentence by the Sanhedrin at the end of the trial (so also Gnilka, Juel, Klostermann, Taylor, and Winter). The contemptuous spitting on Jesus that follows in Mark (14:65) is the treatment of a condemned blasphemer. John's Sanhedrin trial also ended on the note of a decision against Jesus (11:53: "From that day they decided [*ebouleusanto*] to put him to death"), although John makes clear that the decision had no legal status with the Romans (18:31). On pp. 527–28 above I indicated that Luke also thought "the authorities gave him over to a death judgment [*eis krima thanatou*]" (24:20), even if, for reasons of a smoother story flow into the Roman trial, he does not spell that out here (his sense of "order").

Thus, in the last third of the century the evangelists, who knew perfectly well that the Romans sentenced and crucified Jesus, were sharing with their readers the view that the Jewish Sanhedrin also decided on Jesus' death. The evangelists make clear that in the actions of the two parties, Jewish and Roman, different reasons were involved for the death sentence. But even if the Romans carried out the judgment and did the execution, there was greater intensity on the part of the Jewish authorities to get Jesus out of the way. The issues dealt with in the Sanhedrin stories were religious, and for the evangelists they were the most important.

ANALYSIS

Just as the ANALYSES of §20–22 treated the historicity of the preceding parts of the Sanhedrin proceedings, so will this ANALYSIS evaluate the historicity

of the main topic of Part Four, namely, the charge of blasphemy.[16] Beginning
with the trial, I shall ask whether blasphemy could have been punished by
handing the blasphemer over to crucifixion and whether any motif associated
with Jesus at the trial could have been considered blasphemous (Messiah,
Son of God, Son of Man, destroying the sanctuary, false prophet). Then I
shall investigate briefly whether outside the trial, the general implications of
Jesus' words and works were blasphemous. Throughout it is important to be
clear about what constituted blasphemy.

Is it historically possible that in AD 30/33 Jewish authorities came to the
conclusion that Jesus was a blasphemer and for that reason wanted his death?
Certainly the blasphemy issue arose in *Jewish* circles (whether directed
against Jesus or Jewish Christians), for blasphemy over issues of Jewish theology would not have arisen as a serious criminal charge among pagans. In
the COMMENT I presented evidence accumulated from studying all the words
of the stem *blasphēm-* in the LXX, Josephus, and Philo. That survey makes
it clear that these words basically do not refer to naming the divine Name;
and so the issue of whether Jesus mentioned YHWH can be dropped from
the discussion—it has nothing to do with the claim in the Greek preGospel
tradition that in Jesus' lifetime those opposed to him accused him of blasphemy.[17] *Blasphēmos, blasphēmia,* and *blasphēmein* do at times refer to
cursing God, making fun of God, or belittling God. That too can be dropped
from the discussion because nothing in the tradition suggests a deliberately
irreverent attitude toward God by Jesus. From the attested meanings of the
blasphēm- words, *the only likely historical charge would have been that Jesus arrogantly claimed for himself status or privileges that belonged properly to the God of Israel alone and in that sense implicitly demeaned God.*[18]
If there was something Jesus said or did that caused the authorities to think
he blasphemed in that sense, one could point to the antecedents for the plausibility of their tearing their garments when such audaciousness was affirmed.[19] The death penalty would have been an appropriate punishment for

[16]Of the four elements discussed in the COMMENT, this is the only one that can be subjected to a
historical inspection on the basis of considerable outside evidence.

[17]Occasionally the suggestion has been made that the stricter mishnaic restriction of blasphemy
(= abuse of the divine name) arose because of the misapplication of a broader understanding against
Jesus. However, in the early centuries there is no evidence of Jewish defensiveness about the way
Jesus was judged.

[18]Kosmala ("His Blood" 101–2) exaggerates slightly: "Most certainly *hybris* in any form, deeds
done or words said in defiance of God's law or will, discrediting God's power and/or placing oneself
besides Him, was considered blasphemy."

[19]The Greek of II Kings 19:4,6,22 calls blasphemous the claims of the Assyrian general that the
God of Israel will not be able to defeat the king of Assyria, and twice we are told of garments being
torn at hearing such a claim. As for the Gospel account, however, while the high priest could actually
have torn his garments if he heard blasphemy, the intent is obviously to dramatize the charge; and
there is no way historicity can be established for that detail.

such blasphemy.[20] Many scholars, however, reject the historicity of the blasphemy charge, offering two principal objections: that crucifixion was not the appropriate penalty for blasphemy, and/or that nothing Jesus said at the trial was itself blasphemous.

A. The Punishment for Blasphemy

The first objection against the historicity of the blasphemy charge runs thus: Lev 24:16 specifies stoning as the death penalty to be enforced for blasphemy; Jesus was not stoned; and so blasphemy was not the charge. Sometimes the stoning of Stephen for blasphemy is offered as an example of what should have happened, although it is often then forgotten that the blasphemous words charged against Stephen concerned what Jesus of Nazareth had said (Acts 6:11,14)—a fact that paradoxically supports the thesis that Jesus would have been considered blasphemous! Several observations about this argument must be made. *First,* Stephen was not turned over to the Romans and Jesus was; and that would have been a major factor determining the kind of death Jesus died.[21] *Second,* although this change may not have affected the death of Jesus, stoning began to be replaced as a punishment in the 1st cent. as the Pharisee belief in the resurrection of the dead asserted more influence—stoning damaged the body that might one day be raised. *Third,* Josephus (*Ant.* 4.8.6; #202) reports an interesting adaptation of the ancient laws about execution: "Let the one who has blasphemed God, having been stoned, be hung for a day and buried without honor and without recognition [i.e., in an unknown grave]." The specific stoning penalty for blasphemy (which in Josephus' word use would mean insulting God) has been combined with the more general penalty of Deut 21:22–23: "If there shall be against someone a crime judged worthy of death and he be put to death and you hang him on a tree, his corpse shall not remain all night on the tree."[22] Now we know from texts in the Dead Sea Scrolls and Gal 3:13 that in Jesus' time crucifixion was understood as meeting the Law's description of being hanged on a tree (see also Acts 5:30; 10:34). Thus theoretically it would have been possible to combine stoning and crucifixion as the penalty

---

[20]Philo (*De fuga et inventione*) 16; #83–84) says that anyone who reviles father or mother should die; a fortiori for anyone who blasphemes (= reviles) God, the father and maker of the universe, there is no pardon. Indeed Philo states (*De vita Mosis* 2.38; #206) that the penalty of death is mandated for anyone who blasphemes the Lord of gods and human beings or even dares to utter the Name—notice the distinction, with the implication that blasphemy is more serious.

[21]Notice the odd combination of penalties in the famous TalBab *Sanhedrin* 43a passage (p. 376 above). Although it was announced that Jesus would be stoned, he was hanged on Passover eve. Perhaps "stoned" is generically equivalent to "executed." In any case the accompanying explanation that the (Roman) government was involved clarifies why Jesus was crucified ("hanged").

[22]Josephus reads Deut to mean that the body was to be hanged *after* execution.

for blaspheming.[23] *Fourth,* the Qumran Temple Scroll (11Q *Miqdaš* 64:7–13) indicates that in the Qumran interpretation of Deut 21:22 hanging/crucifixion did not follow the putting to death but led to death: "Then you shall hang him on the wood so that he dies." This passage is related to 4QpNahum (4Q 169) 3–4 i 7–9 that has been understood to state that such a form of execution had existed in Israel *of old.* Previously we had known of a few examples of crucifixion carried out by Jews, without an indication that this was an approved practice, e.g., the high priest Alexander Jannaeus crucified 800 Jewish enemies (*War* 1.4.6; #97), and his contemporary Simeon ben Sheṭaḥ is supposed to have crucified 80 witches in Ashkelon (TalJer *Sanhedrin* 23c). Yet apparently at Qumran crucifixion was thought to be a punishment mandated by the Law![24] If the Sadducees also thought that this is what was done in Israel of old (and the 4QpNahum text apparently pertains to what a Jerusalem high priest did when he crucified Pharisees and others), they might have had little problem in seeing Jesus crucified by the Romans. *Fifth,* the Hebrew of Deut 21:22–23 goes on to say that "cursed of God is the one hanged," and the LXX clarifies that by speaking of one "cursed *by* God." But Mishna *Sanhedrin* 6.4 seems to understand Deut to mean "curser of God" rather "cursed by God"; and Wilcox ("Upon" 87–90) shows that this interpretation was held by the Symmachus Greek translation, Targum Onqelos, and the Syriac Peshitta. (See the long discussion of the passage in van Unnik, "Fluch," and an exposition of the complexities by M. J. Bernstein, JQR 74 [1983], 21–45.) A curser of God would be a blasphemer by the standards of the Greek literature we have been discussing (even if the Mishna itself applies blasphemy to naming the divine Name). If this interpretation was shared by the Sanhedrin (it was not shared at Qumran, which speaks of "the one cursed of God and of men"), then the hanging (i.e., crucifying) of Jesus for blasphemy would have been a penalty fully justified by the Law (thus Betz, "Jesus" 88). I

[23]Mishna *Sanhedrin* 6.4 gives as the majority opinion that the double penalty of stoning and hanging should be applied only to the blasphemer and the idolater.

[24]See Y. Yadin, "Pesher Nahum (4QpNahum) Reconsidered," IEJ 21 (1971), 1–12, esp. 9–12 on crucifixion; also Ford, "Crucify"; Betz, "Jesus." Fitzmyer, "Crucifixion," presents a clear treatment; on 505 he offers reasons for rejecting the interpretation by Baumgarten ("Does") that the Temple Scroll refers to hanging (as a form of strangulation). Díez Merino ("Crucifixion" 16–24) invokes Targum Neofiti of Num 25:4 (i.e., the leaders as judges shall crucify on the cross those meriting death) for the Sanhedrin's crucifying the condemned, arguing that this evidence is pre-AD 30! Even more adventurously he assigns a premishnaic date to the tradition in the Targum of Ruth 1:17 that lists crucifixion in place of strangulation as the fourth form of capital punishment.

Simeon ben Sheṭaḥ is discussed by J. Efron in *Jews and Hellenistic Cities in Eretz-Israel,* ed. A. Kasher (Tübingen: Mohr [Siebeck], 1990), 318–41. The execution carried out by him was directed against pagan witches and was an example of zealotry by pious Hasidim in Hasmonean times. Betz ("Jesus" 85–87), following Hengel, thinks it was an execution of Sadducees by Pharisees after the death of Alexander Jannaeus (69 BC).

mention all these factors (of differing value) to show that the "no blasphemy because no stoning" argument is very weak indeed.

B. Was Anything Alleged at the Trial Blasphemous?

Far more serious is the second objection, that nothing raised by or concerning Jesus at the trial was itself blasphemous. We shall have to proceed point by point.

The claim to be the Messiah and blasphemy. I argued in the ANALYSIS of §21 that it is unlikely that publicly or privately Jesus clearly claimed to be the Messiah. But I also argued that it is very likely that some of his followers thought him to be the Messiah and that there is no evidence that Jesus ever denied that designation. Could the hailing of Jesus as the Messiah by his followers have been considered by the Jewish authorities to be blasphemy worthy of death, i.e., arrogance infringing on God's privileges? (Readers are reminded that we are *not* now talking about the exalted reinterpretation of "Messiah" in postresurrectional faith, as apparent in the Gospel-level discussions presented above in the COMMENT.) Most scholars recognize that we have no real evidence that the charge of blasphemy would have been warranted by the assertion that Jesus was the anointed king of the House of David raised up by God as part of the culmination planned for Israel.[25] I strongly favor the negative phrasing of the last sentence ("no real evidence") as true to the situation rather than "*we know* that the claim to be the Messiah was not blasphemous." Because we cannot find the term "Messiah" applied to any other historical figure than Jesus of Nazareth between 150 BC and AD 100, we do not "know" how people would react to the term. Some point to a hundred years after Jesus' death when Rabbi Aqiba designated the rebel Simon ben Kosiba as the Messiah king. Unfortunately the supporting rabbinic documentation stems from centuries later, and there is vigorous debate about the historicity of the designation.[26] As Marcus ("Mark" 128) points

---

[25]W. Beilner ("Prozess" 238) argues that the issue of Jesus being hailed as the Messiah was responsible for Pharisee bitterness toward him. I would agree that a major element of contention between Jesus and some of the religious authorities was his role in God's plan, implicitly claimed by the way he acted and spoke; but I see no way to be sure that this role found expression in a widely known acclamation of him as the Messiah during his lifetime.

[26]TalJer, *Ta'anit* 68d (4:5); TalBab *Sanhedrin* 93b; *Midrash Rabba* 4 on Lam 2:2. Aqiba's designation would explain "Bar Cochba," the patristic name for Simon, reflecting an application of the messianic "prophecy" in Num 24:17 concerning the star (*kôkāb*) rising out of Jacob, and would also explain Simon's persecution of those who hailed Jesus as the Messiah, as reported by Justin (*Apology* 1.31.6) writing some twenty years after Simon's revolt. A. Reinhartz, "Rabbinic Perceptions of Simeon bar Kosiba," JSJ 20 (1989), 171–94, describes well the divided state of Jewish scholarship on Aqiba's messianic designation of Simon. Some totally reject historicity; others posit it but think Simon was regarded only as a political, not an apocalyptic, Messiah (and indeed Simon's coins and letters show a strong political self-conception). Reinhartz's own views are helpfully nuanced. She

out, in rabbinic tradition there are two reactions to the claim about Ben Kos-iba. In TalJer *Ta'anit* Aqiba's designation is regarded as ridiculous: Aqiba will be dead before the Messiah comes. In TalBab *Sanhedrin* a test is proposed for whether Simon is the Messiah. (The further report that Simon failed the test and was put to death is not historical, but reflects later condemnation of the failed revolutionary leader.) Neither reaction is favor-able; but although the claim is not taken lightly, there is no suggestion of blasphemy.

Some have fastened on a specific aspect of the Messiah-blasphemy issue. Jesus was of modest Galilean origins. His insignificance was made visible in that he had been taken prisoner so easily, and he now stood as an accused criminal. If he were condemned and crucified, he would die accursed of God (Deut 21:23; Gal 3:13). Under these circumstances for him not to deny that he was the Messiah was to subject God to ridicule by saying that the ultimate divine plan to deliver the people of the covenant through an anointed king was reduced to sending this accursed ineffectual. Gal 3:13 does point to something like this in Paul's experience, perhaps being the heart of why at first he persecuted those who proclaimed Jesus to be the Messiah. But more likely such a rejection of Jesus' messiahship as blasphemous came *after* his condemnation and crucifixion, not as the cause for condemnation. It came with the proclamation of the risen Jesus as the Messiah–Son of God. Overall, then, if Jesus was accused of blasphemy in AD 30/33, it is not likely that the sole or even principal basis for that accusation was that his followers hailed him as the expected Messiah of the House of David.[27]

The claim to be the Son of God and blasphemy. This can also be an-swered negatively, for I argued above that it is unlikely that this title was used of Jesus during his lifetime either by himself or by his followers.[28]

---

doubts that Simon proclaimed himself the Messiah; but whether or not he accepted it, some in the revolt thought he was the Messiah, and already in his lifetime there were different conceptions of the Messiah.

[27]Stauffer ("Messias" 94) makes the point that until the appearance of the *Toledot Yeshu* (some five hundred years after Jesus' death) there was no strong opposition in Jewish documents to Jesus as the would-be Messiah. (However, that may be in part because the divine elements in Christian affirmations about Jesus were more objectionable). Early Jewish references give little importance to the Roman role in the execution of Jesus, and the charge of being the Messiah king would have been of more importance to the Romans than to the Jews. Blinzler ("Trial" 104–7) was a major scholar who would trace the blasphemy to the Messiah issue, but his discussion was marred by a failure to distinguish adequately between the Gospel level (where "Messiah" means unique Son of God) and the historical level. For his time this Christian scholar showed a perceptively critical sense in the use of rabbinic documents but was insufficiently critical in his approach to the NT.

[28]O'Neill ("Charge" 77), drawing on the Q statement in Matt 11:25–27; Luke 10:21–22, states imaginatively, "The technical charge upon which Jesus was condemned to death by the Sanhedrin may well have been that he blasphemed in making himself God (John 10:33) by presuming to say that he was the Son when the Father alone knew who the Son was." If the Q statement (which is an isolated phenomenon in the Synoptic tradition of Jesus' sayings) was historically made by Jesus, it could have been meant/understood parabolically of a son's relation to a father, without producing the

The claim to be the Son of Man and blasphemy. Of the three Marcan titles mentioned at the trial, in my judgment only this one is favored by the evidence as having been used by Jesus himself in his lifetime. In the Mark/Matt account, "the Son of Man" is Jesus' real addition to the trial; it seems to intensify the offensiveness, and the charge of blasphemy follows it immediately. In Mark 2:7–10 Jesus' first reference to the Son of Man was in response to a charge of blasphemy over forgiving sins. It is not surprising, then, that on the historical level many respectable scholars suggest that Jesus' use of this title was what produced the charge of blasphemy (see those listed by Catchpole, *Trial* 140–41). A major difficulty is our uncertainty as to what this title meant for Jesus' self-understanding or for the understanding of him by those who heard it. In the statement at the trial where Jesus calls himself the Son of Man (Mark 14:62; Matt 26:64; Luke 22:69), he implicitly employs biblical texts to interpret what he means. On the historical level we must ask whether if those texts were used, they would produce a picture able to be interpreted by Jesus' enemies as blasphemous.[29] Since Jesus speaks of seeing "the Son of Man sitting at the right of the Power and coming with the clouds of heaven," the two texts usually invoked in the discussions are Ps 110:1 and Dan 7; and we should explore the possibilities of each.

Jesus' statement about seeing the Son of Man sitting at the right of the Power echoes Ps 110:1 (as we saw in the COMMENT of §22) with its theme of sitting at the right of the Lord (perhaps combined with Ps 80:18, which has a son of man at God's right).[30] Elsewhere in the Gospel Jesus is reported

---

charge that he was making himself God. Aicher (*Prozess*) is another who thinks "Son of God" in the divine sense was what led to Jesus' death.

[29]In the ANALYSIS of §22 I offered two possibilities about 1st-cent. Jewish use of "the Son of Man" in reference to a specific figure. Possibility A was that in apocalyptic circles reflection on Dan 7 had produced an image of a Son of Man, a figure with human likeness whose origins were in heaven and whom God would raise up to heaven, enthrone, and constitute judge over the just and the evil. As I pointed out there, Jesus' use of the term for himself against the background of such a development could easily be considered arrogant (and thus blasphemous) and threatening by those opposed to him. Nevertheless, that approach to the title is probably not dominant among scholars, and so here I shall discuss the blasphemy issue in the context of Possibility B, i.e., that among 1st-cent. Jews there was no established concept of the Son of Man, and that Jesus and/or his followers developed the portrait of that figure we find in the Gospels. Could features in that portrait or its development have been considered blasphemous?

[30]For Flusser ("At the Right") the phrase "at the right of the Power" is the source of the offense taken by the high priest, but the issue is not the echo of Ps 110. In Isa 9:5 two consecutive titles for the Davidic king are "Wonderful Counselor" (lit. "Wonderful of Counsel") and "Mighty God" (lit. "God of Might"). Evidently later generations found the second title disturbing when applied to a human being (the LXX renders as "angel"; see the equation between God and an angel implied in Gen 22:11–12; 32:29–31). Flusser sees the two titles rephrased in 1QH 3.10 (a very obscure passage): "Wonderful Counselor *with* his power" used as a messianic title. Imagining that such an interpretation was widely known, Flusser contends that the high priest understood Jesus as claiming to be the Wonderful Counselor with God's power. I would judge this approach too speculative to be depended on in this discussion.

to have used that text in debating with scribes about the Messiah as the son of David (Mark 12:35–37), so it is not inconceivable that he reflected on the psalm during his lifetime. Would the self-application of "sitting at the right of the Lord" be considered blasphemous in the sense that Jesus was thereby claiming to be on an equal level with God? Lövestam ("Frage" 107) responds affirmatively, once Ps 110 had been joined with Dan 7. Linton ("Trial" 260–61) would respond affirmatively if the image was meant literally (which is how Christians came to understand it after the resurrection), but negatively if it was meant metaphorically. After all, in I Chron 29:23 there seems to be no difficulty in describing Solomon as sitting "on the throne of YHWH." Second-cent. AD rabbinic exegesis (Justin, *Dialogue* 83.1) applied this psalm to King Hezekiah of Judah without seeing anything blasphemous in it. In TalBab *Sanhedrin* 38b Rabbi Aqiba raises the possibility of a Davidic Messiah who would be seated next to God in heaven, but R. Jose objects, "Aqiba, to what degree would you profane the Glory?" Thus in a later period the relationship to God implied in the image of a heavenly session was debated. Yet even if Aqiba was reminded of the perils of his interpretation, there is no suggestion that a rabbinic tribunal was convened against him for blasphemy.

More scholars turn to the use of Dan 7 as the possible basis for a charge against Jesus of blasphemous arrogance in speaking of "the Son of Man" in celestial exaltation.[31] When one looks for OT background for apocalyptic elements in Jesus' vision of the kingdom of God as portrayed in the Gospels, Dan in general and Dan 7 in particular come to mind. If Jesus saw himself as the human figure, "one like a son of man," who would be taken to the Ancient of Days[32] on clouds of heaven, and given glory and an everlasting dominion and a kingdom never to be destroyed, he would certainly have had

---

[31]Lamarche ("Blasphème" 80) localizes the blasphemy in the conjunction of the Ps 110 verse with Dan 7 since the latter leads to the conclusion that the session in heaven makes Jesus the equal of God. Héring (*Royaume* 116–20), having rejected the idea that Jesus would identify himself before the high priest as the Messiah (king), accepts the historicity of the blasphemy charge attached to Jesus' claiming to be the divine Son of Man. Since that expression means "man," the claim is being made that a mere mortal can be placed at God's right. Of interest is Héring's suggestion that a Sadducee high priest would not accept Dan as Scripture because of its portrayal of the resurrection of the dead (12:2).

[32]While the Theodotion rendering of Dan 7:13 has the preposition *heōs* ("as far as") governing "the Ancient of Days," a different construction in the LXX uses *hōs* ("like"). Reconstructing the Old Greek on the basis of Origen's *Hexapla*, F. F. Bruce has argued for reading "One like a son of man appeared *like* the Ancient of Days." Familiar with such an interpretation, the high priest would have perceived Jesus as using a Son-of-Man designation that was equivalent to claiming to be like God. However, in discussing that view of the Old Greek of Daniel in the *Bulletin of the International Organization for Septuagint and Cognate Studies* 17 (1984), 15–35, esp. 28–32, S. Pace has argued persuasively that *heōs* was the original reading and *hōs* a corruption. Since that corruption is a Greek development, it could scarcely have been involved in a historical scene involving Jesus and the high priest.

an exalted view of himself. There is a violently hostile reaction to the portrait of the arrogant King of Babylon in Isa 14:13–14 who says, "I will mount the heavens . . . I will set up my throne on high . . . I will ascend above the tops of the clouds . . . I will make myself like the Most High." Nevertheless, since in Dan 7:14 such privilege is given to one like a son of man voluntarily by the Ancient of Days, would it have been blasphemous arrogance for Jesus to claim to be *the* Son of Man who receives this? The imagery of being taken on the clouds of heaven to meet the Lord is applied to all living believers in I Thess 4:17.

Stauffer ("Messias" 82) thinks he has evidence that Judaism did find offense in Jesus' use of the Son-of-Man title in a rabbinic comment on Num 23:19, "God is not man that He should speak falsely, nor (is He) a son of man that he should change His mind." According to TalJer *Ta'anit* 2.1 (Neusner: XII[L-M]), R. Abbahu said, "If a man should tell you, 'I am a god,' he is lying; if he says, 'I am the son of man,' he will regret it." Abbahu lived in Caesarea ca. 300 and was known to associate with heterodox outsiders, so he may well be criticizing claims made for Jesus by Christians. But that late passage (where "I am a god" increases the offensiveness of "I am the son of man") casts little light on whether the self-designation "the Son of Man" was considered blasphemous in Jesus' time. Overall, then, while it is *possible* that Jesus' use of "the Son of Man," if interpreted by exaltation passages in the OT, could have been considered blasphemous arrogance in his lifetime, one would be imprudent to base the historicity of the Jewish charge of blasphemy on that alone.

The destruction of the sanctuary and blasphemy. In Matt's account of the trial, "I am able to destroy the sanctuary of God, and within three days I will build (it)" is legal testimony and presumably comes under the statement in 26:65: "Behold now you heard the blasphemy." While for Mark the comparable sanctuary statement is false and inconsistent testimony, the blasphemy hurled at Jesus over it in 15:29 may mean that in Mark's understanding his opponents thought there was something blasphemous about that claim. Acts 6:11,13–14 also points to blasphemy in the statement that Jesus of Nazareth would destroy this (holy) place. Many have thought, therefore, that the key to the blasphemy charge against Jesus might lie in his words and attitude toward the Temple/sanctuary.[33]

---

[33]Among the scholars who concentrate on the Temple/sanctuary as the factor that made the authorities want Jesus dead are Flusser, Jülicher, Schubert, and Wellhausen. It is not always possible to discern the extent to which they are considering the issue of blasphemy, however; but see Kilpatrick, *Trial* 10–13. Historically the high priest would have looked on the sanctuary claim as part of a general hostility toward the Temple and not have isolated it from hostile actions (the cleansing) by Jesus.

In the ANALYSIS of §20 I gave arguments for deeming it plausible that besides acting symbolically to cleanse the Temple, Jesus spoke prophetically about imminent Temple destruction because of the hostility shown by the Jerusalem authorities to his proclamation of the kingdom of God. Historically, criticism of the Temple did bring violent reaction. Jer 26:6–8 reports the outcry of priests and court prophets for Jeremiah's death because he predicted that the Jerusalem Temple of Solomon would become like the destroyed shrine at Shiloh. Jeremiah was saved by the argument that the prophet Micah had predicted that the Temple Mount would become a ridge covered by trees and had not been put to death by King Hezekiah (26:18–19). Whether or not the story Josephus tells of the debate in Egypt ca. 150 BC about the merits of the Samaritan and Jerusalem Temples is accurate, it contains the picture that those who defended the Samaritan Temple against the Jerusalem Temple lost and *were put to death* (*Ant.* 13.3.4; #79). The Hasmonean high priest John Hyrcanus (in 128 BC) destroyed the Samaritan holy site which had been modeled on the sanctuary of the Jerusalem Temple (Josephus, *Ant.* 13.9.1; #254–56). Several passages at Qumran (1QpHab 9:9–10; 11:4–8; 4QpPs 37 4:8–9) describe how the wicked Hasmonean high priests at Jerusalem attempted to kill the Qumran priest Teacher, even pursuing him to Qumran on the Essene Day of Atonement. Surely much of the Hasmonean hatred for the Qumran Teacher was based on Qumran criticism of the Jerusalem Temple and the priesthood. After AD 6, however, public intraJewish violence over the Temple was restrained by the Roman prefects.

Theissen's sociological analysis ("Tempelweissagung"), drawing largely from incidents in the thirty-five years after Jesus' death, points to a particular hostility between country people who idealized the Temple and the Sadducean priestly aristocracy. Did Jesus' Galilean origins bring him into that conflict? On the basis of figures supplied by Josephus (*Ant.* 20.9.7; #219), Theissen estimates that some 20 percent of Jerusalem's population depended on the Temple for livelihood, and therefore, like the priests, would have been upset at threats to it. We saw on p. 366 above that the Jews had received from the Romans the right to execute any Gentiles who violated the Temple precincts. Büchsel ("Blutgerichtsbarkeit" 206–7) argues that as an extension of this right, they were able to stone Stephen because he advocated the destruction of the Temple sanctuary.[34]

Serious reaction to woes uttered against the Temple is confirmed by the story of Jesus son of Ananias (Josephus, *War* 6.5.3; #300–9—I have mentioned this several times before but here it could be useful to have a longer

---

[34]Indeed, Büchsel thinks that if the witnesses had agreed against Jesus on the sanctuary issue, the Sanhedrin could have executed him.

description so that readers can see how many parallels there are with the Gospel accounts, despite the somewhat bizarre character of bar Ananias). He was a crude peasant who at the Feast of Tabernacles in the early 60s cried out in the Temple a message of woeful portent, included in which was "a voice against Jerusalem and the sanctuary."[35] This annoyed the leading citizens (in Gospel language, the elders). The *archontes* or authorities (surely including the chief priests), thinking he was under some supernatural or demoniacal drive, had him beaten and led him before the Roman governor Albinus (AD 62–64). Although he was flayed to the bone with scourges, he did not sue for mercy but kept repeating "Woe to Jerusalem." He would not respond a word to Albinus, who finally decided he was a maniac and let him go. Years later, at the time of the siege, he was killed crying out, "Woe again to the city and to the people and to the sanctuary, and woe to me also."

This last case shows that not only the priests and the Jerusalemites but also *the Romans* could get involved in a threat to the Temple. John 11:48 makes that last danger all-important to the priests and Pharisees gathered in a Sanhedrin against Jesus: "If we permit him (to go on) thus, all will believe in him. And the Romans will come and take away from us both the place [i.e., the Temple] and the nation." They seem to be worried (honestly or dishonestly) that the following attracted by Jesus would cause a public disturbance, leading the Romans to send troops into the Temple precincts. That cultic matters could lead to disturbances and provoke the Romans to act is well attested in Josephus, at least for the years after Jesus' lifetime (see the caution on p. 459 above). In AD 36 a major incident occurred in Samaria when a man persuaded a multitude that he would show them where Moses had buried the sacred Temple vessels on Mount Gerizim. Pilate interfered in a bloody suppression that led to his removal (*Ant.* 18.4.1–2; #85–89). In AD 66 Josephus (*War* 2.15.4; #321–22) reports a procession, mourning, and prayers on the part of the priests in Jerusalem, beseeching the people not to provoke the Romans lest they violate the Temple. Slightly later, when Eleazar, the priest captain of the Temple, had successfully argued for the daring step of ceasing sacrifices on behalf of the emperor, the citizens with influence (*dynatoi*), the chief priests, and the Sanhedrin came together to deliberate how they might avert the disaster that the Romans would wreak on the Temple (*War* 2.17.3; #411). In *Ant.* 20.8.5–6; #166–67, describing how religious impostors led the people astray with promises of marvels and signs, Josephus judges that such behavior was why God sent the Romans to

---

[35]In the last decades before the destruction of the Temple there were several threats to Jerusalem. In the 50s a prophet from Egypt tried from the Mount of Olives to cause the walls of Jerusalem to fall down. TalBab *Giṭṭin* 56a reports that R. Zadok began fasting ca. 30 to forestall the destruction of Jerusalem.

burn the city—the Temple was no longer a clean divine dwelling place. Rome and the Temple are associated in Paul's statement of innocence in Acts 25:8: "I have committed no offense against the Jewish Law, the Temple, or the Emperor."

All this becomes more important in relation to Jesus because of a passage in the Qumran Temple Scroll that involves an application of Deut 21:22–23, dealing with hanging someone for a crime judged worthy of death—a passage that we saw (pp. 532–33 above) was interpreted in the light of crucifixion and joined to the penalty for blasphemy. One of the crimes that the scroll (11Q *Miqdaš* 64:7) judges worthy of crucifixion is to betray one's people to a foreign nation and thus to bring evil on one's people. Betz ("Temple" 7) has argued, in the light of John 11:48, that imperiling the Temple and bringing evil on the nation was the charge against Jesus and the reason why he was handed over to be crucified. There are reasons to be cautious about that theory, not the least of which is our ignorance about how widespread this Qumran interpretation was. But it does heighten the already ample evidence that a fear of Roman intervention over actions or threats to the Temple could have been translated into a strong religious antipathy toward those responsible for the threats and actions. Overall I would judge that the attitude of Jesus toward the Temple/sanctuary may very well have been among the religious legal reasons offered to the Sanhedrin in making a case for a death sentence. *But none of the parallels* cited above where serious action was taken on Temple issues *states that blasphemy was involved.*

The false prophet and blasphemy. The mockery by the Sanhedrists that culminates the trial in Mark/Matt and the mockery by Jesus' captors that precedes the Sanhedrin inquiry in Luke centers on a challenge to Jesus to prophesy. As I shall stress in the COMMENT of §26 below, the parallelism with the Roman mockery at the end of the Roman trial with its focus on "King of the Jews" gives the impression that for Mark the key issues in the two trials were (respectively) prophet and king; and God would verify that the Son was both. Thus there is a highly theological thrust in the Marcan mockery of Jesus as prophet, and one should not simply assume historicity. We are made cautious too by the lack of the prophet theme in John's account of the Jewish proceedings against Jesus (although earlier in 7:52 the chief priests and the Pharisees have used a scriptural test to prove that Jesus cannot be a prophet). Nevertheless, major scholars have suggested that historically for the truly religious opponents of Jesus, the charge that underlay all else was that Jesus was a false prophet. This figure is described by Deut 13:2–6 as one who with signs and wonders leads people astray from the path in which the Lord has directed Israel, and by Deut 18:20–22 as one who presumes to speak in the name of God an oracle that God has not commanded him to speak (to be tested by fulfillment and nonfulfillment). This prophet "shall die." It is interesting that in the Qumran Temple Scroll the section on crucifixion that was important for our discussion above of the penalty for blasphemy (11Q *Miqdaš* 64:7–13) follows shortly after an interpretation (61:1–5) of the false prophet of Deut 18. The false prophet who leads the people astray is a major theme of cols. 54–56, with the advice that people should be guided by approved levitical teachers, while the misleading prophet should be killed. Tosepta *Sanhedrin* 14.13 shows a deep continuing hostility toward the prophet who leads people to idolatry. Jeremias (JEWJ 78–79), who thinks Jesus was executed on Passover, cites this "shall die" as the justifying reason for the activities of the religious leaders that would otherwise be forbidden on a feast day—it overrode all other duties.[36]

As we begin to consider the possibility that Jesus was looked on and condemned as a false prophet, minor encouragement comes from the fact that Josephus offers examples of would-be prophets in Jesus' century (whereas he offered no parallels for would-be Messiahs, Sons of God, or Sons of Man). I shall discuss these examples in detail in §31, A2d below. But those prophets lived after Jesus' lifetime, mostly in the latter phase of the prefecture (after 44) when times were much more troubled; they were associated with leading large crowds so that divisions of Roman soldiers were sent against them. Jesus was arrested as a solitary, without any real interest shown by the Roman authorities in his few followers; and he complained that no force whatsoever was necessary despite the weapons of the arresting party. He was put on trial by the Romans; those others perished in battle or escaped. One possible similarity is that some could have understood the claim to be able to destroy the sanctuary of God along the lines of the promises of those prophets to be able to part the Jordan or bring down the walls of Jerusalem.[37]

In critical studies of christology, sometimes the historical question about the role that Jesus assigned to himself in God's plan is answered in terms of the prophet of the endtime. The Gospel evidence is mixed. Jesus is acknowledged by others as a/the prophet in passages like Matt 21:11; Luke 7:16; 9:8; 24:19; and John 7:40, without guidance from the evangelist as to

---

[36]Among those who think that the false-prophet issue played a major role in the decision that Jesus must die are P. E. Davies, Easton, D. Hill ("Jesus"), Strobel (*Stunde*), J. Weiss; see also P. Stuhlmacher, "Warum musste Jesus sterben?" *Theologische Beiträge* 16 (1985), 273–85.

[37]Would Jesus' miraculous actions have been looked on as magic by some who therefore demeaned him as a false prophet? Juel (*Messiah* 124) wonders if Jesus' opponents thought that he would destroy the sanctuary by magic. Acts 13:6 joins the two ideas: "a certain magician, a Jewish false prophet." According to Justin (*Dialogue* 69.7) 2d-cent. Jews accused Jesus of being a magician and a deceiver (= false prophet). See C. H. Kraeling, "Was Jesus Accused of Necromancy?" JBL 59 (1940), 147–57.

whether this is an adequate insight. In John 4:19; 9:17, from the flow of the following narrative, we can tell that "prophet" is a correct but only inchoative insight. In Mark 8:28 and par. it is an inadequate evaluation when contrasted with "the Messiah," while in John 6:14–15 Jesus wants to avoid the crowd that hails him thus. In Mark 6:4; Matt 23:37; and John 4:44 Jesus makes a comparison between himself and prophets in general. In Luke 13:33 he compares his destiny to die in Jerusalem to that of the prophets, a theme echoed in Acts 7:52. (See also Acts 3:22 and 7:37 for Jesus as the prophet-like-Moses.) Thus, while there is no doubt that according to the Gospels Jesus can do many things that prophets (especially Elijah and Elisha) did, and his behavior and attitudes are often like theirs (especially like Jeremiah's), there is no text that indicates a wholehearted approval by him of "prophet" as a satisfactory evaluation; and even his followers know that it is inadequate. Obviously all those texts were written in the last third of the century by evangelists who knew Jesus to be the Son of God, and so we are handicapped in discerning whether "prophet" was ever considered satisfactory.

The fact, however, that Jesus acted like a prophet and thus caused some to think he was one could also have caused others to think he was a false prophet. One of the damnable aspects of the Deut figure is his ability to lead people astray from God and to deceive them by pretending he is speaking for God. Luke 19:48; 20:19,26; 22:2 show the fear of the Jewish authorities about Jesus' hold on the people; and 23:2,5,14 report a charge continuing throughout the Pilate trial that Jesus perverted the nation and stirred up the people.[38] The discussion in John 7:17–18 (also 12:48–50—BGJ 1.491–92) as to whether Jesus speaks on his own or on the authority of the One who sent him echoes Deut 18:20–22.[39] The charge of being a deceiver (*planan*, *planos*) is made against Jesus in John 7:12,47 and Matt 27:63–64. It continues into the Christian additions to (or editions of) the *Testaments* (*Test. Levi* 16.3) and into Justin's *Dialogue* (69.7; 108.2). The latter author (*Dial.* 108.2; see 17.1) reports that everywhere Jews accused Christians of being a "godless sect," perhaps reflecting the theme that Jesus had led them away from the true God of Israel. Strobel (*Stunde* 81–94) points out that opposition to a false prophet would have been something on which Sadducees and Pharisees could agree. All of this comes to a head in the *baraita* reported in TalBab

---

[38]Hill ("Jesus" 185) points out that this is one religious charge that could alarm the Romans as well.

[39]In Acts 6:13–15 the (false) charge is made that Jesus of Nazareth "will change the customs that Moses delivered to us." Plausibly this reflects a charge being made by Jews in Luke's time; it resembles the charge of leading people from the path in which the Lord had directed Israel, i.e., Moses' description of the false prophet (Deut 13:6).

Sanhedrin 43a (p. 376 above). Yeshu is clearly accused of being the false prophet of Deut 13:2–6 who entices Israel to apostasy, and the punishment decreed for him is to be stoned and eventually hung. That is the punishment for blasphemy, and so certainly by the standards of that later period (3d cent.?) Jesus was considered a blasphemous false prophet.[40]

G. Stanton, in discussing early Jewish-Christian polemic (NTS 31 [1985], 377–92), points out this whole train of thought about Jesus. Acknowledging that, Schneider ("Verfahren" 121–25), nevertheless, uses it to challenge the claim of Stuhlmacher and Strobel that "false prophet" was a major historical issue in Jesus' life, for he points out that all this evidence, including that found in Matt, Luke-Acts, and John, is post-70. Was it precisely some of the experiences of the Jewish War with its failed fanatics that caused postwar Jews to regard Jesus as a false prophet? Schneider would find little of the false-prophet motif in Mark and thus in the older strains of Christian memory. Yet the great test of the false prophet in Deut is the fulfillment or nonfulfillment of what he says will happen. In the Marcan trial scene Jesus is mocked and challenged to prophesy in reference to his predictions concerning the destruction of the sanctuary and the vindication of him as the Son of the Blessed—predictions that provoked the charge of blasphemy. Even this possible echo of the false prophet motif, however, one must judge with care, for Mark is writing to prepare readers for Jesus' exactly fulfilling his predictions as he dies. In summation, it is possible that the main blasphemous charge against Jesus, especially in the mind of religious Jews, was that he was a false prophet; but once again the evidence falls far short of establishing this point.

C. Were Implications of Jesus' Ministry Blasphemous?

Thus far, in considering whether it is historically likely that Jesus would have been considered a blasphemer by the Jewish religious authorities, I have concentrated on titles (or, in the case of the sanctuary, an issue) mentioned in the Sanhedrin trial (described by Mark/Matt) where the charge of blasphemy is made. That is the logical and necessary place to start; yet such a starting point handicaps the discussion, for without doubt that trial is phrased in the light of later Christian experience. In it we are hearing how Christians in the last third of the 1st cent. understood Jewish adversaries who considered Christian claims about Jesus to be blasphemous. From the

---

[40]Some would assimilate to the false prophet the rebellious elder of Mishna *Sanhedrin* 11.2–4, noting that his punishment was to take place in Jerusalem before the crowd on one of the three great feasts and that his trial was to begin and end on the same day (Tosepta *Sanhedrin* 10.11)—features true of Jesus' death. But are these later rules relevant to Jesus' time?

trial scene we may conclude that (in Christian eyes) Jewish adversaries thought blasphemous the exaltation of Jesus as the Messiah, the Son of God (only beloved, begotten of a virgin, pre-existent—however that Sonship was phrased in a given place). Perhaps too (in this Christian picture), Jewish adversaries of that period would have considered blasphemously arrogant the Christian evaluation of the destruction of God's Temple as a judgment upon Jews by Jesus, the Son of Man, because those adversaries knew that all such things lay in the hands of the God of Israel alone—"Blessed be He." In the eyes of those Jewish adversaries, their coreligionists who followed Jesus had been led astray from Israel and were no longer disciples of Moses but disciples of "that one" (John 9:28–29). Looking back, many Jews of the late 1st cent. (like their descendants of subsequent centuries who produced TalBab *Sanhedrin* 43a) may have already come to the judgment that Jesus was a false prophet who deserved to be hanged from the tree (of the cross), accursed by God.

I emphasized in n. 10 above that all this is a Christian picture of attitudes held by adversaries; we have little access to how Jews would have expressed themselves in their own words. Rarely in such a conflict does one side do justice to all the nuances of the other side. Even more important, I emphasize that this is a picture some thirty to seventy years after the events, in a period when the issues separating those who believed in Jesus from those (Jews) who did not had become more clearly and hostilely articulated. If we are interested in the issue of whether in his lifetime Jesus was considered a blasphemer, we cannot let the trial scene that was written so much later dictate all the issues to be discussed. That scene is the evangelists' distillation from the wide range of Jesus' ministry, including conflicts depicted therein. As an attempt to do justice to that wider ministry and its contribution to the blasphemy issue, let me list almost without comment Jesus' actions, stances, or words that could well have appeared religiously arrogant or presumptuous (and thus blasphemous)[41] to those whom the Gospels describe as not having ears to hear or eyes to see. What I list below are, in my judgment, possibly or plausibly historical items selected from the Gospel accounts:[42]

- Jesus spoke with great authority and by his "Amen" almost demanded acceptance.

[41]I am concerned here only with blasphemy. Psychologically, however, that charge might have been facilitated by other factors that caused Jesus to be disliked, e.g., his association with tax collectors, prostitutes, and public sinners (see Reichrath, "Prozess" 143–44). The Herodians would not have liked his praise of JBap, whom Herod Antipas had executed. Ritt ("Wer" 170–72) holds that Jesus' Galilean origins would have made him suspect (because of the revolutionary history of Judas the Galilean some twenty years before), as well as his solidarity with the poor.

[42]The order in which the points are listed is topical and does *not* reflect a gradation in importance or plausibility.

- Jesus claimed to have the power to forgive sin. It seemed almost as if the association of sinners with Jesus exempted them from standards of holiness imposed by other religious authorities.[43]
- Jesus performed extraordinary deeds and healings and related them to his making God's rule/kingdom present to people.[44]
- Jesus implied or even stated that people would be judged by God according to how they reacted to his proclamation of the kingdom. Other Jews proclaimed the gracious outreach of God; but in Jesus' proclamation there was a stated element of unique opportunity, which he proclaimed to be unlike any that had ever come before or would come again (parables of the pearl of great price and treasure in the field). Jesus' language of entrance into the kingdom had a tone of eschatological newness that went beyond prophetic calls to repentance.
- Jesus took stances on the Law, especially concerning the Sabbath, that would have seemed highly disputable to Sadducees, Pharisees, or Essenes. Although these disputes must be evaluated cautiously,[45] opponents who were neither legalists nor lacking in religious imagination could still have deeply resented Jesus' freedom toward what Moses had commanded and the piety that flowed from it. To a disciple who asked to be allowed to go first and bury his father, Jesus answered "Follow me, and let the dead bury the dead." That response might appear to nullify the commandment (word) of God, "Honor your father and your mother," and the pious imperative to bury the dead (notice how Tobit 4:3 joins these two duties). God had spoken mouth to mouth to Moses, and one should not feel free to override Moses' authority (Num 12:7–8). Even Sanders (*Jesus* 267) admits that Jesus "did not consider the Mosaic dispensa-

---

43J. Jeremias held that Jesus insulted the Pharisees (*haberim*), whose standards of fellowship were determined by laws of purity. E. P. Sanders (*Jesus*, 176–77) contends that more than ritual purity was involved, for Jesus accepted the wicked without demanding their repentance or obedience to the Law (p. 207). B. D. Chilton (*Tyndale Bulletin* 39 [1988], 3–18) argues that Sanders's doing away with cultic issues so easily is an oversimplification.

44In themselves healings were not blasphemous, and frequently Jesus is compared to wonderworkers like Honi the rain-making Circle-Drawer (1st cent. BC) or R. Hanina b. Dosa (1st cent. AD). Yet those figures did not attach their deeds to the coming of the final kingdom from God and their essential role in it. Healing with the wrong implication could be seriously offensive: In Tosepta *Hullin* 2.22–23 R. Ishmael praises R. Eliezer b. Damah, who died rather than let Jacob from Kefar Sama heal him in the name of (Jesus) ben-Pantera.

45On the one hand Moule ("Gravamen" 177) argues that the heart of the opposition to Jesus stemmed from the way he offended the Judaism of his day. On the other hand, in general the Gospels do not show Jesus arrogantly disregarding or having contempt for the Law. Most of the disagreements were over interpretations of accepted laws; and in his books *Jesus* and *Jewish Law* E. P. Sanders maintains that the historically verifiable legal differences between Jesus and other groups were not startlingly beyond the endurable disputes of the time. For instance, Sanders thinks that all Jews agreed that sufficient human needs overrode Sabbath obligations, but argued as to what constituted sufficiency, with CD (presumably Essene) often showing the narrowest outlook. Though they might make bitter remarks about interpretations of the Law made by other groups, Jewish groups in Jesus' time normally did not use physical compulsion to make others agree with them or kill others over legal interpretations.

tion to be final or absolutely binding." Thus not differences of interpretation but authority over the Law may have been the important issue in relation to Jesus.[46]

- Jesus, a layman, acted in criticism of Temple customs and indicated that rejection of him imperiled Temple survival.[47]
- Jesus never explained his authority in terms that would make him identifiable against an OT background, e.g., as if he were a prophet who had received his power when the word of God came to him. His authority seemed to be part of what he was.[48]
- Jesus addressed God with familiarity as "Abba," an otherwise unattested prayer practice.[49]
- At certain times Jesus spoke of himself in relation to God as the son, e.g., in the parables in Mark 12:6; John 5:19 (see BGJ 1.218); in the Q saying of Matt 11:27; Luke 10:22; and in Mark 13:32, where there is a limitation on the son's knowledge.[50]

If in his lifetime Jesus plausibly did or said most of these things, I see little reason to doubt that his opponents would have considered him blasphemous (i.e., arrogantly claiming prerogatives or status more properly associated with God), even as the Gospels report at the trial.

Before treating the aftermath of the Sanhedrin proceedings in Mark/Matt, namely, the abuse and mockery of Jesus by the Sanhedrin authorities (§25), I shall stop to give a section reflecting on how the narrative of the Sanhedrin proceedings was composed.

(Bibliography for this episode is found in §17, Part 5.)

[46]In point of fact, Christian memory did not report that a negative or outrageous stance toward the Law was mentioned as a reason why the Sanhedrin wanted Jesus dead. Saul, an observant Pharisee, persecuted Jesus' followers shortly after Jesus' death; but we are not sure whether this extreme religious hostility involved interpretation of the Law. Other religious factors could produce lethal hostility. About a hundred years before Jesus' death people stoned to death a miracle worker, Honi (Onias) the rain maker, when he asked God not to hear the prayers of contending Jewish high priests against each other (*Ant.* 14.2.1; #24). Rabbinic tradition (Mishna, *Ta'anit* 3.8) reflects hostility almost to the point of excommunication toward this figure because of his petulance before God in his rain-making prayer. Thirty years after Jesus' death Jerusalem authorities wanted Jesus son of Ananias put to death for his apocalyptic warnings (*War* 6.5.3; #300–8).

[47]That phrasing is true whether his action in the Temple be seen as cleansing or prophetic gesture of doom (Moule, "Gravamen" 183–84); it also does justice to the simplest form of the destroy/rebuild claim about the sanctuary. For Jeremiah, a priest, what imperiled the Temple was a failure to keep God's moral demands.

[48]From this insight came the logic of the Prologue of John: The word of God did not come to Jesus because he is the word.

[49]On pp. 172–75 above I cautioned against exaggerating the familiarity in this address or its christological import. One may also wonder whether Jesus' usage was public enough to be known by his adversaries—similarly for the next point in the list above.

[50]See Catchpole, *Trial* 141–48. Note that Mark and Q do not put "the Son of God" on Jesus' lips.

§24. ANALYSIS COVERING THE COMPOSITION OF ALL FOUR PARTS OF THE SANHEDRIN PROCEEDINGS

(Mark 14:55–64; Matt 26:59–66; Luke 22:66–71)

We have now finished commenting on the central narrative of the Sanhedrin proceedings, which was divided into four parts. In the respective sections (§§20–23) the COMMENT portion concentrated on the portrayal that each of the evangelists wanted to paint of Jesus being interrogated, while the ANALYSES concentrated on evaluating the historicity of what was being recounted. It is now time to turn to the composition of that Sanhedrin trial as described in Mark 14:55–64.[1] While "composition" is primarily concerned with how the trial narrative came together, many of the theories advanced are closely related to the issues of historicity I have been discussing. In generating theories of composition, this scene rivals and even surpasses the Gethsemane scene. Indeed, many 20th-cent. theses about the composition and the historicity of the whole PN have made their focal point this trial. The books of Donahue and Juel are examples of that in the 1970s, but the debate begins earlier. A survey of how scholarship on the trial scene has developed and of some representative current approaches will be given first below. Then I shall offer what I regard as more helpful: a survey of what the Gospels have in common and how that might give us an entrée to a preGospel arrangement.

A. The Development of Scholarship and Some Current Approaches

There have been comments on the trial of Jesus since Josephus at the end of the 1st cent. As Catchpole, *Trial,* has documented, in the 19th cent., when Jewish historians became increasingly aware of Christian higher criticism of

---

[1]Throughout the COMMENT in order to understand the present accounts I had to face the claim that Luke had a source or tradition separate from Mark. I found insufficient evidence for a continuous source, and only in the conditional sentences related to the Messiah issue (Luke 22:67–68—there because of parallels with John) did I see convincing evidence of any such tradition. I saw nothing to suggest that Matt had a separate source. John does not have a Sanhedrin trial at this point. Therefore, for all practical purposes the Marcan account is the main focus in compositional studies. Verses within Mark 14:55–64 will sometimes be referred to without chapter designation.

the NT, there was a growth in their discussions of the reliability of the long-accepted Synoptic picture in which there had been a Sanhedrin trial on the night before Jesus died. Yet in a judgment on all previous Christian and Jewish studies, Easton ("Trial" 430) wrote in 1915: "The first thoroughly critical treatment of the trial of Jesus that was supported by adequate historical knowledge was W. Brandt's *Die evangelische Geschichte und der Ursprung des Christenthums* which appeared in 1893." Following upon that work critical, largely German, scholarship went in two directions: Wellhausen, Klostermann, and Norden found their basic historical nucleus in Mark's account; J. Weiss and Spitta turned toward Luke (considered independent of Mark). Easton himself thought that Mark's central account (minus minor details) rested on a solid historical base, while Luke drew partly from Mark and partly from a separate tradition.

A major development occurred in 1931 when, reacting against liberal skepticism about the PN, Hans Lietzmann published "Der Prozess Jesu." He argued that Mark was the only primary source for the passion and that the Marcan account (14:26–16:8) could be divided into nine scenes. Lietzmann put great emphasis on Peter as the eyewitness source for much of the material, but Peter was not at the Sanhedrin trial. And so amid a rather conservative approach to the PN, Lietzmann argued vigorously that 14:55–64 was inserted by Mark and was not historical. He perceptively invoked the real problems in the scene (those that plagued us in the COMMENT), e.g., prepared false witnesses who then do not agree; the difficulty in understanding how Jesus would destroy the sanctuary; the parallels with the Stephen story in Luke; Christian creedal expressions on the lips of the high priest; the blasphemy issue in light of the Mishna. He followed J. Juster (p. 363 above) in arguing that the Sanhedrin had the right to execute criminals and that therefore the very fact there was a Roman trial proved the unhistorical character of the Jewish trial. The Pharisees and other Jewish leaders disliked Jesus but did not want a religious trial ("Prozess" 321), and so they handed Jesus over to the Romans. Christians knew the real issue was religious and made up the trial narrative to dramatize that.

Lietzmann's paper soon became the focus of a vigorous discussion.[2] (The interest was not only academic; in a sense Lietzmann could be considered

---

[2]In addition to scholars to be discussed above, Kosmala ("Prozess") challenged the arguments that Christians could have had no information about what happened within the Sanhedrin, that Jesus' silence was a creation from Isa 53:7, and that mishnaic rules were applicable. Kosmala's ideas about christological titles (pp. 30–33) are dated. Fiebig ("Prozess") regarded as weak the Juster-Lietzmann claim that the Sanhedrin could execute for crimes that affected Roman interests. The charge against Jesus was not a purely inner-religious issue, and the Romans had to be consulted. Two decades afterward, Jeremias ("Geschichtlichkeit") added further arguments against the Juster-Lietzmann position on Sanhedrin competence (see §18D above).

as being proJewish in Berlin in the early 1930s.) Burkitt in a review brought Lietzmann's views to the attention of the English-speaking world. While he agreed with much of "Prozess," he suggested that Mark might be describing a Jewish investigation carried out for the Romans.[3] Büchsel ("Blutgerichts-barkeit") concentrated his attack on the right of the Sanhedrin to execute capital sentences and (effectively, in my judgment) eliminated that as an argument against the historicity of the Marcan trial.[4] In France, Goguel ("À propos") disagreed with Lietzmann on a host of issues: too much emphasis on Peter; ignoring Johannine evidence; not recognizing that the sanctuary saying was difficult for Christians and scarcely created by them.[5] Goguel (p. 298) proposed as authentic the response of Jesus about being the Messiah because it is so undeveloped; and he suggested that Pilate wanted to protect himself in executing Jesus by getting a Sanhedrin opinion, lest there be trouble during the feast. Complete freedom for the Sanhedrin to execute would have been too dangerous for the Romans.

Probably the major response came from Dibelius ("Historische"), who was provoked into discussing the historicity of the whole PN, taking a position both more radical and more conservative than Lietzmann. He argued for a preMarcan narrative but placed far less emphasis on eyewitnesses; much of the narrative grew out of reflection on the OT. Lietzmann gave two alternatives, historical or Marcan; Dibelius argued strongly for the preMarcan non-historical.[6] In particular Dibelius (p. 200) argued that 14:62–66; 15:1–2 were preMarcan.

While those were the most important contributions to the discussions in the early 1930s, some of the postwar contributions were much in the same line. In two articles in the late 1950s Burkill ("Competence,"[7] "Trial") re-hearsed the historical objections against the Marcan account (with more sophistication than Lietzmann about the utility of mishnaic material) and opted for the reliability of the brief statement in Mark 15:1—that statement shows no knowledge of 14:55–65, which is a Marcan creation. (In some of this

---

[3]Lietzmann ("Bemerkungen II" 84) answered Burkitt correctly that Mark describes a trial, not an investigation, and that none of the issues discussed is used by Pilate.

[4]Most of Lietzmann's "Bemerkungen II" answered Büchsel, who then responded with "Noch Einmal." Büchsel has the better arguments about the instances of capital punishment, but Lietzmann (p. 83) correctly contends that the disproof of this one argument against historicity does not establish historicity.

[5]Goguel ("À propos" 296) thinks it offended Jewish Christians loyal to the Temple, for which reason it was attributed to false witnesses.

[6]Dibelius ("Historische" 199) protested that Lietzmann could not treat Gethsemane as historical and the trial as unhistorical, for in both Jesus speaks of his claims; they stood together in the tradition and are heavily influenced by scriptural motifs. Lietzmann answered Dibelius in "Bemerkungen I," pointing out that scriptural coloring does not militate against historicity. Curiously, Dibelius would accept the naked youth of Mark 14:51–52 as a witness to what happened but would not accept Peter.

[7]This defends the Lietzmann position against Jeremias, "Geschichtlichkeit."

reasoning Mark becomes an extremely incompetent writer, not noticing his own contradictions.) Winter's many writings on the subject began in this period, and articles like "Marginal" and "Markus" reproduced the Lietzmann combination of historical impossibility and free Marcan creation (when the evangelist was writing in Rome to show that Jesus was not a revolutionary of the type just seen in the Jewish Revolt). Defenses of the historical possibility of the Sanhedrin trial were mounted with erudition[8] against Lietzmann and his more recent adherents by Blinzler ("Geschichtlichkeit," "Probleme") and K. Schubert (two "Juden" articles; "Verhör," "Kritik"). It is interesting, however, to find more recently Aguirre ("Poderes") repeating Lietzmann's arguments to prove that the Sanhedrin could sentence people to death, but with a new twist: There actually was a Jewish trial of Jesus; yet the judges could not agree (something for which there is no Gospel evidence whatsoever), and so they had to hand him over to a Roman decision.

In many of the more recent technical discussions the emphasis has shifted away from the historicity of the trial to the techniques of Marcan composition. In addition to the select authors representing different positions whom I shall mention below, I remind the reader of the many authors surveyed by Soards (APPENDIX IX). Sloyan ("Recent") reviews the literature of the 1960s and 1970s. Currently there are at least three important positions about the Marcan Sanhedrin trial in 14:55–64.

A back-formation from the Pilate Trial. In 1961 Braumann defended a theory already advanced by E. Wendling[9] a half century earlier. There is a very close similarity pattern between Mark 14:55–64 and the Pilate trial in 15:2–5, especially if one rearranges the order:[10] charges against Jesus by others; emergence of an authoritative main questioner who points out the number of charges and who asks, "Have you nothing at all to answer?"; Jesus answers nothing at all; "Are you the ————?"; Jesus responds with an affirmative. Although some (Norden) have thought that the Pilate trial was conformed to the Sanhedrin trial, Wendling and Braumann argue that the Sanhedrin trial is entirely a secondary composition on the basis of the Pilate trial. There can be no question about a strong parallelism between the two trials. Some of it, of course, comes from the nature of trials (charges, questioning, response), but much of it stems from Mark. There are many parallelisms within Mark's PN (e.g., the disciples found sleeping three times, comparable to Peter denying three times, etc.); parallelism is a parenetic

---

[8]The evidence from the decrees of Augustus that at Cyrene the death penalty remained within the competence of the Roman prefect had become widely known since their publication in 1927.

[9]*Die Enstehung des Markus-Evangeliums* (Tübingen: Mohr, 1908), 178–80. Lietzmann also drew on this idea.

[10]Braumann proposes the order 15:3,4,5,2. But then the *palin* ("again") in 15:4 is difficult.

technique to highlight theological points. But the parallelism between the two trials tells us nothing about the origin of the material thus shaped, and imperfections in the parallelism (without the benefits of modern re-arrangements) suggest that Mark was being controlled by some traditional material he felt obliged to report. Schneider ("Vorsynoptische" 34) makes an interesting case for a parallelism between the Sanhedrin trial and the de-nials by Peter, e.g., three sections of mounting importance in the questions asked and what happens.[11] This parallelism cautions us against a simplistic theory of the shaping of the Sanhedrin trial by the Pilate trial.

The combination of two narratives. Many have noted that 14:57–59 seems to duplicate 55–56 (Bultmann) and that 61b–62 could be omitted (Well-hausen). If we take the idea that two narratives have been amalgamated, Valentin ("Comparutions" 233) has a simple theory (but one that solves none of the repetition problems): Two trials were put together, one (55–61a) dealing with the witnesses (absent from Luke), the other (61b–64) dealing with the high priest. Taylor (*Mark* 566), concentrating on the first part of the trial, suggests that 55–56 and 57–59 were two parallel narratives joined by Mark, both having "false" and "not consistent" testimony.[12] Quite complex is the thesis of Linnemann (*Studien* 129–34): One account (14:55,57,58,61b,60b,61a) had the theme of Jesus silent before false wit-nesses; another account (14:55,56,60a,61c,62,63,64) had Jesus condemned because he claimed to be the Messiah.[13] Mark would have added 14:59 about the inconsistent testimony, and perhaps the adjectives pertaining to "made by hand" in v. 58. Juel (*Messiah* 24–29) offers a strong critique, and the theory has been found wanting by most because it shows little appreciation of Marcan stylistic techniques. One is hard put to believe that Mark found, each in a ready-made narrative needing only minor alteration, the two main motifs of sanctuary destruction and Messiah/Son of God and that he then made a leitmotif of the two running through the passion to the cross and to the aftermath of Jesus' death.

The glossing of an earlier tradition or narrative. This glossing can be in a preMarcan stage or by Mark himself. The object of the glossing can be a

---

[11]In the Sanhedrin trial the three questions/issues concern the false witnesses in general (14:55–56), the false witnesses about the sanctuary (14:57–59), and the high priest's questioning (14:60–64). Gerhardsson ("Confession" 50–51) finds much the same threefold trial/Peter parallelism in Matt, pointing out additionally that each part ends with a symbol: tearing clothes and cock crowing.

[12]Many composition theories wrestle with the relationship of 55–56 to 57–59 as to which is the older or preMarcan. The tendency to regard 57–59 as secondary (e.g., Vögtle, "Markinische") in-volves passages that are related to it: 15:29b,38.

[13]Here she is consonant with her general thesis that there was no preMarcan PN, only traditions. Note that she has to rearrange verse order and use the hostile-witness motif of v. 55 in both traditions. The first of the two traditions is arranged with an eye on 15:1–5 (thus she has some agreement with the Braumann hypothesis).

complete preGospel PN or only scattered traditions (in which case Mark himself becomes the author of the original PN). Some of the theories are extremely complicated. For instance, Pesch (*Markus* 2.428–29) argues strongly against ten additions to the text posited by Schenke, who sees in every duplication (which Mark uses for narrative emphasis) the sign of an addition. The theory of Gospel formation and Synoptic relationships advocated by Benoit and Boismard finds the earliest tradition in 14:55–56, 61b–64.[14] From another early document were added v. 58 (while 57 and 59 were created from v. 56) and vv. 60–61a. Mark personally contributed only phrases, e.g., "We have heard him saying"; "[not] made by hand." With this one may compare the theory of Donahue (*Are You*), who would recognize as the basic *tradition* 14:53a,56a,60–61a (material already shaped by OT references)—he and Benoit have only part of one verse in common! To this Mark added other traditional worked-over material: 14:54,57–58,63–65— again Donahue has only one verse in agreement with Benoit. Mark himself composed 14:53b,55,56b,59,61b–62 (using Ps 110:1 and Dan 7:14), i.e., much of what Benoit attributes to the oldest tradition.[15] Juel (*Messiah* 30– 35), who offers a critique of Donahue, points out skeptically that in this theory Mark introduced the false witnesses' charge about the sanctuary (57– 58) and then composed 59 so the charge would not seem so false.

Three prominent German commentators on Mark, Pesch (1976), Gnilka (1979), and Lührmann (1987), all posit a preMarcan passion *narrative* but differ widely about how much of this scene was in it. Looking just at the problematic 14:57–59, we find that Pesch attributes it (and the whole Sanhedrin trial) to the preMarcan PN; Gnilka would have it added (along with 61–62) by an apocalyptically minded editor who worked over the preMarcan PN before it came to Mark; and Lührmann would have it added by Mark.

B. *Common Factors in the Gospels*

The history of theories and the diverse views just described (a diversity that is just the tip of the iceberg) give rise, in my judgment, to a few unexception-

---

[14]See M.–E. Boismard et al., *Synopse des Quatres Évangiles* (3 vols.; Paris: Cerf, 1972–77), 2.404–5. In favorably reporting this theory, Prete ("Formazione" 7) contends that v. 56 is secondary. Somewhat close to Benoit's results are the independent theories about the original account by Mohr (*Markus* 275: 14:53a,55–56,61b-64,65b) and L. Schenke (*Gekreuzigte* 26–46: 14:53a,55–56,60– 61,63–65).

[15]Schneider ("Gab"), who has done major studies on the PN and has his own approach, emerges closer to Benoit than to Donahue: Original were 61b–63a,64a; added were 57–59; possibly from Marcan redaction were 55–56,60–61a. Style factors often enter into the decisions. For instance, Donahue argues that 53b is Marcan, marked by *kai* parataxis and the use of "all." (Yet is *synerchesthai*, "to come together" particularly Marcan?) He considers 55 also Marcan, despite the fact that distinctly it does not use *kai* parataxis and uses *thanatoun* for destroying Jesus whereas in all previ-

able observations. No reconstruction of the preGospel history commands enough agreement to serve as a basis for an interpretation of the Marcan PN that would be reliably useful for a large number of readers. Therefore, it was entirely justifiable in the COMMENT to remain on the Gospel level of what the evangelist intended, despite the fact that one might be virtually certain that an earlier arrangement of the material existed. The whole passage 14:55–64 is Marcan in outlook, fitted carefully into Mark's overall theological schema. Though in this scene Mark used earlier material, whether traditions or consecutive narrative, *our best methods do not give us the ability to isolate confidently that material in its exact wording, assigning preMarcan verses and half-verses* from the existing, thoroughly Marcan account.

Once more, then, it may be more helpful to pay attention to what the evangelists have in common as a possible guide to what preceded them. The utility of such a method, of course, depends in part on the observation that John (and at rare times Luke) is so different from Mark that they probably drew on independent material and so agreement between them can be a key to the preGospel situation. Since Johannine independence of Mark is a key issue, a few words might be said about the argumentation that questions this in relation to the Jewish trial/interrogation of Jesus. Dauer ("Spuren" 3–7) gives a good illustration of an attempt to make John 10:22–38 dependent on the Synoptic Sanhedrin questioning. Actually Dauer thinks the dependency was already on the preJohannine level, but the thrust of the argumentation is applicable on the evangelist's level as well. He contends that in John's source there was a Sanhedrin trial of Jesus which was drawn from the Synoptic Sanhedrin trial. To see this, all one has to do is to recognize the equivalence between the Synoptic Sanhedrists and John's "the Jews"; between the Synoptic "They said, 'He is guilty, to be punished by death'" and John's "They took up stones to stone him" (John 10:31—or better, 11:53: "From that day they decided to put him to death"); and between the Synoptic Sanhedrin meeting hall and John's Temple courts. Dauer then goes on to speculate whether this Johannine Sanhedrin trial once stood where the interrogation by Annas now stands. Actually all that Dauer has done is to take scattered parallels between John and the Synoptics and create a Johannine scene; it is a classic exercise in *a posse ad esse:* moving from what could be to what was. Why even more logically could not one move in the other direction, and instead of Johannine disintegration of a scene suppose Marcan integrative creation of a scene from once scattered elements? One could supply a motive for Mark's integration: a more effective, unified presentation just before Je-

---

ous references (3:6; 11:18; 12:12; 14:1) the verbs have been *apollynai* and *kratein*. Dormeyer (*Passion* 299) regards 14:55 as the most primitive element in the Sanhedrin trial!

sus died. A motive for Johannine disintegration is harder to discern. That both Mark and John are drawing on preGospel elements is far easier to imagine.

The reader is reminded that already in the ANALYSIS of §19A features of sequence common to the Gospels were discussed, and remarks made here suppose that previous discussion. We shall begin with indisputable facts, and then turn to a possible explanation of those facts. *In the factual part,* however, as I speak of the four evangelists, I am making one supposition: The trial of Stephen in Acts 6:11–15; 7:1–2a; 7:54–60 is by deliberate Lucan intention a parallel to the trial of Jesus; and, both overtly (by quoting Stephen about Jesus) and more subtly, this parallelism has been fostered by moving some of what Luke found in the Marcan Sanhedrin trial to the Stephen scene. I have made this point again and again in the COMMENT (see also Hasler, "Jesu").

It was noted in §19B (p. 425 above) that all four Gospels[16] have a Sanhedrin session that dealt with Jesus. There is fourfold agreement that the charge that Jesus would cause the destruction of the sanctuary (Mark/Matt) or the holy place (John, Acts[17]) featured prominently in that session. According to John and Acts, Jesus was not present when this charge was made; according to Mark/Matt, he was. Yet in Mark/Matt the charge was made by others quoting him, and he never spoke in relation to that charge. Mark and Acts brand as false the charge that Jesus would destroy the sanctuary or holy place. In John the readers would understand as at least exaggerated the fear expressed by the Pharisees that Jesus will cause the Romans to act against "the place," because they have read in 2:19 what Jesus actually said about the destruction of the sanctuary (the Jews will destroy the sanctuary, i.e., his body). Only Matt looks on the sanctuary testimony as legal and seemingly true.[18] For all four writers the Sanhedrin session ended with a decision that Jesus had to be put to death.[19]

All four Gospels (during the ministry in John) have Jesus questioned by Jewish contemporaries about being the Messiah. In no Gospel did he deny this. His response was affirmative in Mark; qualifiedly affirmative in Matt; evasive through the use of conditional sentences in Luke and John. All four

[16]Is there logic in stressing the agreement of the four Gospels if one maintains, as I do, that Matt and Luke used Mark? Yes—because those two evangelists were certainly aware of Christian tradition before they began to use Mark as an overall guide in composing their Gospels and showed themselves perfectly capable of departing from the Marcan account where they had a different outlook.

[17]John 11:48 has *ho topos* as does Acts 6:14, while 6:13 has *ho topos ho agios.*

[18]In the COMMENT I contended that this was a deliberate theological change of Mark's difficult wording.

[19]The decision, absent from Luke 22:71, is present in Luke 24:20; Acts 13:27–28 (cf. Acts 4:10, addressed to the Sanhedrin). In Acts 6–7 Stephen is put to death for having testified about Jesus.

Gospels closely relate that question to the issue of whether he was the Son of God. On this issue Jesus spoke affirmatively in Mark, John (10:36), and Luke;[20] with a qualified affirmative in Matt.[21] All four Gospels contain a statement about the Son of Man that in some way adds a glorified dimension to the titles "Messiah" and "Son of God." (It should be remembered that John 1:51 is the denouement of a scene where Jesus has been hailed as the Messiah [1:41] and the Son of God [1:49].) All four writers describe a reaction of blasphemy to one or all of these titles applied to Jesus: in Mark/Matt to all three; in John (10:35–36) to the Son of God; in Acts to the Son of Man.[22]

All four Gospels have, after Jesus was arrested and before he was handed over to the Romans, a Jewish interrogation of Jesus. It was conducted by the high priest in Mark/Matt and John, at night while Peter was denying Jesus; in Luke it was by the Sanhedrists in the morning after the conclusion of Peter's denials. (In §19 where I discussed this, I contended that here Luke is secondarily reshuffling Mark and is not drawing on preGospel material.) All four Gospels have Jesus physically maltreated (slapped, beaten) in the night following his arrest. In Mark/Matt and John this took place at the end of the interrogation; in Luke before the interrogation that was secondarily shifted. In the three Synoptics the maltreatment was joined with the mockery of Jesus as a prophet; that is absent from John.

If one looks back at the last three paragraphs, there is an astounding amount of common material. The major difference is in arrangement. For Mark/Matt and (in part) Luke the material of all three paragraphs is joined in one scene; for John and (in part) Luke it is separate. How does one explain that? *I move now from facts to some proposals about preGospel arrangements*[23] that in my judgment best account for the facts listed. In what follows please note that I am speaking about a sequence of material before the Gospel writers rearranged it to fit their theological purposes. I am not proposing that what I describe is necessarily history, although at most times it would be closer to history than the Gospel rearrangements.[24]

---

[20]That is how I interpreted "You yourselves say that I am" in Luke 22:70.

[21]In the COMMENT I contended that this was a deliberate change from Mark by Matt 26:64 to show that Jesus was aware of the trap laid for him.

[22]In Acts 6:11,14 the words attributed to Stephen containing Jesus' assertions are said to be "blasphemous"; in 7:55–58 Stephen is stoned (a punishment for blasphemy) after he says that he has seen Jesus, the Son of Man, standing at the right of God.

[23]In all that follows, "preGospel" describes the era before the written Gospels, i.e., chiefly in the period from 30 to 60 when orally (and probably in writing) there were being formed the traditions that were reshaped and incorporated (with additions) by the evangelists in AD 60–100.

[24]Pesch (*Markus* 2.442–43), for whom the whole Marcan scene was taken virtually unchanged from the preMarcan PN, thinks that almost everything described therein occurred historically on the night before Jesus died!

Before the simplification attested in Mark[25] whereby Jesus' public career has been grouped neatly in two parts (everything in Galilee and its environs, until at the end of his life he comes for the first and only time to Jerusalem), more of Jesus' activities were described as taking place in Jerusalem (clear in John; hinted at in Luke 13:34). Even in the Marcan simplification early in the ministry scribes are said (3:22) to have come to Galilee from Jerusalem and expressed sharp hostility toward Jesus. Thus in the preGospel tradition Jesus did not come to Jerusalem at the end of his life as an unknown; he had some popularity among the Jerusalemites but was already disliked by the religious authorities there. Whether earlier or near the end, it was his preaching in the very Temple precincts, his actions there, including the cleansing of the Temple, and his speaking about its destruction that focused on him the hostility of the chief priests and their allies.

In the last period when Jesus was active in Jerusalem a Sanhedrin was called together to discuss what to do about him.[26] During this session the threat he presented to the Temple (sanctuary, holy place) was discussed.[27] This was probably not a courtroom trial in the technical sense of Jesus being present; but some "testified" to the kinds of things he said and stood for, and there was a decision that he should be put to death. There is never a suggestion in the Gospels that the Jewish authorities thought of executing him themselves; they are remembered only as planning to catch or arrest him without causing a disturbance. From the Gospel unanimity that eventually they gave Jesus over to the Roman governor, without a hint that this was a change of plan, we have every reason to believe that in the preGospel tradition this outcome was envisioned from the beginning. That this picture is not an implausibility can be seen from Josephus' description of how in the 60s (thus in the Gospel formation period) the leading citizens (= the elders) of Jerusalem dealt with Jesus son of Ananias when he threatened the destruction of Jerusalem and the sanctuary (*War* 6.3.5; #300–9). They arrested this Jesus and had him beaten; then the "rulers" (*archontes* or Sanhedrin leaders; see APPENDIX V, B6) brought him before the Roman governor.

[25]I am eschewing the issue of whether Mark himself made the simplification. Some or all of it may already have been done for preaching purposes, and Mark may simply have followed it in writing. I suspect the latter.

[26]John 11:47 describes a Sanhedrin meeting in this period. But before jumping to the conclusion that John gives us a historical reminiscence, one must note that John deliberately makes a sequence between Jesus' giving life to Lazarus and the Sanhedrin's decision to put Jesus to death. His arrangement is theological; yet that does not exclude the possibility of some history. Three times during this period (11:18; 12:18; 14:1) Mark portrays the authorities who would have taken part in a Sanhedrin session as having made up their minds against Jesus that he must be put to death. Are these echoes of the session that I am positing?

[27]In Christian memory, while Jesus did speak about the impending destruction of the Temple or its sanctuary, the way his words were presented or understood by the Jerusalem authorities was a distortion, even to the point of falsehood.

Besides the Temple sanctuary, Christian tradition reported two other important issues relevant to the last period of Jesus' life in Jerusalem. His opponents looked on him as blaspheming, i.e., acting and speaking in such an arrogant way that he infringed on the uniqueness of the God of Israel. This supplied a religious reason why he should be put to death.[28] Also the tradition portrayed Jesus being asked the question, "Are you the Messiah?" In the postresurrectional decades when the preGospel tradition was being formed, the issue of Jesus' identity was the great divider between the Jews who believed in Jesus and those who did not. Consequently in describing Jesus' answer to proposals that he was the Messiah, the tradition reflects Christian sensibilities caused by debates with nonbelievers. In particular, the "Messiah" title is often glossed by "Son of God," a formulation from Christian confessions. One finds unanimity that Jesus did not deny that he was the Messiah and unanimity that he affirmed that he was the Son of God; but affirmations about his being the Messiah vary to the extent to which the Son-of-God interpretation becomes dominant.[29] A form of the Messiah question and answer was presented in the tradition as leading to Jesus' death; for when combined with the Son-of-God (and Son-of-Man) evaluation it was looked on as blasphemous. There is no uniformity in the existing Gospels as to whether the Messiah/Son of God/blasphemy issue was formally part of the Sanhedrin session that decided to put Jesus to death or was part of the atmosphere that contributed to the felt need to call a Sanhedrin to deal with Jesus.

Finally, through the help of Judas, Jesus was seized in a secluded spot on the Mount of Olives and brought to the palace of the high priest. In the tradition it was remembered that Jesus' disciples did not accompany him to lend support in this dark hour, and indeed in the aftermath of the arrest Peter denied him. (The various evangelists have in different ways dramatized this by bringing such behavior into contrast with Jesus' own stance.) Thus in the tradition Jesus was a solitary figure throughout the rest of his passion, and there is a memory that he was beaten by those who now had charge of him (see the parallel in the Jesus son of Ananias account above). During this period after his arrest he was interrogated by the high priest,[30] preparatory

---

[28]The tradition does not quote but assumes an interpretation of the law of Lev 24:16 about putting to death one who blasphemes (and not only one who names the Name).

[29]This is an inadequately brief description of a more complicated situation; see the greater detail in §21 above, which spells out the difference between the historical situation of Jesus' ministry and the preGospel tradition that is being discussed here.

[30]Caiaphas according to Matt 26:57; Annas according to John 18:13,19; perhaps both were remembered in the tradition (Luke 3:2; Acts 4:6 mentions them together). In the COMMENT I expressed my distrust of any restructuring of John 18 whereby on a preGospel level Caiaphas would have done the questioning. The reason Caiaphas is mentioned by John in 18 is to remind the reader that he was the high priest who presided over the Sanhedrin that decided on Jesus' death (11:49). Quite wrong,

to his being given over to the Romans. Whether or not in the preGospel tradition other Sanhedrin members were present is not clear;[31] but there is unanimity that some of them joined the high priest in the morning, taking Jesus to Pilate in order to press the Roman governor to put Jesus to death.

The problems that have been seen in the Gospel accounts of this interrogation (and that give rise to the various theories of composition described above) become more intelligible if we recognize how the individual evangelists have reshaped the preGospel tradition. John has kept his description of the interrogation simple; but the wording of the questioning (about his disciples and his teaching) may well reflect the investigations of followers of Jesus in the synagogue, investigations that were a vivid memory of the Johannine community. Mark, followed by Matt and (in part) by Luke, has combined with the interrogation echoes of the Sanhedrin session that had taken place earlier and had decided on the death of Jesus, thus causing his arrest. That combination caused the following awkwardnesses: A main topic of that earlier session, the Temple sanctuary issue, now occurs here but in a strangely third-person fashion—spoken about Jesus but not answered by him.[32] While from the beginning of the interrogation there is already a decision that Jesus must be convicted, the Sanhedrists are asked to make up their minds at the end, with the resultant impression of playacting. The Messiah/Son of God/blasphemy issues appear as the substance of the interrogation; yet they do not seem to function among the charges against Jesus brought forward by the Sanhedrists in the Roman trial that follows. (The one possible exception is if "the Messiah" is brought over to the Roman trial as "the King of the Jews";[33] in which case the Johannine and Lucan accounts may be closer to the preGospel tradition by keeping "Messiah" distinct from "Son of God" and from blasphemy.) There is a death decision at the end, but then Jesus is handed over to the Romans.

I have pointed out awkwardnesses that were created by the pulling to-

---

in my judgment, are theories that the reference to Caiaphas in 18 shows John's knowledge of or dependence on the Marcan tradition of a Sanhedrin session on the night of Jesus' arrest. Mark does not refer to Caiaphas; John never mentions the Sanhedrin on this night.

[31]In John 18:19–24 they are not; but John likes one-to-one confrontations, so that could be by omission. In the "they" who take Jesus to Pilate after the night arrest and interrogation (18:28) are the chief priests and the nation (18:35), so there is an aura of an official delegation.

[32]Luke knew of this Temple sanctuary issue from Mark but moved it to Acts (the Stephen trial). Was he aware that in the preGospel tradition this did not occur on the night of the arrest? He preserves from the tradition a form of the Messiah question and answer similar to that known by John, and so he may also have been aware of another setting for the Sanhedrin discussion of Jesus and the Temple.

[33]It is tempting to speculate that Jesus' claim to be the Messiah was an issue in the postarrest interrogation, as the high priest sought for material that could make an impression on Pilate. Yet both the Johannine and Synoptic accounts of the interrogation are so overlaid by later theology that it is very difficult to detect *common preGospel tradition* about the subject of the interrogation.

gether of incidents that were separate in the tradition. Why did Mark (or his immediate predecessor) do this? Again I would see this as simplification that served kerygmatic purposes and is the hallmark of Mark's Gospel. If there were in the tradition three or four separate items in the overall Jewish proceedings against Jesus (a Sanhedrin session with the decision to get rid of him, questioning about being the Messiah, a charge of blasphemy, and an interrogation by the high priest after the arrest), are they not all connected? Why not present them forcefully as one dramatic scene where the interaction of motives and decisions can be easily understood? Is what (in my suggestion) was done here much different from Mark's narrating once separated conflict stories all together, joining events that were isolated in the tradition to make one dramatic day at the beginning of the ministry, or collecting parables into a unit? The clarity and force of the unified trial presentation has moved and been remembered by hundreds of millions; the awkwardnesses have bothered a handful of scholars subjecting the narrative to microscopic examination.

(Bibliography for this section may be found in §17, particularly Part 1.)

CONTENTS OF ACT II, SCENE TWO

§25. SECTIONAL BIBLIOGRAPHY
for Scene Two of Act II
Jewish Mockery, Peter's Denials, Judas' Suicide (§§26–29)

This bibliography deals with three episodes that occur in the context of the Jewish trial/interrogation of Jesus; respectively they will be commented on in §§26, 27, 29. Part 1 treats the Jewish abuse and mockery of Jesus that is an adjunct of the questioning of Jesus. Part 2 contains writings on the three denials of Jesus by Peter. Part 3 concentrates on the peculiarly Matthean scene of Judas and the price of innocent blood. Some of these episodes are also treated in works that discuss the whole Jewish trial, already listed in §17, Part 1, above.

Part 1: The Jewish Abuse and Mockery of Jesus (§26)
(Bibliography on the Roman mockery and abuse of Jesus is found in §30, Part 6; comparative treatments of both mockeries are listed here.)

Benoit, P., "Les outrages à Jésus Prophète (Mc xiv 65 par.)," in *Neotestamentica et Patristica* (O. Cullmann Festschrift; NovTSup 6; Leiden: Brill, 1962), 92–110. Reprinted in BExT 3.251–69.

Flusser, D., "Who Is It That Struck You?" *Immanuel* 20 (1986), 27–32.

Gundry, R. H., "*LMṬLYM.* 1QIsaiah[a] 50,6 and Mark 14,65," RevQ 2 (1960), 559–67.

Miller, D. L., "*Empaizein:* Playing the Mock Game (Luke 22:63–64)," JBL 90 (1971), 309–13.

Neirynck, F., "*Tis estin ho paisas se?* Mt 26,28/Lk 22,64 (diff. Mk 14,65)," ETL 63 (1987), 5–47. Reprinted in NEv 2.95–138.

Rudberg, G., "Die Verhöhnung Jesu vor dem Hohenpriester," ZNW 24 (1925), 307–9.

Schmidt, K. L., "*Iēsous Christos kolaphizomenos* und die 'colaphisation' der Juden," in *Aux sources de la tradition chrétienne* (Mélanges Goguel; Neuchatel: Delachaux & Niestlé, 1950), 218–27.

Soards, M. L., "A Literary Analysis of the Origin and Purpose of Luke's Account of the Mockery of Jesus," BZ 31 (1987), 110–16.

van Unnik, W. C., "Jesu Verhöhnung vor dem Synedrium (Mc 14,65 par.)," ZNW 29 (1930), 310–11. Reprinted in his *Sparsa collecta I* (NovTSup 29; Leiden: Brill, 1973), 3–5.

Part 2: The Three Denials of Jesus by Peter (§27)
(Frequently the denials are treated along with Jesus' predictions of the denials, which were commented on in §5; but all the bibliography pertinent to the denials has been kept till here.)

Balagué, M., "Las negaciones de San Pedro," CB 8 (1951), 79–82.

Boomershine, T. E., "Peter's Denial as Polemic or Confession: The Implications of Media Criticism for Biblical Hermeneutics," *Semeia* 39 (1987), 47–68.

Boyd, W. J. P., "Peter's Denial—Mark xiv.68, Luke xxii.57," ExpTim 67 (1955–56), 341.

Brady, D., "The Alarm to Peter in Mark's Gospel," JSNT 4 (1979), 42–57.

Brunet, G., "Et aussitôt le coq chanta," CCER 27 (108; 1979), 9–12.

Buchanan, G. W., "Mark xiv.54," ExpTim 68 (1956–57), 27.

Dassmann, E., "Die Szene Christus-Petrus mit dem Hahn. Zum Verhältnis vom Komposition und Interpretation auf frühchristlichen Sarkophagen," in *Pietas,* eds. E. Dassmann and K. S. Frank (B. Kötting Festschrift; Münster: Aschendorff, 1980), 509–27.

Derrett, J. D. M., "The Reason for the Cock-crowings," NTS 29 (1983), 142–44. Reprinted in DSNT 4.129–31.

Dewey, K. E., "Peter's Curse and Cursed Power (Mark 14:53–54,66–72)," in PMK 96–114.

———, "Peter's Denial Reexamined: John's Knowledge of Mark's Gospel," SBLSP 1979, 1.109–12.

Drum, W., "The Disciple Known to the High Priest," ExpTim 25 (1913–14), 381–82.

Ernst, J., "Noch einmal: Die Verleugnung Jesu durch Petrus (Mc 14,54.66–72)," *Catholica* 30 (1976), 207–26.

Evans, C. A., " 'Peter Warming Himself': The Problem of an Editorial 'Seam,' " JBL 101 (1982), 245–49.

Gardiner, W. D., "The Denial of St. Peter," ExpTim 26 (1914–15), 424–26.

Gewalt, D., "Die Verleugnung des Petrus," LB 43 (1978), 113–44.

Goguel, M., "Did Peter Deny his Lord? A Conjecture," HTR 25 (1932), 1–27.

Guyot, G. H., "Peter Denies His Lord," CBQ 4 (1942), 111–18.

Herron, R. W., Jr., *Mark's Account of Peter's Denial of Jesus: A History of Its Interpretation* (Lanham, MD: University Press of America, 1992).

Hunter, J., "Three Versions of Peter's Denial," *Hudson Review* 33 (1980), 39–57.

Klein, G(ünther), "Die Verleugnung des Petrus," ZTK 58 (1961), 285–328. Reprinted in his *Rekonstruktion und Interpretation. Gesammelte Aufsätze* (Beiträge zur evangelischen Theologie 50; Munich: Kaiser, 1969), 49–98.

Kosmala, H., "The Time of the Cock-Crow," ASTI 2 (1963), 118–20; "The Time of the Cock-Crow (II)," ASTI 6 (1967–68), 132–34.

Kosnetter, J., "Zur Geschichtlichkeit der Verleugnung Petri," in *Dienst an der Lehre* (Cardinal F. König Festschrift; Wiener Beiträge zur Theologie 10; Vienna: Herder, 1965), 127–43.

Krauss, S., "La défense d'élever du menu bétail en Palestine et questions connexes," REJ 53 (1907), 14–55, esp. 28–37 in ref. to Mark 14:72.

Lampe, G. W. H., "St. Peter's Denial," BJRL 55 (1972–73), 346–68.

Lattey, C., "A Note on Cockcrow," *Scripture* 6 (1953–54), 53–55.

LaVerdiere, E., "Peter Broke Down and Began to Cry," *Emmanuel* 92 (1986), 70–73.

Lee, G. M., "St. Mark xiv.72: *epibalōn eklaien,*" ExpTim 61 (1949–50), 160.

———, "Mark 14,72: *epibalōn eklaien,*" *Biblica* 53 (1972), 411–12.

Lehmann, M., *Synoptischen Quellenanalyse und die Frage nach den historische Jesus* (BZNW 38; Berlin: de Gruyter, 1970), 106–12 on Luke 22:31–34, 54b–62.

Linnemann, E., "Die Verleugnung des Petrus," ZTK 63 (1966), 1–32. See also her *Studien* 70–108.

McEleney, N. J., "Peter's Denials—How Many? To Whom?" CBQ 52 (1990), 467–72.

Masson, C., "Le reniement de Pierre. Quelques aspects de la formation d'une tradition," RHPR 37 (1957), 24–35.

Mayo, C. H., "St Peter's Token of the Cock Crow," JTS 22 (1921), 367–70.

Menestrina, G., "Nota: *katathema, katathemazein,*" BeO 21 (1979), 12 (in ref. to Matt 26:74).

Merkel, H., "Peter's Curse," TJCSM, 66–71.

Murray, G., "Saint Peter's Denials," DRev 103 (1985), 296–98.

Neirynck, F., "The 'Other Disciple' in Jn 18,15–16," ETL 51 (1975), 113–41. Reprinted in NEv 1.335–64.

Pesch, R., "Die Verleugnung des Petrus," in *Neues Testament und Kirche,* ed. J. Gnilka (R. Schnackenburg Festschrift; Freiburg: Herder, 1974), 42–62.

Politi, J., "'Not (Not I),'" *Literature & Theology* 6 (1992), 345–55.

Ramsay, W. M., "The Denials of Peter," ExpTim 27 (1915–16), 296–301, 360–63, 410–13, 471–72, 540–42; 28 (1916–17), 276–81.

Riesenfeld, H., "The meaning of the verb *arneisthai,*" ConNT 11 (In honorem A. Fridrichsen; 1947), 207–19, esp. 213–14.

Rothenaicher, F., "Zu Mk 14,70 und Mt 26,73," BZ 23 (1935–36), 192–93.

Schneider, G., "'Stärke deine Brüder!' (Lk 22,32). Die Aufgabe des Petrus nach Lukas," *Catholica* 30 (1976), 200–6.

Seitz, O. J. F., "Peter's 'Profanity'. Mark 14,71 in the Light of Matthew 16,22," StEv I, 516–19.

Smith, P. V., "St. Peter's Threefold Denial of our Lord," *Theology* 17 (1928), 341–48.

Soards, M. L., "'And the Lord Turned and Looked Straight at Peter': Understanding Luke 22,61," *Biblica* 67 (1986), 518–19.

Thomson, J. R., "Saint Peter's Denials," ExpTim 47 (1935–36), 381–82.

Tindall, E. A., "John xviii.15," ExpTim 28 (1916–17), 283–84.

Walter, N., "Die Verleugnung des Petrus," TV–VIII (1977), 45–61.

Wenham, J. W., "How Many Cock Crowings? The Problem of Harmonistic Text-Variants," NTS 25 (1978–79), 523–25.

Wilcox, M., "The Denial-Sequence in Mark xiv.26–31,66–72," NTS 17 (1970–71), 426–36.

Part 3: Judas' Suicide and the Price of Innocent Blood: Matt 27:3–10 (§29)
(This bibliography contains treatments of the Matthean account of Judas' death, sometimes in comparison to the different description of his death in Acts 1:15–26.

Writings dealing more broadly with Judas are found in the bibliography of APPEN-DIX IV.)

Bauer, J. B., "Judas' Shicksal und Selbstmord," BibLit 20 (1952–53), 210–13.

Benoit, P., "The Death of Judas," BJG 1.189–207. French orig. in *Synoptische Studien* (A. Wikenhauser Festschrift; Munich: Zink, 1953), 1–19.

Bernard, J. H., "The Death of Judas," *Expositor* 6th Ser.; 9 (1904), 422–30.

Colella, P., "Trenta denarii," RivB 21 (1973), 325–27.

Conard, A., "The Fate of Judas: Matthew 27:3–10," TJT 7 (1991), 158–68.

Desautels, L., "La mort de Judas (*Mt* 27,3–10; *Ac* 1,15–26)," ScEsp 38 (1986), 221–39.

Escande, J., "Judas et Pilate prisonniers d'une même structure (Mt 27,1–26)," FV 78 (3; June 1979), 92–100.

Follet, R., "'Constituerunt ei trigenta argenteos' (ad Mt 26,15)," VD 29 (1951), 98–100.

Harris, J. R., "Did Judas Really Commit Suicide?" AJT 4 (1900), 490–513.

Hatch, H. R., "The Old Testament Quotation in Matthew xxvii. 9,10," BW NS 1 (1893), 345–54.

Hill, G. F., "The Thirty Pieces of Silver," *Archaeologia* 59, part 2 (or Series 2, 9 [1905]), 235–54.

Jervell, J., "Jesu blods aker. Matt. 27,3–10," NorTT 69 (1968), 158–62.

Lake, K., "The Death of Judas," in *The Beginnings of Christianity, Part I: The Acts of the Apostles,* eds. F. J. Foakes Jackson and K. Lake (5 vols.; London, 1920–1933), 5.22–30.

Luke, K., "The Thirty Pieces of Silver," *Indian Theological Studies* 19 (1982), 15–32.

Menken, M. J. J., "The References to Jeremiah in the Gospel according to Matthew (Mt 2,17; 16,14; 27,9)," ETL 60 (1984), 5–24.

Moeser, A. G., "The Death of Judas," TBT 30 (1992), 145–51.

Moo, D. J., "Tradition and Old Testament in Matt. 27:3–10," in *Gospel Perspectives III,* eds. R. T. France and D. Wenham (Sheffield Univ., 1983), 157–75.

Munro, J. I., "The Death of Judas (Matt. xxvii.3–8; Acts i.18–19)," ExpTim 24 (1912–13), 235–36.

Murmelstein, B., "Die Gestalt Josefs in der Agada und die Evangeliengeschichte [Matt 27:3; John 19:23]," *Angelos* 4 (1932), 51–55.

Niedner, F. A., "The Role of Judas in Matthew's Economy of Forgiveness," SBLA (1989), S156, pp. 176–77.

Quesnel, M., "Les citations de Jérémie dans l'évangile selon saint Matthieu," EstBib 47 (1989), 513–27 (in ref. to Matt 27:9–10).

Reiner, E., "Thirty Pieces of Silver," in *Essays in Memory of E. A. Speiser,* ed. W. W. Hallo (New Haven: American Oriental Society, 1968), 186–90.

Schwarz, W., "Die Doppeldeutung des Judastodes," BibLit 57 (1984), 227–33.

Senior, D., "A Case Study in Matthean Creativity: Matthew 27:3–10," BR 19 (1974), 23–36.

———, "The Fate of the Betrayer. A Redactional Study of Matthew xxvii, 3–10," ETL 48 (1972), 372–426. Also in SPNM 343–97.

Sparks, H. F. D., "St. Matthew's References to Jeremiah," JTS NS 1 (1950), 155–56.

Sutcliffe, E. F., "Matthew 27,9," JTS NS 3 (1952), 227–28.

Torrey, C. C., "The Foundry of the Second Temple at Jerusalem," JBL 55 (1936), 247–60 (in ref. to Matt 27:5).

Upton, J. A., "The Potter's Field and the Death of Judas," *Concordia Journal* 8 (1982), 213–19.

Vaccari, A., "Le versioni arabe dei Profeti," *Biblica* 3 (1922), 401–23, esp. 420–23 in ref. to Matt 27:9–10.

van Tilborg, S., "Matthew 27:3–10: an Intertextual Reading," in *Intertextuality in Biblical Writings* (B. van Iersel Festschrift; Kampen: Kok, 1989), 159–74.

van Unnik, W. C., "The Death of Judas in St. Matthew's Gospel," ATR Supp. Ser. 3 (March 1974), 44–57.

§26. THE JEWISH ABUSE AND MOCKERY OF JESUS

(Mark 14:65; Matt 26:67–68; Luke 22:63–65; John 18:22–23)

Translation

Mark 14:65: And some began to spit on him, and to cover his face and strike him and say to him, "Prophesy"; and the attendants got him with slaps.

Matt 26:67–68: 67Then they spat in his face and struck him. But there were those who slapped him 68saying, "Prophesy for us, Messiah, who is it that hit you?"

Luke 22:63–65: 63And the men who were holding him were mocking him, beating him; 64and having covered him, they were questioning him saying, "Prophesy, who is it that hit you?" 65And blaspheming, they were saying many other things against him.

John 18:22–23: 22 . . . one of the attendants who was standing by gave Jesus a slap, saying, "In such a way do you answer the high priest?" 23Jesus answered him, "If I have spoken badly, give testimony about what is bad. If (I have spoken) well, why do you beat me?"

COMMENT

This scene, narrated by John before the sending of Jesus to Caiaphas and by Luke before the Sanhedrin investigation, follows in Mark/Matt immediately on the judgment by the Sanhedrists that Jesus is guilty, punishable by death. Accordingly there was a strong temptation to entitle it "Sanhedrin Proceedings, Part Five"—and for Mark/Matt that is what this episode is. Nevertheless, partly from a desire to do justice to Luke and John as well, I chose a title that would draw the readers' attention in advance to the parallel "Roman Mockery and Abuse of Jesus" (§36 below[1]) that will immediately follow the

---

[1]Notice that in the two titles the sequence of the two nouns differs; that sequence reflects the proportionate space given to mockery and abuse in the respective scenes.

Roman trial and condemnation. The mockery here concerns Jesus as a (false) prophet; the mockery there will concern Jesus as a (false) King of the Jews. In addition to the parallelism between these two mockeries, scholars bring into this discussion the Synoptic accounts of the mockery of Jesus on the cross and the Lucan account of a mockery by Herod. (*GPet* has no Roman trial of Jesus, and so it transfers to the aftermath of a trial by Herod the mockery that the canonical Gospels associate with the Romans.) Some of these mockeries echo the abuse heaped on the Suffering Servant in Isa 50 and 53, and to an extent the treatment of the suffering just one in Ps. 22. I supply in an accompanying table comparisons of all these mockeries; only after a discussion of the comparisons will there be a subsection devoted to commenting separately on each Gospel report of the mockery associated with the Jewish trial.

COMPARISONS PROVOKED BY THE GOSPEL ACCOUNTS
OF THE JEWISH MOCKERY

Comparisons between the Jewish and Roman Scenes of Abuse/Mockery. Only Mark/Matt have the elaborate parallel sequence in which both Jewish and Roman trials conclude with a scene wherein Jesus is abused as mocking words of evaluation are addressed to him (respectively, "prophet" and "the King of the Jews"). Obviously there is deliberate (Marcan) structuring in this parallel. Even though in Mark/Matt the Jewish and Roman abuse/mockery of Jesus have only one detail in common (spitting), relatively few scholars (e.g., Goguel!) accept the historicity of both, and some deny both. The most common position is that one was fashioned in imitation of the other, usually the Jewish in imitation of the Roman (Winter, Gnilka, etc.), without much commitment about the historicity of the more original. Sometimes Luke and John are invoked as evidence for this theory, but that cannot be done so easily. Luke's portrayal is complicated. He has a Jewish abuse and mockery of Jesus before the Sanhedrin trial, a brief mockery by Herod and his troops in the course of the Roman trial, and finally a mockery of Jesus by soldiers (implicitly Roman) not at the end of the Roman trial but while Jesus hangs on the cross. John has a Jewish abuse (no mockery) of Jesus at the end of the high priest's interrogation, and a Roman mockery and abuse in the middle of the Roman trial.[2] In summation, then, the four Gospels, immediately before or after the Jewish trial/interrogation, have a Jewish abuse of Jesus (plus mockery of him as a prophet in the Synoptics). All four,

[2]Bertram and Loisy are among those who would posit that John drew his account of the Jewish abuse from Mark; Hahn would see Mark's account of the Jewish abuse and mockery as a developed pendant of John's brief reference to abuse. Yet Mark and John agree only on the slapping.

TABLE 2. COMPARING THE VOCABULARIES OF THE VARIOUS ACCOUNTS OF MOCKERY/ABUSE

Vocabulary employed in describing mocking and abuse (Greek and my translation) grouped thematically	I Servant in Isa 50; 53	II Third Passion Prediction Mark 10:33–34 Matt 20:18–19 Luke 18:31b–33	III Context of Jewish Trial Mark 14:64–65 Matt 26:65–68 Luke 22:63–65 John 18:22	IV Herod Trial Luke 23:11 GPet 4:13–14	V Context of Roman Trial Mark 15:15b–20a Matt 27:26b–31a John 19:1–3	VI On the Cross Mark 15:29–32 Matt 27:39–44 Luke 23:35b–39 GPet 4:13–14	COMMENTS
#1. *blasphēmein, blasphēmia:* blaspheme, blasphemy			Mark/Matt* Luke**			Mark/Matt** Luke**	* = Jesus accused of blasphemy (also John 10:33–36—a parallel to III); ** = Jesus is blasphemed against
#2a. *empaizein:* mock		Mark/Matt Luke	Luke	Luke	Mark/Matt	Mark/Matt Luke	
#2b. *ekmyktērizein:* sneer at						Luke	Ps 22:7: Forsaken psalmist is sneered at; In NT elsewhere only Luke 16:14: Pharisees sneer at Jesus
#2c. *oneidizein:* revile				GPet		Mark/Matt	Ps 22:7: Psalmist is object of reviling; Matt 5:11: "Blessed . . . when they revile you"
#2d. *hybrizein:* arrogantly mistreat		Luke					
#2e. *exouthenein:* disdain, treat with contempt or as nothing				Luke			Biform *exoudenein* in Aquila Greek of Isa 53; Ps 22:7: Psalmist is object of contempt; Mark 9:12: "The Son of Man must . . . be treated with contempt"
#3a. *trechein:* push (running)				GPet			
#3b. *syrein:* drag				GPet			
#4a. *phragelloun:* flog					Mark/Matt		

	I	II	III	IV	V	VI	COMMENTS
#4b. *mastigoun, mastizein, mastix*: scourge	✓	Mark/Matt Luke		*GPet*	John		✓ = Presence of word in Isa 50; 53
#4c. *paideia, paideuein*: chastisement, chastise (whip)	✓						Luke 23:16,22: Pilate offers to chastise Jesus
#5a. *derein*: beat			Luke John				Servants in vineyard parable (Mark 12:3,5 and par.); in synagogues (Mark 13:9)
#5b. *paiein*: hit			Matt Luke				Mark 14:27: bystanders hit servant of high priest
#5c. *typtein*: strike					Mark/Matt		
#5d. *kolaphizein*: strike			Mark/Matt				
#5e. *nyssein*: prick, stab, jab				*GPet*		John	*GPet* with a reed; John with a lance Ps 22:17: *oryssein* for piercing hands and feet
#5f. *rapisma, rapizein*: slap	✓		Mark/Matt John	*GPet*	John		
#5g. *emptyein, emptysma*: spit	✓	Mark Luke	Mark/Matt	*GPet*	Mark/Matt		
#6a. *kephalē*: head (of Jesus)	✓			*GPet*	Mark/Matt	Mark/Matt	Mark/Matt head struck; Matt, John, *GPet* thorn-crown on head; Matt inscription over head
#6b. *opsis*: face				*GPet* (spit)			
#6c. *prosōpon*: face	✓		Mark (cover) Matt (spit)				
#6d. *siagōn*: cheek	✓			*GPet* (slap)			

during or after the Roman trial, have mockery of him as "the King of the Jews" by Roman soldiers (plus abuse of him by Roman soldiers in Mark, Matt, and John). A *superficial* impression would be that the common elements in the tradition were a Jewish abuse and a Roman mockery and that the combinations resulted from assimilating the one to the other. We shall have to test that.

Comparison of the Differing Gospel Accounts of the Jewish Scene. A spate of variant textual readings in the ancient Greek mss. and in the versions shows that the scribes of that period were already troubled by the Gospel differences. In the Greek underlying my translation, for instance, Mark has "spit on him" and "cover his face," while Matt has "spat in his face." But Codex Bezae and some versions (OL Vercellensis, Syriac peshitta, Bohairic) read "spit in his face" in Mark, omitting the covering; and Codex Koridethi and some minuscules combine the two readings into "spit in his face and cover his face"! The Codex Koridethi reading of what is said to Jesus in Mark includes "Who is it that hit you?" in agreement with Matt and Luke. There are other examples of what would normally be recognized as attempts to harmonize. Yet serious modern scholars argue that unless one accepts these rather poorly attested readings of Mark, one cannot explain Matt and Luke as dependent on Mark. Others accept the Synoptic readings that are better attested (my translation follows the judgment of the Nestle-Aland Greek NT, 26th ed.) but, at least in this instance, give up the thesis of Matthean and Lucan dependence on Mark and emerge with the most diverse theories. BHST (271), for instance, dismembers Luke thus: 22:63 from a Lucan source; 22:64 composite from Mark *and Matt;* 22:65 Lucan redaction. Benoit ("Outrages" 102–6) in a very complicated theory makes Luke more original than Mark or Matt. (See §19, n. 28 above.) Mark for him would be composed of three traditions: The first (spitting at him) reflects Isa 50:6, which is absent from Luke; the second ("Prophesy") is a secondary form of Luke; the third (attendants getting him with slaps) is a secondary form of John. As for Matt, 26:67 is borrowed from Mark, while 26:68 is borrowed from Luke or a common source. Flusser ("Who"), confusingly mixing the historical and Gospel levels, gives preference to Luke because it makes better sense historically (and spares the Sanhedrists). The idea that the better Lucan order is the product of Luke's professed purpose to establish order and comes from tampering with Mark is not adequately dealt with. Mark for Flusser becomes a rather confused and bungling rewrite of Luke. Yet on the level of the Gospels as theological documents, as we shall see below, Mark makes very good sense.

Normally I have been leaving complicated compositional discussions to a brief treatment in the ANALYSIS on the principle that a commentary should comment on what exists and not on what might have been. Yet since here the compositional theories affect the very text (particularly of Mark) on which one needs to comment, it seems wiser to discuss compositional issues as I treat each evangelist. They will also give me a chance to highlight the message each evangelist wishes to convey. To avoid suspense, the approach here is consistent with the compositional approach taken in the rest of this volume: Matt and Luke can be explained as dependent on Mark if recognition is given to the fact that in certain well-remembered phrases, oral tradition perdured. Mark's account is the oldest of the three but still theological and far from simply historical.

THE MARCAN ACCOUNT

While (when one has looked at Matt) one can see that there are certain awkwardnesses in Mark, the basic text I have translated makes good narrative sense. For instance, despite nit-picking cavils, it is easy to surmise that the reason for covering Jesus' face is because the challenge to "Prophesy" has to do with guessing who struck him—even without the background of a well-known game that shall be explained below. True, commentators, horrified that Mark's "some" seems to refer to the Sanhedrists who have just condemned him, express doubt that distinguished Jewish figures would have acted so callously. That is to confuse historical issues with the intended thrust of a Gospel narrative that has had a hostile view of the chief priests, scribes, and elders from the start. The Marcan Sanhedrists have been seeking Jesus' death for several chapters: They formulated plans to seize him by stealth lest there be a riot among the people; they bought the services of Judas who would give him over; they sent a crowd with swords and clubs against him; they sought testimony against him, listening to patently false testimony that did not agree. That they would now express their contempt for Jesus in a dramatic gesture harmonious with the high priest's tearing his garments is not surprising.[3] Indeed, the only surprise is that Mark would speak of "some" instead of his usual "all." Incidentally, this storyline militates against the theory of those who wish to exculpate the Sanhedrists by arguing that Mark's "some" refers not to them but to the attendants mentioned at the end of the verse (see Blinzler, *Prozess* 164; K. L. Schmidt, *"Iēsous"* 218). That suggestion runs against the grammar, the thought pattern, and the Matthean interpretation as well.

The "began to" is typically Marcan style (some twenty-six times) and

---

[3]In the (*Martyrdom and*) *Ascension of Isaiah* 5:1–2 after Isaiah has been sentenced to death, the false prophets who accused him mock him.

effectively combines this with what has preceded. Probably the main impression of the action of spitting is contempt (Job 30:9–10), and it is the only action of mockery/abuse from this scene that will be shared with the Marcan account of the Roman mockery/abuse of Jesus (15:19). Nevertheless in the OT, spitting in the face is also a punishment for the guilty, e.g., administered by the father to a daughter who has done something wrong (Num 12:14) or by the aggrieved widow to a brother-in-law who refuses levirate marriage (Deut 25:9). Theoretically one might even invoke the Qumran interpretation of Deut 21:23 (11Q *Miqdaš* [Temple Scroll] 64:7–13) wherein the hanged (crucified) is to be cursed by God *and by human beings* in support of the thesis that it was *a duty* for the Sanhedrists to express contempt for this criminal condemned to death (on the cross). Mark 14:63–64; Matt 26:65; and Luke 22:71 make the Sanhedrists witnesses/testifiers to the guilt of Jesus; and Deut 17:7 would have the witnesses the first to be involved in the execution of the guilty. I doubt, however, that Mark's readers would have had such knowledge and that we should invoke it in interpreting what Mark means. Yet the fact that the spitting follows the conviction and is done by those who condemned Jesus moves it from the realm of random abuse to a connection with expressing outrage for one judged guilty of blasphemy, even if Mark's readers would suspect that the outrage, like the tearing of the garments, was theatrical.[4]

Exotic and complicated comments have been evoked by the next action of covering Jesus' face. Was it to make him look like a pagan temple diviner and thus explain the challenge to prophesy? (Wellhausen mentions the Arab *kâhin*.) Was Mark's description a botched derivation from Luke's "covered him," since the verb *perikalyptein* normally involves covering large objects?[5] Yet the verb may refer to covering only the head in Codex Alexandrinus of I Sam 28:8 [since other garments are mentioned], and it is related to *kalymma*, a word for "face veil." The absence of a comparable expression in Matt has convinced many scholars[6] that this phrase was absent from Mark. When I discuss the Matthean account, I shall offer arguments to the contrary (see also Blinzler, *Prozess* 164–65).

There is a good possibility, in my judgment, that the Marcan phrase about covering the face is quite intelligible in light of a game that would have been known to the readers. A series of articles by Rudberg, van Unnik, and D. L.

---

[4]If one were to discuss this on the level of history, a point made by Pesch (*Markus* 2.441) is interesting: According to the Law the Sanhedrists had a duty to stone this man found guilty of blasphemy. Under Roman rule seemingly that power of execution was denied them, and so this is an "ersatz" punishment fulfilling their duty.

[5]E.g., the ark of the covenant in Heb 9:4, or the ephod (how big was that?) in the LXX of Exod 28:20; see also Josephus, *War* 2.8.9; #148.

[6]Benoit, Catchpole, Gundry, Hauck, Kilpatrick, Schneider, Senior, Streeter, Tucker, Taylor, etc.

Miller have thrown light on the ancient background; and Flusser ("Who") mentions modern parallels. The 2d-cent.-BC *Onomasticon* of Pollux (a dictionary of synonyms arranged according to subject matter) mentions three games involving covered or blindfolded eyes: (1) In 9:113 *myinda* or blind tag, where a player shuts his eyes and searches for others to tag or touch them. The verb *manteuesthai,* "to divine, prophesy," is used in this context, so that an element in the game was the ability to detect without seeing. (2) In 9.129 *kollabismos* or guessing game, where a player covers his eyes with his hand, so that when another slaps him, he has to guess which hand was used. Van Unnik cites this as a parallel for what Mark describes. (3) In 9.123 *chalkē myia* or "blindman's buff," where a player is blindfolded and tries to find others while being hit with husks of papyrus. This last, which Miller (*"Empaizein"*) suggests for the background of the present scene, could grow quite nasty at times, depending on the severity of the blows. Mark uses *kolaphizein,* which can run the range from a light cuff to a beating (I Cor 4:11; I Pet 2:20–21—the latter connects it with the sufferings of Christ, and so it may have been set passion vocabulary).[7]

Although a few scholars (Hauck, Wellhausen) have thought the purpose of the scene was to warn Jesus not to prophesy anymore, the analogy of the game makes it clear that we have here a burlesque of his ability to prophesy (Dibelius, Juel, Klostermann, Loisy, Taylor). Two prophecies were narrated in the trial: that Jesus would destroy the sanctuary and within three days build another, and that an aspect of his being the Son of God would involve the Sanhedrists seeing him seated at the right hand of the Power and coming on the clouds of heaven. Although he can prophesy such marvelous things, has he even the ability of prophesying demanded by a child's game? Miller (*"Empaizein"* 313) is correct in insisting that in dealing with Jesus, the child's game has become quite adult.

The mocking attitude manifests indignation at the audacity of Jesus' pretensions. We are not too far, then, from the atmosphere of I Kings 22, the scene with the prophet Micaiah ben Imlah, already invoked as a parallel to Matt's having Jesus put under oath (in 22:16 King Ahab of Israel put Micaiah under oath to tell the truth). Micaiah predicted that lying prophets would mislead Ahab to fight at Ramoth Gilead, where he would die. Zedekiah, one of the false prophets, slapped Micaiah and challenged him whether he spoke in the spirit of the Lord (22:24). Mark expects the Christian reader to see irony in Jesus being mocked in this way as a prophet. Although blindfolded,

---

[7]Schmidt (*"Iēsous"* 221–26) gives an interesting study of *kolaphizein* in Christian Greek, in Latin (*colaphizare, colaphis caedere*), and in French. *Colaphiser le juif* was an expression used for the Passiontide ceremony in the 9th–11th cents. in which a Jew was brought into the cathedral of Toulouse to be given a symbolic blow by the count—an honor!

he is the one who sees while his enemies are the ones blinded.[8] Jesus' prophecies about betrayal by Judas and the scattering of the disciples have already
been fulfilled. Indeed, even as he is being mocked—and that is why Mark
will interrupt the trial, leaving the summing up until 15:1—Peter is denying
him three times before the cock crows twice, just as Jesus prophesied. And
more irony is involved in what is yet to come, for at the moment of Jesus'
death the destruction of the sanctuary will begin and he will be confessed as
Son of God, the two derided prophecies made at the trial.

The scene closes in Mark with slaps by the attendants, figures who have
not hitherto been mentioned in the trial even though they were in the courtyard in 14:54. The presence of such figures at a trial is quite appropriate, for
Matt 5:25 has the judge handing over an offender "to the attendant." Their
role may be traditional since they are mentioned also by John and by Luke
("the men who were holding him"); and, as we shall see, their absence from
Matt is editorial. The readers of Mark would probably think of those who
arrested Jesus (as does Luke), even though at Gethsemane Mark mentioned
only the crowd and the slave of the high priest. The Jewish texts cited above
(p. 273) about the brutality of the servants of the high priest are often invoked here as well. Flusser ("Who" 29) would add the speculation ("far
more probably"!) that these were Gentile slaves; he points to the Syrian
name Malchus found in John. We can know nothing of that historically, but
on the Gospel level it is the diametrical opposite of what Mark (and probably
the other evangelists) intended in this unfortunately prejudicial description.
These are Jewish attendants imitating their Jewish masters; Gentile brutalities will be just as bad but are kept until after the Roman trial.

How to translate the expression Mark uses for what they did (*rapismasin
auton elabon:* "with slaps him they took/received" [*lambanein*]) has been a
problem. To illustrate opposite ways of interpreting these three words, we
have W. Barclay's prolix: "The guards slapped him across the face as they
took him into custody" and the New Jerusalem Bible's: "The attendants
struck him too." The first combines the active and passive aspects of *lambanein,* so that the attendants *take* charge of Jesus, *receiving* him as a condemned criminal from the Sanhedrin. "With slaps" serves as a dative of manner, indicating that as they took custody, they added their own insulting
brutality (so also Pesch, *Markus* 2.442). However, BDF 198[3] and BAGD
464[1e] insist that *lambanein* does not mean that at all but is a "completely
vulgar" Latinism rendering literally *accipere,* "to receive, get, treat," as in
Cicero's description of Spartan boys receiving lashes (*verberibus accipi-*

---

[8]I see little need to introduce, as does Gnilka ("Verhandlungen" 13), the idea that the Messiah
would have the Spirit that gives knowledge (see Isa 11:2).

untur) to toughen them (*Tusculan Disp.* 2.14.34). The colloquial use of English "to get someone" has the same idea, whence my "got him with slaps." I favor this over the attendants' receiving custody of Jesus, since in the Marcan storyline Jesus remains in the control of the Sanhedrists themselves; and in 15:1 they ("the chief priests with the elders and scribes"), having bound Jesus, take him away and give him over to Pilate.

Why does Mark end the scene with the attendants' slaps? Most scholars recognize in the Marcan account several echoes of the description of the suffering servant in the LXX of Isa 50:6–7: "I gave . . . my cheeks to *slaps;* I did not turn my *face* from the shame of *spitting.* And the Lord God became my helper, and so I was not ashamed." Parallels to the three italicized words are found in Mark, two of them at the beginning of the scene and the other at the end.[9] This arrangement could call attention to still another piece of irony. In their contemptuous treatment of Jesus as a false prophet, with their spitting and covering his face, and their attendants' slaps, the Sanhedrists are unconsciously fulfilling a prophecy—the great Isaian prophecy revealing that by self-giving a victim can turn the signs of human rejection into victory through God's help. In the center of the Marcan scene, then, is the challenge to Jesus to prophesy, issued at the very moment that he is being shown to be a true prophet. Framing him on either side are the echoes of Isaiah the prophet. If that analysis is correct, Mark's scene is artistic as well as theological.

THE MATTHEAN ACCOUNT

Matt's readers would encounter a scene of about the same length as Mark's with much of the same theology in a somewhat different arrangement. Since they would presumably not have Mark to compare with Matt, they would not be distracted by the discrepancies that take up most of the space scholars devote to the Matthean passage. As I attempt to show that Matt's rearrangement of Mark is intelligible, I shall seek also to point out the slight variants exhibited by Matthean theology.

The opening "Then" and the avoidance of the Marcan "began" are typical Matthean touches. Matt's love for more balanced sentences often causes him to improve grammatically on Mark's free-flowing (but narratively effective) style. Matt would not appreciate Mark's row of four infinitives (to spit, to cover, to strike, to say). He would recognize that Mark's "some" referred to Sanhedrists, but might well be bothered by the sudden appearance of "the

---

[9] Gundry points out that the 1QIsaª ms. varies from the MT by reading *lmṭlym* and that if this reading is understood as the hiphil of *ṭll* ("to cover"), it too may have influenced the description that now appears in Mark.

attendants." A more pedagogical organizer, Matt might also be bothered by the fact that Mark splits up the physical abuse of "strikes" and "slaps" (the latter in a Latinism) by the command to "prophesy." More logical arrangement could simplify by turning Mark's Sanhedrists and attendants into two groups of Sanhedrists, with each performing two actions. The first group "spat" and "struck" (notice the coordination, instead of infinitives); and then there were those who "slapped" and were "saying, 'Prophesy.'" (Matt's second clause begins with *hoi de,* "But [there were] those who," a construction suggesting that part of the whole group mentioned in the first clause was involved.[10]) This arrangement keeps the physical actions in sequence and has the challenge "Prophesy" bring the scene to its culmination.

The general Matthean rearrangement that I have proposed needs little defense. (Matt will also rearrange slightly Mark's Roman mockery and abuse.) But now let us turn to the first of two features that have greatly puzzled both ancient copyists and modern Synoptic theorists. Why did Matt omit Mark's "cover his face"? Even Senior (SPNM 187), so devoted to explaining all of Matt by Mark, has to yield to the desperate theory that the original Mark never read "to cover his face." The strange argument for this thesis, which as I mentioned earlier is followed by many, is that if Matt saw the phrase in Mark, he would never have omitted it since the phrase helps to make the challenge to prophesy intelligible. But then our solving the problem by omitting the phrase from Mark would make two evangelists somewhat less intelligible instead of one! Equally desperate is the suggestion (Grundmann, Lagrange, Loisy) that Matt left the face of Jesus uncovered because he wanted to shift the test of prophesying from detecting the unseen to detecting the unknown—as if Jesus were supposed to guess the identity of the Sanhedrists whom he could see slapping him. There is a simpler solution in my judgment. Mark has the unusual expression "spit on him"; but the normal idiom, found in the biblical texts I cited in discussing the spitting and especially in the all-important Isaian servant passage, is "spit in the face." Evidently Matt wanted to use that phrase to emphasize the Isaian parallelism; but having changed to "spat in his face," he could not keep "cover his face" (even though Codex Koridethi has that incredible combination in Mark). Not only would the double mention of "face" be stylistically awkward, but one could scarcely spit in a covered face. (Luke, who chooses to retain the covering, deletes the spitting.) In any case, for Matt the phrase "cover his face" was quite dispensable, for Mark was only spelling out a well-known game that could be signaled far more easily.

That leads to the second puzzling feature in relating Matt to Mark: Where

---

[10]See Neirynck (*"Tis estin"* 33–36); he accepts the partitive sense here if not elsewhere.

did Matt get the question "Who is it that hit you?" especially when Luke has verbatim the same question? Codices Koridethi and Washingtonensis, family 13 of minuscules, various versions, and Augustine follow the solution of reading that question in Mark as well.[11] Senior once more opts for a desperate solution (SPNM 189) in proposing that it was added to Matt by an early scribe harmonizing with Luke.[12] He goes that route in part because he does not sufficiently allow that oral tradition may have influenced both Matt and Luke. Yet the oral approach, for which Soards ("Literary" 113) has argued here, is the key to important agreements between Matt and Luke who scarcely worked on texts totally isolated from the way these stories continued to be narrated orally among Christians. And this is exactly the kind of vivid story, involving a brutalizing game, that would have been attractive for popular retelling. Games, instead of being described, can often be quickly signaled by a key phrase in the game. In different American playgrounds one may hear the question "Who's it?" and know the tag game that is being played, without the least necessity of positing the influence of one playground group on the other. The question is so set that it immediately signals the name of the game. (Neirynck, *"Tis estin"* 29, fails to recognize this possibility when he asks by way of rejection, "Can a common oral tradition be restricted to these five words?") I suggest that Matt could drop Mark's "to cover his face" because when he added "Who is it that hit you?" he was giving the readers perfectly clear information about the game in a way more familiar to them; and it is no great surprise that Luke took the same path without dependence on Matt. Plausibly that path had been taken before either evangelist's time in the popular way this story about the mockery of Jesus was told among people who knew the game under the rubric of the question.

Having reluctantly indulged in the distraction of arguing that one need not adopt poorly attested readings of Mark or extraordinary procedures by Matt to explain the present text of Matt, let me now return to commenting on the Matthean text, which has much the same import as Mark's scene, albeit organized more pedagogically according to Matt's standards. The three echoes of Isa 50:6 ("spat," "face," "slapped") are closer together and more obvious since the spitting, not the covering, affects the face. The challenge to prophesy, the key to the theological irony of the trial, is now the terminating line of the trial before Matt turns to Peter's denials that illustrate Jesus' real status as a prophet. The familiar game question, "Who is it that hit you?" constitutes a dramatic ending—unanswerable to the mockers but

[11] An approach defended by G. D. Kilpatrick, JTS 44 (1943), 29–30.
[12] A solution also favored by his teacher Neirynck, *"Tis estin"* 41–47.

shown to be meaningless child's play when compared to the true power of the prophet affirmed by God, as Isa 50:6 had predicted.

Peculiar to Matt is the address "Messiah." (The vocative address *Christe* is unique in the Bible. It heightens the parallel to the Roman mockery of Jesus in Matt 27:29, where Jesus is addressed by the vocative title "King of the Jews.") Some would explain the logic of the addition on the grounds that the ability to prophesy was a well-known test for the Messiah.[13] As proof there is offered TalBab *Sanhedrin* 93b, where Aqiba's claim that Simon ben Kosiba was the Messiah is tested by whether he could judge by scent; he could not and was killed. That much later account is explicable, however, *after* the failure of Kosiba's revolt: Would-be Messiahs now needed to be tested. As pointed out, we have no evidence of men designated Messiah in the 1st cent. (except Jesus), and so one can doubt that a standard test had yet been developed. True, people join the notions of prophet and of king (Messiah?) in John 6:14–15, and a standard test was mandated for the prophet in Deut 18:21–22; but the joining in John is on the basis of miraculous signs, not on predictions. Another explanation, advanced by Benoit ("Outrages" 106–7), draws on attestation in Josephus and John 11:51 that the anointed (hence messianic) high priest was believed able to prophesy. Benoit[14] argues that the Matthean Jesus presented himself as the Messiah priest and as such was expected to be able to prophesy. We discern from Qumran, however, that the expected Messiah priest (from Aaron, i.e., Levi) was distinguished from the Davidic Messiah (from Israel); and certainly beginning with Matt 1:1 (including the PN with its Judas/Ahithophel parallelism), Jesus is emphatically the *Davidic* Messiah with no suggestion of a levitical role.

More simply, I would contend, Matt has the same understanding as Mark that the prophecy test is related to the contents of the trial, namely, that Jesus had made futuristic statements related to the sanctuary, to "the Messiah, the Son of God," and to "the Son of Man" at the right hand of the Power, and therefore his prophetic abilities were being mocked. Yet while in Mark one has to make that connection by analysis, Matt by mentioning the Messiah makes the connection clearer.[15] Interestingly, while Mark will have Jesus mocked as the Messiah on the cross, a mockery closely related to the trial motifs, Matt will not; and so one wonders if Matt has preferred to present that Messiah mockery here. One can debate whether the "Prophesy for us,

---

[13]Catchpole, *Trial* 175–76.

[14]He cites G. Friedrich, ZTK 53 (1956), 265–311.

[15]And if one could show that at this time the destruction of the sanctuary and the rebuilding were the expected roles of the Messiah (distinct from God), as many scholars claim, the connection would be closer—but, as already indicated (pp. 442–43 above), more proof of that is required.

Messiah" makes the Sanhedrists more malevolent, a touch of the harshness found elsewhere in the Matthean PN (27:25; 28:14–15). In any case, since Matt began his Gospel on the theme of the Davidic Messiah, the recognition of Jesus under that title is for him crucial. SPNM (191) affirms: "The central issue for Matthew is . . . to reveal the Christ"; but with irony Matt will now turn to the (predicted) denials by Peter, who was the first one (16:16) to confess Jesus as the Christ (Messiah).

THE LUCAN ACCOUNT

Luke's timing and locale of the mockery scene differ from that of the other Gospels. In the others it comes at the end of the night trial or interrogation of Jesus by the authorities; in Luke it comes at night, just after cockcrow but before the morning Sanhedrin trial. In the other Gospels the mockery or abuse occurs in the place where Jesus is being interrogated; in Luke it occurs near a blazing fire in the middle of the *aulē* of the house of the high priest (see 22:54–55). In that same place, with Jesus present, Peter has just three times denied him; and the Jesus who turned and looked (forgivingly) at Peter will now stand silent, undergoing mockery and blasphemy by captors. (The translation of the Lucan account of Peter's denials, namely, Luke 22:54b–62, which immediately precedes this account of the abuse and mockery in 22:63–65, may be found in §27.)

Theories about how the Lucan scene was composed have ramifications for history. Bussmann, Grundmann, Plummer, Streeter, Taylor, and Winter are among the many who think that here Luke had a source independent of Mark; and that idea has led others (Benoit, Catchpole, Flusser) to judge that Luke's account is more historical than those of the other Gospels. On the other hand, Creed, Finegan, Schneider, and Soards doubt or firmly deny a special Lucan source; and though conservative, K. Schubert ("Juden und die Römer" 239) challenges the originality of the Lucan account, evaluating it as a rearrangement of borrowed material. As for interSynoptic relationships, only nine of twenty-seven words[16] in the Lucan passage are found in Mark's account of the Jewish mockery; but that figure is a bit deceptive, for we must take into account Luke's habit of drawing upon the vocabulary of other Marcan passages that he has omitted. Let us consider the details of the Lucan narrative, using the compositional issue to discuss features in Lucan thought.

Luke begins by speaking of "the men who were holding him" as the agents who will perform the mockery. Already, in my judgment, that expression tilts the discussion away from original source toward secondary compo-

---

[16]Neirynck's count in *"Tis estin"* 17 vs. Taylor.

sition. The verb *synechein* ("to hold") occurs six times in Luke as compared
with once in the other Gospels. With the subject "men," the phrase might
seem the equivalent of the Marcan and Johannine attendants, and Fitzmyer
(*Luke* 2.1461) states that they are "underlings." Yet Luke never mentions
attendants, and the last named people that this could refer to are "the chief
priests and captains of the Temple and elders" of 22:52. Because of the way
he shifted around material, already in 22:55 Luke's sequence gave the logical
problem that those worthies appear to be the ones seated comfortably with
Peter near the fire; now they appear to be the ones holding Jesus physically.
Indeed, should the "him" they are holding be Jesus, since the last mentioned
person (22:62) to whom the pronoun would grammatically refer is Peter?[17]
Actually, if one reads the narrative without paying attention to such niceties,
one can get the true impression Luke intended; but in rearranging he has left
telltale marks by not attentively naming the subjects of the actions he has
borrowed from Mark.

Luke tells us that the men holding Jesus "were mocking" (or "began to
mock" if the impf. is conative [BDF 326; Fitzmyer, *Luke* 2.1465]). In being
the sole evangelist to use *empaizein* Luke is still working out implications
in Mark. The third Marcan passion prediction spoke of the Son of Man being
given over to the chief priests and the scribes, who would condemn him to
death and give him over to the Gentiles (Mark 10:33–34, describing what
will happen in 14:64 and 15:1): "And they will mock him and spit on him
and scourge him and kill (him)." Those four verbs describe what will happen
in Mark after Pilate tries Jesus: Jesus will be flagellated (15:15); he will be
spat on and mocked (*empaizein*) by Roman soldiers (15:19,20) and then led
out and crucified. Luke is not going to narrate a Roman mockery immediately after the Pilate trial, and so he reinterprets the application of the third
passion prediction. In 18:32–33 Luke reads: "For he will be given over to
the Gentiles, and he will be mocked, and he will be arrogantly mistreated
[passive of *hybrizein*], and he will be spat on; and having scourged (him),
they will kill him." Luke has dropped the Marcan mention of being condemned by the chief priests and scribes because he will omit the Sanhedrin
condemnation of Jesus. He has changed the initial verbs (including the
added "arrogantly mistreated") to the passive because the Gentiles will not
do those things (as they do in Mark). Thus for Luke the action of the men
who hold Jesus in the *aulē* of the house of the high priest fulfills at least part
of the predicted abuse: It is *here* that Jesus is "mocked" and by equivalence
"arrogantly mistreated," whence Luke's addition in the current scene of

---

[17]Catchpole (*Trial* 174) and others would solve the problem by omitting Luke 22:62 from Peter's
denials; but that is too easy a solution (Fitzmyer, *Luke* 2.1457–58).

"were mocking" at the beginning and "blaspheming, they were saying many other things against him" at the end. There is no need to posit a special source for such additions.

Indeed, Luke will have a certain artistic arrangement of the theme of mocking running through the PN, using the verb *empaizein* three times (see Table 2): for the action here of the men who hold him, for the action in 23:11a of Herod and his troops who treat Jesus with contempt; and for the action at the cross in 23:36 of the (Roman) soldiers who come forward, as though with respect, to offer him the sour wine and challenge him, if he is the King of the Jews, to save himself. (The last, for Luke, substitutes for the Roman mockery immediately after the Pilate trial.)

Mockery so dominates this scene for Luke that he has eliminated the physical abuse narrated in Mark that is not related to the mockery, e.g., the spitting that Mark has at the beginning and the slaps at the end. The only physical abuse that Luke mentions is "beating," which is essential for the question that identifies the blindman's buff game, "Who is it that hit you?"[18] Mark does not mention blasphemy in the Jewish mockery of Jesus, but he does have Jesus accused of blasphemy by the high priest. Luke will omit that from his version of the Sanhedrin trial, presumably horrified by the thought that the chief authority among God's people accused God's Son of blaspheming God. Rather he turns around the charge and regards the mockery of Jesus as blasphemy *against* God's Son. What Luke writes literally in 22:65 is: "And many other things, blaspheming, they were saying"—a grammatical construction he used previously in 3:18: "So and many other things, exhorting, he preached." It identifies all that happened as blasphemy. That term (p. 523 above) means to curse or revile, but often in a religious context has the tone of arrogance infringing on God's dignity. In the third passion prediction Luke (alone) used the verb *hybrizein,* and *hybris* is an arrogance by which one sets oneself up against God. That is how Luke looked upon this outrage against Jesus.

If I agree, then, with those who think the Lucan scene can be explained as a free rewriting and reorganization of the Marcan account (plus the added use from set oral usage of the identification of the game as "Who is it that hit you?"), there remain two puzzling issues.

First, I suggested that Luke mentioned neither Mark's beginning "spit on" nor Mark's ending "with slaps" because they were extraneous to the mocking game of covering Jesus, beating him, and then asking "Prophesy, who is

---

[18]The verb *derein* ("to beat," used also by John) is one Luke uses with some frequency (eight times in Luke/Acts vs. four times in all the other Gospels); and presumably he prefers it to Mark's *kolaphizein* ("to strike," which I suggested might have been early passion vocabulary, but is never used by Luke).

it that hit you?" Yet by this omission Luke has also removed the echoes of Isa 50:6, the description of the Suffering Servant who gave his cheeks to slaps, who did not turn his face from the shame of spitting.[19] Did Luke feel that he did not need an oblique reference to Jesus as the Suffering Servant here when he would have a scene in Acts (8:26–39) with the Ethiopian eunuch explicitly applying the Isaian servant image to Jesus? Luke moved part of the Marcan Sanhedrin trial of Jesus to the Stephen trial in Acts 7, so the suggestion is not impossible. (The suggestion that Luke has given us an earlier form of the Jewish mockery, reflecting the period before Christians glossed it with a reference to Isa 50:6, runs up against too many other indications that the Lucan scene is not primitive.) Here Luke may have been interested primarily in another image of Jesus, namely, as a model for martyrdom. Luke has just told the story of Peter's denials where Peter did not stay steadfast under hostile questioning; but now Jesus yields not, even under the blows of blaspheming mockery. That model of the martyr had been offered to Greek-speaking Judaism (in the language of which Luke was well versed) by II Macc 6–7 and by *IV Macc* 6 and 8–14. In Acts Luke will describe the steadfastness of Stephen, Peter, and Paul; and for them the Lucan Jesus is an example and forerunner.

Another issue in the Lucan account that is puzzling is the exact logic of "Prophesy." For Mark/Matt that challenge made sense on the storytelling level because Jesus was connected with prophecies at the trial, but in Luke the trial is yet to come. On the level of ironic theology, of course, Jesus has been proved a true prophet because Peter has just denied him three times before a cock crowed, but on the narrative level the men who held Jesus would scarcely have known that. In Luke, perhaps more than in the other Gospels, Jesus has been hailed publicly as a prophet (7:16; 9:8,19; see 24:19); and publicly and to his disciples Jesus has compared himself to the prophets (4:24,27; 13:34). Significant is 13:33: "It is impossible that a prophet should perish outside Jerusalem." When the Pharisee expressed his doubts about Jesus, he did so in these terms: "If this man were a prophet, he would have known" (7:39). Would that be enough to explain why, when his captors wanted to mock Jesus, they did so as a prophet? Or has Luke simply

---

[19]Parenthetically, one would also have to recognize that Luke has removed the fulfillment of his own third passion prediction "will be spat upon." As I pointed out, both "spit on" and "scourge" were fulfilled for Mark in the post-Roman-trial mockery that Luke eliminated. It is a problem for every theory of Lucan composition that Luke has retained these two items in his third passion prediction when they never happen in the Gospel! *The Lucan Jesus is never spat upon and never scourged, even though he says he will be.* Some might contend that Luke covers these under the blasphemy done to Jesus. A more likely explanation is that Luke's sensitivities and his sense of order dictated rearrangements of Marcan material to the point that at times inequities have been created. I shall point out more of them when I discuss the end of the Pilate trial.

taken this over from Mark and (since it made sense as theological irony) not worried too much about the exact logic of the narrative line? Or are we looking in the wrong direction when we search what has *preceded?* Those men who hold Jesus mock him as a prophet; the Sanhedrists in the morning will query unbelievingly whether Jesus is the Messiah and the Son of God. Is this an ascending depiction of the unbelief of his enemies wherein, ironically, they grow closer to the truth?

John's account of the slapping of Jesus by an attendant after Jesus has responded to the high priest was discussed above in §19. We saw that it was an act not of mockery, but of indignation reflecting the command of Exod 22:27(28) about not speaking badly of the ruler of God's people, i.e., in this instance, of the high priest. I left open there whether in this slapping John expected the reader to see a reflection of Isa 50:6 (granted, however, that the Johannine Jesus, unlike the Suffering Servant of Isa 53:7, does indeed open his mouth to speak majestically).

ANALYSIS

The simpler Johannine scene brings us to a discussion of historicity. (That will be the only topic in this analytic section, since we had to discuss compositional issues in the COMMENT.) Can we discover what and whose actions underlay the varying Gospel accounts of the Jewish abuse and mockery of Jesus? Who performed them and when? Let me list some brief observations pulling together what we have seen and then state an evaluative conclusion:

- The Mark/Matt scene after the Jewish trial with its challenge to Jesus to prophesy and the closely parallel Mark/Matt scene after the Roman trial with its challenge to Jesus as the King of the Jews represent a theological structuring calling attention to motifs in the respective trials. Details in the two scenes are for the most part different, and one should not jump to the facile conclusion that one has been created out of nothing to imitate the other. But surely both are not historical simply as described; any underlying tradition has been heavily reshaped.
- One should reject the contention that the Lucan scene is more historical because the mocking is not done by the Sanhedrists but by captors as they hold a prisoner waiting for the Sanhedrin trial. The shift of the Sanhedrin trial to the morning is a Lucan reordering; the identity of the captors, when examined critically, shows the telltale marks of problems caused by that reordering. Luke's account throughout is most probably dependent on Mark (with a minor influence from oral tradition).

▪ John's account too shows the marks of theological interpretation, e.g., the sovereignty of Jesus. Yet John's basic action remains simple: a slap from one of the attendants. It is useless to speculate whether John derived this from the last part of Mark 14:65 or whether that part of Mark (which some think to be appended) was derived from a tradition similar to John's. It would require less imagination to think that both evangelists were dependent on similar older traditions.

Behind all the accounts, when one examines their origin critically (including what one or the other Synoptic evangelist omitted), may lie a slapping or beating of Jesus by one or more attendants in the aftermath of his being interrogated by the high priest during the night of his arrest. (Such abuse is not at all implausible historically: When Jesus son of Ananias was arrested in the 60s by the leading citizens of Jerusalem because he stood in the Temple and prophesied destruction, they gave him many bruises (*plēgē*), as he stood silent, before they handed him over to the Romans [Josephus, *War* 6.5.3; #302].) This violence has been depicted by the Christian tradition and by the evangelists (perhaps through the inclusion of other traditions, e.g., mockery of claims about Jesus) in a way that shows how such a horrendous insult to the person of God's Son fits in with God's will as revealed in OT descriptions of the suffering just one and of the arrogance of the wicked. Mark's and Matt's accounts whereby the abuse was done by the Sanhedrists themselves may be unhistorical, especially for those who think (as I do) that the Sanhedrin meeting pertinent to Jesus took place some time before Jesus was arrested. Nevertheless, the evangelists (or the developing tradition before them) were not seeking to calumniate the Sanhedrists.[20] They were expressing their judgment that the Sanhedrists by their decision against Jesus (even if historically it was made earlier) were responsible not only for Jesus' death but for all the other evil that befell him.

In portraying negative roles in the PN, the evangelists do not confine themselves to Jesus' enemies. A major component of the Jewish legal action against Jesus is the threefold denial of him by Peter, the one of the Twelve who still seeks to come after him when the others are no longer part of the scene. While the sequential relation to the Jewish trial or interrogation varies, the denials of Peter receive as much attention as the questioning and mockery of Jesus. It is to that dramatic threefold denial we now turn.

(*Bibliography for this episode may be found in §25, Part 1.*)

[20]H. C. Waetjen, *A Reordering of Power: A Socio-political Reading of Mark's Gospel* (Minneapolis: Fortress, 1989), 16, points out that the picture of the abuse of Jesus by the Sanhedrin may reflect the pejorative evaluation that the lower class had of the rulers, an evaluation not without basis in experience.

§27. THE THREE DENIALS OF JESUS BY PETER

(Mark 14:66–72; Matt 26:69–75; Luke 22:54b–62;
John 18:15–18,25–27)

Translation

Mark 14:[54]66–72: [⁵⁴And Peter followed him from a distance until inside the court of the high priest, and he was seated together with the attendants and warming himself near the blazing flame.]

(*1st Denial*) ⁶⁶And Peter being below in the court, one of the servant women of the high priest comes; ⁶⁷and having seen Peter warming himself and having looked at him, she says to him, "You too were with the Nazarene, Jesus." ⁶⁸ᵃBut he denied, saying, "I don't know nor understand what you are saying."

(*2d Denial*) ⁶⁸ᵇAnd he went outside into the forecourt [and a cock crowed]. ⁶⁹And the servant woman, having seen him, began again to say to the bystanders that "This is one of them." ⁷⁰ᵃBut again he was denying it.

(*3d Denial*) ⁷⁰ᵇAnd after a little, the bystanders again were saying to Peter, "Truly you are one of them, for indeed you are a Galilean." ⁷¹But he began to curse and swear that "I don't know this man of whom you speak." ⁷²And immediately a second time a cock crowed; and Peter remembered the word as Jesus had spoken it to him, that "Before a cock crows twice, three times you will deny me." And having rushed out, he was weeping.

Matt 26:[58]69–75: [⁵⁸But Peter was following him from a distance until the court(yard) of the high priest; and having entered inside, he sat with the attendants to see the end.]

(*1st Denial*) ⁶⁹But Peter sat outside in the court(yard); and one servant woman came up to him saying, "You too were with Jesus the Galilean." [70]But he denied before all, saying, "I don't know what you are saying."

(*2d Denial*) [71]But after his having gone out into the entranceway, another woman saw him and says to those there, "This one was with Jesus the Nazorean." [72]But again he denied with an oath that "I don't know the man."

(*3d Denial*) [73]But after a little, those present, having come up, said to Peter, "Truly you too, you are one of them, for indeed your speech makes you obvious." [74]Then he began to curse and swear that "I don't know the man." And immediately a cock crowed; [75]and Peter remembered the word spoken by Jesus that "Before a cock crows, three times you will deny me." And having gone outside, he wept bitterly.

Luke 22:54b–62: [54b]But Peter was following at a distance. [55]But when they had kindled a fire in the middle of the court and had sat down together, Peter sat down in their midst.

(*1st Denial*) [56]But having seen him seated near the blazing flame and having stared at him, a certain servant woman said, "This one too was with him." [57]But he denied, saying, "I don't know him, Woman."

(*2d Denial*) [58]And after a short time another man, having seen him, said, "You too are one of them." But Peter said, "Man, I am not."

(*3d Denial*) [59]And after about one hour had passed, a certain man was insisting, saying, "In truth this one too was with him, for indeed he is a Galilean." [60]But Peter said, "Man, I don't know what you are saying." And at that moment while he was still speaking, a cock crowed. [61]And the Lord, having turned, looked at Peter; and Peter remembered the saying of the Lord as he had spoken it to him, that "Before a cock crows today, you will deny me three times." [62]And having gone outside, he wept bitterly.

John 18:15–18,25–27: [15]But following Jesus was Simon Peter and another disciple. But that disciple was known to the high priest, and he entered together with Jesus into the court of the high priest. [16a]But Peter was standing at the gate outside.

(*1st Denial*) [16b]Accordingly the other disciple, the one known to the high priest, came out and spoke to the gatekeeper and brought Peter in. [17]And so the servant woman, the gatekeeper, says to Peter, "Are you too one of the disciples of this man?" He says, "I am not." [18]But the servants and the attendants were standing around, having made a charcoal fire because it was cold; and they were warming themselves. But Peter too was with them, standing and warming himself. [18:19–24 describes the interrogation of Jesus by Annas.]

(*2d Denial*) [25]But Simon Peter was standing there and warming himself. So they said to him, "Are you too one of his disciples?" And he denied and said, "I am not."

(*3d Denial*) [26]One [masc.] of the servants of the high priest, being a relative of him whose ear Peter had cut off, says, "Didn't I see you in the garden with him?" [27]And so Peter denied again, and immediately a cock crowed.

COMMENT

As I shall stress in the ANALYSIS where I shall deal with the composition and antiquity of this scene, ironically this episode of the PN exhibits contrasting aspects. On the one hand it is the episode on which the four Gospels agree most; on the other there are infuriatingly different minor details in the narrative of the setting and of the three denials. I present on adjacent pages Table 3 incorporating those details, and readers will again and again be recommended to consult that table in order to follow the discussion of minutiae.

GENERAL SETTING

In Luke and John, after Jesus has been arrested on the Mount of Olives across the Kidron and has been brought to the high priest or his house, we are immediately told how Peter, who was following, began to be confronted and thus was led to deny Jesus. In those two Gospels, then, there is nothing that separates the general setting describing Peter's location and the denials. In Mark/Matt, however, there is a separation, for the Sanhedrin trial comes between the description of Peter's whereabouts and the account of the denials. As we saw in §19 above, Mark 14:53–54/Matt 26:57–58 constitutes a double introduction, with the first verse readying the readers for the Sanhedrin trial and the second verse (repeated in brackets in my translation here)

TABLE 3. COMPARING ACCOUNTS OF THE THREE DENIALS OF JESUS BY PETER

General	Mark	Matt	Luke	John
#1. Time	In the night when J. (= Jesus) has been seized at Gethsemane on the Mt of Olives and led away to the h.p. (= high priest)	In the night when J. has been seized at Gethsemane on the Mt of Olives and led away to Caiaphas, the h.p.	In the night when J. has been led to the house of the h.p.	In the night when J. has been taken in a garden across the Kidron and led to Annas, father-in-law to Caiaphas, h.p. that year
#2. Sequence of scenes	After Sanhedrin trial when J. was interrogated by the h.p. and abused by Sanhedrin members	After Sanhedrin trial when J. was interrogated by the h.p. (Caiaphas) and abused by Sanhedrin members	Before J. was mocked by the men holding him, and before (as day began) J. was led to a Sanhedrin inquiry to be interrogated by its members	*First Denial:* Before J. was interrogated by the h.p. (Annas) and slapped by guard *Second and Third Denials:* After above; when J. was sent bound to Caiaphas
First Denial	Mark 14:54,66–68a	Matt 26:58,69–70	Luke 22:54b–57	John 18:15–18
#3. Place	Peter followed J. from a distance until inside *aulē* of the h.p., below where J. was	Peter was following J. from a distance until inside *aulē* of the h.p., outside where J. was	Peter was following at a distance. Was in the middle of the *aulē* of the h.p. where J. also was	Simon Peter and another disciple were following J. Disciple entered into the *aulē* of the h.p. with J.; Peter left standing at the gate outside
#4. Peter's position	Seated together with attendants, warming himself near the blazing flame (*phōs*)	Seated with attendants to see the end	Seated in the midst of arresting party near blazing flame (*phōs*) of fire (*pyr*) that they had kindled	Brought in by other disciple, Peter stood with servants and attendants warming himself at a charcoal fire (*anthrakia*) made by them
#5. Questioner	One (*mia*) of the servant women of the h.p.	One (*mia*) servant woman	A certain (*tis*) servant woman	The servant woman who was the gatekeeper
#6. Accusation or question	"You too were with [*meta*] the Nazarene, Jesus."	"You too were with [*meta*] Jesus the Galilean."	"This one too was with [*syn*] him."	"Are you too one of the disciples of this man?"
#7. Reply	But he denied, saying, "I don't know nor understand what you are saying."	But he denied before all, saying, "I don't know what you are saying."	But he denied, saying, "I don't know him, Woman."	He (that one) says, "I am not."

	Mark 14:68b–70a	Matt 26:71–72	Luke 22:58	John 18:25
Second Denial				
#8. Setting	Peter went outside into the forecourt (*proaulion*)	Peter has gone out into the entranceway (*pylōn*)	After a short time (still in the *aulē*)	No indicated interval (still standing in the *aulē* warming himself)
#9. Questioner	Same woman servant, having seen him, began again to say to the bystanders:	Another woman saw him and says to those there:	Another man, having seen him, said:	They (servants and guards of v. 18) said to him:
#10. Accusation or question	"This is one of them."	"This one was with [*meta*] Jesus the Nazorean."	"You too are one of them."	"Are you too one of his disciples?"
#11. Reply	But again he was denying it.	But again he denied with an oath that "I don't know the man."	But Peter said, "Man, I am not."	And he denied and said, "I am not."
Third Denial	**Mark 14:70b–72**	**Matt 26:73–75**	**Luke 22:59–62**	**John 18:26–27**
#12. Setting	After a little (still in forecourt)	After a little (still in entranceway)	After about one hour (still in the *aulē*)	No indicated interval (still at charcoal fire)
#13. Questioner	The bystanders again were saying to Peter:	Those present, having come up, said to Peter:	A(nother) certain (*tis*) man was insisting, saying:	One (masc.) of the servants of the h.p., a relative of him whose ear Peter had cut off, says:
#14. Accusation or question	"Truly you are one of them, for indeed you are a Galilean."	"Truly you too, you are one of them, for indeed your speech makes you obvious."	"In truth this one too was with [*meta*] him, for indeed he is a Galilean."	"Didn't I see you in the garden with [*meta*] him?"
#15. Reply	But he began to curse and swear that "I don't know this man of whom you speak."	Then he began to curse and swear that "I don't know the man."	But Peter said, "Man, I don't know what you are saying."	And so Peter denied again.
#16. Cockcrow	Immediately, a second time, a cock crowed	Immediately a cock crowed	At that moment while he was still speaking, a cock crowed	Immediately a cock crowed
#17. Reaction of Peter	Peter remembered the word as J. had spoken it to him, that, "Before a cock crows twice, three times you will deny me." Having rushed out, he was weeping.	Peter remembered the word spoken by J. that "Before a cock crows, three times you will deny me." Having gone outside, he wept bitterly.	The Lord, having turned, looked at Peter; and Peter remembered the saying of the Lord as he had spoken it to him, that "Before a cock crows today, you will deny me three times." Having gone outside, he wept bitterly.	

preparing for the denials—a preparation separated by some dozen verses from the actual account of the denials. As they begin the present section, both Mark and Matt have to draw upon that preparatory verse which placed Peter seated together with the guards inside the *aulē* (court[yard]) of the high priest. Indeed, Mark's opening in 14:66 ("And Peter being below") and Matt's repetition in 26:69 of "sat" (with the implication of "was sitting") serve to underline the simultaneity of Peter's denials and the Sanhedrin trial which has been described in the verses that separate the preparation from the denials.

In place of a Sanhedrin trial, after the arrest John describes an interrogation of Jesus by Annas; and he too stresses simultaneity by placing Peter's first denial before that interrogation, and the second and third denials after it. (More precisely they come after John 18:24, where Annas sends Jesus bound to Caiaphas; but the *de* at the beginning of 18:25 is equivalent to "In the meantime," so that the second and third denials go on while Jesus is being interrogated and sent away.) Undoubtedly (see ANALYSIS) the primary aim of the simultaneity is theological, dramatically contrasting Peter's denial with Jesus' confession. Only Luke breaks the pattern of simultaneity by having the denials stand alone—after Jesus encountered the chief priests and elders on the Mount of Olives at the time of his arrest, and before the morning meeting of the Sanhedrin. Luke's sense or order would abhor Mark's introducing Peter in 14:54 and then returning to him only in 14:66–72. As McEleney ("Peter's" 469) points out, Luke prefers to "clear the stage" by giving the full treatment of a character before he moves on to another issue. For example, in 3:1–20 Luke describes JBap's ministry up to and including his imprisonment, even before he writes of the baptism of Jesus in 3:21–22, although that baptism had to take place before JBap's imprisonment. So also here Luke has consolidated the Marcan description of Peter in the *aulē* into a consecutive piece, but we notice that he has not changed the time of the denials. If they are historical, they surely took place in the time frame where all the Gospels place them, i.e., in the darkest hours of the night on which Jesus was arrested. The cockcrow motif assures that.

All the Gospels have Peter "follow" the arrested Jesus, a sequence that is surprising in three of the Gospels. In Mark 14:50/Matt 26:56 we were told that all the disciples left Jesus and fled when he was seized in Gethsemane; in John 18:8 Jesus insisted on having his disciples let go without being detained as the price of his own arrest. (Here again Luke is the exception, for that Gospel has not told what happened to the disciples who were with Jesus on the Mount of Olives.) Nevertheless the indication in Mark/Matt (and in Luke too, showing the evangelist's awareness of the issue) that Peter followed "from a distance," while it may have theological overtones,[1] was meant to deal with the seeming contradiction between flight and following. Peter has followed because he claimed to be an exception. A following truly characteristic of discipleship would not be at a distance but unto the cross (Gnilka, *Markus* 2.278). Plummer (*Luke* 513) observes pithily that Peter follows out of love, but at a distance out of fear. John implicitly affirms the tradition of "from a distance" since Peter is shown as arriving at the gate *after* Jesus (with another disciple) is already inside. Actually no attempt to arrest the followers of Jesus was reported during the scene of his arrest, but on the level of the story it is hypercriticism to claim that the hint of fear on Peter's part is unintelligible or illogical (pace Gardiner, "Denial"). Violence was reported during the arrest of Jesus, and three of the four Gospels clearly identified the one who struck off the servant's ear as a disciple of Jesus. Indeed, the Johannine Peter would have had special reason to fear, once inside the *aulē* of the high priest, since it was he who had wounded the servant of the high priest. Moreover, in John the high priest Annas had interrogated Jesus about his disciples (18:19); that this inquiry may have made them suspect is implied in 20:19 where the disciples have locked the door of the place in which they were "for fear of the Jews." *GPet* 7:26 dramatizes this, as Peter speaks: "But I with my companions was sorrowful; and having been wounded in spirit, we were in hiding, for we were sought after by them [the Jews, the elders, and the priests] as wrongdoers and as wishing to set fire to the sanctuary."[2] These reports in John and *GPet* reflect the increasing antiJudaism of the post-70 period. Historically there is no recorded early Christian memory of an attempt to have Jesus' followers put to death with him.

The four Gospels agree in placing the denials in or about the *aulē* of the high priest. This term can refer to the whole of a palatial building (a court), to a room (hall) within it, or to a courtyard outside. Matt (26:69) clearly envisions the last meaning: The *aulē* of the denials is outside the place where Jesus is being tried by the Sanhedrin; but one should remember that Matt 26:3 mentioned the *aulē* of the high priest as the place where the chief priests and the elders gathered—an example of the first or second meanings of the term. Mark imagines the house of the high priest to be of more than one story, so that while Jesus is tried by the Sanhedrin in one place, Peter is denying him "below" (14:66). Probably for Mark *aulē* means a hall or court within the building, while the *proaulion* of 14:68b

---

[1]Ps 38:12[11] portrays the kin of the suffering just one standing at (from) a distance.

[2]The last clause is *GPet*'s echo of the charge against Jesus at the Sanhedrin trial in Mark/Matt that he was planning to destroy the sanctuary.

is the forecourt or courtyard outside the *aulē*, into which Peter goes for the second denial.

It is much harder to guess what Luke and John mean by the *aulē*. Some have thought of a building *with two wings* in order that the movements that these two Gospels posit during the Jewish procedures may be harmonized with the Mark/Matt picture of all the procedures having taken place adjacent to the *aulē* of the denials. After the denials and the mockery of Jesus in the *aulē* of the house of the high priest, Luke 22:66 has Jesus led away to the Sanhedrin of the chief priests and scribes; and after the interrogation of Jesus in the *aulē* of Annas the high priest, John 18:24 has Jesus sent bound to Caiaphas, the high priest. Obviously, however, Luke and John could be envisaging another building in another section of Jerusalem. Harmonizations suppose that one or all the evangelists preserved precise and accurate memories of the setting. Far more likely is that in the tradition there came down to them a general setting for the denials (the *aulē* of the high priest) and a pattern in which the denials were set outside and/or inside that *aulē*. Each evangelist made his own adaptation. As to historicity, the principal issue in regard to the *aulē* of the high priest (presumably at the Hasmonean palace on the western hill; see p. 404 above) would be whether it was originally associated with the Jewish interrogation of Jesus, or with the denials, or with both.

Whether the *aulē* is depicted as outside or inside, three evangelists envision Peter as positioned near a fire (seated in Mark and Luke; standing in John). Mark 14:54, the preparatory verse, had already situated Peter "near the blazing flame." Matt's corresponding preparatory verse (26:58), however, omitted all reference to the fire and had Peter sitting with the attendants "to see the end." Although there has been an attempt to relate "the end" (*to telos*) to a phrase in the Greek title (*eis to telos*) of about one-third of the psalms (and to see a messianic implication), more simply it echoes the Matthean Peter's determination expressed in 26:35, "Even if it be necessary for me *to die* with you, I will not deny you." The phrase "to see the end" also prepares the readers for a prolonged account that will narrate the Sanhedrin trial of Jesus before attention is once more focused on Peter. Still it is curious that when Matt returns to describe Peter's denials in 26:69–75, he never mentions the flame or fire described in Mark. Nights in March and early April in Jerusalem can be very chilly, so that there is nothing implausible in the Marcan depiction.[3] Moreover, the custom of soldiers to keep fires burning through

---

[3] Yet to demonstrate this one may not resort to the frequently cited Jer 36:22, which mentions the need for a fire in the royal palace in the ninth month: That month is December measured from spring, rather than March measured from autumn.

the night is attested by I Macc 12:28–29. Different vocabulary for the fire is used by the evangelists (#4 in table); but the attempt of Buchanan ("Mark") to appeal to Hebrew *'wr* (*'ôr,* "light"; *'ûr,* "fire") to explain the *phōs/pyr* alternation is unnecessary. Both terms are used for "fire" in the Greek of this period, and they appear in successive verses in Luke (22:55–56). Mark and Luke, who both employ *phōs,* "light, flame," stress that the servant woman was able to see Peter clearly by its illumination; John's *anthrakia* is more appropriate for his image of Peter warming himself.

Peter is not described as alone in the *aulē:* Mark/Matt mention *hypēretai* ("attendants, guards"[4]), as does John (along with *douloi,* "servants"); and we shall hear of a servant woman (*paidiskē*). Luke's picture is not clear since he refers simply to a vague "they," the last antecedent for which would be "the chief priests and captains of the Temple and elders who were arrived against him" of 22:52. In any case it is probable that all the evangelists (John more clearly than the others) imagine that in the *aulē,* alongside those who had played a police role in arresting Jesus, there were other servants and attendants who had not been on the Mount of Olives. This, plus the fact that according to three of the Gospels the disciples of Jesus had fled or been let go, helps to explain the flow of the narrative. The charge against Peter produces no hysteria; and even though he is suspect, he is let go. Those who query him or who overhear the queries are not police charged with the responsibility of seeking out adherents. It is never made clear what they would have done if Peter had confessed. Would they have arrested him (probably so in John since he had inflicted injury with a sword) or simply have ejected him from the premises? The story has its basic logic; we should not press too hard for every eventuality.

First Denial

The four evangelists agree in identifying the first person to challenge Peter as a servant woman (*paidiskē*); in the other two denials the Gospels will not be in harmony on the identity of the challenger(s) (compare #5, 9, 13 in table). Mark uses a partitive expression, "one [*mia*] of the servant women," which both Luke and Matt simplify. Luke, who likes indefinite demonstratives, renders this as "a certain [*tis*]" servant woman; Matt has "one [*mia*]" servant woman.[5] John further specifies that the servant woman is the gate-

---

[4]On pp. 249–50, 402–3 above I discussed what the different evangelists intended by *hypēretai.*

[5]There has been an attempt to interpret Matt's usage as a Semitism for "*a* servant woman"; but SPNM 197 points to a Matthean tendency to use the cardinal number in the contrasting pair "one . . . another"—in this instance the "another" appears in the second denial of Matt 26:71.

keeper.[6] Some have questioned that: Would a woman be allowed to tend the gate of the priest's palace late at night? Was that the difficulty that caused the scribe of OS[sin] to use a masculine article: "the woman servant of the man gatekeeper"? One should be cautious, however: Unless theological symbolism moves him otherwise, John respects plausibility, and that evangelist was much closer to what would seem plausible in the 1st cent. than we are. (Acts 12:13 has a servant woman [*paidiskē*] responsible for the gate of a private home at night; and Josephus [*Ant.* 7.2.1; #48] saw nothing inconsistent in picturing a woman gatekeeper at the house of King Saul's son Ishbosheth.) Perhaps the location of one of the denials in the entrance to the *aulē* was fixed in the tradition: It is the setting for the first denial in John, and for the second in Mark/Matt (see #8 in table).

For an evaluation of John a more serious problem than the woman gatekeeper is the presence of "another disciple" (*allos mathētēs,* lacking the definite article in the best mss.), one known to the high priest (18:15). The solution that this "another disciple" was derived by the evangelist from a preJohannine source and that the evangelist knew nothing more about him is possible, but a bit desperate. Most scholars have thought that this "another disciple" is the same as a known Johannine figure, the beloved disciple. In the chronology of John, a few hours before the present scene "one of his disciples, the one whom Jesus loved, was reclining on Jesus' bosom" at the Last Supper; and Simon Peter signaled him to ask whom Jesus meant by speaking of the betrayer (John 13:21–26). Some hours after the denial scene standing near the cross of Jesus will be "the disciple whom he loved" (19:25–27). A sense of economy about the Johannine dramatis personae would cause us to think of one unnamed beloved disciple, close to Jesus at the Supper, staying with him when he was arrested, and still with him when he was put to death, rather than positing at the denials a different, unnamed disciple who is not otherwise mentioned in the text. Support for such an identification may be drawn from the combined designation in John 20:2: "the other disciple [*ho allos mathētēs*], (the one) whom Jesus loved." Scribes saw this similarity, for a number of Koine Greek mss. harmonizingly read the *ho* (definite article) of 20:2 into 18:15.[7]

An objection to identifying "another disciple" of 18:15 with "the disciple

---

[6]The noun *thyrōros* can be masculine or feminine; most mss. of John use a feminine article here. John has used this noun earlier in 10:3 where the (masc.) gatekeeper opens to the (true) shepherd of the sheep. A claim that because the woman gatekeeper in 18:16–17 does not want to allow Simon Peter to enter, he is to be equated with the thief and bandit in 10:1 who does not enter through the gate represents a failure to recognize John's evaluation of Simon Peter. He is weak but scarcely one who cannot serve as shepherd of the sheep (21:15–17).

[7]By way of influence in the other direction, the article in 20:2 may refer back to a previous use of the designation *allos mathētēs* in 18:15: "that other disciple [mentioned previously]."

whom Jesus loved" stems from the supposition that the latter was John son of Zebedee. How would a Galilean fisherman be known to the Jerusalem high priest? Imaginative but hardly persuasive are explanations (some of them ancient) that the Zebedees were purveyors of fish by appointment to the high priestly palace, or were of the nobility, or were of priestly lineage.[8] Influenced in part by the problem of 18:15, some would identify as the beloved disciple another candidate who would have had a better chance of being known by the high priest, e.g., John Mark, whose mother had a house in Jerusalem (Acts 12:12), or Lazarus, who lived at Bethany near Jerusalem (John 11:1,18). The problem partially disappears if we acknowledge that the identity of the beloved disciple (and hence of "another disciple") cannot be established with plausibility—other than negatively: not one of the Twelve, and not purely symbolic.[9]

There is a more serious problem than that of the personal identity of "another disciple." How could any disciple of Jesus (and a fortiori the one whom he especially loved) who was known to the high priest gain entrance to the *aulē* at the very moment when the arresting party was delivering Jesus there?[10] How could such a disciple get in at the moment when Peter's entry was being challenged because he might be a disciple? It helps if one pays precise attention to the text here: John does not say that the disciple was *well or favorably* known to the high priest (although Nonnus, in his 5th-cent. poetic paraphrase [PG 43.892], understood John to mean that the disciple was "well known to the accustomed [famous, well established?] high priest"; see Drum, "Disciple"). Indeed, it is not clear that he is *known as a disciple* of Jesus, even though that may be the more likely implication. Thomson ("Saint" 381) contends that the "so" (*oun*) in John 18:17 is deductive: The servant woman asked Peter if he was a disciple of Jesus because she knew that "the other" was Jesus' disciple. *Oun* is so frequent in John as a simple continuative, however, that one cannot be certain that it is truly meaningful, and the Greek of the question she asks Peter does not imply that an affirmative answer is expected. As for the "too" in that question, "Are you *too* one of the disciples of this man?" it is not necessarily counterposed

---

[8]The last suggestion is often fortified by a complicated theory that John's mother was the sister of Mary mother of Jesus (see BGJ 2.906), who, as Elizabeth's relative, was of levitic, Aaronic descent (Luke 1:5,36).

[9]Parenthetically, there is little to recommend the identification of John's "another disciple" with the man in Mark 14:51–52 who followed Jesus after the others forsook him, only to run away naked (an identification favored by Bacon, Schenk; see Neirynck, "Other" 135–36). Even if one could hope that he had replenished his wardrobe before he approached the woman gatekeeper, nothing by way of vocabulary or action favors the theory.

[10]The solution that "another disciple" was Judas, who had given over Jesus to the high priest, defended by E. A. Abbott (*Expositor* 8th Ser.; 7 [1914] 166–73), avoids that objection; yet it is utterly implausible that John would describe the traitor so obliquely.

to her knowledge that the unnamed figure is a disciple. All the Synoptic Gospels have a "too" in the first challenge to Peter (#6 in table), and they report nothing of an unnamed figure who might be reflected in the "too." The adverbial stress is to be understood as reflecting a general knowledge that Jesus had disciples (see John 18:19) who were with him when he was arrested but are still at large. Thus we cannot discern with certitude whether John means readers to think that the woman gatekeeper was aware that this other man, who had been admitted to the *aulē* as one known to the priestly household, was a disciple of Jesus.[11] John describes Nicodemus as a member of the Sanhedrin (and hence implicitly as one known to the high priest) who is secretly disposed toward Jesus. In this *aulē* we may have another acquaintance of the high priest who, unbeknownst to that worthy, had become a favorite disciple of Jesus.

In any case these elements pertinent to the identity and background of this man are incidental; the main point of the description is the contrast between that other (beloved) disciple and Peter. "Disciple" is an important category in Johannine theology. In being asked at the beginning of the scene if he is a disciple too, Peter is being offered a chance to show himself as a true disciple who will go with Jesus to the cross. By denying he fails, while the other disciple will go on to stand at the foot of the cross (see Giblin, "Confrontations" 228–29).

As for the woman servant, in Matt 26:69 she is reported to have "come up" to Peter.[12] In Mark and Luke she is said to have seen and have looked or stared at[13] Peter by the flaming fire. In John, as the gatekeeper, she challenges Peter as he tries to enter the *aulē*. The words addressed to Peter by the woman are quite similar in the four Gospels, once one notes that the challenges in the Synoptics are always in the form of an accusation, and in John always in the form of a question (#6, 10, 14 in table). In Mark's accusa-

---

[11]Two attempts to discern this are failures in my judgment. (a) Some have tried to argue from John's use of negatives in the challenging questions posed to Peter. The first question contains a *mē*, and in classical usage *mē* indicates that a negative answer is expected: "You are not, are you?" But John also uses a *mē* in the second question to Simon Peter, and a negative answer is scarcely expected there. And John 18:26, the third question to Peter, uses *ouk*, which in classical usage would expect a positive answer. Probably all that the *mē/ouk* interchange represents is John's love of stylistic variation, especially in patterns of three, e.g., John 21:15–17; I John 2:12–14. (b) Some would argue that since Peter is recognizable (by his speech: Matt) as a Galilean (Synoptics) and hence as a disciple of Jesus, if the "another disciple" is not recognized, he must not have been a Galilean. One cannot use information from the Synoptics to decide a Johannine issue in this manner.

[12]"To come up" is *proserchesthai*, used fifty-two times by Matt, especially for the movement of people to Jesus (p. 253 above); it does not offer real precision about motion that could help us envision Matt's mental picture of the *aulē* here or of the *pylon* in the third denial ("entranceway": Matt 26:71). J. R. Edwards's thesis that *proserchesthai* describes a reverential approach to a figure of distinction breaks down in this instance.

[13]Luke's *atenizein* (twelve of fourteen NT uses are Lucan) is more intensive in connotation than Mark's *emblepein*.

tion[14] Jesus is called "the Nazarene" (*Nazarēnos*), while in Matt's he is called "the Galilean" (a designation that appears only here for Jesus in the NT). A reversed pattern will be seen in the accusations leading to Matt's second denial ("the Nazorean": *Nazōraios*) and to Mark's (and Luke's) third denial ("Galilean" in reference to Peter). Both *Nazarēnos* (4 times in Mark, 2 in Luke, never in Matt or John) and *Nazōraios* (8 times in Luke/Acts, 3 in John, 2 in Matt, never in Mark; see BBM 209–13) refer to Jesus' originating from Nazareth in Galilee, and so being a Galilean is an identifying factor in the Synoptic denial scene. Theissen ("Tempelweissagung" 149) finds plausible an apprehension about Galileans in Jerusalem at a time when many such rural people had come up for the feast and disturbances were feared (Mark 14:2). Luke 13:1–3 records that Pilate had trouble in the Temple area with Galileans apparently at a previous feast.

Describing Peter's reply to the servant woman, the three Synoptics say that "he denied" (*arneisthai,* expanded in Matt to a denial "before all"). That verb will appear again in the second reply in Mark/Matt and John (#11 in table), and in John's form of the third reply (#15). However, in Jesus' prediction of the threefold denial (§5 above) and in Peter's recalling that prediction at the end of this scene, the Synoptics consistently use *aparneisthai,* while John uses *arneisthai* in the prediction (and has no recall). No difference of innuendo should be found in this variation of verbs. (In the Greek of this period *arneisthai* can bear the meaning of denying that one has a personal involvement with or relation to someone; eventually it came to have the innuendo of apostatizing.[15]) A difference that is noteworthy is found in the actual wording of Peter's first denial (#7 in table):

Mark: I don't know nor understand what you are saying.
Matt: I don't know what you are saying.
Luke: I don't know him, Woman.
John: I am not (a disciple of this man).

John's negation is the gravest since from the start Peter denies his discipleship. His "I am not" (*ouk eimi*) is a dramatic contrast to the "I am" (*egō eimi*) spoken by Jesus before the arresting party in the garden. Matt has simplified Mark's complex statement by attributing to Peter only an evasion, as he pretends not to understand what the woman is saying.[16] Luke's simpli-

---

[14]In Mark/Matt "You too were . . ." employs the verbal form *ēstha*, an old Attic perfect tense used as an imperfect. This is the only NT instance of this form, and a few minuscules substitute in Mark the regular imperfect form *ēs*.

[15]Riesenfeld, "Meaning," esp. 213–14.

[16]For the Mishnaic Hebrew equivalent of Matt's simplified form, see *Šebu'ot* 8.3, where it is also an evasion.

fication of Mark has Peter do something more serious, since he lies by saying that he does not know Jesus. A peculiarity in Luke's form of all three replies by Peter (#7, 11, 15) is the inclusion of a vocative address to the questioner, respectively, Woman, Man, Man (*anthrōpos*)—perhaps a narrative touch to portray sincerity. Luke 5:20 and 13:12 also have such a vocative.

The truly complex reply attributed to Peter is found in Mark. I have translated it into imperfect English ("don't know nor understand") to reflect a problem in the Greek. By using *oute . . . oute* for "not . . . nor" the evangelist is technically ungrammatical since these particles should not connect synonyms such as "know" and "understand"; and so it is not surprising that the scribes whose sense of more elegant Greek is enshrined in the Koine tradition have left evidence of a change to *ouk . . . oude* (BDF 445²). Some modern interpreters would improve the normal rendering of Mark by reading: "I don't know nor understand. What is it you are saying?" Yet it seems clear from Matt's "I don't know what you are saying" that he did not read Mark that way. Others would argue that Luke understood Mark as an anacoluthon, meaning, "I don't know *him* nor understand what you are saying," and then copied only the first half. Rather, just as Matt selected a simpler statement from Mark's complication, so also Luke simplified with "I don't know him," which is totally harmonious with his phrasing of Jesus' prediction to Peter in 22:34: "A cock will not crow today until you have three times denied *knowing me.*"[17] The most appropriate judgment is that Mark's phrasing catches the repetitiveness of common speech to get across a point—in the language of grammatical analysis, an intensive hendiadys. Yet the popularist style should not disguise the fact that among the evangelists Mark may have the most careful psychological and theological progression in the phrasing of Peter's responses, moving from claimed lack of understanding and knowledge (#7 in table) to denial (#11), on to the cursing rejection of Jesus (#15; see ANALYSIS).

SECOND DENIAL

While for purposes of organizing information we may find it useful to divide a treatment of the denials in this manner, the Gospels do so only in varying degrees. The division is sharpest in John, where Peter's first denial is separated from the second and third denials by the (intervening but simultaneous) actions of Annas, who questions Jesus and sends him bound to Caiaphas. Continuity is kept, however, by repeating vocabulary from the first

---

[17]Surely this is a more plausible analysis than the unnecessary appeal of BAA 79–81 to a misunderstanding of a putative Aramaic original in Mark, presumably undone by the later evangelists.

denial at the beginning of the second: "But Simon Peter was standing there and warming himself." Among the Synoptics, Luke's "after a short time" separates the first and second denials by time, while Mark/Matt have a change of locale. Peter's move from the *aulē*, "court," to the *proaulion*, "forecourt," in Mark 14:68b in a sense brings the first denial to a conclusion and could have been placed with the preceding section, as the versification suggests.

That sense of termination in Mark is fortified in some mss. of the Koine Greek tradition (plus the OL, Vulgate, and Syriac Peshitta) by the addition of "and a cock crowed." Some scholars argue for the likelihood of that reading (e.g., Pesch, *Markus* 2.447), suggesting that it was later dropped to make Mark correspond with the other Gospels. More likely, however, the scribal "improvement" went in the other direction: Since Mark 14:72 mentions that the cock crowed a second time, scribes felt that a first time should be mentioned. The omission (Vaticanus, Sinaiticus, OS[sin]) is the "harder" reading and should be preferred. It is not illogical that Mark mentions the second cockcrow without mentioning the first, for it is the second that fulfills Jesus' prediction. To mention a cockcrow after the first denial would have hurt the plausibility of the narrative: Would it not already have reminded Peter of Jesus' words?

The first of Peter's denials was placed by John at the gate (*thyra*) to the *aulē* and by the Synoptics harmoniously in the *aulē*.[18] There is more diversity in the localization of the second denial. Luke and John place it in the *aulē;* Mark places it in the *proaulion* (forecourt) into which Peter has gone outside from the *aulē;* Matt places it in the *pylōn* (entranceway) into which Peter has gone out from the *aulē*. Both Mark and Matt use *exerchesthai* for the action of going out; in addition Mark has an *exō* ("outside").[19] Matt's omission of that adverb probably stems from an attempt to avoid tautology. Architectural harmonization of the Gospel information has been attempted in the articles of Ramsay ("Denials," 541) and Balagué ("Negaciones" 79). In a rectangular building was there a continuous path that led one from the *pylōn* entrance into the forecourt (*proaulion*) and then through the gate (*thyra*) into the *aulē*, whether that be a courtyard or a hall of the building? Or were *pylōn, proaulion,* and *thyra* variant names for the one entrance into the *aulē?*[20] Such queries are sometimes based on the unlikely assumption

---

[18]Let us recall that the evangelists may have envisioned the *aulē* differently.

[19]The use of *exō* here is the sole instance of Mark's employment of it in the denials. Matt uses it twice in the present scene: The *aulē* of the first denial is outside, and Peter goes farther outside after the third denial. Luke has it only after the third denial; John has it only before the first denial.

[20]In particular, Ramsay ("Denials" 411) argues that the house was a rectangle with towers on the four corners (*tetrapyrgion*), and on one side a passage constituting an entrance gateway (*pylōn* or *proaulion*), with the gate (*thyra*) at the outer end.

that each Gospel has preserved exact historical memories of the locale, rather than an unspecified tradition about an *aulē* and an entrance to it. Much closer to likelihood is the prosaic suggestion (SPNM 201) that Matt prefers *pylōn* as a more common word for Mark's unusual *proaulion* (not found in the LXX or elsewhere in the NT).

Why does Mark have Peter move outside into the *proaulion* for the second denial? Some scholars see here the traces of an earlier story which had Peter leaving after the one and only denial. I do not think the evidence favors that thesis, as I shall explain in the ANALYSIS. Rather, the move dramatizes Peter's weakness: He wants to avoid further, dangerous confrontation, but he is still not willing to give up altogether his halfhearted attempt to fulfill the boast that he would not be like the other disciples who were scattered sheep (Mark 14:27). Objections of scholars to the logic of the scene, e.g., Peter has moved outside but the same servant woman is involved, often do not do justice to the subtlety of the Marcan picture. Mark does not report in the second denial that the servant woman looked (carefully) at Peter or that she spoke to him, as reported in the first denial. The woman is not in the *proaulion* next to Peter but back in the *aulē*, seeing him from a distance and talking about him aloud to the bystanders. The woman's nagging persistence has foiled Peter's ploy to escape attention. Both Matt and Luke choose to simplify the complexity of the Marcan picture. Matt preserves the movement of Peter; but in the *pylōn* there is another audience ("those there"), and in Peter's presence another servant woman is the accuser.[21] Thus Matt gives greater distinctness to the denials (similar to Matt's procedure in regard to Jesus' second visit to his sleeping disciples in Gethsemane; pp. 204–5 above). Luke avoids the complication of moving Peter from the *aulē* and has another (a man)[22] as the accuser. At least that explanation seems more probable than positing that here Luke is following a nonMarcan tradition witnessed also in John, who has the second denial take place in the *aulē*—in Table 3 Luke is closer to Mark in #9, closer to John in #8, 11. Perhaps the denial before a man makes Peter's stance legally more grave.

As for the actual denial by Peter (#11 in table), since for Mark the accusing woman servant is still back in the *aulē*, Peter does not address words directly to her. Yet despite the repetitive character of this second denial scene in Mark ("again" in 14:70a), Peter's stance has become more reprehensible; for he is shown as repeatedly denying (impf. tense) the woman's charge that

---

[21]The possibility of another servant woman may have been suggested by Mark's description of the challenger in the first denial (14:66): "one of the servant women." McEleney ("Peter's" 468, 471) sees this as an example of Matt's penchant for pluralizing items that Mark presents in the singular.

[22]*Heteros* ("another") is five times more frequent in Luke-Acts than in the other three Gospels together.

he is "one of them" (14:69), i.e., one of those who were "with the Nazarene, Jesus" as previously in 14:67—a precision that Matt 26:71 spells out. The Marcan Peter is no longer evading by claiming not to understand: Jesus had appointed the Twelve to be *with him,* and first among those so honored was Simon to whom he assigned the name Peter (Mark 3:14,16); now this Peter "was denying" all that. Matt's Peter fortifies the denial with an oath and in direct speech says that he does not even know Jesus.[23] (Notice a similar contrast in Gethsemane [§11 above] between Mark's Jesus who has no direct speech in his second prayer, and Matt's Jesus whose prayer involves new direct speech, developed in nuance beyond the first prayer.) The words of Luke's Peter, "I am not [*ouk eimi*]," besides denying discipleship, forms by anticipation an interesting contrast with the words Jesus will speak (22:70) before the chief priests who challenge him about being the Son of God: "You yourselves say that I am [*eimi*]." I pointed to a similar contrast in John, who used "I am not [*ouk eimi*]" for Peter's first denial and repeats it here; it is counterposed to the words spoken in 18:5 by Jesus to those who came with Judas looking for the Nazorean, "I am he [*eimi*]." The wording in both Luke and John shows the readers that Peter's behavior is the opposite of Jesus'.

THIRD DENIAL

Unlike the second denial, there is no change of locale here to offer difficulties. Yet the three Synoptics postulate a time interval (#12 in table), with Luke positing "about one hour."[24] Once again there are variant descriptions of the challenger of Peter in the Gospels (#13 in table). John is specific: a servant of the high priest, a relative of the servant whose ear Peter had cut off. (This identification has the function of tying the denials to a previous Petrine scene in John; the Synoptics will accomplish the same result by having Peter recall Jesus' previous prediction [#17 in table].) Mark refers to the bystanders (*parestōtes*) as the challengers of Peter, while Matt refers to those present (*estōtes*). Both seem to envision a group of people in the *proaulion* or *pylōn* similar to the audience that there had been in the *aulē*.[25] Gerhardsson ("Confession" 52) makes the point that the gradation to a plural audience in the Mark/Matt third denial causes the denial to become more public and thus legally more grave.

---

[23] In all three denials the Matthean Peter says, "I don't know."

[24] *Hōsei* ("about") occurs fifteen times in Luke-Acts, versus four times in the other Gospels. The "hour" helps to fill in the night left vacant when Luke moved Mark's trial to the morning.

[25] Indeed, without evidence in the text some scholars would move the Mark/Matt scene back to the *aulē* where the scene occurs for Luke and John. That move would destroy the progressive distancing of Peter from Jesus; he is ever farther outside. This is an important motif for Mark/Matt, running throughout the denials.

The third Synoptic accusation (#14 in table) implies that Peter was easily detectable as a Galilean, stemming from his manner of speech according to Matt. (In fact Peter had spoken few words thus far; but such a free-flowing narrative should not be pressed for minute exactitude, and one does not need to suppose that Peter had said more than is recorded.) Matt probably means nothing more specific than that Peter, like Jesus, had a regional accent characteristic of Galilee.[26] The challenge to the Lucan Peter is phrased in such a way that he will have to deny "in truth" that he was with (*meta*) Jesus; ironically in 22:33 Peter had insisted, "Lord, I am ready to go with [*meta*] you both to prison and to death."

Peter's reply (#15 in table) is of note in Mark/Matt, for it involves two intensifying actions: he began "to curse" (respectively *anathematizein* and *kathanathematizein*[27]) and "to swear" (respectively *omnynai* and *omnyein*[28]). The second verb is clear: Denial has reached such a stage of intensity that Peter is willing to take an oath that he does not know Jesus. (In Matt this has the added gravity of defying Jesus' command not to take oaths [5:34].) The first verb needs clarification, however. Some take "curse" and "swear" as a hendiadys, so that nothing more is involved than a sworn oath. But Matt 26:72 already had an oath in the second denial, and so the addition of "curse" here probably refers to another action. What separate action would be covered by *anathematizein?* The verb, normally transitive, means to place something under a curse or to bind someone with an oath that, if broken, would involve a curse. In Acts 23:12,14,21 it is used with a reflexive pronominal object: "The Jews bound themselves by an oath." In Mark 14:71 no object, reflexive or otherwise, is expressed for Peter's cursing (the only biblical example of such a construction); and so it is very dubious that it should be read intransitively as simply "curse" or, more precisely, as "bound himself under a curse" (RSV: "invoke a curse on himself").[29] Even more dubious is the contention (SPNM 206, citing Schlatter) that Matt's *katanathematizein* may

---

[26]Rothenaicher ("Zu Mk") correctly challenges the thesis of Holtzmeister that Mark changed Matt's "Your speech makes you obvious" to "You are a Galilean" because Mark's Roman audience would not understand that the dialect of Peter's Galilean area might be different from that of Jerusalem. Certainly Italian-peninsula Romans had experienced dialectal differences! To the contrary, Matt is spelling out pedagogically Mark's implication. The "Western" text of Matt 26:73 (Codex Bezae, OL, OS^sin) clearly joins Peter's speech style to that of Jesus, "Your speech is similar." J. C. James (ExpTim 19 [1907–8], 524) and others have tried to identify the speech pecularity as a Galilean tendency to slur Semitic gutturals (e.g., '*ayin* becomes *aleph*), as attested in TalBab '*Erubin* 53b.

[27]Merkel ("Peter's" 66) contends that these two verbs do not differ significantly in meaning.

[28]*Omnynai* is a more classical usage, and *omnyein* (which appears also in the Koine witnesses of Mark) is more popular.

[29]Some invoke in the discussion a variant description of Peter's action in an apocryphal Jewish gospel: "He denied and he swore and he cursed [*katarasthai*]." Often this is attributed to the *Gospel of the Hebrews* (16) and rendered transitively (JANT 7). But HSNTA 1.149 (rev. ed., 1.162) attributes it to the *Gospel of the Nazarenes* (19) and renders it intransitively: "damned himself."

intensify the intransitive force: "call down curses [on himself]." Lampe, Gerhardsson, Menestrina, Merkel, and Seitz are among the many scholars who argue forcefully that "curse" should be taken transitively with "Jesus" understood as the object: Peter cursed Jesus and took an oath that he had no personal acquaintance with him.[30] The importance of this interpretation will be discussed in the ANALYSIS. Granted the harshness of Mark's picture here, it is no surprise that Luke's account of the third denial modifies it—the Lucan denials do not mount in intensity.

COCKCROW

All the Gospels follow Peter's third denial with a notice that "immediately a cock crowed" (#16 in table; Luke uses his favorite *parachrēma*, "at that moment"). Mark 14:72 alone mentions that this was happening "a second time." Above in discussing the termination of the first denial that constitutes a transition to the second (Mark 14:68b: see bracketed phrase in the translation), I mentioned that some scribes added a (first) cockcrow there in order to explain how this could be the second. Occasionally it has been suggested that the reference in 14:68b was not only original but the only Marcan reference to cockcrow, and that later scribes added a cockcrow here after the third denial to harmonize Mark with the other Gospels[31]—a cockcrow that logically had to become the second cockcrow. In some mss., on the other hand, scribes omitted "second" here precisely to harmonize Mark with the other Gospels that do not have the word and also because Mark has never mentioned a first cockcrow (an indication that they found no cockcrow in 14:68b). I would judge that what later scribes did, Matt and Luke had done earlier: They eliminated the Marcan "a second time" because it made little sense to them.[32] As I pointed out on p. 137 above, that phrase may be an implicit precision equivalent to "before the next dawn" since the dawn was associated with the second cockcrow.[33]

[30]The obscure Did 16:5 seems to speak of Jesus as "the one cursed" (*to katathema*).

[31]Still another thesis is that of Wenham ("How Many") that the interpolation of the first cockcrow in 14:68b led to still another interpolation of "second" here. His article is useful for seeing the variants even if I do not accept the thesis that "second" is an interpolation.

[32]I find quite implausible the thesis of G. Murray ("Saint") that Mark drew on Matt and Luke. Strangely unable to find a reason why Matt and Luke would have omitted "a second time" if they were using Mark (whereas, in my judgment, they would have seen it as an unnecessary complication, even as did textual scribes), he offers no reason for why Mark would have added "a second time" if he was using Matt and Luke, neither of which had it. Moreover, there is little reason to think that Mark used Luke throughout for the denials, for about the only item shared by Mark and Luke that is not shared by Mark and Matt is having Peter "near the blazing flame" (#4 in table). To my mind this passage is another example of the unlikelihood of the Griesbach hypothesis.

[33]Deprecatory of Wenham's efforts (n. 31 above) because he does not draw on Jewish background, Derrett ("Reason") appeals to Jewish evidence ranging *from 500 to 1,000 years after* Jesus' time to argue that evil spirits moved about at night until the second cockcrow!

Beyond the difficulty created by Mark's peculiar reading, there are several other problems raised by the reference to cockcrow. Are the evangelists describing an actual cockcrow or simply a designated time of night? Were there cocks in Jerusalem? If so, at what time did they usually crow?

Mayo ("St. Peter's" 367–70) exemplifies the thesis that the evangelists in general, or Mark in particular, or even the preMarcan tradition was referring not to the crowing of a domestic bird aroused from sleep but to the third watch of the night by Roman reckoning (12–3 A.M.), called "cockcrow" (*gallicinium, alektōrophonia*). More specifically in this thesis the cockcrow is identified as the signal given on the curved trumpet or horn (*buc[c]ina*) at the end of the watch. More specifically still, Mark's two cockcrows have been identified as the signals at the beginning and the end of that watch (Balagué, "Negaciones" 80). It is factual that in this era in Jerusalem the four watches (*vigilia, phylakē*) of the night, reflecting Roman military discipline, had become a standard way of reckoning time, probably more used than the older Hebrew division of the night into three watches.[34] In Mishna *Yoma* 1.8 four watches are listed. Each of the four Roman watches consisted of three hours: *opse*, "the late hour" (6–9 P.M.); *mesonyktion*, "midnight" (9–12 A.M.); "cockcrow" (12–3 A.M.): *prōi*, "early" (3–6 A.M.); they are listed in Mark 13:35. Yet there is *no* evidence that the evangelists were thinking here of such a set time period. The abstract temporal designation *alektōrophonia* does not occur in the PN, unless one accepts the very slim evidence for it in Matt 26:34,75 collected by Zuntz (p. 136 above); and even then the word in that context can refer to the bird's cry. Consistently the Gospels refer to *a* cock crowing; the lack of a definite article suggests that if the original reference was to the watch of cockcrow, all the evangelists misunderstood it.

Accepting the likelihood that the Gospels were referring to the cry of a bird, we now must ask whether there were cocks in Jerusalem. Mishna *Baba Qamma* 7.7 forbids the rearing of fowl in Jerusalem and further forbids priests to rear them anywhere in Israel. (We remember that the Gospels have the cock heard crowing in or adjacent to the *aulē* of the high priest.) One cannot be certain, however, that this law recorded in the late 2d cent. was in force in Jesus' time or even was observed rigorously at any time (see JJTJ 47–48[44]). TalJer *'Erubin* 10.1 supposes the presence of cocks in Jerusalem; and Krauss ("Défense" 28–25) wonders whether the restriction did not apply only to the Temple area. References to cocks in the OT are disputable:[35] Prov 30:31 can have in mind any bird; Job 38:36 may refer to a cock. In a

---

[34]On night watches cf. Lam 2:19; Judg 7:19; Exod 14:24; Matt 24:43; and Luke 12:38.
[35]See Brunet, "Et aussitôt"; Fitzmyer, *Luke* 2.1427.

Hellenistic setting, *III Macc* 5:23 alludes to cocks crowing in the morning. A *baraita* (older tradition) in TalBab *Berakot* 60b states that God gave "to the cock understanding to distinguish between day and night"; and TalBab *Yoma* 21a imagines that evil spirits are about at night until the cock crows. None of this evidence is particularly pertinent for the Jerusalem of Jesus' time; and perhaps all we can argue is that the evangelists who were close to the customs of the time (and John in particular seems to preserve some accurate detailed information about Jerusalem) did not hesitate to report a cock's crow being heard.

When did cocks normally crow at this time of the year? It is humorous to think of scholars sitting up at night in 20th-cent. Jerusalem listening for cocks to crow, but that has been done! Lattey ("Note") argues that the first light gets the cocks crowing, and reports that M. J. Lagrange experienced the earliest cockcrow in April at 2:30 A.M., with most of the cries coming between 3:00 and 5:00 A.M. Kosmala ("Time") argues that regular crowing of the cock was known since antiquity and that there is evidence for three distinct nocturnal cockcrows throughout the year in Palestine (about 12:30, 1:30, and 2:30) with the second as traditionally the most important. W. M. Ramsay (ExpTim 28 [1916–17] 280) places cockcrowing between 2:00 and 5:15 A.M. Despite all this, Cicero (*De Divinatione* 2.26.56) may well be right: "Is there any time, night or day, that cocks do not crow?" The evangelists are imagining the early hours of the morning before dawn; nothing more definite can be concluded.

PETER'S REACTION

All the Gospels correlate the cockcrow with Peter's third denial, and so the evangelists wish readers to be struck by the exact fulfillment of Jesus' prophecy of threefold denial before cockcrow—a prophecy that the Synoptics have Peter recall almost verbatim.[36] The Greek verb "remember" differs in the account of each Synoptic Gospel, but the description of what was remembered is smoother in Matt and Luke than it is in Mark's awkward: "Peter remembered the word as Jesus had spoken it to him" (14:72). J. N. Birdsall (NovT 2 [1957–58], 272–75) argues that *hōs* ("as") can be used in constructions such as Mark's when more is the object of reference than the mere existence of the antecedent. He would have Peter recall not only the words of the prediction but the warmer context of the Last Supper that preceded it.

[36]When an action that John narrates fulfills something that has been said previously, he normally points that out (in the PN: John 18:9,14,32; 19:39). It is surprising that he leaves readers on their own to remember the fulfillment of Jesus' prediction in Peter's denials.

Granted the Synoptic evangelists' emphasis on Peter's recall of Jesus' prophecy, how do they envision Peter's final state of mind? All three use the word *klaiein* (Mark: impf. tense; Matt and Luke: aorist, plus *pikrōs,* "bitterly"). In about half of the twenty-one other Gospel uses of the verb, it refers to wailing over the deceased, so that a very emotional reaction seems to be implied here (LaVerdiere, "Peter"). Indeed, one can see the lamentation developed imaginatively in *Acts of Peter* (Vercelli) 7:20: "I bitterly lamented and bewailed the weakness of my faith because I was deceived by the devil and did not keep in mind the word of the Lord."

The drama of Peter's going outside and weeping bitterly in Matt and Luke suggests a man overcome by remorse and now distanced from any possibility of fulfilling his promise, "Lord, I am ready to go with you both to prison and to death" (Luke 22:33) or "Even if it be necessary for me to die with you, I will not deny you" (Matt 26:35). Jesus' prediction, not Peter's, had proved true. Now all that Peter can hope is that Jesus' other predictions would come true as well: "Simon, Simon . . . I have prayed for you that your faith might not fail. And you, when you have turned around [*epistrephein*], strengthen your brothers" (Luke 22:31–32) and "After my resurrection I shall go before you into Galilee" (Matt 26:32). To treat Peter's action in Matt and Luke as one of despair without hope is not to do justice to the whole picture in those Gospels. Both Matt 12:32 and Luke 12:10 promised the possibility of forgiveness even if one spoke against the Son of Man. In both Matt 28:16 (within "the Eleven") and Luke 24:34 Peter will be remembered as having seen the risen Jesus.

In Luke before Peter's exit from the *aulē* there is a unique scene in which "the Lord" (Luke tends to use this title), whom we now have to presume to have been present through all these denials, "having turned [*strephein*], looked at Peter" (22:61). It is this action, not the cockcrow, that is the primary impetus for Peter to remember "the saying of the Lord." Are we to think that in seeing Jesus turn, the Lucan Peter remembered also the prophecy that he himself in the future would turn, this time in strength, not in weakness?[37] According to Mark 14:66 Jesus has been upstairs in the high priest's house while Peter was below in the *aulē;* and so an artistic attempt to harmonize Mark with Luke has been to imagine that Jesus turned and looked out of the window of an upper room and caught Peter's eye in the courtyard (see Schweizer, *Luke* 347). As we shall see in the ANALYSIS, more likely we are dealing with a deliberate Lucan change: He has Jesus together with Peter in the *aulē* to show Jesus' enduring care for his follower at this moment when Satan has tested him (22:31).

---

[37]In Luke-Acts *strephein* ("to turn") is used ten times, often with theological import.

John diverges from the other Gospels at the end of the third denial, not only by reporting no recall by Peter of Jesus' prediction, but also by no mention of weeping by Peter. Functionally this last omission will be compensated in John 21:15–17, where Jesus' threefold questioning of Peter's love causes Peter hurt—all of this before Peter is given a favorable postresurrectional role.

We have not yet discussed Mark's description of Peter's reaction after recalling Jesus' prediction of the denials. Its very obscurity, which will be the subject of the next paragraph, helps to explain why neither Matt nor Luke saw fit to copy it (cf. the last lines of #17 in Table 3). But how then did both evangelists fasten on a verbatim identical substitution: "And having gone outside, he wept bitterly," since in the theory of their dependence on Mark, neither Matt nor Luke is thought to have known the other's work? One solution for this troubling "minor agreement" draws on the fact that Luke 22:62 (and hence this clause) is missing from a 9th-cent. minuscule Greek ms. (0171) and from some OL witnesses. Later scribes of Luke, it is theorized, copied the clause from Matt; and thus it got into most textual witnesses. More plausibly, Soards (*Passion* 102) suggests that even after drawing upon Mark, in a popular narrative like this which was surely told and retold, both evangelists were influenced by oral tradition, and in that tradition an emotional phrase like this was already fixed. (*Pikrōs*, "bitterly," is not characteristic of either Matt or Luke.)

Mark's description of Peter's reaction terminating 14:72 is a famous problem: *kai epibalōn, eklaien*, "And ———, he was weeping." The imperfect tense of *eklaien* can be rendered inchoatively (cf. aorist BDF 331), "he began to weep"; but the force of *epibalōn* remains obscure. The form is the aorist participle of *epiballein*, "to throw over/on; to put on," which can be either transitive or intransitive. In order to have the proposed meaning of the verb make sense with the main clause about Peter's weeping, imaginative supplementation has been required. The logic of the supplementation is often uncertain, but here are proposals:

(a) having thrown (himself), i.e., broke down (RSV)
(b) having thrown (himself down), i.e., to the ground[38]
(c) having thrown (himself out), i.e., rushed outside; this interpretation might be confirmed by Matt's and Luke's "having gone outside" and was favored by T. Beza.
(d) having thrown (himself into), i.e., begun (to cry); burst into (tears).[39] It

---

[38]See C. H. Turner, *The Gospel According to St. Mark* (London: SPCK, 1928), 74.
[39]In articles on Mark 14:72 in ExpTim and *Biblica*, Lee cites examples from Diogenes Laertius and Athenaeus; see also Papyrus Tebtunis 1.50.12.

is an interpretation mentioned by Theophylact and favored by Luther. Perhaps it is reflected by the Western reading of Mark 14:72: "He began [*ērxato*] to weep," but that might simply represent an inchoative interpretation of *eklaien,* as mentioned above.[40] See also BDF 308.

(e) having thrown (his mind to it), i.e., thought of Jesus' prediction.[41] This was the KJV and RV reading.

(f) having cast (his eyes), i.e., on Jesus. This would bring Mark close to Luke, but one must remember that Mark 14:66 separates Jesus from Peter in an upstairs/downstairs arrangement.

(g) having thrown (back), i.e., answered. Usages from Polybius (*Histories* 1.80.1; 22.3.8) are cited.

(h) having thrown (a piece of clothing on), e.g., "and covering his head" (Theophylact), perhaps to disguise himself (cowardice) or to hide his face (shame).

(i) having beat on himself, i.e., the gesture of striking the chest (Boomershine, "Peter's" 59).

Gnilka (*Markus* 2.294) argues that only (d) "begun" and (e) "thought" are likely, but I find both of those tautological (especially if *eklaien* is inchoative). With great hesitation I have chosen (c); however, this is one more of the very obscure phrases in Mark's passion narrative (see APPENDIX III, A).

ANALYSIS

A. **The Gospel Accounts and Tradition**

Perhaps nowhere else in the PN do the Gospels agree so much in the overall flow of the story as in the denials of Jesus by Peter. Perusal of the table given at the beginning of the COMMENT shows that the minor details vary widely (who challenged Peter, in what words, where, and how he responded[42]), but in sixteen of seventeen points of comparison there is a comparability of sequence. Even in details Matt hews close to Mark, and so there is no reason to posit an independent source for Matt. Competent scholars (Bultmann, Catchpole, Dodd, Grundmann, G. Klein, Rengstorf) have argued that Luke's account of the denials differs significantly enough from Mark's to

---

[40]That simpler solution would make unnecessary the proposal of F. Bussby (BJRL 21 [1937], 273–74), who posits a misunderstanding based on reading Aramaic *šd'/šdy* ("to pour out") for the correct *šr'/šry,* which in Syriac means "to begin."

[41]J. M. Danson (ExpTim 19 [1907–8], 307–8) cites classical examples in support.

[42]The details vary so much that determined harmonizers, trying to preserve the historical accuracy of the various Gospels, sometimes posited six denials, or even nine (three groupings of three)!

allow Lucan dependence on an independent source. More scholars, however (including Finegan, Fitzmyer, Linnemann, Schneider, and Soards) judge Luke to be derivative from Mark. Taylor (*Passion* 77–78), who is normally a strong adherent of Lucan independence, points out that about 50 percent of the Lucan wording here is found in Mark, scattered throughout. He judges, "Luke's source is manifestly Mark," and variations can be adequately explained from inferences in Mark. Minor vocabulary differences are generally understandable as Lucan stylistic preference (Fitzmyer, *Luke* 2.1457). Over against Perry and Osty, Soards (*Passion* 77) is correct in arguing that in the account of Peter's denials Luke is closer to Mark than to John. As the COMMENT above indicates, I too judge Luke to be dependent on Mark in this scene and see no need for an independent source.[43]

John offers the only likelihood of a Gospel account of the denials independent of Mark. N. Perrin and others who contend that Mark originated the PN will logically conclude that here John depends on Mark. Fortna ("Jesus") has studied the denials with the supposition that although Perrin overestimates the case for the Marcan composition of the Sanhedrin night trial, Donahue's study of that scene (which is the basis of Perrin's thesis) can be relied on in its detection of Marcan elements. (See §19 above where I expressed disagreement with aspects of Donahue's approach, and so I would have more reason than Fortna to challenge Perrin's thesis.) Even with this concession, Fortna ("Jesus" 381) argues for the independence of John in this scene,[44] as do Boismard and Schneider.

A principal argument for John's dependence on Mark is that both of them place Peter's denials contemporaneous with the Jewish interrogation of Jesus. Let me repeat, however, the reasoning that negates the force of that argument. It was fixed in the tradition that Jesus was given over (into the hands of his captors) at night (I Cor 11:23), and equally fixed that he was crucified publicly (Gal 3:1) and therefore in the daytime. Any Jewish interrogation of Jesus in this period before he was given over to Pilate had to happen either at night after the arrest or in the early morning before the crucifixion—the very two positions in which we find it in the various Gospels. If

---

[43]See the careful argumentation of Linnemann (*Studien* 97–101) on this. I had not studied the issue in detail when, in a passing comment, I favored the opposite stance in BGJ 2.837. As mentioned above in the COMMENT on Matt 26:75 and Luke 22:62, I think that an oral memory of the preGospel tradition survived even after Mark's written account, and that memory explains the "minor agreement" between Matt and Luke on "And having gone outside, he wept bitterly."

[44]Fortna's argument is complex because he thinks he can reconstruct John's Greek source and that John's source can be shown to be independent of Mark. I am not sure that either John's source or Mark's can be reconstructed with accuracy, and so I shall compare the existing Gospels. I particularly reject the use of the OS^{sin} text of John 18:15–27; that ms. betrays a very early attempt to improve on Johannine order; it witnesses the scribe's ingenuity, not the original order of John. See p. 407 above.

there was a tradition that in connection with the arrest all the disciples failed Jesus and that in particular, Peter denied knowing him or being a disciple, that had to take place at night when or just after he was arrested (a time further necessitated if cockcrow was involved in the denial of Peter). Therefore, those Gospels that placed the Jewish interrogation at night had no choice about somehow interrelating it with the denials. (A Gospel that put the interrogation in the early morning would have to put the denials before, and that is exactly what Luke did.[45]) Thus the *fact* of correlation between the Jewish interrogation and Peter's denials reveals nothing of where an evangelist got the detailed account of either scene; the *manner* of correlation might. John's form of correlation (one denial before, two after) is different from Mark's, even as John's account of the Jewish interrogation is different from Mark's; and so the structure of the scene lends no clear support to John's dependence on Mark.[46]

What about details? Mark and John agree on Peter's having followed the arrested Jesus and having denied him three times before cockcrow in a setting that involves a fire in the *aulē* of the high priest and a woman servant. These are basic details that one could easily attribute to a simple preGospel story.[47] But the two Gospels vary widely in how they combine these details (more widely than Matt or Luke varies from Mark). John places the first denial outside before Peter enters the *aulē*, and the second and third denials at the fire in the *aulē;* Mark places the first denial in the *aulē* at the fire, and the second and third denials outside the *aulē* and away from the fire. Except for key terms like *aulē*, *paidiskē* ("servant woman"), "cock," "warming," and "deny," there is no real vocabulary agreement. It is hard to see that John preserves any clearly Marcan features, and so I find no convincing reason to think that John drew on Mark for his account.[48] More plausible is the theory

[45]The Marcan order in chap. 14 is Sanhedrin trial, mockery, denials; the Lucan order in chap. 22 is denials, mockery, Sanhedrin interrogation. Luke's shift of the mockery to before the interrogation by the Jewish authorities matches the sequence of suffering before rejection by Jewish leaders in Jesus' prediction in Luke 9:22. Also the pattern of martyr stories, which is important to Luke, places abuse first so that the confession is seen to be more noble (II Macc 7:1–12; *IV Macc* 6:3–30; 8:12ff.).

[46]Dewey ("Peter's Denial") argues that the fact that both Mark and John intercalate the denials amid an inquiry by the high priest shows dependence of John on Mark; he does not make allowance for how different the intercalation or correlation is. Dewey's other arguments do not deal with the possibility that independently Mark and John drew on an earlier form of the story. The major argument proposed by him that offers difficulty for Johannine independence of Mark is that each Gospel uses "warming himself" twice, with the second instance as part of the repetition when the evangelist returns to the Peter story (Mark 14:54,67; John 18:18,25). However, resuming a story by picking up the language from the last reference is not an unusual technique.

[47]Fortna ("Jesus" 378) quite correctly challenges the assignment of the pattern of three and of cockcrow to *Marcan* redaction, as in the analysis by Dewey ("Peter's Curse" 100–2). See below.

[48]One cannot *disprove* a theory of John's dependence on Mark that would attribute to John editorial freedom or a major addition of nonMarcan material; the issue is one of likelihood and of Johannine practice in general.

that John, like Mark, drew his story from earlier tradition—not necessarily the same preGospel form of the tradition but one that had the basic details that I listed at the beginning of this paragraph. Each evangelist would have made adjustments in the respective preGospel form he used.

We must now consider the issue of *one or three denials*. In §11, A2, we saw how K. G. Kuhn theorized that the Gethsemane scene in Mark represented a combination of two parallel sources and that only through that combination did there emerge *three* visits of Jesus to his sleeping disciples. Similarly here some would argue that in the core of what came to Mark there was only one denial, and that three denials appeared in the Marcan form of the story only through combination or editing. For instance, Masson ("Reniement" 28–29) suggests that Mark combined parallel separate traditions represented in 14:66–68 and 14:69–72. In the last verse of the first Peter went outside and a cock crowed; in the second (which before Mark's editing took place in the *aulē*), again the conclusion had a cockcrow and Peter going outside.[49] Other scholars, like Dewey, think that Mark received from tradition an account of only one denial and that he edited it to consist of three denials. The contention that John's account may well be independent of Mark's obviously works against these approaches, but let us discuss the issue in more detail.

Two possibilities are involved that should be kept distinct. The *first possibility* is that in the earliest formulation of the tradition there was only the specification that Peter denied Jesus and that later, under the influence of Jesus' prediction which had in a generalizing way mentioned reiterated denials, there evolved three denials. When we come below to the discussion of Peter's denials as an effective narrative and an encouragement for persecuted Christians, I shall point to parabolic qualities. Thus, even as with the Gethsemane story, the parabolic thrust may have brought into play "the rule of three" so common in parables (pp. 11–12 above). I judge this theory plausible, although impossible to prove, for it postulates an early stage of the tradition that cannot be reconstructed with surety. G. Klein ("Verleugnung" 309–10), although he does not think the denials are historical, is probably correct in arguing that the traceable preGospel tradition already has the threefold pattern.[50]

The *second possibility* is that Mark was responsible for developing three

---

[49]This is only one of the imaginative theories of combination. Walter ("Verleugnung" 49) asks whether the original form of the denials contained only two (the present first and last), with the awkward middle denial inserted later.

[50]In BGJ 2.1094–95, 1110–14, I argued that the scene involving a threefold questioning of Simon Peter by Jesus in John 21:15–17 may represent a very old tradition. The threefold pattern there is related to the threefold pattern here.

denials from one, leaving seams of editing or combining. (Obviously, then, the three-denial story could not have existed before 70; it would have quickly become so sacrosanct that within the next thirty years it was copied by the other three evangelists.) What positive arguments support this approach? References to Marcan style in the second and third denials (14:68–72) prove nothing, for they would be expected whether Mark created or rewrote. Moreover, there are elements of Mark's style in the first and supposedly original denial (see COMMENT).[51] More important is the issue whether Mark 14: 66–68 is a self-contained unit that Mark could have received from the tradition and expanded in one way or another. The presence of a (first) cockcrow in 14:68 is extremely dubious textually and more likely a scribal correction.[52] The idea that Peter's going outside in 14:68 is clearly the end of the denials, causing awkwardness for a continuation, is in my judgment a failure to read correctly the subtlety of the Marcan storyline (see COMMENT). Thus, while it is not unreasonable to suspect that the earlier verses of the Marcan scene may contain much of what I regard as the most ancient tradition about Peter's denial of Jesus, I find no hard evidence that this tradition came to Mark in the form of one denial (either as a totality that he would edit, or as a separate tradition that he would combine with another tradition to reach three denials). While, as indicated in n. 44, I am not as sanguine as Fortna about the possibility of reconstructing a preJohannine source, I judge it important that his reconstruction of that source (*Gospel* 117–22) posits a three-fold denial (= John 18:16b–18,25b–27).

B. Historicity

If the earliest traceable tradition already contained a threefold denial, that still takes us back only to the way early Christians related the story. In actual fact did Peter deny Jesus on this fateful night? How many times?

1. Discussion of Various Answers. In §5 we saw that the prediction by Jesus that Peter would deny him was related to two other prophecies about his followers attributed to Jesus on the night before he died: the prediction

---

[51] I remind the reader of my general skepticism about our ability to detect the difference between Mark's style and that of his source (§2, C2, above). Therefore, I am speaking of what many scholars consider features of Marcan style.

[52] On pp. 136–37 above (Mark 14:30) I discussed the four passages that support the genuineness of the reference to a second cockcrow. Only this passage which introduces the first cockcrow is, in my judgment, truly dubious. It was added precisely because a second cockcrow was promised and fulfilled with no reference to a first (see COMMENT on 14:68b above). But even if the mention of the first cockcrow were genuine, it would scarcely constitute a convincing "seam." The whole appeal to "awkward" sequence as a sign of editorial joining is dubious: It assumes that an ancient editor could not join material smoothly. Also, often the awkwardness is in the eye of the technical analyst.

of betrayal (by Judas) and the prediction of a scattering/scandalizing of the disciples. I postponed until here the issue of the factuality of the prediction about Peter so that it might be treated together with the issue of the factuality of the denials themselves. In such questions we may hope for a range of judgment that runs from possibility through probability to likelihood, rather than for definitive proof.

The majority of scholarship attributes a factual basis to the denials, including such diverse figures as J. Weiss, E. Meyer, Schniewind, Loisy (early opinion, 1912), Lietzmann, Dibelius, Bertram, Taylor, Dinkler, and Greeven. The dominant argument for this position is that Christians would scarcely have invented a story that brought disgrace on one of their most prominent leaders. Origen (*Contra Celsum* 2.15; SC 132.326) used this story to show the trustworthiness of the Gospels: They did not hide such a disgrace. Other Church Fathers, embarrassed by it, sought to interpret away the shame of Peter's denials, e.g., Peter said he did not know the man; but that was a mental reservation, for he knew the Son of God![53] We may ask whether this story about Peter would have been reported by all four evangelists (with great harmony on essentials), who clearly exercised freedom in what they preserved and who wrote after Peter had died a martyr's death on Vatican Hill, unless it was ineradicably established as tradition.

While I find this general reasoning persuasive, let me disown the exaggerated conclusions that have sometimes been drawn from it. An example of these is found in Taylor (*Mark* 550, 572). In reference to the prediction of Peter's denials, he asserts, "Christian tradition would not have preserved it except on the highest testimony, namely that of Peter himself." In reference to the denials, he cites with favor Loisy: "If there is an actual reminiscence from Peter anywhere in the second Gospel it is most certainly in the story of the denial in the form in which it is found in Mark." It is not implausible that Peter was the ultimate source of the tradition that he denied Jesus (if the tradition is factual), but others could have known and reported it. Often the real reason for appealing to Peter is to claim historicity for the "vivid" details of the denials, as Taylor does when he writes of the candor of the denial story, the psychological appropriateness of the responses to increasingly direct accusations, and Semitisms. (As the COMMENT above points out, many of the Semitisms are dubious.) Pesch goes further, arguing not only for a Petrine source but also for the writing of this material while Caiaphas was high priest (thus before AD 36), whence the Marcan reluctance to mention

---

[53] Another unpersuasive patristic judgment based on the scene is that it was a woman who led Peter to fall, even as women led into trouble Adam, Joseph, Samson, David, Solomon, and John the Baptist (see Kosnetter, "Geschichtlichkeit" 128–29). That Peter was forgiven after denying Jesus was used as an argument against the rigorism of the Novatianists and Donatists.

Peter's name! All such reasoning ignores the likelihood that the artistry and vividness of the narrative probably arose from developments in storytelling both during the stage of oral tradition and during Marcan rewriting of that tradition. From the coincidence of time that both the Jewish interrogation and the denials by Peter took place at night, Mark has made the denials a dramatic contrast to Jesus' own confession—a fulfillment of Jesus' prophecy at the moment he was being mocked as a false prophet. From a general note that the denials were associated with the *aulē* of the high priest, Mark has shaped a movement of Peter from inside near Jesus to outside away from Jesus as the denials are made more vehement. In short, a persuasive argument for a basis in fact does nothing to guarantee the total scene, which is clearly the product of development as the denials became a parable about the failure of the chief disciple when challenged and his ultimate rehabilitation through repentance.

Before I turn to the major arguments against a basis in fact for Peter's denials, let me note that too often objections are offered against minor details that are irrelevant to a nuanced understanding of historicity, e.g., would a woman be gatekeeper at the palace of the high priest, or would Peter not have remembered Jesus' prediction the *first* time he denied Jesus. In what follows I shall ignore such objections, which often have been dealt with in the COMMENT.

A number of scholars deny or seriously doubt the historicity of Peter's denying Jesus, e.g., Goguel, Bultmann, Loisy (later opinion, 1924), G. Klein, and Linneman. Sometimes they do this by challenging the main argument used to support factuality, namely, that Christians would not have invented a scene so unfavorable to Peter, a revered preacher and martyr. Is the story so unfavorable to Peter? Is it not clearly suggested that he repented, and does it not then have a positive thrust, offering readers courage in their trials and failures? Would a religion that preached a crucified-but-risen Messiah be embarrassed by a once-denying-but-now-proclaiming disciple? This counterargument is not really persuasive. Historically Jesus was crucified, and so his followers had to learn how this could be theologically significant. By analogy they learned how to draw parenetic value from the failure of Peter, but that does not mean they would have felt free to invent the scene. As to whether Peter's denying Jesus would have been seen as an embarrassing disgrace, it certainly was presented as such, for it is foretold in the context of Mark 14:27–29, which presents such failure of the disciples as scandal. In Matt how could it not be a problem in light of 10:33: "Whoever denies me before others, I also will deny before my Father who is in heaven"?

If one accepts that Peter's denials were a disgrace, could they not have been invented as antiPetrine propaganda? As mentioned above (pp. 48–50,

141), some scholars (including Kelber and Weeden) see Mark as an attempt to challenge the christology preached by Peter or in his name. Applying that thesis to the present scene, Dewey ("Peter's Curse" 108) states, "Mk reintroduces Peter into the narrative to climax the theme of Petrine opposition to Jesus and to serve as a negative model." It has been proposed that this story explains why Peter (Cephas) is not listed among the apostles by Paul in I Cor 9:5. But did not Paul himself once persecute Jesus, and did he not hold up Cephas as a standard of apostolic evangelizing in Gal 2:7? Boomershine ("Peter's" 57) points out that throughout Mark, after each instance of wrongdoing or wrong thinking by Peter, the evangelist takes explicit steps to reestablish sympathy for him, so that "Kelber's exegesis is improbable as a description of Mark's intention" (47). The other evangelists did not understand the story of Peter's denials to have a final negative thrust, since they all assigned Peter a very positive role in the postresurrectional life of the church (Matt 16:16–18; Luke 22:31–33; John 21:15–17). Indeed Herron's book (*Mark's*) provides through the centuries an interesting history of Peter's denials, a history which he sees as a refutation of the interpretation by Weeden and K. E. Dewey whereby this scene would constitute the utter rejection of Peter. And, of course, if the tradition of the denials is preMarcan or if John had an independent account, this whole theory of Marcan antiPetrine invention falls to the ground. As for the exegesis of Mark, independently of all other evidence, if the Marcan attitude toward Peter is absolutely negative, why does Mark show Peter's remorse and hint at his repentance at the end of the denials narrative (14:72) and give Peter a postresurrectional eminence in 16:7? (The suggestion that 16:7 is a postMarcan insertion has no textual support.) Herron (*Mark's* 143) would translate 16:7 so that the angelic good news is directed to "even Peter" as a sign that his singularly failed discipleship could be resuscitated. As Herron phrases it, the Marcan church was undoubtedly facing persecution and this narrative offered its apostates encouragement: "If the possibility [to be reconciled] exists for him [Peter], it exists for all *before the parousia.*"

Even more imaginatively than Kelber, G. Klein sees a relationship between Peter's three (fictional) denials and three changes in Peter's status or relationship to the Jerusalem church that Klein detects in Acts (from first of the Twelve to apostle, from apostle to pillar of the church, from subordinate to James to independent missionary). All this is highly speculative. Other theories of nonfactual origin for the denials do not rely on such a dubious reconstruction of Marcan ideology. Bertram sees the whole PN as having arisen and being preserved in cult, an idea related to I Cor 11:23–25, where the eucharist is an *anamnēsis* ("remembrance, *re*-presentation") of the sufferings of the Lord. Schille applies this to the denials of Peter with the sug-

gestion that cockcrows accompanied the yearly celebration of the Last
Supper as a Christian Passover (evidenced in the 2d-cent. [?] *Epistula Apostolorum* 15). This is highly tenuous. The basic eucharistic remembrance in
I Cor 11 is presented as recalling something that happened; what evidence
is there for the liturgy's having created the story of Peter's denying? The
tradition of what the Lord Jesus did on the night he was handed over was
something that Paul "received" from earlier tradition, and many suspect that
a font of that was Cephas or Peter from whom Paul got information after his
conversion (Gal 1:18: *historēsai;* see PNT 23). Nothing in that background
would a priori favor the invention of a story that disgraces Peter.

If we leave aside as unprovable and tenuous the various theories about
what might have caused the invention of the denials, there is still the basic
argument that the story contradicts the context. Mark 14:50 reports, "And
having left him, they all fled." Yet here is Peter not fleeing but still following
Jesus. Two observations need to be made. First, the fleeing of the disciples
is the fulfillment of Jesus' prediction in Mark 14:27, "You will all be scandalized." Peter's denials are treated in Mark 14:29–30 as an example or specification of that prediction. (The contention that Mark did not notice that
within four verses he had joined two contradictory passages dubiously supposes that at the distance of two millennia we are more capable of recognizing the import of a passage than the person who first used it.) Second, by
having Peter follow Jesus at a distance, Mark 14:54 correlates the denials
with the flight of the disciples: Peter too fled from Gethsemane, but now he
is cautiously following the arresting party only to fail again.

Another claim is that Peter's denials contradict Luke 22:31–32: "Simon,
Simon, behold Satan asked to test you [pl.] like wheat. But I have prayed for
you [sg.] that your faith might not fail. And you [sg.], when you have turned
around, strengthen your brothers." In particular, G. Klein argues that Luke
gives us the older tradition (without "when you have turned around") in
which Jesus' prayers made Peter an exception who did not fail when the
other disciples did. Klein has argued against the historicity of the denials on
this basis.[54] Again several observations need to be made. First, Luke reported side by side this statement of Jesus and his prediction of Peter's denials (22:34) and so obviously saw no contradiction between the two but rather
a total picture of Peter's fate and role. Second, in Klein's hypothesis the text
has to be gerrymandered to remove the phrase that takes cognizance of the
denials. But even without "when you have turned around," would not Jesus'
special concern for Peter suggest that his faith would be threatened in the

---

[54]He points out that the PN makes sense without Peter's denials. That extremely weak argument
is applicable to many scenes in the PN; one could make sense of it without the betrayal by Judas,
without Barabbas, without the co-crucified bandits, etc.

sifting by Satan, and so leave room for the denials? Third, few would argue that Luke 22:31–32 (peculiar to one Gospel) was more original to the Last Supper and its aftermath than the prediction of Peter's denials (four Gospels). It has the clear characteristic of a Lucan addition to soften the attitude of Jesus toward his disciples. If the saying is not in its original context, did it originally have direct relevance to Peter's denials?[55] Fourth, it is one of three famous sayings that deal with Peter's ecclesiastical role after the resurrection. Matt 16:16–18 constitutes Peter as the rock on which the church will be built, but 16:21–23 shows Peter's lack of understanding and calls him Satan. John 21:15–17 gives Peter a very important pastoral role of feeding Jesus' sheep, but only after Peter's love for Jesus has been queried three times. On that analogy of underlining a weakness or failure in Peter's past as part of predicting his positive future role, is Klein (and Bultmann) justified in regarding "when you have turned around" (with its implication of a lapse) as secondary? Clearly the objections to factuality based on inconsistency with other passion material are not strong.[56]

Involved in the study of historicity is the relationship of Peter's denials (related in all four Gospels) to the prediction by Jesus of those denials at the Last Supper (Luke, John) or on the way to the Mount of Olives (Mark/Matt). Some scholars who accept the historicity of the denials regard the prediction as formulated after the event (*vaticinium ex eventu*) to give Jesus status as a prophet.[57] A model for this theory is the supposition that Jesus' predictions of his own death and resurrection were formulated after the event. That they were completely so formulated is quite uncertain (APPENDIX VIII). Moreover, one can understand a Christian desire to know whether Jesus anticipated in any way his horrible death and how it fitted into his vision of the kingdom; thus there is a context that could have helped to develop Jesus' predictions of his death. It is not clear why a *vaticinium ex eventu* would have been created for Peter's denials when so many other passion incidents were left without one. The notion that it was needed for the reinstatement of Peter is not persuasive, since a postresurrectional dialogue with Jesus (as in John 21:15–17) would have made his rehabilitation clearer. I commented under §5 above that doubt about Jesus' prophecies often smacks of modern

[55]There is solid evidence for thinking that the saying is preLucan, not a Lucan creation (Fitzmyer, *Luke* 2.1421). On this saying, see W. Foerster, ZNW 46 (1955), 129–33.

[56]Unpersuasive too is the argument that if Peter had denied or cursed Jesus, he could not have become a pillar of the church (Goguel). The history of Paul shows what is possible.

[57]Schenke (*Studien* 41) and Wilcox ("Denial" 431–32) give priority to the form of the prediction that Peter remembers in Mark 14:72 (without "today" and "this night") and think this was read back into the setting of Mark 14:30. But the immediacy of "today" or "this night" is very much part of the force of the prediction. If the cockcrow was part of the prediction, implicitly it had to be the same night.

rationalism, a poor optic for viewing how 1st-cent. Christians thought and proceeded. When one studies the denials, one wonders whether the prediction is not a major factor in why the story was formulated and preserved.[58]

Accordingly, priority is sometimes given to the prediction as having produced the *story* of the denials (thus, with different nuances, Goguel, Linnemann, Gewalt). There is much that is perceptive in this approach if one can lay aside the unnecessary complication advanced by its main supporters (Gewalt is uncertain) that there is no factuality in Peter's denying Jesus at the time of the arrest. Why would such a prediction be preserved if it was not fulfilled? This prediction is quite different from Jesus' prediction of the destruction of the Jerusalem Temple, which had no time limit built in. The cockcrow statement was too immediately linked to Jesus' arrest to have any meaning, even as a specification of the failure of the disciples, without a basis in fact. But if we combine a basis in fact with some of the observations of Linnemann, drawing as well on the important article of Wilcox, the broad lines (I claim no more) of a workable theory emerge.

2. Working Hypothesis. When Jesus came to Jerusalem and encountered the exacerbated antagonism of the authorities, he recognized that should there be an attempt to seize him, there would be failure among his disciples leading to desertion and betrayal. Sayings to that effect, perhaps uttered at various moments in his last days, were preserved in the tradition in a Last Supper context that had become a locus for Jesus' words to his followers about their share in his future. (In §5 above, I urged that it was Mark who moved the sayings about the disciples and Peter to a setting on the way to the Mount of Olives.) Of the three sayings preserved in Mark (Judas, the disciples, Peter), only the saying pertinent to Peter with its reference to cockcrow (which cannot have been *any* cockcrow) need have been related to the night on which Jesus was given over (I Cor 11:23) and arrested; but the instinct of the tradition to relate that saying to the overall anticipation of the failure of the disciples may be quite historical.[59]

In the saying about Peter, some (e.g., Gnilka, *Markus* 251) would regard the "two times" as Mark's own creation; but if one understands the prediction as having a parabolic or proverbial tone, the numerals may have been an appropriate part: "Before a cock crows twice, thrice you will deny me."[60]

---

[58]Wilcox ("Denial" 434–35) makes this point forcefully.

[59]In §5 I stressed that the failure of the disciples was predicted in a context evocative of the last chapters of Zechariah. Wilcox ("Denial" 431) suggests that reflection on Zechariah may stem from Jesus himself.

[60]Brady ("Alarm" 54) points to a parallel to the "twice/thrice" pattern in the "three/four" pattern of proverbs (Prov 30:15,18,21,29). Yet this latter pattern involves three/four ways of describing the same phenomenon; and two cockcrows and three denials are different items.

Indeed, the numerals may have been meant figuratively and not literally, even as we have seen the possibility (p. 444 above) that the "three days" in the prediction of the destruction of the Temple was an idiom for a short while.[61] Jesus may have been stressing the swiftness and totality of failure through denial on the part of a Peter whom paradoxically tradition presents as the one of the Twelve most likely to draw attention by his assertiveness.

The earliest form of a consecutive passion account presumably mentioned the betrayal of Jesus by Judas and the failure of the disciples. Included in the latter by way of example could have been a brief mention of Peter's particular failure in denying that he was associated with Jesus when challenged by a woman servant at a fire in the *aulē* of the high priest where Jesus had been taken. The separating out of this denial by Peter into a self-standing *narrative*[62] would have come later as Peter's role in Christianity became more visible (leader of the Twelve, a pillar of the Jerusalem church [Gal 2:9], and evangelist of the circumcised [Gal 2:7]). Accompanying that separation would have been the fleshing out of the predicted behavior in a literal way so that Peter denied Jesus exactly three times, with the last occurring the moment a cock crowed. This development led to preMarcan and preJohannine forms of the narrative where there is a certain agreement about the first denial but greater differences in the second and third denials. Such a theory does justice to the two basic issues that must be faced in discussing the historicity of the denials by Peter: The survival of the story without a basis in fact seems incredible; yet the Gospel narratives reflect strongly an imaginative storytelling style. Basic fact and imaginative description, however, are not an impossible combination. Gewalt ("Verleugnung" 142–43) points out that the long march of the Chinese Red Army was historical, but Mao, who was an eyewitness and major participant, made a poem out of it.

C. The Function of the Denial Narratives

These last observations lead us from a discussion of the historical value of the tradition underlying the stories of the denials to the more important issue of the impact of those tales on the PNs of the different Gospels. They are extraordinarily effective stories that catch the imagination.[63] Among the

---

[61]E. A. Abbott (AJT 2 [1898] 6) points to the Hebrew idiom in Job 33:29, "All these things God does two times, three times with a human being," as a parallel to Mark's two/three. See n. 60.

[62]That a historical memory can be developed into a narrative based on that memory is illustrated in the instance of the empty tomb of Jesus.

[63]Gewalt ("Verleugnung" 114–16) begins by discussing the use of the categories of classical literature, like comedy, to classify a scene such as this. On p. 121 he sees it as a form of tragic parable. Some of the protrayals in art are discussed by Hunter, "Three." Dassmann ("Szene") shows how frequently the motif of the cock shows up in early Christian sarcophagus art, often as the key

elements that contribute to the vividness are Peter's implicit hesitancy exemplified in his following at a distance; his being identified by the light of the fire; his slipping outside to get away from the persistent woman servant (Mark); the progressive arrangement of the three denials from evasion to denial of discipleship to cursing (Jesus?) and taking an oath (Mark and, with variations, Matt); Peter being betrayed by his Galilean background or speech (Matt); the cockcrow occurring precisely at the last denial, bringing to Peter a remembrance of Jesus' word; the final pathetic reaction of Peter when he realizes what he has done.[64]

For Mark these denials took place at the moment Jesus stood before the Sanhedrin. There a Jesus who in his ministry had been very reticent about his identity says, "I am" (Mark), in response to the high priest's question "Are you the Messiah, the Son of the Blessed?" In the denials, a Peter who previously had confessed Jesus as the Messiah (Mark 8:29) now denies under oath that he knows him. (In Matt the contrasted wording is even more precise: Jesus gives a qualified affirmation to the high priest's question, "Are [you] the Messiah, the Son of God?" whereas Peter had once confessed Jesus as "the Messiah, the Son of the living God" [16:16].)

Luke's setting of the scene may be even more dramatic. Instead of the irony of Peter denying downstairs/outside while Jesus is confessing upstairs/inside, the Lucan Jesus is present at the time that Peter has been denying him.[65] Luke's "And the Lord, having turned, looked at Peter" is effectively dramatic, but more important it illustrates Jesus' care for his disciple. Jesus had prayed for Peter that his faith might not fail; and now Jesus is leading his disciple to repentance so that having turned around, he may strengthen others (22:32). In the Lucan sequence, having seen his chief disciple deny him, Jesus will next be mocked and brought before the priests to be interrogated. Yet we are not meant to ask how what others did affected Jesus; Luke wants us to know how amid his sufferings Jesus was thoughtful of others.

In the Synoptics, Jesus' words about denial are recalled by Peter, and so the readers have their attention drawn to a fulfillment of Jesus' prophecy just as he is being mocked by the Sanhedrin (Mark/Matt) or soon will be mocked

---

feature in the iconography of Peter. It is a sign not primarily of the denial but of promised forgiveness and hope of reconciliation, whence the use in the place of burial. This is important in the light of a thesis I have been rejecting, viz., that the denials were meant by Mark as the definite failure of Peter.

[64]Older commentators used such details to establish historicity, stemming from eyewitness participation. Verisimilitude, however, can be the product of imagination as well as of history.

[65]Under the influence of the Marcan account on which Luke is dependent, the presence of Jesus is never alluded to throughout the denials until the very end. Even then, Jesus must turn to look at Peter. We are left to deduce that he must have been present all along, and thus that (the part of) the house (*oikia*) to which Jesus was led in 22:54a was identical with the *aulē* where Peter sits by the fire. See Soards, "And the Lord" 518.

by the attendants (Luke) as a false prophet. This is the fulfillment of the third of Jesus' predictions about his disciples made at the Last Supper or on the way to the Mount of Olives: Judas has already handed him over; the disciples have already been scattered. In §5 above I discussed the major impact of Scripture on the betrayal and flight, e.g., the story in II Sam 15 about how David, abandoned by many of his followers and by his trusted advisor (who later hanged himself), went across the Kidron to the Ascent of Olives, where he wept and prayed to God; and another Mount of Olives context in the last chapters of Zechariah with references to the blood of the covenant, a slain shepherd, and thirty shekels of silver cast into the Temple treasury. The denials of Peter are part of this same general atmosphere, but the "Scripture" that is most influential here is not an OT passage but Jesus' own predictive word. The divine imperative, the "must" that dominates the passion and resurrection (see APPENDIX VIII), is revealed not only in the prophets of Israel but in Jesus' own prophecy. Facing the future, the Marcan Jesus had said (13:23): "Take heed, I have told you all these things beforehand"; and now what Jesus had told beforehand was taking on the force of Scripture and having the same role in developing and coloring passion scenes that OT prophecy had.[66]

On this point John's approach to the denials is different. He does not remind the reader of Jesus' predictive words,[67] even though he (alone) did so previously at the time of the arrest, in reference to betrayal by Judas and the departure of the disciples (18:8–9), where Jesus' words were placed on the level of Scripture. Here as Annas asks Jesus about his disciples, John shows us the behavior of two disciples who follow Jesus even after the arrest, namely, Peter and another disciple (i.e., the disciple whom Jesus loved; see COMMENT). In describing Peter, John reports the traditional story with minor dramatic touches, e.g., having shown himself brave in cutting off the servant's ear in the garden, Peter now denies that he was even in the garden with Jesus when challenged by a relative of the same servant (18:26–27). But Peter in John is not denigrated. In fact, some of the harsh Marcan elements are absent, e.g., progression in the wording of the three denials; going outside and thus leaving Jesus; cursing (Jesus) and swearing that he does not know Jesus. Rather the tradition about Peter serves as a foil for the behavior of another disciple who is never deflected from his following of Jesus. He

---

[66]Wilcox ("Denial" 434) is persuasive on this point. Gewalt ("Verleugnung" 135) discusses the view of W. Schenk that what was once a fulfillment of Jesus' word has become a personal legend. Rather the story is both. In my judgment discussion of the denials of Peter has been plagued by excessively strict form criticism, not recognizing the flexibility of tradition.

[67]A Johannine tradition (21:15–17) where Jesus encounters Peter face to face and asks him three times "Simon Peter, do you love me?" is the functional equivalent of Peter being reminded of Jesus' prediction of threefold denial, especially in the Lucan form where Jesus looks at Peter.

enters the *aulē* of the high priest without opposition,[68] and without him Peter would not have been able to follow that far. He does not deny Jesus; rather he will reappear at the cross of Jesus where there is no other male disciple (19:25–27). There is no way to test the historicity of the disciple's appearance, for only John reports it.[69] Indeed, invisibility to the other evangelists (recognizable to readers of the four Gospels) helps to highlight that this disciple has to be seen in the light of Johannine community faith. He does not appear in John's account of the public ministry but only in the context of the Last Supper, where Jesus is manifesting his love for his own (13:1). Contrast with Peter (at the supper, here, and in two postresurrectional scenes) exalts a disciple who is close to Jesus in a priority of love and who never failed. John's Gospel reflects a life situation in which Christians were thrown out of the synagogue for confessing Jesus as the Messiah (9:22; 12:42). The fear of expulsion and of being put to death created a danger of falling away (16:1–2). Against this background the model of an ideal disciple who did not deny Jesus or desert him as he was led to the cross was important for the Johannine Christians.

Mark's purpose in narrating Peter's denials, besides showing the fulfillment of Jesus' prophecy, involves the theology of the cross that we discussed in relation to the failure of the disciples at Gethsemane. Mark shows that even the disciple who was the first to be named in the Gospel (1:16) and would be the last named (16:7), and who had been the most forward in confessing Jesus, could not remain faithful until after Jesus had died on the cross. The other disciples had fled; now Peter seeks on his own to follow[70] at a distance, exemplifying his boast, "Even if all are scandalized, not I" (Mark 14:29). But Peter has not digested the words that Jesus spoke just after rebuking him as Satan, "If anyone wishes to follow me, let him deny himself, take up his cross, and follow me" (8:34). Peter was not meeting this criterion by following at a distance and seeking to avoid the cross.

The story of the denials of Jesus by Peter may have been very useful for Christian exhortation after Peter died a martyr's death in the mid-60s, thus eventually giving witness to taking up the cross to follow Jesus (p. 226, n. 19 above). Yet inevitably during persecution many Christians were not

---

[68]In the COMMENT I insist that one should not make too much of a mystery of his being known to the high priest; that is simply the explanation of how he got in easily while Peter was challenged.

[69]One can make a serious argument that John's disciple, despite his clear symbolic value, is a real figure, even as the unnamed mother of Jesus has for John symbolic value and yet is a real figure. Such reality, however, does not guarantee the historicity of his appearance in an individual scene. See Schnackenburg, *John* 3.385–86.

[70]Often in Mark "follow" refers to discipleship, e.g., 1:18; 2:14–15; 6:1; 9:38; 10:21,32,52; 15:41. Especially significant for this scene are the words spoken by Peter in 10:28: "We have left everything and followed you."

that brave, and both *I Clem.* 5 and Tacitus (*Annals* 15.44) suggest that in the persecution by Nero in which Peter died some Christians denounced others to the Romans. Was all hope lost for those who failed and denied Christ? A Peter who had once denied and later borne witness could constitute an encouragement that repentance and a second chance were possible.[71] For that reason it may have been important to underline the seriousness of what Peter had done. Before his arrest Jesus had warned his disciples, "Keep on ... praying lest you enter into trial/testing/temptation [*peirasmos*]," precisely because they were not yet sufficiently strong. But with bravado, Peter by attempting to follow had entered into *peirasmos* and failed. (Luke, however, implies that while sifted, his faith did not fail because of Jesus' prayer.) He had denied Jesus, despite Jesus' very dire warning of the consequences of denying him before others (Matt 10:33; Luke 12:9). In Luke that denial was made solemn because it was not only before a woman but before two men who could serve as legal witnesses (Deut 19:15; Josephus, *Ant.* 4.8.15; #219); in Mark/Matt he had taken an oath (despite Jesus' forbidding oaths [Matt 5:34]) and had cursed (Jesus).[72] Some of this, as we shall now see, may have evoked in the minds of the readers the trials of Christian martyrdom.

The verb "to deny" was already part of the testing of martyrs in preChristian Judaism, for *IV Macc* 8:7; 10:15 show the Maccabee brothers challenged to deny the ancestral Law and their brotherhood. In Christian times Rev 2:13 refers to a persecution at Pergamum when Antipas, a faithful witness (*martys*), was killed, and congratulates the other Christians who did not deny the faith. I Tim 6:13 shows how Jesus' own death had been patterned on martyrdom in persecution: "Christ Jesus who made the model confession in his witness [*martyrein*] before Pontius Pilate."[73] II Tim 2:13 promises: "If we are faithless, he remains faithful, for he cannot deny himself." Pliny (*Epistles* 10.96–97) reports that in interrogating those suspected of being Christians, he offered them three opportunities to deny. If they did deny, they had to revile or curse Christ (*male dicere*) to prove the sincerity of the denial; no true Christian would do this. Justin (*Apology* 1.31.6) reports that Bar Cochba in the Second Jewish Revolt (AD 132–135) punished Christians cru-

---

[71]If Mark was written at Rome, the example of Peter would be even more persuasive in the place where he died. On Rome as the possible place of Marcan composition, see R. E. Brown and J. P. Meier, *Antioch and Rome* (New York: Paulist, 1983), 191–201; D. Senior, BTB 17 (1987), 10–20. However, nothing need depend on that; there were other circumstances in which Christians were tested for their faith (Mark 13:9).

[72]The evil that an oath could do is illustrated in Mark 6:23 where Herod swears to Herodias that he will give her whatever she wishes: an oath leading to the beheading of John the Baptist. As for cursing (and cursing Jesus), one should note the obscure I Cor 12:3, "No one speaking by the Spirit of God ever says 'Jesus be cursed!'"

[73]For the death of Jesus depicted as martyrdom, see P. E. Davies, "Did Jesus"; de Jonge, "Jesus"; Downing, "Jesus"; and Gnilka, *Jesu.*

elly "unless they would deny Jesus and utter blasphemy." We hear in the *Martyrdom of Polycarp* 9:2–3 that the proconsul tried to persuade him to deny, to swear, and to revile Christ.[74] We cannot be sure that all these demands were placed on the persecuted Christians of the 1st cent., but there is enough evidence to make it plausible that they would have understood Peter's testing in light of their own.

(Bibliography for this episode may be found in §25, Part 2.)

[74]Lampe ("St. Peter's" 351) sees the influence of the accusations of the persecutors of Christians in the accusation addressed to Peter, "Truly you are one of them" (Mark 14:70).

§28. END OF THE SANHEDRIN PROCEEDINGS; TRANSFER TO PILATE

(Mark 15:1; Matt 27:1–2; Luke 23:1; John 18:28a)

Translation

Mark 15:1: And immediately, early, having made their consultation, the chief priests with the elders and scribes and the whole Sanhedrin, having bound Jesus, took him away and gave him over to Pilate.

Matt 27:1–2: [1]And when the early hour had come, all the chief priests and the elders of the people took a decision against Jesus that they should put him to death. [2]And having bound him, they led him away and gave him over to Pilate the governor.

Luke 23:1: And the whole multitude of them, having stood up, led him to Pilate.

John 18:28a: Then they lead Jesus from Caiaphas to the praetorium. Now it was early.

COMMENT

This short notice that ends the Jewish proceedings against Jesus and serves as a transition to the Roman proceedings requires discussion under several headings: time, the meeting, the participants, and the transfer to Pilate.

TIME

Mark's "And immediately" is stereotypic (twenty-three times). D. Daube[1] overinterprets when he argues that it expresses the inevitable, after-the-other result: "in due course, accordingly, as had to happen." To the contrary, it

[1]*The Sudden in the Scriptures* (Leiden: Brill, 1964), 59–60.

supplies little information and simply continues the narrative; from it we cannot know whether what is described was simultaneous with what preceded or came after a brief interval. If taken with the next adverb, at most it can mean: "And as soon as it was morning." Mark's _prōi_ (which here gives the time for taking Jesus to Pilate after the consultation was over) can refer to the fourth watch of the night (3–6 A.M.), but more frequently it is less specific: "early (in the morning)." Matt 27:1 uses _prōia,_ a feminine form that modifies an unexpressed _hōra:_ "the early hour." (Matt's phrasing, "when the early hour had come" is more elegant than Mark's, avoids the overused "immediately," and matches "when evening had come," which frames Matt's PN in 26:20; 27:57). There is no time indication in Luke's description of the transfer of Jesus to Pilate. Yet Luke's understanding of Mark is reflected in the borrowed time indication (22:66) with which he began the Sanhedrin session (p. 431 above): "And _as it became day,_ there was brought together the assembly of the elders of the people, both chief priests and scribes; and they led him away to their Sanhedrin." John 18:28a, like Mark, has _prōi._

Can we be more specific about the intended time for the transfer to Pilate? Few today would have the confidence of W. R. Ramsay (ExpTim 27 [1915–16], 363) in reconstructing a precise horarium: Before 4 A.M. Jesus reached the house of Caiaphas; by 5:30 the nocturnal interrogation and maltreatment were over; at 6 Jesus was led to Caiaphas in the Sanhedrin council hall; and at 7 he was led to Pilate's praetorium for a trial that would last until noon. One must recognize that Mark's _prōi_ fits into a time sequence that he uses as a frame for the PN events. Mark 13:35 shows a consciousness of the _four watches_ of the night (three-hour stretches from 6 P.M. to 6 A.M.), and in the PN Mark uses terms evocative of them even if he does not mean precise three-hour periods of time. "Evening" was specified by Mark 14:17 as the time when Jesus came with the Twelve to eat the Last Supper; although "midnight" was not mentioned specifically, in 14:30 between the supper and the denials, Jesus spoke of "this very night"; "cockcrow" served as the climax of Peter's denials (14:72); and "early" is mentioned here. In the daytime that will follow, "the third hour" (9 A.M.) will specify the time of the crucifixion (15:25); "the sixth hour" (noon) will mark the coming of darkness over the earth (15:33); "the ninth hour" will be the time of Jesus' final cry (15:34); and "evening" will mark the burial in 15:42 and complete the cycle. Many have puzzled over the significance of this stylized arrangement. Was it so that Christians could pray at set times on this sacred day? More prosaically, does it just reflect Mark's love of numerals?[2] Gnilka ("Verhhandlungen" 9) speaks of a secondary historicizing of an original parenetic ac-

---

[2]C. H. Turner, JTS 26 (1924–25), 337–45.

count; but that judgment pretends to more knowledge of the preMarcan original than is possible (in my view). In any case the times are general and do not supply horological precision.

No other evangelist has such a complete sequence. Indeed, the Gospels disagree among themselves about where Jesus was at a mentioned hour, e.g., for John 19:14 Jesus was still before Pilate at noon, while for Mark he was hanging on the cross. Perhaps all that can be asserted in relation to the present passage, then, is that since Mark/Matt and John use a form of "early" (and Luke signals knowledge of it, in a modified form, attached to the Sanhedrin session), in the tradition this time tag was fixed to the transfer of Jesus to Pilate.[3] An early hour for this would fit the contention already defended that (before Lucan reordering) the tradition was unanimous in placing the Jewish legal proceedings at night. How early? The tradition also spoke of the cock crowing in relation to Peter's denials, and so the period 3–5 A.M. may have been envisioned. Although some modern writers have doubted that Pilate would have been imagined to be available at such an hour, it does not lack versimilitude. Seneca (*De ira* 2.7.3) indicates that Roman trials did begin at daybreak. Sherwin-White ("Trial" 114) observes that the workday of most Roman officials (many of them trained in the army) began in the earliest morning hours: The emperor Vespasian finished his desk work before dawn; and Pliny as prefect of the fleet had completed his whole working day by 10 A.M. Herod Agrippa I entered the theater at Caesarea to celebrate a spectacle before the first rays of sunlight (Josephus, *Ant.* 19.8.2; #344). I have gone into this question in some detail because it is not unrelated to the next issue of whether Mark envisioned a second session of the Sanhedrin in the daytime. If he meant that Jesus was taken to Pilate so very early, his sense of time may not have included a second session.

THE MEETING

Three principal readings are attested in Mark 15:1 pertinent to this issue:

symboulion hetoimasantes: Codices Sinaiticus, Ephraem Rescriptus
symboulion poiēsantes: Codices Vaticanus, Alexandrinus, Koine texts
symboulion epoiēsan: Codices Bezae, Koridethi, OL, Origen

The problem of which is more ancient is compounded by scholarly disagreement about the meaning of *symboulion*. Certainly it can mean "council, con-

---

[3]In my judgment Matera (*Kingship* 12) wrongly argues that it is a *Marcan* addendum because of Mark's fascination with time indications just discussed. A distinction should be made between an occasional time indication confirmed by other evidence (as "early" is by John) and Mark's expansion of it to become part of a complete sequence.

sultation, meeting"; but many contend that it can also refer to what goes on in or emerges from such a meeting: "counsel, plan, decision." Benoit ("Jesus" 1.150) challenges the latter meaning and the evidence offered for it by the Liddell-Scott and BAG dictionaries. Yet that meaning reappears in BAGD 778. In fact, a sharp line between "council" and "counsel" is hard to draw. In the Theodotion translation of Prov 15:22 *symboulion* seems to mean "decision," rendering *sôd* (which has both meanings). The only other Marcan use of *symboulion* is in 3:6, where it is virtually impossible to distinguish between the Pharisees' "holding a council" with the Herodians and "taking counsel" with them.[4]

A choice as to which textual reading is preferable and whether *symboulion* can mean "decision" affects what is being described by Mark/Matt. Probably the majority of scholars have assumed that a new or second meeting of the Sanhedrin is involved. Some would contend that it is this second, morning meeting that Luke 22:66–71 reports, and that such a second meeting brings Mark/Matt into conformity with Mishna *Sanhedrin* 4.1 with its rule that another trial session was necessary for imposing a capital sentence. Both of those observations are invalid. Luke's morning session contains much of the same material as the Mark/Matt night session and is almost surely the product of Lucan rewriting; Luke offers no support for reading a second session into Mark. We have already seen that most likely the mishnaic rules are not applicable to Jesus' time (§18, C3). In any case the rule cited here requires that the second session be held on *another* day; and since in Jewish reckoning late night and early morning are the same day, the rule would not be met no matter how one interprets Mark 15:1 (Blinzler, *Trial* 145). Barton's contention ("On the Trial" 210) that the second session was mandatory but not the day in between is a bit desperate. A variant of the second-session theory is that there was a continuation of the first session where a new matter was discussed, namely, how to have Jesus executed, and that this discussion led to handing him over to the Romans. In the Marcan storyline is that plausible? The Sanhedrin has been plotting to put Jesus to death for some time now (11:18; 12:12; 14:1,10–11). Surely Mark's readers are not meant to think that the Sanhedrists had never considered how this could happen until after they condemned him! Some interpreters who would answer that objection confuse history and the Marcan storyline. For instance, they argue that it had become necessary for the Sanhedrists to come together again to take Jesus to Pilate because they now realized the illegality of their night session (Buss) which was held on a feast day (Lengle, Millar). However, Mark never

---

[4]Matt uses the phrase *symboulion lambanein* five times (a Latinism reflecting *consilium capere*) for Jewish leaders conferring and deciding on a course of action (SPNM 214).

suggests any illegality about the Jewish trial or calls attention to either time factor as objectionable. Bickermann ("Utilitas" 194) argues that the Sanhedrists needed an interval and another session after the main trial in order to draw from it material to phrase the official charge to be brought against Jesus before Pilate. Yet Mark never reports any official charge, and the Marcan Pilate's question to Jesus has no surface relationship to the trial just conducted by the Sanhedrists. Thus there is little in the Marcan narrative that would make a second Jewish trial (or a separate concluding session of the original trial) necessary or even intelligible. Jesus was condemned to death by the Sanhedrists in Mark 14:64; why should there be further Sanhedrin deliberations?

Does the Greek of Mark 15:1 favor a second session?[5] *Hetoimasantes,* which is preferred by an impressive number of scholars, [6] is often understood in the sense of "having prepared their decision," referring to the judgment made previously in 14:64; and so it does not favor a second trial.[7] But that very fact has caused some to suggest that the *hetoimasantes* reading was created by copyists who were anxious to avoid the difficulty of a second trial; they prefer *poiēsantes* with the connotation of "having held a meeting." (Benoit's contention that *symboulion* means "meeting," not "decision," is sometimes invoked in their argument.) Yet even if one prefers *poiēsantes* (of which *epoiēsan* is just a variant for smoother syntax) because it is the better attested and the more difficult reading (and therefore likely to have been changed by copyists), does it necessarily refer to a new meeting? The verb is in the aorist and could simply serve as a recapitulative, referring to the night session. If *symboulion* means only "meeting, council," then the translation would be: "having made [held] their consultation," i.e., finished the Sanhedrin session of 14:55–65. If *symboulion* can mean "counsel, resolution," then the translation would be: "having made [taken] their decision," i.e., passed the judgment of 14:64. A resumptive or recapitulative would be necessary at this stage because Mark interrupted his narrative of the Sanhedrin session to tell of Peter's denials. (When Mark began describing those denials in 14:66–67, he recapitulated what the reader had been told in 14:54 of Peter warming himself at the fire in the *aulē*.) In this understanding *poiein,* "to do, make," assumes the connotation "to be done with." Schneider ("Gab" 27–28) argues for the recapitulative meaning of 15:1 from the *hetoimasantes*

---

[5]Among those who think that the text does *not* imply a second session are Blinzler, Easton, Klövekorn, Léon-Dufour, Lührmann, Matera, Schmid, Schneider, Sherwin-White, and Sickenberger.

[6]E.g., Easton, Holtzmann, Klostermann, Mann, Tischendorf, B. and J. Weiss, and Wellhausen.

[7]Easton ("Trial" 432, 444) argues that the Sanhedrin members had not dispersed and reassembled, but in the continuing assembly there was now renewed deliberation on how to present Jesus to the Romans.

reading; Matera (*Kingship* 9) and Lührmann ("Markus 14" 463) argue for that meaning from the reading *poiēsantes*. I deliberately chose the more difficult *poiēsantes* reading with *symboulion* as "meeting, consultation" in my translation to make clear that my firm rejection of a second meeting needs no crutch. In the ANALYSIS of §19A above I show that a recapitulative 15:1 makes perfect sense in a Marcan outline.

Matt 27:1 offers no objection to reading Mark 15:1 as a recapitulative. Indeed Senior (SPNM 211–12), who recognizes Mark 15:1 to be composed by Mark on the basis of material in 14 but curiously then finds a reference to a second trial, contends that Matt 27:1 does not refer to a second trial but concludes the first. Although like Mark 14:64, Matt 26:66 shows that the Sanhedrists considered Jesus guilty, punishable by death, Matt did not reproduce the Marcan statement "They all judged against him." Now, after having narrated the simultaneous denials by Peter, Matt 27:1 mentions that judgment under the form "took a decision" (*symboulion elabon*). Thus, while Mark 15:1 recapitulates the decision already taken or the trial session already narrated, Matt has kept the last step of the trial until here (27:1 is meant to be immediately consecutive to 26:68, since Peter's denials in 26:69–75 have been going on during the trial). That the *symboulion elabon* of Matt 27:1 is equivalent to the *katekrinan* of Mark 14:64 is made clear when two verses later Matt 27:3 describes Judas as "having seen that he [Jesus] was judged against [*katekrithē*]." By changing Mark's recapitulation into a consecutive description, Matt has created a smoother narrative flow and provided an introduction to the Judas story. As for Luke, his modification of the time details of Mark 15:1 and reuse of them to introduce a morning session of the Sanhedrin (22:66) may have been an act of editorial freedom or may mean that he (mis)understood Mark to refer to a new session.

THE PARTICIPANTS

The interpretation of Mark 15:1 not as a second session, but as a recapitulation, is implicitly a firm rejection of the thesis of Bultmann, Taylor, J. Weiss, Winter, and others that the brief notice in 15:1 preserved the original preMarcan account of the Jewish trial of Jesus, so that 14:53,55–65 was Mark's own filling out of that notice. In the ANALYSIS of §24 above we saw that much of the trial account in Mark 14 represents earlier tradition even if Mark has reshaped and reinterpreted it, placing it on the night before Jesus died. On the other hand, as recapitulation, the first part of Mark 15:1 is totally a Marcan creation.[8] Senior (SPNM 211, summarizing H. Van der

---

[8]This is against the view of Légasse ("Jésus" 191, 196–97) who, in arguing for two Sanhedrin sessions, admits that 15:1 is clearly redacted by Mark but perhaps not created.

Kwaak) argues for that on the basis of vocabulary. In particular, the list of participants in 15:1 ("the chief priests with the elders and scribes and the whole Sanhedrin") is really an inclusion picking up the listing of participants that began the trial: "the chief priests, and the elders, and the scribes" of 14:53, and "the chief priests and the whole Sanhedrin" of 14:55.

At both the beginning and the (recapitulative) ending of the Jewish trial, after mentioning the individual groups of components, Mark adds "and the whole Sanhedrin." That is not simply tautology; for it has the effect of making clear that the agents who condemned Jesus were not acting as individual groups but as the representative Jewish governing body, and that as a collectivity they gave him over to Pilate. Matt's "*all* the chief priests and the elders *of the people*" retains this emphasis on representative collectivity while avoiding even the appearance of tautology. Such an emphasis is indicative that both Mark and Matt envision Christian readers. If the evangelists were writing for neutral outsiders, they might have reflected that having *all* the responsible leaders of Jesus' own people reject him could create the suspicion that he must have been a criminal. But the evangelists are portraying Jesus against a biblical background of the just one standing alone (except for God's help) against all adversaries.

Since Luke's description of the denials by Peter (22:54b-62) and the mockery of Jesus (22:63–65) preceded the morning Sanhedrin session (22:66–71), the verse being considered here (23:1) follows immediately on that session. Indeed, despite the change of chapter number, it is an unbroken part of that session where the last sentence (22:71) was: "What further need of testimony do we have? For we ourselves have heard from his own mouth." That sentence described no judgment, and so it is from this standing up of the whole multitude in 23:1 to lead Jesus to Pilate that we come to know what was decided. In Mark's trial scene false witnesses and the chief priest "stood up" (14:57,60); often the verb is pleonastic, expressing no more than the beginning of an action, but in a courtroom context it may have a legal nuance, indicating a decisive moment. "The whole *multitude* of them" employs *plēthos,* which is used some twenty-four times in Luke-Acts (five of them with "whole").[9] Here it refers to "the assembly of the elders of the people, both chief priests and scribes" whom Luke 22:66 described as leading Jesus away to their Sanhedrin. More broadly three verses later Luke 23:4 will describe "the chief priests *and the crowds*" as present before Pilate.

In John 18:28 those who lead Jesus to Pilate are simply "they." There were Jewish attendants present when Jesus was interrogated by Annas (18:22),

---

[9]In Acts 6:5, 15:12,30 it describes the Christian assembly and may be related to the term (*rabbîm,* "the many") the DSS use to describe the voting assembly at Qumran.

and later Annas sent him bound to Caiaphas (18:24), and so the reader would be thinking of the "they" as the chief priests and the attendants. This is confirmed in John 19:6, which mentions those two groups dealing with Pilate. Yet in the Pilate context a wider group is also envisioned as accusing Jesus, i.e., "the Jews."[10]

TRANSFER TO PILATE

The second part of Mark 15:1 ("having bound Jesus, [they] took him away and gave him over to Pilate") continues abruptly without a connective. Matt in 27:2 adds an "and" (as do some copyists in Mark) because he substituted in the first part a finite verb for Mark's participle. Several actions are described. This is the first time in Mark/Matt that Jesus is bound. A convicted criminal now, Jesus is treated as one (similar to Barabbas in Mark 15:7). Binding will help to show Pilate how dangerous Jesus is; theologically it will remind readers of the fate of the just one who is bound (Isa 3:10 [LXX]) and given over (Isa 53:6,12 [LXX]; Ps 27:12; etc.). Luke apparently cannot bring himself to narrate such an indignity, and so nowhere in the Lucan PN is Jesus described as being bound. Some scholars suggest as another reason for the omission the Lucan desire to picture Jesus as acting freely and spontaneously in the PN. John has had no formal trial of Jesus during this night of his arrest. Rather the Sanhedrin convicted Jesus earlier (11:47–53) before the beginning of the PN, and so Jesus was bound as a criminal from the moment of his arrest (18:12) and was transferred to Caiaphas bound (18:24).

Next Mark 15:1 reports that they "took him away" (*apopherein*). Matt 27:2 uses the compound verb *apagein,* and Luke and John use the simple verb *agein* for leading Jesus away. *Agein* and its compounds are not unusual for delivering a criminal; Josephus (*War* 6.5.3; #303) tells us that the Jerusalem leaders, thinking Jesus son of Ananias was under a supernatural impulse, "led [*anagein*] him to the Roman eparch." In particular the *epi* that Luke uses for leading Jesus *to* Pilate is employed in the context of delivering criminals to legal officers in Matt 10:18; Luke 12:11,58; Acts 25:12.

Finally Mark 15:1 speaks of the giving over of Jesus to Pilate. The sequence fulfills Jesus' prediction in Mark 10:33: "The Son of Man will be given over to the chief priests and the scribes, and they will judge against him (condemning him) to death; and they will give him over to the Gentiles." Mark 14:64 fulfilled the first part of the predicted action by priests and scribes: "They all judged against him as being guilty, punishable by death";

_____

[10]John 18:31; 19:12,38; also "the chief priests of the Jews" in 19:21, and "your own nation and the chief priests" (18:35).

15:1 deals with the second part. By using *paradidonai* (pp. 211–13 above) Mark is fashioning a chain wherein Judas gives Jesus over to the Jewish authorities (14:41–44), who now give him over to Pilate, who will give him over to be crucified (15:15). Matt follows Mark in all this, both in fulfilling the third passion prediction (Matt 20:18–19) and in the chain usage of *paradidonai*. John uses *paradidonai* for Judas (John 18:2,5) and for the transferal to Pilate (not here, but in 18:30,35); Pilate will give Jesus over to be crucified (19:16), and Jesus will give over his own Spirit (19:30). Luke uses the verb for Judas (Luke 22:48) and for Pilate (23:25) as they give Jesus over, but breaks the chain by not using it of the Jewish authorities in the PN.

This is our first reference to Pilate, whom we shall discuss in detail in §31. Mark makes no effort to identify him, presumably since Mark's readers already knew his name as the one under whom Jesus was crucified (cf. I Tim 6:13). Only Matt specifies that Pilate is the "governor" (*hēgemōn*), a designation he uses six times in chap. 27; also 28:14, and one that Josephus uses for the imperial procurators or prefects in the provinces (*Ant.* 18.3.1; #55 for Pilate; see §18, A3b above). Luke 3:1 uses the related verb *hēgemoneuein* for Pilate's rule in Judea (and for Quirinius in Syria in 2:2) and will use the noun for the Roman procurators of Judea, Felix and Festus, in Acts 23–26. John does not mention Pilate until the next verse (18:29) and there, like Mark, without introductory information.

John alone is concerned with first telling the readers where Pilate is, i.e., the praetorium, because the scenario of the interior and exterior of the building will be important for John's theological dramatization (§32D ANALYSIS). In the Synoptics no localizing information is given until the Roman trial is over. Then in Mark 15:16 and Matt 27:27 the soldiers to whom Jesus is given over for crucifixion will first lead him away or bring him into the praetorium. By implication one would get the impression that the trial of Jesus before Pilate had taken place outside the praetorium—a scenario different from John's, where Pilate questions Jesus inside. In §31C pages will be devoted to discussing which building in Jerusalem served as the praetorium. Most likely it was the Herodian Palace, standing with three great towers on the top of the western hill of the city (and not the Fortress Antonia of the medieval and modern "Way of the Cross"). The exact site is not important for Gospel commentary. What is important is that now Jesus is being given over to the domain of the Gentiles.

(Bibliography for this episode may be found in §17, Part 1.)

§29. JUDAS, THE CHIEF PRIESTS, AND THE PRICE OF INNOCENT BLOOD

(Matt 27:3–10)

Translation

Matt 27:3–10: ³Then Judas, the one who gave him over, having seen that he [Jesus] was judged against, having changed with remorse, returned the thirty silver pieces to the chief priests and elders, ⁴saying, "I sinned in having given over innocent blood." But they said, "What is that to us? You must see to it." ⁵And having cast the silver pieces into the sanctuary, he departed; and having gone away, he hanged himself.

⁶But having taken the silver pieces, the chief priests said, "It is not permitted to throw these into the treasury since it is the price for blood." ⁷Having taken a decision, they bought with them the potter's field for a burial ground of strangers. ⁸Therefore that field has been called "Field of Blood" to this day.

⁹Then there was fulfilled what was spoken through Jeremiah the prophet saying, "And they took the thirty silver pieces, the price of the one priced, whom the sons of Israel priced. ¹⁰And they gave them for the potter's field, according to what the Lord directed me."

Acts 1:16–20 (Excerpt from Peter's speech in Acts 1:15–26, placed between Jesus' ascension forty days after the resurrection, and before the descent of the Spirit at Pentecost [fifty days after Passover]; Peter addresses the men of the community whom he calls brothers):

¹⁶"It was necessary that the Scripture be fulfilled that the Holy Spirit spoke beforehand through the mouth of David concerning Judas who was the leader of those who took Jesus, ¹⁷because he was numbered among us and was allotted a share of this ministry. (¹⁸Accordingly this man acquired acreage with the wages of his wickedness; and laid prostrate, he burst open in the middle, and all his entrails poured out. ¹⁹And it became known to all the inhabit-

ants of Jerusalem with the result that his acreage was called in their language Hakeldamach, that is 'Acreage of Blood.'*) [20]It is written in the book of Psalms: 'Let his habitation become a desert, and let there be no dweller in it' and 'Let another take his superintendency.'"

(There follows in 1:21–26 the account of the choice of Matthias "to take the place of the service and apostolate from which Judas turned aside to go to his own place" [v. 25].)

*Many scholars consider vv. 18–19 to constitute a parenthesis, rather than words spoken by Peter. Certainly he cannot be imagined as saying "in their language [dialect]" while speaking in Jerusalem. Irenaeus (*Adv. Haer.* 3.12.1) seems to have recognized the problem; he cites the passage without vv. 18–19.

COMMENT

Only Matt interrupts the story of the transfer of Jesus to Pilate to tell the readers of the fate of Judas or, more precisely, of his attempt to throw off responsibility for the innocent blood of Jesus by paying back to the chief priests the thirty silver pieces he had received from them, and how they in turn tried to rid themselves of this blood money by buying a potter's field. The most consistent element found here in all three subsections is the thirty silver pieces (27:3,6,9). This is the price for *innocent blood;* and that is Matt's real interest, to which he will return in the Roman trial (27:24–25), where Pilate tries to acquit himself as "innocent of the blood of this man," forcing "all the people" to accept responsibility for it. This haunting Judas scene of blood that cannot be easily eradicated anticipates in its theme the Shakespearean portrait of Lady Macbeth's anguish.

On the night before he died, the Matthean Jesus uttered three prophecies pertinent to his disciples. Two of them have been fulfilled: They have all fled (Matt 26:56); Peter has denied him three times (26:69–75). There remains the prediction about the one who, although he ate with Jesus at table, would give him over (26:21): *Woe to that man . . . for whom it would have been better not to have been born* (26:24). Judas has given him over; now we see the dramatic woe that afflicted Judas.

Despite this general pertinence to the sequence of events, the scene in Matt 27:3–10 is clearly an awkward interruption. Matt 27:1–2 (also 27:12) has the chief priests and elders leading Jesus away to give him over to Pilate. Yet here are the chief priests and elders in the area of the Temple sanctuary, picking up scattered silver pieces and then taking the time to buy a field with them. Too perceptive a writer to have overlooked such an inconsistency, Matt probably tells the story here not because it happened at this moment in the PN but because it was the direct result of the decision to give Jesus over. To have related this story after the resurrection would have been a negative anticlimax for the Gospel. (Luke does narrate a story of Judas' death after the resurrection, but not at the end of the Gospel—he places it in the opening of Acts, where, since it leads to the filling out of the Twelve, it prepares for beginnings of the church and the Christian mission.) Moreover, in Matt's story, at the moment when Jesus is judged against by the Jewish authorities, the reactions of Peter and Judas, placed in parallelism before and after the judgment (27:1–2), constitute an interesting contrast.

JUDAS AND THE PRICE OF INNOCENT BLOOD (27:3–5)

The story of Judas is really confined to the first few verses, and even there his principal role is to bring the blood money onto center stage. No longer does Matt remind us that Judas is one of the Twelve as in 26:14,47. What he did to Jesus has removed him from that position (cf. Acts 1:17,25), and now he is known simply as the one who gave Jesus over.[1] Judas *saw* that Jesus was judged against, viz., in the decision taken in 27:1; Matt's description could give readers the impression that Judas was present for that Sanhedrin decision, and that it produced an on-the-spot change of outlook.[2]

How are we to interpret that change of outlook? I have translated the form of the verb *metamelesthai* as "having changed with remorse"; the verb means "to have a different feeling toward, to change one's concern" (see O. Michel, TDNT 4.626–29). The change involved in *metamelesthai* can be unacceptable to God (Exod 13:17). *Metanoein* is the normal NT verb for "to repent, to change one's heart/mind"; and the failure to use it has caused considerable debate whether repentance is intended by Matt here.[3] Two of the other four NT uses of *metamelesthai* were in Matt 21:29,32 for the son who changed his mind about obeying his father's command: Was that a change of feeling by recognizing that more respect was due, or was it true sorrow for disobedience? Has Judas changed his heart toward Jesus to believe in him (*metanoein* would include that), or is he simply one who regrets

---

[1]This was also his designation in the list of the Twelve in Matt 10:4.

[2]One needs to be cautious, for the same grammatical construction with "then" plus an aorist participle of "see" appears in Matt 2:16 to imply immediate consequence; and there a deduction rather than physical sight is involved.

[3]Origen (*Contra Celsum* 2.11) understood the repentance as genuine, despite Judas' previous covetousness: "See, when he repented of his sins, how he was overcome by such agonizing remorse that he could no longer bear even to live."

that his action has brought about consequences that he had not fully foreseen (so Halas, *Judas* 146)? If the latter, had he not listened to Jesus who three times had predicted that the Son of Man, when given over to the chief priests, elders, and scribes, would be killed (Matt 16:21; 17:22–23; 20:18–19)? And when Judas went to the chief priests to arrange to give Jesus over (26:14–16), did he not know that they had taken counsel to kill Jesus (26:3–4) and that was why they were purchasing his help?

On that occasion (only Matt tells us) Judas had asked for money and received thirty silver pieces.[4] Now his remorseful change is expressed by bringing back those coins.[5] Throughout this section, including the OT citation in 27:9, Matt will use (four times) the plural of *argyrion* for "silver pieces," even as he did in the initial reference in 26:15. Indeed, Matt's nine uses of that noun constitute almost half the total NT usage (twenty-one times). The LXX frequently employs *argyrion;*[6] but in the key Zech 11:12–13 passage that Matt draws on, it uses *argyrous,* a contracted form of *argyreos* (see BDF 45).

Colella ("Trenta") discusses what coins would have been paid; but we should remember that Matt wrote some fifty years after Jesus died and would have been thinking of the coinage of his own time, devalued several times in the interval. In the general Roman coinage, between the gold aureus and the bronze sestertius (and lower coins) stood the denarius, which in Nero's time contained 3.45 grams of silver. In Syria and Palestine, circulated from the mint at Tyre, an equivalent was the silver drachma (3.66 grams) and its larger multiples, the didrachma and tetradrachma (= stater). Matt's term *argyrion* (pl.) is not precise;[7] but in the Murabba'at Papyrus 114 (DJD 2.240–43) *argyrion* of Tyre is used to describe a sum consisting of staters and denarii. The Hebrew shekel often stands for a drachma or the larger stater, and many hold that Matt was thinking of thirty silver shekels. That sum constituted recompense for serious injury done to a slave in Exod 21:32. Also Zech 11:12, which influenced the Judas passage, uses the related verb *šql* for weighing out wages consisting of thirty silver pieces; and Jeremiah (32:9) paid silver shekels in purchasing a field. If Matt was thinking of tetradrachmas/staters/shekels (four times more valuable than silver denarii),

---

[4]Reiner ("Thirty," followed by Luke, "Thirty") points out that in Sumerian thirty shekels is a contemptuous sum and in Amarna letter EA 292 thirty silver shekels is a ransom for low-class people; she contends that the contemptuous tone may still be echoed in the OT and NT. Yet while the authorities had contempt for Jesus, the logic of the story is that Judas was adequately paid.

[5]*Strephein,* "to turn" (the best attested reading here), governs "silver pieces" as an object. It is not used elsewhere in the NT in the transitive sense of "return"; accordingly ms. copyists often preferred here the compound *apostrephein* used for "return" in Matt 26:52.

[6]In the singular, however, not the Matthean plural; Mark 14:11 also uses the singular.

[7]A variant Western reading of Matt 26:15 has Judas paid thirty staters.

those minted at Tyre had the Phoenician god Melcart (laureate as Hercules) on the front side, while those minted at Antioch had the laureate head of Augustus (Hill, "Thirty" 254).[8]

Accompanying Judas' remorseful change and return of the silver are his words that tilt the interpretation toward serious repentance: "I sinned in having given over innocent blood." Although he thus indirectly testifies that Jesus is innocent, Judas' primary concern is that he himself is guilty. By giving Jesus over to Pilate, the Jewish authorities have sealed Jesus' fate; yet Judas does not charge them but himself with the sin of judicial murder. Curiously the gravity of the sin does not seem to be increased by the fact that Judas has been unfaithful to one who was his friend and master, and who was God's special agent; the issue is responsibility for the death of an *innocent* (*athōos*) person.[9] By his words, then, Judas indirectly bears witness to Jesus as innocent of guilt. Thus Jesus' blood is associated with "all the just [*dikaios*] blood spilled on earth from that of the just Abel to the blood of Zechariah, the son of Barachiah" that Matt 23:34–35 invokes on the scribes and the Pharisees who were persecuting Jesus' followers. We see the influence of that passage (plus possibly Matt 27:19 where Pilate's wife calls Jesus *dikaios*) in the reading of 27:4 found in Codex Koridethi and an OL witness with "just blood" instead of "innocent blood."[10]

How are we to judge Matt's evaluation of Judas in this scene? In APPENDIX IV we shall encounter much theorizing about the motives of Judas and about what information he gave to the chief priests. Obviously those theories, some of which are highly imaginative, could affect the behavior of Judas described in the present Matthean scene. Some scholars argue that Judas was a conscientious figure, e.g., Bornhäuser (*Death* 50–52) holds that *exomologēsen* in Luke 22:6 does not mean that Judas "promised" to give Jesus over to the chief priests but that he "confessed" that Jesus had blasphemed by claiming to be the "Son of Yahweh"! Niedner ("Role") contends that Judas received the forgiving eucharistic cup at the Last Supper and that Jesus was not ironical in calling Judas "Friend" at the time of the arrest (Matt 26:50). Judas' repentance in the present scene was sincere, and there is a real possi-

---

[8]Hill also has fascinating information on how these thirty pieces functioned in later legend. They were identified with the coins for which Joseph the patriarch was sold into slavery—coins brought to Palestine by the Queen of Sheba, plundered and taken away by Nebuchadnezzar, but brought back by the magi, etc. Six European cities claim to have them among their treasured relics; most often those are silver coins from Rhodes (perhaps because the imprint "Rodion" was related to King Herod), with the image of the sun god. If there were legendary developments of the Judas story already in the NT, they did not cease with the NT.

[9]*Athōos* appears only here in the NT; Daniel (13:46) proclaims himself *athōos* of the blood of Susanna.

[10]See also Lam 4:13, where the false prophets and priests shed "just blood."

bility he was forgiven by God—a view that goes back at least to Origen. (Such a view is often combined with the thesis to be discussed below that Judas' suicide was judgment that he executed on himself as a reparation.) I find that this whole approach runs against Matt's sequence where clearly the death of Judas is described to fulfill Jesus' prediction about him: "Woe to that man . . . for whom it would have been better not to have been born" (26:24).

Yet if Judas' expression of remorse is looked on as ineffective and his death is regarded negatively, does that impinge on the mercy of Jesus or of God? This issue often comes to a head with modern readers when a comparison is made between Judas and Peter. Is the triple denial and cursing of Jesus by Peter much less a crime than the giving over by Judas? Peter never says "I have sinned" or tries to undo his denials by coming back immediately to the servant woman and confessing Jesus. Why is Judas looked upon as unforgiven in Christian tradition (see APPENDIX IV) while Peter is venerated? Some focus their response on Judas' suicide contrasted with Simon Peter's regaining his courage and going on to become a great apostle. Certainly that is a factor; but much more important in the comparison is that Peter was not responsible for Jesus' death and Judas was. Judas had a part in the shedding of "innocent blood," and in Jewish thought responsibility for that was a horror.[11] This was something that would haunt the perpetrator (Jer 26:15 [LXX 33:15]); a pollution was caused by it (Ps 106:38–39), and the Lord would not pardon it (II Kings 24:4). "You shall purge from your midst [the guilt of shedding] innocent blood," commands Deut 21:9. "Cursed be whoever accepts bribes to take the life of innocent blood" (Deut 27:25). Josephus (*Ant.* 1.2.1; #58) reports that God cursed Cain and threatened his descendants till the seventh generation. *Protevangelium of James* 14:1 has Joseph state that if he had denounced the pregnant Mary for adultery, he would "have given over innocent blood to the sentence of death." Thus Judas has done something so heinous that no ordinary repentance affects it. Besides this awe of blood that would have been very convincing to those who shared Matt's theology, one can mention a point that may be more convincing to modern readers, namely, that Judas has come to the chief priests, Jesus' enemies, seeking a form of absolution from his sin. He has not sought out Jesus, who had forgiven many sinners; and thus one may well suspect that in the psychology of the Matthean story his remorse has not really meant belief.

---

[11]I Sam 19:5; 25:26 (LXX); I Kings 2:5; II Macc 1:8; Jer 7:6; 19:4; 22:3; Ps 94:21; *Testament of Zebulon* 2:2; Philo, *De specialibus legibus* 1.37; #204.

Matt gives a very hostile description (27:4b) of the reaction of the chief priests and elders to Judas.[12] Although Judas gave Jesus over to them, they are the ones who have given Jesus over to be crucified by Pilate's orders (27:2). Yet they show no remorse or even interest in either the sin of Judas or the innocence of Jesus. Of all those who will be stained with innocent blood, for Matt they are the most callous. The elliptic expression "What to [*pros*] us?" is a disclaimer of concern (see John 21:22) and thus the opposite of Judas' newly gained concern. "You will see" is also elliptic, and my translation, "You must see to it," fleshes it out. (Van Unnik, "Death," thinks it may be a Latinism reflecting *videris*.) The same expression will occur in 27:24 as Pilate attempts to pass responsibility to the people. Acts 18:15 places it on the lips of Gallio as he refuses to become involved in an issue of Jewish law.

The callousness of the reply forces Judas to two violent actions. The *first violent action* consists of casting the silver pieces into the Temple sanctuary.[13] The original payment of the money to Judas in Matt 26:15, "They set for him thirty silver pieces," echoed Zech 11:12 (LXX): "They set my wages [see Acts 1:18] at thirty silver pieces." The action here echoes by anticipation Zech 11:13 (to be cited by Matt in v. 9 below: "And the Lord said to me, 'Throw it into the potter [?]. . . .' And I took the thirty (pieces) of silver, and I threw them into the House of the Lord into the potter." Some major problems emerge from comparing the MT, LXX, and Matt. First, Matt speaks of "the sanctuary" (*naos*) rather than of "the House of the Lord"; but only the priests could enter the sanctuary. Matt's verb "to cast" (*riptein*) implies a strong action,[14] but surely Matt does not mean that Judas threw the coins from a great distance. Indeed, some mss. of Matt have "in" instead of "into," making it explicit that Judas was in the sanctuary. Did Matt not know the rules of the Temple, or was he deliberately exaggerating Judas' action to communicate the horror of profanation? Or does *naos* stand for the whole Temple precinct, or even "the treasury" specifically?[15] This last suggestion

[12]Van Tilborg (*Jewish* 88–89), who thinks there was a preMatthean narrative, argues that the declaration of repentance by Judas in 27:4 was added to sharpen the contrast of the enduring hostility of the Jewish leaders. He thinks it may have been shaped by Jer 2:34–35, where one who is stained with blood of the innocent says, "I am innocent; I have not sinned."

[13]To explain the way in which Judas returns the money, Jeremias, Gnilka, and Moo are among those who point to the custom cited in Mishna '*Arakin* 9.3–4: X who sold a house has twelve months to redeem it by paying back the money received; if Y who paid the money hides from X, according to Hillel, X can deposit the money in the Temple chamber. However, Matt's picture of Judas casting the money into the sanctuary would scarcely evoke this procedure.

[14]While the LXX uses *emballein* ("to throw into"), Aquila and Symmachus use *riptein*, so that Matt may be affected by an alternative Greek rendering.

[15]That *naos* here means the whole Temple precinct is held by many (e.g., Joüon, Lagrange, McNeile, Zahn); see BAGD 533[1]. For the use of *naos* for the Olympia temple treasury, see *Journal of Hellenic Studies* 25 (1905), 311.

leads us into another problem. The *yôṣer* of the MT of Zech means "potter," but the LXX translates by *chōneutērion* "smelter, foundry," and Targum Jonathan has "sanctuary." Many scholars would emend the MT from *yôṣer* to *'ôṣar,* "treasury," a reading consonant with the mention of "treasury" in Matt 27:6 and supported by the Syriac Peshitta. Torrey ("Foundry") makes an ingenious suggestion that may be considered independently of his implausible thesis that Matt 27:3–10 was translated from an Aramaic document that quoted the Scriptures in Hebrew. Torrey proposes that there was a foundry in the Temple to melt down metal gifts into sacred vessels, and that "the Potter" was the chief craftsman of the foundry, who got his name from the shape of the sacred vessels into which the metal was fashioned. Presumably the sacred vessels would have been preserved in the treasury.[16] That may be helpful in explaining diverse forms of the Zech passage; but we are primarily interested in the usage of the passage by Matt, and we cannot assume that Matt had such knowledge of Temple customs. Rather most who have studied Matt's use of Scripture agree that this author had the ability to utilize the Hebrew, Aramaic, and Greek forms of the Scriptures according to his purpose (BBM 102–3). It may well be that here, with his reference to the treasury and the potter, Matt is drawing on different understandings of Zech 11:13 (combined with Jeremiah as we shall see).

The *second violent action* by Judas is summarized in the description: "He departed; and having gone away, he hanged himself." Several times above (pp. 125, 257, 623) we have seen how the PN was influenced by the story of David's flight from Jerusalem and Absalom in II Sam 15–17. When Ahithophel, who had been the trusted advisor of David but now had tried to give him over into the hands of Absalom, saw that his advice was not being followed and that the revolt against David would fail, "he *went away* to his own house . . . and *hanged himself*" (II Sam 17:23). The vocabulary is the same as in Matt; indeed the verb *apagchesthai* ("to hang oneself"), beyond these two passages, is found in the Greek Bible only in Tob 3:10.[17]

Josephus (*Ant.* 7.9.8; #228–29) reports Ahithophel saying that it was better for him to withdraw from life freely and high-mindedly (by choosing hanging rather than being punished later). Similarly some scholars would interpret Judas' choice of death as a positive action; e.g., Conard ("Fate" 164) speaks of "the fact that Judas removes the curse from himself by his suicide." Isorni (*Vrai* 39–40) speaks of the suicide of Judas as an act of hope

---

[16]Others have theorized that the Temple potter sold his handiwork to people to hold grain or oil offerings and that the profits went into the treasury.

[17]Since the verb in the active means "to strangle," some would translate it in Matt 27:5 as "he strangled himself," with the harmonizing understanding that this attempt was unsuccessful and was followed by the death described in Acts 1:18.

and faith like the Japanese hara-kiri. (Actually, closer to that simile would
be the choice made by those who plunged into the Temple fire in AD 70
rather than surrender to the Romans: Josephus *War* 6.5.1; #280.) Appeal has
been made to biblical passages dealing with atoning for innocent blood and
doing away with the attendant curse to prevent it from spreading. Among
other texts,[18] one may cite II Sam 21:1–6, where the blood of the Gibeonites
shed by Saul and his relatives is atoned for by hanging seven of his descendants. However, the Jewish attitude toward suicide as infringing on God's
rights makes it extremely unlikely that Judas' hanging himself would have
been considered a divinely acceptable expiation (so Desautels, "Mort" 227,
against Derrett). To those who say that for various reasons it is noble to
destroy oneself, Josephus (*War* 3.8.5; #369) replies with indignation, "It is
an act of impiety towards God who created us." The darkest regions of the
nether world receive the souls of suicides, and God punishes even their pos-
terity. Josephus cites the Jewish law that a suicide's body should be exposed
unburied until sunset, even though Jews bury even enemies slain in war. In
later Judaism the minor talmudic tractate *Semahot* (*'Ebel Rabbati*) 2 gives
further evidence of repugnance for suicides: For them one does not rend
garments, bare the head, or mourn openly. More specifically pertinent to the
Judas suicide, Mishna *Sanhedrin* 10.2 states the belief that Ahithophel
would have no place in the world to come. Acts 1:20 gives evidence independent of Matt that Judas' violent death was treated as an additional disgrace
of the former apostle and a divine judgment against him.[19] A self-giving in
death could take away a curse (Gal 3:13), but not a self-inflicted death. Probably Matt intended his final words about Judas in 27:5, "And having gone
away, he hanged himself," to contrast unfavorably with his final words about
Peter in 26:75, "And having gone outside, he wept bitterly."

THE CHIEF PRIESTS AND THE PRICE OF INNOCENT BLOOD (27:6–8)

Despite the callous reply he received from the chief priests (and elders),
Judas by casting the coins into their realm has now visibly entangled the
chief priests in guilt attached to the giving over of Jesus. He has contaminated them with the curse of blood, and they too become indirect witnesses
of Jesus' innocence by their unwillingness to keep the price for his blood.
(Clearly the story is written from a Christian point of view, or the chief

[18]Van Unnik ("Death" 57) cites Deut 27:25. Niedner ("Role") points to Jeremiah's field as a field
of hope (see Jer 32:15). But the burial place near the Potsherd Gate in Jer 19:2,11 is scarcely a
good place.
[19]That divine punishment can be manifested in sudden, violent death is illustrated by the Ananias
and Sapphira story of Acts 5:1–11.

priests would have reacted by justifying their condemnation of Jesus.) The legal analogue for their statement, "It is not permitted to throw these [silver pieces] into the treasury [*korbanas*]" is probably Deut 23:19(18) about not bringing the wages of prostitution into the House of the Lord. In Matt's acid portrayal, their propriety about the blood money is sheer legalism, for they show no concern about the greater crime of shedding the blood.

The word korbanas for Temple treasury is found only here in the NT; it is related to the word *korban* or "dedicated to God" employed in Mark 7:11, and both reflect Hebrew *qorbān* (see J. A. Fitzmyer, JBL 78 [1959], 60–65). The two ideas are joined in a Josephus reference (*War* 2.9.4; #175) that calls the contents of the sacred treasury (*hieros thesauros*) *korbanas*.[20] Presumably the money to pay Judas came from the Temple treasury, and that is why Judas threw it back there; but impurity acquired through usage has halted the return. An impression from this popular story is that the treasury was in or near the sanctuary.[21]

The expression that the silver pieces constituted a "price [*timē*] for blood" (27:6) already anticipates the language of the Jeremiah/Zechariah passage to be cited in 27:9.[22] Acts 1:18 speaks of the (unspecified) money as the "wages [*misthos*] of his wickedness," and Nellessen ("Tradition" 211) argues that both Greek words come from the same Semitic source, Hebrew *měḥîr*, Aramaic *dāmîn*—a thesis that to some extent supposes a consecutive pre-Gospel story that can be reconstructed. In an attempt to avoid contaminating the Temple treasury by blood money, the chief priests "take a decision." Matt 27:7 uses the same Greek expression that 27:1 employed to describe the decision of the Sanhedrin against Jesus—a repetition that gives the impression that all these actions are quite deliberate. Presumably we are to think that this consultation took place near the sanctuary where they picked up the silver pieces. The wording of the decision about buying a potter's field is once more dictated by the Scripture to be cited in v. 10. "Field" is *agros* in Matt 27:7 and 10 (cf. *chōrion* ["acreage"] in Acts 1:18,19).[23] Desautels ("Mort" 228) argues that the vocabulary in Matt 27:7 came from the tradition, but in part that judgment depends on whether Matt or preMatt tradition

[20]Accordingly I see no need for Moo's contention ("Tradition" 164) that in this scene Matt may mean not the treasury but the sacred gifts deposited in the Temple, to which, however, this money could not be added because of its profane purpose. Matt is probably thinking of the treasury as the place where such gifts were kept.

[21]Yet Mark 12:41–44 describes a type of treasury (*gazophylakeion*) outside the sanctuary area that could be reached by the laity (including women) for contributions; see also John 8:20; Josephus, *War* 5.5.2; #200; Mishna, *Šeqalim* 6.5.

[22]This will be important for our discussion in the ANALYSIS of the composition of this story.

[23]Munro ("Death") would see *agros* as a worthless plot and *chōrion* as an estate or farm. However, Luke 23:26 pictures Simon of Cyrene coming into Jerusalem from an *agros;* and Acts 4:36–37 has Barnabas of Cyprus selling an *agros* in Jerusalem—clearly these are farms, not worthless plots.

first employed the Scripture passages. Matt speaks literally of "the field of the potter," with definite articles suggesting a well-known field. But known as of when? Was it famous at the time of the purchase, either as a place in Jerusalem bearing that name or (in the writer's mind) as the field mentioned in the Scriptures? Or was it known at the time of the writing because of the Judas history? (Yet "Field of Blood," not "The Potter's Field," seems to be the name closest to the Judas story.) In the "bought with them" of 27:7 Matt uses *ek* plus a genitive of price, as previously in 20:2 (also in Acts 1:18: "with the wages").

The major element in Matt's description of the purchase that is not derived from the Scripture cited in 27:9–10 is that the field would serve as a burial ground (*taphē*) of strangers. (We note also the total absence of the burial motif in Acts.) In the public forum[24] presumably the "strangers" would not be Gentiles, for their burial would be the concern of the Romans. Rather, Jewish visitors to Jerusalem or proselytes would be in view. Does the combination of Judas' suicide and the use of the money returned by him suggest that he was looked on as a stranger to Jerusalem who could be buried there, e.g., because he was a Jew from Galilee?[25] Would a suicide, however, be given such a burial plot? Others have thought that the field was intended to serve as the burial place for Judas' victim, Jesus from Nazareth, after his execution in Jerusalem.[26] Most likely, however, the "strangers" to be provided with burial were meant by Matt as a general group with reference neither to Judas nor to Jesus. Matt, therefore, offers no support for the thesis that Judas was remembered as buried in this field; nor does Acts 1:25 with its statement that "Judas turned aside to go to his own place"—that is, not his burial place but his destined place (of punishment) in the next world.[27]

Matt 27:8 is introduced by a "therefore" which suggests that the "Field of Blood" designation for the burial ground comes from the blood money returned by Judas that was used to purchase it. The name stands as a reminder of the innocent blood of Jesus, making those guilty who gave him over.[28]

---

[24]Matt seems to speak of a field that would be known *publicly* as "a burial ground of strangers." It is unlikely that Matt is playing upon Judas' having been estranged from the body of the disciples, since here Judas is no longer called "one of the Twelve" as he was previously (Matt 26:47).

[25]That would militate against the theory that explains "Iscariot" in terms of Judas being a man from the town of Kerioth in Judea (see APPENDIX IV, B1).

[26]This explanation assumes that the Jewish authorities would arrange Jesus' burial; in §46 below I shall suggest that in fact Joseph of Arimathea, who buried Jesus, was a member of the Sanhedrin, but (at the time of the crucifixion) not a disciple (even though Matt would give that impression).

[27]See *I Clement* 5:4, which tells how Peter, "having thus given his testimony, went to the glorious place due him."

[28]An explanation of the name "Acreage of Blood" is never given in Acts 1:19, for there has been no mention of blood by Acts in relation to Judas. Are we to make two assumptions: that Judas died on the acreage he had bought and that his violent death (bursting open) involved his shedding blood there so that the acreage recalls his blood?

Matt records that the field has been called "Field of Blood" *to this day* and so indicates an early origin for the story. ("To this day" is employed by the OT in giving etiological explanations of place names, e.g., Gen 26:33; Josh 7:26; II Sam 6:8; and it will be encountered again in peculiarly Matthean material in 28:15.) Antiquity is also implied in Acts, where in Peter's Greek speech the name is first given *in their language* (the Semitic tongue of the Jerusalemites) as "Hakeldamach."[29] That is an accurate Greek transcription of Aramaic *ḥăqēl dĕmā'*, "field [or acreage] of blood," since *aleph* was often transliterated by Greek *chi*. The suggestion (Klostermann, Bernard, and others) that it is an imaginative corruption of the original name "field [or acreage] of sleep" [*dĕmak* = Greek *koimēterion*, "cemetery, sleeping place"] is not necessary.[30]

Where was this place? The site remembered in tradition since Jerome is in the SSW region of Jerusalem, outside the present walls, where the valleys of the Kidron, Tyropoeon, and Hinnom meet. Here there were available both water and wind draft for potters' kilns.[31] (Of course, Matt's reference is to the field owned by the potter, not necessarily to where he worked.) This area receives support from some biblical references. With his pottery vessel Jeremiah (19:1) descended toward the Valley of Hinnom through the Potsherd Gate (so called perhaps because it went out to the Potter's Quarter). This area of the Kidron valley was the site of "the burial ground [*taphos* or *mnēma*] of the common people" (II Kings 23:6; Jer 26[33]:23) in which things or people rejected by the monarchs of Judah were buried. Water carrying blood spattered in the sacrifices of the Temple seems to have been channeled into this same region (Qumran Temple Scroll [11Q *Miqdaš*] 32; Mishna *Me'ila* 3:3; *Yoma* 5:6). This causes Y. Yadin (*The Temple Scroll* [New York: Random House, 1985], 134) to suggest that "Field of Blood" was a preChristian name of the area that Matt took over and interpreted in light of the Judas story—a well-attested technique in biblical etiologies.

THE FULFILLMENT CITATION (27:9–10)

These verses bring the scene to its culmination. At the beginning, the scandalous death of Judas fulfilled Jesus' utterance of woe against the one who would give him over (Matt 26:24). At the end, Matt makes clear that the dominant theme of the scene (the price paid for innocent blood) fulfills

---

[29]A designation also interpolated into the Vulgate of Matt 27:8.

[30]Moreover, as Bernard ("Death" 427) admits, the corruption would already have had to occur before Acts was written.

[31]Schick, "Aceldama," reports that at the end of the 19th cent. potters had moved farther up the slope of the hill because the original loam pit had been exhausted.

what God spoke through Jeremiah the prophet. Here Matt writes out the specific words of the OT citation, something that he did earlier (26:31) in citing Zech 13:7 (from Mark 14:27) at the beginning of the PN as Jesus went to the Mount of Olives. That earlier reference is worth remembering since Zech is also in mind in the present passage. Matt introduces the present passage by a fulfillment formula (German: *Reflexionszitate, Erfüllungs-zitate*): "Then there was fulfilled what was spoken through Jeremiah the prophet saying." There are some fourteen of these formulae in Matt,[32] as compared with one instance in Mark (15:28), three in Luke (18:31; 22:37; 24:44), and nine in John (see BBM 96–104). In the Matthean formulae only two prophets are mentioned by name: Isaiah (five or six times) and Jeremiah (twice). The formula citation in Matt 26:56 was, as noted there, parallel in wording to a citation formula in the infancy narrative (Matt 1:22). Here the formula is parallel to another infancy narrative formula (2:17), the other Jeremiah reference. (At the end of his Gospel Matt is making deliberate inclusions with the beginning of his Gospel; we shall point out more in sections to come.) The two Jeremiah citations have exactly the same wording in their introductory formulae, being the only Matthean examples of starting with "then" (*tote*). They are probably to be kept distinct from the other fulfillment formulae that begin with a *hina* or *hopōs* purpose clause: These two passages describe evil actions of Jesus' enemies (Herod in 2:17; the chief priests here), and so cannot be said to accomplish the purpose of God (BBM 205). There is also a storyline effect if the "Then" is describing another major event in the continuation of the narrative (SPNM 365–66).

Coming now to Matt's citation itself, to facilitate discussion let me divide it into five parts, numbered by letters:

27:9   a. And they took the thirty silver pieces [*argyria*],
       b. the price of the one priced,
       c. whom the sons of Israel priced.
27:10   d. And they gave them for the potter's field,
       e. according to what the Lord directed me.

That conglomeration of words cited by Matt exists *nowhere* in the standard OT. Despite Matt's attribution to Jeremiah, a passage in Zech comes closest to much of the wording, a passage that is not a prediction of the future but an obscure symbolic description of events that took place in the author's own time. Above (p. 643) I called attention to differences between the Hebrew and Greek of Zech 11:13 and to how Matt seems to choose

---

[32]The only previous instance in the PN is 26:56, but there no specific citation was given.

between these witnesses for his own purposes. Let me translate each literally:

MT   a. And the Lord said to me:
      b. Throw it into the potter,
      c. the dignity of price by which I was priced by them.
      d. And I took the thirty of silver
      e. and I threw it into the house of the Lord into the potter.

LXX a. And the Lord said to me:
      b. Set them into the furnace,
      c. and I will see if it is genuine in the manner in which I was tested for their sake.
      d. And I took the thirty silver pieces [*argyrous*]
      e. and I threw them into the house of the Lord into the furnace.

Only Matt's *a, b,* and *e* have close similarities to Zech; and even there the sequence is different: Matt's *a* = Zech's *d;* Matt's *b* = Zech's *c;* Matt's *e* = Zech's *a*. Let us now turn to a line-by-line study of Matt's wording.

Matt's a is close to line *d* of Zech, which is virtually the same in both MT and LXX, except that in Matt the subject apparently is not the "I," who is a heroic shepherd figure in Zech (pp. 129–30 above), but the Jewish authorities, who are hostile figures.[33] Judas, the dominant figure in 27:3–5, has been dispatched from the stage; and the scene has become an implicit judgment on the chief priests.

Matt's b is, in word and content, closer to the MT of Zech *c* than to the complex LXX. The similarity to the Hebrew is enhanced when we note that Matt's *timē* means both "price" and "dignity" and accordingly "the price of the one priced" can be a free translation of the MT "the dignity of price." For Matt "the one priced" is Jesus, who thus becomes the victimized shepherd described by Zech. Yet Zech uses "the dignity of price" ("the lordly price") sarcastically and is expressing indignation at the insignificant wages (repayment for an injured slave). Matt's indignation is not at the sizable amount but at the idea that the innocent blood of Jesus has been paid for.

Matt's c is literally "whom they priced, (some) from the sons of Israel." Since neither Zech nor any other OT text pertinent to Matt mentions "the sons of Israel" as an agent (Jervell, "Jesu" 159), in Matt it is probably an interpretation of the "by them" in the MT of Zech *c*. Although Matt's narrative has directed its ire against the chief priests (and the elders), the citation extends the guilt more widely to Israel, anticipating 27:25 where *all the people* will say, "His blood on us and on our children."

---

[33]I say "apparently" because Matt's *elabon* can mean both "I took" and "they took"; preference for "they" is suggested by the presence of the third plural in *c* and *d* (also 27:6 above).

Matt's d shows little relation to Zech except for the reference to "the potter" in the MT of Zech *b* and *e*. Matt knew those lines but used them in the narrative part of the scene (27:5). Codex Sinaiticus, the minuscule family 13, and OS^{sin} increase the resemblance to Zech in Matt *d* (27:10) by reading "I gave" for "they gave," but that is clearly a scribal attempt to prepare for the first person in the next line.

Matt's e resembles in part Zech *a*, employing the stronger *syntassein* ("directed"), a verb that Matt alone in the NT uses (three times).[34]

The attribution to Jeremiah. With such substantial similarities to Zech, why does Matt 27:9 refer to the citation as "what was spoken through Jeremiah the prophet"? This problem was recognized early, for some minuscule mss. and ancient versions (e.g., OS^{sin}) omit the name of Jeremiah. Eusebius (*Demonstratio Evangelica* 10.4.13; GCS 23.463) as one possibility suggested that Matt wrote "Zechariah" and scribes changed it. A modern suggestion is that Matt wrote simply "the prophet" and a scribe wrongly supplied the name of Jeremiah.[35] Such solutions are too facile, granted the overwhelming ms. evidence for reading "Jeremiah."

Matt is the only NT writer to use Jeremiah's name (three times). Has memory betrayed the evangelist so that he confusedly has attributed to the prophet to whom he appeals more frequently a passage from Zech (thus, with different nuances, Klostermann, Stendahl, and, in antiquity, Augustine and Jerome)? One could argue for possible Matthean confusion from 23:35 where, although Matt means Zechariah the son of Jehoiada (the martyred prophet described in II Chron 24:20–22), he describes him as Zechariah the son of Berechiah, the writing prophet (Zech 1:1) who is being cited here. Yet given the care with which Matt reflects on the citation in 27:9–10, only by last resort should we consider the attribution to Jeremiah simply a mistake.

Was Matt citing a lost work or form of Jeremiah that had in it a passage similar to that cited in Matt 27:9–10?[36] Origen held this view; and Jerome (*Comm. in Matt IV* on 27:9; CC 77.205) claimed that he had seen such a Jeremiah work among the Jewish-Christian Nazarenes. A variation of this thesis is another possibility raised by Eusebius in the same *Demonstratio Evangelica* passage: that the text was in Jeremiah but the Jews removed it.[37]

---

[34]The clause "according to what the Lord directed" appears in Exod 9:12 in the context of Pharaoh not listening to Moses.

[35]In 21:4–5, where Matt cites Zech, he simply calls him "the prophet." Although Hatch ("Old" 347) mentions the possibility of a misread abbreviation (*Zriou* for *Zachariou* read as *Iriou* for *Ieremiou*), he points out that here the mss. do not abbreviate this name.

[36]Jeremiah's prophecies certainly existed in different forms, for the LXX version is one-eighth shorter than the MT.

[37]For supposed Jewish deletion of Jeremiah passages used by Christians, see Justin, *Dialogue* 72.

A pertinent Jeremiah apocryphon is known in Ethiopic, Coptic, and Arabic. Vaccari ("Versioni") reports on a 9th-cent.-AD Arabic codex of the prophets where in Jeremiah's speech to Pashhur (Jer 20) the text cited by Matt is found but with clear Christian flavoring: The one who is priced heals sickness and forgives sins; eternal perdition is invoked on those involved in the potter's field "and on their sons after them because innocent blood will be condemned."[38] All this evidence stems from the Christian era, raising the likelihood that the Jeremiah texts have been influenced by Matt 27:9–10. We have no evidence that such a Jeremiah writing was in circulation in Matt's time.

Quesnel ("Citations") argues that Matt is not citing Zech but Lamentations 4:1–2 (which mentions silver, pricing, the sons of Zion, and the potter), a work that was joined to Jeremiah in the LXX. Another suggestion is offered by Sparks ("St. Matthew's"): Matt used a canon of the writing prophets in which Jeremiah stood first, so that a reference to a passage in the collection could be made by referring to Jeremiah. This solution, however, depends not solely on the existence of such a canon[39] but on a way of citing it. The only other Matthean formula citation mentioning Jeremiah (Matt 2:17–18) cites the Book of Jeremiah, and we should assume that that book is being cited here.

The simplest explanation and the most plausible is that in 27:9–10 Matt is presenting a mixed citation with words taken both from Zech and Jer, and that he refers to that combination by the one name. Matt does use combined citations (even if in the instances to be cited he does not attach a specific name): Matt 2:5–6 cites Micah 5:1 with an intermingled line from II Sam 5:2; Matt 21:4–5 cites Isa 62:11 and Zech 9:9; Matt 2:23b is probably citing Isa 4:3 and Judg 16:17 (BBM 223–25).

What passages from Jer can one detect (intermingled with Zech) in Matt 27:9–10?[40] There is no doubt that Jer 19:1–13 has a conglomeration of themes that have echoes in the whole Judas scene. God directs Jeremiah to take the elders of the people to the Valley of Hinnom and to speak judgment against the Jerusalemites who have filled the place with innocent blood. God will turn Hinnom into the Valley of Slaughter; and it will be a place of burial (see also Jer 26[33]:23), for there will be no other place to bury. As a sign of all this Jeremiah is to break a pottery flask. While some scholars offer this passage of Jer 19 as the best candidate for involvement in Matt

---

[38] A. Resch, *Agrapha* (TU 15³/⁴; Leipzig: Hinrichs, 1906) logion 42, pp. 317–19, has the same type of passage translated from Sahidic.

[39] Some would invoke the old Jewish list in a *baraita* in TalBab *Baba Bathra* 14b, giving the order of the writing prophets as Jer, Isa, Ezek, and the Twelve. See also Sutcliffe, "Matthew," for five Hebrew mss.

[40] For the passages used from the two prophets, see Upton, "Potter's" 216–17.

27:9–10,[41] it really does not cast much light on the key line *d* in Matt's citation, which has little parallel in Zech: "And they gave them [thirty silver
pieces] for the potter's field." For that line one may combine elements from
two famous scenes in Jeremiah: chap. 18, where God speaks to Jeremiah at
length about the potter, beginning in 18:3, "I went down to the potter's
house"; and chap. 32 (LXX: 39), which is centered parabolically on the purchase of a field: "And I bought the field . . . and weighed [*šql*] out the silver
to him, seventeen shekels of silver" (32[39]:9).

The memory of such vivid stories from Jeremiah could easily have led to
Matt's description of giving silver for the potter's field, which then was combined with a section from Zech—a section that also had themes of silver
coins and the potter. Still, why would Matt attribute the combination to Jer
rather than to Zech? Was it because Jer was more important? Or because
Matt wanted an inclusion with the Jer citation that he had employed in the
infancy narrative (Matt 2:17–18)? Or because Jesus was a Jeremiah-like figure (Matt 16:14) who was rejected by the leaders of Judah because he spoke
against the Temple? SPNM (365–66) points out that a citation such as this,
besides applying to the immediate context, furthers the "lifeline" of the Messiah. Zech supplied a whole chain of texts that enable early Christians to
vocalize their interpretation of Jesus (Bruce, "Book" 348–50), but that
prophet in his book had no personal story. Jeremiah both in his message and
in his personal "passion" was a more vivid introduction to God's plan for
the Messiah. The combined prophetic passage with the words of Zech and
the career of Jeremiah serves to show the readers that even the most difficult
aspects of the passion (betrayal by Judas, the refusal of the chief priests and
elders to be swayed by innocent blood) lay within God's plan. All of it is
according to what the Lord directed (Matt 27:10), even as was the hostile
refusal of Pharaoh dealing with Moses (Exod 9:12).

ANALYSIS

In writing on the PN, one must decide whether to place this scene before an
initial discussion of the Roman trial of Jesus (§31 below) or after it. Matt
27:2 reports: "And having bound him [Jesus], they led him away and gave
him over to Pilate the governor." This might indicate that what follows in

---

[41]R. H. Gundry, *The Use of the Old Testament in St. Matthew's Gospel* (NovTSup 18; Leiden:
Brill, 1967), 124.

27:3–10 should come under the framework of the proceedings before Pilate. Yet, as we saw in §28, the deliberations of the Sanhedrin authorities in 27:1–2 constituted for Matt the last step in the Jewish proceedings: The decision of the Jewish authorities to take Jesus to Pilate was reached contemporaneously with Peter's last denial. The Judas scene with its highlighting of the chief priests and the scribes belongs to the same context; the Jewish authorities take a decision (*symboulion*) here (27:7) even as in 27:1. In the earlier passage the decision was what to do with Jesus; the decision here is to slough off the guilt for Jesus' innocent blood. Logically this takes place before Matt turns attention to Pilate.

At the opening of my COMMENT above, I indicated that in one way the sequence is awkward, for the chief priests and the elders should be leading Jesus to Pilate; yet they are now in the Temple precincts, seemingly near the sanctuary and the treasury. In another way, however, to depict a dramatic death of Judas, absent from Mark, is consonant with Matt's consistent glossing of the Marcan Judas stories by adding dramatic features. In the scene where Judas makes contact with the chief priests to help in their plan to arrest Jesus (Matt 26:14–16=Mark 14:10–11), Matt has added the demand of Judas: "What will you give me if I give him over?"—a touch of avarice. In the scene at the Last Supper where Jesus foretells that one of those at table will give him over (Matt 26:21–25=Mark 14:18–21), Matt has added the question posed by Judas (who is never mentioned at the supper in Mark): "Is it I, Rabbi?"—a defiance of Jesus' command to call no one rabbi (Matt 23:8). In the Gethsemane scene when Judas arrives to give Jesus over (Matt 26:47–50=Mark 14:43–46), Matt has added a statement by Jesus that unmasks Judas' intention: "Friend, that's what you are here for." Mark never mentions Judas again after that scene, but Matt must give the denouement of him of whom Jesus has warned, "Woe to that man . . . for whom it would have been better not to have been born" (Matt 26:24).[42]

A. Comparison with Other Accounts of Judas' Death

Where did Matt get this scene? An answer to that inevitably involves a discussion of the other accounts of Judas' death in Acts 1:16–20,25[43] and in citations from Papias, a 2d-cent. writer. In APPENDIX IV, which is devoted to all that we can know about Judas, I shall discuss those other accounts (giving a translation of the long and short form of Papias), analyze how they were composed, and attempt to discern what might be historical. Here I am inter-

---

[42]The history of dramatic Matthean embellishments of Mark has led some scholars to classify the Judas scene as legend (e.g., Wrede, "Judas" 146).

[43]The translation of the Acts scene is given at the beginning of this section.

ested only in the light they throw on the composition of Matt 27:3–10. As an illustration of the range of scholarly opinion,[44] Haugg (*Judas* 160) argues that form-critically Matt's account is older than that in Acts;[45] but how effective is a form-critical comparison between a narrative (Matt) and a notice contained in a speech (Acts)? Moreover, that speech is embedded in a story about the election of Matthias as a replacement of Judas that most scholars think represents ancient tradition (see Menoud, "Additions"). Indeed, there are those who think of a written Aramaic original underlying Acts (Kilpatrick), perhaps known also to Papias (Schweizer) and even to Matt through oral tradition. As for Matt, Jeremias thinks of an ancient written source that is substantially historical,[46] while Kilpatrick and Strecker posit an oral tradition that is preMatthean. Others like Senior think of Matt 27:3–10 as almost totally a Matthean creation.

Internally two major issues come into this decision: First, was there an original account to which the formula citation in 27:9–10 was added as a comment, or did the formula citation give rise to the basic narrative? Second, how important is the number of words in 27:3–8 that are found nowhere else in Matt; do they prove the existence of a preMatthean account?

We may treat the *second* point (vocabulary) briefly. Peculiar to this narrative in Matt are *apangchesthai* ("to hang oneself") in v. 5; *korbanas* ("treasury") and *timē* ("price") in v. 6; *kerameus* ("potter") and *taphē* ("burial ground") in v. 7. The singularity of all those words is explicable because of the special subject matter of the narrative, and tells us nothing about the origin of the story.[47] A possible exception to that judgment is *strephein* in v. 3 in the sense of "return"; but overall the peculiarity of the language is not a major key to the composition of the Matthean scene. Indeed, Vogler (*Judas* 66) is probably correct in observing that if one considers all the language in the scene, vocabulary favors Matthean composition (or, at least, rewriting).

Turning to the *first* point, let me begin the discussion of composition by listing features that Matt and Acts have in common on the principle that since clearly neither copies from the other on the death of Judas (so diverse

---

[44]Further information on some of the opinions I list here may be found in Vogler, *Judas* 67.

[45]See also Benoit ("Death" 1.195), who attributes greater probability to Matt.

[46]Desautels ("Mort" 230) may be one of the most generous scholars in the amount of material he attributes to the preMatthean composition, but he regards 27:5b (Judas hanging himself) as a later insertion.

[47]*Timē* and *kerameus* could also be explained as borrowed from the formula citation in 27:9–10 if this citation gave rise to the narrative. As we saw in the COMMENT, the reference to treasury could reflect an interpretation of the *yôṣer* of the MT of Zech 11:13 as *'ôṣar.* A clause in Zech 11:13 that Matt 27:9–10 has chosen not to repeat is echoed in the narrative itself: "And I threw it into the house of the Lord into the potter/treasury."

are the accounts), common features may point to tradition that antedates both. I shall mention here pertinent matter from the Papias accounts (see APPENDIX IV, A6) but with the warning that the Papias material is preserved indirectly and without its original context, so that the failure of the Papias accounts to mention certain details may not be easily invoked.

- Judas, having given over Jesus to the Jewish authorities, is no longer considered one of the Twelve (implicitly in Matt where all Jesus' disciples have fled; explicitly in Acts 1:25).
- In Christian memory Judas died in close proximity to the death of Jesus (Matt tells of Judas' death before he tells of Jesus' death; Acts tells of it in Peter's speech given before Pentecost).
- Judas died a violent death: hanging himself in Matt; bursting open in Acts;[48] swelling in Papias, so that he was crushed by a wagon (short form) and contracted a loathsome disease (longer form).
- Involved with his death was the use of the money he received from his evil deed in order to purchase land (purchase of a field by the chief priests in Matt; acquisition of acreage by Judas himself in Acts and implicitly in Papias [long form] which speaks of "his own acreage").
- That land was called "the Field/Acreage of Blood": *agros* in Matt, and *chōrion* in Acts and Papias (long form[49]) translating Aramaic *ḥăqēl děmāʾ*. The "Blood" designation in Matt stems from the field being purchased with blood money; in Acts it may stem from Judas' having died there (although his death is not described as bloody; see n. 28 above).[50]
- His death is explicitly related to some Scripture passages (Jer/Zech in Matt; Pss 69 and 109 in Acts) and implicitly related to others.[51]
- Elements in the story are presented as ancient: The field in Matt 27:8 has had its name "to this day";[52] the acreage in Acts 1:19 was called Hakeldamach "in their language" (i.e., Aramaic, of the Jerusalemites).

[48]Here I shall work with the "laid prostrate" translation of *prēnēs genomenos* of Acts 1:18. In APPENDIX IV, A6, attention will be called to another translation; "having swollen up"; that would bring Acts and Papias into harmony.

[49]See n. 23 above. Although Papias uses the term *chōrion*, he mentions nothing about blood. The acreage described by Papias would be remembered not because of its connection with blood but because of its stench.

[50]Papias (long form) is specific on this point: "His life, they say, came to a close in his own acreage." The stench of the acreage may imply that Judas was buried in it.

[51]Among those detected in Matt are II Sam 17:23, where Ahithophel hangs himself; perhaps Gen 37:26–28, where Judah (Judas) arranges the sale of Joseph to the Ishmaelites for twenty/thirty pieces of silver; perhaps Gen 4:10, where Abel's blood cries out to God against Cain. Suggestions about those detected in Luke will be discussed in APPENDIX IV.

[52]Nellessen ("Tradition" 209–10) argues that Matt's "to this day" was part of the original Semitic narrative but was omitted by Luke because he put the story in a speech given by Peter a few weeks after the event.

We shall need frequently to recall this list in what follows.

B. Impact of Scripture on Formation of Matt's Story

Mark's report (14:21) that at the Last Supper Jesus pronounced a horrendous woe against the one who would give him over (better for him not to have been born) could have given rise to stories of a horrible fate for Judas. Yet to explain Matt 27:3–10 one must move from the inevitability of a violent death for Judas to a specific account, none of the details of which are explicable from Mark. (If one points to the silver paid to Judas in Mark 14:11, that still lacks the Matthean specification of thirty pieces.) Clearly Scripture had a major role in developing this Judas story.[53] Matt would not be in disagreement with Acts 1:16 that the Scripture spoken beforehand by the Holy Spirit concerning Judas had to be fulfilled,[54] or with John 17:12: "Not one of them perished except the son of perdition—in order to have the Scripture fulfilled."

In evaluating the impact of Scripture on the formation of the Matthean story, let us begin with the implicit influence of the suicide by hanging of Ahithophel who conspired against David (II Sam 17:23).[55] A simple solution to composition would be that historically Judas did hang himself and that the report of such a death reminded Matt of the Ahithophel suicide, which then he used to color the narrative. My conclusion in APPENDIX IV, where I discuss the four different deaths attributed to Judas in early Christianity, is that prima facie only two have any plausibility (suicide [Matt], and accident [short form of Papias]) but that all correspond to the death of the notoriously wicked in the Scriptures (and in classical writings). Thus the likelihood is that while early Christians knew that Judas had died soon and violently, *the manner of his death entered the various narratives through the instinct to compare him to others who had resisted God or God's anointed.* Probably,

---

[53]Indeed there may already have been a scriptural interplay in the Marcan woe at the supper since in *I Enoch* 38:2 one finds a similar woe against sinners: "It had been good for them if they had not been born." (This section of *I Enoch* has not been found at Qumran but is probably preChristian [see also *I Enoch* 95:7]; this book is treated as Scripture in Jude 14–15.) John 13:18 glosses the supper warning about betrayal thus: "The purpose is to have the Scripture fulfilled, 'He who feeds on bread with me has raised his heel against me'" (Ps 41:10[9]).

[54]When Acts 1:16 says, "It *was* necessary that the Scripture be fulfilled ... concerning Judas," to what aspect of Judas' demise is Acts referring? Most assume the reference is to his replacement among the Twelve because 1:16 mentions Davidic Scripture and because psalms pertinent to Judas' replacement are given in 1:20. But Haugg (*Judas* 177–78) points to the past tense and the fact that in the storyline the replacement has not yet happened. He thinks the reference is to the death of Judas.

[55]Van Unnik ("Death" 96) challenges the relation to Ahithophel because it is based on only one clause: "He hanged himself." But throughout the PN we have seen a series of implicit references to the David-Absalom-Ahithophel story of II Sam 15–17: a close advisor treacherously giving David/Jesus over; going across the Kidron to the Mount of Olives; weeping and praying there; etc.

therefore, the Ahithophel story generated Matt's account of suicide by hanging.

Turning now to the explicit Scripture that Matt cites in 27:9–10, we remember that it consisted of most of Zech 11:13 combined with echoes of Jer 18, 19, and 32 (LXX 39). Elements in the Matthean narrative that are paralleled in (the whole of) Zech 11:13 are hostile Jewish authorities, thirty silver pieces, casting them into the sanctuary (house of the Lord), the price, and treasury/potter. Elements in the narrative that are paralleled in the three Jer passages are the potter, buying a field, silver pieces, innocent blood, and a burial place, plus the implied setting in the Valley of Hinnom. Once again we must inquire about the sequence: Did a story that had some or all of what is in Matt 27:3–8 remind Christians of parallels in Scripture, which were then used to flesh out the story; *or* was the story created from Scripture? If the latter, how did those Scripture passages come to mind? Did, for instance, the mention of silver being promised to Judas in Mark 14:11 call Matt's attention to OT passages that referred to the payment of silver? By way of general observation it should be noted that explicit Scripture citations obviously play an important part in aspects of the Judas story in Acts 1:16–20,25; and yet the overall Acts narrative is quite different from Matt's narrative. This fact scarcely favors the notion that a complete original narrative stood behind Matt and Acts and was simply glossed by Scripture.

Perhaps one may gain insight from Matt's general practice: Are the formula citations of Scripture usually added by him to an already existing story, or do they generate the essential storyline? There are five formula citations in the infancy narrative of 1:18–2:23 (also a popular-style story peculiar to Matt); and there, although some scholars think that the citations gave rise to the narrative, I agree firmly with others (Bultmann, Dibelius, Hirsch, Strecker) who hold that a preMatthean story was glossed by these citations as it was brought into the Gospel (BBM 99–101). My chief argument is that the infancy narrative citations deal only with minor aspects that are tangential to the main storyline. Here, however, the Zech and Jer passages deal with details that are essential to the storyline, so essential that without them there would scarcely be a story. Thus I would judge that Rothfuchs, Gnilka, and Senior (SPNM 371–73, 392) are correct over against Strecker in attributing to the Scripture passages a major generative role in 27:3–8. That would mean that for the most part, the story of Judas' suicide and the price of innocent blood was composed by combining a few traditional items with Scripture.[56]

[56]The use of Scripture may have been in stages; e.g., to a preMatthean story that had echoes of Zech and Jer woven into it, Matt may have added the formula citation in 27:9–10 (so Strecker, *Weg* 76–82; van Tilborg, *Jewish* 86–88).

Now let me be more specific in suggesting how these Scripture passages were brought into play, treating Zech first and then Jer. The last chaps. of Zech play an important role in the PN, as we saw at the very beginning with the explicit citation of Zech 13:7 in Matt 26:31–32 (Mark 14:27–28) in reference to striking the shepherd and scattering the sheep. Since seemingly[57] it was the same shepherd whose pay or price was set at thirty silver pieces in Zech 11:12–13, the leap from Mark's promise of silver to Judas to a reflection on Zech's thirty silver pieces may not have been too great. Also, intermediary texts of Scripture may have facilitated this connection. In the COMMENT attention was called to thirty shekels of silver as the set recompense for injury done to a slave (Exod 21:32). Adaptations of Gen 37:26–28 also fasten on that sum in an evil context.[58] There Judah (= Judas) suggested that rather than killing Joseph and concealing his blood, he be sold into captivity; accordingly, "They sold Joseph to Ishmaelites for twenty shekels of silver." *Test. Gad* 2.3 has that patriarch say, "I and Judah sold him to Ishmaelites for *thirty* pieces of gold; and hiding the ten, we shared [twenty] evenly with our brothers."[59] Origen (*In Exod. Hom.* 1.4 [GCS 29.149]) reports that Joseph was sold for thirty silver pieces by one of his brothers. Ambrose (*De Joseph Patriarcha* 3.14 [CSEL 32 II 81B]) comments on this point: "We find the purchase price of Joseph sometimes twenty gold [sic] pieces, sometimes twenty-five, sometimes thirty." If the variant of Judah's price for Joseph as thirty silver pieces already existed in NT times, it may well have helped the Matthean movement from Mark's vague reference to silver to the more precise thirty silver pieces in Matt 26:15 and to the passage in Zech 11:12–13, which could then have contributed creatively to a story of what happened to this price for innocent blood.

A number of Jer passages have also contributed to Matt's story, indeed to the extent that Matt describes the fulfilled Scripture of vv. 9–10 as "spoken through Jeremiah the prophet." One way in which those prophecies could have come to the fore is a resemblance between Jeremiah and Jesus, both maltreated by the ruling authorities of the nation. Another possible connection is that the potter motif in Zech 11:13 is found in Jer 18 and 19. But another factor may be even more important. If we look back to the list of

---

[57]See remarks on pp. 129–30 above about the complex logic of these obscure Zech passages. In addition to the difficulty of discerning what the author of (Deutero-)Zech meant, one needs to take into account how the chaps. were understood in NT times.

[58]See Murmelstein ("Gestalt" 54) for the possible influence of Gen 37 on the Judas story. To some extent applicability depends on whether in NT times Jesus was seen as a Joseph-like figure. The evidence is slim; e.g., some point to the much later *Midrash Rabbah* 84.8 on Gen 37:3, describing Joseph's cloak (among other interpretations), which has lots cast over it, as background for Jesus' tunic in John 19:23.

[59]*Test. Judah* 17.1; 18.2 stresses that Judah did not intend Joseph to die; this could be another parallel with his namesake Judas, who in Matt 27:3–4 did not want Jesus to die.

common features shared by Matt 27 and Acts 1, thus far all that we have presumed in explaining the composition of Matt's story is an early Christian tradition that Judas died a violent death in close proximity to the death of Jesus. The argument has been that in Matt's account that tradition was combined with the Marcan woe against the traitor to fashion a story of how Judas died—a story weaving together Ahithophel's suicide by hanging and Zech's account of how the shepherd was priced at thirty pieces of silver which were thrown to the potter/treasury in the house of the Lord. But we have not yet taken into account the agreement between Matt and Acts that the money given to Judas was used to purchase land, and that the land was called a place "of Blood." Matt and Acts are not influenced by each other in this detail, for they differ as to whether the purchase was made before or after Judas' death, made by him or by the chief priests, and whether the designation was "Field [*agros*] of Blood" or "Acreage [*chōrion*] of Blood." Thus one may posit that preMatthean tradition contained not only the early violent death of Judas but also the use of his ill-gotten money for the purchase of land that bore the name of "Blood."[60] That tradition may have moved Matt to concentrate on Jer texts about the purchase of a field (Jer 32[39]) and the Valley of Slaughter made profane by innocent blood (Jer 19)—a burial place that was in the same Hinnom area with which the Judas field was associated.

One other factor should be mentioned as part of Matthean composition. Although Jer 19:4 mentions "innocent blood," this has become a major motif running through Matt's Judas story (27:4,6,8) into the Pilate trial (27:24–25). Escande ("Judas") has called attention to a remarkable number of parallels between the peculiar Matthean material on Judas and Pilate: (a) Judas tries to get rid of guilt by saying, "I sinned in having given over innocent blood"; Pilate tries to get rid of guilt by saying, "I am innocent of the blood of this man"; (b) the Jewish chief priest and elders respond to Judas, "You must see to it"; Pilate says to the Jewish chief priests and elders and crowds, "You must see to it"; (c) Judas illustrates his attempt to get rid of guilt by throwing the money away; Pilate illustrates his attempt to get rid of guilt by washing his hands; (d) Judas' action involves the authorities with blood since they must use the blood money; Pilate's action involves all the people with blood since they cry out: "His blood on us and on our children." Both Judas and Pilate profess innocence; both give Jesus over; neither can control the action

---

[60]For Matt the "Blood" designation stems from the field's being purchased with money given for Jesus' innocent blood; Acts does not explain the "Blood" designation but leaves one to imagine it may be related to Judas' death in this acreage. In the COMMENT I gave reasons for thinking that this piece of land in the Hinnom valley may already have borne the name "Field/Acreage of Blood," and that Christians may have reinterpreted that name in the story of Judas, whose death was associated in one way or another with this region.

of those more directly responsible for Jesus' blood, and so the effects of the blood remain. As Escande remarks, both Judas and Pilate are prisoners of a system. The system has judged against Jesus, and they cannot escape from the system. Did this haunting quality of the blood of Jesus already involve Judas and Pilate on a preMatthean level? At this juncture in the commentary it is too early to answer that question, but eventually I shall argue that Matt drew on a popular, imaginative preMatthean body of material where Scripture (but not necessarily Scripture quotations) played a very formative role. For now I simply remark that this parallelism between Judas and Pilate helps to make intelligible Matt's placing of the Judas scene just before the Pilate trial. It is to that trial we now turn our attention.

(*Bibliography for this episode may be found in §25, Part 3.*)

COMMENTARY
ON ACT III:

JESUS BEFORE PILATE, THE ROMAN GOVERNOR

(Mark 15:2–20a; Matt 27:11–31a; Luke 23:2–25; John 18:28b–19:16a)

The third Act of the Passion Narrative describes how Jesus, having been given over to Pilate, was interrogated by him about being the King of the Jews. Although Pilate was not convinced of Jesus' guilt, the crowds preferred the release of Barabbas, a criminal, demanding that Jesus be crucified. Pilate acceded, had Jesus scourged, and gave him over to be crucified by Roman soldiers who first mocked and abused him.

CONTENTS OF ACT III

§30. SECTIONAL BIBLIOGRAPHY
for Act III:
The Roman Trial of Jesus (§§31–36)

Writings that treat *both* the Jewish and the Roman trials are included in §17 (Part 1), the SECTIONAL BIBLIOGRAPHY for the Jewish Trial. The seven subdivisions of this bibliography are listed in the immediately preceding Contents.

Part 1: Jesus as a Revolutionary and Figures on the Political Scene (§31A)
Alonso Díaz, J., "El compromiso político de Jesús," ByF 4 (1978), 151–74.
Bammel, E., "The Revolutionary Theory from Reimarus to Brandon," JPHD 11–68.
Bammel, E., and C.F.D. Moule (eds.), *Jesus and the Politics of His Day* (Cambridge Univ., 1984). Abbreviated as JPHD.
Barnett, P. W., "The Jewish Sign Prophets—A.D. 40–70: Their Intention and Origin," NTS 27 (1980–81), 679–97.
————, "'Under Tiberius all was Quiet,'" NTS 21 (1974–75), 564–71.
Baumbach, G., "Die Stellung Jesu im Judentum seiner Zeit," FZPT 20 (1973), 285–305.
Borg, M., "The Currency of the Term 'Zealot,'" JTS NS 22 (1971), 504–12.
Brandon, S.G.F., *Jesus and the Zealots* (Manchester Univ., 1967).
Carmichael, J., *The Death of Jesus* (London: Penguin, 1966).
Crespy, G., "Recherche sur la signification politique de la mort du Christ," LumVie 20 (1971), 89–109.
Daniel, C., "Esséniens, zélotes, et sicaires et leur mention par paronymie dans le N. T.," *Numen* 13 (1966), 88–115.
Freyne, S., "Bandits in Galilee: A Contribution to the Study of Social Conditions in First-Century Palestine," in *The Social World of Formative Christianity and Judaism*, eds. J. Neusner et al. (Philadelphia: Fortress, 1988), 50–68.
Giblet, J., "Un mouvement de résistance armée au temps de Jésus?" RTL 5 (1974), 409–26.
Guevara, H., *Ambiente político del pueblo judío en tiempos de Jesús* (Madrid: Cristiandad, 1985).
————, *La resistencia judía contra Roma en la época de Jesús* (S.S.D. Dissertation at Pontifical Biblical Institute, 1981; printed at Meitingen, Germany).
Hengel, M., *Was Jesus a Revolutionary?* (Philadelphia: Fortress, 1971).
————, *The Zealots* (Edinburgh: Clark, 1989; German orig. 1961).

Hill, D., "Jesus and Josephus' 'messianic prophets,'" in *Text and Interpretation*, eds. E. Best and R. McL. Wilson (M. Black Festschrift; Cambridge Univ., 1979), 143–54.

Horbury, W., "Christ as a Brigand in Ancient Anti-Christian Polemic," JPHD 197–209.

Horsley, R. A., *Jesus and the Spiral of Violence: Popular Jewish Resistance in Roman Palestine* (San Francisco: Harper & Row, 1987).

———, "Josephus and the Bandits," JSJ 10 (1979), 37–63.

———, "'Like One of the Prophets of Old': Two Types of Popular Prophets at the Time of Jesus," CBQ 47 (1985), 435–63.

———, "Popular Messianic Movements around the Time of Jesus," CBQ 46 (1984), 471–95.

———, "The Sicarii: Ancient Jewish 'Terrorists,'" *Journal of Religion* 59 (1979), 435–58.

Horsley, R. A., and J. S. Hanson, *Bandits, Prophets, and Messiahs* (Minneapolis: Winston, 1985).

Jensen, E. E., "The First Century Controversy over Jesus as a Revolutionary Figure," JBL 60 (1941), 261–72.

Kealy, S. P., *Jesus and Politics* (Collegeville: Liturgical Press, 1990).

Kingdon, H. P., "Had the Crucifixion a Political Significance?" HibJ 35 (1936–37), 556–67.

Maccoby, H. Z., *Revolution in Judea. Jesus and the Jewish Resistance* (New York: Taplinger, 1980).

Morin, J.-A., "Les deux derniers des Douze: Simon le Zélote et Judas Iskariôth," RB 80 (1973), 332–58, esp. 332–49 on the Zealots.

Smith, M., "Zealots and Sicarii: Their Origins and Relation," HTR 64 (1971), 1–19.

Stern, M., "Sicarii and Zealots," SRSTP 263–301, 404–05.

Sweet, J.P.M., "The Zealots and Jesus," JPHD 1–9.

Vargas-Machuca, A., "¿Por qué condenaron a muerte a Jesús de Nazaret?" EstEcl 54 (1979), 441–70.

Winter, P., "The Trial of Jesus as a Rebel against Rome," *The Jewish Quarterly* 16 (1968), 31–37.

Ziesler, J., *The Jesus Question* (Guildford: Lutterworth, 1980), esp. 28–39 on Jesus and the Zealots.

Part 2: Background: Pilate's Career (Josephus, Philo); Praetorium; Trial Law (§31B, C, D)

Aline de Sion, Mère, *La Forteresse Antonia à Jérusalem et la question du prétoire* (Thèse de l'Université de Paris; Jerusalem: Franciscan Press, 1956), esp. chap. 14, "Les lusoriae tabulae," 119–42.

Bagatti, B., "La tradizione della chiesa di Gerusalemme sul pretorio," RivB 21 (1973), 429–32.

Bammel, E., "Pilatus' und Kaiphas' Absetzung," *Judaica. Kleine Schriften I* (WUNT 37; Tübingen: Mohr, 1986), 51–58.

———, "Syrian Coinage and Pilate," JJS 2 (1951), 108–10.

Benoit, P., "L'Antonia d'Hérode le Grand et le Forum Oriental d'Aelia Capitolina," HTR 64 (1971), 135–67. Reprinted in BExT 4.311–46.

———, "Praetorium, Lithostroton and Gabbatha," BJG 1.167–88. French orig. in RB 59 (1952), 531–50.

———, "Le Prétoire de Pilate à l'époque byzantine," RB 91 (1984), 161–77.

Bible et Terre Sainte 57 (1963). Whole issue on Pilate.

Blinzler, J., "Der Entscheid des Pilatus—Exekutionsbefehl oder Todesurteil?" MTZ 5 (1954), 171–84.

———, "Die Niedermetzelung von Galiläern durch Pilatus," NovT 2 (1958), 24–49.

Chilton, C. W., "The Roman Law of Treason under the Early Principate," JRS 45 (1955), 73–81.

Colin, J., *Les villes libres de l'Orient gréco-romain et l'envoi au supplice par acclamations populaires* (Coll. Latomus 82; Brussels-Berchem: Latomus, 1965).

———, "Sur le procès de Jésus devant Pilate et le peuple," REA 67 (1965), 159–64.

Erhardt, A., "Pontius Pilatus in der frühchristlichen Mythologie," EvT NS 9 (1949–50), 433–47.

———, "Was Pilate a Christian?" CQR 137 (1944), 157–67.

Frova, A., "L'Inscrizione di Ponzio Pilato a Cesarea," *Rendiconti* 95 (1961), 123–58.

Hirschfeld, O., *Die kaiserlichen Verwaltungsbeamten bis auf Diocletian* (2d ed.; Berlin: Weidmann, 1905).

Jones, A.H.M., *Studies in Roman Government and Law* (Oxford: Blackwell, 1960).

Kindler, A., "More Dates on the Coins of the Procurators," IEJ 6 (1956), 54–57.

Klostermann, E., "Die Majestätsprozesse unter Tiberius," *Historia* 4 (1955), 72–106.

Kraeling, C. H., "The Episode of the Roman Standards at Jerusalem," HTR 35 (1942), 263–89.

Kreyenbühl, J., "Der Ort der Verurteilung Jesu," ZNW 3 (1902), 15–22.

Lattey, C., "The Praetorium of Pilate," JTS 31 (1930), 180–82.

Leclercq, H., "Flagellation (Supplice de la)," DACL 5 (1923), 1638–43.

Lémonon, J.-P., *Pilate et le gouvernement de la Judée* (EBib; Paris: Gabalda, 1981).

Liberty, S., "The Importance of Pontius Pilate in Creed and Gospel," JTS 45 (1944), 38–56.

Lohse, E., "Die römischen Statthalter in Jerusalem," ZDPV 74 (1958), 69–78.

McGing, B. C., "The Governorship of Pontius Pilate: Messiahs and Sources," PIBA 10 (1986), 55–71.

———, "Pontius Pilate and the Sources," CBQ 53 (1991), 416–38.

MacMullen, R., *Enemies of Roman Order* (Cambridge, MA: Harvard, 1966).

Maier, P. L., "The Episode of the Golden Roman Shields at Jerusalem," HTR 62 (1969), 109–21.

Müller, G. A., *Pontius Pilatus* (Stuttgart: Metzler, 1885).

Oestreicher, B., "A New Interpretation of Dates on the Coins of the Procurators," IEJ 9 (1959), 193–95.

Overstreet, R. L., "Roman Law and the Trial of Christ," BSac 135 (1978), 323–32.

Pflaum, H. G., *Essai sur les procurateurs équestres sous le Haut-Empire romain* (Paris: Maisonneuve, 1950).

Pixner, B., "Noch einmal das Prätorium. Versuch einer neuen Lösung," ZDPV 95 (1979), 56–86.

———, "Where Was the Original Via Dolorosa?" *Christian News from Israel* 27 (1979), 7–10.

Revuelta Sañudo, M., "La localización del Pretorio," EstBib 20 (1961), 261–317.

———, "La polémica del Pretorio de Pilato," *Lumen* 10 (1961), 289–321.

Reyero, S., "Los textos de Flavio Josefo y de Filón sobre la residencia de los procuradores romanos en Jerusalén," *Studium* 1–2 (1961–62), 527–55.

Riesner, R., "Das Prätorium des Pilatus," BK 41 (1986), 34–37.

Rogers, R. S., "Treason in the Early Empire," JRS 49 (1959), 90–94. Response to Chilton.

Schwartz, D. R., "Josephus and Philo on Pontius Pilate," *The Jerusalem Cathedra* 3 (1983), 26–45.

Smallwood, E. M., "The Date of the Dismissal of Pontius Pilate from Judaea," JJS 5 (1954), 12–21.

———, "Philo and Josephus as Historians of the Same Event," JJC 114–29.

Staats, R., "Pontius Pilatus im Bekenntnis der frühen Kirche," ZTK 84 (1987), 493–513.

Stauffer, E., "Zur Münzprägung des Pontius Pilatus," *La Nouvelle Clio* 1–2 (1949–50), 495–514.

Steele, J. A., "The Pavement," ExpTim 34 (1922–23), 562–63.

van Bebber, J., "Das Prätorium des Pilatus," TQ 87 (1905), 209–30.

Vanel, A., "Prétoire," DBSup 44 (1960), 513–54.

Vardaman, J., "A New Inscription which Mentions Pilate as 'Prefect,'" JBL 81 (1962), 70–71.

Vincent, L.-H., "L'Antonia et le Prétoire," RB 42 (1933), 83–113.

———, "L'Antonia, palais primitif d'Herode," RB 61 (1954), 87–107.

———, "Le lithostrotos évangélique," RB 59 (1952), 513–30.

Volkmann, H., "Die Pilatusinschrift von Caesarea Maritima," *Gymnasium* 75 (1968), 124–35, plates XIII-XV.

Part 3: Gospel Accounts of the Trial of Jesus before Pilate

Alegre, X., "'Mi reino no es de este mundo' (Jn 18,36)," EstEcl 54 (1979), 499–525. Eng. summary in TD 29 (1981), 231–35.

Allen, J. E., "Why Pilate?" TJSCM 78–83.

Balagué, M., "Y lo sentó en el tribunal (Jn 19,13)," EstBib 33 (1974), 63–67.

Baldensperger, G., "Il a rendu témoignage devant Ponce Pilate," RHPR 2 (1922), 1–25, 95–117.

Bammel, E., *"Philos tou Kaisaros,"* TLZ 77 (1952), 205–10 (on John 19:12).

———, "The Trial before Pilate," JPHD 415–51.

Bartina, S., "Ignotum *episèmon* gabex (cf. PG 85,1512B) (Io 19,14: hora sexta an hora tertia?)," VD 36 (1958), 16–37.

Baum-Bodenbender, R., *Hoheit in Niedrigkeit: Johanneische Christologie im Prozess Jesu vor Pilatus (Joh 18,28–19,16a)* (Forschung zur Bibel 49; Würzburg: Echter, 1984).

Blank, J., "Die Verhandlung vor Pilatus: Joh 18,28–19,16 im Lichte johanneischer Theologie," BZ 3 (1959), 60–81.

Boismard, M.-E., "La royauté universelle du Christ (Jn 18,33–37)," AsSeign 88 (1966), 33–45; reprinted in AsSeign 2d series, 65 (1973), 36–46.

Bonsirven, J., "Hora Talmudica: La notion chronologique de Jean 19,14 aurait-elle un sens symbolique?" *Biblica* 33 (1952), 511–15.

Brüll, A., "Die Ergreifung und Überlieferung Jesu an Pilatus," TQ 83 (1901), 161–86, 396–411.

Cantinat, J., "Jésus devant Pilate," VSpir 86 (1952), 227–47.

Charbonneau, A., " '*Qu'as-tu fait?*' et '*D'où es-tu?*' Le procès de Jésus chez Jean (18,28–19,16a)," ScEsp 38 (1986), 203–19, 317–29.

Corssen, P., "*Ekathisen epi bēmatos*," ZNW 15 (1914), 338–40.

Creed, J. M., "The Supposed 'Proto-Lucan' Narrative of the Trial before Pilate: A Rejoinder," ExpTim 46 (1934–35), 378–79.

de la Potterie, I., "Jésus roi et juge d'après Jn 19,13 *ekathisen epi bēmatos*," *Biblica* 41 (1960), 217–47. Eng. summary in *Scripture* 13 (1961), 97–111.

Derrett, J.D.M., "Christ, King and Witness (John 18,37)," BeO 31 (1989), 189–98.

———, "Ecce homo Ruber (John 19,5 with Isaiah 1:18; 63:1–2)," BeO 32 (1990), 215–29.

Derwacter, F. M., " The Modern Translators and John 19,13: Is It 'Sat' or 'Seated'?" *The Classical Journal* 40 (1944–45), 24–28.

Dewailly, L.-M., " 'D'où es tu?' (Jean 19,9)," RB 92 (1985), 481–96.

Eager, A. R., " 'The Greater Sin.' A Note on S. John xix.11," *Expositor* 6th Ser., 12 (1905), 33–40.

Ehrman, B. D., "Jesus' Trial before Pilate: John 18:28–19:16," BTB 13 (1983), 124–31.

Escande, J., "Jésus devant Pilate: Jean 18,28–19,16," FV 73 (3; 1974), 66–82. Structural analysis.

Flourney, P. P., "What Frightened Pilate?" BSac 82 (1925), 314–20.

Flügel, H., "Pilatus vor Christus," *Eckart* 16 (1940), 58–63 (on the Johannine account).

Flusser, D., "What Was the Original Meaning of *Ecce Homo*?" *Immanuel* 19 (1984–85), 30–40.

Foulon-Piganiol, C.-I., "Le rôle du peuple dans le procès de Jésus," NRT 98 (1976), 627–37.

Genuyt, F., "La comparution de Jésus devant Pilate. Analyse sémiotique de Jean 18,28–19,16," RechSR 73 (1985), 133–46.

Giblin, C. H., "John's Narration of the Hearing Before Pilate (John 18,28–19,16a)," *Biblica* 67 (1986), 221–39.

Grey, H. G., "A Suggestion on St. John xix.14," *Expositor* 7th Ser., 2 (1906), 451–54.

Guillet, P.-E., "Entrée en scène de Pilate," CCER 24 (98; 1977), 1–24.

Haenchen, E., "Jesus vor Pilatus (Joh 18,28–19,15)," TLZ 85 (1960), cols. 93–102. Reprinted in his *Gott und Mensch* (Tübingen: Mohr, 1965), 144–56.

Heil, J. P., "Reader-Response and the Irony of the Trial of Jesus in Luke 23:1–25," ScEsp 43 (1991), 175–86.

Hill, D., " 'My Kingdom is not of this world' (John 18.36)," IBS 9 (1987), 54–62.

Horvath, T., "Why Was Jesus Brought to Pilate?" NovT 11 (1969), 174–84.

Houlden, J. L., "John 19.5: 'And he said to them, Behold, the man,'" ExpTim 92 (1980–81), 148–49.

Irmscher, J., *"Sy legeis* (Mk. 15,2; Mt. 27,11; Lk. 23,3), *Studii Clasice* 2 (1960), 151–58.

James, E. H., *The Trial Before Pilate* (2 vols.; Concord, MA: self-published, 1909).

Jaubert, A., "La comparution devant Pilate selon Jean. Jean 18,29–19,16," FV 73 (3; 1974), 3–12.

Kastner, K., *Jesus vor Pilatus* (NTAbh 4/2–3; Münster: Aschendorff, 1912).

Kinman, B., "Pilate's Assize and the Timing of Jesus' Trial," *Tyndale Bulletin* 42 (1991), 282–95.

Kolenkow, A., "The Trial before Pilate," KKS 2.550–56.

Kurfess, A., *"Ekathisen epi bēmatos* (Io 19,13)," *Biblica* 34 (1953), 271.

Lampe, G.W.H., "The Trial of Jesus in the *Acta Pilati*," JPHD 173–82.

Lührmann, D., "Der Staat und die Verkündigung," in TCSCD 359–75.

Marin, L., "Jesus before Pilate," TNTSJ 97–144. French orig. in *Langages* 22 (1971), 51–74.

Matera, F. J., "Luke 23, 1–25: Jesus before Pilate, Herod, and Israel," in *L'Évangile de Luc,* ed. F. Neirycnk (BETL 32; rev. ed.; Leuven: Peeters, 1989), 535–51.

Merlier, O., *"Sy legeis, hoti basileus eimi* (Jean 18,37)," *Revue des Études Grecques* 46 (1933), 204–9.

Michaels, J. R., "John 18.31 and the 'Trial' of Jesus," NTS 36 (1990), 474–79.

Mollat, D., "Jésus devant Pilate (Jean 18,28–38)," BVC 39 (1961), 23–31.

Nicklin, T., "'Thou Sayest,'" ExpTim 51 (1939–40), 155 (on Mark 15:2).

Oliver Roman, M., "Jesús proclamado rey por un pagano en Juan 18,28–19,22," *Communio* 19 (1986), 343–64.

O'Rourke, J. J., "Two Notes on St. John's Gospel. Jn 19:13: *eis ton topon*," CBQ 25 (1963), 124–26.

Panackel, C., *Idou ho Anthrōpos (Jn 19,5b). An Exegetico-Theological Study of the Text in the Light of the Use of the Term Anthrōpos Designating Jesus in the Fourth Gospel* (Analecta Gregoriana 251; Rome: Gregorian Univ., 1988).

Porteous, J., "Note on John xix.11: 'The Greater Sin,'" ExpTim 15 (1903–4), 428–29.

Quinn, J. F., "The Pilate Sequence in the Gospel of Matthew," *Dunwoodie Review* 10 (1970), 154–77.

Ramsay, W. M., "The Sixth Hour," *Expositor* 5th Ser., 3 (1896), 457–59.

Rau, G., "Das Volk in der lukanischen Passionsgeschichte, eine Konjektur zu Lc 23.13," ZNW 56 (1965), 41–51.

Rensberger, D., "The Politics of John: The Trial of Jesus in the Fourth Gospel," JBL 103 (1984), 395–411.

Robert, R., "Pilate, a-t-il fait de Jésus un juge? (Jean, xix, 13)," RThom 83 (1983), 275–87.

Roberts, A., "On the proper rendering of *ekathisen* in St. John xix.13," *Expositor* 4th Ser., 8 (1893), 296–308.

Robinson, W. C., *The Way of the Lord* (University of Basel, 1962), 43–56 (on Luke 23:5).

Sabbe, M., "The Trial of Jesus before Pilate in John and Its Relation to the Synoptic Gospels," in DJS 341–85. Also in his *Studia Neotestamentica: Collected Essays* (BETL 98; Leuven Univ. 1992), 467–513.

Schlier, H., "Jesus und Pilatus nach dem Johannesevangelium," *Die Zeit der Kirche* (Frieburg: Herder, 1956), 56–74. Orig. published in 1940.

———, "Der königliche Richter (19,8–16a)," SuS 29 (1964), 196–208.

———, "The State according to the New Testament," *The Relevance of the New Testament* (New York: Herder & Herder, 1968), 215–38 (on John's account of the Roman trial).

Schmidt, D., "Luke's 'Innocent' Jesus: A Scriptural Apologetic," PILA 111–21.

Schnackenburg, R., "Die Ecce-Homo-Szene und der Menschensohn," in *Jesus und der Menschensohn*, eds. R. Pesch and R. Schnackenburg (A. Vögtle Festschrift; Freiburg: Herder, 1975), 371–86.

Schneider, G., "The Political Charge against Jesus (Luke 23:2)," JPHD 403–14.

Schwank, B., "Ecce Homo," ErbAuf 65 (1989), 199–209.

Suggit, J., "John 19:5: 'Behold the man,'" ExpTim 94 (1982–83), 333–34.

Thibault, R., "La réponse de Notre Seigneur à Pilate (Jean xix,11)," NRT 54 (1927), 208–11.

Tolman, H. C., "A Possible Restoration from a Middle Persian Source of the Answer of Jesus to Pilate's Inquiry 'What is Truth?'" *Journal of the American Oriental Society* 39 (1919), 55–57.

Trebolle Barrera, J., "Posible substrato semítico del uso transitivo o intransitivo del verbo *ekathisen* en Jn 19,13," *Filología Neotestamentaria* 4 (#7, 1991), 51–54.

Vicent Cernuda, A., "La aporía entre Jn 18,31 y 19,6," EstBib 42 (1984), 71–87.

———, "La condena inopinada de Jesús. II. La agresividad obtusa de Pilato y política ignorada de Caifás," EstBib 49 (1991), 49–96.

———, "Nacimiento y Verdad de Jesús ante Pilato," EstBib 50 (1992), 537–51 (on John 18:37).

von Campenhausen, H., "Zum Verständnis von Joh. 19,11," TLZ 73 (1948), cols. 387–92.

von Jüchen, A., *Jesus und Pilatus. Eine Untersuchung über das Verhältnis von Gottesreich und Weltreich im Anschluss an Johannes 18,v.28–19,v.16* (Theologische Existenz heute 76; Munich: Kaiser, 1941).

Wansbrough, H., "Suffered Under Pontius Pilate," *Scripture* 18 (1966), 84–93.

Wead, D. W., "We have a Law," NovT 11 (1969), 185–89.

Zabala, A. M., "The Enigma of John 19:13 Reconsidered," *SE Asia Journal of Theology* 22 (2; 1981), 16–28; 23 (1; 1982), 1–10.

Zumstein, J., "Le procès de Jésus devant Pilate," FV 91 (1992), 89–101 (on John's account).

Part 4: Jesus before Herod in Luke 23:6–12 (§33)

Blinzler, J., *Herodes Antipas und Jesus Christus* (Stuttgart: KBW, 1947).

———, "Herodes und der Tod Jesu," *Klerusblatt* 37 (1957), 118–21.

Bornhäuser, K., "Die Beteiligung des Herodes am Prozesse Jesu," NKZ 40 (1929), 714–18.

Bruce, F. F., "Herod Antipas, Tetrarch of Galilee and Peraea," *The Annual of Leeds University Oriental Society* 5 (1963–65), 6–23.

Buck, E., "The Function of the Pericope 'Jesus before Herod' in the Passion Narrative of Luke," in *Wort in der Zeit*, eds. W. Haubeck and M. Bachmann (K. H. Rengstorf Festgabe; Leiden: Brill, 1980), 165–78.

Corbin, M., "Jésus devant Hérode. Lecture de Luc 23,6–12," *Christus* 25 (1978), 190–97.

Darr, J. A., " 'Glorified in the Presence of Kings'; A Literary-Critical Study of Herod the Tetrarch in Luke-Acts," (Ph.D. Dissertation; Nashville: Vanderbilt, 1987), esp. 278–305.

Derrett, J.D.M., "Daniel and Salvation-History," DRev 100 (1982), 62–68 (in ref. to Luke 23:1–16). Reprinted in DSNT 4.132–38.

Dibelius, M., "Herodes und Pilatus," ZNW 16 (1915), 113–26. Also in DBG 1.278–92.

Harlow, V. E., *The Destroyer of Jesus: The Story of Herod Antipas, Tetrarch of Galilee* (Oklahoma City: Modern, 1954).

Hoehner, H. W., *Herod Antipas* (SNTSMS 17; Cambridge Univ., 1972), esp. 224–50 on Luke 23:6–12.

———, "Why did Pilate hand Jesus over to Antipas?" TJCSM 84–90.

Jervell, J., "Herodes Antipas og hans plass i evangelieoverleveringen," NorTT 61 (1960), 28–40.

Joüon, P., "Luc 23,11: *esthēta lampran*," RechSR 26 (1936), 80–85.

Manus, C. U., "The Universalism of Luke and the Motif of Reconciliation in Luke 23:6–12," *African Theological Journal* 16 (1987), 121–35.

Müller, K., "Jesus vor Herodes. Eine redaktionsgeschichtliche Untersuchung zu Lk 23,6–12," in *Zur Geschichte des Urchristentums*, eds. G. Dautzenberg et al. (QD 87; Frieburg: Herder, 1979), 111–41.

Parker, P., "Herod Antipas and the Death of Jesus," in *Jesus, the Gospels, and the Church*, ed. E. P. Sanders (Honor of W. R. Farmer; Macon: Mercer, 1987), 197–208.

Soards, M. L., "Herod Antipas' Hearing in Luke 23,8," BT 37 (1986), 146–47.

———, "The Silence of Jesus before Herod," *Australian Biblical Review* 33 (Oct. 1985), 41–45.

———, "Tradition, Composition, and Theology in Luke's Account of Jesus before Herod Antipas," *Biblica* 66 (1985), 344–64.

Streeter, B. H., "On the Trial of Our Lord before Herod—a Suggestion," in *Studies in the Synoptic Problem*, ed. W. Sanday (Oxford: Clarendon, 1911), 228–31.

Tyson, J. B., "Jesus and Herod Antipas," JBL 79 (1960), 239–46.

Verrall, A. W., "Christ Before Herod," JTS 10 (1909), 321–53.

Part 5: Barabbas; Pilate's Wife (§34)

Aus, R. D., "The Release of Barabbas (Mark 15:6–15 par.; John 18:39–40), and

Judaic Traditions on the Book of Esther," *Barabbas and Esther and Other Studies* (Atlanta: Scholars, 1992), 1–27.

Bajsić, A., "Pilatus, Jesus und Barabbas," *Biblica* 48 (1967), 7–28.

Bauer, J. B., "'Literarische' Namen und 'literarische' Brauche (zu John 2,10 und 18,39)," BZ NS 26 (1982), 258–64.

Chavel, C. B., "The Releasing of a Prisoner on the Eve of Passover in Ancient Jerusalem," JBL 60 (1941), 273–78.

Cohn, H. M., "Christus = Barabbas," *Jahrbuch für jüdische Geschichte und Literatur* 8 (1905), 65–75.

Couchoud, P. L., and R. Stahl, "Jesus Barabbas," HibJ 25 (1926–27), 26–42.

Davies, S. L., "Who Is Called Bar Abbas?" NTS 27 (1980–81), 260–62.

Davis, W. H., "Origen's Comment on Matthew 27:17," RevExp 39 (#1, 1942), 65–67.

Derrett, J.D.M., "Haggadah and the Account of the Passion, 'Have nothing to do with that just man!' (Matt. 27,19)," DRev 97 (1979), 308–15. Reprinted in DSNT 3.184–92.

Dunkerley, R., "Was Barabbas also Called Jesus?" ExpTim 74 (1962–63), 126–27. See reply by R. C. Nevius, ibid 255.

Fascher, E., *Das Weib des Pilatus (Matthäus 27,19). Die Auferweckung der Heiligen (Matthäus 27,51–53)* (Hallische Monographien 20; Halle: Niemeyer, 1951), respectively 5–31, 32–51.

Gillman, F. M., "The Wife of Pilate (Matthew 27:19)," LS 17 (1992), 152–65.

Herranz Marco, M., "Un problema de crítica histórica en el relato de la Pasión: la liberación de Barrabás," EstBib 30 (1971), 137–60.

Husband, R. W., "The Pardoning of Prisoners by Pilate," AJT 21 (1917), 110–16.

Langdon, S., "The Release of a Prisoner at the Passover," ExpTim 29 (1917–18), 328–30.

Maccoby, H. Z., "Jesus and Barabbas," NTS 16 (1969–70), 55–60.

Merkel, J., "Die Begnadigung am Passahfeste," ZNW 6 (1905), 293–316.

Merritt, R. L., "Jesus Barabbas and the Paschal Pardon," JBL 104 (1985), 57–68.

Oepke, A., "Noch einmal das Weib des Pilatus. Fragment einer Dämonologie," TLZ 73 (1948), 743–46.

Ott, E., "Wer war die Frau des Pilatus?" *Geist und Leben* 59 (1986), 104–6.

Rigg, H. A., "Barabbas," JBL 64 (1945), 417–56.

Scholz, G., "'Joseph von Arimathäa' und 'Barabbas,'" LB 57 (1985), 81–94.

Soltero, C., "Pilatus, Jesus et Barabbas," VD 45 (1967), 326–30.

Twomey, J. J., "Barabbas was a Robber," *Scripture* 8 (1956), 115–19.

Vaganay, L., *Initiation à la critique textuelle néotestamentaire* (Paris: Bloud & Gay, 1934), esp. 162–66 on Matt. 27:16–17.

Vicent Cernuda, A., "La condena inopinada de Jesús. I. Pesquisa sobre la identidad de Barrabás," EstBib 48 (1990), 375–422.

Waldstein, W., *Untersuchungen zum römischen Begnadigungsrecht: Abolitio-Indulgentia-Venia* (Commentationes Aenipontanae 18; Innsbruck: Universitätsverlag Wagner, 1964).

Williams, C.S.C., *Alterations to the Text of the Synoptic Gospels and Acts* (Oxford: Blackwell, 1951), 31–33 (on Matt 27:16–17).

Wratislaw, A. H., "The Scapegoat-Barabbas," ExpTim 3 (1891–92), 400–3.

Part 6: Matt 27:24–25: "His blood on us" (§35)

Bowman, J., "The Significance of Mt. 27:25," *Milla wa-Milla* 14 (1974), 26–31.

Cargal, T. B., "'His blood be upon us and upon our children': A Matthean Double Entendre?" NTS 37 (1991), 101–12.

Cohn, H. M., "'Sein Blut komme über uns,'" *Jahrbuch für jüdische Geschichte und Literatur* 6 (1903), 82–90.

Fitzmyer, J. A., "Anti-Semitism and the Cry of 'All the People' (Mt 27:25)," TS 26 (1965), 667–71.

Frankemölle, H., *Jahwebund und Kirche Christi. Studien zur Form- und Traditionsgeschichte des 'Evangeliums' nach Matthäus* (NTAbh NS 10; Münster: Aschendorff, 1974), 204–11 (on "all the people" in 27:25).

Haacker, K., "'Sein Blut über uns.' Erwägungen zu Matthäus 27,25," *Kirche und Israel* 1 (1986), 47–50.

Joüon, P., "Notes philologiques sur les Évangiles," RechSR 18 (1928), 349–50 (on Matt 27:25).

Kampling, R., *Das Blut Christi und die Juden. Mt 27,25 bei den lateinischsprachigen christlichen Autoren bis zu Leo dem Grossen* (NTAbh NS 16; Münster: Aschendorff, 1984).

Koch, K., "Der Spruch 'Sein Blut bleibe auf seinem Haupt' und die israelitische Auffassung vom vergossenen Blut," VT 12 (1962), 396–416.

Kosmala, H., "'His Blood on Us and Our Children' (The Background of Mat. 27,24–25)," ASTI 7 (1968–69), 94–126.

Lovsky, F., "Comment comprendre 'Son sang sur nous et nos enfants'?" ETR 62 (1987), 343–62.

Matera, F. J., "'His blood be on us and on our children,'" TBT 27 (1989), 345–50.

Mora, V., *Le Refus d'Israël. Matthieu 27,25* (LD 124; Paris: Cerf, 1986).

Pfisterer, R., "'Sein Blut komme über uns. . . .'" in *Christen und Juden*, eds. W.-D. Marsch und K. Thieme (Mainz: Grünewald, 1961), 19–37.

Rabinowitz, J. J., "Demotic Papyri of the Ptolemaic Period and Jewish Sources," VT 7 (1957), 398–99 (in ref. to Matt 27:25).

Reventlow, H. G., "'Sein Blut komme über sein Haupt,'" VT 10 (1960), 311–27.

Sanders, W., "Das Blut Jesu und die Juden. Gedanken zu Matt. 27,25," *Una Sancta* 27 (1972), 168–71.

Schelkle, K. H., "Die 'Selbstverfluchung' Israels nach Matthäus 27,23–25," AJINT 148–56.

Smith, R. H., "Matthew 27:25. The Hardest Verse in Matthew's Gospel," CurTM 17 (1990), 421–28.

Sullivan, D., "New Insights into Matthew 27:24–25," *New Blackfriars* 73 (1992), 453–57.

Part 7: The Roman Mockery and Abuse of Jesus (§36)

Bonner, C., "The Crown of Thorns," HTR 46 (1953), 47–48.

Delbrueck, R., "Antiquarisches zu den Verspottungen Jesu," ZNW 41 (1942), 124–45.

Geffcken, J., "Die Verhöhnung Christi durch die Kriegsknechte," *Hermes* 41 (1906), 220–29.

Goodenough, E. R., and C. B. Welles, "The Crown of Acanthus (?)," HTR 46 (1953), 241–42.

Ha-Reubéni, E., "Recherches sur les plantes de l'Évangile: l'épine de la couronne de Jésus," RB 42 (1933), 230–34.

Hart, H. St. J., "The Crown of Thorns in John 19.2–5," JTS NS 3 (1952), 66–75.

Kastner, K., "Christi Dornenkrönung und Verspottung durch die römische Soldateska," BZ 6 (1908), 378–92.

———, "Nochmals die Verspottung Christi," BZ 9 (1911), 56.

Lübeck, K., *Die Dornenkrönung Christi* (Regensburg: Pustet, 1906).

Reich, H., "Der König mit der Dornenkrone," *Neue Jahrbücher für das klassische Altertum* 13 (1904), 705–33.

Schlier, H., "Der Dornengekrönte (18,38b–19,7)," SuS 29 (1964), 148–60.

Vollmer, H., *Jesus und das Sacäenopfer, Religionsgeschichtliche Streiflichter* (Giessen: Töpelmann, 1905).

———, "'Der König mit der Dornenkrone' [H. Reich]," ZNW 6 (1905), 194–98.

———, "Nochmals das Sacäenopfer," ZNW 8 (1907), 320–21.

Wendland, P., "Jesus als Saturnalien-Koenig," *Hermes* 33 (1898), 175–79.

§31. INTRODUCTION: BACKGROUND FOR THE ROMAN TRIAL OF JESUS BY PONTIUS PILATE

We have already seen (§18, A2, 3 above) that at the time of the passion Judea was a lesser imperial province administered by a prefect. In the previous discussion we concentrated on the rights of Jewish courts during the prefecture and the likelihood of a Jewish legal procedure with regard to Jesus. Now we turn to the Roman legal procedure, which we shall discuss under these headings:

A. Roman Procuratorial Rule in Judea/Palestine
    1. Differences in the Two Periods of Roman Rule (AD 6–41, 44–66)
    2. Jesus as a Revolutionary and Figures on the Political Scene
       (a) "Charismatic leaders"
       (b) Messiahs
       (c) Would-be kings
       (d) Prophets and charlatans
       (e) Bandits
       (f) *Sicarii*
       (g) Zealots
B. The Prefecture of Pontius Pilate in Judea (AD 26–36)
    1. The Context and Data of Pilate's Career
    2. Estimations of Pilate, Favorable and Unfavorable
    3. Six Incidents or Items Involving Pilate
C. The Site of Jesus' Trial: The Praetorium
    1. Meaning and Nature of a Praetorium
    2. Two Candidates for the Praetorium of the Passion
D. The Type of Roman Trial
    1. The Legal Quality of the Gospel Record of the Trial
    2. Relation of the Roman Trial to the Jewish Trial/Interrogation
    3. Legal Status of Selected Features in the Roman Trial of Jesus
       (a) The Charge against Jesus and the Crime It Represented
       (b) The Responses of Jesus
       (c) The Role of the Crowd (*Acclamatio*)

We begin by recognizing that the years of direct Roman rule in Palestine were not all of equal quality in governance.

A. *Roman Procuratorial Rule in Judea/Palestine*

In AD 6 Judea, formerly an ethnarchy under Herod Archelaus (a son of Herod the Great), came under the direct rule of an imperial prefect. The era of prefects/procurators ended sixty years later in AD 66 when the first Jewish Revolt broke out, and Roman armies had to reconquer the land.

1. Differences in the Two Periods of Roman Rule (AD 6–41, 44–66)

The Roman prefecture was divided into two periods by the interim in AD 41–44 when Judea was restored to the rule of a Jewish king, Herod Agrippa I.[1] Seven Roman prefects ruled Judea in the 35-year period before Agrippa; seven procurators ruled the whole of Palestine in the 22-year period after Agrippa. These statistics suggest that the postAgrippa period, which led directly to the Revolt, was more troubled, requiring a higher frequency of changes in administration. M. Stern ("Status" 277) makes the interesting point that preAgrippa prefects came from Italy and thus the Western section of the empire, while at least three of the postAgrippa procurators came from the more Greek Eastern section of the empire and may have been tainted with antiJewish attitudes prevalent there. In any case, the combination of an acquired taste for Jewish kingship under Agrippa and the incompetent dishonesty of postAgrippa procurators made the populace much more restive in the second part of the prefecture.

The different atmosphere in Judea/Palestine between the preAgrippa and postAgrippa periods must be emphasized.[2] Too often the final years before the Revolt with their seething discontent and Zealot terrorism have been thought characteristic of the earlier period in which Jesus lived. This has facilitated the creation of the myth that Jesus was a political revolutionary, either the Che Guevara type gathering a band of armed followers, or the Gandhi type practicing and encouraging nonviolent resistance. Such an impression has been furthered on the popular level by what may be called "me-

---

[1] A major study of this ruler is D. R. Schwartz, *Agrippa I* (Tübingen: Mohr, 1990); see the detailed, challenging review by N. L. Collins, NovT 34 (1992), 90–101. Herod Antipas, the tetrarch of Galilee, was removed in AD 39 and his territory added to the realm of Herod Agrippa I, who already ruled over the NE territories around Ituraea formerly administered by (Herod) Philip. In 41 Claudius added Judea to Agrippa's domain, so that from 41–44 Agrippa ruled virtually the whole expanse of territory that had constituted the kingdom of his grandfather Herod the Great before 4 BC. When Roman procuratorial rule was restored in 44, it was over this larger territory (at least until 53–54, when the former tetrarchy of Philip was given to Agrippa II).

[2] See Barnett, "Under." Alonso Díaz ("Compromiso") is an example of a study that does not make this distinction; he assumes that there was massive Roman oppression during the time of Jesus, so that Jesus' entry into Jerusalem may have been a protest against those directing Israel, and "Hosanna" a cry of rebellion against Rome. This is *not* what the Gospels portray.

dia hype," since the view of Jesus as an advocate of Jewish or peasant liberation can be presented with enthusiasm and does not require radio,
newspaper, or TV presenters to take a stance about Jesus' religious claims
that might offend viewers.

Factual data, however, show that the preAgrippa period was more pacific
because the advent of direct Roman prefecture in Judea was not simply
a hostile occupation. The previous century had seen vicious interJewish
struggles between representatives of various religious and political views.
Alexander Jannaeus, the Hasmonean high priest king (107–76 BC), crucified
hundreds, including Pharisees. Even within the Hasmonean priestly heritage, the sons of Alexander, Hyrcanus II and Aristobulus II, strove against
each other, tearing the land apart. Herod the Great (40/37–4 BC) exterminated many of the Hasmonean remnants who would have had a claim to rule,
killed a number of his own family, and executed Pharisees (Josephus, *Ant.*
17.2.4; #44–45). Numerous revolts marked his last years and the time of his
death, leading to the advent of his son Archelaus as ruler in Judea (4 BC–AD
6).[3] The latter was such a bad ruler that at the request of his Jewish subjects
the emperor removed him and appointed Coponius the first prefect of Judea
(Josephus, *War* 2.7.3 to 8.1; #111–17). Although Judas the Galilean resisted
the fiscal census by Quirinius, the legate in Syria, which accompanied this
transition in the government of Judea in AD 6, Smallwood (*The Jews* 153)
judges: "The trouble over the census was apparently not serious in itself and
was quickly suppressed." After such a baneful history of Jewish rule, the
Roman prefecture represented a more sane and orderly administration, even
if foreign rulers are rarely liked. The reign of the Emperor Tiberius (AD
14–37) coincided with much of the preAgrippa period of the prefecture in
Judea. That reign was described in relation to Judea as a time when all things
were quiet (Tacitus, *History* 5.9: "sub Tiberio quies"). Just before Tiberius
died and Gaius Caligula (37–41) began his reign, there was a resistance worthy of concern, as there had been in AD 6.[4] But that was after Jesus' lifetime.
Thus, if we think of Jesus' adult years as from after age twelve to his death
(from ca. AD 7 to 30/33), our sources for the prefecture of Judea *in that
period* supply no evidence of an armed revolt or of *Roman* execution of

---

[3]Judas, son of Ezechias, a brigand chief (*archilēstēs*—note that John 18:40 calls Barabbas a
lēstēs, or even an *archilēstēs* in some mss.) caused trouble in Galilee (*War* 2.4.1; #55–56). Simon,
a would-be king, was troublesome in Perea (*War* 2.4.2; #57–59). The royal pretender Athrongaeus
disturbed Judea even into the reign of Archelaus (*War* 2.4.3; #60–65).

[4]Pilate's harsh suppression of a misguided Samaritan movement in AD 36 (to be discussed below)
caused Vitellius, the legate in Syria, to remove him (*Ant.* 18.4.1–2; #85–89). Arriving from Syria to
provide interim administration, Vitellius was well received in Judea. In 37 without opposition he
administered the oath promising loyalty to the new emperor, Gaius Caligula (*Ant.* 18.5.3; #124). Yet
in 40 in Judea there was resistance to Caligula's command that a statue of him be placed in the
Jerusalem Temple. Fortunately the emperor was assassinated before the matter came to a head.

notorious brigands, would-be kings, prophets, or revolutionaries.[5] Guevara (*Ambiente* 259) concludes his most detailed study of the political context in Judea with these words: "The response of the sources is very clear: The epoch of the public life of Jesus was a peaceful epoch."

2. Jesus as a Revolutionary and Figures on the Political Scene

Before discussing in particular the years crucial to Jesus' ministry and passion (27–30/33), let me discuss scholars' attempts to portray Jesus and/ or his followers as representatives of a revolutionary movement.[6]

The posthumously published work of H. S. Reimarus, *Vom dem Zwecke Jesu und seine Jünger* (1778), argued that both JBap and Jesus were revolutionaries and that Jesus' disciples created the myth of a spiritual savior to disguise this. Historically Jesus hoped to be proclaimed king by the Jews who had come to Jerusalem for Passover; but only the rabble applauded him, and he lost his nerve, aborting the attempt. In the 19th cent. this view of Jesus influenced such diverse German figures as Goethe and Wellhausen, and by the early 20th cent. the Marxist socialist K. Kautsky portrayed Jesus as a rebel against both Jewish and Roman authorities in planning an assault on the Temple.[7] Prominent in the more recent history of this thesis have been Jewish writers, e.g.: R. Eisler,[8] drawing on the Slavonic form of Josephus, called attention to Jesus' attempt to "capture" Jerusalem and occupy the Temple;[9] Carmichael (*Death*), in dependence on Eisler, revived this thesis; and Winter (*On the Trial*), having rejected the historicity of the Sanhedrin

[5]Some scholars, like Rivkin, call up the example of the execution of JBap by Herod Antipas, but that neglects the important distinction between the reign of the Jewish tetrarch/king in the Transjordan (Perea) and Galilee and the Roman prefecture in Judea. As for Jesus' dealings with Herod, see §33 below.

[6]For a survey see Catchpole, *Trial* 116–20; Kealy, *Jesus* 38–47; and especially Bammel, "Revolutionary." Some of those who portray Jesus thus are interested in using his fate as an anticipation of modern dissenters tried politically by oppressive governments. An extreme example is offered by O'Meara ("Trial" 454): "What an accomplishment was that dissent—to be capitally executed at the same time by both temple and state. . . . This drama has as its theme not Jesus' disobedience of Moses and/or Caesar, but the *new religio-human dignity of man preached by the Christ*"! See the response of Wallace, "Trial."

[7]In some of this theorizing Christians become a secret society planning revolution. The ancient report (EH 3.5.3) suggesting that the Jewish Christians were pacifists who fled to Pella across the Jordan rather than join the Jewish Revolt of 66–70 against Rome is dismissed as an invention. See the defense of this tradition by S. Sowers, TZ 26 (1970), 305–20.

[8]*Iēsous Basileus Ou Basileusas* (Heidelberg: Winter, 1929–30); Eng. transl. *The Messiah Jesus and John the Baptist* [New York: Dial, 1931]).

[9]Jesus' entry into the Temple and attack upon the money changers plays a major role in all the attempts to describe him as a revolutionary. If that was the connotation, it is remarkable that no memory is preserved of an intervention of the Temple police or the Roman soldiers, who would have interfered had there been a disturbance in the Temple court (see Acts 4:1–3; 21:29–33). On the contrary, there would have been no reason to interfere with a symbolic prophetic gesture, which is the most obvious meaning of what Jesus did. See Harvey, *Jesus . . . Constraints* 129–34.

proceedings, could portray the charge on which Jesus was crucified as almost totally political. Winter ("Trial . . . Rebel") argues that Jesus was arrested as a rebel and executed by the Romans as such. Mark hid this, not as antiJewish propaganda, but to be sure that Christians would not be seen as a threat by the Roman government. The English-speaking media, however, paid greater attention to the British scholar Brandon (*Jesus* and *Trial*), who also drew on the Slavonic form of Josephus as possibly reflecting an Aramaic draft in which Jesus was portrayed as a Zealot sympathizer challenging the priestly authorities and the Roman governance in Jerusalem. Beneath Mark's fictionalizing[10] Brandon would find that the Jewish authorities arrested Jesus because they regarded him as a menace to the peace of the Jewish state for which they were held responsible by Rome. They handed him over to the Romans for seditious teaching and action; Pilate already knew something of how Jesus was considered and so accepted the charge. Some advocates of liberation theology have latched on to this view of Jesus. Yet within scholarly circles less susceptible to media attention, rejections (often detailed) of the thesis that Jesus was a violent revolutionary have been commonplace, e.g., Catchpole, Guevara, Haufe, Hengel, H.-W. Kuhn, and Ziesler.

This discussion has suffered from imprecision and/or unrestrained imagination in reading the evidence of Josephus about the Roman prefecture in Judea. A major element has consisted of designations that might have revolutionary import, namely, "charismatic leaders," messiahs, would-be kings, prophets and charlatans (pl. of *goēs*), bandits (pl. of *lēstēs*), knife-wielders (pl. of *sicarius*), and Zealots. These have been intermingled as if they belonged to the period of Jesus' lifetime and interchangeably referred to the same candidates, whether or not Josephus juxtaposes those designations in the same time frame or even uses them. Let us consider the designations one by one.

(a) "Charismatic leaders." We may begin the discussion with the modern assignment of this role to numerous Jewish figures of the 1st cent., often with the connotation that they were revolutionaries. Such a designation, which does not appear in Josephus, is open to various interpretations. If it means a persuasive person who attracts followers to a proclaimed message, it is a term applicable to many people of any era and would be applicable to Jesus (or to Paul) without any revolutionary connotation. Set in the biblical background, a talented leader or visionary would be looked on as sent or raised up by God and thus "graced" for the task God wanted accomplished

---

[10]Mark (and the other evangelists) would not only have hidden that Jesus' entry into Jerusalem and cleansing of the Temple were revolutionary acts, but have totally reversed facts, e.g., Jesus did forbid tribute to Caesar despite Mark 12:13–17.

(*charis,* "grace," is related to *charisma,* "gift"). However, we should be careful in reading the NT attitudes toward Jesus. True, in the Gospels people are shown as looking with amazement on Jesus as having unique powers, e.g., of healing, of speaking with authority, and of extraordinary knowledge. But if charism is meant in a more precise sense similar to that found in I Cor 12, i.e., a gift of the Spirit for a particular role (e.g., to be a prophet or the Messiah), it is dubious that Jesus' followers would think of him thus, for they do not describe him as receiving from the Spirit a gift that established his identity or role. They may think that he was conceived through the Spirit and that the Spirit came to rest on him; but it is never indicated that they thought he was endowed by the Spirit with a role that he did not already possess.[11]

(b) Messiahs. If we turn to ancient terms, the scholarly literature about the political situation is filled with references to Jewish "messianic" figures in the 1st cent. even though, as I have stressed above in the ANALYSIS of §21(A), the term "Messiah" (*christos*) is never applied by Josephus to any Jew except Jesus. Apparently some scholars would call "messianic" any leader or movement that produced social or political unrest, at times making this designation equivalent to eschatological. Reacting to such an overly broad usage, Horsley ("Popular" 473) carefully distinguishes prophets and bandit leaders from messianic figures. Nevertheless, although he recognizes that references to an expected Messiah are relatively few in the 1st cent. BC and AD, he would apply "messianic" to charismatic would-be kings and their movements even if they claim no Davidic heritage.[12] By way of support he points out that the ideology of the Davidic dynasty which developed through Solomon was only part of Israel's experience with kingship. Saul (and even David himself) was a charismatic popular figure who by his gifts brought the people to accept him as king; and this pattern continued in the Northern Kingdom despite short-lived attempts to create dynasties there. I have no problem with such an analysis of kingship in pre-exilic Judah and Israel, nor with the fact that would-be kings emerged at the head of popular followings in late-Second-Temple times. My problem is with the wisdom of using "messianic" to describe nonDavidic manifestations of charismatic kingship *for this latter period.* Even though Davidic dynastic kingship was only part of the history, we can see from the DSS, the *Psalms of Solomon,* and the

---

[11]Similarly, although Jesus is thought to speak authoritatively what God wants people to hear, the word of God is never said to come to Jesus—a silence quite significant in the light of the OT pattern. Rather, at least in Johannine language, Jesus is said to be the word.

[12]McGing, for instance, who has made a solid contribution to the study of Pilate's prefecture, is very free on this score: The movement begun by Judas the Galilean "probably had some Messianic flavour to it, even if Judas did not claim to be a king or prophet" ("Governorship" 57–58). Similarly on p. 59, "during the Great Revolt [66–70] Messianic figures, not surprisingly, are again in evidence."

14th (and Babylonian form of the 15th) of the "Eighteen Benedictions" that there had developed an expectation of an anointed, royal son of David who would restore the glory of the Davidic kingdom. There is no clear evidence that the would-be kings of the later Second Temple period claimed such a Davidic role or were hailed as Davidids by their followers. An application of "messiah" to them creates the false impression that these kings claimed to be the Messiah or that their movements closely resembled the following of Jesus, even though there is no sign that their followers said that they were the Messiah. Jesus' followers did hail him as Messiah (perhaps already during his public ministry) and claimed Davidic lineage for him. I would argue, then, that Horsley's laudable caution in narrowing "messianic" should be pushed further so that term is not employed for *nonDavidic* would-be kings.[13]

(c) Would-be kings. If we leave aside the issue of messianic terminology, how do the Jewish would-be kings of "the time of Jesus" compare to Jesus? At the death of Herod the Great ca. 4 BC Josephus (*War* 2.4.1–3; #55–65) mentions three men with royal pretensions who tried to succeed Herod (none of them claiming to be a Davidid): Judas son of Ezechias (the chief bandit/brigand), Simon a slave, and Athrongaeus the shepherd.[14] At a later period, about AD 66, Menahem, the son/grandson of Judas the Galilean, armed a band of bandits/brigands and entered Jerusalem like a king and wore royal robes (*War* 2.17.8–9; #433–48). Josephus' fullest account of a would-be king concerns Simon son of Giora, a military hero who also began to be of noticeable importance in AD 66. Eventually he gathered a considerable army of the discontented, on whom he imposed martial discipline, and ultimately they recognized him as king. When he entered Jerusalem, he became the de facto chief of state during the Roman siege (*War* 4.9.3–4; #507–13). Having failed to escape when the city fell, he emerged from a passage beneath the Temple ruins, dressed in white with an outer purple mantle. Finally he was put on exhibit in the triumphal return of the victors to Rome, where he was executed (*War* 7.2.2; #26–36; and 7.5.6; #153–54). If one seeks to analyze these would-be kings, the earlier three were active in the countryside; and, according to Horsley ("Popular" 485–86), they attracted peasantry made desperate by the tightening economic circumstances. Their goal was to achieve liberation from Herodian domination and to reestablish a more egal-

---

[13]Horsley ("Popular" 484) gives a partial formulation of the difference: "The popular kings at the time of Jesus appear to have been different from the spiritualized or formalized 'anointed ones' expected in Pharisee or Essene traditions, whose *modus operandi* was to be pedagogical or ceremonial."

[14]Notice that I skip over Judas the Galilean in AD 6, who should not be called either a messiah or a would-be king; he was not interested in earthly kings, Jewish or Roman, but only in the rule of God.

itarian and just social structure. The latter two (Menahem and Simon ben Giora) came to Jerusalem and were involved in the great Jewish Revolt against the Romans.

In comparing them to Jesus, we should note first of all that one group functioned thirty years before his public ministry in a period when there was as yet no Roman prefecture, and the other group functioned more than thirty years after his death in an attempt to terminate the Roman prefecture. It is somewhat loose, then, to speak of the would-be kings of the time of Jesus. Judea was better run under Pilate and in the early prefecture than it had been in the last years of Herod the Great or would be in the last years of the Roman prefecture—the two periods that gave rise to the would-be kings.[15] All these "kings" surrounded themselves with large groups of armed troops and perished or were seized while involved in military actions backed by their followers. What had Jesus in common with such figures? His critique of the rich in Luke was not part of an advocated economic restructuring; his most intimate followers were not peasants but, so far as we know, people with independent employment (including fishermen and tax collectors); they were not numerous and certainly not an organized armed group; no military campaign was conducted against him; he was arrested alone and unarmed (see Mark 14:48 and par.); his followers were not pursued; he was put on trial and condemned in an orderly way, not killed in or after a battle. As for Jesus' attitude toward kingship, although we cannot be certain how people understood his references to the kingdom *of God,* none of his preserved statements suggest any intention of establishing a political kingdom on this earth. Although in Christian memory, people associated Jesus' entry into Jerusalem with the coming of "the kingdom of our father David" (Mark 11:10) and he was hailed as "Son of David" (Mark 10:47), he is also remembered as playing down the importance of Davidic descent (12:35–37). The Johannine Jesus resisted an attempt to make him king (6:15) and affirmed that his kingdom was not of this world—indeed, he commented on the lack of armed defense as proof that he was not an earthly king (18:36). Advocates of the revolutionary approach to Jesus often use as an argument the statement of Jesus, "I have not come to bring peace but a sword" (Matt 10:34; the parallel in Luke 12:51 has Jesus come to bring division), and the presence of a sword in the hands of his disciples when he was arrested (Matt 26:51; John 18:10). That argument, however, neglects counterarguments. The three Synoptics (Mark 12:17 and par.) preserve a saying where Jesus insists on rendering to Caesar the things that are Caesar's. The oldest preserved form

[15]The above-mentioned assurance by Tacitus (*History* 5.9) that under Tiberius (therefore during the adult lifetime of Jesus) things in Judea were quiet is by contrast with the report three lines before that at the time of Herod's death Simon (the slave) grasped at (*invaserat*) the name of king.

of the story of the cutting of the servant's ear does not state that it was a follower of Jesus who drew the sword (Mark 14:47); the Gospels that do identify the sword-wielder as a disciple have Jesus correct his follower (Matt 26:52; John 18:11); and the longest treatment of this issue has Jesus twice indicate that possession and use of swords were irrelevant to what was happening and not the right solution (Luke 22:38,49–51). To make Jesus one who planned on being a political king, one must resort to the thesis of a massive Christian cover-up manifested in lies reported in all the Gospels.[16]

(d) Prophets and charlatans. Again Horsley ("Like" 436) has been helpful in warning both against broad references to "prophecy" (and prophetic) without close attention to the figures actually called "prophets" in the 1st cent. and against mixing those figures with Zealots and *sicarii.* Let us consider the various figures called prophets in this period.

(i) There are seers who exhibit the ability to interpret the future. Josephus (*War* 2.8.12; #159) writes of learned Essenes who could detect in the sacred books guidance for what was now happening; and the Righteous Teacher of Qumran was remembered as unlocking the secrets in what the ancient prophets wrote (without understanding) about Qumran history (1QpHab 7:4–5). A parallel might be found in the picture of Jesus' seeing prophecies from the Scriptures fulfilled in his passion (e.g., Mark 14:27; Luke 22:37). In other instances offered by Josephus, without clear reference to the Scriptures, Essenes or Pharisees are credited with the ability to tell what was yet to happen (*Ant.* 13.11.2; #311; 17.2.4; #41–45; 17.13.3; #346–47). That too has a parallel in pictures of Jesus' ability to foretell the future (e.g., Mark 14:13; 14:30 and par.; John 21:18–19).[17]

(ii) More important for our purposes here, however, is another type of prophet, who issued dire oracles about impending divine intervention that would punish the people or Jerusalem and its Temple. That had been done in antiquity by prophets like Amos, Isaiah, Micah, Jeremiah, and others;[18] and especially in the cases of Amos and Jeremiah the oracles brought violent reactions from those in authority, including the priests. Oracular prophetic warnings continued in NT times: Previously I mentioned that Jesus son of Ananias came into Jerusalem in the early 60s with a message of divine judg-

[16]Baumbach ("Stellung" 285–96) is good on the differences between Jesus and revolutionaries. None of the would-be kings mentioned above was brought before a Sanhedrin; an issue of religious import provoked that trial/interrogation in the instance of Jesus (301), even as speaking against the Temple brought Jesus son of Ananias to Jewish authorities before he was handed over to the Romans.

[17]Believers in Jesus were also thought to have the ability to prophesy in this sense: Acts 21:9–11; probably in I Cor 14:1–6.

[18]Horsley ("Like" 450–51) mentions that some of these came from the peasantry, but their origin is so diversified that they are not easily fitted into any socioeconomic class or movement.

ment against the city and the Temple, a message dangerous enough to cause the authorities to seize and beat him and to hand him over to the Romans to be executed (*War* 6.5.3; #300–9). JBap with his words about the ax laid to the root of the tree and the murderous fear he inspired in Herod Antipas would fit into this pattern, as would Jesus with his action of cleansing the Temple and his warning about the coming destruction of the sanctuary (which is seen as threatening in Mark/Matt, John, and Acts). According to Matt 16:14 and Mark 8:28 one of the identifications of Jesus circulating among the people was "(Jeremiah or) one of the prophets."

(iii) Still a third type of prophet led large movements of followers, sometimes armed, by way of initiating a destruction and deliverance that he foretold. In assembling people such prophets promised signs (often resembling those of Moses leading the Hebrews out of Egypt and through the desert) but failed to deliver in the face of armed repression—a failure that led to many deaths. Understandably, Josephus scathingly describes them as charlatans and deceivers.[19] Ca. AD 36, at the end of the prefecture of Pontius Pilate (and thus three to six years after Jesus died), a Samaritan prophet gathered the populace to go to Mount Gerizim where he would show them the site in which Moses had deposited the sacred vessels, a movement Pilate suppressed with bloodshed (*Ant.* 18.4.1–2; #85–89; see B3 #6 below). Ca. 45, under the procurator Cuspius Fadus, a self-designated prophet named Theudas persuaded the masses to gather their possessions and follow him to the Jordan river, the waters of which he promised to part so that they could walk across dryshod; he was captured, and his head was cut off and brought to Jerusalem (*Ant.* 20.5.1; #97–98). More simply, according to Acts 5:36, he was slain and the 400 with him were dispersed. The procurator Felix (AD 52–60) had to punish some unnamed people who got a mob to follow them into the desert, promising them marvels "according to God's design" (*War* 2.13.4; #258–60). In particular there came to Jerusalem an Egyptian who claimed to be a prophet and duped 30,000 (or 4,000) to go out with him to the Mount of Olives from which he promised by command to cause the walls of Jerusalem to fall; over 400 were killed (*War* 2.13.5; #261–63; *Ant.* 20.8.6; #167–72; in this instance Acts 21:38 speaks of *sicarii*). The procurator Festus (AD 60–62) pursued and destroyed an unnamed charlatan and those who followed him into the desert in response to his promise to bring them salva-

---

[19]Besides Horsley ("Like" 454ff.), see Barnett ("Jewish") and Hill ("Jesus") on these prophets. The latter unfortunately calls them "messianic prophets," a practice that Horsley rightly criticizes. Barnett (686–87) argues that they were not Zealots, *sicarii*, messiahs, or pious charismatics. On 681 he points out that Moses, a true prophet, was contrasted in the exodus story with the charlatans and magi of the Egyptian court (*Ant.* 2.13.3; #286).

tion (*Ant.* 20.8.10; #188). In August of 70, at the end of the Roman siege when the Temple was on fire, 6,000 refugees fled to the portico in the outer court, where they perished because a "false prophet" had promised them that they would see signs of their deliverance (*War* 6.5.2; #284–86).

According to Josephus, these "prophets" of the third group all functioned in a time period subsequent to Jesus' lifetime; and so perhaps only in retrospect after his death when his followers grew numerous might Jesus and his followers be compared to them (by Gamaliel in Acts 5:34–38).[20] The brutality and venality of some of the postAgrippa procurators in whose governorships most of these prophets arose may have reminded people of the wicked Pharaohs against whom Moses worked signs. During his public ministry Jesus worked Moses-like miracles, e.g., walking on the water and feeding the crowds of 5,000 or 4,000 miraculously with bread in a desert place. In John 6:14 the latter "sign" led the people to hail him as "the prophet who is to come into the world." There was also a pattern of Elijah/Elisha-like signs[21] that caused Jesus to be hailed as a prophet (Luke 7:11–16; 4:23–27). Yet Jesus is never remembered as gathering crowds or leading them to symbolic places with promises that he was going to perform miraculous signs; indeed, his recorded attitude toward "show-off" miracles was disdainfully uncooperative (Matt 12:38–39; 16:1–4; 27:42). Eventually his opponents may have come to think of Jesus as a deceiver who promised miracles (Matt 27:63), but there is little in the Gospel record that would make Jesus resemble this third group of Josephus' "prophets." Rather Matt distinguishes Jesus' activities from those who would take the kingdom of heaven by force (11:12), and has Jesus warn against false prophets (7:15) who would perform signs and wonders so great as to deceive even the elect and who urge people to go out into the desert (24:24–26). Josephus himself, who spoke often about these charlatan prophets, did not call Jesus one; in an undoubtedly genuine passage he identified James as the brother of "Jesus called the Messiah [Christ]" (*Ant.* 20.9.1; #200). Also neither the would-be kings of the preceding subsection (Judas son of Ezechias, Simon, Athrongaeus, Menahem, and Simon son of Giora) nor the prophets of the third type (the Samaritan, Theudas, and the Egyptian) are remembered as having been subjected before execution to a legal trial, Jewish or Roman, such as the Gospels report for Jesus.

(e) Bandits. The designation *lēstēs* (pl. *lēstai*) occurs fourteen times in the Gospels, half of which are in the PN. The latter instances consist of Jesus' indignant protest when he is arrested on the Mount of Olives (Mark

---

[20]Barnett ("Jewish" 690–91) raises the possibility that Theudas was influenced by some of the traditions surrounding Jesus.

[21]One can debate whether in John the multiplication of the loaves is more clearly Moses-like or Elijah/Elisha-like; see BGJ 1.245–46.

14:48 [= Matt 26:55; Luke 22:52]: "As if against a *lēstēs* have you come out with swords and wooden clubs to take me?"); the designation of Barrabas as a *lēstēs* (John 18:40); and the report that those crucified on either side of Jesus were *lēstai* (Mark 15:27; Matt 27:38,44). Thus the Gospels give the impression that although Jesus disclaimed being a *lēstēs*, his enemies in putting him to death associated him with *lēstai* or treated him as one. These references have encouraged those who argue that Jesus was a political revolutionary, and their interpretations or translations of *lēstēs* run the gamut from thief through terrorist to freedom fighter, with visions of Pancho Villa and Che Guevara in the background. Much of the abundant discussion has not been precise, e.g. K. H. Rengstorf in TDNT 4.258–29 virtually identifies *lēstai* with Zealots (to be discussed below) but cites as examples texts of Josephus in which "Zealot" never occurs.[22]

As I pointed out in §14 in reference to the first PN occurrence, the designation *lēstēs* could have had different connotations in AD 30/33 and after AD 66. That is an important distinction if one is asking historically how Pilate might have considered Jesus. Certainly at any time in 1st-cent. Judea the term covered violent, armed men (not of official police or military status) whom others (including Josephus) often thought of as no better than bandits or thugs.[23] In particular, *lēstai* covered bands of marauders and robbers in the countryside,[24] and troublemakers in the cities who fomented riots. At the time of Jesus' death the Synoptic accounts of the Barabbas incident indicate that recently there had been a riot in Jerusalem, and Barabbas is identified as a *lēstēs* in John 18:40. Perhaps this background is also to be associated with the Mark/Matt designation of those crucified with Jesus as two *lēstai*.

Of major importance, however, is the fact that we have no evidence in the Roman prefecture *of Jesus' lifetime* that *lēstai* were equivalent to revolutionaries. Josephus uses *lēstēs* 78 times, plus *archilēstēs* 11 times; of those, only 39 instances describe enemies of Rome. Among the 39, 1 occurs at the death of Herod the Great; 4 occur in the period AD 44 to 66; and 34 occur during the Jewish Revolt of 66–70. In other words, during Jesus' lifetime and the

---

[22]Alonso Díaz ("Compromiso" 173–74), who thinks of Jesus as a revolutionary against Rome, posits that there was a connection between Jesus and Barabbas that has been glossed over; yet in his view Jesus was not a Zealot but an apocalyptic Pharisee. Maccoby, *Revolution*, also portrays Jesus as a fiery Pharisee involved in political activities who announced the end of Roman rule. Neither the silence of the Gospels (dismissed as Christian suppression) nor the lack of evidence in Jewish sources about the Pharisees of this period lends credibility to such flights of imagination.

[23]Gospel hostility toward *lēstai* is portrayed in Mark 11:17 (= Matt 21:13) and John 10:1,8.

[24]Horsley ("Josephus" and *Bandits*) provides much information on this subject but points out that in the 20s and 30s there was no great brigand activity. The parable Jesus constructs in Luke 10:30,36 has a man who is going from Jerusalem to Jericho fall among robbers (*lēstai*).

preAgrippa segment of the Roman prefecture Josephus never uses *lēstēs* to describe a revolutionary against Rome.[25] That befits the situation already noted that there were no revolutions in the prefecture of AD 6 to 41 (after the resistance of Judas the Galilean which preceded the prefecture). But even in the later prefecture of 44–66 distinctions between *lēstai* and such revolutionaries as *sicarii* and Zealots are in order. In *War* 2.13.2–3; #253–54 Felix (the Roman procurator in 52–60) gets rid of Eleazar the *archilēstēs,* crucifying many of the *lēstai* who had been with him, only to have another type of *lēstai* appear, the knife-wielding terrorists known as *sicarii*. Menahem, who had *lēstai* with him, is described a few lines later as having a coterie of armed *zēlōtai* (*War* 2.17.9; #441,444), perhaps the first mention in Josephus of the Zealots,[26] unless the term still means simply "zealous." *War* 4.3.12; #198–99 shows that others consider the Zealots, despite their religious (nationalistic?) pretensions, to be no better than *lēstai;* yet the Zealots bitterly resist Simon bar Giora when he gathers his *lēstai* from Masada and comes against them. Thus, if we follow Josephus closely, even in the revolutionary period, decades after Jesus' lifetime, *lēstai* are a wider class of violent men of different types and motivations.

I would grant that in the period from ca. 70 onward the evangelists and their audiences may have made no such precise distinction and mentally may have associated Barabbas and those crucified beside Jesus on Golgotha with the revolutionaries of the great Jewish Revolt of AD 66–70, types from whom they carefully distinguished Jesus.[27] Hostile antiChristian propaganda of the post-70 period surely equated Jesus with the Jews who made trouble for Roman order.[28] But none of that supports the view that Barabbas or the co-crucified associated with events of AD 30 or 33 were in fact revolutionaries or that Jesus was looked on as a revolutionary by the enemies of his own time.

(f) Sicarii. This is the plural of *sicarius,* literally, a "knife-wielder," i.e., one who infiltrated a crowd and by stabbing indiscriminately created public disturbance and thus provoked Roman reaction. As will be seen in APPENDIX IV, "*sicarius*" has been invoked (probably incorrectly) as an explanation of the Iscariot designation of Judas. Proof that *sicarii* were among Jesus' fol-

[25]For the statistics, see Guevara, *Ambiente* 122–23.

[26]As we shall see below, before Book 4 of the *War* (which covers AD 67) there are few references to Zealots; accordingly some think the present reference is to fanatics, and that only later do Zealots in the proper sense make their appearance (*War* 2.22.1; #651). Despite the confusing tendency of Rengstorf and others almost to equate *lēstai* with Zealots, *lēstai* constitute a much wider category.

[27]Whatever the charge of Jesus in Mark 11:17 ("You have made it [God's house] a den of *lēstai*") might have meant in his lifetime, after AD 70 people may have thought of the violent figures who used the Temple almost as a stronghold for their cause during the Jewish Revolt against Rome (see Juel, *Messiah* 134, citing G. Vermes).

[28]The late-2d-cent. adversary of Christianity Celsus envisions Jesus as a *lēstēs* punished for violence (Origen, *Adv. Celsum* 2.44) or as the author of an insurrection (*stasis;* 3.7,14; 8.14).

lowers has been offered by calling attention to the sword used to cut off the man's ear during the arrest of Jesus. Such an isolated instance of spontaneous defense that could have occurred in a melee of any period is scarcely indicative of belonging to a resistance movement. Moreover, Josephus' references to these terrorists places them in the time of the procurator Felix (AD 52–60) and later. The brigands who came into Jerusalem with daggers in Felix's time (*Ant.* 20.8.5; #164–65) practiced selective assassinations, eliminated Jewish gentry, and set villages on fire (*War* 2.13.3; #254–57). They flourished under Festus (AD 60–62; *Ant.* 20.8.10; #186–87), but were divided and losing popularity by the time of the First Jewish Revolt (*War* 7.8.1; #254–58).[29] Only by anachronistic analogy does Josephus mention them earlier, in relation to the revolt in AD 6 by Judas the Galilean against the census of Quirinius (*War* 7.8.1; #254). He never mentions them in the period of Pilate or under Tiberius.

(g) Zealots. The Greek *zēlōtēs* means one who is zealous; it renders Hebrew words associated with the root *qn'*. Reflecting Israelite belief that God does not like the halfhearted, "zealot, zealous" could be used of those who ardently protected God's interest, e.g., of Phinehas who massacred violators of the Law (Num 25:6–13), of the Maccabees who resisted Hellenistic syncretism (I Macc 2:24,26), of Paul when he was attached to the traditions of his ancestors (Gal 1:13–14), and of Jews who were fiercely antiChristian (*zēlos* in Acts 5:17–18; *zēloun* in 17:5). Notice that in the examples of this usage during the Roman prefecture before the Jewish Revolt of 66–70, the ire of those called "zealous" was against lawbreakers, not against the Romans (Morin, "Deux" 343–47).

There was, however, also a more specific use of *zēlōtēs* to refer to the Zealots, a group of people, mostly young, who had taken an oath to act fanatically and without mercy against every person who stood in the way of their vision of cultic purity in relation to the Law and to the Temple (*War* 4.6.3; #381–88). Josephus thinks that despite their intentions the actions were reprehensible; and certainly they were violent revolutionaries. The ref-

---

[29]Barnett ("Under" 564) wonders whether the *sicarii* lasted into the heart of the Revolt against Rome after the death of Menahem, the son of Judas the Galilean in AD 66. See Horsley and Hanson, *Bandits* 200–16, for details. Yet Josephus (*War* 7.8.1; #252–53) reports that Eleazar and the *sicarii* were in control of Masada (ca. AD 73). Guevara (*Ambiente* 124–30) offers a new solution. Josephus uses *sicarii* 19 times, of which 5 occur in the period AD 52–64; 3 during the Revolt of 66–70; and 12 in Book 7 of the *War*, where he is concerned with the period 70–74 after the Revolt. That last batch of occurrences portrays the *sicarii* as antiRoman revolutionaries in Masada, Egypt, and Cyrene (North Africa). Guevara thinks that Josephus came across a document at Rome written in Latin that completed his knowledge of the postwar period and had this special use of *sicarius* which differed somewhat from his previous usage. This would serve to reinforce the thesis that the term did not describe a group of revolutionaries against Rome founded by Judas the Galilean in AD 6 and active in Jesus' time.

erences in Josephus point to the existence of the Zealot party only at the time of the Jewish Revolt in late AD 67 and immediately afterward.[30] Indeed, most of the references are in Book 4 of the *War,* in the period from July of 67 to July of 69.

(Parenthetically we may note that before that Book only three instances in Josephus' *War* are possible references to the Zealots.[31] *War* 2.22.1; #651, describing Jerusalem in AD 66–67, mentions the so-called Zealots, and this may be the first reference to the party as such. *War* 2.17.9; #444 describes *zēlōtai* surrounding Menahem, the son [grandson] of Judas the Galilean, in the spring of AD 66 as he went to the Temple in royal robes, but these might be just armed fanatics.[32] If the designation does mean Zealots in the technical sense, the time range of their activity is not changed significantly. Sometime after November of 66, the priest Eleazar, son of Simon, is mentioned in *War* 2.20.3; #564 as surrounded by a bodyguard of Zealots in Jerusalem.)

Analyzing some thirty-nine instances of *zēlōtēs* in Book 4 of the *War,* Guevara (*Ambiente* 135–39) concludes that the group described by Josephus had their origin in Jerusalem at a time when other competing groups during the Revolt (those of John of Gischala, Simon son of Giora, the Idumeans, and Menahem) came to Jerusalem from the outside. They were the smallest group in the city (2,400 according to *War* 5.6.1; #250), the only one led by priests, and were fortified within an interior court of the Temple. They aligned themselves with John of Gischala and fought against Simon son of Giora and the aristocratic high priests.

Despite that evidence some would push the existence of the Zealots back far earlier in history to Herodian or even Maccabean times.[33] Much discussion has centered on *War* 2.8.1; #118 (= *Ant.* 18.1.6; #23–25), which men-

---

[30]This is the majority view: Barnett, Baumbach, Borg, Giblet, Guevara, Horsley and Hanson, Lake, M. Smith, Zeitlin (see bibliography in §30, Part 1). Interestingly, the reference to Zealots in the minor talmudic tractate *'Abot de Rabbi Nathan* 21a (6.1) also associates them with this late period: When Vespasian came to destroy Jerusalem, they sought to burn his stores. B. Salmonsen (NTS 12 [1965–66], 164–76) cautions against sweepingly identifying as Zealots those referred to as zealous for the Law in rabbinic literature; e.g., Mishna *Sanhedrin* 9.6 says that if someone has stolen a sacred vessel or has had sexual relations with an Aramean idolatress, the zealots (= zealous) may lay hold of him.

[31]See above under A2e for the usage of *lēstēs* that sometimes is erroneously looked on as equivalent to *zēlōtēs.* Morin ("Deux" 332–49) is very good on the necessary precisions about Zealots.

[32]Guevara (*Ambiente* 131–34) makes a very strong case against identifying these as Zealots. We should remember that a relative of Menahem, Eleazar, who was also a descendant of Judas the Galilean, is associated by *War* 7.8.1; #253 with the *sicarii,* whom Josephus keeps distinct from the Zealots (*War* 7.8.1; #268–70).

[33]Baron, Bousset, Graetz, Hengel, K. Kohler, E. Meyer, Schlatter, Yadin. W. R. Farmer (*Maccabees, Zealots, and Josephus* [New York: Columbia Univ., 1956]) contends that to protect Jews under Rome Josephus disguised the relation between the Zealots of the Revolt and the ancient Maccabean rebels: The Pharisees were the heirs of the Hasidim of that period, and the Zealots were the heirs of the Maccabees.

tions a fourth philosophy or sect (in addition to Pharisees, Sadducees, and Essenes) founded by Judas of Galilee (or Gaulanitis). Of him we know little more than that he resisted the Roman census and taxation under Quirinius in AD 6 and that he led the fourth group, although they were convinced that God alone should be the ruler (*despotēs*). Except for their extraordinary love of liberty, they were very like the Pharisees (*Ant.* 18.1.6; #23)—even though 18.1.1; #9 associates with Judas a Saddok, whose name might suggest priestly and Sadducee contacts. Acts 5:37 says that this Judas perished and his followers were scattered.[34] The claim that this fourth group were Zealots is *not* affirmed by Josephus, but is largely based on the dubious reference (mentioned above parenthetically) to the "zealous" (Zealots?) who surrounded Judas' son or grandson Menahem sixty years later. Josephus in *Ant.* 18.1.1; #9 says that Judas planted the roots of later troubles; and *Ant.* 18.1.6; #25 describes the flowering of those roots under the worst of the procurators, Gessius Florus (AD 64–66). Yet although in the sixty years separating Judas from Menahem there may have been people of similar apocalyptic idealism about how God should govern Judea, nothing in Josephus points to a continuous, sizable revolutionary movement connecting the two men; indeed, his language of "roots" suggests a period of dormancy between them.[35] M. Smith ("Zealots" 13) states: "None of the major political and religious disturbances between the suppression of Judas in [AD] 6 and the rise of the *Sicarii* after 54 has any reported connection with Judas' party." Borg ("Cur-

---

[34]Scholars have interpreted Judas through both what followed him and what preceded him. After him, two of his sons, Jacob and Simon, were crucified in AD 46 by the procurator Tiberius Alexander (Josephus, *Ant.* 20.5.2; #102); and another son (or grandson) was killed in the Jerusalem troubles of 66 (*War* 2.17.8–9; #433–48). As for what preceded, Josephus' description of "a man of Galilee named Judas" (*War* 2.8.1; #118) would not prima facie encourage us to identify this troublemaker with Judas, son of Ezechias, who had caused trouble at Sepphoris in Galilee a decade earlier (ca. 4 BC: n. 3 above) and broke into the royal arsenals after the death of Herod the Great. Yet M. Black, "Judas of Galilee and Josephus' 'Fourth Philosophy,'" in *Josephus-Studien,* eds. O. Betz et al. (O. Michel 70 Geburtstag; Göttingen: Vandenhoeck & Ruprecht, 1974), 45–53, not only identifies the two figures but makes them the remnant of Hasmonean resistance in Palestine—perhaps as a cadet branch of the priestly royal family! However, Josephus' description of the fourth philosophy as agreeing in almost all respects with the Pharisees (*Ant.* 18.1.6; #23) would scarcely fit the Hasmonean princes. For arguments against identifying the two Judases, see Smallwood, *The Jews* 153.

[35]Pace B. Witherington, *The Christology of Jesus* (Minneapolis: Fortress, 1990), 81–88, who attempts to support Hengel's thesis of continued activity throughout the 1st cent. Although M. Stern, "Sicarii and Zealots," in SRSTP 263–301, 404–5, recognizes that there is no real proof that there were Zealots at the time of Judas the Galilean, he argues that Judas and the antiRoman revolutionaries of the later period were connected by an ideology of freedom—a rather vague concept. Kealy (*Jesus* 36) goes too far in arguing that Zealot armed resistance was a real option in Jesus' lifetime and "indeed in the human situation of every age." Historically, a greater manifestation of unjust oppression than existed in the early prefecture in Judea was required to cause a substantial number of people to risk their lives in this manner. Kealy introduces too much modern imagery in his whole discussion, as exhibited in his perplexing statement on p. 37: "The trouble with Zealots of every age and their theocratic model, is that they have little real understanding of the complexities of a modern state." Has the modern state existed at every age?

rency" 505–6) points out that there is no reason why Josephus would have suppressed all mention of the Zealots before AD 66 if they had been in circulation.

"Zealot" is of importance in our discussion here because the designation *zēlōtēs* was attached to one of Jesus' Twelve (Simon) in Luke 6:15; Acts 1:13.[36] Almost surely this had the general sense of "zealous," even as it does in its two other uses in the Lucan corpus (Acts 21:20; 22:3). Nevertheless, on the basis of that designation, some would associate Jesus and/or his followers with the Zealot movement.[37] To support this, Jesus' triumphal entry into Jerusalem and his cleansing of the Temple are cited. Yet there is no evidence that "Zealots" in the more specific sense existed in Jesus' lifetime; nor does he fit Josephus' description of them: He was not a fanatic about the Law. He related positively to pro-establishment tax collectors who were in the service of an earthly ruler (e.g., Matthew and Zacchaeus; see Smallwood, *The Jews* 151–53). After his death some of Jesus' followers were not loyal to the Temple (Acts 7:47–50), whereas that Temple was a center of Zealot activities and aspirations in the Jewish Revolt. The fact that the Romans crucified Jesus alone rather than with his followers, and did this at a potentially volatile moment (during a feast when there were probably at least 100,000 people in Jerusalem; see §18, n. 98 above), suggests that they did not consider themselves faced with a group of dangerous revolutionaries.[38]

If we may judge from Josephus' usage, then, neither the category of *sicarius* nor that of Zealot would have been applicable to Jesus or his followers. This is not only because those technical terms are not attested in Jesus' time, but more important because in the pertinent part of the preAgrippa period (after 6 until 30/33) the style of Roman governance in Judea did not yet spawn such violent revolutionary movements.[39] That does not mean all things were perfect politically or socially. Burdensome taxation was always an issue.[40] There were absentee landlords who caused economic distress

---

[36]Actually, as Borg ("Currency" 507) points out, the designation of Simon as Cananaean in Mark 3:18 and Matt 10:4 is plausibly more original. Yet since Greek *Kananaios* probably is not derived from a place name but reflects the Hebrew/Aramaic stem for "zealous" (*qn'*), the basic issue is not significantly changed.

[37]Daniel ("Esséniens" 91) would use highly dubious etymologies to find indications that JBap and Nathanael were Zealots.

[38]H.-W. Kuhn ("Kreuzesstrafe" 735) judges it historically certain that Jesus was not a Zealot or revolutionary.

[39]Two generalizations that enter the discussion need caution. S. Freyne, *Galilee from Alexander the Great to Hadrian* (Notre Dame Univ., 1980), 208–55, warns about the exaggerated thesis that Galilee, Jesus' homeland, was seething with revolutionaries. MacMullen, *Enemies*, alerts us that in the earlier period the revolutionary thrust came more often from the upper classes than from the peasants.

[40]In AD 17 the provincial populace of Judea and Syria petitioned for a reduction in the tribute (probably the head tax) to be paid to the Romans (Tacitus, *Annals* 2.42.5).

among tenant farmers. Eschatological visionaries and holy men appealed to the ordinary people and aroused their fervor.

B. *The Prefecture of Pontius Pilate in Judea* (AD 26–36)

Let us turn now to factors involving the emperor Tiberius and the prefect Pontius Pilate in the time of Jesus' public ministry and death (27 to 30/33).

1. The Context and Data of Pilate's Career

Within the twenty-three year reign of Tiberius (AD 14–37), the period from 26 to 31 was peculiar. Lucius Aelius Sejanus, a Roman noble, had gradually risen in importance in the emperor's estimation, even though already in the early 20s Sejanus was engaged in plots with and against members of the imperial family. In 26–27 Tiberius left Rome, eventually to settle on a promontory dominating the isle of Capri, leaving Sejanus in Rome to deal with the ordinary details of administering the empire. Sejanus amassed more and more power until in 31 he was virtually co-ruler. When at last his treasonous ambitions became known, Sejanus was rejected by Tiberius; and he perished on Oct. 18, 31. If Jesus died at Passover in 30 or 31, Sejanus was still in power; if he died in 33, Sejanus had fallen. (For the date of Jesus' death, see APPENDIX II.) The possible correlation of Jesus' death with Sejanus' administration could be important if two other possibilities were verifiable.

First, was the praetorian prefect Sejanus the patron of Pilate, who was appointed prefect of Judea in 26?[41] If so, Pilate could have been more confident of having backing in Rome in 30–31 than in 33. In John 19:12, the challenge that were he to release a king who could become the emperor's rival, he would be no "friend of Caesar" implies that Pilate might be reported to Rome. Obviously such a complaint might have impact if his patron had recently fallen from power, and Sejanus' clients were under suspicion. However, among the list of six historical incidents or items in Pilate's career to be given immediately below, both in #5 and #6 Pilate was in fact denounced to higher Roman officials (for behaving harshly); and John could have fashioned the implied threat in 19:12 on the basis of such memories without any background of a Sejanus-Pilate relationship.

Second, was Sejanus strongly antiJewish, as Philo reports (*Ad Gaium* 24;

---

[41]So Maier, "Episode" 114–15. Lémonon (*Pilate* 275) disagrees with those scholars who relate Pilate to Sejanus.

#160–61; *In Flaccum* 1)? Those who think that Pilate exhibited great severity toward the Jews during his governorship sometimes contend that he was aping his patron in this matter or at least trying to please him. However, no other ancient writer suggests that Sejanus was antiJewish; and many scholars doubt Philo on this point. In a work designed to be persuasive to the Emperor Gaius Caligula and (subsequently) to the Emperor Claudius, Philo had to be very careful in criticizing Tiberius for antiJewish actions;[42] and so he may have shifted the blame to Sejanus to whom, once disgraced, all evil could be attributed. While the Sejanus issue makes us conscious that the Pilate who tried Jesus had to be mindful of political realities (as he did in other matters of governance), there are just too many "ifs" for us to explain Pilate's acquiescence to demands for crucifying Jesus by speculating that a relationship to Sejanus was one of those realities.

Let us move from the Roman political scene at large to some pertinent biographical facts about the prefect. Pontius Pilate was of equestrian rank, that is, of the lower Roman nobility, as contrasted with senatorial rank—a status in life that suggests that he must have had a military career before being appointed prefect. His nomen Pontius (representing the *gens* or tribe) was of Samnite origin; his cognomen Pilatus (representing the *family*) took its origin from *pileus,* "cap, helmet," or *pilum,* "spear." His praenomen or personal name is not preserved in Roman, Jewish, or Christian records. Rosadi (*Trial* 215–17) is an example of those who present as fact legendary material about Pilate: His praenomen was Lucius; he came from Seville; he married Claudia, the youngest daughter of Julia (the daughter of Augustus), with the approval of Tiberius, who immediately sent him to Judea.

Serving as the fifth of the seven preAgrippa prefects in Judea, Pilate is the best known because of the number of references to him in Josephus and Philo. Indeed, of the fourteen prefects/procurators in Judea in the era AD 6–66, Pilate, who ruled from 26 to 36, was equalled in administrative longevity only by his predecessor, Valerius Gratus, who served eleven years. Three legates[43] ruled in Syria during Pilate's term in Judea. It is noteworthy that in his decade-long prefecture Pilate never removed a Jewish high priest—Caiaphas had that religious role from 18 to 36/37, being removed finally by Vitellius, the legate of Syria, seemingly just after Pilate's own removal. Such stability was quite unusual, e.g., four high priests were deposed during the decade of Valerius Gratus' rule (Josephus, *Ant.* 18.2.2; #34–35). Moreover, when we evaluate Pilate's performance as governor, we

---

[42]Wansbrough ("Suffered" 88). In AD 19 Tiberius had the Jews expelled from Rome; Cassius Dio (*History* 57.18.5) gives as the reason for this the success of Jewish proselytism.

[43]L. Aelius Lamia, L. Pomponius Flaccus, and L. Vitellius. In all that follows I give the usual dating for Pilate's prefecture. The revisionist position of D. R. Schwartz (*Studies in the Jewish Back-*

should bear in mind that although after 31 Tiberius dismissed many who had been appointed by Sejanus, Pilate remained in office another five years. These statistics caution against prejudging Pilate as irresponsible or extremely controversial.

We have already shown (#18, A3b) that in Pilate's time the formal or dominant title of the Roman governor was *praefectus* (Gk: *eparchos*). In excavations at Caesarea on the Palestinian coast (the seat of Roman gubernatorial control) an inscription was discovered in 1961 mentioning Pilate.[44] This inscription pertains to the erection (ca. 31) and dedication of a building in honor of Tiberius (the Tiberieum), presumably one that contained a statue of him and served civic, not necessarily religious, purposes. The inscription was later reused in the construction of a theater. The left side of the inscription has been lost; what remains of it is a little over two feet long (68 cm.) and 2½ feet high (82 cm.). From the few surviving lines of the inscription these are the key words that at least tell us how this man referred to his own office:

> PON]TIUS PILATUS   Pontius Pilate
> PRAEF]ECTUS IUDA[EA]E[45]   Prefect of Judea

2. Estimations of Pilate, Favorable and Unfavorable

There were in antiquity diametrically opposite views of Pilate. Even if Mark's portrait of him is not flattering—Pilate knows that Jesus was handed over because of the zealous envy of the Jewish authorities but does little to help him[46]—the three other evangelists portray a nobler Pilate, seeking to deliver Jesus from patently exaggerated and even false charges. In subsequent Christian theology Pilate served primarily as a Greco-Roman chronological signpost for the reality of the death of Jesus. A leading example is the creedal phrase "suffered under Pontius Pilate";[47] sometimes there is an

---

ground of Christianity [Tübingen: Mohr, 1992], 182–201) dates Pilate's accession to 26/27 rather than 18/19, and the dismissal of both Pilate and Caiaphas to just before Passover in AD 37.

[44]See Frova, Vardaman, and Volkmann in the SECTIONAL BIBLIOGRAPHY (§30, Part 2); also Lémonon, *Pilate* 29–31. It is depicted in *Bible et Terre Sainte* 57 (1963) 15 (plate).

[45]There is a debate about the word(s) that would have preceded *praefectus*. Imbert (*Procès* 64) would supply *procurator Augusti;* others disagree; see §18, n. 21.

[46]Many have recognized that there is no exculpation of Pilate in Mark. In a step beyond that, Guillet ("Entrée") imaginatively argues that the reference in Tacitus to Jesus' death under Pilate is a Christian interpolation, and that Mark (written in 135–38) is the oldest attempt by Christians (actually hostile to Hadrian) to blame Pilate and the Romans. Thus Mark becomes an example of the inculpation of Pilate!

[47]Ignatius, *Magn.* 11 ("at the time of the governorship of Pontius Pilate"); *Trall.* 9:1 ("under Pontius Pilate"); *Smyrn.* 1:2 ("under Pontius Pilate and Herod the tetrarch"). Also Justin, *Apology* 1.13; 2.6; Augustine, *De Fide et Symbolo* 5.11 (CSEL 41.14). See Liberty, "Importance." The refer-

added note of Jesus' bravery ("before Pontius Pilate" in I Tim 6:13[48]) or of Pilate's responsibility (Jesus was crucified at the sentence of Pilate). A variant reading of I Pet 2:23, attested in a Latin tradition,[49] reports that Jesus "handed himself over to an unjust judge," obviously referring to Pilate. Yet the popular echoes of the favorable portrayal dominated. Tertullian (*Apologeticum* 21.18,24; CC 1.126–27), who mistakenly identifies Pilate as Procurator of Syria, esteems him as a Christian at heart. *Didascalia Apostolorum* (5.19.4; Funk ed. 290) from 3d-cent. Syria confirms that Pilate did not consent to the wicked deeds of the Jews. Hippolytus (*On Daniel* 1.27; SC 14.121) deems Pilate to be as innocent of the blood of Jesus as Daniel was in relation to Susanna. The *Acts of Pilate* (n. 87 below) are favorable to him, showing him sympathetic to that portion of the Jewish multitude who weep and desire that Jesus not be put to death (4.5). Some of the church writers even began to classify Pilate as a prophet of the kingdom of God.[50] Pilate's wife, identified as Procla in some of the apocryphal Pilate literature (JANT 155), is especially honored in hagiography, sometimes with and sometimes without her husband. Ethiopic homilies quoting sections of a 5th-6th cent. *Gospel of Gamaliel* describe the martyrdom of Pilate; and in the 6th–7th cents. "Pilate" appears as a baptismal name among Copts. In a later Ethiopic Synaxarion Pilate and his wife are mentioned to be venerated on June 19. The Greek church has honored Pilate's wife on Oct. 27. A Latin apocryphon, *Paradosis,* describes how Pilate came before the emperor and was decapitated.[51] By the 9th cent. Vienne was thought to be the place of his death, and later, Switzerland. A memory of the prefect of Judea is preserved by the 4,700-foot Mount Pilat near Vienne and the 7,000-foot Mount Pilatus near Lucerne.

Outside Christian tradition the picture of Pilate given by Josephus is not favorable; Philo's depiction is extremely hostile; and even Roman sources do not ennoble Pilate. Most often this harsh portrayal has been accepted as

---

ence to Pilate in the ancient creeds may have come from Western Christianity to the East (Staats, "Pontius" 508). In those creeds the motif for including "born of the virgin Mary . . . suffered/crucified under Pontius Pilate" was partly antidocetic, but that was not a major factor in these early witnesses or in I Tim 6:13.

[48]Blinzler, *Trial* 287, presents different interpretations of this verse. Baldensperger ("Il a rendu") argues correctly that the primary thrust is the witness Jesus bore when called on to testify before an examining authority, as help to a community that had to do the same (Matt 10:18; Luke 12:8; II Tim 1:8; Heb 12:4; Rev 2:13; *Hermas, Sim.* 9.28.4).

[49]Vulgate, Cyprian, and the Latin of the *Adumbrationes* of Clement of Alexandria.

[50]Augustine, *Sermon* 201 (PL 38.1031–32).

[51]JANT 154–55. A contrary tradition involving Pilate's suicide is found in Eusebius (EH 2.7). For more on these developments, see HSNTA 1.481–84 (rev. ed. 1.530–33); JANT 157–61; Lémonon, *Pilate* 266–71; and the articles by Erhardt and Staats on Pilate's role in Christian thought. Erhardt reminds us that in the Western Church the image of Pilate was less favorable than in the Eastern Churches. He became a damned and haunted figure in medieval plays on the passion.

history over against Christian amelioration, but now revisionist scholars are being more cautious.[52] They point out that the Roman historian Tacitus disliked the equestrian class to which Pilate belonged and did not always do justice to members of that class who held public office. In his *Ant.* Josephus added to the Pilate stories hostile details absent from the earlier *War*, thus raising the issue of accuracy and veracity.

Philo's *Ad Gaium*, which is the most hostile to Pilate, needs to be understood from the viewpoint of its literary genre. The introduction to it in the Loeb series (10.xxiii) describes it as "essentially a Philippic and not a sober history." (Smallwood, "Philo," who describes the background of the work, has a somewhat better estimate of Philo's veracity, even though she admits [*The Jews* 160] that Philo probably blackened Pilate rhetorically as a foil to Tiberius.) While Philo's work concerns the attempts of Gaius Caligula to have himself honored as a god and to set up a statue that would make the Jerusalem Temple a shrine for the imperial cult, it was finally committed to writing in AD 41 after Caligula had been assassinated in January and Claudius had become emperor, in order to impress the new ruler. Thus there are two levels of persuasive address: the original trying to persuade Gaius Caligula to change his plans about the statue in Jerusalem, and a second trying to persuade Claudius to be more favorable to the Jews than his predecessor had been. The main reference to Pilate occurs therein as part of a letter purportedly written ca. 39–40 by King Agrippa I to Caligula (*Ad Gaium* 36–41; #276–329). Agrippa did write to the emperor, but Philo's letter is a free composition on the same theme. Agrippa's rule in Judea replaced that of the Roman prefects beginning in the year 41, and so it is not surprising that the negative portrait of Pilate's governance had a self-serving role—Agrippa wanted to portray a real need for his own accession. Philo's Agrippa decries Pilate's "briberies, insults, robberies, outrages, wanton injuries, constantly repeated executions without trial, ceaseless and supremely grievous cruelty" (*Ad Gaium* 28; #302).

Nor did the debate over Pilate end in antiquity. He has continued to capture imagination to this day. Over a hundred years ago a prestigious figure in French literature, Anatole France, in his collection *Mother-of-Pearl Box*, wrote a rationalistic short story "The Procurator of Judea" in which the aged Pilate could not even remember that he had dealt with a minor figure named Jesus. In 1961 R. Caillois composed a French novel (English transl. *Pontius Pilate* [New York: Macmillan, 1963]) in which Pilate, tired of the image of being one who washed his hands in indecision, let Jesus go. In German

---

[52]Earlier scholars who worked toward the rehabilitation of Pilate included G. A. Müller, H. Peter, and E. von Dobschütz. Thoughtful contributions are made by Blinzler (*Prozess* 267–71), Lémonon, McGing, and Wansbrough.

A. Lernet-Holenia, a composer of a wide variety of literature, ranging from fantasy novels through poetry to a study of Greta Garbo, wrote *Pilatus. Ein Komplex* (Vienna: Zsolnay, 1967) imaginatively drawing on "The Passion of the Lord in a Version by an Unknown" and involving a discussion between the presiding officer of the court and a cardinal.[53]

Looking back at the preceding paragraphs, we see an abundance of portrayals of Pilate, favorable and unfavorable, marked respectively by generalization, caricature, and imagination. That coloring increases the need to look soberly at six items of evidence about Pilate that may help to nuance our judgment, three from Josephus, one from Philo, one from the NT, and one from coinage.

3. Six Incidents or Items Involving Pilate

#1. The Iconic Standards: AD 26 (Josephus, *War* 2.9.2–3; #169–74; *Ant.* 18.3.1; #55–59). Shortly after arriving in Palestine,[54] Pilate sent troops into Jerusalem with iconic medallions or busts of Caesar attached to their standards. It is not totally clear to what extent and how such iconic standards were implicitly religious in character.[55] Seemingly the newly arrived governor wished to show his loyalty to the emperor by having the soldiers act in Judea as they would anywhere else. Pilate was publicly loyal to Tiberius; the inscription discovered with his name, as reported above, was erected in a building at Caesarea dedicated to that emperor. The account in the *War* admits that Pilate had the soldiers make their entry at night, hinting that he knew that it was a controversial gesture that needed caution. The *Ant.* account, however, is silent on that point and stresses that Pilate was doing something not done by his predecessors in the prefecture. In any case, Pilate had miscalculated the intensity of Jewish feelings against imagery in the holy city.[56] Jews came all the way to his headquarters at Caesarea on the

---

[53]Worth mentioning also is K. A. Speidel, *Das Urteil des Pilatus* (Stuttgart: KBW, 1976), which is a popularized account of the passion, interwoven attractively with citations ancient and modern, and illustrated by striking photos.

[54]The dating of the episode is suggested by the sequence in which Josephus places it, but this part of *Ant.* 18 is not notable for the logic of its order. If this is the same as incident #5 below, it could have occurred later.

[55]Kraeling, "Episode" 269–75, discusses these standards (one with the likeness of Caligula has been found in Germany); he argues that the standards represented the numina or the divinity venerated by the unit that bore it. A. D. Nock (HTR 45 [1952], 187–252, esp. 239–40) discusses the veneration of standards. Josephus, *War* 6.6.1; #316, describes how the Romans celebrated their victory over the Temple (and implicitly over the God of the Jews) by offering sacrifices to their standards at the east gate. Earlier, in the DSS, 1QpHab 6:1–6 refers hostilely to the Kittim (Romans) sacrificing to their standards.

[56]This is the reason offered in the *War,* but *Ant.* speaks of the law forbidding even the making of images. Actually, the Jewish anti-iconic attitude seems to have gone beyond the commandment that forbade images of other gods (Exod 20:4–5). Josephus (*Ant.* 17.6.2-3; #150–57) reports an attempt

coast in order to demand the removal of the standards from Jerusalem. Pilate was reluctant to remove them—perhaps not merely out of stubbornness, for Tacitus (*Annals* 3.70) tells us of Ennius who was accused of treason for having melted down a silver statue of Tiberius.[57] On the sixth day of Jewish protest Pilate surrounded the suppliants with armed soldiers, threatening to kill the Jews if they did not go home. Astonished when they lay down ready to die, Pilate did not carry through with his threat, but yielded and removed the offensive standards. This incident suggests an unsubtle man who without native diplomatic skill was following general Roman procedure known elsewhere and perhaps trying to establish a reputation and precedent at the beginning of his prefecture. It does not suggest a tyrant stubborn to the point of savagery.[58]

#2. Coins with Pagan Cultic Symbols: AD 29–31. Imperial coins for the Syro-Palestinian region were minted in Antioch; there were hiatuses, however, and at times coins were minted in Judea. In particular, during the Roman prefecture there were Judean coins depicting a *simpulum* (i.e., a dipper-shaped ladle used for pouring wine in libation sacrifices) and often a *lituus* (a bent staff for auguring). A. Kindler (IEJ 5 [1956], 54–57) argued that these coins with the pagan cultic symbols were already being produced in the prefecture of Valerius Gratus (15–26), Pilate's predecessor. That early dating was challenged by B. Oestreicher (IEJ 9 [1959], 193–95) and others, and Kindler subsequently changed his views. It is now generally conceded that only under Pontius Pilate were these coins issued. Seemingly there was a set die that could be used in various areas, and thus not necessarily one first engraved in Palestine. On that die the place for the date was often left blank to be filled in locally, whence the controversy about the frequently illegible dating on the Judean issue of these coins. Three dates for the coins are attested: coins of the 16th year of Tiberius (= AD 29) with the *simpulum* depicted on one side and wheat on the other, and a reference to Julia/Livia (thus before her death in that year); coins of the 17th and 18th years of Tiberius (= 30–31) with the *simpulum* and the *lituus*. Were such coins an anti-Jewish gesture designed to force Pilate's subjects to handle representations

---

at the time of Herod the Great's death to remove the golden eagle from over the gate to the Temple. See C. Roth, "An Ordinance against Images in Jerusalem," A.D. 66," HTR 49 (1956) 169–77. The early Jewish *Fasting Scroll,* which frequently contains memories from the 1st cent., reports: "On the 3rd of Kislev the [Roman?] ensigns were removed from the Temple court" (*Megillat Ta'anit* 18). Later church writers note the antireligious aspect of Pilate's having iconic standards brought into the Temple area: Origen, *In Matt.* 22:15, #25 (GCS 40.653–54); Eusebius, *Demonstratio Evangelica* 8.2.122–23 (GCS 23.390); Jerome, *In Matt.* 4.24.15 (CC 77.226).

[57]For sensitivity in Tiberius' time about insults to images of the emperor, see Tacitus, *Annals* 3.36; Seneca, *De Beneficiis* 3.26.

[58]McGing ("Governorship" 62): "This episode shows in Pilate a curious mixture of provocation, indecision, stubbornness and finally weakness."

of pagan cult? Stauffer ("Münzprägung" 507) argues strongly in the affirmative; Lémonon (*Pilate* 112–14) is more cautious. Under Herod the Great, it is worth noting, Tyrian shekels with the head of Heracles were minted at Jerusalem; thus there was a history of uncomfortable coins in Judea. Moreover, the pagan cultic symbols were not peculiar to Judea. Once again, then, Pilate may have been expecting to follow in the territory of Judea general Roman procedure from elsewhere. We have no evidence of riots or disturbances over these coins; but if they did give rise to opposition, Pilate would have been guilty once more of underestimating the sensitivity of the Jews.[59] Those who think of Pilate as an appointee of Sejanus have noted that the coins ceased in the year of Sejanus' death. Others point out that the Antioch mint seems to have taken over a more monopolistic role in coinage beginning with AD 32, suspending Judean-prefecture mintage for the following twenty-three years.[60] The latter suggestion is more plausible.

#3. The Aqueduct Riot (Josephus, *War* 2.9.4; #175–77; *Ant.* 18.3.2; #60–62). Later, in order to build a twenty-to-forty-mile-long aqueduct into Jerusalem,[61] Pilate started spending the wealth kept in the sacred Temple treasury, money known as *qorban* (Gk: *korbōnas*). This was audacious, for even the great Pompey had not stripped that treasury (*War* 1.7.6; #153).[62] Yet the money was destined for social welfare and public works to maintain Jerusalem (JJTJ 16[30]), so that Pilate was not simply being greedy. Crowds (or "tens of thousands" according to *Ant.*) ringed the tribunal of Pilate in Jerusalem and besieged him. (The fact that he was in Jerusalem suggests that the demonstration took place at a feast.) In reaction Pilate sent among the people soldiers dressed as civilians "with orders not to use their swords" (omitted in *Ant.*) but to beat any rioters with cudgels. When Pilate gave the signal,

[59]Thus Y. Meshorer, *Ancient Jewish Coinage* [Dix Hills, NY: Amphora, 1982], 2.180, and "Jewish Numismatics," EJMI 216: "This appears to have been done out of ignorance of Jewish culture rather than deliberately to irritate the Jews."

[60]Bammel ("Syrian" 109) explains why the Syrian mint had not been producing coins for a decade before 32, namely, the absence of a Roman governor. L. Aelius Lamia was appointed governor ca. 20 but prevented by Tiberius from traveling to Syria. Only when he got another job in 32 was a new governor sent.

[61]Smallwood (*The Jews* 162) thinks Pilate built the "high-level" aqueduct from Bir al-Daraj, 4 mi. SW of Bethlehem. A. Mazar, "The Aqueducts of Jerusalem," in *Jerusalem Revealed*, ed. Y. Yadin (Jerusalem: Israel Exploration Society, 1975), 79–84, thinks Pilate was improving an existing system (the "low-level" aqueduct) from Ain Arrub to Etam. It is not possible to date this incident; but among the three incidents from Josephus (#1, #3, #6) that I include here, the *Testimonium Flavianum* about Jesus' death (p. 373 above) is placed after the first two and before the third. Would that indicate that the aqueduct incident (#3) took place before Jesus' death? Smallwood (p. 163) thinks #4 may have taken place in protest over #3.

[62]Pompey, however, entered the Holy of Holies and there is no suggestion that Pilate entered the Temple precincts. McLaren (*Politics* 86) thinks the money may have been given over to Pilate by the priests. Such cooperation would make more intelligible the failure to protest at the moment the money was taken and Pilate's (aggrieved) use of coercion against the later protestors.

however, large numbers of Jews perished, some from blows, some trampled in ensuing confused flight. *Ant.* reports that the soldiers inflicted much harder blows than Pilate had ordered, punishing alike those who were rioting and those who were not.[63] Obviously Pilate had underestimated the brutality of his own soldiers, but on Pilate's part there was no calculated savagery against the innocent. The scene reminds us that granted the personnel at Pilate's disposition,[64] the violence of repressive actions during his prefecture need not have reflected his own wishes.

#4. Bloodied Galilean Sacrifices: ca. AD 28–29 (Luke 13:1–2). During Jesus' ministry (and therefore probably before AD 30) Pilate was reported to have mingled the blood of the Galileans with their sacrifices. The reference to sacrifices locates the event in Jerusalem, probably at a pilgrimage feast that would have brought a number of Galileans up to the Temple.[65] Although the numbers involved may have been too few to get attention from Josephus or Philo, some scholars have wondered whether Luke is not referring to one of the incidents mentioned by the Jewish writers. Certainly this is not Incident #1, for that took place in Caesarea and no bloodletting is mentioned. Incident #3 is a possibility; but that incident did not involve Galileans specifically, or sacrifices. More profitably one may wonder whether this incident narrated by Luke explains a fact mentioned later in the same Gospel: There was enmity between Herod Antipas, the Tetrarch of Galilee, and Pilate (Luke 23:12). But the incident I next mention may also have contributed to that enmity.

#5. The Golden Shields: date uncertain but perhaps after AD 31 (Philo, *Ad*

---

[63]In the *Ant.* account Josephus calls this a *stasis*, the same terminology that appears in Mark's and Luke's description of the trouble in Jerusalem that led to the arrest of Barabbas.

[64]See Smallwood, *The Jews* 146–47. In the 40s (Josephus, *Ant.* 19.9.2; #365) the Roman soldiers in Judea available for the prefect/procurator's use consisted of five cohorts (at least some 2,500–3,000 troops), plus a squadron of cavalry (*Ala I gemina Sebastenorum;* see Acts 23:23–24,32) recruited from Samaria (Sebaste) and Caesarea. (*War* 2.3.4; #52 mentions Sebastenian troops much earlier; on *cohortes equitatae* see R. W. Davies, *Historia* 20 [1971], 751–63.) Plausibly the cohorts included the *Secunda Italica Civium Romanorum* (Acts 10:1; Tacitus, *Annals* 1:8) and the *(Prima) Augusta* (Acts 27:1). Kraeling ("Episode" 268, 278–79) suggests that one cohort was stationed in Jerusalem (see Acts 21:31–32) at the Fortress Antonia overlooking the Temple area, while the other four were in Caesarea. Inevitably our information comes from different time periods, but the overall picture is clear. Since the Jews had been exempted from the military service (Josephus, *Ant.* 14.10.6; #204), these cohorts would have been made up of some troops from Italy and many nonJewish soldiers from the Syro-Palestinian area. (See G. L. Cheesman, *The Auxilia of the Roman Imperial Army* [Oxford: Clarendon, 1914].) Many of the latter may have been antiJewish. Higher-quality imperial legionaries were at the disposition of the legate in Syria (Legions *VI Ferrata, X Fretensis, III Gallica, XII Fulminata*—HJPAJC 1.362), but they would have been sent to intervene in Palestine only at moments of serious difficulty.

[65]Blinzler, "Niedermetzelung" 31, stresses "their sacrifices" as indicating the feast to be Passover, since on the 14th of Nisan the laity had an interest in the killing of the animals to be eaten at their tables after sundown. He would date it to AD 29. Luke implies that Jesus had not been in Jerusalem when it happened, for he had to be told about it.

Gaium 38; #299–305). This is the only one of the six Pilate incidents/items drawn from Philo, and readers are reminded of what was said above about the difficulty of evaluating the letter from Herod Agrippa I to Gaius Caligula in which the incident is narrated. In the Herodian palace at Jerusalem Pilate dedicated shields coated with gold. He did this, we are told, to anger the multitude; yet Philo admits that the shields did not have imagery or other details forbidden to Jews, except that they named the person honored and the one who made the dedication. Lémonon (*Pilate* 212–16) thinks that the reference to dedication and the term for "shield" (*aspis,* with the possible implication of a painted portrait) suggest a religious context. McGing ("Governorship" 64) thinks that the dedication would have referred to the *divine* Augustus, a description abhorrent to monotheistic Jews. In response, a protest about an infringement of Jewish tradition was made to Pilate by a multitude with four Herodian princes at their head. The princes, literally "sons of the king," are not named; but they may have included such sons of Herod the Great as Herod Antipas, Philip of Iturea, and Herod "Philip," father of Salome. When Pilate resisted, they warned him that he was provoking an uprising and even war: "Do not take Tiberius as your pretext for outraging the nation; he does not wish any of our customs to be overthrown." Pilate became afraid lest they send an embassy to the emperor against him, as they threatened. When they did so, the emperor rebuked Pilate and ordered him to take the shields from Jerusalem to Caesarea. We may well suspect that the account presented by Philo/Agrippa is not objective. It is narrated against the background of Gaius Caligula's impudent attempt to set statues of himself in Jerusalem; and the author is implicitly encouraging the Emperor Claudius (who is now reigning when Philo writes) to take the same position as Tiberius did when Pilate set up the shields. If historically Tiberius was really so angry with Pilate as Philo/Agrippa reports, why did he not remove the prefect?

A question has arisen whether this incident of the shields is to be identified with #1 above, narrated by Josephus: the incident of the iconic standards—a blending that appears already in Eusebius (*Demonstratio Evangelica* 8.2.122–23; GCS 23.290). Most scholars (e.g., Doyle, Maier, Smallwood) argue for separate incidents on the grounds that Pilate's action in the Philo story is much less offensive in itself than his action in the Josephus story; indeed, his subjects in the Philo story seem almost to be picking a quarrel with him. Moreover, in the Philo story Pilate seems to have no support in Rome, as both the multitude and the Herodian princes know. On the (unverifiable) assumptions that Pilate was appointed by Sejanus and that Sejanus was antiJewish, some would assign the incident to a period after the fall of Sejanus in AD 31, a date at least five years after the likely date of the incident of the iconic standards narrated by Josephus.[66] D. R. Schwartz ("Josephus and Philo"), however, would identify the two incidents[67] by taking into account the limitations of Josephus and of Philo. Josephus may be inaccurate about the time sequence. Philo may help to clarify that the offensive articles were not busts but shields attached to the tops of the standards, and that the spokesmen for the Jewish multitude were the Herodian princes. As for there being no images on them, however, that could fit in with the apologetic emphasis in Philo/Agrippa that Caligula was doing something never done before when he insisted on setting up images in Jerusalem. Also the claim that there had been an appeal to Tiberius, who had countermanded Pilate, could help Philo/Agrippa to get Claudius to change Caligula's directive.

In terms of NT applicability, if taken at face value, the bullying of Pilate by his Jewish adversaries in the incident of the shields resembles strongly the bullying of Pilate in John's account of the passion, including the threat of appeal to the emperor. As for the Herodian princes, it will be remembered that Luke brings Herod Antipas into dialogue with Pilate in the decision about Jesus.

#6. The Samaritan Prophet: AD 36 (Josephus, *Ant.* 18.4.1–2; #85–89). A false prophet announced to the Samaritans that if they would go to Mount Gerizim with him, he would show them where Moses had deposited the sacred vessels.[68] They gathered at Tirathana (possibly Khirbet ed-Duwara or Dawerta at the foot of Gerizim) with arms; but Pilate, perhaps apprehensive of eschatological fanaticism, blocked their ascent to the mountain with cavalry and heavily armed infantry. There was an encounter; some Samaritans were killed, many imprisoned, and the leaders executed. The Samaritan Council protested to Vitellius, the legate in Syria, who ordered Pilate to leave Judea and return to Rome.[69] By the time he got there Tiberius had died

[66]Maier ("Episode" 114) and Doyle ("Pilate's" 191–92) suggest the date of Passover 32. Philo's comment that Pilate feared a denunciation of all the abuses of his governorship implies that he had been prefect for quite a while. Smallwood (*The Jews* 166) thinks the shields incident probably preceded the crucifixion (AD 33).

[67]Also McLaren (*Power* 82–83), who asks why Pilate would make an effort to introduce the shields when the standards had made so much trouble. Pilate backed down in the instance of the standards; and McLaren contends that would make more sense if the Herodian princes were involved, as reported in the instance of the shields.

[68]For Samaritan belief about hidden vessels, see the discussion between M. F. Collins and A. Zeron in JSJ 3 (1972), 97–116; and 4 (1973), 165–68.

[69]What precisely did Vitellius do to Pilate: remove him permanently or suspend him till the emperor judged? Some would argue that a sitting governor could not be tried: He had to retire or be removed before a trial was possible. On the other hand, McGing ("Governorship" 65) contends: "It certainly cannot be the case that Vitellius on his own authority brought Pilate's governorship to an end; it was the emperor who decided that." See §18, A3a above for the peculiar relationship between the Roman legate in Syria and the Roman prefect in Judea.

(March 17, 37). Thus the dismissal seems to have taken place between Dec. 36 and Feb. 37.[70] What Pilate did in this incident does not seem reckless, and one wonders of Vitellius' promptness in removing him was disinterested responsibility. Tacitus (*Annals* 4.6) reports that (at least in his earlier period) Tiberius did not want the cruelty of governors to upset old, accepted patterns; and Vitellius may have been seeking to impress the emperor by siding with the Samaritans against what they regarded as cruel repression. But other explanations are possible. As Bammel ("Pilatus" 58) points out, although Pilate himself should have had little interest in cultic discoveries on Mount Gerizim, the Jerusalem high priesthood had a long-standing hatred for Samaritan worship there from the time that John Hyrcanus had destroyed the Samaritan holy site on Gerizim in 128 BC.[71] Had Caiaphas put pressure on Pilate to act, and was this why Caiaphas was removed in 36 almost immediately after the dismissal of Pilate?

The Pilate who emerges from these six incidents,[72] when one reads between the lines, is not without very serious faults; but he is certainly a much better governor than the caricature Philo describes by way of summary. How does this Pilate compare to NT portrayals? John, with its customary technique, presents Pilate as a dramatic character-type, namely, the person who on being faced with Jesus tries to avoid having to decide between truth and falsehood. Both John and Luke are stylized in having Pilate three times declare Jesus innocent. With those exceptions, however, the NT descriptions of Pilate with their variations are not patently implausible. (The subsequent canonization of him is!) That does not mean any one of them is historical, but the theory that the Gospels exculpate the Romans by creating a totally fictional, sympathetic Pilate has been overdone. Leaving aside the authentic part of the *Testimonium Flavianum* (p. 373 above) which in Josephus comes after #3 and before #6, let us suppose that Josephus had narrated (in slightly different versions in *War* and *Ant.*) another incident to be added to those above. Namely, on the occasion of a feast the Jerusalem authorities handed over to Pilate for punishment a man who threatened the Temple sanctuary and pretended to be a king. After examining him, Pilate thought him to be inconsequential and the Jewish leaders to be acting for their own reasons. A

---

[70]So Smallwood, "Date"; Lémonon, *Pilate* 241–45. Others think Pilate was dismissed in 35 and it took him almost a year to get to Rome (HJPAJC 1.387–88; Bammell, "Pilatus").

[71]However, a revisionist essay by R. T. Anderson ("The Elusive Samaritan Temple," BA 52 [1991], 104–7) calls into doubt the whole tradition of this sanctuary.

[72]I have tried to read them carefully. Vicent Cernuda ("Condena II") is much more adventurous in his reconstruction from much the same evidence. He speaks of Pilate's antiJewish aggressiveness and traces it to the circumstances of his appointment and his incompetence for the post. The passivity of Caiaphas before Pilate conceals a very effective strategy to stop the governor's abuses. Far from being dismissed about the same time as Pilate, Caiaphas resigned his office and eventually embraced the Christian faith! (See pp. 410–11 above for evidence against that thesis.)

Herodian prince became involved in the case since the man was a Galilean, and Pilate announced that he was not going to execute the fellow. Yet when he saw that a riot was breaking out in Jerusalem because of the announcement, Pilate backed down and acceded to the demands of the Jewish leaders. Who would have been moved to query this hitherto unknown Josephus story on the grounds that it did not coincide with the behavior of Pilate in the other incidents?[73]

C. *The Site of Jesus' Trial: The Praetorium*

The Synoptics all give the impression that Jesus stood before Pilate in public and outdoors. The chief priests, the elders, the scribes, and the people seem to be close by and able to converse with Pilate, reacting to his words to and about Jesus. In Mark 15:8 a crowd can "come up" and join the scene. Only after Jesus has been sentenced and flogged do we hear in Mark 15:16 (= Matt 27:27) that the Roman soldiers "led him away inside the court/ palace [*aulē*] i.e., the praetorium." According to John 18:28ff., however, from the start of the trial Jesus was brought into the praetorium, where he was interrogated by Pilate privately while all "the Jews" remained outside the building—a localization that forced Pilate to keep going back and forth, out of and into the praetorium (18:29,33,38; 19:4,9). Finally (19:13) Pilate "led Jesus outside [from the praetorium] and sat on the judgment seat [*bēma*] in the place called Lithostrotos [Stone Pavement], but in Hebrew Gabbatha." There Pilate addressed "the Jews" and sentenced Jesus. Matt 27:19 is the only other canonical Gospel to mention that Pilate "was sitting on the judgment seat [*bēma*]," seemingly outside, for he addressed the chief priests, the elders, and the crowds. *GPet* 3:7 has the Jewish people, seemingly outside and in a context of mockery and scourging, seat Jesus on a chair of judgment (*kathedra kriseōs*). What and where was this praetorium, which Mark identifies with the court or palace, in the vicinity of which stood the judgment seat?

1. Meaning and Nature of a Praetorium

The term "praetorium" is associated with "praetor," a Roman official who often served as a general leading the army (*prae-itor:* the one who goes

[73]Haufe ("Prozess" 97) judges that the Gospels describe Pilate as a weak creature who acts against his better judgment and that this picture is the very opposite of what is described in Josephus and Philo. It may well be the opposite of the summary description of Pilate in Philo (which many regard as a distortion), but it is not the opposite of Josephus' portrayal, Incident #1 is an example of how Pilate reacted when his judgment on an issue had been forcibly called into question: He backed

before).[74] The place he occupied in the camp was the praetorium. When praetors began to serve as governors of Roman-controlled territories, the praetorium was the governor's residence in the main city, often the palace of the former king whom the Romans had replaced. The public might have access to the governor at the praetorium since it served as an administrative headquarters and not only as a residence; but it was not normally the place where justice was administered. That would more likely take place in a basilica, in the forum, or in a public square or court (often in front of the praetorium). An important element was a raised platform (Lat *tribunal;* Gk *bēma*) to which access-steps would be erected and upon which was placed a seat or bench where the appropriate official sat when he gave judgment.[75] (The technical Latin name for the judgment seat became the *sella curulis;* the Greek *bēma* could be used for the seat as well as the platform.)

Since Caesarea on the coast was the center for Roman administration of Judea, the prefect normally resided there at the praetorium. Acts 23:35 calls it the praetorium of Herod, perhaps because the prefects/procurators had taken over the building where the Herodian king or tetrarch once lived. As we have seen from Josephus and Philo, the prefect/procurator of Judea came up to Jerusalem from Caesarea on certain occasions, often Jewish feasts, probably for combined purposes of administration, supervision, and manifesting Roman presence. Where did he reside on these occasions? In the Pilate incidents just narrated, where in Jerusalem did the people or the Herodian princes come when they wished to see Pilate or to make a protest? Knowledge of this would cast light on the building envisaged by the evangelists when they spoke of the praetorium at Jerusalem (Mark: the "palace"). There is no convincing evidence that there could be two praetoria in the same city. Neither Josephus nor Philo use "praetorium" for a building in Jerusalem, but they do offer information about two buildings of Herodian origin that are plausible candidates for what was meant by "praetorium" in the Gospels.

2. Two Candidates for the Praetorium of the Passion[76]

The first is the Fortress Antonia, a castle of the Hasmonean priest-kings that was refurbished by Herod the Great ca. 37–35 BC and named after Mark

---

down and did what the Jewish populace wanted even though he had threatened to do the opposite. That is almost a description of what he did in the case of Jesus.

[74]Two articles by Benoit ("Antonia" and "Praetorium") are very helpful in clarifying the notion of a praetorium.

[75]Of course, the platform could be used for other purposes as well. Acts 12:21 describes Herod Agrippa I taking his seat on the *bēma* to deliver an oration.

[76]A third candidate is proposed by early Christian tradition. (We shall see that *medieval* tradition strongly favors the Fortress Antonia.) In a series of articles (§30, Part 2) Bagatti, Pixner, and Riesner

Antony.[77] It stood on the eastern hill of Jerusalem, on a high rock formation dominating the NW corner of the Temple area, and seems to have been an intrinsic part of the northern defenses, serving as the terminus of the Second Wall (Josephus, *War* 5.4.2; #146), the wall that was the boundary of the city in Jesus' time. The refurbishing by Herod was done lavishly at great expense, so that the Antonia was comparable to a royal dwelling (*War* 1.21.1; #401; 5.5.8; #238–46); and for a while it served as one of Herod's dwelling places. Yet Josephus does not call it an *aulē*, "palace," but a *pyrgos*, "tower," and *phrourion*, "fortress." Its primary importance in Roman times was as quarters for a Roman cohort, giving the soldiers access to the Temple area at festivals: "For if the Temple was situated as a fortress over the city, Antonia dominated the Temple; and those who were in that post dominated all three" (*War* 5.5.8; #244–45). The Antonia figured prominently in the riots under the procurator Florus (*War* 2.15.5–6; 16.5; #328,330,403–4). Kept there was the robe which the high priest wore when he offered sacrifice (*Ant.* 15.11.4; #403).

The second is "the Palace" [aulē] *of the king'* (*War* 5.4.4; #176–83), on the western hill of the city—another fortress dwelling of Herod the Great, but built over Hasmonean ruins on the highest spot within the walls.[78] It too was part of the northern defenses, the fortress (*phrourion*) of the upper city, even as the Antonia was the fortress of the Temple (*War* 5.5.8; #245). Its exterior included three immense towers built by Herod and named after friends and family (Hippicus, Phasael, Mariamme; *War* 5.4.3–4; #161–75). Josephus (*War* 1.21.1; #402; *Ant.* 15.9.3; #318) says that in luxury and extravagance it was indescribable; accordingly, after 23 BC this larger edifice seems to have become the main Herodian residence. The summary descrip-

---

point out that the earliest traceable Christian tradition (4th cent.) claimed to preserve a carefully studied memory of the place where Jesus was condemned and located it at the traditional site of the old Hasmonean (later Herodian) palace on the lower slope of the western hill facing the Temple, marked by the church of St. Sophia, destroyed in 614. Yet this is often thought to be the site of the high priest's palace where Jesus had been tried/interrogated by the Jewish authorities (§18, C1). When tradition localized the house of Caiaphas at another spot (farther up the hill, to the SW), did the memory of a trial having taken place here get shifted to the Romans? In any case, it is dubious that Pilate would reside here when the other two candidates offered more commodious accommodations. Certainly Josephus gave much more attention to the other two.

[77]The naming helps to date the completion; obviously it was not thus dedicated after Antony was defeated at Actium in 31 BC. The earlier name was Baris (*War* 1.3.3; #75; *Ant.* 15.11.4; #403), representing Hebrew *bîrâ*, "fortified place." Hyrcanus I is thought to have built it ca. 134 BC as a fort-residence. In Maccabean times a citadel (Gk *akra*) was built by the Syrian Seleucid king Antiochus IV Epiphanes "in the city of David with a great strong wall and strong towers" (I Macc 1:33)—a citadel so strong that only the third Maccabee brother, Simon, was finally able to conquer it in 141 BC (13:49–52). The exact site of the citadel has been disputed. Was it the forerunner of Baris and Antonia?

[78]For the excavation of this Herodian Palace area in the late 1960s, see R. Amiran and A. Eitan, *IEJ* 20 (1970), 9–17.

tion in *Ant.* 15.8.5; #292 catches the difference between the two buildings we have been discussing: "The city had been made safe for him [Herod] by the Palace in which he lived, and the Temple made safe by the strong fortress called Antonia which had been built by him."

Although there were Roman soldiers in both the Fortress Antonia and the Herodian Palace, Benoit ("Praetorium" 174) is probably correct in judging it incredible that when the prefect/procurator came to the city, he would choose the Antonia as a dwelling place, leaving the tribune who headed the Jerusalem cohort the superior quarters in the Palace. On pp. 175–76 Benoit argues that the descriptions in Josephus and Philo fit best the Palace as the residency of the prefect/procurator, in comparison to the Antonia. Of the many passages the clearest for NT comparison in my judgment is Josephus' description of the last procurator (AD 64–66) in *War* 2.14.8; #301: "Florus lodged [*aulizein*] at the royal residence and on the following day had a tribunal [*bēma*] placed in front and took his seat. The chief priests, the most powerful and best-known citizens, then came forward before the *bēma*." Reyero, however, doubts that the Jewish texts are probative as to the identity of the residence.[79] He admits that Florus was at the Palace, but contends that this was because Florus was blocked by the people from going to the Antonia as he had intended (*War* 2.15.5; #328–29). However, that disturbance occurred later; and he wanted to go to the Antonia as part of his military strategy, not because he desired to reside there.

What do two crucial Pilate incidents tell us about the customs of that prefect when he was in Jerusalem? In #3 above (Aqueduct) we are told that "the populace surrounded the tribunal [*to bēma*] of Pilate, who was then on a visit to Jerusalem" (*War* 2.9.4; #175). There Josephus uses the same language that he would shortly use of Florus in the passage just quoted above;[80] and so he may well be thinking of the Herodian Palace as Pilate's dwelling place and tribunal. In #5 Pilate dedicated in Herod's "royal residence" (*basileia*) some golden shields (Philo, *Ad Gaium* 38; #299). That designation could be used for the Antonia (Josephus, *War* 1.21.1; #401), even though it seems more normal for the Herodian Palace. Overall, a reasonable estimate is that the Jewish descriptions favor the Herodian Palace on the western hill as the dwelling place of Pilate and the other prefects/procurators.

As for the NT, in the Barabbas scene Mark 15:8 describes the crowd in Jerusalem as "coming up" (*anabainein*) to make a request to Pilate about

[79]For instance, Benoit tries to show from *War* 2.3.1–4; #39–54 that the Roman official Sabinus was in the Palace, while Reyero, "Textos" 528–29, argues that Sabinus was not a governing procurator but a quaestor or treasurer who would collect taxes at the Palace.

[80]Yet Reyero, "Textos" 530–31, (over)emphasizes that the article is used with *bēma* in the Pilate scene but not in the Florus scene.

releasing a prisoner. True, standard biblical language has pilgrims going up or coming up to Jerusalem, which was pictured as a mountain. Yet if one wishes to press the Marcan verb as a geographical description of motion within the city, it would fit the "Hebrew" name Gabbatha[81] that John 19:13 gives to the place where Pilate passed sentence on Jesus. By its geographical location and architecture the Palace had the highest altitude of any official building in Jerusalem. Mark 15:16 describes the praetorium as the *aulē*, a term used by Josephus of the Herodian Palace but not of the Antonia. Matt 27:19 writes of Pilate seated on *to bēma*, while John 19:13 uses the same term without the article; both evangelists imagine it as set up outside the praetorium. The quotation given above from Josephus' *War* describing Florus at the Palace has the *bēma* located in exactly the same position relative to the Herodian Palace. Mark 15:15 and Matt 27:26 have Jesus flogged publicly outside the praetorium and then delivered to be crucified. In the Florus scene just mentioned, a few lines later (*War* 2.14.9; #306—therefore, presumably, in the same setting outside the Palace) citizens are brought before the procurator, scourged, and crucified. John 19:13 pictures a *Lithostrōtos*, "Stone Pavement," outside the praetorium. Actually the name tells us only that the stones were notable enough to catch the eye and imagination. Were they particularly large, or cut and designed with care, or laid out in an uncommonly attractive arrangement, or were they especially valuable?[82] Josephus does not mention stones in reference to the Antonia, but a notable variety of precious stone (*lithos*) is mentioned in reference to the Palace (*War* 5.4.4; #178). Acts 21:27–32 shows the Roman tribune with the soldiers of the cohort hurrying to prevent the beating of Paul, who had got into trouble in the Temple area; Paul was led into the barracks (*parembolē*: 21:34–37; 22:24; 23:10,16). Surely that account envisions the Antonia, which stood adjacent to the Temple court; but on this occasion the prefect was at Caesarea on the coast (23:32–33), not at Jerusalem, and so the account does not tell us where the prefect resided when in the holy city. Overall, then, the limited NT evidence favors the Herodian Palace on the western hill as the temporary Jerusalem praetorium of Pilate during the Passover when he encountered Jesus. Indeed, the unintentional agreements between the scenes in the Gospels and those in Josephus and Philo enhance the plausibility of the NT setting of the trial.

[81]The "Hebrew" (Aramaic) *Gabbatha* is not a translation of *Lithostrōtos*. It means a high place or hill, and may be more applicable to the Palace than to the Antonia.

[82]Steele ("Pavement") imagines a movable pavement (laid down and picked up again as the praetor or Roman official came and went) composed of little colored cubes or tesserae arranged to depict pagan gods. He does not offer real proof for this type of stone pavement as judicial equipment for Roman governors; and the proposed irony that Jesus, when he was judged, was standing on a portrait of Jupiter is fanciful.

Before moving on, however, we may ask why the Fortress Antonia has been so often identified as the praetorium.[83] Two major factors have been influential. First, since the 12th cent., Christian tradition has honored the general area of the Antonia as the scene of Jesus' trial. Even today the "Way of the Cross" proceeds station by station westward from the Antonia to the Church of the Holy Sepulchre (the traditional site of Calvary). One should not divorce this tradition, however, from the sites that passed into Christian hands and thus reinforced the tradition. Second, in 1870 in the Antonia area (in what is now the basement of the Sisters of Sion convent, adjacent to the *"Ecce Homo"* arch) a pavement of massive stone slabs was discovered. The famous Jerusalem archaeologist L.-H. Vincent identified this as the *Lithostrōtos* or "Stone Pavement" of John 19:13. The dissertation of Aline de Sion in the mid-1950s marshaled the evidence impressively, including the presence of graffiti of the "king game" that fitted the mockery of Jesus as king which Mark 15:16–20 and Matt 27:27–31 place in the praetorium (p. 875 below). More recent archaeology, however (Benoit, "Antonia"), indicates that the pavement was probably part of a forum related to a triumphal arch at the eastern entry-gate to Aelia Capitolina, the Roman city built on the site of Jerusalem after the Second Jewish Revolt (AD 132–35). The pavement, then, would not have existed in Jesus' lifetime. If this archaeological conclusion holds up, the identification of the Palace as the praetorium becomes almost certain, since the most impressive argument for the Antonia will have disappeared.

D. *The Type of Roman Trial*

In §18, D3 above we saw that the traditional explanation of why Jesus was brought to Pilate is still the most likely, namely, that except for some agreed-upon, automatically punishable crimes, the execution of capital punishment was under the control of the Roman prefect/procurator, not of the Sanhedrin authorities. Yet that explanation does not tell us what type of Roman legal procedure was followed in interrogating and sentencing Jesus. A decision on this issue must be based on the combination of information: general information about Roman trials in similar circumstances and the special NT

---

[83]Those who have favored Antonia include Albright, Aline de Sion, Flusser, Lagrange, Lattey, Meistermann, Olmstead, Revuelta Sañudo, Ricciotti, J. Starcky (DBSup 5.398–405), Vincent, and Vosté. Those who have favored the Palace as the site include Abel, Belser, Benoit, Billerbeck, Blinzler, Boismard, Bornkamm, Dalman, Dibelius, Edersheim, Kastner, Kopp, Kraeling, Kreyenbühl, Lémonon, Lohse, Rostovtzeff, Schürer, van Bebber, and Vanel. To harmonize John with Mark 15:16, Reicke suggests that Jesus was sentenced in the Antonia (John) and then taken to the praetorium (Mark), which was Herod's Palace.

information about Pilate's dealings with Jesus. We shall begin with remarks about the legal quality of the Gospel evidence and then turn to the relationship between the Roman and Jewish trials and to the legality of certain features in the Roman trial.

1. The Legal Quality of the Gospel Record of the Trial

From the outset, we must be cautious about the NT reports. What the Gospels narrate has the goal of dramatizing the *religious* meaning of the condemnation of Jesus. Differences among the Gospel accounts are often representative of diverse theological outlooks. For instance, while Jesus is virtually silent in the Synoptic accounts of the Roman trial, in John Jesus speaks at some length to Pilate.[84] To explain this difference one cannot appeal simply to ampler Johannine historical detail. What the Johannine Jesus says to Pilate reflects an issue that the Christians of John's time faced in relation to Rome, viz., Were they advocating a dangerous, separatist political kingdom? The answer is no: Jesus' kingdom is not of this world and his followers did not fight in his defense. The conversation also reflects issues stemming from John's theology: Jesus has come into the world to testify to the truth, and Pilate must face this judgment as he stands before the truth. Luke may have had independent tradition supporting his inclusion of Herod Antipas in the Roman trial of Jesus, but his main interest may have been to establish a parallel between this scene aligning the prefect Pilate and Herod as judges of Jesus and the scene in Acts 25–26 aligning the procurator Festus and the Herodian Agrippa II as judges of Paul. Such heavy religious coloring means that the few trial features that are recounted in the Gospels cast little light on the historical motives of those involved.[85]

More important, as might be expected from the character and goal of the Gospel accounts, practically no legal details of Pilate's trial of Jesus are in fact reported. To fit that trial into the pattern of Roman judicial procedures attested elsewhere jurists would want documents from the trial or at least an eyewitness report. Nothing remotely resembling a court record of Jesus' trial has survived or can be reconstructed from the Gospel narratives. Indeed we have no reason to think that the evangelists drew on such a record. Even Luke, who in Acts 21–25 gives considerable detail about the trial of Paul, betrays no detailed knowledge about the trial of Jesus. Nor do the evangelists

---

[84]Note that in the Synoptics the interrogation of Jesus is public and outside; yet the Synoptic account is briefer than John's account, where the interrogation is inside and therefore private.

[85]Is Jesus' silence before Pilate in the Synoptics a historical fact, namely, he answered the legitimate question of the governor about his identity as a king but was contemptuously silent about the false charges that the Sanhedrin members urged on Pilate? Or is it a theological motif, e.g., Isa 53:7: "He opened not his mouth"? Or is it both historical and theological?

claim that anyone sympathetic to Jesus was present at the Roman trial to supply an eyewitness account. Whatever historical information they had about the trial would have ultimately been derived from hearsay, from explanations offered post factum by the Roman and Jewish authorities, and from shrewd guesses as to likelihood. As with the Jewish trial of Jesus (#18E above), so here also given the involvement of soldiers, servants, and opponents, it is unbelievable that some word about the contents would not have circulated. At the public execution of Jesus the charge "the King of the Jews" would have been published, and that charge was surely related to the trial that had preceded. Accordingly, despite the absence of court records, no extreme skepticism about the basic issue of the Roman trial is warranted; and the evangelists were in a position to narrate truthfully to their readers the innocence of Jesus before his Roman judge.

Failing to recognize the limited reporting of legalities imposed by the Gospel genre, Rosadi (*Trial* 293–94) recites procedural features that should have been observed (e.g., oaths, a written account of the transgression, witnesses, speeches for the defense) and concludes that this was no legal trial in which there was a miscarriage of justice but judicial murder. Ancient church writers took a different but equally misleading route. Although they recognized that Gospels did not supply a court record, they imagined that one should have existed.[86] This imagining was influenced by their familiarity with standard Roman legal processes of their own times and eventually with the *Acts of the Martyrs* (which were more attentive to Roman legalities than were the evangelists). Church writers thought that Pilate had written a record of the proceedings to Rome. Justin (*Apology* 1.35) stated: "And you can learn these things [the happenings of the crucifixion] from the Acts done by Pontius Pilate" (also 1.48). Justin, however, also thought the Roman archives contained the registry records from the census of Quirinius (*Apology* 1.34)! No major Christian writer claims himself to have seen the document in the Roman archives or to have copied it.[87] Related to that was the creation of the apocryphal *Acts of Pilate,* favorable to the prefect, preserved in several Greek versions. This work was known already by Epiphanius (*Panarion* 50.1.5; GCS 31.245). (In Latin mss. after the 10th cent., under the title of

---

[86]Blinzler, *Trial* 22, argues that a Roman governor did not have to send a report to Rome on all capital cases. We must remember that Jesus was not a Roman citizen, so that under the law he did not possess rights. He was rather an object of the law (see Overstreet, "Roman Law" 326, 330).

[87]See discussion by Steinwenter, "Processo" 472–76; Blinzler, *Trial* 22–23. R. Eisler in his imaginative *Messiah Jesus* (n. 8 above), 15–16, maintained that there really was in the Roman archives an Acts of Pilate, but that the archetype disappeared during the reign of Maximinus Daia in 311 to prevent it from being further used against the church. (Eusebius [EH 9.5.1] does mention a blasphemous *Acts of Pilate* in that context, but regards it as a forgery.) All this is most implausible. If the Roman archives possessed anything pertinent to the death of Jesus, it was a Christian apologetic composition of the sort described in the text above.

the *Gospel of Nicodemus,* the *Acts* was combined with a work on Christ's descent into hell.) Supposedly it contains the testimony of Nicodemus preserved in Hebrew and found by Ananias, a converted Roman guard.[88] Clearly it is an imaginative expansion of the Gospel tradition: Miracles occur during the trial as the imperial images on the Roman standards do homage to Jesus, and Pilate gains much more information about Jesus' life. Also beginning in the 2d cent. there appeared spurious letters of Pilate to Tiberius or Claudius. Tertullian affirmed: "Pilate, now in fact a Christian in his own conscience, sent word of all these things pertinent to Christ to the then-reigning Caesar, Tiberius."[89] A letter of Pilate to Claudius, found in the late *Acts of Peter and Paul* (40), is translated in JANT 146. None of this has value for the historical trial.

Acknowledging, then, the confines imposed by the evidence, let us proceed with limited observations about the legal status of the Roman trial of Jesus. The quest is not without drama, for at this moment Jesus was standing before a representative of the greatest legal system history had known.

2. Relation of the Roman Trial to the Jewish Trial/Interrogation

As for the style of the Roman trial of Jesus, to what extent was it dependent on the preceding Jewish trial or interrogation?[90] If in both Jewish and Roman estimation that Jewish action constituted an acknowledged investigation of Jesus, Pilate should have proceeded to examine him on the basis of what the Jewish authorities reported from their questioning. Only in Luke and then only partially[91] is there a specific verbal echo in the Roman trial of

[88]JANT 94–146. Lampe ("Trial") argues that it is quite late, probably spawned by Tertullian's report. Lémonon (*Pilate* 262) dates it to ca. 310–20. Others opt for an earlier date, e.g., Mommsen (against whom Lampe argues) would have it composed from the four Gospels and noncanonical material, without any real knowledge of Roman law. Erhardt ("Pontius" 446) thinks it stems from a 1st-cent. Ebionite midrash on Dan 13:46 and Ps 2:1. HSNTA 1.444–49 (rev. ed. 1.501–5) also opts for early (2d-cent.?) origins.

[89]*Apology* 21.24; CC 1.127 (also 5.2; CC 1.94–95). This is commented on in EH 2.2. T. D. Barnes, JRS 58 (1968), 32–33, rejects the historicity of Tertullian's claim. For later Pilate correspondence with Tiberius (and Herod), see JANT 153–57. P. Winter, "A Letter from Pontius Pilate," NovT 7 (1964–65), 37–43, reports a 4th-cent. composition found at Liverpool. Also see §32, n. 17 and §35, n. 61 below for the 13th-cent. text of the sentence pronounced by Pilate as reported on a copper tablet.

[90]Blinzler, "Entscheid," treats this in detail. Steinwenter ("Processo" 484) points out that later, under Constantine, whenever in the provinces the local authorities were permitted to make the accusation (Justinian, *Code* 12.22.1), the presiding official had to be all the more vigilant in testing what was charged.

[91]In Luke 23:2, the third charge against Jesus presented by the Jewish multitude to Pilate is: "Saying that he is Messiah king," and this may echo Luke 22:67, where the elders, the chief priests, and the scribes have challenged Jesus: "If you are the Messiah, say to us." Yet Jesus answered them ambiguously ("If I shall say to you, you will never believe"); and the Lucan Pilate completely ignores this reference to the Messiah when he asks, "Are you the King of the Jews?" (23:3). Except for Luke

the interrogation by the Jewish authorities; in no Gospel was the principal issue of Pilate's concern, "the King of the Jews," mentioned as such in the Jewish questioning of Jesus. Thus to our general lack of information about the style of Roman *cognitio* in the provinces we must add the peculiarity of the Gospel separation of issues in the Jewish and Roman interrogations. Specific issues will be treated below in the commentary on individual episodes, and only more general remarks will be made here.

In 1674 J. Steller proposed that Pilate was simply carrying out the Jewish judgment on Jesus; and a surprising number of scholars and jurists (including Bammel, Doerr, Lippert, J. Merkel, Mommsen, Siefert, and von Mayr) have agreed that the Roman trial was little more than a confirmation of the Jewish trial—an *exsequatur,* "Let it be carried out."[92] In discussing this issue, however, we first note that only in Mark/Matt (and not in Luke or John) was there an immediately preceding Jewish trial *with an explicit death sentence* that Pilate might be confirming. Beyond the fact that the two trials (Jewish and Roman) have different subject matter as mentioned in the previous paragraph, Pilate's offer of Barabbas as an alternative to Jesus (all four Gospels) and his sending to Herod for a decision (Luke; cf. *GPet*) would give the impression of independent decision-making. Matt and John have Pilate seated on the judgment seat as he condemns Jesus, as if he were passing his own sentence. Those who support the confirmation or *exsequatur* approach to the Roman trial argue that otherwise the whole Jewish investigation becomes pointless and irrelevant. From the somewhat arrogant Roman point of view, however, is not a judgment of irrelevancy toward the preceding Jewish trial or investigation reconcilable with both the Gospel accounts and our other information about Roman procedures with Jews? All the evangelists show Pilate as ignoring to some degree the urging of the Jewish authorities, as if he did not trust them. In John 18:30–31 his refusal to accept a Jewish determination of guilt is explicit. Acts (18:12–16; 23:26–29) shows Roman officials declining to judge those handed over to them by Jews as

---

neither the motifs of the destruction of the sanctuary and the Messiah Son of God (Mark/Matt Jewish trial) nor the motifs of the disciples and teaching (Johannine Annas interrogation) are repeated in the Pilate trials of those Gospels. Blinzler (*Trial* 170) argues without proof that the Jewish authorities (Mark/Matt) tried unsuccessfully to find material to present to Pilate, viz., the destruction of the Temple sanctuary would have been a plausible issue, but the witnesses did not agree. Finally they derived political possibilities from the religious issue of the Messiah.

[92]Some speak of what Pilate did as a *recognitio causae:* not an independent investigation but an inquiry to see if the accusation in the previous trial was justified and a determination of the details of the penalty. For practical purposes the imaginative theory of James (*Trial* 1.226–29) might be considered a variant of this approach: Fearing the unification of the Jewish people by a great leader, Pilate conspired against Jesus by having the real legal process taken care of by the Sanhedrin. He admitted to his own hearing of Jesus only those hostile to the Nazarene (1.250) and introduced Barabbas to distract the people from Jesus and force a choice against him (1.256).

criminal offenders against Jewish religious law—the Roman officials would be willing to deal with those cases only if something they considered a real crime were involved. That did not mean that such a crime could have no religious aspect, but it had to include an element that Romans would consider legally culpable. Josephus (*Ant.* 20.5.4; #115–17) shows us the procurator Cumanus (AD 48–52) executing a soldier for tearing up publicly a copy of the Law of Moses, blaspheming against it. This was not because Cumanus believed in that Law but because the soldier had committed a public outrage. A more ambiguous case was tried by the procurator Albinus (AD 62–64) when the magistrates of Jerusalem brought to him Jesus son of Ananias, who had cried out against Jerusalem and the Temple. Albinus had him scourged but let him go as a religious maniac (*War* 6.5.3; #300–9). Thus even when the Jews or their leaders had come to a decision about a prisoner, Roman independence was preserved. From these analogies a Roman trial of Jesus conducted independently of a preceding Jewish trial/interrogation and keeping open the possibility of release or condemnation is not implausible. There is nothing in the Gospels to suggest a mere confirmation of the Jewish sentence.

If we judge with the scholarly majority that Pilate was remembered as conducting an independent trial of Jesus, there remain problems. A mere confirmation of the Jewish proceedings might explain why the trial described in Mark/Matt is so brief with no narrated accusation, why an ambiguous answer to the basic question is all the evidence presented, and why Pilate consents to the cries for crucifixion by the crowds. Are these factors explicable as part of a regular Roman trial? Some commentators have answered in the negative, maintaining that the Pilate of the Gospels acts in a totally arbitrary manner, ignoring the juridical elements essential to legality. Such an illegal procedure might be consonant with the picture of Pilate as a brutal tyrant capable of major crimes against the people he was governing; but that picture has not been confirmed in the analysis given above of the six incidents concerning Pilate known to us from early sources. If a priori one is not willing to assume that Pilate as a Roman prefect would be indifferent to legalities,[93] another, more plausible course is to contend that since Jesus was not a Roman citizen, the trial was conducted *extra ordinem*.[94] This means that the full specifications of the ordinary law of Rome did not need

---

[93]E. Bickermann ("Utilitas"), a Jewish scholar, studied the Gospel accounts of the Roman trial and found them legally plausible except for the Barabbas episode, which was a "coup de théâtre" (p. 190). Steinwenter ("Processo" 481) argues that even the Barabbas incident was not illegal.

[94]Mommsen (*Römisches* 193–94) points out that the legal context at the end of the Roman republic and the beginning of the empire (reigns of Augustus and Tiberius) contributed to treating cases *extra ordinem*, especially in a new imperial province like Judea where most were not Roman citizens.

to be observed since Pilate had the right to conduct a more simple *cognitio* or investigation. As Jones (*Studies* 85) stresses, the *ordo* was cumbersome and the *cognitio* was expeditious. The governor could seek out the facts concerning Jesus: why the Jewish leaders wanted this man put to death; whether there was legal matter for Roman punishment; and what an appropriate punishment might be. Using his delegated imperial authority, the prefect of Judea would have few limitations placed upon him in this inquiry.[95] He could draw information from local authority without requiring the kind of proof demanded by the ordinary law.

Josephus narrates many judicial actions by Roman prefects/procurators involving capital punishment, and none of them have much more detail than the Gospel accounts of the trial of Jesus. I am not referring to Josephus' narratives wherein armed terrorists and insurrectionaries were seized and summarily executed with their followers.[96] The treatment of Jesus in the Gospels has little in common with such executions, and that lack of resemblance constitutes proof that Jesus was not looked upon as a violent revolutionary (see A2 above). I think rather of instances in Josephus when the prefect/procurator had to reach a decision about guilt or punishment in a case that came before him.[97] The descriptions in these cases are quite summary, missing many of the detailed legalities that the Gospels also neglect. Part of this brevity may flow from narrative style in both Josephus and the Gospels, but part of it may also reflect the abbreviated procedures of the *cognitio*. In any case, against such a background, the Gospel accounts of the prefect's treatment of Jesus do not seem unusually truncated. But let us now turn to the details of the Roman trial of Jesus to examine legalities.

3. Legal Status of Selected Features in the Roman Trial of Jesus

We begin with some minor features. It is a reflection of Gospel selectivity that Pilate seems to be the only Roman dealing with Jesus throughout the trial, until he hands him over to Roman soldiers at the end after sentencing. Although a Roman judge did function in a highly individual way, in a formal trial, as Blinzler (*Trial* 170–71) points out, there would normally have been *assessores* (junior barristers) and *comites* (attendants) present for consultation. Even if one were to argue that the trial of Jesus was not a major trial, the parallel trial of Paul (a Roman citizen, to be sure) shows his judge, the procurator Festus, consulting with his council before passing judgment

---

[95]Certainly such a legal, administrative procedure would not have been limited by the supervision of the legate of Syria.

[96]*Ant.* 18.4.1; #87; 20.5.1; #98; 20.8.5–7; #161,171,177; 20.9.2; #204.

[97]*Ant.* 18.3.1; #57–59; 20.5.2; #102; 20.5.4; #117; 20.6.2; #127–32.

(Acts 25:12). On the analogy of the edicts of Augustus for Cyrene (§18, D1 above), the prefect in capital cases could make his own *cognitio* (investigation) or assign others to do so. Nothing in either Josephus or the NT suggests that in the province of Judea, the prefect needed the vote of a jury. A final figure who presumably would have been at hand is a translator (Cicero, *In Verrem* 2.3.37; #84; Josephus *War* 5.9.2; #361). The failure of the Gospel accounts to mention technicalities invalidates the supposition of J. A. Fitzmyer (BARev 18 [5; 1992], 60–61) that Jesus and Pilate spoke to each other in Greek. The evangelists offer no way at all of judging what language was used for the interrogation and answers.

(a) The Charge against Jesus and the Crime It Represented. Mark probably shows us the earliest preserved stage of the Christian narrative of the judicial procedures that brought Jesus before Pilate. Though no explicit presentation of the charge is recounted, Pilate is aware of the principal issue, just as without formal presentation the prefect/procurator knows the charge in many of the Josephus accounts. (Matt follows Mark closely in this picture.) More developed stages of the narrative are found in Luke 23:2 with its formal presentation of charges (drawn from ministry issues), and in John 18:29–32, which dramatizes the absence of a formal presentation in order to have "the Jews" unconsciously fulfill the word of Jesus about the kind of death he was going to die. These developments are secondary for our purposes here. The Mark/Matt picture is consonant with the realization that at times of pressure (a busy feast, recent riots) the Roman procedure could be summary, begun with the equivalent of a police report (*elogium*) derived from local magistrates.[98]

The charge against Jesus in the trial is that he claimed to be King of the Jews. Under Roman law that might seem to be sedition, and the later evidence of DJ 48.8.3,4 is sometimes invoked: Those who are authors of sedition or move the people to upheaval are liable to crucifixion. More specifically, most scholars assume that a claim to be a king would be an offense against the *Lex Iulia de maiestate,* which bore a death penalty.[99] The situation is complicated, however. First, let me explain this Roman law and then discuss whether it was applied to Jesus. (In what follows it is important to remember that most of our evidence pertains to Roman citizens and Italy.)

---

[98]Thus Bickermann, "Utilitas" 194–96. On p. 198 he castigates as lacking in sense the objection of critics that the Marcan Pilate could not have known enough about Jesus to ask questions since he has not received a list of charges. Mark is simply not spelling out the details of how Pilate was informed. I am dubious, however, of Bickermann's thesis that Jesus was an officially wanted fugitive at the time of his arrest (see pp. 289–90 above).

[99]Innes (*Trial* 85) speaks of *crimen laesae aut imminutae maiestatis* or *crimen adversus maiestatem populi Romani*. Some like Kennard ("Jewish" 51) think that in itself the claim to be the Messiah would have been an offense against the *maiestas* of the empire.

Experts in Roman law are not in agreement about the relationship between *perduellio* and the various *leges de maiestate,* or about the punishments attached to these by statute.[100] In part, the difficulty arises from a changing legal situation, especially in this transitional period from republic to empire. A term stemming from early times, *perduellio* comprised any malicious offense against the Roman people and could be punished by a range of penalties from death to fines. In 100 BC Saturninus passed his *Lex Appuleia de maiestate,* which would punish by death or voluntary exile incompetent magistrates for culpable negligence. Sulla combined both *perduellio* and *Lex Appuleia* offenses in his new *Lex Cornelia de maiestate,* expanding the applicability, e.g., to private war, to tampering with the loyalty of the troops, to leaving a province without permission. Death was still the penalty, even though never applied to citizens, who were allowed to go into exile and forbidden to return to Italy (*interdictio aquae et ignis*). The wide-ranging concept of offenses *de maiestate* (lese majesty)[101] now virtually replaced *perduellio* (which became archaic and obsolescent). With the initiation of the empire the *princeps* or ruler, as the holder of the *imperium* and the head of the state religion, symbolized the majesty of Rome; consequently the lese majesty laws began to cover insults to him. We are not certain what was covered by the *Lex de maiestate* of Julius Caesar, but now for citizens punishment by exile became compulsory. The major enlargement of *maiestas* came under Augustus with the famous *Lex Iulia de maiestate* (an expansion of Julius Caesar's law[102]). While the exact law has not been preserved, it covered slander of the emperor and his family. Under Augustus and especially under Tiberius (who was singularly sensitive about treason) banishment was made harsher, and summary execution became more common.[103] Tacitus comments (*Annals* 2.50): "The *Lex maiestatis* was growing

[100]C. W. Chilton ("Roman") lays out the problems in great detail. R. S. Rogers ("Treason"), who had earlier (1935) written *Criminal Trials and Criminal Legislation under Tiberius,* has responded in partial disagreement. Basically they agree that *perduellio* became obsolete even though the term continued to appear in later (Ulpian) writing. Although one must be careful about assuming that Ulpian's statements in the 3d cent. are applicable to the 1st cent., law tends to be extremely conservative, as Rogers observes ("Treason" 90).

[101]Cicero (*De inventione* 2.17; #53) writes: "Diminishing *maiestas* consists of taking away something from the dignity or the fullness or the power of the people or from those to whom the people have given power." Several centuries later Ulpian (DJ 48.4.1.1) writes: "The crime of *maiestas* is that which is committed against the Roman people or their safety." For him treason is closest to sacrilege.

[102]Differences between the law of Augustus and the law of Julius are a point of dispute between Chilton and Rogers, with the former contending that the legal penalty remained the same, and Rogers insisting that numerous death sentences had been imposed under Augustus. For Chilton both Augustus and Tiberius were arbitrary in the administration of this law, whereas Rogers insists that development in the law meant the applications were legal.

[103]Chilton ("Roman" 76): "From the very beginning of Tiberius' reign the death penalty was frequently exacted," especially for plotting against the emperor. See also Klostermann, "Majestäts-prozesse" 75–79.

stronger." In the judgment of that Roman historian, Tiberius was abusive in appealing to it (*Annals* 3.38; also Suetonius, *Tiberius* 58).

Let us turn now to applicability to Jesus. There seems little doubt that if Jesus was setting himself up as a rival king in a Roman province, this could constitute lese majesty against the emperor and/or the Roman people.[104] But in only one narrative (John 19:12) is that connection ever made. Is this Johannine passage preserving historical detail; or in retrospect is John working out the implications of the tradition (centered on "Are you the King of the Jews?"), even as he alone works out an explanation of why, having condemned Jesus, the chief priests brought him to Pilate? The narratives in Josephus of the actions of the Roman prefects against various Jewish figures do not spell out the legal basis for condemnation. These people are troublemakers or out of order, and the prefect deals with them. A general principle of maintaining order in a subject province rather than a specific law may have governed the treatment of a noncitizen such as Jesus. In retrospect, of course, one can find a relationship between that general principle and Roman laws against treason; but it would be wrong to imagine that the prefect consulted law books every time he had to deal with a provincial accused of a crime.

(b) The Responses of Jesus. Given that very serious caution, let us look at the questioning of Jesus in the Mark/Matt account of the trial, pointing out parallels to Roman law where they exist. Once we have recognized that we are not dealing with a court record or precise history, there is nothing implausible in the initial question which, even if it has dramatic import, forthrightly raises the basic issue: "Are you the King of the Jews?" Found in all four Gospels, this question may be the oldest component in Christian tradition about the Roman trial of Jesus. True, some would explain it as a back-formation from the charge on the cross (Mark 15:26); but that is not a major qualification, since the charge published at the execution would have been the charge involved in the questioning and condemnation. The follow-up question in Mark 15:4 is: "Do you answer nothing at all? Behold how much they have accused you of." In itself that is not an implausible judicial reaction, as we see from Papyrus Oslo 16 where in a similarly brief account of an interrogation the question is: "What have you to say on this subject?" Thus, though obviously an abbreviated and popular account, the Marcan questioning by Pilate shows no signs of theological creation. (John's account is another matter!)

A more serious difficulty is whether a Roman judge would have been

---

[104]In later commentaries on the *Lex Iulia de maiestate* (DJ 4.48.4.3–4), Marcian includes among the offenders one who, though a private person, acts as if he had an office or magistracy; Scaevola includes a king of a foreign nation who fails by malicious intent to make submission to the Roman people.

satisfied to pass sentence granted the type of responses by Jesus recorded in Mark (since no other evidence is mentioned). The COMMENT on Mark 15:2 (§32) will discuss in detail the exact import of "You say"; but, if I may anticipate, it is not a denial nor is it an unambiguous affirmative. In Mark 15:5 we are told that Jesus made no further answer. And so to the only question addressed to him, Jesus is shown as refusing a clear answer. (His silence surely has a theological aspect, but here I am asking about the legal effect of such an attitude. For detailed discussion, see pp. 734–35 below.) Cato (Sallust, *Bellum Catalinae* 52.36) argues for the principle that a magistrate should punish on the basis of what has been confessed. Jesus, however, has confessed little. What is a judge to do in the instance of an accused criminal who has not pleaded guilty but does not assert innocence or deny the basic charges against him when he is questioned? Is it not lawful to find such a difficult and unresponsive person guilty? True, according to Mark 15:10 Pilate was aware that the chief priests had handed Jesus over to him out of zeal or envy. (That observation surely has the theological goal of assuring the reader of Jesus' easily recognizable innocence, but again here I am asking whether knowledge of envy necessarily made Pilate's verdict illegal.) Could the judge take refuge in passing sentence on evidence brought forth in the trial itself, especially when he was under political pressure to find the accused guilty?

(c) *The Role of the Crowd (Acclamatio).* What is one to make of the outcry of the Jewish crowds, "Crucify him," almost as if they have a say in the decision to be rendered by the Roman judge? (Their say is even more evidence if they chose between Jesus and Barabbas, especially in the option offered in Matt 27:17. But the Barabbas scene is a special problem to be treated in §34 below.) In comment on this, some scholars have appealed to the custom of decision by *acclamatio populi* ("acclamation of the people").[105] In particular, Colin has discussed the polity of the "free cities." The Ten Cities constituting the Decapolis were outside the prefecture of Judea and related to the province of Syria; along with several cities within the prefecture of Judea (Caesarea and Samaria [Sebaste]), they were highly Hellenistic, often with a majority of pagan population. Colin argues that in these cities cases were often decided by the acclamation of the people.[106] For instance, at Caesarea on the coast Herod the Great brought three hundred

---

[105]For instance, Strobel, *Stunde* 124–29. In varying degrees: Blinzler, *Trial* 169; J. Merkel, "Begnadigung" 309, Colin, *Villes.* Yet Lémonon (*Pilate* 96) points out the sparsity of examples of acclamation being used to decide capital punishment for an individual.

[106]The Greek vocabulary in such acclamation includes the verbs of outcry *epiphōnein, epiboan, anaboan,* and the nouns *ekboēsis, epiboēsis, anaboēsis.* Latin correspondences are *clamare, acclamare, acclamatio.*

accused military leaders before the assembly, and the crowd killed them
(*Ant.* 16.11.7; #393–94). At Jericho Herod turned to a crowd in the amphi-
theater to decide the fate of some forty young men who had torn down the
golden eagle from the Temple; those present said they should be punished
(*Ant.* 17.6.3–4; #157–64). Almost two centuries later (AD 174) in Tyre under
Marcus Aurelius the assembly voted by acclamation. Such decision of cases
by crowd acclamation seems to have been an Eastern custom. Frequently the
Romans respected local customs (perhaps more during the transition from
republic to empire than later).[107] But is this "juridical process" really an
explanation of the decision given against Jesus at Jerusalem? Jerusalem was
not a free city; the populace was dominantly Jewish, not pagan. Decision of
cases by popular acclamation was scarcely a Jewish custom that the Romans
could be respecting, for in the Israelite understanding law came from God
and punishments were divinely appointed. The cries of the crowd against
Jesus in the Gospel accounts are mob pressure on the prefect, not the voice
of a recognized jury. Such a distinction is clear in Acts 25:23–27 where,
although Jews in Jerusalem and Caesarea have shouted that Paul should not
live, the procurator Festus insists on a formal, legal inquiry.

Yet even if not part of the legalities, the presence of a hostile crowd is not
an infrequent ingredient in accounts of a condemnatory trial written by those
who sympathize with the accused and against the sentence. The *Martyrdom
of Polycarp* 11–12 shows the proconsul at Smyrna determined on Polycarp's
death unless he recants; the cries of a crowd of pagans and Jews determine
the manner of death. As for whether historically such an outcry of crowds
occurred during the trial of Jesus by Pilate, we can speak only of verisimilitude. In three of the six Pilate incidents discussed above (section B) crowds
of Jews gathered to protest to Pilate (#1,3,5). Thus in evaluating the trial of
Jesus as the Gospels describe it, we find ourselves again not far from the
portrayal of Pilate's prefecture that emerged in the discussion of his career
above on the basis of Josephus, Philo, and coins. A Pilate anxious to assert
Roman prerogatives in responsibility for death sentences wishes to ascertain
for himself the guilt of Jesus, even though Jewish authorities have brought
Jesus to him as one who is guilty. Pilate has learned from his past experiences with the people and rulers in Jerusalem that he and they often do not
agree on what should be done.[108] The virtual silence of the Synoptic Jesus

---

[107]Steinwenter ("Processo" 481) points out that later Roman law was not favorable to acclamation. Justinian's Code (9.47.12) denies it, and Diocletian remarks on the "foolish voices of the
people."

[108]Lémonon (*Pilate* 189) contends that the Gospel accounts, perceptively examined, give us neither a Pilate who cedes to fear nor a Pilate who scrupulously defends the accused but a Pilate who
does not wish to be manipulated by the Jews.

does not help the case legally—if he is innocent, why does he not affirm that? Yet Pilate suspects that the real issue is an internal Jewish religious matter rather than a political crime against the majesty of the emperor. The crowd puts pressure on Pilate; and he does not want the case to blow up into another riot in Jerusalem, especially in the Passover context. Legally, the innocence of the accused is not so clear that Pilate should take a chance, and so he accedes to the crowd's pressure as he did in the instance of the Iconic Standards. This stance of the Pilate portrayed in the Gospels, then, was not a noble or a brave one; yet it was not illegal. In AD 37, when Pilate arrived in Rome to be investigated by the emperor, having been ordered there by the legate in Syria (*Ant.* 18.4.2; #88–89), there were imprudences that could be cited. This trial of Jesus, however (besides being insignificant in Pilate's career), need not have been mentioned as an abusive violation of Roman law. Jesus had not met either the best or the worst of Roman judges.

(*Pertinent bibliography may be found in the preceding section [§30]; in particular, see §30, Part 1 for the theme of Jesus the revolutionary [A2 above], and §30, Part 2 for general background pertinent to Pilate, the praetorium, and Roman law.*)

§32. THE ROMAN TRIAL, PART ONE: INITIAL QUESTIONING BY PILATE

(Mark 15:2–5; Matt 27:11–14; Luke 23:2–5; John 18:28b–38a)

Translation

Mark 15:2–5: ²And Pilate questioned him, "Are you the King of the Jews?" But in answer he says to him, "You say (so)." ³And the chief priests were accusing him of many things. ⁴But Pilate tried to question him again, saying, "Do you answer nothing at all? Behold how much they have accused you of." ⁵But Jesus answered nothing further, so that Pilate was amazed.

Matt 27:11–14: ¹¹But Jesus stood in front of the governor; and the governor questioned him, saying, "Are you the King of the Jews?" But Jesus said, "You say (so)." ¹²And although he was being accused by the chief priests and elders, he answered nothing. ¹³Then Pilate says to him, "Do you hear how much they are testifying against you?" ¹⁴And he did not answer him, not to even one word, so that the governor was greatly amazed.

Luke 23:2–5: ²But they [the whole multitude of them] began to accuse him, saying, "We have found this fellow misleading our nation, both forbidding the giving of taxes to Caesar, and saying that he is Messiah king." ³But Pilate asked him, saying, "Are you the King of the Jews?" But in answer, he said to him, "You say (so)." ⁴But Pilate said to the chief priests and the crowds, "I find nothing guilty in this man." ⁵But they were insistent, saying that "He stirs up the people, teaching through the whole of Judea, having begun from Galilee even to here."

John 18:28b–38a: ²⁸ᵇAnd they did not enter into the praetorium lest they be defiled and in order that they might eat the Passover (meal). ²⁹So Pilate went out to them and says, "What accusation do you bring against this man?" ³⁰They answered and said to him, "If this fellow were not doing what is bad, we would not have given him over to you." [31]So Pilate said to them, "Take him yourselves, and according to your law judge him." The Jews said to him, "It is not permitted us to put anyone to death," [32]in order that there might be fulfilled the word of Jesus that he spoke, signifying what kind of death he was going to die.

[33]So Pilate went again into the praetorium, and called Jesus and said to him, "Are you the King of the Jews?" [34]Jesus answered, "Of yourself do you say this, or have others told you this about me?" [35]Pilate answered, "Am I a Jew? Your nation and the chief priests have given you over to me. What have you done?" [36]Jesus answered, "My kingdom is not of this world. If my kingdom were of this world, my attendants would have struggled lest I be given over to the Jews. But as it is, my kingdom is not from here." [37]So Pilate said to him, "So then you are a king." Jesus answered, "You say that I am a king. The reason for which I have been born and for which I have come into the world is that I may bear witness to the truth. Everyone who is of the truth hears my voice." [38a]Pilate says to him, "What is truth?"

COMMENT

The previous section (§31) supplied background on the Roman trial for *the readers of this book*. Since, to the best of our knowledge, none of the four Gospels was addressed to a pre-70 community *in Judea*, it is very doubtful that the respective Gospel readers would have known much of that background, i.e., Christians living in Antioch, Ephesus, or Rome between 60 and 100 would not have been acquainted in detail with Pilate's prefecture in Judea or with the site of the praetorium in Jerusalem thirty to seventy years before. (Only on the last point in §31, namely, how Romans conducted trials, would they have had more experiential knowledge than is now available to us from written sources; but even then they might have had little experience of trials *extra ordinem* in a small imperial province like Judea.) This is an important point to remember when we have to judge how they would have understood the Gospel accounts of the Roman trial.

I shall devote the ANALYSIS of this section to the outline of the whole Roman trial in each Gospel, for the overall structure contributes to the meaning of each segment. Here in the COMMENT, however, I wish to begin by discussing briefly the various approaches that have governed scholarly research into the trial. (For an outline list giving the order of the subsections, see p. 662 above.)

DIFFERENT APPROACHES TO THE PILATE TRIAL

Historicity. Many have let issues of history combined with logic govern their outlook. Most often they address their questions to Mark's narrative as the shortest and most basic account, and with surprising frequency those questions produce skeptical conclusions. Would a prefect like Pilate interview personally a Galilean Jew of no great social standing accused of a crime? If so, would the trial have been centered around one simple issue ("the King of the Jews") without a detailed Roman investigation of Jesus' background, and would Pilate have been likely to settle for Jesus' silence? Indeed, why would "the King of the Jews" ever have come up in the Roman trial since we have no evidence that this title was ever applied to Jesus during his ministry, never mind claimed by him before the Roman trial. (Matt 2:2, with its use of that title for the infant Jesus, is the one exception, and not many would care to appeal to that in a historical discussion.) Even if one does not insist on the precise title, how would Pilate have known about anything related to Jesus' self-claims, since no introductory information was relayed to him by the Jewish leaders? (Here Luke 23:2 is the exception among the Gospels; but, as we shall see, that listing of several charges is almost surely a Lucan attempt to meet that problem.) Why is there no clear relationship between the issue raised by Pilate and the issues raised at the just-concluded Sanhedrin trial (Synoptics: destroying the sanctuary and being the Messiah, the Son of the Blessed/God) or Annas interrogation (John: about his disciples and his teaching)?[1]

In my judgment many of these questions are inappropriately addressed to the type of narrative the Gospels present which, as I have insisted, is neither a legal report on the trial nor an eyewitness summary. As will become apparent, I think there is a historical kernel in the Roman trial: Pilate sentenced Jesus to die on the cross on the charge of being "the King of the Jews." The evangelists, however, are interested in making that dramatically effective as a vehicle of proclaiming who Jesus is, not in telling readers how Pilate got his information, why he phrased it as he did, or with what legal formalities he conducted the trial. In its brevity Mark's account of the Roman treatment

---

[1]There are other historical questions to be asked, e.g., about Barabbas and the custom of releasing a prisoner at the feast; but these are sufficient for the moment to illustrate the approach.

of Jesus of Nazareth is not too different from Josephus' account of the Roman treatment of Jesus son of Ananias thirty years later (*War* 6.5.3; #303–5). Each Jesus had been handed over to the Roman governor by the Jewish leaders in Jerusalem who were uneasy about his religious implications (in the instance of Jesus son of Ananias, whether his outcries were of supernatural or even demonic [*daimonios*] origin), but those implications do not seem to play a role in the questioning that the governor conducted personally. In neither case are we told that the Jewish authorities reported to the governor the charges against the respective Jesus. Each Jesus is interrogated about a central issue by the governor (in the instance of Jesus son of Ananias, about why he uttered his cry of "Woe to Jerusalem"); and each Jesus refuses to answer, even though he is scourged. Nevertheless, the governor comes to a decision about the prisoner (in the instance of Jesus son of Ananias, he is let go as a maniac). One could raise against the historicity of the Josephus story most of the issues of logic and plausibility that are raised against the Gospel accounts. I know of no instance of that having been done; rather, accepting its basic historicity, most would easily recognize that the genre of Josephus' account does not permit detailed reconstruction of the legal procedure.

Source Criticism. Others reconstruct stages in the development of the Marcan narrative precisely because, as it now stands, they find it illogical. Asking some of the same questions of the Marcan account that I have listed above, Braumann, Bultmann, and Wendling in various ways give primacy not to Mark 15:2 ("the King of the Jews") but to Mark 15:3: "And the chief priests were accusing him of many things." The latter is considered the oldest tradition; and sometimes it is placed ahead of Mark 15:2 so that Pilate's "Are you the King of the Jews?" becomes a specification of it.[2] Gnilka ("Verhandlungen" 10) contends that the trial originally consisted of only the rebuke by the opponents on one side and the sovereign silence of Jesus on the other. Then on a secondary level "the King of the Jews" was added; and it became of major importance, being developed in the Barabbas incident. Eventually it was placed first in the account even if then it illogically preceded the more general accusation of 15:3.

Previously I have manifested little confidence in such source reconstruction because others who attempt it would produce totally different results (see APPENDIX IX). In a rejection of this approach to the Roman trial in particular, Dahl (*Crucified* 23) points out that such an approach has to mean that only latterly was the inscription on the cross, "The King of the Jews" (expressing the charge on which Jesus was found guilty by the Romans),

---

[2]This solution is related to the thesis of Wendling and Braumann (rejected on pp. 551–52 above) that Mark 15:3–5 is the oldest trial tradition from which the Sanhedrin trial was a back-formation.

introduced into the Roman trial that had hitherto been narrated without it. Also a series of verses strung over several episodes all have to be deemed as secondary since kingship is the motif that holds them together (Mark 15:9,12,16–20a,32). Dahl would argue to the contrary that "the King of the Jews" is a very old motif, so old that it has been spiritualized in John and even partially toned down in Matt. (Compare Matt 27:17 to Mark 15:9; and Matt 27:22 to Mark 15:12.) Throughout this commentary I have contended that the thesis of John's dependence on Mark is not convincing. If John was not dependent on Mark, then "the King of the Jews" motif shared by both must predate the Gospels. Indeed, in my judgment one of the strongest arguments for the antiquity of that motif is that all four Gospels have identical Greek for Pilate's question *Sy ei ho Basileus tōn Ioudaiōn* ("Are you the King of the Jews?") and Jesus' response *Sy legeis* ("You say [so]"). That is almost unique in the PN, and I find minimally credible the explanation that it came into the Marcan PN late and was so effective that all the other evangelists adopted it verbatim. Surely both question and answer were so much a part of the tradition that they had to be preserved, even by an evangelist like John who separated them (18:33 and 18:37b) by an expanded interpretation.

The Narratives at Face Value. The observation just made above moves me toward a different approach to the Roman trial based neither on speculation about historical elements (even though I accept their presence) or on sources (even though I think Mark and John drew on earlier traditions). This approach, consonant with my treatment of the two previous "Acts" of the Passion, concentrates on the meaning conveyed by the narratives as they now stand—a meaning that flows from asking what the readers/hearers of the Gospels would most likely have understood from what the evangelists told them. Before I begin calling attention to that meaning, let me illustrate the difference such an approach makes by returning to the last question raised in the first paragraph under *Historicity* above. Why is there no clear relationship between the issues raised at the just-concluded Jewish trail/interrogation and the basic "Are you the King of the Jews?" asked initially by Pilate in the Roman trial? The range of speculation among those who work out a logic in terms of historicity or sources includes:

(a) Pilate knew the details of the religious accusations made in the Sanhedrin against Jesus and

- was simply rephrasing or accepting a Jewish rephrasing (Messiah = King); or
- regarded them as irrelevant or legally unusable in a Roman trial; or
- was seeking his own way in a new situation since no previous Roman prefect of Judea had to deal with a religious figure who was not a brigand at the head of armed outlaws; or

▪ knew also that they were based on false evidence and distortion, and needed valid evidence to judge Jesus.

(b) Pilate never took the trouble to find out what happened at the Jewish trial

▪ because he regarded it as illegal or nil; or
▪ because he preferred to deal with what he himself had heard or could find out about Jesus.

(c) Pilate was deceived or not informed by the Jewish authorities about what had happened at the Sanhedrin.

In part scholars' views of those possibilities are determined by their judgments on whether Pilate conducted a legal trial or a charade, whether he knew that Jesus was not guilty or thought that there was a reasonable case against him, whether Pilate's conduct can be judged according to the juridical patterns summed up in DJ (e.g., Goldin, Innes, Powell), and whether (no matter what the legality of the proceedings) Pilate gave an honest or pressured judgment. Too many of those questions are unanswerable.

Let me suggest how Gospel readers/hearers might have understood the Roman trial as judged from the narratives as they now exist. Since Pilate is Roman governor, there is nothing to suggest to them that his putting Jesus on trial is illegal, even though all the evangelists create the impression that Pilate's condemnation of Jesus was under public coercion and against the prefect's better judgment. Although Mark, Matt, and John do not tell us how Pilate got his information, the presence of the Jewish priests (and in the Synoptics of the Sanhedrin members) would suggest to the readers that *they* supplied Pilate with information about Jesus when they gave Jesus over to him as a prisoner to be tried and condemned. (Accordingly Luke would be only making explicit what was already implicit.) The fact that in all the narratives Pilate phrases the issue as "Are you the King of the Jews?"—language which has not been used previously either in the ministry or in the Jewish trial/interrogation of Jesus—would probably suggest two things. First, there would be a hint that the Jewish authorities were deceptive since they had not told Pilate what they really held against Jesus as reflected in their own questioning of him. (John would be dramatizing this by having "the Jews" at first reluctant to tell Pilate the real issue [18:30] and then finally admitting that it was Jesus' making himself God's Son [19:7].) Second and more important, from the new phrasing that Pilate employs, readers/hearers would get the impression that there was now being introduced an issue the Romans were really interested in. The matters of concern to the Jewish authorities in the immediately preceding trial/interrogation were clearly religious; the Roman issue has a political tone.[3] The qualified reply of Jesus, "You say [so]," would alert the readers that such politicizing was not an accurate understanding of his kingship. (Once again John makes this dramatically explicit [18:36–37].) It should be apparent that such an approach based on what readers/hearers were likely to derive from the narratives shows that much of the speculation listed above is inapplicable as *a meaning of the Gospel passages*.

After this theorizing about approaches to the Roman trial, let us move on to comment on the first part of that trial, beginning by paying attention to a pattern common to all the Gospels, and then studying each Gospel account separately.

A Common Pattern in the Interchanges between Pilate and Jesus

Common to all four Gospels in the Roman trial are two short interchanges in the direct interrogation of Jesus by Pilate. First, Pilate asks him, "Are you the King of the Jews?"; and Jesus answers, "You say (so)" (in John, see 18:33,37). I have already called attention to the remarkable fact that the Greek of the question and answer is identical in the four Gospels. Second, when Pilate continues with questioning, Jesus answers him nothing. This question-and-answer constitutes one of the most fixed elements in the PN. In Mark/Matt these two interchanges are both in this first part of the trial and make up the whole direct interrogation of Jesus by Pilate. In Luke and John the first interchange is prefaced with introductory material that enhances intelligibility, and the second interchange is extended into later parts of the trial.[4] After studying the pattern of the two interchanges in Mark/Matt, we shall analyze the import of the first and more important interchange.

To appreciate this pattern in Mark/Matt, attention must be paid to the similarity between questioning by the high priest at the Sanhedrin trial in Mark 14:60–62 and questioning by Pilate in the Roman trial. In 14:60–62 the high priest begins his questioning by pointing to what is being testified against Jesus, but Jesus answers nothing at all. Then the high priest asks a specific question about Jesus' *identity*, "Are you the Messiah [*Sy ei ho Christos*], the Son of the Blessed?"; and Jesus answers, adding a qualification (cf. also Matt 26:62–64). In Mark 15:2–5 the contents are similar but the order is reversed. Pilate first asks the specific question about Jesus' *identity:* "Are

---

[3]Historically the situation may have been far more complicated, for both the destruction of the sanctuary and the claim to be the Messiah would have had political implications. Synoptic Gospel readers, however, would probably not have recognized such implications from what the evangelists have told them. Contrast with this John 11:48.

[4]Luke 23:9 has moved the silence to the interrogation by Herod; and John had postponed it till 19:9.

you the King [*Sy ei ho Basileus*] of the Jews?" and Jesus answers in a qualified way. Then Pilate asks a general question pointing out what Jesus has
been accused of, but Jesus answers nothing at all. Obviously we are not
hearing excerpts from legal court records or even direct accounts of the
trial(s). We are hearing Christian tradition about the basic issue of Jesus'
identity vocalized respectively between Jesus and the Jewish authorities and
Jesus and the Roman governor. That issue has in each case been shaped into
a simple question format and made central in a dramatized trial setting. The
second interchange wherein there are many more accusations to which Jesus
does not respond has the effect of dismissing such issues (besides the respective Messiah or King question) as irrelevant. As for Jesus' qualified answer
to the main question, that is meant to hint that Christians see both true and
false aspects in identifying Jesus as the Messiah and as the King of the Jews.
Both titles have their truth, but they must be understood with nuance when
applied to Jesus. The nuance is more complex with regard to the first title
and, as we saw, differs in the different Gospels, precisely because Jesus'
identity as the Messiah has been an ongoing religious issue debated between
Jews who believe in Jesus and those who do not—a debate made more sharp
as "Messiah" was interpreted in terms of divine sonship. The more political
issue of the sense in which Jesus was the King of the Jews evidently did not
undergo such active debate, for all four Gospels preserve "You say (so)" as
the nuanced response, with only John choosing to comment on the sense of
"king/kingdom."

In evaluating the logic of the Marcan trial narrative, we must take into
account this understanding of the scene as a kerygmatic dramatization of
formulae preserved in the tradition. Accordingly the question of how Pilate
knows what to ask is irrelevant. On the level of simple consecutive narrative
one could argue that Mark/Matt give us an abbreviation in which they have
skipped the obvious, namely, that the Jewish authorities gave Pilate information about Jesus.[5] In terms of composition, however, another answer is the
key: In Christian tradition the Roman charge against Jesus was preserved in
terms of his being "the King of the Jews"; and so that question was placed
on Pilate's lips. As we saw, Dahl (*Crucified* 10–36) has argued that it came
into the tradition from the statement of the crime attached to the cross, which
in Mark 15:26 and par. contains an element common to all: "the King of the
Jews." This phraseology may well be historical. Taylor (*Mark* 579), working
with the hypothesis that the trial narrative is basically historical, thinks the
chief priests would have phrased the charge in terms of Jesus' claiming to

___

[5]That may be implicit in Mark 15:12 ("him whom *you* call 'the King of the Jews'") and is explicit
in Luke's dramatization where the authorities give Pilate information about Jesus.

"the King of Israel," a term that appears on their lips in Mark 15:32; Matt 27:42 and becomes the title both in the condemnation/mockery of Jesus and on the cross in *GPet* 3:7; 4:11. In the compositional theory I have advanced, however, "the King of the Jews" is the primary remembrance as the Roman political charge (see also Mark 15:12,18), and "the King of Israel" becomes a secondary, religious rendering—a title that Jews would mock when applied to Jesus but that Christians of all stripes could accept since they regarded themselves as the renewed Israel.

The history of the title "the King of the Jews" is interesting. NT commentators point out that most often it appears on the lips of nonJews (John 19:21 is not really an exception). This supports the surface impression that we are hearing how a Roman would understand Jesus, and the past employment of the title detected from Josephus shows why the prefect might consider its use threatening. The Hasmonean high priests, descended by family and political heritage from the leaders of the Maccabean revolt, established an independent Jewish state in Palestine and began to designate themselves as kings; and they are the first recorded users of the title "the King of the Jews." Josephus (*Ant.* 14.3.1; #36, citing an otherwise unpreserved passage from Strabo) reports that a golden vine bearing the inscription "From Alexander, the King of the Jews" was set up in the temple of Jupiter Capitolinus in Rome. Herod the Great was called "King of the Jews" both prophetically as a boy (*Ant.* 15.10.5; #373) and later as a ruler (16.10.2; #311); and Matt 2:1–18 shows him murderously jealous when the infant Jesus is given that title by the magi. Thus in 1st-cent. Palestine the charge that Jesus was claiming that title might well be understood by the Romans as an attempt to reestablish the kingship over Judea and Jerusalem exercised by the Hasmoneans (like Alexander Jannaeus) and Herod the Great.[6]

What about the objection mentioned above that during the ministry Jesus had never spoken of himself as a king, and so even by way of the storyline Mark is implausible in portraying him as being charged with claiming such a title? The Marcan readers, however, know that Jesus has spoken very frequently of the kingdom of God, seemingly with the underlying assumption that he himself would have a special place in that kingdom. Two of the most prominent members of the Twelve whom he had appointed to be with him (3:14), James and John, implied this when they asked to sit at his right hand and his left, in his glory (Mark 10:37). In 11:10 the crowds hailed Jesus in terms of their anticipation of the kingdom *of David,* a salutation that gives Jesus royal status. Matt strengthens the implication that Jesus is a king. The

---

[6]As a parallel some point to the Roman military reaction against would-be kings like Simon and Athrongaeus after the death of Herod the Great (Josephus, *Ant.* 17.10.6–7; #273–84); but the similarity is weak, for those men were engaged in violent actions accompanied by armed bands.

magi of 2:1–2 came looking for the newborn child who was "the King of the Jews." In Matt 13:37–42 the community planted in this world by the Son of Man is called "his kingdom," a kingdom distinct from the kingdom of the Father. In Matt 21:5 Jesus' entry into Jerusalem is specifically compared to the prophecy in Zech 9:9: "Behold your king is coming to you . . . mounted on an ass." Matt 25:34 has Jesus envisioning (himself as) the Son of Man seated in regal judgment over those arrayed to his right and left. Thus it is not really illogical in the storylines of Mark/Matt that Jesus' enemies might distort such sayings and happenings into a claim on his part to be a king.

The lack of verbal connection between the charges in the Sanhedrin trial and the charge known to Pilate probably would give the impression that Pilate was deceived by the Sanhedrin authorities. Yet the gap is not so sharp as to make the storyline implausible, for in a way "the Messiah" and "the King of the Jews" can be looked on as diverse facets of a common theme. True, Mark never explains to his readers that "Messiah" (*Christos*), in its basic applicability to Jesus, means the *anointed* king of the house of David; but that information may have been elementary knowledge for Christians since the very designation given to them involved confessing Jesus as the Messiah (Christ). A presupposition that readers would equate the Messiah and the Davidic king is reinforced by Mark 15:32, which places "the Messiah" and "the King of Israel" in apposition without any explanation. Matt's readers would even more easily make a connection between the Sanhedrin question about the Messiah and the Roman question about the King of the Jews; for in the infancy narrative after seeing Jesus four times described as "the Messiah" (1:1,16,17,18: *Christos*), they are told in 2:2 of the birth of "the King of the Jews."

THE MARCAN ACCOUNT OF THE QUESTIONING (MARK 15:2–5)

After these general remarks about the dramatization of the basic Christian tradition preserving the Roman charge, let us look at the Marcan scene verse by verse. In §28 we discussed Mark 15:1 as a transitional verse concluding the Sanhedrin trial and describing a transfer to Roman control: "The chief priests with the elders and scribes and the whole Sanhedrin, having bound Jesus, took him away and gave him over to Pilate." Strung together by a series of alternating *kai* ("and") and *de* ("but") particles, 15:2–5 will now describe Pilate's dealing with this prisoner brought to him by the chief priests.

In v. 2 "to question" is *eperōtan*.[7] While theoretically this compound form

---

[7]The verb occurs 25 times in Mark, as compared with 8 in Matt, 17 in Luke, 2 in John.

with the preposition *epi* could be more intensive than the simple *erōtan* (used by Luke in 23:3, with the compound kept for 23:6), in Koine Greek they are virtually interchangeable. "Are you the King of the Jews?" is a question employing a personal pronoun but not necessarily in an intensive way ("Are you ... ?"). E. Norden (*Agnostos Theos* [Leipzig: Teubner, 1913; reprint 1956], 194–200) would relate it to a revelatory formula like "You are my Son" (Mark 1:11; cf. 3:11); but Jesus' response here warns that this is a human evaluation that requires nuance, not like the divine evaluation as Son that can be taken at face value. Similarly I would not favor the interpretations given by Nicklin ("Thou"): a sneering question, "You are the King of the Jews, are you?" and a reply, "Is it you who say this?" Those renditions are closer to John's development of basic tradition, but Mark's account is singularly free of such psychological tone.

With a strong narrative sense Mark employs the historical present in introducing Jesus' response even though it gives the awkward "he says ... 'You say'" (*legei ... sy legeis*—both Matt and Luke "improve" by using the past tense [*ephē*]). As for the *sy legeis,* we discussed this type of response above (pp. 489–93) and its variants in reference to Matt 26:64, "*You* have said it" (*sy eipas*) and Luke 22:70, "You [pl.] say that I am" (*hymeis legete*). The connotation is that what has been phrased as a question is true;[8] yet the one who phrased it must take responsibility for it—in this case, must take responsibility for any political interpretation that would have Jesus overthrowing the Roman administration of Judea. Readers would know that Jesus is not affirming such a distortion of his words, even if he is a king.[9] Mark's Jesus was much less ambiguous in responding "I am [*egō eimi*]" to the question about being *the* Messiah, the Son of the Blessed (14:62; contrast Matt 26:64: "*You* have said it"). Marcan readers would have to assume that Jesus is more the Messiah than the King of the Jews. In any case Pilate does not probe Jesus with further questions about this title.

In the next verse the chief priests seize on the ambiguity of Jesus' response to Pilate in order to press their case. They know that by not denying the title Jesus has left himself open to an implication that could seem threatening to the Romans. The scene Mark paints is evocative of the OT picture of the suffering just one who is surrounded by enemies who speak with lying tongues, and who is encompassed with words of hate (Ps 109:2–3). By

---

[8]Certainly the Marcan storyline (15:12) shows that Pilate did not understand it as a negative (pace Pesch, *Markus* 2.458).

[9]As we shall see below, John spells out the appropriate distinction. One should not historicize the nuance, as does Blinzler (*Trial* 190–91) when he argues that Pilate understood the reservation and that is why he did not immediately find Jesus guilty. Pilate's not-guilty judgment flows from the transparent innocence of Jesus, not from the ambiguity of Jesus' "You say (so)."

mentioning the chief priests alone, Mark makes them the insistent, aggravating factor in the trial.[10] While the *polla* in Mark 15:3 could be translated adverbially ("accusing him much"), the literal "of many things" is preferable since Pilate seems to understand that implication in 15:4.[11] The theory (rejected above) that would place 15:3 before 15:2 and make "the King of the Jews" one of the "many things" would falsify Mark's intention. There is only one real question and that is the theme of the whole trial; beyond the King issue the many other things are subordinate and irrelevant, and that is why Jesus answers to them nothing at all (15:4). With similar contempt, in 14:61 Jesus answered nothing at all when the high priest brought forward the many things the *false* witnesses had testified against him.[12]

Pilate's reaction is recorded in 15:4–5, where he ignores the protesting chief priests and addresses himself directly to Jesus. The reaction has features harmonious with Marcan style (proving at least that Mark has rewritten the tradition): *palin*, "again"; *ide*, "behold" (nine times in Mark [four in Matt], always in direct address), and two double negatives (lit., "Do you not answer nothing?" and "Jesus no more answered nothing"). In 15:4 the verb "to question" is imperfect (cf. aorist in 15:2), matching the continuous (impf.) accusation of the chief priests in 15:3. The conative translation ("tried to question"; see BDF 326) catches the effect of Jesus' silence. That Pilate alerts Jesus ("Behold") about the danger of keeping silent in the face of so many accusations gives an impression of fairness, an impression lacking in the Jewish trial in the importuning (14:60) by the high priest who conspired in the testimony against Jesus. In accordance with his conspiracy the high priest did not express amazement at Jesus' silence as Pilate does. Clearly Mark portrays a Pilate who had no part in the Jewish plot against Jesus, despite some modern reconstructions to that effect.[13]

Legally, what was the value of Jesus' refusal to answer? Some have argued that this refusal warranted Pilate's judgment of guilt, appealing to the principle that silence is equivalent to acquiescence. Several times in the English Reformation, e.g., Thomas More to his accusers, or Cranmer to Gardiner, we find the (common or general) law enunciated: *Qui tacet, consentire vide-*

---

[10]All the other Gospels enlarge the cast of accusers: Matt 27:12 adds the "elders"; Luke 23:1–2 had "the whole multitude of them" make the charges; John 18:31,35 involves "the Jews" and "your nation and the chief priests."

[11]Luke 23:2 spells out the "many things."

[12]While rejection is the main thrust of Jesus' refusal to answer, there are possible OT echoes, as we saw above (p. 464). Also there is the parallel in Josephus' account of how Jesus son of Ananias "answered nothing whatsoever" to the procurator Albinus (*War* 6.5.3; #305).

[13]The portrayal of Pilate's amazement may strengthen the case for seeing in Jesus' refusal to answer an echo of the Suffering Servant in Isa 53:7 who did not open his mouth. Eight verses before that Isaian passage (52:14) many nations are *amazed* at the servant. Gnilka (*Markus* 2.300) sees in Pilate's amazement here and in Mark 15:44 a reaction to the presence of the divine.

tur, i.e., "The one who is silent is considered to have consented."[14] One can trace it back to the 13th-cent. and Pope Boniface VIII's *Sextus Liber Decretalium* 3.444, and to ca. 1200 and Thomas Becket, but seemingly not to early Roman law. Of course, in ordinary experience the embarrassed silence of the one accused is often a sign of guilt (Euripides, *Iphigenia in Aulis* 1142: "Silence itself constitutes your admission"). Yet a court requires more than impressions; and "silence means consent" would not explain Pilate's amazement—he is not amazed that Jesus is acting guiltily as charged but that Jesus holds himself aloof from the charges. Moreover, in Mark Jesus' silence does not follow the charge about being "the King of the Jews" (which reappears on Pilate's lips) but the many other charges that Pilate ignores. One gets the impression that Pilate takes the many other charges no more seriously than Jesus does.

THE MATTHEAN ACCOUNT OF THE QUESTIONING (MATT 27:11–14)

By comparison with the Lucan and Johannine expansions of the basic interchanges between Pilate and Jesus that we shall discuss below, Matt's changes of Mark are very modest. Most are either stylistic or adaptations to Matt's sequence. In 27:2 Matt described the transfer from the Sanhedrin thus: "They [the chief priests and the elders of the people] led him away and gave him over to Pilate the governor." But after this Matt interrupted the sequence with the story of Judas. In that story the chief priests and elders heard Judas confess that he gave over innocent blood, and that knowledge makes their continued accusations against Jesus before Pilate more hypocritical. In order to resume the interrupted sequence from 27:2, Matt 27:11 adds to the material taken over from Mark 15:2 a preface: "But Jesus stood in front of the governor," reintroducing the two main protagonists. The language of that clause echoes Mark 13:9 (cf. Matt 10:17–18): "They will give you up to sanhedrins ... and you will stand before governors ... for my sake." The followers of Jesus are having their future fate foreshadowed by what happens to their master. That parallel may be one of the reasons Matt prefers in 27:11 "the governor" (twice) to Mark's "Pilate." Also the use of "the governor" increases the official atmosphere, even as the verb "to stand" increases the trial atmosphere.[15]

As far as the first interchange between Pilate and Jesus, Matt follows Mark's quotations of Pilate and Jesus exactly. But Matt introduces Jesus'

---

[14]See *The Oxford Dictionary of English Proverbs,* ed. F. P. Wilson (Oxford: Clarendon, 1970), 733. One can debate the applicability of such a principle to criminal trials.

[15]See the use of "stand" in Acts 24:20–21; 25:10; 26:6. Matt's description may also hint at defiant dignity on Jesus' part.

response more gracefully than does Mark, clarifying the subject and using the past tense (*ephē:* "Jesus said") in preference to Mark's historical present ("he says"). SPNM 95 suggests that in Matt *ephē* is reserved for more solemn proclamation. The "You say (so)" (*sy legeis*) resembles the "You have said (so)" (*sy eipas*) addressed by Jesus to Judas in 26:25 and to Caiaphas in 26:64. There was deceit in the questions proposed by them, but that is not apparent here. In the next verse (27:12), "And although he was being accused by the chief priests and elders, he answered nothing," Matt subordinates verbs for a more gracious writing style and adds "elders" in conformity with 27:1. More logical than Mark 15:4, which makes one deduce indirectly (from Pilate's statement) that Jesus answered nothing, Matt states that directly. The "Then" of 27:13 is the usual Matthean *tote.* The "Do you hear" which introduces Pilate's question gives the impression that the Roman wants to be sure that Jesus' silence does not flow from an impediment or misunderstanding. "Testifying against" avoids Mark's double use of "accuse" in 15:3–4, and Matt simplifies Mark's repetitive "many things" and "how much" in favor of the latter. Matt 27:14, beginning with "And he did not answer him," offers the same picture as Mark 15:5; but the exact translation of Matt's following words, *pros oude hen rēma* (lit. "to nothing one word"), has offered difficulty. No matter how this heightening of the negation is translated,[16] the Matthean Jesus is refusing to deal seriously with even one of the accusations. Pilate's amazement at this is intensified in Matt.

THE LUCAN EXPANSION OF THE BASIC INTERCHANGE (LUKE 23:2–5)

General Remarks. In Luke the trial of Jesus by Pilate follows immediately upon a Sanhedrin interrogation that passed no explicit sentence on Jesus and seemingly reached only the decision recounted in 23:1, namely, to lead Jesus to Pilate. In fact, as I have argued above (pp. 527–28), it is apparent from passages elsewhere in Luke-Acts that Luke understood that there was a Sanhedrin trial and that the Jewish authorities condemned Jesus to death. Moreover, his readers probably assumed that. Nevertheless, in the PN storyline the Lucan Sanhedrin proceedings lead more smoothly than those in Mark/Matt into the formal Roman trial.

Respected scholars contend that all or most of Luke's account of the Roman trial (23:1–25) is derived from another passion source—one better or-

---

[16]SPNM 232–34. Codex Bezae simplifies by omitting *pros oude,* leaving "did not answer him one word." If one prefers to struggle with all four words, one rendition is "not even to a single word," where *pros* governs *rēma* ("word" = charge against Jesus; see Matt 18:16). Another rendition is "a word not even to one (of them)," where the verb "answer" governs *rēma* (cf. Matt 15:23; 22:46), and "one" means one of the charges. Compare Exod 14:28: "There was not left among them unto one."

ganized than Mark 15 and perhaps more historical. Let me list the individual arguments for this position and with each, a query as to its validity. Vocabulary counts constitute an important argument, e.g., Taylor (*Passion* 86) reports that of the 373 words in Luke 23:1–25 only 52 appear in Mark 15:1–15, or 13.9 percent. If one omits from the comparison the Herod scene in Luke 23:6–15 (a scene absent from Mark), the percentage of common vocabulary goes up to only 27.2 percent. Indeed, sixteen words common to Luke and Mark, almost a third of the common vocabulary, are concentrated in Luke 23:3 (= Mark 15:2), a verse Luke may have drawn from Mark. (Query: Is the presence of so much nonMarcan vocabulary proof of Luke's use of a passion source other than Mark? Could not the Lucan expansion beyond Mark have come from reusing material found elsewhere in Luke-Acts?) Another argument offered for the theory of an independent preLucan PN is the greater intelligibility of Luke 23:2–5, where, unlike Mark, a set of charges is offered before Pilate begins to ask questions. (Query: Did Luke find this intelligibility in a separate source; or did he rearrange Mark as part of his stated intent to make the story more orderly [1:3]? In addition, was part of this reshaping in order to make the Roman trial of Jesus resemble more closely the style of Roman trials of Paul in Acts?) Tyson ("Lukan") and others think that in the preLucan source, Herod was the main magistrate; and he found Jesus guilty (see *GPet* 2:5c). In this approach, Luke has modified what he got from the source about Herod by combining it with Marcan material that made Pilate the magistrate. (Query: If Luke is our entrée to the Herod material in the source, is it wise to discount so much of what Luke actually tells us about Herod [he happened to be in Jerusalem, and only by Pilate's initiative was he consulted] in favor of a differing account reconstructed from a putative source? In §33 below I shall contend that Herod conducted an *anakrisis* or preliminary investigation, in which procedure he would return the prisoner to the governor with an evaluation.) Those who would assign Luke 23:2–5 (or 23:2,4–5) to a special source include Ernst, Grundmann, Marshall, Rengstorf, and Taylor.

As my parenthetical queries in the preceding paragraph suggest, I think of Luke 23:2–5 as a Lucan expansion of Mark 15:2–5, and thus agree with Creed, Dibelius, Fitzmyer, Klostermann, and Schneider. But we must test that thesis verse by verse.

Luke 23:2–5 in Detail. Although we discussed Luke 23:1 in §28 as involving the termination of the Sanhedrin session and the transfer to Pilate, Luke combines that transition very closely with the trial that follows. For instance, "the whole multitude of them," which is the subject of 23:1, becomes the antecedent of the "they" who began to accuse (*katēgorein*) Jesus in 23:2. Although this "multitude" should refer to the group specified in

22:66 ("the assembly of the elders of the people, both chief priests and scribes"), 23:4 shows that Luke thinks of "the chief priests *and the crowds*" as present before Pilate. Yet in the two detailed descriptions of the participants, the chief priests are the common denominator (also 23:10,13). Thus the Lucan "whole multitude" that began to accuse Jesus is not too different from those described in Mark 15:3: "And the chief priests were accusing him of many things." Mark does not elaborate the "many things," but Luke 23:2 does exactly that.

A major factor in Luke's presentation of the Roman trial of Jesus is conformity with Acts' presentations of the various trials of Paul. For instance, in Acts 17:6–7 the Jews of Thessalonica accuse Paul and Silas of *overturning* the world, acting against the decrees of *Caesar,* and saying that there is another *king,* Jesus. The italicized words bear a strong resemblance to the charges against Jesus in Luke 23:2. On a wider scale Radl (*Paulus* 211–20) points to a whole series of passion parallels in the trial of Paul before the Palestinian procurators Felix and Festus in Acts 24–25 ca. AD 58. In Acts 24:1–2 the high priest Ananias comes with some elders to accuse (*kategorein*) Paul. Their spokesman says, "We have found this man . . . arousing revolts among all the Jews throughout the world. . . . By conducting an investigation you yourself can learn about all these things of which we have accused him" (Acts 24:5,8). Luke may have had a source for the trial of Paul; certainly he had popular knowledge of how Roman gubernatorial trials were conducted; and he is following that pattern for both Jesus and Paul. The basic idea that Jesus' own countrymen "delated" him to the Romans would have seemed very plausible if we may judge from Pliny, *Epistles* 10.97.2.

Having seen what guided the overall pattern of listing charges in 23:2, let us now study those charges in detail.[17] The RSV translation gives the impression that three charges are involved, and that may well be the most common interpretation.[18] However, the Greek favors the structure of one overall charge of "misleading [*diastrephein*] our nation [*ethnos*]," which is subdivided into two examples about not giving taxes and saying he is Messiah king (so Büchele, Fitzmyer, Grundmann, Schneider). In slightly different words the first charge (misleading) is repeated in 23:5,14, suggesting that it is the principal accusation. Since this is a political charge, Luke is showing

---

[17]Once Luke established a pattern of listing several charges against Jesus, a combination of imagination and reflection on the Gospels tended to increase the number. In the copper tablet text of Pilate's sentence discovered ca. 1200 (§35, n. 61 below), there are six charges: (1) He is a seducer; (2) Seditious; (3) Enemy of the Law; (4) Calls himself falsely the Son of God; (5) and the King of Israel; (6) Entered into the Temple with a multitude bearing palm.

[18]Cassidy ("Trial" 167) argues for a pattern of three with the third (that he is Messiah king) as the culmination, since that is the one Pilate picks up on.

that those who accuse Jesus to Pilate have departed almost entirely from the more patently religious subjects of the Sanhedrin interrogation.

The initial word in the main charge is the demonstrative *touton* that I have interpreted as contemptuously employed: "this fellow" (BDF 290[6]; also in John 18:30). One may hesitate as to whether here the primary meaning of *diastrephein* is "to pervert" (BAG) or "to twist [=mislead]" (Liddell and Scott Dictionary). The root meaning ("to turn aside") and the Lucan context favor the latter. Misleading the people is a charge that tyrants make of their opponents, e.g., Pharaoh charges Moses and Aaron with misleading the people from their work (Exod 5:4), and the wicked king Ahab charges Elijah with misleading Israel (I Kings 18:17). In Luke two other equivalent descriptions of this overall charge are "stirring up" (*anaseiein*) the people in 23:5 and "leading astray" (*apostrephein*) the people in 23:14.[19] In Acts a similar charge is made against Paul in varying vocabulary: "disturbing our city" (16:20: *ektarassein*); "overturning the world" (17:6: *anastatoun*); "teaching against the [Jewish] people, and the Law, and this place [Jerusalem Temple]" (21:28]; "arousing revolts [pl. of *stasis*] among all Jews" (23:5). The "our nation" in Luke 23:2 is clearly the Jewish people of the parallels in 23:5,14.[20] The phrase is Lucan language, for in 7:5 the Jewish elders of Capernaum tell Jesus that the Roman centurion loves "our nation." Kosmala ("His Blood" 116-17) relates this main charge to the language used for the false prophet in Deut 13:2-6; 18:20-22, the one who turns people away from the Lord God. He points to the *baraita* in TalBab *Sanhedrin* 43a (p. 376 above) charging Yeshu with having enticed Israel to apostasy. Above (pp. 541-44) we discussed the issue of whether Jesus was condemned as the false prophet, but found that all the evidence linking Jesus to this figure belongs to the later sections of the NT, after the Jewish Revolt. (By possibly deliberate irony, what Luke would have Jesus accused of in 23:2 was quite true of the leaders in the Jewish Revolt four decades later.) Luke is writing the charges in 23:2 from the atmosphere of Jewish versus Christian polemics of the 70s-80s. In any case the Lucan readers know that this is a false charge: Jesus frequently taught people (Luke 4:14b-15,31-32; 5:1-3; etc.), but he did not mislead them in any way that threatened Rome. The truth is that he has led the people in a way displeasing to those who accuse him (Luke 19:47-48; 20:6,19,26; 21:38; 22:2).[21]

Luke's readers would also recognize falsity in the subordinate charges.

---

[19]Kosmala ("His Blood" 117) would trace these Greek vocabulary variants to the hiphil conjugation of such Hebrew verbal roots as *swt* and *ndḥ*.

[20]The fact that there is no possessive pronoun in those other verses may explain why scribes in the Koine textual tradition omitted "our" from 23:2.

[21]Luke 9:41 spoke of a "misled" (passive of *diastrephein*) generation, but Jesus tried to correct it.

The first of these concerns taxes paid to Caesar. Both head taxes and poll taxes were part of the Roman system. "Caesar" was the cognomen of Julius (Gaius Julius Caesar), and the adopted name of Augustus (a great-nephew by marriage of Julius) and of Augustus' successors.[22] As for Jesus' forbidding "the giving of taxes to Caesar," Luke 20:22 (alone among the Synoptics) uses the same expression *dounai phoron* in the trap question proposed to Jesus, "Is it permitted for us *to give tax* to Caesar or not?" In that interchange Jesus did *not* forbid giving tax to Caesar.[23] Indeed, he was notorious for associating with tax collectors (Luke 5:27–30; 7:34; 15:1; 18:9–14).

The second subordinate charge is that Jesus was saying "he is Messiah king." *Christos basileus* could be translated as "anointed king," but so soon after the issue of Jesus as the Messiah (22:67: *ho Christos*) in the Jewish interrogation, surely "Messiah king" is meant here. In the Sanhedrin scene Jesus gave a most ambiguous answer as to whether he was the Messiah. Yet earlier in 19:38–40 he refused to rebuke those in Jerusalem who hailed him as king, even if in 22:25 he expressed disdain for the lordship of kings. D. Schmidt ("Luke's"), trying to analyze the innocence of Jesus with regard to these charges, has introduced an important nuance into the picture by showing that in the stances of Jesus there are ambiguities that could be exploited. In my judgment, however, his claim that the accusers of Jesus would not necessarily be seen by Luke's readers as liars (p. 116) is too lenient. Those who accuse Jesus have used ambiguities in a way that most readers would recognize as distortion. They are playing on the fears of a Roman governor that this Jew may be trying to restore a kingdom that Rome had supplanted twenty-five years before, and by so doing challenge the emperor.[24] We find in Tacitus (*Hist.* 5.9) a condemnatory attitude toward Simon who after Herod the Great's death assumed the name of king without waiting for Caesar's decision. In Acts 17:5–7 Jews try to alarm the authorities at Thessalonica by claiming that Paul and Silas acted against the decrees of Caesar by saying that there is another king, Jesus. Through their manipulations against Jesus the Jewish authorities are causing the suffering of an *innocent,* and that is what Luke would have the readers recognize (so also Schmidt, "Luke's" 118).

[22]For Luke and his audience "Caesar" would have been understood as "the emperor." If the Lucan usage goes back to Jesus' own time, "Caesar" may have been a more specific reference to Tiberius Caesar. See p. 844, n. 39 below.

[23]S. Talavero Tovar, CTom 108 (1981), 3–40, contends, nevertheless, that Jesus would not have been a paragon of loyalty to Rome, for these occupiers were levying taxes on land dedicated to God. Readers of the Gospels, living outside Palestine, would not have had the same problems or sensibilities about taxes.

[24]This is more plausible than Fitzmyer's suggestion (*Luke* 2.1475) that Pilate might dislike a king because of tyrannical kings in early Roman history.

After hearing in 23:2 a main charge, subdivided into two specific charges,[25] Pilate in 23:3 pays attention to only part of the last charge, i.e., the "king" part of "Messiah king" expanded to "the King of the Jews." (Thus Pilate appears interested not in abstract kingship, but in what affects Judea.) In other words, despite Luke's expanded introduction, when it comes to the direct interchange between Pilate and Jesus, Luke falls back on the exact language of Mark 15:2.[26] The Westcott-Hort Greek NT raises in the margin the possibility that *sy legeis*, "You say (so)," should be translated as a question, "Do you say (so)?" Others urge that it must be negative here since it leads Pilate to find nothing guilty in Jesus. However, if the phrase serves as a qualified affirmative (rather than as a question or a negative), then in the storyline from such a qualification Pilate recognizes that Jesus is not guilty as a threatening political adversary. Many scholars contend that as one moves from Mark to the later Gospels, there is a tendency to inculpate the Jews and exculpate the Romans. However, since in Luke 22:70 a plural form of *sy legeis* was Jesus' response to the chief priests, Jesus does not show himself more friendly to Pilate than to them.

In 23:4 Pilate addresses himself to the chief priests and the crowds,[27] something he does not do in the comparable Mark/Matt passage. The "crowds" are presumably part of the "multitude" of 23:1 and are "the people" of 23:13. But one cannot press too exactly where the crowds came from and their exact contour; nor is it necessary to identify those here with the crowd that came to arrest Jesus in 22:47.[28] The introduction of crowds is Luke's form of a phenomenon I shall discuss in APPENDIX V A: Besides describing the Jewish authorities, all the Gospels include a collectivity that was hostile to Jesus. In his response to the chief priests and the crowds, Pilate makes the first of three solemn statements of Jesus' innocence.[29] All three involve the negative "nothing," plus the verb "to find," plus *aition*, plus

---

[25]There is a notable series of textual variants in these charges. Above I suggested that in formulating them Luke was aware of attacks on Jesus in the last third of the 1st cent. In the OL of 23:2 the charges multiplied: "and destroying the Law and the prophets" (cf. Matt 5:17) and "leading astray the women and the children." The latter is continued in some OL mss.: "for they are not washed [or baptized] as we are, nor do they clean themselves." (See n. 17 above.) Such additions are often attributed to Marcion, reflecting his dislike of Jewish attitudes and exemplifying his rejection of the Law, of marriage, and/or of Jewish washings. See Blinzler, *Prozess* 280; also Epiphanius, *Panarion* 42.11.6; GCS 31.108ff.

[26]Only the introductions to the quoted words vary. Luke's "asked" is *erōtan*, substituted for Mark's *eperōtan* ("questioned"), which Luke saves for 23:6; and Luke's "said" is *ephē*, used by preference for Mark's historical present ("says").

[27]The expression *eipen pros* ("said to") is very Lucan.

[28]Fitzmyer (*Luke* 1.467) finds that throughout the Gospel Luke's use of "crowd" and "crowds" is "baffling."

[29]See 23:14–15,22. Some would find a fourth in 23:20, but that verse has no direct statement of not guilty.

the preposition *en*. I have translated this combination as "I find nothing guilty," understanding *aition* to be an adjectival form modifying *oudeis*. However, the neuter *aition* can also mean "cause, case," and some (dealing freely with *oudeis* and *en*) would render it "I find no case against this man" (see John 18:38b, where that is more appropriate). Since three similar statements may be found in John 18:38b; 19:4,6, Luke and John may be drawing on a common tradition not used by Mark (see pp. 86–92, 486 above).

Why does Pilate react thus to Jesus' somewhat uncooperative "You say (so)," unless he interprets that statement as a negative? I have already cited Albinus' decision to release an even more uncooperative Jesus bar Ananias (Josephus, *War* 6.5.3; #305) simply because the procurator thought the man a politically harmless religious fanatic. But the Lucan logic should be seen on a different level: Jesus is transparently innocent to anyone whose eyes are not closed by prejudice. Besides Pilate, we shall find these others witnessing to his innocence: Herod will judge Jesus, who answers nothing at all, to be not guilty of the charges (23:9,15); a criminal on the cross who has simply seen Jesus will declare that this man has done nothing disorderly (23:41); and a centurion who has seen what took place when Jesus was on the cross will state: "Certainly this man was just" (23:47). In that sequence it would have been incongruous for Pilate to find Jesus not guilty because of argumentation! Pilate's instinct in 23:4 is equivalent to his perception in Mark 15:10 (Matt 27:18): "For he had knowledge that it was out of envy/zeal that the chief priests had given him over."

Even as in Mark 15:3, we are told in Luke 23:5 that "they" persist in their charges, i.e., the chief priests and the crowds, who are not daunted by Pilate's declaration of not guilty. In their strong insistence (impf. of *epischyein*), they reiterate their main charge of 23:2 in slightly different vocabulary: "He stirs up [*anaseioun*] the people."[30] This time the charge has an appended geographical note: "teaching through the whole of Judea, having begun from Galilee even to here." (Compare the geographical note in the charge against Paul before Felix in Acts 24:5.) The same language is found in Acts 10:37, where Peter speaks of Jesus' preaching the word "through the whole of Judea, having begun from Galilee."[31] How does Luke understand the geography of the land? Why does he omit Samaria, which separated Galilee from Judea? Is it because he is interested only in Pilate and Herod, and since Pilate controlled Judea and Samaria, mention of Judea is sufficient (as in 3:1)? Is it because Jesus did not preach there (9:52–53), passing only along

---

[30]*Laos* ("people") is used 84 times in Luke-Acts, 2 in Mark, 14 in Matt, 2 in John.

[31]Robinson (*Way* 43) contends that the formula is preLucan. Such a description may have arisen in imitation of the set OT geographical dimension "from Dan to Beersheba" (Judg 20:1; I Sam 3:20; etc.).

the border between Samaria and Galilee (17:11)? In any case "through the whole of Judea, having begun from Galilee" does not mean that Luke confusedly thought Galilee a part of Judea nor that we have to understand Judea as a broad designation of the larger "land of the Jews." The formula "having begun from Galilee" is meant to signal the point of origin of Jesus' ministry, even as in Luke 24:47 "beginning from Jerusalem" signals the point of origin of the ministry of the Christian preachers. If with this formula in Acts 10:37 Peter is praising the whole of Jesus' ministry, in Luke 23:5 Jesus' opponents are condemning the whole of Jesus' ministry. Some have thought that by mentioning Galilee these opponents are playing on the memory of Judas the Galilean (Acts 5:37), who came from Galilee to stir up revolt against the Romans in AD 6. In the Lucan narrative, however, "Galilee" stirs up the possibility of sending Jesus to Herod (Antipas) the tetrarch of Galilee (Luke 3:1) and asking that ruler to conduct a preliminary investigation (see §33 below).

THE JOHANNINE EXPANSION OF THE BASIC INTERCHANGE (JOHN 18:28B–38A)

In the ANALYSIS below I shall sketch the elaborate structure of seven episodes in the Johannine account of the Roman trial, one of the master dramatic constructions in this Gospel. The first two of those episodes (commented upon here) are so elaborate a development of the basic interchange between Pilate and Jesus that if one did not know the elements from Mark 15:2–5, one would not be able to recognize them in John 18:33,37 and 19:9 (the latter in Episode 6).[32] Fortna, in his reconstruction of the source that John used (*Fourth* 163), identifies elements in 18:28a,29,33,37b, i.e., basically what is in Mark. However, the danger of reconstructing a preJohannine source by eliminating all that is Johannine is that logically one is forced to posit a source that is extraneous to the Johannine community. If the source (or, I prefer, tradition) developed within the Johannine community of which the evangelist was a part, then what is Johannine would have been shared by both the tradition and the evangelist. Baum-Bodenbender (*Hoheit* 238) is more generous than Fortna in recognizing as preJohannine here 18:28ac,33,36–38, which she thinks comes from a source anterior to Mark as well. I remain skeptical about exact reconstructions of the source or tradition; but I would judge that it included elements not in Mark, e.g., the core of the statement in 18:36: "If my kingdom were of this world, my attendants

---

[32]Theoretically one could argue that John used Mark (very freely) as a source; but what we have seen elsewhere suggests that here Mark and John are independent witnesses to preGospel tradition (Dodd, *Historical* 120; Hahn "Prozess" 26–27; B. Ehrman, "Jesus'" 125).

would have struggled lest I be given over to the Jews." The fourth evangelist contributed to the final phrasing but used elements like "my kingdom" and "my attendants" that have not occurred previously—the resemblance in theme to Matt 26:53 (Jesus' ability to call upon the Father for angelic help) suggests a common preGospel tradition that Matt and John have developed in different ways.

Episode 1: Pilate and Those outside the Praetorium (18:28b–32). As with the other Gospels, we must not forget the transitional verse treated in 18:28a: "Then they lead Jesus from Caiaphas to the praetorium. Now it was early." At the beginning of the Roman trial John has introduced the praetorium,[33] which Mark/Matt will not mention till the Roman mockery after the trial (§36 below; Mark 15:16). The Synoptic postponement of setting means that in none of the first three Gospels does one have any idea where the trial takes place. The ability of the crowd to come up and talk to Pilate (Mark 15:8; Luke 23:4) and of the chief priests to interrupt (15:3) almost gives the impression that all of this took place in a public square. John's more precise setting of locale may be historical—at least it is not implausible—but the precision is primarily in service to Johannine theological symbolism. "The Jews" are outside the praetorium refusing to enter; Jesus is inside the praetorium; these are the separated forces of darkness and light. Pilate must shuttle back and forth, for he is the person-in-between who does not wish to make a decision and so vainly tries to reconcile the opposing forces. For John, however, one must decide for light or darkness and thus judge oneself as one faces the light come into the world (3:19–21). By not deciding for the truth, Pilate is deciding for falsehood and darkness.

The "they" who do not enter into the praetorium in 18:28b are, at least in part, to be identified with the high priest(s) and the Jewish attendants of 18:12–27, i.e., the protagonists of the nighttime interrogation that took place simultaneously with Simon Peter's denials.[34] Yet in 18:31 we shall find them described simply as "the Jews," and that is how John means readers to think of them. The chief priests are still a specific agent in the Johannine trial account (19:6,15), but they have been joined to the nation (18:35); and some ten times there are references to "the Jews."

Granted such a generalization of the "they" in 18:28b, there has been speculation about what would make them (the chief priests in particular or "the Jews" in general?) defiled if they entered into the praetorium. The thesis that Jews in Palestine of the 1st cent. AD thought all Gentiles to be impure

---

[33]For the locale of this site in Jerusalem, see §31C above.

[34]These two scenes, nighttime interrogation by the high priest and early-morning Roman trial, are visibly connected by the opening sentences: "They led (him) first to Annas" (18:13) and "They lead Jesus from Caiaphas to the praetorium" (18:28a).

ritually is rejected by A. Büchler (JQR 17 [1926–27], 1–81), who argues that even the Pharisees, the stricter party, did not hold this view. Was impurity calculated according to the more demanding Jewish attitudes condemnatory of Gentile women who ignored the laws of Lev 15:19–33 involving impurity during menstruation? John, however, unlike Matt 27:19, mentions nothing about the presence of Pilate's wife. Another possibility stems from the fact that Jews were subject to defilement by a corpse (Num 19:16; 31:19), so that houses or rooms built over burial places were considered unclean (Mishna *Oholot* 17.5). We have testimony at Qumran about disliking Gentiles because they buried corpses (foundation sacrifices?) beneath their homes: "You shall not do as the Gentiles do: they bury their dead everywhere; they bury them even in their houses" (11Q *Miqdaš* [Temple Scroll] 48:11–12). Whatever the cause of the impurity,[35] it is likely that John was aware of an existing attitude; but the very fact that the specific defilement is not spelled out suggests that John's reason for mentioning impurity may be theological irony. Those who stand outside the praetorium are careful about ritual purity; yet they wish to put Jesus to death!

The reason for avoiding impurity is "in order that they might eat the Passover (meal)." Ezra 6:19–22 describes a Passover: The Levites had purified themselves, and among the participants were those who had separated themselves from the uncleanness of the peoples of the land. Philo (*De specialibus legibus* 2.27; #145) explains Passover: All the people are involved with the animal victims and "the whole nation functions in a priestly manner with pure hands." The reference in 18:28b means that for John the next day (Fri. night/Saturday) would be the 15th of Nisan involving the Passover meal, and that therefore Jesus was sentenced by Pilate and died on the 14th of Nisan.[36] I find quite implausible the explanation of Story ("Bearing") that for John Jesus had eaten his Passover meal on Thursday night but the Jewish attendants who arrested him and the priests had not yet had time to eat their meal. According to Story's interpretation of Exod 12:10 they had till 6 AM Friday to eat it, and outside Pilate's praetorium they were concerned to keep open that possibility. However, John does not report that—for him their worry was defilement. Logically they would have lost their chance to eat the Passover, for the trial lasted till noon (19:14) and they were still there. Moreover, the group before the praetorium were "the Jews," not just the arresting party. When Jesus was eating Thursday night, it was made clear that the feast had not yet come (13:29); and 19:14,31 confirm that only the next day (Fri. night/

---

[35]Another thesis is based on the date: From noon on the 14th of Nisan (the eve of Passover) there was to be no contact with leaven (Deut 16:4), and Gentiles might have leaven in their houses.

[36]See APPENDIX II B for arguments that this date was historical over against the Synoptic implication that Jesus died on the 15th after having eaten a Passover meal on Thursday evening.

Saturday) would be Passover. At most John may be making a theological play on the fact that "the Jews" had not yet eaten the Passover; once Jesus had been put to death as the Lamb of God who takes away the sin of the world (1:29), the Passover meal to be eaten by "the Jews" would have been replaced in its redemptive significance.

John 18:28b does not explain exactly how ritual impurity would *prevent* the eating of the Passover meal. According to Num 9:6–12 if Israelites contracted impurity and could not eat the Passover meal at the regular time, they had to postpone the celebration for a month. Random exposure to contamination by ritually impure Gentiles would have been a danger only for priests on Temple duty or for Jews who had already been prepared for participation in a sacrificial meal. If others contracted impurity from entering the praetorium, it could have been removed before the meal by a bath at sunset. Impurity from contact with a corpse, however, was a seven-day contamination (Num 19:11).[37] In any case we are once more encountering theological irony: Those who are so careful about the Passover meal will demand the death of the Lamb of God (John 1:29,36). This will happen at noon, just as lambs for Passover begin to be slaughtered in the Temple precincts (see pp. 846–48 below on 19:14).

In 18:29 Pilate appears without previous introduction, even as in the Synoptics. The question "What accusation [*katēgoria*]?" functions in the same introductory role as Luke 23:2: "They began to accuse [*katēgorein*]"; both authors are familiar with Roman trials where accusations are presented first. Some would create a scenario wherein the Jews are offended by this question because they have set the sentence themselves and have come looking simply for the license (*exsequatur*) to carry it out (see §31, D2 above). The fatal objection to that scenario is that in John there has been no Jewish trial during the night. Rather the uncooperativeness that greets Pilate's question is part of the Johannine dialogue technique: It creates a tension that will be used to uncover what lies beneath the surface. In the Jewish answer of 18:30, just as in Luke 23:2, there is a contemptuous use of the demonstrative ("this fellow"). "Doing what is bad [*kakon poiein*]" echoes partially Jesus' defiant statement before the high priest in 18:23: "If I have spoken badly [*kakōs lalein*], give testimony about what is bad [*kakou*]." In Johannine irony those outside the praetorium are the ones who have done what is bad or evil, for they have refused to come to the light (3:19–20). Although previously in John (eight times) *paradidonai*, "to give over," has had only Judas as an agent, now (three times: 18:30,35, 19:11) it will be used with "the Jews" as

---

[37]It is noteworthy that according to Josephus in *Ant.* 18.4.3; #93–94 Jews went to get the high-priestly vestments from Roman custody seven days before the festival, and then the vestments were purified; but in *Ant.* 15.11.4; #408 Josephus mentions only one day before the festival.

the agents; and here they use the verb of themselves as if it were a praise-worthy action.

Pilate's response in 18:31 offers difficulties: The Roman prefect tells "the Jews" to judge Jesus, only to be informed *by them* that they have no power to do so! The dialogue, however, is obviously for the information of the readers, not of Pilate. More difficult is the decision whether Pilate speaks in irony, putting "the Jews" in their place: If they will not follow Roman proce-dures (or cannot, since they have no serious case), they can take care of the matter themselves—all the while knowing that they are legally impotent to do that. One would then also have to posit irony in 19:6, "Take him your-selves and crucify (him)." Others, understanding Pilate's challenge to be seri-ous, not irony, suggest that the prefect had no idea that these people wanted Jesus' death and was telling them they could judge him guilty of (lesser) punishment under their own law. Only when "the Jews" answered would Pilate have found out that they were demanding a death penalty. In the sto-ryline, however, Pilate seems to know what "the Jews" are about, and so the irony explanation is more likely.

Equally difficult is what is meant by "It is not permitted us to put anyone to death."[38] What law or custom does not permit execution? In John 5:10 "it is not permitted" refers to the tenets of the Mosaic Law, and Pilate has just spoken of "your law"; but clearly the law given by Moses (John 1:17) allows execution. If one takes the law to be the Mosaic Law (Allen, Liberty, Mi-chaels, etc.), should a qualification be understood? Augustine, Chrysostom, and modern scholars, like Millar, think of a qualification of time: not permit-ted on the eve of a feast or at Passover. In Acts 12:3–4, although Peter is seized during the days of the Unleavened Bread, his fate is postponed until after Passover. Yet JEWJ 78 challenges whether such a limitation was opera-tive. Certainly TalBab *Sanhedrin* 43a (p. 376 above) shows no embar-rassment in reporting that "on the eve of Passover Yeshu was hanged." Others have suggested a qualification of the charge: not permitted to put anyone to death on a political charge. In John 8:59 and 10:31 there were Jewish at-tempts to stone Jesus; in 10:33 the reason was specified as blasphemy; but

---

[38]The verb *apokteinein* means "to kill"; but although in Johannine polemic "the Jews" may be considered as wanting to kill Jesus, here in the legal atmosphere of the trial the less tendentious "to put to death" seems appropriate. Michaels ("John") argues for the meaning "kill" (contending that *thanatoun* would be the judicial term for "put to death") and sees a reference to the Decalogue, "Thou shalt not kill" (Exod 20:13). In favor of his view he quotes the statistic that *exestin* (or its equivalent) for "permitted/lawful" refers in twenty-five of thirty-one NT uses to what God forbids or allows, with Acts (16:21; 22:25) supplying the unusual instances of what was legal by Roman standards. Yet *apokteinein* is not used in the Exodus commandment (LXX 20:15), and most of the NT references using *exestin* are not in conversation with a Roman judge. Nowhere else does John have "the Jews" forthrightly acknowledge that what they wanted done to Jesus would violate God's law, as Michaels would have them doing here.

there was no suggestion that Roman permission was needed for that. Thus it is possible that here Jesus is brought to the Romans because the charge is not religious. Vicent Cernuda ("Aporía") has a subtle variant of this approach: They are not permitted to put *just anyone* to death. (For this meaning of *oudeis,* he points to Prov 27:4; Wis 1:8; Sir 40:7.) While they could put Jesus to death on religious grounds, they could not put him to death as a would-be king rebelling against the emperor—and that is how they want him remembered.

Against that approach, however, and favoring the idea that John 18:31 means Roman law is the fact that the next verse concentrates on the *kind* of death which (seemingly) could come only from the Romans. That kind of death is the lifting up of Jesus on a cross, as 12:32–33 makes clear. The idea that crucifixion is what "the Jews" want but are not able to accomplish by themselves is suggested also in 19:6.[39] The more widely held view that Roman rather than Jewish law is meant gives an easier solution, but can one prove that the Romans forbade the Jews "to put anyone to death"? For arguments pro and con, see §18D above; there I concluded that according to the better evidence, except for certain specified religious and moral crimes where death was the automatic penalty, the Jews in Judea were not allowed to execute. This imposed limitation caused "the Jews" frustration in dealing with Jesus as they imply when they do cite the Mosaic Law in 19:7: "We have a law, and according to the law he ought to die."[40] Roman authority underlies Pilate's braggadocio in 19:10 as he reminds Jesus that *he* has the power to release and the power to crucify.

The technical dispute among interpreters about which law is meant should not distract us from two major Johannine points in 18:32: "in order that there might be fulfilled the word of Jesus that he spoke, signifying what kind of death he was going to die." John's major concern is not which law forbids putting to death but the fulfillment of Jesus' word about death. Both Jewish accusers and Roman judge are actors in a drama scripted by a divine planner. We saw in reference to John 18:9 (p. 290 above) that the necessity to have Jesus' word fulfilled was the same as the necessity to have fulfilled the word

---

[39]We saw on p. 533 above that a Qumran interpretation of Deut 21:22 mandated crucifixion as a form of execution; but we do not know that this was ever put into effect by Jews or permitted to them by the Romans.

[40]I find implausible Michaels's contention ("John" 478) that this clause represents the Jews' *opinion* that Jesus should die, but for them to execute him themselves would violate the commandment to kill (n. 38 above) because they had not put Jesus on trial (in John—Michaels casts doubt on the Synoptic tradition of a trial). Yet the various OT *commands* to execute a blasphemer or seducer do not specify a trial or what the investigation would consist of; moreover in John a decision that Jesus must die had been taken by the Sanhedrin, consisting of the highest religious authorities (11:47–53). Far from violating the command to kill, the execution of Jesus would be seen by some as a religious duty (15:20; 16:2).

spoken by God through the prophets. The "word" is surely that of 12:31–32, where the evangelist explained that in saying "When I am lifted up from the earth," Jesus was "signifying what kind of death he was going to die." (The latter is the same phrase used in 18:32.) Jesus is not going to die a death like stoning, the usual punishment for blasphemy, that would cast him down to the earth, but a death that would elevate him. The Romans may present his crucifixion as the punishment of a reputed king who would rebel against Caesar, but believers will recognize it as the triumphant lifting up of Jesus in return to the Father. Ironically, "the Jews" want to force the Roman to contribute to the glorification of Jesus.

Episode 2: Pilate and Jesus inside the Praetorium (18:33–38a). The dialogue between Pilate and "the Jews" has made clear that the latter are not interested in a trial to determine Jesus' guilt. They know that he is "doing what is bad" and must be put to death. Still, they have not yet told Pilate their precise accusation; and so there is no more preparation in John 18:33 than in Mark 15:2 for Pilate's "Are you the King of the Jews?" To ask this question Pilate goes "again" into the praetorium and summons Jesus.[41] Above I rejected the idea that in the Synoptics the "you" of the question is emphatic, expressing incredulity. Despite the longer context in John and greater interest in portraying Pilate, the idea of incredulity probably should be rejected here too; Pilate is not yet demeaning Jesus. Some have wondered whether "the King of the Jews" takes on special coloring from John's hostility toward "the Jews"; one can find some support for that in the sarcastic "your king" in 19:14,15. The Synoptic answer to the question, "You say (so)," will appear in John four verses further on (18:37), but only after ambiguity about the implications of the title has been cleared up. The first ambiguity concerns the origin of the title, and 18:34–35 shows that none of this was a Roman idea. Beyond that it would be unJohannine to have the crucial dialogue based on hearsay. The *mēti* in "Am I a Jew?" expects a negative answer (but it is not clearly contemptuous). All the opposition has come from the Jewish nation (*ethnos* as in Luke 23:2) and the chief priests (cf. Luke 23:13: "the chief priests . . . and the people"). Schnackenburg (*John* 3.248) is wrong in arguing that John does not mean the whole Jewish nation, which had not as a totality given Jesus over to Pilate, but refers to their representatives, the elders, who are never mentioned in John. Such a historical argument is irrelevant; John is generalizing, for he sees "the Jews" of his time who have expelled Christian believers from the synagogue as the heirs of the hostile authorities of Jesus' time.

[41]*Palin* ("again," found in most mss. in 18:32 but in different sequences) can be rendered "back." Was Jesus already inside the praetorium as Pilate spoke outside, or is he now brought inside as in Mark 15:16? More plausibly the former.

Are John's readers to think that Jesus is truly "the King of the Jews" when the title came from his enemies and is being used against him? In 6:15, when Jesus realized that the people would come to carry him off and make him king, he fled to the mountain alone. Yet Jesus did not reject Nathanael's hailing him as "the King of Israel" in 1:49. He was acclaimed by that title again in 12:13 and did not deny it, even if he qualified it by his reaction in 12:15. In any case Jesus answers Pilate's question about being a king by discussing his kingdom. Pilate understands being a king in terms of what Jesus has done that would cause Jesus' nation and the chief priests to make such a charge. We must remember that this dialogue was written after the Revolt of AD 66–70 when the world had seen Jewish revolutionaries overthrow Roman control for a brief while. Accordingly, in 18:36 Jesus tries to clear up Pilate's misunderstanding by stressing that his attendants had not struggled on his behalf. I pointed out above (p. 744) that the presence of a saying in Matt 26:53 with somewhat the same thrust may mean that we have here, in Johannine rewriting, an argument from an earlier tradition combating the portrait of Jesus as a dangerous figure. Jesus' words are phrased as a contrary-to-fact condition: "If my kingdom were of this world, my attendants . . ." We have never heard of his attendants before; all the previous references have been to the hostile attendants of the Jewish authorities. It is not clear whether we are to think that because his kingdom is of another type, so are his attendants, or to think that he does not have attendants (but only friends: 15:15).[42] The verb "to struggle" is *agōnizesthai,* of the same root as the *agōnia* that came upon Jesus in Luke 22:44—both Gospels echo the language of the last time with its cataclysmic struggle. "Lest I be given over to the Jews" curiously ignores Pilate's assessment in the previous verse that Jesus has been given over *to him* by the Jews ("your nation and the chief priests"). Perhaps Jesus is being diplomatic in not stressing the Romans in this hostile context. In any case, 18:36 is very Johannine in having Jesus speak of "the Jews" in such an alienated way that one would not suspect that he himself was Jewish. This is the language of the Johannine Christians expelled from the synagogue.

The most important aspect of 18:36 is Jesus' three-times-reiterated affirmation that his kingdom is not of this world, not from here—the affirmation of an incarnate Word who has come into this world from above. One should not too easily identify Jesus' kingdom in John with the kingdom of

---

[42]The situation is complicated by the apparent overlooking of the fact that Simon Peter had cut off the ear of the servant of the high priest in John 18:10. Seemingly this action was too insignificant to be considered a struggle made by Jesus' attendants. Above (pp. 268, 290) I found implausible the thesis that this action meant that Simon Peter could no longer be considered a disciple (= attendant?) of Jesus.

God in the Synoptic Gospels. Throughout John Jesus has struggled to prevent people from misunderstanding gifts he brings them, in part because those gifts bear the same name as elements well known in human experience (light, bread, water, etc.). But Jesus' gifts are not of this world; what makes them true or real (*alēthinos*) is that they are of God. They come into this world with Jesus and are possibilities because he offers them freely. Indeed, he can identify himself with them: I am the light, I am the bread of life, etc. Similarly Jesus' kingdom has come with him into the world, but like him it is not of this world (17:14). If it has attendants, i.e., disciples of Jesus, "They are not of the world any more than I am of the world" (17:16). While what John tells us of Jesus' kingdom is meant to offset any secular charge that he was trying to establish an earthly kingdom to rival Caesar's, one may wonder whether it was not also meant to offset the ideas of other Christians who too simply identified the kingdom of the Son (of Man, or of God) with the visible church, e.g., directions opened up by Matt 13:14 and Col 1:13. John would have disagreed with the answer that Jesus' relatives in Palestine are supposed to have given to the Emperor Domitian's question about Christ's kingdom: "It was not worldly on earth, but heavenly and angelic, and it would be established at the end of the world when he would come in glory to judge the living and the dead" (Eusebius, EH 3.20.4). The Johannine Jesus would say that since he has already come as the light into the world, judgment is taking place as people decide for or against him; his kingdom is not solely in heaven or angelic—rather it is in this world but not of it.

"So then" (*oukoun:* unique in the NT) in 18:37 returns the dialogue to the main theme. Despite all the nuances about kingdom Pilate deduces that after all Jesus is a king. This offers John the opportunity to use the fixed response of the tradition: *sy legeis*. To this "You say" a clause is appended: "that I am a king." Note that the full title "the King of the Jews" has been modified by Jesus, for his response is no simple affirmative (pace Bultmann, *John* 654). Nor is it negative. Although what Pilate asks constitutes truth, it is not phrased the way Jesus would wish.[43] In presenting his own phraseology, Jesus, who has spoken negatively to clarify what his kingdom is not, now speaks positively to proclaim who he is. "I have been born" and "I have come into the world" are not separate moments; rather they stand in parallelism with the second clause interpreting the first. In 9:39 Jesus said, "I came into this world for judgment," and confrontation with the truth is judgment. The reason why Jesus can bear witness to the truth is because he has come down from above (3:13), and sees what the Father does (5:19), and has heard

---

[43]Merlier ("*Sy legeis*"): "It is you who say it, not I"; also see BDF 441³. That rendition is to be favored over attempts to read a question; "Do you say that I am a king?" or to divide it differently; "You say it. Because I am a king, I have been born . . ."

what the Father said (8:26). Jesus can bear witness because *he is the truth* (14:6), a phrase that is an unqualifiedly acceptable assessment of Jesus, while *he is king* needs qualification. (Interestingly, later speculation echoed in a Middle Persian Manichaean fragment has Jesus answer Pilate's question in the next verse [18:38a] "What is truth?" by "I am the truth"—see Tolman, "Possible.")

The idea that Jesus bore witness before Pilate is found in I Tim 6:12–13; but the witness in John is more than not denying. It is a witness that explains the nature and extent of Jesus' kingship. Does the connection between being king and bearing witness have OT background? Some have pointed to Isa 55:3–4, where David is made both a witness and a chief and commander to the peoples; and Derrett ("Christ" 192ff.) would add Ps 89:36–38, where the royal offspring of David on his throne continue forever as a faithful witness to God's promise to David. Von Jüchen (*Jesus* 11) would regard Jesus' "You say that I am a king" in 18:37 as an answer not only to Pilate but to all people who have waited for a Messiah. Jesus chooses to explain the sense in which the Messiah is a king not in dialogue with "the Jews" (10:24–25) but to a Roman as evidence that he has come for "everyone who is of the truth."

Pilate will not be able to understand a kingdom that is not established by human endeavor but by God; and his failure to understand will stem not primarily from the fact that he is a representative of earthly dominion but also and primarily because he is not of the truth. That becomes clear as Jesus explains how a kingdom that "is not of this world" does not threaten Caesar's ruling authority. Instead of attendants of a worldly kingdom, Jesus thinks of those who are of the truth and for that reason hear his voice. (*Akouein* with the genitive signifies listening with understanding and acceptance.) Jesus has spoken before of the sheep who hear the voice of the Good Shepherd (10:3) and follow him. Some of this may echo OT language, e.g., "The Lord shall raise up for you a prophet like me [Moses] . . . you shall listen to his voice" (Deut 18:15); and the willingness to hear is related to the way one lives. Good deeds prepare one to listen (or to come to the light: 3:21) and also manifest that one is truly adhering to the truth (I John 3:18–19). Nevertheless, in the Johannine dualism of those who are *of* the truth and *of* falsehood, there is a predisposition to one or the other that goes beyond deeds. The sheep who hear Jesus are waiting for him and recognize his voice (John 10:4–5); they are those whom the Father has given him out of the world (17:6). In a sense, then, Jesus' statement, "Everyone who is of the truth hears my voice" is a test of Pilate; the judge is being judged. Pilate's response, "What is truth?" is not to be understood as a profound philosophical question. It does echo the imperiousness of the Roman when challenged (see also 19:22); but ironically it is a self-condemnation: His failure to recognize truth and hear Jesus' voice shows that he does not belong to God. This is the last time in John that Jesus shall speak of truth, and his voice has not been heard.

ANALYSIS

The Roman trial of Jesus is treated differently in each Gospel. We are dealing in no Gospel with a complete eyewitness account of what happened (especially in John, where Jesus is inside the praetorium away from the public eye or even from the eye of a disciple who might have remembered). As we have seen (§31, D1), the thesis that a written record of the trial existed in the Roman archives is fiction, despite later patristic references to it. Rather there are elements of Christian tradition that are common to the four Gospels—elements that arose in different ways and are of different historical value (as will be discussed in each scene).[44] Those elements include two short interchanges between Jesus and Pilate (this section), a scene involving Barabbas (§34), and the condemnation to the cross (§35). Yet the extent to which these elements are dramatized and others are introduced varies considerably among the Gospels. Even the portrait of Pilate is not consistent.[45] To see this let us look at the organization of the whole Roman trial in each Gospel.[46]

A. The Marcan Roman Trial (Mark 15:1–15)

This very brief account is only about 60 percent of the length of the Marcan account of the Jewish proceedings, and dramatically and theologically

---

[44]In the COMMENT above I mentioned the thesis that "Are you the King of the Jews?" stems from the title on the cross, thought to be historical. In §34 I shall contend that the release of a criminal named Barabbas may be a historical memory; however, that need not include the custom of a release during the feast or the close relationship between the release of Barabbas and the condemnation of Jesus.

[45]The thesis that the later the Gospel, the better the image of Pilate is not so simply established. For instance, in the latest of the four Gospels, according to Rensberger ("Politics" 402) the Johannine Pilate is a strong figure using Jesus to accomplish his purpose of making the Jews publicly accept the kingship of Jesus, a ridiculous figure, thus discrediting their nationalism. I would judge John's Pilate indecisive and weak to the point of failure in this moment of crisis. When challenged to be of the truth by hearing the voice of Jesus, he shows himself condemned by asking what is truth—that means he is not one of those given by God to Jesus. Pilate's attempt to salvage political gain is by petulant afterthought.

[46]I shall include in outlines here the transitional verses Mark 15:1, Matt 27:1–2; Luke 23:1; John 18:28a (discussed in §28 above) where the Jewish proceedings are closed and Jesus is transferred to Roman custody.

it is not nearly so engrossing. The machinations of the Sanhedrin authorities held together the Jewish trial, but here neither the character nor the motives of Pilate emerge clearly. His range of only mildly interested and even callous behavior includes being amazed when Jesus refuses to answer (15:5); recognizing that it is out of envy/zeal that Jesus was given over (15:10); asking what evil has he done (15:14); giving him over to be crucified in order to satisfy the crowd (15:15). The Marcan Pilate is not exculpated: He is not so malevolent as the chief priests, but he is a poor excuse for Roman justice.

The Jewish trial offered Peter's denials as an interesting counterpart to Jesus' fidelity under questioning. In the Roman trial Barabbas is the counterpart: Although he is guilty of violent political disturbance, he is released, while Jesus, who is innocent of the same charge, is condemned. But there is no development of Barabbas' personal participation comparable to that of Peter's increasing desperation. Theologically what one perceives in the Marcan Roman trial is the persistent hostility of the chief priests, the ease with which the crowd is swayed against Jesus, and Jesus' political innocence. (The latter is transparent even to Pilate; never is there a clarification about Jesus' attitude toward being called "the King of the Jews.") In working with tradition Mark was more impressive in constructing the Sanhedrin trial than he is here. (The other evangelists improve on the situation.) While for the purposes of commenting on all four Gospels, I shall break up the Marcan Roman trial into three segments, 15:2–5; 15:6–11 (Barabbas); and 15:12–15 (condemnation), it is really all a unit. Gnilka (*Markus* 2.297) is correct in arguing that there is no break between vv. 5 and 6; and Soltero ("Pilatus" 327) is correct that there is none between vv. 11 and 12.

B. The Matthean Roman Trial (Matt 27:1–26)

Almost twice as long as the Marcan account, Matt's Roman trial is longer than his Jewish trial. While using Marcan material as the backbone, Matt has supplemented it with dramatic incidents that greatly enliven the account and heighten the theological import. The comparison with Mark is sketched in the accompanying Table 4 (with the Matthean supplements marked by the sign ▪). If one keeps together Mark 15:2–5 and 6–11 as a unit, there are three segments in each of which Matt has supplemented Mark. The Judas scene that constitutes the supplement in the first segment (§29) points in one way back to the Sanhedrin trial, for Peter and Judas embody the predicted responses of disciples to what was done to Jesus in that trial. In another way it points forward to the Roman trial: The chief priests have begun to transfer

TABLE 4. COMPARING THE MARCAN/MATTHEAN ACCOUNTS
OF THE ROMAN TRIAL

Mark 15:1–15		Matt 27:1–26
15:1:	End of Sanhedrin Proceedings and Transfer to Pilate	27:1–2
		▪ 27:3–10: Judas— innocent blood
15:2–5:	Trial: Initial Questions by Pilate	27:11–14
15:6–11:	Trial: Barabbas or Jesus	27:15–18,20–21
		▪ 27:19: Dream of Pilate's wife
15:12–15:	Trial: Condemnation of Jesus	27:22–23,26
		▪ 27:24–25: Pilate washes hands; innocent blood

Jesus to Pilate, but the innocent blood of Jesus haunts Judas, who attempts to shift responsibility to the chief priests. The innocence of Jesus haunts the dreams of Pilate's wife in the Matthean supplement in the second segment, and innocent blood is a subject of debate between Pilate and "all the people" in the supplement in the third segment. Thus there is a common theme threaded through the three segments,[47] a theme dramatized with unforgettable touches: thirty pieces of silver and the Field of Blood in the first, a pagan woman's dream in the second, and washing the hands and "His blood on us and on our children" in the third.

Matt is using popular, almost folkloric, motifs to teach the theological lesson that God's justice is not mocked but is visited on each party involved in shedding the blood of God's Son. A major focus in the trial of Jesus becomes not the judgment passed on him but judgment on those who gave him over. Pilate becomes a more tortured figure, a man forced to condemn Jesus against his better judgment and still seeking to be found innocent by those who will hear what he did. A final touch of Matthean skill is to use the dream

---

[47]Marin ("Jesus"), in a structural analysis, divides Matt 27:1–31 into twelve parts which he then arranges chiastically. To do this he has to rearrange v. 11b after 11a,12–14, and *to omit the Judas scene in 27:3–10!* Thus he cannot capitalize on the flow of thought just described. Besides obvious features that one could recognize without such complexities, I find little of real interpretative contribution in such a complex effort that does not follow the text exactly as it now stands.

motif, the greater Gentile perceptivity of truth, and the hostility of the Jewish authorities and people during the Roman trial to form an inclusion with similar motifs in the infancy narratives, so that there are parallels between the beginning and end of Jesus' life.

C. The Lucan Roman Trial (Luke 23:1-25)

Luke's account is about the same length as Matt's, and that is once again about twice the length of Mark's. Luke too has drawn basic subject matter from Mark; yet just as he reshaped in a major way the Marcan material he used in the Sanhedrin interrogation,[48] here too Luke has reorganized drastically. As a result a comparison with the Marcan outline, similar to that given above for Matt, is not meaningful. Three major points in which Luke differs from Mark include the detailed presentation of charges (23:2); Pilate's sending Jesus to Herod for investigation, only to have Herod find him innocent (23:6–15); and three statements by Pilate that he finds nothing guilty in Jesus (23:4,14,22). The last feature Luke shares with John and probably reflects tradition common to both. The first two features have been strongly influenced by patterns in the trials of Paul before Roman officials described in Acts.[49] In particular when Paul is arrested in Jerusalem and the Jewish authorities plot to kill him (Acts 23–25), Paul is made to stand before a Roman procurator (Felix) as detailed charges are brought against him by the chief priests and elders. Yet the Roman procurator (now Festus), seeking help because he finds Paul not to be guilty, invites a Herodian king to investigate Paul; and that king finds him innocent. Within Luke-Acts the influence most likely came from Paul's trial to Jesus' trial, rather than vice versa. (See S. G. Wilson, "The Jews" 162–64; of course, historically Luke may have imposed a set Roman pattern on both trials.)

As for the arrangement of Luke 23:1–25, there are diverse theories. Büchele ("Tod") has tried to find in this section of the PN an elaborate pattern of threes in which the Roman trial is part one (23:1–25), the crucifixion is part two (23:26–49), and the burial is part three (23:50–56).[50] Each of these in turn is divided into three, and each of those three divisions is further subdivided into three. Büchele relates all of this to Deut 19:15 (cf. 17:6–7) de-

---

[48]For instance, Luke placed Peter's denials and the Jewish mockery of Jesus before the questions posed to Jesus by the Sanhedrin. Are they, then, for him really part of the Jewish proceedings?

[49]The account in Acts of the Sanhedrin trial of Stephen similarly had parallels to Luke's account of the Sanhedrin interrogation of Jesus. Thus the readers would recognize that whether their early Christian heroes stood before Jewish or Roman courts, what happened to them had a parallel in what happened to Jesus.

[50]Notice the unequal length of the parts, especially of the third. Often that is a sign that one is forcing material into a mold or pattern that does not fit.

manding the testimony of two or *three* witnesses. Since we shall see in the Marcan crucifixion narrative several patterns of three,[51] one cannot reject this theory in principle, even though such a consistent pattern as Büchele proposes is very hard to discern. Tyson (*Death* 117) is correct in objecting that Deut 19:15 is never cited here, and finding the theme of witnesses in all these divisions is forced. A very different proposal made by Neyrey (*Passion* 69, 98) would find four trials of Jesus in Luke 22:66–23:25, namely, (a) Jesus before the Sanhedrin (22:66–71); (b) Jesus before Pilate (23:1–5); (c) Jesus before Herod (23:6–12); (d) Jesus before the assembled Jewish crowds (23:13–25).[52] Treating the last three as distinct trials is artificial: Pilate functions in all three, and he alone passes a sentence on Jesus (23:24: *epikrinein*). The parallel with Acts 25:17–26:32 militates against treating the investigation by Herod as a separate trial.

For convenience in order to describe the four Gospels side by side, I shall break Luke 23:1–25 into three segments (23:1–5; 23:6–12; 23:13–25—the division that is probably the most commonly proposed by scholars). Yet such a division disguises transitional elements. In §28 I have already discussed 23:1 as transitional between the Jewish interrogation and the Roman trial. Within 23:1–5, vv. 4–5 (which are not parallel to Mark) point to what follows: They contain the first of three "not guilty" statements and the reference to Galilee that prompts Pilate to send Jesus to Herod, the tetrarch of Galilee, and thus lead into the Herod interrogation. If one assigns 23:6–12 to the Herod interrogation, one does not find the evaluation given by Herod until 23:15, so that 23:13–16 can as well be placed with what precedes.[53] The Barabbas story, which is almost one-third of the Marcan account, becomes in Luke (23:18–19,25a) a passing reference within Luke's finale centered on Pilate's judgment against Jesus. The best conclusion, therefore, may be to stress the overall unity in 23:1–25, so that subdivisions are more our perception than Luke's.

D. The Johannine Roman Trial (John 18:28–19:16a)

John presented the shortest account of Jesus before the Jewish authorities (18:13–27),[54] one that is only about 60 percent the length of Mark's account. John's Roman trial, however, is almost three times the length of Mark's. In

---

[51]In Mark we have already seen several of these patterns, e.g., in Gethsemane Jesus prayed three times and came and found his disciples sleeping three times; Peter denied Jesus three times.

[52]This proposal is very different from an approach that I have already rejected (p. 528 above), i.e., that Luke did not think that the Sanhedrin session was a real trial; accordingly there was for Luke only one trial, the Roman.

[53]Fitzmyer (*Luke* 2.1483) treats 23:13–16 as separate among *four* scenes in the Roman trial.

[54]That is because for John the Sanhedrin trial of Jesus took place earlier in 11:47–53.

TABLE 5. CHIASTIC STRUCTURE OF JOHN'S ACCOUNT OF THE ROMAN TRIAL

1. *Outside* (18:28–32) Jews demand   =   7. *Outside* (19:12–16a) Jews obtain
   death   death
2. *Inside* (18:33–38a) Pilate and Jesus on =   6. *Inside* (19:9–11) Pilate and Jesus on
   kingship   power
3. *Outside* (18:38b–40) Pilate finds no   =   5. *Outside* (19:4–8) Pilate finds no guilt;
   guilt; choice of Barabbas   "Behold the man"
                            4. *Inside* (19:1–3) Soldiers scourge Jesus

dramatic quality only the story of the man born blind in John 9 matches the skill exhibited in this Roman trial scene. If at most there are three steps traceable in the development of the common Synoptic material (initial questioning, Barabbas, condemnation), many exegetes agree in recognizing seven episodes in John in a chiastic arrangement,[55] involving alternating settings outside and inside the praetorium. (Chiastic means that the 1st matches the 7th, the 2d matches the 6th, the 3d matches the 5th, with the 4th a middle episode.) Table 5 illustrates this arrangement.[56]

There can be no doubt that this is deliberate artistry, expanding and rearranging what came down in the tradition.[57] The episodes are chiastically balanced not only in setting and theme but even (partially) in length, for $2+3 = 5+6$. Pilate appears as a major actor in every episode except 4, the middle episode containing the scourging and mockery of Jesus. His lesser presence there is intelligible if we remember that in Mark/Matt those actions take place after Pilate has sentenced Jesus and transferred him to the custody of the soldiers who take him away inside the praetorium. For his own dramatic purposes John has shifted the scourging to the middle of the trial, but he has not violated the tradition by having Pilate prominent during it.

In the outside-inside settings there are contrasting atmospheres. Inside Jesus is serene in a sovereign manner reflecting his conviction, "I lay down

[55]In discussing structure in §8, I rejected an example of exaggerated chiasm-detection because it involved a simple, commonly found pattern easily explicable on other grounds. That is not true here.

[56]The schema I give is influenced by the proposals of Janssens de Varebeke ("Structure"), as explained in BGJ 2.803,858–59. Bultmann (*John* 648) speaks of six episodes because he treats 19:1–7 (my 4th and 5th) as one. Haenchen (*John* 2.185) would detect an introduction (18:28–32 = my Episode 1), a central section with four subsections (18:33–38a = my 2; 18:38b–40 = my 3; 19:1–3 and 19:4–11 = my 4, 5, 6), and a closing scene (19:12–16a = my 7). Obviously one's judgment in treating 19:1–11 will depend on whether one thinks the outside-inside alternation should mark subdivisions. That is a difficult decision because the movements are not all expressly indicated even though they are implied, e.g., Pilate, who has been outside in 18:38b–40 must have gone inside in 19:1–3 because he goes outside again in 19:4.

[57]On pp. 729–32 above I discuss what may have been in the tradition for Episodes 1 and 2, along with the debatable criteria for determining that. Sherwin-White (*Roman* 47) contends that the legal and administrative details peculiar to John are by no means implausible.

my life ... no one has taken it away from me; rather I lay it down of my own accord" (John 10:17–18). He does not treat Pilate as an equal, much less as a superior; rather Jesus pronounces oracular statements that leave Pilate befuddled. Outside "the Jews" bully Pilate and begin to shout at him as he frustrates their demand that he "rubber-stamp" their decision that this fellow (Jesus) must die. The dialogue inside reveals Pilate's inability to recognize the truth standing incarnate before him; the dialogue outside reveals the true motive behind the hostility of "the Jews": not Jesus' claim to be "the King of the Jews" but his claim to be God's Son.[58]

In summation, then, if Mark has done little by way of dramatizing the basic elements received from Christian tradition about the Roman trial and has not woven them into a significant theological drama, the other Gospels have done both. Matt's pursuit of the theme of guilt for innocent blood has illustrated the issue of responsibility in vignettes of theatrical power. Luke, reshaping the trial of Jesus from the model of the trial of Paul, has supplied a paradigm to be imitated by Christians dragged before Roman judges. If the Lucan Jesus exhibits a confident tranquillity that forces even the Roman governor to recognize his innocence, Christians must be able to do likewise. But when all this is said, the judgment of Haenchen (*John* 2.185) is correct even if overstated: "The Johannine version of the scene with Pilate is far superior to that of Matthew and Luke." John has given us the chef d'oeuvre of early Christian drama, unfolding with perspicacity the confrontation of the divine and human.

(Bibliography for this episode may be found in §30, especially Part 3.)

---

[58]Notice the double Johannine clarification of the motives of the Jews in bringing Jesus to Pilate: the theological motive described above, and the practical motive that it was not permitted them to put anyone to death—a motive that paradoxically has the theological result of fulfilling Jesus' word signifying what kind of death he was going to die (18:32). As stressed throughout the COMMENT of the sections dealing with the Roman trial, John's hostile portrayal of "the Jews" here is shaped by the inimical relations that have separated Johannine believers in Jesus from the synagogue(s), a separation seemingly effected by bringing them to trial in synagogue courts (9:24–34; 12:42; 16:2). See J. L. Martyn, *History and Theology in the Fourth Gospel* (rev. ed.; Nashville: Abingdon, 1979).

§33. THE ROMAN TRIAL, PART TWO:
JESUS BEFORE HEROD

(Luke 23:6–12)

Translation

Luke 23:6–12: ⁶But having heard (this), Pilate questioned whether this man was a Galilean; ⁷and having ascertained that he was from Herod's (sphere of) power, he sent him off to Herod who was himself in Jerusalem in these days. ⁸Now Herod, having seen Jesus, rejoiced greatly since for much time he had been wishing to see him because of what he had heard about him; indeed he was hoping to see some sign done by him. ⁹Accordingly with much talking he tried to question him; but Jesus answered nothing to him, ¹⁰even though the chief priests and the scribes had been standing there insistently accusing him. ¹¹But having treated him with contempt and made a mockery, Herod with his troops, having clothed him with a splendid garment, sent him back to Pilate. ¹²But both Herod and Pilate on this same day became friends with each other, for previously they were at enmity toward the other.

COMMENT

Granted the unified Lucan structure of chap. 23 (p. 757 above), this can be looked on as an isolated episode only by comparison with the Marcan outline, from which it is absent. (That absence is significant because much of what precedes and follows in Luke's trial account is present in Mark.) If one should judge that Luke has glossed the outline of Mark 15 by adding the Herod episode even as Matt glossed it by adding the death-of-Judas episode, there is a significant difference between the two additions. Matt's episode, while it fits his theology and outlook, is clearly an interruption even in Matt's own sequence (see beginning of §29); Luke's episode fits smoothly within the Lucan sequence. If the other Gospels by their silence about Herod in the trial of Jesus had not alerted us to a problem, few if any difficulties would be detected in the Lucan sequence. True, scholars acquainted with Roman legal procedures might ask questions about the rationale, but those questions would scarcely occur to ordinary readers. The very smoothness of the sequence makes it difficult to decide whether to start the episode with 23:4 or 23:6. As explained in §32, however, since Pilate's reaction to Jesus' behavior is part of the initial trial scene in Mark/Matt, I made the decision in Luke as well to put Pilate's reaction in 23:4–5 with that initial scene. But from another perspective Luke 23:4–5 points ahead, and there is a smooth flow from the Galilean reference in 23:5 to the Galilean reference in 23:6.

As Manus ("Universalism" 122–25) documents, this Herod episode has generated very different interpretations. In the ANALYSIS I shall discuss historicity, composition, and sources; but one area of discussion cannot be postponed till then, for it contributes to a verse-by-verse discussion as well, namely, the issue of Lucan style in the Herod scene. Writing and vocabulary heavily attested elsewhere in Luke-Acts are very much in evidence here, and there is virtually nothing in the episode that could be called nonLucan. Indeed, were this scene taken over as a whole by Luke from a special source, one would have to judge that the source had the same style as Luke! Below at the beginning of each of the subsections (outlined in the Contents on p. 663 above) I shall point out Lucan stylistic features before commenting on the verses. For more detail, see K. Müller, "Jesus vor Herodes" 114–16; Fitzmyer, *Luke* 2.1479; Soards, "Tradition . . . Herod" 347–58.

SENDING JESUS TO HEROD (23:6–7)

Among Lucan stylistic features, "ascertained" in v. 7 translates *epiginōskein,* which occurs some twenty times in Luke-Acts, i.e., about half the NT usage. The "himself" modifying Herod renders *kai autos,* a Septuagintism favored by Luke. "In these [*tautais*] days" occurs a half-dozen times in Luke-Acts. "Jerusalem" here is *Hierosolyma;* in 23:28 it will be *Hierousalēm*—two of the three references to the city by name in the PN (see Mark 15:41). The spelling more adapted to Hellenistic ears, *Hierosolyma,* is the only one used by Mark, John, and Matt (with the single exception of a saying of Jesus in Matt 23:37). The other, *Hierousalēm* (which is virtually a transliteration from Hebrew *Yĕrûšālēm*), appears with *Hierosolyma* in Luke-Acts in a mixed pattern: In the Gospel *Hierosolyma* occurs 3 or 4 times, and *Hierousalēm* 27 or 26 times; in Acts *Hierosolyma* occurs 23 times, and *Hierousalēm* 36 times. Although some have appealed to situational or theological

differences in the context to explain the Lucan variation, it is probably meaningless and supplies no proof that Luke is using a special source here.[1]

In Luke 23:5 the chief priests and scribes reiterated to Pilate their opposition to Jesus, and from their words what he has retained selectively is that
Jesus' teaching began *from Galilee*. While that reference is "planted" as a
lead into the Herod scene, it also reminds the readers that Jesus is being
judged on his whole ministry and not just on one issue ("the King of the
Jews") that was never mentioned until he came before Pilate. Indeed the
appearance of Herod will be a living connection between Jesus' ministry
and his passion, for Herod was mentioned at the beginning of the ministry
in 3:1,19–20. The Galilee reference provokes a question on Pilate's part.[2]
The verb "to question" (*eperōtan*), while it often has no special function
(22:64), is favored by Luke for legal interrogation, e.g., in Acts 5:27; 23:34.

What Pilate ascertains in Luke 23:7 (that Jesus "was from Herod's [sphere
of] power") is meant to affirm that Jesus is a Galilean. That designation
exemplifies the fact that material appearing in the Lucan infancy narrative,
e.g., Jesus' birth at Bethlehem in Judea, has had no major influence on the
picture of Jesus' ministry derived by Luke from Mark (see BBM 240). Perhaps in this instance one could argue that there is no inconsistency since
before the birth Jesus' parents dwelt in Nazareth.[3] In Luke 4:16,24 Nazareth
is Jesus' *patris*, "hometown."

Those who attribute no historicity to the present Lucan scene contend that
the question posed by Pilate is implausible, for surely he would have been
informed that the accused was Jesus *of Nazareth*. In fact, the Nazareth designation is *not* found in the Lucan form of the Roman charge against Jesus
placed over him on the cross (23:38). More fundamentally, however, such a

---

[1]J. Jeremias (ZNW 56 [1974], 273–76) considers some of the variation to lack significance. J. M.
Ross (NTS 38 [1992], 474–76) thinks that Luke had a plan as to where and when each spelling
should be used but forgot it, so that the final usage is not consistent. The thesis that Luke used
Hierousalēm in Jewish contexts requires the choice of poorly attested scribal variants and a great
deal of imagination. For instance, what makes the context here, which involves Herod's presence in
Jerusalem (*Hierosolyma*), less Jewish than the context in Luke 23:28 (where *Hierousalēm* is used),
especially since Acts 4:25–27 shows that Luke contrasted Pilate and the Gentiles with Herod and
the peoples of Israel? I. de la Potterie (RechSR 69 [1981], 57–70) has defended the thesis that Luke
uses *Hierosolyma* in negative and profane contexts, and *Hierousalēm* in positive and sacred contexts.
That such precision cannot be verified will be argued in reference to Luke 23:28 below. Here, while
Herod himself may be a negative figure, he will decide for Jesus; and so the context is either neutral
or positive.

[2]Some have seen a relationship between this question asked by the Lucan Pilate as to whether
Jesus was a Galilean and the question asked by Pilate of Jesus in John 19:9, "From where are you?"
They theorize that in a source common to Luke and John there was a question about Jesus' origin;
Luke kept it on the geographical level of Herod's *exousia* or power in Galilee, while John in his
theology of "above and below" turned it into an opportunity for Jesus to answer in terms of Pilate's
exousia being given from above (19:11). Such a relationship is possible but no more than that.
Boismard ("Royauté" 39) insists that the question in John 19:9 really means "Who are you?"

[3]Luke 1:26; 2:4, unlike Matt 2:8,11, where they had their house in Bethlehem.

historical objection is *à coté* since the Galilee-Galilean motifs in 23:5–6 are for Lucan storytelling purposes. While the Galilean background of Jesus and his disciples is a theme in all the Gospels (cf. Luke 22:59 and Mark 14:70b), a major emphasis on the transition from a ministry in Galilee to a denouement in Jerusalem is very Lucan. The women who look on from afar at Jesus' death and burial are twice identified by Luke as women who had accompanied Jesus "from Galilee" (23:49,55); on Easter morn they are reminded by the angelic men of what Jesus had told them "while he was still in Galilee" (24:6). In Acts 13:31 the appearances of the risen Jesus are said to have been directed to "those who came up with him from Galilee."

The Galilee motif brings onto the scene Herod, called by Luke "the tetrarch" of Galilee (3:1; 9:7). This is Herod Antipas, son of Herod the Great through Malthace his Samaritan wife.[4] He and his elder brother Archelaus and his half-brother Philip were the appointed heirs of the subdivisions of the kingdom of Herod the Great after his death ca. 4 BC. More adept than the blundering Archelaus who in AD 6 was deposed by the Romans from ruling in Judea, Herod Antipas remained ruler of Galilee and Perea (Transjordan) until AD 39 when he was deposed by the Emperor Gaius Caligula and exiled to Lyons in Gaul. That deposition should not be interpreted to indicate that Antipas was a bad ruler from the Roman viewpoint, for in part it stemmed from Caligula's favoritism toward Herod Agrippa, who was eventually to be given the realm of Antipas. Rather, during four decades of the reign of Augustus and Tiberius, Galilee under Antipas saw no revolt against the Romans. (The revolt of Judas the Galilean concerned the census in Judea.) Antipas showed his loyalty by building Tiberias on the Lake of Galilee in honor of the emperor.[5] In his own territory the tetrarch Herod's powers would not be much different from Pilate's powers as prefect in Judea and Samaria. Although Acts 4:26–27 will identify Herod Antipas as one of "the kings of the earth" in array against Jesus, technically he was not a king.[6] "The King of the Jews" was a title associated with Herod the Great (*Ant.* 16.10.2; #311); and some scholars, wondering if there was ambition among his offspring for that title, have pointed out that in Luke 23:6–12 Pilate is handing over to the mercies of Herod Antipas a person who would be crucified as "the King of the Jews" (Bajsić, "Pilatus" 21). That connection, however, may be overly imaginative.

---

[4]For details on Antipas, see Bruce, "Herod"; S. Perowne, *The Later Herods* (New York: Abingdon, 1958), 43–57.

[5]In two passages (*Ant.* 18.2.3; #36 and 18.4.5; #104–5) Josephus speaks of the closeness and private communication between Herod Antipas and Tiberius.

[6]Ironically, the reason for Antipas being deposed was his overambition to be named a king, in imitation of the privilege given to Herod Agrippa, who had been made king over the territories of the deceased Philip.

As for the NT, Herod Antipas is named 8 times in Mark (7 of them in the beheading of JBap in 6:14–29), 4 times in Matt, 13 times in Luke, and 2 times in Acts. Those statistics indicate Luke's particular interest in this Herod and his relations *with Jesus*[7]—he reduces Mark's story about Herod's beheading JBap to two one-verse notices (3:20; 9:9). In comment on v. 8 below I shall present the Lucan passages pertinent to Herod's attitude toward Jesus, but a saying of Jesus that never mentions Herod is also important for the present scene. In Luke 21:12 he warns his followers that they would be led "before kings and governors for the sake of my name." It is not surprising, then, to find Jesus himself led before a king as well as a Roman governor.

Turning now from this general information about Herod, let us concentrate on the description in Luke 23:7 of what Pilate does; for many it is the key to Pilate's motive. For instance, does "ascertained" (*epiginōskein*, rather than simple *ginōskein*, "to know" by observation) imply an investigation? ZBG #484, however, observes that Koine Greek often prefers verbs compounded with prepositions over simple forms, without any implication of special significance.

What Pilate ascertains is that Jesus is from (*ek*) Herod's *exousia* ("power"). Some would render this as "jurisdiction," a translation that raises the issue of who had the legal authority to try Jesus. Mommsen (*Römisches* 356–57) suggested that in the early period of the empire the prevailing jurisdiction was *forum domicilii* (i.e., determined by where the accused came from; also *forum originis*), not *forum delicti* (i.e., determined by where the crime was committed or the accused was apprehended; also *forum apprehensionis*). A modified form of this theory would be the possibility mentioned by Blinzler (*Trial* 195) that Herod had the right to judge people from his territory when he was dwelling in his own palace in Jerusalem. On the whole, however, this reasoning has had little support from experts in Roman law, e.g., Steinwenter and Sherwin-White. The latter (*Roman* 28–31) argues for the opposite sequence: *forum delicti* (the simpler procedure) in the early empire, and only later the introduction of *forum domicilii*. That Luke did not think of an obligatory *forum domicilii* is clear from Acts 23:34, after Paul has been brought before the procurator Felix. Although the Roman asks "to what province [*eparcheia*]" does Paul belong, the answer that he comes from Cilicia does not prevent his being tried at Caesarea in Judea for his supposed crime. Paulus, who lived ca. AD 200, states (DJ 1.18.3) that it is only over people of his own province that the prefect has *imperium* (§18, A1 above)

---

[7]Two characters mentioned solely by Luke, Joanna the wife of Chuza, Herod's steward (8:3; see 24:10), and Manaen, Herod's *syntrophos* (Acts 13:1: "foster brother"? "companion"? "custodian"? "steward"?), have been invoked as possible channels of Luke's information.

and even then he has *imperium* only while he himself is within the confines of the province—once he exits he becomes a private person. According to that model (if it was applicable to 1st-cent. Judea and Galilee), no matter what his political importance, while in Jerusalem Herod Antipas would be a private person without jurisdiction over Jesus.

Related to this issue is the meaning of *anapempein* (literally "to send up") in v. 7. Is it another instance of the Koine Greek preference for verbs compounded with prepositions, so that there is no major difference from *pempein*, having the meaning of "to send off, back" (Philemon 12)? Or does it have a technical sense of remanding (Latin *remittere*) a prisoner to a different (often higher) jurisdiction (Bickermann, Creed, Harlow, Verrall)? The verb has that sense in Josephus (*War* 2.20.5; #571) and in Acts 25:21 where Paul is sent for judgment from the procurator Festus to the emperor in Rome. But if one argues that Pilate is formally remanding Jesus to the jurisdiction of Herod in 23:7, then the use of the same verb in v. 11 would mean that Herod is formally remanding Jesus back to the jurisdiction of Pilate. That seems an unnecessary complication. Important scholars (Blinzler, Steinwenter, Sherwin-White) argue against giving a technical sense to *anapempein*. Perhaps the best solution is to avoid either extreme (whereby it would mean either simply "to send" or legally "to remand" a prisoner) and to recognize that Luke uses it to enhance the legal atmosphere.

Since I do not think of a technical transfer of Jesus to another jurisdiction, if we may come back to the original issue, a more ordinary translation of *exousia* as Herod's "power" rather than "jurisdiction" is preferable. There may be a threatening theological tone to that word, which Luke has employed in evil contexts. In 4:5–6, where the devil tempts Jesus by showing him all the kingdoms of the world, he says, "I will give to you all this *exousia* . . . for it has been given over to me; and I will give it to whomever I wish." We have seen that for Luke the passion is the time of Satan's return to test Jesus (22:3), so that 22:53 can characterize it as "your hour and the *exousia* of darkness." Thus Lucan readers might well think that there is a Satanic threat when Jesus is sent into Herod's *exousia*.

Verse 7 ends on the note of Herod's being in Jerusalem in those days. That provides a hint of a spur-of-the-moment decision by Pilate made possible by a fortunate occasion—a hint to which I shall return below. There is nothing implausible about Herod Antipas being in Jerusalem for Passover, even if one suspects that like his father, Herod the Great, he may have come not primarily from piety, but from the political importance of a correct religious gesture. Josephus (*Ant.* 18.5.3; #122) shows Herod and Vitellius (Roman governor of Syria) at Jerusalem during Passover of AD 37 "to sacrifice to God." In the course of the golden shields incident (p. 702 above) Philo (*Ad*

Gaium 38; #300) shows four sons of Herod the Great present at Jerusalem, plausibly in the context of a feast, placing themselves at the head of a protest demonstration against Pilate. Where in Jerusalem would Antipas have been? Josephus (*War* 2.16.3; #344; *Ant.* 20.8.11; #189–90) mentions a palace built by the Hasmoneans strategically on the western hill above the Xystus, surveying the city and giving a vantage point on the sacred sections of the Temple. Although Herod the Great married into the Hasmonean family, he gradually eliminated the high priests and replaced their line. Did the high priests of Jesus' time, Annas and Caiaphas, occupy the palace even though they were not Hasmoneans? Are we to imagine that Jesus had been brought there in Mark 14:53 and par.? Or did the Herods take over the palace of these priest-kings, and were Herodian princes allowed to reside there even after the Romans took over direct control of Judea and Jerusalem? The Josephus passages show Agrippa II there in the 60s, much to the annoyance of the eminent men of Jerusalem, who built a wall to block his view of the Temple.

Why would Pilate have sent Jesus to Herod Antipas? One can deal with that question on three levels of response: (1) on a historical level that presumes this to be a factual scene so that one must deal with Roman legalities and maneuvers by Pilate consonant with his reputation; (2) on a level of surface-reader reaction on which one asks how readers with no historical background would understand the scene; (3) on the level of readers in the Greco-Roman world addressed by Luke who would know something about Roman procedures and understand the scene in that light. The third level combines some of the first level (with history ceding to verisimilitude) and the second. The comments below engage the scene on this third level.

In Papyrus Oxyrhynchus II 237 (eds. B. P. Grenfell and A. S. Hunt, pp. 146–48) the Roman prefect in Egypt delegates the *stratēgos* or magistrate of the district to which the accused belongs to investigate a crime. This is a form of *anakrisis* or preliminary investigation that Roman provincial officials employed precisely because they did not bring a large bureaucracy with them and had to depend on locals of various sorts. Pilate may well have regarded the Sanhedrin proceedings relevant to Jesus as an *anakrisis;* but since his first questioning pointed to Jesus' innocence, he can now be seen as wanting an independent evaluation from someone who had a legal relationship to Jesus, because Jesus was from the region of Herod's authority and because (if there is any truth in the Jewish charge of 23:5) Jesus began stirring up people when he was in Galilee. Nothing in history or in Luke's Gospel would cause readers to think of Herod as an expert in religious issues, but he would be highly competent in detecting insurrectionists.

That Luke is thinking of an *anakrisis* (understood as delegated investigation), rather than a formal ceding of jurisdiction is suggested by the parallel in Acts 25:23–27 where the procurator Festus is trying to prepare a document of charges against Paul that will go along with him to the emperor, to whom Paul has appealed. The "whole multitude of the Jewish people" has demanded death, but Festus has found nothing warranting such a judgment. He takes advantage of the presence in Caesarea of the Herodian king Agrippa II thus: "I have brought him ... before you, King Agrippa, so that once the *anakrisis* has been done I may have something to write."[8] In each of these two scenes the Roman governor (Pilate, Festus) spontaneously takes advantage of the presence of a Herodian ruler at the time of the trial of a man (Jesus, Paul) accused as a religious and political troublemaker by the Jerusalem Jewish authorities. In each the Herodian, who had wanted to see or hear the prisoner (Luke 23:8; Acts 25:22), having interrogated him, does not make the final decision (nor is it clear that he is expected to), so that the prisoner must once more stand before the Roman governor. But in each interview the Herodian's evaluation confirms the Roman's that the prisoner need not be executed (Luke 23:14–15; Acts 26:30–32). I see no reason to agree with Blinzler (*Trial* 195–96) that in the logic of the story Pilate had to expect an innocent judgment from Herod Antipas or else his own judgment of innocence would look foolish. Given the overall attitude of Romans in Luke-Acts that internal Jewish squabblings are impenetrably complicated (Acts 18:14–15; 23:29), in the storyline there would have been no great embarrassment to Pilate if Herod had discovered in the *anakrisis* something to cause Pilate to change his mind.

From the Lucan narrative and from history we can detect additional factors that could have made this *anakrisis* by Herod seem wise policy to Pilate. Luke 13:1–2 tells of Pilate having mingled the blood of Galileans with their sacrifices—presumably pilgrims who had come to Jerusalem to sacrifice at a feast (p. 701, #4 above). Luke 23:12 reports that enmity had existed between Herod and Pilate. Does Luke mean the readers to connect these two statements, so that Pilate might not want to increase the enmity by spilling the blood of another Galilean at a feast? If the incident mentioned by Philo (*Ad Gaium* 38; #300) in relation to the golden shields had already taken place, Pilate had seen Herodian princes place themselves at the head of a mob during a feast to make protest against him. Thus, inviting Antipas to do an *anakrisis* about Jesus might have been an ingenious diplomatic way to neutralize the tetrarch and prevent further trouble.[9] In any case Luke 23:12 makes it clear to the readers that Herod regarded Pilate's action as friendly.

---

[8]Later in Acts 28:18, using a related verbal form, Paul regards even Festus' proceedings as an *anakrisis* or preliminary investigation in respect to his being judged by the emperor.

[9]Justin (*Dialogue* 103.4) speaks of it as a gracious gesture.

Other suggestions about Pilate's motives, e.g., he was trying to avoid moral guilt, lack adequate support in the Gospel and in history.

HEROD INTERROGATES JESUS (23:8–10)

Once more we begin with features of Lucan style in this subsection. In v. 8 *chairein* (19 times in Luke-Acts) has the sense of "rejoice" rather than "greet." *Hikanos* ("sufficient," but with the extended meaning of "considerable, much, many") is used in v. 8: "for much time [pl. of *chronos*]" and in v. 9: "with much talking [words]," employing *en* instrumentally.[10] It is found 27 times in Luke-Acts, as compared with 6 times in the other three Gospels together. In the NT only Luke-Acts uses *hikanos* with *chronos* (6 times), and among the Gospels only Luke uses *chronos* in the plural (3 times + 3 in Acts). As for "had been wishing" in v. 8, the periphrastic combination of the verb "to be" ("was" = "had been") plus the present participle occurs 33 times in Luke.[11] The construction catches the intensity of Herod's wish. *Dia* ("because") with the accusative of the articular infinitive ("hear") is a construction that appears some 16 times in Luke-Acts. Soards ("Herod") makes a case for translating it to bring out content: "because of what he had heard," rather than simply "because he was hearing." In the somewhat awkward repetitiveness of v. 8, "rejoiced" and "was hoping" are the main verbs describing Herod's state of mind at the moment of the encounter; the rest describes his previous attitude. The last phrase "sign done by him" seems prolix to some, for "sign" would suffice; it may echo 9:9 where Herod "heard of all that was being done" by Jesus.

There is an overuse of the particle *de* in this scene (7 in 7 verses; 548 times in Luke; 558 times in Acts). In the literal translation style I have adopted I have normally rendered it "but"; that is impossible here, however. Soards ("Tradition . . . Herod" 352) argues that the awkward three instances of *de* in vv. 9–10, related to three different subjects (Herod, Jesus, priests), should be rendered coordinatively, whence "Accordingly . . . but . . . even though." To break up the confusing repetition of "he" and "him" I have introduced the subject "Jesus" in v. 9. The Greek is *autos de,* used as a literary touch at the beginning of a sentence some nine times in Luke. *Eutonōs* ("insistently") is found elsewhere in the NT only in Acts 18:28.

As for the narrative in this subsection, Darr ("Glorified" 288) thinks he can find here a recognition-response pattern that has a rhetorical function.

---

[10]Here Luke reflects the later LXX books that tend to substitute *hikanos* for *megas* and *polys.*

[11]Fitzmyer (*Luke* 1.122–23) judges that eighteen of them may be influenced by Semitic usage, but this one is more likely a Septuagintism than the product of direct Hebrew/Aramaic influence (which might point to a source).

More simply, the emotions that Jesus provokes in Herod (rejoicing greatly, wishing for much time to see him, hoping to see some sign, much talking, repeated questioning) are in sharp contrast to the totally unemotional behavior to be exhibited by the Roman prefect (even in the face of urgently shouted demands: 23:21–22). Indeed, in v. 8 Herod's enthusiastic reaction to seeing Jesus is described before Luke narrates the background that makes the reaction intelligible! The triple use of "see" in that verse and the repetitiveness of "wishing . . . hoping" give a frenetic thrust. If there were just this scene, Herod's attitudes might be classified in a range between childish and petulant; but earlier Lucan statements gave the impression of an unstable character capable of homicidal violence. I shall quote three statements now, italicizing lines pertinent to our discussion: 3:19–20; 9:7–9; and 13:31–33.[12]

The first pertinent action by Antipas is narrated by Luke (3:19–20) in the context of JBap's preaching the gospel to the people: "But Herod the tetrarch, who had been reproved by him [JBap] about Herodias, his brother's wife, and about *all the evil things Herod had done,* added this too to them all: He locked up John in prison." The cause that Josephus reports for Herod's striking against JBap (*Ant.* 18.5.2; #118–19) is the enthusiasm JBap aroused among the crowds.[13]

The next important Lucan notice (9:7–9) about Antipas is in the context of Jesus' sending out the Twelve to preach in the villages of Galilee: "Now Herod the tetrarch *heard of all that was being done,* and he was greatly perplexed because it was said by some that John had been raised from the dead, but by others that Elijah had appeared, and still by others that one of the ancient prophets had risen. But Herod said, 'John I beheaded, but *who is this* about whom I hear such things?' *And he was seeking to see him.*" (This is all that one reads of JBap's death in Luke!) The strong "all that was being done" suggests that Antipas was upset by the whole of Jesus' ministry, including the mission of the disciples. The issue of Jesus' identity dominates Herod's mind, and no one of the three proposals could have set him at ease. This passage attributes to Herod Antipas the only words he speaks in any Gospel, viz., a rhetorical question so that readers may come to know his thinking.

The last pertinent Lucan text is 13:31–33, where, as Jesus makes his way from Galilee toward Jerusalem, certain Pharisees tell him, "Get out and go away from here because Herod wishes to kill you." And he says to them, "Going, tell this fox, 'Behold I cast out demons and perform cures today and

---

[12]For the composition of these statements, see n. 41 below.

[13]Some have tried to compare Herod's (and Herodias') persecution of JBap with Ahab's (and Jezebel's) persecution of Elijah; the evil things that Ahab had done are emphasized in I Kings 16:30–33; 21:25–26.

tomorrow; then on the third day I shall be finished. But it is necessary that today and tomorrow and the next day I go on, for it is not possible that a prophet perish outside Jerusalem.'" Who are these Pharisees? Are they telling the truth? Are they trying to help Jesus, or to get rid of him? Is the image of the fox meant to portray Herod as sly or destructive or both? A. Denaux,[14] holding that in Luke the Pharisees are bad figures and Herod is curious but not homicidal, argues that this is another example of Pharisee hypocrisy and lying. But M. Rese[15] argues for the opposite viewpoint: The Pharisees are telling the truth. In my judgment Darr ("Glorified" 264) argues correctly that the readers are meant to believe the Pharisees but distrust their motive; accordingly Herod does seek to kill Jesus. In classical and Hellenistic Greek and in rabbinic literature the fox has the reputation of being crafty (Fitzmyer, *Luke* 2.1031), but there are also references in which foxes are destructive (Cant 2:15; Ezek 13:4–5). Herod's slyness may be destructively exhibited in the way he gets rid of those who make him uneasy. Here (with the connivance of the Pharisees?) he may be trying threats and, if that fails, planning violence. Jesus takes the menace seriously: Herod beheaded JBap, and Jesus responds to Herod by foretelling his own death as a prophet in Jerusalem.

All this background should make the readers of Luke uneasy when they read in 23:8 that Herod is rejoicing to have seen Jesus at last. This is something he has been trying to do with malicious intent, and now it has been accomplished without any cost to him. If 23:8 speaks of what Herod has "heard" about Jesus as a motive for wanting to see him, nothing that he was said to have "heard" in 9:7–8 would be reassuring to a tetrarch who had found JBap too outspoken a prophet and had him killed. Herod is hoping to see a "sign"; but how would he react if a sign were done for him by Jesus? Would he applaud the marvelous, only on second thought to brood about whether such a performer might gain a dangerously large following? In Luke 11:16 a request to Jesus for a sign is seen by him as the mark of an evil generation (11:29) that should be refused. Requests for the marvelous (without the word "sign") constitute for Jesus a diabolic testing in 4:9–12 and a lack of faith in 4:23–24. Here, as there, a sign will not be granted; and so the tetrarch will not see what is granted only to those of faith: "Many . . . kings have wished to see what you see and have not seen, and to hear what you hear and have not heard" (10:24).

The frenzied aspect of Herod's behavior continues in 23:9 as he questions Jesus "with much [*hikanos*] talking." Harlow would attribute to *hikanos* the tone of "harsh" or "hostile," but it scarcely means something different in

    [14]In *L'Évangile de Luc*, ed. F. Neirynck (BETL 33; Gembloux: Duculot, 1973), 245–85.
    [15]In *Jésus aux origines de la christologie*, ed. J. Dupont (BETL 40; Gembloux: Duculot, 1975), 201–25.

v. 9 from what it means in v. 8, "for *much* time." Derrett ("Daniel" 66) wants to render *eperōtan* as "consult," so that Herod would be approaching Jesus as a prophetic oracle.[16] Yet *eperōtan* did not have the sense of consulting a prophetic oracle three verses before when used of Pilate's questioning, and it probably does not have that sense here either. Many have speculated about the subject matter of the questioning by Herod. Is it related to the charges brought against Jesus as he stood before Pilate, e.g., did Jesus claim to be "the King of the Jews"? Or is it related to previous issues that Herod had raised about Jesus, e.g., "Who is this about whom I hear such things?" (9:9)? The fact that Luke does not answer these questions suggests that his main emphasis is on the frustrated effort of Herod implied in the conative use of the imperfect (BDF 326: "tried to question").

That atmosphere of frustration is increased by the chorus of chief priests and scribes (23:10) who try to force Herod's hand by their continued charges against Jesus. The adverb *eutonōs,* literally "well stretched," translated as "insistently," may have the connotation "at full pitch"; and the *eis* in *eis + stanai* ("standing there") may have an adversative thrust. This gives the picture of the chief priests and scribes as an insistent and shouting presence. (In Acts 25:7 when Paul appears before Festus, his Jewish enemies from Jerusalem stand around [*peri + stanai*], bringing against him many and weighty charges.) The last mention of chief priests and scribes was in Luke 22:66, when, as components of "the assembly of the elders of the people," they led Jesus away to their Sanhedrin. Implicitly these worthies have been part of "the whole multitude of them" who led Jesus to Pilate and accused (*katēgorein*) him on three charges. Presumably the accusation in 23:10 (*katēgorein*) is of the same nature. Pilate's finding no crime in Jesus (23:4) did not stop the chief priests and the multitude from repeating one of the charges against Jesus in 23:5, and now these adversaries have pursued Jesus to Herod. Perhaps one could appeal to the meticulous Roman care to have the accusers personally confront the accused (Acts 23:30,35) in order to argue that Pilate has sent them along. But the prima facie impression is that they have come on their own as part of their continued malevolence. Theoretically "the scribes" might be mistaken by Greco-Roman readers for court scribes, but the presence of the chief priests should make clear to all that the opposition to Jesus is on a religious level and not simply on political issues that could have been of concern to both Pilate and Herod (Delorme, "Procès" 143).

To all this Jesus answers nothing—in startling contrast to Herod's verbos-

---

[16]This is part of a larger attempt by Derrett to portray Jesus before Pilate and Herod as a parallel to Daniel before Cyrus and Darius, an attempt characterized by Fitzmyer (*Luke* 2.1480) as "sheer eisegesis."

ity. This silence is also a major departure from the usual pattern of the Jewish
and Christian martyrs.[17] Luke's phrase is *ouden apekrinato.* The *ouden* could
be translated adverbially as "not at all," but the parallelism of similar statements (below) supports rendering it as an object. The rare aorist middle form
of the verb "to answer" reminds many of the similar description of Jesus'
silence before the high priest in Mark 14:61, "But he stayed silent [*siōpan*]
and answered nothing at all [*ouk apekrinato ouden*]," and less directly of his
silence before Pilate in Mark 15:5, "But Jesus answered nothing further [aor.
pass.: *ouketi ouden apekrithē*]." Luke reported neither of those two Marcan
silences; has he chosen to move the theme to here?[18] Was Luke's motivation
that he did not wish to portray Jesus as uncooperatively silent before figures
who had proper legal standing, viz., the Jewish Sanhedrin and the Roman
prefect, but felt no compunction about having him refuse to answer Herod's
curiosity? Luke can have Paul in Acts speak before Agrippa II, but here he
may have felt bound by Mark's tradition of silence. Besides, in the public
ministry Jesus had already sent an answer to "this fox" (Luke 13:32), and
that may have been thought to obviate the need for further response.

How would readers react to Jesus' silence? Would it make him seem more
majestic? Grundmann (*Lukas* 425) answers affirmatively for pagan readers,
pointing to silence in the Mithras liturgy 6:42. Wis 8:12 relates silence to
divine Wisdom; and Ignatius stresses reverentially the silence of Jesus (*Eph.*
15:2), who is the "Word proceeding from silence" (*Magn.* 8:2). We have
already mentioned the silence of the Suffering Servant of Isa 53:7, who did
not open his mouth, as possible background for previous (Mark/Matt) instances of Jesus' silence, but always with the warning that the vocabulary
was not the same. (Perhaps one can make a better case for Isaian influence
on Luke since in 22:37 Luke has cited Isa 53:12.) A wider pattern of victims
suffering before their accusers in silence (unlike the martyrs with their eloquent professions of faith) may have made the Lucan scene intelligible, e.g.,
Josephus' description (*Ant.* 15.7.6; #235) of the dignified death of Mariamme, the Hasmonean wife of Herod the Great, who "spoke not a single
word." Yet none of these themes is openly developed by Luke, and so the
most obvious impression is the contrast between Pilate's calm interrogation
to which Jesus answers and Herod's emotional display before which Jesus is

---

[17]The martyr too stood before a tyrannical questioner, surrounded by troops (cf. 23:11) and insistent accusers (Darr, "Glorified" 165–71), but usually made a defiant defense speech (II Macc
6:23–28; 7:2,9,11; *IV Macc* 5:14–38; 9:1–9; 11:1–9; *Mart. Polycarp* 10–12). The silence of Jesus
disturbed ancient copyists, who made emendations: OS^{cur} adds "as if he were not present"; the Latin
Colbertinus ms. adds "as if he did not hear."

[18]The idea that an early tradition of Jesus' silence could be attached to different situations by
different authors is reinforced by *GPet* 4:10, where Jesus is silent (*siōpan*) on the cross—see Cambe,
"Récits" 23–24.

silent. The answer Jesus gave to Herod during the ministry (13:32–33) showed Jesus' determination not to be deflected from his work that on the third day would come to a termination related to prophets perishing in Jerusalem. Now the termination has come and Jesus is in Jerusalem; a further answer would be irrelevant, for no matter what Herod decides, Jesus will perish.

SENDING JESUS BACK TO PILATE (23:11–12)

Again we begin by mentioning stylistic features, but this time heavily intermixed with grammatical problems. These two verses continue the frequent Lucan use of *de* (one *de* ["But"] at the beginning of each). There are three aorist nominative singular participles in v. 11 before the main verb of the sentence ("sent") is given. The first two participles (from *exouthenein*, "to treat with contempt," lit. "to treat as nothing"; and *empaizein*, "to mock," lit. "to make fun of") are coordinated. *Exouthenein* (three times in Luke-Acts) is used in the other Gospels only in Mark 9:12 in reference to the predicted sufferings of the Son of Man. This is the second of three Lucan uses of *empaizein* in the PN to describe the mocking of Jesus (p. 582 above): The first mockery was by those who held Jesus during the night of his arrest (22:63); the third will be by the soldiers as Jesus hangs on the cross (23:36). The mockeries correspond to the prediction of the Lucan Jesus that the Son of Man would be given over to the Gentiles and mocked (18:32). These two participles modify "Herod";[19] but the phrase "with [*syn*] his troops [pl. of *strateuma*]" brings Herod's soldiers into the action.[20] *Syn* occurs some 75 times in Luke-Acts, compared with 6 times in Mark, 4 times in Matt, and 3 in John. Here, although virtually equivalent to "and" (BAGD 782, 4b), the prepositional construction leaves Herod as the sole subject of the sending. Skepticism that the Romans would have allowed Herod Antipas to bring an army into Jerusalem (Loisy) is irrelevant, since we need think of no more than a small entourage. I have translated the second participle (from *empaizein*) more generally than the first because there is no direct object following it and I want to make explicable why a few scholars think that Luke is describing a mockery made of the whole process rather than of Jesus. Verrall ("Christ" 340–44) would go further in finding no contempt for Jesus in v. 11a, but the *auton* in the opening clause surely points to Jesus as the object

---

[19]Or "even Herod" if one accepts the additional *kai* in P[75] and Codex Alexandrinus.

[20]The only other Lucan uses of *strateuma* (three of eight NT times) are in Acts 23:10,27 to refer to the troops of the tribune who arrested Paul and saved him from being killed by the Jews in Jerusalem. Although the noun is collective, it is used in the plural (also *IV Macc* 5:1; Matt 22:7).

of the first participle; and those who think of him as the object of the second are probably right.

A major issue is the third participle *peribalōn*, "having clothed," also an aorist nominative singular (lit. "having thrown around").[21] If the implicit object is Jesus and if Herod with his troops is putting on him a garment, how in terms of logic and grammar are we to understand what *peribalōn* modifies? Although it is a normal verb "to clothe" (e.g., it is used in Mark 14:51 for the young man clothed with linen over his nakedness), John 19:2 uses it in the Roman mockery of Jesus where he is clothed with a purple *himation*. Is the clothing here the content of the participle derived from *empaizein*, which it follows immediately: "made a mockery by clothing"? (Thus Delbrueck, Grundmann, Marshall.) Some who hold this view see the mockery in terms of putting royal clothes on Jesus; others think regular clothes were put on one who claimed to be a king. Grammatically, however, there is a difficulty in having one aorist participle subordinated to the other in this manner; and most scholars[22] think *peribalōn* is to be connected with "sent," even as I have translated it.

Esthēs ("garment") occurs 7 times in the NT, 4 of which are in Luke-Acts (never in another Gospel). Two of the Lucan references (24:4; Acts 10:30) refer to angelic clothing. It is a waste of time to debate (as does Delbrueck, "Antiquarisches" 136–37) what garment is meant, e.g., *chitōn, chlamys, himation;* what is important is the thrust of the adjective. *Lampros* ("splendid") occurs 9 times in the NT (2 in Luke-Acts; 0 in the other Gospels); it has the notion of "shining." It is clothed with this shining garment that Herod sends (*anapempein*) Jesus back to Pilate. The use of the same verb of sending as in v. 7 where Jesus was sent to Herod constitutes an inclusion.[23]

Lucan grammatical features continue in v. 12, putting stress on the mutuality of Herod and Pilate. A "both . . . and" function is played by *te* (almost 150 times in Luke-Acts, compared to 0 in Mark, 3 in Matt, 3 in John), and placing it after the definite article that accompanies *Hērōdēs* is quite Lucan. "On this same day" (with a proleptic use of *autos,* also in Luke 24:13) reflects Aramaic grammar but probably through LXX translation from Aramaic (so Fitzmyer, *Luke* 1.117–18); this type of phrase occurs in Luke-Acts 11 times but not in the other Gospels. *Philos* ("friend") occurs 18 times in

---

[21]Bornhäuser ("Beteiligung" 715–17) argues that this is self-reflexive and so describes Herod dressing himself to go back with Jesus to Pilate: "having thrown on himself the royal robe." Blinzler ("Herodes" 121) and Hoehner (*Herod* 242) object that in the NT *periballein* in the active is always transitive. K. Müller ("Jesus vor Herodes" 133) calls the Bornhäuser translation absurd.

[22]Blinzler, Fitzmyer, Joüon, Klostermann, Merk, Nestle, Rudberg, Verrall, Vogels.

[23]That rules out Bornhäuser's attempt ("Beteiligung" 716) to equate *anapempein* with *propempein* in Acts 20:38, so that Herod accompanies Jesus to Pilate. *Anapempein* is always transitive in the NT.

Luke-Acts compared with 0 in Mark, 1 in Matt, 6 in John. The last line of v. 12 (lit. "for they existed before, being in hostility toward themselves") employs *prohyparchein* plus a participle; a similar construction occurs in Acts 8:9 but not elsewhere in the NT.

As we turn from style and difficult grammar to meaning, scholars disagree on how to interpret Herod's treatment of Jesus in v. 11. In 23:14–15 Pilate will interpret Herod's sending Jesus back as a sign of Jesus' innocence. How does Jesus' silence lead Herod to that conclusion, and is Herod's contemptuous treatment and mockery of Jesus consonant with it? At one extreme Verrall ("Christ" 340–44), taking advantage of some of the grammatical obscurities mentioned above, argues that there is no real contempt for Jesus in the scene, only contempt for the political process. The clothing of Jesus with a splendid garment becomes a positive gesture treating him respectfully as king. As for past hostility on Herod's part, Verrall (327) argues that if only reluctantly and under pressure from Herodias, Herod put JBap to death, Jesus should have had nothing to fear from him. That really does not deal with specific passages in Luke (9:7–9; 13:31–33) where Herod is hostile to Jesus and wants to kill him, and we remember that Luke does not explain JBap's death through pressure from Herodias and her daughter. Can one really think that in the storyline Jesus' silence in the face of Herod's frenzied enthusiasm is likely to have produced benevolence on Herod's part?

At the opposite extreme Harlow (*Destroyer* 172–79, 229–42) interprets (or overinterprets) almost every word to confirm extreme hostility toward Jesus on Herod's part. For instance, at the beginning of v. 11, "That word [*exouthenein*], expressing the intense contempt and valuation at less than nothing whatever, is undoubtedly an expression of the attempt of Herod to destroy him, if not a paraphrase of a formal judgment of condemnation" (224). Herod has wanted to kill Jesus for a long time, but Jesus' silence in the face of a stern examination frustrates him. Jesus is dressed in a royal robe to show that Herod found him guilty of claiming to be king—a usurper worthy of punishment.[24]

Intermediary between these extremes is a view that both mockery and declaration of innocence are meant. Luke uses *exouthenein* in 18:9 to describe people who despise others, and that is how the frustrated Herod responds to Jesus' silence—a reaction consonant with the volatile emotions described in preceding verses of Luke. Indeed, Herod lowers himself to join his troops in a mockery of this laughable Jesus. Herod, however, has to react not only to Jesus but to Pilate and in the latter reaction to deal with political

---

[24]Many scholars who do not agree with Harlow's overall view agree on this last point, that the garment is a mockery of royal claims (Blinzler, Hoehner, Kastner, Schneider).

realities. Pilate, who thinks Jesus innocent, has made a friendly gesture by sending a Galilean to Herod for investigation. The chief priests and the scribes want Herod to find Jesus guilty; but it is more important to please Pilate and restore good relations by finding this wretch innocent, thus confirming Pilate's judgment.

This intermediary interpretation hangs on seeing the clothing of Jesus in a splendid garment as a statement of not guilty. The logic for such an interpretation comes indirectly from 23:14–15, where Pilate takes Herod's sending Jesus back as a confirmation of innocence. Since Jesus has said nothing that Herod can report, the only interpretative factor in the sending back has to be the garment with which Herod has clothed Jesus. Can *esthēs lampra* carry a connotation of innocence? The use of *periballein* suggests that this clothing envelops Jesus. *Esthēs* is a garment but often with connotation of a better type of garment, e.g., of the rich in James 2:2–3.[25] I listed above scholars who think that Herod was putting a royal robe on Jesus, but often they assume two factors, both unlikely: *first,* that the "having clothed" in v. 11 develops "(having) made a mockery"—grammar that, as I indicated above, is unlikely; *second,* that this is the "purple" of Mark 15:17, or the "scarlet cloak" of Matt 27:28; or the "purple robe" of John 19:2, all of them part of the mockery of Jesus as king by the Roman soldiers—something that finds no support whatsoever in the Lucan language or setting.

Joüon ("Luc 23" 83–84) has made a very careful study of *esthēs lampra* and argues that the color most appropriate for the shining or splendid character of the description is white, so that the Latin rendition as *vestis alba,* not the Syriac Peshitta rendition as scarlet, is correct. He points to white as a symbol of nobility, joy, and purity, with the Essenes wearing white habitually (Josephus, *War* 2.8.3; #123), whereas the accused come before the Sanhedrin wearing black (*Ant.* 14.9.4; #172). Further afield and in a somewhat opposite direction, pointing toward nobility, Grundmann, Hoehner, and Derrett argue that the *esthēs lampra* is the *toga candida* of Roman candidates for office, citing a passage in Polybius (*History* 10.4.8 combined with 10.5.1) where the two are equivalent. All of this is very tenuous evidence, as Darr ("Glorified" 298) points out in relation to Derrett's theory, and as Fitzmyer (*Luke* 2.1482) observes about the interpretation as "white." Not a particular color, but the description as "splendid, shining" establishes innocence or purity or sanctity. The adjective befits the attire of angels in Acts 10:30 and Rev 15:6, and of the bride of the lamb (Rev 19:8). Here it acquires its force from the context: Jesus was sent a prisoner to Herod (Justin, *Dia-*

---

[25]Some point to Acts 12:21, where it is used of the royal clothing of Herod Agrippa I, clothing that Josephus (*Ant.* 19.8.2; #344) describes as woven of silver and gleaming in the sun. However, in that passage of Acts it is the adjective *basilikos* that makes the garment regal.

logue 103 has Jesus sent "bound"); Herod sends him back in a splendid garment. Apparently in his *anakrisis* the Lucan Herod has found nothing that warrants a continuance of the treatment of Jesus as a prisoner. Contrary arguments that Herod could not deduce innocence from Jesus' silence or that a benevolent decision was out of character for Herod do not do justice to the indication given in v. 12. (Whether Luke's indirectness in keeping Herod's judgment till that verse is controlled by a tradition in which Herod's stance was ambiguous [cf. Acts 4:27] is hard to say.) Luke shows a Herod who is acting to please Pilate; undoubtedly he would have judged another way if that were to his advantage.

For Luke (23:14–15) the important final effect is that two persuasive witnesses, the Jewish tetrarch and the Roman prefect, attest to Jesus being innocent of the charges advanced—persuasive not because Jewish law required two witnesses (Deut 19:15), but because of their status. The facts that Herod had been ill-disposed toward Jesus (9:7–9; 13:31–33), that Jesus had not responded to him to win his favor, and that Herod had treated him with contempt and mockery make Herod's refusal to condemn him all the more impressive. Indeed, from Herod's past evil and his beheading of JBap one could argue that if Herod had thought Jesus a real danger, he would have destroyed the prophet from Nazareth, no matter what Pilate thought.

Luke goes beyond joining Herod and Pilate in a judgment of innocence; he reports that these former enemies became mutual friends. Fitzmyer (*Luke* 2.1482) considers v. 12 to be "one more of Luke's inconsequential explicative notes," but that may not be an adequate assessment. The paucity of historical data means that we cannot verify either the enmity or the subsequent friendship, but neither is implausible. As to the previous enmity, we have already mentioned the tradition that Pilate had killed Galileans in Jerusalem, probably during a feast (Luke 13:1), and Philo's report (*Ad Gaium* 38; #300) that Herodian princes had led a popular demonstration against Pilate in Jerusalem during a feast. Walaskay ("Trial" 89–90) thinks that the friendship might be a Lucan deduction from the fact that Pilate and Herod were deposed about the same time (AD 36 and 39 respectively). It should be noted, however, that Acts 4:26–28 and Luke 23:6–12, while they give different pictures of how Jesus was dealt with, agree on cooperation between Pilate and Herod, so that Luke did not waver on that point. There was a practical reason for Roman governors to remain friendly with Herodian reigning princes: The latter had good relations with the Julio-Claudian imperial family in Rome. Josephus (*War* 1.20.4; #399) tells us that already in the time of Herod the Great the Roman governors in Syria were forbidden to take measures without his concurrence, and later the future Emperor Vespasian sent to Agrippa II Jewish captives who were from his realm as a gift (*War* 3.10.10; #541).

Acts 25:13ff. may well be historical in describing a friendship between Agrippa II and the procurator Festus ca. 60.

Yet neither plausibility nor history is Luke's goal in 23:12. That verse reflects Luke's theology of the passion as forgiveness and healing (p. 281 above). Herod has shown himself Jesus' enemy in a previous desire to kill him and in an exercise of contempt and mockery during the trial; but Jesus has provided the occasion of grace for both Herod and Pilate by healing their enmity, even as he healed the ear of the servant who came to arrest him. Soards ("Tradition . . . Herod" 363) is correct in judging this to be another instance where the Jesus of the PN is consistent with the Jesus of the ministry in "doing good" (Acts 10:38). Darr ("Glorification" 304) may also be correct in seeing the friendship motif as preparing the reader for the linkage of Herod and Pilate in Acts 4:27, even if that linkage scene will take the overall view that by not letting Jesus go both men were gathered against him.[26] Some would find here an echo of the LXX of Prov 15:28 (= MT 16:7): "The ways of the righteous are received by the Lord, and through them enemies become friends." I do not see sufficient reason, however, to interpret the reconciliation of Herod and Pilate as abstractly symbolic, e.g., the reconciliation of Jews and Gentiles (E. Schweizer, Talbert), or the reconciliation of Jewish religion based on Law and Gentile paganism (Manus).

ANALYSIS

The complete absence of any reference to Herod Antipas in the PNs of the other Gospels raises acutely two problems: Where did Luke get this material? How historical is it? To those two questions we now turn.

A. Formation of the Story

There are basically three possibilities:[27] (1) Luke took over the whole story from an earlier source that scholars describe in various ways[28] (Ellis,

[26]"Gathered together" does not mean they met physically (pace Bornhäuser); it is language conformed to Ps 2:2 and indicates no more than that their efforts were harmonious.

[27]While in principle these three approaches are quite distinct, variations and nuances given to them by some adherents blur the line of demarcation. The assignment of a scholar's name to one of the theories is subject to that limitation. Also there are scholars who have changed their views: Schneider was originally under (1), but in "Verfahren" 127 the most he allows behind the story is a legendary or anecdotal note.

[28]For some the thrust of the source has the same thrust as Luke; for others in the source Herod condemned Jesus and sent him back to Pilate to be executed. Some scholars speak of an independent Lucan source for part of the scene, e.g., holding that the mockery of Jesus in 23:11 was not derived from Mark (Benoit, Delbrueck).

Grundmann, Hoehner, Perry, Rehkopf, Rengstorf, Tyson, Wente); (2) Luke composed the scene himself on the basis of an early tradition of Herodian involvement in the death of Jesus, combined with material drawn from Mark, etc. (Dodd, Ernst, Fitzmyer, Kratz, Loisy, Pesch, Schneider, Soards); (3) Luke created the whole scene himself without drawing substantially on a source or early tradition relating Herod to Jesus (F. C. Baur, Beare, Bultmann, Cadbury, Creed, Dibelius, Finegan, Hendrickx, H. Klein, Klostermann, Leaney, K. Müller, Radl, Sloyan). Sometimes Luke is thought to have got the idea for the scene from Psalm 2 or from the involvement of Agrippa II in the trial of Paul.

We begin with solution (1). In the COMMENT I gave more than usual attention to the amount of Lucan style in the passage, agreeing with K. Müller ("Jesus vor Herodes" 114–16) that the Lucan elements are found throughout. If the story was taken over whole from a source, either that source was written almost entirely in Lucan style (and so the source really becomes an earlier form of Lucan composition), or Luke rewrote in his own style the complete story that he had taken over from the source. The latter is not an impossibility; but the agreement of Luke 23:6–12 with other Lucan material on Herod[29] and the parallels with the scene of Paul before Agrippa II suggest considerably more Lucan activity than simply retranslating into his own style a ready-made story. We have already discussed several other Lucan PN sections that some would trace to a source and have found consistently that a tradition, not a source, is an adequate point of origin. Let us see whether that works as well here.

Before turning to solution (2), however, we must look at a major factor in solution (3)—a factor that many think makes an appeal to a tradition unnecessary. Acts 4:24–28 describes an early Christian group praying by citing Ps 2:1–2 according to the LXX:[30]

Why did the Gentiles [*ethnē* = nations] act arrogantly,
and the peoples think of empty things?
The kings of the earth came to take their stand,
and the rulers [pl. of *archōn*] gathered together in the same place
against [*kata*] the Lord and against His Messiah [*Christos*].

[29]Earlier in 3:19–20; 9:7–9; 13:31–33 Herod had heard about Jesus, had been wishing to see him, had questions about him, etc.

[30]According to Hebrew parallelism, as visible in the poetic lines, "the Gentiles" are the same as "the peoples" and the kings are the same as the rulers, so that only one hostile group and its authorities are involved. By ignoring the parallelism, the Acts interpretation comes out with two hostile groups and two different authorities. Ignoring parallelism in OT poetry, however, seems to be more the rule than the exception in the NT, e.g., Matt 21:4–7 (two animals); John 19:23–24 (garments read as distinct from clothing/tunic).

This is followed by an application of the psalm: "For in truth in this city there were gathered together against [*epi*] Your holy servant Jesus, whom You did anoint, both Herod and Pontius Pilate with the Gentiles and the peoples of Israel, to do whatever Your hand and Your[31] will [or plan: *boulē*] had predestined to take place." Dibelius ("Herodes" 124–25) contends that the citation of Ps 2:7 in early christology (e.g., Acts 13:33; Heb 1:5) points to the fact that this was a psalm reflected on by Christians and used in cult; and this reflection spread to Ps 2:1–2 and produced the involvement of Herod in the passion. One of his arguments is drawn from Justin, *Apology* 1.40, which cites Ps 2:1–2 and Ps 2:7 and which states that David foretold "the conspiracy formed against Christ by Herod the king of the Jews and the Jews themselves, and Pilate, who was procurator [*epitropos*] among them and his soldiers." Dibelius contends that Justin did not get this from Luke but from meditation on the psalm. However, Dibelius's line of thought can be challenged on several scores. The interpretation of the psalm in Acts involves ingenious stretching to fit the facts of the passion. To understand "the peoples" of the psalm to refer to "the peoples [pl.!] of Israel" is extraordinary. Elsewhere Luke refers to Herod Antipas as a tetrarch, never in the Gospel as a king;[32] he does not refer to Pilate as an *archōn*.[33] If there were not already a tradition of Herod's involvement against Jesus, how would reading the psalm suggest such interpretations? As for Justin, if his interpretation is not dependent on Luke (even through oral memory),[34] he could be dependent on the same type of tradition about Herod that Luke drew from.

A further objection to complete Lucan creation of Herodian involvement on the basis of Psalm 2 is the difference in the portrayals of Herod's role in Acts 4:24–28 and Luke 23:6–15. In Acts 4 Herod and Pontius Pilate are gathered together against Jesus, as are the peoples of Israel. In Luke 23:14–15 both Herod and Pilate find Jesus not guilty, and in Luke 23:27,35 the "people" are not particularly hostile. If there were a preLucan tradition of

---

[31]The "Your" is omitted in important textual witnesses.

[32]In various ways scholars bring into the discussion the Idumean background of Antipas' grandfather (Antipater II), and the designation of his father (Herod the Great) as "half-Jewish" (Josephus, *Ant.* 14.15.2; #403), so that Antipas might be considered neither Jewish nor Gentile. None of that appears in the NT: For early Christians, Herod was a Jewish figure, whom Acts 4:27 clearly aligns with "the peoples of Israel," counterposed to the Gentiles.

[33]In reference to the passion, the plural of *archōn* refers to Jewish authorities (Luke 23:13,35; 24:20; Acts 3:17, etc.).

[34]Too often the question of the dependency of 2d-cent. writers on the NT is debated only on the level of their having written documents before them; at this period, with few copies of NT works, oral memory would have been important. In *Dialogue* 103 Justin says, "When Herod received the *exousia* assigned to him, Pilate as a gracious favor sent Jesus to him bound." Can it be pure chance the two references in Justin to Herod (*Dialogue* and *Apology*) resemble closely the differing tones of Luke 23 and Acts 4?

Herodian hostility toward Jesus, one can see how Luke might adapt it in the Gospel to make Herod bear witness to Jesus' innocence.[35] But would Luke *create* a psalm relationship in Acts that is the opposite of the way he is describing Herod in the Gospel? And if the psalm passage was the point of origin of the whole Herod Antipas picture, why does it not appear in the many references to Antipas in the Gospel, instead of being kept till the end of the descriptions of Herod, in Acts?

Still another argument against pure Lucan creation of Herodian involvement comes from other early references to the involvement of Herod in the death of Jesus. Ignatius (*Smyrnaeans* 1.2) speaks of Jesus being nailed to a tree in the flesh for our sake "under Pontius Pilate and Herod the tetrarch." Surely this is not based on Ps 2, since "king" is not the title given to Herod; nor is there major evidence that here Ignatius draws on Luke or Acts, neither of which in the PN reference to Herod calls him "tetrarch." There is no evidence at all that *GPet* 1:1–2:5, describing the role of King Herod in the death of Jesus, is the source of Luke's knowledge about Antipas' role.[36] Nor is there evidence that *GPet* draws on Ps 2, the interpretation of which puts Herod Antipas and Pontius Pilate on the same level. In *GPet* Herod the king is the chief magistrate in the trial of Jesus; he refuses to wash his hands (of the innocent blood of Jesus); he commands that Jesus be marched off; he receives Pilate's request for Jesus' body; he delivers Jesus to the people who mock him as "King of Israel," clothing him (*periballein*) with purple. I shall contend in APPENDIX I that while the author of the 2d-cent. *GPet* was familiar with the canonical Gospels, he also knew independently some popular traditions employed by the canonical Gospels—in fact, knew those traditions at a more developed level than we can see in the canonical Gospels. In the continuing growth of the tradition about Herod's seeking the death of Jesus, he becomes the tool of the diabolic serpent, along with Caiaphas, in opposition to Jesus in the *Acts of Thomas* 32; and it is he who gives the order that Jesus be crucified in the Syriac form of the *Didascalia Apostolorum* 21.5.19 (Connolly ed. p. 190). In these later developments, however, it is impossible to decide whether one is still hearing mutations of the early Herod tradition, or developments of the Luke-Acts variations on that theme, or even developments of *GPet*.[37]

---

[35]While the approaches to Herod's role in Luke 23 and Acts 4 are different, one should not treat them as contradictory (see the final paragraph of the COMMENT). The fact that Justin has both approaches (preceding note) suggests that they were not seen as in total conflict.

[36]See Brown, "Gospel of Peter" over against the extravagant theory of Crossan that would make *GPet* the most ancient PN on which the canonical Gospels drew. This issue will be treated in detail in APPENDIX I.

[37]Irenaeus, *Proof of Apost. Preaching* 77 (SC 62.144), retells the story of Luke 23:6–12, whereas Tertullian, *Adv. Marcion* 4.42.2–3 (CC 1.659), draws on both Acts 4:24–28 and Luke 23. Blinzler

All this points to the existence of an early tradition about lethal Herodian opposition to Jesus and therefore supports the second solution I listed at the beginning of this ANALYSIS. That tradition did not arise from reading Psalm 2 but led to interpreting the psalm in the manner we see in Acts 4. The story we encounter in Luke 23:6–12 is not simply a Lucan adaptation of the Ps 2 and Acts 4 interpretation but another Lucan variation of the early Antipas tradition, fleshed out by three addenda:[38] (a) material from Mark about the questioning of Jesus during the trial (in Mark by Pilate), about the silence of Jesus before the questioner, and about the mockery of Jesus;[39] (b) a schema of the Roman governor inviting a Herodian prince to examine a Jewish prisoner accused by the leaders of his own people—a schema similar to that in the account of Festus inviting Agrippa II to examine Paul in Acts 25:13–26:32;[40] (c) sayings pertinent to Herod, preserved especially in Luke 13:31–33.[41]

The early tradition had Herod hostile to Jesus. It is not clear to what extent the Jewish people were mentioned alongside Herod (as in Acts 4 and *GPet*). Luke has taken over into 23:11a part of that hostility by having *Herod with his troops* treat Jesus with contempt and make (of him) a mockery. These troops take the place of the "peoples of Israel" associated with Herod in

---

("Herodes" 120) lists a whole group of apocryphal works that he judges to be directly or indirectly dependent on *GPet,* including the Syriac *Didascalia.*

[38]In much of this I agree substantially with Soards ("Tradition . . . Herod" 358–59), who is more precise, however, in the allotment of every Lucan verse.

[39]Mark 15:16–20 (= Matt 27:27–31) recounts a mockery of Jesus as "the King of the Jews" by Roman soldiers (at the end of the Pilate trial) which includes putting a mock regal garment on him and physical abuse. (John 19:1–3 has elements of this scene but in the middle of the Roman trial.) Luke has chosen not to narrate the Marcan scene as a whole or to substitute for it at the end of the Roman trial. Rather Luke 23:36–37 tells of the mockery of Jesus by Roman soldiers as "the King of the Jews" as Jesus hangs on the cross. In the Herod scene Luke has used other elements from the Marcan account of the mockery of Jesus: namely, *empaizein* ("to mock"), and the clothing of Jesus with a splendid garment. This last element, however, is kept clear of the mockery.

[40]Was the direction of the influence from Acts 24–26 to Luke 23, or vice versa, or did Luke create both? Acts constitutes our only evidence for how Paul was treated. Clearly in the speeches of Paul there has been Lucan development; but it is very plausible that Acts preserves tradition about *the facts* of Paul's trial. In listing charges against Jesus, Luke 23:2 seems to have been influenced by Acts 24:5–6; and similarly Luke 23:6–7,11b–12 (sending of the Galilean to Herod, sending him back, friendship between Herod and Pilate) seems to have been influenced by Acts 25:13ff.

[41]Again one must ask about the direction of the influence: from Luke 9:7–9 and 13:31–33 to Luke 23:6–12 or vice versa? Blinzler (*Herodes*) relativizes the issue by taking all the passages as historical. Fitzmyer (*Luke* 1.756–58) treats 9:7–9 as a Lucan modification of Marcan material, and from that modification some motifs have been taken over into 23:8, e.g., having heard about Jesus, wondering who he is, wishing to see him. Basically, then, both 9:7–9 and 23:8 would be free Lucan composition inspired by themes in Mark. Fitzmyer (*Luke* 2.1028) reports a consensus that in 13:31–32 "the report of the Pharisees to Jesus about Herod's attitude toward him is a piece of authentic tradition rooted in Stage I [Jesus' ministry] of the Gospel material." The image of the crafty, destructive fox sums up that tradition, and Luke has used it to paint Herod in 23:6–12.

Acts 4:27 (perhaps under the influence of the Marcan mockery scene, which involves Roman soldiers). The omission of direct reference to the Jewish people is suited to the major change Luke makes in 23:11b,14–15 whereby, despite the contempt and mockery, Herod becomes an affirmer of Jesus' innocence.[42] In the COMMENT I underlined the import of this change: The readers see that both the Jewish tetrarch and the Roman prefect think Jesus not guilty of arousing the people against Caesar and being a royal pretender. But one must still ask what prompted Luke to change the hostile Herod tradition in this way. Was the content of the Marcan Roman trial a major factor? To introduce a Herod who played a major role in condemning and killing Jesus (as in *GPet*) would be a very drastic revision of Mark, perhaps more than Luke wished.[43] Another important factor may have been the tradition of the trial of Paul, where the involvement of Agrippa II at the invitation of the procurator Festus resulted in Agrippa's judgment that Paul was not guilty as charged (Acts 26:31). In any case what Luke has done is a compromise. He has changed the Marcan outline by introducing Herod, but he has not changed the flow of the trial: Pilate remains the controlling judge making the final decision. In Acts 4:24–28, Luke has taken over an early tradition about lethal Herodian hostility to Jesus and kept the tone of it with an adaptation to Ps 2:1–2. But in the Gospel, where he is working from Marcan guidelines, Luke has adapted that Herod tradition, preserving only part of the hostility and using it for a different effect. That change in the Gospel presentation of Herod was in preparation for the last words that will be spoken about Jesus in the Lucan PN: "Certainly this man was just [*dikaios*]."

B. Historicity of the Herod Tradition

The theory of formation just expounded indicates that the scene in Luke 23:6–12(14–15) is scarcely a direct historical account. But there remains the question whether the tradition of Herod's deadly hostility toward Jesus—the tradition that Luke drew upon and interpolated into the trial—is historical.[44] Obviously those who hold for solution (3) about the formation of the Lucan narrative, in which the whole is created by Luke, would deny the historicity

---

[42]Too often Luke's introduction of Herod in the trial of Jesus is treated as an antiJewish gesture. If anything it complicates the picture of Jewish responsibility, for a Jewish ruler (see n. 32 above) has taken a different stance from that of the chief priests and the scribes.

[43]Respecting Mark's outline, Luke has not made the Herod scene a separate trial; what Herod decided is known only through the words of Pilate in 23:15, so that clearly Pilate remains the presiding judge.

[44]Among those who judge that there is a historical substratum are Blinzler, Marshall, Rengstorf, Taylor, and Verrall.

of a tradition the very existence of which they have challenged. Solutions (1) and (2) presume preLucan material about Herod, but that material is not necessarily historical; and the absence of it in Mark, Matt, and John shows that a serious issue remains. Yet Mark (followed by Matt) supplies a simplified preaching outline of the PN and may not do justice to popularly preserved oral tradition about minor incidents of the passion that could be historical. The silence about Herod in John may be a greater problem; yet the Johannine tradition is idiosyncratic in what it preserves as useful, and its failure ever to mention any Herod means that John is not a particularly sure guide on this point.

Some scholars are convinced that the Lucan notice about Herod's role in Jesus' death is just the tip of the historical iceberg. For them Herod was the major opponent of Jesus, a master plotter who had the decisive role in the death of Jesus (e.g., Harlow, Parker). In the NT references to Herod, Harlow gives optimal value to every phrase that can point to hostility, as I pointed out in discussing "treated him with contempt" in 23:11; and from this emerges his imagery of Herod, the destroyer of Jesus. Parker pulls together the scattered NT references to shape a plot worthy of a novel involving the Sanhedrin, Pilate, and the Herodians against Jesus.[45] There are obscure references to opposition to Jesus by the Herodians in Mark 3:6; 12:13 (= Matt 22:16). Luke, however, never mentions the Herodians, and they may represent merely the Marcan form of the Herodian tradition that Luke has used in another way. If so, they really offer no additional evidence.

That leads me to a factor that is often not taken into account in assessing the historicity of the hostility of Herod Antipas to Jesus. Three men in the NT are called *Hērōdēs:* Herod the Great, Herod Antipas, and Herod Agrippa I. This enumeration of three is by *our* informed counting, for no such distinctions as "the Great," or "Antipas," or "Agrippa" ever occur as modifications of *Hērōdēs* in the NT.[46] To compound the confusion all three men are called "king": Herod the Great is king in Matt 2:1,3,9; Luke 1:5; Herod Antipas is

---

[45]In Parker's theory there is much use of the imagination and an appeal to silence. The appearance of the cohort in John 18:3 is treated as historical without any discussion that it could be a feature introduced to serve John's theology of Jesus' supremacy. The fact that Antipas and the Herodians do not appear in that Johannine context is "doubtless [!] because, however much trouble they may stir up, they have no *legal* authority in Jerusalem" ("Herod" 199). Pilate's decision to send Jesus to Herod and the words the Sanhedrists spoke to Herod were "all according to plan"—thus Parker treats the Lucan scene as history but denies what Luke indicates about the haphazardness of Herod's presence.

[46]"Agrippa" does occur in Acts 25–26 for Agrippa II, but never for Herod Agrippa I who appears (only) in Acts 12, five times as *Hērōdēs.*

king in Matt 14:9; Mark 6:14,22,25,26,27; Acts 4:26–27;[47] Herod Agrippa I is king in Acts 12:1,20. What would early Christians have understood when they heard "Herod the king," since they scarcely had at hand a Herodian family tree? Matt 2 shows Herod the king, advised by the chief priests and the scribes, seeking to kill Jesus who is being hailed as "the King of the Jews." A combination of Luke 13:31; 23:10; Acts 4:26–27 shows a Herod identified as a king seeking to kill Jesus, and being advised to do so by the chief priests and scribes after Jesus has been asked about being "the King of the Jews." Acts 12 shows a Herod ("the king") pleasing the Jews by killing James (the brother of John) and planning to do the same to Peter. How many hearers or readers would have known that these were three different men?

When I wrote above of an early tradition about a Herodian role in the death of Jesus or a lethal Herodian opposition to Jesus, I was deliberately using a broadly phrased description. I think this same tradition may show up in Mark as Herodians seeking to kill Jesus; in Matt's infancy narrative as Herod (the Great) trying to kill Jesus at Bethlehem; in Luke-Acts as Herod (Antipas) wanting to kill Jesus and taking part in his trial, and perhaps even as Herod (Agrippa I) putting Jesus' leading follower(s) to death. With so many echoes in the NT and added echoes in Ignatius and *GPet*, it is very probable that there was a historical nucleus in the tradition. Yet the very accounts that preserve the tradition show considerable imaginative elaboration, so that it becomes difficult, if not impossible, to know whether one, two, or three Herods was/were hostile to Jesus (and to his followers).[48] Even if one were to center on Antipas, the references are not at one as to what moment in Jesus' career the lethal opposition came into play. Jesus' admiration for JBap would certainly have made him distrust Herod who killed that prophet; vice versa Antipas would have had no love for Jesus who praised JBap and attracted some of the Baptist's followers. Having killed one religious figure, Antipas may have had to act with more discretion toward another whom he wanted to rid himself of, perhaps settling for getting Jesus out of Galilee. In my judgment we must settle for a Lucan author of 23:6–12 who is neither a simple recorder of historical fact nor totally a creative, imaginative novelist. He transmits early tradition about Herod Antipas— tradition that had a historical nucleus but had already developed beyond simple history by the time it reached Luke. By weaving this tradition and

---

[47]He is also called a tetrarch in Matt 14:1; Luke 3:19; 9:7; Acts 13:1.

[48]The Matthean infancy narrative and *GPet* evidence a popular legendary development of the Herod tradition whereby he comes to embody Jewish opposition to Jesus and becomes Jesus' chief adversary.

other items into the narrative of 23:6–12, Luke not only made an important theological statement about Jesus' innocence and the healing power of his passion;[49] he also contributed to the further development of the picture of Herodian involvement.[50]

(Bibliography for this episode may be found in §30, Part 4.)

---

[49]Fitzmyer (*Luke* 2.1480) states: "In the Lucan passion narrative this scene is actually a minor one. It has no significance for the understanding of Jesus' person or fate." As indicated above, I would have a more generous evaluation of the scene.

[50]Just as the early tradition about Herod brought an interpretation of Ps 2:1–2 as we see in Acts 4:24–28, so also the development of the Herod tradition in Luke 23:7 called attention to another OT text, as cited by many church writers (Irenaeus, Tertullian, Cyril of Jerusalem): "And having bound him, they brought him to Assyria for a gift to King Jarim" (variation on the LXX of Hosea 10:6).

§34. THE ROMAN TRIAL, PART THREE: BARABBAS

(Mark 15:6–11; Matt 27:15–21; Luke 23:13–19; John 18:38b–40)

Translation

Mark 15:6–11: ⁶But at a/the feast he used to release to them one prisoner whom they requested. ⁷But there was someone called Barabbas imprisoned with the rioters, those who had done killing during
the riot. ⁸And the crowd, having come up, began to request (that he
do) as he used to do for them. ⁹But Pilate answered them, saying,
"Do you will that I release to you 'the King of the Jews'?" ¹⁰for he
had knowledge that (it was) out of envy/zeal that the chief priests
had given him over. ¹¹But the chief priests stirred up the crowd that
he should rather release Barabbas to them.

Matt 27:15–21: ¹⁵But at a/the feast the governor was accustomed to
release to the crowd one prisoner whom they willed. ¹⁶But at that
time they had a notorious prisoner called [Jesus] Barabbas. ¹⁷So
when they had gathered together, Pilate said to them, "Whom do
you will that I release to you: [Jesus] Barabbas or Jesus who is
called Messiah?" ¹⁸For he was aware that (it was) out of envy/zeal
that they gave him over. ¹⁹But while he was sitting on the judgment
seat, his wife sent to him, saying, "Let there be nothing between
you and that just man, for many things have I suffered today in a
dream because of him." ²⁰But the chief priests and the elders persuaded the crowds that they should request Barabbas, but Jesus
they should destroy. ²¹But in answer the governor said to them,
"Which of the two do you will that I should release to you?" But
they said, "Barabbas."

Luke 23:13–19: ¹³But Pilate, having called together the chief priests
and the rulers and the people, ¹⁴said to them, "You brought to me
this man as leading astray the people; and behold, having investi-

gated him in your presence, I have found nothing in this man (making him) guilty of what you charged against him. ¹⁵Neither did Herod, for he sent him back to us; and behold there is nothing worthy of death that has been done by him. ¹⁶Having chastised him (by whipping), therefore, I shall let him go." ⁽¹⁷*⁾ ¹⁸But all together they shouted out, saying, "Take this fellow but release to us Barabbas," ¹⁹who was someone thrown into prison because of a certain riot that had taken place in the city and (because of) killing.

John 18:38b–40: ³⁸ᵇAnd having said this, again he went out to the Jews and says to them, "I find no case at all against him. ³⁹You have a custom that I release to you one person at Passover. So do you desire that I release to you 'the King of the Jews'?" ⁴⁰So they yelled back, "Not this fellow but Barabbas." But Barabbas was a bandit.

Acts 3:14 [Peter speaking in the Temple precincts to the men of Israel, having mentioned Pilate's decision to release Jesus, says:] "But you denied the holy and just one, and requested that a man who was a killer be granted to you."

*In the Koine Greek mss. and some versions (OL, Vulgate, Peshitta) there is a v. 17 (or in Codex Bezae a verse after 19) that is probably a copyist's addition to make Luke correspond to Mark/Matt: "But he had the obligation to release one person to them at a/the feast."

COMMENT

While for the convenience of obtaining digestible units I treat the Barabbas episode separately, only in John with its technique of outside/inside does it approach being a distinct entity. Among the Synoptics Mark's account is basic. The longer account in Matt is for the most part a close following of Mark[1] with two exceptions. In the middle Matt (27:19) interrupts to recount a message to Pilate emanating from the dream of his wife, a message that underlines the innocence of Jesus, "that just man." At the end Matt (27:21) has a question addressed by Pilate to the Jewish authorities and people forcing them to spell out in direct address their preference for Barabbas over Jesus the Messiah, a preference that has already been indicated indirectly.

[1]Matt 27:15–18 = Mark 15:6–10; Matt 27:20 = Mark 15:11.

The contrast between their choice and the advice given by Pilate's wife intensifies the miscarriage of justice.

Luke's account is also longer than Mark's, but what it covers is quite different. If we leave out Luke 23:17 as a later copyist's gloss, what pertains to Barabbas in 23:18–19 is a major abbreviation of Mark. The custom of the release has disappeared, and Barabbas is identified only by afterthought. The dominant feature is the preface (23:13–16) to the choice of Barabbas, consisting of a transition from the interrogation before Herod (23:6–12 = §33 above). This transitional preface contains Pilate's reaction to Herod's decision, with an emphasis on Pilate's statement (second of three) that he finds nothing in Jesus that would make him guilty and so he will let him go. Functionally, then, Pilate has the role in Luke that Pilate's wife has in Matt: Gentile proclamation of Jesus' innocence while the Jewish authorities and crowds/people are opting for the release of the guilty Barabbas.

John's account is by far the shortest. His transitional preface (18:38b), while much shorter than Luke's, also contains a statement by Pilate (first of three) that he finds no case at all against Jesus. The Barabbas material is as short as Luke's even if it mentions the custom of a release; and again only at the end is Barabbas identified, but with dramatic force. Let us discuss these accounts section by section (see the outline on p. 663 above).

THE TRANSITIONAL PREFACES (LUKE 23:13–16; JOHN 18:38b)

Luke 23:13–16. In the Lucan sequence, Jesus, clothed with a splendid garment, has just been sent back by Herod to Pilate (23:11); and Pilate makes that the occasion of calling together (to himself: aorist middle voice, BDF 316[1]) "the chief priests and the rulers and the people."[2] Scholars have paid minute attention to details in this verse. The verb *sygkalein* ("to call together") is found seven times in Luke/Acts vs. one use in the rest of the NT (in Mark 15:16: the cohort for the mockery of Jesus). In Acts 5:21 it describes the convocation of the Sanhedrin. Foulon-Piganiol ("Rôle" 631) sees in *sygkalein* a decisive, formal intervention by Pilate, exercising jurisdiction. Bickermann ("Utilitas" 318) points out that in the judicial papyri the accusers had to wait until they were summoned, and at times the judge could convoke the public to render judgment. In itself, however, the calling together of the people need not give them a judicial function, e.g., II Macc 15:31 has the multitudes convened (*sygkalein*) to see a barbarous spectacle.

---

[2] Jaubert (*Date* 104–5, 112–15) wants to place the Herod interrogation of Jesus on Thursday afternoon and this convocation on Friday morning, but there is nothing in 23:13 to support that.

As for those called together, Luke 23 introduces with increasing detail the Jewish adversaries of Jesus who stand before Pilate. At the beginning, 23:1 speaks of one collectivity, "the whole multitude of them" (presumably referring back to "the assembly of the elders of the people, both chief priests and scribes" of 22:66); then 23:4 speaks of two groups, "the chief priests and the crowds." Now 23:13 has three groups: Inevitably the chief priests are the most prominent, but next to them appear "the rulers" (*archontes*), a designation in the PN peculiar to Luke (the same twosome is found in 24:20). As explained in APPENDIX V, B6, lexicographically the plural of *archōn* covers a wide range of officials and men of import; but in the Luke-Acts descriptions of those who are opposed to Jesus or to his followers, *archontes* is an umbrella term for all or part of the chief priests, the captains of the Temple, the elders, and the scribes (see Acts 3:17; 4:5–8; 13:27–29)—in short, in the present sequence (from 22:66), members of the Sanhedrin.

Greater attention has been focused on the third group mentioned in 23:13, "the people" (*laos*). In one direction Codex Bezae aggravates the situation by reading "all the people," making Luke's scene comparable to Matt 27:25, where "all the people" answer, "His blood on us and on our children."[3] In the other direction some modern scholars are puzzled that Luke should mention "the people" in 23:13 in a context that makes them unfriendly to Jesus, namely, being among those who will cry out rejecting him in 23:18. Except for the usage cited on p. 431, n. 4 above, in a strong sequence of passages (19:47–48; 20:6,19,45; 21:38; 22:2), Luke has shown (all) the people favorable to Jesus, protecting him against the authorities; and in the crucifixion the people will not act hostilely (23:27,35; cf. 24:19–20). Rau ("Volk" 48) is so impressed by the Lucan consistency in portraying the *laos* favorably that he emends 23:13 to read "the rulers *of* the people" (as in Acts 4:8), a reading that Winter (*On the Trial* 141) favors as part of his effort to show that in the original trial of Jesus (best preserved by Luke) there was a minimum of antiJudaism. Alas, that suggestion (lacking in textual support) must be rejected, for Luke is not that consistent and like the other Gospels he portrays a Jewish collectivity opposed to Jesus. In Acts 4:27 "the peoples of Israel" are described as gathered together with the Gentiles against Jesus; and similar hostility toward Jesus is attributed to "the men of Israel" in Acts 2:22–23; 3:12–15, to "the Jews" in Acts 10:39, and to the Jerusalemites in Acts 13:27–28. "The people" in Luke 23:13 is surely not significantly different from "the crowds" in 23:4–5 who were insistent on accusing Jesus before

---

[3]Rice ("Role") points out that this is consistent with Bezae's tendency to increase the role of the Jewish people against Jesus, e.g., by including them in the arrest in 22:52 ("to those *of the people* who were arrived against him"), even as Bezae intensifies the hostility of the Jewish authorities.

Pilate.[4] "The people" have become part of "the whole multitude of them" who have been involved since 23:1.[5] But if "the people" is equivalent to "the multitude" or "the crowds," as I contend, why has Luke shifted to this term here? One should not discount a stylistic desire to vary vocabulary, but more likely Luke wants "the people" present to hear Pilate in the next verse recall the charge made against Jesus that he led *the people* astray. Pilate's rejection of that charge will be witnessed not only by the authorities but by those who reputedly were misled.

In 23:14 we find much Lucan vocabulary: *eipen pros* for "said to" (see 23:4); *kai idou,* "and behold" (26 times in Luke; not in Mark, but in a Q saying: Fitzmyer, *Luke* 1.121); *enōpion (hymōn),* "in (your) presence" (a Septuagintal equivalent of a preposition, used some 35 times in Luke-Acts, once in the other Gospels); and *apostrephein* ("to lead astray"), which is just a variant for *diastrephein* ("to mislead") in 23:2 and *anaseiein* ("to stir up") in 23:5. "Having investigated" is the verb *anakrinein,* from which comes the noun *anakrisis* discussed on pp. 766–68 above as a legal description of part of the Roman process. We have been noting parallels in the trials of Paul in Acts: The procurator Felix "investigates" Paul in Acts 24:8, while in Acts 25:26 the procurator Festus speaks of the "investigation" of Paul that he and Agrippa II are making.

The official tone of Pilate's introductory words in 23:14, repeating the charge and insisting that he had made a public investigation, gives solemnity to his judgment. In 23:4 Pilate already said, "I find nothing guilty in this man"; but that was after only one question, and inevitably the Jewish accusers protested that Pilate had not taken seriously enough their charge that they reiterated in 23:5. Now he has made a full investigation and his judgment is identical: "I have found nothing in this man . . . guilty." Indeed, Pilate affirms that the "not guilty" refers specifically to what they had charged against Jesus. No longer can they say Pilate has ignored their charges.

Then in 23:15 Pilate points out that Herod's investigation came to the same result. Many interpreters, ancient and modern, have found this report on Herod a surprise, granted that Jesus showed no respect for him and that Herod had mocked Jesus—all the more a surprise if they misunderstood Herod's clothing of Jesus with a splendid garment as continued mockery instead of as a statement of innocence. The possibilities of confusion are increased by Luke's elliptic *alla oude Hērōdēs* (literally, "However not Herod"). Harlow (*Destroyer*) interprets this to mean that Herod did not agree with Pilate about Jesus' innocence; otherwise he would not have sent Jesus

---

[4]For the equivalence of *laos* and *ochlos,* see 22:2 and 6; also Tyson, *Death* 32,35.

[5]In my judgment such evidence refutes the thesis of Cassidy ("Luke's" 151), who suggests that Pilate has brought the people in to halt the momentum of the chief priests against Jesus.

back for further trial. Such an interpretation, however, makes Pilate illogical: Why would he weaken his own position by citing Herod's judgment if it were contradictory, and thus offer the Jewish adversaries of Jesus an argument against a not-guilty decision? Rather the Greek means "Neither did Herod (find him guilty)," wherein the logic of the *alla* ("However") is against the implicit insistence of the Jewish adversaries of Jesus that he is guilty.[6]

Confusion about how to interpret Pilate's attitude toward Herod is visible in variant readings of the second clause in 23:15. The first and best attested (Codices Vaticanus and Sinaiticus, P[75], Coptic) is "for he sent him back to us," i.e., Herod sent Jesus back to Pilate and the Jewish accusers.[7] The accusers are included because they had gone to Herod (23:10). A minor variant (family 13, some Vulgate and Syriac mss.) is "he sent him back to you"; Verrall ("Christ" 351) and others opt for this, understanding it to mean that Herod sent Jesus back to his Jewish accusers, signifying that he refused to prosecute their complaint. (This assumes that Pilate had turned complete jurisdiction over to Herod.) In the opposite direction, Harlow (*Destroyer* 225) argues that Herod's sending Jesus back represents a desire to have Jesus prosecuted; for if Herod thought Jesus innocent, he would have kept him under his protection. Still another implicit variant is Bornhäuser's theory ("Beteiligung" 715) that in 23:11 Herod did not *send* Jesus to Pilate but *went* with Jesus to Pilate (supposing an unattested NT use of *anapempein* as an intransitive)—yet if Herod were present, why did Pilate have to speak for him? The best-attested reading, explained first above, is the most persuasive.

The last part of 23:15 ("nothing worthy of death") reinforces Pilate's judgment of 23:14 that Jesus is not guilty of the charge.[8] That reinforcement makes all the more startling Pilate's compromise offer to have Jesus chastised before releasing him. *Paideuein* means "to discipline, chastise, teach a lesson"; in I Kings 12:11,14 Rehoboam speaks of chastising and mentions various types of whips. Here most assume that the chastisement is to be whipping even though no such instrument is specified. This is not the flogging (*phragelloun* = Latin *flagellare*) of which Mark 15:15; Matt 27:26 will

[6]See ZAGNT 1.276 ("nor Herod either") and BAGD 38[3] (explaining that the usage indicates "that the preceding is to be regarded as a settled matter").

[7]The "us" is not a royal plural as if Jesus were sent back to Pilate alone, for in this passage Pilate speaks as "I," not as "we." A prominent variant (Koine tradition; Codices Alexandrinus, Bezae, most Latin witnesses) is "I sent you to him," i.e., Pilate sent the chief priests and scribes to Herod (but there is no reference to sending them in 23:7,10). A third phrasing (minuscules; see MTC 179) is "I sent him [Herod] to you."

[8]It contains another *kai idou,* and in the "done by him" an extremely rare, if not unique, NT dative of agency (BDF 191; ZBG 59).

speak and which was part of the sentence of crucifixion. Rather Luke refers to a minor beating that would be the whole penalty.[9] This is close to a form of plea-bargaining seeking a lesser sentence. Several factors are noteworthy. Luke knew Mark's account where Jesus is flogged by the Romans; he softens that to an offer by Pilate (seemingly not carried out) of whipping. To maintain that this exculpates Pilate forces one to face the objection that Pilate, who has twice said Jesus is not guilty, is willing to punish him—scarcely a noble image of justice. The Pilate who emerges, while not malevolent, is placating "the chief priests and the rulers and the people." Overall, however, the main import for the readers from this preface that Luke places before the mention of Barabbas is not Pilate's shortcomings but his witness (and Herod's) to Jesus' innocence.

John 18:38b. The much briefer transition to Barabbas in John requires little commentary. Because Pilate has been challenged to hear Jesus' voice and thus to show that he is of the truth, in a certain sense he is escaping Jesus' judicial presence when, after his question "What is truth?" he goes outside to "the Jews." As the man-in-between he is not willing to give to Jesus the hearing that the truth demands; but neither, as he now shows, is he willing to give to "the Jews" what they demand. The Johannine Pilate, unlike the Lucan, does not have to call together Jesus' adversaries; "the Jews" (i.e., the "nation and the chief priests" of 18:35) are already gathered outside. Pilate's statement "I find no case at all against him," with *heuriskein* ("to find") and *oudemian aitian* ("no [guilty] case: noun *aitia*), is quite close to the Greek of Luke 23:14 that has *heuriskein* and *outhen aition* ("nothing guilty": adj. *aitios*). As I have already noted, a tradition of three similarly worded denials of guilt has been drawn on independently by Luke and John.

THE CUSTOM OF RELEASING A PRISONER AT THE FEAST (MARK 15:6; MATT 27:15; JOHN 18:39A)

If the Lucan Pilate calls together the chief priests, rulers, and people, and the Johannine Pilate goes outside the praetorium to speak to the already gathered "Jews," in Mark 15:8, the crowd now comes up to add its presence to the whole Sanhedrin (15:1) before Pilate.[10] Matt 27:17, with a reflexive

---

[9]For distinctions among chastisements by whips, see p. 851 below. Hengel (*Crucifixion* 34) points to an inscription from Myra in Lycia in the time of Claudius (AD 41–54) wherein an imperial legate has a slave scourged with the warning that another offense would bring more severe punishment (crucifixion?). See also the example of G. Septimius Vegetus in Egypt (p. 816 below).

[10]Verbs of "going up" or "coming up" are idiomatic for a journey to Jerusalem, but some have used the expression here to locate the praetorium at Herod's palace on the top of the western hill of the city; see §31C.

use of the passive of *synagein,* has "when they had gathered together," without specifying the "they"—the pronoun would include "all the chief priests and the elders of the people" from 27:1,12, as well as "the crowd(s)" of 27:15,20. Matt's *synagein* gives a more official tone to those present than Mark's *anabas* ("having come up"); but for the latter there is an interesting textual variant in the Koine tradition and the OS[sin]: *anaboēsas* ("having screamed/cried out"), related to *epiboēsis* ("acclamation"). Colin (*Villes* 14) accepts this reading as part of his thesis that the verdict in the Roman trial was by acclamation of the crowd/people (§31, D3c above); copyists would have misunderstood this rare verbal form and substituted *anabas.* Matt's "gathered," however, means that he read a verb of motion in Mark, not a verb of calling out. Probably the copyist's change went in the other direction, i.e., removing "having come up" because it contradicted the picture in Luke and John where the addressees were already present.

Mark explicitly and Matt implicitly give as the purpose of the coming up or gathering of the crowd(s) before Pilate the custom of releasing a prisoner at a/the feast. John 18:39a also mentions the custom. But before we discuss this custom, let us note that Luke 23:17, which refers to it, is absent from the best textual witnesses to Luke (P[75], Codices Vaticanus, Alexandrinus, Sahidic). Some scholars who think that the custom mentioned in Mark 15:6–8 is a secondary addition by Mark to an original tradition that lacked it (Dibelius, "Herodes") evaluate Luke 23 without v. 17 as closer to that original tradition. Others doubt that Luke had special access to such an original tradition and explain his text (without v. 17) as a deliberate shortening of Mark to facilitate the storyline. The opposite approach is to affirm 23:17, "But he had the obligation *to release one* person *to them at a/the feast,*" to have been originally written by Luke (despite its weaker, Koine attestation[11]) and to have been omitted by a copyist's error as his eye skipped from the *anagkēn de* that began v. 17 to the *anekragon de* beginning v. 18. To the more common thesis that v. 17 is a copyist's insertion in imitation of Mark and Matt (because all the words I have italicized are in those two Gospels) an objection is raised that neither of them speaks of an "obligation" (*anagkē*), something an imitative copyist would not have introduced. Recognizing the difficulty of settling the issue, although I shall follow the majority view that 23:17 is a copyist's addition, I will not speculate about Luke's reason for omitting all reference to the custom. His silence cannot with surety be used as an argument that he thought the custom incredible (see p. 819 below).

---

[11]G. D. Kilpatrick in *The New Testament in Historical and Contemporary Perspective,* eds. H. W. Anderson and W. Barclay (Honor of G.H.C. Macgregor; Oxford: Blackwell, 1965), 189–205, esp.

In the three Gospels that mention the custom of release there is a combination of agreements and disagreements. John attaches the custom specifically to Passover; but Mark/Matt (and Luke 23:17) use *kata heortēn* anarthrously, which could mean "at a feast" (every or any: *kata* as a distributive). The same expression, however, in Josephus (*War* 1.11.6; #229) means "at the feast."[12] Now, in the last instance of *heortē* ("feast") in each Synoptic (Mark 14:1–2; Matt 26:2,5; Luke 22:1) the reference has been to Passover. Thus it seems likely that Mark/Matt refer to every year's occurrence of *the* feast, i.e., Passover, and thus implicitly agree with John. No evangelist, however, necessarily places the release on Passover day itself.

To describe the habitual character of the custom, Mark 15:6 employs the imperfect of *apolyein* ("used to release"); and in 15:8 the Koine ms. variant has "as he *always* used to do for them." Matt 27:15 uses the verb *eiōthein* ("to be accustomed"); John 18:39a has the noun *synētheia* ("custom"). The dubious Luke 23:17 hardens it to an obligation. Mark (along with Luke 23:17) indicates that this is Pilate's custom. In speaking more generally of "the governor," Matt 27:15 is not necessarily describing every governor's custom, since he equates Pilate with the governor in 27:2 and 27:13–14. On the other hand, the "You have a custom" in John 18:39a makes it a custom of "the Jews." All the Gospels agree that the content of the custom is to release one person or prisoner—one whom they requested (Mark: *paraiteisthai*), or willed (Matt: *thelein*),[13] or desired (John: *boulein*).

The release is "to you" (= for you) in Mark, Matt, and John.[14] The crowd constituted by the Jewish or Jerusalem populace is the main agent in choosing the one to be released. In John (and in Luke 23:17) the chief priests are part of the choosing group, whereas in Mark/Matt the chief priests have to lobby the crowd(s).

By way of summary, then, the Gospels agree on a festal custom attached to Passover (explicitly in John, implicitly in Mark/Matt) whereby a prisoner was released whom the Jewish crowds chose. The major disagreement is whether it was a custom of Pilate the governor or a Jewish custom recognized by Pilate.

195, treats v. 17 in the light of a general thesis that sometimes the Koine or *Textus Receptus* is to be preferred over the Alexandrian tradition, represented by P[75] and Vaticanus.

[12]Codex Bezae of both Mark 15:6 and Matt 27:15 reads the article.

[13]Mark's *paraiteisthai* has a juridical tone (see Acts 25:11). Matt probably changed it to *thelein* to agree with the use of that verb two verses later in both Mark 15:9 and Matt 27:17 in Pilate's "Do you will?" (see also Matt 27:21, so that Matt has absolutely consistent vocabulary). Mark's sequence of *paraiteisthai* in 15:6 followed by *thelein* in 15:9 echoes a sequence in 6:22.

[14]This phrase is missing in Tatian's use of John 18:39a and appears as a genitive in some minor textual witnesses.

THE IDENTITY OF BARABBAS (MARK 15:7; MATT 27:16; LUKE 23:19; JOHN 18:40B)

All the Gospels agree that the Romans had in custody[15] a prisoner named Barabbas. (The words for "prisoner" and "imprisoned" in Mark 15:6–7 are related to the verb used for Jesus' being "bound" [*deein*] in 15:1—vocabulary creating an atmosphere in which "release" [*apolyein:* 15:6,9,11,14] is very important.) Mark's periphrastic Greek in 15:7 is somewhat awkward, literally: "But there was the one called/said to be Barabbas with the rioters imprisoned."[16] Gnilka (*Markus* 2.301) raises the possibility that if Barabbas means "son of the Father" (see ANALYSIS), Mark may mean "the one so-called Barabbas," with the idea that Jesus of Nazareth is truly "the son of the Father." Pesch (*Markus* 2.463) has another possibility: The one *nominated* (for release) was Barabbas. Probably it is best to interpret Mark simply to refer to someone called Barabbas. We are not told whether, having been apprehended, Barabbas had already been tried and even convicted (see the two different legal situations in Matt 5:25 and 14:3).

There is not perfect uniformity among the Gospels as to why Barabbas had been apprehended. John simply refers to him as a *lēstēs* (pp. 686–88 above), one of those violent lawless men, often bandits, whom Josephus describes in Palestine in the century from Herod the Great's reign to the Jewish Revolt. No other Gospel uses that term for him, although what they describe about him would be consonant with that description. Mark 15:27 and Matt 27:38,44 will describe Jesus as crucified between two *lēstai* (plural of *lēstēs*); and so the evangelists have the same overall outlook on the imprisonment of *lēstai* at the time of Jesus' arrest and execution, even if no evangelist explicitly connects Barabbas who was released with the other two who were crucified. Perhaps Mark prepares for the latter when he speaks of other rioters imprisoned with Barabbas (or in the Koine tradition "co-rioters" [*systasiastēs*]). Both Mark and Luke associate Barabbas' arrest with a *stasis* ("insurrection, disturbance, riot"). Mark also uses the term *stasiastēs* ("rioter"), employed by Josephus (*Ant.* 14.1.3; #8; *War* 6.2.8; #157) to describe a range from a troublemaker to a rebel. Luke specifies that the *stasis* took place in Jerusalem. The text does not demand that we think of a widespread revolution (something not attested in Jesus' time); a local riot may be all Mark and

---

[15]Actually Matt's "they" in "they had a notorious prisoner" (27:16) grammatically should refer to the crowd—see "they willed" at the end of v. 15—but logically it must refer to the Romans controlled by the governor. Is Matt writing carelessly, or is the ambiguity meant to prepare us for the negative role of the crowd?

[16]We shall see that some mss. of Matt have the personal name "Jesus" before "Barabbas"; and some think that the Marcan text used by Matt had that name ("But there was Jesus called Barabbas")—a guess not supported by Marcan ms. evidence. See n. 23 below.

Luke intend. (See p. 777 above for troubles during feasts.) Mark prefaces *stasis* with the definite article as if it were a well-known event, but perhaps only to Christians because traditionally for them it constituted part of the context of Jesus' passion. Both Mark and Luke indicate that killing (*phonos,* "murder") had marked the riot; but neither suggests that Roman soldiers were the victims, as some scholars suppose in their attempts to make this a major insurrection.

As for Barabbas, although Mark does not specify that he took part in the riot or did any killing,[17] Mark's purpose in the scene is to contrast the release of a guilty rioter and the crucifixion of one innocent of any such political offense. Luke understood that, for he spells out the involvement of Barabbas in three passages. In 23:19 he introduces Barabbas "who[18] was someone thrown into prison because of a certain riot that had taken place in the city and (because of) killing." In 23:25 Luke writes that Pilate "released the one who had been thrown into prison for riot and murder." In Acts 3:14 he bluntly calls Barabbas "a man who was a killer." Probably independently of Mark, John's designation of Barabbas as a *lēstēs* shows that in the tradition Barabbas was no innocent. (Yet John's choice of the designation may reflect more than violence. In 10:1–2 he contrasted Jesus, the [good] shepherd of the sheep, with all others who were only *lēstai.* Now "the Jews" prefer a *lēstes* to Jesus!)

Interestingly, Matt does not repeat Mark's reference to a riot, perhaps reflecting a post-Jewish-Revolt sensitivity that the memory of Jesus should not be associated even indirectly with political disturbance. But Matt does describe Barabbas as "notorious" or "notable" (*episēmos*).[19] The fact that the name of Barabbas was preserved in the tradition while the names of the crucified *lēstai* were not could easily have led to the conclusion that he was the most famous of the troublemakers at the time of Jesus' death and indeed the ringleader. In the rewriting of the Gospel story by Bajsić and Soltero whereby Pilate is primarily interested in executing Barabbas, the fact that Matt calls him "notorious" becomes important evidence.

"Barabbas" is a patronymic, i.e., a father's name used to make a distinction among men who bear the same personal names. For instance among the

---

[17]A. Menzies forces Mark's silence by theorizing that Barabbas was an innocent bystander apprehended by mistake during the riot (*The Earliest Gospel* [London: Macmillan, 1901], 273). Imagination in the opposite direction is illustrated by Isorni (*Vrai* 96–104), who tells us that Barabbas had killed a Roman soldier. In choosing him over Jesus the populace was preferring a freedom fighter who resisted over an apparent collaborator who had urged them to pay Roman taxes!

[18]*Hostis,* in place of the simple relative, as thirty other times in Luke-Acts.

[19]This term is used by Josephus (*War* 2.21.1; #585) to describe the bandit leader John of Gischala. In the same vein some minor textual witnesses of John 18:40b read *archilēstēs* or chief of the *lēstai.* Davis ("Origen's" 66) paints Barabbas as a would-be messiah heading a band of soldiers.

many men named Jesus in 1st-cent.-AD Palestine (Josephus mentions about a dozen), the one of most interest to us would be distinguished as Jesus of/ from Nazareth; and if there were several men named Jesus at Nazareth, he would be further identified as Jesus *Bariōsēph* ("son of Joseph": John 1:45; 6:42). Not infrequently only the patronymic is used in a description, e.g., an 8th-cent.-BC Bar-Rekub inscription, and the NT Bartholomew and Barti- maeus. More usual is the combination of a personal name with the patro- nymic: Simon Barjona (Matt 16:17); Joseph Barnabas (Acts 4:36); John and James, sons of Zebedee (Mark 1:19).

What was Barabbas' personal name? Lesser textual witnesses to Matt read in v. 16, in v. 17, or in both, "*Jesus* Barabbas."[20] Is the name Jesus the origi- nal reading in either Matthean verse? Those who answer no (formerly the majority) point to the tendency of later generations to supply names for those left nameless by the NT (see pp. 804, 969, 1148 below). Moreover, the neat pattern in v. 17, "Jesus Barabbas or Jesus who is called Messiah," could reflect a copyist's dramatic touch to heighten the parallelism of the two fig- ures whom Pilate faced. Those who answer yes point out that over against Mark, names are sometimes added or changed in Matt (9:9: "Matthew"; 26:3,57: "Caiaphas").

Yet if the name Jesus did appear in the original text of Matt, why would later scribes have omitted it so that it is absent from many important mss.? At least in the case of v. 17 haplography has been proposed (Streeter, Metzger): namely, the omission of *īn* (abbreviation of *Iēsoun*, "Jesus") following the last syllable of *hymin*. More common is the suggestion that theological judg- ment caused deliberate excision. Ca. AD 250, and thus before all preserved Greek copies of Matthew, Origen (*In Matt.* 27:16–18, #121; GCS 38.255– 56) argued defensively, "In many copies it is *not* stated that Barabbas was also called Jesus." He insisted that it is not proper that the name of Jesus be given to an iniquitous person; and since no sinner is ever given the name Jesus elsewhere in the Scriptures, Origen thought the name might have been added to the Matthean text by heretics. Origen's authority and attitude make it unlikely that Christian scribes of later centuries would have added "Jesus" to Barabbas' name in Matthean mss. that lacked it. Indeed they would have been encouraged to delete it as an impiety where it already appeared.[21] Yet probably most scholars now argue for the originality of the "Jesus Barabbas"

---

[20]These include Codex Koridethi, Lake family of minuscules, OS[sin], along with other codices manifesting variations that may imply that the scribes who wrote them were aware of the "Jesus" reading.

[21]Similarly Ephraem and the Peshitta omit "Bar-Jesus" as the name of the magician in Acts 13:6, preferring "Bar-Shema" ("Son of the Name").

reading in Matt,[22] and indeed many go beyond the textual issue to assert that this represents historical tradition lacking in Mark.[23]

What does "Barabbas" mean? One explanation has it reflect Bar-Rabban (a reading reflected in the "rr" spelling found in some mss.). "Rabban" was an honorific title for an eminent teacher or head of the Sanhedrin, built upon "rabbi." The medieval *Epistle of Sherira Gaon* claimed that the first person to bear the title "rabban" was Gamaliel at the end of the 1st cent. AD; more frequently, however, it was applied to Rabbi Judah ha-Nasi a century later. In this same vein some have taken "Barabbas" to mean "son of the [eminent] teacher," or even simply "teacher" (on the analogy that "son of man" means "man").[24] A further variant is the suggestion that in the 2d cent. *bĕrabbî* meant "attached to the rabbi." In a 10th-cent. uncial ms. of the NT (S) and in about twenty minuscule mss. there appears a marginal comment: "In many ancient copies I have dealt with, I found that Barabbas himself was likewise called Jesus ... apparently the paternal name of the robber was 'Barabbas' which is interpreted 'son of a/the teacher.'"[25] Overall, the rabban/teacher interpretation of "Barabbas" is not truly probable because of lack of proof that this title was in use in the early 1st cent., because the best attested orthography has one "r," and also because one would expect a patronymic to contain a personal name and "rabban" is not such a name.

A more plausible interpretation relates "Barabbas" to "Bar-Abba" ("son of [a person named] Abba"). "Abba" appears as a personal name with frequency in the Gemara section of the Talmud (ca. AD 200–400). In TalBab *Berakoth* 18B we find: "'I am looking for Abba.' They said to him, 'There are many Abbas here.' He said, 'I want Abba bar Abba.' They said, 'There are several Abbas bar Abba here.' He then said to them, 'I want Abba bar Abba, the father of Samuel.'" In the same TalBab the only example of "bar Abba" as a personal name applied to a figure of the Tannaitic period before AD 200 is Rabbi Hiyya bar Abba (*Berakoth* 48A,B). Yet "Abba" has now

---

[22]Allen, Bertram, Burkitt, Couchoud, Gaechter, Goguel, Grundmann, Klostermann, Lohmeyer, MacNeile, Maccoby, Moffatt, Rigg, Streeter, Trilling, Vaganay, Zahn, plus the NEB and the majority of the UBSGNT committee.

[23]A few like Taylor and Vincent argue that while no ms. of Mark has "Jesus," the Marcan Greek is awkward without it, and so originally there was a personal name in Mark too before *ho legomenos Barabbas* in 15:7, on the analogy of Matt 1:16; 4:18; 10:2; 27:22.

[24]W. Brandt (p. 549 above) suggests romantically that he was the son of a famous lawyer and that the father's argumentation aroused a popular demand for his release (Merkel, "Begnadigung" 300).

[25]This scholion is attributed variously to Anastasius (late-6th-cent. bishop of Antioch), or to Chrysostom, or to Origen (MTC 67). Jerome (*In Matt.* 27:16–17; CC 77.265) reports that the *Gospel according to the Hebrews* (= Nazoraeans) interpreted Barabbas as "son of their teacher" (also CC 72.135). One must remember, however, that this patristic interpretation may represent knowledge by Christians of later centuries that "rabban" had become a rabbinic title.

appeared as a name in a pre-70-AD burial at Giv'at ha-Mivtar (E. S. Rosenthal, IEJ 23 [1973], 72–81). Of course, Aramaic *'abbā'* means "father," as NT authors were aware because of the usage associated with Jesus (see Mark 14:36). Accordingly some scholars think "Barabbas" did not contain a proper name but meant "son of the father." See ANALYSIS below.

PILATE'S OFFER OF RELEASE (MARK 15:8–10; MATT 27:17–18; JOHN 18:39B)

In Mark the initiative that brings into the trial of Jesus the custom of releasing a prisoner comes from the crowd that has come up for the very purpose of making a request.[26] In Luke 23:18 (without any reference to a festal privilege) the Jewish authorities and the people whom Pilate has called together show initiative, responding to Pilate's offer to release Jesus (23:16) by demanding that a substitute be released. In Matt and John (an unusual agreement) the initiative for a release corresponding to the custom comes from Pilate. In John that makes sense, for Pilate has found no case against Jesus and is looking for a way to release him. In Matt it makes sense because the custom is the governor's own. Since we have heard that he was greatly amazed (Matt 27:14), we must presume that his offer is an attempt to resolve his perplexity.

Looking more closely at the individual passages, we find some obscurities. Mark 15:8 does not make clear whether those who constitute the crowd that comes up already have a candidate for release, but in what follows nobody has to explain to them who Barabbas is. Using the imperfect as in 15:6, Mark's verbal construction is awkward: "to request as he used to do for them." Presumably this is an ellipsis for "to request (that he do) as he used to do for them," although some resort to a putative Aramaic original.[27] The "he" of Mark 15:8 is also awkward, for the logical antecedent is not "Barabbas" of 15:7 but the "he" (Pilate) of 15:6. BAA 92[1] points out that often Semitic is not specific about the impersonal subject, so that in Greek translation the effect might be "to request just as *one* was used to do."

Matt 27:17 is less awkward than Mark; yet ungrammatically the antecedent of "they" who had gathered is not the "they" of 27:16 (implicitly the Romans) but the crowd of 27:15. The sequence of John 18:39b is smoother, for the "you" to whom the release will be made are "the Jews" of the preceding verse. While in Luke and John those who will be involved in the choice

---

[26]The "began to request" (*archesthai* helping an infinitive) is typical Marcan style; see 14:33,65,69,71.

[27]Herranz Marco, "Problema" 150; G. M. Lee, NovT 20 (1978), 74. The Koine textual tradition reads the adverb "usually, always" before the imperfect, thus stressing the notion of custom.

are already hostile to Jesus, the Mark/Matt crowd seems to have gathered recently and not yet to be partisan since, after Pilate has spoken, they will have to be persuaded by the chief priests to opt against Jesus. Preachers have sometimes ignored the precision of the text to paint a crowd that was enthusiastically for Jesus at his entry into Jerusalem a week before but has now turned against him (e.g., Mode, "Passionsweg"). In fact, "crowd" does not appear in Mark's account of the entry into Jerusalem (contrast Matt 21:8–9); and Marcan readers would have no reason to identify this crowd that has come up with any that has gone before, even with the crowd that came out to Gethsemane to arrest Jesus (Mark 14:43; Matt 26:47,55).

The question that the Marcan Pilate poses to the crowd in 15:9 is almost equivalent to a condition: "If you will, I shall release to you 'the King of the Jews'" (so Pesch, *Markus* 2.464). Both Mark and John use that title; and I have placed it in quotation marks not because the usage is sarcastic as "your king" would have been, but because it is the designation that has been the issue throughout the Roman trial. The Marcan Pilate seems to know little else about Jesus. The Johannine Pilate knows already that Jesus has no political ambitions; but in trying to work with "the Jews," Pilate employs the title they supplied. Matt 27:17 has Pilate employ the designation "Messiah" (*Christos*) that thus far has not been mentioned in the Roman trial but was central to the earlier Sanhedrin trial (26:63). Evidently the Matthean Pilate has penetrated to the religious issue that lay beneath the political title "the King of the Jews." Also Matt achieves a dramatic contrast missing from the other Gospels by having Pilate mention both figures: "Barabbas" who is a notorious prisoner and "Jesus who is called Messiah"—a contrast heightened if both men were named Jesus.[28]

Mark 15:10 and Matt 27:18 now take the important step of revealing to the readers Pilate's mind (Luke and John do that by the not-guilty statements). The reason Pilate includes Jesus in the release is that he knows why Jesus was given over, a knowledge that reflects on the character of those who have done this. Mark uses the imperfect of *ginōskein* as if Pilate had the knowledge for a while; Matt uses *ēdein;* but neither makes it clear whether the knowledge springs from a general acquaintanceship with the character of the chief priests or from knowing something about Jesus before they arrested him. The Marcan statement that the chief priests gave Jesus over out of envy/zeal creates the impression that Pilate hopes for greater honesty

---

[28]The fact that Matt's Pilate brings up Barabbas is a key point in Bajsić's reconstruction of the history: Pilate's goal was to get Barabbas convicted and not to have his release requested by the crowd. Underestimating the hostility against Jesus of Nazareth, he thought the crowd could be persuaded to accept "the King of the Jews." Besides depending on what is not said, this fanciful theory gratuitously supposes the historicity of the release custom (see ANALYSIS).

from the crowd in deciding about "the King of the Jews."[29] The Matthean
"they" who gave Jesus over out of envy/zeal seems to refer to the crowd who
had gathered, and that makes problematic the question posed to them about
which one they would want released. Some scholars would follow Codex
Vaticanus and OS[sin] in omitting "the chief priests" from Mark 15:10 and thus
read "they" in Mark too. C. H. Turner (*JTS* 25 [1923–24], 385–86) thinks
that the implication of "they" was equivalent to a passive: "that he had been
given over out of envy/zeal," without specifying who had done it. Such
hypotheses may not be necessary. The omission of "the chief priests" in
some mss. of Mark 15:10 is probably a copyist's improvement to avoid repetition with "the chief priests" that begins the next verse. Matt 27:18 has deliberately omitted the Marcan reference to the chief priests because this
evangelist holds all the people responsible (27:20,25). John 19:11 will exhibit similar Christian reflection on the responsibility for Jesus' death.

The idea of "giving over" (*paradidonai*) has been discussed above
(p. 211). While Mark is very consistent in showing how one party gives
Jesus over to the next and no one takes a stance for Jesus, Matt 27:4 has
increased the notion of guilt through the horror of the sin of giving over
innocent blood.[30] By specifying *phthonos*, "envy, jealous zeal," as the cause
of giving Jesus over, Mark may intend a paronomasia with *phonos* ("killing") that was the cause for the imprisonment of Barabbas. *Phthonos* covers
the spectrum of violent dislike for good, even to the point of homicide:
"Through the *phthonos* of the devil, death entered the world, and those who
belong to his party experience it" (Wis 2:24). In Josephus (*Ant.* 10.11.5–6;
#250–57) the satraps are afraid Darius will pardon Daniel and are envious
(*phthonein*) of Daniel; *III Macc* 6:7 specifies that it was through *phthonos*
that Daniel was cast to the lions. Yet Herranz Marco ("Proceso" [1975],
90–111) is helpful in pointing out that the envy or jealousy covered by
phthonos is often closely related to zeal. (I Macc 8:16 equates *phthonos* and
zēlos; Hebrew *qn'* means "to be jealous of" or "zealous for"; and English
"jealous" and "zealous" are from the same root.) The *zēlos* that made Paul
a persecutor of the church (Philip 3:6) may have involved envy of the success
of the Christian preachers but certainly involved zeal for the Law to which
he was devoted as a Pharisee (3:5). Most of the conflicts between Pilate and
his subjects in Judea, as described by Josephus and Philo (§31, B3 above),

---

[29]Blinzler (*Trial* 208–9) regards this as the historical situation.

[30]Some scholars would add another element: the Jewish authorities or crowd giving over a fellow
Jew to the Romans (p. 541 above). Yet in Mark/Matt the evil of giving over does not seem to be
affected by the fact that the governor is a foreigner (explicit only in John 18:35) but from the finality
of the crucifixion: Jesus is given over to die. The passion prediction in Mark 10:33 and par. emphasizes the Gentile element.

stemmed from the Jews' intransigent zeal for God's Law as they understood it. In the present scene, Mark/Matt have Pilate recognizing that the Jewish authorities gave Jesus over to him out of *envy and zeal,* i.e., both shades of the meaning of *phthonos.* They were envious of Jesus' hold on the people and they were zealous for the Law violated by his threats against the Temple/sanctuary and his blasphemy.

In pointing out that *phthonos* brought Jesus to his death, Mark/Matt may be warning their readers against a similar threat among Christians. When Paul (Philip 1:15) speaks of some of his Christian competitors proclaiming Christ out of *phthonos,* he is pointing to a spirit of jealous rivalry that sprang from zeal for their understanding of the gospel. The fear of *phthonos* in the Christian community (I Tim 6:4; Titus 3:3; I Pet 2:1) is probably a fear of divisive competitiveness among groups struggling for their own viewpoint. That same understanding may underlie *I Clement* 5:2 and its explanation of how Peter and Paul were betrayed to their death in the Neronian persecution: "Through jealousy and *phthonos* the greatest and most righteous pillars [of the church] were persecuted and their death desired." *Phthonos* killed the master and his most famous apostles.

THE MESSAGE FROM PILATE'S WIFE (MATT 27:19)

If for both Mark and Matt the knowledge that Jesus was given over out of envy causes Pilate to propose releasing him, Matt adds another reason: the message about Jesus' innocence that Pilate receives from his wife.[31] Whatever older tradition is preserved in 27:19 Matt has rewritten in his own style, as SPNM 242–48 shows, following Trilling, e.g., "sitting on" as in 24:3; *dikaios* ("just, righteous") corresponding to *dikaiosynē; sēmeron* ("today"), used eight times in Matt to Mark's one; "in a dream," found only in Matt (six times) in the NT.

A dramatic setting is given to the message: Pilate is sitting on the *bēma,*[32] about to render a life-or-death sentence. That sense of drama has caused this brief notice to be the subject of much imaginative reconstruction and has caused Pilate's wife to take her place alongside the young man who fled away naked as PN characters most likely to serve the insatiable desire of interpreters to make whole stories out of one verse.[33]

First, who was she? Both Church Fathers and Christian apocrypha began

---

[31]Some have thought that Pilate's dealing with this message also supplies time in the storyline for the chief priests and elders to persuade the crowds (27:20).

[32]This judgment seat or platform is mentioned elsewhere in the PN only in John 19:13 and will be discussed there.

[33]As I discuss various elements in the developments about Pilate's wife, I acknowledge that Fascher (*Weib*) has supplied much useful information.

very early to identify Pilate's wife, making her both noble and saintly. In an appendix to the *Acts of the Pilate* she is identified as Procla, and G. A. Müller (*Pontius* 5) defends the historicity of Claudia Procla as her name. An even fuller form appears: Claudia Vilia Procula; and Rosadi (*Trial* 215–17) argues that she was the youngest daughter of Julia, the daughter of Augustus. (Indeed, sometimes the whereabouts of the imperial family at the time of Jesus' death is brought into answering the second point below, e.g., Drucker, *Trial* 24). Origen would see her conversion to Christ beginning here (see *In Matt.* 27:19, #122; GCS 38.257–58). Apocryphal Pilate literature tells us that years later she witnessed her husband's beheading before the emperor in Rome and rejoiced to see an angel taking the head (HSNTA 1.483–84; rev. ed. 1.532). Eventually she came to be listed as a saint in some of the Orthodox churches. On the other side of the picture, in the *Acts of Pilate* 2.1 the Jewish opponents of Jesus explain to Pilate that his wife's dream was caused by Jesus' sorcery. A form of this approach appears in subsequent Christian tradition[34] which attributes her dream to the devil on the curious logic that if she had been successful in getting Pilate to release Jesus, salvation would not have been accomplished.

Second, is it possible that Pilate's wife was in Jerusalem with him? Suetonius (*Augustus* 24) reports that Augustus had not permitted governors to take their wives with them to their posts but allowed only a visit during the winter months. That strictness seems to have broken down under Tiberius, for the emperor's adopted son, Germanicus, brought his wife Agrippina to Germany and to the East (Tacitus, *Annals* 1.40; 2.54). In AD 21 Caecina, a former legate, tried to have the policy affirmed whereby magistrates would not take their wives to assignments; but he did not prevail in the senate (Tacitus, *Annals* 3.33–34).

Third, does she embody OT symbolism? Augustine (*Sermo* 150 [121 *De tempore*]; PL 39.2038) contrasts Eve who incited her husband to make a decision that would lead to death, and Procula who tried to persuade her husband to make a decision that would lead to life.[35]

---

[34]Rhabanus Maurus, Bernard of Clairvaux, and especially the 9th-cent. Old Saxon alliterative poem, the *Heliand*. This life of Jesus in the tradition of heroic songs was part of a rendering of the Bible into the vernacular in the missionary enterprise of Emperor Louis the Pious to convert the Saxons. It enters biblical discussions because of its sources (which go back to the Diatessaron) and because it was popularized in 1562 by the ardent Lutheran classicist (Matthias) Flacius Illyricus. To Fascher's discussion of it Oepke ("Noch" 743) adds a version found in a late medieval passion play where the devil disguises himself as one of the Seraphim and pleads Jesus' case over against the Jews.

[35]Derrett ("Haggadah" 314), attempting to use the Joseph tradition (largely represented in post-1st-cent. sources) to explain elements in the PN (see p. 658 above), would compare her to the wife of Potiphar, the chief baker, who objected to her husband's having Joseph stripped and beaten, saying "Your judgment is unjust" (*Test. Joseph* 13:9–14:1). The dating of the tradition is uncertain, and the goal of that wife was to sin with Joseph (14:4). Adopting a similar approach, despite the statement

Fourth, how did she know about Jesus so that she was able to dream about him at the very moment Pilate was first encountering him? In part this type of question reflects the thesis that the dream had natural origins. Some argue that after a three-year ministry in Galilee Jesus' name would have been known all over Palestine including Judea. Or else Pilate, having heard at night of the arrest of Jesus, shared this with his wife, causing her to dream of Jesus. (So with variants Paulus, B. Weiss, Zahn, etc.) In this same vein, one might then ask why she did not tell Pilate of her dream before he set out for the trial, or are we to posit that she was a late sleeper and dreamer?

Fifth, how did she know that Jesus was *dikaios* ("just, righteous")? Some Church Fathers thought that she could recognize this because she was a holier person than Pilate and so more spiritually perceptive (Chrysostom, Theophylact).

With due respect for the effort expended on the above issues, I would judge that the solutions and even the questions are far from Matt's thought patterns. The imaginative affirmation of the innocence of Jesus ties this episode to other special Matthean episodes in the PN, e.g., to Judas and the innocent blood, and Pilate's washing his hands—episodes that reflect the development of the passion story through symbolism and imagination in popular circles. (A fuller expansion of this attribution to a special tradition is found in Gillman, "Wife," which would localize it in the Caesarea Maritima region where Pilate made his headquarters.) As for the dream medium, in the Matthean infancy narrative there are four examples of divine revelation given in a dream. Besides the three dreams of Joseph there is in 2:12 a dream revelation extended to the Gentile magi, who had already received revelation through a star about the identity of Jesus and had come and worshiped him, while Herod, the chief priests, and the scribes of the people tried to kill him (2:3–4,20 ["those who sought the child's life"]). This revelation through a dream to Pilate's wife stems from the same type of popular narrative wherein God uses extraordinary means to reveal Jesus to the Gentiles since they do not have the Scriptures, and wherein their promptness to accept the revelation is contrasted with the hostile rejection of Jesus by those who do have the Scriptures. That the dream of Pilate's wife was of divine origin was recognized by most church writers (Origen, Jerome, Augustine, Calvin). This type of parallel with the infancy narrative at the beginning of Matt is a type of inclusion already noticed on several occasions (pp. 288, 648 above).

Why has Pilate's wife rather than Pilate become the recipient of the revelation? The exotic story of the magi, sages from the East seeing the birth star

---

in Esth 5:14 that the wife of Haman wanted Mordecai hanged, Aus ("Release" 21) would appeal to much later Jewish tradition to have her advise her husband not to do evil to that "just" man. Thus she is supposed to have given rise to the story of Pilate's wife.

of the Davidic king, had its main coloration from the OT account of Balaam, a magus from the East who saw the star of David rise (Num 22–24; see BBM 193–96). This story would not have seemed naively romantic to 1st-cent. readers because of several contemporary instances of exotic envoys coming from the East with gifts and pageantry (BBM 174), especially the visit of the Armenian king Tiridates to Rome in the time of Nero. So here too Matt's readers would have had as a parallel the image of noble Roman pagan women who were favorable to Judaism. Josephus (*War* 2.20.2; #560) reports that in Nero's time, even though the pagan men of Damascus were virulently antiJewish, their wives "with a few exceptions had all become converts to the Jewish religion." In *Ant.* 20.8.11; #195 he describes Poppaea, Nero's wife, as a God-fearer, pleading on behalf of the Jews. These pictures may not be strictly historical,[36] but in discussing reader response to the Matthean portrayal of Pilate's wife we are on the level of verisimilitude. The *Acts of Pilate* 2.1 catches this atmosphere by making Pilate's wife a worshiper of God and an adherent of the Jewish religion.

By way of overview, then, if in Luke and John Pilate three times judges Jesus not guilty, on a more popular dramatic level in Matt, Pilate's wife proclaims *dikaios* ("just, righteous") a Jesus who at the beginning of Matt (3:15) stated that it is fitting to fulfill all *dikaiosynē* ("righteousness"). Matt is continuing the haunting motif of innocent blood that runs from Judas (27:4) through this verse (27:19) to Pilate's attempt to wash his hands of it (27:24). Some scholars have thought that Matt's goal is primarily apologetic, to convince Romans after AD 66 that Jesus was not at all like the fanatics of the Jewish Revolt. In 27:19, however, the motif of Pilate's wife came into Matt's picture primarily as a sign of the evangelical openness of the Gentiles who could recognize the truth about Jesus. (Comparably a Roman centurion will proclaim that Jesus was *dikaios* immediately after Jesus dies in Luke 23:47.)

Would the fact that Pilate's wife declared Jesus innocent create in Matt's readers a more negative view of Pilate who ignored her advice, released Barabbas, and gave Jesus over to be crucified (27:26)? Rather, the primary impression, I believe, would be that her testimony was what led Pilate to make the extraordinary effort in 27:24–25 not to become tainted by innocent blood (see Broer, "Prozess" 107). He was following her advice, "Let there be nothing between you and that just man." In 27:4,6–8 the chief priests also wanted to avoid Judas' attempt to shift the responsibility for Jesus' innocent blood to them. But they were touched by the blood even as Pilate will be touched.

Elisabeth Ott ("Wer") would stress the sufferings of Pilate's wife ("many

---

[36]See E. M. Smallwood, JTS 10 NS (1959), 329–35.

things I have suffered today in a dream because of him"), raising the issue of whether she was the first Gentile to suffer for Christ. Gnilka (*Matthäus* 2.456) suggests that her suffering was on behalf of her husband lest he make a judgment against the guidance given her in the dream. He points to another parallel in the Greco-Roman world: the dream of Julius Caesar's wife on the night before his assassination (Cassius Dio, *History* 44.17.1). The main motif in the suffering of Pilate's wife, however, may be that she is sharing some of the anguish brought on by innocent blood.

THE CHOICE MADE FOR BARABBAS (MARK 15:11; MATT 27:20–21; LUKE 23:18 [ACTS 3:14]; JOHN 18:40A)

At the outset we should take note of the second Lucan description of this choice, namely, Acts 3:14 where, speaking to the men of Israel, Peter mentions Pilate's decision to release Jesus and then condemns the audience for denying the holy and just one (*dikaios* as in Matt 27:19) and requesting that a killer be granted them. In all four Gospels the set verb in reference to Barabbas is *apolyein* ("to release"), but Acts uses *charisthēnai* ("to grant") by way of variation from "release" in the previous verse. It also sharpens the portrait of Barabbas by bluntly calling him a killer. If we join the Acts passage to Luke, then there are *two basic approaches* to the making of the choice, one represented by Luke and John, the other by Mark/Matt, both involving the populace. From the outset we should recognize that the role of the people in legal judgment, so foreign to the exercise of much modern jurisprudence, is commanded in the OT. Num 35:12 insists that a homicide shall not be put to death before he is tried in the presence of the community. Schinzer ("Bedeutung" 145) notes that the official judges are the representatives of the community.

For Luke and John the chief priests are with the people or are part of "the Jews"; these parties cry out their choice without one group needing to persuade the other. The antagonism expressed against Jesus is surprisingly strong in Luke 23:18, which uses the adverb *pamplēthei* ("all together"— the only instance in the Greek Bible) to stress the unanimity of the opposition. (It evokes Luke's use of *plēthos* in "the whole multitude of them" in 23:1.) Also Luke employs *anakrazein,* which has previously referred to the shouting out of the demon-possessed (4:33; 8:28).[37] The imperatives ("take," "release") with which all those called together by Pilate reject his plan to release Jesus have the psychological effect of beginning to force him. "Take" has a destructive connotation also in the trials of Paul in Acts 21:36; 22:22;

---

[37]The pleonastic use of "saying" after "cried out" is a feature of Lucan style.

in the latter instance it is used with the contemptuous "such a fellow," even as here. Some scholars argue that without the reference to the festal custom in the dubious v. 17, Luke 23:18 is scarcely intelligible. Rather, without that reference the audacious demand in 23:18 that Pilate release Barabbas turns around Pilate's proposal to release Jesus, with the implication of a preference for anyone other than Jesus, even a killer. Pilate's ultimate act of releasing such a man as Barabbas (23:25) would be total appeasement since no custom required this.

As for John 18:40, the adverb *palin* modifies the yelling out (*kraugazein*). Although there has been no previous outcry, the meaning "again" is occasionally defended as a sign that John is digesting a longer account. More likely *palin* means "back," as "the Jews" answer Pilate. Both Luke and John begin with the rejection of Pilate's offer to release Jesus; only secondarily is Barabbas chosen. If in Luke they have chosen by preference a killer, in John they have chosen a *lēstēs* or man of violence. Giblin ("John's" 228) cannot be followed in arguing that "the Jews" accept Barabbas *as* their king in place of Jesus—a mistake that stems from equating *lēstēs* with "Zealot" and, furthermore, understanding it to mean messianic leader.[38] For John, it is Caesar whom "the Jews" choose as king in place of Jesus (19:15); here they are choosing a bandit instead of a king.

Mark/Matt at the beginning attribute less hostility to the crowd(s) since they are misled by the chief priests. Yet once "stirred up,"[39] the crowd will assume a major role among the adversaries of Jesus. In 15:11 the Marcan Greek once more is elliptic: "stirred up the crowd that he should release." Obviously one must suppose after "the crowd" the clause "that they should ask."[40] We are never told in Mark that the crowd carried out such a request, but the action of Pilate in the next verse implies that they did.

Besides adding "the elders" to Mark's chief priests to describe the manipulators,[41] Matt 27:20 fills in the Marcan ellipsis by specifying that they exercised persuasion on the crowds. Notice the switch to the plural "crowds" from the singular in 27:15; a similar shift was made in the Gethsemane scene in 26:47,55; the plural aids the sense of mass persuasion. In both Mark and Matt the swiftness with which the chief priests win the crowd(s) over is an impressive touch. Somewhat in the same direction as Luke and John, Matt

---

[38]On p. 475 above I pointed out that Josephus never calls any revolutionary figure a messiah; indeed he never calls any Jew except Jesus *"christos."*

[39]*Anaseiein* in Mark 15:11, a verb used by Luke 23:5 in the charge made by the chief priests against Jesus that he had stirred up the people.

[40]The Bobbio Latin ms. *k* for Mark 15:11 has seemingly been conformed to Matt: "persuaded the people that all the more they should say [*aiere* for *agere*], 'Deliver Barabbas to us'"; see D. DeBruyne, RBen 27 (1910), 498.

[41]See APPENDIX V, B3, for Matt's frequency in mentioning the elders among Jesus' enemies.

goes beyond Mark in having the choice not only for Barabbas but against Jesus who is called Messiah (27:21, referring back to 27:17). Indeed, the goal is the destruction of Jesus; and in the grammar of Matt 27:20 *they*, not Pilate, will do the destroying. The degree to which hostility toward Jesus dominates in all the Gospel pictures is apparent when we consider two details on which there is curious silence: No Gospel explains why the populace wanted Barabbas, who was scarcely a desirable character, and none mentions even one voice being raised in favor of Jesus, who hitherto had fared well in his public relations. In all the Gospels the mass opposition to him is what ultimately forces Pilate to accede to the crucifixion.

ANALYSIS

I shall begin with a brief discussion of composition and then turn to two major issues of historicity, i.e., the historicity of Barabbas and of the custom of a release at Passover.

A. Composition of the Scene

Matt is dependent on Mark, which he complements with items from popular tradition, viz., the personal name (Jesus) of Barabbas and the dream of Pilate's wife. The end of the Lucan scene (23:18–19) is a modification of Mark; the first part (23:13–16) is a Lucan composition. It combines an item from the tradition to which John also witnesses, i.e., one of the three not-guilty statements, which it combines with a transition from the Herod scene. (We saw in §33 that the Herod scene draws on tradition about Herodian opposition to Jesus, with a modification to make Herod a reluctant witness of Jesus' innocence.) The first part of John's account has a similar not-guilty statement. The second part, which deals with Barabbas, is so brief that considering it in isolation, one would not be able to tell whether it was dependent on Mark or on other tradition. It does contain the description *lēstēs* absent from Mark, but that could be deduction from the Marcan reference to *lēstai* crucified with Jesus. Fortna (*Gospel* 124) attributes most of 18:38b–40 to the independent Johannine source; and granted that elsewhere in the passion we have found it more probable that John did not draw on Mark, we should probably take that approach here as well. The issue is not without importance, for Johannine independence of Mark in this scene means that both Barabbas and the paschal privilege of releasing a prisoner were part of the preGospel tradition.

As for the composition of the Marcan scene, there is, as always, little agreement among scholars who would reconstruct exactly the preMarcan account of the trial. The theory that would have Mark combining two sources (p. 54, n. 45 above) would maintain that the Barabbas story in 15:6–11, taken by Mark from a source different from that which supplied him with the rest of the Pilate trial, was inserted by him into that trial. Obviously Christians could have told less detailed versions of the trial, as well as more detailed ones involving Barabbas; but can one reconstruct such a source history from Mark? Those who answer yes point to awkwardnesses in the narrative flow that are for them proof of an insertion, e.g., the antecedent for the "them" of 15:6 is vague.[42] One must remember, however, that often Mark is not a meticulously logical writer. Moreover, when one tries to excise the Barabbas incident of 15:6–11 as if it had been added, there are even more problems in the flow of the account: V. 6 follows v. 5 more smoothly than would either v. 12 or v. 15 (which mentions Barabbas).[43]

Another theory is that only part of 15:6–11 was added by Mark to an older, briefer account. As a sign some point to a pattern of postpositive *de* ("but") in vv. 6,7,9,11 (and 12) which is interrupted by a *kai* ("and") in v. 8 and a *gar* ("for") in v. 10. Such a feature, however, which may simply reflect a desire to vary style, can scarcely be a guide to composition, e.g., the answer in v. 9 supposes the action in v. 8. Matera (*Kingship* 17ff.) would regard vv. 6,9,11–12 as older, with vv. 7–8,10 as Marcan editing.[44] The older account had a hostile crowd, but Mark introduced the envy of the chief priests in v. 10 to soften the picture. I find the criteria for such a judgment extremely subjective, for there are elements of Marcan style in verses attributed to the primitive layer.[45] As I pointed out above, if John is independent of Mark, then the preMarcan layer of the tradition contained a reference to Barabbas and the custom of releasing a prisoner; but Mark has so rewritten the trial that one can no longer reconstruct the preMarcan account exactly. Even as in the Sanhedrin trial Mark wrote two verses (14:53–54) to preface what would follow, so here Mark has written 15:6–7 as a short preface to the

---

[42]Dibelius ("Herodes" 116) thinks that Mark 15:1 and 15:8 represent two different localizations of the trial, so that originally 15:1–5 and 6–15 were not together. But can the vague setting Mark gives to the Pilate trial really support this view?

[43]Gnilka (*Markus* 2.296–98) points out the close unity of 15:1–15 as it now exists in Mark.

[44]I am choosing a sample theory. Gnilka, ibid., thinks vv. 12–14 cannot be broken up and may have undergone Marcan rewriting. Dormeyer (*Passion* 300) attributes 6–7,11 to the oldest source, 9–10 to the next stage, and finally 8 to Mark. Lührmann (*Markus* 257) attributes 1–15 to the source, with redaction in 7 and 10.

[45]There are ellipses in Matera's supposedly Marcan v. 8 and preMarcan 11; words used only once in Mark occur in the Marcan v. 7 and in the preMarcan 6 and 11.

scene, and that explains the somewhat intrusive nature of those verses.[46] Be that as it may, although using different methodologies, many scholars would agree on the preMarcan existence of a tradition about Barabbas and about a paschal custom. We must now turn to the issue of the historicity of either or both of those points.

B. Historicity of Barabbas

I shall confine the discussion to the historicity of what is described in the text about Barabbas and the circumstances of his imprisonment, and not attempt to investigate dramatizations not even hinted at in the text. Some scholars, interpreting Mark and Luke to be talking about an insurrection (*stasis, stasiastēs*), seek to identify it with one of the public demonstrations during Pilate's rule mentioned by Philo or Josephus.[47] The evangelists may be describing no more than a local riot not worthy of the pages of history. If *at most* Jesus was noticed in a small paragraph in Josephus' *Antiquities* (p. 373 above) should one expect the appearance there of a character that even the Gospels treat as very minor?

We begin with the most fundamental question: Did Barabbas ever exist? On the surface that should be no more a problem than that of the existence of other minor figures in the Gospels known only by patronymics, e.g., Bartimaeus. But as indicated in the COMMENT, the situation is complicated by two facts: There is Matthean tradition that his personal name was Jesus, and his patronymic is susceptible of being translated figuratively as "son of the father." One could form the mental image of a confused Pilate faced with two prisoners named Jesus. In one romantic reconstruction, when the crowd came asking for Jesus to be released, Pilate could confidently have assumed that they were asking for Jesus of Nazareth, only to be trapped when it was Jesus Barabbas they sought. More radically, scholars like Cohn, Rigg, Maccoby, and S. L. Davies interpret the scene as if originally there was only one person named Jesus who stood before Pilate, namely, Jesus of Nazareth. Barabbas, then, would not have been another person but only an aspect of Jesus' identity, e.g., under a religious charge Jesus was called Barabbas, the

---

[46]The problem of the vague "them" in v. 6 is eased, for the evangelist is preparing for the larger group he will mention in vv. 8ff. The "he" of v. 8 is also clarified as being the Pilate of v. 5 (before the parenthetic introduction).

[47]Of the events described in §31, B3 above, *stasis* is used by Josephus in #3, the aqueduct riot; but there is nothing in the account to cause us to identify it with the Barabbas riot. Since we are discussing historicity, I am concerned with what *stasis* and *lēstēs* might reflect ca. 30, leaving aside how the readers of the Gospels might have understood them after the much more troubled period in the 50s and 60s.

son of the Father,[48] and under a political charge he was called the King of the Jews. Pilate is supposed to have dismissed the Barabbas or religious charge as beyond Roman competence but to have sentenced Jesus on the political charge. (A further dramatization adds the idea that the crowd was on the side of Jesus religiously over against the priests, and that is why they supported the Barabbas title.) Either by confusion or deliberate antiJewish stratagem the evangelist then would have made a separate person of (Jesus) Barabbas and turned the crowd's support for Barabbas to a condemnation by them of Jesus of Nazareth.

This novelistic reconstruction does not hold up under critical analysis. The proposed change from a twofold designation of one person to designations for two different people could have happened no later than Mark (late 60s) and almost surely must have gone back into preMarcan days since it appears in all the Gospels, even in John, which is not provably dependent on Mark's Barabbas account. Can one show similar historical confusion to the point of creating a nonexistent person so early in the Gospel tradition? Moreover, no form of the religious charge in the passion deals with the "son of the father." In the earliest Gospel tradition (as distinct from developments in Matt and John) Jesus does not speak frequently of God as his Father or call himself "the Son" and "the Son of God." He never calls himself "the Son of the Father"; and only once in the Gospels (Mark 14:36) does he ever use the word *Abba*. Thus there is little likelihood that by AD 30 "Barabbas" had become a title of Jesus. If it were a title of Jesus, then it should have been under the aspect of Barabbas that his enemies within Judaism wanted to kill him, e.g., John 5:18: "For this reason the Jews sought all the more to kill him . . . he was speaking of God as his own father"; also Mark 12:6–8 and par. The proposed Christian plot to hide the enthusiasm of the Jewish crowd for Jesus by using the Barabbas figure is most implausible. (There is sufficient antiJudaism in what is narrated without aggravating it reprehensibly by such theorizing.) In the Gospel of Luke, as distinct from Acts, the populace is more often treated as favorable and sympathetic to Jesus; yet that does not prevent Luke from presenting Barabbas as a separate figure and a killer.

Another attempt to interpret Barabbas figuratively draws upon evidence found in Philo (*Flaccus* 6; #36–39) describing the events surrounding the visit of the Jewish King Herod Agrippa I to Alexandria in AD 38. AntiJewish rioters in Alexandria expressed their contempt for this visit by setting up for

---

[48]If the title were used by his followers, the Father would be God; if the title were used by his adversaries (who thought he worked by the power of Beelzebub), the father could be sarcastically understood as the devil. The polemic in John 8:38,44 suggests that having the devil as a father was a charge thrown back and forth.

public display in the gymnasium a lunatic named Karabas. He had been the butt of many jokes since he wandered around the streets naked day and night. They dressed Karabas with a rug-robe, a mock diadem, and a papyrus-reed scepter; then they approached and hailed him as lord. We shall discuss this scene later in relation to the Roman mockery of Jesus as king, to which it has clear parallels. S. Reinach[49] and others have suggested that the name of the figure hailed by the crowd as king has been brought over as Barabbas into the Jesus story. A variant of this proposal is that Karabas and Barabbas are forms of a title given to a role played in the mockery game. The basic objection, however, to all forms of the proposal is that there is little similarity (other than a partial likeness of name) between the figure/role at Alexandria and the Barabbas of the Gospel accounts. There is no mockery of Barabbas by the Jerusalem crowd, no reference to him as king—that is much closer to what happens to Jesus. Is it likely that something that happened in Alexandria in AD 38 would have become so massively confused that by AD 65–70 in Mark (or much earlier in the preGospel tradition underlying both Mark and John) Karabas had become Barabbas and what happened to him had been shifted to Jesus? Certainly none of the evangelists show any awareness of the supposed Karabas origins.

Still another interpretation of Barabbas as a purely fictional character draws on Scripture. In other writing Aus has attributed the changing of water to wine, the beheading of JBap, and much of the crucifixion to a midrashic or popular interpretation of the Book of Esther. In "Release" he would explain the Barabbas account as a midrash on Esth 2:18–23. Drawing on the Midrash on the Psalms (4th to the 9th cents. AD) and the two 7th-cent. targums of Esther, Aus relates Esther to Passover, Ps 22, the *Aqedah* or Binding of Isaac, and *sicarii* assassination. If we leave aside all that as unprovable for the preMarcan period, Aus's connections that can be dated to the 1st cent. become much more tenuous, e.g., the frequency of the verb "to hang" in Esth (nine times, with occasional connotations of crucifixion in the LXX), and an understanding of the holiday or remission of taxes in Esth 2:18 as equivalent to the release of prisoners in the Barabbas story. Josephus (*Ant.* 11.6.4; #207) mentions Barnabazos, a Jew who revealed the plot against the king to Mordecai. For Aus (17) it was "only a small step" to have this name become Barabbas—even though the functions of the two figures are not at all the same!

Rather than such fanciful theories, it is far less demanding on the imagina-

[49]See Couchoud, "Jesus" 32: Reinach combines the Karabas scene with the Sacaean drama (p. 876 below). H. Box, in his ed. of Philo's *In Flaccum* (London: Oxford, 1939), 91–92, lists others who find background for the mockery of Karabas (and Jesus) in the mockery of the Saturnalia-king (also p. 876 below). He states that the name Karabas means "cabbage," presumably thinking of

tion to posit that historically a real man with the patronymic "son of Abba" and the personal name Jesus was arrested during a riot in Jerusalem but spared by Pilate.[50]

C. Historicity of the Paschal Release

There is a further question. At the time when Jesus of Nazareth was executed, was clemency extended to Barabbas because there was a set custom of releasing a prisoner during Passover?[51] Once again there are fanciful theories that go beyond the Gospel evidence. For instance, Bajsić would make Barabbas the center of interest for Pilate. In his theory the governor knew that the Jewish crowd would want this dangerous revolutionary released; and even though he had to observe the custom of the festal pardon, he was trying to avoid releasing Barabbas. Obviously Jesus of Nazareth was politically harmless, so Pilate tried to offer Jesus to the crowd in order that Barabbas would not get off. While well intentioned, this theory is just as contrary to the Gospel evidence as is the totally fictional approach to Barabbas.

Studying the Gospel accounts, one must ask what legal procedure of pardon the evangelists had in mind. In any developed legal system there are distinct forms of clemency, e.g., terminating a trial and dismissing a prisoner because of lack of evidence; suspending a sentence and dismissing the prisoner even when there is sufficient evidence of guilt because there are mitigating circumstances; after a sentence has been passed, granting pardon from punishment—an action often performed by a higher authority. The last of these (pardon), we might note, is often the most difficult to obtain; and in later Roman law there was reluctance to have governors of provinces reverse their decisions. Unfortunately, the evangelists are not precise about Barabbas: Is he in prison because he has not yet been tried, or because he has been tried and is awaiting sentence, or because he has been sentenced and is awaiting execution? Normal Roman procedure would not suggest intervals in the trial, sentence, and execution pattern. In Justinian's _Code_ (9.4.5) a principle that seems to have gone back to early imperial and even republican times is enunciated: "One who is convicted should quickly undergo punish-

---

Hebrew _kĕrûb_, Aramaic _kĕrûbāʾ_, which have that meaning and to which the Greek word for "cabbage," _krambē_, is related. Are we dealing then with a contemptuous nickname?

[50]A much larger claim is made by Vicent Cernuda ("Condena I"). In a very learned but highly idiosyncratic presentation he argues from _lēstēs_ and _stasis_ that a foreign charioteer named Abas performed at Jerusalem's hippodrome and involuntarily ran over a pedestrian, causing a disturbance. Later Christian thought understood him as a revolutionary.

[51]Among those who opt for the historicity of the custom of paschal release may be mentioned Bammel, Blinzler, Bruce, Chavel, Cole, Flusser, Merritt, and Strobel. Among those who deny or doubt it are Aus, Beare, H. Cohn, Gordis, Watson, and Winter.

ment." Nevertheless, for various reasons including political expediency, normal Roman procedure would not always have been followed. How careful we need to be is suggested by Josephus (*Ant.* 20.9.5; #215), who reports that the procurator Albinus had many imprisoned in Judea who deserved death but had not been executed. Since presumably Pilate would have had to handle capital punishment trials in relation to a riot, judgment on Barabbas might have waited upon Pilate's arrival in Jerusalem from Caesarea at the time of the Passover feast. The fact that several criminals were executed with Jesus suggests that Pilate was sentencing and executing judgment during the feast. (Of uncertain applicability is the directive later attested in Tosepta *Sanhedrin* 11.7 that certain types of criminals should not be executed immediately but kept in Jerusalem until they could be executed more publicly at the feast.)

How would clemency fit into the Roman legal procedure? Remembering that Rome had just shifted from a republic to an empire, we must be aware that there is uncertainty in our knowledge of procedures in Pilate's time,[52] especially in a province like Judea. Although some commentators speak of amnesty, the Greek legal term *amnēstia* appears rather seldom in Latin literature and mostly as a loan word. The true Latin equivalent would be *abolitio,* most often in the sense of a mass pardon, sometimes setting aside a controversial legal procedure (Quintillian). *Indulgentia,* again often on a mass scale, tended to cover the nonapplication of a punishment because an appeal had been made; in Jesus' lifetime it would largely have been extended as an act of the emperor. More applicable to individuals would have been *venia,* sometimes extended because mitigating circumstances took away guilt, but also extended independently of guilt—indeed to one known to be guilty (*poenae meritae remissio:* Seneca, *De clementia* 2.7.1). All things considered, what the Gospels describe might best be classified as *venia* to be extended either to Jesus before sentencing (leaving aside the value of the case against him) or to Barabbas wherever he was in the legal process.

The Gospels differ as to the background of the custom of pardoning; it pertained to the Roman governor according to Mark/Matt, and to "the Jews" according to John. (Because of the Passover setting this custom has come to be known as the *privilegium paschale.*) Scholars have sought parallels to the custom in attested Greco-Roman practice of clemency and in Jewish practices.

GRECO-ROMAN PARALLELS. *(1) Festal amnesties.* The Gospel atmosphere pertaining to the custom involves a feast (not specified by Mark/Matt but specified as Passover by John). Grotius (+ 1645) suggested a parallel in the

---

[52]I draw here on the invaluable study of Waldstein, *Untersuchungen.*

Roman Lectisternia. Livy (*History* 5.13.7–8) reports that on the first historic celebration of this type of eight-day feast in 399 BC prisoners were unbound, and such was the religious awe inspired by the proceedings no one dared afterward to rechain them. Dionysius of Halicarnassus (*Roman Ant.* 12.9.10) reports that there was a release of slaves who had been placed under arrest by their masters. The Lectisternia were not celebrated annually but only on the occasion of thanksgiving in time of special stress. It is not clear that the unbindings were repeated, or that the concessions went much beyond parole. Other scholars (J. Gothofredus) appeal to clemency extended at the Greek feast of Thesmophoria (a feast associated with Demeter the lawgiver, insuring the fertility of the earth). The Panathenae, involving a procession to the acropolis in honor of Athena, has also been proposed as a parallel. Merritt ("Jesus" 62, 65) mentions a prisoner release during the greater Dionysia celebrated in early April at Athens since the 6th cent. BC, and at the Greek festival of Kronia (= Roman Saturnalia; see p. 876 below) celebrated widely in December. Scholars have studied Papyrus Tebtunis 5.1–5 where, following the Greek model of the gracious king, the Hellenistic Egyptian monarchs Ptolemy and Cleopatra proclaimed "an amnesty to all their subjects for errors, crimes. . . ." At most, however, these are mass amnesties of varying scope; none of them is truly parallel to the custom of a judicial pardon granted to an individual by a Roman governor ruling over subject people.

(2) Common practices by imperial officials. There is no doubt that these officials granted pardons. The Pilate of John 19:10 states, "I have the authority to release you and the authority to crucify you." Cynically, Origen (*In Matt.* 27:15, #120; GCS 38.254) comments, "So they grant some favors to people whom they subject to themselves, until their yoke over them is made firm." Pliny in correspondence with the Emperor Trajan (*Epistles* 10.31–32) reports that by order of proconsuls and legates, condemned criminals who had become intermingled with slaves working in the public service had been released; Trajan wanted this abuse corrected by insisting that sentences could be reversed only by proper authority. In particular, Florentine Papyrus 61.59ff. (LFAE 267–69) narrates an incident in Egypt in AD 85 when G. Septimius Vegetus released to the crowds a prisoner who was guilty of having sent to prison an honest family and who accordingly deserved to be scourged (*mastigoun*). Josephus (*Ant.* 20.9.5; #215) reports that in AD 64 the procurator of Judea Albinus, when he heard that Florus was coming to succeed him, in a final effort to gain a name for himself cleared the prisons. He had those executed who deserved death, but for a bribe released those convicted of trifling crimes. Yet all these examples tell us nothing about a regular custom on a feast; at most they are isolated instances of humane behavior. Another Josephus story about Albinus (*Ant.* 20.9.3; #208–9) is set on a feast

(probably Passover) when the procurator had to let ten bandits (*lēstai*) go in order to ransom the secretary of the high priest's son, who had been kidnapped by terrorists (*sicarii*). Obviously, despite the festal setting, no benevolent custom was involved. Under this same general heading might be treated the thesis that the release of Barabbas was in the pattern of "acclamation" or *anaboēsis* (§31, D3c above).[53] Justinian's Code (9.47.12) insists, "When the populace speaks viva voce, they are not to be heard; nor should one believe their voices when they desire that someone guilty of a crime be dismissed, or that someone innocent be condemned." Would such a maxim have bound Pilate? Suetonius, *Tiberius* 47, tells us that the emperor himself was forced to release a slave who had done well in the arena because the crowds cried out for it. Yet this is far from the custom described in the Gospels. Would release by acclamation have been a regular festal custom? Was it extended to a subject populace when a riot had recently occurred?

(3) A special Roman concession to Jews as a safety valve. J. Spencer (1727) thought that the Seleucid kings in the 3d or 2d cents. BC might have begun such a custom and that the Romans continued it. True, I Macc 9:70–72; 10:23 give us examples of the release of captives taken in war as part of an attempt by Syrian rulers to gain peace with the Maccabean leaders. Once again, however, this is quite different from releasing a single prisoner from jail at Passover. Other scholars have thought that the Roman emperors might have begun such a custom. Josephus (*Ant.* 14.10; #185–267) gives a long list of imperial and local Roman concessions to the Jews, beginning with those of Julius Caesar; but none of these concessions mentions releasing a prisoner on a feast. Still another suggestion (or guess) is that Pilate might have introduced the custom to make amends for his heavy-handed behavior and mistakes as prefect (pp. 698–705 above). The weaknesses of all these parallels are obvious, and one is left with the enduring doubt that Roman governors could ever have committed themselves to a custom that would require them to release a killer in the midst of a recent riot in a volatile province.

JEWISH PARALLELS. Some have thought that the Romans or Pilate might have had to accept a Jewish custom already in place. The Passover theme of release from Egypt might feasibly have led to a Jewish custom of releasing a prisoner at that feast. Merritt ("Jesus" 59, 61) mentions occasional releases of prisoners as part of the *šigû* rite of pardon, and points to the influence of the Babylonian calendar and customs on the Jews. Evidence that the Babylonian king released a prisoner on the 6th, the 16th, and 26th days of the 8th

---

[53]See Colin, *Villes;* Steinwenter, "Processo" 481; but also Merkel, "Begnadigung" 309–11. The variant reading *anaboēsas* in Mark 15:8 (p. 794 above) may mean that later scribes understood the Barabbas release as an instance of acclamation.

month of the year has been adduced to explain why Jews would have moved toward such a practice (Langdon, "Release"). Some of this theorizing, however, neglects the mentality of biblical law which presents its punishments as set by God and therefore not to be dispensed from. Num 35:31 affirms: "You shall accept no ransom for the life of a murderer who is guilty of death, but he shall be put to death." Heb 10:28 is no less firm: "One who has violated the Law of Moses dies without mercy. . . ." Thus it is not surprising that the Bible offers no evidence of a Passover-release custom, not even extended by a Jewish king. Was there a change in attitude when serious cases were decided not according to the biblical law but according to the law of the Hellenistic or Roman conquerors? Chavel ("Releasing" 277–78) thinks that in the 1st cent. BC, when there were many political prisoners because of inner Jewish struggles, the Hasmonean priest-kings of Jerusalem introduced this custom of pardoning to please the excitable pilgrim throngs. Josephus (*War* 2.2.5; #28) tells us that Archelaus liberated those whom his father had imprisoned for the gravest crimes. Such evidence establishes only a possibility; the talmudic literature gives almost an hour-by-hour description of Passover and never mentions the custom; nor do Josephus and Philo mention it. Indirect evidence has been sought in Mishna *Pesaḥim* 8:6 governing the slaughtering of the Passover lamb (see Blinzler and Chavel). The legal issue concerns those who may and may not be counted as members of a Passover company (*ḥaburah*), for whom a lamb can be prepared by sacrifice. The discussion includes "someone who has received a promise to be released from prison." The accountability for this person is a problem, for the promise might not be fulfilled. (TalBab *Pesaḥim* 91a notes that someone in an Israelite prison is a special case since a temporary release for Passover would be given by Jews.) The citation deals with a series of possible cases, including the sick and the aged (see also Tosepta *Pesaḥim* 7.11); it concerns someone who might be eligible for permanent or temporary release; it has nothing to do with the right of the populace to have one prisoner released.

The conclusion from this discussion of Roman and Jewish amnesty/pardon parallels is that there is no good analogy supporting the historical likelihood of the custom in Judea of regularly releasing a prisoner at a/the feast (of Passover) as described in three Gospels.[54] Already in the early 3d cent. Origen (*In Matt.* 27:15, #120; GCS 38.253–54) betrayed surprise at such a

---

[54]Herranz Marco ("Problema" 150–55), recognizing that the evidence for a custom of pardoning is weak, appeals to reconstructed Aramaic to provide a translation that would drop it from Mark 15:8: "They began to request as it was customary for them [to do]"—a custom of petitioning which the subsequent tradition misunderstood as a custom of pardoning. Rather than resorting to a very dubious Aramaic original, I judge it easier to postulate that an instance of pardon was misunderstood as a custom.

custom. Luke's omission of the custom, even though he knew Mark, has been thought to represent an earlier skepticism.[55] Can one reconcile the possible nonhistoricity of the Passover privilege with the existence of a historical Barabbas who was released from prison by Pilate (all four Gospels)? One might suspect that the evangelists (or their predecessors in the tradition) assumed that the release was a reflection of a regular custom when in fact it was an isolated incident. What might have led the evangelists to assume that there was a custom? Wratislaw ("Scapegoat") suggests that the description might have been influenced by the Israelite liturgical custom of the two goats described in Lev 16:7–22: One goat was let go, the other killed for a sin offering. Other scholars have theorized that already there may have been a *Christian* custom of pardoning at Easter time.[56] Merritt ("Jesus") points to general similitude: The existence of various amnesties and pardons in the diverse cultures described above would have made the idea of a regular custom of release at a feast seem plausible to narrators and hearers who had no exact knowledge of Judea ca. 30. Bauer ("Literarische") gives examples where something that happened was freely explained as coming from a custom.

If we lay aside the custom as a secondary development, the historical substratum of the Barabbas incident may have been relatively simple. The following outline could be reconstructed on the basis of the Gospel reports: A man with the name Barabbas was arrested in a roundup after a riot that had caused some deaths in Jerusalem. Eventually he was released by Pilate when a feast brought the governor to Jerusalem to supervise public order. Presumably this took place at the same time that Jesus was crucified, or not far from it, or at another Passover. In any case, this release struck Christians as ironic: The same legal issue was involved, sedition against the authority of the emperor.[57] Although they knew Jesus was innocent, he was found guilty by Pilate, while Barabbas was let go. (As seen in the COMMENT on Mark 15:7, that verse never states that Barabbas rioted or killed. Even if the evangelist judged Barabbas guilty, in a preMarcan stage, closer to the original story, Barabbas' guilt may not have been established—a fact that would have allowed Pilate to release him.) The storytelling tendency to contrast the released Barabbas and the crucified Jesus by bringing them together at the

---

[55]In Acts 25:16 Luke betrays knowledge of a contrary Roman custom; for the prefect Festus asserts that it is not the custom of the Romans to give up a prisoner before proper legal procedures.

[56]Roman emperors of the 4th cent. gave mass amnesties at Easter, but we cannot verify an intraChristian *abolitio paschalis* mentality in the 1st cent.

[57]The *stasis* of Mark 15:7 and Luke 23:19 is the normal Greek equivalent of the Latin *seditio*. Paulus (ca. AD 200) writes even of Roman citizens (DJ 48.19.38.2): "Authors of sedition and inciters of the people are, according to their rank, to be crucified, or to be exposed to the beasts, or to be deported to an island."

same moment before Pilate's "justice"[58] would have been enhanced if both had the same personal name, Jesus.

Inevitably, one would have wished a historical investigation to produce more certain results than the above-described likelihoods. (Of course, there is the beneficial effect of showing that some of the plot approaches to Barabbas, often involving antiJewish creation by the evangelists, are fiction with little likelihood.) Yet historical criticism cannot overcome the lack of comparative material, and the Barabbas case is particularly frustrating on that score.[59] Nevertheless, the real import of the Barabbas motif is on another level, namely, the truth that the evangelists wished to convey about the death of Jesus. For them conviction of the innocent Jesus had a negative side, the choice of evil. The story of Barabbas with a basis in fact was dramatized to convey that truth.

(Bibliography for this episode may be found in §30, Part 5.)

---

[58]The oldest recorded form of the contrast between the two men involved the patronymic Barabbas and the title "the King of the Jews." Dibelius ("Herodes" 117–20) suggests a combination between the memory of a known malefactor, Barabbas, and reflection on the charge on the cross (Mark 15:26).

[59]A badly skewed picture can emerge from ignoring the doubts raised by historical criticism. Besnier ("Procès" 203–5) sees three gambits tried by the governor before he acceded to Jewish demands for crucifixion: (1) sending Jesus to Herod; (2) appeal to the festal amnesty; (3) offer of a lesser punishment, e.g., whipping. Besnier goes on to theorize that Pilate would have had the sense not to try such foredoomed gambits (especially 2) if he knew that Jesus had already been tried and condemned by the Sanhedrin. This theorizing ignores that gambits 1 and 3 are found only in Luke (dubiously a primary source for history), and the historicity of gambit 2 is highly debated. One could even argue the other way: Only because Jesus had been condemned by the Sanhedrin did Pilate finally agree to his crucifixion, for that knowledge assured him that Jesus would not be looked on as a hero whose death might cause riots.

§35. THE ROMAN TRIAL, PART FOUR: CONDEMNATION OF JESUS

(Mark 15:12–15; Matt 27:22–26; Luke 23:20–25;
John 19:1,4–16a)

Translation

Mark 15:12–15: 12But in answer again, Pilate kept saying to them, "What therefore shall I do with him whom you call 'the King of the Jews'?" 13But they shouted back, "Crucify him." 14But Pilate kept saying to them, "For what has he done that is bad?" But they shouted even more, "Crucify him." 15But Pilate, desiring to satisfy the crowd, released to them Barabbas; and he gave over Jesus, having had him flogged, in order that he be crucified.

Matt 27:22–26: 22Pilate says to them, "What therefore shall I do with Jesus called the Messiah?" All say, "Let him be crucified." 23But he said, "For what that is bad has he done?" But they kept shouting even more, saying, "Let him be crucified." 24But Pilate, having seen that nothing was of use, but rather a disturbance was taking place, having taken water, washed off his hands before the crowd, saying, "I am innocent of the blood of this man. You must see to it." 25And in answer all the people said, "His blood on us and on our children." 26Then he released to them Barabbas; but having had Jesus flogged, he gave (him) over in order that he be crucified.

Luke 23:20–25: 20But again Pilate cried out in addressing them, wishing to release Jesus. 21But they kept crying out in return saying, "Crucify, crucify him." 22But he said to them a third time, "For what that is bad has this fellow done? I have found nothing in him (making him) guilty of death. Having chastised him (by whipping), therefore, I shall release him." 23But they were pressing with loud cries, demanding him to be crucified; and their cries were getting stronger. 24And Pilate made the judgment that their demand should be put into effect; 25so he released the one who had been thrown into prison for riot and murder whom they had been demanding, but Jesus he gave over to their will.

John 19:1,4–16a: ¹Then Pilate took Jesus and had him scourged. [*For 19:2–3, where the soldiers, having put on Jesus a crown of thorns and a purple robe, hail him as "the King of the Jews" and give him slaps, see §36 below.*] ⁴And again Pilate went outside and says to them, "Look, I lead him out to you so that you may know that I find no case at all [against him]." ⁵Therefore, Jesus went outside bearing the thorny crown and the purple robe; and he [Pilate] says to them, "Behold the man." ⁶So when the chief priests and the attendants saw him, they yelled out saying, "Crucify, crucify." Pilate says to them, "Take him yourselves and crucify, for I do not find a case against him." ⁷The Jews answered him, "We have a law, and according to the law he ought to die, because he has made himself God's Son." ⁸So when Pilate heard this statement, he was more afraid.

⁹And he went back into the praetorium and says to Jesus, "From where are you?" But Jesus did not give him an answer. ¹⁰So Pilate says, "Do you not speak to me? Do you not know that I have power to release you and power to crucify you?" ¹¹Jesus answered, "You have no power over me at all except what was given to you from above. Therefore the one who gave me over to you has the greater sin."

¹²From this Pilate was seeking to release him. But the Jews yelled out saying, "If you release this fellow, you are not a friend of Caesar. Anyone who makes himself a king contradicts Caesar." ¹³Now Pilate, having heard these words, led Jesus outside and sat on the judgment seat in the place called Lithostrotos, but in Hebrew Gabbatha. ¹⁴Now it was preparation day for Passover; it was the sixth hour. And he says to the Jews, "Look, your king." ¹⁵So they yelled out, "Take (him), take (him), crucify him." Pilate says to them, "Shall I crucify your king?" The chief priests answered, "We have no king but Caesar." ¹⁶ᵃSo then he gave him over to them in order that he be crucified.

COMMENT

In the Synoptic Gospels Pilate reacts to the choice of Barabbas by the populace either by asking what to do with Jesus (Mark/Matt) or by expressing a wish to release Jesus (Luke). (Some scholars would argue that Pilate still hopes to use the paschal privilege on Jesus' behalf, for he does not release Barabbas until the end of the trial when he condemns Jesus. The "again," however, in Mark and Luke suggests a new initiative.) This tactic brings from the populace the first outcry to crucify Jesus. When Pilate still resists by asking what Jesus has done that is bad, there is a second outcry even more insistent on crucifixion. Then Pilate acquiesces (in Matt after washing his hands to shed the guilt for innocent blood): He releases Barabbas, but Jesus (after having him flogged: Mark/Matt) he gives over to be crucified.

John's account is far longer and more dramatic. Yet one can still detect a pattern of two outcries for crucifixion (19:6,15) and a final giving over of Jesus to be crucified (19:16a). Indeed, guided by the briefer Marcan account, Fortna (*Gospel* 243) reconstructs the Johannine source as 19:6,12(?),13,15 (which he moves around), and 16a. I have previously expressed my doubt about this method of reconstructing the source. Baum-Bodenbender (*Hoheit* 239–41) considers preJohannine 19:7–11a,13,14b,15,16a.

Since a basic pattern of a first and a second outcry for crucifixion and a final giving over of Jesus can be found in all the Gospels, I shall follow the pattern of those three parts in commenting. The second part (= second outcry), however, will have to be subdivided because of the length caused by Matt's addition of Pilate washing his hands and John's dialogue between Pilate and Jesus. The divisions are outlined on pp. 663–64 above.

FIRST OUTCRY FOR CRUCIFIXION AND PILATE'S RESPONSE
(MARK 15:12–14A; MATT 27:22–23A; LUKE 23:20–22; JOHN 19:1,4–8)

Only in John is this scene partially distinct from the populace's choice of Barabbas that has immediately preceded. That choice leaves Pilate with the problem of dealing with Jesus.

Mark 15:12–14a. Just as in the previous section,[1] the postpositive *de* is very prominent here (each verse—I continue to translate it mechanically as "But," even if sometimes it could more smoothly be read as "And" or ignored). Throughout, the "to them" means to the crowd that has been stirred up by the chief priests to ask for the release of Barabbas, as is made specific

---

[1] For the use of postpositive *de* in Mark 15:6–11, see pp. 732, 810 above.

in 15:15. To this crowd Pilate poses directly the question of what to do with Jesus. This makes sense in 15:12 because, despite the baneful influence of the priests on the choice for Barabbas, the mind of the crowd toward Jesus is not yet clear in Mark. The *palin* ("again") in 15:12 shows that Pilate's question is related to the previous question in 15:9, which was directed toward the release of "the King of the Jews."[2] By posing a question to the crowd about the fate of Jesus, Pilate is beginning to show that he will be swayed by them. The phrase "whom you call" in 15:12 does not mean that they acknowledge that Jesus is "the King of the Jews"; rather it suggests that they used the title in the charge when they first brought Jesus to Pilate (and thus clarifies 15:2, i.e., how Pilate got the information to ask Jesus about this title). The phrase is omitted by Koine textual witnesses;[3] but it fits Pilate's tendency to probe beneath the appearances of the Jewish charge, as he did in 15:10, for it suggests that the accusers, not Jesus, used the title. Perhaps by this stage "the King of the Jews" is being used with a tinge of sarcasm; yet it remains all that the Marcan Pilate knows about this man, whom he never calls "Jesus."

Even though the chief priests have been active, the brutal imperative of the shout of the crowd against Jesus in 15:13 is shocking in the flow of the story. There is another *palin*, and some have objected against the Marcan logic since the crowd has not previously shouted. One might respond that there is an implicit (shouted) response to Pilate in 15:11; but here the implication is probably "back," as the crowd gives its definitive answer to the second initiative of Pilate. Ironically, the verb *krazein* ("to shout") was last used in Mark when those who went before and after Jesus as he entered Jerusalem seated on a colt shouted Hosanna and blessed him (11:9). In the present instance the shout contains the first reference to crucifixion in Mark.[4] Below (pp. 946–47) we shall consider the brutality of crucifixion, and so the demand of the crowd pertinent to Jesus is barbarous indeed.

That second rebuff does not yet convince the prefect. The imperfect tense ("kept saying") in 15:14 catches the continued force in his third attempt to

---

[2]A number of Koine textual witnesses add a *thelete* here ("What therefore *do you will* that I shall do . . . ?"), heightening the conformity to the question in 15:9. If the reading were original, it would make more deliberate the reaction of the crowd in 15:13.

[3]Probably again in conformity with 15:9, which does not have it.

[4]In the three Marcan predictions by Jesus of the death of the Son of Man (8:31; 9:31; 10:34), the verb used was *apokteinein*, "to put to death, kill." The basic NT verb for crucifixion is *stauroun*, a denominative from *stauros* ("stake"); Josephus normally uses *anastauroun* (*War* 1.4.6; #97; *Ant.* 13.14.2; #380). The root idea is to put someone on a stake, and P.-E. Guillet ("Les 800") tries to interpret Josephus as referring to impalement. Now, however, we know from contemporary documents that some Jews did contemplate hanging certain types of condemned criminals alive (p. 533 above), and that makes stronger the probability that crucifixion was meant, rather than a shaft going up vertically through the body which would most likely kill the victim.

deal appropriately with Jesus. (The pattern of three questions by Pilate and three responses by the crowd[5] fits in with other triads in the Marcan PN: three prayers in Gethsemane; three denials, etc.) "For what has he done that is bad?" is as close as Mark comes to the theme of not-guilty found in the thrice-reiterated not-guilty statements by Pilate in Luke and John, a theme that appears in Matt in the reference to innocent blood. Allusions to doing something "bad [*kakos*]" have appeared in John 18:23, where Jesus challenged the attendant of Annas to give evidence if he had spoken anything bad, and in 18:30, where "the Jews" had arrogantly answered Pilate, "If this fellow were not doing what is bad, we would not have given him over to you." Despite the question form, then, Mark is using a traditional phrase to proclaim Jesus' sinlessness (see Isa 53:9). Thus from the question one can neither assume that this was a trial by acclamation (p. 720 above) nor reconstruct Pilate's psychological outlook as if he had hoped for a more favorable response from Jesus' adversaries. If anything, in the storyline he is losing control of the outcome.

Matt 27:22–23a. In this part of the scene Matt stays very close to Mark and even is slightly briefer. That may be because Matt has already taken the suspense out of how the crowds would deal with Pilate's new initiative by telling us in 27:20 that the chief priests had persuaded them not only to ask for Barabbas (as Mark reports) but to destroy Jesus. We are forewarned what will be the answer to Pilate's "What therefore shall I do with Jesus?"[6] As already in 27:17, so also here Matt prefers "Messiah" (*Christos*) as a title for Jesus over Mark's "the King of the Jews." The harsher implication, therefore, is that not only do the crowds prefer Barabbas to the Messiah but also they want to crucify the Messiah.[7] The logic of asking what to do with "Jesus called the Messiah" makes better sense if the crowds have chosen for the release of *Jesus* Barabbas (27:16–17). Another Matthean difference is that while in Mark 15:13 the crowd shouts back, "Crucify him," in Matt 27:22 *all say,* "Let him be crucified." The "all" prepares for "all the people" in 27:25 who will take on themselves and their children the responsibility for Jesus' blood. The use of "say" instead of "shout" suggests a less emotional and more deliberate rejection of the Messiah.[8]

Luke 23:20–22. Luke has the same overall pattern as Mark 15:12–14a, namely, another postBarabbas attempt on Jesus' behalf by Pilate; the shout/

---

[5]So Foulon-Piganiol, "Rôle" 628; cf. Mark 15:9,12,14a and 15:11,13,14b.

[6]If we compare Matt 27:22 to Mark 15:12, Matt has already used Mark's introductory "in answer" in 27:21, as he created direct discourse in the Barabbas scene.

[7]A variant in Codex Bezae and the OL of 27:22, "What therefore shall *we* do with Jesus?" brings the crowds more intimately into the decision.

[8]The "Let him be crucified" is not theologically significant as to responsibility but represents Matt's preference for the passive or impersonal form of this verb (SPNM 251).

cry to crucify; Pilate's reaction to this demand for crucifixion. Yet the (very Lucan) phrasing is quite different from Mark's, so that if Luke used Mark here (as I think), he has indulged in considerable rewriting. In the PN the regular Marcan verb "to shout" is *krazein* (three times; Matt two times). John uses *kraugazein* which, for the purpose of distinguishing, I have translated "to yell." In 23:18 Luke (alone) has already used *anakrazein* ("to shout out"). Here, however, Luke employs an intricate pattern: in 23:20 of Pilate, the verb *prosphōnein* ("to cry toward" = "to cry out in address"); in 23:21 of the Jewish authorities and people, the verb *epiphōnein* ("to cry out against" = "to cry out in return");[9] and in 23:23 two nominal references to their "cries" (*phōnē*) against Jesus. Thus in terms of vocabulary both Pilate and the Jewish opponents of Jesus are on the same level of emotion. In 23:21 Luke's doubled outcry, "Crucify, crucify him," not only is a much stronger response than that given in 23:18 by Jesus' adversaries to Pilate's earlier proposal, but is more intensive than the single shout for crucifixion in Mark 15:13 and Matt 27:22. Büchele (*Tod* 37) points to a Lucan penchant for double words, vocatives, sentences, and pericopes. However, the yell is also doubled in John 19:6 ("Crucify, crucify"), and some think this is another instance where Luke adds elements from a tradition similar to that used by John. As with Mark/Matt, this is the first reference to crucifixion in Luke.

Pilate's response (Luke 23:22) to the outcry combines the question taken from Mark 15:14 ("For what that is bad has this fellow done?") with the Lucan Pilate's third not-guilty statement,[10] the latter being another feature that Luke shares with John. The "I have found nothing in him guilty of death" appears to be a composite of "I have found nothing in this man ... guilty" of 23:14 and "worthy of death" of 23:15. "Having chastised him (by whipping), therefore, I shall release him" echoes the same phrasing in 23:16. (For whipping, see p. 851 below.) The result of all this combined language is that the Lucan Pilate reacts more strongly against the outcry for crucifixion than the Marcan/Matthean Pilate, almost as if he is going to ignore it and release Jesus. Subsequently, then, Pilate's rapid acquiescence after some stronger cries for crucifixion (23:23b–24) is surprising in the storyline.

John 19:4–8. In this section of the Roman trial it is very difficult to compare to the relatively lean Synoptic accounts John's longer and more powerful dramatization. The same basic elements that are in Mark 15:12–14a can be found in John (19:4,6), but they are part of an expanded framework that gives them new meaning. In particular, there is a new preface: Two elements

---

[9]*Prosphōnein* and *epiphōnein* are overwhelmingly Lucan in the NT, and each is used twice in Acts' account of the Judean trial of Paul.

[10]Luke himself notes that this is "a third time," even if curiously that enumeration seems to govern the question borrowed from Mark as well.

that Mark 15:15b–20 places at the end of the trial, i.e., a flogging and a Roman mockery of Jesus, appear in John 19:1–3 in the middle of the trial as Pilate's immediate reaction to the choice for Barabbas. Scourging, instead of being part of the crucifixion punishment (as is the flogging in Mark/Matt), becomes in John a lesser punishment that Pilate hopes will satisfy "the Jews" by causing them to give up on this wretched Jesus. (Here John's Pilate is not unlike the Lucan Pilate of 23:16: "Having chastised him (by whipping), therefore, I shall let him go"; but in John the scourging takes place, whereas in Luke the offer is rejected.) The mockery described in 19:2–3 (see §36 below) is part of the same strategy. In the seven-episode arrangement of John's Roman trial (p. 758), 19:1–3 is the middle Episode 4, implicitly set inside the praetorium (see 19:4). Pilate has a lesser role in this than in any other episode, for the soldiers carry out the brutality.

The narration in 19:1–3 is meant to preface and support the dramatic Episode 5 (19:4–8), where the scourged Jesus is led outside the praetorium to face "the Jews." There he is still clothed in the mock royal robe and wearing the thorny crown,[11] demonstrating the lack of seriousness that Pilate has found in the charge that he is "the King of the Jews." In 19:4, with Jesus standing before his accusers, Pilate states that he finds no case at all against him. This is the second of John's three not-guilty affirmations, phrased in almost the same Greek as the first (18:38).[12]

In Mark/Matt Pilate's second challenge to the populace is "What therefore shall I do with him whom you call 'the King of the Jews' [or 'Jesus called the Messiah']?"; Luke 23:20 describes the challenge indirectly as Pilate cries out, wishing to release Jesus. Neither of these efforts matches in drama what Pilate does in John 19:5 as he presents the scourged and mocked Jesus with the words: "Behold the man."[13]

What is meant by *anthrōpos* ("man")? Some give it no particular theological meaning, so that the phrase is equivalent to "Look at this poor fellow," either by way of eliciting pity (Bernard), or by way of ridiculing any attempt

---

[11]John never tells us that the apparel of mockery was taken off Jesus, but by 19:23 he has his own clothes.

[12]In most mss. the negative modifies the noun ("find no case"), but in P66 and Codex Sinaiticus of 19:4 it modifies the verb ("not find a [guilty] case"); and mss. vary on the presence and placing of "against him."

[13]By way of minor detail, *idou* ("behold") is used by John here and three other times, as contrasted with fifteen uses of *ide* ("look"), to be employed in 19:14. G. D. Kilpatrick (JTS NS 18 [1967], 426) would read *ide* here as well, making the two proclamations of chap. 19 parallel. Curiously P66, the OL, and the sub-Achmimic Coptic omit "Behold the man." That omission may be a sign that already early interpreters were puzzled about the import of this enigmatic statement, known often by its Latin rendition *Ecce homo*. An odd interpretation (discussed and rejected by Houlden,"John") is that the "he" who says this is not Pilate but Jesus, who is commenting on those who judge him: "See what man is like" (cf. John 2:25). The partial parallel with John 19:14 militates against this.

to take this hapless figure seriously as a royal claimant (Bultmann, Blinzler, Charbonneau, Flusser), or by way of contempt to goad the crowd into demanding Jesus' release (Bajsić). Along the lines of the last suggestion, the question has been raised whether the scourging was part of the amnesty process, so that this is the amnesty formula, i.e., "Behold the man who should be released" (see Soltero, "Pilatus" 329–30). Lohse (*History* 93) takes it as an indication of the strong impression Jesus has made on Pilate: "Here is a *man!*"

Others give *anthrōpos* a christological meaning. Suggit ("John 19") points to the number of times "man" has a pregnant meaning in John, e.g., 9:11, where the blind man's knowledge of "the man called Jesus" is the first step on the road to faith; 10:33, "You who are a man are making yourself God"; 11:50, "It is better that one man die for the people" (also 18:14). This type of association is also defended by Derrett ("Ecce" 229, 216), who with almost unbridled imagination combines references in both Hebrew and Greek with the assurance that he has discovered a symbolism that "has passed unnoticed for centuries." Some think the formula here is by contrast with the charge of Jesus' making himself God's Son two verses later. Others (including Barrett) appeal to the myth of the primal Man that has been dubiously proposed as a background for John's christology (discussed in Schnackenburg, *John* 1.543–57). More common is the equation of "man" with the Son of Man whom Jesus thrice predicted would be lifted up (3:14; 8:28; 12:32–34; thus Blank, de la Potterie, Dodd). But why would John in this one instance change the title to "man"? Meeks (*Prophet-King* 70–72) contends that "Man" was an eschatological title in Hellenistic Judaism and points to Zech 6:12, "Behold a man [*anēr*, not *anthrōpos*] whose name is the Branch . . . he shall build the house of the Lord." It is generally recognized that "the Branch" is a title with Davidic and messianic implications, so that Pilate's "Behold the man" would be connected with the issue of being "the King of the Jews."[14] We cannot resolve this question, but solutions that at this stage in the trial have Pilate acknowledge truth about Jesus' heavenly identity make meaningless what follows in 19:7–8. Clearly the Jewish reaction to the proclamation implies that through it Pilate would commend Jesus' release. Personally I favor the simplest explanation, that Pilate was demonstrating Jesus to be pathetic and no challenge to either Rome or "the Jews."

In Mark 15:13 Pilate's initiative on Jesus' behalf is met by the shout "Crucify him" coming from the crowd whom the chief priests had influenced.

---

[14]Schwank, "Ecce homo," gives a strongly theological interpretation: Pilate is answering his own question, "What is truth?" (18:38a) by pointing to the man who is the way for all human beings who seek the truth (cf. 8:12).

John 19:6 places the yell[15] "Crucify, crucify" (doubled as in Luke 23:21) directly on the lips of the chief priests and the attendants. Yet "the Jews" will take part in the dialogue in the next verse, so John too thinks of a collectivity acting unanimously. The intensity of the double "Crucify" is most intelligible in John since from the very beginning of the trial (18:31–32) "the Jews" have expressed insistently their demand for Jesus' death and indeed for this kind of death.

In John 19:6b Pilate's answer to the demand for crucifixion is more exasperated than that given in the other Gospels. "Take him yourselves and crucify" echoes the tone and words of 18:31 at the beginning of the trial, "Take him yourselves, and according to your law judge him." The Jewish reaction to the earlier challenge was in terms of Roman law (p. 748 above): "It is not permitted us to put anyone to death"; the Jewish reaction in 19:7 is in terms of Jewish law: "We have a law, and according to the law he ought to die, because he has made himself God's Son."[16] During Jesus' ministry we were told that "the Jews" sought to kill Jesus because he was speaking of God as his own Father, thus making himself God's equal (5:18), and that they were planning to stone him for blasphemy since, although only a man, he was making himself equal to God (10:33). Accordingly most think that the law invoked here is Lev 24:16 about putting the blasphemer to death.[17]

By changing Mark's "the King of the Jews" to "the Messiah" Matt 27:22 made it clear that Jesus was rejected as a religious figure; similarly John makes it clear that the Son of God is rejected.[18] In Mark/Matt the persuasion of the chief priests got the crowd to demand Jesus' crucifixion. Blinzler (*Trial* 211–12) suggests that these authorities had great religious influence and that the crowd began to think that Jesus really was religiously evil. Yet the Synoptics do not introduce the Law into the issue. John is looking back on the trial of Jesus with the insights of the last third of the 1st cent. when, with the destruction of the Temple, the Law became an even greater factor in Jewish life. At that time the chief priests were less important in Jewish life; and so in the Johannine trial the chief priests, while present and active, are for the most part subsumed into "the Jews." By the end of the century the divinity of Jesus as a threat to the unicity of God was emerging as the

---

[15]On p. 826 above I discussed the varied Gospel vocabulary translated as "shout," "yell," and "cry out."

[16]This statement, attributed by John to "the Jews," shows that for him "the Jews" cannot simply be equated with the world or with a geographical designation (Judeans).

[17]Wead ("We have") would also appeal to the condemnation of the false prophet in Deut 13:1–5 who does signs (see John 11:47–48) and teaches rebellion against the Law of Israel (John 18:19: "his teaching"), and must be put to death. See also Meeks, *Prophet-King* 47–57. I discussed the false prophet issue on pp. 541–44 above, suggesting that it appears largely in the later sections of the NT.

[18]The parallelism of the motifs is heightened when we remember that Matt 16:16; 26:63 interpret "the Messiah" as "the Son of God."

great issue between Jews and Christians, and John describes it as the factor beneath the surface in the Roman trial.

As already indicated, John places Pilate on trial before Jesus. Consequently, as the true issue why "the Jews" want Jesus crucified is unveiled, Pilate sees that he cannot hope to accomplish a political compromise by which he would be delivered from rendering an offensive judgment. He will have to decide not only whether the so-called "King of the Jews" will die but whether the Son of God will die. And so (19:8) Pilate "was more afraid." The "more" has puzzled interpreters, since there was no previous reference to fear. Bultmann and Schnackenburg would interpret Pilate's hesitance in dealing with Jesus earlier in the scene as a manifestation of fear, but more likely the "more" has the force of an elative (Barrett) and means simply that Pilate was very afraid. Some think the fear is political since these intransigent people will put his governing ability in a bind (along the lines of 19:12 below). However, most think of it as a religious fear. Flourney, Haenchen, and others understand John's Pilate as exhibiting pagan superstition in encountering a deity or the numinous.[19] Yet although John portrays Pilate with the coloration of an imperious Roman, one can doubt that he tries to give Pilate pagan religious sensibilities. He is rather for John the type of human being who does not want to make a decision between light and darkness, between truth and falsehood. The Jewish charge that Jesus claims to be God's Son is consonant with Jesus' own statement to Pilate that he has come into the world to bear witness to the truth (18:37). Pilate is afraid because it becomes clearer and clearer that he will not be able to escape making a judgment about truth.

SYNOPTIC SECOND OUTCRY FOR CRUCIFIXION; MATTHEW'S PILATE WASHES HIS HANDS (MARK 15:14B; LUKE 23:23; MATT 27:23B–25)

While a second outcry for crucifixion is a common element in all four Gospels, there are three different treatments of how Pilate responds: In Mark and Luke he immediately acquiesces; in Matt he washes his hands and forces the people to take the responsibility for the innocent blood of Jesus. As we shall see in the next subdivision, in John the second outcry is embedded in further dialogue with Jesus and with "the Jews," as Pilate forces them to acknowledge Caesar as king.

Mark 15:14b and Luke 23:23. In these two Gospels the second sharp outcry for crucifixion responds to Pilate's renewed attempt to spare Jesus,

---

[19]Frequently there is cited a passage from Philostratus' *Life of Apollonius* (4.44) where in Nero's time the Roman official Tigellinus, having interrogated Apollonius, thinks he is divine and wants no more to do with him lest he be fighting a god. See also on John 19:9 below.

and the outcry brings to an end Pilate's efforts. In Mark 15:14b the second shout of the crowd is stronger (*perissōs*, "even more"), and that presumably is why Pilate immediately proceeds to satisfy their demands and have Jesus crucified (15:15). Luke 23:23 describes the second crucifixion outcry by using the verb *aitein*. When Mark 15:8 used this verb to describe the action of the crowd that came up, I translated it as "request"; for there was as yet no aggravating antagonism apparent between Pilate and the crowd. Here in Luke it takes on the tone of "demand"; it is a participle complementing *epikeisthai* ("to press on"), expressing urgency. Luke further underlines the intensity of the demand by the duplication "loud cries"[20] and "their cries were getting stronger." (The last expressed antecedent for the "their" was in v. 13: "the chief priests and the rulers and the people"; and some Koine textual witnesses remind the readers of that by an addition in v. 23: "their cries and those of the chief priests.") That pressure will lead Pilate in the next verse to pass sentence that their request for crucifixion should be carried out.

Matt 27:23b–25. With the minor exception of a different imperative form ("Let him be crucified"), Matt's phrasing of the second outcry for crucifixion is identical with Mark's; but Matt has a unique episode by way of Pilate's reaction to that second outcry. In commenting on this passage, one cannot ignore its tragic history in inflaming Christian hatred for Jews.[21] While the whole PN has been (mis)used in antiJewish ways, this text with all the people crying, "His blood on us and on our children," has had a special role. It has been treated as if it were a self-curse by which the Jewish people brought down on themselves Jesus' blood for all times (a view correctly rejected by Schelkle, "Selbstverfluchung").[22]

Let us hope that no modern exegete would read such later prejudices into Matt's mind. By reaction, however, some well-meaning interpreters would try to defuse antisemitism by making Matt's text meaninglessly bland, abstracting it from the polemics of the late 1st cent. The Christians of Matt's church had struggles with the synagogue and, as they understood it, had been persecuted by Jewish authorities. Inevitably they interpreted disasters that befell Jews as God's wrath for rejecting Jesus.[23] God's anger at the chosen

---

[20]*Phōnē megalē:* 6 uses in Luke, 6 in Acts, 4 in Mark, 2 in Matt, 1 in John.

[21]See the discussion of antiJudaism in §18F. In the bibliography of §30, Part 6, see Kampling for the history of the interpretation of "his blood" in the Western church; also Fitzmyer, Lovsky, Matera, Mora, and Sanders for some modern issues.

[22]Pfisterer ("Sein Blut") says that since the 4th. cent. it has been the *locus classicus* for establishing God's rejection of Israel. C. G. Montefiore, *The Synoptic Gospels* (2 vols.; New York: Ktav, 1947, reprint of 1927 ed.), 2.346, calls it a terrible verse whereby seemingly all the atrocities ". . . wrought upon the Jews were accepted and invoked upon their own heads by the Jews themselves. This is one of those phrases which have been responsible for oceans of human blood and a ceaseless stream of misery and desolation."

[23]For background for the above, see Mora, *Refus* 156–65; Pfisterer, "Sein Blut" 25.

people for resisting the divine plan is an established biblical category. Six hundred and fifty years before Matt wrote, the prophets interpreted the destruction of the First Temple by the Babylonians as God's punishing Israel (and Judah: Ezek 9:8–11). Christians and Jews alike interpreted the destruction of the Second Temple by the Romans the same way, differing only in why they thought God was angry. Josephus (*War* 4.6.3; #386–88) traced the fall of the city and the burning of the Temple to the brutalities of the Jewish groups against one another and their impieties; Matt traced it to Jewish involvement in Jesus' crucifixion. But one should add a corollary about this supposition of God's anger. The biblical understanding is that God's anger endures but a brief moment while God's mercy endures forever (Pss 30:6; 100:5). Thus Origen went drastically beyond the judgment Matt had passed when ca. 240 he wrote, "For this reason the blood of Jesus is not only on those who lived at the moment but on all the generations of Jews that followed till the end of time" (*In Matt.* 27:22–26, #124; GCS 38.260—unfortunately he was followed in his evaluation by some of the greatest names in Christendom.) While Paul and Matt may not have had the same outlook, Rom 9–11 shows how a NT writer could speak of God's wrath toward "His people" and still contend that God had not permanently rejected them.

Even without later distortions, Matt's hostility toward the synagogues and his attribution of the responsibility for Jesus' blood to the "us" and "our children" of "all the people" would be regarded as problematic by most today, and indeed Luke 23:34a ("Father forgive them, for they do not know what they were doing") may show that some in Matt's own time would not share his attitude. Nevertheless, our sensibilities on that score should not blind us to the dramatic power of this episode. Taken together with previous episodes about Judas' guilt over innocent blood and the tormenting dream of Pilate's wife about this just man, it raises Matt's PN to the level of supplying the most effective theater among the Synoptics, outclassed in that respect only by the Johannine masterpiece.

Understanding that Matt is dramatizing theology is very important in the exegesis of the scene. True, a number of scholars think of this episode as basically historical (Blinzler, Goppelt, Lagrange), and sometimes an appeal to history has been used to blunt Matt's message. For instance, obviously "all the [Jewish] people" could not have been present in a given locale in Jerusalem on a Friday in AD 30 or 33, and so some would apply the responsibility only to the handful who were present (see Kosmala, "His Blood" 95–96). But since it is Matt's dramatic intent to generalize the responsibility, that historical limitation is irrelevant to the meaning of the text. On the other hand, some would argue that the episode is purely drama without historical basis and that since the words were never spoken by a group of Jews, the text has no real import. This outlook ignores the point that the episode is a textually certain passage of Scripture representing an evangelist's outlook in the 80s, and that very fact gives it import for most Christians. In my comments below I shall try to be sensitive to the various facets of the scene; but in terms of historicity let me observe that I think that this episode represents a Matthean composition on the basis of a popular tradition reflecting on the theme of Jesus' innocent blood and the responsibility it created. It is of the same derivation and formation as the episodes of Judas (27:3–10) and Pilate's wife (27:19). (Indeed, I suspect that the tradition behind the story of the magi came out of the same Jewish-Christian circles.) Some of the elements that went into such tradition were quite old, and there may have been a small historical nucleus; but the detection of that nucleus with accuracy is beyond our grasp. As an example of the cautious judgment I would apply to the present episode, let me note that SPNM 256–61 has shown that the language, which is similar to that found in 27:3–10, is not foreign to Matt and is heavily colored by OT themes. SPNM, however, does not go beyond such indications of Matthean formation or rewriting to discuss older tradition. The existence of such tradition is suggested by a parallel with Acts 5:28, where the Sanhedrin authorities angrily make an accusation against the apostolic preachers: "You desire to bring upon us the blood of this man." Reflection about the responsibility created by the blood of Jesus did not originate with Matt.

The episode begins in 27:24 by describing the atmosphere created by the second cry for crucifixion in 27:23b. Pilate was now convinced that nothing he could do was of use, and that because of his resisting the crowd(s) a disturbance (*thorybos*) was taking place. In Mark and Luke a riot (*stasis*) had already taken place leading to the arrest of Barabbas; Matt never mentioned that, but he reflects the same milieu in which the Romans were alarmed by disturbances in Jerusalem (perhaps especially during a feast). Previously, the chief priests and elders had also shown themselves anxious to dispose of Jesus without a disturbance (Matt 26:5); now paradoxically they seem to have shifted tactics, for by stirring up the crowd they have created a disturbance that works against Jesus. This developing situation has convinced Pilate that he will have to accede to shouts for crucifixion; but before he does, he will attempt to free himself from the guilt of putting an innocent man to death. In what follows Pilate acts and speaks as if he has read the OT and is following Jewish legal customs. For some that proves the account is not historical; others who support historicity argue that Pilate had learned Jewish practices and was using them, even if contemptuously, to demonstrate his innocence. Such reflections about what Pilate would have known are distractions that scarcely occurred to Matt, who on the level of the storyline was presenting a scene intelligible to both Jewish and Gentile readers. (Cargal ["His blood" 101–3] reinforces the point of paying attention to narrative intelligibility.) Jewish-Christian circles, from which I think Matt drew the building blocks of material in 27:3–10,19,24–25, would have been saturated with an OT outlook, so that the implausibility of a Gentile judge having deuteronomical sensibilities would not have occurred to them. As for Gentile Christians, we have seen that Matt is not indifferent to the plausibility on a wider level of what he relates. Despite the cavils of some scholars, and the fact that the *Letter of Aristeas* (305–6) seems to think it necessary to explain that Jews wash their hands as a token that they have done no evil, there are adequate parallels for washing as protective purification in a wide range of Greco-Roman literature, as Broer ("Prozess" 106) has pointed out: Homer (*Iliad* 6.266–68), Sophocles (*Ajax* 654–55), Herodotus (*History* 1.35), and Virgil (*Aeneid* 2.718–20).

We turn to the OT background that is the key to Matt's meaning. Pss 26:6 and 73:13 illustrate washing the hands in innocence. In relation to violent death the image of washing the hands is especially appropriate because of the staining property of blood. Deut 21:1–9 presents the procedure to be followed when one does not know who committed a murder. (Frankemölle [*Jahwebund* 208–9] is particularly emphatic on Deut as the background for Matt's scene.) With the presupposition that the blood of an innocent victim creates responsibility, in the presence of the priests, the elders of the area are to wash their hands over a slain heifer and declare, "Our hands did not shed this blood" (21:7). They shall ask the Lord, "Let not (the guilt for) innocent blood be deposited in the midst of your people Israel"—notice the possibility of the guilt contaminating the whole people. Pilate's words interpret his hand-washing in the same vein as Deut 21:7, but now the blood that Matt's Pilate does not wish his hands to shed will be deposited in the midst of God's people. An intensification of this imagery is seen in *GPet* 1:1: "But none of the Jews washed his hands, neither Herod nor one of his judges. And since they did not desire to wash, Pilate stood up." This work, which is sharply more antiJewish than the canonical Gospels, indicates not only that the Jews did not wash their hands of Jesus' blood, but that they did not wish to wash their hands. Also *GPet* separates Pilate's statement claiming innocence from his washing his hands; only in 11:46 does he say, "*I* am clean of the blood of the Son of God." (There Pilate echoes the charge of "the Jews" in John 19:7: "He has made himself God's Son.") The interpretation in *GPet* has clearly developed beyond that in Matt.

In describing Pilate's action Matt uses *aponiptein,* combining *niptein* ("to wash"[24]) with the preposition *apo* ("from"). The verb is in the middle voice, so that one catches the innuendo of Pilate's attempt to wash off from himself. In his statement he uses *athōos,* employed previously in 27:4 (only two NT uses) in Judas' confession, "I sinned in having given over *innocent* blood." The Koine textual witnesses have Pilate say he is "innocent of this *just* man's blood," increasing the closeness to the message from Pilate's wife in 27:19, "Let there be nothing between you and that just man." Staats ("Pontius" 498–99) points out that Pilate washing his hands was a favorite motif in early Christian art, and that sometimes his wife appears. That appearance shows that the connection between 27:19 and 27:24 was quickly perceived and that Pilate was thought to be attempting to fulfill his wife's command, even if in 27:26 he will condemn Jesus.

The words that Pilate speaks to his audience directly in 27:24 are literally, "*You* [pronoun] will see." Some would understand this almost as a threatening promise: Ultimately those present would see that Jesus is innocent and they are guilty; and there is a precedent for this in the words Jesus speaks to the high priest in 26:64: "From now on you [no pronoun] will see the Son of Man sitting at the right of the Power." More likely, however, we are to think of the identical construction used by the chief priests and scribes in addressing Judas after he had sought to evade the responsibility for innocent blood; they said, "What is that to us? *You* [pronoun] will see." In that context it had to mean "You must see to it," and that is what it means here as well. The priests sought to throw the responsibility back upon Judas, and Pilate seeks to throw it on the crowds who have demanded crucifixion. Of course, he really cannot do that; as the supreme political authority in Judea, he has ultimately to see to it himself. Even if "all the people" will respond by taking responsibility, Pilate cannot escape some guilt. He may use the language of the judge Daniel in the Susanna story (Dan 13:46), "I am innocent of the blood of this woman,"[25] but unlike Daniel (13:64) he will not be praised for being the instrument in saving those who hope in God (13:60).

It is worth pausing for a moment to reflect on the responsibility of the various dramatis personae as sketched in these closely related Matthean episodes about Judas and Pilate. (Caution: This discussion pertains to the responsibility implied in the storyline of these popular narratives, not to historical responsibility, which was discussed in §18D–E.) Judas acquired

---

[24]This verb is used in *GPet;* in the LXX it is frequent for ritual purity.

[25]Other parallels to the Daniel story of Susanna are pointed out by van Tilborg, *Jewish Leaders* 91: the condemnation of the sin of "judging unjust judgments and condemning [*katakrinein*] the innocent and freeing the guilty, although the Lord says, 'The innocent and the just [*dikaios*] you shall not put to death.'" (13:53). However, "Thus was innocent blood saved on that day" (13:62) constitutes a contrast between the fates of Susanna and Jesus.

responsibility for shedding innocent blood by making it possible for Jesus' adversaries to seize him. Despite his gesture with the money, he could not escape guilt for having set in motion a destructive process that could not be reversed. God's punishment for that guilt was evidenced in Judas' suicide. Although the chief priests by rejecting the money tried to escape Judas' transfer of responsibility to them, they were in fact most responsible for innocent blood because of the death sentence they had just passed on Jesus, after having sought false testimony against him (26:59,66). Jesus had warned that divine judgment would come upon them, for they would see the Son of Man (26:64). As for Pilate's attempt to avoid responsibility while passing a sentence on an innocent man, the washing ritual of Deut 21 is efficacious only if the elders who performed it had no share in the murder either by doing it themselves or knowing who did. Pilate's responsibility may not have been the principal responsibility, but he cannot wash himself clean any more than Lady Macbeth can wash out the "damned spot." Matt does not stop to tell us, as he did for Judas, how God's judgment came upon Pilate. If one had to choose, however, among the legends of different fates that befell Pilate (§31, B2 above) one can be sure that the man haunted in life and death would have been closer to Matt's instinct for Grand Guignol than the portrait of Pilate confessor and saint.

But let us turn to 27:25, where Matt attributes great responsibility to "all the people," the only ones in the story who are willing to accept it. There has been a debate among scholars about the relationship of "all the people" to the crowd(s) Matt has previously mentioned, e.g., Mora (*Refus* 38) maintains they are never synonymous. However, they can scarcely be divorced. Since the crowd was first mentioned in the trial (27:15), Pilate has regularly addressed his questions to those who constituted it, and they have responded (27:17,20–21; 27:22; 27:23). We were told in 27:24 that he washed off his hands before the crowd, and addressed them with a "you" plural. Simply for the sake of the storyline "all the people" has to have the crowd(s) as a constituent. Nevertheless, "all the people" is a more collective term with several plausible implications. The chief priests and the elders were last mentioned in 27:20 as persuading the crowds; since the demand for crucifixion embodies their persuasion that Jesus should be destroyed, surely Matt would include them in "all the people" who accept responsibility for Jesus' death. Matt's attitude toward the responsibility of such authorities can be guessed from the harsh words Jesus speaks in 23:29–35 to the scribes and Pharisees who will kill, *crucify*, and *scourge* the prophets, the wise men, and the scribes whom Jesus will send: "in order that there may come on you all the just blood shed on earth from the blood of the just Abel to the blood of Zechariah." But Matt has a reason for speaking of "all the people" rather than of the crowds and the chief priests. In Lev 24:10–16 we are told that a blasphemer is to be put to death by "the whole community"; see also Num 35:12. The Sanhedrin authorities condemned Jesus to death for blasphemy; the crowds have allowed themselves to be persuaded by those authorities to become the chief instrument in moving Pilate to give Jesus over to crucifixion. The whole community has therefore participated in the blasphemy judgment, and from Matt's view that makes "all the people" responsible for innocent blood.

The final and most important reason for Matt's use of "all the people" lies in the OT usage of "the people" for Israel, God's people. In Deut 27:14–26, where levites address a series of curses to the whole of Israel, there is a set pattern in which "all the people" answer (see also Josh 24:16). Fitzmyer ("Anti-Semitism" 699) points out that in most instances *laos* in Matt means the Jewish people ethnically; and one of the first Matthean formula citations of the OT contained God's word through the prophet (Micah) describing Jesus as "a ruler who would govern my people Israel." Other OT passages were employed by Matt with a judgmental tone, e.g., Matt 13:14–15 in reference to a people that never understands God's word, and 15:8–9 in reference to a people far in heart from God. With hindsight from the post-70 period, Matt sees those in Jerusalem who cry for Jesus' death as representative of the whole Jewish people who suffered God's punishment in the Roman suppression of the Jewish Revolt. Compare Acts 2:36, where Peter speaks to Jerusalemites as representative of "the whole house of Israel" and accuses them of having crucified the Lord and Messiah.[26]

Let us look now at the phrase "His blood on us and on our children."[27] One should note that there is no verb in the Matthean formula. It is not wrong to supply a verb as many translations do ("come" or "be"); but that creates the danger of misreading the phrase as a self-curse, a prophecy, or a bloodthirsty wish. Primarily it is a formula of Israelite holy law dealing with responsibility for death. Sometimes the ensuing punishment is specified, sometimes it is left in God's hands. Behind it lies a deep sense that the extermination of life or the shedding of blood is such an infringement on God's authority over life and death that it must be accounted for. Lev 20:9,11 describes crimes that should be punished by execution. For example, if someone curses his parents or commits adultery with his father's wife, "his blood

---

[26]Notice how Acts 5:28 translates this when the high priest speaks to the apostles before the assembled Sanhedrin, "You have filled Jerusalem with your teaching, and you wish to bring on us the blood of this man [Jesus]."

[27]While I shall concentrate on the biblical usage, the phrase is attested throughout the Near East (Mora, *Refus* 30; also Rabinowitz, "Demotic"). For varieties in the biblical usage, see Koch, "Spruch."

on him," i.e., by his action he had made himself responsible for his own blood being shed in punishment (also Ezek 18:13). An equivalent expression is found in II Sam 1:16 in reference to the execution of the Amalekite who dispatched the wounded King Saul: Even though the king requested mercy killing, the Amalekite should not have laid hands on God's anointed: "Your blood is on your head." In 26:15 Jeremiah warns the princes and "all the people": "If you put me to death, you are bringing innocent blood on your-selves, on this city . . . ," i.e., they will be held responsible and (implicitly) God will punish them. The destruction of Jerusalem by the Babylonians or Chaldeans causes Zion to say, "My blood on the inhabitants of Chaldea" (Jer 51:35). Thus, with a variety of prepositions (*bĕ, 'el, 'al*) there is a set phrase, "blood on (someone)" or "blood on (someone's) head," indicating who is responsible for death in the eyes of God.

A lucid distinction is made in Josh 2:19, where Rahab is told that she can protect her family during the Israelite conquest of Jericho by keeping them indoors: "If anyone goes out of the door of your house, his blood on his head; and we shall be guiltless"; but if someone inside the house is injured or killed, "his blood on our head" (also Num 35:27; TalBab *Yoma* 21a). In II Sam 3:28–29 and I Kings 2:33 we see the problem caused when Joab, David's general, kills Abner without David's knowledge or consent. David exclaims that he and his kingdom are without guilt for the blood of Abner: "Let it fall on the head of Joab and on all the house of his father." That comes to pass when Solomon has Joab executed. Mishna *Sanhedrin* 4:5 judges that in capital cases the blood of the wrongfully condemned, as well as that of the children he would have had if he lived, is on the false witness whose testimony condemned him. It should be noted that here and elsewhere the responsibility affects a whole household including descendants. Although Jer 31:29–30 and Ezek 18:1–4 reacted against the children being punished for the sins of their fathers, the biblical notion of solidarity remained strong, holding that the descendants are affected by what the ancestor does. For "us and our children," see Gen 31:16; Exod 17:3; and the variant in II Kings 9:26.

This background makes Matt 27:25 clear. Pilate is going to condemn to crucifixion a man whom he considers just or innocent (as his wife had re-ported from a dream revelation), and he washes his hands to demonstrate his unwillingness to bear the responsibility for shedding this man's blood. He says to the crowd(s) persuaded by the chief priests to destroy Jesus "You must see to it," i.e., take the responsibility. By the expression "His blood on us and on our children," the crowds speaking (in Matt's view) for all the people accept the responsibility. They are not being bloodthirsty or callous; for they are persuaded that Jesus is a blasphemer, as the Sanhedrin judged him. But in Matt's outlook ironically they are the ones who finally have accepted responsibility whereas all others have attempted to avoid it. Jesus is innocent; for Matt that means that God has visited or will visit his blood on all involved, and that most surely includes "all the people" who accepted the responsibility.

How far does the "us and our children" extend? In at least three of fourteen Matthean uses, *tekna* ("children") has the broad sense of descendants; and here it includes those who underwent the destruction of Jerusalem and the Temple, that period that Matt 24:21 calls the "great tribulation, such as has not been seen since the beginning of the world until now." (See exactly the same situation in Luke 23:28, where Jesus on the way to be crucified urges the Daughters of Jerusalem not to weep for him, but because of the terrible things to come, "For yourselves weep, and *for your children.*") In an early Christian development beyond Matt, we read in *Test. Levi* 16:3–4: "You give the name 'Deceiver' to a man who in the power of the Most High renews the Law; and finally you will kill him, as you suppose, not knowing that he would be raised up. Thus in wickedness you take innocent blood on your heads; and because of him your holy place will be desolate, razed to the ground." Like Dahl, we can see an etiological element in the Matthean story, designed to explain why the destruction of Jerusalem did not occur until some forty years after Jesus' death. Frankemölle (*Jahwebund* 210) would extend the etiological element in Matt 27:24–25 so that this punishment constitutes the rejection of the former Israel in favor of the new people of God constituted by the Christian believers, in harmony with the replacement motif in 21:28–32,33–41; 22:1–10. That is why Jesus' directive not to go into the paths of the Gentile nations but to the lost sheep of the house of Israel (10:5–6) has been changed by the time the Gospel ends (28:19) into "Going, make disciples of all nations." (With a somewhat different sense Eph 2:13 will tell the Gentiles who once were far off that they have "become near by the blood of Christ.") But is this an everlasting rejection, and would Matt extend the responsibility and the punishment beyond his own time to the indefinite future? SPNM 260 is inclined to think so, even if it makes the point firmly that Matt did not intend to curse the Jews, or to provide fuel for antisemitism, or to suggest that each generation would pay with blood (see also Sanders, "Blut" 170). Yet for Matt as for the rest of the Bible, where punishment is attributed to God, there must always be God's sovereignty to forgive and to break the chain of responsibility seen as guilt (Reventlow, "Sein Blut" 327). And after all there is in Matt 26:28 another significance given to the blood of Jesus: "This is my blood of the covenant which is poured out on behalf of many [= all] for the forgiveness of sins" (see Cargal, "His blood" 109–10).

JOHN'S PILATE SPEAKS TO JESUS; SECOND OUTCRY FOR CRUCIFIXION
(JOHN 19:9–15)

In this Gospel the second outcry ("yelled out") for crucifixion does not occur until 19:15a. Instead of describing at length Pilate's reaction to that cry (as does Matt), John dramatizes what builds up to it. As we saw above, in 19:5–7 Pilate sought to release Jesus after scourging him, only to be met with insistence of "the Jews" that according to their law Jesus must die because he made himself God's Son. Now, more afraid in the presence of the divine, Pilate returns inside the praetorium to see what can be done with Jesus. In the Johannine outline (p. 758 above), 19:9–11 constitutes Episode 6, a second interrogation of Jesus by Pilate, comparable chiastically to Episode 2, the first interrogation. These are the two episodes in the Roman trial where Johannine elaboration in the dialogue pattern is the most obvious and probably the most extensive.

In v. 9 Pilate begins by asking, "From where are you?" Haenchen (*John* 2.182) and others go to Philostratus' *Life of Apollonius* of Tyana (4.44) to explain this question, for there the judge inquires about Apollonius' identity as a divine being.[28] Perhaps more simply we may recall Jesus' statement to Pilate in 18:36–37: "My kingdom is not of this world . . . I have come into the world." Boismard ("Royauté" 39) insists that in the Near East the question "Where are you from?" is one of identity since people are known by where they are from (e.g., Jesus *of Nazareth*); see the questions about origin asked of Jonah in Jon 1:8. Working with that idea, we recall that in the first interrogation of Jesus, Pilate asked about Jesus' identity in terms of the question handed down in the tradition, "Are you the King of the Jews?" In the second interrogation with "From where are you?" Pilate would be asking about Jesus' identity as "God's Son," the title that, as Pilate has just learned, constitutes the real charge against Jesus. Pilate has grown during the trial: The identity of Jesus is a more profound issue than what Jesus has done (18:35).

As a further indication of parallelism between the two interrogations, we note that in Mark 15:5 and Matt 27:14 Jesus refused to answer Pilate's attempt to probe deeper after the question about the King of the Jews. John has kept that refusal until the second interrogation, as Pilate probes deeper into the charge that Jesus is God's Son. Through all the references in both Jewish and Roman trials I have been very cautious about appealing to the silence of the Suffering Servant in Isa 53:7; that is secondary at most, for in

---

[28]See n. 19 above. Yet, while the Johannine Pilate is a Roman official, there is no emphasis given to his pagan religious background. Like the other partners in the Johannine dialogues with Jesus, he is "of the earth" and "from below," rather than pagan.

each instance Jesus' refusal is intimately related to the context in the storyline. In Mark/Matt the silence before Pilate showed Jesus' contempt for
the many accusations that were hurled against him by the authorities. (A
similar contempt for Herod was signaled by the refusal to answer him in
Luke's transferal of this motif to the interrogation by Herod: 23:9.) In John,
however, the refusal to answer may be a recognition that Pilate, who could
not understand when Jesus explained about his being a king, will never understand his origins from above.[29]

In 19:10 Pilate, who understands that by not answering Jesus is somehow
looking down on him, presses on with a question that exhibits the extent to
which he thinks "from below." (In the first interrogation Jesus spoke to Pilate
about a kingdom not of this world; now he will have to speak to Pilate about
a power from above.) The Roman governor bluffs to cover his fear, "Do you
not know that I have power [*exousia*] to release you and power to crucify
you?" The *imperium* (Latin equivalent of *exousia*) given to Pilate by Caesar
enables him to impose the death penalty even on a man who would make
himself God's Son![30] Scholars have been intrigued by Jesus' answer in
19:11: "You have no power over me at all except what was given to you from
above."[31] Hill ("My Kingdom" 59) wonders whether *exousia* has the same
meaning in the two vv. 10 and 11. Or does Pilate claim the *right* to do something, and Jesus allow him only the *ability*? Although some would have John
making a point here about the origins or limitations of civil authority (see
Rom 13:1), the Johannine Jesus is scarcely interested in abstract discussions
of power.[32] The issue is Pilate's claim to have power over Jesus' life—a

---

[29]Most of the Johannine Jesus' dialogue partners misunderstand him; and to Nicodemus Jesus
said, "If you do not believe when I tell you about earthly things, how are you going to believe when
I tell you about heavenly things?" (3:12).

[30]If in John, Pilate thinks he has *exousia* over Jesus, in *GPet* 3:6, the Jewish people say, "Let us
drag along the Son of God now that we have *power* over him."

[31]"From above" means "from God"; cf. John 3:31 with 3:34. Quite implausible is the thesis of
Eager ("Greater") that "from above" refers to the Sanhedrin which, as a higher court, gave to Pilate
jurisdiction over Jesus. John has not mentioned any Sanhedrin on the night when Jesus was arrested
and given over to Pilate.

[32]The issue of the power of the state, whether it was from above, and how it compared to the
power of Jesus often underlay discussions of John 19:11 at the height of Nazi power in Germany.
That implicit context gives a tone to the treatments of Flügel (1940) and von Jüchen (1941). E.
Hirsch (see Lührmann, "Staat" 367-68) interpreted John to mean that God gave to the state power
over the Jews, but the Jews perverted this power against Jesus. Bultmann (*John* 660) and Schlier
("Jesus" 71) reacted against such a potentially antisemitic interpretation by maintaining that the
political state is distinct from the kingdom-not-of-this-world. The state's power comes from God,
but it can misuse that power. When it does, however, it acts in a different way from the world
(represented here by "the Jews"), which has a personal hatred of the truth. More recently most have
abandoned this approach (so von Campenhausen, Lührmann), recognizing that for John's time the
whole discussion of the state is anachronistic. Nor do "the Jews" simply represent the world. As von
Jüchen (*Jesus* 21-27) insists, the kingdom of God is embodied in the Johannine Jesus; it is not future
or otherworldly but here already in Jesus; it is not of this world because Jesus is not of this world

claim that must be contrasted with Jesus' own claim, "I lay down my life
... no one has taken it away from me; rather I lay it down of my own accord"
(John 10:17–18). Hahn ("Prozess" 46) would have Jesus allot to Pilate no
power except that of judging; he cannot have real dominance over Jesus, who
is from above. As Thibault ("Réponse" 210) points out, any power Pilate has
over Jesus is precariously conditioned: only usable to the degree that the
accused, who has divine origin, agrees. Here Pilate's sentencing of Jesus to
crucifixion and Jesus' laying down his own life are harmonious because Pilate's role in the trial of Jesus has been given him from above, i.e., from the
Father; and Jesus is from above and one with the Father. In 11:51 we learned
that Caiaphas could have a prophetic role in Jesus' death not on his own but
because in God's plan he was high priest that fateful year. Pilate's judicial
position comes under the same rubric, all in harmony with 3:27: "No one
can take anything unless heaven gives it to him."

In 19:11b Jesus concludes this final dialogue with Pilate by once more
making it clear that because he is the light come into the world people are
judged by their reaction to him (3:12–21); he is not judged by them. Pilate
may have the power (given from above) to crucify and release; Jesus has the
power to discern sin. Even though Pilate has been placed by God in the
judicial position in this trial, he does not escape sin, for he does not choose
the truth. The greater sin,[33] however, belongs to those who have placed themselves against the truth by giving Jesus over. Those who fit that description
were named in 18:35: "Your nation and the chief priests have given you over
to me."[34] On another level (that of "above" and "below") that is always present in the Johannine dialogue, John would consider those who have given
him over as the representatives of the Prince of This World. Pilate, with all
the power he thinks he has, is a secondary figure, only the man-in-between
in a titanic battle between Jesus and the world (16:33).

Jesus' statement pushes Pilate to the finale of the Roman trial, constituting
Episode 7 in John's structure (19:12–16a, in its entirety; p. 758 above). The

---

(17:14). Jesus is in conflict with the Prince of the World; to the extent that earthly rulers are the
instruments of that Prince, Jesus' power and kingdom are in conflict with them.

[33]"Greater" presumably than the sin of Pilate. Porteous ("Note") argues that John means
"greater" than it would have been: Caiaphas who gave over Jesus to Pilate committed more than an
ordinary sin of injustice because he got his power from above (God) and was misusing that power.
This is to warn Pilate that if he misuses the power he has from God, his sin will be greater also.
However, it would be hard to apply this interpretation if the "nation and chief priests" gave Jesus
over to Pilate, for the nation was not given power from above.

[34]Some have suggested that the reference was to Judas, traditionally the one who gave Jesus over.
Yet, as Eager ("Greater") points out, Judas did not give Jesus over *to Pilate,* as Jesus' description
states. It is not clear whether that objection is avoided by Boismard ("Royauté" 35), who would
include Judas functioning as an agent of Satan (13:2,27), the Prince of this World who is behind the
giving over to Pilate.

"From this" that begins 19:12 refers partially to temporal sequence ("after this"), partially to result. The implications of the statement of Jesus about the origins of Pilate's power over him and of Pilate's sinfulness in the way he was using it makes the governor seek (*zētein*) to release Jesus.[35] John does not state when Pilate went outside again. Many scholars assume that it was not until v. 13 and so would start Episode 7 with that verse (Giblin, "John's" 223). The response in 19:12b of "the Jews" who are outside, however, assumes that Pilate's search to release Jesus has been audible.[36] The dialogue of Pilate with Jesus in 19:9–11 inside should be kept separate from the Jews' dialogue with Pilate outside (19:12–15). "The Jews" in v. 12 can respond to Pilate's seeking to release Jesus because he has gone outside and vocalized it. The new action in v. 13 is not Pilate's going outside but, as the text specifically states, his having Jesus led outside.

The hostility of the Jewish reaction to Pilate in 19:12b is underlined by the use of the verb *kraugazein* ("to yell"), used earlier in 19:6 for "Crucify, crucify." "The Jews" threaten Pilate with the consequences of releasing "this fellow"—the same contemptuous *houtos* as in 18:30 in the first episode of the trial, where "the Jews" also answered Pilate in a conditional sentence. The chiastic parallelism between the opening and the closing episodes goes beyond style. In Episode 1 John (alone among the Gospels) made clear why Jesus was brought to Pilate: The Jewish accusers could not crucify "this fellow" themselves. In Episode 7 John (alone among the Gospels) makes clear why Pilate acceded to the demand of the populace: If he did not do as they wished, they would portray him as disloyal to the emperor. They phrase this in terms of his not being a "friend of Caesar." That may mean no more than friendly to Caesar or loyally representing him; yet in later Roman usage "friend of Caesar" was an honorific title bestowed in recognition of service. If Pilate had this title,[37] "the Jews" are accusing him of not being faithful to it.

This brings us to an issue that haunts many discussions of this scene. Tacitus (*Annals* 6.8) says, "Whoever was close to Sejanus had a claim on the friendship of Caesar." In §31, B1 I raised the issue of whether Pilate was appointed by Aelius Sejanus, the all-powerful vicegerent of Tiberius (until AD 31), and whether the trial of Jesus took place before or after Sejanus'

---

[35] Luke 23:20 uses *thelein* in "wishing to release him."

[36] Haenchen (*John* 2.183) lamely assumes "that the Jews on the outside learned of Pilate's decision on the inside."

[37] Some would date the use of the title to no earlier than the reign of Vespasian (69–79); others argue for an earlier usage (BAGD 395; LFAE 378; and especially Bammel, "*Philos*"). In the early Roman empire the "friends of Augustus" were a well-known group. Coins of Herod Agrippa I (AD 37–44) bear the inscription *philokaisar*, "friend of Caesar," a designation that Philo also gives him (*In Flaccum* 6; #40).

fall. If Sejanus was Pilate's patron and Sejanus had fallen from power, Pilate would have been more vulnerable to a denunciation to the emperor, especially since Tiberius turned suspicious about the appointees of Sejanus (see Maier, "Sejanus"). (Philo [*In Flaccum* 1–4; #1–2,16,21–24] shows how a prefect of Alexandria, who was appointed by Tiberius and lived into Caligula's reign, felt insecure when his patron at Rome died and gave in to the inappropriate demands of the local citizens.) Unfortunately there are too many "ifs" to draw any conclusions from the Sejanus connection. Even without that, John's Pilate fits one part of Philo's description (*Ad Gaium* 38; #301–2): Pilate was naturally inflexible and stubbornly resisted when the Jews clamored against him for violating their customs; "The final point that particularly exasperated him was that he feared that if they actually sent an embassy [to the emperor], they would also expose the rest of his conduct as governor."[38]

To the "friend of Caesar" sarcasm, "the Jews" add: "Anyone who makes himself a king contradicts Caesar." The initial charge of the trial, "the King of the Jews," now returns and dominates the finale. The competition with Caesar[39] would be more apparent in the Near East, where the emperor was often referred to as a king. The verb *antilegein*, while it literally involves speaking against, covers a hostile attitude toward someone.

In 19:13 Pilate acts, now that he has heard the threat (*akouein* with the gen. implies listening); they have forced his hand. There is considerable debate about how to translate the action that Pilate takes once he has led Jesus out: Does *ekathisen epi bēmatos* mean that (intransitively) Pilate sat on the judgment seat (as I have translated it) or that (transitively) Pilate seated Jesus on the judgment seat? (In either translation *bēma* can have a larger meaning of "on the platform" where the judicial action was taking place). Those who favor the transitive translation picture Jesus almost as if he were enthroned, so that Pilate can mock him as a king or judge. In APPENDIX III D, I shall explain the reasons why I reject it. The issue is important, for in my judgment this is not a scene where Pilate mocks Jesus or indulges in buffoonery. Rather Pilate, who has been shuttling back and forth to see if he could avoid

---

[38]The last clause may embody exaggeration, as pointed out on p. 697 above. Yet that Pilate was afraid of being denounced to an unpredictable emperor may be historically accurate. Nonhistorical possibilities are that John created his image of Pilate's dealing with Jesus out of charges about Pilate similar to those of Philo or out of a remembrance that Pilate was removed when the Samaritans complained about him to his Roman superiors.

[39]"Caesar" was the cognomen of Julius (Gaius Julius Caesar), and the adopted name of Augustus (a great-nephew by marriage of Julius) and of Augustus' successors. When did "Caesar" shift in connotation from a proper name to a title equivalent to "emperor"? Certainly the shift came by the time of Vespasian and the Flavian emperors, who had no family relationship to Julius, but probably earlier. The prefect coinage of Judea under Augustus bore the name *kaisaros* and a date—possibly a reflection of looking on "Caesar" as the ruler's title.

crucifying a man who he knows is innocent, is now about to render judgment—a decision about God's Son that will change the whole status of those who have demanded crucifixion. John indicates the solemnity of the moment by describing Pilate taking a position on the *sella curulis* or judgment seat to make the action official. He also sets the place and time with great precision—a precision that would be meaningless were simple mockery meant.

The place where judgment was rendered seems to have come to the evangelist from his tradition, i.e., a locale remembered not because the names have theological symbolism but because something important happened there.[40] *Lithostrōtos* literally means "Stone Pavement," although Benoit ("Praetorium" 185) points out that it covers a range of pavements from marble slabs to mosaics.[41] As discussed on p. 710 above, in Jerusalem today a Roman pavement of colossal stone slabs is visible under the convent of the Sisters of Sion, near where once stood the Fortress Antonia, one of the two main sites proposed (the less likely) as having served Pilate as praetorium (§31C above). It is a favorite spot for tourist visits. Archaeology, however, has shown that this pavement dates to the century after Jesus and thus could not have been the Lithostrotos of his sentencing. *Gabbatha* is an Aramaic (not Hebrew) noun from the root *gbh* or *gbʿ*, "to be high, to protrude." Josephus (*War* 5.2.1; #51) interprets a place name involving Gabath as "hill." The designation could fit either of the two main sites proposed for the praetorium: The Fortress Antonia stood on a rocky elevation in NE Jerusalem (*War* 5.5.8; #246); the Herodian Palace stood on the uppermost part of the high west hill of the city (*War* 5.4.1; #137). Boismard ("Royauté" 39; also Ehrman, "Jesus" 130) sees a theological meaning: Jesus is being lifted up (John 12:32–33) on this elevation; but that is unlikely since John, who translates important Aramaic words ("Hebrew"; see 1:38,41), offers no translation of "Gabbatha" that would enable the audience to catch the play on its meaning.[42] Moreover, it is Pilate, not Jesus, who takes his seat on this elevated site.

The time indication for the judgment rendered by Pilate seated on the *bēma* is more plausibly theological: "It was the preparation day [*paraskeuē*] for Passover; it was the sixth hour" (19:14). The Greek noun, related to *paraskeuein*, "to prepare," probably represents Hebrew *'ereb*, Aramaic *'ărûbā'*,

---

[40]At times John seems to have a detailed knowledge of sites in Jerusalem not exhibited by the other evangelists, e.g., of Bethesda by the Sheep Pool with five porticoes (5:2).

[41]See Steele's interpretation in §31, n. 82. Esther 1:6 pictures a *lithostrōtos* of porphyry, marble, mother-of-pearl, and colored stones. In II Chron 7:3 (LXX) *lithostrōtos* describes the pavement of Solomon's Temple, and monumental pavements would not have been rare in the Greco-Roman world.

[42]Bornhäuser (*Death* 136–37) has had little following in his thesis that "Gabbatha" was the name given to the raised platform on which the seat (*bēma*) was built.

which has the connotation of "vigil, day before." But Bonsirven ("Hora" 513) is probably correct in arguing that in most instances the Greek has kept the element of preparation, so that *paraskeuē* refers not only to "the day before" but the day preparing for a next day that has an importance. A frequent use of it is as the vigil day before the Sabbath, namely, Friday; and it has this meaning in the Synoptic PNs.[43] Some scholars have tried to understand it similarly in John in order to make this Gospel harmonious with the Synoptics and not have Jesus die on the day before Passover. They render John's phrase: "It was the Friday of Passover [Week]."[44] (Inevitably this interpretation is combined with an attempt to get around John 18:28b, which indicates that the Passover meal remains to be eaten when the daytime of Jesus' trial ends.) In my judgment Zeitlin ("Date") has refuted this; the Johannine expression is the equivalent of '*ereb pesaḥ*, (St-B 2.834ff.); and unlike the Synoptics John is stressing the vigil day before Passover, and not simply the day before the Sabbath. The fact that the next day was both Sabbath and Passover makes that a great day (John 19:31).

Precisely because this Friday was the vigil day before Passover, the fact that Jesus is sentenced at the sixth hour, i.e., noon, is significant. But before we discuss that significance, let me mention the many attempts to change the time indication. Part of the uneasiness with the noon interpretation is the discord with Mark 15:25, where Jesus is crucified at the third hour (9 A.M.).[45] To avoid the conflict some minor textual witnesses of John 19:14 read the "third" rather than the "sixth" hour.[46] Grey ("Suggestion") proposes a modern emendation: "There was preparation for Passover at about the sixth hour," as if at an early hour of the morning John would have had the Jews who stood before Pilate thinking about what should happen at noon. However, the subject of the surrounding sentences is Pilate, not "the Jews." Others try to reread Mark, e.g., Mahoney ("New . . . Third") argues desperately that the third hour in Mark 15:25 refers to the time when Jesus was stripped

---

[43]Mark 15:42; Matt 27:62; Luke 23:54. See also *Didache* 8:1; *Martyrdom of Polycarp* 7:1.

[44]C. C. Torrey, JBL 50 (1931), 227–41; Story ("Bearing" 318); and E. A. Abbott, *Johannine Grammar* (London: Black, 1906), #2048, who argues for a possessive genitive ("of" = "within" Passover) over an objective genitive ("of" = "for").

[45]One of the most popular attempts to harmonize is to contend that although Mark calculates hours from 6 A.M., John reckons from midnight, so that his sixth hour is 6 A.M. and paradoxically earlier than Mark's third hour. Thus N. Walker (NovT 4 [1960], 69–73), Belser, Bornhäuser; also Westcott (*John* 282). In my judgment this has been convincingly refuted (in defense of John's reckoning from 6 A.M.) by J. E. Bruns, NTS 13 (1966–67), 285–90; and Ramsay ("Sixth").

[46]This reading is upheld by Bartina ("Ignotum") on the grounds that when letters were used for numbers, an original gamma (= 3) may have been confused with an open sigma (= old digamma, called gabex or episēmon; = 6). Jerome (*Tractatus/Brevarium* in Ps 77; CC 78.67) worked the episēmon theory in the opposite direction by maintaining that a scribe mistook Mark's original 6th hour for the 3d hour (despite the fact that in a later verse Mark will mention the 6th hour, obviously for the first time).

and scourged, not to the time of crucifixion. E. Lipinski (see NTA 4 [1959–60], #54), working with the idea that the third hour covers from 9 to 12 noon, points out that in Mark 15:21 Simon of Cyrene is coming in from the fields, an action more appropriate at the noon end of the span. But even if one argues that crucifixion at the third hour means toward noon, that is not reconcilable with John's indication that at the sixth hour or noon Jesus was still at the praetorium being judged. Instead of such attempted harmonizations, one should recognize that the time indications in both Mark and John are preserved for theological purposes (see below on Mark 15:25 for Mark's third, sixth, and ninth hours), and that as to hours we receive little historical precision from the Gospels beyond the indication that Jesus died on the cross on Friday afternoon.

What theological significance does John give to noon on this preparation day for Passover? The dialogue with the Samaritan woman as Jesus sat tired at the well was also at noon (John 4:6), and some church hymns and writers have connected the two scenes; but that is by interpreters' accommodation. Certain rabbinic references (Mishna *Pesaḥim* 1.4; 4.1,5; see Bonsirven, "Hora") point to noon on Passover Eve as the time for beginning some preparatory observances, e.g., no more leavened bread. Most commonly scholars point to noon as the hour when the priests in the Temple began slaughtering the lambs for the Passover meal to be eaten that night.[47] One may wonder whether John's readers would have understood this symbolism, but it is commonly held that leading members of the Johannine community had been ejected from the synagogue and knew Jewish customs well. Two factors favor this interpretation. First, in 7:37–39; 9:5; and 10:36 John has played upon the symbolism of the feasts of Tabernacles (water and light ceremonies) and of Dedication or Hanukkah (consecration of the Temple altar) without stopping to explain the symbolism. Second, John has several passages that seem to be related to the paschal lamb motif: 1:29,36 (Lamb of God); 19:29 (hyssop); 19:36 (no bone broken). That Jesus the Lamb of God was sentenced to death at the very hour when lambs for the Jewish Passover began to be killed would constitute a replacement theme (i.e., Jesus in place of a significant

---

[47]The issue concerns an interpretation of "between two evenings" in Exod 12:6. The strictest interpretation (Sadducees, Samaritans) is the very brief time between the sun's dropping below the horizon and darkness. That was not practical when large numbers of animals had to be sacrificed. *Jubilees* 49:12 mentions the period bordering on evening, but 49:10 allows the third part of the day, presumably from 2 P.M. to 6 P.M.; and a midafternoon beginning for sacrifice is supported by Josephus (*War* 6.9.3; #423); Philo *Questions and Answers on Exodus* 1.11; and Mishna *Pesaḥim* 5.1. But Mishna *Pesaḥim* 5.3 says that an animal slaughtered before noon is invalid; and Philo (*De specialibus legibus* 2.27; #145) reports that many myriads of animals were sacrificed beginning from midday (*mesēmbria*). The logic is that the sun begins to decline after noon, and "evening" may be said to begin then.

festal motif) quite at home in John's treatment of Jewish feasts (BGJ 1.*cxli*, *cxliv*).

At this solemn moment Pilate says, "Look [*ide*], your king." Previously (19:5), in reference to a Jesus attired in mock regalia, he had proclaimed "Behold [*idou*] the man," in an attempt to gain sympathy for Jesus. Many regard the present scene as a repetition of the earlier scene (Bultmann, *John* 665), and would interpret the thrust either as mockery or as a final, feeble attempt to dissuade "the Jews" (Schnackenburg, *John* 3.265). But there is no element of mockery (John does not report that Jesus is wearing the imitation regalia), and the scenario with "the Jews" is no longer at a point where Pilate could avoid passing sentence (he has mounted the judgment seat). Other scholars who correctly recognize that 19:14b cannot be interpreted by the tone of 19:5[48] still misinterpret the thrust. Jensen ("First" 270–71), for example, thinks Pilate has recognized the reasonableness of Jesus' claim to be king in a spiritual sense; and Blinzler (*Prozess* 350–52) takes "Look, your king" as a formula of judgment as if Pilate were saying that Jesus is guilty as charged of claiming to be "the King of the Jews." In my judgment the Johannine Pilate by mounting the *bēma* indicates that he has made up his mind; he will yield to the threats of denunciation before Caesar and will condemn Jesus. But Pilate has not forgotten that the one who claimed to be God's Son has pointed to the sinfulness of making such a decision. Therefore, very much like Pilate in Matt 27:24–25,[49] John's Pilate will maneuver to clarify who has true responsibility for this condemnation. He will draw from "the Jews" a statement of full awareness that Christians will see as a self-condemnation, a statement similar in function to that in Matt 27:25. John employs his usual dialogue technique of statement, response, and further probing to accomplish his goal in this final episode of the Roman trial.

The import of 19:14b, "Look, your king," is to make explicit that they are asking a Roman to destroy one who is their king. The response in 19:15 is the harsh yell (*kraugazein*),[50] "Take, take [*airein*], crucify him."[51] John is drawing deliberate parallels to 19:6, where there was also a yell with a doubled verb to crucify. That was in response to Pilate's request for pity; this is an even stronger response to his indication of what is really at issue. In dialogue style Pilate spells out the responsibility: Do "the Jews" want their own king crucified? And this question leads into the line with which John

---

[48]Charbonneau ("Qu'as-tu" 325) is correct: "Look, your king" is a more advanced proclamation than "Behold the man."

[49]*GPet* 11:46 draws a connection between the episode in Matt and the episode in John by combining Matt 27:24 and John 19:7: "I am clean of the blood of the Son of God."

[50]In place of "they yelled out" (or in addition to it) various textual witnesses in the Koine tradition have a verb of saying; and some scholars consider original that less dramatic description.

[51]Luke 23:18 also employs this verb *airein* in the outcry "Take this fellow."

culminates Jesus' relationship to "his own people who did not accept him" (1:11). The affirmation "We have no king but Caesar," vocalized by the chief priests as spokesmen for "the Jews," may not be as dramatic or as historically harmful as "His blood on us and on our children"; but theologically it is even more devastating. J. W. Doeve (*Vox Theologica* 30 [1961], 69–83) argues that this answer could have fitted in with the attitude of some Jews who were tired of nationalistic movements and uprisings and who preferred Roman rule to internecine struggles. John's statement, however, does not primarily concern a political situation, but is echoing a theme that runs through many centuries of Israelite self-consciousness. In Isa 26:13 we find, "O Lord our God, other lords besides you have ruled over us; but your name alone we acknowledge." The Eleventh Benediction of the *Shemoneh Esreh* prays, "May you rule over us, you alone." A Passover hymn of somewhat later Judaism (*Nišmat kol ḥay*) states, "Besides You, we have no king." Actually in the Jewish writings it is not clear that God's kingship over the world would necessarily exclude earthly dominance by a Caesar; but in Johannine polemic "We have no king but Caesar" is meant to suggest a denial of the kingship of God in Jesus. In the implications of Johannine irony both Pilate and the chief priests have spoken the truth. As understood according to 18:36–39 Jesus is truly "the King of the Jews"; by rejecting him the chief priests have given up their hope for the Messiah king to be sent by God and have settled for Roman civil kingship. In Matt 27:24–25 the acceptance by all the people of the responsibility for Jesus' death is related to God's taking away the kingdom from them (21:43). There is a similar result in John's thought: By their own choice and words "the Jews" have become like other nations, subject to Rome; they are no longer God's special people. Mishna *Roš Haššana* 1.2 portrays Passover as one of the times when the world is judged. Whether or not that tradition was known in John's time, at noon on this day before the Passover meal John portrays "the Jews" judging themselves by forcing Pilate to condemn the one whom God has sent into the world. If they have maneuvered Pilate to accomplish their will, he has also maneuvered them to take some of the responsibility for the "greater sin" (19:11).

JESUS GIVEN OVER TO (FLOGGING AND) CRUCIFIXION (MARK 15:15; MATT 27:26; LUKE 23:24–25; JOHN 19:16A + 19:1)

All four Gospels in a single sentence describe the decision that terminates the Roman trial, a decision that follows closely upon the second cry for crucifixion. John has the shortest sentence because, unlike the Synoptics, he does not mention the release of Barabbas. This Gospel brevity in describing

Pilate's decision has the psychological impact of portraying a man making a decision under pressure.

In the brief description only Mark includes a clause explaining Pilate's decision. That is understandable because the other three Gospels previously had episodes absent from Mark that probed Pilate's psychology. (*Matt:* Pilate's washing his hands plus the acceptance of responsibility by all the people; *Luke:* the interrogation by Herod and its aftermath as Pilate draws upon Herod's decision; *John:* the scene with Pilate on the *bēma*.) Mark's explanatory clause is "desiring to satisfy the crowd." The governing verb is *boulesthai,* a verb that conveys a strong desire (see John 18:39). The Greek *to hikanon poiēsai* ("to do enough"), while found in writers like Appian and Polybius, is a Latinism equivalent to *satisfacere* ("to satisfy"; BAGD 374). Mark will use another Latinism, *phragelloun* (*flagellare,* "to flog"), in this same verse, and so this is probably a deliberate imitation of Latin style to supply atmosphere for the Roman governor's legal decision. Some scholars would argue that since only one prisoner could be released by the paschal privilege, Pilate had to condemn Jesus, whom he had acknowledged as guilty by twice calling him "the King of the Jews" (15:9,12); but Mark insists that the reason for Pilate's decision was to satisfy the crowd[52] who had asked both for the release of Barabbas and the crucifixion of Jesus. The close relation of the two clauses in Mark 15:15 and the presence of a Latinism in each militate against the view of Matera (*Kingship* 20) and others who assign v. 15a to the preMarcan source and v. 15b to Mark. On the other hand one can challenge the view of Dormeyer, followed by Pesch (*Markus* 2.467), that this verse could have come from the court record of the trial; it is too imprecise legally for that.

Although the three Synoptics agree in placing Pilate's release of Barabbas alongside Pilate's giving over of Jesus, Luke 23:25 increases the contrast by repeating here Barabbas' full identity: "one who had been thrown into prison for riot and murder"—information given previously in 23:19 (see also Acts 3:14–18). Luke is simply making explicit the contrast that Mark/Matt imply: a criminal released and an innocent man given over. The concise style in Matt 27:26 has a sardonic effect: His initial "Then" calls attention to a conclusion, and the two figures are set chiastically ("He released to them Barabbas, but Jesus . . . he gave over").

We are never told the specific Roman crime for which Pilate gave over Jesus to crucifixion (whether or not he believed Jesus was guilty). Most scholars suspect that Jesus could have been seen as offending against the *Lex Iulia de maiestate.* I discussed this law above (p. 717) but warned that

---

[52]The responsibility of the populace is affirmed also by Matt 27:25; Luke 23:23; John 19:12.

in maintaining order in a province like Judea the prefect scarcely consulted lawbooks. Indeed, as pointed out in §31, n. 94 above, the judicial procedure for dealing with a serious crime by one who was not a Roman citizen in a province like Judea at this period may have been *extra ordinem* and thus not written out in the lawbooks. Even much later Ulpian (DJ 48.19.13) says: "Nowadays [a judge] who is hearing a criminal case *extra ordinem* may lawfully pass the sentence he wishes, provided that he does not exceed what is reasonable in either direction." Were there any threat that Pilate would be denounced to the Emperor Tiberius if he released Jesus (so John), he could scarcely be reprimanded if he went in the other direction of applying too severely the *lex de maiestate,* since Tiberius himself did that (Tacitus, *Annals* 3.38; 4.6.2; Suetonius, *Tiberius* 58).

Let us turn now to three items that need detailed examination: the flogging, the condemnation, and the issue of those to whom Jesus was given.

The Flogging. Only Mark/Matt mention that Jesus was flogged at the end of his trial. Somewhat awkwardly, Mark 15:15 places Pilate's having Jesus flogged between "he gave over Jesus" and "in order that he be crucified." Matt makes the flow smoother by putting "having had Jesus flogged" before "he gave (him) over in order that he be crucified." Each evangelist is wrestling with the understanding that flogging was part of the sentence of crucifixion. Although no details of this flogging are given, it has influenced popular piety and artistic imagination. Normally the delinquent was stripped, and bound to a low post or pillar or thrown to the ground. Occasionally the flogging took place as he carried the cross beam to the place of execution.[53] Rods were used on freeman; sticks on military personnel; and scourges on others. These scourges were generally leather thongs fitted with pieces of bone or lead or with spikes.[54] Sherwin-White (*Roman* 27), following DJ (see 40.19.7), offers a distinction in Roman uses of the whip: *fustigatio* (beating), *flagellatio* (flogging), and *verberatio* (scourging), in ascending gradation. That information is probably of little use in interpreting the NT. Even if this tripartite distinction were already in effect in Jesus' time, we can well doubt that either the evangelists or their readers had such precise knowledge. Walaskay ("Trial" 90) argues that not even Roman writers distinguish sharply between *flagellatio* and *verberatio.*

Less technical distinctions among these chastisements probably could be made by popular writers simply from knowing what happened to accused prisoners in the Roman world. We may distinguish the following: (a) a chas-

[53]Dionysius of Halicarnassus (*Roman Antiquities* 7.69) describes how those who trailed a slave to his place of punishment tore his naked body with whips.

[54]For detailed information on the whole procedure, see Blinzler, "Trial" 222–35, and (with pictures) Leclercq, "Flagellation."

tisement that would constitute a punishment for lesser crimes (*crimen leve*) and serve as a pedagogical warning not to cause further trouble; (b) a chastisement bordering on inquisitional torture to extract information from the prisoner or to get him to confess; (c) a chastisement that was part of the crucifixion punishment, adding to the condemned's suffering and enabling the executioners to control how long he would survive (the heavier the whipping, the shorter the survival). One can debate whether deaths caused by this last type were themselves decreed punishments (whipping as a death penalty) or were the unintended results of brutality (as in Philo, *In Flaccum* 10; #75). Of these chastisements type (a) is probably illustrated by Luke 23:16 where Pilate offers to chastise (*paideuein*) Jesus, presumably with whips, before he releases him.[55] (The Lucan Jesus never is whipped, although he predicted his own scourging [*mastigoun*] in 18:33.) Harder to classify is the scourging of Jesus in John 19:1; Pilate's motive seems to be to make Jesus look wretched so that "the Jews" will be satisfied and accept his release. Type (b) is represented in Josephus' description of Jesus son of Ananias before the procurator Albinus in the early 60s (*War* 6.5.3; #304): "Although he was lacerated to the bone with scourges [*mastix*], he neither asked for mercy nor wept." In Acts 22:24–25 a Roman tribune has Paul tied and prepares to scourge (*mastizein*) him as part of the examination, until Paul invokes his Roman citizenship. Type (c) is attested in the Mark/Matt account of Jesus being flogged by the Roman soldiers, and in the *GPet* account (3:9) of Jesus being scourged (*mastizein*) by the Jewish populace. There are other examples in Josephus: The procurator Florus in the 60s has people scourged (*mastix*) and then crucified, causing a comment on his cruelty toward even Jews of the highest rank.[56] The variety of terms used above for functionally the same type of chastisement shows that the vocabulary is not set precisely; indeed, although in Mark 10:34; Matt 20:19 Jesus predicts that the Gentiles will scourge (*mastigoun*) him, they actually flog (*phragelloun*) him.

In terms of historicity no harmonization of a scourging in mid-trial (John) followed by a flogging at the end (Mark/Matt) should be attempted (pace Bruce, "Trial"), even if a double whipping would explain why Jesus died so quickly. Despite Luke's omission of all chastisement of Jesus (perhaps from a delicate preference not to have Jesus undergo such physical violence), the tradition contained reference to one whipping of Jesus that Mark/Matt and John used in different ways. In John's highly theological arrangement of the Roman trial in seven episodes (p. 758 above) the scourging is part of the

[55]For examples of this form of chastisement in Lycia and in Egypt, see pp. 793, 816 above.

[56]*War* 2.14.9; #306, 308; also 5.11.1; #449; 7.6.4; #200, 202; Seneca, *De consolatione ad Marciam* 20.3; Livy, *History* 33.36.3. The Jewish revolutionary Simon bar Giora was flailed (*aikizein*) as he was led through the Forum in Rome to execution.

middle episode; the Mark/Matt localization is historically more probable, as the examples of type (c) cited in n. 56 indicate. The sequence in John 19:1,5 implies that the scourging was done inside the praetorium; the sequence in Mark 15:15–16; Matt 27:26–27 implies that the flogging was done outside the praetorium, perhaps in Pilate's presence, before the *bēma* (Matt 27:19). The latter is where scourgings take place in Josephus' account of the crucifixions carried out in Jerusalem thirty-five years later by the procurator Florus (*War* 2.14.9; #308).

Condemnation of Jesus. All four Gospels use *paradidonai* to describe what Pilate did to Jesus ("to give over"; p. 211 above; Isa 53:6,12), a theological term, not a juridical one. In Roman trials resulting in crucifixion a sentence would probably have been addressed to the accused: *Ibis in crucem* (Petronius, *Satyricon* 137) or *Abi in crucem,* with the force: "You shall go on the cross" or "On the cross with you." Indirect descriptions in Latin often use *iussit* ("he ordered") governing the leading away (*duci*) or affixing (*adfigi*) of the criminal to the cross (Sherwin-White, *Roman* 27). In Greek the verb governing the death penalty is often *katakrinein*,[57] and that is used of Jesus in the third passion prediction: "And they [the chief priests and the scribes] will condemn him to death" (Mark 10:33; Matt 20:18). Yet in the Pilate trial only Luke (23:24) uses a comparable description: "And Pilate made the judgment [or decision: *epikrinein*] that their demand should be put into effect." Schneider (*Lukas* 2.479) would not give *epikrinein* the force of *krisis* ("judgment"); but in 24:20 Luke evaluates the action against Jesus thus: "Our chief priests and rulers gave him over to a judgment [*krima*] of death." Fitzmyer (*Luke* 2.1492) says *epikrinein* "could have the technical nuance of issuing an official sentence." MM 240 reports that in the papyri the verb is a common term for the decisive examination for military service, and *epikrima* is an edict. In II Macc 4:47 *epikrinein* is used to render a formal royal condemnation to death (as opposed to a release, even as in Luke 23:24–25). Thus Luke does mean to describe a formal judgment here, just as at the beginning of the trial he added a set of charges. He is fleshing out the tradition taken from Mark in order to make it conform to the familiar pattern of Roman trials.[58]

Many scholars deem it very important that the other three Gospels do not use a verb like *katakrinein* or *epikrinein* in describing a sentence by Pilate. Some have thought that the absence means that for those evangelists this is

[57]Josephus, *Ant.* 10.7.6; #124; John 8:10–11; Rom 8:3.

[58]This is contrary to the view of Walaskay ("Trial" 91) and Hendrickx (*Passion* 88) that Luke did not consider the appearance before Pilate to be a complete or regular Roman trial (e.g., Luke does not mention a scourging in the sentence). Neyrey (*Passion* 81) is correct: Luke, "more so than the Marcan source, presents a formal trial scene."

really not a trial[59] but a lesser procedure like *coercitio,* an exercise of the power to punish. That is surely a wrong evaluation of the intent of Matt and John since they have Pilate seated on the *bēma,* a position assumed in an official trial. Nor do I think it true of Mark, since I have rejected the thesis that the Sanhedrin passed sentence and Pilate is just carrying it out (see Gnilka, *Markus* 2.303). These are popular accounts, not legal records. Their theological language of "giving over" assumes a sentence. The "in order that he be crucified" is tantamount to "You will go to the cross." One can cite a whole series of examples of trials with condemnatory sentences that use a variety of verbs but not the technical one. For instance, Josephus (*War* 6.5.3; #305) reports in reference to Jesus son of Ananias: "Albinus pronounced against [*kataginōskein*] him as a maniac and released him [*apolyein* as in the Gospels]." The *Testimonium Flavianum* (*Ant.* 18.3.3; #64; p. 373 above) says that Pilate punished/condemned (*epitiman*) Jesus to the cross. Tacitus (*Annals* 15.44.4) says that Jesus was executed ("had capital punishment inflicted on him": *supplicio adfectus erat*) by Pontius Pilate.[60]

Since I think there is an implicit death sentence in Mark/Matt and John (explicit in Luke), I do not agree with those scholars who, finding no sentence, assume that the absence of it has the purpose of exculpating the Romans and inculpating the Jews for the crucifixion of Jesus. Winter (*On the Trial* 79) thinks that the evangelists found it difficult to state plainly that the sentence of death was pronounced by the Romans.[61] In response to such a thesis, I judge it lucidly clear that all the evangelists would identify those who plainly wanted Jesus dead as the chief priests and the Jewish populace who stood with them. But there is really no exculpation of the Romans. All Gospels use *paradidonai* of Pilate, and so he joins the chain of those described by this verb: Judas gave Jesus over to the Jewish authorities; the Jewish authorities gave Jesus over to Pilate; now Pilate gives Jesus over to be crucified. That chain scarcely delivers Pilate from participation. For Matt, by washing his hands Pilate can no more get rid of responsibility for innocent blood than Judas could get rid of it by returning the coins. For John, the chief priests and the nation have the greater sin, but that still means Pilate has the lesser sin. For Luke and John, the Pilate who has three times said Jesus is not guilty cannot be considered blameless

---

[59]Millar ("Reflections" 378): "Since no Gospel represents Pilate's decision as a formal verdict, there is a very clear sense in which the entire notion of 'the trial of Jesus' is a modern construct."

[60]Besides the vocabulary issue, the fact that Jews and pagans knew that Pilate had passed a judgment against Jesus makes quite implausible the thesis that Christian preachers, as represented in the Gospels, were avoiding saying that.

[61]Also "Marginal" 241–42. He adds the evidence from Justin (*Dialogue* 16.4; 133.6), who accuses Jews of having killed the Just One or Christ, and Melito of Sardis (*On the Pasch* 74; 79; 92;

when he proceeds to give Jesus over to crucifixion. Indeed, in the overall Lucan picture Pilate may be contrasted to the noble Roman officials in Acts who refuse to find Christians guilty.

Leaving aside exaggerated interpretations of what the Gospels do not say, we should appreciate the impact of what they do say. The flogging of Jesus described by Mark/Matt might well evoke in 1st-cent. readers a reaction such as that of Horace (*Satire* 1.3.119), who speaks of *horribile flagellum*. Reading that Jesus was given over in order that he be crucified would evoke horror; Origen (*In Matt.* 27:22–26, #124; GCS 38:259) speaks of "the most foul [*turpissima*] death of the cross." To that Jews would add the word of Deut 21:23 that God's curse rests on him who is hanged on a tree, so that Jesus was becoming a curse (Gal 3:13). Laconically the Gospels are telling us that Jesus has been sent to one of the most terrible deaths known to antiquity.

Assignment of Jesus to Whom? The Gospels are not of equal clarity about those to whom Jesus is given over:

Mark 15:15: he gave over Jesus in order that he be crucified
Matt 27:26: he gave (him) over in order that he be crucified
Luke 23:25: he gave over Jesus to their will
John 19:16a: he gave him over to them in order that he be crucified

Mark/Matt do not leave the readers in suspense as to the recipients, for in each the very next verse mentions the soldiers (Matt: of the governor) who bring Jesus into the praetorium. Thus clearly Jesus is given over to Roman soldiers who will crucify him. The problem is more complicated in Luke and John, where there is no scourging/mocking by Roman soldiers between the giving over and the crucifixion.

In John 19:16a the last-mentioned antecedent for the "to them" would be the chief priests at the end of 19:15. This is an example of careless narrative style, for in the subsequent narrative of the crucifixion (the topic of 19:16a) we read in 19:23: "So the soldiers, when they crucified Jesus." Johannine

---

96). However, Justin and Melito are exaggerating one side of the Gospel picture (Jewish responsibility); they are not denying Roman involvement. Justin (*Apology* 1.13; 2.6) says in an almost creedal phrase that Jesus was crucified under Pontius Pilate, and Melito (*On the Pasch* 92) mentions that Pilate was involved in the trial. Although one branch of later Christian legend makes Pilate more sympathetic and even penitent (§31, B2), practically never is it denied that he condemned Jesus— GPet, which has Herod sentence Jesus to death (1:2), disappeared from mainline Christian memory. The copper tablet found ca. AD 1200 at Aquila (Amiturnum), as reported by Cheever ("Legal" 507– 8), formalizes the issue: "*Sentence Rendered by Pontius Pilate That Jesus of Nazareth Shall Suffer Death on the Cross:* In the year 17 of the empire of Tiberius Caesar, and the 24th of March, the city of holy Jerusalem, Annas and Caiaphas being priests, sanctificators of the people of God, I, Pontius Pilate, governor of the praetory, condemn Jesus of Nazareth to die on the cross between two thieves." There follows a list of six justifying charges (§32, n. 17 above), four witnesses, and instructions to the centurion Quintus Cornelius to lead him to the place of execution through the city gate Struenus.

Christians knew perfectly well that Roman soldiers did the crucifying, and so the evangelist's "to them" would not be likely to be misread. One should not press grammatical antecedents as if the readers knew nothing of the passion before the Gospel was written. The total Johannine PN is clear about the involvement of Roman soldiers (in addition to 19:23, see 19:31–34). The situation here is quite different from that of *GPet* where the Jewish king Herod gives the order for Jesus to be marched off (1:2), and the people or the Jews mock Jesus, scourge and crucify him, and Roman soldiers do not appear until Pilate orders them to watch the sepulcher (8:31).

Luke 23:24–25 is more complicated. In v. 24 Pilate makes the judgment that "their demand [*aitia;* see *aitein* in v. 23] should be put into effect" and in v. 25 "he gave over Jesus to their will." (Contrast to the latter 22:42: "Not my will but yours be done"; here there is a third will.) The "their" in both vv. 24 and 25 has as its last specified antecedent "the chief priests and the rulers and the people" of 23:13. Thus the phrases in vv. 24 and 25 are Luke's clarification of Jewish responsibility, rendering equivalently Mark's "desiring to satisfy the crowd."

However, Luke seems to go beyond Mark, for in v. 26 the "they" lead Jesus off to crucifixion,[62] and one does not hear of Roman soldiers until ten verses later. Does Luke want his readers to think that "the chief priests and the rulers and the people" physically crucified Jesus? All the Gospels have Jewish participation in the death of Jesus and indeed even primary responsibility for it. But if Luke actually has Jews crucify Jesus in the sense of nailing him to the cross, he would be closer to *GPet* than to the other canonical Gospels. Those who tend to answer affirmatively point to passages like Acts 2:36 and 3:12–15 where the "House of Israel" or "men of Israel" are the "you" who crucified Jesus or killed the author of life, and 10:39 where the Jews and the Jerusalemites are the "they" who put Jesus to death by hanging him on a tree. I myself have cited such texts to show that Luke's failure to mention a death sentence at the Sanhedrin trial did not mean that he denied Jewish responsibility for the death of Jesus. But here the issue is more precise: Was the physical execution carried out by Jews or Romans? The Acts texts establish responsibility but not physical causality. More difficult is Luke 24:20: "Our chief priests and rulers gave him over to a judgment of death and crucified him." Although some scholars would argue that this means the priests did the crucifying, we should pay attention to the sequence "gave him over to a judgment [*krima*] . . . and crucified." Granted 23:1 where

---

[62]Fitzmyer (*Luke* 2.1496) argues against Caird, Marshall, and Schmid that the "they" who act here are the Jewish authorities and people.

the whole multitude of them led him to Pilate and 23:24 where Pilate made the judgment (*epikrinein*), one could argue that readers would understand: "gave him over to Pilate's judgment which led to his being crucified." Luke 18:31–33 has the same sequence of giving over and killing, and there it is clear that the Son of Man is given over to the Gentiles and that they are the ones who kill him.

In evaluating the total Lucan picture, I think it more likely that when Luke wrote in 23:25 that Pilate "gave Jesus over to their will" and in 23:26 "they led him away," he meant and his audience would have understood that Pilate acceded to Jewish wishes about Jesus, and Roman soldiers took him off to be crucified—the soldiers Luke abruptly mentions for the first time in 23:36–38. Let me list arguments that support that. (1) This is an issue of the antecedent of a pronoun. Antecedents are a problem in writing, as anyone with experience in correcting composition knows; they are even a greater problem in an oral context. In §2 I insisted that the Gospels emerged from an oral transmission of material about Jesus, that orality remained a live factor even in the writing of the Gospels, and that in the early days the written Gospels were more often heard than read. It is possible for modern scholars to look back from the "they" of Luke 23:26 thirteen verses to "the chief priests and the rulers and the people" of 23:13 and equate them; but no one sitting in a church hearing the PN read will make that connection. The audience will understand the "they" in light of what they already know about the crucifixion and will think of Roman soldiers leading Jesus out to crucify him. The antecedent thirteen verses before will not be a factor in their interpretation of what they have heard. As for the 1st-cent. audience, the general Lucan picture of Romans governing Judea, Pilate passing judgment, crucifixion as a Roman punishment, and the subsequent reference to soldiers around the cross and clearly involved in the crucifixion could plausibly move hearers to think of the Romans, not the Jews, as physically crucifying Jesus. Moreover, as I have insisted before, there is no reason to think Luke's audience was hearing of the crucifixion for the first time. Therefore the fact that the other Gospels have Roman soldiers do the deed creates the possibility that Luke's audience would have been influenced by a general Christian picture of the crucifixion scene.[63]

(2) I anticipate an objection that while orality may have had its influence on the audience, surely Luke knew what he was writing and would be aware

---

[63] I do not know how this would affect the understanding of later writing, e.g., when Tertullian (*Apology* 21.18; CC 1.126) reports that Jews extorted from Pilate a sentence giving Jesus "up to them" to be crucified. I suspect that given general Christian knowledge, it would mean to Tertullian's readers that Pilate acceded to their request but not that they nailed Jesus to the cross.

of his antecedent. Even good writers can be careless about antecedents; and we have just seen that John is careless in 19:16a about the "them," for although the grammatical antecedent should be the "chief priests," the sequence shows that the Roman soldiers are meant. I do not think that Luke the writer escaped the influence of orality, and here we have a particular reason why he may not have noticed the grammatical import of his own pronoun. In following Mark, Luke is at this juncture omitting the flogging of Jesus in Mark 15:15 and the whole mockery scene in Mark 15:16–20a. Mark 15:20b, where Luke picks up the story, also has a "they" ("they lead him out in order that they might crucify him"); but there is no ambiguity in Mark because of the presence of the Roman soldiers in the preceding verses which Luke omitted. In other words, Luke may not have noticed that his omission of a Marcan passage now meant that the "they" he mentions when he picks up the Marcan narrative has lost its Marcan antecedent and now has grammatically a new Lucan antecedent from thirteen verses earlier. That Luke was unobservant in such situations can be documented by two examples. First, Luke (18:31–33) copied from Mark 10:33–34 the third passion prediction where Jesus stated that the Son of Man would be given over to the Gentiles and spat upon and scourged. By rewriting the end of the Roman trial, as I have just indicated, Luke deletes the Marcan scene where Jesus is flogged and spit upon. Therefore Luke carelessly leaves Jesus' prediction unfulfilled! Second, we have a previous example of carelessness when Luke tampers with the Marcan sequence. Mark's order was Sanhedrin trial, mockery of Jesus, Peter's denials. Luke reverses the order: Peter's denials, mockery of Jesus, Sanhedrin trial. The join between Peter's denials and the mockery of Jesus in the new Lucan order takes place in 22:61–63: Peter remembered the Lord's saying about cockcrow, and he went out and wept bitterly; and the men who were holding him were mocking him, beating him. Luke means that they mocked and beat Jesus, but he does not notice that his shift of the material means that grammatically the antecedent would appear to be Peter. Thus I would argue that Luke is influenced by his Marcan source and in his writing supposes information in that source even when he has actually failed to convey it.

(3) If elsewhere Luke has generalizing statements about the Jews killing Jesus, he also gives indications that he expected his audience to know that the Gentiles (Romans) crucified him. Not only does Acts 4:25–28 specify that Pilate and the Gentiles were arrayed against the Lord and his anointed (Christ), but Jesus himself predicted in 18:31–33 that the Son of Man would be given over to the Gentiles and they would kill him. Given all this, I think that Luke would be quite surprised to find commentators claiming that his careless "they led him away" was written to imply that the Jewish priests,

rulers, and people nailed Jesus to the cross.[64] Luke had the same view of the crucifiers as the other evangelists.

ANALYSIS

As we come to the end of the Roman trial and summarize a discussion that has been spread over four sections (§§32–35, plus §29 on Judas and §31 devoted to background), the basic components that came from preGospel tradition seem relatively clear. Jesus was "given over" to the Roman prefect by the Jewish Sanhedrin authorities, foremost among whom were the chief priests. The charge on which he was interrogated and ultimately condemned and crucified concerned a pretension to be "the King of the Jews," a title seemingly derived from that period in the 2d and 1st cent. BC when Jewish kings ruled in Judea. According to the tradition Jesus did not bother to deny this charge, keeping silence except for a vague "You say (so)." The prefect recognized that this was not the real basis for the antagonism toward Jesus on the part of the Jewish authorities, but under orchestrated pressure Pilate yielded to the will of those authorities rather than have public trouble over an issue in which he had little interest. Even before the evangelists added their own touches, the pressure on Pilate had been dramatized in a fixed way by having the crowd (containing the chief priests or instigated by them) cry out several times for crucifixion. (That this dramatization had verisimilitude we can see from the role of protesting crowds in several Pilate incidents narrated by Josephus; see §31, B3 above.) Pilate in turn was pictured as vocalizing his perception that the charge against Jesus was a sham. In one form of the tradition known to Luke and John, Pilate's unease had been stylized into three not-guilty statements. (The import of this stylization was not to exculpate Pilate, but to show the transparent falsehood of the pretense that Jesus had threatening royal ambitions.) Also the memory of a figure named Barabbas had entered the preGospel tradition of the trial. Historically he may have been someone released during a feast when the crowd gave him support, but already on the preGospel level of Christian tradition he was set side-by-side in contrast with Jesus (the guilty man released and the innocent

---

[64]Some who admit that the attempt to take the antecedent literally is weak still claim that Luke wrote ambiguously in order to bring the Jews into closer cooperation with the Romans in the crucifixion and thus to prepare the way for the statements in Acts that the men of Israel crucified Jesus. That view depends on the interpretation of the antiJudaism of Acts (see p. 390 above).

man condemned), and the procedure explained as a custom involving the release of one criminal during the feast.

Other touches in the Gospel accounts of the trial were made by the individual evangelists as they expanded some of the motifs already present in the tradition (which reached Matt and Luke through Mark). Popular reflection on the real responsibility for Jesus' death was expressed in OT terms of innocent blood being "on" someone, a guilt that from the Christian viewpoint touched all involved: Judas, the Jewish authorities, Pilate, and the people. Matt drew from that popular reflection (which probably already existed as romanticized characterizations) and wove it into the Marcan outline in tales of Judas' suicide, the stigma attached to thirty pieces of silver, a dream of Pilate's wife, and a vivid washing of the hands to escape blood guilt.

Luke added to the trial a dramatization drawn from traditions of Herodian opposition to Jesus, an opposition that appears elsewhere in the NT in various forms. In the Lucan addition Herod, an enemy of Jesus, finds him not guilty and thus becomes another witness to the fallacy of the political charge, even as in the trial of Paul in Jerusalem a Herodian king and a Roman prefect declare him not guilty (Acts 26:31–32). In this same vein of parallels to the Roman trials of Paul, Luke also made the trial of Jesus appear more formally proper by listing charges against Jesus at the beginning (charges echoing themes in the account of Jesus' ministry) and by supplying a recognizable sentence of condemnation (*epikrinein*) at the end.

John drew on a tradition similar to the one that came to Mark, but more generously endowed with geographic and temporal details that may well be historical, e.g., the praetorium as a setting for the trial, the Lithostrotos, the day before the Passover meal. More radically than any of the Synoptists, John reshaped what he received into a seven-episode drama, impressive in its theological analysis of what was happening. Pilate, shuttling back and forth between "the Jews" outside the praetorium and Jesus inside, is placed on trial before the personification of divine truth. A man-in-between who wishes to avoid a judgment for or against truth, Pilate enters into dialogues that enable John to have both Jesus and his adversaries explain what lies beneath the surface—a loquacity far beyond the "You say (so)" or the "Crucify, crucify" of the tradition. The themes of Jesus in his dialogue with Pilate inside the praetorium include the otherworldliness of his kingdom, his role as truth come into the world, the from-above character of authority, and the guilt of those who gave him over. Among the themes drawn forth from "the Jews" in their dialogue with Pilate outside the praetorium are that they were incapable of putting Jesus to death in the way he predicted (lifting up on the cross), that the real issue was not Jesus' claim to be "the King of the Jews" but his claim to be God's Son, and that in rejecting Jesus those for whom God was sovereign were now willing to acknowledge that they had no other king but Caesar. John's added dialogues, like Matt's added actions, reflect the theological controversies between Christians and Jewish synagogue leaders of the late 1st cent.—controversies seen presumably by both sides as a continuation of the opposition between Jesus and Jewish leaders (especially the chief priests) that occurred in Jerusalem in the early 1st cent. and led to his death at Roman hands.

(*Bibliography for this episode may be found in §30, with a special bibliography for Matt 27:24–25 ["His blood"] in §30, Part 6.*)

§36. THE ROMAN MOCKERY AND ABUSE OF JESUS

(Mark 15:16–20a; Matt 27:27–31a; John 19:2–3)

Translation

Mark 15:16–20a: [16]But the soldiers led him away inside the court, that is, the praetorium, and called together the whole cohort. [17]And they put purple on him; and having woven a thorny crown, they put it on him. [18]And they began to salute him, "Hail, King of the Jews." [19]And they were striking his head with a reed and spitting on him; and bending the knee, they worshiped him. [20a]When they had mocked him, they undressed him of the purple and dressed him with his own clothes.

Matt 27:27–31a: [27]Then the soldiers of the governor, taking Jesus into the praetorium, gathered together the whole cohort against him. [28]And having undressed him, they put a scarlet cloak around him; [29]and having woven a crown of thorns, they put it on his head and a reed into his right hand. And kneeling before him, they mocked him, saying, "Hail, King of the Jews." [30]And having spit at him, they took the reed and were striking at his head. [31a]And when they had mocked him, they undressed him of the cloak and dressed him with his own clothes.

John 19:2–3: [2]And the soldiers, having woven a crown of thorns, put it on his head; and they clothed him with a purple robe. [3]And they were coming up to him and saying, "Hail, O King of the Jews." And they gave him slaps.

Luke 23:11 [during the Roman trial]: But having treated him with contempt and made a mockery, Herod with his troops, having clothed him with a splendid garment, sent him back to Pilate.

23:36–37: [while Jesus was on the cross]: [36]Moreover, also the soldiers mocked, coming forward, bringing forward to him vinegary wine, [37]and saying, "If you are the King of the Jews, save yourself." (Codex Bezae, OS add: having put on him also a thorny crown.)

GPet 3:7–9: [7]And they [the people] clothed him with purple and sat him on a chair of judgment, saying, "Judge justly, King of Israel." [8]And a certain one of them, having brought a thorny crown, put it on the head of the Lord. [9]And others who were standing there were spitting in his face, and others slapped his cheeks. Others were jabbing him with a reed; and some scourged him saying, "With such honor let us honor the Son of God."

COMMENT

At the beginning of §26 on "The Jewish Abuse and Mockery of Jesus," I pointed out the strong parallels between that scene and this, especially in Mark/Matt where each scene comes immediately after Jesus has been condemned (respectively by the Jewish Sanhedrin and the Roman prefect) and where in each the words addressed mockingly to Jesus ("Prophesy," "King of the Jews") are related to a theme in the preceding trial. John also has two scenes but without so close a parallelism: In the midst of the interrogation of Jesus by the high priest, he was abused (not mocked) by an attendant (18:22–23); in the midst of the Roman trial he is abused and mocked. Luke's treatment of the two themes is the most complicated: Immediately after the denials by Peter but before the Sanhedrin session Jesus was mocked and abused by the men who held him; there is no mockery of Jesus by Romans during or immediately after the Roman trial; yet in the midst of the Roman trial (similar to John's timing) Jesus is mocked by Herod with his troops; and as Jesus hangs on the cross he will be mocked by Roman soldiers as "King of the Jews" (see n. 6 below). *GPet* seems to have combined echoes of the Jewish and Roman mockeries from the canonical Gospels: The mockery is done by the Jewish people; it is done after a trial in which Herod and Pilate are featured; the contents are much the same as the canonical Roman mockery; and the theme of seating Jesus on a chair of judgment and mocking him to judge justly seems to echo a tradition close to both Matt 27:19 and John 19:13.

With that general background, let us turn to commenting on the scene verse by verse.

THE SOLDIERS AND THE PRAETORIUM (MARK 15:16; MATT 27:27)

Both Mark's "But" and Matt's "Then" connect this verse to what has preceded: Jesus has just been given over to crucifixion, and through this verse we learn to whom, namely, the (Roman) soldiers. Matt, by subordination, improves on Mark's string of finite verbs; he also identifies the soldiers as "of the governor" and identifies Mark's "him" as Jesus. In the PN of Mark/ Matt this is the first mention of soldiers (*stratiōtēs*).[1] This is also the first of six instances of *stratiōtēs* in John (all in chap. 19); as in Mark, they are soldiers under Roman command. Luke will use *stratiōtēs* in the PN for the first time during the mockery of Jesus hanging on the cross (23:36). Previously Luke wrote of the captains of the Temple (22:4,52: *stratēgoi*) associated with the chief priests in the apprehension of Jesus, even as John 18:3,12,18,22 wrote in the same context of attendants (*hyperētēs*) of the chief priests and the Pharisees who seemed to serve as a type of police.[2] A third group of military appears in Luke 23:11: the troops (*strateuma*) of Herod.

Mark/Matt have the soldiers assemble "the whole cohort" (*speira*). Earlier in John (18:3,12) a cohort with a centurion (*chiliarchos*) came to the garden to arrest Jesus. While Mark's "the whole cohort"[3] may be simply a generalization of guilt, like "the whole Sanhedrin" of Mark 14:55 and 15:1, the presence in the Jerusalem praetorium of one of the five cohorts at Pilate's disposal is easier to imagine than their presence in a garden across the Kidron. This is the only instance of "call together" (*synkalein*) in Mark. The same verb is used in Luke 23:13 for Pilate's calling together the Jewish antagonists of Jesus (see also Acts 5:21; 10:24; 28:17).

The action in Mark has now moved[4] inside the praetorium—the first time this locale has been mentioned in the Synoptics. John has placed the whole Roman trial alternately inside the praetorium or outside in front of it; in particular the soldiers mocked Jesus *inside* as can be seen from 19:4–5. *GPet* has the mockery and scourging done by the Jewish people in a public place where they drag Jesus around and seat him on a chair of judgment. In Luke, Herod and his troops mock Jesus presumably in a building or part of Jerusalem other than where Pilate is, for Jesus has to be sent back and forth from one to the other (Luke 23:7,11). All the evangelists have used *aulē* for the

---

[1]In either Gospel the only earlier instance is the reference to the soldiers the centurion had under his control in Matt 8:9.

[2]Presumably the latter would now be with "the Jews" outside the praetorium; see John 19:6.

[3]See pp. 248, 701 above for the size of the *speira* (600 to 1,000 men) and the ethnic makeup of Roman soldiery in Judea.

[4]"Led away"; see 14:53–54; 15:1; 15:20b for verbs of motion changing the scene in the Marcan PN. To harmonize John's outside localization with Mark's "inside," Kreyenbühl ("Ort" 16) thinks of outer and inner rooms in the praetorium.

courtyard/palace of the chief priests (p. 593 above), but only Mark uses that term for the Roman site, taking care to explain it by its Greco-Latin equivalent (see similar equivalency in 12:42). Probably the scene that Mark/Matt envisage takes place in the courtyard inside the palace,[5] a place large enough to gather a whole body of troops. Matt specifies what is implicit in Mark, namely, that the gathering is hostile to Jesus.

THE ROYAL GARMENT AND CROWN OF THORNS (MARK 15:17; MATT 27:28–29A; JOHN 19:2)

Luke does not report these dramatic elements of Roman mockery.[6] Matt improves on Mark's Greek, eliminating historical presents and imaginatively extending the paraphernalia beyond robe and crown to include a reed scepter, thus anticipating the use of a reed to strike Jesus (Mark 15:19).[7] In his description John is very close to Mark and Matt (to Matt in putting on the crown; to Mark in the clothing). Either there was Johannine dependence on the Synoptics, or in this scene the vocabulary was very fixed in Christian tradition. *GPet* is close to Mark/Matt (combined with Johannine elements in the total scene); its reference to "the head of the Lord" increases the outrage. In Mark/Matt this mockery, following the flogging, has not been ordered by Pilate and is seemingly spontaneous buffoonery by the soldiers. In John scourging and mockery occur in the middle of the trial and are arranged by Pilate as a ploy to win the sympathy of "the Jews" for a Jesus thus pitiably disfigured.

As for the garment of mockery, Mark and *GPet* mention simply *porphyra*, which John expands to *himation porphyroun* "purple robe." Delbrueck ("Antiquarisches" 124–28) reports that *porphyra* was a technical name for the Macedonian-style *chlamys* or cloak, circular in form and pinned at the right shoulder. If the color is emphasized, Tyrian purple dye obtained from shellfish was expensive, and beyond the means of ordinary soldiers (Blinzler, *Prozess* 326). Therefore, it suggests royal or even imperial attire. The Seleucid king Alexander Balas extended to the Maccabee leader Jonathan the high priesthood and royal status; this involved a purple robe and a golden crown

[5]The use of *aulē* for the Roman locale may help to confirm that the tradition envisaged the Herodian Palace rather than the Fortess Antonia as the site of the praetorium, since Josephus uses *aulē* for the former but *phrourion* or *pyrgos* for the latter (see p. 707 above).

[6]Evidently copyists felt acutely the lacuna in Luke, for in Codex Bezae and the OS a clause "having put on him also a thorny crown" appears at the end of Luke 23:37 after the first Lucan mention of soldiers in 23:36—with the result that a mock coronation takes place on the cross!

[7]Because of the contrast with Mark, scribes have produced many variant readings of Matt, e.g., adding "of his clothes" to "undressed"; or changing "undressed" to "dressed"; or adding "purple clothing and" before "a scarlet cloak." See J. M. Bover, "Un caso típico de crítica textual, Mt. 27,28," SBE 15 (1954), 221–26.

(I Macc 10:20; also 10:57–62; 11:58). Josephus (*Ant.* 11.6.10; #256) has honored ministers of the Persian court wearing purple. In the magnificent funeral of King Herod the Great, his body was wrapped in purple (*Ant.* 17.8.3; #197). Yet sometimes this adjective can shade over into scarlet, e.g., to describe the prostitute in Rev 17:4; 18:16, and for Caesar's military cloak in Appian, *Bellum civile* 2.21; #150. Matt substitutes "scarlet *chlamys,*" which probably means the ordinary red military cloak, but could also refer to the scarlet *paludamentum* worn by upper Roman officials, such as the lictor (outside Rome) and even the emperor.[8] Perhaps this means that Matt's readers would have caught the note of royal mockery so clear in Mark, but also more plausibly could have thought that the garment of mockery was a cloak supplied by a soldier. The Lucan scene involving Herod describes a splendid, shining garment (perhaps white; p. 776 above); it was primarily a sign of innocence, not of mockery.

As for the crown, since the evangelists mention "thorns" (Mark, John 19:5, and *GPet* use the adjective *akanthinos;* Matt and John 19:2 use the pl. of *akantha* ["thorn plant"]), in Christian thought it became an image of pain and suffering.[9] In the Gospels, however, there is no stress on torture; and the crown is part of the royal mockery, like the robe and the scepter. Inevitably, scholars have wondered what type of thorn plant and what style crown were imagined by the evangelists. Delbrueck ("Antiquarisches"135) warns that at this time "crowns" were diadems or wreaths, not the crowns of later royalty. In part the answers given by scholars have been determined by whether mockery or torture dominated their understanding, by the practical realization that stiff thorns cannot be woven (even if the branches can be entangled), and even by an analysis of the thorns that appeared as relics of Christ in medieval times.

Let me mention some of the theories. (1) Influenced by relics, Linnaeus the 19th-cent. botanist tendentiously named a plant with long thorns and dark green, oval leaves *Ziziphus spina Christi L.* Yet F. Lundgreen (NKZ 27 [1916], 840–41) points out that while this plant's need for heat may have enabled it to survive in the Jordan valley, it would not be found in the mountainous Jerusalem area. (2) Ha-Reubéni thinks of a very common Palestinian thornbush, *Poterium spinosam L.,* the *sîrâ* of Isa 34:13 and other OT passages. It has small thorns, and entangled clumps of it could have been pushed

---

[8]In general, the *chlamys* of Matt was a smaller cloak used by travelers and soldiers, while the *himation* of John was a robe used more widely. The scarlet/purple issue may not be a significant difference. Hebrew *'argāmān* covers a range of dark reddish purple, as distinct from *tĕkēlet,* which covers the violet or cerulean purple range.

[9]Tertullian, *De corona* 14.3; CC 2.1063; Clement of Alexandria, *Paedagogus* 2.8.73–75; SC 108.144–50.

onto Jesus' head to look like a cap or helmet. That fits the fresco in the catacombs of Praetextatus (ca. 200) of a man from whose head spikes seem to go out in every direction (illustration 4141 in DACL 5, facing col. 188). If that figure is Christ, we have an idea of how early Roman Christians imagined the crown.[10] (3) Hart draws inspiration from the tetradrachma coins of Rhodes (called Judas pennies in the Middle Ages), for they show on one side a radiate head of the sun god, which was thought to be a head of Christ, and on the other side the rose of Sharon/Jericho. The divinity of a ruler could be suggested by having him wear a diadem from which the rays of the sun radiated on all sides.[11] This radiate (*aktinōtos*) depiction is attested for the Emperors Augustus, Tiberius, and Caligula. Hart wonders if the Marcan *akanthinos* might not be a play on that, and suggests that the thorns that constitute the beginnings of new leaves on the stem of the date palm might have offered the imagery of rays. The soldiers who do homage to Jesus would then be mocking not only the royal claim associated with him but also the divine (emphasized in John). (4) Delbrueck, Goodenough and Welles think that the reader of the Gospels would not have thought immediately of *akantha*, "thorn," but of *akanthos*, the acanthus plant. One variety, *acanthus mollis*, supplies the shiny leaves so well known from Corinthian-style capitals (still to be seen in Palestine on the later synagogue remains at Capernaum and Chorazin). There is also a thorny variety, *acanthus spinosus*, and of its leaves the soldiers could have woven a wreath to serve as a mock crown. Other suggestions beyond these four have been made, but all fit with the obvious Gospel theme of burlesquing royalty. In choosing among them one must ask how the ordinary Greek reader of the 1st cent. would have understood the Gospel accounts and, if one thinks the basic story is historical, what was possible in the setting of hasty action by soldiers in Jerusalem.

Presumably the Matthean reed scepter would be patient of as much discussion as the thorny crown; fortunately, however, that has not happened. The general royal symbolism of a scepter makes very dubious the claim of Daniel ("Esséniens" 97) that it would have been meant or seen as a Zealot symbol. From the historical viewpoint a reference to the Zealots would have

---

[10]Barbet (*Doctor* 84–85) offers a citation from Vincent of Lerins (*Sermo in Parasceve*—a citation I have unsuccessfully tried to verify) describing the crown of thorns as being "in the shape of a *pileus* [cap, helmet] so that it touched and covered his head in every part." He seeks to combine this description with the crown of plaited rushes preserved at Notre Dame in Paris which St. Louis got from the Venetians; he suggests that the *pileus* of thorns was bound to the head by plaited rushes.

[11]The oldest preserved portrayal of the crucified Christ, on a red jasper gem from Gaza in Syria (dated to the 2d cent.; DACL 3.3049), seems to depict a radiate crown. Bonner picks up on this and points to a 2d-cent. passage from Apuleius (*Metamorphoses* 11.24) where the initiate to the mysteries of Isis is shown as the sun god with the head crowned with palm spikes in the manner of protruding rays. (The most familiar depiction of a radiate crown in our times is the one on the Statue of Liberty.)

been anachronistic for the time of Jesus (§31, A2g above), and for the later period of Gospel composition we have no evidence that either Matt or his readers were so minutely knowledgeable about the Zealots as to find such a reference meaningful.

THE SALUTATION OF THE KING OF THE JEWS AND THE ABUSE (MARK 15:18–19; MATT 27:29B–30; JOHN 19:3)

Mark's salutation makes likely that he intends the scene as a burlesque of the "Ave Caesar" acclamation of the emperor. Here as elsewhere Matt avoids the characteristic Marcan (twenty-six times) "began to"; and he fills in Mark's abruptness with a verb of saying. Also Matt changes the Marcan "salute" (*aspazesthai*) by using the two verbs "kneeling" (cf. the similar substitution in Matt 17:14 from Mark 9:15) and "mocked" (*empaizein*). Both those ideas will appear at the end of Mark's scene ("worshiped" and "mocked"); Matt has "mocked" at both the beginning and the end of the salutation.[12] Mark/Matt and *GPet* use the classical vocative for "King"; John uses the nominative with an article (a usage classified as a Semitism by BDF 147[3]); the address is derogatory, equivalent to "Hail, you King." Scribes who insert the article before "King" in Mark or Matt are probably harmonizing with the presence of that article in other passion instances of the title (Mark 15:2,12,26). *GPet* prefers "(the) King of Israel" both here and in the title on the cross (4:11). This work is quite hostile to the Jews, and its author may have wished that "the Lord" be given a totally acceptable title. Also, the mockery in *GPet* "Judge justly" (addressed by the people to a Jesus seated on a chair of judgment) brings in the judging aspect of kingship, an important function of the ancient Israelite king, e.g., I Kings 3:9,28.[13] John's iterative imperfect, giving the impression that the soldiers did this burlesque time and time again, heightens the mockery. Mark does not mention kneeling in homage here, but only later after violence has been done to Jesus. Matt thinks it goes better here as a preface to the nonviolent buffoonery and thus, like John, sharpens the mockery.

The mockery of the king soon turns to *physical abuse*. Mark's iterative imperfects in 15:19, "were striking . . . and spitting" (*etypton, eneptyon*), are comparable to John's usage in the preceding description (19:3: "were coming

[12]There is a variant reading in Koine mss. of Matt 27:29, "were mocking," to match the imperfect in the next verse, "were striking." The presence of *empaizein* in Luke's Herod scene is not a significant agreement with Matt; it echoes the use of the verb by all three Synoptics in the third prediction of the passion (Mark 10:34 and par.). To compare vocabulary in the Jewish and Roman mockeries and in Jesus' prediction, see Table 2 in §26.

[13]A similar mockery, "Judge us," appears in Justin (*Apology* 1.35.6), giving witness that the details of the mockery were still flexible in the mid-2d cent. (see also *GPet*).

up . . . and saying"). Matt 27:30 has made the Marcan grammar more formal and switched Mark's order of the striking/spitting so that the more harmful action concludes. Matt speaks of "the reed" because he has already mentioned its use as a scepter. As we saw, Matt's sense of orderliness caused him to move earlier in the scene the genuflection that Mark places here.[14] Even though Mark is less orderly than Matt in listing the details of the mockery and abuse, dramatically Mark culminates the hostile action with mock worship (*proskynein*).[15] The only other Marcan use of "worship" (5:6) has been to describe the demoniac who at the impulse of the possessing spirits rendered homage to Jesus as the "Son of the Most High God." *Proskynēsis* or worshipfully bending the knee was an essential part of Hellenistic homage to the ruler.

John makes no reference to spitting or striking with a reed but has the equivalent in the slaps given to Jesus. Here John is probably influenced by Isa 50:6, "I gave . . . my cheeks to slaps"; yet the Johannine failure to include the spitting, which is also in Isa, is curious. *GPet* seems to join the Marcan spitting (imperfect tense) and striking with a reed to the Johannine slapping (more closely conformed to Isa). It has placed the scourging after all this as the final and most severe physical indignity. The malevolence of the apocryphal gospel's picture is seen in the distribution of these actions to "others, others, some," as if it wishes to emphasize that all took a role; moreover, the Jewish people who do this are making fun of the Son of God. The *GPet* account of the mockery began in 3:6 with the statement, "Let us drag along the Son of God now that we have power over him"; that beginning and the ending in 3:9, "with such honor let us honor the Son of God," show the author's real interest. In a different way the scourging and mocking in John underline the malevolence of "the Jews": the actions may be done by the Roman soldiers, but the display of the scourged and mocked Jesus leads "the Jews" to admit that their real hostility to Jesus is not on the issue of kingship but on his pretense to be the Son of God (19:5). Obviously, as Christian reflection on the mockery continued, theological motifs were being developed, sometimes with a polemic thrust.

UNDRESSING AND DRESSING JESUS AFTER THE MOCKERY (MARK 15:20A; MATT 27:31A)

Here is Mark's first use of "mock" (*empaizein*—is there a play on the similar-sounding *emptyein*, "spit," which has just preceded?). The verb sums

[14]In describing the genuflection, Matt also simplified the Marcan Greek, for bending (literally "to place") the knee is an awkward Greek equivalent to the Latin *ponere genua* (BDF 5[3]).

[15]It is not clear why Matt chose to omit this act, even though elsewhere Matt used *proskynein* thirteen times; perhaps the evangelist wished to avoid the pleonasm of genuflecting and worshipping.

up his evaluation of the whole scene. Matt has anticipated the verb earlier in the scene (27:29) but reuses it here. The two Gospels are alike in this verse except for their descriptions of the garment of mockery, for which each uses the language it had employed earlier ("purple"; "cloak"). Neither John nor *GPet* mentions taking off the clothing of mockery and resuming normal dress. John, however, which had the mockery in the middle of the trial, clearly imagines that at the moment of crucifixion (19:23) Jesus is wearing ordinary clothes, including a tunic, and not royal purple. Resumption of ordinary clothes before crucifixion seems likely in *GPet* (4:12) as well, even though *GPet* allows less time between mockery and the crucifixion. No evangelist mentions the deposition of the crown of thorns. Perhaps the reader is meant to assume in Mark/Matt that all the instruments of mockery were removed; and in most early art of the crucifixion (DACL 3.4047–50) Jesus is depicted without a crown. The scribal addendum in Luke 23:37 where Jesus *on the cross* is crowned with thorns (n. 6 above) may have influenced the change in later portrayals of the crucifixion. (See Reich, "König" 106–9.)

Even though Jesus has been flogged, Mark/Matt have Jesus dressed again before he sets out to the place of crucifixion. Normally the criminal, carrying the lateral beam of the cross behind his neck with his arms fastened to it, would go naked to the place of crucifixion, being scourged as he went. We know this from passing references in Dionysius of Halicarnassus (*Roman Antiquities* 7.69.2) and Valerius Maximus (*Facta* 1.7.4). Indeed, Josephus (*Ant.* 19.4.5; #270) reports that even Roman nobles involved in the assassination of Gaius Caligula had their clothes removed before being taken to the place of execution. In having the final disrobing of Jesus only at the place of execution (Mark 15:24 and par.), the evangelist may reflect a local concession that the Romans made to the Jewish abhorrence of public nudity. Josephus reports that the Roman tribune Celer, who was executed in Jerusalem by imperial order, was dragged across the whole city as a public spectacle before being beheaded; but there is no mention of his being disrobed (*War* 2.12.7; #246; *Ant.* 20.6.3; #136).

ANALYSIS

At the beginning of the COMMENT to this section I called attention to two notable factors in the Roman mockery and abuse of Jesus. First, in Mark/ Matt between the Jewish mockery and abuse that occurs at the end of the Sanhedrin trial and this scene at the end of the Roman trial there are clear parallels in placing and thrust.[16] Table 2 in §26, which gives a detailed comparison of the two scenes (as well as of other mockeries and of Jesus' prediction of mockery), should be studied carefully as background for this discussion. Second, there is a sharp disagreement between Mark/Matt and John as to when during the trial the Roman mockery of Jesus took place. Luke, moreover, goes his own way by substituting for it a mockery before Herod and one while Jesus is on the cross. Inevitably we must wonder whether there were two mockeries (Jewish and Roman). If so, has one been conformed to the other to increase the parallelism; if not, which was the more original,[17] and would even the more original have already been dramatized in the tradition, echoing OT motifs and/or burlesquing patterns in Greco-Roman feasts, theater, and literature? To such questions we now turn under two headings: composition of the scene and source of the mockery imagery.

A. Composition of the Scene

Let us begin by discussing the relation of the Roman mockery to the flogging/scourging. In Mark/Matt and John the mockery follows the flogging/scourging, while in Luke mockery (both by Herod with his troops and by Roman soldiers while Jesus hangs on the cross) stands by itself without any whipping. In *GPet* and in the third passion prediction (Mark 10:34 and par.) scourging follows mocking. Separating the two actions, Benoit ("Outrages" 109) suggests that Mark/Matt have the most plausible location for the scourging, namely, at the end of the Roman trial and after Jesus has been sentenced, so that the scourging is part of the crucifixion penalty. On the other hand, in his view, Luke and John have the most plausible location for the mockery, namely, in the midst of the trial. Indeed, Benoit would argue that mockery was more likely to have been done not by Roman soldiers, but by Herod's less tightly disciplined troops, as in Luke. Benoit's solution is harmonistic, but it does answer a major objection against the historicity of the Roman mockery scene: Under orders to crucify Jesus and with a certain press of time to have the execution finished by evening (in order not to rile the Jewish populace so sensitive about the oncoming Sabbath), would the Romans have held up the execution to play games victimizing Jesus?

Source criticism has lent indirect support to the movability of the Roman

---

[16]There are also minor parallels of context, e.g., the "they" who abuse Jesus in Matt 26:67 are presumably "the whole Sanhedrin" of 26:59, while "the whole cohort" does that here. The *aulē* of the high priest functions as a setting in the Sanhedrin proceedings (Mark 14:54,66) and that term recurs here in Mark 15:16.

[17]Winter (*On the Trial* 150–51) thinks the Jewish mockery was developed (orally) from the Roman mockery as part of the general inculpation of the Jews in the Gospels. Yet there are major differences between the two mockeries, not easily explained in the duplication approach.

mockery scene. Those who posit two sources behind the Marcan PN posit that while the scourging comes from the A source, the mockery comes from the B source (§2, n. 45 above). Matera (*Kingship* 21) argues that the end of Mark 15:15 (Pilate "gave over Jesus, having had him flogged, in order that he be crucified") fits in smoothly with 15:20b ("And they lead him out in order that they might crucify him"[18]). Thus the intervening mockery (15:16–20a) would have been a redactional insertion (even as the mockery of Jesus on the cross in 15:29–32 is an insertion). For Gnilka (*Markus* 2.306), however, most of the mockery material (15:19a excepted) would have been pre-Marcan tradition with occasional signs of Marcan editing, e.g., in v. 16 the clarification of the *aulē* (court/palace) as the praetorium.[19] Trying to be consistent with his theory of Marcan insertion, Matera has to explain John's joining of scourging to mockery as evidence of John's dependence on Mark.[20] That conclusion is not so obvious. The Johannine sequence may have been influenced by the description of the Suffering Servant in Isa 50:6: "I gave my back to *scourges,* and my cheeks to *slaps*"—the italicized vocabulary begins and ends John 19:1–3. To discuss the issue further we must look at the unity of Mark's mockery scene.[21]

While insulting buffoonery is the overall motif in Mark 15:16–20a, two sets of actions are involved. The FIRST SET in 15:18 and 19b, which includes the purple clothing, the crown, and kneeling (plus the scepter in Matt), consists of nonviolent actions. The SECOND SET in 15:19a, which includes striking (slapping in John) and spitting, consists of violent actions. To the latter in particular Mark gives the name "mockery."[22] *Parallels between this Roman scene and the mockery that follows the Jewish trial in Mark/Matt are only in the second set of actions (i.e., spitting and the idea [but not the vocab-*

---

[18]In the present Marcan sequence "out" means out from the praetorium where Jesus was mocked (cf. 15:16: "inside"). If the mockery is an insertion, the "out" would mean out of the city, beyond the walls. In John 19:17 "out" means both. Luke 23:26 had "led away."

[19]Yet there are "Marcan stylistic features" in the preMarcan material, e.g., historical present tenses, overuse of *kai* ("and"), and "begin" as an auxiliary in 15:18.

[20]Similarly Borgen ("John" 252) thinks that here John "consists almost only of combinations and agreements with Matthew and Mark," plus additional reworking. Details, however, are once again difficult: If John knew Matt, why change the more plausible military *chlamys* ("cloak") of Matt 27:28 to the more general *himation* ("robe"—John 19:2)?

[21]Matt adds little to Mark except minor details (the scepter) and improvements in grammar and logical arrangement. Luke's mockery before Herod has been discussed already (§33) and is not really identical with this scene.

[22]By using *empaizein* ("to mock") twice, in 27:29b and 31a, Matt thinks of both sets of actions as having the same import. D. L. Miller (*"Empaizein"*) suggests that the notion of a mock game is intrinsic to the verb. Although John does not use *empaizein,* mockery is clear in John's form of the scene. That plus the identity of the agents as Roman soldiers makes implausible the contention of Derrett ("Ecce") that John's "purple robe" (19:2,5) echoes Isa 1:18 (sins like scarlet, crimson red) and 63:1–2 (the one who comes in crimson garments, red apparel), and that all this sets Jesus in the context of a propitiatory sacrifice fulfilling the law for Israel's cleansing.

ulary] of striking). Accordingly, Gnilka (*Markus* 2.306) can suggest that 15:19a, which contains the second set of actions, was a Marcan addition to a preMarcan tradition.

John 19:2–3a has a much shorter second set of actions with only slapping specified (the same expression John 18:22 used in the brutalization of Jesus before Annas). If John was following Mark here, he did an amazingly subtle adaptation: He would have recognized the difference between the two sets of actions, keeping the first set (crown, purple, "Hail, O King of the Jews") very close to Mark, but resisting the Marcan elements in the second set and going back to his own preferred language.[23] More likely John drew on a preJohannine level for the first set of actions, in which the description was similar to that of the preMarcan level of those actions.[24] Then both evangelists or their tradition would have added elements echoing the language of Isa 50 that describes the mocking of the Suffering Servant. Since that same Isaian scene gave inspiration to the description of the Jewish mockery of Jesus, in their final form both the Marcan and Johannine Roman mockery scenes have parallels to their respective Jewish mockery scenes. An added note: The third prediction of Jesus' passion (Mark 10:32–34 and par.) speaks of mocking, spitting, and scourging—elements in Isa 50:6 and 53:5, in the Jewish mockery of Jesus, and in the second set of Roman actions (§26, Table 2:##2a,4b[cf.4a],5g). Yet the prediction seems to attribute these actions to the *Gentiles*.[25] However one explains that phenomenon, it indicates that very quickly in Christian memory what we have called the second set of actions (the violent abuse) became an intrinsic part of what the Romans did to Jesus.

B. The Source of the Imagery for Mocking

Be all this as it may, what has caught Christian literary and artistic imagination through the ages is the first set of actions that are not primarily violent: the buffoonery of cloaking and crowning Jesus, giving him a scepter, and then kneeling before him in mock homage as "the King of the Jews."

---

[23]*GPet* 3:7–9 seems dependent on the canonical Gospels: In the first set of actions *GPet* agrees closely with Mark/Matt and John; in the second set it combines Mark/Matt with the diverse elements in John.

[24]Buse ("St. John . . . Marcan" 218) thinks that John drew on the preMarcan B source rather than on an independent preJohannine tradition. While not an impossible solution here (if there was a preMarcan B source), that theory is very difficult to verify throughout the PN (see BGJ 2.816–17). This is one of the few scenes in the PN where John is very close to Mark in vocabulary; yet in the crowning with thorns John 19:2 is closer to Matt 27:29 than to Mark 15:17. In oral tradition there may have been set ways of describing such a dramatic incident, and these may have influenced the evangelists without written interdependence.

[25]Mark 10:33–34: "And they [chief priests and scribes] will give him over to the Gentiles. [34]And they will mock him, and they will spit on him, and they will scourge him." The "they" of v. 34 might include the "they" of v. 33, but the Gentiles are primarily in focus.

There is no way of knowing whether this happened historically; at most one can discuss the issue of verisimilitude. Is this buffoonery a plausible action? Is there any reason (other than haste in the execution) for thinking that it could not or would not have happened? The scene represents preGospel tradition: If it was historical, what inspired Roman soldiers to act in this way? (Once again, however, we should keep in mind that these are not first-class imperial legionaries, but auxiliary troops from the Syro-Palestinian region, many of whom could very well have been antiJewish.) If the scene was not historical, what inspired Christian preachers to imagine and portray this type of Roman action? There is little likelihood that the scene took its inspiration from Israelite tradition: The classical mocking of the servant in Isa 50:6 does not have these features, nor do the mockeries of the just one in Ps 69 and Wis 2. By the time of Jesus, however, Jewish ideas of royal paraphernalia would have been shaped by Hellenistic and Roman models, for even the Jewish kinglets aped their more powerful patrons. The regal clothing of Herod Agrippa I in AD 44 (Acts 12:21) is described as a marvelous garment woven of silver (Josephus, *Ant.* 19.8.2; #344).[26] Not surprisingly, then, a variety of Greco-Roman episodes and customs have been offered as possible background for the Gospel description. I now group these:[27]

1. HISTORICAL INCIDENTS: (a) Mockery of Karabas. On p. 813 above I mentioned the incident in Alexandria in AD 38 mocking the Jewish king Herod Agrippa I. It involved an idiot named Karabas (Philo, *In Flaccum* 6; #36–40). Elevating him in the gymnasium, the antiJewish mobs put on his head a sheet of papyrus spread out as a diadem. They threw around his body a rug as a royal robe and gave him a papyrus reed as a scepter. And when "as in theatrical mimes" he had received the insignia of kingship, young men stood on either side as an imitation bodyguard. Others proceeded to salute him or to petition him for justice while the crowd hailed him in Aramaic as lord. Notice that there is no element of physical violence done to Karabas.

(b) Death of Herod Agrippa I. In AD 44 this Jewish king who had dressed splendidly and acted like a god died. The people of Caesarea on the Palestinian coast and of Samaria quickly forgot his benefactions and indulged in

---

[26]In the last days as Jerusalem fell to the Romans, Simon bar Giora, as a final act of braggadocio, paraded himself dressed in white tunics (*chitōn*) with a purple mantle (*porphyra chlanis*) over them (Josephus, *War* 7.2.2; #29); eventually he was executed in Rome after having been incorporated in Titus' triumphal procession (7.5.6; #153–55). Later Midrash *Tehillim* on Ps 21:1 (#2) describes the clothing of the Messiah as purple. S. Ben-Chorin, *Zeitschrift für Religions- und Geistesgeschichte* 5 (1953), 211–12, points to a talmudic story attributed to R. Levi where a commander wearing a purple mantle delivers people from taxes and oppression.

[27]Besides what I describe, harmonizations among the Gospels have been suggested, e.g., Herod sent Jesus back in mock royal clothing, and this gave the Roman soldiers the idea of mocking him. But the evangelists who describe this Roman mockery (Mark/Matt, John) show no awareness of the Lucan Herod story.

public mockery of him, wearing garlands and using perfumes (Josephus, *Ant.* 19.9.1; #356–59). See also n. 30 below.

(c) Mockery of a prisoner. Plutarch (*Pompey* 24.7–8) tells us how pirates treated a prisoner who insisted on his rights as a Roman citizen. They dressed him up, made fun of him with all honors, and finally made him walk the plank.

2. GAMES OF MOCKERY. (a) The 2d-cent.-AD writer Pollux (*Onomasticon* 9.110) has a reference to *basilinda,* the game of the king, in which a person was selected as king and all had to obey his orders. Herodotus (*History* 1.114) reports that King Cyrus of Persia as a child played such a king game with others. Horace (*Odes* 1.4.18) indicates that it was played with dice, and *basilicus* was a Latin term for the best throw of the dice. This game was interdicted by the *Lex talaria* against gambling. Excavations under the convent of the Sisters of Sion in Jerusalem, in the general area where once stood the Fortress Antonia (§31, C2), have uncovered in the NE section designs of various games of skill and chance (Aline de Sion, *Forteresse* 119–42), and at places on the flagstones there is a "B" that some would relate to *basileus* ("king"), proposing that we are seeing the *basilinda* game board (Miller, "*Empaizein*" 311). It has been surmised but not established that the games were played by Roman soldiers stationed at the Antonia. Now, however, these designs have lost some of their importance, since there is an increasing archaeological consensus that the pavement in question belongs to the early 2d cent. AD, and that the Antonia was probably not the praetorium of the trial and mockery of Jesus.

(b) In Rome on the Palatine Hill in the rooms of the Domus Gelotiana, which served as a training school for imperial pages, there was discovered a graffito from ca. AD 225 with a crucified ass and a figure worshiping it. Crude letters read: "Alexamenus worships god." Seemingly those in imperial service sometimes mocked the religion of their confreres, especially a minority superstition involving the worship of a crucified Christ. For pagan mockery of the crucified, see Tertullian, *Apologeticum* 16.6–8 (CC 1.115–16); *Ad Nationes* 1.12 (CC 1.30–32).

3. THEATRICAL MIMES. Comic plays and mimes enacted in the theater were a part of Greco-Roman life, and both soldiers and populace would have been familiar with them. (This background has been stressed by Kastner.) In describing the staging of the Karabas incident discussed above, Philo mentions the influence of *theatrikoi mimoi* on the way the idiot received the insignia of kingship. Jews were the object of satire both in poetry and in plays. Mimes of kings are somewhat harder to find, probably because they would have been politically dangerous for the participants (Reich, "König" 728); yet Oxyrhynchus Papyri, Fragment 413 (Part III [= vol. 5], pp. 46–47,

lines 66–106) does give a burlesque of a drunk king. True, there is no extant ancient mime of the Jewish king, but both the ideas and some of the components of mocking Jesus as king could well have been suggested by what was seen on the comic stage. Reich's article has interesting details about later mimes satirizing both Christian and Jewish beliefs.

4. CARNIVAL FESTIVALS. (a) The Sacaean Feast. (This background has been stressed by Frazer, Reinach, Vollmer, and others.) Several accounts describe the *Sakaia*, an ancient Persian festival perhaps borrowed from the Babylonians. Ca. AD 225 Athenaeus of Naucratis (*Deipnosophistai* 14.639c), drawing from the Babylonian historian Berossus, describes a five-day Sacaean feast during which masters were ruled over by slaves, with one slave made master and dressed in a royal robe. At the beginning of the Christian era Strabo (*Geography* 11.8.4–5; #512) tells how Cyrus the Persian caught his Sacae enemies by surprise during a drunken orgy; in honor of this victory the Sacaean feast was celebrated in bacchanalian style with drunken sexual orgies. Ca. AD 100 Dio Chrysostom (*De Regno* 4.66–70) describes another feature of the feast: A prisoner condemned to death was set on the king's throne,[28] given royal apparel, and allowed licentious behavior. After that he was stripped, spit upon, scourged, and killed. We do not know how well this feast would have been known to Roman soldiers, and when or how widely the abuse and killing of the honored one became part of the feast.

(b) The Saturnalia. (This background has been expounded by Wendland.) This feast was supposed to have begun in 217 BC (Livy, *History* 22.1.20); in fact it is older and possibly of Etruscan origin. Cicero (*Ad Atticum* 5.20.5) shows that it was known in the army. Later, Seneca (*Apocolocyntosis* 8.2) in a satirical context speaks of the mock king.[29] Despite the orgiastic character, there is a basic idea of joyous freedom anticipating the golden period of Saturn. Given this context, when a soldier was involved as king of the feast, he was allowed to indulge himself and to give orders, but then later return somewhat shamefaced to his regiment (Geffcken, "Verhöhnung" 221). Except by contamination with the Sacaean feast or with the Kronia or with Oriental motifs (Vollmer, "König" 195), there is no real evidence of putting anyone to death as part of the feast. We can be reasonably certain that no Roman officer allowed one of his soldiers to be put to death each year.

(c) The Kronia. Romans identified their god Saturn with the Greek god

---

[28]Those who accept this as background for the Roman mockery of Jesus often opt for the transitive reading of John 19:13 whereby Pilate set Jesus on the judgment seat. However, not only is there no Johannine reference to a throne, but also the custom of mock enthronement may be what caused ancient interpreters to misread the Johannine verse transitively.

[29]Other details are supplied by Lucian (*Saturnalia* 2–4,9), Epictetus (*Dissertationes* 1.25.8), and Tacitus (*Annals* 13.15).

Kronos. The latter is supposed to have swallowed the other gods and then have been forced to yield them up again; thus there is a dark aspect to his character. On the feast in his honor, masters and slaves feasted together. Ca. AD 300 Porphyry (*De Abstinentia* 2.54,56) reports a human sacrifice to the god at Rhodes, under Phoenician influence. In the *Martyrdom of Dasius* (MACM 272–73) we hear of Roman soldiers in the Danube area in AD 303 choosing someone to play the kingly role in honor of Kronos/Saturn: "Clad in royal clothing, he would go forth in public in the guise and semblance of Saturn with a shameful and immoral reputation among all the people." On the third day he offered himself as a sacrifice by the sword. There is no other evidence for such self-immolation. In all these feasts, the elements of orgiastic buffoonery and of a king or master for a time seem to be original. Physical abuse and execution of the honored person seem later and much less certain, most often appearing when a prisoner became the participant. In such reports one must allow for hostile exaggeration by contemptuous philosophers and disapproving Christians.

Some earlier scholars who uncovered these parallels[30] operated with a simplistic comparative-religion bias, assuming that similarities proved the early Christians to have invented the Roman mockery. Rather, the parallels establish verisimilitude: The content of what is described in the Gospels about the Roman mockery is not implausible, whether historical or not. Readers in the 1st cent. could have comprehended the scene as an effective capsulizing not only of the issue that interested the Romans (kingship), but also of the Gentile attitude toward a crucified king—just as the Sanhedrin mockery dramatized the Jewish horror at a false prophet. In a concise way the two mockeries illustrate the twofold element in I Cor 1:23: "Christ crucified, to the Jews a stumbling block, to the Greeks [Gentiles] foolishness." If we reflect on parallelism, the whole Sanhedrin condemned Jesus to death and some began to mock him as a prophet (Mark 14:64–65); Pilate has condemned Jesus to crucifixion and the whole cohort is called together to mock Jesus as king. The claim that the Gospels excuse the Gentiles but condemn the Jews is scarcely supported by the equally negative portrayal of the two sets of mockers.

(Bibliography for this episode may be found in §30, Part 7.)

---

[30]I have concentrated on four types of proposed Greco-Roman parallels to the mockery of Jesus by Roman soldiers. V. K. Robbins in the ms. of a paper distributed to the SBL Seminar on the Passion and elsewhere has insisted on the possibilities of a Jewish-Hellenistic background. In particular he has pointed to *IV Macc* 6, where guards take Eleazar, strip off his clothes, scourge him, and subject him to verbal abuse and blows, while people urge him to save himself by yielding to the king's command. Before the martyr dies, he speaks in prayer to God.